WEBSTER'S WORD POWER

English
Dictionary

GEDDES & GROSSET

WEBSTER'S WORD POWER

Betty Kirkpatrick, a graduate of Edinburgh University, has a long career in reference publishing. She has edited *Chambers Twentieth Century Dictionary, Roget's Thesaurus*, the concise edition of *Brewer's Phrase and Fable*, and was language consultant to the *Encarta World English Dictionary*. She has compiled various other reference books, including the *Oxford Paperback Thesaurus* and the *Bloomsbury Dictionary of Clichés*. She acts as a consultant to the *Bloomsbury Good Word Guide*. Betty is author of an extensive list of publications on various aspects of the English language for learners of English.

Compiled By Betty Kirkpatrick
Pronunciation scheme by Scott and Bettina Montgomery

Published 2013 by Geddes & Grosset, an imprint of DC Thomson Books Group Ltd.,
144 Port Dundas Road, Glasgow G4 0HZ

ISBN 978-1-84205-762-9

Printed and bound in the EU

ENGLISH DICTIONARY

This book is an accessible and comprehensive modern dictionary. As well as providing over 35,000 concise, up-to-date dictionary definitions, it has a specially commissioned, crystal-clear pronunciation guide.

The pronunciation system in this book is a readable one. There are no phonetic symbols, and there is even no need for a key as there is in some other dictionaries with "spelled-out" pronunciation. To achieve this, each entry in the dictionary includes a syllable-based "spelling pronunciation". This means that the pronunciation of the word stays as close to the original spelling of the word as is usefully possible and uses the conventions of English spelling to provide an easy-to-understand guide to pronunciation. Research has shown that pronunciation guides that stay as close as possible to the actual spelling of a word provide the most accessible guide for the reader. To help our readers pronounce the words in our dictionary, we have used the norms of the English sound/spelling system broken into manageable syllables. Syllables break down words into smaller units. Our words often have more than one syllable, with one syllable in each word more prominent than others. This is known as the stressed syllable. We have produced, for each word, a series of syllable blocks divided by hyphens (-) which when read, reveal the pronunciation of the word. The main stress is marked in bold.

Thi re-**zult** is a clear and in-**choo**-wi-tiv **spe**-ling pro-nun-see-**ay**-shun which is baist on thi sound and **spe**-ling normz ov thi **ing**-glish **lang**-gwidge at a si-**la**-bic **le**-vel and which iz i-**mee**-dee-it-lee in-**choo**-wi-tiv.

Other features:

Strict alphabetical order is followed. All compound words and hyphenated words are alphabetized as if they are one word.

Variant spellings appear in bold type next to the headword.

Parts of speech are indicated in italic, after the bold headword by the abbreviations shown on the following page. Other parts of speech after the main headword are indicated by a full point (.) and •. Other terms, of a **different part of speech**, that are related to the headword are given at the end of an entry in bold preceded by •.

Inflected forms of verbs and **plural form**s of nouns appear in bold following the headword.

Different senses within parts of speech are numbered. Parts of speech are separated by full points (.) and •.

Words of **different origins** but with the same spelling are given separate, numbered entries.

Registers are indicated by the following labels: *fml, inf, sl, derog, dial*.

Abbreviations or **acronyms** appear with the label *abbr* and are followed by an equals sign (=).

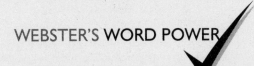

WEBSTER'S **WORD POWER**

Abbreviations

abbr	abbreviation	*neut*	neuter
adj	adjective	*npl*	noun plural
adv	adverb	*NT*	New Testament
approx	approximately	*obs*	obsolete
astron	astronomy	*old*	old fashioned, archaic
aux	auxiliary	*off*	offensive
Br	Britain, British	*orig*	original, originally, origin
c	circa, about	*OT*	Old Testament
cap	capital, capitalised	*p*	participle
Cdn	Canadian	*pers*	person, personal
cent	century	*pl*	plural
compar	comparative	*poet*	poetical
comput	computing	*poss*	possessive
conj	conjunction	*pp*	past participle
derog	derogatory, derogatorily	*prep*	preposition
dial	dialect	*pres t*	present tense
e.g.	exempli gratis, for example	*pron*	pronoun
etc	etcetera, and so on	*prp*	present participle
esp	especially	*pt*	past tense
f	feminine	*RC*	Roman Catholic
fig	figuratively	*reflex*	reflexive
fml	formal	*Scot*	Scotland, Scottish
gram	grammar	*sing*	singular
hum	humorous	*sl*	slang
i.e.	id est, that is	*TM*	trademark
incl	including	*TV*	television
inf	informal	*UK*	United Kingdom
interj	interjection	*US*	United States
lit	literary	*USA*	United States of America
m	masculine	*usu*	usually
math	mathematics	*var*	variant
med	medicine	*vb*	verb
mus	music	*vulg*	vulgar, vulgarly
myth	mythology	*zool*	zoology
n	noun		

A

A, a /ay/ *n* **1** the first letter of the English alphabet. **2** (*mus*) the sixth note of the scale of C major. **3** a human blood type.

a /a/ *indefinite article* (**an** before a vowel) **1** any, some, one. **2** one single thing. **3** per, for each.

aardvark /ard-vark/ *n* an African mammal with a long snout that feeds on ants.

abacus /a-ba-kus, a-**ba**-kus/ *n* a counting frame with beads.

abalone /a-ba-**lo**-nee/ *n* an edible sea snail with a shell that is shaped like an ear.

abandon /a-**ban**-don/ *vb* **1** to give up. **2** to depart from forever, desert. • *n* freedom from care.

abandoned /a-**ban**-dond/ *adj* **1** deserted. **2** immoral, shameless.

abattoir /a-ba-twar/ *n* a place where animals are killed for food.

abate /a-**bate**/ *vb* to lessen. • *n* **abatement**.

abbess /a-bess/ *n* the chief nun in a convent.

abbey /a-bee/ *n* **1** a monastery or convent. **2** a church, once part of a monastery or convent.

abbot /a-bot/ *n* the chief monk in a monastery.

abbreviate /a-**bree**-vee-ate/ *vb* to shorten. • *n* **abbreviation**.

abdicate /**ab**-di-kate/ *vb* to give up high office, especially a throne. • *n* **abdication**.

abdomen /**ab**-do-men/ *n* the part of the body between your chest and your thighs. • *adj* **abdominal**.

abduct /ab-**duct**/ *vb* to kidnap. • *n* **abduction**, **abductor**.

abhor /ab-**hor**/ *vb* to loathe. • *n* **abhorrence**.

abhorrent /a-**hor**-rent/ *adj* loathsome.

abide /a-**bide**/ *vb* to put up with. • **abide by** to obey, to remain true to.

abiding /a-**bide**-ing/ *adj* lasting.

ability /a-**bil**-it-ee/ *n* **1** skill or power to do a thing. **2** cleverness.

ablaze /a-**blaze**/ *adj, adv* on fire, in flames.

able /**ay**-bl/ *adj* **1** having skill or power to do a thing. **2** clever. • *adv* **ably**.

able-bodied /ay-bl-**bod**-eed/ *adj* able to walk; physically healthy.

abnormal /ab-**nor**-mal/ *adj* different from the usual. • *adv* **abnormally**.

abnormality /ab-nor-**mal**-it-ee/ *n* an unusual quality.

aboard /a-**board**/ *adv, prep* on board, on a ship, train, aeroplane, etc.

abode /a-**bode**/ *n* (*fml or hum*) house, home.

abolish /a-**bol**-ish/ *vb* to put an end to, to do away with. • *n* **abolition, abolitionist**.

abominable /a-**bom**-in-na-bl/ *adj* hateful.

aboriginal /a-bor-**ri**-ji-nal/ *adj* **1** describing a feature that is native to a country. **2** (*cap*) describing the native peoples of Australia. • *n* (*cap*) a descendant of the people who inhabited Australia before the arrival of the Europeans.

aborigine /a-bor-**ri**-ji-nee/ *n* **1** one of the original inhabitants of a country, who has been there since the earliest times. **2** (*cap*) another name for an Australian **Aboriginal**. • *adj* **aboriginal, Aboriginal**.

abort /a-**bort**/ *vb* **1** to have an abortion or miscarriage. **2** to perform an abortion on. **3** to stop something, especially in the early stages.

abortion /a-**bor**-shun/ *n* a miscarriage, usually induced.

abortive /a-**bor**-tive/ *adj* unsuccessful because done too soon.

abound /a-**bound**/ *vb* to be plentiful.

about /a-**bout**/ *adv, prep* **1** concerning. **2** around. **3** near to. **4** nearly. **5** on the point of.

above /a-**buv**/ *adv, prep* **1** over. **2** higher (than).

aboveboard /a-**buv**-board/ *adj* honest, fair.

abrasion /a-**bray**-zhen/ *n* **1** the act of rubbing away at something. **2** an area of skin that has been scraped.

abrasive /a-**bray**-ziv/ *adj* **1** causing abrasion. **2** harsh or irritating. • *n* something that causes abrasion.

abreast /a-**brest**/ *adv* side by side. • **abreast of the times** up-to-date.

abridge /a-**bridge**/ *vb* to make shorter. • *n* **abridg(e)ment**.

abroad /a-**brawd**/ *adv* **1** out of your own country. **2** far and wide.

abrupt /a-**brupt**/ *adj* **1** sudden, hasty. **2** discourteous. • *adv* **abruptly**. • *n* **abruptness**.

abscess /**ab**-sess/ *n* a boil, a gathering of pus in some part of the body.

abseil /**ab**-sail/ *vb* to go down a very steep slope, such as a cliff face or a very tall building, using a rope secured at the top and passed around the body in a kind of harness.

absence *see* **absent**.

absent /**ab**-sent/ *adj* not present. • *n* **absence**.

absentee /ab-sen-**tee**/ *n* someone who is not present.

absentminded /ab-sent-**mind**-ded/ *adj* not thinking of what you are doing.

absolute /**ab**-so-lute, ab-so-**lute**/ *adj* **1** complete. **2** free from controls or conditions. • *adv* **absolutely**.

absolution *see* **absolve**.

absolve /ab-**solve**/ *vb* to set free, as from guilt or punishment. • *n* **absolution**.

absorb /ab-**sorb**/ *vb* **1** to soak up. **2** to take up all the attention of.

absorbed /ab-**sorbd**/ *adj* giving the whole mind to.

absorbent /ab-**sor**-bent/ *adj* drinking in.

absorption /ab-**sorp**-shen/ *n* **1** act of absorbing. **2** full attention.

abstain /ab-**stain**/ *vb* **1** to keep yourself from, to hold back from. **2** not to vote. • *n* **abstainer, abstention**.

abstract /**ab**-stract/ *n* a summary. • *adj* **1** existing in the mind only. **2** portraying ideas rather than realistic images.

absurd /ab-**surd**/ *adj* foolish. • *n* **absurdity**.

abundance /a-**bun**-dance/ *n* more than enough, plenty. • *adj* **abundant**. • *adv* **abundantly**.

abuse /a-**byooz**/ *vb* **1** to make wrong use of. **2** to ill-treat, to maltreat, especially physically or sexually. **3** to use insulting language. • *n* /a-**byooss**/ **abuse**.

abusive /a-**byoo**-sive/ *adj* **1** ill-treating, cruel. **2** insulting. • *adv* **abusively**.

abysmal /a-**biz**-mal/ *adj* very bad.

abyss /a-**biss**/ *n* a very deep pit or ravine.

academic /a-ca-**de**-mic/ *adj* **1** of or concerning education, especially in a college or university. **2** not practical or useful; theoretical. • *n* teacher in a college or university.

academy /a-**ca**-de-mee/ *n* **1** a school for special studies. **2** a society for advancing arts and sciences.

accelerate /ac-**sel**-le-rate/ *vb* to increase speed. • *n* **acceleration**.

accelerator /ac-**sel**-le-ray-tor/ *n* a device that controls the speed of a car.

accent /**ac**-sent/ *n* **1** a special emphasis given to part of a word. **2** the mark that indicates such emphasis. **3** a way of speaking peculiar to certain persons or groups. • *vb* to emphasize a certain part of a word.

accentuate /ac-**sen**-choo-ate/ *vb* to emphasize.

accept /ak-**sept**/ *vb* **1** to receive something offered. **2** to regard as true, reasonable, satisfactory, etc. • *n* **acceptance**.

acceptable /ak-**sep**-ta-bl/ *adj* **1** pleasant to receive. **2** satisfactory, good enough. **3** allowable, tolerable.

access /**ak**-sess/ *n* a way or means of approach. • *vb* to find on a computer file.

accessible /ak-**sess**-i-bl/ *adj* **1** easily approached. **2** easily reached. **3** easily obtained or understood. • *n* **accessibility**.

accessory /ak-**sess**-or-ee/ *n* **1** an assistant, especially in crime. **2** an additional part or tool. **3** an additional item worn with clothing.

accident /**ak**-sid-ent/ *n* **1** an unexpected happening. **2** an unexpected event that causes damage or injury. • *adj* **accidental**.

acclaim /a-**claim**/ *vb* to greet with applause • *n* recognition and praise; applause.

acclamation /ak-la-**may**-shun/ *n* a shout of joy or approval.

acclimatize /a-**clime**-a-tize/ *vb, also* **acclimatise** to accustom to a new climate or situation. • *n* **acclimatization, acclimatisation**.

accolade /a-ko-**lade**/ *n* **1** the touching on the shoulder with a sword in the ceremony of making someone a knight. **2** praise or approval.

accommodate /a-**com**-o-date/ *vb* **1** to provide lodgings for. **2** to have space for. **3** to supply with. **4** to make suitable, to adapt.

accommodating /a-**com**-o-date-ing/ *adj* obliging.

accommodation /a-com-o-**day**-shun/ *n* **1** lodgings. **2** adaptation.

accompaniment /a-**com**-pan-ee-ment/ *n* the music played with a singer or player.

accompanist /a-**com**-pan-ist/ *n* someone who plays the accompaniment for a singer or player.

accompany /a-**com**-pan-ee/ *vb* **1** to go with. **2** to join a singer or player by playing a musical instrument.

accomplice /a-**com**-pliss/ *n* a helper, especially in crime.

accomplish /a-**com**-plish/ *vb* to perform successfully, to finish.

accomplished /a-**com**-plisht/ *adj* **1** finished. **2** skilled.

accomplishment /a-**com**-plish-ment/ *n* **1** something which is done successfully. **2** completion.

accord /a-**cord**/ *vb* **1** to agree. **2** to give. • *n* agreement. • **of your own accord** by your own wish.

accordance /a-**cor**-dans/ *n* agreement.

accordingly /a-**cor**-ding-lee/ *adv* therefore.

according to /a-**cor**-ding to/ *prep* **1** in keeping with. **2** as stated by.

accordion /a-**cor**-dee-on/ *n* a portable musical instrument played by keys and worked by bellows. • *n* **accordionist**.

accost /a-**cost**/ *vb* to approach and speak to in an aggressive way.

account /a-**count**/ *vb* (*fml*) to consider, to reckon. • *n* **1** a statement of money received and paid, a bill. **2** a report, description. • **account for** give an explanation of. • **of no account** of no importance. • **on account of** because of.

accountable *adj* /a-**count**-a-bl/ responsible.

accountancy /a-**count**-an-see/ *n* the work of an accountant.

accountant /a-**count**-ant/ *n* someone who keeps or examines money accounts.

accumulate /a-**kyoom**-yoo-late/ *vb* **1** to increase, to heap up. **2** to collect.

accumulation /a-kyoom-yoo-**lay**-shun/ *n* growth, a large collection.

accuracy /ak-yoo-**rass**-ee/ *n* exactness, precision.

accurate /ak-yoo-rit/ *adj* **1** correct, exact. **2** correct, careful. • *adv* **accurately**.

accursed /a-**curst**/ *adj* **1** under a curse, doomed. **2** hateful.

accusation /a-kyoo-**zay**-shun/ *n* a charge brought against anyone.

accuse /a-**kyooz**/ *vb* to charge with wrongdoing. • *n* **accuser**.

accused /a-**kyoozd**/ *n* someone charged with wrongdoing.

accustom /a-**cuss**-tom/ *vb* to make well known by use.

accustomed /a-**cuss**-tomd/ *adj* **1** usual. **2** used (to), familiar with.

ace /ace/ *n* **1** the value of 'one' in games of cards, dice, or dominoes. **2** someone good at sports. • **within an ace of** on the very point of.

acetic /a-**set**-ic/ *adj* sour, of vinegar.

acetylene /a-**set**-ill-een/ *n* a gas used for giving light and heat, and commonly used with oxygen for welding or cutting metal.

ache /ake/ *vb* to be in or to give prolonged pain. • *n* a prolonged or throbbing pain.

achieve /a-**cheev**/ *vb* **1** to succeed in doing. **2** to gain.

achievement /a-**cheev**-ment/ *n* **1** something done successfully. **2** a feat.

acid /a-sid/ *n* a sour or corrosive substance. • *adj* sour; sharp to the taste; bitter.

acid rain /a-sid rane/ *n* rain that has been polluted by acid from factory waste, car exhausts, etc. and is harmful to the environment.

acid test /a-sid test/ *n* a test that indicates the worth or value of something.

acidity /a-**sid**-it-ee/ *n* sourness.

acknowledge /ak-**naw**-ledge/ *vb* **1** to admit as true. **2** to admit the receipt of. • *n* **acknowledg(e)ment**.

acne /ak-nee/ *n* a skin condition that causes pimples.

acorn /**ay**-corn/ *n* the fruit or seed of the oak tree.

acoustic /a-**coos**-tik/ *adj* **1** having to do with hearing and sound. **2** making its natural sound, not electric.

acoustics /a-**coos**-tiks/ *npl* the science of sound.

acquaint /a-**kwaint**/ *vb* **1** to make familiar with. **2** to inform.

acquaintance /a-**kwain**-tanse/ *n* **1** a person you know. **2** knowledge.

acquire /a-**kwire**/ *vb* to gain, to obtain.

acquit /a-**kwit**/ *vb* **1** to declare innocent. **2** to conduct yourself.

acquittal /a-**kwi**-tal/ *n* a setting free.

acre /**ay**-kr/ *n* an imperial measure of land (= 4840 square yards or 4046.9 square metres).

acrobat /a-cro-bat/ *n* a high-wire or trapeze artiste. • *adj* **acrobatic**. • *npl* **acrobatics**.

acronym /a-cro-nym/ *n* an abbreviation, made from the initial letters, or from combinations of letters from a word, which itself can be pronounced as a word.

act /act/ *vb* **1** to do. **2** to conduct yourself. **3** to perform on the stage, in films, or on television. **4** to produce an effect. • *n* **1** a deed. **2** a law. **3** a part of a play.

action /ac-shon/ *n* **1** something done. **2** a movement. **3** the producing of an effect. **4** the events in a narrative or drama. **5** a battle. **6** a lawsuit.

active /ac-tiv/ *adj* **1** energetic. **2** taking part, involved. **3** being in action, working, operative.

activity /ac-**ti**-vi-tee/ *n* **1** energy. **2** occupation or pastime.

actor /ac-tor/ *n* a man who performs in a play or film or on television.

actress /ac-tress/ *n* a woman who performs in a play or film or on television.

actual /ac-chul/ *adj* **1** real, not imaginary. **2** true.

actuality /ac-chu-**wa**-li-tee/ *n* reality.

actually /ac-cha-lee/ *adv* really, as a matter of fact.

acupuncture /a-kyoo-punk-cher/ *n* a treatment used in alternative medicine in which fine needles are inserted into the skin at certain points along energy paths known as meridians.

acute /a-**kyoot**/ *adj* **1** coming to a sharp point. **2** sharp-witted. **3** (*of emotions or* *diseases*) intense but short-lasting. • *adv* **acutely**.

acute angle /a-**kyoot** ang-gl/ *n* an angle less than 90°.

AD /ay dee/ *abbr* = **Anno Domini**: a Latin phrase meaning 'in the year of our Lord', used to describe the years following the birth of Jesus.

ad /ad/ *n* short for **advertisement**.

adage /a-didge/ *n* a proverb, an old wise saying.

adamant /a-da-mant/ *adj* determined, firm.

adapt /a-**dapt**/ *vb* 1 to make suitable, to fit to a different use. 2 to change, adjust.

adaptable /a-dap-ta-bl/ *adj* easily fitted to new uses or conditions. • *n* **adaptability**.

adaptation /a-dap-**tay**-shun/ *n* the action or result of adapting.

adapter /a-dap-ter/ *n* a device for connecting electrical plugs with a socket.

add /add/ *vb* 1 to join one thing to another. 2 to increase. 3 to say more.

adder /a-der/ *n* a small poisonous snake, a viper.

addict /a-dict/ *n* a person who is dependent on and so unable to give up a habit, especially a harmful one such as drug-taking.

addicted /a-**dic**-ted/ *adj* dependent on, unable to give up. • *n* **addiction**.

addition /a-**di**-shen/ *n* 1 act of adding. 2 something added. • *adj* **additional**.

additive /a-di-tiv/ *n* a substance added to another, especially to add flavour or colour.

address /a-**dress**/ *vb* 1 to speak to. 2 to direct a letter. 3 to direct your attention or energy to. • *n* 1 the place where a person lives or works. 2 the directions on a letter or envelope. 3 a formal talk.

adenoids /a-de-noids/ *npl* glands at the back of the nose that if enlarged can hinder breathing.

adept /a-**dept**/ *adj* very skilful. • *n* someone who is skilled.

adequate /a-de-kwit/ *adj* 1 enough. 2 satisfactory. 3 able. • *adv* **adequately**. • *n* **adequacy**.

adhere /ad-**heer**/ *vb* 1 to stick (to). 2 to remain loyal to. • *n* **adherence**.

adhesive /ad-hee-ziv/ *adj* sticky. • *n* a sticky substance, glue.

adieu /a-**dyoo**/ *interj* the French word for farewell, goodbye. • *n* (*pl* **adieus** or **adieux**) a farewell.

adjacent /a-jay-sent/ *adj* lying near (to).

adjective /a-jec-tiv/ *n* a word that describes a noun. • *adj* **adjectival**. • *adv* **adjectivally**.

adjourn /a-jurn/ *vb* 1 to put off to another time. 2 to go to another place. • *n* **adjournment**.

adjust /a-**just**/ *vb* 1 to set right. 2 to put in order. • *adj* **adjustable**. • *n* **adjuster**, **adjustment**.

administer /ad-mi-ni-ster/ *vb* 1 to manage, to govern. 2 to carry out. 3 (*fml*) to give.

administration /ad-mi-ni-**stray**-shun/ *n* 1 the management of a business or a government. 2 people involved in this. • *adj* **administrative**.

administrator /ad-**mi**-ni-stray-tor/ *n* a person who works in administration.

admirable /ad-mi-ra-bl/ *adj* deserving admiration or praise. • *adv* **admirably**.

admiral /ad-mi-ral/ *n* the highest rank of naval officer.

admiration /ad-mi-**ray**-shun/ *n* a feeling of respect for another person.

admire /ad-**mire**/ *vb* to think very highly of. • *n* **admirer**.

admission /ad-mi-shen/ *n* 1 permission to enter. 2 the amount payable for entry. 3 a confession.

admit /ad-**mit**/ *vb* 1 to allow to enter. 2 to accept as true or just. 3 to confess.

admittance /ad-mi-tanse/ *n* right or permission to enter.

admittedly /ad-**mi**-ted-lee/ *adv* it cannot be denied.

admonish /ad-mo-nish/ *vb* to give a warning or scolding to. • *n* **admonition**. • *adj* **admonitory**.

ado /a-doo/ *n* fuss, trouble.

adobe /a-**doe**-bee/ *n* 1 a building material made of sun-dried earth and straw. 2 a building made of this material.

adolescent /a-doe-**less**-sent/ *adj* growing up from youth to adulthood. • *n* a person of either sex when adolescent. • *n* **adolescence**.

adopt /a-**dopt**/ *vb* 1 to take as your own. 2 to take over and use. 3 to choose formally. • *n* **adoption**.

adorable /a-doe-ra-bl/ *adj* lovable.

adore /a-**dore**/ *vb* 1 to worship. 2 to love or like very much. • *n* **adoration**.

adorn *vb* /a-**dorn**/ to decorate, to make beautiful. • *adj* **adorned**.

adornment /a-**dorn**-ment/ *n* an ornament.

adrift /a-**drift**/ *adj* and *adv* floating without control.

adrenalin /a-dre-na-lin/ *n, also* **adrenaline** a chemical produced by your body when you are scared or excited.

adulation /a-je-**lay**-shun/ *n* extreme praise, flattery.

adult /a-**dult**, a-dult/ *adj* grown-up. • *n* a grown-up person.

adulterate /a-dul-te-rayt/ *vb* to lower in value by mixing with something of less worth (e.g. to mix wine with water, gold with tin, etc). • *n* adulteration.

advance /ad-**vanse**/ *vb* **1** to put forward. **2** to go forward. **3** to help promote. **4** to lend. • *n* **1** a forward movement. **2** progress. **3** a loan (of money), especially a payment made before the normal time. **4** increase. • **in advance** in front; before.

advanced /ad-**vanst**/ *adj* **1** far on (in life, time, etc). **2** at a high level, not elementary. **3** modern and new and sometimes not yet generally accepted.

advantage /ad-**van**-tidge/ *n* **1** a better position or something that puts someone in a better position. **2** gain, profit, benefit.

advantageous /ad-van-**tey**-jess/ *adj* profitable; helpful. • *adv* advantageously.

advent /ad-vent/ *n* a coming, an arrival.

Advent /ad-vent/ *n* in the Christian church, the period from the fourth Sunday before Christmas to Christmas Day.

adventure /ad-**ven**-cher/ *n* an exciting or dangerous deed or undertaking.

adventurer /ad-**ven**-cher-rer/ (*m/f*), **adventuress** /ad-**ven**-che-ress/ (*f*) *n* **1** someone who seeks adventures. **2** someone who lives by his or her wits.

adventurous /ad-**ven**-che-russ/ *adj* **1** daring, eager for adventure. **2** dangerous, involving risk.

adverb /ad-verb/ *n* a word that modifies the meaning of a verb, an adjective, or another adverb. • *adj* adverbial.

adversary /ad-ver-se-ree/ *n* an enemy.

adverse /ad-**verse**, ad-verse/ *adj* acting against, unfavourable. • *adv* adversely.

adversity /ad-**ver**-si-tee/ *n* misfortune.

advertise /ad-ver-tize/ *vb* to make known to the public. • *n* advertiser.

advertisement /ad-**ver**-tiss-ment/ *n* an announcement to the public, often for the purpose of selling something.

advice /ad-**vice**/ *n* **1** a helpful opinion offered to another. **2** a formal letter, etc, giving information.

advisable /ad-**vie**-za-bl/ *adj* wise; correct in the circumstances. • *n* advisability.

advise /ad-**vize**/ *vb* **1** to give advice. **2** to inform.

adviser /ad-**vie**-zer/ *n* someone who gives advice.

advisory /ad-**vie**-zo-ree/ *adj* for the purpose of giving advice.

advocate /ad-vo-cat/ *n* **1** someone who speaks for another. **2** a lawyer who pleads a cause in court. • *vb* to recommend, to speak in favour of.

aeon *also* **eon** (*US*) /ee-on/ *n* **1** (*inf*) a period of time so long it is impossible to measure. **2** (*astron*) one thousand million years. • *adj* aeonian.

aerial /ae-ree-al/ *adj* of or from the air. • *n* a wire or rod for receiving radio waves or television signals.

aerie /ee-ree/ *n*, *also* **eyrie** the nest of a bird of prey.

aerobatics /ae-ro-**ba**-tics/ *npl* difficult exercises performed by an aircraft.

aerobics /ae-ro-bics/ *n* a type of physical exercise that strengthens the heart and lungs by temporarily increasing the heart rate. • *adj* aerobic.

aerodynamic /ae-ro-die-**na**-mic/ *adj* streamlined for smooth movement through the air.

aeronautics /ae-ro-**naw**-tics/ *n* the science of the operation and flight of aircraft.

aeroplane /**air**-plane/ *n*, *also* **airplane** (US) a heavier-than-air flying machine with wings.

aerosol /ae-ro-sol/ *n* **1** a liquid under pressure in a container, which is released in a fine spray. **2** the container for this.

aesthetics /ess-**theh**-ticks/ *n*, *also* **esthetics** (*US*) the science or philosophy of art and the beautiful.

affable /a-fa-bl/ *adj* pleasant, polite, easy to talk with. • *n* affability. • *adv* affably.

affair /a-**fair**/ *n* **1** business. **2** a matter, a concern. **3** happenings or events connected with a particular person or thing. **4** a romantic or sexual relationship.

affect /a-fect/ *vb* **1** to act upon. **2** to move the feelings. **3** to pretend.

affected /a-**fec**-ted/ *adj* full of affectation.

affectation /a-fec-**tay**-shun/ *n* manner or behaviour that is not natural; pretence.

affection /a-**fec**-shun/ *n* fondness, love.

affectionate /a-**fec**-shi-nit/ *adj* loving. • *adv* affectionately.

affiliate /a-**fi**-lee-ate/ *v* to be joined or be connected with something. • *n* affiliation.

affinity /a-**fi**-ni-tee/ *n* **1** relationship. **2** attraction.

affirm /a-**firm**/ *vb* to state with certainty.

affirmation /a-fir-**may**-shun/ *n* **1** a statement. **2** a solemn statement of the truth.

affirmative /a-**fir**-ma-tiv/ *adj* answering 'yes'. • *n* an answer meaning 'yes'. • **answer in the affirmative** to say 'yes'.

afflict /a-**flict**/ *vb* to cause pain, distress, etc, to. • *n* affliction.

affluence /a-**floo**-ents/ *n* wealth.

affluent /a-floo-ent/ *adj* wealthy.

afford /a-ford/ *vb* **1** to be able to pay for. **2** to be able to do, spend, etc, something without trouble, loss, etc. **3** (*fml*) to give.

afloat /a-**float**/ *adj*, *adv* floating.

aforesaid /a-fore-said/ *adj* already mentioned.

afraid /a-**frade**/ *adj* frightened.

afresh /a-**fresh**/ *adv* again.

African American /a-fri-can a-**me**-ri-can/ *n* a United States citizen who has African ancestors. • *adj* describing African Americans, or their culture, history, etc.

aft /aft/ *adj*, *adv* at or near the stern of a ship.

after /af-ter/ *adv*, *prep* **1** later in time (than). **2** behind.

aftermath /af-ter-math/ *n* the period of time, or consequences, following an unpleasant or unfortunate event.

afternoon /af-ter-**noon**/ *n* the time from noon to evening.

afterthought /af-ter-thot/ *n* **1** a fresh thought after an act or speech. **2** something added or done later, not part of an original plan.

afterwards /af-ter-wards/ *adv* later.

again /a-**gen**/ *adv* once more.

against /a-**genst**/ *prep* **1** in opposition to. **2** supported by.

agate /a-get/ *n* a very hard precious stone.

age /ayj/ *n* **1** the length of time a person or thing has lived or existed. **2** (*inf*) a long time. **3** the state of being old. **4** a particular period in history. • *vb* **1** to become old. **2** to make old.

aged /ayjd/ *adj* **1** at the age of. **2** /ayj-ed/ old.

ageless /ayj-less/ *adj* never becoming old.

agency /ay-jen-see/ *n* the office or business of an agent.

agenda /a-jen-da/ *n* a list of matters to be discussed at a meeting.

agent /ay-jent/ *n* **1** someone or something that acts. **2** a person who acts on behalf of someone else.

aggravate /a-gra-vate/ *vb* **1** to make worse. **2** (*inf*) to make angry. • *adj* **aggravating**. • *n* **aggravation**.

aggression /a-gre-shun/ *n* **1** an attack. **2** hostile feelings.

aggressive /a-gre-siv/ *adj* **1** always ready to attack, quarrelsome. **2** forceful, determined. • *adv* **aggressively**.

aggressor /a-gre-sor/ *n* the first to attack.

aggro /ag-gro/ *n* (*inf*) *abbr* = **aggravation**: **1** aggressive behaviour. **2** annoying problems or difficulties.

agile /a-jile/ *adj* quick of movement, nimble. • *n* **agility**.

agitate /a-ji-tate/ *vb* **1** to excite, to make anxious. **2** to try to stir up public feeling. **3** (*fml*) to shake. • *n* **agitation**.

agitator /a-ji-tay-tor/ *n* someone who tries to cause public discontent or revolt.

agnostic /ag-**naw**-stic/ *n* someone who believes that the existence of God cannot be proved.

ago /a-go/ *adv* in the past.

agonizing /a-gon-eye-zing/ *adj*, *also* **agonising** **1** causing great pain. **2** causing great distress.

agony /a-gon-ee/ *n* **1** great pain. **2** great distress.

agree /a-gree/ *vb* **1** to be of the same opinion. **2** to be alike. **3** to suit.

agreeable /a-gree-a-bl/ *adj* **1** pleasant. **2** ready to agree. • *adv* **agreeably**.

agreement /a-gree-ment/ *n* **1** sameness of opinion. **2** likeness. **3** a contract.

agriculture /a-gri-cul-cher/ *n* the science of cultivating the land, farming. • *adj* **agricultural**.

aground /a-ground/ *adj*, *adv* on or on to the sea bed.

ahead /a-hed/ *adv* **1** in front. **2** forward, for the future.

AI /ay eye/ *abbr* = **artificial intelligence**: the study of the capacity of computers to simulate human intelligence.

aid /aid/ *vb* to help. • *n* help.

aide /aid/ *n* = **aide-de-camp** (*pl* **aides-de-camp**) an officer in attendance on a king, general or other high official.

AIDS, Aids /aidz/ *abbr* = **Acquired Immune Deficiency Syndrome**: a serious disease that affects the body's immune system, greatly reducing resistance to infection.

ailing /ay-ling/ *adj* **1** unwell. **2** weak.

ailment /ayl-ment/ *n* a minor health problem.

aim /aim/ *vb* **1** to point a weapon (at). **2** to intend, to try. • *n* **1** the act of aiming a weapon. **2** intention, goal, purpose.

aimless /aim-less/ *adj* without purpose.

air /air/ *n* **1** the mixture of gases composing the earth's atmosphere. **2** a light breeze. **3** a tune. **4** manner. **5** *pl* a manner that is not genuine. • *vb* **1** to expose to fresh air. **2** to expose to warm air, to dry. **3** to speak openly about.

air bag /air-bag/ *n* an inflatable safety device in automobiles that inflates on impact to cushion the driver.

air-conditioning /air-con-**dish**-un-ing/ *n* a system for controlling the temperature and quality of the air in a building. • *adj* **air-conditioned**. • *n* **air-conditioner**.

aircraft /air-craft/ *n* (*pl* **aircraft**) a flying machine.

airfield /**air**-feeld/ *n* a starting and landing place for aircraft.

airily /**air**-ill-ee/ *adv* in an airy manner.

airing /**air**-ing/ *n* **1** act of exposing to fresh or warm air. **2** an outing in the open air.

airless /**air**-less/ *adj* stuffy.

airline /**air**-line/ *n* a company providing regular aircraft services.

airliner /**air**-line-er/ *n* a large passenger aircraft.

airmail /**air**-male/ *n* a postal service where mail is carried by aeroplane.

airplane US variant of **aeroplane**.

air pocket /**air** pock-it/ *n* a stream of air that carries an aircraft suddenly up or down.

airport /**air**-port/ *n* a station for passenger aircraft.

air raid /**air** rade/ *n* an attack by aircraft.

airship /**air**-ship/ *n* an aircraft kept aloft by a gas-filled balloon and driven by a motor.

airtight /**air**-tite/ *adj* so sealed that air can pass neither in nor out.

airy /**ay**-ree/ *adj* **1** with plenty of fresh air. **2** lacking seriousness.

aisle /ile/ *n* **1** the side part of a church, often separated from the central part by a row of pillars. **2** a passage in a church. **3** a passageway in a theatre or store.

ajar /a-**jar**/ *adv* partly open.

akimbo /a-**kim**-bo/ *adv* with the hand on the hip and the elbow outward.

akin /a-**kin**/ *adj* similar.

alabaster /a-la-**bas**-ter/ *n* a soft marble-like stone.

alarm /a-**larm**/ *n* **1** a warning of danger. **2** sudden fear. • *vb* to frighten.

alarm clock /a-**larm** clock/ *n* a clock that can be set to ring or buzz to wake you.

alarming /a-**larm**-ing/ *adj* frightening. • *adv* **alarmingly**.

alarmist /a-**larm**-ist/ *n* someone who needlessly spreads frightening news or rumours. • *adj* causing needless fear.

alas /a-**las**/ *interj* a cry of grief or pity.

albatross /**al**-ba-tross/ *n* a large white seabird.

albino /al-**bee**-no/ *n* a person or animal with white skin and hair and pink eyes because he or she has no natural colouring.

album /**al**-bum/ *n* **1** a blank book into which may be put autographs, photographs, stamps, etc. **2** a collection of songs on a CD or other recording.

alcohol /**al**-co-hol/ *n* **1** pure spirit, also called ethanol. **2** an intoxicating drink containing such spirit.

alcoholic /al-co-**hol**-ic/ *n* someone who is addicted to alcohol. • *adj* having to do with alcohol.

alcove /**al**-cove/ *n* a recess, a section of a room, etc, that is set back from the main part.

ale /ale/ *n* a light-coloured, bitter beer.

alert /a-**lert**/ *adj* **1** attentive. **2** quick. • *n* a warning of danger. • *n* **alertness**.

alfalfa /al-**fal**-fa/ *n* a green plant used as cattle food.

algebra /**al**-ji-bra/ *n* a method of calculation in which letters and symbols are used to represent numbers. • *adj* **algebraic**.

alias /**ay**-lee-ass/ *adv* otherwise. • *n* a false name.

alibi /**a**-li-buy/ *n* the plea that you were elsewhere when a crime was committed.

alien /**ay**-lee-an/ *adj* **1** foreign. **2** different, strange. • *n* **1** a foreigner, a person who is not a naturalized citizen of the country where he or she is living. **2** a being from another world.

alienate /**ay**-lee-an-ate/ *vb* to make unfriendly.

alight[1] /a-**lite**/ *vb* **1** to get down (from). **2** to settle upon.

alight[2] /a-**lite**/ *adj*, *adv*, *adj* on fire.

align /a-**line**/ *vb* **1** to put in line, to straighten. **2** to join, ally yourself with. • *n* **alignment**.

alike /a-**like**/ *adj* like, similar. • *adv* in the same way.

alimentary canal /a-li-**men**-tree ca-**nal**/ *n* the passage through the body by which food is received and digested.

alimony /**a**-li-mone-ee/ *n* the money payable regularly by a man or woman to his or her former spouse after legal separation or divorce.

alive /a-**laiv**/ *adj* **1** living. **2** lively. **3** aware of.

alkali /**al**-ka-lie/ *n* a substance such as potash or soda that neutralizes acids and unites with oil or fat to form soap.

all /ol/ *adj* **1** every one of. **2** the whole of. • *n* **1** everyone. **2** everything. • *adv* wholly, entirely.

Allah /a-la, a-**lah**/ *n* the Islamic name for God.

allay /a-**lay**/ *vb* to calm.

allege /a-**ledge**/ *vb* to state without proof. • *n* **allegation**. • *adj* **alleged**.

allegiance /a-**lee**-jance/ *n* loyalty.

allegory /**a**-li-go-ree/ *n* a story with a hidden meaning different from the obvious one. • *adj* **allegorical**.

allegro /a-**le**-gro/ *adv* (*mus*) briskly.

allergy /**a**-ler-jee/ *n* a reaction of the body to some substance. • *adj* **allergic**.

alleviate /a-**lee**-vee-ate/ *vb* to lessen. • *n* **alleviation**.

alley /a-lee/ *n* **1** a narrow walk or passage. **2** a lane for bowling. **3** a building containing lanes for bowling.

alliance /a-lie-anse/ *n* a union between families, governments, etc.

allied *see* **ally**.

alligator /a-li-gay-tor/ *n* a reptile related to the crocodile found in North America, South America and China.

alliteration /a-lit-er-ay-shon/ *n* the repetition of a sound at the beginning of words especially in poetry, for example, 'Peter Piper picked a peck of pickled pepper'.

allocate /a-lo-cate/ *vb* to share out, to distribute. • *n* **allocation**.

allot /a-lot/ *vb* (**allotted, allotting**) to give a share, to distribute.

allotment /a-lot-ment/ *n* **1** act of allotting. **2** a small piece of land for growing vegetables, etc.

allow /al-ow/ *vb* **1** to permit. **2** to provide, to set aside.

allowable /al-ow-a-bl/ *adj* permissible.

allowance /al-ow-anse/ *n* a sum of money granted for a special purpose. • **make allowance for** take into consideration.

alloy /a-loy/ *n* a mixture of metals.

all right /ol rite/ *adj* **1** acceptable or satisfactory. **2** safe or well. • *adv* an expression of agreement.

allude /a-lood/ *vb* to refer to, to mention. • *n* **allusion**. • *adj* **allusive**.

allure /a-loor/ *vb* to attract. • *n* attraction, charm. • *n* **allurement**. • *adj* **alluring**.

allusion *see* **allude**.

ally /a-lie/ *vb* to join with another for a special purpose (e.g. by marriage or by treaty). • *adj* **allied**. • *n* **1** a helper. **2** a nation bound to another by treaty of friendship.

almanac /ol-man-ac, al-man-ac/ *n*, *also* **almanack** (*old*) a book containing a calendar and information about anniversaries, tides, stars and planets, etc.

almighty /ol-mite-ee/ *adj* **1** (*often cap*) all-powerful. **2** (*inf*) very great, strong, loud, etc. • *n* **The Almighty** God.

almond /a-mond/ *n* an oval nut.

almost /ol-most/ *adv* nearly.

aloe /a-loe/ *n* a plant with a bitter juice used in medicines, especially for the skin.

aloft /a-loft/ *adv* high up in the air.

alone /a-lone/ *adj*, *adv* **1** without company. **2** taken by itself.

alongside /a-long-side/ *adv*, *prep* by the side of.

aloof /a-loof/ *adv* apart, distant. • *adj* distant, cool. • *n* **aloofness**.

aloud /a-loud/ *adv* so as can be heard.

alp /alp/ *n* a high mountain.

alphabet /al-fa-bet/ *n* the set of letters used in writing a language. • *adj* **alphabetical**.

alpine /al-pine/ *adj* having to do with high mountains, especially the Swiss Alps.

already /ol-red-ee/ *adv* **1** before this time, previously. **2** now or before the expected time.

altar /ol-ter/ *n* **1** a raised place or table on which sacrifices are offered. **2** a Communion table.

alter /ol-ter/ *vb* to change. • *n* **alteration**.

alternate /ol-ter-nit/ *adj* **1** first one coming, then the other. **2** every other. **3** (*esp US*) alternative. • *vb* **1** to do, use, cause, arrange, etc, by turns. **2** to happen by turns. • *adv* **alternately**. • *n* **alternation**.

alternative /ol-ter-na-tiv/ *n* **1** a choice between two things. **2** (*inf*) a choice of two or more possibilities. • *adj* **1** available, used, etc. instead of something else. **2** not conventional or traditional. • *adv* **alternatively**.

although /ol-tho/ *conj* though.

altitude /al-te-tood/ *n* height.

alto /al-toe/ *n* **1** the highest male singing voice. **2** a low female singing voice, properly called **contralto** /con-**tral**-toe/. **3** a singer having this voice. • *also adj*.

altogether /ol-te-ge-ther/ *adv* **1** wholly. **2** including everything. **3** on the whole.

altruism /al-troo-izm/ *n* acting to please others rather than yourself. • *n* **altruist**. • *adj* **altruistic**.

aluminium /al-yoo-**min**-ee-em/, *also* **aluminum** /al-**oo**-min-em/ (*US*) *n* a soft, white, light metal.

Alzheimer's (disease) /olts-hime-ers/ *n* a brain disease mainly affecting elderly people and causing memory loss and confusion.

always /ol-waze/ *adv* at all times.

am /am/ *vb* the form of the verb **to be** used with 'I'.

a.m. /ay em/ *abbr* = **ante meridiem** /an-tee mer-**id**-ee-um/: a Latin phrase meaning before midday.

AM /ay em/ *abbr* = **amplitude modulation** /am-pli-tyood mod-you-**lay**-shun/: transmitting information via a radio wave.

amalgam /a-mal-gam/ *n* a mixture, especially of mercury with another metal.

amalgamate /a-mal-ga-mate/ *vb* to unite, to join together. • *n* **amalgamation**.

amass /a-mass/ *vb* to collect a large amount of.

amateur /a-ma-ter, a-ma-cher/ *n* **1** someone who takes part in any activity for the love of it, rather than for money. **2** a person without skill or expertise in something. • *n* **amateurism**.

amateurish /a-ma-te-rish, a-ma-che-rish/ *adj* inexpert, unskilful.

amaze /a-maze/ *vb* to astonish. • *n* **amazement**.

ambassador /am-**bass**-sa-dor/ *n* a high-ranking official appointed to represent his or her government in a foreign country. • *adj* **ambassadorial**.

amber /am-ber/ *n* a clear yellowish substance used for ornaments. • *adj* **1** made of amber. **2** brownish yellow.

ambidextrous /am-bi-**dek**-strus/ *adj* able to do things equally well with either hand.

ambiguous /am-**bi**-gyoo-uss/ *adj* having more than one meaning. • *n* **ambiguity**.

ambition /am-**bi**-shen/ *n* **1** desire for power, determination to succeed. **2** a goal, aim. • *adj* **ambitious**.

amble /am-bl/ *vb* to walk at an easy pace. • *n* **1** an easy pace. **2** a slow walk. • *n* **ambler**.

ambulance /am-byoo-lanss/ *n* a vehicle for carrying the sick or injured.

ambush /am-boosh/ *n* **1** a body of people so hidden as to be able to make a surprise attack on an approaching enemy. **2** the place where such people hide. **3** a surprise attack made by people in hiding. • *vb* to lie in wait, to attack from an ambush.

ameba US variant of **amoeba**.

ameliorate /a-**meel**-ye-rayt/ *vb* **1** to make better. **2** to grow better. • *n* **amelioration**.

amen /ay-men, ay-men/ *interj* may it be so!; so be it!

amenable /a-**mee**-na-bl/ *adj* ready to be guided or influenced.

amend /a-mend/ *vb* **1** to correct. **3** to alter slightly. • **to make amends** to make up for a wrong done.

amendment /a-mend-ment/ *n* **1** an improvement. **2** an alteration (e.g. in a law).

amenities /a-**mee**-ne-tees, a-**meh**-ne-tees/ *npl* things that make life easier or more pleasant.

American Indian /a-**me**-ri-can **in**-dee-an/ *n* a native person of the United States or Canada. • *adj* describing the native people of the United States and Canada and their languages, customs, etc.

amethyst /a-me-thest/ *n* a precious stone of a bluish-violet or purple colour.

amiable /ay-mee-abl/ *adj* friendly, pleasant. • *n* **amiability**.

amicable /a-mi-ca-bl/ *adj* friendly.

amid, amidst /a-mid, a-midst/ *prep* in the middle of, among.

amiss /a-miss/ *adv* wrong. • **take amiss** to take offence at.

ammonia /a-mo-nee-a/ *n* **1** a strong-smelling, colourless gas. **2** a solution of ammonia gas and water.

ammunition /am-ye-**ni**-shen/ *n* **1** gunpowder, bullets, shells, etc. **2** facts, etc, used against someone in an argument.

amnesia /am-nee-zha/ *n* loss of memory.

amnesty /am-ne-stee/ *n* a general pardon.

amoeba /a-mee-ba/ *n*, *also* **ameba** (*US*) (*pl* **amoebae, amebae** a tiny living creature found in water. • *adj* **amoebic, amebic**.

among, amongst /a-mung, a-mungst/ *prep* **1** in the middle of. **2** in shares or parts to each person. **3** in the group of.

amorous /a-mo-rus, am-rus/ *adj* feeling or expressing love or sexual desire.

amount /a-mount/ *vb* **1** to add up to. **2** to be equal to. • *n* the sum total.

amp *see* **ampere**.

ampere /am-pir/ *n* the unit used in measuring electric current, usually shortened to **amp**.

ampersand /am-per-sand/ *n* a character (&) that stands for 'and'.

amphibian /am-fi-bee-an/ *n* **1** a creature that can live both on land and in water. **2** a vehicle designed to move over land or water. **3** an aircraft that can take off from or land on either land or water. • *adj* **amphibious**.

amphitheatre /am-fe-thee-e-ter/ *n*, *also* **amphitheater** (*US*) an oval or circular theatre or building in which the seats rise in tiers around and above a central stage or arena.

ample /am-pl/ *adj* **1** large. **2** enough, sufficient, more than enough.

amplification *see* **amplify**.

amplifier /am-ple-fie-er/ *n* an instrument for making sounds louder.

amplify /am-ple-fie/ *vb* **1** to enlarge. **2** to make louder. • *n* **amplification**.

amplitude /am-pli-tood/ *n* size, extent, abundance.

amply /am-plee/ *adv* fully, sufficiently.

amputate /am-pye-tate/ *vb* to cut off. • *n* **amputation**.

amulet /am-ye-let/ *n* an ornament worn as a charm against evils.

amuse /a-myooz/ *vb* **1** to entertain, to give pleasure. **2** to make laugh or smile. • *adj* **amusing**.

amusement /a-myooz-ment/ *n* **1** pleasure, entertainment. **2** entertainment, pastime.

an *see* **a**.

anaconda /a-na-**con**-da/ *n* a large snake of South America.

anaemia /a-nee-mee-a/ *n*, *also* **anemia** (*US*) a condition caused by lack of red corpuscles in the blood, which causes pallor and fatigue.

anaemic /a-nee-mic/ *adj*, *also* **anemic** (*US*) **1** suffering from anaemia. **2** pale, colourless. **3** lifeless, lacking spirit.

anaesthesia /a-ness-**thee**-zha/ *n*, *also* **anesthesia** (*US*) loss of feeling.

anaesthetic /a-ness-**thet**-ic/ *n*, *also* **anesthetic** (*US*) a substance that causes loss of feeling for a time, either in the whole body (**general anaesthetic**) or in a limited area of the body, such as a leg (**local anaesthetic**). • *also adj.* • *vb* **anaesthetize, -ise**, *also* **anesthetize** (*US*).

anaesthetist /a-nes-the-tist/ *n*, *also* **anesthetist** (*US*) a medical doctor specializing in anaesthetics.

anagram /a-na-gram/ *n* a word or words formed by arranging the letters of a word or phrase in a new order (e.g. *mite* from *time*).

analogue /a-na-log/ *n*, *also* **analog** (*US*) an object, e.g. such as a pointer on a dial, used to measure something else.

analogous /a-na-lo-gus/ *adj* similar.

analogy /a-na-lo-jee/ *n* **1** likeness. **2** the process of reasoning based on such similarity.

analyse /a-na-lize/ *vb*, *also* **analyze** (*US*) to break a thing up into its parts or elements.

analysis /a-na-li-siss/ *n* (*pl* **analyses**) **1** the process of analysing. **2** a statement of the results of this. **3** *short for* **psychoanalysis**. • *adj* **analytical**.

analyst /a-na-list/ *n* **1** someone who analyses, especially in chemistry. **2** short for **psychoanalyst**.

analytical *see* **analysis**.

anarchist /a-nar-kist/ *n* who wishes to do away with all government.

anarchy /a-nar-kee/ *n* **1** lawlessness. **2** absence of government.

anathema /a-**na**-the-ma/ *n* **1** a solemn curse. **2** a thing that is accursed or hateful. **3** something or someone that one detests or strongly disapproves of.

anatomy /a-**na**-ta-mee/ *n* **1** the study of the way the body is put together. **2** the cutting up of a body to study its parts and their relation to one another. **3** the body. • *adj* **anatomical**. • *n* **anatomist**.

ancestor /an-sess-tor/ *n* forefather, a person from whom you are descended. • *adj* **ancestral**.

ancestry /an-sess-tree/ *n* line of forefathers.

anchor /ang-kor/ *n* **1** a heavy iron hook that grips the sea bed and holds a ship at rest in the water. **2** a person or thing that provides support, stability or security. • *vb* **1** to hold fast by an anchor. **2** to drop an anchor. • **to weigh anchor** to take up an anchor before sailing.

anchorage /ang-ko-ridge/ *n* a place where a ship can anchor.

anchovy /an-tcho-vee/ *n* a small strong-tasting fish of the herring family.

ancient /ayn-shent/ *adj* **1** old, existing since early times. **2** belonging to old times. **3** (*inf*) very old. • **the ancients** those who lived long ago, especially the Greeks and Romans.

ancillary /ant-si-le-ree/ *adj* supporting, helping, subsidiary.

andante /an-**dan**-tay/ *adj* (*mus*) with slow and graceful movement.

anecdote /a-nec-dote/ *n* a short, interesting or amusing story about a person or event.

anemia US variant of **anaemia**.

anemic US variant of **anaemic**.

anemone /a-ne-me-nee/ *n* the wind-flower, a kind of garden plant with red, purple, or white flowers.

anesthesia US variant of **anaesthesia**.

anesthesiologist US variant of **anaesthetist**.

anesthetic US variant of **anaesthetic**.

anesthetist US variant of **anaesthetist**.

anew /a-**nyoo**/ *adv* (*fml or old*) again, in a new or different way.

angel /ayn-jel/ *n* **1** in Christianity, a spirit created to serve God. **2** a very good and helpful person. • *adj* **angelic**.

anger /ang-ger/ *n* a feeling of rage or fury. • *vb* to enrage.

angina /an-jie-na/ *n* a disease of the heart, causing sudden, sharp pains.

angle¹ /ang-gl/ *n* **1** the space between two meeting lines. **2** a corner. **3** point of view.

angle² /ang-gl/ *vb* **1** to fish with hook and bait. **2** to try to get by indirect means.

angling /ang-gling/ *n* the art of fishing with a rod. • *n* **angler**.

angora /ang-**go**-ra/ *n* wool from a long-haired goat.

angry /ang-gree/ *adj* feeling or showing anger. • *adv* **angrily**.

anguish /ang-guish/ *n* very great pain, of body or mind. • *adj* **anguished**.

angular /ang-gyoo-lar/ *adj* **1** sharp-cornered. **2** thin and bony.

animal /a-ni-mal/ *n* **1** a living being with the

power to feel and to move at will. **2** such a living being other than human beings. **3** a four-footed creature, as distinct from a bird, fish, or insect. **4** a wild or uncivilized person.

animate /a-ni-mate/ *vb* **1** to give life to. **2** to enliven, to make lively and interesting. • *adj* /a-ni-mit/ living.

animation /a-ni-**may**-shun/ *n* liveliness, excitement.

animosity /a-ni-**mo**-si-tee/ *n* strong dislike, hatred.

ankle /**ang**-kl/ *n* the joint that connects the foot with the leg.

annex /a-**neks**, **a**-neks/ *vb*, *also* **annexe 1** to add to the end. **2** to take possession of. • *n* a part added to or situated near a building. • *n* **annexation**.

annihilate /a-**nie**-e-late/ *vb* to destroy completely. • *n* **annihilation**.

anniversary /an-ni-**ver**-sa-ree/ *n* the yearly return of the date on which some event occurred and is remembered.

annotate /**an**-no-tate/ *vb* to write notes upon. • *n* **annotation**.

announce /a-**nounse**/ *vb* to make known. • *n* **announcement**.

announcer /a-**noun**-ser/ *n* in broadcasting, someone who makes known the programmes or reads news items.

annoy /an-**noy**/ *vb* to vex; to tease; to be troubled by something you dislike. • *n* **annoyance**.

annual /**an**-ye-wel/ *adj* **1** yearly. **2** happening every year or only once a year. • *n* **1** a plant lasting only for one year. **2** a book of which a new edition is published yearly. • *adv* **annually**.

anoint /a-**noint**/ *vb* to put oil on, especially with the intention of making holy.

anomaly /a-**nom**-a-lee/ *n* something unusual, irregular or not normal. • *adj* **anomalous**.

anon[1] /a-**non**/ *adv* (*old or hum*) soon.

anon[2] /a-**non**/ *abbr* = **anonymous**.

anonymous /a-**non**-ni-muss/ *adj* nameless, of unknown name. • *n* **anonymity**.

anorak /**an**-o-rak/ *n* **1** a light waterproof jacket with a hood and zip. **2** a person who is so interested in a particular subject that other people regard them as a bore.

anorexia /a-ne-**rek**-see-a/ *n* an eating disorder in which someone refuses to eat in order to lose weight, although already very thin. • *adj* **anorexic**.

answer /**an**-ser/ *vb* **1** to reply to. **2** to be suitable, to fit. **3** to accept blame for or punishment. **4** to be responsible to. • *n* **1** a reply. **2** a solution (to a problem).

answerable /**an**-se-re-bl/ *adj* open to blame for.

answering machine /**an**-se-ring ma-**sheen**/ *n* a machine that records telephone messages while someone is out.

ant /ant/ *n* a small, social insect, that lives in a colony.

antagonism /an-**ta**-ge-nizm/ *n* opposition, ill feeling.

antagonist /an-**ta**-ge-nist/ *n* an opponent.

antagonistic /an-ta-ge-**nis**-tic/ *adj* opposed to, hostile.

antagonize /an-**ta**-ge-nize/ *vb*, *also* **antagonise** to make an enemy of.

antacid /an-**ta**ss-id/ *n* a medicine that makes the stomach less acidic and relieves pain caused by acid.

Antarctic /ant-**arc**-tic/ *adj* of south polar regions. • *n* **the ~** Antarctica, the continent around the South Pole.

anteater /**an**-tee-ter/ *n* a mammal with a long snout that feeds on ants and termites.

antecedent /an-te-**see**-dent/ *adj* (*fml*) going before. • *npl* **antecedents** the previous family, history, etc, of a person.

antelope /**an**-te-lope/ *n* a graceful, delicate animal like the deer.

antenatal /an-ti-**nay**-tal/ *adj* before birth.

antenna /an-**ten**-na/ *n* **1** (*pl* **antennae**) the feeler of an insect. **2** (*esp US*) (*pl* **antennas**) a wire or rod, etc, for receiving radio waves or television signals.

anthem /**an**-thum/ *n* a hymn or song of praise to God.

anthology /an-**tho**-le-jee/ *n* a collection of pieces of poetry or prose by different authors.

anthracite /**ant**-thre-site/ *n* a type of coal that burns almost without flame or smoke.

anthrax /**an**-thraks/ *n* a disease attacking sheep or cattle and sometimes infecting humans.

anthropology /an-thre-**po**-le-jee/ *n* the study of human beings in relation to their surroundings.

anti- /**an**-tie, an-ti/ *prefix* against.

antibiotic /an-ti-bie-**o**-tic/ *n* a substance used in medicine to destroy bacteria that cause disease. • *also adj*.

antibody /**an**-ti-bo-dee/ *n* a protein your body produces to fight infections and illnesses.

anticipate /an-**ti**-si-pate/ *vb* **1** to expect. **2** to take action in advance of. **3** to foresee. • *n* **anticipation**.

anticlimax /an-ti-**clie**-maks/ *n* an unexpectedly dull ending to a striking series of events.

anticlockwise /an-ti-**clock**-wise/ *adj* going

around in the opposite direction from the hands of a clock.

antics /an-tiks/ *npl* absurd or exaggerated behaviour.

antidote /an-ti-dote/ *n* a medicine that counteracts the effects of poison or disease.

antipathy /an-**ti**-pa-thee/ *n* dislike, opposition to.

antiquated /an-te-kway-ted/ *adj* old-fashioned, out of date.

antique /an-**teek**/ *adj* 1 made in an earlier period and usually valuable. 2 (*fml*) connected with ancient times. • *n* a piece of furniture, jewellery, etc, made in an earlier period and considered valuable.

antiquity /an-**ti**-kwe-tee/ *n* 1 ancient times, especially those of the Greeks and Romans. 2 great age.

antiseptic /an-ti-**sep**-tic/ *adj* having the power to kill germs. • *n* an antiseptic substance.

antithesis /an-**ti**-thi-sis/ *n* (*pl* **antitheses**) 1 contrast of ideas, emphasized by similarity in expressing them. 2 the exact opposite. • *adj* **antithetical**.

antler /ant-ler/ *n* a branch of a stag's horn. • *adj* **antlered**.

antonym /an-ti-nim/ *n* a word meaning the opposite of.

anxious /**ang**-shus/ *adj* worried about what will happen or has happened. • *n* **anxiety**.

any /en-ee/ *adj* 1 one out of many. 2 some. 3 every. • *adv* at all.

anybody /en-ee-baw-dee/ *pron* any person.

anyhow /en-ee-how/ *adv* 1 in any way, whatever. 2 in any case.

anyone /en-ee-won/ *pron* any person, anybody.

anything /en-ee-thing/ *pron* any object, event, fact etc. • *n* a thing, no matter what kind. • *adv* at all.

anytime /en-ee-time/ *adv* at any hour, day, week, etc.

anyway /en-ee-way/ *adv* in any case. • *adv* **any way** in any manner.

anywhere /en-ee-ware/ in, at, or to any place.

aorta /ae-or-ta/ *n* the great artery leading from the heart, carrying blood to all parts of the body.

apart /a-**part**/ *adv* separately.

apartheid /a-**part**-hide/ *n* a policy where different races are kept apart.

apartment /a-**part**-ment/ *n* 1 a room. 2 (*esp. US*) a set of rooms rented as a dwelling.

apathy /a-path-ee/ *n* lack of feeling or interest. • *adj* **apathetic**.

ape /ape/ *n* a mammal resembling a tailless monkey (e.g. gorilla, chimpanzee, orangutan, gibbon). • *vb* to imitate exactly.

aperture /a-per-choor/ *n* an opening, a hole.

apex /ay-peks/ *n* (*pl* **apexes** *or* **apices**) the top or highest point.

aphid /ay-fid/ *n* an insect that lives on the sap of green plants.

aphorism /a-for-iz-um/ *n* a short, wise saying.

apiary /ay-pee-ar-ee/ *n* a place where bees are kept.

apiece /a-**peess**/ *adv* to or for each one.

apocalyptic /a-poc-a-**lip**-tic/ *adj* 1 telling of great misfortune in the future. 2 relating to an event of great importance, particularly an event of disastrous or catastrophic importance.

apocryphal /a-**poc**-ra-fal/ *adj* not likely to be genuine; doubtful or untrue.

apologetic /a-pol-o-**je**-tic/ *adj* making excuses, expressing regret.

apologize /a-**pol**-o-jize/ *vb*, *also* **apologise** to express regret for a fault or error, to say you are sorry.

apology /a-**pol**-o-jee/ *n* an admission that wrong has been done, an expression of regret.

apostle /a-**pos**-l/ *n* 1 someone sent to preach the gospel. 2 one of the twelve disciples of Christ.

apostrophe /a-**pos**-tro-fee/ *n* a mark (') indicating the possessive case or omission of certain letters.

appal /a-**pawl**/ *vb*, *also* **appall** (*US*) to shock, to horrify. • **appals**, **appalled**, **appalling** *also* (*US*) **appalls**, **appalled**, **appalling**.

appalling /a-**paw**-ling/ *adj* shocking, terrible, horrific.

apparatus /a-pa-**ra**-tus/ *n* tools or equipment for doing work.

apparel /a-**par**-el/ *n* clothing. • *vb* (*old*) to dress.

apparent /a-pa-rent/ *adj* 1 easily seen, evident. 2 seeming but not necessarily real.

apparently /a-pa-rent-lee/ *adv* evidently, seemingly.

appeal /a-**peel**/ *vb* 1 to make an earnest and strong request for. 2 to carry (a law case) to a higher court. 3 to interest, to please. • *also n*.

appear /a-**peer**/ *vb* 1 to come into sight. 2 to seem. • *n* **appearance**.

appease /a-**peez**/ *vb* 1 to calm, to make peaceful. 2 to satisfy by giving what is wanted. • *n* **appeasement**.

append /a-pend/ *vb* to add, to attach.

appendage /a-**pen**-dige/ *n* 1 something added or attached. 2 something forming a part or attached to something larger or more important.

appendicitis /a-pend-ih-**sie**-tis/ *n* a painful disease of the appendix, requiring surgical removal.

appendix /a-**pen**-diks/ *n* (*pl* **appendixes** *or* **appendices**) **1** information added at the end of a book. **2** in your digestive system, a short, closed tube leading off the bowels.

appetite /a-pe-tite/ *n* desire to have something, especially food or pleasure.

appetizer /a-pe-tize-er/ *n*, *also* **appetiser** something eaten or drunk to stimulate the appetite.

appetizing /a-pe-tize-ing/ *adj*, *also* **appetising** increasing the desire for food.

applaud /a-**plod**/ *vb* **1** to praise by clapping or shouting. **2** to praise. • *n* **applause**.

apple /a-pl/ *n* **1** a tree with many varieties, and pink or white blossom. **2** the sweet fruit of this tree.

appliance /a-**plie**-anse/ *n* an instrument intended for some particular use.

applicable /a-pli-ca-bl/ *adj* that may be applied, suitable under the circumstances. • *n* **applicability**.

applicant /a-**plic**-ant/ *n* someone who asks for, a person who applies for or makes a formal request for.

application /a-pli-**cay**-shon/ *n* **1** the act of applying. **2** a formal request. **3** perseverance, hard work.

apply /a-**ply**/ *vb* **1** to put or spread on. **2** to use. **3** to pay attention (to), to concentrate. **4** to ask for, to put in a formal request for. **5** to concern or be relevant to.

appoint /a-**point**/ *vb* **1** to choose for a job or position. **2** (*fml*) to fix or decide on.

appointment /a-**point**-ment/ *n* **1** a post or position. **2** a meeting arranged for a certain time.

appraisal /a-**prase**-al/ *n* the assessment of the value or quality of.

appraise /a-**prase**/ *vb* to judge the value, quality, ability, etc, of.

appreciable /a-**pree**-sha-bl/ *adj* enough to be noticed. • *adv* **appreciably**.

appreciate /a-**pree**-shee-ate/ *vb* **1** to recognize the value or good qualities of, to enjoy. **2** to understand fully, to recognize. **3** to be grateful for. **4** to rise in value.

appreciation /a-**pree**-shee-**ay**-shon/ *n* **1** a good or just opinion of. **2** gratitude. **3** understanding. **4** increase in value.

appreciative /a-**pree**-sha-tive/ *adj* **1** willing to understand and praise justly. **2** grateful. • *adv* **appreciatively**.

apprehend /a-pre-**hend**/ *vb* (*fml*) to arrest, to seize.

apprehension /a-pre-**hen**-shon/ *n* **1** fear, dread. **2** (*fml*) arrest, seizure. **3** (*fml*) understanding.

apprehensive /a-pre-**hen**-sive/ *adj* afraid of what may happen.

apprentice /a-**pren**-tiss/ *n* someone who is learning a trade or skill while working at it. • *vb* to bind by agreement to serve as an apprentice.

apprenticeship /a-**pren**-tiss-ship/ *n* the time served as an apprentice.

approach /a-**proch**/ *vb* **1** to move nearer (to). **2** to seek an opportunity to speak to someone. • *n* **1** act of approaching. **2** the way leading to a place.

approachable /a-**pro**-cha-bl/ *adj* **1** able to be approached. **2** easy to speak to.

approbation /a-pro-**bay**-shon/ *n* praise, approval.

appropriate /a-**pro**-pree-ate/ *vb* **1** to take and use as your own. **2** to set apart for a particular purpose or use. • *adj* /a-**pro**-pree-it/ suitable. • *adv* **appropriately**. • *n* **appropriation**, **appropriateness**.

approve /a-**proov**/ *vb* **1** to think well of, to accept as good. **2** to agree to, to accept. • *n* **approval**. • **on approval** for a period of trial before purchase.

approximate /a-**prok**-si-mat/ *vb* to come near to. • *adj* nearly correct.

approximately /a-**prok**-si-mat-lee/ *adv* nearly.

approximation /a-prok-si-**may**-shon/ *n* a nearly correct result.

apricot /**ay**-pri-cot, **a**-pri-cot/ *n* an orange-yellow fruit of the peach family.

April /**ay**-pril/ *n* the fourth month of the year.

apron /**ay**-pron/ *n* a garment or cloth worn in front to protect the clothes.

apt /apt/ *adj* **1** suitable, appropriate. **2** ready to learn. **3** having a tendency to.

aptly /apt-lee/ *adv* appropriately.

aptitude /**ap**-ti-tood/ *n* skill, cleverness.

aptness /apt-ness/ *n* suitability.

aquarium /a-**kwa**-ree-um/ *n* (*pl* **aquariums** *or* **aquaria**) a tank for (live) fish and water animals and water plants.

aquatic /a-**kwa**-tic/ *adj* **1** living or growing in water. **2** taking place in water.

aqueduct /**a**-kwi-duct/ *n* **1** a man-made channel for carrying water. **2** a bridge built to carry water.

aqueous /**ay**-kwee-us/ *adj* of or like water, watery.

aquiline /**a**-kwi-leen/ *adj* hooked like the beak of an eagle.

Arabic /a-ra-bic/ *n* a language spoken by people in North Africa and Middle Eastern countries. • *adj* describing the language and the countries in which it is spoken.

Arabic numerals /a-ra-bic nyoo-mer-als/ *n* the numbers 0, 1, 2, 3, 4, 5, 6, 7, 8 and 9.

arable /a-ra-bl/ *adj* suitable for ploughing.

arbiter /ar-bi-ter/ *n* someone chosen by the parties concerned to settle a dispute, an umpire.

arbitrary /ar-bi-tre-ree/ *adj* **1** not decided by rules, laws, etc, but by a person's own opinion. **2** uncontrolled, unrestrained. • *adv* **arbitrarily**.

arbitrate /ar-bi-trate/ *vb* to act as an umpire or referee, especially in a dispute. • *n* **arbitrator, arbitration**.

arbour /ar-bor/ *n, also* **arbor** (*US*) a shady recess in a garden.

arc /ark/ *n* **1** a curve. **2** a part of the circumference of a circle.

arcade /ar-cade/ *n* **1** a covered walk. **2** a covered street containing shops.

arch- /arch/ *prefix* chief.

arch[1] /arch/ *n* a curved structure, usually supporting a bridge or roof.

arch[2] /arch/ *adj* cunning, roguish. • *adv* **archly**. • *n* **archness**.

archaeology /ar-kee-aw-lo-jee/ *n, also* **archeology** (*US*) the study of the remains and monuments of ancient times. • *adj* **archaeological,** *also* **archeological** (*US*). • *n* **archaeologist,** *also* **archeologist** (*US*).

archaic /ar-kay-ic/ *adj* **1** old-fashioned. **2** (*of words*) no longer in current use.

archaism /ar-kay-ism/ *n* a word or expression not in present-day use.

archbishop /arch-bish-op/ *n* a chief bishop, with other bishops under his rule.

archeology US variant of **archaeology**.

archer /ar-cher/ *n* someone who uses a bow and arrow.

archery /ar-cher-ee/ *n* the art of shooting with bow and arrow.

archipelago /ar-ki-pe-la-go/ *n* (*pl* **archipelagos** *or* **archipelagoes**) **1** a sea dotted with many islands. **2** a group of islands.

architect /ar-ki-tect/ *n* **1** someone who plans buildings. **2** someone who plans, designs or creates something.

architecture /ar-ki-tect-choor/ *n* **1** the art or science of planning or designing buildings. **2** a special fashion in building. • *adj* **architectural**.

archives /ar-kives/ *npl* **1** historical records. **2** the place where they are kept. • *n* **archivist**.

arctic /arc-tic/ *adj* very cold.

Arctic /arc-tic/ *adj* of north polar regions.

ardent /ar-dent/ *adj* eager, enthusiastic, passionate. • *adv* **ardently**.

arduous /ar-joo-us/ *adj* difficult, requiring a lot of effort.

are /ar/ *vb* the form of the verb **be** used with 'you', 'we' and 'they'.

area /ay-ree-a/ *n* **1** any open space, place, region. **2** a subject, topic or activity. **3** the extent of a surface.

area code /ay-ree-a code/ *n* a number dialled to identify a particular area when telephoning.

arena /a-ree-na/ *n* **1** an open space of ground for contests or games. **2** area of activity or conflict.

argue /ar-gyoo/ *vb* **1** to give reasons for believing something to be true. **2** to discuss in an unfriendly or quarrelsome way. **3** to quarrel. • *adj* **arguable**.

argument /ar-gyoo-ment/ *n* **1** reasons for holding a belief. **2** a dispute, an unfriendly discussion. **3** a quarrel. **4** a summary of a book.

argumentative /ar-gyoo-men-ta-tive/ *adj* given to discussing or disputing.

arid /a-rid/ *adj* **1** very dry. **2** unproductive, uninteresting. • *n* **aridity**.

arise /a-rise/ *vb* (*pt* **arose**, *pp* **arisen**) **1** to come into being, to appear. **2** to result from. **3** (*old*) to get up.

aristocracy /a-ri-stock-ra-see/ *n* **1** government by the nobility of birth. **2** the nobility.

aristocrat /a-ri-sto-crat/ *n* a person of noble birth. • *adj* **aristocratic**.

arithmetic /a-rith-me-tic/ *n* the science of numbers; the art of working with numbers. • *adj* **arithmetical**.

ark /ark/ *n* **1** a wooden chest. **2 the Ark** in the Old Testament of the Bible, the vessel in which Noah was saved from the Flood.

arm /arm/ *n* **1** one of the upper limbs, the part of the body from the shoulder to the hand. **2** anything resembling this. **3** the part of a garment that covers the arm. **4** power. **5** *pl* **arms** weapons or armour used in fighting. **6** *pl* the badge of a noble family, town, etc. • *vb* **1** to take up weapons. **2** to provide with weapons.

armada /ar-ma-da/ *n* a fleet of armed ships.

armadillo /ar-ma-dil-ow/ *n* a South American animal with a bony protective shell.

armament /ar-ma-ment/ *n* the guns on a ship, tank, etc. • **armaments** *pl* all the weapons used in war.

armistice /ar-mi-stis/ *n* in war, an agreement to stop fighting for a time.

armlet /arm-let/ *n* a band worn round the arm.

armour /ar-mor/ *n, also* **armor** (*US*)
1 protective covering. **2** (*old*) a metal
covering worn by soldiers to protect their
bodies. **3** the tank force of an army.

armoury /arm-ree/ *n, also* **armory** (*US*) a
place for keeping weapons or armour.

armpit /arm-pit/ *n* the hollow under the
shoulder, between the arm and the body.

army /ar-mee/ *n* **1** a large number of soldiers
organized for war. **2** a large number of
persons engaged on a common task.

aroma /a-rome-a/ *n* a pleasant smell.

aromatic /a-rome-at-ic/ *adj* sweet-smelling.

aromatherapy /a-rome-a-ther-a-pee/ *n*
therapy involving the use of aromatic oils,
such as lavender oil.

around /a-round/ *prep* **1** on all sides of or in
a circle, about. **2** here and there, at several
places in. **3** approximately. **4** near to. • *adv*
1 on every side, here and there. **2** in the
surrounding area. **3** available. **4** in the
opposite direction.

arouse /a-rouz/ *vb* **1** to stir up. **2** to make
awake or active.

arrange /a-range/ *vb* **1** to put into order. **2** to
make plans, to make preparations for. • *n*
arrangement.

arrant /a-rant/ *adj* thoroughly (bad), out-
and-out.

arras /a-ras/ *n* a hanging of ornamental cloth
on a wall.

array /a-ray/ *vb* **1** to set in order. **2** to dress
up. • *n* **1** order. **2** dress.

arrears /a-rirz/ *npl* that which remains
unpaid or undone.

arrest /a-rest/ *vb* **1** to take as prisoner,
especially in the name of the law. **2** (*fml*)
to catch or attract. **3** to stop. • *n* **1** the act
of stopping. **2** the act of arresting in the
name of the law.

arrival /a-rive-al/ *n* **1** the act of arriving.
2 someone who arrives.

arrive /a-rive/ *vb* **1** to come. **2** to reach.

arrogant /a-ro-gant/ *adj* proud, haughty. • *n*
arrogance.

arrow /a-ro/ *n* a pointed stick or similar
missile for shooting from a bow.

arrowroot /a-rò-root/ *n* a West Indian plant
from which an edible starch is obtained.

arsenal /ar-snal/ *n* a place where weapons of
war are made or stored, usually on behalf
of a government.

arsenic /ar-snic/ *n* a toxic chemical.

arson /ar-son/ *n* the crime of setting fire to
property on purpose.

art /art/ *n* **1** a particular ability or skill.
2 (*fml*) cunning, trickery. **3** the practice
of painting, sculpture and architecture,
etc. **4** examples of painting, sculpture,
etc. • **the Arts** subjects of study that are
intended to broaden the mind rather than
(or as well as) to teach practical skill.

artery /ar-te-ree/ *n* a tube carrying blood
from the heart.

artful /art-ful/ *adj* deceitful, cunning. • *adv*
artfully.

art gallery /art ga-le-ree/ *n* a public building
where works of art are displayed.

artichoke /ar-ti-choke/ *n* **1** (**globe artichoke**)
a tall plant, somewhat like a thistle, part
of the leaves of which can be eaten.
2 (**Jerusalem artichoke**) a type of sunflower
with edible underground stems.

article /ar-tic-l/ *n* **1** a thing. **2** an essay on
a single topic in a newspaper, periodical,
or encyclopedia. **3** a single item in a list
or statement (e.g. a treaty). **4** *pl* a written
agreement.

articulate /ar-tic-yoo-lit/ *adj* **1** distinct, clear.
2 able to express yourself clearly. • *vb* **1** to
join together. **2** to speak distinctly.

articulation /ar-tic-yoo-lay-shon/ *n* **1** a joint.
2 the act of joining. **3** forming of sounds
in speech.

artifice /ar-ti-fis/ *n* **1** a trick. **2** trickery.

artificial /ar-ti-fish-al/ *adj* **1** man-made and
so not natural. **2** not genuine, unnatural.
• *n* **artificiality**.

artillery /ar-til-ree/ *n* **1** big guns. **2** the part of
an army that cares for and fires such guns.

artisan /ar-ti-zan/ *n* a skilled manual worker.

artist /ar-tist/ *n* **1** a professional painter.
2 one skilled in some art. **3** an artiste.

artiste /ar-teest/ *n* a public entertainer, such
as a professional singer or dancer.

artistic /ar-tis-tic/ *adj* **1** having to do with
art or artists. **2** having or showing love for
what is beautiful.

artistry /ar-tis-tree/ *n* artistic skill.

artless /art-less/ *adj* simple, sincere. • *adv*
artlessly.

asbestos /as-bes-tos/ *n* a soft white mineral
that cannot burn.

ASBO, Asbo /az-bo/ (*UK*) *abbr =* **anti-social
behaviour order**: an order made against a
person who persists in anti-social behaviour.

ascend /a-send/ *vb* (*fml*) **1** to go upward. **2** to
climb.

ascent /a-sent/ *n* (*fml*) **1** act of going up. **2** an
upward slope.

ascribe /a-scribe/ *vb* to explain as the result
of something else.

ash[1] /ash/ *n* a type of forest tree.

ash[2] /ash/ *n or* **ashes** /ash-iz/ *npl* the dust left
after anything has been burned.

ashamed /a-**shaymd**/ *adj* feeling shame.

ashore /a-**shore**/ *adv* on or to land.

ashtray /**ash**-tray/ *n* a small dish for cigarette ash.

aside /a-**side**/ *adv* **1** on one side. **2** to one side, apart.

ask /ask/ *vb* **1** to request. **2** to inquire.

askew /a-**skyoo**/ *adv* to one side, crookedly.

asleep /a-**sleep**/ *adj*, *adv* sleeping.

asp /asp/ *n* a small poisonous snake.

asparagus /a-**spa**-ra-gus/ *n* a plant, the tops of which can be eaten as a vegetable.

aspect /**a**-spect/ *n* **1** (*fml*) appearance. **2** the direction in which a building, etc, faces. **3** a particular part or feature of something.

Asperger's syndrome /as-**per**-gerz **sin**-drome/ *n* a disorder in which people have difficulty with social relationships.

aspen /**a**-spen/ *n* a type of poplar tree.

asphalt /**ass**-folt/ *n* a type of pitch used in road-making.

asphyxiate /ass-**fik**-see-ate/ *vb* to choke, to suffocate. • *n* **asphyxiation**.

aspiration /ass-pi-**ray**-shon/ *n* eager desire, ambition.

aspire /a-**spire**/ *vb* to try very hard to reach (something ambitious, difficult, etc).

aspirin /**a**-sprin/ *n* a drug that relieves pain.

ass[1] /ass/ *n* **1** a long-eared domestic animal of the horse family; also known as a **donkey**. **2** a foolish person.

ass[2] /ass/ *n* (*sl*) the bottom.

assail /a-**sale**/ *vb* (*fml*) to attack.

assailant /a-**sale**-ant/ *n* an attacker.

assassin /a-**sass**-in/ *n* someone who kills by surprise or secretly.

assassinate /a-**sass**-in-ate/ *vb* to murder by surprise or treachery, often for political reasons. • *n* **assassination**.

assault /a-**solt**/ *n* a sudden violent attack. • *vb* to attack.

assay /a-**say**/ *n* a test of the quality of a metal, to find out whether it is pure or an alloy. • *vb* to test the quality, especially of metals.

assemble /a-**sem**-bl/ *vb* **1** to bring or put together. **2** to come together. • *n* **assemblage**.

assembly /a-**sem**-blee/ *n* a gathering of people to discuss and take decisions.

assent /a-**sent**/ *vb* to agree. • *n* consent; permission.

assert /a-**sert**/ *vb* to state firmly. • **assert yourself** to stand up for your rights.

assertion /a-**ser**-shon/ *n* a firm statement.

assertive /a-**ser**-tive/ *adj* confident, tending to assert yourself.

assess /a-**sess**/ *vb* **1** to fix an amount payable. **2** to estimate the value, worth, quality, etc, of. • *n* **assessor**.

assessment /a-**sess**-ment/ *n* the amount or value fixed.

asset /a-**set**/ *n* a help, an advantage.

assets /a-**sets**/ *npl* the entire property of a person or company.

assign /a-**sine**/ *vb* **1** to give as a share, duty, task, etc. **2** to appoint. **3** to fix, to name.

assignment /a-**sine**-ment/ *n* **1** the share or amount (of work, etc) given to a person or group. **2** a piece of homework.

assimilate /a-**sim**-i-late/ *vb* to take in and absorb. • *n* **assimilation**.

assist /a-**sist**/ *vb* to help.

assistance /a-**sis**-tanse/ *n* help, aid.

assistant /a-**sis**-tant/ *n* a helper.

associate /a-**so**-she-ate/ *vb* **1** to keep company with, to join with. **2** to join or connect in the mind. • *n* a companion, a partner, a colleague.

association /a-so-she-**ay**-shon/ *n* **1** act of associating. **2** a group of persons meeting for a common purpose. **3** the bringing together of connected ideas.

assorted /a-**sor**-ted/ *adj* mixed. • **ill-assorted** badly matched.

assortment /a-**sort**-ment/ *n* a mixed collection.

assume /a-**soom**/ *vb* **1** to take for granted. **2** to take over. **3** (*fml*) to put on, to pretend. **4** (*fml*) to take on, to begin to have.

assumption /a-**sum**-shon/ *n* **1** act of assuming. **2** something supposed, but not proved, to be true.

assurance /a-**shoo**-ranse/ *n* **1** confidence. **2** a promise.

assure /a-**shoor**/ *vb* **1** to make certain. **2** to tell as a sure fact, to state positively.

assuredly /a-**shoo**-rid-lee/ *adv* certainly.

aster /**as**-ter/ *n* a flower with the shape of a star.

asterisk /**a**-ster-isk/ *n* a star-shaped mark (*) used in printing.

asthma /**az**-ma/ *n* a disease marked by difficulty in breathing. • *adj* **asthmatic**.

astonish /a-**ston**-ish/ *vb* to surprise greatly, to amaze. • *n* **astonishment**.

astound /a-**stound**/ *vb* to shock with surprise, to surprise greatly.

astral /**a**-stral/ *adj* belonging to the stars.

astray /a-**stray**/ *adv* out of the right way.

astride /a-**stride**/ *adv* with the legs apart or on each side of a thing.

astringent /a-**strin**-jent/ *adj* **1** helping to close open wounds, cuts, or pores. **2** stern, severe. • *n* **astringency**.

astrology /a-strol-o-jee/ *n* the study of the stars in order to learn about future events. • *n* **astrologer.**

astronaut /a-stre-nawt/ *n* a member of the crew of a spaceship.

astronomical /a-stre-**no**-mi-cal/ *adj* **1** connected with astronomy. **2** extraordinarily large.

astronomy /a-**straw**-ne-mee/ *n* the scientific study of the stars. • *n* **astronomer.**

astute /a-styoot/ *adj* clever, shrewd. • *n* **astuteness.**

asylum /a-**sie**-lem/ *n* **1** a place of refuge or safety. **2** (*old*) a home for the care of helpless or mentally ill people.

ate *pt of* **eat.**

atheism /ay-thee-izm/ *n* the belief that there is no God.

atheist /ay-thee-ist/ *n* someone who believes that there is no God. • *adj* **atheistic.**

athlete /ath-leet/ *n* someone good at sports, especially outdoor sports.

athletic /ath-**let**-ic/ *adj* **1** having to do with sport or athletics. **2** physically strong and active.

athletics /ath-**let**-ics/ *npl* **1** sporting activities. **2** competitive athletic events that involve running, jumping or throwing.

atlas /at-lass/ *n* a book of maps.

ATM /ay-tee-em/ *abbr* = **automated/automatic teller machine:** a cash machine that allows you to take money from your bank account using a card and a PIN.

atmosphere /at-mes-fear/ *n* **1** the air surrounding planet Earth. **2** the gas surrounding any star. **3** the air in a particular place. **4** the feelings given rise to by an incident, place, story, etc; mood.

atmospheric /at-mes-**fer**-ic/ *adj* **1** connected with the air. **2** creating a certain atmosphere or mood.

atoll /a-tawl/ *n* a ring-shaped coral island.

atom /a-tom/ *n* **1** the smallest possible particle of an element that can be shown to have the properties of that element. **2** anything very small.

atomic /a-tom-ic/ *adj* connected with atoms.

atomic energy /a-**tom**-ic e-ner-jee/ *n* the power obtained by separating the electrical units in an atom.

atone /a-tone/ *vb* to make up for, to pay for a wrong. • *n* **atonement.**

atrocious /a-tro-shess/ *adj* **1** very cruel or wicked. **2** very bad.

atrocity /a-**traw**-se-tee/ *n* a very cruel act.

attach /a-tach/ *vb* to join (by tying, sticking, etc).

attaché /a-ta-**shay**/ *n* an official at an embassy.

attaché case /a-ta-**shay** case/ *n* a small case for papers, etc.

attached /a-**tachd**/ *adj* **1** joined onto. **2** fond of.

attachment /a-**tach**-ment/ *n* **1** something joined on. **2** fondness.

attack /a-tack/ *vb* **1** to use force against, to begin to fight against. **2** to speak or act strongly against. **3** to begin to deal with vigorously, to tackle. • *also n.* • *n* **attacker.**

attain /a-tane/ *vb* to reach.

attainable /a-**tay**-na-bl/ *adj* able to be reached.

attainment /a-tane-ment/ *n* **1** act of attaining. **2** something, such as a skill or ability, learned successfully.

attempt /a-**tempt**/ *vb* to try to do. • *n* an effort.

attend /a-tend/ *vb* **1** to be present at. **2** to take care of. **3** (*fml*) to fix the mind on. **4** to wait on.

attendance /a-ten-dense/ *n* **1** presence. **2** the persons present.

attendant /a-ten-dent/ *n* **1** someone who waits on another. **2** a servant.

attendee /a-ten-**dee**/ *n* someone who is present.

attention /a-ten-shen/ *n* **1** care. **2** heed, notice. **3** concentration.

attentive /a-ten-tiv/ *adj* giving attention, paying heed.

attest /a-test/ *vb* to bear witness to, to vouch for. • *n* **attestation.**

attic /a-tic/ *n* a room just under the roof of a house.

attire /a-tire/ *vb* to dress. • *n* dress.

attitude /a-ti-tood/ *n* **1** position of the body. **2** way of thinking or behaving.

attorney /a-ter-ney/ *n* (*US*) a lawyer. • **power of attorney** the legal right to act on another's behalf.

attract /a-**tract**/ *vb* **1** to cause to come nearer. **2** to cause to like or desire. **3** to arouse.

attraction /a-tract-shen/ *n* **1** act of attracting. **2** the power to attract. **3** something that attracts.

attractive /a-trac-tiv/ *adj* **1** having the power to attract, interesting, pleasing, etc. **2** good-looking, pretty, handsome.

attributable /a-tri-byoo-ta-bl/ *adj* able to be attributed.

attribute /a-**tri**-byoot/ *vb* **1** to think of as being caused by. **2** to regard as being made, written, etc, by. • *n* **attribute** /a-tri-byoot/ a quality, a characteristic.

attune /a-tyoon/ *vb* to make to agree, bring into harmony.

ATV *abbr* = **all-terrain vehicle**: a vehicle like a motorcycle but with three wheels or more that can be driven over rough ground.

aubergine /oh-ber-dzjine/ *n* a vegetable with a shiny, dark purple skin, often egg-shaped or long and pear-shaped, used in cooking.

auburn /aw-bern/ *adj* reddish brown.

auction /awk-shen/ *n* a public sale at which an object is sold to the person offering the highest price or bid.

auctioneer /awk-she-neer/ *n* the person who conducts the sale at an auction.

audacious /aw-day-shess/ *adj* **1** bold, daring. **2** bold, shameless. • *n* **audacity**.

audible /aw-de-bl/ *adj* able to be heard. • *n* **audibility**.

audience /aw-dee-ense/ *n* **1** the people who listen (e.g. to a speech, concert, etc.). **2** an interview granted by a ruler or person of high authority.

audition /aw-di-shen/ *n* a test given to an actor or musician to see how good he or she is.

auditorium /aw-di-to-ree-um/ *n* the part of a hall open to the audience.

auditory /aw-di-to-ree/ *adj* having to do with the sense of hearing.

augment /awg-ment/ *vb* to increase. • *n* **augmentation**.

august /aw-gust/ *adj* (*fml*) noble, worthy of reverence.

August /aw-gust/ *n* the eighth month of the year.

auk /awk/ *n* a northern sea bird expert at swimming and diving.

aunt /ant/ *n* the sister of someone's mother or father.

au pair /aw pair/ *n* a young person from abroad who helps with childcare and domestic work in exchange for board and a small salary.

aural /aw-ral/ *adj* having to do with the ear or hearing.

aurora /aw-ro-ra/ *n* **1** an atmospheric phenomenon creating waves of light moving across the sky. **2** (*lit*) the dawn.

aurora australis /aw-ro-ra/ *or* **the southern lights** the aurora sometimes seen in the sky around the South Pole.

aurora borealis /aw-ro-ra/ *or* **the northern lights** the aurora sometimes seen in the sky around the North Pole.

auspicious /aw-spi-shess/ *adj* promising future good.

austere /aw-steer/ *adj* **1** simple and severe. **2** stern. **3** plain, without decoration. • *n* **austerity**.

authentic /aw-then-tic/ *adj* true, genuine. • *n* **authenticity**.

authenticate /aw-then-ti-cate/ *vb* to show the authenticity of, to prove genuine.

author /aw-ther/ *n* **1** a writer of books, etc. **2** (*fml*) a person who creates or begins something. • *n* **authorship**.

authoritative /a-tho-re-tay-tiv/ *adj* **1** having or showing power. **2** reliable, providing trustworthy information.

authority /a-tho-re-tee/ *n* **1** the power or right to rule or give orders. **2** a person or group of persons having this power or right.

authorize /aw-the-rize/ *vb*, *also* **authorise** to give to another the right or power to do something.

autism /aw-ti-zum/ *n* a condition in which someone has unusual difficulty in communicating or in relating to other people or the world around him or her. • *adj* **autistic**.

auto- /aw-toe/ *prefix* self.

autobiography /aw-to-bie-aw-gre-fee/ *n* the story of a person's life written by himself or herself.

autograph /aw-to-graf/ *n* a person's own handwriting or signature.

automated/automatic teller machine *see* **ATM**.

automatic /aw-to-ma-tic/ *adj* **1** working by itself. **2** done without thought. • *adv* **automatically**.

automation /aw-to-may-shun/ *n* the act of replacing human labour by machines.

autopsy /aw-top-see/ (*esp US*) *n* an examination of a dead body to discover the cause of death. • *also* **postmortem**.

autumn /aw-tum/ *n* the season between summer and winter. • *also* **fall** (*US*).

autumnal /aw-tum-nal/ *adj* having to do with the autumn.

auxiliary /og-zil-ye-ree/ *n* a person or thing that helps. • *also adj*.

avail /a-vail/ *vb* to make use of. • *n* use, help.

available /a-vail-e-bl/ *adj* at hand if wanted.

avalanche /a-ve-lansh/ *n* **1** a great mass of snow, earth and ice sliding down a mountain. **2** a great amount.

avarice /a-va-riss/ *n* greed for gain and riches. • *adj* **avaricious**.

avenge /a-vendge/ *vb* to take revenge for a wrong. • *n* **avenger**.

avenue /a-ven-yoo/ *n* **1** a way of approach. **2** a broad street. **3** a double row of trees, with or without a road between them.

average /a-ve-ridge/ *n* the figure found by dividing the total of a set of numbers by

the number of numbers in the set. • *adj*
1 calculated by finding the average of
various amounts, etc. **2** ordinary. • *vb* to
find the average.

averse /a-**verse**/ *adj* not in favour of.

aversion /a-**ver**-shen/ *n* **1** dislike. **2** something disliked.

avert /a-**vert**/ *vb* to turn away.

aviary /ay-vee-a-ree/ *n* a place for keeping
birds.

aviation /ay-vee-**ay**-shun/ *n* the science of
flying aircraft.

aviator /ay-vee-ay-tor/ *n* an airman.

avid /a-vid/ *adj* eager, keen. • *n* **avidity.**

avocado /a-ve-**ka**-do/ *n* a pear-shaped fruit
with a hard, dark green skin, soft, pale
green flesh and a large stone, used in
salads, etc.

avoid /a-**voyd**/ *vb* to keep away from. • *adj*
avoidable. • *n* **avoidance.**

await /a-**wate**/ *vb* (*fml*) to wait for.

awake /a-**wake**/ *vb* (*pt* **awoke,** *pp* **awoken**)
1 (*fml*) to rouse from sleep. **2** (*fml*) to stop
sleeping. **3** to stir up, to rouse. • *adj* **1** not
sleeping. **2** aware of, conscious of.

awaken /a-**way**-ken/ *vb* **1** to awake. **2** to rouse.

award /a-**ward**/ *vb* to give after judgment or
examination. • *n* what is awarded, a prize.

aware /a-**ware**/ *adj* **1** having knowledge of,
interested, concerned. **2** conscious of.

awe /aw/ *n* fear mixed with respect or
wonder.

awesome /aw-sum/ *adj* **1** causing awe.
2 (*inf*) excellent, marvellous.

awful /aw-ful/ *adj* **1** very bad or unpleasant,
terrible. **2** (*inf*) very great. **3** (*old or lit*)
causing awe.

awfully /aw-ful-lee/ *adv* (*inf*) very.

awkward /aw-kward/ *adj* **1** clumsy,
unskilled. **2** difficult to use or deal with.
3 inconvenient. • *adv* **awkwardly.**

awoke /a-**woke**/ *pt* of awake. • *pp* **awoken.**

axe /aks/ *n, also* **ax** (*US*) a tool for hewing
or chopping. • *n* **1** to dismiss someone
suddenly. **2** to end or cancel something
suddenly.

axiom /ak-see-em/ *n* a statement accepted
as true without need for proof.

axis /ak-sis/ *n* (*pl* **axes**) the straight line, real
or imaginary, on which a body turns.

axle /aks-l/ *or* **axle-tree** *n* the pole on which
a wheel turns.

Aztec *n* an ancient Mexican Indian people
who created a great civilization.

azure /a-zher/ *adj* sky-blue. • *n* **1** a bright
blue colour. **2** the sky.

B

B, b /bee/ **1** the second letter of the English alphabet. **2** the seventh note of the scale of C major.

babble /ba-bl/ *vb* **1** to make indistinct sounds. **2** to chatter continuously and without making a lot of sense. **3** to make a sound as of running water. • *n* **1** indistinct sounds. **2** foolish chatter. **3** murmur, as of a stream.

babe /babe/ *n* **1** a baby. **2** (*sl*) a pretty young woman.

baboon /ba-**boon**/ *n* a type of large African monkey.

baby /bay-bee/ *n* the young of a person or animal.

babysitter /bay-bee-sit-er/ *n* a person who is paid to look after someone else's children for a short time. • *vb* **babysit**.

bachelor /bach-lor/ *n* **1** an unmarried man. **2** someone who has passed certain university examinations.

back /back/ *n* the part of the body, from the bottom of the neck to the base of the spine. **2** the rear or hind part of something. • *also adj*, *adv*. • *vb* **1** to go or move backward. **2** to support.

backbone /back-bone/ *n* **1** spine. **2** firmness, determination. **3** chief support.

backer /back-er/ *n* a supporter or helper.

backfire /bak-fire/ *n* an explosive noise made by a motor vehicle. • *vb* **1** to explode. **2** (*of a plan*) to go wrong in such a way that it harms its maker.

backgammon /back-ga-mon/ *n* a board game played with counters and dice.

background /back-ground/ *n* **1** the area behind the principal persons in a picture, scene, or conversation. **2** a series of events leading up to something. **3** a person's origins, upbringing, education, etc.

backhand /back-hand/ *n* **1** writing in which the letters slope backward. **2** in tennis, a stroke played with the back of the hand turned outward.

backhanded /back-hand-ded/ *adj* **1** made with the back of the hand. **2** indirect and sometimes with a double meaning.

backpack /back-pack/ *n* a large bag with straps, carried on the back by hikers, etc to hold their luggage. • *vb* to travel from place to place with your belongings in a backpack. • *n* **backpacker**.

backstroke /back-stroke/ *n* in swimming, a stroke where the swimmer floats on his or her back.

backward /back-ward/ *adj* behind others in progress or development. • *variant of* **backwards**. • *n* **backwardness**.

backwards /back-wards/ *or* **backward** *adv* **1** towards the back. **2** in reverse of the usual orientation or order. **3** towards the original starting point.

backwater /back-wat-er/ *n* **1** a piece of water supplied by a river, but away from its current. **2** a remote place, unaffected by modern progress.

backwoods /back-woods/ *npl* land not cleared of forest.

bacon /bay-con/ *n* meat taken from the back and sides of a pig, often salted or smoked.

bacteria /back-**tee**-ree-a/ *npl* (*sing* **bacterium** /bac-**tee**-ree-um/) very tiny living things that are often the cause of disease.

bacteriology /bac-tee-ree-ol-o-jee/ *n* the study of bacteria. • *n* **bacteriologist**.

bad /bad/ *adj* **1** not good. **2** naughty, mischievous. **3** serious. **4** rotten or spoiled. **5** sorry, apologetic. • *adj* **worse**, **worst**.

badge /badge/ *n* something worn as a sign of membership, office, rank, etc.

badger /ba-jer/ *n* a night animal that lives in a burrow. • *vb* to worry, to pester.

badminton /**bad**-min-ton/ *n* a game played with shuttlecocks batted with rackets across a net.

bad-tempered /bad-**tem**-perd/ *adj* frequently cross.

baffle /ba-fl/ *vb* **1** to puzzle, to bewilder. **2** to make someone's efforts useless. • *n* **bafflement**.

bag /bag/ *n* a container for carrying things. • *vb* (**bagged**, **bagging**) **1** to put into a bag. **2** (*inf*) to take possession of. **3** to catch or kill. **4** to hang loosely, to bulge.

bagel /bay-gl/ *n* a ring-shaped bread roll that has a shiny surface.

baggage /ba-gidge/ *n* luggage.

baggy /ba-gee/ *adj* **1** loose. **2** out of shape.

bagpipes /bag-pipes/ *npl* a musical wind instrument in which a bag serves as bellows.

baguette /ba-**get**/ *n* a long crusty loaf of bread.

bail[1] /bale/ *n* **1** someone ready to pay a sum of money to obtain freedom for a person charged with a crime until the day of his or her trial. **2** money paid to release someone from jail, which is lost if the person does not appear for trial. • *vb* **bail out** to help someone out, usually by giving them money.

bail[2] /bale/ *n* a small bar placed on the top of the stumps in cricket.

bail[3] /bale/ *vb* to throw water out of a boat, a little at a time.

bailiff /bay-lif/ *n* an official who takes charge of prisoners when they appear in court.

bait /bate/ *n* **1** food to trap or attract animals or fish. **2** a temptation. • *vb* **1** to put bait on a hook or in a trap. **2** to torment.

bake /bake/ *vb* **1** to dry, to harden by fire. **2** to cook in an oven.

baker /bay-ker/ *n* one who makes or sells bread.

bakery /bay-ker-ee/ *n* a place where bread is made.

baking powder /bay-king pow-der/ *n* a powder, usually containing baking soda and an acid, used instead of yeast in baking to make bakery products rise.

baking soda /bay-king so-da/ *n* another name for the alkaline chemical sodium bicarbonate, or sodium hydrogen carbonate, used in cookery as a raising agent. • *also known as* **bicarbonate of soda**.

balalaika /ba-la-lie-ka/ *n* a type of guitar used in Russia.

balance /ba-lanse/ *n* **1** a pair of weighing scales. **2** equality of weight, power, etc. **3** a state of physical steadiness. **4** a state of mental or emotional steadiness. **5** the difference between the amount of money possessed and the amount owed. • *vb* **1** to make equal. **2** to keep steady or upright. **3** to add up two sides of an account to show the difference between them. • **in the balance** doubtful; about to be decided.

balcony /bal-co-nee/ *n* **1** a railed platform outside a window or along the wall of a building. **2** an upper floor in a hall or theatre.

bald /bawld/ *adj* **1** without hair. **2** bare, without the usual or required covering. **3** plain. • *n* **baldness**.

bald eagle /bawld ee-gl/ *n* an eagle with a brown body and white feathers on its head.

balderdash /bawld-er-dash/ *n* senseless talk, nonsense.

bale /bale/ *n* a large bundle or package.

balk /bawlk/, *also* **baulk** *n* a large beam of timber. • *vb* to stop short of, to be reluctant or unwilling to be involved in.

ball[1] /bawl/ *n* **1** anything round in shape. **2** a round or roundish object used in games. **3** a rounded part of something.

ball[2] /bawl/ *n* a party held for the purpose of dancing. • *n* **ballroom**.

ballad /ba-lad/ *n* **1** a simple poem relating a popular incident. **2** a short, romantic song.

ballast /ba-last/ *n* heavy material carried in a ship or other vehicle to keep it steady.

ball-bearings /bawl-bay-rings/ *npl* small metal balls that help a machine to work more smoothly.

ballerina /ba-le-ree-na/ *n* a female ballet dancer.

ballet /ba-lay/ *n* a performance in which dancing, actions and music are combined to tell a story.

ball game /bawl game/ *n* **1** any game played with a ball. **2** a baseball game. **3** (*inf*) any situation.

ball park /bawl park/ *n* **1** a field where baseball is played. **2 ball park figure** a number that is close to, but not exactly the same as, the correct amount. • **in the right ball park** a figure that is close to the right amount.

balloon /ba-loon/ *n* **1** a small brightly coloured rubber bag that can be blown up and used as a toy or as a decoration at parties, etc. **2** a large bag of light material that floats in the air when filled with air or light gas, with a large basket hanging below for carrying passengers. • *n* **balloonist**.

ballot /ba-lot/ *n* a way of voting secretly by putting marked cards into a box. • *also vb*. • *n* **ballot box**.

ballpoint /bawl-point/ *n* a pen that writes by means of a small rotating ball fed by a tube of ink.

balm /bahm/ *n* **1** a sweet-smelling oil. **2** a pain-relieving ointment. **3** something that heals or soothes.

balmy /bahm-ee/ *adj* gentle, soft.

balsa /bawl-sa/ *n* a tree with light, corky wood.

balsam /bawl-sam/ *n* **1** a flowering plant. **2** a sweet-smelling, healing oil.

bamboo /bam-boo/ *n* a giant tropical reed from which canes, etc, are made.

ban /ban/ *n* an order forbidding something. • *vb* (**banned, banning**) to forbid.

banal /ban-al/ *adj* unoriginal, commonplace; uninteresting. • *n* **banality**.

banana /ba-na-na/ *n* a tropical fruit that is yellow in colour, long and curved.

banana split /ba-na-na split/ *n* a dessert that includes a banana, halved lengthwise, with ice cream, whipped cream, nuts and syrup.

band[1] /band/ *n* **1** anything used to bind or tie together. **2** a strip of cloth round anything.

band[2] /band/ *n* a group of persons united for a purpose, especially to play music together. • *vb* to join.

bandage /ban-dage/ *n* a strip of cloth used in dressing a wound or injury. • *also vb*.

bandanna, bandana /ban-da-na/ *n* a brightly

coloured handkerchief often worn over the head or around the neck.

bandit /ban-dit/ *n* an outlaw, a robber.

bandy[1] /ban-dee/ *vb* **1 to bandy words** to quarrel. **2 to bandy about/around** to mention something.

bandy[2] /ban-dee/, **bandy-legged** /ban-dee leg-(e)d/ *adj* having legs curving outward.

bane /bane/ *n* a cause of ruin or annoyance.

baneful /bane-ful/ *adj* causing harm, hurtful.

bang /bang/ *n* **1** a sudden loud noise. **2** a blow or knock. • *vb* **1** to close with a bang. **2** to hit or strike violently, often making a loud noise. **3** to make a sudden loud noise. • *npl* (*US*) a fringe of hair over the forehead. • *see also* **big bang.**

bangle /bang-gl/ *n* a ring worn around the wrist or ankle.

banish /ban-ish/ *vb* **1** to order to leave the country. **2** to drive away. • *n* **banishment.**

banister /ban-iss-ter/ *n* a post or row of posts supporting a rail at the side of a staircase.

banjo /ban-jo/ *n* a stringed musical instrument played with the fingers.

bank /bangk/ *n* **1** a ridge or mound of earth, etc. **2** the ground at the side of a river, lake, etc. **3** a place where money is put for safekeeping. • *vb* **1** to heap up. **2** to cover a fire with small coal to make it burn slowly. **3** to put money in a bank. **4** to make an aeroplane slope one wing tip down when turning.

banker /bang-ker/ *n* **1** one who runs or manages a bank. **2** one who holds the money staked in gambling games.

banking /bang-king/ *n* the business of a banker.

bankrupt /bang-krupt/ *n* one who is unable to pay his or her debts. • *also adj.* • *n* **bankruptcy.**

banner /ban-ner/ *n* a flag.

banns /bannz/ *n* an announcement in a church or other public place of an intended marriage.

banquet /bang-kwet/ *n* a feast.

banter /ban-ter/ *vb* to poke fun at, to tease. • *also n.*

baptism /bap-tiz-um/ *n* **1** the ceremony by which one is received into the Christian church. **2** a first experience of something, an initiation. • *adj* **baptismal.**

baptize /bap-tize/ *vb*, *also* **baptise 1** to dip in or sprinkle with water during a baptism. **2** to christen or give a name to.

bar /bar/ *n* **1** a solid piece of wood, metal, etc, that is longer than it is wide. **2** a length of wood or metal across a door or window to keep it shut or prevent entrance through it. **3** an obstacle. **4** a bank of sand, etc, at the mouth of a river which hinders entrance. **5** a counter at which food or drink may be bought and consumed. **6** a counter at which alcoholic drinks are served. **7** a place where alcoholic drinks are sold, a public house. **8** the rail behind which a prisoner stands in a courtroom. **9** a division in music. • *vb* (**barred, barring**) **1** to fasten with a bar or belt. **2** to hinder or prevent. **3** to forbid, to ban. • *prep* except.

barb /barb/ *n* **1** one of many sharp points facing in more than one direction. **2** a backward-curving spike on a fish-hook or arrow.

barbarian /bar-bay-ree-an/ *n* **1** an uncivilized person. **2** one who does not respect the arts or learning.

barbaric /bar-ba-ric/ *adj* connected with barbarism.

barbarism /bar-bar-izm/ *n* the state of being uncivilized.

barbarity /bar-ba-ri-tee/ *n* savage cruelty.

barbarous /bar-ba-russ/ *adj* **1** savage, uncivilized. **2** cruel.

barbecue /bar-bi-kyoo/ *n* **1** a framework on which meat, etc, may be cooked over a charcoal fire, usually outside. **2** an outdoor party where food is cooked on a barbecue. • *vb* to cook on a barbecue.

barbed /barbd/ *adj* **1** having a barb or barbs. **2** intended to hurt someone's feelings.

barber /bar-ber/ *n* a man's hairdresser.

bar code /bar code/ *n* a pattern of vertical lines of differing widths, that represent numbers, printed on an item for sale, and containing information, such as the price.

bard /bard/ *n* **1** a Celtic minstrel. **2** a poet.

bare /bare/ *adj* **1** uncovered. **2** empty. **3** naked. • *vb* to uncover, to expose.

barefaced /bare-fayst/ *adj* shameless.

barely /bare-lee/ *adv* **1** only just. **2** scarcely.

bargain /bar-gin/ *n* **1** an agreement about buying and selling. **2** an agreement. **3** something bought cheaply. • *vb* **1** to argue about the price before paying. **2** to make an agreement. • **to bargain for** to expect. • **into the bargain** in addition.

barge /barge/ *n* a flat-bottomed boat for carrying cargoes on inland waters. • *vb* to move clumsily and often rudely.

baritone /ba-ri-tone/ *n* a male singing voice that can go neither very high nor very low.

bark[1] /bark/ *n* the outer covering of a tree. • *vb* to scrape the skin off.

bark[2] /bark/ *n* the noise made by a dog, wolf, etc. • *also vb.*

barley /**bar**-lee/ *n* a grain used for making malt.

barmaid, barman see **barperson**.

bar mitzvah /bar **mits**-va/ *n* a ceremony held on the 13th birthday of a Jewish boy whereby he becomes an adult.

barn /**barn**/ *n* a farm building for the storage of grain, hay, etc.

barnacle /**bar**-ni-cl/ *n* a type of shellfish.

barn dance /**barn** dance/ *n* a country dance.

barometer /ba-**rom**-i-ter/ *n* **1** an instrument for measuring air pressure, thus showing what the weather may be. **2** something that indicates change.

baron /**bar**-on/ *n* a nobleman of the lowest rank. • *f* **baroness**.

baronet /**bar**-on-et/ *n* a titled rank just below that of a nobleman. • *n* **baronetcy**.

barperson /**bar**-per-son/ *n* (*also* **barman**, **barmaid**) someone who serves drinks at a public bar.

barracks /**bar**-aks/ *n pl* a building for housing soldiers.

barracuda /ba-ra-**coo**-da/ *n* a fish with a long body and many sharp teeth.

barrage /**bar**-azh/ *n* **1** a bar across a river to make the water deeper. **2** a concentration of heavy gunfire on a certain area. **3** a large number (of questions, etc.) made rapidly one after the other.

barrel /**bar**-el/ *n* **1** a round wooden cask or container with flat ends and curved sides. **2** the tube of a gun.

barren /**bar**-en/ *adj* **1** producing no fruit or seed. **2** (*old*) unable to produce young, infertile. **3** unable to produce crops. **4** useless, not productive. • *n* **barrenness**.

barricade /ba-ri-**cade**/ *n* a barrier, often temporary and quickly constructed, to prevent people from passing or entering. • *also vb*.

barrier /**bar**-ee-er/ *n* **1** a fence put up to control or restrain. **2** an obstacle or obstruction. **3** something that separates or keeps people apart.

barrister /ba-**ris**-ter/ *n* a lawyer with the right to plead a case in court.

barrow /**bar**-oe/ *n* **1** a small handcart. **2** (*old*) a mound over a grave.

barter /**bar**-ter/ *n* trade by exchange of goods instead of money payments. • *vb* to trade by barter, to exchange.

basalt /bi-**solt**, **bay**-solt/ *n* a dark volcanic rock.

base[1] /**base**/ *n* **1** that on which a thing stands or is built up. **2** the place in which a fleet or army keeps its main stores and offices. **3** a fixed point in certain games. • *vb* **1** to use

as a foundation or grounds. **2** to establish, to place.

base[2] /**base**/ *adj* low, worthless, vile. • *adv* **basely**.

baseball /**base**-bawl/ *n* **1** a game played with bat and ball and two teams of nine players. **2** the ball used in this game.

baseless /**base**-less/ *adj* without foundation, groundless.

basement /**base**-ment/ *n* the ground floor, below ground level.

bash /**bash**/ *vb* to beat, to hit with great force.

bashful /**bash**-ful/ *adj* modest, shy.

basic /**base**-ic/ *adj* **1** providing a foundation or beginning. **2** without more than is necessary, simple, plain.

basin /**base**-in/ *n* **1** a deep broad dish. **2** a hollow place containing water. **3** a dock. **4** the land drained by a river.

basis /**base**-iss/ *n* (*pl* **bases**) that on which a thing is built up, the foundation or beginning.

bask /**bask**/ *vb* **1** to lie in the sun. **2** (*fml*) to enjoy.

basket /**bas**-ket/ *n* a container made of thin sticks or coarse grass plaited together.

bas mitzvah see **bat mitzvah**.

bass[1] /**base**/ *n* **1** the lowest part in music. **2** the lowest male voice.

bass[2] /**bass**/ *n* a type of fish.

bassoon /ba-**soon**/ *n* a musical wind instrument, with low notes only.

baste /**baste**/ *vb* **1** to drip or pour fat on meat while roasting. **2** to sew with long, loose stitches.

bastion /**bas**-chen/ *n* **1** a tower jutting out from the wall of a fort to allow the defenders to aim arrows, bullets, etc, at the flanks of the attackers. **2** a person or thing that provides strong support or defence.

bat[1] /**bat**/ *n* a piece of wood prepared for striking a ball in certain games. • *vb* to use the bat for striking the ball

bat[2] /**bat**/ *n* a flying creature with a body like a mouse and large wings.

batch /**batch**/ *n* **1** a quantity of bread, etc, baked at one time. **2** a set or group.

bath /**bath**/ *n* **1** act of washing the body. **2** a large vessel in which the body is washed, bathtub. **3** a large tank in which one can swim. • *vb* to wash the body in a bath.

bathe /**bathe**/ *vb* **1** to go for a swim. **2** to wash the body in a bath. **3** to apply water to in order to keep clean. • *n* act of swimming or playing in water.

bathtub see **bath 2**.

bat mitzvah /bat **mits**-va/ *n* , *also* **bas mitzvah**

/bas-**mits**-va/ a ceremony for a Jewish girl similar to a **bar mitzvah**.

baton /ba-**ton**/ n **1** a short stick used by the director of a band or choir. **2** a short club carried by policemen as a weapon. **3** a stick passed by one member of a team of runners to the next runner in a relay race.

battalion /ba-**tal**-yen/ n a body of infantry, about 1000 strong.

batten[1] /**ba**-ten/ n **1** a long board or strip of wood. **2** a strip of wood used to fasten down the hatches of ships. • vb to close firmly with battens.

batten[2] /**ba**-ten/ vb. • **to batten on** to live well or thrive by taking advantage of someone else.

batter /**ba**-ter/ vb to beat with violence. • n a mixture of flour and liquid combined for cooking.

battering ram /**ba**-te-ring ram/ n a heavy piece of wood with an iron head formerly used for battering down castle walls or doors.

battery /**ba**-te-ree/ n **1** a group of guns and the people who serve them. **2** a number of connected cells for providing or storing electric current. **3** a violent attack.

battle /**ba**-tl/ n **1** a fight between armies, fleets, etc. **2** a struggle. • vb to fight or struggle.

battlement /**ba**-tl-ment/ n the top wall of a castle, with openings through which weapons can be aimed.

bauble /**baw**-bl/ n a small, worthless ornament or piece of jewellery.

baulk *see* **balk**.

bawl /bawl/ vb to shout or cry loudly. • *also* n.

bay[1] /bay/ adj reddish-brown. • n a bay horse.

bay[2] /bay/ n **1** an inlet of the sea. **2** a recess in a wall.

bay[3] /bay/ n the laurel tree.

bay[4] /bay/ n the bark of a dog, the low cry of a hunting dog. • **to stand at bay** to stop running away and turn to defend oneself. • **to keep at bay** to keep at a safe distance. • vb to give the bark or cry of a dog.

bayonet /**bay**-o-net/ n a weapon, like a dagger, for fixing on to a rifle. • vb to stab with a bayonet.

bay window /bay **win**-doe/ n a window built into a section of the wall that juts out.

bazaar /be-**zar**/ n **1** in the East, a marketplace or group of shops. **2** a sale of articles held to raise money for a special purpose.

BC /bee see/ abbr = **before Christ**: referring to a date occurring before the birth of Jesus Christ.

be /bee/ vb (pr p **being**, pt p **been**) **1** to live. **2** to exist. **3** to have a specified state or quality.

beach /beech/ n the shore of a sea or lake. • vb to run or pull.

beachcomber /**beech**-comb-er/ n **1** in the Pacific, one who lives by what he or she finds on the beach (e.g. pearls, wreckage). **2** a vagrant who lives around harbours or beaches.

beacon /**bee**-con/ n **1** a signal fire. **2** a high hill on which a beacon could be lighted. **3** a signal of danger or hope.

bead /beed/ n **1** a small object, usually round, of glass or other material, with a hole through it for a string. **2** a drop or bubble. **3** pl a rosary.

beady /**bee**-dee/ adj small and bright.

beagle /**bee**-gl/ n a small hunting dog.

beak /beek/ n the bill of a bird.

beaker /**bee**-ker/ n **1** a glass vessel used in scientific experiments. **2** a cup usually with a lip from which to pour or drink liquid.

beam /beem/ n **1** a thick piece of wood. **2** a main timber in a building. **3** the greatest breadth of a ship. **4** a ray of light. **5** radio waves sent out in one particular direction, as a ray. • vb to smile brightly.

bean /been/ n a plant whose seed or seed pod is eaten as a vegetable.

bear[1] /bare/ vb (pt **bore**, pp **borne**) **1** (fml) to carry. **2** to put up with. **3** to support. **4** to have or show. **5** to move. **6** (pp **born**) to bring into existence, give birth to. **7** (pp **borne**) to produce.

bear[2] /bare/ n a wild animal with thick fur and claws.

bearable /**bare**-a-bl/ adj able to be put up with.

beard /beerd/ n the hair on the chin and lower jaw. • vb to defy openly.

bearer /**bare**-rer/ n a carrier.

bearing /**bare**-ring/ n **1** the way a person holds himself or herself or behaves. **2** (usually pl) direction. **3** connection, influence.

beast /beest/ n **1** a four-footed animal. **2** a person who behaves in an animal-like way, a hateful person. • adj **beastly**. • n **beastliness**.

beat /beet/ vb (pt **beat**, pp **beaten**) **1** to strike several times. **2** to defeat or win against. **3** to throb. • n **1** a repeated stroke. **2** a policeman's round. **3** a regular rhythm (e.g. the pulse, a drum).

beau /bo/ n (pl **beaux**) (old or fml) a male sweetheart.

beautify /byoo-ti-fie/ *vb* to make beautiful.

beauty /byoo-tee/ *n* 1 that which is pleasing to the senses. 2 a beautiful woman. 3 (*inf*) a very fine specimen. 4 (*inf*) advantage. • *adj* beautiful.

beaver /bee-ver/ *n* an animal with a wide, flat tail that can live both on land and in water.

because /be-coz/ *conj* a word meaning 'for the reason that'.

beckon /be-kon/ *vb* to make a sign inviting a person to approach.

become /be-come/ *vb* (*pt* became, *pp* become) 1 to come to be. 2 to suit.

becoming /be-come-ing/ *adj* 1 (*fml*) fitting, suitable, appropriate. 2 suiting the wearer.

bed /bed/ *n* 1 a thing to sleep or rest on. 2 the channel of a river. 3 a piece of ground prepared for growing flowers, plants, etc.

bedclothes /bed-cloe(th)z/ *npl* the coverings on a bed.

bedding /bed-ing/ *n* bedclothes.

bedraggled /bi-drag-geld/ *adj* wet and dirty, muddy.

bedridden /bed-rid-n/ *adj* having to stay permanently in bed.

bedrock /bed-rock/ *n* 1 the solid rock underlying the broken rock formations near the earth's surface. 2 basic facts or principles.

bedroom /bed-room/ *n* a room in which to sleep.

bedspread /bed-spred/ *n* a quilt used as a bed covering.

bedstead /bed-sted/ *n* a frame for supporting a bed.

bee /bee/ *n* a flying, honey-making insect.

beech /beech/ *n* a type of tree. • *n* beechnut.

beef /beef/ *n* the flesh of an ox or cow.

beehive /bee-hive/ *n* a place, often dome-shaped, where bees are kept.

beeline /bee-line/ *n* the shortest way. • make a beeline for to go directly and quickly towards.

been *vb, pp* of be.

beer /beer/ *n* an alcoholic drink made from barley and hops.

beeswax /beez-waks/ *n* the wax made by bees for their honeycombs. • *vb* to polish with beeswax.

beet /beet/ *n* a vegetable with an edible root, often cultivated to make sugar, *varieties include* sugar beet, spinach beet and beetroot. • *also* red beet (*US*) beetroot.

beetle[1] /bee-tl/ *n* a common insect. • *vb* (*inf*) to hurry, to scurry.

beetle[2] /bee-tl/ *n* a heavy wooden tool, like a mallet, used to beat such things as paving stones into place.

beetle[3] /bee-tl/ *vb* to jut, to hang over.

beetroot /beet-root/ *n* the root of the beet.

befall /bi-fol/ *vb* (*pt* befell, *pp* befallen) (*fml*) to happen.

befit /bi-fit/ *vb* (befitted, befitting) to suit, to be appropriate for. • *adj* befitting suitable. • *adv* befittingly.

beforehand /bi-fore-hand/ *adv* earlier.

befriend /bi-frend/ *vb* to act as a friend to, to be kind to.

beg /beg/ *vb* (begged, begging) 1 to ask for money or food. 2 to ask earnestly. • to beg the question to take a fact for granted without proving its truth.

beggar /beg-er/ *n* one who begs.

begin /bi-gin/ *vb* (*pt* began, *pp* begun, *prp* beginning) 1 to start. 2 to be the first to do or take the first step in doing.

beginner /bi-gi-ner/ *n* one starting to learn.

begonia /bi-goan-ya/ *n* a plant with brightly coloured flowers.

behalf /bi-half/ *n* 1 interest. 2 benefit. • on behalf of in the name of.

behave /bi-hayv/ *vb* 1 to conduct oneself. 2 to conduct oneself well. 3 to act.

behaviour /bi-hay-vyer/ *n*, *also* behavior (*US*), conduct.

behead /bi-hed/ *vb* to cut off the head.

behold /bi-hold/ *vb* (*pt, pp* beheld) to see; to watch. • *n* beholder.

being /bee-ing/ *n* 1 existence. 2 a thing existing. • *adj* existing, present.

belated /bi-lay-ted/ *adj* too late.

belch /belch/ *vb* to send out forcefully, especially gas through the mouth.

belfry /bel-free/ *n* a bell tower.

belief /be-leef/ *n* 1 faith. 2 trust. 3 opinion.

believe /be-leeve/ *vb* 1 to accept as true or real. 2 to trust. 3 to have faith, especially in God. 4 to think. • *adj* believable. • *n* make-believe pretence.

believer /be-lee-ver/ *n* one who has faith, especially in God.

belittle /bi-li-tl/ *vb* to make to seem small or unimportant.

bell /bell/ *n* 1 a hollow metal vessel that gives a ringing sound when struck. 2 a device that gives a ringing or buzzing sound as a signal of some kind.

belle /bell/ *n* a lady of great beauty.

bellow /bell-o/ *vb* 1 to shout loudly. 2 to roar. • *also n.*

bellows /bell-oez/ *n* or *npl*, *also* a pair of bellows an instrument that makes a draught of air by forcing wind out of an airtight compartment.

belly /bell-ee/ *n* 1 the part of the human body between the breast and thighs. 2 the under part of an animal's body. • vb to bulge out.

belly button /**bel**-lee bu-ton/ (inf) the informal name for the navel.

belong /bi-**long**/ vb **1** to be the property. **2** to be a member. **3** to be connected with.

belongings /bi-**long**-ing-z/ npl the things that are one's own property.

beloved /bi-**luvd**, bi-**luv**-ed/ adj greatly loved. • n one who is greatly loved.

belt /belt/ n **1** a strap or band for putting round the waist. **2** a leather band used to carry the motion of one wheel onto another in a piece of machinery. **3** a space that is much longer than it is broad. **4** an area that has a particular quality or characteristic. **5** (inf) an act of hitting, a blow. • vb **1** to put on a belt. **2** to hit with a strap. **3** to hit, to attack with blows. **4** (inf) to go very quickly. • **below the belt** unfair.

bemused /bi-**myoozd**/ adj confused, bewildered.

bench /bench/ n **1** a long seat. **2** a worktable. **3** the seat of a judge in court. **4** all the judges, as a body.

benchmark /**bench**-mark/ n **1** a mark on a fixed object indicating height. **2** a standard for judging or measuring.

bend /bend/ vb (pt, pp bent) **1** to curve. **2** to make to curve. **3** to incline the body, to stoop. • n **1** a curving turn on a road. **2** an angle.

benediction /be-ne-**dic**-shen/ n blessing. • adj benedictory.

benefactor /**be**-ne-fac-tor/ n one who gives help to another. • f benefactress.

beneficial /be-ne-**fi**-shal/ adj helpful, having a good effect.

beneficiary /be-ne-**fi**-shee-ree/ n **1** one who receives money or property by will. **2** one who benefits from another's kindness.

benefit /**be**-ne-fit/ n **1** advantage, gain. **2** the money to which an insured person has the right when unemployed, ill, etc. • vb **1** to do good to. **2** to be of advantage to.

benevolence /be-**ne**-vol-ense/ n kindness, generosity.

benevolent /be-**ne**-vol-ent/ adj kindly, generous.

benign /bi-**nine**/ adj **1** kindly, gentle. **2** not malignant, not cancerous. • adv benignly.

bent[1] /bent/ pt, pp of bend.

bent[2] /bent/ adj (inf) dishonest.

bent[3] /bent/ n a natural skill in.

bequeath /bi-**kweeth**/ vb to leave by will.

bequest /bi-**kwest**/ n the money or property left by will; a legacy.

berate /bi-**rate**/ vb to scold.

bereave /bi-**reev**/ vb (pt, pp bereaved or bereft) to take away. • n bereavement.

bereaved /bi-**reev**-d/ adj having lost, by death, a near relative. • n one who has lost a relative by death.

bereft /bi-**reft**/ adj having been deprived of something.

beret /be-**ray**/ n a round flat cap with no peak or brim.

berry /**be**-ree/ n a small fruit containing seeds.

berserk /ber-**serk**/ adj uncontrollably angry.

berth /berth/ n **1** the place where a ship lies when at anchor or in dock. **2** a place for sleeping in a ship or train. • vb to moor a ship. • **to give a wide berth to** to keep well clear of.

beseech /bi-**seech**/ vb (beseeched) (fml) to ask earnestly, to beg for. • adv beseechingly.

beset /bi-**set**/ vb (beset, besetting) to attack from all sides.

besiege /bi-**seedge**/ vb **1** to surround a fortress with soldiers in order to bring about its capture. **2** to surround, to crowd round. **3** to overwhelm. • n besieger.

besom /**be**-zom/ n a broom.

besotted /bi-**sot**-ted/ adj silly, muddled.

bespatter /bi-**spat**-ter/ vb to sprinkle (with dirt, etc).

best /best/ adj (superl of good) good in the utmost degree. • vb to do better than, to win against.

bestial /**bes**-chal/ adj like an animal, beastly, disgusting.

bestiality /bes-chee-a-li-tee/ n animal-like behaviour.

bestow /bi-**sto**/ vb (fml) to give (to).

bestride /bi-**stride**/ vb to sit or stand across something, with a leg on either side of it.

bet /bet/ n money put down in support of an opinion, to be either lost or returned with interest, a wager. • vb (bet, betting) to stake money in a bet.

betide /bi-**tide**/ vb (fml or lit) to happen.

betoken /bi-**to**-ken/ vb to be a sign of, to indicate.

betray /bi-**tray**/ vb **1** to give up to an enemy. **2** to be false to, to be a traitor to. **3** to reveal, to show. • n betrayer.

betrayal /bi-**tray**-al/ n act of betraying.

betroth /bi-**troth**/ vb to promise in marriage. • n betrothal /bi-**troth**-al/.

between /bi-**tween**/ prep **1** at or in the space, time, etc, separating. **2** connecting from one to the other.

betwixt /bi-**twikst**/ prep between.

bevel /**be**-vel/ vb (bevelled, bevelling) to cut to a slope. • n a sloping edge.

beverage /**bev**-ridge/ *n* a drink.

bevy /**be**-vee/ *n* **1** a group. **2** a flock of birds.

bewail /bi-**wale**/ *vb* (*fml*) to lament aloud, to regret.

beware /bi-**ware**/ *vb* to be cautious or careful of.

bewilder /bi-**will**-der/ *vb* to puzzle, to confuse. • *adj* **bewildering**. • *n* **bewilderment**.

bewitch /bi-**wich**/ *vb* **1** to put under a spell. **2** to charm, to fascinate.

bewitching /bi-**wich**-ing/ *adj* charming, fascinating.

beyond /bi-**yond**/ *prep* on the farther side of. • *adv* at a distance.

bias /**bie**-ess/ *n* **1** an unreasonable dislike. **2** a preference. **3** in dress-making, a line across the weave of a fabric. • *vb* to incline to one side, to prejudice.

bias(s)ed /**bie**-esst/ *adj* prejudiced.

bib /bib/ *n* a cloth tied under a child's chin to keep him or her clean while eating.

Bible /**bie**-bel/ *n* the Holy Scriptures of the Christian religion. • *adj* **biblical**.

bibliography /bi-blee-**og**-ra-fee/ *n* a list of books dealing with a particular subject. • *n* **bibliographer**. • *adj* **bibliographical**.

bibliophile /**bi**-blee-o-file/ *n* (*fml*) a lover of books.

bicarbonate of soda *see* **baking soda**.

bicentennial /bie-sen-**te**-nee-al/ *n* the 200th year.

biceps /**bie**-seps/ *n* a muscle in the upper part of the arm.

bicker /**bik**-er/ *vb* to quarrel frequently over unimportant things.

bicycle /**bie**-si-cl/ *n* a machine with two wheels that can be ridden on. • *also vb.*

bid /bid/ *vb* (*pt* **bid** *or* **bade**, *pp* **bidden** *or* **bid**, *prp* **bidding**) **1** to offer. **2** to ask, to order. • *n* **1** an offer of money, especially at a sale. **2** a strong effort.

bidder /**bid**-der/ *n* one offering a price.

bide /bide/ *vb* (*old, pt, pp* **bided** *or* **bode**) **1** to dwell. **2** to endure. • **bide one's time** to wait for a good opportunity.

biennial /bie-**en**-ee-al/ *adj* **1** lasting for two years. **2** happening every second year. • *n* a plant that flowers only in its second year, then dies. • *adv* **biennially**.

bier /bir/ *n* a stretcher for carrying a dead body or coffin to the grave.

big *adj* **1** large or great. **2** pregnant. **3** pompous.

big bang /big **bang**/ *n* (*inf*) the name of the theory that the whole universe was created by the explosion of one tiny superdense mass, and that the universe is still expanding. • **big-bang theory**.

bigamy /**bi**-ga-mee/ *n* the state of having two wives or two husbands at the same time. • *n* **bigamist**. • *adj* **bigamous**.

bigot /**bi**-get/ *n* one who accepts without question certain beliefs and condemns the different beliefs held by others. • *adj* **bigoted**. • *n* **bigotry**.

bikini /bi-**kee**-nee/ *n* a two-piece swimsuit for women.

bilateral /bie-**la**-te-ral/ *adj* **1** two-sided. **2** concerning two parties.

bilberry /**bil**-bi-ree/ *n* a small blue berry.

bile /bile/ *n* **1** a fluid, coming from the liver, that aids digestion. **2** (*fml*) anger.

bilingual /bie-**ling**-gwel/ *adj* able to speak two languages.

bilious /**bil**-i-yes/ *adj* **1** relating to bile. **2** sick. • *n* **biliousness**.

bilk /bilk/ *vb* to cheat, to defraud.

bill[1] /bill/ *n* the beak of a bird.

bill[2] /bill/ *n* **1** a note of money owed at a restaurant or bar. **2** the form of a proposed law, as put before government for discussion. **3** (*US*) a piece of paper money. **4** a printed notice. • *vb* **1** to present a note of money owed. **2** to advertise by bills.

billboard /**bill**-board/ *n* a large sign that is pasted with advertisements.

billet /**bill**-let/ *n* a lodging, especially for soldiers. • *vb* to lodge (e.g. soldiers) in people's houses.

billiards /**bill**-yardz/ *n* a game played on a cloth-covered table, with cues and balls.

billion /**bill**-yon/ *n* **1** in America, and often now in Britain, one thousand millions. **2** in Britain, one million millions.

billow /**bill**-low/ *n* a great wave of the sea. • *vb* to swell out. • *adj* **billowy**.

billy goat /**bill**-lee goat/ *n* a male goat.

bin /bin/ *n* **1** a large box for corn, meal, etc. **2** a container for rubbish or litter. • *vb* to throw something away as rubbish.

bind /biynd/ *vb* (*pt, pp* **bound**) **1** to tie. **2** to fasten together. **3** to cover. **4** to put an edging on. **5** (*fml*) to put under an obligation. • **bind oneself** to promise.

binding /**biynd**-ing/ *n* the cover and sewing of a book.

bin man /**bin** man/ *n* a person whose job is to empty rubbish bins.

binoculars /bi-**nok**-ye-lers/ *npl* a pair of field glasses.

biochemistry /bie-o-**ke**-me-stree/ *n* the chemistry of living things. • *adj* **biochemical**. • *n* **biochemist**.

biodegradable /bie-o-di-**gray**-da-bl/ *adj* decaying naturally as the result of the action of bacteria and so not causing pollution to the environment.

biodiversity /bie-o-die-**ver**-si-tee/ *n* the variety of animal and plant life in a particular environment or in the world.

biographer /bie-**og**-re-fer/ *n* a writer of biography.

biography /bie-**og**-re-fee/ *n* the written life story of a person. • *adj* **biographical**.

biology /bie-**ol**-le-jee/ *n* the study of life and living creatures. • *adj* **biological**. • *n* **biologist**.

biotechnology /bie-o-tek-**nol**-o-jee/ *n* the use of living things, such as cells and bacteria, in scientific processes and industrial production.

biped /**bie**-ped/ *n* an animal with two feet.

biplane /**bie**-plane/ *n* an aeroplane with two wings, one above the other, on each side.

birch /berch/ *n* **1** a type of deciduous tree with thin bark. **2** a bundle of sticks tied together at one end and used for flogging.

bird /berd/ *n* a creature with feathers and wings that usually flies.

birth /berth/ *n* **1** the act of being born. **2** the beginning.

birthday /**berth**-day/ *n* the day on which one is born, or its anniversary.

birthmark /**berth**-mark/ *n* a mark on the body from birth.

birthright /**berth**-rite/ *n* any right one possesses by birth.

biscuit /**bis**-ket/ *n* a small, sweet cake, usually either crispy or chewy.

bisect /**bie**-sect/ *vb* (*fml*) to cut into two equal parts.

bishop /**bi**-shep/ *n* **1** in the Roman Catholic Church, Anglican Church, or Eastern Orthodox Church, the chief clergyman of a district. **2** a chess piece.

bison /**bie**-sen/ *n* a type of wild ox.

bit /bit/ *n* **1** a small piece. **2** a piece of. **3** part. **4** a tool for boring holes. **5** the metal bar attached to the bridle and put in the mouth of a horse.

bite /bite/ *vb* (*pt* bit, *pp* bitten) **1** to cut, pierce, etc, with the teeth. **2** to take the bait. • *n* **1** the amount bitten off. **2** the wound made by biting. **3** a taking of the bait by fish.

biting /**bite**-ing/ *adj* **1** sharp. **2** hurtful. • *adv* **bitingly**.

bitter /**bit**-ter/ *adj* **1** sharp to the taste. **2** severe, piercing. **3** painful. **4** feeling or showing hatred, hostility, envy, disappointment, etc. • *n* a beer with a strong, rather bitter taste. • *adv* **bitterly**. • *n* **bitterness**.

bivalve /**bie**-valve/ *n* an animal or fish whose shell is in two parts joined by hingelike cartilage. • *adj* **bivalvular**.

biweekly /bie-**week**-lee/ *adj* **1** happening once every two weeks. **2** twice in one week.

bizarre /be-**zar**/ *adj* strange, peculiar, weird.

black /black/ *n* a dark colour like coal. • *adj* (*sometimes cap*) belonging to a race with dark skin. • *vb* **1** to make black. **2** to clean with black polish. • *n* **blackness**.

blackbird /**black**-berd/ *n* a type of thrush.

blackboard /**black**-board/ *n* a dark-coloured board used for writing on with a light-coloured chalk.

blacken /**black**-en/ *vb* **1** to make black. **2** to become black or dark.

blacklist /**black**-list/ *n* a list of persons suspected of doing wrong.

blackmail /**black**-male/ *vb* to obtain money by threatening to reveal a secret. • *also n.* • *n* **blackmailer**.

blackout /**black**-out/ *n* **1** a sudden putting out of all lights. **2** a period when all lights must be put out or covered. **3** a sudden, short loss of consciousness.

blacksmith /**black**-smith/ *n* a metal-worker who works with iron.

bladder /**bla**-der/ *n* **1** a part of the body in which urine collects. **2** a bag of thin leather, rubber, etc, containing air.

blade /blade/ *n* **1** a leaf (of grass, corn, etc.). **2** the cutting part of a sword or knife. **3** the flat part of an oar.

blame /blame/ *vb* **1** to find fault with. **2** to regard as guilty or responsible. • *n* **1** fault. **2** guilt. • *adj* **blameless, blameworthy**.

blancmange /ble-**mandge**/ *n* a jelly-like milk dessert.

bland /bland/ *adj* **1** so mild as to be almost tasteless. **2** so mild or gentle as to be without personality or emotion.

blank /blank/ *adj* **1** not written on or marked. **2** empty, without expression. • *n* an empty space.

blanket /**blang**-ket/ *n* **1** a woollen, etc, bed covering. **2** a covering. • *vb* to cover.

blare /blare/ *vb* to make a loud sound. • *also n.*

blaspheme /blass-**feem**/ *vb* **1** to speak mockingly or disrespectfully of God. **2** to swear or curse. • *n* **blasphemer**. • *adj* **blasphemous**. • *n* **blasphemy**.

blast /blast/ *n* **1** a sudden, strong gust of wind. **2** a loud sound. **3** an explosion. • *vb* **1** to blow up or break up by explosion. **2** to make a loud noise. **3** (*old or lit*) to cause to wither. **4** to ruin. **5** (*inf*) to criticize severely.

blatant /**blay**-tant/ *adj* very obvious, shameless.

blaze[1] /blaze/ n **1** a bright fire or flame. **2** a bright glow of light or colour. **3** a large, often dangerous, fire. **4** an outburst. • vb **1** to burn brightly. **2** to shine like a flame.

blaze[2] /blaze/ n a mark, especially as made on a tree by cutting off a piece of bark. • vb to show a trail by such marks.

blazer /blay-zer/ n a kind of jacket.

bleach /bleech/ vb **1** to make white or whiter. **2** to become white. • n a substance that bleaches.

bleak /bleek/ adj **1** dreary, cold. **2** not hopeful or encouraging. • n **bleakness**.

bleat /bleet/ vb to cry, as a sheep. • also n.

bleed /bleed/ vb (pt, pp **bled**) **1** to lose blood. **2** to take blood from. **3** (inf) to take money from illegally or dishonestly.

blemish /blem-ish/ n a stain, a fault. • vb to stain; to spoil.

blend /blend/ vb to mix together. • n a mixture.

bless /bless/ vb **1** to pronounce holy. **2** to ask God's favour for.

blessed /blest/ adj **1** holy. **2** happy, fortunate.

blessing /bless-ing/ n **1** a thing that brings happiness. **2** a prayer.

blight /blite/ n **1** a disease in plants that causes them to wither. **2** a cause of ruin. • vb **1** to cause to wither. **2** to ruin.

blind /blinde/ adj **1** having no sight. **2** unable or unwilling to understand. **3** closed at one end. • n **1** a window screen. **2** (inf) a pretence. • vb **1** to make blind. **2** to dazzle. • adv **blindly**. • n **blindness**.

blindfold /blinde-folde/ vb to cover the eyes with a bandage. • also adj.

bling /bling/ n (slang) showy expensive jewellery.

blink /blink/ vb **1** to wink. **2** to twinkle. • n **1** a glimpse. **2** a quick gleam of light.

blinkers /bling-kers/ n a piece of leather put over a horse's eyes to prevent them seeing sideways.

bliss /bliss/ n **1** great happiness. **2** the happiness of heaven.

blissful /bliss-ful/ adj very happy.

blister /bliss-ter/ n a bag of skin containing watery matter. • vb to raise a blister.

blizzard /bli-zard/ n a violent storm of wind and snow.

bloated /blow-ted/ adj blown out, swollen.

blob /blob/ n a drop, a small round mass.

block /block/ n **1** a solid piece of wood, stone, etc. **2** the piece of wood on which people were beheaded. **3** a group of connected buildings. **4** a piece of wood in which a pulley is placed. **5** an obstacle. • vb to stop the way.

blockade /block-ade/ n the surrounding of a place with soldiers and/or ships to prevent people and food from going in or leaving. • also vb.

blockhead /block-hed/ n a stupid fellow.

blog /blog/ n short for **weblog**, a website on which someone regularly gives information about their personal experiences, opinions and interests.

bloke /bloke/ (inf) n a man.

blond /blond/ adj having fair hair and skin. • f **blonde**. • also n.

blood /blud/ n **1** the red liquid in the bodies of people and animals. **2** family or race.

bloodhound /blud-hound/ n a large dog often used in tracking.

bloodless /blud-less/ adj **1** without blood or killing. **2** pale, anaemic. **3** without spirit or energy.

bloodshed /blud-shed/ n the spilling of blood, slaughter.

bloodshot /blud-shot/ adj (of the eye) red and inflamed with blood.

bloodthirsty /blud-thur-stee/ adj eager to shed blood, taking pleasure in killing.

blood vessel /blud-vess-l/ n a vein or artery.

bloody /blud-ee/ adj **1** bleeding, covered with blood. **2** stained with blood. **3** with a lot of wounding or killing.

bloom /bloom/ n **1** a blossom, a flower. **2** the state of flowering. **3** freshness, perfection. • vb to blossom.

blot /blot/ n **1** a spot or stain, often of ink. **2** disgrace. **3** something that spoils something beautiful or good. • vb (**blotted**, **blotting**) **1** to spot, to stain, especially with ink. **2** to dry ink with blotting paper.

blotch /blotsh/ n a large spot or mark.

blouse /blouse/ n a loose upper garment.

blow[1] /blo/ vb (pt **blew**, pp **blown**) **1** to cause air to move. **2** to breathe hard. **3** to pant. • vb **blow up 1** to fill with air. **2** to destroy by explosives.

blow[2] /blo/ n **1** a stroke. **2** a misfortune.

blow[3] /blo/ vb (pt **blew**, pp **blown**) to bloom.

blowlamp /blo-lamp/ n a lamp producing heat by a rush of air.

blowy /blo-ee/ adj (inf) windy.

blubber /blub-er/ n the fat of whales, etc. • vb (**blubbered**, **blubbering**) to weep noisily.

bludgeon /blud-zhen/ n a short club. • vb to strike repeatedly with something heavy.

blue /bloo/ n a primary colour, as that of the sky on a clear day. • also adj.

bluebell /bloo-bel/ n **1** the harebell. **2** in Scotland, the wild hyacinth.

blueberry /bloo-ber-ee/ n a round, sweet blue berry grown on a bush.

bluebottle /**bloo**-botl/ *n* a large bluish fly.

blue jeans /**bloo** jeenz/ *n* trousers made of blue denim material.

blueprint /**bloo**-print/ *n* **1** a photographic print of a plan for a structure. **2** a detailed plan or scheme.

bluff /bluf/ *n* **1** a cliff, a steep headland. **2** a pretence. • *adj* frank and abrupt but good-natured. • *vb* to try to deceive by a show of boldness.

blunder /**blun**-der/ *vb* **1** to make a foolish mistake. **2** to stumble about or into something. • *also n*.

blunt /blunt/ *adj* **1** not sharp. **2** short and plain in speech. **3** outspoken. • *vb* **1** to make less sharp. **2** to weaken.

blur /blur/ *n* **1** an indistinct mass. **2** a stain, a blot, a smear. • *vb* (**blurred, blurring**) to make unclear.

blurb /blurb/ *n* a short description of something written to promote it.

blurt /blurt/ *vb* to speak suddenly or thoughtlessly.

blush /blush/ *vb* to become red in the face from shame, modesty, etc. • *n* the reddening of the face so caused. • *adv* **blushingly**.

bluster /**blust**-er/ *vb* **1** (*of wind*) to blow violently. **2** to talk boastfully, noisily or threateningly. • *n* boastful, noisy or threatening talk.

boa /**boe**-a/ *n* **1** a snake that kills by crushing its victim. **2** a scarf of fur or feathers.

boa constrictor /**boe**-a con-**stric**-ter/ *n* a type of boa snake.

boar /bore/ *n* **1** a male pig. **2** a wild pig.

board /bored/ *n* **1** a long, broad strip of timber. **2** food. **3** a group of people who meet, for example, for business reasons. **4** the deck of a ship. **5** *pl* the stage. **6** a flat surface, often marked with a pattern, on which certain games are played. • *vb* **1** to cover with boards. **2** to supply with food and accommodation. **3** to take meals, and usually have accommodation, in. **4** to enter a ship. **5** to get on to.

boarder /**bore**-der/ *n* one who receives food and lodging at an agreed price.

boarding house /**bore**-ding house/ *n* a house where food and lodging may be obtained.

boarding school /**bore**-ding skool/ *n* a school in which pupils live as boarders.

boast /boste/ *vb* **1** to speak with too much pride about oneself or one's belongings, etc. **2** to possess. • *n* proud speech; a proud claim.

boastful /**boste**-ful/ *adj* fond of or given to boasting.

boat /bote/ *n* **1** a ship, especially a small one. **2** a dish shaped like a boat. • *vb* to go in a boat. • *n* **boatman**.

boatswain /**boe**-sun/ *n* a petty officer on board ship.

bob /bob/ *vb* **1** to move quickly up and down. **2** to cut hair short. • *also n*.

bobbin /**bob**-in/ *n* a pin or cylinder around which thread is wound, a reel.

bode /bode/ *vb* to foretell, to be an omen of. • **bode ill** *or* **well** to be a bad *or* good sign of future events.

bodice /**bod**-iss/ *n* **1** a woman's tight-fitting, sleeveless garment worn on the upper body. **2** the upper part of a woman's dress.

bodily /**bod**-il-ee/ *adj* having to do with the body. • *adv* by taking hold of the body.

bodkin /**bod**-kin/ *n* **1** an instrument, like a needle, for piercing holes. **2** a blunt needle with a large eye for threading tape through a hem.

body /**bod**-ee/ *n* **1** the physical structure of a human being or animal. **2** the main part of anything. **3** a group of persons. **4** a dead body, a corpse.

bodyguard /**bod**-ee-gard/ *n* a guard to protect a person from attack.

body piercing /**bod**-ee **peer**-sing/ *n* the piercing of part of the body, such as the lip or nose, in order to insert a ring or stud.

bog /bog/ *n* soft, wet ground, a marsh.

bogey, bogy /**boe**-gee/ *n* **1** (*also* **bogeyman**) a goblin, an imaginary evil spirit. **2** an object of fear. **3** in golf, one stroke over par on a hole.

bogie /**boe**-gee/ *n* **1** a four-wheeled truck supporting the front of a railway engine. **2** a low truck.

bogus /**boe**-gus/ *adj* not genuine, sham.

bogy *see* **bogey**.

bohemian /boe-**hee**-mee-an/ *n* anyone who pays little heed to the customs or conventions of the time.

boil[1] /boil/ *vb* **1** to bubble from the action of heat. **2** to cook in boiling water. • *n* **boiler**.

boil[2] /boil/ *n* a painful swelling containing pus.

boisterous /**boy**-struss/ *adj* **1** stormy. **2** noisy and cheerful.

bold /bolde/ *adj* **1** daring, brave. **2** large and clear.

boldness /**bolde**-ness/ *n* courage.

bole /bole/ *n* the trunk of a tree.

boll /bole/ *n* a seed-container, as of the cotton or flax plant.

bollard /**bol**-ard/ *n* a short, thick post used to prevent vehicles from going on part of a road.

boll weevil /**bole** wee-vil/ *n* an insect that destroys cotton bolls.

bolster /**bole**-ster/ *n* a long pillow. • *vb* to hold up, to support.

bolt /**bolte**/ *n* **1** an arrow. **2** a thunderbolt. **3** a bar of a door. • *vb* **1** to fasten with a bolt. **2** to run away. **3** to eat too quickly.

bomb /**bom**/ *n* a hollow metal missile containing explosive, gas, etc. • *vb* **1** to attack with bombs. **2** (*inf*) to go very quickly.

bombard /**bom-bard**/ *vb* **1** to fire many guns at. **2** to direct many questions, statements of criticism, etc, at. • *n* **bombardment**.

bombshell /**bom**-shell/ *n* a very surprising piece of news, often bad news.

bonbon /**bon**-bon/ *n* (*fml*) a sweet.

bond /**bond**/ *n* **1** that which binds. **2** a written agreement, especially to pay money. **3** (*fml*) *pl* chains, fetters.

bondage /**bon**-dage/ *n* slavery.

bone /**bone**/ *n* **1** the hard substance forming the skeleton of human beings and animals. **2** any one of the pieces of this. • *vb* to take out the bones from.

bonfire /**bon**-fire/ *n* a large, open-air fire.

bonk /**bongk**/ (*inf*) to have sex with.

bonnet /**bon**-et/ *n* **1** a headdress. **2** the hinged front part of a car that covers the engine.

bonny /**bon**-ee/ *adj* **1** pretty. **2** healthy-looking.

bonus /**boe**-nus/ *n* an extra payment, made for a special effort or services.

bony /**boe**-nee/ *adj* **1** having many bones. **2** having protruding bones.

booby /**boo**-bee/ *n* a stupid person.

booby prize /**boo**-bee prize/ *n* a prize given to the worst performer.

booby trap /**boo**-bee trap/ *n* a trap hidden in a place so obvious that no one suspects it.

book[1] /**book**/ *n* printed matter, bound between covers.

book[2] /**book**/ *vb* to reserve in advance.

bookish /**boo**-kish/ *adj* fond of reading or study.

bookkeeper /**book**-kee-per/ *n* one who keeps accounts. • *n* **bookkeeping**.

bookmaker /**book**-may-ker/ *n* (*also inf*) **bookie** /**boo**-kee/) one who makes his or her living by accepting and paying out on bets.

bookworm /**book**-wurm/ *n* one who reads a great deal.

boom[1] /**boom**/ *n* **1** a long pole to stretch the bottom of a sail. **2** a barrier set up across a harbour entrance or river.

boom[2] /**boom**/ *n* a long deep sound. • *also vb*.

boom[3] /**boom**/ *n* a time of rapid increase or growth. • *vb* to increase or grow quickly.

boomerang /**boo**-me-rang/ *n* a curved throwing stick that returns to the thrower, used by Australian Aboriginals. • *vb* (*of an action, plan, etc.*) to go wrong in such a way that harm or damage is caused to the person responsible.

boon /**boon**/ *n* **1** (*old*) a favour, a special request. **2** an advantage, a blessing.

boor /**boor**/ *n* a rough, ill-mannered person. • *adj* **boorish**.

boot /**boot**/ *n* **1** a covering for the foot and lower leg. **2** the compartment to the rear of a car used for carrying luggage. • *vb* to kick.

booth /**booth**/ *n* **1** a tent at a fair. **2** a covered stall at a market. **3** a small, enclosed structure.

booty /**boo**-tee/ *n* **1** goods seized and divided by the victors after a battle. **2** goods taken by thieves. **3** (*slang*) the human bottom.

booze /**booz**/ *n* (*inf*) alcoholic drink.

border /**bor**-der/ *n* **1** the outer edge of anything. **2** the boundary between two countries. **3** a flowerbed round a lawn, etc. • *vb* to be next to. • **border** (**up**)**on** to come close to.

bore[1] /**bore**/ *vb* to make a hole in. • *n* **1** the hole made by boring. **2** the greatest breadth of a tube, especially of a gun.

bore[2] /**bore**/ *vb* to weary by uninteresting talk, etc. • *n* a person whose talk is wearisome. • *adj* **boring**.

bore[3] /**bore**/ *n* a large tidal wave.

bored /**board**/ *adj* weary and dissatisfied with one's circumstances.

boredom /**bore**-dom/ *n* the state of being bored.

born /**born**/ *pp of* **bear**, sense 6.

borne /**born**/ *pp of* **bear**, senses 1–5, 7.

borrow /**bor**-o/ *vb* to ask or receive as a loan. • *n* **borrower**.

bosom /**boo**-zum/ *n* **1** the breast. **2** (*lit or fml*) the heart, considered as the seat of desires and feelings. • *adj* close, well-loved.

boss[1] /**boss**/ *n* a knob.

boss[2] /**boss**/ *n* (*inf*) a master, a manager(ess). • *vb* **1** to be in charge. **2** to order about.

bossy /**boss**-ee/ *adj* (*inf*) fond of ordering others about.

botany /**bot**-(a)-nee/ *n* the science or study of plants. • *adj* **botanic**, **botanical** /bo-**ta**-nic-al/. • *n* **botanist** /**bot**-a-nist/.

bother /**baw**-ther/ *vb* **1** to annoy. **2** to trouble oneself. • *n* **1** a trouble, an inconvenience. **2** trouble.

Botox /boe-tox/ *n* (*TM*) a drug used in medicine to relax muscles and in beauty treatment to reduce wrinkles.

bottle /baw-tl/ *n* **1** a container, usually of glass, with a narrow neck. **2** (*inf*) courage, boldness. • *vb* to put into bottles.

bottleneck /baw-tl-neck/ *n* **1** a narrow or busy part of a road where traffic has to slow down or stop. **2** something that slows down progress.

bottom /bot-um/ *n* **1** the lowest part. **2** the buttocks. • *adj* lowest. • *adj* **bottomless**.

botulism /boch-oo-liz-um/ *n* a dangerous form of food poisoning.

boudoir /boo-dwar/ *n* (*fml*) a lady's private room.

bough /ba-oo/ *n* (*fml*) the branch of a tree.

bought /bot/ *pt of* **buy**.

bouillon /bool-yon/ *n* a strong broth.

boulder /bole-der/ *n* a large smooth stone.

boulevard /boo-le-vard/ *n* a wide street, with trees planted along either side.

bounce /bounse/ *vb* to jump or rebound suddenly. • *also n*.

bouncer /boun-ser/ *n* (*inf*) a door supervisor; a security person employed at a nightclub to exclude or remove unwanted customers.

bouncing /boun-sing/ *adj* big, strong.

bound[1] /bound/ *n* a limit or boundary beyond which one must not go. • *vb* to form a limit or boundary.

bound[2] /bound/ *vb* to jump, to leap. • *also n*.

bound[3] /bound/ *adj* **1** on the way to. **2** (*pt of* **bind**). **3** obliged. **4** sure. **5** tied. **6** covered.

boundary /boun-dar-ee/ *n* **1** an outer limit. **2** a border.

boundless /bound-less/ *adj* without limit, endless.

bountiful /boun-tee-ful/ *adj* (*fml*) giving generously.

bounty /boun-tee/ *n* (*fml*) **1** generosity, kindness. **2** a gift of money above what is earned.

bouquet /boo-kay/ *n* **1** a bunch of flowers. **2** perfume of wine.

bout /bout/ *n* **1** a period of action. **2** an attack (of illness). **3** a contest.

boutique /boo-teek/ *n* a small shop selling fashionable clothes.

bovine /boe-vine/ *adj* **1** of or like a cow. **2** slow and stupid.

bow[1] /bow/ *vb* **1** to bend, especially in respect or greeting. **2** to lower. • *n* a bending of the head or body in respect or greeting.

bow[2] /boe/ *n* **1** a weapon for shooting arrows. **2** a looped knot. **3** a stick for playing a stringed instrument (e.g. the violin).

bow[3] /bow/ *n* the curved front part of a ship.

bowed /bode/ *adj* bent, stooping.

bowels /ba-wels/ *npl* **1** the inside of the body, the intestines. **2** the organ by means of which waste matter is expelled from the body.

bowie knife /baoo-wee nife/ *n* a long curved hunting knife.

bowl[1] /bole/ *n* a roundish dish or basin.

bowl[2] /bole/ *n* **1** a heavy, wooden ball. **2** *pl* the game played with such balls. • *vb* **1** to play bowls. **2** to deliver the ball at cricket.

bowlegged /boe-le-ged/ *adj* having legs wide apart at the knees.

bowler[1] /boe-ler/ *n* one who bowls.

bowler[2] /boe-ler/, **bowler hat** *n* a stiff felt hat with a rounded crown, also known as a **derby** in the US.

bowline /boe-lin, boe-leen/ *n* **1** a rope on a sailing ship. **2** a knot that does not slip.

bowling /boe-ling/ *n* a game where you attempt to knock down 10 pins by rolling a large, heavy ball down an alley.

bow tie *n* /boe tie/ a tie, tied in the shape of a bow, usually for formal occasions.

bow window /bow win-doe/ *n* a window built into a section of wall that curves out and back.

box[1] /boks/ *n* a type of hardwood tree.

box[2] /boks/ *n* **1** a case or container. **2** in a theatre, a separate compartment with seats, overlooking the stage. • *vb* to put in a box.

box[3] /boks/ *vb* **1** to strike. **2** to fight in sport, wearing padded gloves. • *n* **boxer**.

boxing /bok-sing/ *n* the sport of fighting with padded gloves on.

Boxing Day /bok-sing day/ *n* the day after Christmas Day.

box room /boks room/ *n* a storage room in a house.

boy /boy/ *n* **1** a male child. **2** a young male person. • *n* **boyhood**.

boycott /boy-cot/ *vb* to refuse to have any dealings with. • *also n*.

Boy Scout /boy scout/ *n* formerly the name given to a member of an international youth organization for boys, now **Scout**.

bra /bra/ *n abbr* = **brassiere** /bra-zeer/: underwear worn by women to support the breasts.

brace /brase/ *n* **1** a support. **2** a pair or a couple. **3** a boring tool. **4** (*pl*) elastic straps for holding up trousers. **5** (*often* **braces**) a wire device used to straighten the teeth. • *vb* to steady or prepare oneself.

bracelet /brase-let/ *n* an ornament for the wrist.

bracing /bray-sing/ *adj* giving strength.

bracket /bra-ket/ *n* **1** a support for something fixed to a wall. **2** *pl* marks in printing to enclose a word, as {}, //, (), or <>. • *vb* **1** to enclose in brackets. **2** to link or connect.

brag /brag/ *n* a boast. • *vb* (**bragged, bragging**) to boast.

braid /brade/ *vb* to twist together into one. • *n* **1** a plait of cords or of hair so twisted together. **2** a narrow edging of decorated tape.

braided /bray-did/ *adj* edged with braid.

Braille /bray-el/ *n* a system of printing for blind people in which the letters of the alphabet and numbers are printed as raised dots that can be read by touching them.

brain /brane/ *n* **1** the soft matter within the skull, the centre of the nervous system. **2** *pl* cleverness, intelligence. **3** (*inf*) someone very clever or intelligent. • *vb* to dash the brains out.

brainless /brane-les/ *adj* stupid.

brainy /bray-nee/ *adj* (*inf*) clever.

brake[1] /brake/ *n* **1** a fern. **2** a clump of bushes or undergrowth.

brake[2] /brake/ *n* **1** a large wagon. **2** an apparatus for slowing or stopping a vehicle. • *vb* to apply the brake.

bramble /bram-bl/ *n* **1** a prickly bush, especially the blackberry bush. **2** the berry from this bush.

bran /bran/ *n* the husks of grain when separated from the flour.

branch /branch/ *n* **1** a shoot growing out of the trunk or one of the boughs of a tree. **2** any connected part of a larger body (e.g. office, store, bank, etc.). • *vb* to divide into branches. • **branch out 1** to begin something new. **2** to expand.

brand /brand/ *n* **1** (*fml*) a burning piece of wood. **2** a mark made with a hot iron to identify cattle, etc. **3** a trademark, a special make of article. **4** variety. • *vb* **1** to mark with a hot iron. **2** to mark down.

brandish /bran-dish/ *vb* to wave, to shake.

brandy /bran-dee/ *n* a strong, alcoholic drink made from wine.

brass /brass/ *n* **1** an alloy of copper and zinc. **2** (*inf*) impudence. • *adj* **brassy**.

brassiere *see* **bra**.

brat /brat/ *n* an ill-mannered child.

bravado /bre-va-do/ *n* pretended courage, boastful talk.

brave /brave/ *adj* courageous, daring. • *vb* **1** to defy. **2** to face with courage. • *n* a North American Indian warrior.

bravery /bray-ve-ree/ *n* courage, daring.

brawl /brawl/ *vb* to quarrel noisily. • *n* a noisy row. • *n* **brawler**.

brawn /brawn/ *n* muscle, strength.

brawny /braw-nee/ *adj* muscular, strong.

bray /bray/ *vb* to make a loud, harsh sound, as an ass. • *also n*.

brazen /bray-zen/ *adj* **1** made of brass. **2** impudent, bold. • *vb* to face boldly and impudently.

breach /breech/ *n* **1** act of breaking. **2** (*fml*) a gap. **3** a fault. **4** a quarrel, separation. • *vb* to make a gap or opening in.

bread /bred/ *n* a food made from flour or meal and baked.

breadth /bredth/ *n* the distance from side to side, width.

breadwinner /bred-win-er/ *n* the person whose earnings supply the needs of the family.

break /brake/ *vb* (*pt* **broke**, *pp* **broken**) **1** to separate into two or more parts, usually by force. **2** to become unusable or in need of repair. **3** to tame. **4** to fail to keep. **5** to tell gently. **6** to go with force. **7** to do better than. • *n* **1** an opening. **2** a separation. **3** a pause. **4** a short rest. • *adj* **breakable**.

breakage /brake-idge/ *n* **1** a breaking. **2** the thing broken.

breaker /bray-ker/ *n* a wave broken by rocks.

breakfast /brek-fast/ *n* the first meal in the day. • *vb* to eat breakfast.

breakthrough /brake-throo/ *n* an important new development.

breakwater /brake-wa-ter/ *n* a wall to break the force of the waves.

breast /brest/ *n* **1** (*fml*) the front part of the body from the neck to the stomach, the chest. **2** each of the milk-producing glands in a female. • *vb* **1** to face. **2** to touch. **3** to come to the top of.

breastplate /brest-plate/ *n* armour for the breast.

breath /breth/ *n* **1** the air taken into and put out from the lungs. **2** a gentle breeze.

breathe /breethe/ *vb* **1** to take air into one's lungs and put it out again. **2** (*fml*) to live. **3** (*fml*) to whisper.

breathless /breth-less/ *adj* **1** out of breath, panting. **2** excited, eager. • *adv* **breathlessly**.

breech /breech/ *n* **1** the back part of a gun barrel. **2** *pl* **breeches** trousers that fasten just below the knee.

breed /breed/ *vb* (*pt, pp* **bred**) **1** to produce young. **2** to keep. **3** to be the cause of. • *n* a type, variety, species.

breeding /bree-ding/ *n* **1** the bearing of offspring. **2** good manners.

breeze /breez/ n a light wind.

breezy /bree-zee/ adj 1 windy. 2 lively. • adv **breezily**.

brethren /breth-ren/ npl (old or relig) brothers.

brevity /bre-vi-tee/ n (fml) shortness.

brew /broo/ vb 1 to make beer. 2 to make tea. 3 to be about to start. • n the mixture made by brewing. • n **brewer**.

brewery /broo-e-ree/ n a factory where beer is made.

briar see **brier**.

bribe /bribe/ n a reward offered to win favour or preference unfairly. • vb to win over by bribes. • n **bribery**.

bric-a-brac /bri-ke-brak/ n small ornaments.

brick /brick/ n 1 a block of baked clay. 2 (inf) a good or helpful person.

brickbat /brick-bat/ n a piece of criticism.

bricklayer /brick-lay-er/ n one who builds with bricks.

bridal /bride-al/ adj concerning a bride or a wedding.

bride /bride/ n a woman about to be married, or newly married.

bridegroom /bride-groom/ n a man about to be married, or newly married.

bridesmaid /brides-made/ n a girl or woman who attends the bride at a wedding.

bridge[1] /bridge/ n 1 a roadway built across a river, etc. 2 the small deck for a ship's captain. 3 the piece of wood that supports the strings of a violin, etc. • vb 1 to build a bridge over. 2 to close a gap or a pause so as to make a connection.

bridge[2] /bridge/ n a card game.

bridle /bride-il/ n 1 the head straps and metal bit by which a horse is guided. 2 a check. • vb 1 to put a bridle on. 2 to check. 3 to toss the head in anger, etc. 4 to show anger or indignation.

brief /breef/ n a summary of an argument, especially a law case for use in court. • adj short. • vb to provide with a summary of the facts.

briefcase /breef-case/ n a case for carrying papers.

brier, briar /brie-er/ n a thorn bush, the wild rose.

brigade /bri-gade/ n an army unit consisting usually of three battalions.

brigadier /bri-gad-ir/ n an officer commanding a brigade.

brigand /bri-gand/ n (old) a member of a band of robbers.

bright /brite/ adj 1 shining. 2 strong, vivid. 3 lively, cheerful. 4 clever. • n **brightness**.

brighten /brie-ten/ vb to make or become bright.

brill /bril/ n a type of flatfish.

brilliant /bril-yant/ adj 1 sparkling. 2 very bright. 3 very clever. 4 excellent. • n a diamond. • n **brilliance, brilliancy** /bril-yan-see/.

brim /brim/ n 1 the rim. 2 the edge.

brimful /brim-ful/, **brimming** /brim-ing/ adj full to the brim.

brimstone /brim-stone/ n sulphur.

brindled /brin-duld/ adj marked with streaks.

brine /brine/ n salt water. • **the briny** the sea.

bring /bring/ vb (pt, pp **brought**) 1 to fetch, to carry. 2 to cause. • **bring about** to cause to happen. • **bring off** to succeed. • **bring up** 1 to rear, to educate. 2 to raise.

brink /bringk/ n 1 the edge of a steep place. 2 the edge, the point.

brisk /brisk/ adj keen; lively. • adv **briskly**. • n **briskness**.

brisket /briss-ket/ n a cut of meat from the breast of an animal.

bristle /briss-el/ n a short, stiff hair. • vb to stand on end.

bristly /briss-(u)-lee/ adj having bristles, rough.

brittle /bri-tl/ adj hard but easily broken.

broach /broach/ vb 1 (fml) to open up. 2 to begin to speak of.

broad /brawd/ adj 1 wide. 2 not detailed, general. 3 (of speech) with a strong local accent. • n **broadness**.

broadcast /brawd-cast/ vb (pt, pp **broadcast**) 1 to make widely known. 2 to send out by radio or television. 3 to scatter widely. • also n.

broaden /braw-den/ vb to make or become broad or broader.

broad-minded /brawd-mine-ded/ adj 1 ready to listen to and consider opinions different from one's own. 2 liberal.

brocade /bro-kade/ n a silk cloth with a raised pattern.

broccoli /broc-o-lee/ n a green vegetable.

brochure /broe-shoor/ n a small book, a pamphlet.

broke pt of **break**.

broken pp of **break**.

broker /bro-ker/ n 1 one who buys and sells for others for a commission. 2 a stockbroker.

bronchial /brong-kee-al/ adj having to do with the bronchi, the branches of the windpipe to the lungs.

bronchitis /bronk-eye-tis/ n an illness affecting the windpipe to the lungs.

bronco, broncho /brong-co/ n a half-tamed horse.

brontosaurus /bron-to-**saw**-rus/ *n* a very large plant-eating dinosaur.

bronze /bronz/ *n* **1** an alloy of copper and tin. **2** a reddish brown colour. • *vb* to give or become a reddish brown colour.

brooch /broach/ *n* an ornamental pin.

brood /brood/ *vb* **1** to sit on eggs. **2** to think deeply or anxiously about. • *n* **1** children. **2** a family of young birds.

broody /brood-ee/ *adj* **1** hatching eggs. **2** badly wanting to have children.

brook[1] /brook/ *n* a small stream.

brook[2] /brook/ *vb* (*fml*) to bear, to tolerate.

broom /broom/ *n* **1** a plant with yellow flowers. **2** a brush, especially one of twigs.

broomstick /broom-stick/ *n* the handle of a broom.

broth /brawth/ *n* a meat soup with vegetables.

brother /bru-ther/ *n* (*pl* **brothers** *or old or relig*, **brethren** /breth-ren/) **1** a son of the same parents. **2** a member of the same group.

brotherhood /bru-ther-hood/ *n* **1** the relation of a brother. **2** a group with one common purpose.

brotherly /bru-ther-lee/ *adj* of or like a brother.

brought /braw-t/ *pp*, *pt of* **bring**.

brow /braoo/ *n* **1** the forehead. **2** the jutting-out edge of a cliff or hill.

browbeat /braoo-beet/ *vb* to bully.

brown /braoon/ *adj* of a dark colour. • *also n*. • *vb* to make or become brown.

brownie /braoo-nee/ *n* **1** a small, rich, chocolate cake, usually square, with nuts. **2** a kindly fairy. **3** a junior member of the Guides Association.

browse /braooz/ *vb* **1** to feed upon. **2** to glance through a book.

bruise /brooz/ *n* a dark spot on the skin, caused by a knock. • *vb* to cause a bruise on.

brunette /broo-net/ *n* a woman with dark brown hair.

brunt /brunt/ *n* the main force or shock of something, the worst effects.

brush /brush/ *n* **1** an instrument for cleaning, sweeping, or smoothing. **2** an instrument for putting paint on to something. **3** the tail of a fox. **4** small trees and bushes. **5** a short battle. **5** (*inf*) a slight disagreement or hostile encounter. • *vb* **1** to clean with a brush. **2** to touch lightly.

brushwood /brush-wood/ *n* **1** small trees and bushes. **2** a thicket.

brusque /brusk/ *adj* blunt, rude and abrupt in speech or manner. • *adv* **brusquely**. • *n* **brusqueness**.

Brussels sprout /brus-sel sprout/ *n* a small, round, green vegetable like a very small cabbage.

brutal /broo-tal/ *adj* cruel, savage.

brutality /broo-ta-li-tee/ *n* cruelty, savagery.

brute /broot/ *n* **1** an animal. **2** (*inf*) a cruel person.

bubble /bu-bul/ *n* a film of water or other liquid, containing air. • *vb* to form bubbles. • *adj* **bubbly**.

buccaneer /bu-ca-neer/ *n* a pirate.

buck /buck/ *n* **1** a male deer, goat, rabbit, etc. **2** (*old*) a dandy, a lively young man. **3** (*inf*) a dollar. • *vb* to jump straight up with the back arched.

bucket /bu-ket/ *n* a vessel for carrying water, a pail.

buckle /bu-kl/ *n* a fastener for joining the ends of a belt or band. • *vb* **1** to fasten. **2** to bend out of shape.

buckskin /buck-skin/ *n* a soft leather.

bud /bud/ *n* a leaf or flower before it opens. • *vb* (**budded, budding**) to put out buds.

Buddhist /boo-dist/ *n* a person who believes in the religious teaching of Buddha. • *n* **Buddhism**.

budding /bu-ding/ *adj* promising.

budge /budge/ *vb* (*inf*) to move, to stir.

budgerigar /bu-je-ree-gar/ *n* a type of small parrot that can be trained to talk.

budget /bu-jet/ *n* **1** a statement of government taxation and intended spending for the coming year. **2** a plan to ensure that household expenses or those of a firm or organization will not be greater than income. • *vb* **1** to make such a plan. **2** to allow for something in a budget.

buff /buf/ *n* **1** a type of leather. **2** a pale dull yellow colour. • *adj* light yellow.

buffalo /buf-a-lo/ *n* (*pl* **buffalos** *or* **buffaloes**) a type of ox.

buffer /buf-er/ *n* an apparatus to lessen the force of a collision or shock.

buffet[1] /bu-fay/ *n* **1** a sideboard. **2** a counter or bar at which refreshments may be obtained. **3** a meal, often cold, set out on tables so that people can help themselves.

buffet[2] /buf-et/ *n* (*fml*) a blow, a slap. • *vb* **1** to strike. **2** to knock about.

buffoon /bu-foon/ *n* **1** a clown. **2** a person who plays the fool.

bug /bug/ *n* **1** a blood-sucking insect. **2** any insect. **3** (*inf*) an infection. **4** (*inf*) a hidden microphone used to record other people's conversations secretly. **5** a defect or error in a computer program or system. • *vb* (**bugged, bugging**) **1** to install or use a hidden microphone in. **2** (*inf*) to annoy.

bugle /byoo-gul/ *n* a small brass instrument like a trumpet. • *n* **bugler**.

build /bild/ *vb* (*pt*, *pp* **built**) to put together materials in order to make something; to construct. • *n* **builder**.

building /bild-ing/ *n* the thing built.

bulb /bulb/ *n* 1 the round root of certain flowers. 2 a pear-shaped glass globe surrounding the element of an electric light.

bulbous /bul-bus/ *adj* bulb-shaped, swollen.

bulge /bulge/ *n* a swelling. • *vb* to swell out. • *adj* **bulgy**.

bulimia /boo-lee-mee-ya/ *n* an eating disorder in which bouts of over-eating are followed by bouts of vomiting in order to lose weight. • *adj* **bulimic**.

bulk /bulk/ *n* 1 the size, especially of large things. 2 the main part. • **in bulk** in a large quantity. • *vb* to make fuller, to increase in size. • **bulk large** (*fml*) to be important or prominent.

bulkhead /bulk-hed/ *n* an inside wall between one part of a ship or aeroplane and another.

bulky /bul-kee/ *adj* very large and awkward to move or carry.

bull[1] /bool/ *n* 1 the male of cattle. 2 the male ox, elephant, whale, etc.

bull[2] /bool/ *n* a ruling by the pope.

bulldog /bool-dog/ *n* a type of dog.

bulldozer /bool-doe-zer/ *n* a heavy tractor for clearing away obstacles and making land level.

bullet /boo-let/ *n* a small piece of metal shot from a rifle or pistol.

bulletin /boo-le-tin/ *n* 1 a short, official report of news. 2 a printed information sheet or newspaper.

bulletproof /boo-let-proof/ *adj* not able to be pierced by bullets.

bullfrog /bool-frog/ *n* a large frog.

bullion /bool-yon/ *n* uncoined gold and silver in lumps.

bulls-eye /boolz-eye/ *n* 1 the centre of a target. 2 a shot that hits it. 3 a type of candy.

bully /boo-lee/ *n* a person who uses his or her strength to hurt or to terrify those who are weaker. • *vb* to intimidate, oppress, or hurt.

bulrush /bool-rush/ *n* a tall weed.

bum /bum/ (*inf*) *n* a person's bottom, the buttocks.

bumblebee /bum-bel-bee/ *n* a large type of bee.

bump /bump/ *n* 1 a heavy blow, or the dull noise made by it. 2 a lump caused by a blow. • *vb* to knock against. • *adj* **bumpy**.

bumper /bum-per/ *n* 1 (*old*) a full glass or cup. 2 a protective bar at the front and the back of an automobile. • *adj* unusually large or full.

bumptious /bum(p)-shus/ *adj* conceited, too full of oneself.

bun /bun/ *n* 1 a small cake or bread roll. 2 hair styled in a rounded mass.

bunch /bunch/ *n* 1 a group or collection of things of the same kind. 2 (*inf*) a group of people. • *vb* to come or put together in groups or bunches.

bundle /bun-del/ *n* a collection of things tied together. • *vb* 1 to tie in a bundle. 2 to force to go in a hurry.

bungalow /bung-ga-loe/ *n* a low house usually of one storey.

bungee jumping /bun-jee jum-ping/ *n* the act of jumping from a high place while the ankles are secured by an elastic cord.

bungle /bung-gul/ *vb* to do badly or clumsily. • *also n*.

bunion /bun-yon/ *n* a swelling on the foot, especially on the big toe.

bunk /bungk/ *n* 1 a narrow bed, especially in a ship. 2 one of a pair of beds placed one above the other.

bunker /bung-ker/ *n* 1 a ship's coal store. 2 a large chest for storing coal. 3 an indentation full of sand in a golf course.

bunny /bu-nee/ *n* (*inf*) a rabbit.

bunting /bun-ting/ *n* 1 a material used for making flags. 2 flags.

buoy /boy/ *n* an object floating in a fixed position to show ships the safe course. • *vb* 1 to keep afloat. 2 to support, to keep high. 3 to raise the spirits of.

buoyant /boy-ant/ *adj* 1 floating, able to float easily. 2 cheerful, optimistic. • *n* **buoyancy**.

bur, burr /bur/ *n* the prickly seed container of certain plants.

burden /bur-den/ *n* 1 a load. 2 the chorus of a song. 3 the leading idea. • *vb* to load heavily. • *adj* **burdensome**.

bureau /byoo-ro/ *n* (*pl* **bureaux** *or* **bureaus**) 1 a writing desk with drawers. 2 an office.

bureaucracy /byoo-rok-ra-see/ *n* 1 a system of government by paid officials working for a government. 2 these officials taken as a group. 3 a system of doing things officially, often unnecessarily complicated and time-consuming.

burger *n see* **hamburger**.

burglar /bur-glar/ *n* a thief who breaks into a house.

burglary /bur-gla-ree/ *n* the crime of breaking into a house.

burgle /bur-gul/ *vb* to commit burglary.

burial /ber-ee-al/ *n* the act of putting into a grave.

burlap /bur-lap/ a course material used in making sacks.

burlesque /bur-lesk/ *n* a comic or mocking imitation, a parody, a caricature. • *also adj and vb.*

burly /bur-lee/ *adj* stout, big and strong.

burn /burn/ *vb* (*pt, pp* **burned** *or* **burnt**) 1 to be alight, to give out heat. 2 to be on fire. 3 to destroy or damage by fire. 4 to hurt or injure by fire. 5 to be very hot. 6 to feel great anger, passion, etc. • *n* a hurt caused by fire.

burner /bur-ner/ *n* the part of a stove, etc, from which the flame comes.

burnish /bur-nish/ *vb* to polish. • *also n.*

burr *see* **bur**.

burrow /bu-ro/ *n* a hole in the earth made by certain animals, e.g. rabbits, foxes, etc. • *vb* 1 to make by digging. 2 to search for something.

burst /burst/ *vb* (*pt, pp* **burst**) 1 to break in pieces. 2 to rush, to go suddenly or violently. • *n* a sudden outbreak.

bury /ber-ee/ *vb* 1 to put into a grave. 2 to put under ground.

bus /bus/ *n* a large road vehicle for carrying passengers (short for **omnibus**). • *vb* (**bussed, bussing**) to transport by bus).

bush /boosh/ *n* 1 a small low tree. 2 wild, uncleared country; forest country.

bushel /boo-shel/ *n* a dry measure (35.3 litres) for grain, etc.

bushy /boo-shee/ *adj* 1 full of bushes. 2 thick-growing.

business /biz-nis/ *n* 1 one's work or job. 2 trade and commerce. 3 a matter that concerns a particular person. • *adj* **businesslike**.

bust /bust/ *n* 1 a statue showing only the head, shoulders and breast of a person. 2 the shoulders and breast.

bustle[1] /bu-sel/ *vb* to move about busily and often fussily. • *n* noisy movement, hurry.

bustle[2] /bu-sel/ *n* a frame or pad once worn to hold out the back of a woman's skirt.

busy /bi-zee/ *adj* 1 always doing something. 2 at work, engaged in a job, etc. 3 full of people, traffic, etc. • *vb* to occupy. • *adv* **busily**.

busybody /bi-zee-bod-ee/*n* one who shows a lot of interest in the affairs of others, a meddler.

butcher /boo-cher/ *n* 1 one who kills and sells animals for food. 2 a cruel killer. • *vb* 1 to kill for food. 2 to kill cruelly.

butchery /boo-che-ree/ *n* cruel slaughter.

butler /but-ler/ *n* the chief manservant in a household, formerly in charge of the wine cellar.

butt[1] /but/ *n* 1 a large barrel. 2 the thicker end of a thing. 3 a cigarette end. • *vb* to strike with the head or horns.

butt[2] /but/ *n* 1 a mark to be shot at. 2 the mound behind the targets for rifle practice. 3 a person who is always being made fun of.

butter /but-er/ *n* a spread made from milk.

buttercup /but-er-cup/ *n* a common yellow wild flower.

butterfly /but-er-flie/ *n* 1 an insect with large colourful wings. 2 a frivolous unreliable person.

buttermilk /but-er-milk/ *n* the liquid that remains after butter has been made.

butterscotch /but-er-scotch/ *n* a hard toffee.

button /but-on/ *n* 1 a knob or disc to fasten one part of a garment to another. 2 something shaped like a button, especially a knob or switch on an electrical appliance. • *vb* to fasten with buttons.

buttonhole /but-on-hole/ *n* 1 a hole for a button. 2 a flower worn in a buttonhole. • *vb* to stop and hold in conversation.

buy /bye/ *vb* (*pt, pp* **bought**) to obtain by paying for.

buyer /bye-yer/ *n* 1 one who buys. 2 one whose job is to buy goods.

buzz /buz/ *n* a humming noise. • *also vb.*

buzzard /bu-zard/ *n* a type of hawk.

by /bye/ *prep* 1 next to. 2 by the means of. 3 through the work of. 2 past.

by and by /bye an bye/ *adv* soon. • *n* **by-and-by** a future occasion or time.

bye /bye/ *n* 1 in cricket, a run made from a ball that is not hit. 2 in a competition, a pass without contest into the next round.

bye-law *see* **bylaw**.

by-election /bye-e-lec-shun/ *n* an election held when the person elected at a general election has resigned or has died.

bygone /bye-gon/ *adj* (*fml*) past.

bylaw, by-law /by-law/ *n* a law made by a local body and applying to the area in which the body has authority.

by-product /by-prod-uct/ *n* something made in the course of making a more important article.

bystander /bye-stan-der/ *n* an onlooker, a spectator.

byte /bite/ *n* the unit of storage in a computer memory.

byway /bye-way/ *n* a side road.

C

C, c /see/ n **1** the third letter of the English alphabet. **2** (*mus*) the first note of the scale of C major.

cab /cab/ n **1** a taxi. **2** (*old*) a horse carriage for public hire. **3** the driver's part of a railway engine or truck.

cabaret /ca-ba-ray/ n a form of light entertainment consisting of songs and dancing, usually performed in a nightclub or restaurant.

cabbage /ca-bidge/ n a common vegetable with edible leaves formed into a bud.

cabin /ca-bin/ n **1** a small, simple house, a hut. **2** a room on a ship for passengers to stay in. **3** the space available for passengers or crew on an aircraft. **4** the covered part of a yacht.

cabinet /cab-net/ n **1** a display case. **2** a piece of furniture with drawers. **3** a case or container for a radio, television, etc. **4** (*cap*) the chief ministers in a government.

cable /cay-bl/ n **1** a strong rope, often of wire. **2** a chain attached to a ship's anchor. **3** an undersea or underground telegraph or telephone line. **4** a bundle of electric wires enclosed in a pipe. **5** a message sent by cable. **6** cable television. • *vb* to send a message by cable, sense 3.

cablegram /cay-bl-gram/ n a more formal name for cable, sense 5.

cable television /cay-bl te-le-vi-zhon/ n a television service that is supplied using underground cables.

cacao /ca-kaow/ n a tropical tree that bears seeds from which chocolate and cocoa are made.

cackle /ca-kl/ n **1** the shrill, broken sound of a hen or goose. **2** noisy chatter. **3** loud unpleasant laughter. • *also vb*.

cacophony /ca-cof-u-nee/ n (*fml*) loud, unpleasant mixture of different sounds. • *adj* cacophonous.

cactus /cac-tus/ n (*pl* cacti /cac-tie/) a desert plant with fleshy stems, reduced or prickly leaves and often bright, colourful flowers.

CAD *abbr* = computer-aided design.

cadet /ca-det/ n **1** someone training in the armed forces. **2** a boy at a military school. **3** (*fml*) a younger son.

café /ca-fay/ n a small restaurant serving coffee and light meals.

cafeteria /ca-fe-tir-ee-ya/ n a restaurant in which a person serves him or herself from a variety of meals that are displayed on or behind a counter.

caffeine /ca-feen/ n a chemical that is a stimulant and is found in tea, coffee and some soft drinks.

cage /cage/ n a box with one or more walls consisting of bars or wire netting in which animals or birds can be kept. • *vb* to shut in a cage or prison.

cake /cake/ n **1** a dessert, made from flour, eggs, milk, sugar, etc, that is baked and usually covered with icing. **2** a small, usually flat amount of dough, or some other food, that is baked or fried. **3** a small, flat lump.

calamity /ca-la-mi-tee/ n **1** a tragedy. **2** a serious misfortune. • *adj* calamitous.

calcium /cal-see-um/ n a soft, silver-white metal found in chalk, marble, etc. and is the basic part of bones, teeth and shells.

calculate /cal-kyu-late/ *vb* **1** to work with numbers and mathematics. **2** to estimate. **3** to plan for a purpose. • *adj* calculable.

calculating /cal-kyu-late-ing/ *adj* scheming, clever, or sly, especially in a selfish way.

calculation /cal-kyu-lay-shun/ n **1** the act or process of calculating. **2** a sum.

calculator n a small electronic machine used to make arithmetical and mathematical calculations.

calendar /ca-len-dar/ n a table showing the relation of the days of the week to the dates of a particular year.

calf[1] /caf/ n (*pl* calves /cavz/) the young of the cow, elephant, whale, etc.

calf[2] /caf/ (*pl* calves /cavz/) the fleshy back part of the leg below the knee.

calfskin /caf-skin/ n a type of leather made from a calf's skin.

calibre /ca-li-bur/ n **1** the diameter of the bore of a gun. **2** quality.

calico /ca-li-co/ n a cotton cloth from India.

calk[1] *see* caulk.

calk[2] n a metal spike on a shoe to prevent slipping.

calk[3] *vb* to trace a pattern using a blunt implement.

call /cawl/ *vb* **1** to say or read in a loud voice; to shout or announce. **2** to give a name. **3** to request or demand. **4** to make a short visit. **5** to ask to come. **5** to telephone. • n **1** a cry. **2** a short visit. **3** a telephone call. **4** need, demand. • **a close call** a narrow escape.

calligraphy /ca-lig-ro-fee/ n **1** handwriting as an art. **2** the art of writing well.

calling /caw-ling/ n (*fml*) **1** profession or employment. **2** an inner urging towards some profession.

callous /**ca**-lus/ *adj* hardened, unfeeling, insensitive. • *n* **callousness**.

calm /**cahm**/ *adj* **1** quiet, still. **2** unexcited, not agitated. • *n* **1** stillness. **2** freedom from excitement. • *vb* to make calm. • *n* **calmness** /**cahm**-nes/.

calorie /**ca**-lo-ree/ *n* **1** a measure of heat. **2** a unit for measuring the energy value of food.

calve /**cav**/ *vb* to give birth to a calf.

calypso /ca-**lip**-so/ *n* songs sung as originally by the native people of Trinidad, with stresses and short emphasized rhythms.

cam /**cam**/ *n* a wheel-like part of a machine that creates a straight movement from a rotating one.

camcorder /**cam**-cor-der/ *n* a portable video camera that records pictures and sound.

came *pt* of **come**.

camel /**ca**-mel/ *n* an animal, found in Asian and African deserts, that has a long neck and one or two humps on its back.

cameo /**ca**-me-o/ *n* **1** a raised carving (usually of the side view of a person's head) on a gem or shell, with a different-coloured background. **2** a precious stone with a raised design carved on it, often of a different colour. **3** a small but important role in a film or play performed by a celebrity.

camera /**ca**-me-ra/ *n* a device for taking photographs or recording images, consisting of a closed box into which light enters through a lens.

camisole /**ca**-mi-sole/ *n* a woman's light undergarment, sleeveless and trimmed in lace, worn on the upper part of the body.

camp /**camp**/ *n* **1** a place where people live in tents, caravans, huts, etc. **2** a group of tents, caravans, huts, or other kinds of temporary shelter. • *vb* to stay in or set up a camp.

campaign /cam-**pane**/ *n* **1** a battle or series of battles in a war. **2** any series of actions, meetings, etc directed to one purpose. • *vb* to take part in or conduct a campaign.

camp bed /**camp** bed/ *n* a folding portable bed.

camphor /**cam**-for/ *n* a strong-smelling chemical mixture used in protecting fabrics from moths, in making plastics and in medicine.

campus /**cam**-pus/ *n* the grounds of a school or college.

can[1] /**can**/ *vb* (*pt* **could**) **1** indicates the ability to do something. **2** indicates permission to do something. **3** indicates the opportunity to do something.

can[2] /**can**/ *n* a small metal container in which food or drink is preserved. • *vb* (**canned**, **canning**) to put into tins to preserve.

canal /ca-**nal**/ *n* a human-made waterway.

canary /ca-**nay**-ree/ *n* a small, yellow bird often kept as a pet. • *adj* bright yellow.

cancel /**can**-sel/ *vb* (**cancelled**, **cancelling**) **1** to cross out. **2** to do away with. • *n* **cancellation**.

cancer /**can**-ser/ *n* **1** a harmful, sometimes fatal growth in the body. **2** a growing evil.

candid /**can**-did/ *adj* very honest or frank in what you say. • *adv* **candidly**.

candidate /**can**-di-date/ *n* **1** someone who seeks a post or position. **2** someone who takes an exam.

candle /**can**-dl/ *n* a mass of formed, shaped wax or tallow containing a wick for lighting.

candlestick /**can**-del-stick/ *n* a holder for a candle.

candour /**can**-dor/ *n also* **candor** (*US*) frankness.

candy /**can**-dee/ *n* **1** sugar hardened by boiling. **2** (*US*) any sweet or sweets. • *vb* to preserve by boiling with sugar.

cane /**cane**/ *n* **1** a usually bendable, slender, jointed, hollow stem, such as bamboo, sugar cane, etc. **2** a walking stick. • *vb* to beat with a cane.

cane sugar /**cane** shu-gar/ *n* sugar obtained from the sugar cane.

canine /**cay**-nine/ *adj* having to do with dogs or other animals in the dog family. • *n* one of the pointed teeth in the front of the mouth (*also* **canine tooth**).

canister /**ca**-nis-ter/ *n* a small box or tin.

cannabis /**can**-a-bis/ *n* a drug made from the dried leaves and flowers of the hemp plant, smoked or chewed, and illegal in many countries.

cannibal /**ca**-ni-bal/ *n* **1** a person who eats human flesh. **2** an animal that eats flesh of its own species. • *n* **cannibalism** /**ca**-ni-ba-li-zum/.

cannon /**ca**-non/ *n* a large, mounted weapon.

cannonball /**ca**-nun-bol/ *n* an iron ball fired from a cannon.

cannot *often shortened to* **can't** *v* to be unable to do something.

canoe /ca-**noo**/ *n* a narrow, light boat moved by paddles.

canon /**ca**-non/ *n* **1** the law or laws of a church. **2** a member of clergy who lives according to the laws in a church.

canopy /**ca**-no-pee/ *n* a hanging cover forming a shelter above a throne, bed, etc.

cant[1] /**cant**/ *n* **1** a special way of speaking used by a particular group of people. **2** meaningless or insincere talk.

cant[2] /**cant**/ *vb* to tilt up. • *n* a tilt.

can't *contraction* a shortened form of **cannot**.

cantaloupe /can-ta-lope/ *n* a type of melon with sweet orange flesh.

canteen /can-**teen**/ *n* **1** a place where food and drink can be obtained in a camp, factory, office, etc. **2** a small metal or plastic container used to carry water. **3** a case containing a set of cutlery.

canter /can-ter/ *vb* to gallop at a smooth, easy pace. • *also n*.

cantor /can-ter/ *n* someone who leads the singing and prayer in a synagogue.

canvas /can-vas/ *n* **1** a coarse cloth of cotton, hemp, or linen, often unbleached, and used for sails, tents, etc, or for painting on. **2** the sails of a ship. **3** an oil painting.

canvass /can-vas/ *vb* **1** to ask for votes or orders. **2** to look at or discuss in detail. • *n* **canvasser**.

canyon /can-yin/ *n* a long, narrow valley between cliffs, often with a river or stream flowing through it.

cap /cap/ *n* **1** a covering for the head with no brim or only part of one. **2** a cover or top piece. • *vb* (**capped**, **capping**) **1** to put a cap on. **2** to improve on. **3** to impose an upper limit on.

capable /cay-pa-bl/ *adj* **1** able to. **2** likely to. **3** able to do things well, efficient. • *n* **capability**.

capacity /ca-pa-si-tee/ *n* **1** ability to hold or contain. **2** ability to produce or perform, experience, etc. **3** (*fml*) position.

cape[1] /cape/ *n* a short cloak for covering the shoulders, a sleeveless cloak.

cape[2] /cape/ *n* a piece of land jutting out into the water.

caper[1] /cay-per/ *vb* to jump about playfully. • *n* **1** a jump or leap. **2** a prank, a mischievous act. **3** a robbery.

caper[2] /cay-per/ *n* a kind of tree or shrub that has tiny, green flower buds that are picked and used to flavour food.

capillary /ca-**pil**-a-ree/ *adj* small and thin, hairlike. • *npl* **capillaries** small blood vessels.

capital /ca-pi-tal/ *adj* **1** chief. **2** punishable by death. **3** (*inf*) excellent. • *n* **1** the top of a column or pillar. **2** the chief city. **3** money, especially when used for business. **4** a large letter, as used first in proper names.

capital punishment /ca-pi-tal **pun**-ish-ment/ *n* punishment by death.

capitalist /ca-pi-tal-ist/ *n* wealthy businessman, a person who owns capital.

capitalism /ca-pi-ta-li-zum/ *n* an economic system where production is privately owned and run to make a profit.

caprice /ca-**preess**/ *n* a sudden desire or fancy,.

capricious /ca-**pri**-shus/ *adj* changeable, unreasonable.

capsize /cap-**size**/ *vb* to overturn or upset.

capsule /cap-sul/ *n* **1** a hollow pill containing medicine. **2** the part of a spacecraft containing the instruments and crew.

captain /cap-tin/ *n* **1** a commander. **2** an officer. **3** a leader. • *also vb*.

caption /cap-shon/ *n* the heading over (or under) a picture or newspaper report.

captivate /**cap**-ti-vate/ *vb* to charm, to fascinate.

captive /cap-tiv/ *n* a prisoner. • *also adj*.

captivity /cap-**ti**-vi-tee/ *n* the state of being a prisoner.

captor /cap-tor/ *n* someone who holds something or someone captive.

capture /cap-shur/ *vb* **1** to take prisoner, to catch. **2** to take control of. • *n* **1** act of catching or taking prisoner. **2** the thing so caught or taken.

car /car/ *n* **1** a wheeled vehicle. **2** a motor car. **3** a carriage.

carafe /ca-raf/ *n* a glass bottle.

caramel /ca-ra-mel/ *n* **1** burnt sugar used as colouring and flavouring in cooking. **2** a type of sweet made with sugar, milk, etc.

carat /ca-rat/ *n* a unit of weight used for jewellery, equal to 200 milligrams.

caravan /ca-ra-van/ *n* **1** a covered vehicle for passengers, circus animals, etc. **2** a road vehicle without an engine and containing living quarters, pulled by a car. **3** a group of people travelling together for safety.

caraway /ca-ra-way/ *n* a plant whose seeds are used to flavour cakes, breads etc.

carbohydrate /car-bo-**hie**-drate/ *n* the compound in foods that gives you energy; examples are sugars and starch.

carbon /cahr-bun/ *n* a natural element, found in coal, charcoal, soot, etc.

carbon dioxide /car-bun die-**oc**-side/ *n* a gas without colour or smell, breathed out by people and animals and absorbed by plants.

carbon footprint /car-bun foot-print/ *n* a means of measuring the carbon dioxide produced by an individual person or an organization.

carbon monoxide /car-bun mon-**oc**-side/ *n* a poisonous gas, without colour or smell, produced by the exhausts of cars, etc.

carbon paper /car-bun pay-per/ *n* thin, prepared paper used to make copies of letters as they are written.

car boot sale /car **boot** sale/ *n* a public sale where people sell things, often unwanted objects, from the backs of their cars.

carburettor /car-bu-ray-tor/ *n* the part of a motor engine in which air is mixed with petrol, etc, to make a vapour that will burn.

carcass /car-cas/ *n* the dead body of an animal.

card[1] /card/ *n* a small piece of thick paper for various purposes.

card[2] /card/ *vb* to comb wool or flax before making it into thread. • *n* an instrument for combing wool or flax. • *n* **carder**.

cardboard /card-bored/ *n* stiff, thick paper.

cardiac /car-dee-ac/ *adj* to do with the heart.

cardigan /car-di-gan/ *n* a jumper that buttons down the front.

cardinal /car-di-nal/ *adj* very important, principal. • *n* **1** in the Roman Catholic Church, a high-ranking official with the right to take part in the election of the pope. **2** a bright red, crested bird.

care /care/ *n* **1** worry. **2** attention. **3** being looked after. • *vb* **1** to be interested. **2** to look after. **3** to have a liking or love.

career /ca-reer/ *n* someone's work or profession in life. • *vb* to move at full speed.

careful /care-ful/ *adj* **1** taking trouble. **2** cautious. • *adv* **carefully**.

care home /care home/ *n* a place where people who are too ill or too old to take of themselves live and are looked after.

careless /care-less/ *adj* taking little or no trouble. • *adv* **carelessly**. • *n* **carelessness**.

carer /cay-rer/ *n* someone who is responsible for looking after someone, such as an ill person, usually in the person's own home.

caress /ca-ress/ *vb* to touch or stroke lovingly. • *also n*.

caretaker /care-tay-ker/ *n* someone who looks after a building or place.

cargo /car-go/ *n* the goods carried by a ship, plane, etc.

caribou /ca-ri-boo/ *n* the North American reindeer.

caricature /ca-ri-ca-choor/ *n* a cartoon picture of a person or thing that exaggerates a particular feature to make others laugh. • *vb* to draw a caricature. • *n* **caricaturist**.

carnage /car-nidge/ *n* widespread killing, slaughter.

carnal /car-nal/ *adj* having to do with the body rather than the spirit.

carnation /car-nay-shun/ *n* a plant with usually double flowers of white, pink, or red that smell of cloves.

carnival /car-ni-val/ *n* **1** a time of feasting and merriment just before Lent, a Christian time of fasting. **2** a circus or fair.

carnivore /car-ni-vore/ *n* a flesh-eating animal. • *adj* **carnivorous**.

carol /ca-rol/ *n* a song of joy, especially one sung at Christmas. • *vb* (**caroled, caroling**) to sing joyfully.

carotid /ca-rot-id/ *n* having to do with the two large arteries in the neck.

carousal /ca-row-zul/ *n* (*fml*) a noisy drinking party.

carouse /ca-rowz/ *vb* (*fml*) to drink freely.

carousel /ca-ro-sel/ *n*, *also* **carrousel 1** a merry-go-round. **2** a rotating conveyor belt.

carp[1] /carp/ *vb* to find fault or complain, often unreasonably.

carp[2] /carp/ *n* a freshwater fish.

carpenter /car-pen-ter/ *n* someone who builds and repairs wooden things, especially for houses, ships, etc. • *n* **carpentry**.

carpet /car-pet/ *n* **1** a thick covering of wool or other material for a floor. **2** a covering. • *vb* **1** to cover with a carpet. **2** to cover. **3** (*inf*) to scold, to reprimand.

carpetbag /car-pet-bag/ *n* an old-fashioned travelling bag made of carpeting.

carriage /ca-ridge/ *n* **1** act of carrying. **2** the price of carrying. **3** the way someone stands or moves. **4** a cart with wheels or other passenger vehicle.

carrier /ca-ree-yer/ *n* **1** someone who carries or transports goods. **2** anyone or anything that carries.

carrier bag /ca-ree-yer bag/ *n* a paper or plastic bag with handles.

carrier pigeon /ca-ree-yer pi-jin/ *n* a pigeon used for carrying letters.

carrion /ca-ree-yon/ *n* rotten flesh.

carrot /ca-rot/ *n* an orange-red root vegetable.

carry /ca-ree/ *vb* **1** to take from one place to another. **2** to go from one place to another. **3** to have or hold. • **carry on 1** to continue to do. **2** to behave badly or in an uncontrolled manner. • **carry out** to perform.

cart /cart/ *n* a two-wheeled vehicle (usually made of wood) for carrying goods. • *vb* to carry by cart. • *n* **carter**.

cartilage /car-ti-lige/ *n* an elastic substance surrounding the joints of bones.

cartography /car-tog-ra-fee/ *n* the art of map making. • *n* **cartographer**.

carton /car-ton/ *n* a cardboard box.

cartoon /car-toon/ *n* **1** a comic drawing. **2** an animated drawing. • *n* **cartoonist**.

cartridge /car-tridge/ *n* **1** the container for the explosive that fires the bullet or shell from a gun. **2** any small container that carries a substance for a larger device.

carve /carve/ *vb* **1** to cut into a special shape. **2** to make by cutting wood or stone. **3** to cut into slices.

carver /car-ver/ n **1** someone who carves. **2** a carving knife.

cascade /ca-scade/ n **1** a waterfall. **2** something like a waterfall. • vb to fall or drop in a cascade.

case[1] /case/ n **1** a box or container. **2** a covering. **3** a suitcase. **4** a piece of furniture for displaying or containing things.

case[2] /case/ **1** an event, instance, or example. **2** a person having medical, etc, treatment. **3** a statement of facts and arguments or reasons. **4** a question to be decided in a court of law, a lawsuit.

cash /cash/ n **1** coins or paper money, not cheques or credit cards, etc. **2** immediate payment rather than by credit. **3** (inf) money generally. • vb to turn into money.

cashier /ca-sheer/ n someone who has charge of money in a store or a bank. • vb to dismiss (an officer from the army, navy, etc.) in disgrace.

cash machine see **ATM**.

cashmere /cazh-meer/ n a fine, soft, woollen material.

casino /ca-see-no/ n a hall for dancing or gambling.

cask /cask/ n a barrel.

casket /cas-ket/ n a jewel case.

casserole /ca-se-role/ n **1** a glass or earthenware dish in which food can be cooked in an oven and then served at table. **2** the food so prepared.

cassette /ca-set/ n a flat plastic case containing tape for recording or playing back sounds or pictures.

cassock /ca-sok/ n a long, close-fitting robe worn by clergymen and those taking part in services.

cast /cast/ vb (pt, pp **cast**) **1** to throw. **2** to throw off. **3** to shape. • n **1** a throw. **2** a squint (in the eye). **3** a model made in a mould. **4** the actors in a play.

castaway /cas-ta-way/ n a shipwrecked person.

caste /cast/ n in India, the social class or rank into which someone is born.

caster /ca-ster/ n, also **castor 1** a small jar or bottle with holes in the top for sprinkling salt, sugar, etc. **2** a small wheel on a piece of furniture, making it easy to move.

castigate /ca-sti-gate/ vb (fml) to scold or criticize severely. • n **castigation**.

cast iron /cast eye-urn/ n iron that has been melted and shaped in a mould. • adj very strong.

castle[1] /ca-sel/ n **1** a large building, usually one strengthened against attack. **2** a piece in chess. • **castles in the air** a daydream.

casual /cazh-yoo-ul/ adj **1** happening by chance. **2** not regular. **3** uninterested. **4** not careful, not thorough. **5** informal. • adv **casually**.

casualty /ca-zhul-tee/ n **1** an accident, especially a fatal one. **2** an injured or wounded person. **3** (inf) the accident and emergency (A&E) department of a hospital. **4** something that is damaged or destroyed as a result of an event.

cat /cat/ n **1** an animal with soft fur and sharp claws, commonly kept as a pet. **2** a family of meat-eating animals.

catacomb /ca-ta-com/ n an underground tomb.

catalogue /ca-ta-lawg/ n, also **catalog** (US) a complete list arranged in a special order so that the items can be found easily. • vb to make a list.

catalyst /ca-ta-list/ n **1** a substance that aids a chemical reaction but is not itself changed. **2** something or someone that causes a change in a situation or has a marked effect on the course of events.

catamaran /ca-ta-me-ran/ n a sailing boat made in long, narrow parts joined by a bridge.

catapult /ca-ta-pult/ n **1** a machine used for hurling heavy stones in war. **2** a Y-shaped stick with elastic for shooting stones, etc.

cataract /ca-ta-ract/ n **1** a large waterfall. **2** a disease of the eye, causing gradual loss of sight.

catastrophe /ca-ta-stro-fee/ n a sudden, great disaster. • adj **catastrophic**.

catch /catch/ vb (pt, pp **caught**) **1** to take and hold. **2** to capture. **3** to become accidentally attached or held. **4** to surprise in the act of. **5** to succeed in hearing. **6** to get by infection. **7** to be in time for, to get on. • n **1** the act of catching. **2** the number of fish caught at one time. **3** a fastener. **4** a snag. **5** a song in which the same words and tune are repeated by several singers starting at different times.

catchy /ca-chee/ adj memorable.

categorical /ca-te-gawr-ic-al/ adj definite. • adv **categorically**.

category /ca-te-go-ree/ n a class or group of things in a system of grouping.

cater /cay-ter/ vb **1** to supply with food and drinks, especially at social occasions. **2** to provide what is needed or desired. • n **caterer**.

caterpillar /ca-ter-pi-lar/ n the wormlike larvae of insects such as the butterfly or moth.

cathedral /ca-thee-dral/ n the main church in a district in which a bishop has his throne.

catholic /cath-lic/ *adj* wide-ranging, broad, including many different things. • *n* **catholicity**.

Catholic /cath-lic/ *n* a member of the Roman Catholic Church. • *also adj*.

catkin /cat-kin/ *n* the furry blossom of the willow, hazel, etc.

CAT scan /cat-scan/ *abbr* = **computerized axial tomography**: a series of x-rays that create a 3D image of the body.

cattle /cat-tl/ *n pl* cows, bulls and oxen.

caught *pt and pp of* **catch**.

cauldron /col-drun/ *n* a large boiling pot.

caulk, calk *vt* to render watertight by pressing a sealant into the seams.

cauliflower /caw-li-fla-wer/ *n* a type of cabbage, of which the white, fleshy flower is eaten as a vegetable.

cause /cawz/ *n* **1** something or someone that produces an effect or result. **2** the reason for an action, a motive. **3** a purpose, aim. • *vb* to make happen.

causeway /cawz-way/ *n* a road or path raised on a mound above the surrounding country, as over wet ground or water.

caustic /caw-stic/ *adj* **1** burning. **2** bitter, severe. • *adv* **caustically**.

caution /caw-shen/ *n* **1** carefulness, especially to avoid risk or danger. **2** warning. • *vb* **1** to warn against possible danger. **2** to give a warning to, often with the threat of future punishment.

cautious /caw-shess/ *adj* careful, showing caution.

cavalcade /ca-val-cade/ *n* a procession.

cavalier /ca-va-leer/ *n* an armed horseman. • *adj* offhand, casual and disrespectful. • *adv* **cavalierly**.

cavalry /ca-val-ree/ *n* originally soldiers on horses, but now often riding in armoured trucks or tanks.

cave /cave/ *n* a hollow place in the earth, as in a hillside extending back. • **cave in** to fall in over a hollow.

cave man /cave man/ *n* **1** (*old*) a human who, in the earliest times, lived in a cave. **2** a man with very rough manners, especially towards women.

cavern /ca-vern/ *n* a large cave. • *vb* to hollow out.

cavernous /ca-ver-nus/ *adj* large and hollow, like a cavern.

caviar(e) /ca-vee-ar/ *n* the eggs of sturgeon, salmon and similar fish eaten as a delicacy.

cavity /ca-vi-tee/ *n* **1** a hollow place. **2** a hole.

cayenne /kie-yen/ *n* a very hot red pepper.

CCTV /see-see-tee-vee/ *abbr* = **closed-circuit** television: a type of surveillance camera system.

CD /see dee/ *abbr* = **compact disc** or **compact disk** (*US*): a small, mirrored, plastic disc that stores music, images, or files that are read optically by a laser beam.

CD-ROM /see-dee-rom/ *abbr* = **compact disc read-only memory**: a disc that holds files that can be read by a computer, but that cannot be altered.

cease /sees/ *vb* **1** to stop. **2** to come to an end.

ceaseless /sees-less/ *adj* endless, continuous.

cedar /see-dar/ *n* a large, cone-bearing tree or its wood.

ceiling /see-ling/ *n* **1** the inside roof of a room. **2** the greatest height to which a particular aircraft can climb. **3** an upper limit.

celebrate /se-le-brate/ *vb* **1** to perform a religious ceremony. **2** to honour an event by feasting and rejoicing. • *n* **celebration**.

celebrated /se-le-bray-ted/ *adj* famous.

celebrity /se-le-bri-tee/ *n* a famous person.

celery /se-le-ree/ *n* a kind of vegetable, of which the green stem is eaten either cooked or raw.

celestial /se-les-chal/ *adj* **1** heavenly. **2** having to do with the sky.

celibacy /se-li-ba-see/ *n* the state of being unmarried, not having sexual relationships.

celibate /se-li-bet/ *adj* unmarried, not having sexual relationships.

cell /sell/ *n* **1** a small, bare room, especially in a prison or monastery. **2** a space in a honeycomb. **3** a single unit of living matter. **4** a unit of an electric battery. **5** a small group of people working towards the same end.

cellar /se-lar/ *n* an area underneath a house, often used for storage.

cello /che-lo/ (*short for* **violoncello**) a musical instrument of the violin family, between the viola and bass in size and pitch. • *n* **cellist**.

cellophane /se-lo-fane/ *n* a thin, transparent wrapping material.

cellular /sell-ye-lar/ *adj* having cells, made up of cells.

cellulose /sell-ye-loze/ *n* a substance obtained from wood or plants and used in making paper, imitation silk, film, etc.

Celsius /sell-see-es/ *adj* a way of measuring temperature so that 0 degrees is the freezing point of water and 100 degrees is the boiling point.

cement /si-ment/ *n* a powdered substance that, mixed with liquid, forms a solid material used to make things stick together. • *vb* **1** to join with cement. **2** to unite closely.

cemetery /se-me-te-ree/ *n* a burial ground, a graveyard.

censer /sen-ser/ *n* a decorated container in which incense is burned.

censor /sen-ser/ *n* someone who examines letters, books, films, etc, to see if they contain anything inappropriate, offensive, or harmful to society. • *also vb*. • *n* **censorship**. • *adj* **censorious**.

census /sen-ses/ *n* **1** an official counting of a country's population. **2** an official counting of other things.

cent /sent/ *n* a coin that is worth one-hundredth of a dollar, euro etc.

centaur /sen-tawr/ *n* in Greek myths, an imaginary creature that is half man and half horse.

centenarian /sen-te-ne-ree-an/ *n* a person at least 100 years old.

centenary /sen-tee-ne-ree/ *n* the 100th year after a certain event.

centennial /sen-ten-ee-al/ *adj* happening once every 100 years.

centimetre /sen-ti-mee-ter/ *n* one-hundredth of a metre, *abbr* **cm**.

centipede /sen-ti-peed/ *n* a small, insect-eating, caterpillar-like animal with a segmented body and many feet.

central /sen-tral/ *adj* **1** in the middle. **2** chief.

centralize /sen-tra-lize/ *vb* *also* **centralise** to bring together to one place. • *n* **centralization** *also* **centralisation**.

centre /sen-ter/ *also* **center** (*US*) *n* **1** the middle point or part of anything. **2** a place where certain activities or facilities are concentrated. **3** a political position that is not extreme. • *vb* **1** to put into the middle. **2** to collect or concentrate at or around.

centrifugal /sen-trif-yew-gul/ *adj* describing a physical force that causes an object that is rotating around a central point to move away from that point.

centripetal /sen-trip-it-ul/ *adj* describing a physical force that pulls something towards the centre point it is rotating around.

centurion /sen-choo-ree-en/ *n* (*old*) the captain of 100 men, especially in an ancient Roman army.

century /sen-choo-ree/ *n* 100 years.

ceramic /se-ra-mic/ *adj* having to do with pottery, earthenware, tile, etc.

ceramics /se-ra-mics/ *n* the art or work of making pottery, earthenware, tile, etc.

cereal /si-ree-al/ *n* **1** any grain that can be eaten. **2** food made from such grain, often eaten at breakfast.

cerebral /se-ree-bral/ *adj* **1** having to do with the brain. **2** intellectual rather than emotional.

ceremonial /se-re-mo-nee-al/ *n* the actions connected with a ceremony. • *adj* having to do with a ceremony.

ceremonious /se-re-mo-nee-es/ *adj* full of ceremony, very formal.

ceremony /se-re-mo-nee/ *n* **1** the performing of certain actions in a fixed order for a religious or other serious purpose. **2** formal behaviour, formality.

certain /ser-ten/ *adj* **1** sure. **2** particular.

certainly /ser-ten-lee/ *adv* **1** undoubtedly. **2** willingly.

certainty /ser-ten-tee/ *n* **1** the state of being certain or sure. **2** that which is certain.

certificate /ser-ti-fi-cate/ *n* a written statement of fact.

certify /ser-ti-fie/ *vb* **1** to confirm formally the truth of a statement. **2** officially to declare a person mentally ill.

chafe /chafe/ *vb* **1** to warm by rubbing. **2** to make sore or wear away by rubbing. **3** to be angry.

chain /chane/ *n* **1** a number of metal rings joined to form a rope. **2** a number of connected facts or events, a series. **3** a measure of length. **4** (*of mountains*) a range. • *vb* to bind or fasten with a chain.

chair /chare/ *n* **1** a movable seat with a back. **2** chairperson. **3** the seat or place of an official (e.g. of a professor in a university or a person controlling a meeting). • *vb* to be in charge of a meeting.

chairman, chairperson, chairwoman /chair-man, chair-per-son, chair-wu-man/ *n* someone who controls a meeting.

chalet /sha-lay/ *n* a wooden house or hut with a steeply sloping roof, common in Switzerland.

chalice /cha-lis/ *n* **1** (*old*) a drinking cup. **2** a cup with a stem, especially used in church services.

chalk /chawk/ *n* **1** a soft, white limestone. **2** a piece of chalk used for writing on a blackboard. • *vb* to mark with chalk. • *adj* **chalky**.

challenge /cha-lenj/ *vb* **1** to call on another to fight or play a match to see who is the better. **2** to doubt the truth of. • *n* **1** the daring of another to a contest. **2** a statement or action that questions something. **3** a difficult or exciting task. • *n* **challenger**.

chamber /chame-ber/ *n* **1** (*old*) a room. **2** a room in which a meeting takes place. **3** an administrative group. **4** the part of a gun in which the cartridge is held.

chamber music /chame-ber myoo-zik/ *n* music written to be played by only a few people (such as a quartet) for a small audience, as in a room rather than a hall.

chameleon /ca-**meel**-ee-en/ *n* a type of lizard that can change the colour of its skin.

champ /champ/ *vb* to chew noisily with the teeth. • *n* short for **champion**.

champagne /sham-**pain**/ *n* a type of sparkling white wine.

champion /**cham**-pee-en/ *n* **1** someone who has beaten all his or her rivals or opponents. **2** someone who fights for a certain cause, or for another person. • *vb* to defend or support.

championship /**cham**-pee-en-ship/ *n* **1** a series of contests or matches to discover the champion. **2** the state of being a champion.

chance /chans/ *n* **1** accident. **2** opportunity. **3** risk. • *vb* **1** (*fml*) to happen. **2** to risk. • *adj* accidental.

chancel /**chan**-sel/ *n* the altar end of a church.

chancellor /**chan**-se-ler/ *n* **1** a country's leader or high government official. **2** the chief judge of England. **3** the head of a university. • **Chancellor of the Exchequer** in Britain, the chief minister of finance in the government.

chandelier /shan-de-**lir**/ *n* a hanging lamp frame with branches to hold lights.

change /change/ *vb* **1** to become different. **2** to make different. **3** to put or take one thing in place of another, to exchange. • *n* **1** a difference or alteration. **2** money given in return for money received. **3** small coin. • *adj* **changeable**. • *adj* **changeless**.

changeling /**change**-ling/ *n* (*myth*) a child put by fairies in the place of another, as told in folk tales.

channel /**cha**-nel/ *n* **1** the course of a river. **2** the deep part of a river where ships can sail safely. **3** a narrow sea. **4** a band of frequencies used in radio and television. **5** a means of communication.

chant /chant/ *vb* **1** to sing. **2** to recite slowly in a singing voice. • *n* **1** a song. **2** a way of singing sacred music.

chaos /**kay**-os/ *n* a state of utter confusion, disorder.

chaotic /kay-o-tic/ *adj* completely without order or arrangement.

chap[1] /chap/ *vb* (**chapped, chapping**) to crack. • *n* a crack in the skin, caused by cold and wet. • *adj* **chapped**.

chap[2] /chap/ *n* (*inf*) a man, a fellow.

chapel /**cha**-pel/ *n* a small church.

chaperon(e) /**sha**-pe-rone/ *n* **1** especially formerly, an older person, usually a woman, who accompanies young unmarried people when they go out. **2** a person who

supervises young people on an outing. • *vb* to act as chaperon to.

chaplain /**cha**-plen/ *n* **1** the clergyman serving a private chapel. **2** a clergyman with the army, navy, or air force.

chapter /**chap**-ter/ *n* **1** a division of a book. **2** a meeting of the canons of a cathedral.

char /char/ *vb* (**charred, charring**) **1** to burn in part. **2** to burn the outside.

character /**ca**-ric-ter/ *n* **1** a letter or figure or, as in Chinese, a symbol standing for a whole word. **2** a person's nature as known by words, deeds, etc. **3** a reputation. **4** a person in a story or play. **5** (*inf*) an odd, humorous, or interesting person. **6** (*inf*) a person.

characteristic /ca-ric-te-**ris**-tic/ *n* a single point in a person's character, a special and recognizable quality in someone or something. • *adj* typical.

characterize /**ca**-ric-te-rize/ *vb*, *also* **characterise** **1** to be characteristic or typical of. **2** (*fml*) to describe as.

charade /sha-**rayd**/ *npl* **1** a word game in which players guess the word clue without saying anything, just using motions. **2** something that is easily seen to be false.

charcoal /**char**-cole/ *n* partly burned wood used as fuel.

charge /charge/ *vb* **1** to ask a price. **2** to accuse. **3** to rush. **4** to attack at speed. **5** to fill with electricity or energy. **6** to tell a person to do something as a duty. • *n* **1** a load of electricity or energy. **2** a price. **3** a duty, especially that of a clergyman. **4** a violent attack. **5** an accusation. • *adj* **chargeable**. • **take charge** to take command, take control.

chariot /**cha**-ree-et/ *n* (*old*) a horse-drawn, two-wheeled cart used in ancient times for war, racing, parades, etc.

charioteer /cha-ree-e-**teer**/ *n* (*old*) the driver of a chariot.

charity /**cha**-ri-tee/ *n* **1** a love of other human beings. **2** kindness to others. **3** generosity in giving to the poor. **4** an organization that raises money to help people in need or other good causes. • *adj* **charitable**.

charity shop /**cha**-ri-tee shop/ *n* a shop that sells second-hand goods to raise money for charity.

charlatan /**shar**-la-tan/ *n* someone who deceives by pretending to have special knowledge or skill.

charm /charm/ *n* **1** a magic spell. **2** an object or words possessing magical power. **3** any small ornament worn as decoration on a necklace, bracelet, or other jewellery.

chart 50 chessmen

4 attractiveness of character, a pleasant quality. **5** *pl* (*fml*) beauty. • *vb* **1** to put under a spell. **2** to delight.

chart /**chart**/ *n* **1** a map, especially one for sailors. **2** a paper showing information in a graph or table.

charter /**char**-ter/ *n* a written document granting certain rights. • *vb* to hire.

chase¹ /**chase**/ *vb* **1** to run after. **2** to drive away. • *n* a pursuit, a hunt.

chase² /**chase**/ *vb* **1** to engrave or cut figures on metal. **2** *n* a groove cut into a wall to provide space for a pipe.

chasm /**ka**-zm/ *n* **1** a wide, deep crack in the surface of the earth, a gorge, a canyon. **2** a wide gap or difference of opinion, attitudes, feelings, etc.

chaste /**chaste**/ *adj* pure, decent, or modest in nature.

chasten /**chay**-sen/ *vb* to teach by suffering or punishment.

chastise /chas-**tize**/ *vb* to punish severely, especially by beating. • *n* **chastisement**.

chastity /**chas**-ti-tee/ *n* purity, the state of being chaste.

chat /**chat**/ *vb* (**chatted, chatting**) to talk about unimportant matters. • *n* a friendly talk.

chat room, chatroom /**chat** room/ *n* an Internet web site that allows several members at once to send each other typed instant messages.

château /sha-**toe**/ *n* (*pl* **châteaux**) a French castle or country house.

chattel /**cha**-tel/ *n* **1** movable belongings, someone's possessions. **2** a slave or slaves.

chatter /**cha**-ter/ *vb* **1** to talk quickly and continuously, usually about something unimportant. **2** to make meaningless sounds. • *also n.* • *n* **chatterer**.

chatterbox /**cha**-ter-boks/ *n* one who chatters a great deal.

chauffeur /**sho**-fer/ *n* a person employed to drive someone's car. • *also vb.*

chauvinism /**sho**-vi-ni-zm/ *n* too great a pride in one's country, race, sex, etc, leading to a dislike or mistreatment of others. • *n* **chauvinist**.

chav /**chav**/ *n* (*inf*, *derog*) a young working-class person who is thought by others to have inferior and vulgar tastes in clothes etc.

cheap /**cheep**/ *adj* **1** of a low price. **2** of little value.

cheapen /**chee**-pen/ *vb* to lessen the price or value of.

cheat /**cheet**/ *vb* to deceive, to use unfair means. • *n* **1** a trick. **2** a swindler.

check /**check**/ *vb* **1** to stop. **2** to slow down. **3** to scold. **4** to look at something to see if it is correct or in order. • *n* **1** a sudden halt or obstacle. **2** a control. **3** US variant of **cheque**. • *adj* **checked** divided into or marked by squares.

checkers /**che**-kers/ *npl* (*US*) draughts.

checkmate /**check**-mate/ *n* the winning move in chess. • *vb* to defeat another's plans.

cheddar /**che**-der/ *n* a variety of cheese.

cheek /**cheek**/ *n* **1** the side of the face. **2** disrespect, impudence.

cheeky /**cheek**-ee/ *adj* rude or impudent, sometimes in an amusing way.

cheep /**cheep**/ *n* a faint squeak, a chirp. • *also vb.*

cheer /**cheer**/ *n* **1** (*old*) mood, disposition. **2** a shout of joy or encouragement. • *vb* **1** to brighten up. **2** to encourage, especially by shouts.

cheerful /**cheer**-ful/ *adj* **1** happy and lively. **2** bright and attractive.

cheerless /**cheer**-less/ *adj* sad, gloomy.

cheese /**cheez**/ *n* a solid food made from milk.

cheetah /**chee**-ta/ *n* a large, wild animal of the cat family that is lean and fast and has a coat with black spots on it.

chef /**shef**/ *n* a cook in charge of a kitchen.

chemical /**ke**-mi-cal/ *adj* having to do with chemistry. • *n* a substance studied in chemistry.

chemist /**ke**-mist/ *n* **1** someone who studies or works in chemistry. **2** someone who is authorized to sell medicines. **3** a shop where medicines, toiletries and cosmetics are sold.

chemistry /**ke**-mis-tree/ *n* the science that separates and studies the substance(s) of which all things are made.

cheque /**check**/ *n*, *also* **check** (*US*) a written order to a bank to pay out a sum of money from one's bank account.

cherish /**cher**-ish/ *vb* **1** to treat lovingly, to hold dear. **2** to keep in the mind or heart.

cherry /**cher**-ee/ *n* **1** a small, pitted fruit. **2** a tree bearing cherries.

cherub /**cher**-ub/ *n* (*pl* **cherubs** *or* **cherubim**) **1** an angel. **2** in art, an angel pictured as a winged child. **3** a beautiful, innocent-looking child.

cherubic /che-**roo**-bic/ *adj* angelic.

chess /**chess**/ *n* a game of skill played on a chequered board by two people with 16 chessmen that are limited in their movements according to kind, the object being to capture the king.

chessmen /**chess**-men/ *n* game pieces used in chess, including a king, a queen, two rooks (or castles), two knights, two bishops and eight pawns.

chest /chest/ *n* **1** a large, strong box. **2** the front, upper part of the body, from the shoulders to the lowest ribs.

chestnut /chest-nut/ *n* **1** a nut. **2** a tree bearing chestnuts. **3** a reddish brown horse. • *adj* reddish brown.

chevron /shev-ron/ *n* **1** a V-shaped strip of cloth worn on the sleeve as a sign of rank in the military. **2** a pattern of horizontal V shapes, like a zigzag.

chew /choo/ *vb* to crush with the teeth.

chic /sheek/ *adj* smart, fashionable.

chicanery /shi-**cane**-ree/ *n* trickery.

chick /chick/ *n* a young bird.

chicken /chi-ken/ *n* **1** a farm bird raised for its eggs and meat. **2** a person who is afraid, not brave, timid.

chickenpox /chi-ken poks/ *n* a disease involving fever and red itchy spots, usually affecting children.

chickpea *n* a large kind of pea.

chicory /chi-ko-ree/ *n* a plant whose leaves are used in salads, and the roasted root is sometimes mixed with coffee.

chide /chide/ *vb* to scold.

chief /cheef/ *adj* **1** highest in rank. **2** most important, main. • *n* a head, a leader. • *adv* **chiefly**.

chieftain /cheef-tin/ *n* a chief, the head of a clan or tribe.

chiffon /shi-fon/ *n* a thin, silky cloth.

child /childe/ *n* (*pl* children /chil-dren/) **1** a young boy or girl, an adolescent. **2** a son or daughter. • *n* **childhood**.

childcare /child-care/ *n* the care of children, especially by people other than the parents, when they are at work.

childish /chile-dish/ *adj* **1** like a child. **2** silly, immature.

childminder /child-mine-der/ *n* a person who is paid to look after other people's children, usually in his or her own home.

children *see* **child**.

chill /chil/ *n* **1** coldness. **2** coldness of manner, unfriendliness. • *vb* **1** to make cold. **2** to make cold without freezing. **3** to discourage. • *adj* cold.

chilli /chi-lee/ *n* (*pl* **chillies**), *also* **chili** (*US*) the small red or green seed pod of a type of hot pepper, used in cooking spicy food.

chilly /chi-lee/ *adj* **1** cold. **2** unfriendly.

chime /chime/ *n* **1** the sound of a bell. **2** the music of bells. **3** *pl* a set of bells. • *vb* to ring musically. • **chime in** to agree.

chimney /chim-nee/ *n* a passage by which smoke may escape from a fireplace.

chimney pot /chim-nee pot/ *n* a pipe at the top of a chimney.

chimney sweep /chim-nee sweep/ *n* someone who cleans chimneys.

chimpanzee /chim-pan-zee/ *n* a type of ape found in Africa with black fur and large ears.

china /chine-a/ *n* **1** a fine, thin porcelain or ceramic ware. **2** cups, plates, ornaments, etc, made of this.

chinchilla /chin-chi-la/ *n* **1** a small rodent valued for its fur. **2** the fur from this animal.

chink /chingk/ *n* **1** a very narrow opening. **2** a ringing or jingling sound. • *vb* to jingle.

chintz /chints/ *n* a gaily patterned cotton material that is usually glazed.

chip /chip/ *n* **1** a small piece. **2** a counter or token used in games. **3** a small piece of deep-fried potato. • *vb* (**chipped, chipping**) **1** to cut into small pieces. **2** to break off a small piece, often accidentally.

chipmunk /chip-munk/ *n* a type of small squirrel with black stripes down its head and back, living mainly in the ground and found in North America.

chiropodist /kir-**op**-od-ist/ *n* someone whose job is to treat feet problems, a podiatrist. • *n* **chiropody**.

chirp /chirp/ *vb* to make a short, sharp whistling sound. • *also n*.

chisel /chi-zel/ *n* a tool used for cutting or chipping wood, stone, etc. • *vb* **chiselled, chiselling**.

chivalry /shi-val-ree/ *n* **1** (*old*) the rules of good behaviour laid down for knights in the Middle Ages; gentlemanly behaviour. **2** good manners, especially towards women. • *adj* **chivalric** /shi-**val**-ric/, **chivalrous** /shi-val-rus/.

chloride /clo-ride/ *n* a mixture of chlorine with another substance.

chlorine /clo-reen/ *n* a chemical used as a bleaching agent or disinfectant.

chlorophyll /**claw**-ro-fil/ *n* the green colouring of plants.

chock-a-block /choc-a-bloc/, **chock-full** /choc-ful/ *adjs* (*inf*) completely full.

chocolate /choc-lat/ *n* a paste, powder, syrup, or bar made from cacao seeds that have been roasted and ground. • *adj* chocolate-coloured, i.e. reddish brown.

choice /choyss/ *n* **1** act of choosing. **2** that which is chosen. • *adj* very good, excellent.

choir /kwire/ *n* **1** a group of singers. **2** the part of a church where the choir sits.

choke /choke/ *vb* **1** to be unable to breathe. **2** to prevent breathing by pressing the windpipe. **3** to block up. • *n* **1** a fit of choking or its sound. **2** a part that controls the flow of air in a carburettor.

cholera /co-le-ra/ *n* a serious stomach illness.

choose /chooz/ *vb* (*pt* **chose**, *pp* **chosen**) to select or take what you prefer.

chop /chop/ *vb* (**chopped, chopping**) **1** to cut with a quick, strong blow. **2** to cut into pieces. • *n* a piece of pork or mutton on a rib bone.

choppy /chop-ee/ *adj* rough.

chops /chops/ *npl* the jaws.

chopsticks /chop-stiks/ *npl* two long, thin sticks held in one hand, used in some Asian countries to eat food.

choral /core-al/ *adj* having to do with a chorus or choir.

chord /cawrd/ *n* a group of several musical notes played at once in harmony.

chore /chore/ *n* a regular job about the house.

chorus /co-rus/ *n* **1** a group of singers and sometimes dancers. **2** a song or part of a song in which all may join. • *vb* to sing or speak together.

chose *pt* of **choose**.

chosen *pp* of **choose**.

christen /cris-en/ *vb* **1** to baptize, or make part of the Christian church. **2** to name. **3** to make use of for the first time. • *n* **christening**.

Christian /cris-chin/ *adj* having to do with Christ and his teaching. • *n* a believer in Christ.

Christian name *see* **first name**.

Christmas /criss-mas/ *n* December 25, the day each year on which the birth of Christ is celebrated.

Christmas cracker /cris-mas crak-er/ *n see* **cracker**.

chromatic *adj* relating to colours.

chrome *n* something plated with an alloy of chromium

chromium *n* a metallic element (symbol Cr).

chromosome *n* a microscopic body responsible for hereditary characteristics.

chronic /cron-ik/ *adj* lasting for a long time.

chronicle /cron-ik-al/ *adj* a record of events, set down in the order in which they happened. • *also vb*. • *n* **chronicler**.

chronological /cron-o-**lodge**-ik-al/ *adj* arranged in order of time.

chrysalis /cris-sa-lis/ *n* an early stage in the life of a flying insect, when it is shut up in a cocoon until its wings grow.

chrysanthemum /cri-**zanth**-e-mum/ *n* a garden plant with a large, bushy flower.

chubby /chu-bee/ *adj* plump.

chuckle /chu-kl/ *vb* to laugh quietly. • *also n*.

chum /chum/ *n* (*inf*) a close friend. • *adj* **chummy**.

chunk /chungk/ *n* a thick piece.

church /church/ *n* **1** a building set aside for worship. **2** a group of people having the same beliefs and religious organization. **3** those in charge of a religious organization.

churn /churn/ *n* a vessel or machine for making butter. • *vb* to shake or stir (cream) so as to make butter.

chute /shoot/ *n* **1** a waterfall. **2** a sloping passage or slide.

chutney *n* a savoury preserve or relish made, usually, from fruit, vegetables and spices.

cider /sie-der/ *n* an alcoholic drink made from pressed apple juice.

cigar /si-**gar**/ *n* a roll of tobacco for smoking, consisting of cut tobacco rolled in a whole tobacco leaf.

cigarette /si-ga-**ret**/ *n* tobacco finely cut and rolled in thin paper for smoking.

cinder /sin-der/ *n* partly burned coal or wood.

cinema /si-ne-ma/ *n* **1** a building in which films are shown. **2** the industry of making films. • *adj* **cinematic**.

cinnamon /si-na-mon/ *n* a yellowish brown spice made from the dried inner bark of several kinds of trees and shrubs of the laurel family, used in cooking.

circle /sir-kl/ *n* **1** a perfectly round figure. **2** a group of people. • *vb* **1** to move round. **2** to draw a circle around.

circlet /sir-klet/ *n* a ring or circular band worn as an ornament.

circuit /sir-kit/ *n* **1** a path round. **2** the act of moving around. **3** the journey of a judge round a district to hold courts of law in several places. **4** the path of an electric current.

circular /sir-kyi-lar/ *adj* round. • *n* a letter, copies of which are sent to many people.

circularize /sir-kyi-la-rize/ *vb, also* **circularise** to send circulars to.

circulate /sir-kyi-late/ *vb* **1** to move in a circle or a fixed path. **2** to pass around, to spread. **3** to move from one person to another.

circulation /sir-cue-**lay**-shun/ *n* **1** the act of circulating. **2** the movement of the blood through the body. **3** the number of readers (of a newspaper, etc).

circumference /sir-**cum**-frense/ *n* the line marking the limits of a circle.

circumnavigate /sir-cum-**na**-vi-gate/ *vb* (*fml*) to sail around.

circumstance /**sir**-cum-stanse/ *n* **1** (*usually pl*) a condition relating to or connected with an act or event. **2** *pl* state of affairs, position.

circus /sir-cus/ *n* **1** a travelling show given

largely by skilled acrobats and trained animals.

cistern /sis-tern/ *n* a tank for storing water.

citadel /si-ta-del/ *n* a fortress above a city for its defence.

cite /site/ *vb* 1 to call to appear in court. 2 to quote. 3 to give as an example.

citizen /si-ti-zen/ *n* 1 an inhabitant of a city. 2 a member of a state.

citizenship /si-ti-zen-ship/ *n* being, or having the rights of, a citizen.

citrus /si-trus/ *adj* of a group of related fruits, including the lemon, orange, lime and grapefruit.

city /si-tee/ *n* a centre of population larger than a town or village.

civic /si-vic/ *adj* 1 having to do with a city. 2 having to do with citizens or citizenship. • *npl* **civics** the study of the rights and duties of citizens.

civil /si-vil/ *adj* 1 having to do with citizens. 2 having to do with those citizens who are members of neither the armed forces nor the clergy. 3 polite. • *adv* **civilly**. • *n* **civility**.

civilian /si-vil-yen/ *n* someone not in the armed forces.

civilization /si-vi-li-zay-shun/ *n*, *also* **civilisation** 1 a well-organized and polished society. 2 the state of being civilized.

civilize /si-vi-lize/ *vb*, *also* **civilise** 1 to bring or come out of a primitive condition. 2 to make more polite and well-mannered. • *adj* **civilized**, *also* **civilised**.

civil war /si-vil wor/ *n* a war between citizens of the same country.

CJD /cee-jay-dee/ *abbr* = **Creutzfeldt-Jakob disease** /kroytz-felt-yak-ob di-zeez/: a fatal degenerative disease that affects the nerve cells of the brain.

clad /clad/ *pp of* **clothe**.

claim /clame/ *vb* to demand as a right. • *also n*.

clam /clam/ *n* a type of shellfish.

clamber /clam-ber/ *vb* to climb with difficulty, to scramble. • *also n*.

clammy /cla-mee/ *adj* damp, cold and sticky.

clamorous /cla-mo-rus/ *adj* noisy.

clamour /cla-mur/ *n*, *also* **clamor** (*US*) loud shouting, a general outcry, especially demanding something. • *vb* to shout.

clamp /clamp/ *n* 1 a device used for holding things firmly together. 2 a device attached to a car to prevent it from being driven away. • *vb* to fasten with a clamp.

clan /clan/ *n* an early social group of families with the same name, thought to be related, who were ruled by a chief. • *n* **clansman**, **clanswoman**.

clang /clang/ *n* a loud ringing sound, as of metal against metal. • *also vb*.

clank /clangk/ *n* a short, sharp ringing sound. • *also vb*.

clap /clap/ *vb* (**clapped, clapping**) 1 to smack the hands together noisily. 2 to slap or tap, usually in a friendly way. 3 to put suddenly and quickly. • *n* 1 the noise made by clapping the hands. 2 a sudden sound (e.g. of thunder).

clarify /cla-ri-fy/ *vb* to make clear or clearer. • *n* **clarification**.

clarinet /cla-ri-net/ *n* a musical wind instrument with a reed in the mouthpiece. • *n* **clarinettist**.

clarity /cla-ri-tee/ *n* clearness.

clash /clash/ *vb* 1 to strike together noisily. 2 to disagree strongly about. 3 to happen at the same time, as in events. • *n* 1 the loud noise of two objects coming violently together. 2 a quarrel.

clasp /clasp/ *n* 1 a metal fastener. 2 a firm hold. • *vb* 1 to fasten. 2 to hold firmly.

class /class/ *n* 1 a group of persons or things of the same kind. 2 a group of pupils or students. 3 a rank, a standard of excellence. 4 the system according to which people are divided into social groups. 5 one of these social groups. • *vb* to put in a class, to regard as being of a certain type.

classic /cla-sic/ *adj* of the best kind or standard. • *n* 1 a great writer or book. 2 *pl* **the classics** ancient Greek and Roman literature.

classical /cla-si-cal/ *adj* 1 classic. 2 having to do with ancient Greek and Roman literature, art, or customs.

classify /cla-si-fy/ *vb* to arrange in classes. • *n* **classification**.

clatter /cla-ter/ *vb* to make rattling noises. • *n* a rattling noise.

clause /clawz/ *n* 1 a group of words forming a part of a sentence. 2 a section of an agreement.

claustrophobia /claw-stri-foe-bee-a/ *n* the fear of being confined in any small enclosed space.

claw /claw/ *n* 1 the hooked nail of a bird or other animal. 2 a foot with such nails. • *vb* to scratch or tear with claws or nails.

clay /clay/ *n* a moist, formable earth that hardens when dried, used to make sculptures and pottery. • *adj* **clayey**.

clean /cleen/ *adj* 1 free from dirt. 2 pure, free from guilt, evil, crime, sickness, etc. 3 complete. • *adv* completely. • *vb* to remove dirt, dust, etc, from. • *n* **cleaner**. • *n* **cleanness**.

cleanly /clen-lee/ *adj* having clean habits. • *adv* in a clean manner, neatly. • *n* **cleanliness**.

cleanse /clenz/ *vb* to make clean or pure. • *n* **cleanser**.

clear /cleer/ *adj* **1** easy to hear, see or understand. **2** bright. **3** free from difficulties or obstacles. **4** obvious. **5** transparent. • *vb* **1** to make or become clear. **2** to prove innocent. **3** to remove difficulties or obstacles from. **4** to pass through or over. • *adv* **clearly**.

clearance /clee-ranse/ *n* **1** act of clearing. **2** permission for something to be done. **3** the distance between two objects.

clearing /clee-ring/ *n* a wide open part of a forest with no trees.

clef /clef/ *n* a mark to show the pitch in music.

cleft /cleft/ *n* a crack, a split.

clench /clench/ *vb* to press tightly together.

clergy /cler-jee/ *n* persons who are in charge of and who lead religious services: ministers, priests, rabbis, etc.

cleric /cle-ric/ *n* a member of the clergy.

clerical /cle-ri-cal/ *adj* **1** having to do with the clergy. **2** having to do with a clerk.

clerk /clark/ *n* an office employee doing written work.

clever /cle-ver/ *adj* **1** able to learn quickly. **2** able to think quickly. **3** able to do things well with the hands, skilful. • *adv* **cleverly**. • *n* **cleverness**.

cliché /clee-shay/ *n* a stock phrase in common use.

click /click/ *n* a light, sharp sound. • *also vb*.

client /clie-ent/ *n* **1** a customer. **2** someone who employs a member of some profession.

clientele /clee-on-tel/ *n* all the clients of a professional or customers of a shopkeeper.

cliff /cliff/ *n* a high, steep rock face.

climate /clie-mit/ *n* the usual weather conditions of a place. • *adj* **climatic**.

climate change /clie-mit change/ *n* long-term changes to global weather patterns, including changes in temperature and amounts of rainfall.

climax /clie-max/ *n* the highest or most exciting point, the most dramatic moment. • *adj* **climactic**.

climb /clime/ *vb* **1** to rise or ascend. **2** to go up, using the feet and often the hands. • *n* **climber**.

clinch /clinch/ *vb* **1** to settle. **2** in boxing, to stand so close that no strong punches may be given. • *also n*.

cling /cling/ *vb* (*pt, pp* **clung**) **1** to stick to. **2** to hold firmly to.

clinic /cli-nic/ *n* a building or a part of a hospital for people needing special medical treatment or advice. • *adj* **clinical**.

clink /clingk/ *n* a sharp, thin ringing sound. • *also vb*.

clip[1] /clip/ *vb* (**clipped, clipping**) to cut. • *n* **1** something that has been clipped. **2** a sharp blow.

clip[2] *n* a fastener. • *vb* (**clipped, clipping**) to fasten.

clipper /cli-per/ *n* **1** an instrument for clipping. **2** a fast sailing ship.

clique /cleek/ *n* a small group of people who keep together, not mixing with others.

clitoris /cli-tu-riss/ *n* a small sensitive erectile organ of the vulva.

cloak /cloke/ *n* **1** a loose outer garment. **2** something that hides or covers. • *vb* **1** to cover as with a cloak. **2** to conceal.

cloakroom /cloke-room/ *n* **1** a room where you can leave outer garments, packages, etc, in a public place. **2** a room containing a toilet.

clock /clock/ *n* an instrument for telling the time. • *vb* to measure time.

clockwise /clock-wise/ *adj* going around in the direction of the hands of a clock.

clockwork /clock-wurk/ *n* machinery like that inside a mechanical clock. • **like clockwork** regularly and smoothly.

clod /clod/ *n* **1** a lump of earth. **2** a clumsy or stupid person.

clog /clog/ *n* **1** a shoe with a wooden sole. **2** something that blocks or gets in the way of. • *vb* (**clogged, clogging**) to block, to choke.

cloister /cloy-ster/ *n* **1** a monastery or other place where religious people choose to be by themselves. **2** a covered walkway that leads to a courtyard. • *vb* (**cloistered, cloistering**) to confine as if in a monastery.

clone /clone/ *n* **1** an animal or plant that has been produced or manufactured from the cells of another and is, therefore, an exact copy. **2** a person or thing that is very like someone or something else. • *vb* to produce an exact copy of an animal or plant from its own cells.

close[1] /cloze/ *vb* **1** to shut. **2** to finish. **3** to bring or come near. • *n* the end.

close[2] /close/ *adj* **1** shut in. **2** stuffy. **3** near, not far.

closed-circuit television *see* **CCTV**.

closet /cloz-it/ (*esp US*) *n* a large cupboard or small room in which clothes are kept. • *vb* to shut up.

closure /clo-zhur/ *n* (*fml*) closing, end.

clot /clot/ *n* a soft lump formed on or in liquid. • *vb* (**clotted, clotting**) **1** to form into clots. **2** to thicken.

cloth /cloth/ *n* a material made by weaving threads of wool, cotton, etc.

clothe /clothe/ *vb* (*pt, pp* **clothed** *or* **clad**) to put clothes on.

clothes /cloze/ *npl* garments.

clothes peg /cloze peg/ *n* a wooden or plastic clip that holds washed clothes on a line to dry, sometimes called clothes pin.

clothing /clothe-ing/ *n* garments.

cloud /cloud/ *n* **1** a mass of water vapour floating high in the sky. **2** a great many. **3** a cause of gloom or trouble. • *vb* to darken. • *adj* **cloudy, cloudless.**

cloudburst /cloud-burst/ *n* a sudden, very heavy rainstorm.

clove /clove/ *n* **1** a plant bud from a tree used as a spice. **2** a part of a bulb, such as garlic.

clover /clo-ver/ *n* a three-leaved plant grown as food for cattle.

clown /cloun/ *n* **1** a fool. **2** one who plays the fool to amuse others. • *vb* to play the fool.

club /club/ *n* **1** a heavy stick. **2** a golf stick. **3** a group of people who meet for a common purpose. **4** their meeting place. **5** a place, usually one selling drinks, where people go to listen to music and dance. **6** *pl* a suit of playing cards. • *vb* (**clubbed, clubbing**) **1** to beat with a club. **2** to go to a club, sense **5**.

cluck /cluck/ *n* a low, sharp, clicking sound, like the sound made by a hen. • *also vb.*

clue /cloo/ *n* a fact that, when understood, helps one to find the answer to a problem; a hint.

clump /clump/ *n* a closely packed group, a cluster. • *vb* to walk heavily.

clumsy /clum-zee/ *adj* **1** awkward in movement, shape, etc. **2** badly done. • *n* **clumsiness.** • *adv* **clumsily.**

cluster /cluss-ter/ *n* a number of things growing close together; a closely packed group. • *vb* to grow or stand close together.

clutch /cluch/ *vb* **1** to seize. **2** to hold tightly. • *n* **1** a firm hold. **2** *pl* power, control. **3** eggs being hatched at one sitting. **4** in a car, a lever that puts an engine in or out of action. **5** a woman's small handbag or purse.

clutter /clu-ter/ *vb* to fill or cover untidily. • *n* an untidy mass.

cm *abbr* = **centimetre.**

co- /co-/ *prefix* together.

coach /coach/ *n* **1** (*old*) a closed four-wheeled horse carriage. **2** a railway carriage. **3** a bus, especially one with comfortable seats, used for long journeys. **4** a private teacher. **5** one who trains athletes. • *vb* **1** to give private lessons. **2** to prepare.

coal /cole/ *n* a black rock dug from a mine, used as fuel for fires.

coalition /co-wa-li-shun/ *n* **1** a joining together. **2** the joining together of different political parties for a special purpose.

coarse /coarse/ *adj* **1** rough. **2** rude, vulgar, unrefined. • *adv* **coarsely.** • *n* **coarseness.**

coarsen /coar-sen/ *vb* to make coarse.

coast /coast/ *n* the side of the land next to the sea. • *vb* **1** to sail alongside the coast. **2** to move without the use of power. **3** to go on without much effort. • *adj* **coastal.**

coast guard /coast-gard/ *n* the coast police.

coastline /coast-line/ *n* the line of the coast or shore.

coat /coat/ *n* **1** an outer garment with sleeves. **2** the natural cover of an animal (e.g. hair, wool, fur). **3** anything that covers. • *vb* to cover.

coating /co-ting/ *n* a covering.

coat of arms /coat of arms/ *n* the design on a shield or badge representing a person, family, country, or organization.

coax /coaks/ *vb* to get someone to do something by speaking kindly or petting.

cob /cob/ *n* **1** a corncob. **2** a male swan. **3** a short-legged, thickset riding horse.

cobble /cob-ul/ *vb* **1** (*old*) to mend. **2** to mend or put together roughly. • *n* a cobblestone.

cobbler /cob-ler/ *n* a mender of shoes.

cobblestone /cob-ul-stone/ *n* a rounded stone used to pave roads.

cobra /co-bra/ *n* a poisonous snake, found in Africa and Asia, that has loose skin behind its head that stiffens into a hood when the snake is excited, scared or angry.

cobweb /cob-web/ *n* a spider's web found in a house and that has collected dust.

cocaine /co-cane/ *n* a drug that deadens pain, but is very addictive and can be fatal.

cock /cock/ *n* **1** a male bird. **2** an adult male chicken. **3** a tap. **4** the hammer of a gun. **5** (*sl*) the penis • *vb* **1** to turn upward, to tilt. **2** to raise, to cause to stand up. **3** (*of a gun*) to draw back the hammer before firing.

cockatoo /cock-a-too/ *n* a type of parrot.

cockerel /cock-rel/ *n* a young cock.

cocker spaniel /cock-er span-yel/ *n* a small, long-haired, long-eared dog.

cockle /cock-ul/ *n* a type of shellfish.

cockleshell /cock-ul-shell/ *n* **1** the shell of the cockle. **2** a small, light boat.

cockpit /cock-pit/ *n* **1** (*old*) a pit in which cocks were made to fight each other. **2** the pilot's place in an aircraft.

cockroach /cock-roach/ *n* a kind of black beetle with long antennae and a flat body.

cocktail /**cock**-tale/ *n* a strong drink made by mixing alcoholic drinks with juice or other drinks.

cocky /**cock**-ee/ *adj* absolutely sure, over-confident.

cocoa /**co**-co/ *n* **1** a powder made from cacao seeds. **2** a drink made from this powder: hot chocolate.

coconut /**co**-co-nut/ *n* the fruit of the coconut palm tree, with a white inside flesh covered in a brown husk surrounded by a hard shell.

coconut palm /**co**-co-nut pam/ *n* a tropical palm tree.

cocoon /co-**coon**/ *n* a silky case spun by many insects as they grow and transform, as from a caterpillar to a butterfly.

COD /**see**-oh-dee/ *abbr* = **cash on delivery**: a method of payment whereby a person receiving a package must pay for it when he or she receives it.

cod /cod/ *n* a large sea fish.

coddle /**cod**-ul/ *vb* **1** to pet, to treat with too much care. **2** to cook gently.

code /code/ *n* **1** a collection of laws, rules, or signals. **2** a method of sending secret messages by using signs, sounds, or words.

coerce /co-**erse**/ *vb* to make to do, to force. • *n* **coercion**. • *adj* **coercive**.

coexist /co-eg-**zist**/ *vb* to live at the same time or in the same place with another, especially peacefully. • *n* **coexistence**.

coffee /**co**-fee/ *n* a dark brown drink brewed from the roasted, ground seeds of the coffee tree or shrub.

coffin /**co**-fin/ *n* a box in which a dead body is put for burial.

cog /cog/ *n* the tooth of a wheel for receiving motion by fitting between the teeth of another wheel, as on the gears for a bicycle.

coherent /co-**hee**-rent/ *adj* clear and logical. • *n* **coherence**.

cohesion /co-**hee**-zhen/ *n* **1** the force that holds the parts of a substance together. **2** coherence. • *adj* **cohesive**.

coil /coil/ *vb* to wind in a series of rings. • *n* a ring or rings into which a rope, etc, is wound.

coin /coin/ *n* a metal piece of money. • *vb* **1** to make money out of metal. **2** to invent.

coinage /**coy**-nage/ *n* **1** the act of coining. **2** all coined money. **3** the coined money in use in a particular country. **4** a newly invented word.

coincide /co-in-**side**/ *vb* **1** to happen at the same time. **2** to be in agreement.

coincidence /co-**win**(t)-si-dense/ *n* the accidental happening of one event at the same time as another. • *adjs* **coincident**,

coincidental /co-**win**(t)-si-**den**-tal/.

coke /coke/ *n* coal from which most of the gas has been extracted by heating, used as industrial fuel.

colander /**col**-an-der/ *n* a strainer.

cold /coald/ *adj* **1** not hot or warm. **2** without emotion or excitement; unenthusiastic. **3** unfriendly. • *n* **1** absence of heat. **2** an illness, usually consisting of a runny or stuffy nose, sneezing, coughing, aches and pains.

cold-blooded /**coald blu**-ded/ *adj* **1** having body temperature that depends on the environment, as fish, snakes, etc. **2** completely unfeeling, cruel.

collaborate /co-**la**-bo-rate/ *vb* **1** to work together, especially in writing, study, art, or science. **2** to work with another to betray secrets, etc. • *n* **collaboration**, **collaborator**.

collapse /co-**lapse**/ *n* **1** a fall. **2** a sudden loss of consciousness. **3** a failure. • *vb* **1** to fall down. **2** to lose consciousness. **3** to fail completely.

collar /**col**-ar/ *n* **1** the part of the clothing that covers or surrounds the neck. **2** a strap or band put round the neck of an animal. • *vb* (*inf*) to take hold of, to seize.

colleague /**col**-eeg/ *n* a fellow worker.

collect /co-**lect**/ *vb* **1** to bring together. **2** to come together. **3** to gather and keep things of the same kind. **4** to obtain money by contributions. **5** to go somewhere to fetch someone or something.

collected /co-**lek**-ted/ *adj* **1** gathered together. **2** calm, cool, in control.

collection /co-**lek**-shun/ *n* **1** act of collecting. **2** the things collected. **3** the gathering of money for a special purpose. • *n* **collector**.

collective /co-**lek**-tive/ *adj* taken as a whole, joint. • *n* a collective enterprise, as a farm. • *adv* **collectively**.

college /**col**-edge/ *n* **1** a society of learned or professional people that have certain duties. **2** a place of further education, especially in a particular field.

collide /co-**lide**/ *vb* to run into, to strike against. • *n* **collision**.

collie /**col**-ee/ *n* a long-haired dog with a long, narrow head, originally bred for herding sheep.

collision *see* **collide**.

colloquial /co-**lo**-kwee-al/ *adj* conversational, having to do with the spoken language of ordinary people.

colloquialism /co-**lo**-kwee-a-li-zum/ *n* a popular expression.

collusion /co-**loo**-zhun/ *n* a secret agreement to do something wrong.

colon /**co**-lon/ *n* **1** a mark of punctuation (:). **2** a part of the bowel, or lower intestine.

colonel /**cur**-n(e)l/ *n* a military officer.

colonial /co-**lo**-nee-al/ *adj* 1 having to do with a colony. 2 relating to a country that rules other countries, often from far away.

colonist /**col**-un-ist/ *n* a settler in a colony.

colonize /**col**-un-ise/ *vb, also* **colonise** to form or set up a colony in.

colonnade /col-un-**ade**/ *n* a row of columns or pillars.

colony /**col**-un-ee/ *n* 1 a community of settlers in a new land. 2 the place in which they settle.

colossal /cu-**law**-sal/ *adj* very big, gigantic.

colour /**cul**-ur/ *n, also* **color** (*US*) 1 a quality that objects have and that can be seen only when light falls on them. 2 paint. 3 redness (of the face). 4 a skin colour varying with race. 5 brightness. 6 *pl* a flag. • *vb* 1 to paint, to put colour on or into. 2 to give interesting qualities to, to elaborate. 3 to affect. 4 to blush.

colourblind /**cul**-ur-blinde/ *n, also* **colorblind** (*US*) *adj* unable to see the difference between colours or certain colours.

colourful /**cul**-ur-ful/ *adj, also* **colorful** (*US*) 1 full of colour, bright. 2 bright and interesting.

colourless /**cul**-ur-less/ *adj, also* **colorless** (*US*) 1 without colour. 2 uninteresting.

colt /colt/ *n* a young, male horse or donkey.

columbine /**col**-um-bine/ *n* a kind of wild flower of the buttercup family.

column /**col**-um/ *n* 1 a pillar used to support or ornament a building. 2 something similar in shape. 3 a body of troops standing one behind the other in one or more lines. 4 a vertical row in a list, table or chart. 5 a narrow division of a page. • *adj* **columnar**.

columnist /**col**-um-nist/ *n* the writer of a regular series of articles for a newspaper or magazine.

coma /**co**-ma/ *n* a long-continuing state of being unconscious or not awake or aware of one's surroundings.

comatose /**co**-ma-toze/ *adj* 1 of, like, or in a coma. 2 (*inf*) very sleepy, drowsy.

comb /coam/ *n* 1 a toothed instrument for passing through and arranging hair, wool, etc. 2 the crest of a cock. • *vb* to pass through or arrange with a comb.

combat /**com**-bat/ *vb* (**combated, combating**) to fight against, to try to defeat, destroy, etc. • *n* a fight.

combatant /**com**-ba-tant/ *n* one taking part in a fight. • *also adj.*

combative /**com**-ba-tive/ *adj* liking to fight.

combination /com-bi-**nay**-shun/ *n* 1 a joining, a union. 2 *pl* a one-piece undergarment covering the upper and lower body.

combine /com-**bine**/ *vb* to join.

combust /com-**bust**/ *vb* to burn.

combustible /com-**bus**-ti-bul/ *adj* able to take light and burn easily.

combustion /com-**bus**-chin/ *n* the process of burning.

come /cum/ *vb* (*pt* **came**, *pp* **come**) 1 to move towards. 2 (*inf*) to have an orgasm • **come across** to discover. • **come to pass** (*old or fml*) to happen. • *n* **coming**.

comedian /cu-**mee**-dee-an/ *n* 1 a performer who tells jokes, a comic. 2 one who is always trying to make others laugh. • *f* **comedienne**.

comedy /**com**-ed-ee/ *n* 1 a light or amusing play with a happy ending. 2 an amusing happening, the amusing side of something.

comely /**cum**-lee/ *adj* (*old or fml*) pleasant-looking, graceful. • *n* **comeliness**.

comet /**com**-et/ *n* a bright heavenly body made up of frozen dust and gas that orbits the sun, seen only rarely, with a tail of light.

comfort /**cum**-furt/ *n* 1 the state of being free from anxiety, worry, pain, etc, and having all one's physical needs satisfied; ease. 2 something that satisfies one's physical needs. 3 strength, hope, sympathy, etc. 4 the cause of comfort to others. • *vb* to give comfort to, to cheer (someone) up.

comfortable /**cumf**-te-bl/ *adj* 1 at ease, free from anxiety, worry, etc. 2 providing comfort, soft and restful, relaxing.

comforter /**cum**-fur-ter/ *n* someone who comforts.

comic /**com**-ic/ *adj* 1 having to do with comedy. 2 amusing, laughable. • *n* 1 a comedian. 2 a magazine of cartoons, or an illustrated story.

comical /**com**-ic-al/ *adj* funny, amusing.

comma /**com**-a/ *n* a mark of punctuation (,).

command /cu-**manned**/ *vb* 1 to order. 2 to be in charge. 3 to control. 4 to overlook. • *n* 1 an order. 2 mastery.

commander /cu-**man**-der/ *n* 1 an officer in charge of troops. 2 an officer in the navy.

commanding /cu-**man**-ding/ *adj* arousing respect.

commandment /cu-**mand**-ment/ *n* an order, a law.

commemorate /cu-**mem**-o-rate/ *vb* to make people remember something by holding a service or doing something special. • *n* **commemoration**.

commence /cu-**mense**/ *vb* (*fml*) to begin. • *n* **commencement**.

commend /cu-mend/ *vb* **1** to praise. **2** (*fml*) to recommend.

commendable /cu-men-da-bl/ *adj* deserving praise.

commendation /com-en-day-shun/ *n* praise.

comment /com-ent/ *vb* **1** to say something about, to remark on. **2** to write notes in explanation of. • *n* **1** a remark. **2** an explanation.

commentary /com-en-te-ree/ *n* **1** a series of remarks or notes. **2** a spoken description of an event as it happens. • **running commentary** a description of an event as it happens, given by an onlooker.

commentator /com-en-tay-tor/ *n* **1** one who comments. **2** the writer or speaker of a commentary.

commerce /com-erse/ *n* the buying and selling of goods, trade.

commercial /co-mer-shal/ *adj* **1** having to do with trade or commerce. **2** profit-making. • *n* (*US*) an advertisement for radio or television.

commiserate /co-miz-u-rate/ *vb* to pity, to sympathize with. • *n* **commiseration**.

commission /co-mi-shun/ *n* **1** act of committing. **2** an order for a work of art. **3** a group of people appointed to study and report on a particular matter. **4** money paid to someone who has helped to arrange a business deal. • *vb* to give an order or request to, to appoint.

commissionaire /co-mi-shun-air/ *n* a uniformed attendant at the entrance of some public buildings.

commit /co-mit/ *vb* (**committed**, **committing**) **1** to perform or do, especially something illegal. **2** to make a definite agreement. **3** to give (someone) into care. **4** (*fml*) to put in or on.

commitment /co-mit-ment/ *n* **1** the act of committing. **2** a promise, a duty, a responsibility. **3** state of being devoted.

committee /co-mi-tee/ *n* a group of people appointed from a larger body to manage its affairs or perform a particular duty.

commodity /co-mod-i-tee/ *n* (*often pl*) anything bought and sold; a useful thing.

common /com-on/ *adj* **1** belonging to everyone, of no special rank or quality. **2** found everywhere. **3** ordinary. **4** frequent. **5** rough, regarded as being low class. • *n* land belonging to or open to the community.

common denominator /com-on di-nom-in-ay-tor/ *n* a denominator shared by two or more fractions.

commonplace /com-on-place/ *n* a well-known remark, an ordinary or unoriginal remark. • *adj* ordinary, not regarded as special.

common sense /com-on sense/ *n* practical knowledge of how to act in everyday matters.

commonwealth /com-on-welth/ *n* **1** a state in which everyone has a say in the type of government. **2** a group of states united by certain common interests.

commotion /co-mo-shun/ *n* confused movement, disorder.

communal /cu-myoo-nal/ *adj* shared by all.

commune /cu-myoon/ *vb* (*fml*) to talk together (with), to exchange thoughts or feelings with.

communicable /cu-myoo-ni-ca-bl/ *adj* **1** able to be passed to others. **2** able to be communicated or explained to others.

communicant /cu-myoo-ni-cant/ *n* one who receives Holy Communion, a religious ceremony practised in some Christian churches.

communicate /cu-myoo-ni-cate/ *vb* **1** to make known to, to tell. **2** to get in touch with. **3** to make information, ideas, feelings, etc, known clearly to others. **4** to pass.

communication /cu-myoo-ni-cay-shun/ *n* **1** a message. **2** a means of communicating.

communicative /cu-myoo-ni-ca-tiv/ *adj* talkative, ready to give information.

communion /cu-myoon-yun/ *n* the act of sharing. • **Holy Communion** a religious ceremony practised in some Christian churches.

communism /com-yoo-ni-zum/ *n* the belief in an economic system that is based on all property being owned by the whole community and not by the individual.

communist /com-yoo-nist/ *n* a believer in communism. • *adj* to do with communism. • *adj* **communistic**.

community /cu-myoo-ni-tee/ *n* the whole body of the people living in a town, district, country, etc.

commute /cu-myoot/ *vb* **1** to travel daily from the place where one lives to the place where one works. **2** to change into something less unpleasant. • *adj* **commutable**. • *n* **commutation**.

commuter /cu-myoo-ter/ *n* one who commutes.

compact /com-pact/ *adj* **1** tightly packed, firm. **2** fitted neatly together in a small space. **3** short, concise. • *n* **compact** a flat case for face powder. • *n* **compactness**.

compact disc /com-pact disc/ *n* a small, hard, plastic disc on which sound or information is recorded in a form readable by a laser, often called **CD**.

companion /com-pan-yon/ *n* **1** a friend, a person, etc, who regularly accompanies another. **2** one who goes with or accompanies.

3 a person employed to live with someone and keep him or her company. **4** one of a matching pair or set of things. • *n* **companionship**.

companionable /com-**pan**-yu-na-bl/ *adj* liking company.

companionway /com-**pan**-yun-way/ *n* stairs on a ship from deck to cabin.

company *n* **1** a number of people gathered together by chance or invitation. **2** being together with another or others. **3** a group of persons who have put together money to run a business. **4** a group of people working together. **5** a body of soldiers commanded by a captain. **6** the crew of a ship.

comparable /com-pa-ra-bl/ *adj* **1** able to be compared. **2** nearly or just as good as.

comparative /com-**pa**-ra-tive/ *adj* judged alongside something else, relative.

compare /com-**pare**/ *vb* **1** to consider things together to see how they are alike and different. **2** to point out the likeness or difference between.

comparison /com-**pa**-ris-son/ *n* **1** act of comparing. **2** likeness, similarity.

compartment /com-**part**-ment/ *n* **1** a part (e.g. of a drawer) divided off from the rest. **2** one of the small rooms in a railway carriage.

compass /com-pass/ *n* **1** a direction-finding instrument containing a magnetic needle that always points north. **2** (*fml*) full extent or range. **3** *pl* **compasses** an instrument for drawing circles, consisting of two pointed legs connected at one end.

compassion /com-**pa**-shun/ *n* pity, deep sympathy.

compassionate /com-**pa**-shu-nate/ *adj* feeling or showing pity or deep sympathy.

compatible /com-**pa**-ti-bl/ *adj* **1** able to exist together peacefully. **2** in agreement with.

compatriot /com-**pay**-tree-ut/ *n* a person from the same country.

compel /com-**pel**/ *vb* (**compelled, compelling**) to make to do, to force. • *adj* **compelling** very interesting, attractive.

compendium /com-**pen**-dee-um/ *n* a summary containing the important aspects of a subject.

compensate /com-pen-sate/ *vb* **1** to give something to make up for harm or injury done. **2** to undo or counteract the effect of a disadvantage, loss, etc.

compensation /com-pen-**say**-shun/ *n* something given, such as a payment, to make up for harm or injury.

compete /com-**peet**/ *vb* **1** to try to do better than one's fellows in work, games, etc. **2** to take part in the hope of winning.

competence /com-pe-tense/, **competency** /com-pe-ten-see/ *n* **1** ability, skill. **2** (*old*) a sufficient amount of money to live on.

competent /com-pe-tent/ *adj* **1** good at one's job. **2** well-done. **3** (*fml*) having the necessary powers. • *adv* **competently**.

competition /com-pe-**ti**-shun/ *n* **1** the act of competing, rivalry. **2** a contest for which a prize is offered. **3** people competing for a prize, etc.

competitive /com-**pe**-ta-tive/ *adj* encouraging competition or rivalry.

competitor /com-**pe**-ti-tor/ *n* **1** one who competes. **2** a rival.

compile /com-**pile**/ *vb* to collect (facts and figures, etc.) and put together in an orderly form. • *n* **compiler**. • *n* **compilation**.

complacence /com-**play**-sense/, **complacency** /com-**play**-sen-see/ *n* satisfaction, especially self-satisfaction, smugness.

complacent /com-**play**-sent/ *adj* smug, satisfied with oneself and one's actions, etc.

complain /com-**plane**/ *vb* **1** to grumble. **2** to say that one is not satisfied.

complainant /com-**play**-nant/ *n* one who accuses another of an offence against the law.

complaint /com-**playnt**/ *n* **1** a grumble. **2** an expression of dissatisfaction. **3** an illness. **4** an accusation.

complaisant /com-**play**-sant/ *adj* agreeable, ready to please. • *n* **complaisance**.

complement /com-**pli**-ment/ *n* **1** that which completes. **2** the number or quantity needed to make something complete.

complementary /com-pli-**men**-ta-ree/ *adj* adding what is necessary to make complete.

complementary medicine /com-pli-**men**-ta-ree me-di-sin/ *n* a range of therapies other than the usual scientific medical treatments, including herbal medicine, homoeopathy and acupuncture.

complete /com-**pleet**/ *adj* **1** finished. **2** whole. **3** perfect. • *vb* **1** to finish. **2** to make whole. • *n* **completion**.

complex /com-**plex**/ *adj* **1** having many parts. **2** not simple. • *n* /**com**-plex/ **1** a group of connected or similar things. **2** an abnormal mental state, often caused by past experiences or suppressed desires or fears, that influences a person's behaviour.

complexion /com-**plek**-shun/ *n* the colour, texture and general appearance of the skin, especially the face.

complexity /com-**plek**-si-tee/ *n* **1** the state of being complex. **2** difficulty.

compliant /com-**plie**-ant/ *adj* giving in easily to others. • *n* **compliance**. • *see also* **comply**.

complicate /**com**-pli-cate/ *vb* to make difficult.

complicated /**com**-pli-cay-ted/ *adj* **1** difficult to understand. **2** confusing because of having many parts.

complication /com-pli-**cay**-shun/ *n* **1** a confused state of affairs. **2** an event or fact that makes things difficult.

complicity /com-**pli**-si-tee/ *n* helping to do something wrong.

compliment /**com**-pli-ment/ *n* **1** praise, a flattering remark. **2** *pl* (*fml*) good wishes. • *vb* to praise, to express admiration.

complimentary /com-pli-**men**-ta-ree/ *adj* **1** flattering, showing admiration. **2** free.

comply /com-**ply**/ *vb* (*usually accompanied by* **with**) **1** to agree to. **2** to obey. • *n* **compliance**.

component /com-**po**-nent/ *n* a part necessary to the whole object. • *also adj*.

comport /com-**poart**/ *vb* (*fml*) to behave.

compose /com-**poze**/ *vb* **1** to make up by putting together. **2** to write. **3** to calm.

composed /com-**pozed**/ *adj* calm.

composer /com-**po**-zer/ *n* one who writes music.

composite /com-**poz**-it/ *adj* made up of several parts.

composition /com-po-**zi**-shun/ *n* **1** act of putting together. **2** the arrangement of parts to form a pleasing whole. **3** the thing composed or written. **4** a mixture.

compost /**com**-post/ *n* rotting vegetable matter, etc, used as a fertilizer.

composure /com-**po**-zhur/ *n* calmness.

compote /**com**-pote/ *n* preserved fruit.

compound¹ /**com**-pound/ *vb* **1** to put together, to mix. **2** to increase greatly. • *adj* /com-pound/ made up of two or more parts. • *n* /**com**-pound/ a mixture of two or more substances.

compound² /**com**-pound/ *n* an enclosed space with a building or buildings in it.

comprehend /com-pre-**hend**/ *vb* **1** to understand. **2** (*fml*) to include.

comprehensible /com-pre-**hen**-si-bl/ *adj* able to be understood.

comprehension /com-pre-**hen**-shun/ *n* the power of understanding.

comprehensive /com-pre-**hen**-sive/ *adj* taking in as much as possible.

compress /com-**press**/ *vb* to press together into a smaller space. • *n* **compression**. • *n* /**com**-press/ a soft pad.

comprise /com-**prize**/ *vb* to be made up of.

compromise /**com**-pro-mize/ *vb* **1** to reach agreement by giving way on certain points. **2** to leave open to suspicion or criticism. • *n* an agreement reached when each party gives way on certain points.

compulsion /com-**pul**-shun/ *n* **1** force. **2** an irresistible urge.

compulsory /com-**pulse**-ree/ *adj* forced, compelled.

compunction /com-**punc**-shun/ *n* regret, feeling of guilt.

compute /com-**pyoot**/ *vb* (*fml*) to calculate or estimate. • *n* **computation**.

computer /com-**pyoo**-ter/ *n* an electronic machine capable of storing and processing large amounts of information and of doing calculations. • *vb* **computerize**, *also* **computerise**. • *n* **computerization**, *also* **computerisation**.

computer-aided design *n* the use of a computer to create plans and drawings, *also known as* **CAD**.

computer graphics *npl* artwork or design that is created on a computer.

comrade /**com**-rade/ *n* a friend, a companion.

comradeship /**com**-rade-ship/ *n* good fellowship.

con¹ /con/ *vb* (**conned, conning**) to deceive, to trick.

con² /con/ *n* a reason, vote, or position in opposition.

concave /con-**cave**/ *adj* hollow, curved inward.

conceal /con-**seel**/ *vb* to hide, to keep from others.

concealment /con-**seel**-ment/ *n* act of concealing.

concede /con-**seed**/ *vb* **1** to admit as true. **2** to give up. • *n* **concession**.

conceit /con-**seet**/ *n* **1** too high an opinion of oneself. **2** (*fml*) a fanciful or imaginative idea.

conceited /con-**see**-ted/ *adj* too proud of oneself, vain.

conceivable /con-**see**-va-bl/ *adj* able to be thought of or imagined.

conceive /con-**seev**/ *vb* **1** to grasp clearly with the mind. **2** to imagine. **3** to become pregnant.

concentrate /con-**sen**-trate/ *vb* **1** to bring together to one point. **2** to bring all the powers of the mind to bear on. **3** to make a substance stronger by reducing its volume. **4** to pack tightly. • *n* a concentrated substance. • *n* **concentration**.

concentric /con-**sen**-tric/ *adj* having the same centre.

concept /**con**-sept/ *n* a general idea. • *adj* **conceptual**.

conception /con-**sep**-shun/ *n* **1** act of conceiving. **2** an idea.

concern /con-**sern**/ *vb* **1** to have to do with. **2** to take interest. **3** (*fml*) to be anxious about. • *n* **1** an affair. **2** interest. **3** anxiety. **4** a business.

concerning /con-**ser**-ning/ *prep* having to do with, about.

concert /con-sert/ *n* a musical entertainment.

concerted /con-ser-ted/ *adj* planned together, worked out together.

concertina /con-ser-**tee**-na/ *n* a musical wind instrument similar to an accordian but with buttons instead of a keyboard.

concerto /con-**cher**-toe/ *n* a musical composition for a solo player accompanied by an orchestra.

concession /con-se-shun/ *n* **1** the act of giving up. **2** a thing conceded, a favour. **3** a reduction on the cost of something, such as a theatre ticket.

conch /conch/ *n* the large, spiral seashell of certain shellfish.

conciliate /con-si-lee-ate/ *vb* **1** (*fml*) to make less angry or more friendly. **2** to create peace between.

conciliation /con-si-lee-**ay**-shun/ *n* the bringing together in peace or friendship of those who have quarrelled.

conciliatory /con-**sil**-ya-toe-ree/ *adj* calming, peace-making.

concise /con-**sice**/ *adj* short and to the point, brief. • *n* conciseness.

conclave /con-clave/ *n* **1** in Catholicism, the meeting of cardinals to choose a new pope. **2** a meeting held in private.

conclude /con-**clood**/ *n* **1** (*fml*) to end, to bring to an end. **2** to arrange, to settle on. **3** to come to believe after consideration of the facts.

conclusion /con-**cloo**-zhun/ *n* **1** (*fml*) end. **2** the idea finally reached after thinking something out.

conclusive /con-**cloo**-siv/ *adj* convincing, putting an end to doubt.

concoct /con-coct/ *vb* **1** to make by mixing. **2** to make up, invent.

concoction /con-**coc**-shun/ *n* something, such as food or drink, made by mixing several things.

concomitant /con-**com**-i-tant/ *adj* (*fml*) accompanying, going together. • *also n*.

concord /con-cord/ *n* (*fml*) **1** agreement. **2** peace and friendship.

concordance /con-**cor**-danse/ *n* **1** agreement. **2** an alphabetical list of the most important words used in a book or by a writer and exactly where they can be found.

concordat /con-**cor**-dat/ *n* a treaty, a formal agreement.

concourse /con-**coarse**/ *n* **1** a large, open space for people. **2** (*fml*) a gathering, a crowd.

concrete /con-**creet**/ *adj* **1** solid, having a real bodily existence. **2** definite. • *n* a mixture of cement, sand and gravel with water.

concur /con-**cur**/ *vb* (**concurred, concurring**) **1** to happen at the same time. **2** to agree.

concurrence /con-**cur**-ense/ *n* **1** happening together at the same place. **2** (*fml*) agreement.

concurrent /con-**cur**-ent/ *adj* **1** in agreement. **2** happening at the same time. • *adv* **concurrently**.

concussion /con-cu-shun/ *n* **1** a violent shaking. **2** an injury that affects the function of an organ, especially the brain, as a result of a violent blow or impact.

condemn /con-**dem**/ *vb* **1** to blame. **2** to find guilty. **3** to name a punishment for a guilty person. • *n* **condemnation**.

condemnatory /con-**dem**-na-toe-ree/ *adj* laying the blame on.

condense /con-**dense**/ *vb* **1** to make shorter or smaller. **2** to make a substance more solid (e.g. to change vapour into liquid). • *n* **condensation**.

condescend /con-di-**send**/ *vb* to descend to the level, regarded as lower, of the person or people with whom one is dealing, usually in an ungracious, proud manner. • *adj* **condescending**. • *n* **condescension**.

condiment /con-di-ment/ *n* a seasoning, sauce, or relish eaten with food to bring out its flavour or enhance its taste.

condition /con-**di**-shun/ *n* **1** state. **2** something that must be or happen before something else can take place.

conditional /con-**dish**-nal/ *adj* depending on something else happening.

condolence /con-**doe**-lense/ *n* (*often pl*) expression of sympathy.

condone /con-**doan**/ *vb* to forgive, to pardon, to overlook a wrong.

condor /con-dor/ *n* a large vulture with black feathers, a bald head and neck and soft, white feathers at the base of the neck.

conducive /con-**dyoo**-sive/ *adj* helping to produce, leading.

conduct /con-**duct**/ *vb* **1** to lead, to guide. **2** to carry. **3** to direct. **4** (*fml*) to behave. • *n* /con-duct/ behaviour.

conductor /con-**duc**-tor/ *n* **1** the director of an orchestra. **2** the person who takes the fares on a bus. **3** a substance that passes on heat or electricity to something else. • *f* **conductress**.

conduit /con-dwit/ *n* **1** a pipe or channel made to carry fluids. **2** tubing or piping that protects electric wires.

cone /cone/ *n* **1** a figure with a circular base and a pointed top. **2** the fruit of pines and firs. **3** any object shaped like a cone.

confection /con-**fec**-shun/ *n* **1** the process of making something by mixing. **2** any kind of sweet or other sugary treat.

confectionary /con-**fec**-shu-na-ree/ *adj* of or like a confection, of confectioners or their work.

confectioner /con-**fec**-shu-ner/ *n* a person whose work is making or selling sweets.

confectionery /con-**fec**-shu-na-ree/ *n* **1** sweets; sweet treats made from sugar, chocolate, etc. **2** the business or work of a confectioner. **3** a sweet shop.

confederate /con-**fe**-de-rit/ *adj* joined together by agreement or common purpose. • *n* a supporter, a helper, often in wrongdoing. **confederation** *n* a group of states or nations that have agreed to act together.

confer /con-**fer**/ *vb* (**conferred**, **conferring**) **1** to talk together. **2** to give.

conference /con-frense/ *n* a meeting held to discuss matters.

confess /con-**fess**/ *vb* to own up, to admit fault or guilt.

confession /con-**fe**-shun/ *n* the act of confessing, an account of the wrong one has done.

confessional /con-**fesh**-nal/ *n* in the Catholic church, the small room in which a priest hears confessions.

confessor /con-**fe**-sor/ *n* **1** a person who confesses. **2** in the Catholic church, a priest who hears confessions.

confetti /con-**fe**-tee/ *n* small pieces of coloured paper thrown during celebrations.

confidant /con-fi-dawnt/ *n* a person trusted with a secret. • *f* **confidante**.

confide /con-**fide**/ *vb* to give or tell something to a person one trusts.

confiding /con-**fie**-ding/ *adj* trusting.

confidence /con-fi-dense/ *n* **1** trust. **2** belief in one's own abilities.

confident /con-fi-dent/ *adj* having no fear of failure. • *adv* **confidently**.

confidential /con-fi-**den**-shal/ *adj* **1** trusted. **2** secret. • *adv* **confidentially**.

configuration /con-fig-yu-**ray**-shun/ *n* (*fml*) shape that is determined by the arrangement of various parts.

configure /con-fi-gyer/ *vb* to arrange in a certain way.

confine /con-**fine**/ *vb* **1** to shut up. **2** to keep within limits. • *n* /con-fine/ a limit, a boundary.

confinement /con-**fine**-ment/ *n* **1** imprisonment. **2** childbirth.

confirm /con-**firm**/ *vb* **1** to say that something is undoubtedly certain or true. **2** to give final approval to.

confirmation /con-fir-**may**-shun/ *n* **1** proof. **2** the ceremony by which one becomes a full member of certain churches.

confirmed /con-firmd/ *adj* settled, habitual.

confiscate /con-fi-skate/ *vb* to seize a person's private property, especially as a punishment. • *n* **confiscation** /con-fi-**skay**-shun/.

conflagration /con-fla-**gray**-shun/ *n* (*fml*) a big, destructive fire.

conflict /con-flict/ *n* **1** a state of disagreement. **2** a fight. • *vb* /con-**flict**/ to disagree, to clash.

conflicting /con-**flic**-ting/ *adj* **1** going against each other, fighting, or quarrelling. **2** clashing, disagreeing.

confluence /con-floo-ense/ *n* **1** a flowing together. **2** the meeting of streams. • *adj* **confluent**.

conform /con-**fawrm**/ *vb* **1** to act or think like most other people, to accept the laws and practices of the time or place. **2** to obey, to be in accordance with.

conformation /con-for-**may**-shun/ *n* the way in which a thing is put together; shape.

conformity /con-**fawr**-mi-tee/ *n* **1** behaviour, attitudes, etc, that are the same as most people's. **2** agreement, obedience.

confound /con-**found**/ *vb* **1** to defeat completely. **2** to confuse, to mix up.

confront /con-**frunt**/ *vb* to meet face to face. • *n* **confrontation**.

confuse /con-**fyooz**/ *vb* **1** to put into disorder, to muddle. **2** to puzzle, to bewilder. **3** to mistake one person or thing for another.

confusion /con-**fyoo**-zhun/ *n* **1** disorder. **2** puzzlement, bewilderment.

confute /con-**fyoot**/ *vb* to prove (someone) wrong, to prove untrue. • *n* **confutation**.

congeal /con-**jeel**/ *vb* **1** to become thick by cooling or freezing. **2** to become solid and stiff.

congenial /con-**jee**-nee-al/ *adj* **1** having the same likes and dislikes. **2** pleasing.

congenital /con-**jen**-i-tal/ *adj* existing from birth.

conger /**cong**-ger/ *n* a saltwater eel with a long fin on its back, sharp teeth and powerful jaws.

congested /con-**jess**-tid/ *adj* **1** overcrowded. **2** too full of blood or mucus. • *n* **congestion**.

conglomerate /con-**glom**-rit/ *adj* stuck together in a lump. • *n* **1** a cluster. **2** a rock made up of different kinds of pebbles sticking together. **3** a large corporation formed by merging several different firms.

conglomeration /con-glom-e-**ray**-shun/ *n* a mixed collection.

congratulate /con-**gra**-chu-late/ *vb* to express pleasure at another's success, a happy event, etc. • *n* **congratulation**. • *adj* **congratulatory**.

congregate /**cong**-gri-gate/ *vb* to meet, to form a crowd.

congregation /cong-gri-**gay**-shun/ *n* a gathering of people, especially at a church service.

congress /**cong**-gress/ *n* 1 a formal meeting of statesmen, etc, to settle certain questions. 2 **Congress** the part of the US government that makes laws, consisting of the Senate and the House of Representatives. • *adj* **congressional**.

congruent /**cong**-groo-ent/ *adj* suitable, agreeing. • *n* **congruity**.

congruous /**cong**-groo-us/ *adj* suitable, agreeing.

conic /**con**-ic/, **conical** /**con**-i-cal/ *adj* cone-shaped.

conifer /**con**-i-fer/ *n* a cone-bearing tree. • *adj* **coniferous**.

conjectural /con-**jec**-che-ral/ *adj* due to guesswork, not certain.

conjecture /con-**jec**-cher/ *vb* to guess, to suppose. • *n* guess.

conjoin /con-**join**/ *vb* (*fml*) to join, unite.

conjoint /con-**joint**/ *adj* (*fml*) joined, united. • *adv* **conjointly**.

conjugal /**con**-ji-gal/ *adj* having to do with marriage or the relationship between husband and wife.

conjugate /**con**-ji-gate/ 1 *adj* joined, especially in a pair, coupled. 2 *vb* to give the forms (i.e. mood, tense, person, etc.) of a verb. • *n* **conjugation**.

conjunction /con-**jung**-shun/ *n* 1 a connection. 2 in grammar, a joining word, such as 'and', 'but', 'or'. • *adj* **conjunctive**.

conjuncture /con-**jungk**-cher/ *n* (*fml*) a combination of events or situations, especially one causing difficulties.

conjure /**con**-jer/ *vb* 1 to do magic; to do tricks so quickly and skilfully that the onlooker cannot see how they are done. 2 to summon, to cause to appear as if by magic.

conjurer /**con**-ju-rer/ *n*, *also* **conjuror** one who entertains by doing tricks, one who performs magic.

connect /co-**nect**/ *vb* 1 to join. 2 to see that a thing or idea is related to another, to associate in the mind. • **well-connected** related to important or powerful people.

connection /co-**nec**-shun/ *n* 1 something that joins. 2 a relation by blood or marriage. 3 something that makes one think of a certain person, place, event, etc, when one sees another.

connive /co-**nive**/ *vb* 1 to pretend not to see wrongdoing. 2 to cooperate secretly with someone, especially in wrongdoing. • *n* **connivance**.

connoisseur /con-i-**sur**/ *n* one with expert knowledge of something and the ability to tell what is bad from what is good.

connotation /con-i-**tay**-shun/ *n* what is suggested by a word in addition to its actual meaning.

connote /co-**note**/ *vb* to suggest in addition to the actual meaning.

connubial /co-**noo**-bee-al/ *adj* (*fml*) having to do with marriage or married life.

conquer /**cong**-ker/ *vb* 1 to win by war. 2 to defeat. 3 to overcome. • *n* **conqueror**.

conquest /**con**-kwest/ *n* 1 act of conquering. 2 a thing gained by force.

conscience /**con**-shense/ *n* one's sense of right and wrong.

conscientious /con-she-en-shus/ *adj* careful to do one's duty. • *n* **conscientiousness**.

conscientious objector /con-she-en-shus ob-**jec**-tor/ *n* one who, in war, refuses to fight because he or she believes it is wrong to do so.

conscious /**con**-shus/ *adj* 1 knowing what is going on around one. 2 aware. • *n* **consciousness**.

conscript /**con**-script/ *n* one made by law to serve in the armed forces.

conscription /con-**scrip**-shun/ *n* the act of making people serve in the armed forces by law.

consecrate /**con**-si-crate/ *vb* 1 to make holy. 2 to devote, to set apart. • *n* **consecration**.

consecutive /con-**sec**-yu-tiv/ *adj* following one after the other, in order.

consensus /con-**sen**-sis/ *n* general agreement.

consent /con-**sent**/ *vb* to agree, to give one's permission. • *n* agreement, permission.

consequence /**con**-se-kwense/ *n* 1 a result, an effect. 2 importance.

consequent /**con**-se-kwent/ *adj* (*fml*) following, resulting.

consequential /con-se-**kwen**-shal/ *adj* 1 following upon. 2 consequential.

conservatism /con-**ser**-va-ti-zum/ *n* dislike of changes, especially in governing.

conservative /con-**ser**-va-tiv/ *adj* 1 disliking change. 2 moderate, cautious, safe. 3 (*cap*) describing a member of the British Conservative political party. • *n* 1 a person with politically conservative views. 2 (*cap*) a member of the British Conservative party.

conservatory /con-**ser**-va-toe-ree/ *n* 1 a room enclosed in glass; a greenhouse. 2 a school of fine arts, usually music.

conserve /con-**serv**/ vb **1** to keep something as it is. **2** to keep from being wasted or spoiled. • n fruits preserved in sugar, a kind of jam. • n **conservation**.

consider /con-**si**-der/ vb **1** to think about. **2** to think seriously. **3** to take into account. **4** to regard as.

considerable /con-**si**-der-a-bl/ adj fairly large, great.

considerate /con-**sid**-rit/ adj thoughtful of others.

consideration /con-si-de-**ray**-shun/ n **1** serious thought. **2** thought for others and their feelings. **3** a payment or reward.

considering /con-**si**-de-ring/ prep allowing for.

consign /con-**sine**/ vb (fml) **1** to deliver to, to put in the care of another. **2** to send.

consignment /con-**sine**-ment/ n the goods sent.

consist /con-**sist**/ vb to be made up of.

consistency /con-**sis**-ten-see/ n **1** degree of density or (of liquids) thickness. **2** the quality of being consistent.

consistent /con-**sis**-tent/ adj **1** fixed, having a regular pattern. **2** agreeing with. **3** always thinking or acting on the same principles.

consolation /con-so-**lay**-shun/ n **1** comfort. **2** a person or thing that brings comfort in sorrow or sadness.

console¹ /con-**sole**/ vb to comfort.

console² /con-**sole**/ n a unit, e.g. between the two front seats in a car, containing switches and/or controls.

consolidate /con-**sol**-i-date/ vb **1** to make solid or firm, to strengthen. **2** to unite or combine into a single whole, to merge. • n **consolidation**.

consonance /**con**-si-nanse/ n (fml) agreement.

consonant /**con**-si-nant/ n a speech sound or letter other than a vowel. • adj in agreement with.

consort /**con**-sort/ n a partner, a husband or wife. • vb /con-**sort**/ (fml) to go out together, to associate with.

conspicuous /con-**spic**-yoo-us/ adj easily seen, very noticeable.

conspiracy /con-**spi**-ra-see/ n **1** a coming together to plan wrongdoing. **2** a plot.

conspire /con-**spire**/ vb **1** to plan secretly together to do something wrong or unlawful. **2** to unite. • n **conspirator**.

constable /**con**-stab-il/ n a police officer of the lowest rank.

constant /**con**-stant/ adj **1** never stopping. **2** unchanging. **3** (fml) faithful, loyal. • n **constancy**.

constantly /**con**-stant-lee/ adv **1** again and again, nearly always, regularly. **2** without stopping.

constellation /con-ste-**lay**-shun/ n a group of stars, usually named for an object or animal that it resembles.

consternation /con-ster-**nay**-shun/ n great surprise, dismay.

constipated /**con**-sti-pay-ted/ adj having difficulty in clearing the bowels.

constipation /con-sti-**pay**-shun/ n a condition in which clearing the bowels is difficult.

constituency /con-**stich**-wan-see/ n the people of a district who vote for a representative, e.g. a member of parliament.

constituent /con-**stich**-wint/ adj being part of, forming. • n **1** a necessary part. **2** a member of a constituency.

constitute /**con**-sti-toot/ vb **1** (fml) to be. **2** to make up, to form.

constitution /con-sti-**too**-shun/ n **1** the way something is made up. **2** the general health of the body. **3** the body of law with which a country is governed.

constitutional /con-sti-**toosh**-nal/ adj having to do with the laws of a country. • n (old) a short walk taken to improve the health.

constrain /con-**strane**/ vb to force, to compel.

constraint /con-**straint**/ n **1** force, compulsion. **2** a limit. **3** strained manner, lack of friendliness.

constrict /con-**strict**/ vb **1** to make smaller or narrower, to make tight. **2** to prevent free movement. • n **constriction**.

constrictor /con-**stric**-tor/ n a large snake that crushes its prey.

construct /con-**struct**/ vb **1** to build. **2** to make by putting the parts together.

construction /con-**struc**-shun/ n **1** act of constructing. **2** the thing constructed. **3** the way of arranging words to give a certain meaning. **4** (fml) meaning.

constructive /con-**struc**-tiv/ adj useful and helpful.

construe /con-**stroo**/ vb **1** to translate into another language. **2** to explain, to interpret.

consul /**con**-sul/ n a person appointed to look after the interests of his or her country in a foreign country.

consular /**con**-si-lar/ adj having to do with a consul.

consulate /**con**-si-lit/ n the office of a consul.

consult /con-**sult**/ vb **1** to ask advice, information, or help from. **2** to discuss matters with. **3** to look up. • n **consultation**.

consultant /con-**sul**-tant/ n one able to advise, especially a doctor who is an expert in a particular branch of medicine.

consume /con-**soom**/ vb **1** to eat. **2** to use up. **3** to destroy, to waste.

consumer /con-**soo**-mer/ n one who buys or uses.

consummate /con-su-mate/ vb **1** to finish, to make complete or perfect. **2** to make a marriage or relationship complete by having sex. • adj complete, perfect. • n **consummation**.

consumption /con-**sum**-shun/ n **1** the act of using. **2** the amount used. **3** (old) a disease of the lungs.

contact /con-tact/ n **1** touch. **2** communication. • vb to get in touch with, to communicate with.

contact lens /con-tact lenz/ n a small convex piece of thin plastic placed on the front of the cornea to help the wearer see better.

contagious /con-**tay**-jus/ adj (of disease) able to be passed on, quickly spreading to others. • n **contagion**.

contain /con-**tane**/ vb **1** to have in it. **2** to keep control of.

container /con-**tay**-ner/ n anything made to hold something else in it.

contaminate /con-**ta**-mi-nate/ vb to make dirty, infected, or impure; to pollute. • n **contamination**.

contemplate /con-tem-plate/ vb **1** to look at thoughtfully. **2** to think deeply about. **3** to think of doing. • n **contemplation**.

contemplative /con-**tem**-pla-tiv/ adj **1** thoughtful. **2** spending time in prayer.

contemporary /con-**tem**-po-ra-ree/ adj **1** belonging to the same time. **2** modern. • n one who lives at the same time as another.

contempt /con-**temt**/ n the feeling that another person or thing is worthless and to be looked down on; scorn.

contemptible /con-**tem**-ti-bl/ adj deserving to be looked down on.

contemptuous /con-**tem**-choo-us/ adj showing contempt or scorn.

contend /con-**tend**/ vb **1** to struggle against. **2** to compete. **3** to maintain, to state. • n **contender**.

content[1] /con-**tent**/ n that which is in something else.

content[2] /con-**tent**/ adj satisfied, pleased, not wanting more than one has. • also vb. • n **contentment**.

contention /con-**ten**-shun/ n **1** disagreement, argument. **2** competition. **3** an opinion.

contentious /con-**ten**-shus/ adj quarrelsome.

contest /con-**test**/ vb **1** to try to prove wrong. **2** to try hard to gain. • n /con-test/ **1** a struggle. **2** a competition.

contestant /con-**tes**-tant/ n one who contests.

context /con-**tecst**/ n **1** the parts of a sentence, book, paragraph, etc, surrounding a word or meaning. **2** circumstances, the whole situation, background, or environment to a particular event.

contiguous /con-**ti**-gyoo-uss/ adj (fml) touching, next to, neighbouring. • n **contiguity**.

continence /con-ti-nense/ n self-control.

continent[1] /con-ti-nent/ adj able to control oneself.

continent[2] /con-ti-nent/ n one of the large land masses in the world (e.g. Africa).

continental /con-ti-**nen**-tal/ adj having to do with a continent.

contingency /con-**tin**-jen-see/ n something that may happen but is not certain to do so.

contingent /con-**tin**-jent/ adj **1** happening only if something else happens first. **2** accidental. • n a body of soldiers, scouts, etc.

continual /con-**tin**-yoo-wal/ adj **1** going on all the time. **2** happening again and again, repeated.

continuance /con-**tin**-yoo-wanse/ n the going on or lasting of.

continuation /con-tin-yoo-**way**-shun/ n **1** act of going on or carrying on. **2** something that continues from something else.

continue /con-**tin**-yoo/ vb **1** to go on doing. **2** to carry on with later. **3** to go or move further. **4** to remain.

continuity /con-ti-**nyoo**-wi-tee/ n uninterrupted connection, a series, the fact or quality of being continuous.

continuous /con-**tin**-yoo-wus/ adj **1** never stopping. **2** unbroken.

contort /con-**tort**/ vb to twist out of shape.

contortion /con-**tor**-shun/ n **1** act of twisting. **2** a twisting of the body.

contortionist /con-**tor**-shu-nist/ n one who entertains people by twisting his or her body into strange shapes; an acrobat.

contour /con-**toor**/ n **1** an outline, a shape. **2** a line drawn on a map through all places of the same height.

contraband /con-tra-band/ n **1** goods that it is forbidden by law to bring into the country. **2** goods brought into the country against the law. • adj (of goods) forbidden by law.

contraceptive /con-tra-**sep**-tiv/ n something which is used to prevent a woman becoming pregnant. • also adj.

contract /con-**tract**/ vb **1** to arrange by agreement. **2** to make or become smaller or shorter. **3** to begin to have. • n /con-tract/ a legal written agreement.

contraction /con-**trac**-shun/ *n* **1** the act of becoming smaller. **2** a shortened form.

contractor /con-trac-tor/ *n* one who undertakes to do certain jobs.

contradict /con-tra-**dict**/ *vb* **1** to say the opposite. **2** to say that something is not true. • *n* **contradiction**.

contradictory /con-tra-**dic**-tree/ *adj* saying the opposite.

contralto /con-**tral**-toe/ *n* **1** a low female singing voice. **2** a singer with a voice in this range. • *also adj*.

contraption /con-**trap**-shun/ *n* an unusual machine or instrument.

contrary /con-tra-ree/ *adj* **1** opposite. **2** /con-**tray**-ree/ always choosing to act differently from others, difficult to deal with. • *n* /con-tra-ree/ the opposite.

contrast /con-**trast**/ *vb* **1** to put things together to show clearly the differences between them. **2** to appear very different from. • *n* /con-trast/ a clear difference.

contravene /con-tra-**veen**/ *vb* to go against (a law or rule), to conflict with. • *n* **contravention**.

contribute /con-**tri**-byut/ *vb* **1** to give part of what is needed. **2** to write something for. • *n* **contribution**. • *n* **contributor**.

contributory /con-**tri**-byu-toe-ree/ *adj* giving a share, helping.

contrite /con-**trite**/ *adj* showing or feeling guilt or sorrow for something one has done. • *n* **contrition**.

contrive /con-**trive**/ *vb* **1** to succeed in, usually with difficulty. **2** to succeed in bringing about, usually with difficulty.

control /con-**trole**/ *n* **1** power over the movements and actions of another person or thing. **2** power over one's own thoughts and feelings. **3** *pl* those parts of a machine that start, stop, or change the movement of all other parts. • *vb* (**controlled**, **controlling**) **1** to have power or authority over. **2** to direct the movements of. **3** to hold back, to restrain. **4** to regulate, to cause to keep to a fixed standard. • *n* **controller**.

control tower /con-**trole** tow-er/ *n* an airport building from which messages are sent by radio to aircraft.

controversial /con-tro-**ver**-shal/ *adj* causing disagreement, discussion, argument.

controversy /con-tro-ver-see, con-**tro**-ver-see/ *n* disagreement, discussion, argument.

controvert /con-tro-vert/ *vb* to argue or reason against.

conundrum /co-**nun**-drum/ *n* a riddle or puzzle, the answer to which is often a play on words.

convalesce /con-va-**less**/ *vb* to recover gradually after an illness. • *n* **convalescence**. • *adj, n* **convalescent**.

convection /con-**vec**-shun/ *n* warming by the spreading of heat from a portion of water or air to that surrounding it until a current of warmth is set up.

convector /con-**vec**-tor/ *n* a heater that works by convection.

convene /con-**veen**/ *vb* **1** to call together. **2** to meet.

convener /con-**vee**-ner/ *n* **1** one who calls members to a meeting. **2** the chairman of a committee.

convenience /con-**veen**-yense/ *n* **1** quality of being convenient or suitable. **2** comfort.

convenient /con-**veen**-yent/ *adj* **1** suitable, not causing trouble or difficulty. **2** easy to reach, accessible. **3** easy to use or manage.

convent /**con**-vent/ *n* a community of nuns or sometimes monks living under strict religious vows. • *adj* **conventual**.

convention /con-**ven**-shin/ *n* **1** a large meeting called for a special purpose. **2** an agreement. **3** a way of behaving that has been in use for so long that it is regarded as necessary; a custom.

conventional /con-**vench**-nal/ *adj* **1** following convention. **2** accepting the manners and ideas of others, not original.

converge /con-**verge**/ *vb* to move from different directions towards one point. • *n* **convergence**. • *adj* **convergent**.

conversant /con-**ver**-sant/ *adj* having knowledge of.

conversation /con-ver-**say**-shun/ *n* talk or speech with others.

conversational /con-ver-**say**-shnal/ *adj* having to do with talk or speech with others.

conversationalist /con-ver-**say**-shna-list/ *n* one who is good at talking easily with others.

converse[1] /con-**verse**/ *vb* (*fml*) to talk together.

converse[2] /**con**-verse/ *n* the exact opposite. • *also adj*.

conversely /con-**verse**-lee/ *adv* looked at in the opposite way.

conversion /con-**ver**-zhun/ *n* a change, especially in belief or way of life.

convert /con-**vert**/ *vb* **1** to change from one state or form to another. **2** to get another to change his or her ideas, especially on religion. • *n* /con-vert/ one who has changed his or her beliefs or way of life.

convertible /con-**ver**-ti-bl/ *adj* able to be changed into something else. • *n* a car whose roof rolls or folds back so that the driver and passengers are riding in open air.

convex /con-**veks**/ *adj* curved outward. • *n* **convexity**.

convey /con-**vay**/ *vb* **1** to carry, to take from one place to another. **2** to pass (e.g. property) from one person to another. **3** to make known.

conveyance /con-**vay**-anse/ *n* **1** any kind of vehicle that carries people or things. **2** the document by which property is passed from one person to another.

conveyancing /con-**vay**-an-sing/ *n* the preparing of the papers to make a change in ownership lawful.

convict /con-**vict**/ *vb* to prove guilty, especially in a court of law. • *n* /**con**-vict/ a person imprisoned for a crime.

conviction /con-**vic**-shun/ *n* **1** a proving of guilt. **2** a strong belief.

convince /con-**vince**/ *vb* to persuade a person that something is true.

convincing /con-**vin**-sing/ *adj* **1** able to convince. **2** clear.

convivial /con-**viv**-yal/ *adj* **1** having to do with a feast or festive activity. **2** fond of eating, drinking and good company. • *n* **conviviality**.

convocation /con-vo-**cay**-shun/ *n* a meeting, especially for religious or academic purposes.

convoke /con-**voke**/ *vb* to call together.

convolution /con-vo-**loo**-shun/ *n* **1** a twisting or winding together. **2** complication. • *adj* **convolute**. • *vb* **convolve**.

convoy /con-**voy**/ *vb* to go with to protect. • *n* **1** warships accompanying other ships to protect them. **2** the ships so protected. **3** a number of army wagons travelling together for protection.

convulse /con-**vulse**/ *vb* **1** to shake violently. **2** to agitate, to disturb.

convulsion /con-**vul**-shun/ *n* a fit, shaking.

convulsive /con-**vul**-sive/ *adj* sudden and jerky.

coo /**coo**/ *vb* to make a soft, murmuring sound as a dove would; to speak gently and lovingly. • *also n*.

cook /**cook**/ *vb* to prepare food by heating it. • *n* one who prepares food for eating.

cooker /**cook**-er/ *n* a kitchen appliance for cooking food.

cookery /**coo**-ke-ree/ *n* the art, practice, or work of preparing food.

cookie /**coo**-kee/ *n* **1** (*US*) **biscuit**, sense 1. **2** a small file placed on a computer by a Web site or online service to store information about the user.

cool /**cool**/ *adj* **1** slightly cold, pleasantly cold. **2** calm, not easily excited. • *vb* **1** to make or become colder. **2** to become calmer or less interested. • *n* **coolness**.

coolly /**cool**-lee/ *adv* without excitement.

coop /**coop**/ *n* a cage for hens or other small animals. • *vb* to shut up in a small space.

cooper /**coo**-per/ *n* one who makes or repairs barrels.

cooperate, co-operate /co-**op**-er-ate/ *vb* to work or act together. • *n* **cooperation, co-operation**.

cooperative, co-operative /co-**op**-er-a-tive/ *adj* **1** willing to work with others, helpful. **2** made, done, etc, by people working together. • *also n*.

co-opt /co-**opt**/ *vb* to elect into a society or committee by the votes of the members.

coordinate, co-ordinate /co-**or**-di-nate/ *vb* to make things work or happen together for the same purpose. • *npl* figures that indicate a position on a map or squared paper. • *n* **coordination, co-ordination**.

coot /**coot**/ *n* a ducklike freshwater bird.

cope[1] /**cope**/ *n* a capelike garment worn by a clergyman on certain occasions.

cope[2] /**cope**/ *vb* to deal with, especially successfully.

coping /**co**-ping/ *n* the top row of stones, bricks, or concrete on a wall, usually sloped to carry off water.

copious /**co**-pee-us/ *adj* plentiful.

copper /**cop**-er/ *n* **1** a reddish brown metal, used to make pennies. **2** a large metal container. **3** (*inf*) a policeman.

copperplate /**cop**-er-**plate**/ *n* **1** a plate of copper on which something has been engraved. **2** a print made from this.

copse, coppice /**cops**/ *n* a group of small trees or bushes growing close together.

copulate /**cop**-yew-late/ *vi* to have sexual intercourse.

copy /**cop**-ee/ *n* **1** a thing done or made in exactly the same way as another. **2** a single example of a newspaper, magazine, book, etc. **3** written material given to the printer for printing. • *vb* to imitate, to make a copy of.

copyright /**cop**-ee-rite/ *n* the right, given to one person, team of people or publisher only, to reproduce and sell a particular book, musical work, or picture for a certain number of years.

coquette /co-**ket**/ *n* a woman who flirts. • *adj* **coquettish**.

coracle /**cawr**-a-cl/ *n* a boat made of basket-work or wicker and covered with animal skins.

coral /cawr-al/ n a rocklike material found under the sea made of the secretions of tiny creatures.

cord /cawrd/ n **1** a thin rope, a thick string. **2** an electric flex. **3** a part of the body resembling this.

cordial /cawr-jal/ adj **1** very friendly. **2** heartfelt. • n a refreshing drink.

cordiality /cawr-jee-a-li-tee/ n friendliness.

cordon /cawr-don/ n a line of soldiers, police, etc, to prevent people from entering an area. • vb to surround with a cordon.

corduroy /cawr-du-roy/ n a strong cotton cloth with raised, cordlike lines running from one end to the other.

core /core/ n **1** the central part of a fruit in which the seeds are stored. **2** the innermost part, the most important part.

cork /cawrk/ n **1** the cork tree or its bark. **2** a stopper made from cork. • vb to stop a bottle with a cork.

corkscrew /cawrk-scroo/ n an instrument for taking the cork out of a bottle.

corn[1] /cawrn/ n **1** a small, hard seed or seedlike fruit, kernel. **2** the seeds of some cereal plants, especially wheat. **3** (US) maize, sweetcorn • vb to put salt on or soak in salt water to preserve.

corn[2] /cawrn/ n a hard, painful growth of skin on the toe or foot.

cornea /cawr-nee-ya/ n the clear covering of the eyeball.

corner /cawr-ner/ n **1** the meeting place of two walls. **2** a bend in a road. **3** a difficult position. • vb **1** to drive into a position from which there is no escape. **2** to put into a difficult situation. **3** to gain total control of.

cornerstone /cawr-ner stone/ n **1** a stone put at the corner of the foundation of a new building. **2** something very important, something on which everything is based.

cornet /cawr-net/ n a musical instrument similar to a trumpet.

cornflour /cawrn-flaoo-wer/ n flour made from maize.

cornflower /cawrn-flaoo-wer/ n a plant with white, pink, or blue flowers that form a round head at the top of the stem.

cornice /cawr-nis/ n **1** a plaster decoration running along the top of a wall of a room. **2** an ornamental line of stone sticking out at the top of a wall of a building.

corollary /cor-ol-la-ree/ n something that must be true if another thing is proved true.

coronation /caw-ro-nay-shun/ n the crowning of a king or queen.

coroner /caw-ro-ner/ n an officer of the law who determines the cause of death when it is not obviously due to natural causes.

corporal[1] /cawr-pral/ adj (fml) having to do with the body.

corporal[2] /cawr-pral/ n an officer in the army.

corporal punishment /cawr-pral pun-ish-ment/ n punishing by beating the body.

corporate /cawr-pe-rit/ adj **1** forming one group. **2** of or shared by all the members of a group. • adv **corporately**.

corporation /cawr-pe-ray-shun/ n a group of people allowed by the law to act as one person in certain cases (e.g. in business matters).

corps /core/ n **1** a large body of soldiers, a division of an army. **2** a group of people working together for one purpose.

corpse /cawrps/ n the dead body of a person.

corpulent /cawr-pyu-lent/ adj (fml) fat, stout. • n **corpulence**.

corral /co-ral/ n enclosure for horses or cattle.

correct /co-rect/ adj right, having no mistakes. • vb **1** to set right, to remove mistakes from. **2** to point out or mark mistakes. • n **correctness**.

correction /co-rect-shun/ n **1** act of correcting. **2** the right thing put in place of a mistake. **3** (old or fml) punishment.

corrective /co-rec-tive/ adj putting right or improving what is wrong. • also n.

correspond /caw-re-spond/ vb **1** to write letters to. **2** to fit in with, to agree with. **3** to be like, to be the equal of.

correspondence /caw-re-spon-dense/ n **1** all the letters a person or office sends or receives. **2** likeness.

correspondent /caw-re-spon-dent/ n **1** one who writes letters to another. **2** one who makes special reports to a newspaper or news service.

corresponding /caw-re-spon-ding/ adj like or similar.

corridor /cawr-i-dore/ n an indoor passage or hallway.

corroborate /co-rob-e-rate/ vb to support or confirm the story or idea of another. • n **corroboration**. • adj **corroborative**.

corrode /co-rode/ vb to eat or wear away slowly. • n **corrosion**.

corrosive /co-roe-siv/ adj able to eat away. • also n.

corrugate /caw-ru-gate/ vb to shape into an uneven, wavy, grooved surface. • adj **corrugated**.

corrupt /co-rupt/ vb to make or become evil or morally bad. • adj **1** evil. **2** ready to act dishonestly for money. • n **corruption**. • adv **corruptly**.

corset /**cawr**-set/ *n* a stiff, tight-fitting undergarment.

cosmetic /coz-**met**-ic/ *n* something used to make the face and/or hair more beautiful. • *adj* 1 intended to improve the appearance. 2 dealing only with outside appearances.

cosmic /**coz**-mic/ *adj* 1 having to do with the universe. 2 (*inf*) very great.

cosmology /coz-**mol**-o-jee/ *n* the study of the universe as a whole.

cosmopolitan /coz-mo-**pol**-i-tan/ *adj* 1 consisting of people from many different parts of the world. 2 having or showing wide experience of different people and places.

cosmos /**coz**-mus/ *n* the whole universe as an orderly system.

cosset /**cos**-et/ *vb* to treat with great or too much kindness, to pamper.

cost /cost/ *vb* (*pt*, *pp* **cost**) 1 to be on sale at a certain price. 2 to cause loss or suffering. • *n* 1 the price. 2 loss. 3 *pl* the money needed to pay for a lawsuit.

costly /**cost**-lee/ *adj* having a high price.

costume /**cos**-toom/ *n* the clothes worn in a special place or at a special time.

costumer /**cos**-too-mer/ *n* a person who makes, sells, or rents costumes.

cosy /**co**-zee/ *adj*, *also* **cozy** (*US*) pleasantly comfortable or warm. • *n* a teapot or egg cover. • *adv* **cosily**.

cot /cot/ *n* a small bed with high barred sides for a baby or young child.

cot death /cot deth/ *n* (Sudden Infant Death Syndrome, SIDS) a sudden unexplained death of a baby in its sleep.

cottage /**cot**-idge/ *n* a small house. • *n* **cottager** a person who lives in a cottage.

cotton /**cot**-on/ *n* 1 a soft white substance from the cotton plant. 2 thread or cloth made of cotton. • *also adj*.

cotton wool /cot-on-**wool**/ *n* raw cotton before it is made into thread or cloth.

couch /couch/ *n* a sofa; a long piece of furniture on which one sits or lies. • *vb* (*fml*) to put into words.

cougar /**coo**-ger/ *n* (*US*) a puma.

cough /cof/ *vb* to force air noisily from the throat, often to clear it of some matter, such as dust or phlegm. • *n* 1 a noisy forcing of the air from the throat. 2 an illness marked by frequent coughing.

council /**coun**-sil/ *n* a group of people chosen to make decisions, to advise, or to discuss issues affecting a larger number.

councillor /**coun**-si-lor/ *n* a member of a council.

counsel /**coun**-sil/ *n* 1 (*fml*) advice. 2 professional advice given by a counsellor. 3 the lawyer who presents a case in a court of law. • *vb* to advise.

counselling /**coun**-sel-ing/ *n*, *also* **counseling** (*US*) the act of listening to people's difficulties or problems and giving professional advice as to how to cope with them or solve them.

counsellor /**coun**-se-lor/ *n*, *also* **counselor** (*US*) an adviser, one who gives counsel.

count¹ /count/ *vb* 1 to number. 2 to consider. 3 to matter. • *n* a numbering.

count² /count/ *n* a European nobleman.

countenance /**coun**-te-nanse/ *n* (*fml*) 1 the face. 2 the expression of the face. • *vb* (*fml*) to tolerate, to allow.

counter /**coun**-ter/ *n* 1 a person or thing that counts. 2 a small flat object used in some games to keep score. 3 the table in a shop across which goods are sold. • *vb* to act in order to oppose or defend onself against.

counter- /**coun**-ter/ *prefix* against, opposite to.

counteract /coun-te-**ract**/ *vb* to undo or prevent the effect of by opposite action.

counterattack /**coun**-ter-a-tac/ *n* an attack made in reply to an enemy attack. • *also vb*.

counterbalance /coun-ter-**ba**-lanse/ *vb* to put something of equal weight or importance on the other side.

counterfeit /**coun**-ter-fit/ *vb* 1 to copy or imitate with intent to deceive. 2 (*fml*) to pretend. • *adj* 1 not real. 2 made alike so as to deceive. 3 pretended. • *n* something copied, not real or true. • *n* **counterfeiter**.

counterpart /**coun**-ter-part/ *n* a person or thing similar to another or having a similar function to another.

counterpoint /**coun**-ter-point/ *n* (*mus*) the art of arranging two different tunes so that they can be played together.

countess /**coun**-tess/ *n* the wife of a count or of an earl.

countless /**count**-less/ *adj* too many to be counted.

country /**cun**-tree/ *n* 1 the land of one nation or people. 2 the land outside and away from towns. 3 an area or stretch of land. • *adj* having to do with the country rather than the town.

countryside /**cun**-tree-side/ *n* country or rural areas.

county /**coun**-tee/ *n* a district of a country or state.

coup /coo/ *n* a sudden successful action.

coupé /coo-**pay**/ *n* a two-door car.

couple /**cu**-pl/ *n* 1 (*inf*) two. 2 husband and wife. 3 two people who are in a committed relationship. • *vb* 1 to join. 2 to link or associate with.

couplet /cu-plet/ *n* two lines of poetry, one after the other, that rhyme.

coupling /cu-pling/ *n* a joining link, as that between two railway carriages.

coupon /coo-pon/ *n* a ticket that can be exchanged for money or goods.

courage /cur-age/ *n* bravery.

courageous /cur-ay-jus/ *adj* brave, fearless.

courgette /coor-jet/ *n* a long thin vegetable with green skin.

courier /coo-ree-yer/ *n* 1 a messenger. 2 a guide in charge of a party of travellers.

course /coarse/ *n* 1 the way along which a thing moves or runs. 2 the ground on which a race is run or golf is played. 3 a number of lectures or lessons given for the same purpose. 4 a row or layer, as of bricks in a wall or shingles on a roof. 5 part of a meal served at one time. • *vb* 1 to chase. 2 (*fml*) to move quickly.

court /coart/ *n* 1 an open area surrounded or partly surrounded by buildings, houses, or walls; a courtyard. 2 a place marked out for tennis, badminton, etc. 3 a king and queen and all their advisers and attendants. 4 the building in which judges hear cases and give decisions. 5 all the judges and officials in a court of law. 6 attentions paid to someone to gain favour. • *vb* 1 to pay attention to someone to try and gain the love of. 2 (*fml*) to try to gain. 3 to act in a way that is likely to bring about.

courteous /cur-tee-us/ *adj* polite, considerate and respectful.

courtesy /cur-ti-see/ *n* politeness, good manners.

courtier /core-tee-yer/ *n* someone who attends the court of a king or queen.

court-martial /court-mar-shal/ *n* (*pl* **courts-martial**) a military court, with officers acting as judges. • *vb* **court-martial** (**court-martialled, court-martialling**) to try by court-martial.

courtship /coart-ship/ *n* courting or wooing in hopes of obtaining love.

courtyard /coart-yard/ *n* an open space surrounded or partly surrounded by buildings, walls, or houses.

cousin /cu-zin/ *n* the child of an uncle or aunt, the child of a parent's brother or sister.

cove /coav/ *n* a small bay or inlet.

covenant /cuv-nant/ *n* a written agreement. • *vb* to enter into written agreement, to promise.

cover /cu-ver/ *vb* 1 to spread over. 2 to protect. 3 to wrap. 4 to include. • *also n*.

covering /cuv-ring/ *n* anything that covers.

covert /coe-vert/ *adj* secret, hidden. • *n* 1 a shelter. 2 a group of bushes or trees in which hunted birds or animals can hide.

covet /cu-vet/ *vb* to want to have something belonging to another. • *adj* **covetous**. • *n* **covetousness**.

cow /cow/ *n* the female of certain animals (e.g. of cattle, oxen, elephants, whales).

coward /cow-ard/ *n* one easily frightened in the face of danger.

cowardice /ca-war-diss/ *n* fear of danger.

cowardly /ca-ward-lee/ *adj* having no bravery, showing fear.

cowboy /cow-boy/ *n* a man who looks after cattle on a ranch on horseback. • *f* **cowgirl**.

cower /cow-er/ *vb* to crouch or shrink back out of fear.

cowherd /cow-herd/ *n* one who looks after cows.

coy /coy/ *adj* 1 shy, bashful, especially excessively so. 2 hesitant to give information. • *adv* **coyly**.

coyote /kie-yo-te/ *n* an animal of the dog family resembling a small wolf, found in North America.

cozy *US* variant of **cosy**.

crab /crab/ *n* 1 a sea creature with eight legs and two pincers, a flat shell and a short, wide belly. 2 the sideways motion of an aircraft. • *vb* to fish for crab.

crabbed /crab-bed/ *adj* bad-tempered, cross.

crab apple /crab a-pl/ *n* 1 very small apples growing wild or grown for making jellies or preserves. 2 a tree bearing crab apples.

crack /crak/ *n* 1 a sudden, sharp noise. 2 a break in which the parts remain together. 3 a sharp blow. 4 (*sl*) a highly addictive form of the drug cocaine. • *also vb*.

cracked /crakt/ *adj* 1 broken, but not in pieces. 2 (*inf*) mad.

cracker /cra-ker/ *n* 1 a crisp, thin wafer or biscuit. 2 (**Christmas ~**) a tube of brightly coloured paper, often containing a small toy, which makes a sharp noise when two people pull it apart. 3 (*inf*) something considered very good.

crackle /cra-kl/ *vb* to make a series of short, sharp, popping noises, to rustle. • *n* the act or sound of crackling.

crackling /cra-kling/ *n* the crisp fatty skin of roast pork.

cradle /cray-dl/ *n* 1 a baby's bed that can be rocked or swung. 2 the frame in which something is cradled, such as the frame under a ship when it is being built or the base of a telephone where the receiver is placed. 3 the place of a thing's early development. • *vb* to hold or rock as in a cradle.

craft /craft/ *n* **1** a special skill, especially with the hands. **2** cleverness, especially in deceiving. **3** a ship. **4** (the ~) (*inf*) witchcraft.

craftsperson /crafts-per-sun/ *n* a skilled worker, especially with the hands. • *n* **craft(s)manship**.

crafty /craf-tee/ *adj* good at deceiving, clever. • *adv* **craftily**.

crag /crag/ *n* a steep, rough rock that rises above others or projects from a rock mass. • *adj* **craggy**.

cram /cram/ *vb* (**crammed, cramming**) **1** to fill very full by pressing or squeezing. **2** to learn many facts immediately before a test.

crammer /cra-mer/ *n* a teacher who prepares someone for a test by making him or her learn many facts in a short time.

cramp /cramp/ *n* a sudden pain in a muscle. • *vb* to prevent free movement, to hinder.

cranberry /cran-be-ree/ *n* a sour, red berry used in making juice, in cooking and in baking.

crane /crane/ *n* **1** a long-legged, long-necked water bird. **2** a machine for lifting or moving heavy weights using a moving beam or arm anchored to its base by an overhead support. • *vb* to stretch out one's neck.

cranium /cray-nee-um/ *n* (*fml*) the skull. • *adj* **cranial**.

crank /crank/ *n* **1** in machines, a part that changes an up-and-down or side-to-side movement into a round-and-round movement (or the other way round). **2** a person with fixed, obsessive ideas, a person with strange ideas. • *vb* to turn or wind.

cranny /cra-nee/ *n* a small narrow opening, a crack.

crash /crash/ *vb* **1** to fall with a loud noise. **2** to dash violently against something. **3** to collide with another vehicle. • *n* **1** the loud noise of a breakage or collision. **2** the sudden failure of a business.

crass /crass/ *adj* very stupid, insensitive.

crate /crate/ *n* a large box, basket, or packing case, made with wooden boards or out of wicker or plastic.

crater /cray-ter/ *n* **1** the bowl-shaped mouth of a volcano. **2** a deep, wide hole in the ground.

cravat /cra-vat/ *n* a piece of cloth worn round the neck.

crave /crave/ *vb* **1** (*fml*) to beg for. **2** to desire very much.

craving /cray-ving/ *n* a strong desire.

crawfish *see* **crayfish**.

crawl /crawl/ *vb* **1** to move with the body on or near the ground, to move on the hands and knees. **2** to move slowly. • *n* **1** act of crawling. **2** a style in swimming.

crayfish /cray-fish/ *n*, *also* **crawfish** small, usually freshwater shellfish that look like little lobsters.

crayon /cray-on/ *n* a stick of coloured chalk, wax, or charcoal used for drawing, colouring, or writing. • *vb* to draw with crayons.

craze /craze/ *n* a popular fashion, a temporary excitement for.

crazy /cray-zee/ *adj* **1** (*inf*) mad. **2** very foolish. **3** excited, liking very much.

creak /creek/ *vb* to make a harsh grating or squeaking sound. • *also n*. • *adj* **creaky**.

cream /creem/ *n* **1** the oily, yellowish part of the milk that rises to the top and from which butter is made. **2** any sweet, smooth substance that is made from cream. **3** the best of anything. **4** a creamlike substance for rubbing into the skin. **5** the colour of cream.

creamery /creem-ree/ *n* a place where milk is made into butter and cheese.

creamy /cree-mee/ *adj* like cream.

crease /creess/ *n* a mark made by folding, crushing, or pressing. • *vb* to make creases in.

create /cree-ate/ *vb* **1** to bring into existence. **2** to make.

creation /cree-ay-shun/ *n* **1** act of creating. **2** anything made or invented.

creative /cree-ay-tiv/ *adj* **1** involving creation. **2** able to create or invent, producing original ideas and works.

creator /cree-ay-tor/ *n* one who creates or invents. • **the Creator** God, the Supreme Being.

creature /cree-chur/ *n* anything created, especially humans, animals and other living things.

crèche /cresh/ *n* a kind of day nursery for small children.

credence /cree-dense/ *n* belief, trust.

credentials /cri-den-shals/ *npl* papers saying that the owner of them may be trusted.

credible /cre-di-bl/ *adj* able to be believed. • *n* **credibility**.

credit /cre-dit/ *n* **1** belief, trust in. **2** approval or praise. **3** a cause of honour. **4** a system of buying goods or services and paying for them later. **5** the quality of being able to pay debts. **6** the money a person has in a bank. • *vb* **1** to believe. **2** to sell or lend in trust. **3** to write in on the credit side of an account. **4** to consider as having.

creditable /cre-di-ta-bl/ *adj* deserving praise.

credit card /cre-dit card/ *n* a plastic card with

which goods can be purchased and paid for later.

credit crunch /**cre**-dit crunch/ *n* (*inf*) a sudden reduction in the availability of credit, such as bank loans and mortgages.

creditor /**cre**-di-tor/ *n* one to whom money is owed.

credulous /**cre**-ju-lus/ *adj* too ready to believe, too trusting. • *n* **credulity**.

creed /**creed**/ *n* **1** that which one believes, especially in religion. **2** a statement of one's faith or beliefs.

creek /**creek**/ *n* long narrow inlet of water that flows from the sea into the land.

creel /**creel**/ *n* a basketlike cage for catching fish.

creep /**creep**/ *vb* (*pt, pp* **crept**) **1** to move with the body on or near the ground. **2** to move slowly and silently. **3** to shiver with horror. • *n* a person regarded as annoying or disgusting.

creeper /**cree**-per/ *n* **1** a person, animal, or thing that creeps. **2** a plant that grows along the ground or up walls, trees, etc.

creepy /**cree**-pee/ *adj* (*inf*) eerie, strange, causing fear or disgust.

cremate /**cree**-mate/ *vb* to burn a dead body to ashes.

cremation /cree-**may**-shun/ *n* act of cremating.

crematorium /cre-ma-**toe**-ree-um/ *n* a place where dead bodies are cremated.

creosote /**cree**-u-zote/ *n* an oily liquid taken from tar and used to disinfect or preserve wood from decay.

crepe /**crep**/ *n* **1** a thin, soft, crinkly cloth. **2** any crinkly material. **3** a thin pancake, generally served rolled or folded with a filling.

crept *pt and pp of* **creep**.

crescendo /cri-**shen**-doe/ *n* **1** a sign used in writing music. **2** a gradual increase in loudness.

crescent /**cre**-sent/ *n* **1** the shape of the moon in its first and last quarter. **2** a narrow, tapering curve. **3** a curving street. • *adj* shaped like a crescent.

cress /**cress**/ *n* an edible water plant.

crest /**crest**/ *n* **1** a tuft or comb on the heads of certain birds. **2** a bunch of feathers on the top of a helmet. **3** a sign or badge of a family, seen on a coats-of-arms, writing paper, etc. **4** the top of a slope, wave, etc. • *vb* to get to the top of.

crestfallen /**crest**-faw-len/ *adj* sad, disappointed.

cretin /**cree**-tin/ *n* (*inf*) a foolish or stupid person.

Creutzfeldt-Jakob disease *see* **CJD**.

crevasse /cri-**vas**/ *n* **1** a deep crack in a glacier.

2 a break in the outside walls of a river.

crevice /**cre**-vis/ *n* a narrow opening caused by a crack or split.

crew /**croo**/ *n* **1** the sailors of a ship. **2** a group of people working or classed together, a gang. **3** the rowers on a rowing team.

crib /**crib**/ *n* **1** a baby's bed. **2** something copied dishonestly from someone else. **3** a translation of a text. **4** the house, apartment, etc where a person lives. • *vb* (**cribbed**, **cribbing**) to copy unfairly the work of another.

cribbage /**crib**-idge/ *n* a card game for up to four players in which the object is to form various combinations for points.

crick /**crick**/ *n* a painful stiffness, especially of the neck. • *vb* to cause this.

cricket[1] /**cri**-ket/ *n* a small, jumping insect that makes chirping noises with its legs.

cricket[2] /**cri**-ket/ *n* an outdoor game played with a flat bat and red leather ball by a team of eleven. • *n* **cricketer**.

crime /**crime**/ *n* a breaking of the law.

criminal /**cri**-mi-nal/ *adj* **1** against the law. **2** wrong, wicked. • *n* one who breaks the law.

crimp /**crimp**/ *vb* **1** to compress into small folds or ridges. **2** to curl.

crimson /**crim**-zon/ *n* a deep red colour. • *also adj*. • *vb* to make or become red.

cringe /**cringe**/ *vb* **1** to shrink back in fear. **2** to behave too humbly towards.

crinkle /**cring**-kl/ *vb* to twist or bend into many folds, to wrinkle. • *n* a fold or wrinkle.

cripple /**cri**-pl/ *vb* **1** to make unable to move freely, to make lame. **2** to make less strong, to cause not to work as well, etc.

crisis /**crie**-sis/ *n* (*pl* **crises** /**crie**-seez/) **1** a turning point at which things must become either better or worse. **2** a very serious state of affairs.

crisp /**crisp**/ *adj* **1** hard but easily broken. **2** tight. **3** fresh and firm. **4** firm and clear. **5** dry and clear. • *vb* to curl or twist. • *adj* **crispy**. • *adv* **crisply**. • *n* a thin, crisp slice of fried potato.

criterion /cri-**tee**-ree-on/ *n* (*pl* **criteria** /cri-**tee**-ree-ya/) a rule or standard with which things may be compared to judge their value; a test.

critic /**cri**-tic/ *n* **1** one who judges something by pointing out its good and bad points. **2** one who finds fault, a person who expresses dislike and disapproval of.

critical /**cri**-ti-cal/ *adj* **1** pointing out both good and bad. **2** hard to please, ready to find fault. **3** having to do with a crisis. **4** most important.

criticism /cri-ti-si-zum/ *n* **1** judgment. **2** fault-finding.

criticize /cri-ti-size/ *vb, also* **criticise 1** to point out the good and bad in. **2** to find fault with.

critique /cri-**teek**/ *n* an essay or discussion in which a criticism is made.

croak /croak/ *vb* to make a low, hoarse noise in the throat. • *also n.* • *adj* **croaky**.

crochet /croa-shay/ *n* a type of knitting done with one hooked needle. • *also vb*.

crock[1] /crok/ *n* a pot or jar.

crock[2] /crok/ *n* an old, broken-down animal, anything useless. • *vb* to injure.

crockery /crok-e-ree/ *n* earthenware or china cups, plates and other dishes.

crocodile /crok-o-dile/ *n* a large, lizardlike reptile with a long snout, long tail, large teeth and a scaly body that lives in or around water.

crocodile tears /crok-o-dile **teerz**/ *npl* pretended sorrow or grief.

crocus /cro-cus/ *n* a spring plant grown from a bulb with yellow, purple, or white flowers that bloom in early spring.

croissant *n* /qua-**song**/ a light, crescent-shaped roll made of flaky pastry, usually eaten at breakfast.

crone /crone/ *n (old)* an old woman.

crony /cro-nee/ *n (inf)* a close friend.

crook /crook/ *n* **1** a bend, curve. **2** a stick, hook-shaped at one end, as carried by a shepherd or bishop. **3** *(inf)* a dishonest person, a criminal. • *vb* to bend, to shape like a hook.

crooked /croo-ked/ *adj* **1** not straight, twisted. **2** dishonest, illegal. **3** dishonest, not to be trusted. • *n* **crookedness**.

croon /croon/ *vb* to sing softly.

crop /crop/ *n* **1** a pocket in the throat of birds in which the food is partly digested before passing to the stomach. **2** a riding whip. **3** the whole amount of grain, fruit, etc. that is grown or gathered at one place or time. **4** a short haircut. • *vb* (**cropped, cropping**) **1** to cut short. **2** to bite off. **3** to sow or gather. • **crop up** to turn up unexpectedly. • **come a cropper 1** to fall heavily. **2** to fail completely.

croquet /cro-kay/ *n* a game in which wooden balls are hit through hoops with long hammer-shaped wooden clubs.

cross /crawss/ *n* **1** a mark made by drawing one straight line across another, e.g. +, x. **2** one piece of wood fastened across another in the shape of a cross. **3** anything made in the shape of a cross. **4** the sign of the Christian religion. **5** *(old)* a cross-shaped wooden frame to which criminals were fixed as a punishment. **6** a place

where roads meet. **7** a monument in the shape of a cross. **8** a source of suffering or sorrow. **9** an animal or plant that is the offspring of different breeds or varieties. • *vb* **1** to draw a line through or across. **2** to go from one side to the other side. **3** to pass across each other. **4** to put or place something across or over something of the same type. **5** to hinder, to obstruct. • *adj* angry, bad-tempered. • *n* **crosser, crossness**. • *adv* **crossly**.

crossbow /crawss-boe/ *n* a bow fixed across a support or stand onto which the string is looped when drawn back, then fired by a trigger.

crossbreed /crawss-breed/ *n* a mixture of two breeds. • *also vb*.

cross-country /crawss-cun-tree/ *adj* going across fields, etc, instead of along roads.

cross-examine /crawss-ig-za-min/ *vb* to ask a person questions about a statement he or she has made to test its truth, especially in a court of law. • *n* **cross-examination**.

cross-eyed /crawss-eyed/ *adj* an abnormal condition in which the eyes are turned towards each other, facing inward.

crossing /craw-sing/ *n* a place at which one may cross a street, river, etc.

cross-purpose /crawss-pur-pus/ *n*. • **to be at cross-purposes** to disagree with another through a misunderstanding.

cross-question /crawss-kwess-chin/ *vb* to cross-examine.

cross-reference /crawss-re-frense/ *n* the mention in a book of another passage in the same book in which the same subject is discussed.

crossroads /crawss-roadz/ *n* the place where two roads cross.

crossword /crawss-wurd/ *n* a word puzzle with squares and clues, in which each answer shares a letter with another answer or answers.

crotchet /croch-et/ *n* **1** a strange desire or idea, a whim. **2** a hook.

crotchety /cro-che-tee/ *adj* **1** *(old)* having strange desires or ideas. **2** cross, bad-tempered.

crouch /crouch/ *vb* to bend low.

croup /croop/ *n* a disease of the throat in children consisting of a swollen throat, a hoarse cough and trouble breathing.

croupier /croo-pee-ay/ *n* the person who takes in and gives out the money at a gambling table.

crow /croe/ *n* **1** a large black bird. **2** the cry of a male chicken. **3** a baby's cry of pleasure. • *vb* **1** to cry like a male chicken. **2** *(of a* *baby*) to make sounds expressing pleasure. **3** (*inf*) to boast. • **as the crow flies** following the straightest and shortest way from one place to another.

crowbar /**croe**-bar/ *n* a bar of iron used to raise heavy objects or open things that are stuck or tightly shut.

crowd /**croud**/ *n* a large number of people gathered together, especially into a small space. • *vb* **1** to come together in large numbers. **2** to fill too full by coming together in.

crowded /**crou**-ded/ *adj* full of people or objects.

crown /**crown**/ *n* **1** an ornamental head-covering worn by a king or queen as a sign of office. **2** a wreath worn on the head. **3** the top of certain things. • *vb* **1** to put a crown on. **2** to finish with a success. **3** (*inf*) to hit on the head.

crows-feet /**croze**-feet/ *npl* the little lines on the face at the outside corners of the eye.

crucial /**croo**-shal/ *adj* of the greatest importance, needing a clear decision.

crucible /**croo**-si-bl/ *n* a melting pot.

crucifix /**croo**-si-fiks/ *n* a figure of Jesus Christ on a cross.

crucifixion /croo-si-**fik**-shun/ *n* act of crucifying. • **the Crucifixion** the crucifixion and death of Jesus Christ.

crucify /**croo**-si-fy/ *vb* **1** to put to death by fastening on a cross and being left. **2** to treat cruelly, to deal with severely.

crude /**crood**/ *adj* **1** rough. **2** in the natural state. **3** vulgar, not civilized. • *n* **crudity**.

cruel /**crool**/ *adj* **1** taking pleasure in making others suffer, hard-hearted. **2** causing pain. • *n* **cruelty**.

cruet /**croo**-et/ *n* a small glass bottle for vinegar, salt, oil, etc.

cruise /**crooz**/ *vb* **1** to sail from place to place, often now for pleasure. **2** to travel at the speed that uses the least amount of fuel. • *also n*.

cruiser /**croo**-zer/ *n* **1** a fast warship. **2** anything that cruises.

crumb /**crum**/ *n* **1** a very small bit, especially of some form of bread. **2** a small piece.

crumble /**crum**-bl/ *vb* **1** to break into small bits or dust. **2** to fall to pieces or into dust. **3** gradually to get into a poor state and come to an end.

crumpet /**crum**-pet/ *n* a small flat cake with holes in it, eaten toasted.

crumple /**crum**-pl/ *vb* **1** to press into many folds, to crush out of shape. **2** to fall down suddenly. **3** to collapse, to fail. • *also n*.

crunch /**crunch**/ *vb* to crush noisily with the teeth. • *also n*.

crusade /croo-**sade**/ *n* **1** an attempt by Christian armies from the eleventh to thirteenth centuries to win back control of the Holy Land from Muslims. **2** any attempt by a number of people to do what is considered to be good or work against what is considered to be evil. • *n* **crusader**.

crush /**crush**/ *vb* **1** to squeeze or press together with force. **2** to press out of shape. **3** to defeat completely. • *n* the crowding together of things or persons. • *adj* **crushing**.

crust /**crust**/ *n* the hard, crispy, or crunchy outside of anything (e.g. bread). • *vb* to cover with a crust.

crusty /**cru**-stee/ *adj* **1** having a distinctive crust. **2** short-tempered. • *adv* **crustily**.

crutch /**cruch**/ *n* **1** a stick, with a top made to fit under the armpits, to support people whose legs have been injured. **2** a person or thing that provides help and/or support.

crux /**cruks**/ *n* the most important or difficult part of a matter, issue, etc.

cry /**craee**/ *vb* (**cried**, **crying**) **1** to make shrill, loud sounds, as of weeping, joy, etc. **2** to weep. **3** to shout. • *also n*.

crying /**craee**-ying/ *adj* dreadful, needing to be put right. • **crying shame**.

crypt /**cript**/ *n* an underground chamber or vault, found in some churches, often used as a burial place.

cryptic /**crip**-tik/ *adj* difficult to understand, sometimes on purpose.

crystal /**cri**-stal/ *n* **1** a clear, bright glass. **2** a hard, glassy-looking stone. **3** one of the regular shapes in which the atoms of certain bodies are arranged. • *also adj*.

crystalline /**cri**-sta-line/ *adj* **1** clear. **2** made of or like crystal.

crystallize /**cri**-sta-lize/ *vb*, *also* **crystallise 1** to form into crystals. **2** to make or become clear or definite. • *n* **crystallization**, *also* **crystallisation**.

cub /**cub**/ *n* the young of certain animals (e.g. bear, fox, etc).

cube /**cyoob**/ *n* **1** a solid body with six equal square sides. **2** the answer got by multiplying a number twice by itself (e.g. 2 x 2 x 2 = 8, therefore 8 is the *cube* of 2, and 2 is the **cube root** of 8).

cubic /**cyoo**-bic/ *adj* **1** cube-shaped. **2** having to do with cubes.

cubicle /**cyoo**-bi-cal/ *n* **1** a small sleeping area in a dormitory. **2** any small compartment in a larger room.

cuckoo /**coo**-coo/ *n* a greyish brown bird with a white underside, whose call sounds similar to its name.

cucumber /**cyoo**-cum-ber/ *n* a creeping plant with a long green fruit used in salads.

cud /**cud**/ *n* the food that certain animals bring up from their stomachs to chew again.

cuddle /**cu**-dl/ *vb* **1** to hug lovingly. **2** to lie close and comfortably.

cue /**cyoo**/ *n* **1** a word or sign that reminds a person of what to say or do next. **2** the long stick used for striking the balls in bllliards and pool.

cuff[1] /**cuf**/ *n* the part of a sleeve near the wrist.

cuff[2] /**cuf**/ *n* a blow. • *also vb.*

cuisine /cwi-**zeen**/ *n* a style of cooking.

cul-de-sac /**cul**-di-sac/ *n* a street closed at one end, a dead-end street.

culinary /**cu**-li-ne-ree/ *adj* having to do with cooking.

cull /**cul**/ *vb* **1** to gather, choose, or select. **2** to select and destroy.

culminate /**cul**-mi-nate/ *vb* to reach the highest point. • *n* **culmination.**

culprit /**cul**-prit/ *n* a wrongdoer, one accused of a crime.

cult /**cult**/ *n* **1** a particular system of beliefs, especially religious. **2** a sect with a particular set of beliefs that separates itself from ordinary life. • *adj* fashionable amongst a minority, often temporarily.

cultivate /**cul**-ti-vate/ *vb* **1** to prepare. **2** to make to grow. **3** to improve. • *n* **cultivation.** • *n* **cultivator.**

culture /**cul**-chur/ *n* **1** the character of an age and people as seen in customs, arts, etc. **2** learning and good taste. **3** the rearing of creatures or growing of plants in conditions not natural to them. • *adj* **cultural.**

cultured /**cul**-churd/ *adj* having learning and good taste.

cumbersome /**cum**-ber-sum/ *adj* **1** heavy and difficult to move. **2** slow and not working to the best ability.

cumulative /**cyoom**-yu-la-tive/ *adj* (*fml*) growing gradually larger by being added to. • *vb* **cumulate.**

cumulus /**cyoom**-yu-lus/ *n* a mass of white rounded clouds. • *adj* **cumulous.**

cunning /**cun**-ing/ *adj* **1** clever, skilful, crafty. **2** good at deceiving. **3** clever. • *n* skill, deceit.

cup /**cup**/ *n* a small drinking vessel. • *vb* (**cupped, cupping**) to put (usually the hands) into the shape of a cup.

cupboard /**cu**-board/ *n* a shelved place for storing food, dishes, etc.

cupcake /**cup**-cake/ *n* a small sponge cake, cooked in a paper case, usually with icing on top.

cupful /**cup**-ful/ *n* the amount a cup holds.

curator /**cyoo**-ray-tor/ *n* one in charge of a museum, art gallery, etc.

curb /**curb**/ *vb* to control, to keep in check. • *n* **1** anything that controls or holds in check. **2** a chain or strap fastened to the bit in a horse's mouth.

curd /**curd**/ *n* a solid substance that forms in sour milk, and from which cheese is made.

curdle /**cur**-dl/ *vb* **1** to thicken. **2** when solids separate from liquid in a mixture.

cure /**cyoor**/ *n* **1** act of healing. **2** that which heals or gives back health. • *vb* **1** to heal. **2** to preserve meat, fish, etc.

curfew /**cur**-fyoo/ *n* **1** (*old*) a bell rung in the evening as a signal to put out all lights. **2** a military order for people to be indoors and keep the streets empty after a certain hour. **3** the time at which people have to be indoors or in their homes.

curiosity /cyoo-ree-**oss**-i-tee/ *n* **1** the desire to learn, or to find out about. **2** a rare or strange object.

curious /**cyoo**-ree-us/ *adj* **1** wanting to learn. **2** wanting to know the private affairs of others. **3** strange.

curl /**curl**/ *vb* **1** to form into ringlets. **2** to twist around. **3** to play at the game of curling. • *n* a ringlet.

curling /**cur**-ling/ *n* a winter game played on ice, involving sliding heavy smooth stones towards a target.

curly /**cur**-lee/ *adj* having curls.

currant /**cur**-ant/ *n* **1** a small dried grape. **2** a type of sour, red, black, or white berry growing on certain shrubs and used in jellies or jams.

currency /**cur**-en-see/ *n* **1** the money in present use in a country. **2** the state of being widely known.

current /**cur**-ent/ *adj* **1** in general use. **2** belonging to the present time. • *n* **1** a stream of water or air moving in a certain direction. **2** a flow of electricity.

curriculum /cu-ri-cyu-lum/ *n* a course of study at a school, university, etc.

curry[1] /**cu**-ree/ *n* a dish of meat, vegetables, etc, cooked with a spicy sauce.

curry[2] /**cu**-ree/ *vb* to rub down a horse with a comb. • **curry favour** to try to win the favour of another by pleasing.

curse /**curse**/ *vb* **1** to use bad language, to swear. **2** to call down harm and evil upon. • *n* **1** the wish that another may suffer harm and evil. **2** a great evil or cause of suffering. **3** a swear word.

cursor /**cur**-sor/ *n* a movable pointer on a computer screen that shows, for example, where the next piece of text would be typed.

cursory /cur-so-ree/ *adj* quick, careless.

curt /curt/ *adj* 1 abrupt, rude. 2 brief, abrupt. • *n* curtness.

curtail /cur-tale/ *vb* (*fml*) to cut short. • *n* curtailment.

curtain /cur-tin/ *n* a cloth hung up, as over a window or stage, to darken, or to hide things behind it. • *also vb*.

curtsy /curt-see/ *n* a bow made by women as a respectful greeting by bending the knees with a slight lowering of the upper body. • *also vb*.

curve /curv/ *n* 1 a line that is not straight and that changes direction without angles. 2 something shaped like this. • *vb* to bend into a curve.

cushion /coo-shin/ *n* 1 a cloth bag filled with soft material, for sitting, leaning, or kneeling on. 2 anything that takes the force of a blow or shock. • *vb* to lessen a blow or shock.

custard /cu-stard/ *n* a dish of milk, eggs and sugar, baked or boiled.

custodian /cu-sto-dee-an/ *n* a keeper, one who takes care, especially of a museum or other public building.

custody /cu-sto-dee/ *n* 1 care. 2 safekeeping. 3 imprisonment.

custom /cu-stom/ *n* 1 the usual way of doing something. 2 something done often as a habit. 3 the buying of certain things at one particular shop, etc. 4 *pl* the taxes payable on goods brought into a country. 5 *pl* the office where such taxes are paid, or the officials collecting them.

customary /cu-sto-me-ree/ *adj* usual.

customer /cu-sto-mer/ *n* one who usually buys things (in a particular shop).

cut /cut/ *vb* (**cut, cutting**) 1 to make an opening with a sharp instrument. 2 to divide into pieces with a sharp instrument. 3 to shorten or shape by cutting. 4 to divide a pack of cards. 5 to lessen. 6 to refuse to look at or speak to. • *n* 1 an opening made by cutting. 2 a wound. 3 the way a thing is shaped. 4 a lessening. 5 a piece of meat.

cutback /cut-back/ *n* a reduction in the amount of something.

cute /cyoot/ *adj* 1 (*inf*) cunningly clever. 2 pretty, attractive, especially in a lively way.

cuticle /cyoo-ti-cl/ *n* 1 the outer skin of a plant or of the body. 2 the hardened skin at the base of the fingernails and toenails.

cutlass /cut-lass/ *n* a short, curving sword.

cutlery /cut-le-ree/ *n* knives, forks, spoons, etc.

cutlet /cut-let/ *n* a thin slice of meat, usually from a rib or leg; a chop.

cutter /cu-ter/ *n* 1 a light sailing boat. 2 a tailor who cuts out a cloth.

cutting /cu-ting/ *adj* hurting the feelings. • *n* 1 a piece of a plant cut off for replanting. 2 a piece cut out of a newspaper. 3 a passage cut through rock for a road or railway.

cuttlefish /cu-tul-fish/ *n* a sea creature with eight legs that gives out a black liquid when attacked.

CV /cee-vee/ *abbr* = **curriculum vitae:** a written account of a person's qualifications and previous employment, often accompanying a job application.

cyber café /sie-bur ca-fay/ *n* a café that provides computer terminals so that customers can browse the Internet.

cyberspace /sie-bur-space/ *n* worldwide communication via computer networks.

cycle /sie-cul/ *n* 1 a series of events that are regularly repeated in the same order. 2 a number of stories, songs, etc, about the same person or event. 3 (*inf*) a bicycle. • *vb* to ride a bicycle.

cyclic /sie-clic/ *adj* happening in cycles.

cyclist /sie-clist/ *n* one who rides a bicycle.

cyclone /sie-clone/ *n* a violent storm of wind that moves in a circular motion, such as a hurricane or tornado.

cygnet /sig-net/ *n* a young swan.

cylinder /si-lin-der/ *n* 1 a solid or hollow shape with circular ends and straight sides. 2 an object or container shaped like this. • *adj* cylindrical.

cymbal /sim-bal/ *n* one of two brass plates used as a musical instrument and struck together to make a clanging noise.

cynic /si-nic/ *adj* one who believes that people do not do things for good or kindly reasons but for their own advantage. • *also adj*. • *adj* cynical. • *n* cynicism /si-ni-si-zum/.

cyst /sist/ *n* a small bag full of liquid that forms on or in the body.

czar /zar/ *n*, *also* **tsar, tzar** the title of former emperors of Russia, or any person having great or unlimited power. • *f* czarina.

D

D, d /dee/ **1** the fourth letter of the English alphabet. **2** (*mus*) the second note of the scale of C major.

dab¹ /dab/ *vb* (**dabbed, dabbing**) to touch or hit gently with something soft or damp. • *n* **1** a gentle touch. **2** a small lump of anything soft or damp.

dab² /dab/ *n* a flatfish.

dabble /da-bul/ *vb* **1** to splash, to wet. **2** to take up in a small way. • *n* **dabbler**.

dachshund /daks-hoont/ *n* a small dog with a long body and short legs.

dad /dad/, **daddy** /da-dee/ *n* (*inf*) father.

daddy long legs /da-dee long-legs/ *n* the informal name for the crane fly, a fly with a long thin body and long spindly legs.

daffodil /da-fo-dil/ *n* a yellow bell-shaped spring flower.

daft /daft/ *adj* (*inf*) foolish, silly.

dagger /da-ger/ *n* a short sharp-pointed sword.

daily /day-lee/ *adj* happening every day. • *also adv*. • *n* a daily newspaper.

dainty /dane-tee/ *adj* small, delicate and pretty. • *n* **daintiness**.

daintily /dane-ti-lee/ *adv* **1** in a dainty way. **2** with very great care.

dairy /day-ree/ *n* a place where milk is sold, or made into butter or cheese.

dais /day-us/ *n* a low platform.

daisy /day-zee/ *n* a usually white, common wild flower with many petals and a yellow centre.

dalmatian /dal-may-shun/ *n* a large black-and-white-spotted dog.

dam¹ /dam/ *n* a wall to stop or control the flow of water. • *vb* (**dammed, damming**) to keep back by a dam.

dam² /dam/ *n* (*of animals*) a mother.

damage /da-midge/ *n* **1** injury, harm. **2** *npl* money paid to make up for loss or harm. • *vb* to harm.

dame /dame/ *n* the status of a lady of the same rank as a knight.

damn /dam/ *vb* **1** in religion, to send to everlasting punishment. **2** to condemn, to declare to be bad. **3** to curse. • *n* a curse.

damp /damp/ *adj* slightly wet. • *n* slight wetness. • *vb* to make slightly wet. • *n* **dampness**.

dampen /dam-pen/ *vb* **1** to make or become damp. **2** to make less strong, etc.

dance /danss/ *vb* **1** to move in time to music. **2** to move in a lively way. • *n* **1** act of dancing. **2** a social gathering for the purpose of dancing. • *n* **dancer**.

dandelion /dan-dee-lie-on/ *n* a wild plant with a yellow flower.

dandruff /dan-druff/ *n* small pieces of dead skin on the scalp.

dandy¹ /dan-dee/ *n* a man who pays what is considered to be too much attention to his appearance and clothes. • *adj* **dandified**.

dandy² /dan-dee/ *adj* great or fine.

danger /dane-jer/ *n* **1** the risk of hurt or harm. **2** something that may cause harm, injury, death, etc.

dangerous /dane-je-russ/ *adj* full of risks.

dangle /dang-gul/ *vb* to hang loosely.

dank /dangk/ *adj* cold and damp.

dapple /da-pel/, **dappled** /da-puld/ *adj* marked with spots of a different shade.

dare /dare/ *vb* **1** to be brave enough (to), to undertake to do. **2** to challenge. • *n* a challenge.

daredevil /dare-de-vil/ *n* a person who is ready to face any danger.

daring /dare-ing/ *adj* brave, fearless. • *n* courage.

dark /dark/ *adj* **1** without light. **2** having black or brown hair. **3** evil. • *n* **darkness**.

darken /dar-ken/ *vb* to make or become darker.

darkroom /dark-room/ *n* a room that is kept dark in which photographs are developed and printed.

darling /dar-ling/ *n* a person who is dearly loved. • *also adj*.

darn /darn/ *vb* to mend holes in clothes. • *also n*.

dart /dart/ *n* **1** a pointed weapon thrown by hand. **2** a sudden quick movement. **3** in needlework, a small pleat. • *npl* a game in which darts are thrown at a target. • *vb* to move quickly.

dash /dash/ *vb* **1** to run quickly. **2** to smash against. **3** to discourage. • *n* **1** a quick movement. **2** a small amount. **3** a mark of punctuation (—).

dashboard /dash-board/ *n* the instrument board in a car.

data /day-ta/ *npl* (*now often regarded as singular*), *sing* **datum** /day-tum/ a known fact or piece of information.

database /day-ta-base/ *n* a collection of data that is stored in a computer.

date¹ /date/ *n* **1** the day and month and/or year in which something happened or is going to happen. **2** (*inf*) an arrangement to meet at a certain time, especially a social meeting with a member of the opposite sex. • *vb* **1** to write the date on. **2** (*inf*) to make a date, often to see a romantic partner. • **date from** to have a beginning at a certain time. • **out of date** no longer in use.

date² /date/ *n* the edible fruit of the date palm.

dateline /date-line/ *n* the line in the Pacific Ocean where one day is regarded as beginning and another as ending.

datum *sing of* **data**.

daub /dawb/ *vb* **1** to put on in lumps or smears. **2** to paint roughly. • *n* a smear.

daughter /daw-ter/ *n* a parent's female child.

daughter-in-law /daw-ter-in-law/ *n* (*pl* **daughters-in-law**) the wife of a son.

daunt /dawnt/ *vb* to make less brave, to discourage. • *adj* **dauntless** /dawnt-less/.

dawdle /daw-dul/ *vb* to move slowly, often stopping; to waste time.

dawn /dawn/ *n* **1** the beginning of day. **2** a beginning. • *vb* to grow light. • **dawn on** to become clear eventually.

day /day/ *n* **1** during daylight. **2** 24 hours.

daybreak /day-brake/ *n* the beginning of day, dawn.

day care /day care/ *n* **1** the taking care of children, during daytime, usually while their parents are at work. **2** the place where children go to be taken care of.

daydream /day-dreem/ *vb* to dream while awake. • *also n*.

daylight /day-lite/ *n* the light of day.

daytime /day-time/ *n* the hours of day.

daze /daze/ *vb* to confuse, to bewilder. • *n* confusion.

dazzle /da-zul/ *vb* **1** to prevent from seeing clearly with strong light. **2** to confuse or impress.

dead /ded/ *adj* **1** without life. **2** dull, lifeless. **3** absolute, complete. **4** not working. • *adv* **1** completely. **2** straight. • *n* **the dead** the quietest time. • *npl* **the dead** dead people.

deaden /de-den/ *vb* to dull, to lessen.

dead end /ded end/ *n* a road that is closed at one end.

deadline /ded-line/ *n* a time by which something must be done.

deadlock /ded-lock/ *n* a complete disagreement.

deadly /ded-lee/ *adj* **1** causing death. **2** (*inf*) very boring. • *n* **deadliness**.

deaf /def/ *adj* **1** unable to hear. **2** unable to hear very well. **3** unwilling to listen. • *n* **deafness**.

deafen /def-en/ *vb* to make deaf. • *adj* **deafening**.

deal /deel/ *n* **1** an amount. **2** the giving out of playing cards. **3** a business agreement. • *vb* (*pt, pp* **dealt**) **1** to give out. **2** to cope with, to handle. **3** to do business with.

dealer /dee-ler/ *n* **1** a person who buys and sells. **2** a person who gives out playing cards in a game.

dealings /dee-lingz/ *npl* acts of business, relations.

dean /deen/ *n* **1** a leader of the church in charge of a cathedral. **2** the head of a university faculty.

dear /deer/ *adj* **1** well-loved. **2** expensive, high in price. • *n* a loved person. • *n* **dearness**. • *adv* **dearly**.

death /deth/ *n* **1** act of dying. **2** state of being dead.

deathly /deth-lee/ *adj, adv* like death.

deathtrap /deth-trap/ *n* (*inf*) a place that is very dangerous.

debate /de-bate/ *n* **1** an argument. **2** the formal discussion of a question in public. • *vb* **1** to argue. **2** to discuss. • *adj* **debatable**.

debilitate /de-bi-li-tate/ *vb* to weaken.

debility /de-bi-li-tee/ *n* weakness.

debit /de-bit/ *n* the written note in an account book of a sum owed. • *vb* to note the sum owed.

debris /de-bree/ *n* **1** the remains of something broken, destroyed, etc, wreckage. **2** rubbish, litter, etc.

debt /det/ *n* anything owed.

debtor /de-tor/ *n* a person who owes.

debug /dee-bug/ *n* to correct the errors in a computer program.

debut /day-byoo, day-**byoo**/ *n* a first appearance in public.

decade /de-cade/ *n* **1** a period of 10 years. **2** (*inf exaggeration*) a long time.

decaffeinated /dee-ca-fi-nay-ted/ *adj* of a drink such as coffee, having had most of the caffeine removed, often abbreviated to **decaf** /dee-caf/.

decagon /de-ca-gon/ *n* a figure with 10 sides. • *adj* **decagonal**.

decamp /di-camp/ *vb* to go away secretly.

decant /di-cant/ *vb* to pour carefully from one vessel to another.

decanter /di-can-ter/ *n* a stoppered bottle in which wine or spirits are served.

decapitate /di-ca-pi-tate/ *vb* to cut off the head of. • *n* **decapitation**.

decathlon /di-cath-lon/ *n* a track-and-field event in which people compete in 10 different sports.

decay /di-cay/ *vb* **1** to go rotten. **2** to fall into ruin. • *also n*.

deceased /di-**seesst**/ *adj* dead. • *n* a dead person.

deceit /di-**seet**/ *n* anything said or done to deceive; trickery. • *adj* **deceitful**.

deceive /di-**seev**/ *vb* to make someone believe what is not true, to trick. • *n* **deceiver**.

December /di-**sem**-ber/ *n* the 12th month of the year.

decency *see* **decent**.

decent /**dee**-sent/ *adj* 1 proper, not shocking. 2 reasonable, satisfactory. • *n* **decency**.

deception /di-**sep**-shun/ *n* 1 act of deceiving. 2 a trick, pretence. • *adj* **deceptive**.

decibel /**de**-si-bel/ *n* a unit for measuring how loud something is.

decide /di-**side**/ *vb* 1 to make up your mind. 2 to settle a question, etc.

decided /di-**sie**-ded/ *adj* 1 firm. 2 definite.

decidedly /di-**sie**-ded-lee/ *adv* undoubtedly.

deciduous /di-**si**-joo-wus/ *adj* having leaves that drop off in the autumn.

decimal /**de**-si-mal/ *adj* counted by tens, hundreds, etc. • *n* a fraction worked out to the nearest tenth, hundredth, etc.

decimalize /**de**-si-mal-ize/, *vb also* **decimalise** to change to a decimal system of money or measurement. • *n* **decimalization**, *also* **decimalisation**.

decimal point *n* a period, or full stop, in a number that is used to show fractions. The numbers appearing to the right of the period are less than 1.

decimal system /**de**-si-mal **si**-stem/ *n* a system of weights, measures, and money based on multiplying and dividing by 10.

decipher /di-**sie**-fer/ *vb* to work out the meaning of.

decision /di-**si**-zhun/ *n* 1 act of deciding. 2 a judgment.

decisive /di-**sie**-siv/ *adj* 1 firm. 2 settling a matter finally.

decisively /di-**sie**-siv-lee/ *adv* firmly, clearly.

deck /**deck**/ *vb* (*fml*) to cover, to decorate. • *n* the covering or floor on a ship.

declare /di-**clare**/ *vb* 1 to make known, to announce. 2 to state firmly. • *n* **declaration**.

decline /di-**cline**/ *vb* 1 to refuse. 2 to slope downward. 3 to become worse or weaker. 4 to give the cases of a noun or adjective. • *n* a gradual worsening or weakening.

decode /dee-**code**/ *vb* to work out the meaning of a message in code.

decompose /dee-com-**poze**/ *vb* to decay, to rot. • *n* **decomposition**.

decontaminate /dee-con-**ta**-mi-nate/ *vb* to free from what is infectious or harmful. • *n* **decontamination**.

décor /**day**-cawr/ *n* the style of decoration in a room or house.

decorate /**de**-cu-rate/ *vb* 1 to make beautiful or ornamental. 2 to put wallpaper, paint, etc, on the walls of. 3 to give a badge or medal of honour to. • *n* **decoration**.

decorative /**de**-cra-tiv/ *adj* ornamental.

decorator /**de**-cu-rate-or/ *n* a person who paints and wallpapers houses.

decoy /**dee**-coy/ *n* anything intended to lead people, animals, etc, into a trap. • *vb* to lead into a trap, to trick into a place of danger by using a decoy.

decrease /di-**creess**/ *vb* to become or make less. • *n* /**dee**-creess/ a lessening.

decree /di-**cree**/ *n* 1 an order or law. 2 a judgment at law. • *vb* to make a decree.

decrepit /di-**crep**-it/ *adj* broken down with age. • *n* **decrepitude**.

dedicate /**de**-di-cate/ *vb* 1 to set apart for a special purpose. 2 to write another's name at the beginning of a book to show that you think highly of him or her. • *n* **dedication**.

deduce /di-**dyooss**/ *vb* to work out a truth from things already known. • *adj* **deductive**.

deduct /di-**duct**/ *vb* to subtract, to take away.

deduction /di-**duc**-shun/ *n* 1 an amount taken away. 2 a conclusion worked out from things already known.

deed /**deed**/ *n* 1 that which is done, an act. 2 a written agreement.

deem /**deem**/ *vb* (*fml*) to judge, to consider.

deep /**deep**/ *adj* 1 going far down. 2 difficult to understand. 3 strongly felt. 4 cunning. 5 (*of sounds*) low in pitch. 6 (*of colour*) strong, dark, intense. • *n* **the deep** the sea.

deepen /**dee**-pen/ *vb* to become or make deep.

deer /**deer**/ *n* (*pl* **deer**) a swift-moving animal with hooves and horns (e.g. the reindeer).

deface /di-**face**/ *vb* to damage, to spoil the appearance of. • *n* **defacement**.

default /di-**fawlt**/ *n* 1 failure to do what is necessary. 2 failure to pay a debt. 3 the action that a computer takes unless you give it a different command. • *also vb*. • *n* **defaulter**.

defeat /di-**feet**/ *vb* 1 to beat in a fight or contest. 2 to make to fail. • *n* a lost fight or contest.

defeatist /di-**fee**-tist/ *adj* expecting or being ready to accept defeat or failure. • *n* a defeatist person. • *n* **defeatism**.

defecate /**deh**-feh-cate/ *vb* to expel faeces from the body through the anus.

defect[1] /**dee**-fect/ *n* a fault or flaw.

defect[2] /di-**fect**/ *vb* to desert a country, army,

group, or political party to join an opposing one. • *n* **defection**.

defective /di-**fec**-tiv/ *adj* **1** below average or normal. **2** faulty, flawed.

defend /di-**fend**/ *vb* **1** to protect or guard against attack. **2** to give reasons in support of your ideas. **3** to present the case for an accused person.

defendant /di-**fen**-dant/ *n* in law, the person accused.

defence /di-**fense**/ *n*, *also* **defense** (*US*) **1** the act of holding off an attack. **2** that which protects. **3** the arguments in favour of an accused person, especially in a court of law.

defenceless /di-**fense**-less/ *adj*, *also* **defenseless** (*US*) without protection.

defensible /di-**fen**-si-bul/ *adj* able to be defended.

defensive /di-**fen**-siv/ *adj* **1** suitable for defence, protecting. **2** ready to defend against attack. • *n* state of defending.

defer[1] /di-**fer**/ *vb* (**deferred, deferring**) to put off till later. • *n* **deferment**.

defer[2] /di-**fer**/ *vb* (**deferred, deferring**) to give in to another's wishes from respect.

defiance /di-**fie**-anse/ *n* defiant behaviour.

defiant /di-**fie**-ant/ *adj* fearlessly and boldly refusing to obey.

deficiency /di-**fi**-shen-see/ *n* lack, want.

deficient /di-**fi**-shent/ *adj* lacking something that should be present.

deficit /de-fi-sit/ *n* the amount by which a sum of money falls short of what is needed; a shortage.

define /di-**fine**/ *vb* **1** to mark out the limits of. **2** to explain exactly.

definite /de-fi-nit/ *adj* fixed, certain. • *adv* **definitely**.

definition /de-fi-ni-shun/ *n* an exact meaning or explanation.

definitive /de-fi-ni-tiv/ *adj* **1** clear and certain. **2** final.

deflate /di-**flate**/ *vb* **1** to let the air out of. **2** to reduce, especially someone's pride, importance, etc. • *n* **deflation**.

deflect /di-**flect**/ *vb* to make to change direction, to turn aside. • *n* **deflection**.

deforest /dee-**faw**-rest/ *vb* to clear a forest by cutting down or burning trees in an area. • *n* **deforestation**.

deform /di-**form**/ *vb* to spoil the shape or appearance of.

deformed /di-**formd**/ *adj* badly or unnaturally shaped. • *n* **deformity**.

defraud /di-**frawd**/ *vb* to cheat.

defrost /di-**frawst**/ *vb* to thaw out frozen food.

deft /deft/ *adj* skilful. • *n* **deftness**.

defunct /di-**funct**/ *adj* dead, out of existence.

defuse /dee-**fyooz**/ *vb* **1** to remove the fuse from. **2** to calm down.

defy /di-**fie**/ *vb* **1** to challenge. **2** to refuse to obey or to respect. **3** to care nothing for.

degenerate /di-**jen**-er-rate/ *vb* to become worse, to lose good qualities. • *also adj.* • *n* a person whose character has become worse. • *n* **degeneracy, degeneration** /di-je-ne-**ray**-shun/.

degrade /di-**grade**/ *vb* **1** to lower in rank or importance. **2** to disgrace. • *n* **degradation**.

degree /di-**gree**/ *n* **1** a step or stage. **2** a unit of measurement for heat, angles, etc. **3** the title given by a university to those who reach a certain standard of learning.

dehydrate /dee-**hie**-drate/ *vb* **1** to take the water out of. **2** to lose water from the body.

de-ice /dee-**ice**/ *vb* to remove ice or frost from a vehicle's windshield, etc. • *n* **de-icer**.

deity /**day**-i-tee/ *n* a god or goddess. • **the Deity** God.

déjà vu /**day**-zha **voo**/ *n* the feeling that you have experienced something before.

dejected /di-**jec**-tid/ *adj* sad, discouraged. • *n* **dejection**.

delay /di-**lay**/ *vb* **1** to put off till later. **2** to make late. **3** to wait before going on. • *also n*.

delectable /di-**lec**-ta-bul/ *adj* (*fml*) delightful, very pleasing.

delegate /de-le-gate/ *vb* **1** to send a person to act or speak for others. **2** /de-le-git/ to give certain powers to another. • *n* a person who acts or speaks for others.

delegation /de-le-**gay**-shun/ *n* a body of delegates.

delete /de-**leet**/ *vb* to rub out, to cross out, to remove. • *n* **deletion**.

deli *see* **delicatessen**.

deliberate /de-li-be-rate/ *vb* **1** (*fml*) to think over carefully, to consider. **2** to talk over. • *adj* /de-li-be-rit/ **1** done on purpose. **2** slow. • *adv* **deliberately**.

deliberation /de-li-be-**ray**-shun/ *n* (*fml*) **1** careful thought. **2** discussion.

delicate /de-li-kit/ *adj* **1** fine, easily hurt, or damaged. **2** fine, dainty. **3** not very healthy, easily made ill. **4** light, subtle. • *n* **delicacy**.

delicatessen /de-li-ca-**te**-sen/ *n* a store, or part of one, that sells cold meats and cheese and speciality foods from other countries. Often shortened to **deli**.

delicious /di-**li**-shus/ *adj* very pleasing, especially to the taste.

delight /di-**lite**/ *n* great joy or pleasure. • *vb* to gladden, to give great joy.

delightful /di-**lite**-ful/ *adj* causing delight, pleasant. • *adv* **delightfully**.

delinquency /di-**ling**-kwen-see/ *n* **1** (*fml*)

failure to do duty. **2** wrongdoing, minor crime.

delinquent /di-ling-kwent/ *adj* **1** (*fml*) not doing your duty. **2** doing wrong, committing minor crimes. • *n* **1** a person who does not do his or her duty. **2** a wrongdoer, especially a young one.

delirious /di-li-ree-us/ *adj* **1** wandering in the mind. **2** highly excited. • *n* **delirium**.

deliver /di-li-ver/ *vb* **1** (*fml*) to set free, to rescue. **2** to hand over. **3** to make. **4** to aim.

delivery /di-li-ve-ree/ *n* **1** childbirth. **2** a giving out of letters, parcels, etc. **3** manner of speaking in public.

dell /dell/ *n* a small valley.

delta /del-ta/ *n* the land between the branches of a river with two or more mouths.

delude /di-lood/ *vb* to deceive, to trick.

deluge /del-yoodge/ *n* a great flood.

delusion /di-loo-zhun/ *n* a mistaken belief.

delusive /di-loo-siv/ *adj* deceiving, misleading.

delusory /di-loo-su-ree/ delusive.

de luxe /di luks/ *adj* luxurious, top-quality.

delve /delv/ *vb* (*old*) to dig, to search deeply.

demand /di-mand/ *vb* **1** to ask for firmly or sharply. **2** require or need. • *n* **1** a claim. **2** a pressing request.

demean /di-meen/ *vb* to lower.

demeanour /di-mee-nor/ *n* (*fml*), *also* **demeanor** (*US*) behaviour, manner.

demi- /de-mee/ *prefix* half.

demigod /de-mee-god/ *n* in fable, a being that is half-human, half-divine.

demise /de-mize/ *n* **1** (*fml*) death. **2** end, often due to failure.

democracy /de-mok-ra-see/ *n* **1** government by the people. **2** a state that is governed by the people or by persons elected by the people.

democrat /de-mo-crat/ *n* a person who believes in democracy. • *adj* **democratic**.

Democrat /de-mo-crat/ *n* a member or supporter of the Democratic Party in the USA. • *adj* **Democratic**.

Democratic Party /de-mo-cra-tik par-tee/ *n* one of the main political parties of the USA.

demolish /de-mol-ish/ *vb* **1** to pull down. **2** to destroy. • *n* **demolition**.

demon /dee-mon/ *n* an evil spirit, a devil.

demonstrate /de-mon-strate/ *vb* **1** to show. **2** to show how something works. **3** to take part in a public show of strong feeling or opinion, often with marching, large signs, etc. • *n* **demonstrator**.

demonstration /de-mon-stray-shun/ *n* **1** a proof. **2** actions taken by a crowd to show their feelings. **3** a display to show how something works.

demonstrative /de-mon-stra-tiv/ *adj* **1** indicating the person or thing referred to. **2** quick to show feelings, showing feelings openly.

demoralize /di-maw-ra-lize/ *vb*, *also* **demoralise** to weaken the courage or self-confidence of. • *n* **demoralization**, *also* **demoralisation**.

demure /di-myoor/ *adj* serious and modest in manner. • *n* **demureness**.

den /den/ *n* **1** the home. **2** a secret meeting place. **3** (*inf*) a small room for studying in.

denim /de-nim/ *n* a cotton material used for jeans, overalls, etc.

denomination /di-nom-in-ay-shun/ *n* **1** a class or unit of measurement or money. **2** all those sharing the same religious beliefs.

denominational /di-nom-in-aysh-nal/ *adj* having to do with a religious group or sect.

denominator /di-nom-in-ay-tor/ *n* the number below the line in a vulgar fraction.

denote /di-note/ *vb* to be a sign of, to mean.

denounce /di-nounse/ *vb* to speak openly against, to accuse publicly. • *n* **denunciation**.

dense /dense/ *adj* **1** thick. **2** closely packed. **3** stupid.

density /den-si-tee/ *n* thickness.

dent /dent/ *n* a hollow made by a blow or by pressure on the surface. • *also vb*.

dental /den-tal/ *adj* having to do with the teeth.

dental floss /den-tal floss/ *n* a fine string used to clean between the teeth. • *also* **floss**.

dentist /den-tist/ *n* a person who takes out or repairs bad teeth, makes false teeth, and in general cares for the teeth of others. • *n* **dentistry**.

denture /den-chur/ *n* a set of artificial teeth.

denunciation *see* **denounce**.

deny /di-nie/ *vb* **1** to say that something is not true. **2** to refuse. • *n* **denial**.

deodorant /dee-oe-de-rant/ *n* a liquid or powder that takes away or hides bad smells.

deodorize /dee-oe-de-rize/ *vb* (*fml*), *also* **deodorise** to take the smell away from something.

depart /di-part/ *vb* **1** (*fml*) to go away, to set out. **2** to cease to follow. **3** (*fml*) to die. • *n* **departure**.

department /di-part-ment/ *n* a separate part.

department store /di-part-ment store/ *n* a large store that has many different sections, each selling a different type of goods.

departure *see* **depart**.

depend /di-pend/ *vb* **1** to be likely to happen only under certain conditions. **2** to trust, to rely on. **3** to need for support.

dependable /di-**pen**-da-bul/ *adj* trustworthy.

dependant /di-**pen**-dant/ *n* a person who looks to another for support or livelihood.

dependence /di-**pen**-dense/ *n* the state of depending.

dependency /di-**pen**-den-see/ *n* a country governed by another country.

dependent /di-**pen**-dent/ *adj* **1** relying on another for support. **2** to be decided by.

depict /di-**pict**/ *vb* **1** to describe. **2** to draw, paint, etc.

deplete /di-**pleet**/ *vb* to lessen in amount, size, or numbers. • *n* **depletion**.

deplorable /di-**plo**-ra-bul/ *adj* very bad, regrettable.

deplore /di-**ploar**/ *vb* to regret, to express disapproval of.

deploy /di-**ploy**/ *vb* to spread out over a wide front. • *n* **deployment**.

deport /di-**poart**/ *vb* **1** to send a person out of the country. **2** (*fml*) to behave.

deportation /dee-pore-**tay**-shun/ *n* act of sending out of the country.

deportment /di-**poart**-ment/ *n* (*fml*) the manner in which you stand, move, etc.

depose /di-**poze**/ *vb* to remove from high office or the throne. • *n* **deposition**.

deposit /di-**poz**-it/ *vb* **1** (*fml*) to lay down. **2** to put in a safe place. • *n* **1** an amount paid into a bank. **2** a first payment towards a larger amount. **3** solid matter in liquid, collecting at the bottom.

depository /di-**poz**-i-toe-ree/ *n* a storehouse.

depot /**de**-pot/ *n* **1** a storehouse. **2** a military station or headquarters. **3** a garage for buses.

depreciate /di-**pree**-shee-ate/ *vb* **1** to lower the value of. **2** (*fml*) to represent as being of little value. • *n* **depreciation**.

depress /di-**press**/ *vb* **1** to press down, to lower. **2** to make sad.

depression /di-**pre**-shun/ *n* **1** gloom, sadness. **2** a hollow. **3** low atmospheric pressure, causing unsettled or stormy weather.

deprivation /de-pri-**vay**-shun/ *n* **1** loss. **2** want, hardship.

deprive /di-**prive**/ *vb* to take away from.

depth /depth/ *n* **1** deepness. **2** strength (of feeling). • *npl* **depths** the deepest or most central part.

depute /di-**pyoot**/ *vb* **1** to send someone to act or speak for others. **2** to hand over to someone else to do. • *adj* /**de**-pyoot/ acting for another. • *vb* **deputize**, *also* **deputise**.

deputy /**de**-pyoo-tee/ *n* a person who acts for another.

derail /dee-**rail**/ *vb* to cause to leave the rails. • *n* **derailment**.

deranged /di-**rainjd**/ *adj* mentally ill or unbalanced.

derelict /**de**-re-lict/ *adj* left as useless.

derivation /de-ri-**vay**-shun/ *n* the history of something back to its earliest known form.

derivative /di-**ri**-va-tiv/ *n* something made or coming from from another thing. • *adj* not original, copying others.

derive /di-**rive**/ *vb* **1** to obtain from. **2** to come from.

dermatology /der-ma-**tol**-o-jee/ *n* the study of the skin and its diseases. • *n* **dermatologist**.

derrick /**der**-ick/ *n* a type of crane.

descend /di-**send**/ *vb* **1** to climb down. **2** to attack. **3** to have as an ancestor.

descendant /di-**sen**-dant/ *n* someone who has a certain person as an ancestor.

descent /di-**sent**/ *n* **1** (*fml*) act of climbing down. **2** a slope. **3** a sudden attack. **4** a line of ancestors.

describe /di-**scribe**/ *vb* **1** to tell what happened. **2** to tell what a thing or person is like. • *n* **description**. • *adj* **descriptive**.

desert[1] /**deh**-zert/ *adj* without inhabitants. • *n* a large area of barren, often sandy, land.

desert[2] /di-**zert**/ *vb* **1** to leave, to run away from. **2** to go away from. • *n* **desertion**.

deserter /di-**zer**-ter/ *n* a person who leaves the army, navy, etc, without permission.

deserve /di-**zerv**/ *vb* to be worthy of. • *adj* **deserving**.

deservedly /di-**zer**-ved-lee/ *adv* justly.

design /di-**zine**/ *vb* **1** to make a plan of. **2** to plan, to intend. • *n* **1** a plan or drawing of something to be made. **2** a plan, a purpose. **3** a pattern.

designate /**de**-zig-nate/ *vb* **1** to name. **2** to point out. **3** to appoint to a particular post or position. • *adj* appointed to a post, but not yet in it.

designation /de-zig-**nay**-shun/ *n* (*fml*) name, title.

designer /di-**zie**-ner/ *n* a person who designs something. • *adj* made by a famous designer and bearing a label with that name on it.

designing /di-**zie**-ning/ *adj* always planning cunningly or to gain advantage.

desirable /di-**zie**-ra-bul/ *adj* **1** much wanted. **2** arousing longing for. • *n* **desirability** /di-zie-ra-**bi**-li-tee/.

desire /di-**zire**/ *vb* **1** (*fml*) to wish for, to long for. **2** to be physically attracted to. • *n* **1** a longing, a wish. **2** a strong physical attraction to someone. **3** something or someone that is desired. • *adj* (*fml*) **desirous**.

desk /desk/ *n* a table for reading or writing at.

desktop /**desk**-top/ *n* **1** the surface of a desk.

2 (*comput*) the backdrop on a computer screen on which icons and windows appear. • *adj* suitable for use on a desk.

desktop publishing /**desk**-top pu-bli-shing/ *n* the act or business of printing and publishing material by means of a desktop computer.

desolate /**de**-so-lit/ *adj* **1** deserted and miserable. **2** miserable, lonely. • *vb* to lay waste.

desolation /de-so-**lay**-shun/ *n* **1** loneliness, grief. **2** a wilderness.

despair /di-**spare**/ *vb* to be without hope, to give up hope. • *n* hopelessness.

despatch *see* **dispatch**.

desperate /**de**-sprit/ *adj* **1** hopeless, and therefore ready to take risks. **2** without hope. **3** urgent and despairing. • *n* **desperation**.

despicable /di-**spi**-ca-bul/ *adj* mean, deserving to be despised.

despise /di-**spize**/ *vb* to look down upon, to consider worthless.

despite /di-**spite**/ *prep* in spite of.

despondent /di-**spon**-dent/ *adj* without hope, downcast. • *n* **despondency**.

dessert /di-**zert**/ *n* the sweet course at the end of a meal.

destination /des-ti-**nay**-shun/ *n* the place to which a person or thing is going.

destined /**des**-tinned/ *adj* marked out for a special purpose.

destiny /**des**-ti-nee/ *n* a power that seems to arrange people's lives in advance; fate.

destitute /**des**-ti-toot/ *adj* in great want, very poor. • *n* **destitution**.

destroy /di-**stroy**/ *vb* **1** to break to pieces. **2** to ruin. **3** to kill.

destroyer /di-**stroy**-er/ *n* **1** a person who destroys. **2** a fast-moving warship.

destructible /di-**struc**-ti-bul/ *adj* able to be destroyed.

destruction /di-**struc**-shun/ *n* **1** the act of destroying. **2** ruin. **3** death.

destructive /di-**struc**-tiv/ *adj* **1** causing ruin. **2** unhelpful.

detach /di-**tach**/ *vb* **1** to unfasten. **2** to take away from the rest.

detachable /di-**ta**-cha-bul/ *adj* able to be detached.

detached /di-**tacht**/ *adj* **1** separate, not joined to others. **2** not influenced by others, impartial.

detachment /di-**tach**-ment/ *n* **1** a group of soldiers taken away from a larger group. **2** freedom from prejudice, impartiality.

detail /di-**tale**, dee-**tale**/ *vb* **1** (*fml*) to give a very full account or description. **2** to set apart for a particular job. • *n* a small part or item.

detailed /di-**taild**, dee-**taild**/ *adj* very full and exact.

detain /di-**tane**/ *vb* **1** to prevent from leaving or doing something, to delay. **2** to arrest, to keep in custody. • *n* **detainee**. • *n* **detention**.

detect /di-**tect**/ *vb* **1** to find out, to notice, to discover. **2** to investigate and solve. • *n* **detection**.

detective /di-**tec**-tiv/ *n* a person whose job it is to find those guilty of crimes.

detention *see* **detain**.

deter /di-**ter**/ *vb* (**deterred, deterring**) to keep from, to discourage.

detergent /di-**ter**-jent/ *n* a chemical material used instead of soap for washing and cleansing.

deteriorate /di-**ti**-ree-o-rate/ *vb* to become worse.

determination /di-ter-mi-**nay**-shun/ *n* strength of will, firmness.

determine /di-**ter**-min/ *vb* **1** to fix, to decide on. **2** to find out exactly.

determined /di-**ter**-mind/ *adj* strong-willed.

deterrent /di-**te**-rent/ *n* something that keeps people from acting in a certain way. • *also adj*.

detest /di-**test**/ *vb* to hate, to loathe. • *adj* **detestable**. • *n* **detestation**.

detonate /**de**-tu-nate/ *vb* to explode. • *n* **detonation**.

detonator /**de**-tu-nay-tor/ *n* a mechanism that sets off an explosion.

detour /**dee**-toor/ *n* a roundabout way.

detox /**dee**-toks/ *n* (*inf*) the process of detoxifying an alcoholic or drug addict. • *also vb*.

detoxify /dee-**tok**-si-fie/ *vb* **1** to remove a poison from. **2** to subject someone to the withdrawal of addictive substances in order to cure their addiction.

detract /di-**tract**/ *vb* to take away from. • *n* **detraction**.

detriment /**de**-tri-ment/ *n* (*fml*) harm, damage, disadvantage.

detrimental /de-tri-**men**-tal/ *adj* harmful, disadvantageous.

devalue /dee-**val**-yoo/ *vb* to reduce the value of. • *n* **devaluation**.

devastate /**de**-va-state/ *vb* **1** to lay waste. **2** to overwhelm with grief or disappointment. • *n* **devastation**.

develop /di-**ve**-lop/ *vb* **1** to grow bigger or better. **2** to make to grow bigger or better. **3** in photography, to treat a film with chemicals to make the picture appear.

developing country /di-**ve**-lop-ing **cun**-tree/ *n* a relatively poor country that is working towards improving its industrial production and living conditions.

development /di-**ve**-lop-ment/ *n* **1** growth. **2** a stage of growth. **3** a new product or invention.

deviate /**dee**-vee-ate/ *vb* to turn aside.

deviation /dee-vee-**ay**-shun/ *n* a turning aside from the normal or expected course.

device /di-**vice**/ *n* **1** a plan, scheme, trick. **2** an invention, tool, or mechanism. **3** an emblem or sign.

devil /**de**-vil/ *n* **1** an evil spirit. **2** (*Bible*) Satan. **3** a very wicked person. **4** a person who does detailed or routine work for some professional people (e.g. a lawyer, printer, etc.).

devilish /**de**-vul-ish/ *adj* very evil.

devilment /**de**-vil-ment/, **deviltry** /**de**-vil-tree/ *n* mischief, naughtiness.

devious /**dee**-vee-us/ *adj* **1** roundabout, indirect. **2** not direct, not straightforward and honest.

devise /de-**vise**/ *vb* to plan, to invent, to work out, especially cleverly.

devoid /de-**void**/ *adj* lacking in, free from.

devote /di-**vote**/ *vb* to give up wholly to.

devoted /di-**vo**-ted/ *adj* loving.

devotee /de-vu-**tee**/ *n* a very keen follower.

devotion /di-**vo**-shun/ *n* **1** great love, dedication. **2** (*fml*) prayer.

devour /di-**vour**/ *vb* **1** to eat greedily. **2** to destroy. **3** to possess completely. **4** to read eagerly.

devout /di-**vout**/ *adj* **1** given to prayer and worship, religious. **2** sincere, deeply felt.

dew /dyoo/ *n* tiny drops of water that fall on the ground when air cools during the night. • *adj* **dewy**.

dexterity /dek-**ste**-ri-tee/ *n* cleverness with the hands, skill. • *adj* **dext(e)rous**.

diabetes /die-a-**bee**-teez/ *n* a disease causing too much sugar in the body. • *adj*, *n* **diabetic**.

diabolic /die-a-**bol**-ic/, **diabolical** /die-a-**bol**-ic-al/ *adj* **1** devilish. **2** very wicked, very cruel. **3** (*inf*) very bad.

diagnose /die-ag-**noaz**/ *vb* to decide by examining a sick person the kind of illness that he or she has. • *n* **diagnosis**.

diagonal /die-**ag**-u-nal/ *adj* going from corner to opposite corner. • *n* a line joining opposite corners. • *adv* **diagonally** at a slant.

diagram /**die**-a-gram/ *n* a plan or sketch, a drawing made to help to explain something.

dial /**die**-al/ *n* **1** the face of a watch or clock. **2** the numbered disc or pad by means of which you ring a telephone number. • *vb* (**dialled, dialling** /**die**-a-ling/) to ring a telephone number.

dialect /**die**-a-lect/ *n* the way of speaking in a particular part of a country.

dialogue /**die**-a-lawg/ *n* a conversation between two or more people.

diameter /die-**a**-me-ter/ *n* a straight line passing from one side of a circle to the other through its centre.

diametrically /die-a-**met**-ri-ca-lee/ *adv*: **diametrically opposed** exactly opposite.

diamond /**die**-mond/ *n* **1** a hard, very valuable precious stone. **2** *npl* a suit of playing cards.

diamond wedding /**die**-mond **wed**-ing/ *n* the 60th anniversary of marriage.

diaper /**die**-per/ *n* the US word for **nappy**.

diaphragm /**die**-a-fram/ *n* a muscle separating the chest from the abdomen.

diarrhoea /die-a-**ree**-a/ *n*, *also* **diarrhea** (*US*) looseness of the bowels.

diary /**die**-a-ree/ *n* a book in which you write something every day.

dice[1] /dice/ *vb* to cut into pieces shaped like cubes.

dice[2] *npl of* **die**[2] sense **2**.

dictate /dic-**tate**, **dic**-tate/ *vb* **1** to speak aloud something to be written down by another. **2** to give orders, to order about. **3** to fix, to determine. • *n* /**dic**-tate/ an order. • *n* **dictation**.

dictator /dic-**tay**-tor/ *n* one person with complete power of government. • *n* **dictatorship**.

dictatorial /dic-ta-**toe**-ree-al/ *adj* **1** like a dictator. **2** liking to order others about.

diction /**dic**-shun/ *n* **1** choice of words. **2** way of speaking.

dictionary /**dic**-shu-ree/ *n* a book in which words are arranged in alphabetical order and their meanings and other information about them given.

did /did/ *vb*, *pt* of **do**.

die[1] /die/ *vb* **1** to stop living. **2** to fade away.

die[2] /die/ *n* **1** (*pl* **dice**) a small cube, its sides marked with numbers from 1 to 6, used in games of chance. **2** (*pl* **dies**) a stamp for marking designs on paper, coins, etc.

diesel /**dee**-zel/ *n* **1** a petroleum oil, heavier than petrol, used as fuel. **2** a vehicle driven by diesel.

diesel engine /**dee**-zel en-jin/ *n* an engine that works by burning diesel oil using heat produced by compressing air.

diet /**die**-it/ *n* **1** food, the type of food on which you live. **2** a course of limited foods designed to help lose weight, treat a medical condition, etc. • *vb* to eat certain foods only, especially in order to lose weight.

dietary /**die**-i-ter-ee/ *adj* concerning diet.

differ /**di**-fer/ *vb* **1** to be unlike. **2** to disagree.

difference /**di**-frense/ *n* **1** unlikeness. **2** a disagreement, a quarrel.

different /**di**-frent/ *adj* **1** unlike, not the same. **2** (*inf*) unusual, special.

differentiate /di-fe-ren-shee-ate/ *vb* **1** to see or point out the difference between. **2** to make different. **3** to treat differently.

difficult /**di**-fi-cult/ *adj* **1** hard to do. **2** hard to please. **3** troublesome. • *n* **difficulty**.

diffident /**di**-fi-dent/ *adj* bashful, not sure of yourself. • *n* **diffidence**.

diffuse /di-**fyooz**/ *vb* (*fml*) to spread widely. • *adj* /di-**fyoos**/ **1** widely spread. **2** long-winded, wordy. • *n* **diffusion**.

dig /**dig**/ *vb* (**dug**, **digging**) **1** to turn up earth or soil. **2** to prod, to poke. **3** (*inf*) to search. • *n* a prod, a sharp push. • *n* **digger**.

digest /die-**jest**/ *vb* **1** to dissolve in the stomach. **2** to think over and understand fully.

digestible /die-**jes**-ti-bul/ *adj* able to be digested.

digestion /die-**jes**-chun/ *n* the process of digesting food.

digestive /die-**jes**-tiv/ *adj* concerning digestion.

digit /**di**-jit/ *n* **1** any figure from 0 to 9. **2** (*fml*) a finger or toe.

digital /**di**-ji-tal/ *adj* **1** showing information in the form of numbers. **2** recording or transmitting information as numbers in the form of very small signals. **3** to do with the fingers or toes. • *adv* **digitally**.

digital television /**di**-ji-tal te-le-vi-zhun/ *n* a system of television in which the picture is transmitted as a digital signal and decoded by a device attached to the viewer's television set.

digital video disk *see* **DVD**.

dignified /**dig**-ni-fied/ *adj* noble in manner, stately.

dignify /**dig**-ni-fie/ *vb* **1** to give grace or nobility to. **2** to make something seem important.

dignitary /**dig**-ni-ter-ee/ *n* a person of high rank.

dignity /**dig**-ni-tee/ *n* **1** goodness and nobleness of character, worthiness. **2** seriousness, calmness, formality.

digress /die-**gress**/ *vb* to speak or write on a subject other than the one being considered. • *n* **digression**.

dike, dyke /**dike**/ *n* **1** a ditch or wall. **2** a bank built up to hold back the sea or floods.

dilapidated /di-**la**-pi-day-ted/ *adj* completely worn out, falling to bits. • *n* **dilapidation**.

dilate /die-**late**/ *vb* **1** to become larger or wider. **2** to cause to become larger or wider. • *n* **dilatation**, **dilation** /die-**lay**-shun/.

dilemma /di-**le**-ma/ *n* a choice between two things or actions, usually equally unpleasant.

diligent /**di**-li-jent/ *adj* very careful, painstaking, hardworking. • *n* **diligence**.

dilly-dally /**di**-lee-da-lee/ *vb* (*inf*) to waste time, to wait about.

dilute /die-**lyoot**/ *vb* **1** to water down, to reduce in strength by adding water or another liquid. **2** to weaken in force, effect, etc. • *n* **dilution**.

dim /**dim**/ *adj* **1** faint, not bright. **2** indistinct. **3** (*inf*) not intelligent, not understanding clearly. • *vb*.

dime /**dime**/ *n* a silver coin that is a 10th part of a dollar, 10 cents.

dimension /di-**men**-shun/ *n* **1** the measure of length, breadth, and depth. **2** (*often pl*) size, extent.

diminish /di-**mi**-nish/ *vb* to make or become less.

diminutive /di-**mi**-nyu-tiv/ *adj* very small, tiny. • *n* a word or part of a word suggesting smallness (e.g. *-kin* in *lambkin*).

dimple /**dim**-pul/ *n* a small hollow, especially on the cheek or chin. • *vb* to show dimples.

din /**din**/ *n* a loud noise that lasts a long time. • *also vb*.

dine /**dine**/ *vb* to eat dinner.

diner /**die**-ner/ *n* **1** one who dines. **2** an informal restaurant.

dinghy /**ding**-ee/ *n* a small boat, a ship's boat.

dingy /**din**-gee/ *adj* dull, dirty-looking, faded. • *n* **dinginess**.

dinner /**di**-ner/ *n* the principal meal of the day.

dinner jacket /**di**-ner jak-et/ *n* a formal black (sometimes white) jacket worn with a bow tie by men on formal occasions in the evening.

dinosaur /**die**-no-sawr/ *n* a very large lizard-like animal of prehistoric times.

dip /**dip**/ *vb* (**dipped**, **dipping**) **1** to put into liquid for a moment. **2** to lower sheep into a liquid that disinfects them or kills insects. **3** to lower for a short time. **4** to take a sudden downward slope. • *n* **1** (*inf*) a quick wetting, a bathe. **2** a liquid or semi-liquid substance into which something is dipped. **3** a cleansing liquid for dipping sheep. **4** a downward slope.

diploma /di-**plo**-ma/ *n* a printed paper showing that a person has passed certain examinations.

diplomacy /di-**plo**-ma-see/ *n* **1** the discussing of affairs and making of agreements with foreign countries. 2 the ability to get people to do things without annoying them.

diplomat /di-plo-mat/ *n* 1 a person who represents his or her country in discussions with foreign governments. 2 a person who is good at managing people.

diplomatic /di-plo-ma-tic/ *adj* 1 having to do with or good at diplomacy. 2 tactful.

dire /dire/ *adj* very great, extreme, terrible.

direct /di-rect, die-rect/ *adj* 1 straight. 2 without any other reason or circumstances coming between. 3 saying openly what you think. • *vb* 1 to point or aim at. 2 to show or tell the way to. 3 to control. 4 (*fml*) to order. 5 to address.

direction /di-rec-shun/ *n* 1 the way in which someone or something is looking, pointing, going, etc. 2 control. 3 an order. 4 an address. 5 *npl* information as to how to do something or how to get somewhere.

directly /di-rect-lee/ *adv* 1 in a direct manner. 2 at once, very soon.

director /di-rec-tor/ *n* 1 one of a group of people who manage a business, etc. 2 a person in charge of putting on a play or making a film.

directory /di-rec-tree/ *n* 1 a book containing people's names, addresses, telephone numbers, etc. 2 in a computer, a folder that contains files.

dirge /durge/ *n* a song of mourning, a lament.

dirt /durt/ *n* 1 anything not clean. 2 (*inf*) gossip, scandal. 3 (*inf*) something obscene.

dirty /dur-tee/ *adj* 1 unclean. 2 mean or unfair. 3 (*inf*) obscene. 4 (*of weather*) rough. • *also vb*.

dis /dis/ *vb* (**dissed** /dist/, **dissing** /di-sing/) (*sl*) to treat with disrespect.

disable /di-say-bul/ *vb* 1 to deprive of some physical or mental ability. 2 to make something unable to work. • *n* **disability**, **disablement** /di-say-bul-ment/.

disabled /di-say-buld/ *adj* describing someone who is physically or mentally restricted in some way.

disadvantage /di-sad-van-tidge/ *n* something unfavourable or harmful to your interests, a drawback. • *adj* **disadvantageous**.

disadvantaged /di-sad-van-tijd/ *adj* suffering from a disadvantage, especially with regard to your economic situation, family background, etc.

disagree /di-sa-gree/ *vb* 1 to differ. 2 to have different opinions, etc. 3 to quarrel. 4 to have a bad effect on. • *n* **disagreement**.

disagreeable /di-sa-gree-a-bul/ *adj* unpleasant.

disallow /di-sa-laoo/ *vb* (*fml*) to refuse to allow.

disappear /di-sa-peer/ *vb* 1 to go out of sight. 2 to leave or become lost, especially suddenly or without explanation. 3 to cease to exist. • *n* **disappearance**.

disappoint /di-sa-point/ *vb* 1 to fail to do what is hoped or expected. 2 (*fml*) to fail to fulfil. 3 to cause sorrow by failure. • *n* **disappointment**.

disapprove /di-sa-proov/ *vb* to believe that something is wrong or bad. • *n* **disapproval**.

disarm /di-sarm/ *vb* 1 to take away weapons from. 2 to do away with weapons of war. 3 to make less angry, to charm.

disarrange /di-sa-range/ *vb* (*fml*) to set in the wrong order, to untidy. • *n* **disarrangement**.

disarray /di-sa-ray/ *n* disorder or untidiness.

disaster /di-za-ster/ *n* 1 a great misfortune. 2 an accident affecting many people or causing a lot of damage. 3 a complete failure. • *adj* **disastrous**.

disband /dis-band/ *vb* to break up and separate. • *n* **disbandment**.

disbelieve /dis-bi-leev/ *vb* to refuse to believe. • *n* **disbelief**.

disc /disk/ *n*, *also* **disk** (*US*) 1 a round flat object. 2 an audio recording, especially a compact disc. 3 a layer of cartilage between the bones of the spine.

disc jockey /disc jock-ee/ *n* a person who introduces and plays recorded pop music on a radio or television show or at a club.

discard /dis-card/ *vb* to throw away.

discharge /dis-charge/ *vb* 1 to unload. 2 to set free. 3 to fire. 4 to send away. 5 to give or send out. 6 to do, to carry out. 7 to pay. • *n* **discharge** 1 act of discharging. 2 the matter coming from a sore or wound.

disciple /di-sie-pul/ *n* a person who believes in the teaching, etc, of another; a follower.

disciplinarian /di-si-pli-nay-ree-an/ *n* a person who controls others firmly or severely.

discipline /di-si-plin/ *n* 1 training of mind or character. 2 ordered behaviour. 3 punishment. 4 a branch of knowledge. • *vb* 1 to train to be obedient. 2 to punish • *adj* **disciplinary**.

disclose /dis-cloaz/ *vb* 1 to make known. 2 to uncover.

disclosure /dis-clo-zher/ *n* the telling or showing of something previously hidden.

disco /dis-co/ *n* a club to which people go to dance to recorded pop music.

discolour /dis-cu-lur/ *vb*, *also* **discolor** (*US*) to spoil the colour of, to stain. • *n* **discolouration**, *also* **discoloration**.

discomfort /dis-**cum**-furt/ *n* the fact or state of being uncomfortable. • *vb* to make uncomfortable.

disconcert /dis-con-**sert**/ *vb* to make uneasy.

disconnect /dis-cu-**nect**/ *vb* **1** to unfasten. **2** to break the connection.

disconnected /dis-cu-**nec**-ted/ *adj* showing little connection between.

disconsolate /dis-**con**-so-lit/ *adj* sad, disappointed.

discontent /dis-con-**tent**/ *n* the state of not being satisfied, displeasure. • *adj* **discontented**. • *n* **discontentment**.

discontinue /dis-con-**ti**-nyoo/ *vb* to stop or put an end to.

discord /dis-cawrd/ *n* **1** two or more notes of music that sound unpleasing when played together. **2** (*fml*) disagreement, quarrelling. • *adj* **discordant**.

discount /dis-count/ *n* a reduction in the cost or price of. • *vb* /dis-**count**/ **1** to give a discount. **2** to regard as unimportant or untrue.

discourage /dis-cu-ridge/ *vb* **1** to dishearten. **2** to persuade not to do. • *n* **discouragement**.

discourse /dis-coarse/ *n* a speech, a lecture. • *vb* /dis-**coarse**/ to talk.

discourteous /dis-**cur**-tee-us/ *adj* rude, impolite. • *n* **discourtesy**.

discover /dis-cu-ver/ *vb* **1** to find. **2** to find out.

discoverer /dis-**cu**-ve-rer/ *n* an explorer.

discovery /dis-**cu**-ve-ree/ *n* **1** act of finding. **2** the thing found.

discredit /dis-**cre**-dit/ *vb* **1** to refuse to believe. **2** to cause to be disbelieved. **3** to damage the good reputation of. • *n* shame, dishonour.

discreditable /dis-**cre**-di-ta-bul/ *adj* shameful.

discreet /dis-**creet**/ *adj* thinking carefully before acting or speaking; cautious; not saying anything that is likely to cause trouble. • *n* **discretion**, **discreetness**.

discrepancy /dis-**cre**-pan-see/ *n* the difference between what a thing is and what it ought to be or is said to be.

discretion /dis-**cre**-shun/ *n* **1** discreetness. **2** judgment, caution.

discriminate /dis-**cri**-mi-nate/ *vb* **1** to see differences, however small. **2** to show judgment. • *n* **discrimination**.

discriminating /dis-**cri**-mi-nay-ting/ *adj* having good judgment.

discus /di-scus/ *n* in track-and-field, a heavy disc-shaped object that is thrown in a field event.

discuss /di-**scus**/ *vb* to talk about, to consider. • *n* **discussion** /di-scu-shun/.

disdain /dis-**dane**/ *vb* to look down upon; to be too proud to; to refuse because of pride. • *n* scorn. • *adj* **disdainful**.

disease /di-zeez/ *n* an illness or unhealthy condition.

diseased /di-**zeezd**/ *adj* suffering from a disease.

disenchant /di-sen-**chant**/ *vb* to free from mistaken positive beliefs. • *adj* **disenchanted**.

disentangle /di-sen-**tang**-gul/ *vb* **1** to take the knots out of. **2** to free from a position that is difficult to escape from. **3** to separate from a confused condition.

disfigure /dis-**fi**-gyur/ *vb* to spoil the appearance of. • *n* **disfigurement**.

disgrace /dis-**grace**/ *n* **1** shame, loss of favour or respect. **2** a person or thing that should cause shame. • *vb* to bring shame or dishonour upon.

disgraceful /dis-**grace**-ful/ *adj* shameful. • *adv* **disgracefully**.

disguise /dis-**gize**/ *vb* to change the appearance of, so as not to be recognized. • *n* changed dress or appearance so as not to be recognized.

disgust /dis-**gust**/ *n* strong dislike, loathing. • *vb* to cause to loathe or hate.

disgusting /dis-**gu**-sting/ *adj* sickening.

dish /dish/ *n* **1** a broad open vessel for serving food. **2** a particular kind of food. **3** food mixed and prepared for the table. • *vb* to put into a dish. • **dish out 1** to distribute and give out. **2** (*inf*) to give out generously.

dishearten /dis-**har**-ten/ *vb* to discourage.

dishevel /di-**shev**-el/ *vb* (**dishevelled**, **dishevelling**) to untidy.

dishevelled /di-**shev**-eld/ *adj* untidy and unkempt.

dishonest /di-**son**-est/ *adj* not honest. • *n* **dishonesty**.

dishonour /di-**son**-ur/ *n*, *also* **dishonor** (*US*) shame, disgrace. • *vb* **1** to bring shame on. **2** (*fml*) to treat in a shameful way.

dishonourable /di-**son**-e-ra-bul/ *adj*, *also* **dishonorable** (*US*) not honourable, shameful.

dishwasher /dish-waw-sher/ *n* a machine for washing dishes and cutlery.

disillusion /di-si-**loo**-zhun/ *vb* to free from a wrong idea or belief. • *n* **disillusionment**.

disinfect /di-sin-**fect**/ *vb* to destroy germs. • *n* **disinfection**.

disinfectant /di-sin-**fec**-tant/ *adj* destroying germs, killing infection. • *n* a disinfectant substance.

disinherit /di-sin-**her**-it/ *vb* to take from someone, especially a son or daughter, the right to receive anything by the will of a dead person.

disintegrate /di-**sin**-ti-grate/ *vb* **1** to break up into parts. **2** to fall to pieces. • *n* **disintegration.**

disinterested /di-**sin**-tre-stid/ *adj* favouring no side.

disjointed /dis-**join**-tid/ *adj* having no clear connection between ideas, rambling.

disk /disk/ *n* **1** US variant of **disc**. **2** a circular plate, coated with magnetic material, on which data can be recorded in a form that can be used by a computer.

dislike /dis-**like**/ *vb* not to like. • *also n.*

dislocate /dis-lo-cate/ *vb* **1** to put out of joint. **2** (*fml*) to throw into disorder. • *n* **dislocation.**

dislodge /dis-**lodge**/ *vb* to move from its place.

disloyal /dis-**loy**-al/ *adj* **1** unfaithful. **2** not true to. • *n* **disloyalty.**

dismal /**diz**-mal/ *adj* dark, gloomy.

dismantle /dis-**man**-tul/ *vb* to take to pieces.

dismay /dis-**may**/ *vb* to make afraid, anxious, discouraged, etc. • *also n.*

dismiss /dis-**mis**/ *vb* **1** to send away. **2** to send someone away from his or her job. • *n* **dismissal.**

dismount /dis-**mount**/ *vb* to get down from a horse, etc.

disobey /dis-o-**bay**/ *vb* to refuse to do what you are told. • *n* **disobedience.** • *adj* **disobedient.**

disorder /dis-**awr**-der/ *vb* to put things out of their places, to make untidy. • *n* **1** untidiness. **2** disturbance, riot. **3** a sickness, disease.

disorderly /dis-**awr**-der-lee/ *adj* **1** untidy. **2** out of control.

disorganize /dis-**awr**-ga-nize/ *vb, also* **disorganise** to put out of order, to throw into confusion. • *n* **disorganization,** *also* **disorganisation.**

disown /dis-**oan**/ *vb* to refuse to have anything to do with, to refuse to acknowledge as belonging to yourself.

disparage /dis-**pa**-ridge/ *vb* to suggest, especially unfairly, that something or someone is of little value or importance. • *n* **disparagement.**

disparate /**dis**-pa-rit/ *adj* unlike, completely different.

disparity /dis-**pa**-ri-tee/ *n* difference, inequality.

dispassionate /dis-**pash**-nit/ *adj* not influenced by emotion, taking no side, impartial.

dispatch, despatch /dis-**patch**/ *vb* **1** to send off. **2** (*old*) to kill. **3** (*fml*) to do quickly. • *n*

1 the act of sending off. **2** a written official report. **3** (*fml*) quickness in doing.

dispel /dis-**pel**/ *vb* (**dispelled, dispelling**) to drive away, to make disappear.

dispensable /dis-**pen**-si-bul/ *adj* able to be done without.

dispensary /dis-**pen**-sa-ree/ *n* a place where medicines are prepared and given out.

dispensation /dis-**pen**-say-shun/ *n* a permission, often from the church, not to do something.

dispense /dis-**pense**/ *vb* **1** (*fml*) to give out. **2** to prepare and give out. • **dispense with** to do without.

dispenser /dis-**pen**-ser/ *n* **1** a person who prepares medicines. **2** a machine from which something can be obtained, sometimes by the insertion of money.

disperse /dis-**perse**/ *vb* to scatter. • *n* **dispersal, dispersion** /dis-**per**-shun/.

dispirited /dis-**pi**-ri-ted/ *adj* discouraged, in low spirits.

displace /dis-**place**/ *vb* **1** (*fml*) to put out of place. **2** to take the place of.

displacement /dis-**place**-ment/ *n* **1** act of displacing. **2** the amount of liquid put out of place when an object is placed in it.

display /dis-**play**/ *vb* **1** to show, to make obvious. **2** to put where it can be easily seen. • *n* **1** show. **2** a parade. **3** an exhibition.

displease /dis-**please**/ *vb* to anger, to annoy.

displeasure /dis-**ple**-zhur/ *n* annoyance.

disport /dis-**port**/ *vb* (*fml*) to play about, to amuse yourself actively.

disposable /dis-**po**-za-bul/ *adj* designed to be used once and then thrown away.

disposal /dis-**po**-zal/ *n* **1** act of getting rid of. **2** the way that people or things are arranged. **3** use.

dispose /dis-**poze**/ *vb* **1** (*fml*) to arrange. **2** (*fml*) to make willing. **3** to get rid.

disposition /dis-po-**zi**-shun/ *n* **1** arrangement. **2** a person's character, as revealed by his or her behaviour.

dispossess /dis-po-**zess**/ *vb* to take away from.

disproportion /dis-pro-**poar**-shun/ *n* lack of proper or usual relation between things.

disproportionate /dis-pro-**poar**-shu-nit/ *adj* too great (or too small) in the circumstances.

disprove /dis-**proov**/ *vb* to prove to be false.

disputation /dis-pyu-**tay**-shun/ *n* an argument, a debate.

dispute /dis-**pyoot**/ *vb* **1** to argue, to quarrel. **2** to refuse to agree with, to question the truth or rightness of. • *also n.*

disqualify /dis-**kwaw**-li-fy/ *vb* **1** to make unable. **2** to put out of a competition, etc, usually for breaking a rule. • *n* **disqualification**.

disquiet /dis-**kwie**-it/ *n* anxiety. • *vb* to make anxious. • *n* **disquietude**.

disregard /dis-ri-**gard**/ *vb* to take no notice of. • *n* neglect.

disrepair /dis-ri-**pair**/ *n* a bad state due to lack of repairs.

disreputable /dis-**rep**-yu-ta-bul/ *adj* having a bad character or reputation.

disrepute /dis-ri-**pyoot**/ *n* disgrace, bad reputation.

disrespect /dis-ri-**spect**/ *n* rudeness, failure to behave in a proper way. • *adj* **disrespectful**.

disrobe /dis-**robe**/ *vb* (*fml*) to take off clothing, especially ceremonious or official clothing.

disrupt /dis-**rupt**/ *vb* to put into a state of disorder. • *n* **disruption**.

disruptive /dis-**rup**-tiv/ *adj* causing disorder.

dissatisfied /di-**sa**-tis-fied/ *adj* not satisfied, discontented.

dissatisfy /di-**sa**-tis-fie/ *vb* to fail to satisfy, to displease. • *n* **dissatisfaction**.

dissect /di-**sect**/ *vb* 1 to cut into separate parts in order to examine. 2 to study carefully. • *n* **dissection**.

dissemble /di-**sem**-bul/ *vb* to pretend not to be what you are, to hide your feelings, intent, etc. • *n* **dissembler**.

disseminate /di-**se**-mi-nate/ *vb* (*fml*) to spread far and wide. • *n* **dissemination**.

dissension /di-**sen**-shun/ *n* disagreement, quarrelling.

dissent /di-**sent**/ *vb* to disagree, to think differently from. • *also n*.

dissertation /di-ser-**tay**-shun/ *n* a lecture or essay.

disservice /di-**ser**-vis/ *n* a bad turn.

dissident /**di**-si-dent/ *adj* disagreeing. • *n* a person who disagrees with a government's policies, especially one who is punished.

dissimilar /di-**si**-mi-lar/ *adj* unlike.

dissipate /**di**-si-pate/ *vb* 1 to scatter. 2 to spend or use wastefully. 3 to waste. • *n* **dissipation**.

dissipated /**di**-si-pay-ted/ *adj* given to living wildly, indulging in drinking and foolish or dangerous pleasures.

dissociate /di-**so**-shee-ate/ *vb* 1 to separate from. 2 to refuse to be connected with. • *n* **dissociation**.

dissolute /**di**-so-loot/ *adj* living wickedly, immoral.

dissolution /di-so-**loo**-shun/ *n* act of dissolving.

dissolve /di-**zolv**/ *vb* 1 to make or become liquid by placing in liquid. 2 to break up, to put an end to.

dissuade /di-**swade**/ *vb* to advise not to do. • *n* **dissuasion**. • *adj* **dissuasive**.

distance /**dis**-tanse/ *n* 1 being far off. 2 the space between two points or places. 3 (*fml*) unfriendliness.

distant /**dis**-tant/ *adj* 1 far off. 2 not close. 3 cold or unfriendly in manner.

distaste /dis-**taste**/ *n* dislike or disgust.

distasteful /dis-**taste**-ful/ *adj* unpleasant.

distemper /dis-**tem**-per/ *n* 1 a disease of dogs. 2 (*old*) an oil-less paint for walls.

distend /dis-**tend**/ *vb* to stretch, to swell. • *n* **distension**.

distil /dis-**til**/ *vb, also* **distill** (*US*) 1 to fall in drops. 2 to purify a substance by heating it until it turns into vapour, and then cooling the vapour until it becomes liquid.

distillation /dis-ti-**lay**-shun/ *n* act of distilling.

distiller /dis-**ti**-ler/ *n* a maker of whisky or other alcoholic liquor.

distillery /dis-**ti**-le-ree/ *n* a factory where whisky, etc, is made.

distinct /dis-**tingkt**/ *adj* 1 separate. 2 easily heard, seen, etc.

distinction /dis-**ting**-shun/ *n* 1 difference. 2 excellence. 3 a special mark of honour.

distinctive /dis-**ting**-tiv/ *adj* different in a special way.

distinguish /dis-**ting**-gwish/ *vb* 1 to see or point out the differences. 2 to make different. 3 to make. 4 to see, to make out.

distinguished /dis-**ting**-gwishd/ *adj* famous.

distort /dis-**tawrt**/ *vb* 1 to twist out of shape. 2 to give a false meaning to. • *n* **distortion**.

distract /dis-**tract**/ *vb* to draw the attention away.

distracted /dis-**trac**-ted/ *adj* almost mad with grief or anxiety.

distraction /dis-**trac**-shun/ *n* 1 anything that draws the attention away. 2 confusion of mind.

distraught /dis-**trawt**/ *adj* almost mad with grief or anxiety.

distress /dis-**tress**/ *n* 1 great pain or anxiety. 2 suffering caused by lack of money. 3 danger. • *vb* to cause anxiety, sorrow, or pain.

distribute /dis-**tri**-byoot/ *vb* 1 to give out, to give each his or her share. 2 to spread out widely. • *n* **distribution**.

distributor /dis-**tri**-byoo-ter/ *n* 1 a person who gives away or shares something. 2 part of a motor engine.

district /**dis**-trict/ *n* 1 part of a country. 2 an area marked off for some special purpose.

distrust /dis-**trust**/ *vb* to have no confidence or belief in. • *n* doubt, suspicion. • *adj* **distrustful**.

disturb /dis-**turb**/ *vb* **1** to throw into disorder. **2** to trouble. **3** to interrupt.

disturbance /dis-**tur**-banse/ *n* **1** disorder, riot. **2** disarrangement. **3** an interruption. **4** mental illness.

disuse /dis-**yoos**/ *n* a state of not being used, neglect. • *adj* disused.

ditch /ditch/ *n* a long narrow trench for carrying away water. • *vb* to make a ditch.

ditto /di-toe/ *n* the same as before, indicated by the sign ". • *abbr* **do**.

ditty /di-tee/ *n* a short simple song.

divan /di-van/ *n* **1** a long low sofa without back or arms. **2** a kind of bed with a thick base and a mattress.

dive /dive/ *vb* (**dived**, **dove** (*US*), **diving**) **1** to plunge into water head first. **2** to move quickly downward. • *n* **1** a plunge. **2** a sudden downward move.

diver /die-ver/ *n* **1** one who, with special equipment, is able to work under water. **2** a diving bird.

diverge /die-**verge**/ *vb* to go off in a different direction, to branch in different directions. • *n* divergence. • *adj* divergent.

diverse /die-**verse**/ *adj* different, unlike.

diversify /die-**ver**-si-fy/ *vb* to make or become different. • *n* diversification.

diversion /die-ver-shun/ *n* **1** (*fml*) amusement. **2** something that distracts the attention. **3** a turning aside from the main route (e.g. to avoid an obstacle).

diversity /die-**ver**-si-tee/ *n* difference, variety.

divert /die-**vert**/ *vb* **1** to turn in another direction. **2** to draw away. **3** to amuse.

diverting /die-**ver**-ting/ *adj* amusing.

divest /die-**vest**/ *vb* **1** to take away, to strip. **2** to take off, especially ceremonial clothes.

divide /di-**vide**/ *vb* **1** to break up into parts. **2** to share out. **3** to separate. **4** in mathematics, to see how many times one number is contained in another.

dividend /di-vi-dend/ *n* **1** in mathematics, a number to be divided. **2** a share of profit. **3** the rate at which the profits of a company are divided among shareholders.

divine /di-**vine**/ *adj* **1** of or belonging to God. **2** (*inf*) extremely good. • *vb* **1** to foretell, to guess. **2** to learn or discover by intuition, insight. • *n* divination.

divining rod /di-**vie**-ning-rod/ *n* a Y-shaped rod, usually of hazel, used to find underground water.

divinity /di-**vi**-ni-tee/ *n* **1** a god. **2** the study of religion.

divisible /di-**vi**-zi-bul/ *adj* able to be divided.

division /di-**vi**-zhun/ *n* **1** the act of dividing. **2** one of the parts into which something is divided. **3** disagreement. **4** a large army group.

divisional /di-vizh-nal/ *adj* having to do with a division.

divorce /di-**voarss**/ *n* **1** legal permission to separate from your married partner and to marry someone else if so desired. **2** separation. • *vb* **1** officially to end a marriage. **2** to separate.

divulge /di-**vulge**/ *vb* to make known, to reveal.

Diwali /di-wa-lee/ *n* a Hindu festival held in the autumn, particularly associated with Lakshmi, the goddess of prosperity.

DNA /dee-en-ay/ *abbr* = **deoxyribonucleic acid**: a substance in your body that stores genetic information.

DNA fingerprinting /dee-en-ay fing-ger-prin-ting/, **DNA profiling** /dee-en-ay-pro-fiel-ing/, *also* **genetic fingerprinting** *n* the process of analysing DNA patterns from body tissues, such as blood and saliva, in order to establish someone's identity, used particularly in crime detection.

DIY /dee-eye-why/ *abbr* = **do it yourself**: the act of making, repairing, or decorating things yourself, as opposed to employing a tradesman.

dizzy /di-zee/ *adj* giddy, having the feeling that everything is spinning around. • *n* **dizziness**.

do[1] /doo/ *vb* (*pt* **did**, *pp* **done**) **1** to perform, to carry out. **2** to attend to. **3** to act or behave. **4** to be enough or suitable. **5** (*inf*) to cheat or swindle.

do[2] *see* **ditto**.

docile /do-siel/ *adj* easily managed, controlled, or influenced, quiet. • *n* docility.

dock[1] /dock/ *n* **1** an enclosure in a harbour where enough water can be kept to float a ship when it is being loaded or unloaded, repaired, etc. **2** the box in which prisoners stand in a court of law. • *vb* to sail into dock.

dock[2] /dock/ *vb* to cut short, to remove part of.

dock[3] /dock/ *n* a common weed.

docket /dock-et/ *n* a label attached to goods.

dockyard /dock-yard/ *n* a place where ships are built and repaired.

doctor /doc-tor/ *n* **1** a person who is qualified by medical training to attend the sick and injured. **2** a person who receives a degree granted by universities to those learned in a certain field. • *vb* **1** to give medical treatment to. **2** to make different in order to deceive; to tamper with.

doctorate /doc-trit/ *n* the degree of doctor.

doctrinal /doc-tri-nal/ *adj* having to do with a

doctrine or set of beliefs held by a religious society.

doctrinaire /doc-tri-**nare**/ *adj* believing in or trying to put into action a system of ideas without considering the practical difficulties of doing so.

doctrine /**doc**-trin/ *n* a set of beliefs held by a person or group.

document /**doc**-yu-ment/ *n* a written or printed paper, often one that can be used as proof. • *vb* to bring forward written evidence.

documentary /doc-yu-**men**-tu-ree/ *adj* 1 having to do with documents. 2 giving facts and explanations. • *also n.*

dodder /**dod**-er/ *vb* to move unsteadily or shakily.

dodge /**dodge**/ *vb* 1 to make a quick movement to avoid someone or something. 2 to avoid by cleverness or trickery. • *n* 1 a quick movement aside. 2 a trick.

dodo /**doe**-doe/ *n* (*pl* **dodoes** *or* **dodos**) a type of flightless bird no longer in existence.

doe /**doe**/ *n* the female of many animals (e.g. deer, rabbit, etc).

doff /**doff**/ *vb* (*fml*) to take off.

dog /**dawg**/ *n* 1 a common domestic animal. 2 (*hum or inf*) a fellow. • *vb* (**dogged** /**dawg**-ed/, **dogging**) to follow closely, to pursue.

dogcart /**dawg**-cart/ *n* a two-wheeled cart or carriage.

dog collar /**dawg** caw-ler/ *n* 1 a collar for a dog. 2 the collar worn by a member of the clergy.

dog-eared /**daw**-geerd/ *adj* with the corners of the pages turned down.

dogfish /**dawg**-fish/ *n* a type of small shark.

dogged /**daw**-ged/ *adj* determined, unwilling to give in. • *n* **doggedness**.

doggerel /**daw**-ge-rel/ *n* bad poetry.

dogma /**dawg**-ma/ *n* a belief or set of beliefs put forward by an authority to be accepted as a matter of faith.

dogmatic /dawg-**ma**-tic/ *adj* 1 relating to dogma. 2 holding your beliefs very strongly and expecting other people to accept them without question. • *n* **dogmatism**.

dog rose /**dawg** roaz/ *n* the wild rose.

Dog Star /**dawg** star/ *n* Sirius, the brightest of the fixed stars.

dogwatch /**dawg**-watch/ *n* on a ship, a short watch of two hours.

doily /**doi**-lee/ *n*, *also* **doyley** a small fancy napkin or mat.

doldrums /**doal**-drumz/ *npl* seas near the equator where there is little or no wind. • **in the doldrums** in a sad mood.

dole /**dole**/ *vb* to give out shares of, often in small amounts. • *n* (*inf*) money paid by the state to unemployed people.

doleful /**dole**-ful/ *adj* gloomy, sad. • *adv* **dolefully**.

doll /**dol**/ *n* a toy in the shape of a person.

dollar /**dol**-ar/ *n* a unit of American, Australian, or Canadian currency (=100 cents).

dolorous /**dol**-o-rus/ *adj* (*fml*) sad, sorrowful. • *n* **dolour**, *also* **dolor** (*US*).

dolphin /**dol**-fin/ *n* a sea animal like the porpoise, belonging to the whale family.

dolt /**doalt**/ *n* a stupid person.

domain /doe-**mane**/ *n* 1 the land that you own. 2 the country that a monarch rules. 3 an area of interest, knowledge, influence, etc.

dome /**dome**/ *n* 1 a rounded top on a building. 2 something of this shape. • *adj* **domed**.

domestic /du-**mes**-tic/ *adj* 1 belonging to or having to do with the house. 2 concerning your personal or home life. 3 tame and living with or used to people. 4 having to do with your own country. 5 (*inf*) interested in and good at cooking, housework, etc. • *n* a house servant.

domesticated /du-**mes**-ti-cay-ted/ *adj* 1 accustomed to living near and being used by people. 2 fond of and/or good at doing jobs associated with running a house.

domesticity /du-mes-**ti**-si-tee/ *n* 1 home life. 2 the state of being fond of and good at running a home.

domicile /**dom**-i-sile/ *n* (*fml*) a house, a home, the place where a person is living.

dominant /**dom**-i-nant/ *adj* 1 controlling others. 2 most important. • *n* **dominance**.

dominate /**dom**-i-nate/ *vb* 1 to have complete control over. 2 to be the most important. 3 to rise high above. • *n* **domination**.

domineer /dom-i-**neer**/ *vb* to bully. • *adj* **domineering**.

dominion /du-**min**-yun/ *n* 1 (*fml*) rule, government. 2 the territory governed.

dominoes /**dom**-i-noaz/ *n* a game played with small flat pieces of wood, ivory, etc, marked with dots.

don[1] /**don**/ *vb* (*old*) (**donned, donning**) to put on (clothing).

don[2] /**don**/ *n* a teacher in a university or college.

donate /**doa**-nate/ *vb* to give, especially to a charity, etc; to contribute. • *n* **donation**.

done /**dun**/ *vb*, *pp* of **do** • *adj* 1 finished, completed. 2 cooked thoroughly. 3 socially acceptable.

donkey /**dong**-kee/ *n* another word for **ass**[1].

donor /doe-nur/ *n* **1** a person who gives or contributes. **2** a person who provides blood for transfusion, organs for transplants, etc.

doodle /doo-dul/ *vb* to draw or scribble casually or absent-mindedly. • *also n.*

doom /doom/ *n* death, ruin, destruction, terrible and inevitable fate. • *vb* to cause to suffer something unavoidable and terrible, such as death, ruin, or destruction.

doomsday /doomz-day/ *n* the day of judgment at the end of the world.

door /dore/ *n* a movable barrier in an entrance to a building or room.

doorway /dore-way/ *n* an entrance to a building or room.

dope /dope/ *n* (*inf*) a fool, a stupid person.

dormant /dawr-mant/ *adj* not at present active.

dormer /dawr-mer/ *n* a small window in a sloping roof.

dormitory /dawr-mi-toe-ree/ *n* a sleeping room with many beds.

dormouse /dawr-mouse/ *n* (*pl* **dormice** / dawr-mice/) a small mouse-like animal that hibernates in winter.

dorsal /dawr-sal/ *adj* having to do with the back.

dory /doe-ree/ *n* a sea fish (often **John Dory**).

dosage /doe-sidge/ *n* the amount to be given in a dose.

dose /doze/ *n* the amount of medicine given at one time. • *vb* to give medicine to.

dossier /doss-ee-yay/ *n* a collection of papers dealing with one particular subject or person.

dot /dot/ *n* a small point or mark. • *vb* (**dotted, dotting**) to mark with dots • **dotted with** having (things) placed here and there.

dotage /doe-tidge/ *n* the weak-mindedness of old age.

dote /doat/ *vb* to show great fondness of, especially in a foolish way.

double /du-bul/ *adj* **1** twice as much as usual or normal. **2** for two people. **3** forming a pair. **4** combining two things or qualities. • *n* **1** twice the amount. **2** a person or thing looking the same as another. **3** a glass of alcoholic liquor holding twice the standard amount. **4** a running pace. • *vb* **1** to multiply by two, to cause to become twice as large or numerous. **2** to fold in two. **3** to have two uses, jobs, etc. • *adv* **doubly**. • **double back** to turn back in the opposite direction, especially unexpectedly.

double-bass /du-bul-base/ *n* a large, low-toned stringed instrument.

double-cross /du-bul-crawss/ *vb* to deceive someone who trusts you and believes that you are their friend.

double-dealing /du-bul-dee-ling/ *n* deceit, dishonesty. • *adj* devious, not to be trusted.

doublet /du-blet/ *n* **1** a close-fitting body garment worn by men in the 14th to 17th centuries. **2** one of a pair of words having the same meaning.

doubt /dout/ *vb* to be uncertain about, to be unwilling to believe or trust. • *n* **1** a feeling of uncertainty. **2** distrust. • *adj* **doubtful**. • *adv* **doubtless**.

douche /doosh/ *n* a stream of water directed on to the body to clean it. • *also vb.*

dough /doe/ *n* **1** flour, etc, moistened with liquid and made into a paste ready for baking. **2** (*inf*) money.

doughnut /doe-nut/ *n* a type of sweet cake, often in the shape of a ring.

douse /douz/ *vb*, **dowse 1** to drench in water. **2** to put out.

dove /duv/ *n* a bird of the pigeon family.

dove-cote /duv-cot(e)/ *n* a pigeon house.

dovetail /duv-tail/ *n* a sticking-out end of wood shaped like a dove's tail made to fit into a hole in another piece of wood to lock the two together. • *vb* to fit neatly or exactly together.

dowager /dow-i-jer/ *n* the title given to the widow of a nobleman.

dowdy /dow-dee/ *adj* badly or shabbily dressed, unfashionable, drab. • *n* **dowdiness**. • *adv* **dowdily**.

down[1] /down/ *prep* in a descending direction in, on, along, or through. • *adv* **1** from a higher to a lower position, to a lying or sitting position. **2** towards or to the ground, floor, or bottom. **3** to or in a lower status or in a worse condition. **4** in cash. **5** to or in a state of less activity. • *adj* **1** occupying a low position, especially lying on the ground. **2** (*inf*) depressed. • *n* **1** a low period. **2** (*inf*) a dislike. • *vb* **1** to go or cause to go or come down. **2** to swallow.

down[2] /down/ *n* the fine soft feathers of a bird. • *adj* **downy**.

down-and-out /dow-nan-dout/ *adj* having no job and no home, and no money. • *n* a down-and-out person.

downcast /down-cast/ *adj* **1** directed downward. **2** sad, in low spirits.

downfall /down-fawl/ *n* ruin, fall from power, prosperity, etc.

down-hearted /down-har-tid/ *adj* discouraged, in low spirits.

download /down-load/ *vb* to copy or transfer data or a program from one computer to another.

downpour /**down**-poar/ n a heavy fall of rain.

downright /**down**-rite/ adj **1** thorough, complete. **2** frank, straightforward, saying exactly what you think. • also adv.

downsize /**down**-size/ vb to reduce the number of people who work in a company, usually in order to reduce costs.

dowry /**dow**-ree/ n the property a woman brings to her husband at marriage.

dowse see **douse**.

doyley see **doily**.

doze /doaz/ vb to be half asleep. • n light sleep.

dozen /**du**-zen/ n twelve.

drab /drab/ adj **1** of a dull greyish brown colour. **2** dull, uninteresting.

draft /draft/ n **1** a written order to pay money to someone. **2** a rough copy or plan of work to be done. • vb **1** to prepare a plan or rough copy. **2** to pick and send off. **3** (US) to conscript.

drag /drag/ vb (**dragged**, **dragging**) **1** to pull along with force. **2** to trail on the ground. **3** (inf) to go very slowly. **4** to search underwater with hooks or a net. • n anything that causes to go slowly.

dragon /**dra**-gon/ n **1** in fables, a winged monster. **2** a fierce, stern person.

dragonfly /**dra**-gon-fly/ n a winged insect.

dragoon /dra-**goon**/ n a horse soldier. • vb to force to obey, to bully into.

drain /drane/ vb **1** to draw off liquid by pipes, ditches, etc. **2** to empty completely. **3** to cause to become dry as liquid flows away. • n **1** a pipe or channel to carry away liquid. **2** metal bars over a drain in the ground.

drainage /**dray**-nidge/ n all the means used to draw water away from a certain area.

drake /drake/ n a male duck.

dram /dram/ n **1** a small measure of weight (1/16 ounce). **2** a small drink of whisky, etc.

drama /**dra**-ma/ n **1** a play. **2** plays as a branch of literature and as a performing art. **3** an exciting event, a series of exciting events. **4** excitement.

dramatic /dra-**ma**-tic/ adj **1** having to do with drama. **2** sudden or exciting. **3** showing too much feeling or emotion. • adv **dram-atically**.

dramatist /**dra**-ma-tist/ n a writer of plays.

dramatize /**dra**-ma-tize/ n, also **dramatise 1** to turn into a stage play. **2** to exaggerate the importance or significance of. • n **dramatization**, also **dramatisation**.

drape /drape/ vb **1** to cover or decorate with cloth, etc, in folds. **2** to cause to hang or rest loosely.

draper /**dray**-per/ n a person who sells clothes.

drapery /**dray**-pe-ree/ n **1** cloth, linen. **2** a draper's shop.

drastic /**dra**-stic/ adj acting with strength or violence; thorough. • adv **drastically**.

draught /draft/ n, also **draft** (US) **1** the amount taken in one drink. **2** a stream of air through a room. **3** the depth a ship sinks in water.

draughts /drafts/ npl a game that is played between two people using 12 round, flat pieces on a board divided into checks, the objective being to capture the other player's pieces.

draughtsman /**draft**-sman/ n a man whose job it is to draw plans for buildings, etc.

draughty /**draf**-tee/ adj cold because of a stream of air.

draw /draw/ vb (pt **drew**, pp **drawn**) **1** to pull along or towards. **2** to move towards or away from. **3** to attract. **4** to receive money. **5** to make a picture or pictures of, usually with a pencil, crayons, etc. **6** (of a game or contest) to end with nobody winning. **7** (of a ship) to sink to a certain depth in the water. • n **1** an attraction. **2** a game or contest won by nobody. **3** the selecting of winning tickets in a raffle, lottery, etc. • **draw the line at** to refuse to have to do. • **draw up 1** to stop. **2** to prepare, especially in writing.

drawback /draw-**back**/ n a disadvantage.

drawbridge /draw-**bridge**/ n a bridge that can be lifted at one end to prevent crossing.

drawer /drawr/ n **1** a sliding box or container in a table, closet, etc. **2** (pl) see **drawers**.

drawers /drawrz/ npl (old) an undergarment with legs for the bottom part of the body.

drawing /**draw**-ing/ n **1** a picture made with a pencil, crayons, etc. **2** the art of making such pictures.

drawing room /**draw**-ing room/ n a sitting room, especially a large one in which guests are received.

drawl /drawl/ vb to speak slowly or lazily. • also n.

dread /dred/ n fear, terror. • adj (fml) causing great fear, terrible. • vb to fear greatly.

dreadful /**dred**-ful/ adj **1** terrible. **2** very unpleasant, bad. • adv **dreadfully**.

dreadlocks /**dred**-loks/ npl hair that is twisted into long thick braids all around the head.

dream /dreem/ n **1** the ideas or fancies passing through the mind of a person sleeping. **2** memories of the past or thoughts of what may happen. **3** state of being occupied by your thoughts, daydream. **4** (inf) a beautiful or wonderful person or thing. • vb (pt, pp **dreamed** or **dreamt**) **1** to have dreams. **2** to imagine.

dreamer /dree-mer/ *n* a person who is more interested in thoughts or fancies than facts.

dreamt *pt and pp* of **dream.**

dreamy /dree-me/ *adj* **1** given to or relating to daydreaming. **2** extremely attractive.

dreary /dree-ree/ *adj* cheerless, gloomy.

dredge[1] /dredge/ *n* a machine for bringing up mud, fish, etc, from the bottom of a river or the sea. • *vb* **1** to bring up with a dredge. **2** to clear with a dredge. **3** to mention something from the past.

dredge[2] /dredge/ *vb* to sprinkle with.

dredger /dre-jer/ *n* a ship fitted to clear mud from the channel in a river or harbour.

dregs /dregz/ *npl* tiny pieces of matter that sink to the foot of a standing liquid.

drench /drench/ *vb* **1** to make very wet. **2** to force (an animal) to drink.

dress /dress/ *vb* **1** to put on clothes. **2** to wear evening or formal dress. **3** to straighten, to set in order. **4** to bandage. **5** to prepare for use. • *n* **1** clothing. **2** a woman's outer garment. • **dress up 1** to put on the clothing of another person, nation, etc. **2** to put on your best clothing.

dress circle /dress sir-cul/ *n* the first-floor gallery in a theatre.

dresser /dre-ser/ *n* **1** a kitchen sideboard. **2** a person who helps an actor to dress.

dressing /dre-sing/ *n* **1** the ointments, bandages, etc, put on a wound. **2** something put on as a covering. **3** sauce for food, especially a mixture of oil and vinegar, etc, for putting on salads.

dress rehearsal /dress-ri-her-sal/ *n* a practice before a performance, in the appropriate costume.

dressy /dre-see/ *adj* **1** (*inf*) fond of nice clothes. **2** elegant, for special occasions.

dribble /dri-bul/ *vb* **1** to fall or let fall in small drops. **2** to allow saliva to run from the mouth. **3** to keep a moving ball under control by little kicks or taps.

driblet /dri-blet/ *n* a small amount.

drift /drift/ *n* **1** that which is driven by wind (e.g. snow, sand) or water (e.g. seaweed). **2** meaning. • *vb* **1** to be driven by wind or water current. **2** to do something aimlessly.

drill[1] /drill/ *n* **1** a tool for boring holes. **2** training practice. **3** procedures to be followed in a certain situation, such as an emergency. • *vb* **1** to make holes with a drill. **2** to teach something by making learners do it again and again. **3** to practise military exercises.

drill[2] /drill/ *n* **1** a machine for sowing seeds. **2** a row of seeds. • *vb* to sow in rows.

drily *see* **dry.**

drink /dringk/ *vb* (*pt* **drank,** *pp* **drunk**) **1** to swallow. **2** to take alcoholic liquor, especially in too great amounts. • *n* **1** an act of drinking. **2** a liquid suitable for drinking. **3** alcoholic liquor. **4** a glass of alcoholic liquor.

drip /drip/ *vb* (**dripped, dripping**) to fall or let fall in drops. • *n* a drop.

dripping /dri-ping/ *n* the fat that drops from roasting meat.

drive /drive/ *vb* (*pt* **drove,** *pp* **driven**) **1** to control or guide. **2** to ride in a car or other vehicle. **3** to force or urge along. **4** to hit hard. • *n* **1** a ride in a car or carriage. **2** a private road up to a house. **3** a hard hit. **4** energy.

drive-in /drie-vin/ *n* a cinema, restaurant, etc. which you can use while staying in your car.

drivel /dri-vel/ *n* (*inf*) foolish talk, nonsense. • *also vb.*

driver /drie-ver/ *n* **1** a person who drives. **2** a golf club with a wooden head.

drizzle /dri-zel/ *vb* to rain in small drops. • *n* a fine rain.

droll /drole/ *adj* amusing, odd.

dromedary /drom-e-de-ree/ *n* a camel with one hump on its back.

drone /drone/ *n* **1** the male or nonworking bee. **2** a lazy person. **3** a humming sound. • *vb* **1** to make a humming sound. **2** to speak boringly.

drool /drool/ *vb* **1** to dribble saliva from the mouth. **2** (*inf*) to admire very enthusiastically.

droop /droop/ *vb* **1** to hang down. **2** to become weak. • *also n.*

drop /drop/ *n* **1** a very small amount of liquid. **2** the act of falling. **3** the distance that a person may fall. • *vb* (**dropped, dropping**) **1** to fall or let fall in drops. **2** to fall or let fall. **3** to fall or cause to fall to a lower level or amount. **4** to stop seeing, talking about, doing, etc.

drought /drout/ *n* a long spell of dry weather, lack of rain, dryness.

drove[1] /drove/ *vb, pt* of **drive.**

drove[2] /drove/ *n* a herd or flock on the move.

drover /dro-ver/ *n* a person who drives cattle.

drown /droun/ *vb* **1** to die under water by water filling the lungs. **2** to kill by keeping under water. **3** to flood, to submerge. **4** to put too much liquid in or on. **5** to prevent from being heard by making a noise.

drowsy /drou-zee/ *adj* sleepy. • *n* **drowsiness.**

drub /drub/ *vb* (**drubbed, drubbing**) to beat, to thrash. • *n* **drubbing.**

drudge /drudge/ *vb* to work hard, to slave. • *n* a person who does hard or boring work.

drudgery /dru-je-ree/ *n* dull or hard work.

drug /drug/ *n* **1** any substance used as or in a medicine. **2** a substance that causes sleep or loss of feeling, especially a habit-forming one. • *vb* (**drugged, drugging**) to give drugs to in order to make insensible.

druid /droo-id/ *n* a priest of the Celts in ancient Britain before the Christian era.

drum /drum/ *n* **1** a musical instrument in which skin is stretched tightly over the ends of a box and then beaten to produce a booming sound. **2** the tight skin across the inside of the ear. **3** something shaped like a drum. • *vb* (**drummed, drumming**) **1** to beat a drum. **2** to make a noise by beating or tapping. • *n* **drummer**.

drumstick /drum-stick/ *n* a stick for beating a drum.

drunk /drungk/ *adj* overcome or overexcited by too much alcoholic liquor. • *also adj* **drunken**. • *n* **drunkenness**.

drunkard /drung-kard/ *n* a person who is often drunk.

dry /drie/ *adj* **1** not wet or damp. **2** with little rainfall. **3** not legally allowed to sell alcohol. **4** not sweet. **5** (*inf*) thirsty. **6** uninteresting. **7** (*of humour*) quiet, not easily noticed. • *vb* to make or become dry. • *adv* **drily, dryly**. • *n* **dryness**.

dryad /drie-ad/ *n* a mythical spirit of the woods.

dry-clean /drie-cleen/ *vb* to clean with chemicals instead of water. • *n* **dry-cleaner**.

dry dock /drie dock/ *n* a dock out of which water can be drained so that a ship may be repaired.

dry rot /drie-rot/ *n* a disease of wood that makes it crumble away.

dual /joo-el/ *adj* consisting of two; double. • *n* **duality**.

dual carriageway /joo-el ca-ridge-way/ *n* a wide road which has a strip of grass or barrier in the middle to separate two lines of traffic moving in opposite directions.

dub /dub/ *vb* (**dubbed, dubbing**) **1** to make someone a knight by touching with a sword. **2** to nickname someone.

dubbin, dubbing /du-bin(g)/ *n* a grease for softening leather.

dubious /dyoo-bee-us/ *adj* **1** feeling doubt. **2** causing doubt, of uncertain worth, etc, possibly dishonest. • *n* **dubiety**.

duchess /du-chess/ *n* the wife or widow of a duke.

duchy /du-chee/ *n* **1** the lands of a duke. **2** a country ruled by a duke.

duck[1] /duck/ *n* a type of common waterfowl, both domestic and wild, whose flesh is used as a food.

duck[2] /duck/ *vb* **1** to plunge or dip under water. **2** to bend to avoid something or to avoid being seen. **3** to avoid or dodge.

duckling /duck-ling/ *n* a young duck.

duct /duct/ *n* **1** a pipe or tube for carrying liquid, gas, electric wires, etc. **2** a tube in the body or in plants through which fluid, etc, passes.

dud /dud/ *adj* (*inf*) of no use. • *also n*.

dudgeon /du-jun/ *n* annoyance, anger.

due /dyoo/ *adj* **1** owed. **2** proper. **3** expected. • *adv* directly. • *n* **1** an amount owed. **2** a right. • *npl* a sum payable. • **due to** caused by.

duel /dew-el/ *n* **1** an arranged fight between two armed people. **2** a contest or struggle between two people. • *also vb* (**duelled, duelling**).

duet /dyoo-wet/ *n* a piece of music for two singers or players.

duffel, duffle /du-ful/ *n* a rough woollen cloth.

dugout /du-gout/ *n* **1** an underground shelter. **2** a boat made from a hollowed-out tree.

duke /dyook/ *n* **1** the highest rank of nobleman. **2** in some parts of Europe, especially formerly, a ruling prince.

dulcet /dul-set/ *adj* sweet, tuneful.

dulcimer /dul-si-mer/ *n* a musical instrument played by small hammers striking strings, the forerunner of the piano.

dull /dull/ *adj* **1** slow, stupid. **2** uninteresting. **3** cloudy, sunless, gloomy. **4** not bright. **5** not sharp. • *vb* to make dull, to blunt. • *n* **dullness**. • *adv* **dully**.

dullard /du-lard/ *n* a dull or stupid person.

duly /dyoo-lee/ *adv* **1** properly. **2** at the due and proper time.

dumb /dum/ *adj* **1** unable to speak. **2** silent. **3** (*inf*) stupid, unintelligent. • *n* **dumbness**. • **dumb down** (*inf*) to make something less intellectually challenging.

dumbbells /dum-belz/ *npl* weights used when exercising the arm muscles.

dumbfound /dum-found/ *vb* to astonish greatly.

dummy /du-mee/ *n* **1** a model of the human figure, used for displaying or fitting clothing. **2** an imitation article. **3** a device containing a rubber or plastic teat given to a baby or young child to suck on in order to soothe them. • *adj* pretended, not real.

dump /dump/ *vb* **1** to throw away. **2** (*inf*) to let fall or set down heavily. **3** to sell goods in another country at a low price. **4** to end a romantic relationship with. • *n* **1** a place where rubbish or waste is left. **2** a military store. **3** (*inf*) a dirty, untidy, or uninteresting place. **4** (*pl*) *see* **dumps**.

dumper truck, dump truck *n* a heavy truck the back of which can be tilted back and up to unload cargo such as earth, gravel, rocks, etc.

dumpling /**dum**-pling/ *n* **1** a food consisting of a thick paste, sometimes rolled into balls, or sometimes filled with fruit or meat, and cooked. **2** thin pastry with a savoury filling, steamed, boiled or fried.

dumps /dumps/ *npl* low spirits.

dun /dun/ *adj* of a pale yellowish or greyish brown colour.

dunce /dunse/ *n* a slow learner, a stupid student.

dune /doon/ *n* a low sandhill, especially on the seashore.

dung /dung/ *n* the waste matter passed from the bodies of animals. • *vb* to mix dung with earth to fertilize it.

dungarees, dungarees /dung-ga-**reez**/ *npl* outer garments worn to protect the clothing.

dungeon /**dun**-jin/ *n* a dark prison, an underground prison cell.

dunk /dungk/ *vb* to dip into liquid for a moment.

duo /**dew**-oe/ *n* a group of two people, especially two musicians.

duodenum /dew-oe-**dee**-num/ *n* part of the bowel. • *adj* **duodenal**.

dupe /dewp/ *vb* to cheat. • *n* a person who is cheated or deceived.

duplicate /**dew**-pli-kit/ *adj* exactly the same, exactly like another. • *n* an exact copy. • *vb* /**dew**-pli-kate/ to make a copy or copies of. • *n* **duplication**.

duplicity /dew-**pli**-si-tee/ *n* deceit, trickery.

durable /**dew**-ra-bul/ *adj* **1** lasting, hard-wearing. **2** lasting or able to last. • *n* **durability**.

duration /dyoo-**ray**-shun/ *n* the time for which a thing lasts.

duress /dyoo-**ress**/ *n* use of force, threats.

during /**dyoo**-ring/ *prep* **1** in the course of. **2** throughout the time of.

dusk /dusk/ *n* partial darkness, twilight. • *adj* **dusky**.

dust /dust/ *n* tiny dry particles of earth or matter. • *vb* **1** to remove dust. **2** to sprinkle with powder. • *adj* **dusty**.

dustbin /**dust**-bin/ *n* a receptacle into which one puts rubbish.

duster /**dust**-er/ *n* a cloth for removing dust, etc.

dutiable /dyoo-tee-a-bul/ *adj* able to be taxed.

dutiful /dyoo-tee-ful/ *adj* obedient, careful to do your duty.

duty /**dyoo**-tee/ *n* **1** that which you ought to do. **2** an action or task requiring to be done, especially one attached to a job. **3** a tax on goods.

duvet /**doo**-vay/ *n* a quilted bed covering.

DVD /dee-vee-**dee**/ *abbr* = **digital video disc**: a kind of compact disc on which particularly large amounts of information, especially photographs and video material, can be stored.

dwarf /dwawrf/ *n* (*pl* **dwarfs** /dwawrfs/ *or* **dwarves** /dwawrvz/) **1** (*sometimes offensive*) a person, animal or plant that is much smaller than average. **2** in fairy tales, a creature like a very small man who has magical powers. • *adj* undersized, very small. • *vb* to make seem small. • *adj* **dwarfish**.

dwell /dwell/ *vb* (*pt, pp* **dwelt** *or* **dwelled**) **1** (*old or lit*) to live in. **2** to talk or think a lot about.

dwelling /**dwe**-ling/ *n* (*fml or old*) a house.

dwindle /**dwin**-dul/ *vb* to grow gradually less or smaller.

dye /die/ *vb* to give a new colour to, to stain. • *n* a colouring substance. • *n* **dyer**.

dyke /dike/ *see* **dike**.

dynamic /die-**na**-mic/ *adj* active, energetic.

dynamics /die-**na**-mics/ *n* the science of forces and movement.

dynamite /**die**-na-mite/ *n* a powerful explosive.

dynamo /**die**-na-mo/ *n* a machine for making electric current.

dynasty /**di**-na-stee/ *n* a line of rulers of the same family. • *adj* **dynastic**.

dysentery /**di**-sen-te-ree/ *n* a disease of the bowels.

dysfunctional /dis-**fung**-shnal/ *adj* not functioning in what is considered the normal fashion.

dyslexia /dis-**lek**-see-a/ *n* difficulty with reading and spelling caused by a slight disorder in the brain.

E

E, e /ee/ **1** the fifth letter of the English alphabet. **2** (*mus*) the third note of the scale of C major.

each /eech/ *pron, adj* every one taken singly or separately.

eager /ee-ger/ *adj* full of desire, keen. • *n* **eagerness.**

eagle /ee-gl/ *n* a large bird of prey.

eagle-eyed /ee-gl-eyed/ *adj* having very keen sight.

eaglet /ee-glet/ *n* a young eagle.

ear[1] /eer/ *n* **1** the organ of hearing. **2** the ability to hear the difference between sounds. **3** attention.

ear[2] /eer/ *n* a head or spike of corn.

earache /ee-rake/ *n* a pain in the ear.

eardrum /eer-drum/ *n* the tight skin across the inside of the ear that enables a person to hear sounds.

early /ur-lee/ *adj* **1** before the time arranged. **2** near the beginning. **3** belonging to the first stages of development, etc. **4** (*fml*) soon. • *adv* **1** near the beginning (of a period of time, etc). **2** sooner than usual, sooner than expected, sooner than often, etc.

earmark /eer-mark/ *vb* to set aside for a special purpose.

earmuffs /eer-mufs/ *npl* pads that fit over the ears to keep them from getting cold.

earn /urn/ *vb* **1** to get money in return for work. **2** to deserve.

earnest /ur-nest/ *adj* **1** serious. **2** determined. • *n* **earnestness.** • **in earnest** meaning what one says.

earnings /ur-nings/ *npl* wages, money paid for work done.

earring /ee-ring/ *n* an ornament worn on the ear.

earshot /eer-shot/ *n* the distance within which one can hear something.

earth /urth/ *n* **1** the planet on which we live. **2** the world as opposed to heaven. **3** dry land, the ground or soil. **4** the hole of a fox, badger, etc. **5** the wire connecting an electric appliance to the ground. • *adj* **earthen.**

earthly /urth-lee/ *adj* having to do with the world, of worldly rather than heavenly things.

earthquake /urth-kwake/ *n* a shaking movement of the surface of the earth.

earthwork /urth-wurk/ *n* a defensive wall of earth.

earthworm /urth-wurm/ *n* a worm that lives in the soil.

earthy /urth-ee/ *adj* **1** like, or of, earth. **2** coarse, not refined.

ease /eez/ *n* **1** freedom from anxiety or pain. **2** lack of difficulty. **3** freedom from work; rest, comfort. **4** naturalness. • *vb* **1** to lessen. **2** to move gently or gradually.

easel /ee-zel/ *n* a stand to hold a picture, blackboard, etc, upright.

east /eest/ *n, adj, adv* one of the four chief points of the compass, the direction in which the sun rises. • *adj* **eastern, eastward** /eest-ward/. • **the East** the countries of Asia.

Easter /ee-ster/ *n* a Christian festival that commemorates the rising of Christ from the dead.

easterly /ee-ster-lee/ *adj* from or towards the east.

easy /ee-zee/ *adj* **1** not difficult. **2** free from anxiety or pain. **3** comfortable. **4** relaxed, leisurely.

easy-going /ee-zee-go-wing/ *adj* not easily worried or angered.

eat /eet/ *vb* (*pt* **ate**, *pp* **eaten**) **1** to chew and swallow, as food. **2** to wear away.

eating disorder /ee-ting di-sawr-der/ *n* an emotional disorder in which the sufferer has an irrational attitude towards food.

eaves /eevz/ *npl* that part of the roof that comes out beyond the walls.

eavesdrop /eevz-drop/ *vb* (**eavesdropped, eavesdropping**) to try to hear what others are saying to each other privately. • *n* **eavesdropper.**

ebb /eb/ *n* **1** the flowing back of the tide. **2** a falling away or weakening. • *vb* **1** to flow back. **2** to grow less, weak, faint, etc.

ebony /e-bu-nee/ *n* a hard black wood. • *adj* **1** made of ebony. **2** black.

eccentric /ek-sen-tric/ *adj* **1** odd, strange. **2** (*of circles*) not drawn round the same centre. • *n* a person who behaves in an odd or unusual manner. • *n* **eccentricity.**

echo /e-co/ *n* (*pl* **echoes** /e-coaz/) **1** the repeating of a sound by the reflection of sound waves from a surface. **2** an imitation. • *vb* **1** to repeat, to throw back a sound. **2** to imitate.

eclipse /e-clips/ *n* **1** the cutting off of the light from the sun by the moon coming between it and the earth. **2** the darkening of the face of the moon by the earth coming between it and the sun. **3** a failure caused by the unexpected success of another. • *vb* **1** to cut off the light from, to darken. **2** to make another seem inferior by outdoing.

ecology /e-**col**-o-jee/ *n* **1** the science of the life of things in their physical surroundings. **2** the relation of plants and living creatures to each other and to their surroundings. • **ecological** *adj*.

e-commerce /ee-com-erse/ *n* electronic commerce, business conducted online.

economic /e-co-**nom**-ic/ *adj* **1** having to do with economics. **2** designed to give a profit.

economical /e-co-**nom**-i-cal/ *adj* careful of money, not wasteful.

economics /e-co-**nom**-ics/ *n* the study of the means of increasing the wealth of a community or nation.

economist /e-**con**-o-mist/ *n* a person who works in or studies economics.

economize, economise /e-**con**-o-mize/ *vb* to spend or use carefully, to save, to be economical.

economy /e-**con**-o-mee/ *n* **1** management of the wealth, money, goods, etc, of a home, business or country. **2** sparing use of money.

ecosystem /e-co-sis-tem/ *n* all the plants and living creatures that live in an area and depend on one another, together with their habitat.

ecstasy /ec-sta-see/ *n* great delight or joy.

ecstatic /ec-sta-tic/ *adj* delighted, carried away by joy.

eczema /ig-zee-ma, eg-ze-ma/ *n* a skin disease.

eddy /ed-ee/ *n* a whirling current of water or air, a whirlpool or whirlwind. • *vb* to move in eddies.

Eden /ee-den/ *n* (*OT*) the garden of Adam and Eve; paradise.

edge /edge/ *n* **1** the sharp side of a blade. **2** a border or boundary. **3** keenness, sharpness. • *vb* **1** to move gradually, especially with small sideways movements. **2** to put a border on.

edgeways /edge-wayz/ *adj* sideways.

edging /e-jing/ *n* a border or fringe.

edible /ed-i-bl/ *adj* able or fit to be eaten.

edit /e-dit/ *vb* to prepare for printing or publication.

edition /e-di-shun/ *n* the number of copies of a book or newspaper published at one time.

editor /e-di-tor/ *n* **1** a person who edits. **2** a person who collects the material for a newspaper or magazine and selects what is to be published or who is in charge of a newspaper or part of a newspaper.

editorial /e-di-**toe**-ree-al/ *adj* of an editor. • *n* an article by the editor or someone chosen by him or her on a matter of immediate interest.

educate /e-ju-cate/ *vb* to teach or train. • *n* **education**.

educational /e-ju-**cay**-shu-nal/ *adj* having to do with education.

eel /eel/ *n* a snakelike fish.

eerie, eery /ee-ree/ *adj* strange and frightening.

effect /i-fect/ *n* **1** result; power to bring about a change. **2** impression. **3** *pl* goods, property. **4** *pl* lighting and sounds used in a play, film, etc. • *vb* to bring about, to succeed in doing, to produce.

effective /i-fec-tive/ *adj* **1** doing what is intended or desired, successful. **2** striking. **3** actual, real. **4** in operation, working.

effeminate /i-fe-mi-nit/ *adj* womanish, unmanly. • *n* **effeminacy**.

effervesce /e-fer-vess/ *vb* to bubble or sparkle. • *n* **effervescence**.

effervescent /e-fer-ve-sent/ *adj* **1** bubbling, sparkling. **2** lively and enthusiastic.

efficient /e-fi-shent/ *adj* **1** able to do what is necessary or intended without wasting time, energy, etc. **2** good at one's job, capable. • *n* **efficiency**.

effigy /e-fi-jee/ *n* **1** a likeness in the form of a picture, statue or carving. **2** the head on a coin. **3** a figure of a person.

effluent /e-floo-ent/ *adj* flowing out from. • *n* **1** the discharge of liquid waste matter, sewage, etc. **2** a stream flowing from a larger stream. • *n* **effluence**.

effort /e-fort/ *n* **1** an energetic attempt. **2** the making use of strength or ability.

effortless /e-fort-less/ *adj* with ease, without trying hard.

effusive /i-**fyoo**-siv/ *adj* expressing one's feelings too freely; pretending to feel more than one really feels. • *n* **effusiveness**.

egg /eg/ *n* **1** object, usually covered with a hard brittle shell, laid by a bird, reptile, etc, from which a young one is hatched. **2** such an object laid by the domestic hen used as food. **3** in the female mammal, the cell from which the young is formed, the ovum.

egg on /eg on/ *vb* to encourage somebody.

eggplant /eg-plant/ *n* the US word for **aubergine**.

ego /ee-go/ *n* **1** the image a person has of himself or herself. **2** self confidence to the point of being conceited, **egotism**.

egoism /ee-gu-i-zum/ *n* **1** selfishness, self-centredness. **2** egotism. **3** a theory that states that self-interest is the foundation for morality.

egoist /ee-gu-wist/ *n* a selfish person, someone who believes in and practises egoism. • *adj* **egoistic**.

egotism /ee-go-tizm/ *n* **1** excessive talking about yourself. **2** an exaggerated opinion of yourself. **3** extreme selfishness.

egotist /ee-gu-tist/ *n* a person always talking of himself or herself. • *n* **egotism**. • *adj* **egotistic, egotistical** /ee-gu-**ti**-sti-cal/.

egress /ee-gress/ *n* **1** (*fml*) a way out. **2** the right or power of going out.

eider /ie-der/ *n* the Arctic duck.

eiderdown /ie-der-down/ *n* a warm bedcovering stuffed with the soft feathers of the eider.

eight *n* a number that is the sum of one and seven. • *adj* **eighth**.

eighteen *n* a number that is the sum of ten and eight. • *adj* **eighth**.

eighty *n* a number that is the product of ten and eight. • *adj* **eightieth**.

either /ee-ther, eye-ther/ *adj, pron, conj* and *adv* one or other of two.

ejaculate /i-jac-yew-late/ *vt, vi* **1** to emit a fluid. **2** to exclaim.

eject /i-ject/ *vb* to throw out.

ejection /i-jec-shun/ *n* act of throwing out.

elaborate /i-la-bo-rit/ *adj* **1** worked out with great care. **2** having many parts. **3** very decorative. • *vb* /i-la-bo-rate/ **1** to work out very carefully, to add to and improve upon. **2** to explain fully. • *n* **elaboration**.

elapse /ee-lapse/ *vb* (*fml*) (of time) to pass.

elastic /ee-la-stic/ *adj* able to stretch or be stretched easily, but returning immediately to its former shape. • *n* a strip of material lined with rubber to make it elastic.

elasticity /ee-la-**sti**-si-tee/ *n* springiness.

elate /ee-late/ *vb* to make very glad or proud. • *n* **elation**.

elated /ee-**lay**-ted/ *adj* to be filled with happiness or pride.

elbow /el-bo/ *n* **1** the joint between the forearm and upper arm. **2** a sharp bend or corner. • *vb* to push with the elbow.

elder[1] /el-der/ *adj* older. • *n* **1** an older member of a community. **2** an official in certain Christian churches (e.g. the Presbyterian).

elder[2] /el-der/ *n* a small tree with dark purple berries.

elderly /el-der-lee/ *adj* old, getting old.

eldest /el-dest/ *adj* oldest.

elect /i-lect/ *vb* **1** (*fml*) to choose. **2** to choose by voting. • *adj* chosen. • *n* **1** those chosen. **2** those chosen by God.

election /i-lec-shun/ *n* act of choosing, especially by vote.

elector /i-lec-tor/ *n* a person with the right to vote.

electoral /i-lec-tu-ral/ *adj* having to do with electors.

electorate /i-lec-tu-rit/ *n* all those having the right to vote on a certain occasion.

electric /i-lec-tric/ *adj* **1** having to do with electricity. **2** exciting, thrilling. • *npl* electric fittings.

electrical /i-lec-tri-cal/ *adj* having to do with electricity, worked by electricity.

electrician /i-lec-**tri**-shun/ *n* a person who works with electricity or electrical apparatus.

electricity /i-lec-**tri**-si-tee/ *n* an energy produced by chemical or other action, a natural force that can be harnessed to give heat, light and power.

electrify /i-lec-tri-fie/ *vb* **1** to put electricity into. **2** to thrill.

electrocute /i-lec-tri-cyoot/ *vb* to kill by electricity. • *n* **electrocution**.

electrode /i-lec-trode/ *n* either of the two conductors through which electricity enters or leaves something, such as a battery.

electron /i-lec-tron/ *n* the negative electrical unit in an atom.

electronic /i-lec-**tron**-ic/ *adj* of a device, having many small parts, such as microchips and transistors, which control and direct an electric current.

electronics /i-lec-**tron**-ics/ *n* the branch of technology that is concerned with electronic devices such as computers and televisions.

elegant /e-le-gant/ *adj* **1** graceful, smart, stylish. **2** stylish, polished. • *n* **elegance**.

elegy /e-le-jee/ *n* a mourning or sorrowful poem.

element /e-le-ment/ *n* **1** a necessary part. **2** a substance that cannot be broken down into any other substances and from which all other things are made up. **3** *pl* knowledge without which a subject cannot be properly understood. **4** *pl* **the elements** nature, the weather.

elemental /e-le-**men**-tal/ *adj* **1** having to do with elements. **2** having to do with the powers of nature. **3** basic.

elementary /e-le-**men**-tu-ree/ *adj* **1** having to do with the beginning. **2** simple, easy.

elephant /e-le-fant/ *n* a large very thick-skinned animal with a trunk and ivory tusks. • **white elephant** a gift or purchase that turns out to be of no use, a useless possession that is troublesome to keep up or retain.

elevate /e-le-vate/ *vb* **1** (*fml*) to make finer, better, more educated, etc. **2** to raise to a higher place or rank.

elevation /e-le-vay-shun/ *n* **1** the act of raising. **2** (*fml*) a hill. **3** height. **4** a plan showing a building as seen from one side. **5** the angle measuring height.

elevator /e-le-vay-tor/ *n* (*esp US*) a lift.

eleven /i-le-ven/ *n* the number that is one more than ten. • *adj* **eleventh**.

elf /elf/ *n* (*pl* **elves** /elvz/) in fairy tales, a mischievous fairy. • *adj* **elfin**, **elfish** /el-fish/, **elvish** /el-vish/.

eligible /e-li-ji-bl/ *adj* able to be chosen, suitable. • *n* **eligibility**.

eliminate /i-li-mi-nate/ *vb* to get rid of. • *n* **elimination**.

elite /i-leet/ *n* a group that is at a higher level or rank, professionally, socially or in ability, etc.

elixir /i-lik-sir/ *n* (*old*) a magic liquid that, alchemists believed, could change any metal into gold, or enable people to live forever.

elk /elk/ *n* a type of large deer.

ellipse /i-lips/ *n* an oval figure.

elm /elm/ *n* a type of tree with rough, jagged leaves.

elongate /i-long-gate/ *vb* **1** to make longer. **2** to stretch out. • *n* **elongation**.

elope /i-lope/ *vb* to leave home secretly with one's lover. • *n* **elopement**.

eloquent /e-lo-kwent/ *adj* **1** able to speak well, especially in public, and express one's ideas and opinions effectively. **2** showing or using such an ability. • *n* **eloquence**.

else /elss/ *adj* **1** besides, also. **2** other than that already mentioned.

elsewhere /elss-where/ *adv* in another place.

elude /i-lood/ *vb* **1** to escape or avoid by quickness, cleverness or trickery. **2** to be difficult, etc, to understand or remember.

elusive /i-loo-siv/ *adj* **1** hard to remember, express, identify, etc. **2** hard to catch or track down.

elves, elvish *see* **elf**.

email, e-mail /ee-male/ *n* **1** electronic mail, a system for sending communications from one computer to another, using a telephone connection and a modem. **2** a message sent by email. • *vb* to send an email to; to send by email.

emanate /e-ma-nate/ *vb* (*fml*) to come from. • *n* **emanation**.

emancipate /i-man-si-pate/ *vb* to free from control. • *n* **emancipation**.

embalm /im-balm/ *vb* to preserve a dead body with spices or chemicals.

embankment /im-bank-ment/ *n* a mound of stones and earth built to shut in a river or to carry a road, railway, etc, over low ground.

embargo /im-bar-go/ *n* (*pl* **embargoes**) an official order forbidding some activity, especially trade, with another country.

embark /im-bark/ *vb* **1** to put or go on board ship. **2** to start. • *n* **embarkation**.

embarrass /im-ba-ras/ *vb* **1** to cause to feel shy or uncomfortable. **2** to involve in difficulties. • *n* **embarrassment**.

embassy /em-ba-see/ *n* **1** the duties of an ambassador. **2** the house of an ambassador. **3** a group of people sent by a country to act for it in another country.

embed /im-bed/ *vb* to fix firmly and deeply into something.

embers /em-berz/ *npl* **1** live cinders of a dying fire. **2** the fading remains.

embezzle /im-be-zul/ *vb* to steal money that one has been entrusted with by other people. • *n* **embezzlement**.

embitter /im-bi-ter/ *vb* to make someone feel bitter, to increase anger or hatred.

emblem /em-blem/ *n* an object that is regarded as a sign of something. • *adjs* **emblematic, emblematical**.

embodiment /em-bod-ee-ment/ *n* a living example.

embody /em-bod-ee/ *vb* **1** to give a solid form to, to express in a real or physical form. **2** to include.

embolden /em-bole-den/ *vb* to give courage, to make bold.

emboss /im-boss/ *vb* to make a raised pattern on.

embrace /im-brase/ *vb* **1** to hold in the arms, to hug. **2** to include. • *n* a holding in the arms, a hug.

embroider /im-broy-der/ *vb* **1** to decorate with needlework. **2** to add interesting or exaggerated details to a story.

embroidery /im-broy-de-ree/ *n* **1** the art of decorating with needlework. **2** the act of adding interesting or exaggerated detail to. **3** decorative needlework.

embryo /em-bree-oe/ *n* **1** the form of any creature before it is born or grows. **2** the beginning stage of anything. • *adj* **embryonic**.

emerald /em-rald/ *n* a bright green precious stone. • *adj* bright green.

emerge /i-merge/ *vb* **1** to come out. **2** to become known. • *n* **emergence**. • *adj* **emergent**.

emergency /i-**mer**-jen-see/ n a state of affairs requiring immediate action.

emery /**em**-i-ree/ n a very hard mineral, made into powder and used for polishing or sharpening metals.

emigrant /e-mi-grant/ n a person who emigrates. • also adj.

emigrate /e-mi-grate/ vb to leave one's country and go to live in another. • n **emigration**.

eminence /e-mi-nense/ n 1 (fml) a high place, a hill. 2 fame. 3 the title given to a cardinal in the Roman Catholic Church.

eminent /e-mi-nent/ adj distinguished, very well-known.

emit /e-**mit**/ vb (**emitted, emitting**) to send or give out. • n **emission**.

emollient /i-**mol**-yent/ adj soothing and softening, usually to the skin.

emolument n /i-**mol**-yew-ment/ 1 salary. 2 remuneration.

emotion /i-**mo**-shun/ n 1 strong or deep feeling. 2 the moving or upsetting of the mind or feelings.

emotional /i-**mo**-she-nal/ adj 1 of the emotions. 2 causing or showing deep feelings. 3 easily moved by emotion.

empathy /**em**-path-ee/ n the ability to imagine oneself in another's situation. • vb **empathize**, also **empathise**.

emperor /**em**-pe-ror/ n the ruler of an empire. • f **empress**.

emphasis /**em**-fa-sis/ n (pl **emphases** /**em**-fa-seez/) 1 the added force with which certain words or parts of words are spoken. 2 special meaning, value, importance, etc.

emphasize /**em**-fa-size/ vb, also **emphasise** 1 to say with emphasis. 2 to call attention to specially, to stress.

emphatic /im-**fa**-tic/ adj forceful, firm and definite.

empire /**em**-pire/ n 1 a group of countries under the rule of one of their number. 2 a large industrial organization controlling many firms.

employ /im-**ploy**/ vb 1 to give work to. 2 to use.

employee /im-**ploy**-ee/ n a person paid to work for another person or for a firm.

employer /im-**ploy**-er/ n a person who gives work to another.

employment /im-**ploy**-ment/ n job, occupation.

emporium /im-po-**ree**-um/ n (pl **emporia** /im-po-**ree**-ya/ or **emporiums** /im-po-ree-umz/) a large store in which many different kinds of things are sold.

empower /im-**pou**-wer/ vb to give the right or power to.

empress see **emperor**.

empty /**em**-tee/ adj having nothing inside. • vb 1 to take everything out of. 2 to become empty. • n **emptiness**.

emu /ee-myoo/ n a large Australian flightless bird.

emulate /**em**-yoo-late/ vb (fml) to try to be like, or as good as or better than.

emulation /em-yoo-**lay**-shun/ n act of emulating, rivalry.

emulsion /i-**mul**-shun/ n 1 a mixture of two liquids that would normally remain separate (e.g. oil and vinegar). 2 a type of paint, used on walls and ceilings.

enable /i-**nay**-bl/ vb to give the power or means to do something.

enact /i-**nact**/ vb 1 to lay down by law, to pass a law. 2 to act, perform.

enamel /i-**na**-mel/ n 1 a smooth, glossy coating put on metals or wood to preserve or decorate them. 2 the outer covering of the teeth. • vb (**enamelled, enamelling**) to cover with enamel.

enamour /i-**na**-mur/ vt to inspire with love.

encase /in-**case**/ vb to put in a case or covering.

enchant /in-**chant**/ vb 1 (old) to put a magic spell on. 2 to delight. • n **enchanter**. • f **enchantress**. • n **enchantment**.

encircle /in-**sir**-cl/ vb to surround; to make a circle around. • n **encirclement**.

enclose /in-**cloaz**/ vb 1 to shut in, to fence in. 2 to send with a letter.

enclosure /in-**cloa**-zher/ n 1 a space shut or fenced in. 2 something sent with a letter.

encompass /in-**cum**-pass/ vb 1 to surround. 2 to include or comprise.

encore /**on**-core or ong-core/ adv again, once more. • n 1 a call to a performer to repeat something or perform something else. 2 the repetition of part of a performance or a further performance by the same person or people given after the main performance. • also vb.

encounter /in-**coun**-ter/ n 1 a meeting, especially an unexpected one. 2 a fight or quarrel. • vb to meet.

encourage /in-**cu**-rage/ vb 1 to make bold. 2 to urge on. • n **encouragement**.

encyclopaedia /in-sie-clo-**pee**-dee-a/ n, also **encyclopedia** a book or set of books containing information about every subject or about every branch of one subject.

encyclopaedic /in-sie-clo-**pe**-dic/ adj very detailed or complete.

end /end/ n 1 the last part of anything. 2 death. 3 purpose or aim. • vb to bring or come to an end.

endanger /in-**dane**-jer/ *vb* to put someone or something in a dangerous or harmful situation. • **endangered** *adj* in danger or at risk, especially of ceasing to exist.

endear /in-**deer**/ *n* to make dear.

endeavour /in-**dev**-ur/ *vb*, *also* **endeavor** (*US*) to try, to try hard. • *n* attempt, effort.

endemic /in-**dem**-ic/ *adj* found specially among one people or in one place.

endless /**end**-less/ *adj* **1** having no end. **2** seemingly having no end.

endorse /in-**dorss**/ *vb* **1** to sign one's name on the back of a cheque or document. **2** to express approval or support. • *n* **endorsement**.

endow /in-**dow**/ *vb* **1** to provide with a permanent income. **2** to give, to grant. • *n* **endowment**.

endurance /in-**joo**-ranse/ *n* the ability to endure or bear patiently.

endure /in-**joor**/ *vb* **1** (*fml*) to last. **2** to bear patiently. **3** to put up with.

enemy /**e**-ne-mee/ *n* **1** a person who is unfriendly, someone who acts against another. **2** those with whom one is at war. • *also adj*.

energetic /e-ner-**je**-tic/ *adj* active, powerful, vigorous.

energize /**e**-ner-jize/ *vb*, *also* **energise** to give energy to.

energy /**e**-ner-jee / *n* active power, force, vigour.

enforce /in-**foarss**/ *n* to cause to be obeyed or carried out. • *n* **enforcement**.

engage /in-**gage**/ *vb* **1** (*fml*) to bind oneself by a promise, to promise. **2** to begin to employ. **3** to begin fighting. **4** to busy. **5** to attract and keep.

engaging /in-**gay**-jing/ *adj* pleasing, attractive.

engagement /in-**gage**-ment/ *n* **1** (*fml*) a written agreement. **2** a promise to marry. **3** an arrangement to meet someone, an appointment. **4** a battle.

engine /**en**-jin/ *n* **1** a machine that produces power. **2** a railway locomotive.

engineer /en-ji-**neer**/ *n* **1** a person who looks after engines. **2** a person who makes or designs machinery, roads, bridges, etc. • *vb* to arrange for or cause something to happen, usually by clever, cunning or secret means.

engineering /en-ji-**nee**-ring/ *n* the science of making and using machines.

engrave /in-**grave**/ *vb* **1** to cut or carve on metal, stone, wood, etc. **2** to cut a picture on a metal plate in order to print copies of it.

engraving /in-**gray**-ving/ *n* a print from an engraved plate.

engross /in-**grose**/ *vb* to take up one's whole time or attention.

engulf /in-**gulf**/ *vb* to swallow up.

enhance /in-**hanse**/ *vb* to increase in amount, value, importance, etc; to increase, to improve. • *n* **enhancement**.

enigma /en-**nig**-ma/ *n* a person or thing that is difficult to understand; a mystery.

enigmatic /en-nig-**ma**-tic/, **enigmatical** /en-nig-**ma**-ti-cal/ *adj* having to do with an enigma, mysterious.

enjoy /in-**joy**/ *vb* **1** to take pleasure in. **2** to possess. • *adj* **enjoyable**. • *n* **enjoyment**.

enlarge /in-**large**/ *vb* **1** (*fml*) to make larger. **2** to reproduce.

enlargement /in-**large**-ment/ *n* **1** act of making larger. **2** a larger copy of a photograph.

enlighten /in-**lite**-en/ *vb* (*fml*) to give more and correct information or knowledge about. • *n* **enlightenment**.

enlist /in-**list**/ *vb* **1** to join the armed forces. **2** to obtain support. **3** to obtain from. • *n* **enlistment**.

enliven /in-**lie**-ven/ *vb* to brighten, to cheer.

enormity /i-**nawr**-mi-tee/ *n* **1** immensity. **2** a great wickedness. **3** a crime, an act of great wickedness.

enormous /i-**nawr**-mus/ *adj* huge, very large.

enough /i-**nuf**/ *adj* as many or as much as is required. • *n* a sufficient amount.

enquire *see* **inquire**.

enrage /in-**rage**/ *vb* to make very angry.

enrapture /in-**rap**-chur/ *n* (*fml*) to fill with delight.

enrich /in-**rich**/ *vb* **1** to make rich. **2** to improve greatly in quality. • *n* **enrichment**.

enrol /in-**role**/ *vb*, *also* **enroll** (*US*) (**enrolled**, **enrolling**) **1** to write. **2** to join or become a member. • *n* **enrolment**.

ensemble /on-**som**-bul/ *n* **1** a group of musicians regularly performing together. **2** clothing made up of several items, an outfit. **3** all the parts of a thing taken as a whole.

enslave /in-**slave**/ *vb* (*fml*) to make a slave of.

ensue /in-**soo**/ *vb* to follow upon, to result from.

ensure /in-**shoor**/ *vb* to make sure.

entail /in-**tale**/ *vb* **1** to leave land or property to be passed down through a succession of heirs. **2** to make necessary, to involve. • *n* land or property so left.

entangle /in-**tang**-gul/ *vb* **1** to cause to

become twisted, tangled or caught. **2** to get into difficulties or complications.

entanglement /in-**tang**-gul-ment/ *n* a difficult situation, involvement.

enter /en-ter/ *vb* **1** to go or come into. **2** to become a member of. **3** to put down in writing.

enterprise /en-ter-prize/ *n* **1** an undertaking or project, especially one that is difficult or daring. **2** willingness to take risks or to try out new ideas.

enterprising /en-ter-prie-zing/ *adj* having or showing enterprise.

entertain /en-ter-**tane**/ *vb* **1** to receive as a guest. **2** to please, to amuse. **3** (*fml*) to consider.

entertainment /en-ter-**tane**-ment/ *n* **1** the act of entertaining. **2** amusement. **3** something that entertains, such as a public performance.

enthral /in-**thrawl**/ *vb* (**enthralled, enthralling**) to delight, to enchant.

enthuse /in-**thewz**/ *vb* to be, become or cause to be enthusiastic, to show enthusiasm.

enthusiasm /in-**thew**-zee-a-zum/ *n* great eagerness, keenness.

enthusiast /in-**thew**-zee-ast/ *n* a person who is very keen.

enthusiastic /in-thoo-zee-a-stic/ *adj* full of enthusiasm.

entice /in-**tice**/ *vb* to tempt, to attract by offering something. • *n* **enticement**. • *adj* **enticing**.

entire /in-**tire**/ *adj* whole, complete. • *adv* **entirely**.

entirety /in-**tie**-ri-tee/ *n* completeness.

entitle /in-**tite**-ul/ *vb* **1** to give a right to. **2** to give a name to.

entity /en-ti-tee/ *n* **1** existence. **2** anything that exists.

entrails /en-traylz/ *npl* the bowels, the internal organs of the body.

entrance[1] /in-**transe**/ *vb* to delight, to fill with wonder.

entrance[2] /en-transe/ *n* **1** coming or going in. **2** a place by which one enters (e.g. a door or gate).

entrant /en-trant/ *n* a person who puts his or her name in for or joins.

entrap /in-**trap**/ *vb* (**entrapped, entrapping**) to catch in a trap or by a trick.

entreat /in-**treet**/ *vb* (*fml*) to ask earnestly.

entreaty /in-**tree**-tee/ *n* an earnest request.

entrée /on-tray/ *n* a main course at dinner.

entrench /in-**trench**/ *vb* **1** to dig ditches around, thus putting oneself in a strong position. **2** to establish firmly or in a strong position.

entrust /in-**trust**/ *vb* to give into the care of.

entry /en-tree/ *n* **1** act of entering. **2** a way in. **3** something written in a diary, cash book, etc.

enunciate /i-**nun**-see-ate/ *vb* to speak or state, to pronounce in a distinct way. • *n* **enunciation**.

E-number /ee-number/ *n* a · number beginning with the letter E given to food and drink additives and printed on packs and containers to show what colours, flavours, etc have been added to the food.

envelop /in-**ve**-lop/ *vb* to cover or surround completely.

envelope /en-ve-lope/ *n* a wrapper or cover, especially one made of paper for a letter.

enviable /en-vee-a-bl/ *adj* causing envy, very desirable.

envious /en-vee-us/ *adj* full of envy, jealous.

environment /in-**vie**-ron-ment/ *n* **1** surroundings. **2** all the conditions and surroundings that influence human character. **3** the natural world in which people, animals and plants live. • **environmental** *adj*.

envisage /in-**vi**-zage/ *vb* (*fml*) to picture to oneself.

envoy /en-voy/ *n* a messenger, especially one sent to speak for his or her government in another country.

envy /en-vee/ *n* **1** a feeling of discontent caused by someone else's good fortune or success, especially when one would like these for oneself. **2** something that causes envy. • *vb* to feel envy towards or at.

eon US variant of **aeon**.

epaulette /e-pu-**let**/ *n* a flap of material, sometimes of another colour, worn on the shoulder of a uniform jacket.

ephemeral /i-**fem**-ral/ *adj* lasting for only a short time.

epic /e-pic/ *n* **1** a long poem telling of heroic deeds. **2** a story, film, etc, dealing with heroic deeds and exciting adventures. • *adj* of or like an epic, heroic, in the grand style.

epidemic /e-pi-**dem**-ic/ *n* a disease or condition that attacks many people at the same time.

epilepsy /e-pi-lep-see/ *n* a disease causing fits of unconsciousness and sudden attacks of uncontrolled movements of the body. • *adj*, *n* **epileptic**.

epilogue /e-pi-log/ *n*, *also* **epilog** (*US*) **1** a speech addressed to the audience at the end of a play. **2** a part or section added at the end of a book, programme, etc. *See also* **prologue**.

Epiphany /e-pi-fa-nee/ *n* the Christian festival that commemorates the revealing of Jesus Christ to the Magi, or three wise men from the East.

episode /e-pi-soad/ *n* **1** a particular event or a series of events that is separate from but forms part of a larger whole. **2** a part of a radio or television serial that is broadcast at one time.

episodic /e-pi-sod-ic/ *adj* consisting of events not clearly connected with one another.

epitaph /e-pi-taf/ *n* words referring to a dead person, inscribed on his or her tombstone.

epitome /i-pi-to-mee/ *n* **1** a person or thing that is a perfect example of a quality, type, etc. **2** something that in a small way perfectly represents a larger or wider idea, issue, etc.

epitomize /i-pi-to-mize/ *vb, also* **epitomise** to be an epitome of.

epoch /e-pok/ *n* **1** a period of time in history, life, etc, especially one in which important events occurred. **2** the start of such a period.

equal /ee-kwal/ *adj* **1** the same in size, number, value, etc. **2** able. • *n* a person the same as another in rank or ability. • *vb* (**equalled, equalling**) to be equal to.

equality /i-kwol-i-tee/ *n* the state of being equal.

equalize /ee-kwol-ize/ *vb, also* **equalise** to make or become equal.

equate /i-kwate/ *vb* **1** to state that certain things are equal. **2** to think of as equal or the same.

equation /i-kway-zhun/ *n* a statement that two things are equal.

equator /i-kway-tor/ *n* an imaginary line round the earth, halfway between the poles.

equatorial /i-kwa-toe-ree-al/ *adj* **1** having to do with the equator. **2** on or near the equator.

equi- /e-kwee/ *prefix* equal.

equilateral /ee-kwi-la-te-ral/ *adj* having all sides equal.

equilibrium /ee-kwi-li-bree-um/ *n* **1** a balance between equal weights. **2** steadiness. **3** balanced state of the mind, emotions, etc.

equinox /eh-kwi-noks/ *n* either of the two times in the year at which the sun crosses the equator and day and night are equal. • *adj* **equinoctial**.

equip /i-kwip/ *vb* (**equipped, equipping**) to provide things necessary for doing an activity, to fit out.

equipment /i-kwip-ment/ *n* the set of things needed for a particular activity.

equity /e-kwi-tee/ *n* fairness, justice.

equivalent /i-kwi-va-lent/ *adj* **1** equal in value, amount, meaning, etc. • *n* an equivalent thing.

era /i-ra/ *n* **1** a long period of time, starting from some important or particular event. **2** a period of time marked by an important event or events.

eradicate /i-ra-di-cate/ *vb* to root out, to destroy completely. • *n* eradication.

erase /i-rase, i-raze/ *vb* to rub out, to remove.

ere /eer/ *adv, conj, prep* (*old or lit*) before.

erect /i-rect/ *adj* standing up straight. • *vb* **1** to build. **2** to set upright. • **3** of a penis, enlarged and stiffened. *n* **erection**.

ermine /er-min/ *n* **1** a type of weasel. **2** its white winter fur.

erode /i-rode/ *vb* to destroy or wear away gradually. • *n* erosion.

erotic /i-rot-ic/ *adj* having to do with love or sexual desire.

err /er/ *vb* (*fml*) to make a mistake, to do wrong.

errand /e-rand/ *n* **1** a short journey made to give a message, deliver goods, etc, to someone. **2** the purpose of such a journey.

errant /e-rant/ *adj* **1** (*old*) wandering. **2** (*fml*) doing wrong.

erratic /e-ra-tic/ *adj* not steady, irregular, uneven, unpredictable.

error /e-ror/ *n* **1** a mistake. **2** the state of being mistaken.

erupt /i-rupt/ *vb* to break or burst out.

eruption /i-rup-shun/ *n* act of breaking or bursting out (e.g. of a volcano).

escalate /e-sca-late/ *vb* **1** to rise or increase. **2** to increase in intensity.

escalator /e-sca-lay-tor/ *n* a moving staircase.

escapade /e-sca-pade/ *n* a foolish or risky adventure.

escape /i-scape/ *vb* **1** to get out of the way of, to avoid. **2** to free oneself from. **3** to leak. **4** to avoid being noticed, remembered, etc. • *n* **1** act of escaping. **2** a leakage.

eschew /is-choo/ *vb* (*fml*) to keep away from, to avoid.

escort /is-coart/ *vb* to go with as a guard, a partner, to show the way, or as an honour. • *n* /es-coart/ **1** a guard, a bodyguard. **2** a partner, a companion.

Eskimo /ess-ki-mo/ *n* one of the original inhabitants of Northern Canada, parts of Alaska, Greenland and parts of Siberia, or their descendants. In North America and Greenland especially, **Inuit** is preferred and 'Eskimo' regarded as offensive.

esophagus US variant of **oesophagus**.

especial /i-**spe**-shal/ *adj* (*fml*) more than ordinary, particular.

especially /i-**spesh**-lee/ *adv* specially, particularly, markedly.

espionage /es-pee-o-nazh/ *n* spying.

essay /e-say/ *vb* (*fml or old*) to try. • *n* **1** (*fml or old*) an attempt. **2** a written composition.

essence /e-sense/ *n* **1** the nature or necessary part of anything. **2** a substance obtained from a plant, etc, in concentrated form.

essential /e-**sen**-shal/ *adj* **1** necessary, very important, that cannot be done without. **2** of the basic or inner nature of something, fundamental. • *n* something that cannot be done without.

establish /i-**sta**-blish/ *vb* **1** to set up. **2** to place or fix in a position, etc, usually permanently. **3** to prove, to show to be true.

establishment /i-**sta**-blish-ment/ *n* **1** act of setting up. **2** a group of people employed in an organization, the staff of a household. **3** a place of business, the premises of a business organization or large institution. • **the Establishment** the people holding important positions in a country, community, etc, and usually supporting traditional ways, etc.

estate /i-**state**/ *n* **1** all one's property and money. **2** area of land with one owner. **3** (*old*) political or social group or class. **4** (*fml or old*) condition.

estate agent /i-**state ay**-jent/ *n also* **real estate agent** (*US*) a person who sells property.

esteem /i-**steem**/ *vb* to think highly of. • *n* respect, regard.

esthetics US variant of **aesthetics**.

estimate /es-ti-mate/ *vb* **1** to judge size, amount, etc, roughly, to guess. **2** to calculate the probable cost of. • *n* /es-ti-mit/ **1** an opinion. **2** a judgment as to the value or cost of a thing.

estimation /e-sti-**may**-shun/ *n* **1** judgment. **2** opinion (of someone).

estuary /e-styoo-a-ree/ *n* the mouth of a river as far as the tide flows up it.

etc /et-se-te-re/ *abbr* = **et cetera**.

et cetera, etcetera /et-se-te-re/ *adv* and all the rest.

etch /ech/ *vb* to cut a picture on a metal plate by use of acids in order to print copies of it.

etching /e-ching/ *n* a picture printed by etching.

eternal /i-**ter**-nal/ *adj* **1** everlasting, without beginning or end. **2** seeming never to stop.

eternity /i-**ter**-ni-tee/ *n* **1** everlasting existence, with no beginning and no end; unending life after death. **2** (*inf*) a very long time.

ether /ee-ther/ *n* **1** the clear upper air. **2** formerly, an invisible substance supposed to fill all space and to pass on electric waves. **3** a colourless liquid, often formerly used as an anaesthetic.

ethical /e-thi-cal/ *adj* **1** having to do with right and wrong. **2** relating to ethics.

ethics /e-thics/ *n* **1** the study of right and wrong. **2** rules or principles of behaviour.

ethnic /eth-nic/ *adj* having to do with human races or their customs, food, dress, etc.

etiquette /e-ti-ket/ *n* the rules of polite behaviour, good manners.

etymology /e-ti-**mol**-o-jee/ *n* **1** the study of the history of words. **2** derivation, an explanation of the history of a particular word. • *adj* **etymological**. • *n* **etymologist**.

EU /ee-yoo/ *abbr* = **European Union**: a group of European countries that have joined together for economic and political purposes.

eucalyptus /yoo-ca-**lip**-tus/ *n* **1** an Australian gum tree. **2** the oil from its leaves, used in the treatment of colds.

euphemism /yoo-fe-mi-zum/ *n* the use of mild words or phrases to say something unpleasant. • *adj* **euphemistic**.

euro /yoo-ro/ *n* the common unit of currency in the following European countries: Austria, Belgium, Cyprus, Estonia, Finland, France, Germany, Greece, Ireland, Italy, Luxembourg, Malta, the Netherlands, Portugal, Slovakia, Slovenia and Spain.

European Union /yoo-ro-pee-an **yoon**-yun/ *see* **EU**.

evacuate /i-va-cyoo-ate/ *vb* **1** to go away from. **2** (*fml*) to make empty. **3** to send to a place of safety in wartime. • *n* **evacuation**.

evade /i-vade/ *vb* **1** to keep oneself away from. **2** to dodge, to find a way of not doing something, especially by using trickery, deception, etc. **3** to refuse to answer directly. • *n* **evasion**.

evaluate /i-val-yoo-ate/ *vb* to work out the value of. • *n* **evaluation**.

evangelic /ee-van-je-lic/, **evangelical** /ee-van-je-li-cal/ *adj* **1** having to do with the Christian Gospels. **2** accepting the Bible as the only guide to faith.

evangelist /ee-van-je-list/ *n* **1** one of the four Gospel writers. **2** a preacher of the Gospel.

evaporate /i-va-po-rate/ *vb* **1** to turn into vapour and disappear. **2** to disappear. • *n* **evaporation**.

evasion *see* **evade**.

evasive /i-vay-siv/ *adj* **1** having the purpose of evading. **2** not straightforward, not frank.

eve /eev/ *n* **1** (*old*) evening. **2** the day before. **3** the time before an important event.

even /ee-vin/ *adj* **1** level. **2** smooth. **3** equal. **4** divisible by 2. **5** calm. • *adv* (*intensifier*) **1** unexpected (*even the boss*). **2** just (*even as we speak*). **3** comparative (*even better*). • *vb* **1** to make smooth or level. **2** to make equal. • *n* **evenness**. • **get even** to get revenge.

evening /eev-ning/ *n* the close of day.

event /i-vent/ *n* **1** anything that happens, an incident. **2** a single race or contest at sports or races.

eventful /i-vent-ful/ *adj* full of interesting or exciting happenings.

eventual /i-ven-sha-wul/ *adj* happening as a result, final.

eventuality /i-ven-cha-**wa**-li-tee/ *n* a possible happening.

eventually /i-ven-cha-wa-lee/ *adv* finally, at length.

ever /e-ver/ *adv* always, at all times.

evergreen /e-ver-green/ *n* a tree or plant that has green leaves all the year round. • *adj* always green.

everlasting /e-ver-la-sting/ *adj* **1** never ending. **2** seemingly without end, frequent.

evermore /e-ver-**more**/ *adv* forever.

every /ev-ree/ *adj* each one.

everybody /ev-ree-bu-dee/ *pron* every person.

everyday /ev-ree-day/ *adj* **1** happening every day. **2** usual, ordinary.

everyone /ev-ree-wun/ *pron* every person.

everything /ev-ree-thing/ *pron* all things being considered as a group.

evict /i-vict/ *vb* to put out of a house or off land by order of a court. • *n* **eviction**.

evidence /e-vi-dense/ *n* **1** information given to show a fact is true. **2** the statement made by a witness in a court of law.

evident /e-vi-dent/ *adj* clear, easily understood, obvious.

evil /ee-vil/ *adj* **1** wicked, bad, sinful. **2** unpleasant, nasty. • *n* **1** wickedness. **2** anything bad or harmful.

evoke /i-**voke**/ *vb* **1** to call up. **2** to give rise to, to cause. • *n* **evocation**.

evolution /e-vu-**loo**-shun/ *n* **1** the belief that life began in lower forms of creature and that these gradually changed over millions of years into the highest forms, such as humans. **2** development.

evolve /i-**volve**/ *vb* **1** to work out. **2** to develop gradually.

ewe /yoo/ *n* a female sheep.

exact /ig-zact/ *adj* **1** absolutely correct, accurate in every detail. **2** showing or taking great care. • *vb* **1** to force to make payment. **2** to demand and obtain.

exacting /ig-zac-ting/ *adj* needing a lot of work or attention.

exaggerate /ig-za-je-rate/ *vb* **1** to speak or think of something as being better or more (or worse or less) than it really is. **2** to go beyond the truth in describing something. • *n* **exaggeration**.

exalt /ig-zolt/ *vb* **1** (*fml*) to raise in power or rank. **2** to praise highly. • *n* **exaltation**.

examine /ig-za-min/ *vb* **1** to look at closely and carefully in order to find out something. **2** to question. **3** to test a learner's knowledge by questions. • *n* **examination**. • *n* **examiner**.

examinee /ig-za-mi-nee/ *n* a person who is being examined.

example /ig-zam-pl/ *n* **1** one thing chosen to show what others of the same kind are like, a model. **2** a person or thing deserving to be imitated.

exasperate /ig-za-spe-rate/ *vb* to make angry. • *n* **exasperation**.

excavate /ek-sca-vate/ *vb* **1** to uncover by digging. **2** to dig up, to hollow out.

excavation /ek-sca-**vay**-shun/ *n* **1** act of excavating. **2** a hole or trench made by digging.

exceed /ik-seed/ *vb* **1** to go beyond. **2** to be greater or more numerous than.

exceedingly /ik-**see**-ding-lee/ *adv* very, extremely.

excel /ik-sel/ *vb* (**excelled**, **excelling**) to do very well at, to get exceptionally good at.

excellence /ek-se-lense/ *n* perfection, great merit.

excellent /ek-se-lent/ *adj* very good, of a very high standard.

except[1] /ik-sept/ *vb* (*fml*) to leave out.

except[2] /ik-sept/, **excepting** /ik-sep-ting/ *prep* leaving out.

exception /ik-sep-shun/ *n* a person or thing that does not follow the rule. • **take exception** to object.

exceptional /ik-sep-shu-nal/ *adj* different from others, unusual, remarkable. • *adv* **exceptionally**.

excerpt /ek-serpt/ *n* a short passage taken out of a longer piece of writing or music.

excess /ik-sess/ *n* **1** too much. **2** the amount by which a thing is too much. **3** bad and uncontrolled behaviour.

excessive /ik-se-siv/ *adj* more than is right or correct.

excessively /ik-se-siv-lee/ *adv* to excess, very.

exchange /iks-**change**/ *vb* to give one thing and receive another in its place. • *n* **1** the act of exchanging. **2** a place where merchants meet to do business. **3** the changing of the money of one country into that of another. **4** a telephone centre where lines are connected to each other.

excise[1] /ek-size/ *n* a tax on certain goods made within the country.

excise[2] /ik-size/ *vb* to cut out, to cut away. • *n* **excision**.

excitable /ik-site-a-bl/ *adj* easily excited.

excite /ik-site/ *vb* **1** to stir up feelings of happiness, expectation, etc. **2** to rouse. • *n* **excitement**. • *adj* **exciting**.

exclaim /ik-sclame/ *vb* to cry out suddenly. • *adj* **exclamatory**.

exclamation /ek-scla-**may**-shun/ *n* a word or words said suddenly or with feeling.

exclamation mark /ek-scla-**may**-shun **mark**/ *n* a mark of punctuation (!).

exclude /ek-sclood/ *vb* **1** to shut out. **2** to leave out. **3** to leave out, not to include. • *n* **exclusion**.

exclusive /ek-scloo-siv/ *adj* **1** open to certain people only. **2** sole. **3** not shared. • *adv* **exclusively**.

excrement /eks-cre-ment/ *n* waste matter put out from the body.

excrete /ik-screet/ *vb* to put out what is useless from the body. • *adj* **excretory**.

excruciating /ik-scroo-she-ate-ing/ *adj* **1** very great, intense. **2** terrible, very bad.

excursion /ik-scur-zhon/ *n* a trip made for pleasure, an outing.

excuse /ek-scyooz/ *vb* **1** to let off. **2** to forgive, to overlook. **3** to give reasons showing or intended to show that someone or something cannot be blamed. • *n* a reason given for failure or wrongdoing. • *adj* **excusable**.

execute /ek-si-cyoot/ *vb* **1** to perform. **2** to carry out. **3** to put to death by law.

execution /ek-si-**cyoo**-shun/ *n* **1** the carrying out, performance, etc, of something. **2** skill in performing music. **3** the act of putting to death by order of the law.

executioner /ek-si-**cyoo**-shu-ner/ *n* an officer who puts condemned criminals to death.

executive /ig-**zec**-yoo-tiv/ *adj* **1** concerned with making and carrying out decisions, especially in business. **2** having the power to carry out government's decisions and laws. • *n* **1** a person involved in the management of a firm. **2** the part of government that puts laws, etc, into effect.

executor /ig-**zec**-yoo-tor/ *n* a person who sees that a dead person's written will is carried out.

exemplify /ig-**zem**-pli-fy/ *vb* **1** to be an example. **2** to illustrate by example.

exempt /ig-**zempt**/ *vb* to free from, to let off. • *adj* free. • *n* **exemption**.

exercise /**ek**-ser-size/ *n* **1** an action performed to strengthen the body or part of the body. **2** a piece of work done for practice. **3** training. **4** use. • *vb* **1** to use, to employ. **2** to perform some kind of physical exercises. **3** to give exercise to, to train.

exert /ig-**zert**/ *vb* to apply. • **exert oneself** to try hard.

exertion /ig-**zer**-shun/ *n* effort.

exhale /eks-**hale**/ *vb* to breathe out. • *n* **exhalation**.

exhaust /ig-**zawst**/ *vb* **1** to use up completely. **2** to tire out. **3** to say everything possible about. • *n* **1** a passage by which used steam or gases are carried away from an engine. **2** these gases.

exhausting /ig-**zaw**-sting/ *adj* very tiring.

exhaustion /ig-**zaw**-schun/ *n* **1** the state of being tired out. **2** lack of any strength.

exhaustive /ig-**zaw**-stiv/ *adj* **1** very thorough, complete. **2** dealing with every possible aspect of a subject.

exhibit /ig-**zi**-bit/ *vb* **1** to show in public. **2** (*fml*) to display, to show. • *n* a thing shown in public.

exhibition /ek-si-**bi**-shun/ *n* **1** act of exhibiting. **2** a collection of many things brought together to be shown to the public.

exhibitionist /ek-si-**bi**-shu-nist/ *n* a person who behaves in such a way as to draw attention to himself or herself.

exhibitor /ig-**zi**-bi-tor/ *n* a person who exhibits at a show.

exhilarate /ig-**zi**-li-rate/ *vb* to make lively or happy. • *n* **exhilaration**.

exile /**eg**-zile/ *n* **1** long or unwilling absence from one's home or country. **2** a person living in a country other than his or her own. • *vb* to send someone out of his or her own country as a punishment.

exist /ig-**zist**/ *vb* **1** to be. **2** to live. • *n* **existence**. • *adj* **existent**.

exit /**eg**-zit/ *n* **1** a way out. **2** a going out. • *also vb*.

exodus /**ek**-so-dus/ *n* a going out or away by many people (e.g. the departure of the Jews from Egypt).

exorcism /**ek**-sawr-si-zum/ *n* act of exorcising. • *n* **exorcist**.

exorcize /**ek**-sawr-size/ *vb*, *also* **exorcise** to drive out evil spirits.

exotic /ig-**zot**-ic/ *adj* **1** foreign, introduced from another country. **2** striking and unusual.

expand /ik-**spand**/ *vb* **1** to make or become larger. **2** to spread out. **3** to become more friendly or talkative.

expanse /ik-**spanse**/ *n* a wide area.

expansion /ik-**span**-shun/ *n* act of expanding.

expansive /ik-**span**-siv/ *adj* **1** wide. **2** ready to talk freely.

expatriate /ek-**spa**-tree-ate/ *vb* to send someone out of his own country. • *n* /ek-**spa**-tree-it/ a person living or working in a country other than his or her own.

expect /ik-**spect**/ *vb* **1** to wait for. **2** to think it likely that something will happen. **3** to require as a right or duty.

expectancy /ik-**spec**-tan-see/ *n* state of being expectant.

expectant /ik-**spec**-tant/ *adj* hopeful, waiting for something to happen. • **expectant mother** a woman who is pregnant.

expectation /ek-spec-**tay**-shun/ *n* **1** hope that something will happen. **2** that which is expected.

expedience /ik-**spee**-dee-ence/, **expediency** /ik-**spee**-dee-en-see/ *n* doing things not because they are right or moral but because they are likely to be successful or to one's advantage.

expedition /ek-spe-**di**-shun/ *n* **1** a journey made for a particular purpose. **2** (*fml*) speed.

expel /ik-**spel**/ *vb* (**expelled, expelling**) **1** to drive out. **2** to force to go away. **3** to dismiss officially from a school, club, etc. • *n* **expulsion**.

expend /ik-**spend**/ *vb* to spend, to use up.

expenditure /ik-**spen**-di-cher/ *n* **1** the amount spent. **2** the act of spending.

expense /ik-**spense**/ *n* **1** cost. **2** spending of money, etc.

expensive /ik-**spen**-siv/ *adj* dear, costing a lot.

experience /ik-**spi**-ree-ense/ *n* **1** a happening in one's own life. **2** knowledge gained from one's own life or work. • *vb* **1** to meet with. **2** to feel. **3** to undergo.

experiment /ik-**spe**-ri-ment/ *n* something done so that the results may be studied, a test. • *vb* to do an experiment. • *adj* **experimental**.

expert /ek-spert/ *adj* very skilful. • *n* a person having special skill or knowledge. • *n* **expertise** /ek-sper-**teez**/.

expire /ik-**spire**/ *vb* **1** (*fml*) to die. **2** (*fml*) to breathe out. **3** to come to an end.

expiry /ik-**spie**-ree/ *n* end.

explain /ik-**splane**/ *vb* **1** to make clear. **2** to give reasons for.

explanation /ek-spla-**nay**-shun/ *n* a statement of the meaning of or the reasons for.

explanatory /ek-**spla**-na-toe-ree/ *adj* helping to make clear.

expletive /ek-**splee**-tiv/ *n* a swear word.

explicable /ek-**spli**-ca-bl/ *adj* able to be explained.

explicit /ek-**spli**-sit/ *adj* **1** stating exactly what is meant. **2** with full details, with nothing hidden.

explode /ik-**spload**/ *vb* **1** to burst or blow up with a loud noise. **2** to show to be untrue, to destroy.

exploit *n* /ek-**sploit**/ **1** a brave or outstanding deed. • *vb* /ik-**sploit**/ to make use of for selfish reasons. • *n* **exploitation**.

explore /ik-**sploar**/ *vb* **1** to examine closely. **2** to travel through a country to find out all about it. • *n* **exploration**. • *n* **explorer**.

explosion /ik-**splo**-zhun/ *n* **1** going off or bursting with a loud noise. **2** an outburst.

explosive /ik-**splo**-siv/ *adj* able to cause an explosion. • *n* any substance that will explode.

exponent /ik-**spo**-nent/ *n* **1** a person who explains and supports a theory, belief, etc. **2** a person who is good at.

export /ek-**sport**/ *vb* to send goods to another country. • *n* export /ek-sport/ an article that is exported. • *n* **exportation**.

expose /ek-**spoaz**/ *vb* **1** to uncover. **2** to make known the truth about. **3** to allow light to fall on.

exposition /ek-spo-**zi**-shun/ *n* **1** (*fml*) a collection of things brought together to be shown to the public. **2** a full explanation.

exposure /ek-**spo**-zher/ *n* **1** act of exposing. **2** the effect on the body of being out in cold weather for a long time.

expound /ik-**spound**/ *vb* (*fml*) to explain fully.

express /ik-**spress**/ *vb* **1** to put into words. **2** to make known by words or actions. • *adj* **1** swift. **2** clearly stated. • *n* a fast train.

expressly /ik-**spress**-lee/ *adv* **1** clearly. **2** specially, with a certain definite purpose.

expression /ik-**spre**-shun/ *n* **1** a word or phrase. **2** the look on one's face. **3** ability to read, play music, etc, with meaning or feeling.

expressive /ik-**spre**-siv/ *adj* with feeling or meaning.

expulsion /ik-**spul**-shun/ *see* **expel**.

expunge /ik-**spunge**/ *vb* to rub out, to wipe out.

expurgate /ek-spur-gate/ *vb* to cut out of a book unsuitable or objectionable passages. • *n* **expurgation**.

exquisite /ek-**skwi**-zit/ *adj* **1** beautiful and delicate, very fine. **2** (*fml*) strongly felt, acute.

extant /ek-stant/ *adj* still existing.

extemporaneous /ek-stem-po-**ray**-nee-uss/ *adj* (*fml*) unprepared.

extempore /ik-**stem**-po-ree/ *adv, adj* without preparation.

extemporize /ik-**stem**-po-rize/ vb, also **extemporise 1** to speak without preparation. **2** to make up music as one is playing.

extend /ik-**stend**/ vb **1** to stretch out. **2** to reach or stretch. **3** to offer. **4** to make longer or bigger.

extension /ik-**sten**-shun/ n **1** an addition. **2** an additional period of time.

extensive /ik-**sten**-siv/ adj **1** large. **2** wide, wide-ranging.

extent /ik-**stent**/ n **1** the area or length to which something extends. **2** amount, degree.

extenuate /ik-**sten**-yoo-ate/ vb (fml) to make excuses for in order to make seem less bad. • n **extenuation**.

extenuating /ik-**sten**-yoo-ay-ting/ adj making a crime, etc, seem less serious by showing there is some excuse for it.

exterior /ek-**sti**-ree-or/ adj outer. • n the outside.

exterminate /ik-**ster**-min-ate/ vb to kill to the last one, to destroy completely. • n **extermination**.

external /ek-**ster**-nal/ adj on the outside.

extinct /ik-**stingt**/ adj **1** no longer found in existence. **2** no longer burning.

extinction /ik-**stingk**-shun/ n **1** act of destroying. **2** the state of being no longer living. **3** the putting out of.

extinguish /ik-**sting**-wish/ vb **1** to put out. **2** to put an end to.

extirpate /ek-**stir**-pate/ vb (fml) to destroy completely, to root out. • n **extirpation**.

extol, extoll /ik-**stoal**/ vb (extolled, extolling) (fml) to praise highly.

extort /ik-**stawrt**/ vb to take from by force or threats. • n **extortion**.

extortionate /ik-**stawr**-shu-nate/ adj **1** far too expensive. **2** asking too much.

extra /ek-stra/ adj additional, more than is usual, expected or necessary. • adv more than usually. • n something additional.

extract /ek-**stract**/ vb **1** to draw, take or pull out. **2** to select a passage from a book. • n **extract** /ek-stract/ **1** a passage taken from a book. **2** a substance drawn from a material and containing all its qualities.

extraction /ek-**strac**-shun/ n **1** act of drawing out. **2** connection with a certain family or race.

extradite /ek-stra-dite/ vb to hand over a foreign criminal to the police of his own country. • n **extradition**.

extramural /ek-stra-**myoo**-ral/ adj **1** organized for those who are not members (e.g. of a university). **2** separate from or outside the area of one's studies.

extraneous /ek-**stray**-nee-uss/ adj having nothing to do with the subject.

extraordinary /ek-**strawr**-di-na-ree/ adj **1** very unusual, remarkable. **2** (fml) additional to what is usual or ordinary.

extraterrestrial /ek-stra-te-re-**stree**-al/ adj existing or happening beyond the earth's atmosphere.

extravagance /ek-**stra**-vi-gense/ n **1** wasteful spending. **2** wastefulness.

extravagant /ek-**stra**-vi-gent/ adj **1** spending or using a great deal, wasteful. **2** spending foolishly. **3** foolish and improbable.

extreme /ek-**streem**/ adj **1** farthest away. **2** greatest possible. **3** far from moderate, going beyond the limits, not sharing the views of the majority. **4** intense, strong, not ordinary or usual. • n **1** the end, the farthest point. **2** something as far or as different as possible from something else. **3** the greatest or highest degree. • adv **extremely**.

extreme sport /ek-streem spoart/ n a sport which is associated with a particularly high risk of injury or death.

extremist /ek-**stree**-mist/ n a person who holds extreme ideas. • also adj.

extremity /ek-**stre**-mi-tee/ n **1** the farthest point. **2** (fml) a situation of great misfortune, distress or danger. **3** (fml) the farther parts of the body, i.e. the hands and feet.

extricate /ek-stri-cate/ vb to set free from a difficult position.

extrovert /ek-stro-vert/ n a person who is extremely outgoing and self-assured. • also adj.

exuberant /ig-**zoo**-ber-ant/ adj **1** vigorous, strong. **2** in high spirits. • n **exuberance**.

exude /ig-**zood**/ vb to ooze out, to give off.

exult /ig-**zult**/ vb to rejoice very much, to express joy. • adj **exultant**. • n **exultation**.

eye /ie/ n **1** the organ by means of which we see. **2** a small hole in a needle. **3** the seed bud of a potato. • vb **1** to watch closely.

eyebrow /eye-brow/ n an arc of hair on the brow bone above the eye.

eye-opener /eye-oa-pe-ner/ n something very surprising.

eyelash /eye-lash/ n each of the short hairs extending from the edge of the eyelid.

eyelid /eye-lid/ n the fold of skin that can be lowered to close the eye.

eyesight /eye-sight/ n a person's ability to see.

eyesore /eye-sore/ n something very ugly.

eyewitness /eye-wit-ness/ n a person who sees an event happen.

eyrie n see **aerie**.

F

F, f /eff/ **1** the sixth letter of the English alphabet. **2** (*mus*) the fourth note of the scale of C major.

fable /**fay**-bl/ *n* a short story, usually about animals, etc, who talk and behave like humans, meant to teach people to do what is right.

fabric /**fa**-bric/ *n* **1** the framework of a building. **2** manufactured cloth.

fabricate /**fa**-bri-cate/ *vb* **1** to make or build, to manufacture. **2** to make up or invent. • *n* **fabrication**.

fabulous /**fa**-byoo-lus/ *adj* **1** (*fml*) existing only in fable or legend, mythical. **2** (*inf*) wonderful, marvellous, very good.

façade /fa-**sad**/ *n* **1** the front of a building. **2** outer appearance.

face /fayss/ *n* **1** the front part of the head, from forehead to chin. **2** the front part of anything. • *vb* **1** to stand looking towards, to turn towards. **2** to meet or encounter boldly. **3** to cover with a surface of different material.

facet /**fa**-set/ *n* **1** one of many small sides, as of a diamond. **2** an aspect.

facial /**fay**-shal/ *adj* having to do with the face. • *n* a treatment to improve the appearance of the skin on the face.

facile /**fa**-sul/ *adj* **1** done with ease, often done too easily. **2** without depth, not sincere.

facilitate /fa-**si**-li-tate/ *vb* to make easy. • *n* **facilitation**.

facility /fa-**si**-li-tee/ *n* **1** (*fml*) ease, skill. **2** *pl* the means or conditions for doing something easily.

facsimile /fac-**si**-mi-lee/ *n* **1** an exact copy. **2** an image produced by facsimile transmission (*also* **fax**). • **facsimile transmission** a system of sending written, printed, or pictorial documents over a telephone line by scanning it and then reproducing the image in a different location.

fact /fact/ *n* **1** something known to be true or to have happened. **2** truth. **3** a deed, an event.

factor /**fac**-tor/ *n* **1** a person who does business for another, someone who manages another's land. **2** a cause, element. **3** a number that divides exactly into another number.

factory /**fac**-to-ree/ *n* a building where large quantities of goods are made.

factual /**fac**-chu-wul/ *adj* having to do with facts.

faculty /**fa**-cul-tee/ *n* **1** a special ability. **2** the power to do something. **3** all the teachers of a school, college, or university or of a school's departments.

fad /fad/ *n* a craze, a short-lived fashion.

fade /fade/ *vb* **1** to wither. **2** to lose colour. **3** to disappear gradually.

faeces /**fee**-seez/ *n* solid bodily waste excreted from the anus.

Fahrenheit /**fa**-ren-hite/ *adj* of a scale of temperature in which the freezing point of water is 32° and the boiling point is 212°, named for a German physicist.

fail /fale/ *vb* **1** not to succeed. **2** to break down. **3** to disappoint. **4** to owe so much money that debts cannot be paid.

failing /**fay**-ling/ *n* a fault, a weakness.

failure /**fale**-yer/ *n* **1** lack of success. **2** a person who has not succeeded. **3** a breakdown.

fain /fane/ *adj* (*old, lit*) glad. • *adv* gladly.

faint /faint/ *vb* to become weak, to fall down unconscious. • *n* act of falling down unconscious. • *adj* **1** weak, dizzy. **2** lacking clearness or brightness. **3** slight.

fair[1] /fare/ *adj* **1** light in colour, having light-coloured hair or skin. **3** quite good. **3** just. **4** (*of weather*) not rainy. **5** (*old, lit*) attractive.

fair[2] /fare/ *n* **1** **fun fair** a type of public entertainment in a park with sideshows and rides. **2** an outdoor event with refreshments, games and small things for sale. **3** an exhibition where businesses show and perhaps sell their products.

fairly /**fare**-lee/ *adv* somewhat.

fairway /**fare**-way/ *n* **1** the deep part of a river where ships usually sail. **2** the part of a golf course where the grass is cut short.

fairy /**fay**-ree/ *n* an imaginary small being, supposed to have magic powers.

fairy tale /**fay**-ree tale/ *n* a story about fairies, giants, magic deeds, etc.

faith /faith/ *n* **1** belief, especially in God. **2** trust, being sure of something. **3** religion. **4** a person's word of honour, loyalty.

faithful /**faith**-ful/ *adj* **1** true to one's friends or one's promises. **2** loyal to one's marriage vows. **3** true to the facts or an original.

faithless /**faith**-less/ *adj* (*fml*) **1** disloyal, dishonest. **2** unreliable.

fake /fake/ *n* someone or something that

deceives by looking other than he, she, or it is. • *vb* **1** to change something so that it falsely appears better, more valuable, etc. **2** to copy something so as to deceive. **3** (*inf*) to pretend.

falcon /**fal**-con/ *n* a bird of prey trained to hunt smaller birds.

falconry /**fal**-con-ree/ *n* **1** the art of training falcons to hunt game. **2** the sport of hunting with falcons.

fall /fawl/ *vb* (*pt* **fell**, *pp* **fallen**) **1** to drop down. **2** to become less or lower. **3** to hang down. **4** to happen or occur. **5** to enter into a certain state or condition. **6** to be taken by an enemy. **7** to be killed in battle. • *n* **1** a drop or descent. **2** a lessening or lowering. **3** loss of power. **4** a waterfall. **5** (*US*) autumn. • **fall back** to go back. • **fall on** *or* **upon** to attack. • **fall out** (*inf*) to quarrel. • **fall through** to fail.

fallacy /**fa**-la-see/ *n* a wrong idea or belief, usually one that is generally believed to be true; false reasoning. • *adj* **fallacious**.

fallen /**faw**-len/ *pp of* **fall**.

fallible /**fa**-la-bl/ *adj* (*fml*) able to make mistakes. • *n* **fallibility**.

fallout /**faw**-lout/ *n* particles of radioactive dust that are in the air and fall to the ground after an atomic explosion.

fallow /**fa**-lo/ *adj* ploughed but left un-planted for a season or more to kill weeds, make soil richer, etc. • *also n*.

false /fawlse/ *adj* **1** not true. **2** disloyal. **3** not real, fake. • *n* **falseness**, **falsity** /**fawl**-si-tee/.

falsehood /**fawlse**-hood/ *n* (*fml*) a lie.

falter /**fawl**-ter/ *vb* **1** to speak or say in an uncertain or hesitant way. **2** to stumble.

fame /fame/ *n* the state of being well-known.

famed /faymd/ *adj* (*fml*) well-known.

familiar /fa-**mil**-yar/ *adj* **1** well-known because often seen. **2** having good know-ledge of. **3** too friendly, disrespectful. • *n* **1** a close friend. **2** in folklore, an evil spirit constantly with someone and usually dwelling within an animal. • *n* **familiarity**.

familiarize /fa-**mil**-ya-rize/ *vb*, *also* **familiarise** to make used to.

family /**fam**-lee/ *n* **1** a household, parents and children. **2** one's children. **3** people descended from the same ancestors. **4** a group of things in some way related to one another (e.g. races, animals, etc.).

family tree /**fam**-lee tree/ *n* a chart that shows the members of a family, their ancestors, and their relationship to one another.

famine /**fa**-min/ *n* a shortage of food.

famish /**fa**-mish/ *vb* to make or be very hungry. • **to be famished** (*inf*) to be very hungry.

famous /**fay**-mus/ *adj* well-known to all.

fan[1] /fan/ *n* an instrument or machine that causes a current of air. • *vb* (**fanned**, **fanning**) to move the air with a fan. • **fan out** to spread out over a wider front.

fan[2] /fan/ *n* a follower or supporter.

fanatic /fa-**na**-tic/ *n* someone who holds a belief, especially a religious or political belief, so strongly that he or she can neither discuss it reasonably nor think well of those who disagree with it. • *n* **fanaticism**.

fanatical /fa-**na**-ti-cal/ *adj* having the views of a fanatic.

fan belt /fan belt/ *n* a tough, thin belt on most car engines.

fanciful /**fan**-si-ful/ *adj* **1** imaginative, inclined to have strange, unreal ideas. **2** imaginary, unreal.

fancy /**fan**-see/ *n* **1** (*fml*) the imagination. **2** a false idea or belief, something imagined. **3** a sudden desire. **4** a liking for, often a romantic one. • *adj* not plain, ornamented. • *vb* **1** (*fml*) to imagine. **2** (*inf*) to like. **3** to be romantically or sexually attracted to.

fanfare /**fan**-fare/ *n* the sounding of many trumpets in greeting.

fang /fang/ *n* **1** a long, pointed tooth. **2** the tooth of a snake that is used to inject venom, or poison, into its prey.

fantasia /fan-**tay**-zha/ *n* a light or fanciful piece of music.

fantastic /fan-**ta**-stic/ *adj* **1** strange or weird. **2** created in the mind, fanciful, unrealistic. **3** (*inf*) very large. **4** (*inf*) very good, excellent.

fantasy /**fan**-ta-see/ *n* **1** an unusual or far-fetched idea, a dream. **2** a story with highly imaginative characters or settings that are not part of the real world.

fanzine /**fan**-zeen/ *n* a magazine for people who are particularly interested in something, such as a football team, a particular type of music, etc.

far /far/ *adj* distant. • *adv* at a distance in time, space, or degree.

faraway /**far**-a-way/ *adj* **1** distant in time, space, or degree. **2** dreamy, distracted.

farce /farse/ *n* **1** a stage play intended only to arouse laughter. **2** a laughable or senseless, unreasonable situation.

farcical /**far**-si-cal/ *adj* laughable, senseless, unreasonable.

fare /fare/ *vb* (*fml*, *old*) to be or do. • *n* **1** food. **2** the cost of a travel ticket. **3** a passenger on a bus or in a taxi.

farewell /far-**well**/ *interj* goodbye.

farfel /for-fel/ *n* noodle dough formed into small grains.

far-fetched /far-fecht/ *adj* so unlikely as to be almost impossible.

farina /fa-ree-na/ *n* a hot cereal made from wheat, potatoes, nuts, etc.

farm /farm/ *n* an area of land prepared for crops and/or herds by the owner. • *vb* to use land as a farm. • *n* **farmer**. • **farm out** to give out to be done by others.

farmstead /farm-sted/ *n* the land and buildings of a farm.

farrow /fa-ro/ *n* a litter of baby pigs.

farseeing /far-see-ing/ *adj* wise, having shown good judgment.

farsighted /far-sie-tid/ *adj* 1 having better vision for distant objects than for near ones. 2 farseeing.

farther /far-ther/ *adj* 1 at or to a greater distance. 2 additional.

fascinate /fa-si-nate/ *vb* to attract or interest very strongly, to charm. • *n* **fascination**.

fascism /fa-shi-zum/ *n* a political movement based on one person/group being in charge of the country in a militaristic way, incorporating nationalist and/or racist views. • *n, adj* **fascist**.

fashion /fa-shin/ *n* 1 the way in which a thing is done or made. 2 the kinds of things, usually clothes, popular at a certain time. • *vb* to shape, to make.

fashionable /fash-na-bl/ *adj* 1 following a style that is currently popular. 2 used or visited by people following a current fashion.

fast[1] /fast/ *vb* to do without food, especially for religious reasons. • *n* act or time of fasting.

fast[2] /fast/ *adj* 1 firm, fixed. 2 quick, swift. • *adv* 1 firmly. 2 quickly. 3 (*old*) near.

fasten /fa-sen/ *vb* 1 to fix firmly. 2 to fix to.

fastener /fa-sner/ *n* a device that joins together or fixes one thing to another.

fastening /fa-se-ning/ *see* **fasten** sense 1.

fast-food /fast-food/ *n* hot food that is prepared and served very quickly, often taken away to be eaten.

fastidious /fa-sti-dee-us/ *adj* hard to please. • *n* **fastidiousness**.

fast lane /fast lane/ *n* a lane on a motorway for moving at a higher speed or for overtaking other automobiles.

fastness /fast-ness/ *n* 1 the quality of being fast or quick. 2 a fort, a stronghold.

fast track /fast track/ *n* a career path offering rapid advancement.

fat /fat/ *adj* well fed, fleshy. • *n* 1 an oily substance in animal bodies. 2 this substance, or the oily substance found in some plants, when in solid or almost solid form, used as a food or in cooking.

fatal /fay-tal/ *adj* 1 causing death. 2 bringing danger or ruin, or having unpleasant results.

fatality /fay-ta-li-tee/ *n* 1 death caused by accident, war, etc. 2 (*fml*) deadliness.

fate /fate/ *n* 1 a power that is supposed to decide future events before they happen. 2 what will happen to someone in the future.

fateful /fate-ful/ *adj* important for one's future.

father /fa-ther/ *n* 1 a male parent. 2 a person who begins, invents, or first makes something. 3 a priest. • *vb* 1 to be the father of. 2 to start an idea or movement.

fatherhood /fa-ther-hood/ *n* the state of being a father.

father-in-law /fa-ther-in-law/ *n* the father of someone's spouse.

fathom /fa-thom/ *n* a measurement of 6 feet or 1.8 metres, especially of the depth of water. • *vb* to understand fully.

fatigue /fa-teeg/ *n* weariness, great tiredness. • *vb* to tire out.

fatten /fa-ten/ *vb* to make fat.

fatty /fa-tee/ *adj* containing fat.

fault /fawlt/ *n* 1 a mistake. 2 a weakness in character. 3 an imperfection, something wrong with something. • *adj* **faulty**. 4 a break in the rock of Earth's crust where one side moves against, above, or below the other.

faun /fawn/ *n* in Roman legend, a minor god, half man and half goat.

fauna /faw-na/ *n* all the animals found in a country or region.

favour /fay-vur/ *n, also* **favor** (*US*) 1 a feeling of kindness or approval towards. 2 an act done out of kindness. 3 something (e.g. a flower, rosette, etc) worn as a sign of good will or support. • *vb* 1 (*fml*) to show more kindness to one person than to another. 2 to prefer. 3 to give an advantage.

favourable /fay-vu-ra-bl/ *adj, also* **favorable** (*US*) kindly, helpful.

favourite /fay-vu-rit/ *n, also* **favorite** (*US*) a person or thing preferred to others. • *also adj*.

favouritism /fay-vu-ra-ti-zum/ *n, also* **favoritism** (*US*) showing more liking for one person than for others.

fawn[1] /fawn/ *n* 1 a young deer. 2 a yellowish brown colour. • *adj* yellowish brown.

fawn[2] /fawn/ *vb* to flatter or behave like a servant to gain another's favour. • *adj* **fawning**.

fax /faks/ *n* **1** a machine that sends and receives documents electronically along a telephone line and then prints them out, *see* **facsimile**, also called **fax machine**. **2** a document sent or produced in this way. • *vb* to send by fax machine.

FBI /ef-bee-eye/ *abbr* = **Federal Bureau of Investigation**: a US governmental organization that investigates crimes.

fear /feer/ *n* dread, terror, anxiety. • *also vb*.

fearful /feer-ful/ *adj* **1** afraid. **2** terrible. **3** (*inf*) very bad, very great.

fearless /feer-less/ *adj* unafraid.

fearsome /feer-sum/ *adj* (*fml*) causing fear.

feasible /fee-zi-bl/ *adj* possible, able to be done. • *n* **feasibility**.

feast /feest/ *n* **1** a meal with plenty of good things to eat and drink. **2** something extremely pleasing. **3** a day or period of time kept in memory, especially in religion, such as in honour of God or a saint. • *vb* **1** to eat well. **2** to provide a good meal for others.

feat /feet/ *n* a deed notable for courage, skill, etc.

feather /fe-ther/ *n* one of the growths that cover a bird's body. • *vb* to line or cover with feathers. • **feather one's nest** to make a profit for oneself by taking advantage of a situation.

feature /fee-chur/ *n* **1** an outstanding part of anything. **2** a special long article in a newspaper. **3** *pl* the face. • *vb* to give or have a position, especially an important one.

February /feb-ye-wa-ree/ *n* the second month of the year.

feces US variant of faeces.

feckless /fec-less/ *adj* helpless, lacking determination or strength of character.

fed /fed/ *pt and pp of* feed.

federal /fe-de-ral/ *adj* united under one central government, but keeping local control of certain matters.

federation /fe-de-ray-shun/ *n* **1** a group of states that give up certain powers to a common central government. **2** a joining of certain groups of people.

fee /fee/ *n* **1** a payment made for special professional services, a charge or payment. **2** money paid for entering or being taught in a school, college, etc.

feeble /fee-bl/ *adj* very weak. • *n* **feebleness**.

feed /feed/ *vb* (*pt, pp* **fed**) **1** to give food to. **2** to eat. **3** to provide what is necessary for. **4** to put into. • *n* food.

feedback /feed-back/ *n* information about how good or bad something or someone has been.

feel /feel/ *vb* (*pt, pp* **felt**) **1** to touch. **2** to find out by touching. **3** to experience or be aware of. **4** to believe or consider. **5** to be moved by, to have pity. • *n* the sense of touch, a quality as revealed by touch.

feeler /fee-ler/ *n* **1** the threadlike organ of touch on an insect. **2** something said to try to get others to give their opinions.

feeling /fee-ling/ *n* **1** the sense of touch. **2** emotion. **3** kindness for others. **4** an impression or belief. • *adj* able to understand the emotions of others.

feet *pl of* foot.

feign /fane/ *vb* to pretend.

feint /faynt/ *n* a pretended movement. • *also vb*.

feisty /fie-stee/ *adj* energetic, full of spirit.

feline /fee-line/ *adj* **1** catlike. **2** of the cat family.

fell[1] /fel/ *pt of* fall.

fell[2] /fel/ *vb* to cut down, to knock down.

fell[3] /fel/ *adj* (*old*) cruel, savage, deadly.

fell[4] /fel/ *n* an animal's hide or skin.

fell[5] /fel/ *n* a rocky, bare hill; a moor.

fellow /fe-lo/ *n* **1** one of a pair. **2** a companion and an equal. **3** a member of a learned society or a college. **4** (*inf*) a man.

fellowship /fe-lo-ship/ *n* **1** company. **2** friendship. **3** an association. **4** a grant of money given to someone to enable him or her to do advanced studies.

felon /fe-lon/ *n* (*fml*) a criminal.

felony /fe-lo-nee/ *n* (*fml*) a serious crime.

felt[1] /felt/ *pt and pp of* feel.

felt[2] /felt/ *n* a cloth made of wool, hair and/or fur being worked together by pressure, heat, etc. instead of by weaving.

female /fee-male/ *adj* **1** consisting of girls or women. **2** of or relating to the sex that produces offspring. • *also n*.

feminine /fe-mi-nin/ *adj* **1** having the qualities considered suitable for a woman. **2** of a woman.

feminism /fe-mi-nis-zum/ *n* the principle that men and women should have equal rights. • *n* **feminist**.

femininity /fe-mi-ni-ni-tee/ *n* the state of being female or womanly.

femur /fee-mur/ *n* (*fml*) the thighbone. • *adj* **femoral**.

fence /fense/ *n* **1** a wall made of wood or of wooden posts and wire to enclose a field or other land. **2** (*inf*) a receiver of stolen goods. • *vb* **1** to put a fence around. **2** to take part in swordplay. **3** to avoid giving direct answers to questions, especially by quibbling over minor points. • **sit on the fence** to give no decision either way, to be neutral.

fencing /fen-sing/ *n* **1** the materials for making a fence. **2** swordplay as a sport.

fend /fend/ *vb* **1** to keep off, to turn aside. **2** to look after. **3** (*US*) the bumper of a car.

fender /fen-der/ *n* **1** a low guard around a fireplace. **2** a pad made of rope, canvas, or wood to protect the side of a ship when at a pier.

feng shui /fung show-ay/ *n* a Chinese method of interior and exterior design with the aim of bringing good fortune.

fennel /fe-nel/ *n* a sweet-smelling plant used as a herb and vegetable.

ferment /fer-ment/ *n* **1** that which causes fermentation. **2** excitement. • *vb* /fer-ment/ **1** to cause or undergo fermentation. **2** to excite.

fermentation /fer-men-tay-shun/ *n* a chemical change that causes solids to break up and mix and liquids to froth and bubble.

fern /fern/ *n* a plant with no flowers and feathery leaves that reproduces by spores.

ferocious /fe-ro-shus/ *adj* fierce, cruel, savage. • *n* ferocity.

ferret /fe-ret/ *n* a small weasel-like animal used in hunting rabbits. • *vb* **1** to search busily and persistently. **2** to find something carefully hidden.

Ferris wheel /fe-ris wheel/ *n* a large, upright wheel that rotates and that has seats on it; used as an amusement-park ride.

ferry /fe-ree/ *vb* **1** to carry over water in a boat or aeroplane. **2** to transport. • *n* **1** a boat that ferries. **2** the place where a ferry crosses.

fertile /fer-tile/ *adj* **1** able to produce a lot of, fruitful. **2** inventive. • *n* fertility.

fertilize /fer-ti-lize/ *vb*, *also* **fertilise** to make fertile or fruitful, to enrich.

fertilizer /fer-ti-lie-zer/ *n*, *also* **fertiliser** a material mixed into soil to make it more fertile.

fervent /fer-vent/ *adj* eager, devoted, sincere.

fervid /fer-vid/ *adj* (*fml*) very strong.

fervour /fer-vor/ *n*, *also* **fervor** (*US*) strength of feeling.

fester /fess-ter/ *vb* **1** (*of a wound*) to become full of poisonous matter, to become infected. **2** to give rise to bitter feelings, to become bitter.

festival /fe-sti-val/ *n* **1** a day or number of days spent in joy, celebrating, etc. **2** a season of plays, films, concerts, etc.

festive /fe-stiv/ *adj* suited to a feast, merry, joyous.

festivity /fe-sti-vi-tee/ *n* joyful celebration, merrymaking.

festoon /fe-stoon/ *n* a drooping chain of flowers, ribbons, etc, put up as a decoration; a hanging wreath. • *v* to decorate with festoons, etc.

feta /fe-ta/ *n* a soft, white cheese first made in Greece.

fetal /fee-tal/ US variant of **foetal**.

fetch /fech/ *vb* **1** to go and bring. **2** to be sold for.

fetching /fe-ching/ *adj* attractive.

fetish /fe-tish/ *n* **1** an object that is worshipped and believed to have magic power. **2** something regarded with too much attention or respect.

fetus /fee-tus/ US variant of **foetus**.

feud /fyood/ *n* a lasting quarrel or strife between persons, families, etc.

feudal /fyoo-dal/ *adj* having to do with feudalism.

feudalism /fyoo-da-li-zum/ *n* a system in mediaeval Europe under which people worked and lived on land in exchange for military or other services.

fever /fee-ver/ *n* **1** a disease causing great heat in the body. **2** an abnormally high body temperature. **3** excitement.

fevered /fee-verd/, **feverish** /fee-ve-rish/ *adjs* **1** hot with fever. **2** excited.

few /fyoo/ *adj* not many, a small number of.

fez /fez/ *n* a brimless red cap with a black tassel.

fiancé /fee-on-say/ *n* a man engaged to be married. • *f* **fiancée** a woman engaged to be married.

fiasco /fee-a-sco/ *n* (*pl* fiascoes *or* fiascos) a complete failure, a laughable failure.

fib /fib/ *n* a not very serious lie or untruth. • *vb* (**fibbed**, **fibbing**) to tell untruths. • *n* **fibber**.

fibre /fie-ber/, *also* **fiber** (*US*) *n* **1** a threadlike part of an animal or plant. **2** a material made of fibres.

fibreglass /fie-ber glass/ *n* finely spun, cottonlike glass.

fibrous /fie-bruss/ *adj* like or made of fibres.

fibula /fi-byu-la/ *n* (*fml*) the outer of the two bones between the knee and the ankle.

fickle /fi-cul/ *adj* quickly changing, not faithful. • *n* **fickleness**.

fiction /fic-shun/ *n* **1** a made-up story. **2** the art of writing stories. **3** novels.

fictitious /fic-ti-shus/ *adj* imaginary, invented.

fiddle /fi-dl/ *n* a violin. • *vb* **1** to play the violin. **2** to play about with. **3** to prepare or alter dishonestly to one's own advantage. • *n* **fiddler**.

fiddlesticks /**fi**-dl-sticks/ *interj* (*old*) nonsense.

fidelity /fi-**de**-li-tee/ *n* 1 faithfulness, loyalty. 2 exactness.

fidget /**fi**-jet/ *vb* to move restlessly. • *also n.*

field /feeld/ *n* 1 open country. 2 an enclosed area of ground. 3 a battlefield. 4 a sports ground. • *vb* 1 to catch and return a ball. 2 to put a team or player in the field for a game. 3 to deal with, or handle.

fiend /feend/ *n* 1 a devil. 2 a very cruel person. • *adj* **fiendish**.

fierce /feerse/ *adj* wild, angry. • *n* **fierceness**.

fiery /**fie**-ree/ *adj* 1 having to do with fire. 2 easily angered or excited.

fiesta /fee-**ess**-ta/ *n* a festival or celebration, especially a religious one.

fife /fife/ *n* a small flute with six to eight finger holes.

fifteen /fif-**teen**/ *n* the sum of ten and five. • *adj* **fifteenth**

fifth *see* five.

fifty /**fif**-tee/ *n* the product of five and ten. • *adj* **fiftieth**.

fig /fig/ *n* 1 a soft fruit with many seeds. 2 the tree bearing such fruit.

fight /fite/ *vb* (*pt, pp* **fought**) 1 to use force against another. 2 to take part in war or battle. 3 to quarrel, to argue. 4 to try hard to succeed. • *n* 1 a struggle in which force is used, a battle. 2 a hard effort.

figure /**fi**-gur/ *n* 1 the shape of the body. 2 a shape of a person or a thing. 3 lines drawn to show a shape. 4 a number. 5 a price. 6 a diagram or illustration. • *vb* 1 to work out the answer to a sum or problem. 2 to appear. 3 (*inf*) to think or consider.

figurehead /**fi**-gur-hed/ *n* 1 a carved figure fixed on the front of a ship. 2 a person who has a high position but no real power.

figure of speech /**fi**-gur ov **speech**/ *n* the use of words in an unusual meaning or order to express ideas with greater understanding or feeling.

figurine /fi-gyu-**reen**/ *n* a small, moulded sculpture.

filament /**fi**-la-ment/ *n* 1 a very thin thread. 2 the thin wire in a light bulb.

file[1] /file/ *n* 1 a number of papers arranged in order. 2 any device that keeps these papers in order. 3 in a computer, a collection of related information stored under a particular name. 4 a row of persons, one behind the other. • *vb* 1 to put in place in a file. 2 to walk in file.

file[2] /file/ *n* a tool with a rough face for smoothing or cutting. • *vb* to smooth or cut away with a file.

filings /**fie**-lingz/ *npl* the small pieces rubbed off by a file.

fill /fil/ *vb* 1 to make full. 2 to become full. 3 to stop up. 4 to occupy. • *n* as much as fills or satisfies, often to a great extent.

fillet /**fi**-let/ *n* 1 a thin strip or band worn around the head to keep the hair in place. 2 a flat, boneless piece of meat or fish. • *vb* to take the bones out of and slice.

filling /**fi**-ling/ *n* 1 the act of one that fills. 2 a thing used to fill something else. 3 the metal, plastic, etc. that a dentist puts into a prepared cavity.

filly /**fi**-lee/ *n* a young female horse.

film /film/ *n* 1 a thin skin or covering. 2 the thin roll of material on which pictures are taken by a camera. 3 a story recorded by a camera and sound equipment and shown in the cinema or on television. • *vb* to take a moving picture.

filter /**fil**-ter/ *n* a strainer; a device through which liquid or air is passed to clean it. • *vb* to clean or separate by passing through a filter.

filth /filth/ *n* 1 dirt. 2 anything considered foul, indecent, or offensive.

filthy /**filth**-ee/ *adj* 1 very dirty. 2 disgusting, foul.

fin /fin/ *n* a small winglike organ by means of which a fish swims.

final /**fie**-nal/ *adj* 1 last. 2 putting an end to. • *n* **finality**. • *adv* **finally**.

finale /fi-**na**-lee/ *n* the last part of a piece of music, a play, etc.

finalist /**fie**-na-list/ *n* a person who takes part in the final round of a contest.

finance /**fie**-nanss/ *n* 1 having to do with money. 2 *pl* money resources. • *vb* to find or provide the money for. • *adj* **financial**. • *n* **financier**.

finch /finch/ *n* one of many kinds of small singing birds.

find /finde/ *vb* (*pt, pp* **found**) 1 to come upon what a person is looking for. 2 to discover. 3 to decide. • *n* a valuable discovery.

finding /**fine**-ding/ *n* a decision or opinion reached.

fine[1] /fine/ *adj* 1 very thin or small. 2 excellent. 3 delicate, beautiful. 4 bright, sunny. 5 healthy. 6 slight.

fine[2] /fine/ *n* money paid as a punishment. • *vb* to punish by fine.

finesse /fi-**ness**/ *n* great skill and cleverness.

finger /**fing**-ger/ *n* one of the five points that extend from the hand or glove. • *vb* to touch with the fingers.

fingering /**fing**-ge-ring/ *n* the use of the fingers in playing a musical instrument.

fingernail /**fing**-ger-nale/ *n* the horny substance growing from the end of the finger.

fingerprint /**fing**-ger-print/ *n* **1** the mark made by the tips of the fingers. **2** an ink print of the lines on the fingertips for identification purposes.

fingertips /**fing**-ger-tips/ *npl* the tips of the fingers. • **have at one's fingertips** to have ready knowledge of.

finicky /**fi**-ni-kee/ *adj* **1** fussy, too particular. **2** needing a lot of attention to detail.

finish /**fi**-nish/ *vb* **1** to bring to an end. **2** to come to an end. • *n* **1** the end. **2** extra touches to make perfect.

finite /**fie**-nite/ *adj* having an end, limited.

fiord *see* **fjord**.

fir /**fur**/ *n* a cone-bearing (coniferous) tree.

fire /**fire**/ *n* **1** the activity of burning, which gives out heat and light. **2** (*fml*) strong feeling, excitement. • *vb* **1** to start a fire. **2** to bake. **3** to cause to explode. **4** to arouse interest and/or excitement. **5** (*inf*) to dismiss from employment.

firearm /**fire**-arm/ *n* a gun, rifle, or pistol.

fire engine /**fire** en-jin/ *n* a vehicle that carries firefighters and equipment for putting out fires.

fire escape /**fire** i-scape/ *n* a long ladder or steps by which people can escape from a burning building.

fire extinguisher /**fire** ex-**ting**-gwish-er/ *n* a portable container used to put out fires.

firefighter /**fire**-fie-ter/ *n* a person who is trained to put out fires.

firefly /**fire**-flie/ *n* any of the beetles that glow in the dark.

fireplace /**fire**-plase/ *n* a framed opening in the wall of a house to hold a fire.

fireproof /**fire**-proof/ *adj* that cannot be set on fire; ovenproof.

fire side /**fire**-side/ *n* the area next to the fireplace in a home.

fire station /**fire**- **stay**-shun/ *n* the building where fire engines are kept and firefighters stay when on duty.

firewood /**fire**-wood/ *n* wood, such as sticks or logs, which will be burned as fuel to heat a home.

fireworks /**fire**-wurks/ *npl* explosives of different colours and styles set off in the dark for a showy celebration.

firm[1] /**firm**/ *adj* **1** steady, not easily moved. **2** determined. • *n* **firmness**.

firm[2] /**firm**/ *n* a business company organized to manufacture or trade in goods.

first /**furst**/ *adj* before all others. • *adv* **1** before all others. **2** before doing anything else.

first aid /**fur stade**/ *n* treatment given to an injured person before the doctor arrives; simple medical attention.

firstborn /**furst**-bawrn/ *n* (*fml*) eldest child.

first class /**furst class**/ *adj* of the highest class, rank, excellence, etc.

first floor /**furst flore**/ *n* the floor just above the ground floor.

first mate /**furst mate**/ *n* a ship's officer next in rank below the captain.

first name /**furst** name/ *n* a personal name that comes before the family name or surname and is given at birth, also called **forename** and sometimes **Christian name**.

fish /**fish**/ *n* a cold-blooded animal with gills and fins that lives in water. • *vb* **1** to try to catch fish. **2** (*inf*) to search for. **3** (*inf*) to try to get by indirect means.

fishhook /**fish**-hook/ *n* a hook, usually barbed, for catching fish.

fishing rod /**fi**-shing rod/ *n* a slender pole with an attached line, hook, and reel used in fishing.

fishmonger /**fish**-mong-ger/ *n* someone who buys and sells fish.

fishy /**fi**-shee/ *adj* **1** of or like fish. **2** doubtful, arousing suspicion.

fission /**fi**-shun/ *n* the splitting into parts.

fist /**fist**/ *n* the hand tightly shut.

fit[1] /**fit**/ *adj* **1** suitable, proper, right. **2** in good health. • *n* the particular way in which something fits. • *vb* (**fitted, fitting**) **1** to be of the right size. **2** to suit. **3** to make suitable.

fit[2] /**fit**/ *n* **1** a sudden attack of illness, fainting, etc. **2** a sudden feeling.

fitful /**fit**-ful/ *adj* occurring in short periods, not regularly or steadily.

fitness /**fit**-ness/ *n* suitability.

fitter /**fi**-ter/ *n* someone who puts the parts of machinery together.

fitting /**fi**-ting/ *adj* suitable, proper. • *n* **1** a thing fixed in position. **2** the trying on of clothes to see if they fit.

five /**five**/ *n* the sum of three and two. • *adj* **fifth**.

fix /**fiks**/ *vb* **1** to make firm. **2** to arrange. **3** to fasten. **4** to repair. **5** (*inf*) to arrange the result of dishonestly. • *n* (*inf*) a difficulty.

fixate /**fik**-sate/ *vb* to focus on. • *n* **fixation**.

fixative /**fik**-sa-tiv/ *n* a substance used to make something permanent, prevents fading, etc.

fixed /**fikst**/ *adj* firm, not moving or changing. • *adv* **fixedly** /**fik**-sed-lee/.

fixture /**fiks**-chur/ *n* **1** anything fastened in place. **2** any person or thing that has remained in a situation so long as to seem fixed there. **3** a sports event fixed to take place at a particular time.

fizz /fiz/ *vb* to release or give off many bubbles. • *n* **1** bubbles of gas in a liquid. **2** the sound of fizzing. **1** (*inf*) enthusiasm, liveliness, excitement. • *adj* **fizzy**.

fizzle /fi-zl/ *vb* to fail, to come to nothing.

fjord /fee-**awrd**/ *n, also* **fiord** a long, narrow bay running inland between steep rocky hills.

flab /flab/ *n* sagging flesh.

flabbergast /fla-ber-gast/ *vb* to astonish. • *adj* **flabbergasted**.

flabby /fla-bee/ *adj* **1** soft, hanging loosely. **2** having soft loose flesh. • *n* **flabbiness**.

flaccid /fla-sid/ *adj* soft and weak, flabby, hanging in loose folds.

flag[1] /flag/ *n* **1** a square or oblong piece of material with a pattern on it representing a country, party, association, etc. **2** a coloured cloth or paper used as a sign or signal. • *vb* (**flagged, flagging**) **1** to signal with flags. **2** to cause a vehicle to stop by signalling to the driver.

flag[2] /flag/ *n* any of the wild irises with flat fans of sword-shaped leaves and white, blue, or yellow flowers.

flag[3] /flag/ *n* a flat paving stone.

flag[4] /flag/ *vb* (**flagged, flagging**) to become tired.

flagpole /flag-pole/ *n* a pole on which a flag is raised and flown.

flair /flare/ *n* **1** a natural ability. **2** style, stylishness, an original and attractive quality.

flake /flake/ *n* **1** a small thin piece of anything, especially a small loose piece that has broken off something. **2** a very light piece (e.g. of snow). • *vb* to come off in flakes. • *adj* **flaky**.

flamboyant /flam-**boy**-ant/ *adj* **1** very brightly coloured or decorated. **2** showy and confident.

flame /flame/ *n* a tongue of fire, a blaze. • *vb* **1** to burn brightly. **2** (*inf*) to become suddenly angry.

flaming /flay-ming/ *adj* **1** burning with flames. **2** excited, violent. **3** very bright.

flamenco /fla-**meng**-co/ *n* a Spanish gypsy style of dance or music featuring stamping, clapping, etc.

flamingo /fla-**ming**-go/ *n* (*pl* **flamingoes**) a brightly coloured water bird with long legs and neck.

flammable /fla-ma-bl/ *adj* likely to catch fire and burn easily.

flan /flan/ *n* **1** a piece of shaped metal ready to be made into a coin by a stamp. **2** an open pastry case with a sweet or savoury filling. **3** a Spanish dessert of custard covered with a burnt-sugar syrup.

flange /flange/ *n* a rim that sticks out, as on a wheel that runs on rails.

flank /flangk/ *n* **1** the fleshy part of an animal's side between the ribs and the hip. **2** the side of anything (e.g. an army, a mountain, etc.). • *vb* to be at the side of, to move to the side of.

flannel /fla-nel/ *n* **1** a soft, loosely woven woollen cloth. **2** a shirt or other piece of clothing made from this material.

flap /flap/ *n* **1** anything fixed at one end and hanging loose at the other. **2** the sound made by such a thing when it moves. **3** (*inf*) panic, agitation. • *vb* (**flapped, flapping**) **1** to flutter, to move up and down, to make a sound as of fluttering. **2** (*inf*) to get into a panic, to become confused or excited.

flapjack /flap-jack/ *n* **1** a sweet cake made from oats. **2** (*US*) a pancake.

flare /flare/ *vb* **1** to blaze up, to burn brightly but unsteadily. **2** to spread out. • *n* **1** a bright, unsteady light. **2** a light used as a signal. **3** a gradual widening, especially of a skirt.

flare-up /flare-up/ *n* a sudden outburst of flame, anger, trouble, etc.

flash /flash/ *n* **1** a quick or sudden gleam. **2** (*inf*) a moment. **3** anything lasting for a very short time. **4** a device for producing a short burst of electric light used to take photographs. • *vb* **1** to shine out suddenly. **2** to move very quickly.

flashback /flash-back/ *n* **1** a section of a story, play, film, etc, telling of something that happened in the past. **2** a sudden, clear, detailed memory of something in the past.

flash flood /flash flud/ *n* a sudden, violent flood, as after a heavy rain.

flashlight /flash-lite/ *n* **1** a short burst of electric light used to take photographs in the dark. **2** (*US*) a torch.

flashy /flash-shee/ *adj* gaudy, showy.

flask /flask/ *n* **1** a kind of bottle with a narrow neck, used in laboratories. **2** a pocket bottle. **3** a Thermos bottle.

flat /flat/ *adj* **1** level. **2** uninteresting, dull, and lifeless. **3** (*of music*) below the right note. **4** lying full length. **5** deflated, without enough air in it. **6** clear, strong, firm. **7** no longer fizzy. • *n* **1** a level area. **2** the flat part or side. **3** a set of rooms on one floor or part of a floor for someone to live in, an apartment. **4** a musical sign (♭) showing that a note is to be played a semitone lower. **5** a flat tyre. • *n* **flatness**.

flatbread /flat-bred/ *n* bread made into thin, circular pieces or sheets, such as pitta or matzo.

flatfish /flat-fish/ *n* a kind of fish, such as a flounder or sole, with a flattened body and both eyes and mouth on one side of its body.

flatten /fla-ten/ *vb* to make flat.

flatter /fla-ter/ *vb* **1** to praise excessively or insincerely. **2** to make appear better than is true. • *n* **flatterer.**

flattery /fla-te-ree/ *n* insincere or excessive praise.

flatulence /fla-chu-lense/ *n* gas in the stomach or bowels. • *adj* **flatulent.**

flaunt /flawnt/ *vb* to show off, to try to draw attention to.

flavour /flay-vor/ *n, also* **flavor** (*US*) **1** a taste. **2** the taste special to a thing. • *vb* to add something to a dish to improve its taste.

flavouring /flay-vor-ing/ *n, also* **flavoring** (*US*) something added to improve the taste.

flaw /flaw/ *n* **1** a crack, a defect, an imperfection. **2** any weakness that makes a person or thing less than perfect, less effective, etc. • *adj* **flawed.**

flawless /flaw-less/ *adj* without any imperfections or defects.

flax /flaks/ *n* a plant with narrow leaves and blue flowers, the fibres of which are made into linen and the seeds of which are made into linseed oil.

flaxen /flak-sen/ *adj* **1** like or of flax. **2** light yellow in colour.

flea /flee/ *n* a small, jumping, bloodsucking insect.

flea market /flee-mar-ket/ *n* a bazaar, usually outdoors, dealing mainly in cheap, secondhand goods.

fleck /flek/ *n* a spot. • *vb* to mark with spots.

fled /fled/ *pt and pp* of **flee.**

fledgling /fledge-ling/ *n* a young bird learning to fly.

flee /flee/ *vb* (*pt, pp* **fled**) to run away, to run away from.

fleece /fleese/ *n* the woolly coat of a sheep or similar animal. • *vb* **1** to cut the wool off. **2** (*inf*) to overcharge.

fleet[1] /fleet/ *n* **1** a large number of ships, motorcars, aeroplanes, etc, together. **2** a large group of warships commanded by an admiral.

fleet[2] /fleet/ *adj* (*fml*) quick-moving. • *vb* (*fml*) to pass quickly.

fleeting /flee-ting/ *adj* (*fml*) passing quickly.

flesh /flesh/ *n* **1** the soft substance that covers the bones of an animal to form its body. **2** this as food. **3** the edible part of fruit. **4** the body. **5** the desires of the body.

fleshly /flesh-lee/ *adj* having to do with the body and its desires.

fleshy /flesh-ee/ *adj* fat.

flew /floo/ *pt* of **fly.**

flex /fleks/ *vb* to bend. • *n* a cord of rubber-covered wires used to carry electric currents.

flexible /flek-si-bl/ *adj* **1** easily bent. **2** easily changed, adaptable. **3** willing and able to change according to the situation, adaptable. • *n* **flexibility.**

flick /flik/ *vb* to strike lightly and quickly. • *also n.*

flicker /fli-ker/ *vb* **1** to shine or burn unsteadily. **2** to flutter, to move quickly and lightly. • *also n.*

flier /flie-er/ *see* **fly.**

flight /flite/ *n* **1** the act of flying. **2** the act of running away. **3** the movement or path of a thing through the air. **4** a journey made by air. **5** a number of birds flying together. **6** a set of stairs or steps.

flight attendant /flite a-ten-dant/ *n* a person whose job it is to look after passengers in an aircraft.

flight control /flite con-trole/ *n* **1** the control from the ground by radio of aircraft in flight. **2** a station using such control.

flighty /flie-tee/ *adj* **1** changeable, unreliable.

flimsy /flim-zee/ *adj* **1** thin. **2** not strong, easily broken or destroyed. **3** weak.

flinch /flinch/ *vb* to draw back in fear or pain.

fling /fling/ *vb* (*pt, pp* **flung**) **1** to throw. **2** to move suddenly and forcefully. • *n* **1** a throw. **2** a brief love affair. **3** a trial effort.

flint /flint/ *n* **1** a hard stone. **2** a piece of hard mineral from which sparks can be made when struck. • *also adj.*

flip /flip/ *vb* (**flipped, flipping**) **1** to turn over lightly but sharply. **2** to toss. • *also n.* • *adj* disrespectful, not serious.

flippant /fli-pant/ *adj* not serious, disrespectful. • *n* **flippancy.**

flipper /fli-per/ *n* a broad, flat part or limb used by certain sea creatures (e.g. seal, turtle, penguin) when swimming.

flirt /flurt/ *vb* **1** to show interest in for a time only. **2** to behave towards another as if attracted by or to attract. • *n* someone who plays at making love. • *n* **flirtation.**

flirtatious /flur-tay-shus/ *adj* fond of flirting.

float /float/ *vb* **1** to remain on the surface of a liquid. **2** to start. • *n* **1** anything that floats (e.g. a raft, a buoy, etc.) or helps to make something else float. **2** a low, flat, decorated automobile for carrying things in a parade. **3** (*US*) a cold beverage with ice cream floating in it.

flock[1] /flok/ *n* **1** a company of birds or animals. **2** a number of people together. **3** a congregation. • *vb* to come together in a crowd.

flock[2] /flok/ *n* **1** a tuft or flake of wool. **2** waste wool used for stuffing cushions, etc.

floe /flo/ *n* a large sheet of floating ice.

flog /flog/ *vb* (**flogged, flogging**) to beat, to thrash • *n* **flogging**.

flood /flud/ *n* **1** an overflowing of water on to dry land. **2** a rush (of water, people, etc.). **3** the flowing in of the tide. • *vb* **1** to overflow, to cover with water. **2** to arrive in great quantities.

floodlight /flud-lite/ *n* a very bright lamp directed on to the outside of a building at night to light it up. • *also vb*. • *n* **floodlighting**.

flood plain /flud-plane/ *n* a plain that borders a river, made up of the soil deposited by the river after it floods.

floor /flore/ *n* **1** the bottom surface of a room on which a person walks. **2** any bottom surface. **3** all the rooms, etc, on the same level in a building. • *vb* **1** to make a floor. **2** to knock down. **3** (*inf*) to astound.

floorboard /flore-board/ *n* the wooden boards that make up the floor to a house or building.

flooring /flore-ing/ *n* a floor, or material for making a floor.

floor plan /flore-plan/ *n* a scaled drawing of the layout of the rooms of a house or building.

flop /flop/ *vb* (**flopped, flopping**) **1** to sit or fall down heavily or loosely. **2** to hang or swing heavily or loosely. **3** to fail completely, to be unsuccessful. • *n* a complete failure.

floppy /flop-ee/ *adj* hanging loosely, not stiff.

flora /flo-ra/ *n* all the plants in a country or region.

floral /flo-ral/ *adj* having to do with flowers.

florist /flo-rist/ *n* someone who grows or sells flowers.

floss /floss/ *n* **1** rough silk. **2** any fluffy substance. **3** waxed thread for cleaning between the teeth. • *vb* to clean teeth with floss.

flotsam /flot-sam/ *n* floating wreckage.

flounce[1] /flounse/ *vb* to move sharply or quickly. • *also n*.

flounce[2] /flounse/ *n* a gathered strip of cloth sewn by its upper edge round a skirt or dress and left hanging. • *n* **flouncing**.

flounder[1] /floun-der/ *n* a type of flatfish; a fluke.

flounder[2] /floun-der/ *vb* **1** to struggle helplessly or awkwardly. **2** to be in doubt as to what to say next, to hesitate, to struggle when speaking.

flour /flour/ *n* grain, especially wheat, ground into powder.

flourish /flur-ish/ *vb* **1** to get on well, to be very successful, to prosper. **2** to grow well, to bloom. **3** to wave about in a showy manner. • *n* **1** spoken words or handwriting that attract attention by being unusual. **2** a sudden short burst of music. **3** a bold, sweeping movement or gesture.

floury /flou-ree/ *adj* **1** covered with flour. **2** like flour.

flout /flout/ *vb* to pay no attention to, to disobey openly and scornfully.

flow /flo/ *vb* **1** to move steadily and easily, as water. **2** to proceed evenly and continuously. **3** to fall or hang down loosely and freely. **4** to be plentiful. • *n* **1** a flowing movement, a stream. **2** the rise of the tide. **3** a continuous stream or supply.

flowchart /flo-chart/ *n* a diagram showing the order of stages in a process or system.

flower /flour/ *n* **1** a blossom, consisting of petals and bearing pollen. **2** the best part of. • *vb* to blossom or bloom.

flowerpot /flour-pot/ *n* a container in which plants can be grown.

flowery /flou-ree/ *adj* **1** full of flowers. **2** patterned with flowers. **3** ornate, over-elaborate.

flown /flone/ *pp of* **fly**.

flu /floo/ *n* short for **influenza**, a sickness caused by a virus.

fluctuate /fluck-choo-wate/ *vb* **1** to rise and fall, as a wave. **2** to vary, to change continually and irregularly. • *n* **fluctuation**.

flue /floo/ *n* a passage in a chimney for carrying away air or smoke.

fluent /floo-ent/ *adj* able to speak or write quickly and easily. • *n* **fluency**.

fluff /fluf/ *n* any soft or feathery material. *vb* **1** **fluff up** make something fuller by shaking. **2** (*inf*) to fail to do something properly.

fluffy /fluf-ee/ *adj* like fluff, soft and downy.

fluid /floo-id/ *adj* **1** able to flow, flowing. **2** able to change quickly. **3** smooth and graceful. • *n* any substance that flows, as liquid or gas.

fluke[1] /flook/ *n* a type of flatfish, a flounder.

fluke[2] /flook/ *n* **1** the part of an anchor that hooks into the seabed. **2** one of the pointed parts on a whale's tail.

fluke[3] /**flook**/ n (inf) a lucky chance.

flume /**floom**/ n a human-made channel or chute for carrying water, usually down a mountainside.

flung /**flung**/ pt and pp of **fling**.

fluorescence /floo-re-sense/ n a quality in certain substances that enables them to give off very bright light.

fluorescent /floo-re-sent/ adj having or showing fluorescence.

fluoride /**flaw**-ride/ n a chemical compound that is sometimes added to toothpaste and water supplies to prevent tooth decay.

flurry /**flu**-ree/ n 1 confused movement. 2 a sudden rush of air, rain, etc. • vb to make anxious or confused.

flush /**flush**/ vb 1 to become suddenly red in the face. 2 to cleanse by a flow of water. • n 1 a sudden redness in the face. 2 a rush of water. 3 freshness, vigour. • adj 1 (inf) having plenty of money. 2 level.

fluster /**flu**-ster/ vb to make confused, to overexcite. • also n.

flute /**floot**/ n 1 a wooden musical wind instrument. 2 a shallow hollow carved in a pillar. • vb 1 to play the flute. 2 to carve hollows and grooves.

flutter /**flut**-er/ vb 1 to move the wings up and down quickly without flying. 2 to move about quickly. • n 1 quick movement. 2 (inf) excitement. 3 (inf) a bet, a gamble.

fly /**flie**/ vb (pt **flew**, pp **flown**) 1 to move through the air on wings. 2 to travel by aeroplane. 3 to move quickly. 4 to run away. • n 1 a common flying insect. 2 a fishing hook covered with feathers to make it look like a fly. 3 a flap, especially one that closes the entrance to a tent. • n **flier**, **flyer**.

FM /**ef**-em/ abbr = **frequency modulation**: a system that uses waves to send and receive sound.

foal /**foal**/ n a young horse, mule, donkey, etc. • vb to give birth to a foal.

foam /**foam**/ n bubbles on the top of liquid, froth. • vb to gather or produce foam.

focaccia /fo-**coch**-ee-a/ n a round, flat Italian yeast bread that has a crispy crust and contains olive oil, herbs, etc.

focal /**fo**-cal/ adj 1 of a focus. 2 central, main.

focus /**fo**-cus/ n (pl **foci** /fo-**kie**/ or **focuses** /**fo**-cu-seez/) 1 a point at which rays of light meet. 2 a centre of interest or attention. • vb 1 to bring to bear on one point. 2 to get a clear image in the lens of a camera before taking a photograph.

fodder /**fod**-er/ n dried food for cattle, horses, sheep, etc.

foe /**fo**/ n (fml) an enemy.

foetal /**fee**-tal/ adj, also **fetal** (US) of a foetus.

foetus /**fee**-tus/ n, also **fetus** (US) the young of a human or animal before it has been born.

fog /**fog**/ n a thick mist.

fogey, fogy /**fo**-gee/ n a person whose ideas are out of date.

foggy /**fog**-ee/ adj 1 misty. 2 confused, vague.

foil[1] /**foyl**/ vb to cause to fail, to defeat.

foil[2] /**foyl**/ n 1 a very thin sheet of metal. 2 the metal coating on the back of a mirror.

foil[3] /**foyl**/ n a long, thin sword with a cap or button on the tip to prevent injury, used in fencing.

fold[1] /**foald**/ vb 1 to bend one part of a thing all the way over to cover another part. 2 to enclose. • n 1 a line or crease made by folding. 2 the part doubled over.

fold[2] /**foald**/ n a place where sheep are kept.

folder /**foal**-der/ n a stiff cover for holding papers, letters, etc.

foliage /**fo**-lee-idge/ n (fml) the leaves of trees or other plants.

folio /**fo**-lee-yo/ n 1 a sheet of paper folded so that it opens to two equal, opposing pages. 2 a book made with large sheets of paper.

folk /**foak**/ n 1 (inf) people. 2 the people of a country or a particular part of a country. (inf) pl relatives, parents.

folklore /**foak**-loar/ n all the stories, songs, beliefs, etc, that have been passed on from one generation of people to another (e.g. **folk dance, folk song, folktale**).

follow /**fol**-oa/ vb 1 to go or come after. 2 to be next in order to. 3 to go along. 4 to accept as a leader or a teacher. 5 to result from. 6 to understand.

follower /**fol**-oa-er/ n a supporter.

following /**fol**-oa-ing/ n all one's supporters. • adj next in order.

folly /**fol**-ee/ n 1 foolishness. 2 a foolish act.

fond /**fond**/ adj 1 having a love or liking for. 2 loving. 3 foolishly loving, indulging, doting. 4 hoped for but not likely to be realized. • n **fondness**.

fondle /**fon**-dl/ vb to stroke, to touch lovingly.

font /**font**/ n 1 the basin holding the water for baptism. 2 a set of type of the same size and style.

food /**food**/ n that which can be eaten.

food chain /**food**-chane/ n a series of living things, each of which feeds on the one below it in the series.

fool /**fool**/ n 1 a silly or stupid person. 2 (old) a jester. • vb 1 to deceive. 2 to behave as if someone were a fool.

foolish /**foo**-lish/ *adj* silly, stupid. • *n* **foolishness**.

foolproof /**fool**-proof/ *adj* unable to go wrong even when foolishly used.

foot /foot/ *n* (*pl* **feet** /feet/) **1** the part of the leg below the ankle. **2** the lowest part of anything. **3** an imperial measure of length equal to 12 inches. **4** foot-soldiers. • *vb* (*inf*) to pay.

football /**foot**-bol/ *n*, *also* **soccer 1** a team game the object of which is to kick a ball into the goal to score points. **2** the ball used to play this game.

foothills /**foot**-hilz/ *npl* low hills at the bottom of mountains.

footing /**foo**-ting/ *n* **1** a safe place for the feet. **2** balance. **3** foundation, basis. **4** relationship.

footlights /**foot**-lites/ *npl* lights on the floor at the front of the stage in a theatre.

footnote /**foot**-note/ *n* a note at the bottom of a page.

footpath /**foot**-path/ *n* a narrow path used by walkers only.

footprint /**foot**-print/ *n* the mark left by a foot.

footstep /**foot**-step/ *n* the sound or mark made by the foot of someone walking.

footstool /**foot**-stool/ *n* a low stool to support the feet of a person seated.

for /for/ *prep* **1** in place of. **2** in the interest of. **3** with the purpose of doing. **4** in search of. **5** as being. **6** the length of.

forage /**faw**-ridge/ *n* food for cattle or horses. • *vb* **1** to gather food for cattle or horses. **2** to go out and look for food. **3** to search, to hunt, to rummage.

forbid /fawr-**bid**/ *vb* (*pt* **forbade**, *pp* **forbidden**) to order not to do.

forbidding /fawr-**bi**-ding/ *adj* frightening.

force /foarse/ *n* **1** strength, power. **2** violence. **3** an organized body of people. **4** *pl* the army, navy, and air force. **5** a person or thing that has great power. • *vb* **1** to make. **2** to get something by strength, violence, or effort. **3** to grow plants out of season under artificial conditions.

forced /foarst/ *adj* **1** brought about by force, **2** unnatural, strained.

forceful /**foarse**-ful/ *adj* strong, energetic. • *adv* **forcefully**.

forceps /**fore**-seps/ *n* an instrument like tongs or pincers used by doctors and dentists to hold, lift, or grip things.

forcible /**fore**-si-bl/ *adj* done by force.

ford /foard/ *n* a place where a river is shallow enough to be crossed. • *vb* to wade across.

fore /fore/ *adj*, *adv* in front. • *interj* (*in golf*) look out!

forearm[1] /**fore**-arm/ *n* the arm from the elbow to the wrist.

forearm[2] /fore-**arm**/ *vb* to arm or prepare in advance.

foreboding /fore-**bo**-ding/ *n* a feeling that evil is going to happen.

forecast /**fore**-cast/ *vb* (*pt*, *pp* **forecast**) to say what will happen in the future. • *also n*.

forefather /**fore**-fa-ther/ *n* an ancestor.

forefinger /**fore**-fing-ger/ *n* the finger next to the thumb; the index finger.

forefront /**fore**-frunt/ *n* the front part.

forego[1] /**fore**-**go**/ *vb* (*pt* **forewent**, *pp* **foregone**) to go before.

forego[2] /fore-**go**/ *see* **forgo**.

foregoing /fore-**go**-ing/ *adj* earlier, previous.

foregone /**fore**-gon/ *adj* previously determined, predicted. • *vb pp* of **forego**[1].

foreground /**fore**-ground/ *n* **1** the nearest objects shown in a picture. **2** the nearest part of a view.

forehead /**fore**-hed/ *n* the part of the face above the eyebrows and below the hairline.

foreign /**fawr**-un/ *adj* **1** belonging to or concerning another country. **2** strange. **3** out of place.

foreigner /**fawr**-u-ner/ *n* a person from a different country from where they are.

foreleg /**fore**-leg/ *n* one of the front legs of an animal.

foremost /**fore**-most/ *adj* **1** most famous, best. **2** most important.

forename /**fore**-name/ *see* **first name**.

forensic /fo-**ren**-zic/ *n* **1** having to do with the law or courts of law. **2** having to do with applying scientific, especially medical, knowledge to legal matters, as in crime investigation.

forerunner /**fore**-ru-ner/ *n* **1** (*old*) someone who goes before with a message or announcement. **2** a person or thing that comes before another. • *vb* **forerun**.

foresee /fore-**see**/ *vb* (*pt* **foresaw**, *pp* **foreseen**) to see what is going to happen.

foreshadow /fore-**sha**-doe/ *vb* to be a sign of future events.

foresight /**fore**-sight/ *n* the ability to guess and prepare for future events.

foreskin /**fore**-skin/ *n* the fold of skin that covers the tip of the penis; this is sometimes removed by circumcision for religious or medical reasons.

forest /**faw**-rest/ *n* a large area covered by trees and undergrowth.

forestall /fore-**stawl**/ *vb* to guess what another is going to do and act before him or her.

forestation /fore-**stay**-shun/ *n* the planting and caring for forests.

forested /**faw**-re-sted/ *adj* covered with trees and undergrowth.

forester /**faw**-re-ster/ *n* a person in charge of a forest.

forestry /**faw**-re-stree/ *n* the study of planting and looking after forests.

foretell /fore-**tell**/ *vb* (*pt, pp* **foretold**) to say what will happen in the future.

forethought /**fore**-thot/ *n* care that the results of actions will be good.

forever /fu-**rev**-er/ *adv* for always, endlessly, at all times.

forewarn /fore-**wawrn**/ *vb* to warn in advance.

foreword /**fore**-word/ *n* a piece of writing at the beginning of a book as an introduction.

forfeit /**fawr**-fit/ *vb* to lose or give up. • *n* that which is so lost or given up, a fine.

forgave /fawr-**gave**/ *pt of* **forgive**.

forge /**foarge**/ *n* 1 a blacksmith's workshop. 2 a furnace for heating metal. • *vb* 1 to beat hot metal into shape. 2 to make by hard effort. 3 to imitate something to deceive.

forger /**fore**-jer/ *n* a person who forges.

forgery /**fore**-je-ree/ *n* 1 act of imitating something dishonestly, especially another's writing. 2 the imitation so made.

forget /fore-**get**/ *vb* (*pt* **forgot**, *pp* **forgotten**) to fail to remember.

forgetful /fore-**get**-ful/ *adj* bad at remembering. • *n* **forgetfulness**.

forget-me-not /for-**get**-me-not/ *n* a small blue flower.

forgive /fore-**giv**/ *vb* (*pt* **forgave**) 1 to pardon. 2 to stop being angry or bitter towards, to stop blaming or wanting to punish. • *n* **forgiveness**. • *adj* **forgivable**.

forgiving /fore-**gi**-ving/ *adj* quick to forgive.

forgo, forego /for-**go**/ *vb* to give up, to do without.

forgot *pt of* **forget**. • *pp* **forgotten**

fork /fork/ *n* 1 an instrument with two or more pointed prongs used for digging, eating, etc. 2 a place where two roads meet. 3 a place where a tree or branch divides. • *vb* 1 to raise or dig with a fork. 2 to divide into branches.

forked /forkt/ *adj* divided into branches or sections.

forklift /**fork**-lift/ *n* a device on the front of a truck for lifting heavy objects.

forlorn /fur-**lawrn**/ *adj* left alone, miserable.

form /fawrm/ *n* 1 shape. 2 a paper so printed that a message or information can be written in prepared spaces. 3 kind.

4 arrangement. 5 a fixed way of doing things. 6 a class or year in a school. • *vb* 1 to make, to cause to take shape. 2 to come into existence, to take shape.

formal /**fawr**-mal/ *adj* 1 following the accepted rules or customs. 2 stiff in manner. • *adv* **formally**.

formality /fawr-**ma**-li-tee/ *n* 1 stiffness of manner. 2 something done only to carry out a rule. 3 care to follow rules and customs.

format /**fawr**-mat/ *n* the general shape and size of anything. • *vb* to prepare a computer disk so that data can be recorded and stored on it.

formation /fawr-**may**-shun/ *n* 1 act of forming. 2 an orderly arrangement.

formative /**fawr**-ma-tiv/ *adj* helping to shape or develop.

former /**fawr**-mer/ *adj* earlier, past. • *pron* the person or thing previously mentioned.

formerly /**fawr**-mer-lee/ *adv* in earlier times.

formidable /fawr-**mi**-da-bl/ *adj* 1 to be feared. 2 difficult.

formless /**fawrm**-less/ *adj* having no definite shape or regular plan.

formula /**fawrm**-yu-la/ *n* (*pl* **formulae** *or* **formulas**) 1 a fixed arrangement of words or numbers. 2 a rule in arithmetic set down with signs or letters so that it can be used for any sum. 3 in chemistry, the use of signs or letters to show how substances are made up.

formulate /**fawrm**-yu-late/ *vb* (*fml*) to express or set down clearly.

forsake /fawr-**sake**/ *vb* (*pt* **forsook**, *pp* **forsaken**) to give up, to abandon.

fort /foart/ *n* 1 a place prepared for defence against an enemy. 2 a permanent military post.

forte[1] /foart/ *n* one's strong point, the thing at which a person is best.

forte[2] /**fawr**-tay/ *adv* (*mus*) loud.

forth *adv* 1 /**foarth**/ onward in time, place, or order. 2 out.

forthcoming /foarth-**cu**-ming/ *adj* 1 about to happen, coming soon. 2 open, responsive.

forthright /**foarth**-rite/ *adj* saying what one thinks.

fortify /**fawr**-ti-fie/ *vb* 1 to strengthen or enrich. 2 to build defences around.

fortitude /**fawr**-ti-tood/ *n* ability to suffer without complaint; courage, patience.

fortnight /**fawrt**-nite/- *n* a period of two weeks. • *adv* **fortnightly**.

fortress /**fawr**-tress/ *n* a place prepared with strong defences against attackers.

fortunate /fawr-chi-net/ *adj* lucky.

fortune /fawr-chin/ *n* **1** luck, chance. **2** wealth, a large amount of money. **3** the supposed power that affects one's life.

forty /for-tee/ *n* the product of four and ten. • *adj* **fortieth**.

forum /fo-rum/ *n* (*pl* **forums** *or* **fora**) **1** (*old*) the market place in a Roman town. **2** any place of public discussion. **3** a meeting involving a public discussion.

forward /for-wurd/ *adv* (*also* **forwards**) towards the front. • *adj* **1** advancing. **2** near the front. **3** in advance. **4** developing more quickly than usual. **5** bold, not shy. • *vb* **1** to help move along. **2** to send on.

fossil /fos-il/ *n* **1** the remains of a plant or animal that have hardened into stone and so been preserved in rock or earth. **2** a person whose ideas are out of date.

fossil fuel /fos-il fyool/ *n* a natural substance, such as coal or oil, found underground and formed in an earlier time, used as a source of energy.

fossilize /fos-il-ize/ *vb*, *also* **fossilise** to change into a fossil.

foster /faws-ter/ *vb* **1** to look after for a time, to bring up a child that is not one's own. **2** to encourage.

foster child /faws-ter child/ *n* (*pl* **foster children**) a child brought up for a time by someone who is not his or her parent. • *also n* **foster brother**, **foster sister**.

foster father /faws-ter fa-ther/, **foster mother** /faws-ter mu-ther/ *n*, **foster parents** /faws-ter pay-rints/ *npl* those who bring up for a time the child(ren) of other parents.

foster home /faws-ter hoam/ *n* a home in which foster children are cared for for a time by people other than their families.

fought *pt and pp of* **fight**.

foul /foul/ *adj* **1** dirty, disgusting. **2** stormy. **3** against the rules. **4** nasty. **5** bad. • *vb* **1** to make or become dirty. **2** to become entangled. **3** to break the rules of a game. • *n* an act against the rules of a game.

foul play /foul play/ *n* **1** unfair play. **2** violence or murder.

found[1] /found/ *pt of* **find**.

found[2] /found/ *vb* **1** to start from the beginning, to set up. **2** to give money to start a school, hospital, etc. • *n* **founder**.

foundation /foun-**day**-shun/ *n* **1** the lowest part of a building on which the walls stand. **2** the amount of money given to start a school, hospital, etc. **3** the place started with such money.

founder[1] /foun-der/ *vb* **1** to fill with water and sink. **2** to come to nothing, to fail.

founder[2] /foun-der/ a person who founds or establishes something.

foundry /foun-dree/ *n* a workshop where metals are melted and shaped.

fount /fount/ *n* **1** (*old*) a spring of water. **2** (*fml*) a cause or beginning.

fountain /foun-tin/ *n* **1** a spring of water. **2** a jet of water thrown into the air from a pipe. **3** (*fml*) a beginning or source.

fountain pen /foun-tin pen/ *n* a pen containing a supply of liquid ink.

four /fore/ *n* the sum of two and two. • *adj* **fourth**.

fourteen /fore-teen/ *n* the product of two and seven. • *adj* **fourteenth**

fourth *see* **four**.

four-poster /fore-poe-ster/ *n* a bed with four tall corner posts that sometimes hold up a decorative drape.

fowl /foul/ *n* a bird, especially the farmyard chicken or rooster.

fox /foks/ *n* **1** a doglike animal with reddish brown or grey fur and a bushy tail. **2** a cunning or deceitful person. • *f* **vixen** /vik-sen/.

foxhound /foks-hound/ *n* a kind of dog with black, tan, and white fur and trained for hunting.

foxy /fok-see/ *adj* **1** cunning. **2** like a fox.

foyer /foy-ay/, /fwa-yay/ *n* an entrance hall.

fraction /frac-shun/ *n* **1** a part of a whole. **2** a small part. **3** in arithmetic, part of a whole number, e.g. $1/2$, $1/4$, etc.

fractional /frac-shnal/ *adj* very small.

fracture /frac-cher/ *n* **1** a break. **2** the breaking of a bone. • *vb* to break, to suffer a fracture.

fragile /fra-jile/ *adj* **1** easily broken. **2** not strong.

fragment /frag-ment/ *n* **1** a part broken off. **2** a small part. • *vb* **fragment** to break into fragments.

fragrance /fray-granse/ *n* **1** scent, sweet smell. **2** perfume.

fragrant /fray-grant/ *adj* sweet-smelling.

frail /frale/ *adj* **1** weak, feeble, delicate. **2** (*old*) easily tempted to do wrong.

frame /frame/ *vb* **1** to make, to construct. **2** to put into a frame. **3** (*inf*) to cause someone to seem guilty of a crime. • *n* **1** the supports around which the rest of a thing is built. **2** the border of metal, wood, etc, placed around a picture. **3** the body.

framer /fray-mer/ *n* a person or thing that frames.

framework /frame-wurk/ *n* the supports around which the rest of a thing is built.

franc /frangk/ *n* a money that was formerly used in France, Belgium, Luxembourg, etc.

franchise /fran-chize/ n 1 the right to vote. 2 a special right given or sold by a company to one person or group of people to sell the company's goods or services in a particular place.

frank[1] /frangk/ adj 1 saying what one really thinks, honest. 2 open, honest-looking. • n frankness.

frank[2] /frangk/ vb to put an official mark on a letter.

frankfurter /frangk-fur-ter/ n a long, thin smoked sausage, a hot dog.

frankincense /frang-kin-sense/ n a gum giving a sweet-smelling smoke when burned.

frantic /fran-tic/ adj 1 very anxious or worried. 2 wildly excited, hurried.

fraternal /fra-ter-nal/ adj brotherly.

fraternity /fra-ter-ni-tee/ n 1 a group of men meeting for a common purpose. 2 (fml) the state of being brothers or like brothers.

fraternize /fra-ter-nize/ vb, also **fraternise** to mix with in a friendly or brotherly way.

fraud /frawd/ n 1 dishonesty. 2 a deceiving trick. 3 a person who deceives.

fraudulent /fraw-ju-lent/ adj dishonest.

fray[1] /fray/ n 1 a fight. 2 a noisy quarrel.

fray[2] /fray/ vb 1 to wear away by rubbing. 2 to become worn at the edges. 3 to upset.

freak /freek/ n 1 a living creature not physically normal. 2 a strange, unexpected happening. 3 (inf) a person with an extremely strong interest in a particular subject • adj strange, unusual.

freakish /free-kish/ adj, also **freaky** /free-kee/ very unusual, strange.

freckle /fre-kul/ n a brownish yellow spot on the skin. • adj freckled.

free /free/ adj 1 at liberty, able to do what a person wants. 2 not forced or persuaded to act, think, speak, etc, in a particular way. 3 not occupied. 4 generous. 5 costing nothing. 6 open, frank. • n 1 to set at liberty. 2 to set free from.

freedom /free-dum/ n 1 the state of being at liberty. 2 the right to act, think, speak, etc, as a person pleases. 3 the state of being without. 4 the unlimited use of something.

freelance /free-lanse/ n someone who works for himself or herself and not any particular company. • vb to work in such a way.

free-range /free-range/ adj of eggs, laid by hens that are allowed to move around freely.

freestyle /free-stile/ adj (sports) not limited to one specific style.

freethinker /free-thing-ker/ n someone who tries to work out his or her own ideas about God, religion, politics, morals, etc.

free trade /free-trade/ n the exchanging of goods without making a customs charge on imports.

free verse /free-verse/ n poetry without rhyme or a standard, regular pattern.

freeze /freez/ vb (pt froze, pp frozen) 1 to harden because of cold. 2 to become or make into ice. 3 to be very cold. 4 to make very cold. 5 to become suddenly still.

freezer /free-zer/ n a piece of electrical equipment or the part of a refrigerator that freezes and preserves food or other things at very low temperatures.

freight /frate/ n 1 the cargo of a ship. 2 the load on a train carrying goods. 3 the cost of transporting goods.

freighter /fray-ter/ n a cargo ship.

French /french/ adj of or relating to France. • n the language spoken in France.

French bread /french bred/ n a long, slender loaf of white bread with a hard, crisp crust.

French windows /french win-doze/ npl two glass doors that are next to each other and hinged at opposite sides so that they open together in the middle.

French dressing /french dre-sing/ n a salad dressing made from oil, vinegar and seasoning; also known as **vinaigrette**.

French fries /french frize/ n chips, especially thin chips, made from potato.

French horn /french hawrn/ n a brass musical instrument consisting of a long, spiral tube ending in a flared bell.

French toast /french toast/ n sliced bread dipped in beaten egg and fried in a pan.

frenzied /fren-zeed/ adj wild, uncontrolled.

frenzy /fren-zee/ n 1 a sudden attack of madness. 2 uncontrollable excitement or feeling.

frequency /free-kwen-see/ n 1 the number of times something happens. 2 the number of waves, vibrations, etc, per second.

frequent /free-kwent/ adj happening often, common. • vb /fra-kwent/ to visit often.

fresh /fresh/ adj 1 new. 2 not tired. 3 cool. 4 not stale. 5 not frozen or canned. 6 not salted.

freshen /fre-shen/ vb 1 to make or become fresh. 2 to cause to become less untidy, etc. • n freshener.

freshwater /fresh-waw-ter/ n not saltwater. • adj of or relating to those things that live in fresh water.

fret /fret/ vb (fretted, fretting) 1 to wear away by rubbing. 2 to worry, to be anxious.

fretful /fret-ful/ *adj* troubled, irritable.

friar /frie-er/ *n* a member of a Roman Catholic religious order.

friary /frie-e-ree/ *n* a house of friars.

friction /fric-shun/ *n* **1** rubbing, a rubbing together. **2** the resistance felt when one object is moved against another. **3** disagreement.

Friday /frie-day/ *n, adv* the sixth day of the week, following Thursday.

fridge /fridge/ *n* a refrigerator.

friend /frend/ *n* a close companion.

friendly /frend-lee/ *adj* **1** kind. **2** fond of or liking one another. • *n* **friendliness**.

friendship /frend-ship/ *n* the state of being friends.

frieze /freez/ *n* a decorative border around the top of a wall.

frigate /fri-git/ *n* a small fast warship.

fright /frite/ *n* a sudden feeling of fear, a shock.

frighten /frie-ten/ *vb* to make afraid.

frightful /friet-ful/ *adj* **1** dreadful, causing fear. **2** (*inf*) very bad, dreadful.

frigid /fri-jid/ *adj* **1** (*fml*) cold, frozen. **2** cold and unemotional, unfriendly. **3** not able to enjoy sex. • *n* **frigidity** /fri-ji-di-tee/.

frill /fril/ *n* **1** a loose ornamental edging of cloth gathered or pleated at one end and sewn on to a garment. **2** an unnecessary ornament. • *adj* **frilly**.

fringe /fringe/ *n* **1** an ornamental edging of hanging threads. **2** part of someone's hair that hangs over the forehead. **3** the edge. • *vb* to border.

Frisbee /friz-bee/ *n* **1** a simple game in which a flat, plastic disc is flung between players. **2** the disc used to play this game.

frisk /frisk/ *vb* **1** to jump and dance about, to play about joyfully. **2** to search quickly.

frisky /fri-skee/ *adj* playful, active.

fritter /fri-ter/ *n* any sweet or tasty food cut small, fried in batter, and served hot. • *vb* to waste.

frivolity /fri-vol-i-tee/ *n* fun, lack of seriousness.

frivolous /fri-vu-lus/ *adj* **1** interested only in amusement. **2** not taking important matters seriously; silly. **3** not serious, playful, light-hearted.

frizz /friz/ *vb* to form into small, tight curls. • *adj* **frizzy**.

fro /fro/ *adv*. • **to and fro** forward and back again.

frog /frawg/ *n* a cold-blooded, four-footed land and water creature that can leap long distances.

frogman /frawg-man/ *n* a person trained and equipped for underwater work.

frolic /frol-ic/ *vb* (**frolicked, frolicking**) to play about, to dance or jump about happily. • *n* a trick played for fun; lively amusement.

from /from/ *prep* **1** beginning at. **2** starting with. **3** out of. **4** with. **5** out of the whole of. **6** as not being like. **7** because of.

frond /frond/ *n* a leaf, especially of a palm or fern.

front /frunt/ *n* **1** the forward part of anything. **2** in war, the place where the fighting is going on. • *also adj*. • *vb* to face, to stand before.

frontier /frun-teer/ *n* **1** the boundary between one country and another. **2** that part of a settled, civilized country that is still underdeveloped and somewhat wild.

frost /frawst/ *n* frozen dew or moisture freezing. • *vb* **1** to cover with frost. **2** to cover with icing. **3** to treat glass so that it cannot be seen through.

frostbite /frawst-bite/ *n* injury caused to the body by very severe cold. • *adj* **frostbitten**.

frosty /fraw-stee/ *adj* **1** covered with frost. **2** cold because of frost. **3** unfriendly.

froth /frawth/ *n* a mass of tiny bubbles on the surface of liquid; foam. • *vb* to throw up froth. • *adj* **frothy**.

frown /froun/ *vb* to wrinkle the forehead, to scowl, to look angry. • *also n*. • **frown on** to discourage, to disapprove of.

froze /froze/ *pt of* **freeze**.

frozen /froe-zin/ *pp of* **freeze**.

fructose /fruke-toze/ *n* a sugar found in fruit and honey.

frugal /fru-gal/ *adj* **1** careful, not wasteful, thrifty. **2** very small, not much. • *n* **frugality**.

fruit /froot/ *n* **1** the part of a plant that produces the seed, often eaten as a food. **2** result.

fruit bat /froot bat/ *n* any fruit-eating bat, such as the flying fox.

fruitcake /froot-cake/ *n* **1** a rich cake containing nuts, fruit, spices, etc. **2** (*sl*) a foolish person.

fruit cup /froot-cup/ *n* mixed diced fruits served in a small bowl as a dessert or appetizer (*also* **fruit cocktail**).

fruit fly /froot-flie/ *n* a small fly that feeds on fruit.

fruitful /froot-ful/ *adj* **1** (*old*) fertile. **2** having good results.

fruition /froo-wi-shun/ *n* fulfilment, a successful ending.

fruitless /froot-less/ *adj* unsuccessful.

fruity /froo-tee/ *adj* like fruit in taste or smell.

frump /frump/ *n* a badly or unfashionably dressed woman. • *adj* **frumpy**.

frustrate /fru-**strate**/ *vb* **1** to make to fail. **2** to cause to have feelings of disappointment or dissatisfaction. • *n* **frustration**.

fry[1] /frie/ *vb* to cook in fat. • *n* anything fried.

fry[2] /frie/ *n* (*pl* **fry**) young fish.

fryer /frie-er/ *n* a person or thing that fries.

frying pan /frie-ing-pan/ *n* a shallow pan with a handle for frying food.

fuchsia /fyoo-sha/ *n* **1** a shrub with long, hanging, bell-shaped flowers of a pink, red, or purple colour. **2** purplish red.

fudge /fudge/ *n* a soft sweet. • *vb* to refuse to commit; to fail to give a direct answer.

fuel /fyool/ *n* **1** material to keep a fire going. **2** material used for producing heat or power by burning.

fugitive /fyoo-ji-tiv/ *n* someone who is running away. • *adj* **1** (*fml*) passing quickly. **2** escaping. • *n* a person who flees from danger, pursuit, or duty.

fugue /fyoog/ *n* a piece of music in which different parts or voices carry the same tune at different times.

fulfil /fool-fil/ *vb, also* **fulfill** (*US*) (**fulfilled**, **fulfilling**) **1** to carry out sucessfully, to complete. **2** to satisfy, to meet. • *n* **fulfilment**, *also* **fulfillment** (*US*).

full[1] /fool/ *adj* **1** holding as much as possible. **2** complete. • *n* **fullness**.

full[2] /fool/ *vb* to clean and thicken cloth. • *n* **fuller**.

full-blown /fool-bloan/ *adj* in full bloom, fully opened.

full-bodied /fool-**bod**-eed/ *adj* having a rich, strong flavour.

fully-fledged /foo-li-flejd/ *adj* having a complete set of feathers, completely developed.

full-grown /fool-groan/ *adj* having reached full size.

full-length /fool-lenth/ *adj* showing or covering the full length of an object or all of a person's figure, said of pictures, mirrors, etc.

full moon /fool-**moon**/ *n* the phase of the moon when its entire face can be seen from Earth.

full stop /fool **stop**/ *n* a punctuation mark (.) used at the end of a sentence.

full-time /fool-**time**/ *adj* engaged in work, study, etc. for the full extent of the working hours of the day.

fulmar /fool-mar/ *n* a type of sea bird.

fulminate /fool-mi-nate/ *vb* to speak loudly and threateningly. • *n* **fulmination**.

fulsome /fool-sum/ *adj* overmuch.

fumble /fum-bul/ *vb* **1** to feel for something not seen. **2** to handle clumsily.

fume /fyoom/ *n* smoke, vapour. • *vb* **1** to give off fumes. **2** (*inf*) to show anger.

fumigant /fyoo-mi-gant/ *n* the substance used in fumigation.

fumigate /**fyoo**-mi-gate/ *vb* to disinfect by means of fumes. • *n* **fumigation**.

fun /fun/ *n* merriment, amusement, enjoyment. • *adj* amusing, enjoyable.

function /funk-shun/ *n* **1** the work that a thing is made or planned to perform; its use. **2** duties. **3** (*fml*) a public ceremony or party. • *vb* **1** to work as intended. **2** to act.

functional /funk-shu-nal/ *adj* designed with a view to its use.

functionary /funk-shu-ne-ree/ *n* (*fml*) an official.

fund /fund/ *n* **1** an amount laid aside till needed. **2** money collected or kept for a purpose.

fundamental /fun-da-**men**-tal/ *adj* having to do with the beginning or most necessary parts of something, of great importance. • *also n*.

fundamentalism /fun-da-**men**-ta-li-zum/ *n* the belief that the whole of the Bible is to be believed and lived by exactly as written.

fundraiser /fund-ray-zer/ *n* an event put together to raise money for an organization, cause, etc.

funeral /fyoon-ral/ *n* **1** burial of the dead. **2** the ceremonies performed at burial.

funeral director /fyoon-ral di-**rec**-tor/ *n* a person who manages funerals.

funereal /fyoo-ni-ree-al/ *adj* gloomy, sad, dark.

funfair *see* **fair**.

fungal /fung-gal/ *adj* having to do with or caused by a fungus.

fungus /fung-gus/ *n* (*pl* **fungi** /fung-gie/ *or* **funguses** /fung-gu-sez/) **1** a mushroom, toadstool, or similar plant. **2** an unhealthy growth on an animal or plant.

funk[1] /fungk/ *n* a state of fear.

funk[2] /fungk/ *n* a style of music with a jerky bassline, popular since the 1970s. • *adj* **funky**.

funnel /fu-nel/ *n* **1** a hollow cone used for pouring liquids into bottles etc. **2** a passage by which smoke etc, escapes.

funnies /fu-neez/ *npl* comic strips.

funny /fu-nee/ *adj* **1** amusing, humorous. **2** strange, odd.

funny bone /fu-nee-bone/ *n* a place on the elbow that gives a strange, tingling sensation when it is hit.

fur /fur/ *n* **1** the short soft hair of certain animals. **2** the skin of an animal with the hair still attached, used as a garment. **3** a coating (e.g. on the tongue). • *adj* **furry**.

furious /fyoo-ree-us/ *see* **fury**.

furl /furl/ *vb* to roll up.

furlong /fur-lawng/ *n* one-eighth of a mile (220 yards).

furlough /fur-lo/ *n* (*fml*) permission to be absent from work for a certain time.

furnace /fur-nis/ *n* an enclosed place in which great heat can be produced by fire.

furnish /fur-nish/ *vb* **1** to provide what is necessary. **2** to put tables, chairs, beds, and other necessary articles in a house.

furnishings /fur-ni-shingz/ *npl* the fittings in a house.

furniture /fur-ni-cher/ *n* the articles (tables, chairs, etc.) needed in a house or office.

furore /fyoo-ror-ri/ *n*, *also* **furor** /fyoo-roar/ (*US*) great excitement, craze, frenzy.

furrier /fu-ree-er/ *n* someone who deals in furs.

furrow /fu-ro/ *n* **1** the trench cut in the earth by a plough. **2** a wrinkle. • *vb* **1** to plough. **2** to wrinkle.

furry /fu-ree/ *adj* covered with fur.

further /fur-ther/ *adv* **1** besides. **2** farther. • *adj* **1** more distant. **2** more. • *vb* to help forward.

furthermore /fur-ther-more/ *adv* besides, in addition.

furthermost /fur-ther-most/ *adj* most distant (*also* **furthest**).

furtive /fur-tiv/ *adj* careful, done secretly.

fury /fyoo-ree/ *n* rage, great anger. • *adj* **furious**.

fuse[1] /fyooz/ *vb* **1** to melt by heat. **2** to melt together as a result of great heat. **3** (*of an electrical appliance or circuit*) to stop working or cause to stop working because of the melting of a fuse. **4** to join together. • *n* easily melted wire used to complete an electric current.

fuse[2] /fyooz/ *n* a tube of slow-burning substance used to explode shells, bombs, dynamite, etc.

fuselage /fyoo-su-lazh/ *n* the body of an aeroplane.

fusible /fyoo-zi-bul/ *adj* that can be fused or easily melted.

fusion /fyoo-zhun/ *n* **1** act of melting. **2** a joining to make one.

fuss /fuss/ *n* anxiety or excitement over unimportant things.

fussy /fu-see/ *adj* worrying over details, hard to please.

futile /fyoo-tile/ *adj* having no useful result. • *n* **futility**.

futon /foo-ton/ *n* a thin cushion placed on a frame that can be used as a bed or folded into a chair or couch.

future /fyoo-cher/ *adj* about to happen, coming. • *n* the time to come.

futuristic /fyoo-che-ri-stic/ *adj* of or having to do with the future; so advanced in design, etc as to seem from the future.

fuzz /fuzz/ *n* a mass of fine, light hair or similar substance.

fuzzy /fu-zee/ *adj* **1** covered in fuzz. **2** not clear, blurred.

G

G, g /jee/ **1** the seventh letter of the English alphabet. **2** (*mus*) the fifth note of the scale of C major.

gab /gab/ *vb* (**gabbed, gabbing**) (*sl*) to chatter or talk idly. • *n* idle chat. • **gift of the gab** the ability to speak well or at length.

gable /gay-bl/ *n* the pointed top of the end wall of a building with a sloping roof.

gadget /ga-jet/ *n* a small useful tool or machine.

gag /gag/ *vb* (**gagged, gagging**) **1** to stop someone speaking by forcibly stopping the mouth. **2** to prevent someone from speaking or writing freely about something. • *n* **1** something put in the mouth to prevent speech. **2** a joke.

gaggle /ga-gl/ *n* **1** a flock of geese. **2** a disorderly group of people.

gaily /gay-lee/ *see* gay.

gain /gane/ *vb* **1** to obtain. **2** to have an increase in. **3** to reduce the distance between oneself and someone or something. **4** (*fml*) to reach. • *n* profit, advantage.

gainful /gane-ful/ *adj* (*fml*) paid, profitable.

gait /gate/ *n* manner of walking.

gala /ga-la/ *n* a day or time of feasting and rejoicing.

galaxy /ga-lak-see/ *n* **1** a belt of stars stretching across the sky (e.g. the Milky Way). **2** a company of well-known, impressive, etc, people.

gale /gale/ *n* a strong wind.

gallant /ga-lant, ga-lant/ *adj* (*fml*) brave, noble. • *adv* **gallantly**.

galleon /gal-yun/ *n* (*old*) a large sailing ship with several decks, as used by the Spaniards in the 15th and 16th centuries.

gallery /ga-le-ree/ *n* **1** a raised floor over part of a church or theatre. **2** a narrow passage in a mine. **3** a room in which pictures, etc. are displayed.

galley /ga-lee/ *n* **1** (*old*) a long low ship with sails and oars. **2** a ship's kitchen.

gallon /ga-lon/ *n* in the imperial system, a measure for liquids or grain (=4 quarts, 3.785 litres, or 231 cubic inches).

gallop /ga-lop/ *n* a horse's fastest speed. • *vb* **1** to go at a gallop. **2** (*inf*) to move or do very quickly.

gallows /ga-loze/ *n or npl* a wooden frame for hanging criminals.

galore /ga-lore/ *adj* in plenty.

galoshes /ga-losh-ez/ *npl* overshoes, usually of rubber, which protect the shoes in wet weather.

galvanize /gal-va-nize/ *vb*, *also* **galvanise** **1** to put on a coat of metal by electricity, to electroplate. **2** to rouse to activity.

gamble /gam-bl/ *vb* **1** to play for money, to bet. **2** to take risks. • *n* a risk. • *n* **gambler**. • *n* **gambling**.

gambol /gam-bl/ *vb* to jump about playfully. • *also n*.

game¹ /game/ *n* **1** a sporting contest. **2** a single part of a set into which a game is divided. **3** an amusement or diversion, a pastime. **4** (*inf*) a scheme, a trick. **5** birds or animals hunted for sport. • *adj* **1** brave, plucky. **2** willing, ready. • *vb* to gamble. • **make game of** (*fml*) to make fun of, mock.

game² /game/ *adj* lame, injured.

gaming /gay-ming/ *n* **1** gambling. **2** the playing of computer games.

gander /gan-der/ *n* a male goose.

gang /gang/ *n* **1** a group of people, especially friends. **2** a group of people working on the same job. **3** a group of criminals working together.

gangrene /gang-green/ *n* the rotting away of a part of the body. • *adj* **gangrenous**.

gangster /gang-ster/ *n* a member of an organized gang of criminals.

gangway /gang-way/ *n* **1** a movable footbridge from a ship to the shore. **2** a passage between rows of seats.

gaol *see* jail.

gap /gap/ *n* **1** an opening. **2** a space between. **3** something missing.

gape /gape/ *vb* **1** to stare open-mouthed. **2** to be wide open.

gap year /gap year/ *n* a year's break taken by students, especially between school and university, usually spent travelling, doing voluntary work overseas etc.

garage /ga-ridge/ *n* **1** a building in which an automobile can be kept. **2** a shop where vehicles are repaired. **3** a petrol station

garb /garb/ (*old*) *n* dress, clothes. • *vb* to clothe.

garbage /gar-bage/ *n* (*esp US*) rubbish.

garbled /gar-buld/ *adj* mixed up and muddled.

garden /gar-den/ *n* a piece of land on which flowers or vegetables are grown. • *vb* to look after a garden, often as a hobby. • *n* **gardener**. • *n* **gardening**.

gargle /gar-gl/ vb to wash the throat with a mouthful of liquid by blowing it up and down in the back of the mouth. • n a liquid prepared for gargling.

gargoyle /gar-goyl/ n a grotesquely carved spout in the form of a person's or animal's head, for carrying away water from a roof gutter.

garish /gay-rish/ adj flashy, unpleasantly bright.

garland /gar-land/ n a wreath of flowers. • vb to decorate with a garland.

garlic /gar-lic/ n a plant with a strong-smelling bulb used in cookery.

garment /gar-ment/ n (fml) any article of clothing.

garnet /gar-net/ n a red mineral, sometimes a precious stone.

garnish /gar-nish/ vb to decorate.

garrison /ga-ri-son/ n the soldiers sent to a place to defend it.

garter /gar-ter/ n a band of elastic to hold up a stocking.

gas /gas/ n 1 matter in the form of an airlike vapour. 2 any of various gases or mixtures of gases used as fuel. 3 the vapour given off by a substance at a certain heat. 4 a feeling of discomfort caused by gases in the digestive tract. 5 (US) gasoline, petrol. • adj gaseous.

gash /gash/ n a wide, deep wound or cut. • vb to cut deeply.

gas mask /gas-mask/ n a mask that enables one to breathe when surrounded by poisonous gas.

gasoline /ga-so-leen/ (US) n petrol.

gasp /gasp/ vb 1 to breathe with difficulty, to pant. 2 to draw in the breath suddenly through the mouth. • n the act or sound of gasping.

gassy /ga-see/ adj full of gas, fizzy.

gastric /ga-stric/ adj having to do with the stomach.

gastronomy /ga-stron-o-mee/ n the art of good eating. • adj gastronomic /ga-stri-nom-ic/, gastronomical /ga-stri-nom-i-cal/.

gate /gate/ n 1 a movable frame of wood, iron, etc, to close an opening in a wall or fence. 2 an entrance or way out, especially in an airport. 3 the number of people who pay to see a game. 4 the total sum of money paid for entrance to a sports ground.

gateau, gâteau /ga-toe/ n (pl gateaux or gateaus) a large cake, often filled and decorated with cream.

gatecrash /gate-crash/ vb to attend a party, etc, without an invitation. • n gatecrasher.

gateway /gate-way/ n 1 the opening closed by a gate. 2 the way or path to.

gather /ga-ther/ vb 1 to bring or come together. 2 to collect, to pick. 3 to draw cloth together in small folds. 4 to come to the conclusion. • n a fold in cloth held in position by thread.

gathering /ga-ther-ing/ n a meeting.

gaudy /gaw-dee/ adj showy, flashy, too bright. • adv gaudily. • n gaudiness.

gauge /gage/ vb 1 to measure. 2 to make an estimate of. 3 to make a judgment about, to judge. • n 1 a measuring rod. 2 a measuring instrument. 3 the distance between the two rails of a railway. 4 a help to guessing accurately.

gaunt /gawnt/ adj very thin, haggard.

gauntlet /gawnt-let/ n 1 (old) an iron glove worn as part of a suit of armour. 2 a type of glove covering the wrist. • **run the gauntlet** to be criticized or attacked from all sides. • **throw down the gauntlet** to challenge.

gauze /gawz/ n a light cloth that one can see through. • adj gauzy.

gave /gave/ pt of give.

gawky /gaw-kee/, **gawkish** /gaw-kish/ adj clumsy, awkward.

gay /gay/ adj 1 (esp of men) homosexual. 2 connected with people who are homosexual. 3 (old) lively, fond of enjoyment, cheerful. • adv gaily. • n a person who is homosexual, especially a man.

gaze /gaze/ vb to look hard at without looking away. • n a fixed look.

gazelle /ga-zel/ n a small antelope.

gazette /ga-zet/ n a government news sheet containing official notices, appointments, etc.

gazetteer /ga-ze-teer/ n a book listing places in alphabetical order and telling where they can be found on a map.

gear /geer/ n 1 the set of tools, equipment, etc, used for a particular job, sport, expedition, etc. 2 any arrangement of levers, toothed wheels, etc, that passes motion from one part of a machine to another.

geese see **goose**.

gel /jel/ n a smooth, soft substance resembling jelly, often used in products for the skin or hair.

gelatine /je-la-tin/ n, also **gelatin** a jellylike substance made from boiled-down bones, etc, used as a thickening agent in jellies, etc.

gelignite /je-lig-nite/ n a powerful explosive.

gem /jem/ n 1 a precious stone. 2 anything

or anyone that is thought to be especially good.

gender /jen-der/ n **1** (gram) grouping of nouns roughly according to the sex (masculine, feminine or neuter) of the things they name. **2** (of a person or animal) the state of being male or female.

gene /jeen/ n any of the basic elements of heredity passed from parents to their offspring, that cause the offspring to have certain features that the parents have.

genealogist /jee-nee-al-o-jist/ n one who studies genealogy.

genealogy /jee-nee-al-o-jee/ n **1** the tracing of the history of a family to discover all its ancestors and branches. **2** a diagram showing this. • adj **genealogical**.

genera see **genus**.

general /je-ne-ral/ adj **1** including every one of a class or group. **2** not specialized. **3** common, usual, normal. **4** taken as a whole, overall. **5** widespread, public. **6** without details. • n **1** a high-ranking army officer. **2** the commander of an army.

generalize /je-ne-ra-lize/ vb, also **generalise 1** to work out from a few facts an idea that covers a great number of cases. **2** to talk in general terms without details. • n **generalization**.

generally /je-ne-ra-lee/ adv in most cases.

generate /je-ne-rate/ vb to bring into life, to produce, to be the cause of.

generation /je-ne-ray-shun/ n **1** the act of bringing into existence or producing. **2** a single step in family descent. **3** people living at the same time.

generator /je-ne-ray-tor/ n a machine for producing electricity, steam, etc.

generic /je-ne-ric/ adj being a member of a group or class (see **genus**). • n (of a drug, etc.) a product not patented or sold with a brand name.

generous /je-ne-rus/ adj **1** giving or given freely and gladly. **2** ready to see the good in others. • n **generosity**. • adv **generously**.

genetic /je-ne-tic/ adj of genes, of genetics.

genetic fingerprinting /je-ne-tic fing-ger prin-ting/ n see **DNA fingerprinting**.

genetically modified see **GM**.

genetics /je-ne-tics/ n the science of breeding and family characteristics.

genial /jee-nee-al/ adj friendly in manner, cheerful. • n **geniality**. • adv **genially**.

genie /jee-nee/ n (pl **genii** /jee-nee-ie/) a good or evil spirit in Eastern tales.

genital /je-ni-tal/ adj having to do with reproduction. • npl **genitals**, **genitalia** the genital organs (penis, testicles, vagina).

genius /jeen-yus/ n **1** extraordinary skill or ability. **2** a person of extraordinary intelligence. **3** (inf) a natural ability.

genome n a full set of chromosomes.

gent /jent/ n (hum, inf) short for **gentleman**.

gentile /jen-tile/ adj non-Jewish. • also n.

gentility /jen-ti-li-tee/ n the state of having good manners or being of good birth.

gentle /jen-tul/ adj **1** (old) well-born. **2** not rough or violent in manner, unwilling to hurt anyone. • n **gentleness**. • adv **gently**.

gentleman /jen-tul-man/ n (pl **gentlemen** /jen-tul-men/) **1** (fml) a man; sometimes considered more polite than 'man'. **2** (old) a man of good birth. **3** a well-mannered and kindly man.

gentlemanly /jen-tul-man-lee/ adj well-mannered.

gentry /jen-tree/ n people of good but not noble birth.

gents /jents/ n (inf) (short for gentlemen) a public toilet for men.

genuflect /jen-yu-flect/ vb (fml) to bend the knee in respect. • n **genuflection**.

genuine /jen-yoo-in/ adj **1** true, real. **2** sincere, without pretence or dishonesty. • adv **genuinely**. • n **genuineness**.

genus /jee-nus/ n (pl **genera** /je-ne-ra/) a kind or class of animals, plants, etc, with certain characteristics in common. • adj **generic**.

geography /jee-og-ra-fee/ n the study of the surface of the earth and its climate, peoples, cities, etc. • n **geographer**. • adj **geographic**, **geographical**.

geology /jee-o-lo-jee/ n the study of the rocks, etc, forming the earth's crust. • n **geologist**. • adj **geological**.

geometry /jee-om-e-tree/ n a branch of mathematics dealing with the measurement of lines, figures, and solids. • adjs **geometric**, **geometrical**.

geranium /je-ray-nee-um/ n a strongly scented plant, with red, pink, or white flowers.

gerbil /jer-bil/ n a small ratlike rodent, often kept as a pet.

germ /jerm/ n **1** a tiny living cell that has the power to grow into a plant or animal. **2** the beginning of anything. **3** a disease-carrying microbe.

German /jerman/ adj of or relating to Germany. • n a language spoken in Germany and Austria.

germicide /jer-mi-side/ n a substance that kills germs.

germinate /jer-mi-nate/ vb to begin to grow.

gesticulate /je-**sti**-cyu-late/ *vb* to make meaningful signs with the hands, especially while speaking, usually for emphasis. • *n* **gesticulation**.

gesture /**jes**-chur/ *n* **1** a movement of the hands, head, etc, to express feeling. **2** an action showing one's attitude or intentions. • *vb* to make a gesture.

get /get/ *vb* (*pt* **got**, *pp* **getting**, *pp* **got** *or* (*US*) **gotten**) **1** to obtain. **2** to reach. **3** to become.

geyser /**gie**-zer/ *n* a hot water spring that shoots up into the air.

ghastly /**gast**-lee/ *adj* **1** (*fml or lit*) deathly pale. **2** horrible, terrible. **3** (*inf*) very bad, ugly, etc. **4** (*inf*) unwell, upset. • *n* **ghastliness**.

gherkin /**ger**-kin/ *n* a small cucumber used for pickling.

ghetto /**ge**-toe/ *n* (*pl* **ghettos** *or* **ghettoes**) a part of a city, often poor, in which a certain group of people, often immigrants, lives.

ghost /**goast**/ *n* the spirit of a dead person appearing to one living. • *adjs* **ghostlike**, **ghostly**. • *n* **ghostliness**.

ghoul /**gool**/ *n* **1** a spirit said to prey on corpses. **2** a person who takes an unusually great interest in death, disaster, and other horrible things. • *adj* **ghoulish**.

giant /**jie**-ant/ *n* **1** in fairy stories, a huge man. **2** a person of unusually great height and size. **3** a person of very great ability or importance. • *f* **giantess**.

gibberish /**ji**-be-rish/ *n* nonsense, meaningless words.

gibbon /**gi**-bon/ *n* a type of ape.

gibe, jibe /**jibe**/ *vb* to mock, to jeer at. • *also n.*

giddy /**gi**-dee/ *adj* **1** dizzy. **2** changeable, not serious in character, fond of amusement. • *n* **giddiness**.

gift /gift/ *n* **1** a present. **2** a natural ability to do something. • *vb* to give as a present.

gifted /**gif**-ted/ *adj* having exceptional natural ability.

gig /gig/ *n* **1** (*inf*) a single booking for a jazz or pop band, etc; a single night's performance. **2** (*old*) a light two-wheeled carriage. • *vb* (**gigs, gigging, gigged**).

giga- *prefix* denoting a factor of 10^9 or a billion.

gigabyte /**gigga**-bite/ *n* (*comput*) 1024 bytes.

gigantic /jie-**gan**-tic/ *adj* huge, giantlike.

giggle /**gi**-gl/ *vb* to laugh quietly, but in a silly way.

gild /gild/ *vb* to cover with gold.

gill[1] /gil/ *n* a quarter of a pint.

gill[2] /gil/ *n* the organ through which a fish breathes.

gilt /gilt/ *adj* covered with gold or gold paint. • *n* the gold or imitation of gold used in gilding.

gimmick /**gi**-mic/ *n* an ingenious gadget or device to attract attention.

gin[1] /gin/ *n* a strong alcoholic drink flavoured with juniper berries.

gin[2] /gin/ *n* **1** a trap or snare. **2** a machine for separating cotton from its seeds.

ginger /**jin**-jer/ *n* **1** a hot-tasting root used as a spice. • *adj* of a reddish yellow colour.

gingerbread /**jin**-jer-bred/ *n* treacle cake flavoured with ginger.

gingerly /**jin**-jer-lee/ *adv* carefully, cautiously.

gingham /**ging**-am/ *n* a striped or checked cotton cloth.

gipsy /**jip**-see/ *see* **gypsy**.

giraffe /ji-**raf**/ *n* an African animal with a very long neck and long legs.

girder /**gir**-der/ *n* a heavy beam of iron or steel used to bridge an open space when building.

girdle /**gir**-dl/ *n* **1** a kind of belt. **2** (*fml or lit*) anything that surrounds. • *vb* to surround as with a belt.

girl /girl/ *n* **1** a female child. **2** a young woman. **3** a daughter. • *n* **girlhood**.

girlfriend /**girl**-frend/ *n* **1** a female friend. **2** a female romantic partner.

girlish /**gir**-lish/ *adj* like or of a girl.

Girl Guide /**girl** gide/ *n* a member of an international youth organization for girls.

girth /girth/ *n* **1** the measurement around the waist. **2** the distance around something cylindrical in shape. **3** a strap that holds the saddle in place on a horse's back.

gist /jist/ *n* the meaning, the most important part.

give /giv/ *vb* (*pt* **gave**, *pp* **given**) **1** to make a present of. **2** to hand over to. **3** to allow. **4** to utter. **5** to produce. **6** to organize, to hold. **7** to yield, bend, break, etc. • *n* **giver**. • **give and take** accepting some of another's views as correct. • **give away 1** to give as a gift. **2** to tell something secret. • **give ground** to go backward. • **give in** to admit defeat. • **give out** to report. • **give up 1** to leave to be taken by others. **2** to stop. **3** to lose hope. • **give way 1** to stop in order to allow someone or something to pass. **2** to be replaced by. **3** to break and fall.

glacial /**glay**-shal/ *adj* **1** of ice. **2** icy, very cold. **3** (*fml*) very cold in manner.

glacier /**glay**-sher/ *n* a large slow-moving river of ice.

glad /glad/ *adj* pleased, cheerful. • *adv* **gladly**. • *n* **gladness**.

gladden /gla-den/ *vb* to make glad.

glade /glade/ *n* (*fml*) a clear space in a wood.

gladiator /gla-dee-ay-tor/ *n* in Ancient Rome, a man trained to fight with other men or wild animals for public entertainment. • *adj* **gladiatorial.**

glamour /gla-mur/ *n*, *also* **glamor** (*US*) apparent charm and attractiveness that depends entirely on the outer appearance, dress, etc. • *adj* **glamorous.** • *vb* **glamorize**, *also* **glamorise.**

glance /glanss/ *n* a quick look. • *vb* **1** to look at for a moment. **2** to hit the side of something and fly off in another direction.

gland /gland/ *n* an organ in the body that produces certain fluids necessary to the health of the body. • *adj* **glandular.**

glare /glare/ *n* **1** a dazzling light. **2** an angry or fierce look. • *also vb.*

glaring /glay-ring/ *adj* **1** having a fierce look. **2** very obvious. • *adv* **glaringly.**

glass /glass/ *n* **1** hard, easily broken transparent material. **2** a mirror. **3** a glass drinking vessel. • *adj* made of glass.

glass ceiling /glass see-ling/ *n* a barrier, based on discrimination, which prevents someone, usually a woman, from getting a senior position in an organization.

glasses /gla-siz/ a pair of lenses set in a frame resting on the nose and ears, used to improve the wearer's eyesight or to protect the eyes from strong sunlight.

glaze /glaze/ *vb* **1** to fit with glass. **2** to cover with a smooth shiny surface. **3** to become fixed or glassy-looking. • *n* a smooth shiny surface.

glazier /glay-zher/ *n* one who fixes glass in windows.

gleam /gleem/ *n* **1** a small ray of light, especially one that disappears quickly. **2** a temporary appearance of some quality. • *vb* **1** to shine softly. **2** to be expressed with a sudden light, to be bright.

glee /glee/ *n* pleasure, joy.

gleeful /glee-ful/ *adj* joyful. • *adv* **gleefully.**

glen /glen/ *n* (*Scot*) a narrow valley.

glib /glib/ *adj* **1** quick to answer, able to find words easily, fluent. **2** spoken fluently and without hesitation. • *n* **glibness.**

glide /glide/ *vb* to move smoothly or without effort.

glider /glie-der/ *n* an aircraft with no engine.

glimmer /gli-mer/ *vb* to burn low and unsteadily, to shine faintly. • *n* **1** a low and unsteady light.

glimpse /glimss/ *n* a quick or passing view of. • *vb* to see for a moment only.

glint /glint/ *vb* to flash, to sparkle. • *n* **1** a brief flash of light. **2** a brief indication.

glisten /gli-sen/ *vb* to sparkle, to give a bright, steady light. • *also n.*

glitch /glich/ *n* something that goes unexpectedly wrong, especially with computers.

glitter /gli-ter/ *vb* to sparkle, to give a bright flickering light. • *also n.* • *adj* **glittery.**

gloat /gloat/ *vb* to look at with greedy or evil enjoyment.

global /glo-bal/ *adj* **1** affecting the whole world. **2** relating to or including the whole of something. • *adv* **globally.**

globalization /glo-ba-li-zay-shun/ *n*, *also* **globalisation** the process by which a business firm or organization begins to operate on an international basis.

global warming /glo-bal wawr-ming/ *n* a gradual increase in the world's temperatures believed to be caused, in part at least, by the **greenhouse effect.**

globe /globe/ *n* **1** a ball, a sphere. **2** anything ball-shaped. **3** the earth. **4** a map of the earth printed on to a ball.

globular /glob-yu-lar/ *adj* ball-shaped.

globule /glob-yul/ *n* a drop, a very small ball.

gloom /gloom/ *n* **1** darkness. **2** sadness.

gloomy /gloo-mee/ *adj* **1** dark, dim. **2** sad-looking, depressed.

glorify /glo-ri-fie/ *vb* **1** to praise or worship. **2** to make seem better, more beautiful, more important, etc. • *n* **glorification.**

glorious /glo-ree-us/ *adj* **1** splendid, magnificent. **2** famous.

glory /glo-ree/ *n* **1** honour, fame. **2** brightness, beauty, splendour. **3** worship, adoration. **4** a special cause for pride, respect, honour, etc. • *vb* to take pride in, to rejoice.

gloss[1] /gloss/ *n* a bright or shiny surface. • *vb* to give a shine to. • **gloss over** to try to make appear pleasing or satisfactory.

gloss[2] /gloss/ *n* **1** a note written in the margin or between lines. **2** an explanation, interpretation. • *vb* to provide with glosses, to annotate.

glossary /gloss-a-ree/ *n* a list of words with their meanings.

glossy /gloss-ee/ *adj* smooth and shining.

glove /gluv/ *n* a covering of cloth or leather for the hand, each finger being separately covered.

glow /glo/ *vb* **1** to give out light and heat but no flame. **2** to look or feel warm or red. • *n* **1** a bright steady light. **2** a warm look or feeling. **3** a good feeling.

glower /glaoo-er/ *vb* to give an angry look.

glowing /glo-ing/ *adj* **1** full of praise. **2** giving out heat.

glow-worm /glo-wurm/ *n* an insect that sends out a light in the dark.

glucose /gloo-cose/ *n* grape sugar, a natural sugar found in fruits and plants.

glue /gloo/ *n* a substance used for sticking things together. • *vb* to stick with glue.

gluey /gloo-ee/ *adj* sticky.

glum /glum/ *adj* **1** sad, gloomy. **2** downcast.

glut /glut/ *vb* (**glutted, glutting**) **1** to fill too full, to supply with more than is needed. **2** to stuff, to gorge oneself. • *n* too great an amount.

gluten /gloo-ten/ *n* a sticky protein found in wheat and some other cereal grains.

glutinous /gloot-nus/ *adj* (*fml*) sticky.

glutton /gluh-ten/ *n* **1** a person who eats too much. **2** (*inf*) a person who is always ready for more.

gluttonous /glut-nus/ *adj* greedy, too fond of food.

gluttony /glut-nee/ *n* a fondness for eating a lot, love of food.

glycerin /glis-rin/ *n* a colourless sweet liquid obtained from fats.

GM /jee-em/ *abbr* = **genetically modified**: food, e.g. from a plant, whose genetic material or structure has been altered by technological means to improve growth or inhibit disease.

gnarled /narld/ *adj* twisted and having a rough surface.

gnash /nash/ *vb* to strike the teeth together, to grind the teeth, often as a sign of emotion.

gnat /nat/ *n* a small biting insect.

gnaw /naw/ *vb* **1** to keep on biting at so as to wear away gradually. **2** to cause continued distress to.

gnome /nome/ *n* in fairytales, a mischievous fairy supposed to live underground.

gnu /noo/ *n* a large African antelope.

go /go/ *vb* (*pt* **went**, *pp* **gone**) **1** to move. **2** to become. • *n* going. • **go for** to attack. • **go hard with** (*fml*) to turn out badly for. • **go in for** to take interest in. • **go under** to fail.

go-ahead /go-a-hed/ *adj* ready to try out new ideas. • *n* permission to proceed.

goal /goal/ *n* **1** an aim, target, object of one's efforts. **2** in some games, the frame through which players try to pass the ball. **3** a score at football, hockey, etc.

goalkeeper /goal-kee-per/ *n* the player who defends a goal.

goat /goat/ *n* an animal with horns, related to the sheep.

goatee /go-tee/ *n* a neat pointed beard on a man's chin.

gobble /gob-ul/ *vb* **1** to eat quickly. **2** to make a noise like a turkey.

gobbledygook /gob-ul-dee-gook/ *n* language which seems meaningless because of the use of difficult words and complicated sentence structures.

go-between /go-bee-tween/ *n* one who arranges an agreement between two other parties.

goblet /gob-let/ *n* a drinking cup without a handle.

goblin /gob-lin/ *n* in fairytales, a mischievous fairy.

god /god/ *n* **1** any being that is worshipped for having supernatural powers. **2** (*cap*) in various religions, the creator of the world, the supreme being. **3** a man of superior charms or excellence.

goddess /god-ess/ *n* **1** a female god. **2** a woman of superior charms or excellence.

godfather /god-fa-ther/ *n* a man who makes the promises for a child at a Christian baptism. • *f* **godmother**. • *also* **godchild, goddaughter, god-parent, godson**.

God-fearing /god-fee-ring/ *adj* deeply religious.

godless /god-less/ *adj* (*fml*) not believing in God; wicked.

godlike /god-like/ *adj* **1** like God. **2** like a god.

godly /god-lee/ *adj* religious, following God's laws. • *n* godliness.

goes form of the verb **go** used with 'he', 'she', 'it' and 'one' or with singular nouns.

goggles /gog-ulz/ *npl* a type of eyeglasses, especially those worn to protect the eyes.

go-kart /go-kart/ *n* a small racing vehicle made of an open frame on four wheels with an engine.

gold /goald/ *n* **1** a precious metal. **2** wealth, money. **3** the colour of gold.

golden /goal-den/ *adj* **1** made of gold. **2** of the colour of gold. **3** valuable.

goldfinch /goald-finch/ *n* a beautiful singing bird.

goldfish /goald-fish/ *n* a small red Chinese carp, often kept in an aquarium or pond.

goldsmith /goald-smith/ *n* a worker in gold.

golf /golf/ *n* an outdoor game played with clubs and a hard ball. • *also vb.* • *n* golfer.

gondola /gon-du-la/ *n* **1** a long narrow boat used on the canals of Venice. **2** the car of an airship.

gondolier /gon-du-leer/ *n* a man who rows a gondola.

gone /gon/ *pp of* go.

gong /gong/ *n* a flat metal plate that makes a ringing sound when struck.

good /good/ *adj* **1** right, morally acceptable, virtuous. **2** of a high quality. **3** pleasant, agreeable, welcome. **4** fit, competent. **5** well-behaved. **6** kindly. **7** clever. **8** fit to be eaten. **9** beneficial.

goodbye, good-bye /good-bie/ *n and interj* a farewell greeting.

Good Friday /good frie-day/ *n* the Friday before Easter.

good-looking /good-loo-king/ *adj* handsome, attractive.

good-natured /good-nay-churd/ *adj* kindly.

goodness /good-ness/ *n* the quality of being good.

goods /goodz/ *npl* **1** movable property. **2** things for buying or selling.

goodwill /good-will/ *n* **1** kindly feeling. **2** the good name and popularity of a store or business.

Google, google /goo-gl/ *vb* (*TM*) to use the search engine Google to look for information on the Internet.

goose /gooss/ *n* (*pl* **geese** /geess/) **1** a web-footed farmyard fowl. **2** (*fml or old*) a foolish person.

gooseberry /gooss-be-ree/ *n* **1** a thorny shrub. **2** its edible berry. **3** an unwanted third person when two people, especially lovers, want to be alone.

goose pimples /gooss pimpels/ *npl* a roughness or bumpiness of the skin due to cold or fear. • *also* **goose flesh** /gooss flesh/, **goose bumps** /gooss bumps/.

gore[1] /gore/ *vb* to wound with a tusk or horn.

gore[2] /gore/ *n* (*fml or lit*) blood from a dead or wounded person, especially when formed into solid lumps. • *adj* **gory**.

gorge /gorge/ *n* **1** (*old*) the throat. **2** a deep narrow pass between hills. • **make one's gorge rise** to sicken, to fill with disgust. • *vb* to overeat, to eat greedily.

gorgeous /gawr-jus/ *adj* **1** (*inf*) very beautiful and glamorous. **2** splendid, magnificent, richly decorated or coloured. **3** (*inf*) giving a lot of pleasure, marvellous.

gorilla /gaw-ri-la/ *n* a large African ape.

gory *see* **gore**.

gosling /goz-ling/ *n* a young goose.

gospel /gos-pel/ *n* **1** (*usually cap*) the teaching of Jesus Christ. **2** in the Christian New Testament, the story of the life of Christ. **3** any complete system of beliefs. **4** (*inf*) the truth.

gossamer /gos-a-mer/ *n* **1** cobweblike threads floating in the air or resting on bushes. **2** any very light material. • *adj* very light.

gossip /gos-ip/ *n* **1** one who likes to hear and spread news about the private affairs of others. **2** idle talk. • *vb* **1** to spread stories about others. **2** to talk idly or chatter, often about other people.

got *pt, pp of* **get**.

Gothic /goth-ic/ *adj* in the pointed-arch style of architecture common in the Middle Ages.

Gouda /gow-da/ *n* a mild, round Dutch cheese.

gouge /gowj/ *n* a chisel with a curving blade for cutting grooves. • *vb* **1** to make a groove or hole in. **2** to scoop out, to force out.

gourd /goard/ *n* **1** a large fleshy fruit (e.g. cucumber, melon). **2** the hollow skin of a gourd used as a bottle or cup.

gourmand /goor-mawnd/ *n* **1** (*fml*) a greedy eater, a glutton. **2** a person who likes good food, often to excess.

gourmet /goor-may/ *n* a person who is a good judge of wines and food.

gout /gout/ *n* a disease causing painful swelling of the joints.

govern /gu-vern/ *vb* **1** to control and direct the affairs of. **2** to control, to guide, to influence. **3** to exercise restraint over, to control, to regulate.

governess /gu-ver-ness/ *n* a woman who looks after and teaches children in their home.

government /gu-ver-ment/ *n* **1** the act or way of ruling. **2** the group of people who direct the affairs of a country. • *adj* **governmental**.

governor /gu-ve-nor/ *n* **1** in the United States, a person who is elected as head of a state. **2** a member of the committee of people who govern a school, hospital, etc. **3** (*old*) a person governing a province or colony.

gown /goun/ *n* **1** a woman's dress, usually formal. **2** a long robe worn by members of clergy, teachers, lawyers, etc.

grab /grab/ *vb* (**grabbed, grabbing**) **1** to take hold of with a sudden quick movement. **2** to get or take something quickly and sometimes unfairly. **3** (*inf*) to affect, to influence, to find favour with. • *also n*.

grace /grase/ *n* **1** the mercy or kindness associated with God. **2** a sense of what is right or decent. **3** a delay allowed as a favour. **4** beauty and effortlessness of movement. **5** a short prayer said at meal times. **6** a title of respect used to dukes, archbishops, etc. • *n* **1** to honour. **2** to adorn.

graceful /grase-fool/ *adj* beautiful in appearance, style, form or movement. • *adv* **gracefully**.

gracious /gray-shus/ *adj* kind, pleasant, polite. • *adv* **graciously**.

grade /grade/ *n* 1 a placing in an order according to one's merit, rank, performance, etc. 2 rank. • *vb* 1 to arrange in grades. 2 to assign a grade to. 3 to pass or change from one thing to another gradually.

gradient /gray-dee-ent/ *n* 1 a slope. 2 the steepness of a slope.

gradual /gra-ju-wul/ *adj* slow and steady, little by little. • *adv* **gradually**.

graduate /gra-ju-wate/ *vb* 1 to receive an academic degree or diploma. 2 (*fml*) to divide into stages or equal spaces. • *n* /gra-ju-wit/ a person who holds an academic degree or diploma. • *adj* relating to people who already hold one academic degree or diploma.

graduation /gra-ju-**way**-shun/ *n* the receiving of an academic degree or dilpoma.

graffiti /gra-**fee**-tee/ *npl* (*sing* **graffito** (*rare*)) writing or drawings, often humorous or rude, scribbled or sprayed unofficially or illegally on walls or other surfaces in public places.

graft[1] /graft/ *vb* 1 to fix a piece cut from one plant onto another so that it grows into it. 2 to put skin cut from one part of the body on to another part. 3 to replace an organ of the body by one belonging to someone else; to transplant. • *n* the cutting or skin so grafted.

graft[2] /graft/ *n* (*inf*) 1 bribery and corruption. 2 wealth made by illegal use of office. 3 hard work.

Grail /grale/ *see* **Holy Grail**.

grain /grane/ *n* 1 the small hard seeds of some food plants, such as wheat or rice. 2 one of these seeds. 3 a very small hard particle. 4 a very small amount. 5 in the imperial system the smallest measure of weight (1 pound = 7000 grains). 6 the pattern of markings in wood, leather, etc. • *vb* to imitate the grain of wood when painting doors, etc.

gram /gram/ *n* the basic unit of weight in the metric system.

grammar /gra-mer/ *n* the science of the correct use of language. • **grammarian**.

grammatical /gra-ma-ti-cal/ *adj* correct in grammar.

granary /gra-na-ree/ *n* a storehouse for grain.

grand /grand/ *adj* 1 noble, magnificent, splendid. 2 important, proud, too proud. 3 pleasant. 4 wonderful, highly respected. 5 dignified.

grandeur /gran-jur/ *n* nobility, magnificence, splendidness.

grandfather /gran-fa-ther/ *n* the father of one's father or mother. • *f* **grandmother**. • *also* **grandchild, grand-daughter, grandparent, grandson**.

grandiose /gran-dee-oas/ *adj* meant to be splendid, intended to be impressive.

grand piano /grand pee-a-no/ *n* a large piano in which the strings are horizontal.

grandstand /grand-stand/ *n* rows of seats built on a rising slope to allow people a good view of a sports contest. • *vb* to show off to the audience or onlookers.

granite /gra-nit/ *n* a hard rock.

granny /gra-nee/ *n* (*inf*) a grandmother.

grant /grant/ *vb* 1 to give, to agree to, to allow. 2 (*fml*) to admit as true. • *n* something allowed or given, especially money given for a certain purpose.

granular /gran-yu-lar/ *adj* 1 of or like grains. 2 rough to the touch, rough in appearance.

granulate /gran-yu-late/ *vb* to break into grains or small pieces. • *adj* **granulated**.

granule /gran-yool/ *n* a small grain.

grape /grape/ *n* the fruit of the vine.

grapefruit /grape-froot/ *n* a large yellowish sharp-tasting citrus fruit.

graph /graf/ *n* a diagram in which different numbers, quantities, etc, are shown by dots and then joined up by lines so that they can be easily compared.

graphic /gra-fic/ *adj* 1 so well told that the events, etc, can be seen in the mind's eye. 2 drawn, concerned with drawing, painting, etc. • **graphics** *npl* information in the form of illustrations or diagrams.

graphite /gra-fite/ *n* a soft black form of carbon used in pencils.

grapple /gra-pl/ *vb* 1 to fight hand to hand, to take hold of and struggle with. 2 to struggle with.

grasp /grasp/ *vb* 1 to take firm hold of. 2 to understand. • *n* 1 firm hold. 2 reach. 3 understanding.

grasping /gra-sping/ *adj* mean, always wanting more money.

grass /grass/ *n* the common plant covering of the ground, usually green. • *adj* **grassy**.

grasshopper /grass-hop-er/ *n* a small jumping insect.

grate[1] /grate/ *n* a metal frame in a fireplace for holding the fire.

grate[2] /grate/ *vb* 1 to break down by rubbing on something rough. 2 to make a harsh sound, as of metal rubbing on metal. 3 to annoy, to irritate.

grateful /grate-ful/ *adj* thankful. • *adv* **gratefully**.

grater /gray-ter/ *n* an instrument with a rough surface for breaking down to crumbs or powder.

gratification /gra-ti-fi-**cay**-shun/ *n* pleasure, satisfaction.

gratify /gra-ti-fy/ *vb* **1** to please, to delight. **2** to satisfy.

grating /gray-ting/ *n* a framework of metal bars.

gratitude /gra-ti-chood/ *n* thankfulness.

gratuitous /gra-**choo**-i-tus/ *adj* **1** unasked-for, unwanted. **2** unnecessary, unjustified.

grave¹ /grave/ *n* the hole dug in the earth for a dead body.

grave² /grave/ *adj* serious, important.

gravel /gra-vel/ *n* **1** small stones or pebbles. **2** a mixture of small stones and sand used to make the surface of roads and paths.

gravestone /grave-stone/ *n* a memorial stone placed over a grave.

graveyard /grave-yard/ *n* a piece of land set aside for graves.

gravitate /gra-vi-tate/ *vb* **1** to move towards the centre. **2** to move in a certain direction as if drawn there by some force. • *n* **gravitation**.

gravity /gra-vi-tee/ *n* **1** seriousness, importance. **2** (*fml*) weight. **3** the force drawing bodies towards the centre of a larger body, e.g. the earth.

gravy /gray-vee/ *n* the juice got from meat when it is being cooked, often thickened and served as a sauce with the meat.

gray /gray/ *adj* US variant of **grey**.

graze¹ /graze/ *vb* **1** to touch or rub against lightly in passing. **2** to scrape along the surface. • *n* **1** a passing touch. **2** a scraping of the skin.

graze² /graze/ *vb* to eat growing grass, to feed on grass.

grazing /gray-zing/ *n* land with grass suitable for feeding cattle.

grease /greese/ *n* **1** fat in a soft state. **2** fatty or oily matter. • *vb* to smear with grease. • *adj* **greasy**.

great /grate/ *adj* **1** large in amount, number, or size. **2** important. **3** famous. **4** long in time. **5** more than is usual. **6** noble. **7** having possessed and made full use of extraordinary ability. • *adv* **greatly**. • *n* **greatness**.

great-grandfather /grate-gran-fa-ther/ *n* the father of one of one's grandparents. • *f* **great-grandmother**. • *also* **great-grandchild**, **great-grandparent**, etc.

greed /greed/ *n* **1** the desire to have more and more for oneself. **2** love of eating.

greedy /gree-dee/ *adj* always wanting more than one has. • *adv* **greedily**. • *n* **greediness**.

green /green/ *adj* **1** the colour of grass. **2** fresh, not ripe. **3** inexperienced. **4** concerned with the protection and conservation of the environment. • *n* **1** green colour. **2** a piece of ground covered with grass. **3** a person who is concerned with the protection and conservation of the environment. • *n* **greenness**. • *npl* green vegetables (e.g. cabbage).

greengrocer /green grow-ser/ *n* a person selling fruit and vegetables.

greenery /green-ree/ *n* green plants, foliage.

greenhouse /green-house/ *n* a glasshouse for growing plants.

greenhouse effect /green-house eh-**fect**/ *n* an increase in the earth's atmosphere of the amount of carbon dioxide and other gases that trap the heat of the sun and prevent it from escaping into space, thought to be a major cause of **global warming**.

greet /greet/ *vb* **1** to welcome. **2** to speak or send good wishes to someone. **3** to receive.

greeting /gree-ting/ *n* **1** welcome. **2** to speak or send good wishes to someone. **3** to receive.

gregarious /gre-**gay**-ree-us/ *adj* **1** fond of company. **2** (*fml*) living in flocks or herds.

grenade /gre-**nade**/ *n* a small bomb thrown by hand.

grew /groo/ *pt of* **grow**.

grey /gray/ *adj*, *also* **gray** (*US*) **1** black mixed with white in colour. **2** of the colour of hair whitened by age. • *also n*.

greyhound /gray-hound/ *n* a lean fast-running dog, used in dog-racing.

grid /grid/ *n* **1** a framework of metal bars. **2** a gridiron. **3** a large number of electric wires, rail lines, roads, etc, crossing and going in different directions. **4** the division of a map into squares to make map-reading easier.

griddle /gri-dul/ *n* a flat iron plate for baking cakes, etc, on a fire or the top of a stove.

gridiron /grid-ie-urn/ *n* a framework of iron bars used for cooking meat over a fire.

grief /greef/ *n* great sorrow. • **come to grief** to fail, to suffer a misfortune.

grievance /gree-vanse/ *n* a cause of complaint.

grieve /greeve/ *vb* **1** to sorrow, to mourn. **2** (*fml*) to cause sorrow.

grievous /gree-vus/ *adj* (*fml*) **1** causing pain or sorrow. **2** severe, serious.

grill /grill/ *n* **1** a framework of metal bars used in cooking that directs heat downward for cooking meat, etc. **2** food cooked on a grill. **3** an informal restaurant or diner. **4** a grille. • *vb* **1** to cook on a grill. **2** (*inf*) to question intensively.

grille /grill/ *n* a framework of metal bars fitted into a counter or door, or outside a window.

grim /grim/ *adj* **1** angry-looking, unsmiling. **2** unpleasant, depressing. **3** severe, harsh. **4** stubborn, determined. • *n* grimness.

grimace /gri-mas/ *vb* to twist the face to show one's feelings. • *also n*.

grime /grime/ *n* dirt, filth. • *adj* grimy.

grin /grin/ *vb* (**grinned, grinning**) to smile widely in pleasure. • *also n*.

grind /grinde/ *vb* (*pt, pp* **ground**) **1** to rub or crush to powder or small pieces. **2** to sharpen by rubbing. **3** to press together noisily. **4** (*inf*) to work hard. • *n* hard and uninteresting work. • *n* a certain grade of coffee.

grinder /grine-der/ *n* a person or thing that grinds.

grip /grip/ *vb* (**gripped, gripping**) **1** to take a firm hold of, to hold very tightly. **2** to seize the attention of. • *n* a firm or tight hold.

gripe /gripe/ *vb* **1** (*fml*) to cause a sharp pain in the stomach. **2** (*inf*) to complain. • *n* **1** a pain in the stomach. **2** (*inf*) a complaint.

grisly /griz-lee/ *adj* dreadful, frightening.

gristle /gri-sul/ *n* a tough elastic substance surrounding the joints of the bones. • *adj* gristly /griss-lee/.

grit /grit/ *n* **1** grains of sand or dust. **2** courage, determination. • *vb* (**gritted, gritting**) **1** to press (the teeth) tightly together. **2** to spread grit on (roads). • *adj* gritty.

grizzled /griz-uld/ *adj* streaked with grey, especially hair.

grizzly /griz-lee/ *adj* grey and grizzled.

grizzly bear /griz-lee bare/ *n* a large North American bear.

groan /groan/ *vb* to utter a low, deep sound expressing pain or anxiety. • *also n*.

grocer /gro-ser/ *n* a person who sells dry and tinned foods, tea, sugar, household supplies, etc.

grog /grog/ *n* (*old*) a mixture of strong alcoholic drink and cold water.

groggy /grog-ee/ *adj* not steady on the feet, weak.

groin /groin/ *n* the part of the body where the legs join the trunk.

groom /groom/ *n* **1** a person who cares for horses. **2** *also* **bridegroom** a man who is being married.

groomsman /groomz-man/ *n* a male friend or relative who accompanies the bridegroom at a wedding.

groove /groov/ *n* a long, narrow hollow, such as that made by a tool in wood. • *vb* to make a groove in.

grope /grope/ *vb* to feel with one's hands for something unseen.

gross /grawss/ *adj* **1** fat and overfed. **2** coarse, vulgar, impolite. **3** (*inf*) disgusting, repulsive. **4** very noticeable, glaringly obvious. **5** whole, complete, total. • *n* **1** twelve dozen, 144. **2** the whole. • *adv* grossly.

grossness /gross-ness/ *n* rudeness, vulgarity.

grotesque /gro-**tesk**/ *adj* **1** strangely shaped, distorted, fantastic. **2** ridiculously exaggerated, unreasonable, absurd, foolish.

grotto /graw-toe/ *n* (*pl* **grottoes**) a cave, often an artificial one in a park or shop.

ground[1] /ground/ *n* **1** the surface of the earth, land. **2** a piece of land used for a particular purpose. **3** (*often pl*) a reason. • *vb* **1** (*of a ship*) to run ashore. **2** (*of an aeroplane*) to come to or keep on the ground. **3** to base. **4** to teach the basic facts to. • *npl* **1** the tiny pieces of matter that sink to the bottom of a liquid. **2** the land surrounding a large house, castle, etc.

ground[2] /ground/ *pt and pp of* grind.

ground floor /ground flore/ *n* the storey of a building on the same level as the ground.

grounding /groun-ding/ *n* knowledge of the elementary part of a subject.

groundless /ground-less/ *adj* without a reason.

groundskeeper /groundz-kee-per/ *n* the person in charge of maintaining a sports field.

groundwork /ground-wurk/ *n* work that must be done well in the beginning if later work on the subject or task is to succeed.

group /groop/ *n* **1** a number of persons or things taken together. **2** a set of people who play music or sing together. • *vb* to put or go into a group.

grouse[1] /grouse/ *n* (*pl* **grouse**) a small fowl hunted on the moors as game.

grouse[2] /grouse/ *vb* (*inf*) to grumble, to complain. • *also n*.

grove /grove/ *n* (*fml*) a small wood.

grovel /gruov-el/ *vb* **1** to lie face downward in humility or fear. **2** to humble oneself, to behave with humility.

grow /gro/ *vb* (*pt* **grew**, *pp* **grown**) **1** to become bigger. **2** (*of plants*) to have life.

3 to become. **4** to plant and rear. **5** to increase the size of. • *n* **growth**.

growl /groul/ *vb* to utter a low harsh sound, as a dog when angry. • *also n*.

grown *pp of* **grow**.

grown-up /gro-nup/ *n* a fully grown person.

growth *see* **grow**.

grub /grub/ *vb* (**grubbed**, **grubbing**) **1** to dig, to root out. **2** to search for by digging. **3** (*inf*) to search around for. • *n* **1** the form of an insect when it comes out of the egg. **2** (*inf*) food.

grubby /gru-bee/ *adj* dirty.

grudge /grudge/ *vb* **1** to be unwilling to give. **2** to be displeased by another's success, to envy. • *n* a deep feeling of ill-will, dislike, resentment, etc.

gruel /grool/ *n* (*old*) a light food made by boiling meal in water.

gruelling /groo-ling/ *adj*, *also* **grueling** (*US*) very difficult and tiring.

gruesome /groo-sum/ *adj* horrible, very unpleasant.

gruff /gruff/ *adj* **1** deep and rough. **2** rough, angry-sounding.

grumble /grum-bul/ *vb* to complain, to express discontent. • *also n*. • *n* **grumbler**.

grumpy /grum-pee/ *adj* (*inf*) cross, ill-tempered.

grunt /grunt/ *vb* to make a noise like a pig. • *also n*.

guarantee /ga-ran-tee/ *n* **1** a promise to pay money on behalf of another person if that person fails to pay money he or she has promised to pay. **2** a person who undertakes to see that another keeps his or her promise, especially to repay money; a guarantor. **3** a promise, usually in the form of a written statement, that if an article bought is unsatisfactory, it will be repaired or replaced. **4** a thing that makes something likely or certain. • *vb* **1** to promise. **2** to undertake to see that a promise is kept.

guarantor /ga-ran-tawr/ *n* one who hands over something as a guarantee and loses it if the promise is not kept.

guard /gard/ *vb* **1** to watch over, to protect. **2** to defend against attack. • *n* **1** something that protects. **2** a person, such as a soldier or prison officer, who watches over a person or place to prevent escape, attack, etc. **3** a group of persons whose duty it is to watch over and defend something or someone. **4** the official in charge of a train. **5** a position in which one can defend or protect oneself, a state of watchfulness.

guarded /gar-did/ *adj* careful, cautious.

guardian /gar-dee-an/ *n* **1** a person who has the legal duty to take care of a child. **2** (*fml*) a keeper.

guava /gwa-va/ *n* a tropical tree or its fruit.

guerrilla, guerilla /gu-ri-la/ *n* a member of an unofficial small military group that makes sudden, unexpected attacks.

guess /ges/ *vb* **1** to put forward an opinion or solution without knowing the facts. **2** (*inf*) to suppose, to consider likely. • *n* an opinion or judgment that may be wrong as it is formed on insufficient knowledge.

guesswork /ges-wurk/ *n* a number of connected guesses.

guest /gest/ *n* **1** a visitor to a house. **2** a person staying in a hotel.

guffaw /gu-faw/ *vb* to laugh loudly or rudely. • *also n*.

guidance /gie-danse/ *n* help and advice.

guide /gide/ *vb* **1** to lead to the place desired. **2** to show the way. **3** to direct, to influence. • *n* **1** a person who shows the way. **2** an adviser, a person who directs or influences one's behaviour. **3** a guidebook. **4** a person who leads people around a place, pointing out things of interest. **5** a thing that helps one to form an opinion or make a calculation.

guidebook /gide-book/ *n* a book describing a place and giving information about it.

guide dog /gide-dog/ *n* a dog trained to lead a blind person.

guild /gild/ *n* a group of people who meet for a particular purpose.

guilder /gil-der/ *n* formerly the currency unit of the Netherlands, until the introduction of the euro in 2002.

guile /gile/ *n* (*fml*) deceit, trickery, cunning skill. • *adjs* **guileful, guileless**.

guillotine /gi-le-teen/ *n* **1** a machine formerly used in France for beheading people. **2** a machine for cutting paper.

guilt /gilt/ *n* **1** the fact of having done wrong, the fact of having committed a crime. **2** blame or responsibility for wrongdoing. **3** a sense of shame, uneasiness, etc, caused by the knowledge of having done wrong. • *adj* **guiltless**.

guilty /gilt-lee/ *adj* **1** having done wrong, having broken a law. **2** responsible for behaviour that is morally wrong or socially unacceptable. **3** feeling or showing a sense of guilt or shame.

guinea fowl /gi-nee foul/ *n* a large spotted edible bird.

guinea pig /gi-nee-pig/ *n* **1** a small tailless rodent, often kept as a pet. **2** a person made use of for the purpose of an experiment.

guise /gize/ *n* **1** dress. **2** appearance.

guitar /gi-**tar**/ *n* a six-stringed musical instrument.

gulf /gulf/ *n* **1** an inlet of the sea, a long bay. **2** a deep hollow. **3** an area of serious difference or separation.

gull[1] /gul/ *n* a long-winged sea bird.

gull[2] /gul/ *vb* (*old*) to cheat, to deceive. • *n* one who has been cheated, one easily deceived.

gullet /gu-let/ *n* the food passage from the mouth to the stomach; the throat.

gullible /gu-li-bul/ *adj* easily deceived.

gully /gu-lee/ *n* a deep channel worn by running water.

gulp /gulp/ *vb* **1** to eat quickly, to swallow in large mouthfuls. **2** to make a swallowing movement. • *also n*.

gum[1] /gum/ *n* the flesh in which the teeth are set.

gum[2] /gum/ *n* **1** the sticky juice of trees. **2** a liquid used for sticking things together. **3** chewing gum • *vb* (**gummed, gumming**) to stick with gum.

gumboil /gum-boil/ *n* a painful swelling on the gum.

gumboot /gum-boot/ *n* a rubber boot.

gummy /gu-mee/ *adj* sticky.

gumption /gum-shun/ *n* common sense, good sense.

gum tree /gum-tree/ *n* a tree from which gum is obtained.

gun /gun/ *n* any weapon that fires bullets or shells by means of explosive. • *vb* (**gunned, gunning**) to shoot or hunt with a gun.

gunboat /gun-boat/ *n* a small warship.

gundog /gun-dog/ *n* a dog trained to accompany hunters and to fetch game that has been shot.

gunfire /gun-fire/ *n* the sound of guns being fired.

gunmetal /gun-met-al/ *n* **1** a mixture of copper and tin. **2** a dull-grey colour.

gunner /gu-ner/ *n* a man trained to fire large guns.

gunpowder /gun-pou-der/ *n* a type of explosive.

gunrunning /gun-ru-ning/ *n* taking guns into a country against its laws.

gunshot /gun-shot/ *n* **1** the firing of a gun. **2** the distance a gun can fire.

gunsmith /gun-smith/ *n* a person who makes or repairs guns.

gurgle /gur-gul/ *vb* **1** to flow with a bubbling sound. **2** to make a noise resembling this. • *also n*.

guru /goo-roo/ *n* a spiritual leader or guide.

gush /gush/ *n* a sudden or strong flow. • *vb* **1** to flow out strongly. **2** to talk as if one felt something very deeply; to speak insincerely.

gusset /gu-set/ *n* a piece of cloth put into a garment to strengthen part of it.

gust /gust/ *n* a sudden violent rush of wind.

gusto /gu-sto/ *n* keen enjoyment, eagerness.

gusty /gu-stee/ *adj* **1** windy. **2** in short violent bursts.

gut /gut/ *n* **1** a tube in the body that takes the waste matter from the stomach. **2** a strong cord used for violin strings, fishing lines, etc. • *vb* (**gutted, gutting**) **1** to take out the inner parts. **2** to remove or destroy all except the walls of a building. • *npl* (*inf*) **1** the bowels, intestines. **2** bravery, courage.

gutter /gu-ter/ *n* **1** a passage at the edge of a roof or at the side of the road to carry away water. **2** the lowest, poorest level of society. • *vb* to run down in drops, as wax on a candle.

guttural /gu-te-ral/ *adj* **1** having to do with the throat. **2** made or seeming to be made in the throat, harsh.

guy[1] /gie/ *n* a rope to steady anything (e.g. a tent).

guy[2] /gie/ *n* **1** a man or boy. **2** (*inf*) a person. **3** a model representing Guy Fawkes, burned on November 5 in memory of his attempted attack on the Houses of Parliament in 1605.

guzzle /gu-zul/ *vb* (*inf*) to eat or drink greedily.

gym /jim/ *n* a gymnasium.

gymkhana /jim-**ka**-na/ *n* a sports meeting for races, horse racing, horse jumping, etc.

gymnasium /jim-**nay**-zee-um/ *n* (*pl* **gymnasia** *or* **gymnasiums**) a room or hall with equipment for physical exercise.

gymnast /jim-nast/ *n* a person who is skilled in gymnastics. • *adj* **gymnastic**.

gymnastics /jim-**nast**-ics/ *npl* exercises to develop the muscles of the body.

gynaecology /gie-ne-**col**-u-jee/ *n*, *also* **gynecology** (*US*) the branch of medicine dealing with the female reproductive system.

gypsy /jip-see/ *n* a member of a travelling people.

gyrate /jie-rate/ *vb* **1** to move in circles. **2** to spin round. • *n* **gyration**.

gyroscope /jie-ro-scope/ *n* an instrument that is sometimes used to keep ships, aircraft, etc steady.

H

H, h /aitch/ the eighth letter of the English alphabet.

ha /ha/ *interj* **1** a sound used to express surprise, wonder, triumph. **2** the sound of a laugh.

habit /ha-bit/ *n* **1** a fixed way of doing something without having to think about it; someone's ordinary way of doing things; something that a person does regularly. **2** dress, especially of a monk or rider.

habitable /ha-bi-ta-bul/ *adj* that may be lived in.

habitat /ha-bi-tat/ *n* the place or surroundings in which a plant or animal is usually found.

habitation /ha-bi-**tay**-shun/ *n* **1** the act of living in a place. **2** the place where a person lives.

habitual /ha-**bich**-wul/ *adj* **1** usual. **2** having formed a certain habit.

habituate /ha-bi-chu-wate/ *vb* (*fml*) to make used to.

hack¹ /hack/ *vb* to cut roughly or unevenly. • *n* **1** a tool for cutting or hacking. **2** a dry, harsh cough.

hack² /hack/ *n* **1** a hired horse. **2** a person hired to do uninteresting written work.

hacker /ha-ker/ *n* **1** a person who hacks. **2** a highly skilled computer user who tries to access unauthorized files.

hacksaw /hak-saw/ *n* a saw for cutting metal.

had /had/ *vb* past tense of have.

haddock /ha-dock/ *n* a sea fish of the cod family, used as food.

haematology /hee-ma-**tol**-u-jee/ *n*, *also* **hematology** (*US*) the study of the blood.

haemoglobin /hee-mo-glo-bin/ *n*, *also* **hemoglobin** (*US*) the red matter that gives blood its colour.

haemophilia /hee-mo-**fil**-ee-a/ *n*, *also* **hemophilia** (*US*) a condition where the blood does not clot properly when a person bleeds.

haemorrhage /hem-ridge/ *n*, *also* **hemorrhage** (*US*) heavy bleeding.

haemorrhoid /hem-a-roid/ *n*, *also* **hemorrhoid** (*US*) a painful swelling of a vein near the anus, usually with bleeding.

haft /haft/ *n* (*fml or lit*) a handle.

hag /hag/ *n* **1** a female demon or evil spirit. **2** an ugly, often mean, old woman.

haggard /ha-gard/ *adj* pale, thin-faced, and tired looking.

haggis /ha-gis/ *n* a Scottish dish in which the heart, liver and lungs of a sheep are minced, mixed with oatmeal and seasoning and boiled in a sheep's stomach.

haggle /ha-gul/ *vb* to try to get a seller to lower his or her price.

haiku /hie-koo/ *n* a Japanese poem of three unrhymed lines of five, seven, and five syllables, often about nature.

hail¹ /hail/ *n* **1** frozen rain. **2** a shower of anything. • *vb* **1** to rain hail. **2** to pour down.

hail² /hail/ *vb* **1** to call to, to greet. **2** to shout to a person to try to catch his or her attention. • *interj* a call of greeting. • **hail from** to come from.

hailstone /hail-stone/ *n* a pellet of hail.

hailstorm /hail-storm/ *n* a storm in which hail falls.

hair /hair/ *n* any or all of the threadlike growths covering the skin of humans and animals. • *adj* **hairless**, **hairy** /hay-ree/. • **to split hairs** to point out differences so slight that they could be overlooked.

hairbrush /hair-brush/ *n* a brush for grooming the hair.

haircut /hair-cut/ *n* a cutting of the hair of the head, or the style in which this is done.

hairdo /hair-do/ *n* the style in which hair is arranged.

hairdresser /hair-dre-ser/ *n* a person who cuts, styles, etc, hair as a job.

hairnet /hair-net/ *n* a net cap for keeping the hair in place.

hairpiece /hair-peess/ *n* a wig.

hairpin /hair-pin/ *n* a small, usually U-shaped, piece of wire for keeping the hair in place or a headdress on. • *adj* shaped like a hairpin.

hair-raising /hair-ray-zing/ *adj* terrifying, thought of as causing the hair to stand on end.

hair spray /hair spray/ *n* a liquid sprayed on the hair to hold it in place.

hairstyle /hair-stile/ *n* a style of hairdressing, often one that is fashionable.

hairy /hay-ree/ *adj* covered with hair.

hajj /hadge/ *n* the religious trip to Mecca that every Muslim is expected to make at least once.

hake /hake/ *n* a fish like the cod, used as food.

halal /ha-lal/ *n* meat from an animal that has been killed according to Muslim law. • *also adj*.

halcyon /hal-see-yon/ *n* the kingfisher. • *adj* calm, peaceful. • **halcyon days** a time of happiness and peace.

half /haf/ *n* (*pl* **halves** /hahvz/) one of two equal parts. • *also adj*.

half brother /haf bru-ther/ *n* a brother by one parent only.

halfhearted /haf-har-ted/ *adj* lacking interest and energy, not eager.

half-hour /haf-our/ *n* 30 minutes.

half-moon /haf-moon/ *n* **1** the moon in its first or last quarter phase. **2** anything shaped like a half-moon or crescent.

half sister /haf si-ster/ *n* a sister by one parent only.

halftime /haf-time/ *n* the rest period between the halves of a football game, etc.

halfway /haf-way/ *adj* equally distant between two places.

halibut /ha-li-but/ *n* a large flatfish, used as food.

hall /hol/ *n* **1** a large public room. **2** the room or passage at the entrance to a house or between rooms.

hallelujah /ha-le-loo-ya/ *n* an exclamation or song of praise to God. • *also interj*.

hallmark /hawl-mark/ *n* **1** an official mark stamped on things made of gold, silver or platinum. **2** a mark or symbol that shows the quality of a person, thing, etc.

hallow /ha-lo/ *vb* **1** to make holy. **2** to treat as being holy.

hallowed /ha-lode/ *adj* sacred or holy.

Halloween /ha-lo-ween/ *n* the eve of All Saints' Day.

hallucinate /ha-loo-si-nate/ *vb* to see something that is not there.

hallucination /ha-loo-si-nay-shun/ *n* **1** the seeing of something that is not there. **2** something imagined as though it is really there. • *adj* **hallucinatory**.

hallway /hawl-way/ *n* a passageway between the entrance and interior of the house or between rooms.

halo /hay-loe/ *n* **1** a circle of light around the Sun or Moon. **2** a coloured ring or ring of light around the head of a holy person, e.g. in a painting.

halt[1] /holt/ *vb* to stop. • *n* a stop.

halt[2] /holt/ *vb* **1** (*old*) to limp. **2** to hesitate. • *adj* lame, limping.

halter /hawl-ter/ *n* **1** a rope or strap fitted on to the head of a horse for leading it. **2** a rope for hanging a person. **3** a dress or top held up by a strap that goes round the wearer's neck leaving the shoulders bare.

halve /hav/ *vb* to cut or break into halves.

halves *see* **half**.

ham /ham/ *n* **1** the back of the thigh. **2** the thigh of a pig salted and dried and used as food. **3** (*inf*) an actor who exaggerates his or her actions and speech.

hambone /ham-bone/ *n* the bone of a ham.

hamburger /ham-bur-ger/ a flat round patty made of ground beef, fried or grilled, and usually eaten in a bun, often known as a **burger** /bur-ger/.

hamlet /ham-let/ *n* a very small village.

hammer /ham-er/ *n* **1** a tool for pounding nails, beating metal, etc. **2** part of a machine or device that strikes. • *vb* **1** to drive or beat with a hammer. **2** to strike hard.

hammered /ham-erd/ *adj* shaped or marked by hammer blows.

hammerhead /ham-er-hed/ *n* any of a family of large sharks with large, mallet-shaped heads.

hammertoe /ham-er-toe/ *n* a condition in which the first joint of a toe is bent downward permanently.

hammock /ham-ock/ *n* a bed made of a strip of canvas or network hung up at the ends.

hamper[1] /ham-per/ *n* a large basket.

hamper[2] /ham-per/ *vb* to prevent from moving freely.

hamster /ham-ster/ *n* a small rodent with large cheek pouches, often kept as a pet.

hamstring /ham-string/ *n* the tendon behind the knee. • *vb* (*pt, pp* **hamstrung**) **1** to make lame by cutting the hamstring. **2** to prevent from acting freely.

hand /hand/ *n* **1** the end of the arm below the wrist. **2** a worker. **3** a sailor on a ship. **4** the cards given to one player in a card game. **5** a person's style of writing. **6** the pointer of a clock or watch. **7** a measure of 0.1 metres, used in measuring a horse's height at the shoulder. • *vb* to give with the hand. **8** a share, a part, an influence. • **hand in glove with** in league with. • **hand-to-hand** at close quarters. • **hand-to-mouth** with only just enough money to live on with nothing for the future. • **out of hand** out of control. • **upper hand** control. • **to wash one's hands of** to refuse to have anything more to do with.

handbag /hand-bag/ *n* a small bag that contains the owner's possessions, usually carried by women.

handball /hand-bol/ *n* **1** a game in which a small ball is batted against a wall by hand by opposing players. **2** the ball used in this game.

handbill /hand-bill/ *n* a small printed notice.

handbook /hand-book/ *n* a small useful book giving information or instructions. •

handcart /hand-cart/ *n* a small cart, often with two wheels, pulled or pushed by hand.

handcraft /hand-craft/ *vb* to make by hand with craftsmanship.

handcuff /hand-cuff/ *vb* to put handcuffs on. • *npl* **handcuffs** metal rings joined by a chain, locked on the wrists of prisoners.

handful /hand-fool/ *n* **1** as much as can be held in one hand. **2** a small number or amount.

hand grenade /hand gri-nade/ *n* a small, round, handheld bomb that is thrown at its target after pulling out a fuse.

handgun /hand-gun/ *n* any firearm that is held and fired while being held in only one hand.

handheld /hand-held/ *adj* small enough to be held in the hand while being used.

handhold /hand-hoald/ *n* a secure grip or hold with the hand.

handicap /han-di-cap/ *vb* (**handicapped, handicapping**) **1** in sports or races, to give a certain advantage to weaker competitors so that they have an equal chance of winning. **2** to obstruct, to put at a disadvantage. • *n* **1** in sports or games, an arrangement that allows all competitors to start with an equal chance of winning. **2** an obstruction, a disadvantage. **3** a physical or mental disability.

handicraft /han-di-craft/ *n* skilled work done by hand. • *n* **handicraftsperson**.

handily /han-di-lee/ *adv* with no trouble, easily.

handiwork /han-di-wurk/ *n* **1** work done with a person's hands. **2** something done or caused by someone.

handkerchief /hang-ker-chif/ *n* a cloth for wiping the nose.

handle /han-dul/ *vb* **1** to feel, use, or hold with the hand. **2** to deal with. • *n* that part of a thing made to be held in the hand.

handlebar /han-dul-bar/ *n* the bent rod with which a person steers a bicycle.

handler /hand-ler/ *n* a person or thing that handles, trains, or manages.

handmade /hand-made/ *adj* made by hand, not by machine.

hand-me-down /hand-mee-down/ *n* something that has been used and then passed along to someone else.

handout /han-dout/ *n* **1** a gift of food, clothing, etc, as to a poor person. **2** a leaflet or printed notice handed out for information.

handpick /hand-pick/ *vb* to choose with care for a special purpose.

hand puppet /hand pu-pet/ *n* a puppet that fits over the hand and is moved by the fingers.

handrail /hand-rail/ *n* a rail used as a guard or support, as along a staircase.

handsaw /hand-saw/ *n* a hand-held saw.

handsel /hand-sel/ *n* a present for good luck.

handset /hand-set/ *n* a telephone mouthpiece, receiver, and dial buttons in a single unit.

handshake /hand-shake/ *n* a gripping and shaking of each other's hand in greeting.

handsome /hand-sum/ *adj* **1** good-looking. **2** generous.

handspring /hand-spring/ *n* a tumble in which a person turns over in midair with one or both hands touching the ground.

handstand /hand-stand/ *n* the act of standing upside down on the hands.

handwriting /hand-rie-ting/ *n* the way a person writes.

handwritten /hand-ri-ten/ *adj* written by hand, with pen, pencil, etc.

handy /han-dee/ *adj* **1** clever in using the hands, skilful. **2** useful and simple. **3** ready, available. **4** near. • *n* **handiness**.

hang /hang/ *vb* **1** (*pt*, *pp* **hung**) to fix one part to something above and allow the rest to drop. **2** to remain steady in the air, as certain birds. **3** to let fall. **4** (*pt*, *pp* **hanged**) to kill a criminal by putting a rope round the neck and then letting him or her drop suddenly so that the neck is broken.

hangar /hang-ar/ *n* a large shelter in which aeroplanes are kept.

hanger /hang-er/ *n* a thing from which a garment is hung.

hanger-on /hang-er-on/ *n* (*pl* **hangers-on**) a person who supports another in the hope of gaining some advantage.

hang gliding /hang glie-ding/ *n* the sport of gliding through the air while hanging from a large kite-like device.

hangman /hang-man/ *n* a person whose job it is to hang criminals.

hangnail /hang-nale/ *n* a bit of torn skin hanging at the side or base of a fingernail.

hangout /hang-out/ *n* a place where a group of people go frequently.

hangover /hang-oa-ver/ *n* the sick feeling a person gets after drinking too much alcohol.

hang-up /hang-up/ *n* a feeling of worry or embarrassment about something, often unjustified.

hank /hangk/ *n* a coil of thread or wool.

hanker /hang-ker/ *vb* to want greatly, to long for.

hankie /hang-kee/ *n* a handkerchief.

hansom /han-sum/ *n* (*old*) a two-wheeled carriage pulled by one horse.

Hanukkah /hon-i-ca/ *n* an 8-day Jewish

festival taking place in November or December.

haphazard /hap-**ha**-zard/ *adj* chance, unplanned. • *adv* **haphazardly**.

hapless /**hap**-less/ *adj* (*fml*) unfortunate, unlucky.

happen /**ha**-pen/ *vb* 1 to take place. 2 to come about by chance.

happening /**ha**-pe-ning/ *n* an event.

happy /**ha**-pee/ *adj* 1 lucky. 2 pleased, joyous. 3 pleasant, joyful. 4 suitable. • *n* **happiness**.

happy-go-lucky /ha-pee-go-**lu**-kee/ *adj* not easily worried, carefree.

happy hour /ha-pee our/ *n* a time when a bar sells its drinks at reduced prices.

harangue /ha-**rang**/ *n* a loud speech. • *vb* to speak loudly and forcefully.

harass /ha-**rass**/ *vb* 1 to attack again and again. 2 to worry or disturb constantly or frequently.

harbour /**har**-bur/ *n*, *also* **harbor** (*US*) 1 a place of safety for ships. 2 a place of shelter. • *vb* 1 to give shelter. 2 to keep in the mind.

hard /hard/ *adj* 1 firm, solid. 2 unfeeling, unkind, cruel. 3 difficult. 4 harsh, severe. • *adv* 1 with force. 2 with great effort. 3 close. 4 with great attention. • **hard of hearing** fairly deaf. • **hard up** (*inf*) having little money.

hardboard /**hard**-board/ *n* a building material made by pressing and heating wood chips.

hard-boiled /hard-**boild**/ *adj* cooked in boiling water until it is solid throughout, as with eggs.

hard copy /hard **caw**-pee/ *n* a computer printout.

hard disk /hard disk/ *n* a computer disk on which data and programs are stored.

hard drive /hard drive/ *n* a computer drive for hard disks.

harden /**har**-den/ *n* to make hard or harder.

hardily /**har**-di-lee/ *adv* in a hardy manner.

hardiness /**har**-dee-ness/ *n* toughness, strength.

hardly /**hard**-lee/ *adv* 1 almost not. 2 only just, not really. 3 with difficulty.

hardness /**hard**-ness/ *n* the state of being hard.

hardship /**hard**-ship/ *n* poor or difficult conditions.

hardware /**hard**-ware/ *n* 1 household articles and tools made of metal. 2 the mechanical and electronic parts of a computer system.

hard-wired /hard-**wirde**/ *adj* directly connected to a computer.

hardwood /**hard**-wood/ *n* any tough, heavy timber with a compact grain.

hardy /**har**-dee/ *adj* 1 strong, tough. 2 (*old*) bold.

hare /hare/ *n* a fast-running animal with rabbit-like ears and long hind legs.

harebell /**hare**-bell/ *n* a bluebell-shaped flower.

harebrained /**hare**-braned/ *adj* thoughtless, careless, hasty.

harelip /**hare**-lip/ *n* an upper lip divided in the centre, like that of the hare.

haricot /**ha**-ri-co/ *n* a type of French bean.

harm /harm/ *n* hurt, damage, wrong. • *also* *vb*. • *adj* **harmful**, **harmless** /**harm**-less/.

harmonic /har-**mon**-ic/ *adj* having to do with harmony.

harmonica /har-**mon**-i-ca/ *n* a mouth organ played to make music.

harmonics /har-**mon**-ics/ *n* the study of harmony in music.

harmonious /har-mo-**nee**-us/ *adj* 1 pleasant-sounding. 2 friendly. 3 pleasant to the eye.

harmonium /har-**mo**-nee-um/ *n* a musical wind instrument, like a small organ.

harmonize /**har**-mo-nize/ *vb*, *also* **harmonise** 1 to cause to be in harmony or agreement, to be in harmony or agreement. 2 to play or sing notes that sound pleasantly with the others.

harmony /**har**-mo-nee/ *n* 1 agreement, friendship. 2 the pleasant effect made by parts combining into a whole. 3 the playing at one time of musical notes that are pleasant when sounded together. 4 pleasant sound.

harness /**har**-ness/ *n* the straps, etc, by which a horse is fastened to its load. • *vb* to put a harness on. • **to die in harness** to die while still doing a job.

harp /harp/ *n* a stringed musical instrument played by the fingers. • *n* **harpist**. • *vb* **harp on** to keep on talking about one subject.

harpoon /har-**poon**/ *n* a long spear used in hunting whales. • *vb* to strike with a harpoon.

harpsichord /**harp**-see-cawrd/ *n* a string instrument played by striking keys.

harpy /**har**-pee/ *n* 1 in Greek legend, a monster with the head and upper body of a woman and the lower body of a bird. 2 a cruel or nasty woman.

harrowing /**ha**-ro-wing/ *adj* very distressing.

harsh /harsh/ *adj* 1 rough and unpleasant to hear, see, etc. 2 unkind, severe, cruel.

hart /hart/ *n* (*old*) a stag or male red deer.

harvest /**har**-vest/ *n* 1 the time when the ripe crops are cut and gathered. 2 the crops so gathered. • *vb* to cut and gather. • *n* **harvester**.

has /haz/ *vb* form of the verb **have** used with 'he', 'she', 'it', 'one' or any singular noun.

has-been /haz-bin/ *n* a person or thing that was popular but is no longer so.

hash /hash/ *n* **1** a dish of finely chopped or shredded meat. **2** (*inf*) something done badly, a mess. • *vb* to finely chop or shred.

hash browns /hash **brounz**/ *n* potatoes that have been chopped and then fried in a pan.

hassle /ha-sul/ (*inf*) *vb* to annoy someone, especially by repeatedly asking them to do something. • *n* a difficult or troublesome situation.

haste /haste/ *n* speed, hurry.

hasten /hay-sen/ *vb* (*fml*) to hurry.

hasty *adj* **1** done in a hurry. **2** done too quickly, rash. **3** quick to lose one's temper.

hat /hat/ *n* a head covering.

hatch[1] /hach/ *vb* **1** to produce. **2** to break out of the egg. **3** to work out in secret. • *n* the young hatched from eggs.

hatch[2] /hach/ *n* **1** an open space in a wall or roof or the deck of a ship. **2** the lower half of a split door.

hatch[3] /hach/ *vb* to decorate (in drawing, stone-carving) with thin lines that cross one another.

hatchback /hach-back/ *n* a car with a rear door or section that swings up to provide access to a storage area.

hatchet /ha-chet/ *n* a small axe. • **bury the hatchet** to end a quarrel.

hatchling /hach-ling/ *n* a recently hatched bird, fish, turtle, etc.

hatchway /hach-way/ *n* **1** an opening in the ship's deck through which cargo is loaded. **2** a similar opening in the floor or roof of a building.

hate /hate/ *vb* to dislike greatly. • *n* great dislike.

hate crime /hate crime/ *n* a crime against a person that has been committed because of race, religion, gender, etc.

hateful /hate-fool/ *adj* deserving or causing hate.

hatred /hate-red/ *n* great dislike.

hatter /ha-ter/ *n* one who makes, sells, or cleans hats.

hat trick /hat-trick/ *n* **1** the scoring of three goals in a game, such as soccer, ice hockey, etc. **2** the act of achieving something three times.

haughty /haw-tee/ *adj* proud, behaving as if better than others. • *n* **haughtiness**.

haul /hawl/ *vb* to pull by force, to drag. • *n* **1** a pull. **2** an amount taken or caught (e.g. of fish).

haulier /hawl-eer/ *n* a company that carries goods in lorries or trains for other companies.

haunch /hawnch/ *n* the thick part of the body around the hips.

haunt /hawnt/ *vb* **1** to visit again and again, to go often to. **2** to visit as a ghost. **3** to be always in the thoughts of someone. • *n* a place often visited. • *n*, *adj* **haunting**.

haunted /hawn-tid/ *adj* visited by ghosts.

haunting /hawn-ting/ *adj* often recurring in the mind, not easily forgotten.

have /hav/ *vb* (*pt*, *pp* **had**; *indicative* **I have, he has; we, they have**) **1** to possess, to own, to hold. **2** to be forced. • **to have to do with** to be concerned in.

haven /hay-ven/ *n* **1** (*old*) a harbour. **2** (*fml*) a place of safety, a shelter.

haversack /ha-ver-sack/ *n* a bag carried on the back, used for carrying food, etc, on a journey.

havoc /ha-voc/ *n* destruction, ruin.

haw /haw/ *n* the berry of the hawthorn.

hawk[1] /hawk/ *n* a bird of prey. • *vb* to hunt with a hawk.

hawk[2] /hawk/ *vb* to sell. • *n* **hawker**.

hawthorn /haw-thawrn/ *n* a thorny tree with white, pink, or red flowers and small berries.

hay /hay/ *n* grass that has been cut and dried.

hay fever /hay fee-ver/ *n* an illness caused by an allergy to dust or pollen.

hayfield /hay-feeld/ *n* a field of grass to be made into hay.

hayloft /hay-loft/ *n* a loft or upper storey of a barn for storing hay.

haystack /hay-stack/ *n* a large pile of hay.

haywire /hay-wire/ *adj* (*inf*) tangled up, mixed up, in a state of disorder.

hazard /ha-zard/ *n* **1** risk. **2** (*fml*) chance. **3** a piece of rough ground or a bunker on a golf course. • *vb* **1** to risk. **2** to put in danger. **3** to put forward.

hazardous /ha-zar-dus/ *adj* risky, dangerous.

haze /haze/ *n* **1** a thin mist. **2** vagueness of mind.

hazel /hay-zel/ *n* **1** a tree with edible nuts. **2** a greenish brown colour.

hazelnut /hay-zel-nut/ *n* the nut of a hazel tree.

hazy /hay-zee/ *adj* **1** misty. **2** not clear. **3** doubtful. • *n* **haziness**.

H-bomb /aich-bom/ *n* hydrogen bomb, a very powerful weapon of mass destruction.

he /hee/ *pron* the man, boy, or male animal previously mentioned.

head /hed/ *n* **1** the top part of the body. **2** a

person's mind. **3** a chief person. **4** the top or front part. **5** the marker of a division in an essay or speech. **6** the beginning of a stream. **7** a piece of high land jutting out into the sea. • *vb* **1** to lead. **2** to be first. **3** to direct. **4** to strike. • *adj* coming from the front.

headache /hed-ake/ *n* pain in the head.

headband /hed-band/ *n* a band worn around the head for decoration.

head cold /hed-coald/ *n* a common cold resulting in a clogged or blocked nose and head.

head count /hed count/ *n* the act of counting people in a certain group.

headdress /hed-dress/ *n* a covering for the head.

header /hed-er/ *n* (*inf*) **1** a fall or dive forward. **2** the act of hitting a ball with the head.

headfirst /hed-**furst**/ *adv* with the head in front, headlong.

headhunter /hed-hun-ter/ *n* **1** a member of certain cultures that remove the heads of enemies and keep them as trophies. **2** an agent whose job it is to find highly skilled people for employment. • *vb* **headhunt**.

heading /hed-ing/ *n* the words written at the top of a page or above a piece of writing.

headland /hed-land/ *n* a piece of high land jutting out into the sea.

headlight /hed-lite/ *n* a light at the front, especially of a car, truck, etc.

headline /hed-line/ *n* **1** the line in large print above a piece of news in a newspaper. **2** the line of print at the top of a page of a book. • *v* **1** to give something a headline. **2** to be the leading performer.

headlock /hed-loc/ *n* in wrestling, a hold in which one person's head is held between the arm and the body of another.

headlong /hed-long/ *adv* **1** hastily and rashly. **2** with the head first. • *adj* **1** rash. **2** headfirst.

headmaster /hed-**ma**-ster/ *n* the man who is head of a school. • *f* **headmistress**.

headmost /hed-moast/ *adj* in the lead.

head-on /hed-on/ *adj*, *adv* with the head or front being first.

headphone /hed-foan/ *n* a listening device made of small speakers held to the ears by a band.

headpiece /hed-peess/ *n* a covering for the head.

headquarters /hed-kwawr-terz/ *n* the office of those who are in control or command.

headrest /hed-rest/ *n* a support for the head, as on a chair.

headroom /hed-room/ *n* the space available above a person's head.

headset /hed-set/ *n* a headphone with a small microphone for two-way communication.

headship /hed-ship/ *n* the position of a leader or person of authority.

headshrinker /hed-shring-ker/ *n* **1** a head-hunter who shrinks the heads of his victims. **2** (*sl*) a psychiatrist.

headspring /hed-spring/ *n* a fountain or source.

headstand /hed-stand/ *n* the act of standing upside down on the head, usually helped by the hands.

headstone /hed-stone/ *n* the stone placed over a dead person's grave in his or her memory.

headstream /hed-stream/ *n* a stream forming the source of another, larger stream or river.

headstrong /hed-strong/ *adj* determined to have one's own way.

head-to-head /hed-to-hed/ *adj*, *adv* in direct confrontation.

headwaters /hed-waw-terz/ *n* the beginnings of a large stream or river.

headway /hed-way/ *n* advance, improvement.

head wind /hed-wind/ *n* a wind blowing directly opposite the direction a person is trying to go.

heady /hed-ee/ *adj* **1** excited. **2** strong, having a quick effect on the senses.

heal /heel/ *vb* to make or become well or healthy, to cure.

healer /hee-ler/ *n* one who heals or cures.

health /helth/ *n* **1** the state of being well. **2** the state of being free from illness.

healthcare /helth-care/ *n* the treatment of illness.

health club /helth club/ *n* a private club for exercise.

healthful /helth-ful/ *adj* (*fml*) causing good health.

health spa /helth spa/ *n* a place people go to exercise.

healthy /helth-ee/ *adj* **1** having good health. **2** causing good health.

heap /heep/ *n* a number of things lying one on top of another. • *vb* to put one on top of another, to pile.

hear /heer/ *vb* (*pt*, *pp* **heard**) **1** to perceive sounds by the ear. **2** to listen.

hearer /hee-rer/ *n* a person or animal who listens.

hearing /hee-ring/ *n* **1** the power to hear sounds. **2** the distance at which a person can hear something. **3** the examining of evidence by a judge.

hearing aid /hee-ring ade/ *n* a small, battery-powered device that helps a person to hear better.

hearing-impaired /hee-ring-im-**paird**/ adj unable to hear properly.

hearsay /**heer**-say/ n what people say though not perhaps the truth; gossip.

hearse /hurss/ n a car or carriage for a coffin at a funeral.

heart /hart/ n 1 the organ that keeps the blood flowing through the body. 2 the central or most important part of anything. 3 the centre of a person's thoughts and emotions. 4 the cause of life in anything. 5 enthusiasm, determination. 6 kindly feelings, especially love. 7 npl a suit of playing cards. 8 a thing shaped like a heart. • **learn by heart** to memorize. • **take to heart** to feel deeply about.

heartache /**har**-take/ n sorrow.

heart attack /hart a-**tack**/ n a sudden, painful, sometimes fatal medical condition in which the heart stops working normally.

heartbeat /**hart**-beet/ n the pulse of the heart pumping blood through the body.

heartbreak /**hart**-brake/ n sorrow, grief. • adj **heartbreaking**.

heartbreaker /**hart**-bray-ker/ n someone or something that causes heartbreak.

heartbroken /**hart**-bro-ken/ adj overcome by sorrow or grief.

heartburn /**hart**-burn/ n a burning feeling in the stomach, caused by indigestion.

hearten /**har**-ten/ vb to encourage, to cheer up.

heart failure /hart **fale**-yur/ n the failure of the heart to beat or to pump blood through the body.

heartfelt /**hart**-felt/ adj sincere.

hearth /harth/ n 1 the floor of a fireplace. 2 the fireside.

heartily /**har**-ti-lee/ adv sincerely, friendly, with zest.

heartland /**hart**-land/ n 1 a geographically central area having importance in politics, strategy, etc. 2 an area that is of particular importance for an activity, political party, etc.

heartless /**hart**-less/ adj having no kind feelings.

heart-rending /**hart**-ren-ding/ adj causing great sorrow or grief.

heartsease /**harts**-eez/ n 1 peace of mind. 2 the pansy.

heartsick /**hart**-sick/ adj (old) very sad or sorrowful.

heartstrings /**hart**-stringz/ n deepest feelings.

heart-to-heart /hart-to-**hart**/ adj intimate.

heartwarming /**hart**-wawr-ming/ adj such as to cause a warm glow of good feelings.

heartwood /**hart**-wood/ n the hard, nonliving, older wood at the centre of a tree trunk.

hearty /**har**-tee/ adj 1 cheerful, sometimes too cheerful. 2 sincere. 3 healthy. 4 large.

heat /heet/ n 1 hotness, warmth. 2 anger, excitement. 3 pressure to do something. 4 a division of a race from which the winners go on to the final. • vb to make or become warm or hot.

heated /**hee**-ted/ adj 1 hot. 2 angry.

heater /**hee**-ter/ n a device for heating a room, car, water, etc.

heath /heeth/ n 1 a stretch of wasteland, especially in Britain, that is covered in low shrubs. 2 a low-growing evergreen shrub.

heathen /**hee**-then/ n 1 a person who is not a member of one of the world's main religions; someone who believes in more than one God. 2 a person who is not religious. • also adj.

heather /**he**-ther/ n a low-growing shrub with purple or white flowers.

heat shield /**heet** sheeld/ n any device protecting against heat, especially those fastened to a spacecraft.

heatstroke /**heet**-stroke/ n a serious failure of the body's ability to regulate its heat, resulting in high fever, dry skin, collapse, and sometimes coma.

heat wave /**heet** wave/ n a long spell of hot weather.

heave /heev/ vb 1 to lift, to raise with effort. 2 to move up and down regularly. 3 to pull hard. 4 to utter with effort. • n 1 an upward throw. 2 a pull. • **heave to** (of a ship) to stop moving.

heaven /**he**-ven/ n 1 the sky. 2 the everlasting presence of God. 3 the dwelling place of the gods. 4 in some religions, the happiness enjoyed by good people after death.

heavenly /**he**-ven-lee/ adj 1 having to do with heaven or the sky. 2 (inf) delightful.

heavy /**he**-vee/ adj 1 having weight, of great weight. 2 of more than the usual size, amount, force, etc. 3 dull, dark, and cloudy. 4 sleepy. 5 sad. 6 difficult to digest. 7 busy, full of activity. • n **heaviness**. • adv **heavily**.

heavy-duty /**he**-vee-**dyoo**-tee/ adj strong and not easily damaged or worn out.

heavy-handed /**he**-vee-**han**-did/ adj 1 without a light touch. 2 cruel.

heavy metal /**he**-vee **me**-tal/ n 1 any metal that has a gravity greater than 5. 2 a form of rock music that features loud rhythms, guitar, and sometimes shouted lyrics.

heavyweight /**he**-vee-wate/ n 1 a person or animal weighing much more than average. 2 an athlete who is in the heaviest weight division. 3 a person of power and importance.

Hebrew /hee-broo/ *n* the language of the Jewish people. • *also adj.* • *adj* **Hebraic**.

heckle /he-cul/ *vb* to put difficult questions to a public speaker. • *n* **heckler**.

hectare /hec-tare/ *n* a unit of measurement equal to 10,000 square metres or 2.471 acres.

hectic /hec-tic/ *adj* 1 feverish. 2 busy, very active.

hedge /hedge/ *n* 1 a fence of bushes, shrubs, etc. 2 means of defence or protection. • *vb* 1 to surround with a hedge. 2 to avoid giving a clear, direct answer.

hedgehog /hedge-hog/ *n* a small animal, covered with prickles, that can roll itself into a ball.

hedgerow /hedge-roe/ *n* a line of bushes, shrubs, etc, forming a hedge.

heed /heed/ *vb* to pay attention to, to notice. • *n* care, attention. • *adj* **heedful, heedless**.

heel[1] /heel/ *n* 1 the back part of the foot. 2 the part of a shoe, etc, under the heel of the foot. • *vb* 1 to strike with the heel. 2 to put a heel on. • **bring to heel** to get control over. • **down at heel** poorly or untidily dressed. • **take to one's heels** to run away.

heel[2] /heel/ *vb* to lean over to one side.

hefty /hef-tee/ *adj* 1 rather heavy, big and strong. 2 large and heavy. 3 powerful. 4 (*inf*) large, substantial. • *n* **heft** weight, heaviness, bulk.

heifer /he-fer/ *n* a young cow.

height /hite/ *n* 1 the distance from top to bottom. 2 the state of being high. 3 a high place. 4 a hill. 5 the highest degree of something.

heighten /hie-ten/ *vb* 1 to make higher. 2 to increase.

Heimlich manoeuvre /hime-lick ma-noo-ver/ *n* a way of stopping a person from choking by which the user puts sudden, sharp pressure to the stomach area to force wind up through the windpipe so as to clear the blockage.

heinous /hey-nus/ *adj* very bad, wicked.

heir /air/ *n* a person who receives property or a title after the death of the previous owner. • *f* **heiress**.

heirloom /air-loom/ *n* a valuable object that has been the property of a family for many generations.

heist /hiest/ *n* a robbery.

held *vb pt, pp of* **hold**.

helicopter /he-li-cop-ter/ *n* a type of aircraft with propellers that enable it to go straight up or down.

helium /hee-lee-um/ *n* a very light gas.

hell /hell/ *n* 1 in some religions, the place where the wicked are punished after death. 2 everlasting banishment from God. 3 a place of great evil or suffering.

hellish /he-lish/ *adj* 1 having to do with or like hell. 2 (*inf*) very bad, extremely unpleasant.

hello /he-low/ *interj* used as a greeting or to attract attention.

helm /helm/ *n* a steering wheel or handle on a ship. • **at the helm** in control or command.

helmet /hel-met/ *n* 1 (*old*) head armour. 2 a protective covering for the head.

help /help/ *vb* 1 to aid, to assist. 2 to give what is needed. 3 to serve someone in a shop. 4 to make it easier for something to happen. 5 to avoid. • *n* aid, assistance. • *n* **helper**.

helpful /help-ful/ *adj* 1 willing to help. 2 useful.

helping /help-ing/ *n* a person's share of a dish of food.

helpless /help-less/ *adj* unable to help oneself.

helter-skelter /hel-ter-skel-ter/ *adj* carelessly hurried. • *adv* in a hurry and confusion. • *n* a spiral slide.

hem /hem/ *n* the border of a garment folded back and sewn. • *vb* (**hemmed, hemming**) to sew a hem. • **hem in** to surround closely.

he-man /hee-man/ *n* a strong man.

hematology *n* US variant of **haematology**.

hemisphere /he-mi-sfeer/ *n* 1 half of the world. 2 a map showing half of the world. 3 half of a sphere.

hemline /hem-line/ *n* the bottom edge of a skirt, coat, etc, which is usually hemmed.

hemlock /hem-lock/ *n* a poisonous plant.

hemoglobin *n* US variant of **haemoglobin**.

hemophilia *n* US variant of **haemophilia**.

hemorrhage *n* US variant of **haemorrhage**.

hemorrhoid *n* US variant of **haemorrhoid**.

hemp /hemp/ *n* 1 a grasslike plant from whose fibres ropes are made. 2 a drug made from the plant.

hen /hen/ *n* a female bird, especially a farmyard fowl.

henchman /hench-man/ *n* a follower, a trusty supporter. • *pl* **henchmen**.

henna /he-na/ *n* 1 a plant with white or red flowers. 2 a dye taken from the leaves of this plant. 3 reddish brown.

hen night /hen nite/ *n* (*inf*), *also* **hen party** /hen par-tee/ a party for women held just before one of the women gets married.

hepatitis /he-pa-tie-tis/ *n* irritation and swelling of the liver.

heptagon /hep-ta-gon/ *n* a seven-sided figure.

heptathlon /hep-tath-lon/ *n* a contest, usually for women, in which there are seven events,

100-metre hurdles, shot put, high jump, 200-metre dash, long jump, javelin throw, and 800-metre run.

her /hur/ *objective pron* **1** the female person or animal being referred to. **2** *poss* of or belonging to her.

herald /he-rald/ *n* **1** (*old*) a person who makes important announcements to the public. **2** a sign of something to come. • *vb* **1** to announce the approach of someone or something. **2** to be a sign of.

herb /herb/ *n* **1** any plant whose stem dies away during the winter. **2** a plant used for medicine or for flavouring food.

herbaceous /her-**bay**-shus/ *adj* having to do with or full of herbs. • **herbaceous border** a flower bed with plants that flower year after year.

herbal /her-bal/ *adj* of herbs.

herbalist /her-ba-list/ *n* a person who studies or sells herbs, often for medical purposes.

herbivore /her-bi-vore/ *n* an animal that eats plants and grasses. • **herbivorous** *adj* eating grass or herbs.

herd /herd/ *n* **1** a flock of animals. **2** a large crowd of people. • *vb* **1** (*inf*) to crowd or collect together. **2** to look after a herd. **3** to drive.

herdsman /herdz-man/ *n* a person who looks after a herd.

here /heer/ *adv* at or in this place.

hereafter /hee-raf-ter/ *adv* after this time. • *n* the life after death.

hereby /heer-bie/ *adv* by or through this, by this means.

hereditary /hi-**re**-di-ta-ree/ *adj* passed on from parents to children.

heredity /hi-**re**-di-tee/ *n* the passing on of qualities from parents to children.

heresy *n* an opinion contrary to the orthodox religious opinion.

heretic /he-re-tic/ *n* a person who teaches a heresy. • *adj* **heretical**.

heritable /he-ri-ta-bul/ *adj* able to be passed on from parents to children.

heritage /he-ri-tage/ *n* **1** that which is passed on to a person by his or her parents. **2** things that have been passed on from earlier generations.

hermit /her-mit/ *n* a person who lives alone or away from other people, originally often for religious reasons.

hernia /her-nee-a/ *n* a break in the wall of muscle in the front of the stomach.

hero /hee-ro/ *n* (*pl* **heroes**) **1** a brave person, someone admired for his brave deeds. **2** the chief character in a play or novel. • *f* **heroine**.

heroic /he-**ro**-ic/ *adj* **1** brave. **2** having to do with heroes. • *adv* **heroically**. • *n* **heroics**.

heroin /he-ro-in/ *n* a habit-forming pain-killing drug obtained from opium.

heroine *see* **hero**.

heroism /he-ro-i-zum/ *n* bravery.

heron /he-ron/ *n* a water bird with long legs and neck.

herpes /her-peez/ *n* a disease that causes small blisters on the skin.

herpetology /her-pe-**tol**-o-jee/ *n* the study of reptiles.

herring /he-ring/ *n* a small sea fish used as food.

herringbone /he-ring-bone/ *adj* with a pattern like the backbone of a herring.

herring gull /he-ring gull/ *n* the common sea gull of the Northern Hemisphere with grey and white feathers and black wing tips.

hers /herz/ *poss pron* of or belonging to her.

herself /her-**self**/ **1** *reflex* form of her. **2** *pron* her real, true, or actual self.

hertz /herts/ *n* a unit of measurement for the number of waves, vibrations, etc per unit of time.

hesitance /he-zi-tanse/, **hesitancy** /he-zi-tan-see/, **hesitation** /he-zi-**tay**-shun/ *n* doubt, act of hesitating, indecision.

hesitant /he-zi-tant/ *adj* doubtful, undecided.

hesitate /he-zi-tate/ *vb* **1** to stop for a moment before doing something or speaking. **2** to be undecided.

hessian /he-shan/ a coarse cloth used for sacks.

heterosexual /he-te-ro-**sek**-shal/ *adj* of different sexes; being attracted to the opposite sex.

hew /hyoo/ *n* (*fml*) to cut by a number of strong blows, to chop as with an axe. • *adj* **hewn**.

hex /heks/ *n* a spell believed to bring bad luck, a jinx.

hexagon /hek-sa-gon/ *n* a six-sided figure. • *adj* **hexagonal**.

hexagram /hek-sa-gram/ *n* a six-sided star.

hey /hay/ *interj* used to attract attention or express surprise or delight; sometimes used as a greeting.

heyday /hay-day/ *n* full strength, the time of life when a person's abilities, etc, reach their full power.

hi /hie/ *interj* hello.

hiatus /hie-ay-tus/ *n* **1** a break in a piece of writing or a speech. **2** a gap.

hibernate /hie-ber-nate/ *vb* to pass the winter in sleep, as certain animals do. • *n* **hibernation**.

hibiscus /hi-**bi**-scuss/ *n* a kind of plant or shrub with large, colourful flowers.

hiccup /hi-cup/ *n* **1** a sudden, short stoppage of the breath. **2** the sound caused by this. **3** a small delay or interruption. • *vb* (**hiccupped, hiccupping**) to have hiccups.

hickory /**hic**-ree/ *n* an North American tree with very hard wood.

hide[1] /hide/ *vb* (**hid, hidden**) **1** to put or keep out of sight. **2** to keep secret. • *n* a camouflaged place used by bird-watchers, hunters, etc.

hide[2] /hide/ *n* the skin of an animal.

hide-and-seek /hide-and-**seek**/ *n* a game in which one player tries to find the other players, who have all hidden.

hideaway /hie-da-way/ *n* a place where a person can hide.

hideous /hi-dee-us/ *adj* **1** frightful. **2** very ugly.

hide-out /hie-dout/ *n* a place to hide.

hiding[1] /hie-ding/ *n* the condition of being hidden.

hiding[2] /hie-ding/ *n* a thrashing, a beating.

hierarchy /hie-rar-kee/ *n* **1** an arrangement in order, putting the most important first. **2** the group of people in an organization who have power or control. • *adj* **hierarchical**.

hieroglyph /hie-ro-glif/, **hieroglyphic** /hie-ro-**gli**-fic/ *n* a picture or sign standing for a word or sound, as in ancient Egyptian writing.

hieroglyphics /hie-ro-gli-fics/ *n* **1** a system of writing that uses hieroglyphs. **2** (*inf*) writing that is difficult to read.

high /hie/ *adj* **1** being a certain distance up. **2** being above normal level. **3** raised above. **4** of important rank. **5** morally good. **6** expensive. • *also adv*. • **on a high horse** wanting to be treated with great respect; haughty.

higher education /hie-er e-joo-**cay**-shun/ *n* college or university education.

high-five /hie-**five**/ *n* the slapping of another person's upraised, open hand in celebration.

high jump /hie jump/ *n* a contest to see who can jump the highest over a bar set up between two posts.

highland /hie-land/ *n* **1** land well above sea level, land containing many hills or mountains. **2** (**the Highlands**) the northern, mountainous part of Scotland.

Highlander /hie-lan-der/ *n* a person who lives in the Highlands.

highlight /hie-lite/ *n* **1** a part on which light is brightest. **2** the most important or interesting part of something • *v* **1** to mark with something to make lighter or brighter. **2** to emphasize.

highlighter /hie-lie-ter/ *n* a pen that is used to highlight parts of text.

highly /hie-lee/ *adv* greatly, very.

highly-strung /hie-lee-**strung**/ *adj* very nervous, easily excited.

highness /hie-ness/ *n* **1** the quality or state of being high. **2** a title of honour given to royalty.

high-rise /hie-**rize**/ *adj* of a tall block of flats, office building, etc. • *also n*.

high school /hie skool/ *n* a secondary school.

high seas /hie seez/ *npl* the open seas.

high-tech /hie-tek/ *adj, also* **hi-tech** using very advanced modern machinery and methods, especially electronic ones.

high tide /hie-tide/ *n* the time of day when the water level is highest.

high-top /hie-top/ *n* a sneaker or athletic shoe that extends over the ankle.

high water /hie **waw**-ter/ *n* high tide.

highway /hie-way/ *n* a public road, a main road.

high wire /hie wire/ *n* a wire stretched high between two supports across which people will walk and perform tricks, as in a circus, fair, etc.

hijack /hie-jack/ *vb* to steal or take control of a car, lorry, train, etc. illegally during a journey. • *n* **hijacker**.

hike /hike/ *vb* to go on a long walk in the country, especially over rough ground. • *n* **hiker**.

hilarious /hi-**lay**-ree-us/ *adj* **1** extremely amusing or funny. **2** noisily merry. • *n* **hilarity**.

hill /hill/ *n* a low mountain, a raised part of the earth's surface.

hillside /hill-side/ *n* the side of a hill.

hilltop /hill-top/ *n* the top of a hill.

hilly /hi-lee/ *adj* having many hills.

hilt /hilt/ *n* the handle of a sword, dagger, or knife.

him /him/ *objective pron* the male person or animal being referred to.

himself /him-self/ • *reflex form of* him. • *pron* his real, true, or normal self.

hind[1] /hinde/ *n* a female deer (esp red deer).

hind[2] /hinde/ *adj* at the back.

hinder[1] /hine-der/ *adj* at the back.

hinder[2] /hin-der/ *vb* to stop or delay the advance or development of, to put difficulties in the way of.

Hindi /hin-dee/ *n* the main language in India.

hindrance /hin-dranse/ *n* something or someone that makes action or progress difficult.

hindsight /hind-site/ *n* the ability to see, after the event, what should have been done.

Hindu /hin-doo/ *n* a believer in Hinduism.

Hinduism /hin-doo-i-zum/ *n* a religion practised by many in India, focused on three things: Dharma, the universal law; Karma, the effects of personal actions; and Samsara, the cycle of rebirth.

hinge /hindge/ *n* a folding joint to which a door or lid is fixed so that it can turn on it. • *vb* **1** to fix hinges to. **2** to depend.

hint /hint/ *vb* to suggest indirectly. • *n* **1** an indirect suggestion. **2** a helpful suggestion. **3** a small amount.

hip[1] /hip/ *n* the upper part of the thigh.

hip[2] /hip/ *n* the fruit of the wild rose.

hip[3] /hip/ *adj* aware, fashionable, stylish.

hip-hop /hip-hop/ *n* a form of music that combines rap, funk, street sounds, and melody.

hippies /hi-peez/ *npl* young people of the 1960s and 1970s who believed in peace, lived together in separate communities, and dressed in a similar, casual way.

hippo /hi-po/ *n* short for **hippopotamus**.

hippopotamus /hi-po-**paw**-ta-mus/ *n* (*pl* **hippopotamuses** *or* **hippopotami**) a large, dangerous, plant-eating river animal found in Africa with thick skin, an almost hairless body, and short legs.

hire /hire/ *n* **1** the renting of something. **2** the money paid for the use of a thing or for the work of another. • *vb* **1** to get the use of a thing by paying for it. **2** to lend to another for payment.

his /hiz/ *poss pron* of or belonging to him.

hiss /hiss/ *vb* to make a sound like that of the letter *s*, often as a sign of disapproval. • *n* the act or sound of hissing.

historian /hi-**sto**-ree-an/ *n* a person who writes about and studies history.

historic /hi-**staw**-ric/ *adj* of lasting importance.

historical /hi-**staw**-ri-cal/ *adj* having to do with history.

history /hi-sto-ree/ *n* **1** the study of past events. **2** an account of past events, conditions, ideas, etc.

hit /hit/ *vb* (**hit, hitting**) **1** to strike. **2** to reach, to arrive at. • *n* **1** a blow. **2** a success.

hit-and-miss /hit-an-miss/ *adj* resulting in both successes and failures.

hit-and-run /hit-an-run/ *adj* of an accident in which the driver involved flees from the scene.

hitch /hich/ *vb* **1** to hook or fasten. **2** to try to get a ride in someone else's car. • *n* **1** a jerk, a pull. **2** a type of knot. **3** a difficulty, a snag.

hitchhike /hich-hike/ *vb* to travel by asking for rides from others along the way.

hi-tech *see* **high-tech**.

hither /hi-ther/ *adv* (*fml or old*) to this place. • **hither and thither** here and there, backwards and forwards.

hitherto /hi-ther-too/ *adv* (*fml*) until now.

hit man /hit-man/ *n* a man paid to kill someone.

hit-or-miss /hi-tor-miss/ *adj* random.

HIV /aych-ie-vee/ *abbr* = **Human Immunodeficiency Virus**: a virus that affects the body's immune system, or its ability to protect itself from infection, and that can lead to **AIDS**.

hive /hive/ *n* **1** a home made for bees. **2** a place of great activity.

hives /hivez/ *npl* an allergic reaction that causes itching, burning, stinging, and red patches on the skin.

ho /ho/ *interj* used to attract attention.

hoard /hoard/ *n* a hidden supply. • *vb* **1** to store secretly. **2** to collect.

hoarse /hoarse/ *adj* having a rough or husky voice.

hoarsen /hoar-sen/ *vb* to make or become hoarse.

hoax /hoaks/ *n* a trick or joke intended to deceive. • *vb* to deceive, to trick.

hob /hob/ *n* **1** the top part of a cooker, on which pans are used for cooking. **2** the shelf at the side or rear of a fireplace for pots, etc.

hobble /hob-ul/ *vb* **1** to limp. **2** to tie the legs of an animal to one another to stop it running away.

hobby /hob-ee/ *n* a favourite subject or interest for a person's spare time, an interesting pastime.

hock /hock/ *n* the joint in the middle of an animal's back leg.

hockey /hock-ee/ *n* **1** (*Br*) a team game played with a ball or puck and sticks curved at the end, played indoors, in a field, or on pavement. **2** (*US*) ice hockey: a game in which the players skate on ice and score by hitting a puck into a goal with a long stick.

hod /hod/ *n* a V-shaped wooden container on a pole used for carrying bricks, etc.

hodgepodge /hodge-podge/ *n* any jumbled mixture or mess.

hoe /ho/ *n* a garden tool with a thin, flat blade at the end of a long handle for loosening the earth around plants. • *vb* to dig with a hoe.

hog /hog/ *n* **1** a pig, especially a male pig that has been castrated. **2** a greedy person.

Hogmanay /hog-man-ay/ *n* in Scotland, the last night of the year, New Year's Eve.

hogwash /hog-wash/ *n* useless talk, writing, etc.

ho-hum /ho-hum/ *interj* used to suggest boredom.

hoist /hoist/ *vb* to lift, to raise, especially by some device. • *n* a lift for goods.

hold /hoald/ *vb* (*pt, pp* **held**) **1** to have or take in the hand(s) or arms. **2** to bear the weight of, to support. **3** to contain or be able to contain. **4** to have. **5** to cause to take place. • *n* **1** grasp. **2** the lowest part of a ship, where the cargo is stored. • **hold forth** (*fml*) to speak in public or at length. • **hold up 1** to attack and rob. **2** to delay, to hinder. **3** to last. **4** to raise. **5** to support. • **hold with** to agree with. • **hold your own** to keep advantages without gaining any more.

holdall /hold-all/ *n* a large bag with handles for carrying clothes, tools, etc.

holder /hole-der/ *n* one who holds or possesses.

hole /hole/ *n* **1** a hollow or empty space in something solid. **2** an opening. **3** an animal's den. **4** (*inf*) a difficulty. • *vb* to make a hole in.

holiday /hol-i-day/ *n* **1** a day of freedom from work, a day set aside for rest or amusement. **2** (*often pl*) a period of rest from work, school, etc, often spent away from home. • *vb* to spend a holiday. • *n* **holiday-maker**.

holiness /hoe-lee-ness/ *n* the state of being holy. • **Holiness** a title given to the pope.

holler /hol-er/ *vb* to shout or yell.

hollow /hol-o/ *adj* **1** not solid. **2** empty inside. **3** worthless. **4** not sincere. **5** sounding as if coming from a hollow place, echoing. • *n* **1** a sunken place, something hollow. **2** a low place between folds, ridges, etc. **3** a valley. • *vb* **1** to make hollow. **2** to take out the inside leaving the outside untouched.

holly /hol-ee/ *n* an evergreen bush with dark green spiky leaves and red berries.

holocaust /ho-lo-cawst/ *n* killing or destruction on a huge scale, often by fire.

hologram /ho-lo-gram/ *n* a 3-dimensional photographic image created by using a laser beam.

holograph /ho-lo-graf/ *n* a document or book in the author's own handwriting.

holster /hole-ster/ *n* a pistol case that can be fixed to a belt.

holy /ho-lee/ *adj* **1** good, and trying to be perfect in the service of God. **2** set aside for the service of God.

Holy Communion /ho-lee cu-myoon-yun/ *n* in the Christian faith, the receiving of bread and wine to remember Jesus's last meal with his followers before his death.

holy day /ho-lee day/ *n* any day set aside for a religious purpose.

Holy Grail *n* **1** (*myth*) the drinking vessel used by Jesus Christ at the last supper. **2** (*inf*) any fantastical goal.

homage /om-idge/ *n* **1** (*old*) the promise to do certain duties for an overlord. **2** respect, things said or done to show great respect.

home /home/ *n* **1** a person's house, the place where a person lives. **2** where a person was born, the place where a person or thing originally comes from. **3** a place where people who need special care, such as children without parents, old people, people who are ill, etc, are looked after. • *adj* **1** having to do with a person's home. **2** made or done at home. • *adv* to or at home.

homeless /home-less/ *adj* having no home.

homely /home-lee/ *adj* **1** plain, simple. **2** like home, comfortable.

homemade /home-made/ *adj* made at home or at the place where it is being offered, sold, etc.

homeopathy /ho-mee-aw-pa-thee/ *n, also* **homoeopathy** a system of medical treatment based on the belief that certain illnesses can be cured by giving the patient small doses of a drug that would cause a mild form of the illness in a healthy person. • *adj* **homeopathic**, *also* **homoeopathic**.

homeowner /ho-moa-ner/ *n* a person who owns the house that he or she lives in.

home page /home page/ *n* the first web page, often with links to other pages, found on an Internet site.

home schooling /home skoo-ling/ *n* the process of teaching children in the home rather than sending them to a school.

homesick /home-sick/ *adj* having a longing for home. • *n* **home-sickness**.

homespun /home-spun/ *adj* plain and simple.

homestead /home-sted/ *n* a house with grounds and outbuildings around it, especially a farm.

hometown /home-town/ *n* the town where a person lives or grew up.

homewards /home-wards/ *adv* (*fml*) towards home.

homework /home-wurk/ *n* work to be done or lessons to be studied at home.

homicide /hom-i-side/ *n* **1** the act of killing another human being. **2** a person who kills another human being. • *adj* **homicidal**.

homogenize /ho-modge-i-nize/ *vb, also* **homogenise** to make the same in texture, mixture, or quality by breaking down and blending the different parts. • *adj* **homogenous**.

homonym /hom-o-nim/ *n* a word sounding the same as another but having a different meaning (e.g. here, hear).

homophobia /ho-mo-**fo**-bee-a/ *n* irrational fear or hatred of homosexuals or homosexuality.

Homo sapiens /ho-mo **sa**-pee-enz/ *n* the scientific name for human beings.

homosexual /ho-mo-**sek**-shwal/ *adj* of or having to do with sexual desire for those of the same sex. • *n* **homosexuality**.

honcho /**hon**-cho/ *n* the person in charge, the boss.

honest /**on**-est/ *adj* **1** free from deceit, upright, truthful; not cheating, stealing, etc. **2** open and frank. **3** typical of an honest person, open. **4** true. • *n* **honesty**.

honey /**hu**-nee/ *n* a sweet fluid made by bees from flowers.

honeybee /**hu**-nee-bee/ *n* a bee that makes honey.

honeycomb /**hu**-nee-coam/ *n* the waxy cells in which bees store their honey.

honeymoon /**hu**-nee-moon/ *n* the holiday taken by a newly married couple immediately after marriage.

honeysuckle /**hu**-nee-su-cul/ *n* a sweet-smelling climbing plant.

honk /hongk/ *n* the call of a wild goose or any similar sound, like that of a car horn.

honour /**on**-ur/ *n, also* **honor** (*US*) **1** good name, reputation. **2** high principles and standards of behaviour. **3** glory. **4** a person or thing that brings pride or glory. **5** a title of respect used when talking to or about certain important people such as judges, mayors, etc. **6** respect. • *vb* **1** to respect. **2** to raise in rank or dignity. **3** to pay (a bill) when due.

honourable /**on**-ur-a-bul/ *adj, also* **honorable** (*US*) **1** worthy of respect or honour. **2** honest, of high principles. **3** just.

honorary /**on**-ur-ra-ree/ *adj* **1** unpaid. **2** given to a person as a mark of respect for his or her ability.

hood /hood/ *n* **1** a covering for the head and neck. **2** anything that looks like a hood or can be used as such.

hoodlum /**hood**-lum/ *n* a wild, lawless person, often a member of a gang of criminals.

hoodwink /**hood**-wingk/ *vb* to deceive.

hoof /hoof/ *n* (*pl* **hooves** *or* **hoofs**) the horny part of the foot in certain animals. • *adj* **hoofed** having hooves.

hook /hook/ *n* **1** a piece of metal or plastic bent for catching hold of or for hanging things on. **2** a short, curved cutting instrument. • *vb* to catch, hold, or fasten with a hook. • *adj* **hooked, hook-shaped**. • **by hook or by crook** by any means, fair or unfair.

hooligan /**hoo**-li-gan/ *n* a wild, lawless person, often a member of a gang of criminals. • *n* **hooliganism**.

hoop /hoop/ *n* **1** a band of metal around a cask. **2** a large ring of wood, metal, etc.

hoot /hoot/ *vb* **1** to cry as an owl. **2** to make a loud noise of laughter or disapproval. • *n* **1** the cry of an owl. **2** a shout of laughter or disapproval.

Hoover *n* (*TM*) a vacuum cleaner. • *also vb.*

hooves *see* hoof.

hop[1] /hop/ *vb* (**hopped, hopping**) **1** to jump on one leg. **2** to jump. • *n* a jump, especially on one leg.

hop[2] /hop/ *n* a plant with bitter-tasting cones used in making beer, ale, etc.

hope /hope/ *vb* to wish for and expect good things in the future. • *n* a wish or expectation for the future.

hopeful /**hope**-ful/ *adj* **1** full of hope. **2** giving cause for hope.

hopeless /**hope**-less/ *adj* **1** without hope. **2** giving no cause for hope. **3** (*inf*) poor, not good.

hopping /**hop**-ing/ *adj* very busy or active.

hopscotch /**hop**-scotch/ *n* a game in which a player tosses a stone or other object into a section of a figure drawn on the ground and hops from section to section to pick to the stone up after the toss.

horde /hoard/ *n* a huge crowd.

horizon /ho-**rie**-zun/ *n* **1** the line along which the earth and sky seem to meet. **2** the breadth of a person's understanding and experience.

horizontal /ho-ri-**zon**-tal/ *adj* parallel to the horizon, flat, level.

hormone /**hawr**-moan/ *n* a substance made in the body that has a specific job or effect.

horn /horn/ *n* **1** a hard, pointed growth on the heads of some animals. **2** anything shaped like a horn (e.g. snail's feelers). **3** a musical brass instrument. **4** on a car, lorry, etc, an instrument that makes a warning noise. • *adj* made of horn.

horned /hornd/ *adj* having horns.

hornet /**hor**-net/ *n* a large, stinging insect of the wasp family coloured yellow and black.

hornpipe /**horn**-pipe/ *n* **1** a lively dance; a sailor's dance. **2** music for such a dance.

horoscope /**haw**-ro-scope/ *n* **1** a plan showing the positions of the stars in the sky at a particular time, especially at the hour of a person's birth, made in the belief that from it features and future events can be foretold. **2** a forecast of a person's future based on such a plan.

horrendous /haw-**ren**-dus/ *adj* horrible, frightful.

horrible /**haw**-ri-bul/ *adj* **1** causing horror, dreadful, terrible. **2** (*inf*) unpleasant, nasty. • *adv* **horribly**.

horrid /**haw**-rid/ *adj* **1** (*fml*) horrible, dreadful. **2** (*inf*) horrible, unpleasant, nasty.

horrify /**haw**-ri-fie/ *vb* to fill with horror; to shock unpleasantly. • *adj* **horrific**.

horror /**haw**-ror/ *n* **1** terror, great fear or dislike. **2** (*inf*) a horrible or disagreeable person or thing. • *also adj*.

horrorstruck /**haw**-ror-struck/ *adj* horrified.

hors d'oeuvre /awr-**durv**/ *n* an appetizer, a small portion of food served before a meal.

horse /**horss**/ *n* **1** an animal that can be used for riding on or pulling loads. **2** a device or frame with legs to support something. **3** a padded block on four legs used by gymnasts in vaulting.

horseback /**horss**-back/ *adv* on the back of a horse.

horsefly /**horss**-flie/ *n* a large fly that typically feeds on the blood of horses and cattle.

horseplay /**horss**-play/ *n* rough play.

horsepower /**horss**-pow-er/ *n* the pulling power of a horse, taken as an imperial unit of power equal to the power needed to raise 33,000 pounds by 1 foot in 1 minute.

horseradish /**horss**-ra-dish/ *n* a plant with a sharp-tasting edible root used for sauce or relish.

horseshoe /**horss**-shoo/ *n* **1** a curved iron shoe for horses. **2** anything of this shape.

horticulture /**hor**-ti-cul-chur/ *n* the art or science of gardening or growing flowers, vegetables, etc. • *adj* **horticultural**.

horticulturist /**hor**-ti-cul-chu-rist/ *n* a person skilled in gardening.

hose /**hoaz**/ *n* **1** (*fml*) stockings, socks, etc. **2** a movable pipe of rubber, plastic, etc, used for carrying water. • *vb* to spray with a hose.

hosier /**ho**-zee-er/ *n* someone who sells stockings.

hosiery /**ho**-zhe-ree/ *n* the articles sold by a hosier.

hospice /**hos**-pis/ *n* **1** (*old*) a place of rest or shelter for travellers. **2** a hospital for sufferers of incurable diseases.

hospitable /**hos**-**pi**-ta-bul/ *adj* kind to guests and visitors.

hospital /**hos**-pi-tal/ *n* a building for the care of the sick.

hospitality /hos-pi-**ta**-li-tee/ *n* kindness to guests and visitors.

hospitalization /hos-pi-ta-lie-**zay**-shun/ *n*, *also* **hospitalisation** the condition of being put into the hospital for a time.

host[1] /**hoast**/ *n* **1** one who receives guests. **2** (*old*) an innkeeper or hotelkeeper. • *f* **hostess**. • *vb* to act as a host.

host[2] /**hoast**/ *n* a very large number.

host[3] /**hoast**/ *n* in some Christian services, the bread taken during Holy Communion.

hostage /**hos**-tidge/ *n* a person held prisoner until certain conditions have been carried out.

hostel /**hos**-tel/ *n* a building in which persons away from home (students, travellers, etc.) can stay if they agree to keep its rules.

hostelry /**hos**-tel-ree/ *n* (*old*) an inn.

hostess *see* **host**.

hostile /**hos**-tile/ *adj* **1** unfriendly. **2** having to do with an enemy.

hostility /hos-**ti**-li-tee/ *n* **1** unfriendliness. **2** *pl* warfare.

hot /**hot**/ *adj* **1** very warm. **2** easily excited. **3** having a sharp, burning taste.

hot air /**hot** air/ *n* writing or speech that claims to be important but really is not.

hotbed /**hot**-bed/ *n* **1** in a garden, a piece of earth kept warm so that plants will grow in it more quickly. **2** a place where things develop quickly.

hotch-potch *see* **hodgepodge**.

hot dog /**hot** dog/ *n* a frankfurter, usually served on a long, soft roll.

hotel /ho-**tel**/ *n* a building where people sleep and eat when away from home; an inn.

hotheaded /**hot**-he-ded/ *adj* easily excited, rash. • *n* **hothead**.

hot plate /**hot** plate/ *n* a small, portable device for cooking food or for keeping it warm.

hot seat /**hot** seet/ *n* any stressful, difficult position to be in.

hotshot /**hot**-shot/ *n* a person who is regarded as an expert at an activity or very important, aggressive, or skilful at something.

hot spring /**hot** spring/ *n* a spring with water that is hotter than the temperature of the human body.

hot-tempered /**hot**-tem-perd/ *adj* easily angered.

hot tub /**hot** tub/ *n* a large tub in which several people soak in hot water together.

hot water bottle /**hot** water bo-tl/ *n* a rubber container holding hot water which is used to warm a person in bed.

hound /**hound**/ *n* **1** a hunting dog. **2** (*inf*) a rascal. • *vb* to hunt. • **hound out** to drive out.

hour /**our**/ *n* **1** 60 minutes. **2** the time fixed for doing something, the time at which something is usually done.

hourglass /**our**-glass/ *n* a sand-filled glass for measuring time.

houri /hoo-ree/ *n* in the Muslim faith, any of the beautiful young women in paradise.

hourly /our-lee/ *adj* happening every hour.

house /howss/ *n* **1** a building in which people, often a family, live. **2** a place or building used for a particular purpose. **3** a theatre audience. • *vb* /howz/ **1** to provide a house for. **2** to shelter.

houseboat /house-boat/ *n* a large, flat-bottomed boat used as a home.

housebreaking /house-bray-king/ *n* the act of illegally gaining entry to a building with the intention of stealing things.

housefly /house-fly/ *n* a kind of fly that feeds on rubbish, food, etc and found around houses.

houseguest /house-gest/ *n* a person who stays at least one night in a person's home.

household /house-hoald/ *n* all who live in a house. • *adj* having to do with a house or those who live in it.

househusband /house-huz-band/ *n* a married man whose primary job it is to manage the home and family.

housekeeper /house-kee-per/ *n* a person in charge of managing a house.

housekeeping /house-kee-ping/ *n* the work of a housekeeper.

house music /house myoo-zic/ *n* a kind of dance music developed in Chicago with a low bass and rap sound.

House of Commons /house of com-ons/ *n* the part of the UK parliament whose members are elected by the people.

House of Lords /house of lords/ *n* the part of the UK parliament whose members are not elected by the people and include peers and bishops.

House of Representatives /house of re-pri-zen-ta-tivz/ *n* a part of the US government responsible for creating laws.

house party /house par-tee/ *n* a party of guests that stay overnight or for a few days.

houseplant /house-plant/ *n* a plant that is grown indoors for decoration.

housesit /house-sit/ *vb* to stay in and care for a house while its owners are absent.

housetrained /house-traned/ *adj* trained to go outside to urinate, etc, said of dogs.

housewife /house-wife/ *n* a married woman whose primary job it is to manage the home and family.

housework /house-wurk/ *n* the work involved in housekeeping, such as cleaning, cooking, etc.

housing /hou-zing/ *n* shelter or lodging, the act of providing shelter.

housing estate /how-zing ih-state/ *n* a large number of houses that have been built together in a planned manner.

hovel /hu-vel/ *n* a small, dirty house.

hover /hu-ver/ *vb* **1** to stay in the air without moving. **2** to stay near.

hovercraft /hu-ver-craft/ *n* a type of car or boat that can skim over the surface of smooth land or water on a cushion of air.

how /how/ *adv* **1** in what manner or way. **2** in what state or condition. **3** for what reason or purpose. **4** at what price.

however /how-ev-er/ *adv* **1** in whatever way. **2** no matter how. **3** yet.

howl /howl/ *vb* to give a long, loud cry, as a dog or wolf. **2** to wail, to cry. • *also n*.

hub /hub/ *n* **1** the central part of a wheel. **2** a centre of interest or activity.

hubcap /hub-cap/ *n* a cap over the centre of a wheel on a car, truck, etc.

huddle /hu-dul/ *vb* to crowd together. • *n* a close crowd.

hue /hyoo/ *n* (*fml or lit*) **1** colour. **2** shade of a colour.

hue and cry /hyoo an cry/ *n* a noisy expression of anger, a noisy protest.

huff /huff/ *n* a fit of temper.

huffy /hu-fee/ *adj* easily angered.

hug /hug/ *vb* (**hugged, hugging**) **1** to hold tightly in the arms; to take lovingly in the arms. **2** to keep close to. • *n* a close grip, an embrace.

huge /hyoodge/ *adj* very big, enormous. • *n* **hugeness**.

huh /hu/ *interj* used to express surprise or used to ask a question.

hula-hoop /hoo-la-hoop/ *n* a light hoop made of plastic that is twirled around the body.

hulk /hulk/ *n* **1** the body of an old ship. **2** anything difficult to move. **3** a big, clumsy person or thing.

hulking /hul-king/ *adj* big and awkward.

hull /hull/ *n* **1** the outer covering of a grain or seed. **2** the frame or body of a ship. • *vb* to strip off the husk.

hullabaloo /hu-la-ba-loo/ *n* noise and confusion.

hum /hum/ *vb* (**hummed, humming**) **1** to make a buzzing sound. **2** to sing without words or with the mouth closed. • *n* **1** a buzzing noise. **2** the noise made by a bee when flying.

human /hyoo-man/ *adj* having to do with people. • *n* person.

humane /hyoo-mane/ *adj* kindly, merciful.

humanism /hyoo-ma-ni-zum/ *n* **1** love of literature and learning. **2** the belief that humans are the most important subject of study. • *n* **humanist**.

humanitarian /hyoo-ma-ni-**tay**-ree-an/ *n* a person who works to lessen human suffering. • *also adj*.

humanity /hyoo-**ma**-ni-tee/ *n* **1** all humankind. **2** kindness, feeling for others.

humanize /hyoo-ma-nize/ *vb, also* **humanise** to make gentler, to make kind.

humankind /hyoo-man-**kind**/ *n* all people as a race.

human resources /hyoo-man ri-**zoar**-sis/ *n* the department in a company which deals with the recruitment and management of staff.

humble /**hum**-bul/ *adj* thinking oneself unimportant, not proud, seeking no praise. • *vb* **1** to make humble. **2** to lessen the importance or power of. • *adv* **humbly**.

humdrum /**hum**-drum/ *adj* dull, ordinary, boring.

humerus /**hyoo**-me-rus/ *n* the bone that extends from the shoulder to the elbow.

humid /**hyoo**-mid/ *adj* moist, damp.

humidify /hyoo-**mi**-di-fy/ *vb* to make damp, to moisten.

humidity /hyoo-**mi**-di-tee/ *n* dampness, the amount of moisture in the air.

humiliate /hyoo-**mi**-lee-ate/ *vb* to embarrass, to lessen the importance or power of, to lower the dignity or pride of. • *n* **humiliation**.

humility /hyoo-**mi**-li-tee/ *n* the state of being humble.

hummingbird /**hu**-ming-burd/ *n* a small, brightly coloured bird whose wings make a humming sound when it is flying.

hummus /**hu**-mus/ *n* a Middle Eastern dish made of mashed chickpeas and eaten as an appetizer.

humour /**hyoo**-mur/ *n, also* **humor** (*US*) **1** any fluid or juice of an animal or plant. **2** a comical or amusing quality. **3** a state of mind, mood.

humorist /**hyoo**-mu-rist/ *n* a person who writes or talks amusingly.

humorous /**hyoo**-mu-rus/ *adj* **1** funny, amusing. **2** having or displaying a sense of humour.

hump /hump/ *n* a rounded lump, especially on the back. • *adj* **humped**, **humpy**.

humpback /**hump**-back/ *n* a person with a lump on his or her back.

humph /humf/ *interj* used to express doubt, disgust.

humus /**hyoo**-mus/ *n* rotted leaves, etc, mixed into the earth.

hunch /hunch/ *n* **1** a rounded hump, especially on the back. **2** (*inf*) an intuitive feeling, a hint.

hunchback /**hunch**-back/ *n* a person with a hunch on his or her back. • *adj* **hunchbacked**.

hundred /**hun**-dred/ *n* 10 times 10, the number after 99. • *adj* **hundredth**.

hung *pt and pp of* **hang**.

hunger /**hung**-ger/ *n* **1** a strong desire for food. **2** lack of food. **3** any strong desire. • *vb* **1** (*old*) to feel hunger. **2** to desire greatly.

hungry /**hung**-gree/ *adj* **1** needing food, feeling or showing hunger. **2** having a strong need or desire for.

hunk /hungk/ *n* (*inf*) a large piece, a chunk.

hunt /hunt/ *vb* **1** to chase wild animals to kill or capture them. **2** to look for. **3** to follow so as to catch. • *n* **1** the act of hunting. **2** a group of people who meet to hunt wild animals.

hunter /**hun**-ter/ *n* a person who hunts.

huntsman /**hunts**-man/ *n* a man who hunts.

hurdle /**hur**-dl/ *n* **1** a gatelike movable frame of wood or metal. **2** a wooden frame over which people or horses must jump in certain races. **3** obstruction, obstacle. • *vb* to jump over hurdles in a race.

hurl /hurl/ *vb* to throw with force.

hurrah /hu-ra/, **hurray** /hu-ray/ *interj* a cry of joy.

hurricane /**hu**-ri-cane/ *n* a violent storm, a very strong wind.

hurried /**hu**-reed/ *adj* done quickly, often too quickly; hasty.

hurry /**hu**-ree/ *vb* **1** to do or go quickly. **2** to make to go quickly. • *n* haste, speed.

hurt /hurt/ *vb* (*pt, pp* **hurt**) **1** to cause pain to, to wound, to injure. **2** to upset. • *n* (*fml*) **1** a wound, an injury. **2** harm.

hurtful /**hurt**-ful/ *adj* harmful.

husband /**huz**-band/ *n* a married man. • *vb* to use or spend carefully.

husbandry /**huz**-ban-dree/ *n* **1** (*old*) farming. **2** (*fml*) careful spending.

hush /hush/ *n* silence, stillness. • *vb* **1** to make silent. **2** to become silent. • **hush up** to prevent something becoming generally known. • *interj* quiet! silence!

husk /husk/ *n* the dry outer covering of a grain or seed, or of certain fruits.

husky[1] /**huss**-kee/ *adj* **1** hoarse, dry, and rough. **2** hefty, strong.

husky[2] /**huss**-kee/ *n* an Arctic sled dog.

hut /hut/ *n* a small, roughly built house; a wooden shed.

hutch /hutch/ *n* a boxlike cage, e.g. for rabbits.

hyacinth /**hie**-a-sinth/ *n* a bulb plant with bell-like flowers and a strong scent.

hybrid /**hie**-brid/ *n* a plant or animal resulting from the mixing of two different kinds or species. • *adj* bred from two different kinds. • *vb* hybridize, *also* hybridise.

hydrant /hie-drant/ *n* a pipe from the main water pipe of a street from which water may be drawn directly.

hydraulic /hie-draw-lic/ *adj* worked by the pressure of water or other liquid.

hydro- /hie-dro/ *prefix* having to do with water.

hydroelectric /hie-dro-we-lec-tric/ *adj* having to do with electricity obtained by water power.

hydrogen /hie-dro-jen/ *n* an invisible gas with no colour or smell that with oxygen forms water.

hydrogen bomb /hie-dro-jen bom/ *n* an extremely destructive nuclear bomb.

hydroplane /hie-dro-plane/ *n* **1** an attachment of an aeroplane that enables it to glide along the water. **2** a speedboat that skims the surface of the water. • *also vb*.

hyena /hie-ee-na/ *n* a doglike animal that eats dead flesh.

hygiene /hie-jeen/ *n* **1** the study of clean and healthy living. **2** clean and healthy living.

hygienic /hie-jee-nic/ *adj* having to do with hygiene, clean.

hymn /him/ *n* a song of praise, especially to God.

hymnal /him-nal/, **hymnary** /him-na-ree/ *n* a book of hymns.

hype /hipe/ *vb* to promote in an extravagant way. • *n* such promotion.

hyperactive /hie-per-ac-tiv/ *adj* too active and unable to sit still for very long.

hyperbole /hie-per-bo-lee/ *n* a figure of speech by which a statement is exaggerated in a striking way. • *adj* hyperbolic.

hypertension /hie-per-ten-shun/ *n* high blood pressure.

hyphen /hie-fen/ *n* a short dash (-) between syllables or between words joined to express a single idea.

hypnosis /hip-no-sis/ *n* an artificially induced trance-like state in which deeper parts of the subject's subconsciousness are reached.

hypnotic /hip-not-ic/ *adj* producing the state of hypnosis.

hypnotism /hip-no-ti-zum/ *n* the art of producing hypnosis.

hypnotist /hip-no-tist/ *n* a person who has the power to hypnotize others.

hypnotize /hip-no-tize/ *vb*, *also* hypnotise to put a person into a sleeplike state and to then control the sleeper's actions.

hypochondria /hie-po-con-dree-a/ *n* a condition in which someone is overanxious about his or her health, constantly believing that he or she is ill when he or she is not. • **hypochondriac** *n* a person who suffers from hypochondria.

hypocrisy /hi-poc-ri-see/ *n* the pretence of being good or of having beliefs or feelings that one does not have.

hypocrite /hi-po-crit/ *n* a person who pretends to be good but is not so, a person who says one thing and does another.

hypocritical /hi-po-cri-ti-cal/ *adj* not sincere, false.

hypotenuse /hie-paw-te-nooz/ *n* the side opposite the right angle of a triangle, the longest side of a right triangle.

hypothermia /hie-po-ther-mee-a/ *n* a serious medical condition in which the body temperature is much lower than normal because of prolonged exposure to cold.

hypothesis /hie-poth-e-sis/ *n* an idea accepted as true for the basis of an argument, something supposed true but not proved so. • *adj* hypothetical.

hysterectomy /hi-ste-rec-to-me/ *n* the surgical removal of all or part of the uterus.

hysteria *n* **1** a disorder of the nerves, causing a person to laugh or cry violently, have imaginary illnesses, etc. **2** lack of control, uncontrolled excitement.

hysterics /hi-ste-rics/ *n* **1** a fit of hysteria. **2** (*inf*) an uncontrollable fit of laughter.

hysterical /hi-ste-ri-cal/ *adj* **1** suffering from hysteria. **2** caused by hysteria. **3** (*inf*) very funny.

I

I, i /eye/ the ninth letter of the English alphabet.

I /eye/ *pron* meaning the person speaking or writing.

ice /eyess/ *n* frozen water. • *vb* **1** to cool in ice. **2** to cover with icing.

Ice Age /eyess age/ *n* a time when large amounts of ice and glaciers cover many areas of the earth.

icebox /eyess-boks/ *n* a cabinet, box, or room with ice in it for keeping things cold.

icebreaker /eyess-bray-ker/ *n* a ship designed for cutting its way through ice.

ice cap /eyess-cap/ *n* a dome-shaped mass of ice that spreads slowly outward from the centre.

ice cream /eyess-creem/ *n* **1** cream or a mixture of creamy substances flavoured, sweetened, and frozen. **2** a portion of ice cream.

ice floe /eyess-flo/ *n* a large sheet of floating ice.

ice hockey /eyess-hock-ee/ *see* **hockey**.

ice pack /eyess-pack/ *n* ice collected and put into a bag or container of some kind, used to cool things down.

ice pick /eyess-pick/ *n* a sharp, pointed metal tool used to chip ice pieces away from a larger block of ice.

ice skate /eyess-skate/ *n* footwear with a blade on the bottom, used for skating on the ice.

ichthyosaur /ic-thee-o-sawr/ *n* a huge fish-like prehistoric reptile.

icicle /eye-si-cul/ *n* a long, hanging, pointed piece of ice formed by the freezing of falling water.

icily /eye-si-lee/ *adv* in an icy manner, very coldly.

icing /eye-sing/ *n* a mixture of powdered sugar with liquid, used to cover cakes.

icing sugar /eye-sing shoo-gar/ *n* finely powdered sugar used to make icing.

icon /eye-con/ *n* **1** a religious picture or statue, an image. **2** a famous person or thing that many people admire and regard as a symbol of a way of life or set of beliefs. **3** a small symbol on a computer screen that represents a program or file. • *adj* **iconic**.

icy /eye-see/ *adj* **1** very cold. **2** covered with ice. **3** unfriendly.

ID /eye-dee/ *abbr* = **identification** sense 2.

idea /eye-dee-ya/ *n* **1** a plan, thought, or suggestion. **2** a picture in the mind. **3** an opinion or belief.

ideal /eye-deel/ *n* **1** a perfect example. **2** high principles or perfect standards, a person's standard of behaviour, etc. • *adj* **1** perfect. **2** extremely suitable. **3** expressing possible perfection that is unlikely to exist. • *adv* **ideally**.

idealism /eye-dee-li-zum/ *n* the desire to achieve perfection, the state of having high principles or perfect standards. • *n* **idealist**. • *adj* **idealistic**.

idealize, idealise /eye-dee-lize/ *vb* to think of as perfect or better than reality.

identical /eye-den-ti-cul/ *adj* **1** the very same. **2** the same, exactly alike.

identification /eye-den-ti-fi-**cay**-shun/ *n* **1** act of recognizing. **2** something that is proof of or a sign of identity, often **ID**. **3** the feeling that one shares ideas, feelings, etc, with another person.

identify /eye-den-ti-fie/ *vb* **1** to think of as being the same. **2** to recognize as being a certain person or thing. **3** to discover or recognize.

identity /eye-den-ti-tee/ *n* **1** (*fml*) the state of being the same. **2** who a person is.

ideology /eye-dee-ol-o-jee/ *n* **1** the study of the nature and origin of ideas. **2** a system of ideas.

idiocy /i-dee-u-see/ *n* **1** the state of being an idiot. **2** a foolish action.

idiom /i-dee-um/ *n* **1** the language or dialect of a certain group of people. **2** a group of words that together have an unexpected meaning different from the exact sense.

idiosyncrasy /i-dee-yo-**sing**-cra-see/ *n* an odd way of behaving. • *adj* **idiosyncratic**.

idiot /i-dee-yot/ *n* **1** a foolish or stupid person. • *adj* **idiotic**. • *adv* **idiotically**. • *see* **idiocy**.

idle /eye-dul/ *adj* **1** doing nothing, not working, not in use. **2** lazy. **3** having no effect or results. • *vb* **1** (*fml*) to be idle, to do nothing. **2** (*of a machine*) to run without doing work. • *n* **idleness**. • *n* **idler**. • *adv* **idly**.

idol /eye-dul/ *n* **1** a statue or other object that is worshipped. **2** a person regarded with too great love and respect.

idolize /eye-dol-ize/ *vb, also* **idolise** to love or admire very greatly.

idyll /eye-dil/ *n* **1** a poem about simple, country life. **2** a beautiful scenic area.

idyllic /eye-**di**-lic/ *adj* **1** perfectly happy, pleasant. **2** charming, picturesque.

if /if/ *conj* on condition that, in case, supposing.

igloo /i-**gloo**/ *n* an Eskimo house or hut, usually dome shaped and made of blocks of frozen snow.

igneous /**ig**-nee-us/ *adj* (*of rocks*) formed from lava from a volcano.

ignite /ig-**nite**/ *vb* **1** to set fire to. **2** to catch fire.

ignition /ig-**ni**-shun/ *n* **1** act of setting fire to. **2** the part of a motor engine that sets fire to the fuel that drives the engine.

ignoble /ig-**no**-bul/ *adj* **1** (*fml*) mean, dishonourable. **2** (*old*) of low birth.

ignoramus /ig-ni-**ray**-mus/ *n* a person with little or no knowledge.

ignorance /**ig**-ni-ranse/ *n* **1** want of knowledge. **2** lack of awareness or knowledge.

ignorant /**ig**-ni-rant/ *adj* **1** having little or no knowledge. **2** unaware of.

ignore /ig-**nore**/ *vb* to take no notice of, to refuse to pay attention to.

iguana /ig-**wa**-na/ *n* any of a large family of lizards with spines along its back and that eats vegetation or insects.

ill /ill/ *adj* **1** sick. **2** bad. **3** evil, harmful. • *n* **1** evil, harm. **2** trouble. • *adv* badly.

I'll /eyel/ *contraction* I will.

illegal /i-**lee**-gal/ *adj* against the law. • *n* **illegality**.

illegible /i-**le**-ji-bul/ *adj* that cannot be read, badly written.

illegitimate /i-le-**ji**-ti-mit/ *adj* born of unmarried parents. • *n* **illegitimacy**.

illicit /i-**li**-sit/ *adj* unlawful, against the law.

illiterate /i-**li**-trit/ *adj* **1** unable to read or write. **2** uneducated. • *n* **illiteracy**.

illness /**ill**-ness/ *n* sickness, the state of being unwell.

illogical /i-**lodge**-ic-al/ *adj* **1** not using reasoning, not reasonable. **2** against the rules of reasoning. • *n* **illogic** the state of being illogical.

illuminate /i-**loo**-mi-nate/ *vb* **1** (*old*) to light up. **2** (*of books, etc.*) to decorate with bright colours. **3** to explain, to make clear.

illumination /i-loo-mi-**nay**-shun/ *n* (*fml*) **1** a lighting up. **2** decorative lights. **3** a picture or decoration painted on a page of a book. **4** explanation, clarification.

illusion /i-**loo**-zhun/ *n* **1** a deception, an unreal image or appearance. **2** a wrong belief, a false idea. • *adj* **illusory**.

illusionist /i-**loo**-zhu-nist/ *n* a person who performs tricks that deceive the eye; a magician.

illusive /i-**loo**-siv/ *adj* unreal.

illustrate /i-**lu**-strate/ *vb* **1** to make clear by examples. **2** to provide pictures for a book or magazine.

illustration /i-lu-**stray**-shun/ *n* **1** an example that makes something easier to understand or demonstrates something. **2** a picture in a book or magazine.

illustrative /i-**lu**-stra-tiv/ *adj* helping to explain.

illustrious /i-**lu**-stree-us/ *adj* (*fml*) famous.

ill will /ill **will**/ unfriendly feeling, hate, dislike.

I'm /eyem/ *contraction* I am.

image /i-**midge**/ *n* **1** a likeness, form. **2** a likeness or copy of a person, etc, made of stone, wood, etc. **3** a statue or picture that is worshipped. **4** a picture formed of an object in front of a mirror or lens. **5** a picture in the mind. **6** the impression that a person or organization gives to the public.

imagery /i-**midge**-ree/ *n* figures of speech, words chosen because they call up striking pictures in the mind.

imaginable /i-**ma**-ji-na-bul/ *adj* that can be imagined.

imaginary /i-**ma**-ji-na-ree/ *adj* existing in the mind only, not real.

imagination /i-ma-ji-**nay**-shun/ *n* **1** the power of inventing stories, persons, etc; creative ability. **2** the power of forming pictures in the mind. **3** the seeing or hearing of things that do not exist.

imaginative /i-**ma**-ji-na-tiv/ *adj* **1** having a good imagination. **2** demonstrating imagination.

imagine /i-**ma**-jin/ *vb* **1** to form a picture in the mind. **2** to form ideas of things that do not exist or of events that have not happened. **3** to suppose.

imam /i-**mam**/ *n* the leader of prayer in a Muslim mosque; any of various Muslim leaders.

imbalance /im-**ba**-lanse/ *n* lack of balance.

imbecile /**im**-bu-sil/ *n* a fool, an idiot. • *n* **imbecility**.

imitate /i-**mi**-tate/ *vb* to copy; to try to be, behave, or look the same as. • *n* **imitator**.

imitation /i-mi-**tay**-shun/ *n* **1** act of imitating. **2** a copy.

imitative /i-**mi**-ta-tiv/ *adj* **1** done as a copy. **2** fond of copying.

immaculate /i-**ma**-cyu-lit/ *adj* **1** (*old*) pure. **2** spotless, perfectly clean. **3** perfect.

immaterial /i-ma-**tee**-ree-al/ *adj* **1** not consisting of matter, spiritual. **2** unimportant.

immature /i-ma-**choor**/ *adj* **1** unripe. **2** not fully grown. **3** lacking experience and wisdom. • *n* **immaturity**.

immeasurable /i-mezh-ra-bul/ *adj* huge, that cannot be measured, vast.

immediate /i-**mee**-dee-it/ *adj* **1** happening at once. **2** direct, without anyone or anything coming between. **3** near, close. • *n* **immediacy** the quality or condition of being immediate.

immediately /i-**mee**-dee-it-lee/ *adv* **1** at once. **2** closely.

immense /i-**mense**/ *adj* huge. • *n* **immensity**.

immerse /i-**merse**/ *vb* **1** to put into water. **2** to give a person's whole attention to. • *n* **immersion**.

immigrant /**i**-mi-grant/ *n* a person who immigrates, or moves to another country. • *adj* of or relating to immigrants.

immigrate /**i**-mi-grate/ *vb* (*fml*) to enter and settle in a new country. • *n* **immigration**.

imminent /**i**-mi-nent/ *adj* just about to happen, near in time. • *n* **imminence**.

immobile /i-**mo**-bul/ *adj* not moving, unable to move. • *n* **immobility**. • *vb* **immobilize**, *also* **immobilise**.

immoderate /i-**mod**-rit/ *adj* more than is proper, uncontrolled.

immodest /i-**mod**-est/ *adj* (*fml*) **1** shameless, indecent. **2** not modest. • *n* **immodesty**.

immoral /i-**maw**-ral/ *adj* wrong, evil, wicked. • *n* **immorality**.

immortal /i-**mawr**-tul/ *adj* **1** living or lasting forever. **2** famous for all time.

immortality /i-mawr-ta-li-tee/ *n* **1** everlasting life. **2** undying fame.

immortalize /i-**mawr**-tu-lize/ *vb*, *also* **immortalise 1** to make immortal. **2** to make famous for all time.

immovable /i-**moo**-va-bul/ *adj* **1** not able to be moved. **2** not changing easily.

immune /i-**myoon**/ *adj* **1** free from, specially protected from. **2** not to be infected by. • *n* **immunity**.

immune system /i-**myoon sis**-tem/ *n* the system that protects the body from disease.

immunize /**i**-myoo-nize/ *vb*, *also* **immunise** to inject disease germs into the blood stream to cause a mild attack of an illness and so make the person immune to it.

immunology /i-myu-**nol**-o-jee/ *n* the study of the immune system.

imp /imp/ *n* **1** in fairy tales, an evil spirit, a devil's child. **2** a mischievous child.

impact /im-**pact**/ *n* **1** the force with which one thing strikes another. **2** a collision. **3** a strong effect or impression.

impair /im-**pair**/ *vb* to make worse, to weaken.

impale /im-**pale**/ *vb* to fix upon something sharp, to pierce.

impart /im-**part**/ *vb* (*fml*) **1** to tell. **2** to give or share.

impartial /im-**par**-shal/ *adj* fair, just, not taking sides.

impartiality /im-par-shee-a-li-tee/ *n* fairness, treating all parties or persons in the same way.

impassive /im-**pa**-siv/ *adj* **1** not showing strong feeling, not feeling pain. **2** calm, unexcited.

impatient /im-**pay**-shent/ *adj* not willing to wait, easily angered by delay. • *n* **impatience**.

impeach /im-**peech**/ *vb* **1** to charge with a crime. **2** to charge an important person with a crime. **3** (*fml*) to raise doubts about. • *n* **impeachment**.

impeccable /im-**pe**-ca-bul/ *adj* faultless.

imperative /im-**pe**-ra-tiv/ *adj* **1** commanding. **2** necessary, urgent.

imperfect /im-**per**-fect/ *adj* having faults, not perfect. • *n* **imperfection**.

imperial /im-**pee**-ree-al/ *adj* **1** having to do with an empire or emperor. **2** of a country that has control over other countries or colonies. **3** a mostly obsolete British system of weights and measures.

impersonal /im-**per**-snal/ *adj* **1** not influenced by personal feelings. **2** (*of verbs*) occurring only in the third person singular, usually with 'it' as the subject. • *vb* **impersonalize**, *also* **impersonalise**.

impersonate /im-**per**-su-nate/ *vb* to pretend to be someone else.

impertinent /im-**pert**-nent/ *adj* not showing proper manners, purposely disrespectful. • *n* **impertinence**.

impetuous /im-**pech**-wus/ *adj* acting without thinking first; rash, hasty. • *n* **impetuousness**, **impetuosity**.

impish /**im**-pish/ *adj* mischievous.

implant /im-**plant**/ *vb* **1** to place in, often to put something into part of the body for a medical purpose. **2** to fix firmly an idea or feeling in someone's mind. • *n* /**im**-plant/ something that is implanted.

implement /**im**-ple-ment/ *n* a tool, an instrument. • *vb* **implement** to put into practice.

implicate /**im**-pli-cate/ *vb* to show that a person is involved or connected with.

implication /im-pli-**cay**-shun/ *n* something hinted at but not said openly.

implicit /im-**pli**-sit/ *adj* **1** understood but not said. **2** unquestioning, without doubts.

implode /im-**plode**/ *vb* to burst or collapse inward. • *n* **implosion**.

implore /im-**plore**/ *vb* to ask earnestly, to beg.

imply /im-**ply**/ *vb* to suggest something without saying it openly, to hint.

impolite /im-pu-**lite**/ *adj* (*fml*) rude, ill-mannered.

import /im-**poart**/ *vb* to bring in goods from abroad. • *n* **import** something brought in from abroad. • *n* **importer**.

important /im-**poar**-tant/ *adj* **1** deserving great attention. **2** having results that affect many people. **3** having a high position. • *n* **importance**. • *adv* **importantly**.

importation /im-poar-**tay**-shun/ *n* an importing or being imported.

impose /im-**poaz**/ *vb* **1** to lay on or place. **2** to force to accept. • **impose on** to take advantage of, to exploit, to make unfair demands on.

imposing /im-**poa**-zing/ *adj* important-looking, stately.

imposition /im-pu-**zi**-shun/ *n* **1** the act of laying on or placing. **2** a tax. **3** an unfair demand.

impossible /im-**poss**-i-bul/ *adj* not able to be done or achieved. • *n* **impossibility**.

impostor *or* **imposter** /im-**poss**-tor/ *n* a person who pretends to be someone else; a deceiver.

imposture /im-**poss**-chur/ *n* the act or practice of an impostor; fraud, deception.

impotent /**im**-pu-tent/ *adj* **1** lacking power, helpless, weak. **2** of a man, unable to achieve an erect penis and so unable to have full sex.

impractical /im-**prac**-ti-cal/ *adj* not practical, not workable or useful.

imprecise /im-pri-**sise**/ *adj* not precise, exact, or definite.

impregnate /im-**preg**-nate/ *vb* **1** to fill with. **2** to fertilize or make pregnant.

impress /im-**press**/ *vb* **1** to mark by pressing into, to stamp. **2** to fix in the mind. **3** to stress, to emphasize the importance of. • *adj* **impressible**.

impression /im-**pre**-shun/ *n* **1** the mark left by pressing or stamping. **2** the number of copies of a book printed at one time. **3** an effect on the mind or feelings. **4** a not very clear idea or memory. **5** an attempt to copy, in a humorous way, someone else's voice, behaviour, appearance, etc.

impressionable /im-**presh**-na-bul/ *adj* easily influenced.

Impressionism /im-**pre**-shu-ni-zum/ *n* **1** a way of painting; the representation of scenes just as they appear at a certain moment by using colour and brush strokes in a specific way. **2** similar attempts in writing and music.

impressionist /im-**pre**-shu-nist/ *n* **1** (*cap*) an artist who practises Impressionism. **2** a person who does impressions of people, especially as a form of entertainment. • *also adj*.

impressive /im-**pre**-siv/ *adj* **1** important-looking. **2** causing deep feeling, such as admiration.

imprint /im-**print**/ *vb* **1** to make a mark by pressing or printing. **2** to fix in the memory. • *n* **imprint** /**im**-print/ **1** that which is imprinted. **2** a publisher's name, address, etc, on a book.

imprison /im-**pri**-zon/ *vb* to put into prison, to shut in.

imprisonment /im-**pri**-zon-ment/ *n* the act of imprisoning or the state of being imprisoned.

improbable /im-**prob**-a-bul/ *adj* not likely to happen or to be true. • *n* **improbability**.

impromptu /im-**prom**-too/ *adj* not prepared. • *adv* without preparation.

improper /im-**prop**-er/ *adj* **1** wrong. **2** not suitable, not polite. **3** indecent.

improper fraction /im-**prop**-er **frac**-shun/ *n* a fraction greater than 1, in which the denominator is less than the numerator (e.g. $5/2$).

impropriety /im-pru-**prie**-i-tee/ *n* (*fml*) incorrect or impolite behaviour, the quality of being improper.

improve /im-**proov**/ *vb* to make or become better. • *n* **improvement**.

improvise /**im**-pru-vize/ *vb* **1** to make something from material that is available. **2** to make something up at the moment required without preparation. • *n* **improvisation**.

imprudent /im-**proo**-dent/ *adj* rash, acting without forethought, unwise. • *n* **imprudence**.

impudent /**im**-pyu-dent/ *adj* disrespectful, shameless, saucy. • *n* **impudence**.

impulse /**im**-pulse/ *n* **1** a force causing movement. **2** a sudden desire or decision to act at once.

impulsive /im-**pul**-siv/ *adj* **1** done without forethought. **2** acting without thinking first. • *n* **impulsiveness**.

impure /im-**pyoor**/ *adj* **1** dirty, polluted. **2** mixed with something else. **3** sinful. • *n* **impurity**.

in /in/ *prep* **1** contained or enclosed by. **2** wearing, clothed by. **3** during the course of. **4** at or before the end of. **5** being a member of or worker at.

inability /i-na-**bi**-li-tee/ *n* lack of power, state of being unable.

inaccessible /i-nac-**se**-si-bul/ *adj* not able to be reached or approached.

inaccurate /i-na-**cyu**-rit/ *adj* **1** not correct. **2** not exact. • *n* **inaccuracy**.

inaction /i-**nac**-shun/ *n* idleness, lack of action.

inactive /i-**nac**-tiv/ *adj* **1** not taking much exercise. **2** no longer working or operating. **3** not taking an active part.

inadequate /i-**na**-de-kwit/ *adj* **1** not good enough. **2** not sufficient. • *n* **inadequacy**.

inadmissible /i-nad-**mi**-sa-bul/ *adj* not able to be allowed.

inadvertent /i-nad-**ver**-tent/ *adj* not on purpose. • *n* **inadvertence**.

inadvertently /i-nad-**ver**-tent-lee/ *adv* not purposely.

inadvisable /i-nad-**vie**-za-bul/ *adj* not wise, not advisable.

inane /i-**nane**/ *adj* foolish, silly, lacking sense. • *n* **inanity**.

inanimate /i-**na**-ni-mit/ *adj* without life.

inappropriate /i-na-**pro**-pree-it/ *adj* not suitable, fitting, or proper.

inapt /i-**napt**/ *adj* not suitable, not appropriate, not proper.

inarticulate /i-nar-**ti**-cyu-lit/ *adj* **1** not clear. **2** unable to express oneself clearly.

inattentive /i-na-**ten**-tiv/ *adj* not attentive, neglectful, absentminded.

inaudible /i-**naw**-di-bul/ *adj* that cannot be heard.

inauspicious /i-naw-**spi**-shus/ *adj* unlucky, being a sign of bad luck to come.

inborn /in-**bawrn**/ *adj* existing in a person since birth, natural.

inbound /in-**bound**/ *adj* travelling or going inward.

inbred /in-**bred**/ *adj* **1** having become part of a person's nature as a result of early training. **2** bred from closely related parents, resulting from inbreeding.

inbreed /in-**breed**/ *vb* to breed by mating closely related parents.

Inca /**ing**-ka/ *n* a member of a group of peoples in ancient Peru who had a highly developed civilization.

incalculable /in-**cal**-cyu-la-bul/ *adj* very great, too many or too much to be counted.

incandescent /in-can-**de**-sent/ *adj* white-hot or glowing with heat. • *n* **incandescence**. • *vb* **incandesce**.

incantation /in-can-**tay**-shun/ *n* words sung or spoken as a spell or charm.

incapable /in-**cay**-pa-bul/ *adj* **1** not good at a job. **2** not able, helpless. • *n* **incapability**.

incapacitate /in-ca-**pa**-si-tate/ *vb* to make unfit or unable.

incapacity /in-ca-**pa**-si-tee/ *n* **1** unfitness. **2** lack of ability.

incarcerate /in-**car**-se-rate/ *vb* (*fml or hum*) to imprison. • *n* **incarceration**.

incense[1] /in-sense/ *n* a mixture of spices burned to give a sweet-smelling smoke.

incense[2] /in-**sense**/ *vb* to make angry.

incentive /in-**sen**-tiv/ *n* something for which someone is prepared to work hard, a reason for action.

incessant /in-**se**-sant/ *adj* not stopping, going on all the time.

incest /in-sest/ *n* sex between people who are too closely related to marry legally. • *adj* **incestuous**.

inch /inch/ *n* in imperial measurements, one-twelfth of a foot in length. • *vb* to move a little at a time.

incidence /in-si-dense/ *n* **1** the extent or rate of frequency of something. **2** the act, fact, or manner of falling on or influencing.

incident /in-si-dent/ *n* **1** a happening, an event. **2** an event involving violence or law-breaking.

incidental /in-si-**den**-tal/ *adj* **1** happening as a result of something, though not the most important result. **2** accompanying.

incidentally /in-si-**den**-ta-lee/ *adv* by the way.

incinerate /in-**si**-ne-rate/ *vb* to burn to ashes.

incinerator /in-**si**-ne-ray-tor/ *n* a furnace for burning anything to ashes.

incise /in-**size**/ *vb* to cut into with a sharp tool. • *adj* **incised**.

incision /in-**si**-zhun/ *n* **1** act of cutting. **2** a cut, a deep cut.

incisive /in-**sie**-siv/ *adj* clear and sharp, to the point.

incisor /in-**sie**-zor/ *n* a cutting tooth in the front of the mouth.

incite /in-**site**/ *vb* to stir up, to urge on. • *n* **incitement**.

inclement /in-**cle**-ment/ *adj* (*fml*) **1** stormy, unpleasant. **2** merciless. • *n* **inclemency**.

inclination /in-cli-**nay**-shun/ *n* **1** a slope. **2** a bow. **3** a liking, preference. **4** a tendency.

incline /in-**cline**/ *vb* **1** to slope. **2** to bend. **3** to move gradually off the straight way. • **be inclined to 1** to feel a desire or preference. **2** to have a tendency to. • *n* /**in**-cline/ a slope.

include /in-**clude**/ *vb* to count as a part or member. • *n* **inclusion**.

inclusive /in-**cloo**-siv/ *adj* including everything mentioned or understood.

incognito /in-cog-**nee**-toe/ *adj* in disguise, under a false name. • *f* **incognita**.

incoherent /in-co-**hir**-ent/ *adj* 1 having no clear connection between the parts, muddled. 2 not speaking or writing clearly, difficult to follow or understand. • *n* **incoherence**.

income /**ing**-cum/ *n* the money earned or gained.

income tax /**ing**-cum-taks/ *n* the tax charged on income.

incomparable /in-**com**-pa-ra-bul/ *adj* 1 that cannot be equalled. 2 having no equal.

incompatible /in-com-**pa**-ti-bul/ *adj* 1 unable to get along. 2 not in agreement. • *n* **incompatibility**.

incompetent /in-**com**-pe-tent/ *adj* 1 unable to do a job well, unskilful. 2 not good enough. • *n* **incompetence**, **incompetency**.

incomplete /in-com-**pleet**/ *adj* unfinished.

incomprehensible /in-com-pre-**hen**-si-bul/ *adj* that cannot be understood. • *n* **incomprehension**.

inconceivable /in-con-**see**-va-bul/ *adj* unable to be imagined.

inconclusive /in-con-**cloo**-siv/ *adj* not final, not leading to a definite result.

inconsiderable /in-con-**si**-der-(a)-bul/ *adj* very small, of no importance.

inconsiderate /in-con-**sid**-(e)-rit/ *adj* having no thought for the feeling of others, thoughtless.

inconsistent /in-con-**sis**-tant/ *adj* 1 not agreeing with what was said or done before or elsewhere. 2 changeable, erratic. 3 contradictory. • *n* **inconsistency**.

inconsolable /in-con-**soe**-la-bul/ *adj* not able to be comforted, broken-hearted.

inconspicuous /in-con-**spic**-yu-wus/ *adj* not easily seen.

inconstant /in-**con**-stant/ *adj* 1 often changing. 2 not always behaving in the same way. • *n* **inconstancy**.

incontinent /in-**con**-ti-nent/ *adj* unable to control the bladder and/or bowels. • *n* **incontinence**.

inconvenience /in-con-**veen**-yense/ *n* trouble, annoyance. • *vb* (*fml*) to cause trouble or difficulty.

inconvenient /in-con-**veen**-yent/ *adj* causing trouble, unsuitable.

incorporate /in-**cawr**-po-rit/ *vb* 1 to bring together in one. 2 to make to form a part of, to include. • *n* **incorporation**.

incorrect /in-caw-**rect**/ *adj* 1 wrong. 2 not according to accepted standards.

increase /in-**creess**/ *vb* to make or become greater in size or number. • *n* /**in**-creess/ a rise in amount, numbers, or degree.

incredible /in-**cre**-di-bul/ *adj* 1 unbelievable, hard to believe. 2 amazing, wonderful. • *n* **incredibility**.

incredulous /in-**cre**-ju-lus/ *adj* not willing to believe, unbelieving. • *n* **incredulity**.

increment /**in**-cre-ment/ *n* an increase in money or value, often in salary.

incriminate /in-**cri**-mi-nate/ *vb* to show that a person has taken part in a crime.

incubate /**ing**-cyu-bate/ *vb* 1 to sit on eggs, to keep eggs warm until the young come out of them. 2 (*of eggs*) to be kept warm until the young birds come out. 3 (*of a disease or infection*) to develop until signs of disease appear. 4 to be holding in the body an infection that is going to develop into a disease.

incubation /ing-cyu-**bay**-shun/ *n* 1 act of incubating. 2 the time between the catching of a disease and the showing of symptoms.

incubator /**ing**-cyu-bay-tor/ *n* 1 an apparatus for hatching eggs. 2 an apparatus for keeping alive premature babies.

incurable /in-**cyoo**-ra-bul/ *adj* that cannot be cured.

indebted /in-**det**-id/ *adj* owing thanks, owing something to someone or something. • *n* **indebtedness**.

indecent /in-**dee**-sent/ *adj* 1 not decent, morally offensive, improper. 2 not suitable, not in good taste. • *n* **indecency**.

indecision /in-di-**si**-zhun/ *n* doubt, hesitation, inability to make up the mind.

indecisive /in-di-**sie**-siv/ *adj* 1 uncertain, having difficulty in making decisions. 2 settling nothing.

indeed /in-**deed**/ *adv* truly.

indefensible /in-de-**fen**-si-bul/ *adj* that cannot or should not be defended.

indefinable /in-de-**fine**-a-bul/ *adj* that cannot be clearly described or explained.

indefinite /in-**def**-nit/ *adj* 1 not fixed or exact, without clearly marked outlines or limits. 2 not clear, not precise, vague.

indelicate /in-**de**-li-kit/ *adj* 1 slightly indecent, improper. 2 lacking in tact. • *n* **indelicacy**.

indent /in-**dent**/ *vb* 1 to make a notch or zigzag in. 2 to begin a line of text inward from the margin. 3 to order goods in writing. • *n* /**in**-dent/ an order for goods.

indentation /in-den-**tay**-shun/ *n* 1 a notch or piece cut out of a straight edge. 2 the starting of a line of text inward from the margin.

independence /in-di-**pen**-dense/ *n* freedom to act or think as one likes; freedom.

independent /in-di-**pen**-dent/ *adj* **1** thinking and acting for oneself. **2** free from control by others. **3** having enough money to live without working or being helped by others.

in-depth /in-**depth**/ *adj* carefully worked out, thorough.

indescribable /in-di-**scrie**-ba-bul/ *adj* that cannot be described.

indestructible /in-di-**struc**-ta-bul/ *adj* that cannot be destroyed.

indeterminable /in-di-**ter**-mi-na-bul/, **indeterminate** /in-di-**ter**-mi-nit/ *adj* not fixed, uncertain.

index /in-deks/ *n* (*pl* **indexes** or **indices**) **1** the pointer on the dial or scale of an instrument. **2** something that indicates or points to. **3** an alphabetical list of names, subjects, etc, at the end of a book.

indicate /in-di-cate/ *vb* **1** to point out, to show. **2** to be a sign of. **3** to show to be necessary or desirable.

indication /in-di-**cay**-shun/ *n* a sign.

indicative /in-**di**-ca-tiv/ *adj* showing, being a sign of.

indicator /in-di-cay-tor/ *n* **1** a needle or pointer on a machine that indicates something or gives information about something. **2** one of the lights on a car, truck, etc. that flashes to show which way the car is turning.

indifference /in-di-frense/ *n* lack of interest.

indifferent /in-**di**-frent/ *adj* **1** taking no interest, not caring. **2** neither good nor bad.

indigenous /in-di-je-nus/ *adj* born or growing naturally in a country. • *n* **indigene**.

indigestible /in-di-**je**-sti-bul/ *adj* not easily digested.

indigestion /in-di-**jes**-chun/ *n* illness or pain caused by failure to dissolve food properly in the stomach. • *adj* **indigestive**.

indignant /in-**dig**-nant/ *adj* angry, annoyed by what is unjust. • *n* **indignation**.

indignity /in-**dig**-ni-tee/ *n* treatment that makes a person feel shame or loss of respect.

indigo /in-di-go/ *n* a blue dye obtained from certain plants. • *adj* deep blue.

indirect /in-di-**rect**/ *adj* **1** not leading straight to the destination, roundabout. **2** not direct, not straightforward, not frank. **3** not intended, not directly aimed at. • *n* **indirection**.

indiscreet /in-di-**screet**/ *adj* unwise, thoughtless, not careful of what you say or do.

indiscretion /in-di-**scre**-shun/ *n* **1** thoughtless behaviour. **2** an act done without thought of its results. **3** lack of good judgment.

indiscriminate /in-di-**scrim**-nit/ *adj* taking no notice of differences, choosing without care. • *n* **indiscrimination**.

indispensable /in-di-**spen**-si-bul/ *adj* that cannot be done without, absolutely necessary.

indisputable /in-di-**spyoo**-ti-bul/ *adj* that cannot be denied or contradicted.

indistinct /in-di-**stingt**/ *adj* not seen or heard clearly, faint.

indistinguishable /in-di-**sting**-gwi-sha-bul/ *adj* that cannot be made out as being different or separate.

individual /in-di-**vij**-u-wal/ *adj* **1** single. **2** intended for, used by, etc, one person only. **3** special to one person. • *n* **1** a single person. **2** (*inf*) a person.

individualism /in-di-**vij**-wa-li-zum/ *n* **1** the belief that the rights of the single person are more important than those of society. **2** a person's individual character.

individualist /in-di-**vij**-wa-list/ *n* a person who believes in doing things in his or her own way.

individuality /in-di-vi-je-**wa**-li-tee/ *n* a person's own character and qualities.

individualize /in-di-**vij**-wa-lize/ *vb*, *also* **individualise** to mark as different from other persons or things, to suit the taste, requirements, etc, of a particular individual.

individually /in-di-**vij**-wa-lee/ *adv* separately, one by one.

indivisible /in-di-**vi**-zi-bul/ *adj* that cannot be divided.

indoctrinate /in-**doc**-tri-nate/ *vb* to bring to accept a system of beliefs unquestioningly.

indoor /in-**dore**/ *adj* done in a house or building.

indoors /in-**dores**/ *adv* within doors, inside a house.

inducement /in-**dyoos**-ment/ *n* something that leads a person to try to do something, an attractive reason for doing something.

indulge /in-**duldge**/ *vb* **1** to take pleasure in something, without trying to control oneself. **2** to give in to the wishes of.

indulgence /in-**dul**-jense/ *n* **1** act of indulging. **2** in the Roman Catholic Church, a release from the punishment that is due to sinners.

indulgent /in-**dul**-jent/ *adj* kindly, easygoing, ready to give in to the wishes of others.

industrial /in-**du**-stree-al/ *adj* having to do with the manufacturing of goods.

industrialism /in-**du**-stree-a-li-zum/ *n* social and economic organization featuring large industries, machine production, concentration of workers in cities, etc.

industrious /in-**du**-stree-us/ *adj* hardworking, busy, skilful, clever.

industry /**in**-du-stree/ *n* **1** (*fml*) the ability to work hard. **2** in trade or commerce, the work that is done to make goods ready for selling, the manufacturing and selling of goods.

inedible /i-**ne**-di-bul/ *adj* that should not or cannot be eaten.

ineffective /i-ne-**fec**-tiv/ *adj* useless, having no effect. • *n* **ineffectiveness**.

ineffectual /i-ne-**fec**-chal/ *adj* **1** not having the desired effect. **2** powerless, not able to get things done.

inefficient /i-ni-**fi**-shent/ *adj* **1** not good at a job, unable to do the job required. **2** not producing results in the best, quickest, and/or cheapest way. • *n* **inefficiency**.

inept /i-**nept**/ *adj* clumsy, awkward.

ineptitude /i-**nep**-ti-tood/ *n* clumsiness, awkwardness.

inequality /i-ne-**kwol**-i-tee/ *n* lack of equality, unevenness.

inert /i-**nert**/ *adj* **1** without the power to move. **2** not wanting to take action, not taking action. **3** not acting chemically when combined with other substances.

inertia /i-**ner**-sha/ *n* **1** unwillingness or inability to move. **2** the inability of matter to set itself in motion or to stop moving.

inescapable /i-ne-**scay**-pa-bul/ *adj* that cannot be avoided.

inevitable /i-**ne**-vi-ta-bul/ *adj* certain to happen. • *n* **inevitability**.

inexact /i-nig-**zact**/ *adj* not quite correct. • *n* **inexactitude**.

inexcusable /i-nik-**scyoo**-za-bul/ *adj* that cannot be forgiven or pardoned.

inexpensive /i-nik-**spen**-siv/ *adj* cheap, not expensive.

inexperience /i-nik-**spee**-ree-ense/ *n* lack of skill or practice. • *adj* **inexperienced**.

inexplicable /i-nik-**spli**-ca-bul/ *adj* that cannot be explained, understood, or accounted for.

infallible /in-**fa**-la-bul/ *adj* **1** unable to make a mistake. **2** that cannot fail. • *n* **infallibility**.

infamous /**in**-fa-mus/ *adj* having a bad reputation, famous for something bad or wicked. • *n* **infamy** the quality of being infamous, an infamous act.

infancy /**in**-fan-see/ *n* **1** babyhood. **2** the early stages of anything.

infant /**in**-fant/ *n* a very young child, a baby.

infantile /**in**-fan-tile/ *adj* **1** childish. **2** having to do with infants.

infantry /**in**-fan-tree/ *n* foot soldiers.

infatuate /in-**fa**-chu-wate/ *vb* **1** to make foolish. **2** to inspire with foolish love or affection.

infatuated /in-**fa**-chu-way-tid/ *adj* loving foolishly or unreasonably. • *n* **infatuation**.

infect /in-**fect**/ *vb* **1** to pass on a disease to another. **2** to make impure by spreading disease into it. **3** to pass on or spread.

infection /in-**fec**-shun/ *n* the passing on or spreading of disease, or anything harmful.

infectious /in-**fec**-shus/ *adj* that can be passed on to others.

infer /in-**fer**/ *vb* (**inferred**, **inferring**) **1** to work out an idea from the facts known. **2** (*inf*) to suggest by hints.

inference /**in**-frense/ *n* an idea or conclusion worked out from the known facts.

inferior /in-**fee**-ree-ur/ *adj* **1** of lesser value or importance. **2** of bad quality. • *n* a person lower in rank.

infertile /in-**fer**-tile/ *adj* not fertile, barren.

infest /in-**fest**/ *vb* to be present in very large numbers in.

infiltrate /**in**-fil-trate/ *vb* **1** to pass through, a few at a time. **2** to enter and secretly, gradually become part of, usually with an unfriendly purpose. • *n* **infiltration**.

infinite /**in**-fi-nit/ *adj* **1** having neither beginning nor end, limitless. **2** (*inf*) very great.

infinitive /in-**fi**-ni-tiv/ *n* the form of a verb that expresses action without referring to a person, number, or tense (e.g. to go, to live, to see).

infinity /in-**fi**-ni-tee/ *n* **1** space, time, or quantity that is without limit or is immeasurably great or small. **2** an indefinitely large number, quantity, or distance.

infirm /in-**firm**/ *adj* weak, sickly.

infirmary /in-**firm**-ree/ *n* a hospital.

infirmity /in-**fir**-mi-tee/ *n* illness, weakness.

inflammable /in-**fla**-ma-bul/ *adj* easily set on fire.

inflammation /in-fla-**may**-shun/ *n* a swelling on part of the body, accompanied by heat and pain.

inflammatory /in-**fla**-ma-toe-ree/ *adj* causing excitement or anger.

inflate /in-**flate**/ *vb* **1** to puff up. **2** to make to swell by filling with air or gas. **3** to increase in price or value. • *adj* **inflatable**.

inflation /in-**flay**-shun/ *n* **1** act of inflating. **2** a situation in a country's economy where prices and wages keep forcing each other to increase. • *adj* **inflationary**.

inflexible /in-**flek**-si-bul/ *adj* **1** that cannot be bent; stiff and firm. **2** not easily changed. **3** not giving in. • *n* **inflexibility**.

inflict /in-**flict**/ *vb* to force something unpleasant or unwanted on someone.

infliction /in-**flic**-shun/ *n* **1** the act of inflicting. **2** punishment.

in-flight /in-**flite**/ *adj* done, occurring, shown, etc. while an aircraft is in flight.

influence /in-**floo**-ense/ *n* **1** the ability to affect other people or the course of events. **2** the power to make requests to those in authority. • *vb* to have an effect on.

influential /in-floo-**en**-shal/ *adj* having power, important.

influenza /in-floo-**en**-za/ *n* a type of infectious illness, usually causing headache, fever, cold symptoms, etc. • *abbr* **flu**.

inform /in-**fawrm**/ *vb* **1** to tell, to give information. **2** to teach, to give knowledge to. **3** to tell facts to the police or authorities about a criminal, etc.

informal /in-**fawr**-mal/ *adj* **1** without ceremony. **2** not bound by rules or accepted ways of behaving. **3** suitable for ordinary everyday situations. • *n* **informality**.

information /in-fur-**may**-shun/ *n* facts told, knowledge in the form of facts, news, etc.

information technology /in-fur-**may**-shun tek-**nol**-o-jee/ *n* the use of computers and other electronic equipment to produce, store, and communicate information.

informative /in-**fawr**-ma-tiv/ *adj* giving news or facts.

informer /in-**fawr**-mer/ *n* someone who gives away the plans of others.

infrequent /in-**free**-kwent/ *adj* not happening often. • *n* **infrequency**.

infuriate /in-**fyoo**-ree-ate/ *vb* to madden, to make very angry.

infuse /in-**fyooz**/ *vb* **1** to put into. **2** to steep in hot liquid.

infusion /in-**fyoo**-zhun/ *n* **1** act of infusing. **2** a liquid given taste or colour by something steeped in it.

ingenious /in-**jeen**-yus/ *adj* **1** having good or new ideas, inventive. **2** cleverly thought out.

ingenuity /in-je-**noo**-i-tee/ *n* **1** cleverness, inventiveness. **2** the ability to invent; cleverness.

ingot /**ing**-gut/ *n* a bar or block of metal, especially gold or silver, got from a mould.

ingrained /in-**graind**/ *adj* fixed firmly in. • *vb* **ingrain**.

ingredient /in-**gree**-dee-ent/ *n* one of the things in a mixture.

ingrown /in-**groan**/ *adj* grown within, inward, or into, especially grown into the flesh. • *n* **ingrowth**.

inhabit /in-**ha**-bit/ *vb* to live in.

inhabitable /in-**ha**-bi-ta-bul/ *adj* that can be lived in.

inhabitant /in-**ha**-bi-tant/ *n* a person who lives in a certain place.

inhabited /in-**ha**-bi-tid/ *adj* having inhabitants, lived in, occupied.

inhalation /in-ha-**lay**-shun/ *n* **1** act of breathing in. **2** something that is breathed in.

inhale /in-**hale**/ *vb* to breathe in.

inhaler /in-**hay**-ler/ *n* a device for giving medicine in the form of a vapour by inhalation.

inherit /in-**he**-rit/ *vb* **1** to receive something from another at his or her death. **2** to receive certain qualities through the parents. • *n* **inheritor**.

inheritance /in-**he**-ri-tanse/ *n* that which is inherited.

inhibit /in-**hi**-bit/ *vb* **1** to prevent or hinder, to hold back from doing. **2** to make someone inhibited. • *n* **inhibitor**.

inhibited /in-**hi**-bi-tid/ *adj* unable to relax and express feelings in an open and natural way.

inhibition /in-hi-**bi**-shun/ *n* a belief or fear of which a person is not aware but which may prevent him or her from performing certain actions.

inhospitable /in-hos-**pi**-ta-bul/ *adj* not welcoming visitors, not kind to strangers. • *n* **inhospitality**.

inhuman /in-**hyoo**-man/ *adj* not having the qualities considered normal to, or for, humans; cruel, brutal, unkind.

inhumane /in-hyoo-**mane**/ *adj* unmoved by the suffering of others, cruel, merciless, brutal, unkind.

inhumanity /in-hyoo-**ma**-ni-tee/ *n* the quality or condition of being inhuman or inhumane.

inimitable /i-**ni**-mi-ta-bul/ *adj* that cannot be copied, too good to be equalled.

initial /i-**ni**-shal/ *adj* first, happening at the beginning. • *adv* **initially**. • *vb* (**initialled**, **initialling**) to mark or write initials. • *npl* the first letters of each of a person's names.

initiate /i-**ni**-she-ate/ *vb* **1** to begin. **2** to teach the ways of a society to a new member. • *n* **initiation**.

initiative /i-**ni**-sha-tiv/ *n* **1** the ability to make decisions and take action without asking for help and advice. **2** the first movement or action that starts something happening.

inject /in-**ject**/ *vb* **1** to put into the bloodstream through a hollow needle. **2** to put in. • *n* **injection**.

injure /in-joor/ *vb* **1** to hurt. **2** to harm, to damage.

injury /in-ju-ree/ *n* **1** damage, harm, hurt. **2** a physical hurt or wound.

injustice /in-**ju**-stiss/ *n* **1** unfairness. **2** an unfair act.

ink /ingk/ *n* a coloured liquid used for writing or printing. • *vb* to mark with ink.

inkblot /**ingk**-blot/ *n* any of a group of irregular patterns made by blots of ink and used in certain kinds of tests, as for the way a person thinks.

inkjet /**ingk**-jet/ *adj* of a high-speed printing process in which ink droplets are formed into printed characters on paper.

inky /**ing**-kee/ *adj* **1** stained with ink. **2** like ink in colour, dark.

inlaid *see* **inlay**.

inland /in-land/ *n* the part of a country away from the sea coast or border. • *adj* **1** having to do with a country's own affairs. **2** away from the coast or border. • *also adv*.

in-law /in-law/ *n* a relative by marriage.

inlay /in-lay/ *vb* (*pt*, *pp* **inlaid**) to decorate by filling carved designs with gold, silver, ivory, etc. • *adj* **inlaid**. • *n* **inlay**.

inlet /in-let/ *n* **1** a way in. **2** a small bay.

in-line skate /in-line skate/ *n* a kind of roller skate having wheels arranged in a straight line like a blade from toe to heel.

inmate /in-mate/ *n* a person living with others in the same house, hospital, prison, etc.

inmost /in-most/ *adj* farthest in.

inn /in/ *n* an establishment where travellers may pay to eat, drink, and/or stay for the night.

innards /i-nerdz/ *n* the inner parts of anything.

innate /i-nate/ *adj* existing naturally rather than being acquired; that seems to have been in a person since birth.

inner /i-ner/ *adj* farther in.

innkeeper /in-kee-per/ *n* the person who is in charge of an inn.

innocence /i-no-sense/ *n* freedom from blame or wickedness.

innocent /i-no-sent/ *adj* **1** not guilty. **2** having no knowledge or experience of evil.

innocuous /i-noc-yu-wus/ *adj* harmless.

innovation /i-no-**vay**-shun/ *n* **1** a new way of doing something, a new thing or idea. **2** the introduction of new things or ideas.

• *vb* **innovate** to renew, to introduce new ways of doing things.

innuendo /i-nyoo-**wen**-doe/ *n* (*pl* **innuendoes** *or* **innuendos**) **1** a way of speaking that makes one understand what is meant without actually saying it. **2** an indirect hint.

innumerate /i-**nyoo**-me-ret/ *adj* unable to do math and arithmetical problems.

inoculate /i-**noc**-yu-late/ *vb* to infect slightly with the germs of a disease to prevent more serious infection. • *n* **inoculation**.

inoffensive /i-no-**fen**-siv/ *adj* not causing harm or trouble.

inpatient /in-pay-shent/ *n* a patient who is kept in a hospital for more than a day.

input /in-poot/ *n* **1** the act of putting in. **2** what is put in, as in the amount of money, material, effort, opinion, etc.

inquire, enquire /in-kwire/ *vb* **1** to ask. **2** to ask for information about. **3** to try to discover the facts of.

inquiring /in-**kwie**-ring/ *adj* seeking information, curious.

inquiry, enquiry /in-**kwie**-ree/ *n* **1** a question. **2** a careful search for information, an investigation.

inquisition /in-kwi-**zi**-shun/ *n* (*fml*) an inquiry involving a long period of detailed questioning or investigation. • *n* **inquisitor**.

inquisitive /in-**kwi**-zi-tiv/ *adj* **1** eager to seek information. **2** asking too many questions, especially about other people; prying.

inroad /in-road/ *n* a raid, a sudden attack.

insane /in-**sane**/ *adj* **1** mentally ill. **2** (*inf*) very unwise, very foolish.

insanity /in-**sa**-ni-tee/ *n* the state of being insane; mental illness.

inscribe /in-**scribe**/ *vb* to write in a book or engrave on stone, etc.

inscription /in-**scrip**-shun/ *n* words written on something, often as a tribute.

insect /in-sect/ *n* any of a large group of small creatures that have a body divided into three sections, six legs, and usually wings.

insecure /in-si-**cyoor**/ *adj* **1** anxious and unsure of oneself, lacking confidence. **2** (*fml*) not safe, likely to be lost. **3** (*fml*) not safe or firmly fixed. • *n* **insecurity**.

insensible /in-**sen**-si-bul/ *adj* **1** unaware. **2** without feeling, indifferent. **3** unconscious.

insensitive /in-**sen**-si-tiv/ *adj* **1** not noticing the feelings of others. **2** not quick to feel or notice.

inseparable /in-**se**-pra-bul/ *adj* that cannot be put apart.

insert /in-**sert**/ *vb* to put in or among.

insertion /in-**ser**-shun/ *n* **1** something inserted. **2** the act of inserting.

inset /in-set/ *n* an extra piece set in (e.g. a small picture in a larger one). • *vb* **inset**.

inside /in-**side**/ *n* **1** the inner side or part. **2** *pl* (*inf*) the internal organs, stomach, bowels. • *adj* /in-side/ **1** internal. **2** known only to insiders, secret. • *adv* **1** on or in the inside, within, indoors. **2** (*inf*) in prison. • *prep* in or within.

insider /in-**sie**-der/ *n* **1** a person inside a given place or group. **2** a person having or likely to have secret information.

insidious /in-**si**-dee-us/ *adj* developing gradually, without being noticed, and causing harm.

insight /in-site/ *n* ability to see the real meaning or importance of something, thorough knowledge. • *adj* **insightful**.

insignia /in-**sig**-nee-ya/ *npl* badges of rank, membership, or honour.

insignificant /in-sig-**ni**-fi-cant/ *adj* of little importance. • *n* **insignificance**.

insincere /in-sin-**seer**/ *adj* not meaning what is said, false, not truly meant. • *n* **insincerity**.

insinuate /in-**sin**-yu-wate/ *vb* **1** to make way gradually and cunningly. **2** to hint in an unpleasant way. • *n* **insinuation**.

insipid /in-**si**-pid/ *adj* **1** having no taste or flavour. **2** uninteresting, dull.

insist /in-**sist**/ *vb* **1** to state firmly, to demand or urge strongly. **2** to keep on saying.

insistent /in-**sis**-tent/ *adj* **1** firm. **2** wanting immediate attention. • *n* **insistence**.

insole /in-sole/ *n* the inside sole of a shoe.

insolent /in-**so**-lent/ *adj* rude, boldly insulting or disrespectful. • *n* **insolence**.

insoluble /in-**sol**-yu-bul/ *adj* **1** impossible to dissolve. **2** that cannot be solved.

insomnia /in-**som**-nee-ya/ *n* sleeplessness.

inspect /in-**spect**/ *vb* to look at closely, to examine.

inspection /in-**spec**-shun/ *n* an examination.

inspector /in-**spec**-tor/ *n* **1** someone who inspects. **2** someone who examines the work of others to see that it is done properly. **3** a rank of police officer.

inspectorate /in-**spec**-taw-rit/ *n* a body or group of inspectors.

inspiration /in-spi-**ray**-shun/ *n* **1** (*fml*) the breathing in of air. **2** a person or thing that encourages a person to use his or her powers, gifts, talent, etc. **3** the encouragement so given. • *adj* **inspirational**.

inspire /in-**spire**/ *vb* **1** (*fml*) to breathe in. **2** to encourage someone with the desire and ability to take action by filling with eagerness, confidence, etc. **3** to be the force that produces something, to be the origin of. **4** to arouse in someone.

instability /in-sta-**bi**-li-tee/ *n* unsteadiness.

install /in-**stawl**/ *vb* **1** to place in office, especially with ceremony. **2** to put in place. • *n* **installation**.

instalment /in-**stawl**-ment/ *n, also* **installment** (*US*) **1** payment of part of a sum of money owed. **2** part of a serial story published or broadcast at one time.

instance /in-stanse/ *n* an example. • **for instance** for example. • *vb* to give or quote as an example.

instant /in-stant/ *adj* **1** immediate. **2** concentrated or precooked for quick preparation. • *n* **1** a moment. **2** the exact moment. • *adv* **instantly** at once.

instantaneous /in-stan-**tay**-nee-us/ *adj* happening or done very quickly.

instate /in-**state**/ *vb* to put in a particular status, position, or rank.

instead /in-**sted**/ *adv* in place of.

instep /in-step/ *n* the upper part of the foot between the ankle and the toes.

instil /in-**still**/ *vb, also* **instill** (*US*) (**instilled**, **instilling**) to put in the mind, little by little.

instinct /in-stingt/ *n* a natural tendency to behave or react in a particular way without having been taught.

instinctive /in-**stink**-tiv/ *adj* done at once without thinking, natural.

institute /in-sti-toot/ *vb* to set up for the first time. • *n* **1** an organization, especially one connected with a particular profession, working to achieve a certain purpose. **2** the building in which such a society meets or works.

institution /in-sti-**too**-shun/ *n* **1** an organization, usually a long-established or well-respected one. **2** the building used by such an organization. **3** an accepted custom or tradition. • *adj* **institutional**.

institutionalize /in-sti-**too**-shna-lize/ *vb, also* **institutionalise 1** to make into an institution. **2** to place in an institution.

instruct /in-**struct**/ *vb* **1** to teach. **2** to order.

instruction /in-**struc**-shun/ *n* **1** teaching. **2** an order. **3** *pl* information on how to use something correctly.

instructive /in-**struc**-tiv/ *adj* giving knowledge or information.

instructor /in-**struc**-tor/ *n* a teacher, a coach, someone who instructs.

instrument /in-stru-ment/ *n* **1** a tool, especially one used for delicate work. **2** a device producing musical sound. **3** a device for measuring, recording, controlling, etc, especially in an aircraft.

instrumental /in-stru-**men**-tal/ *adj* **1** being the cause of. **2** played on musical instruments. • *n* **instrumentality** the state of being instrumental.

instrumentation /in-stru-men-**tay**-shun/ *n* **1** the arrangement of music for instruments. **2** the act of using instruments, especially scientific instruments. **3** the instruments used.

insubstantial /in-sub-**stan**-shal/ *adj* **1** weak or flimsy. **2** not real, imaginary.

insufferable /in-**suf**-ra-bul/ *adj* unbearable.

insufficient /in-su-**fi**-shent/ *adj* not enough. • *n* **insufficiency**.

insular /in-syoo-lar/ *adj* **1** (*fml*) having to do with an island. **2** narrow-minded.

insularity /in-su-**la**-ri-tee/ *n* narrow-mindedness.

insulate /in-su-late/ *vb* **1** to keep apart. **2** to cover with a special material to prevent the loss of electricity or heat. • *n* **insulation**.

insulator /in-su-lay-tor/ *n* a material that does not allow electricity or heat to pass through it.

insulin /in-su-lin/ *n* a substance that if given as a medicine helps to use up the sugar in the body when there is too much of it.

insult /in-**sult**/ *vb* to speak rude or hurtful words to or of. • *n* /**in**-sult/.

insupportable /in-su-**pore**-ta-bul/ *adj* unbearable, not capable of being upheld or supported.

insure /in-**shoor**/ *vb* to pay regular sums to a society on condition that the payer receives an agreed amount of money in case of loss, accident, death, etc. • *n* **insurance**.

insured /in-**shoord**/ *n* a person whose life, property, etc. is insured against loss or damage.

insurer /in-**shoo**-rer/ *n* a person or company that insures others against loss or damage.

insurmountable /in-sur-**moun**-ta-bul/ *adj* that cannot be passed over or overcome.

intact /in-**tact**/ *adj* untouched, unharmed, with no part missing.

intake /**in**-take/ *n* the act or process of taking in.

intangible /in-**tan**-ji-bul/ *adj* **1** that cannot be touched. **2** not able to be clearly defined or understood.

integer /**in**-ti-jer/ *n* a whole number.

integral /**in**-ti-gral/ *adj* necessary to make something complete. • *also n*.

integrate /**in**-ti-grate/ *vb* **1** to join in society as a whole, to mix freely with other groups.

2 to fit parts together to form a whole. • *n* **integration**.

integrity /in-**te**-gri-tee/ *n* **1** the state of being whole and undivided, completeness. **2** honesty, sincerity.

intellect /**in**-ti-lect/ *n* **1** the mind, the power to think and understand. **2** someone with great intellect.

intellectual /in-ti-**lec**-chu-wal/ *adj* **1** having a high intellect. **2** having to do with the intellect. • *also n*.

intelligence /in-**te**-li-jense/ *n* **1** cleverness, quickness of mind or understanding. **2** (*fml*) news.

intelligent /in-**te**-li-jent/ *adj* having a quick mind, clever.

intelligible /in-**te**-li-ji-bul/ *adj* clear, that can be understood.

intemperate /in-**tem**-per-it/ *adj* **1** lacking self-control, given to taking too much, especially strong drink. **2** more than is desirable. **3** excessive, unrestrained. **4** extreme. • *n* **intemperance**.

intend /in-**tend**/ *vb* **1** to have as a purpose. **2** to mean. • *adj* **intended** meant, planned for the future.

intense /in-**tense**/ *adj* **1** very great. **2** very serious.

intensify /in-**ten**-si-fie/ *vb* to make greater or more severe. • *n* **intensifier** a person or thing that makes greater or more severe.

intensity /in-**ten**-si-tee/ *n* **1** strength. **2** seriousness, earnestness. **3** great energy, emotion, thought.

intensive /in-**ten**-siv/ *adj* increasing or degree or amount.

intent /in-**tent**/ *adj* **1** attending carefully. **2** eager, planning or wanting to do something. • *n* (*fml*) purpose.

intention /in-**ten**-shun/ *n* purpose, aim in doing something.

intentional /in-**ten**-shu-nal/ *adj* done on purpose.

inter /in-**ter**/ *vb* (**interred, interring**) (*fml*) to bury.

inter- /in-**ter**/ *prefix* between, among.

interact /in-te-**ract**/ *vb* to act on each other. • *n* **interaction**.

intercede /in-ter-**seed**/ *vb* **1** to try to settle a dispute or quarrel between others. **2** to speak in defence of another.

intercept /in-ter-**sept**/ *vb* to stop or catch on the way from one place to another. • *n* **interception**.

interchange /**in**-ter-change/ *vb* **1** to change places with each other. **2** to give and receive in return. • *n* an exchange.

interchangeable /in-ter-**chane**-ja-bul/ *adj* that which can be exchanged for each other.

intercourse *n* **1** interaction between people. **2 sexual intercourse.**

interest /in-trest/ *n* **1** something in which a person takes part eagerly. **2** advantage. **3** eager attention. **4** concern. **5** the money paid for the use of a loan of money. • *vb* to gain the attention of.

interesting /in-tres-ting/ *adj* arousing interest.

interface /in-ter-face/ *n* the point at which two subjects affect each other or are connected.

interfere /in-ter-fere/ *vb* **1** to get in the way of, to prevent from working or happening. **2** to force oneself into the affairs of others. **3** to touch or move something that is not supposed to be touched or moved.

interference /in-ter-**fee**-rense/ *n* **1** act of interfering. **2** the interruption of radio broadcasts by atmospherics or other broadcasts.

intergalactic /in-ter-ga-**lac**-tic/ *adj* existing or occurring between or among galaxies.

interim /in-te-rim/ *n* the meantime, the time between two events. • *adj* acting for a time only.

interior /in-**tee**-ree-ur/ *adj* **1** inner. **2** inland. • *n* **1** the inner part. **2** the inland part.

interject /in-ter-**ject**/ *vb* **1** to say something short and sudden. **2** to put in a remark when another is speaking.

interjection /in-ter-**jec**-shun/ *n* **1** a short word expressing surprise, interest, disapproval, etc. **2** a remark made when another is speaking.

interlude /in-ter-**lood**/ *n* **1** an interval between the acts of a play, etc. **2** the music or other entertainment provided during such an interval. **3** a period of time that comes between two events or activities.

intermediate /in-ter-**mee**-dee-it/ *adj* coming between two other things, in the middle.

interminable /in-**ter**-mi-na-bul/ *adj* without, or apparently without, end; seeming to last forever.

intermission /in-ter-**mi**-shun/ *n* an interval, a time between two parts.

intermittent /in-ter-**mi**-tent/ *adj* stopping for a time, then going on again; happening at intervals.

intern /in-tern/ *n* a person, especially a student, working in a professional field to gain experience in the work place. • *vb* /in-**tern**/ to detain or confine people, ships, etc. as during a war. • *n* **internment.**

internal /in-**ter**-nal/ *adj* **1** having to do with the inside, especially of the body. **2** of a person's own country.

international /in-ter-**nash**-nal/ *adj* having to do with several or many countries. • *n* a person associated with two different countries.

Internet /in-ter-net/ *n* the worldwide system of linked computer networks.

interplay /in-ter-play/ *n* the action of one thing on another.

interpret /in-**ter**-pret/ *vb* **1** to explain the meaning of. **2** to understand the meaning to be. **3** to translate from one language into another. • *adj* **interpretive.**

interpretation /in-ter-pre-**tay**-shun/ *n* **1** act of interpreting. **2** the meaning given to a work of art by a critic or performer.

interpreter /in-**ter**-pre-ter/ *n* someone who translates from one speaker's language into another's.

interracial /in-ter-**ray**-shal/ *adj* between, among, or involving members of different races.

interrogate /in-**te**-ro-gate/ *vb* to put questions to.

interrogation /in-te-ro-**gay**-shun/ *n* **1** the act of interrogating.

interrogative /in-te-**rog**-a-tiv/ *adj* asking a question, having to do with questions.

interrupt /in-te-**rupt**/ *vb* **1** to break flow of speech or action. **2** to stop a person while he or she is saying or doing something. **3** (*fml*) to cut off. • *n* **interrupter** a person who interrupts.

interruption /in-te-**rup**-shun/ *n* a remark or action that causes a stoppage.

intersect /in-ter-**sect**/ *vb* to cut across each other.

intersection /in-ter-**sec**-shun/ *n* the point at which lines or roads cross each other.

intersperse /in-ter-**sperse**/ *vb* to scatter over, to put here and there.

interstellar /in-ter-**ste**-lar/ *adj* among or between the stars.

intertwine /in-ter-**twine**/ *vb* to twist together.

interval /in-ter-val/ *n* **1** the time or distance between. **2** a break, a spell of free time. **3** a short break in a play, concert, etc. **4** the difference of pitch between two musical sounds.

intervene /in-ter-**veen**/ *vb* **1** to interrupt, to interfere. **2** to be or to happen between (in time). **3** to happen so as to prevent something. • *n* **intervention.**

interview /in-ter-vyoo/ *n* **1** a meeting at which a person applying for a job is questioned. **2** a meeting with a person to get information or to do business. • *also vb*.

intestinal /in-**tes**-ti-nal/ *adj* having to do with the intestines.

intestines /in-**tes**-tinz/ *npl* the inner parts of the body, especially the bowels.

intifada /in-ti-fa-da/ *n* an uprising, specifically the uprising of Palestinian Arabs against Israeli military forces in occupied territories of the Gaza Strip and the west bank of the Jordon River, begun in 1987.

intimacy /in-ti-ma-see/ *n* closeness, close relationship.

intimate /in-ti-mit/ *adj* **1** having a close relationship. **2** having a close knowledge of. • *n* a close friend. • *vb* (*fml*) /in-ti-mate/ to make known.

intimation /in-ti-**may**-shun/ *n* **1** (*fml*) a hint. **2** an announcement.

intimidate /in-**ti**-mi-date/ *vb* to make afraid, e.g. by making threats. • *n* **intimidation**.

into /in-too/ *prep* **1** from the outside to the inside. **2** continuing to the midst of. **3** to the form, substance, or condition of. **4** so as to strike, against. **5** to the work or activity of.

intolerable /in-**tol**-ra-bul/ *adj* that cannot or should not be put up with.

intolerant /in-**tol**-rant/ *adj* not willing to put up with actions or opinions that are different from one's own; narrow-minded. • *n* **intolerance**.

intonation /in-tu-**nay**-shun/ *n* the rise and fall of the voice while speaking.

intoxicate /in-**tok**-si-cate/ *vb* **1** to make drunk or stupefied. **2** to excite greatly. • *n* **intoxication**.

intra- /in-tra/ *prefix* within, inside.

intranet /in-tra-net/ *n* a private computer network using Internet technology but keeping access limited to members of a particular organization.

intransitive /in-**tran**-zi-tiv/ *adj* (*gram*) describing verbs not taking an object.

intravenous /in-tra-**vee**-nus/ *adj* in or directly into a vein or veins.

intrepid /in-**tre**-pid/ *adj* fearless, brave.

intricate /in-tri-cit/ *adj* having many small parts, complicated. • *n* **intricacy**.

intrigue /in-treeg/ *n* **1** a secret plot. **2** a secret love affair. • *vb* /in-treeg/ **1** to plot secretly. **2** to interest greatly. • *adj* **intriguing**.

intrinsic /in-**trin**-zic/ *adj* being part of the nature or character of, belonging to a thing as part of its nature.

introduce /in-tru-**dyoos**/ *vb* **1** to bring in or put forward, especially something new. **2** to make one person known to another.

introduction /in-tru-**duc**-shun/ *n* **1** act of introducing. **2** a short section at the beginning of a book to make known its purpose.

introductory /in-tru-**duc**-tu-ree/ *adj* coming at the beginning, giving an introduction.

introspective /in-tro-**spec**-tiv/ *adj* thinking a lot about one's own actions and ideas. • *n* **introspection**. • *vb* **introspect** to look into one's own mind.

introvert /in-tro-vert/ *n* someone who is always thinking about his or her own ideas and aims.

intrude /in-**trood**/ *vb* to come or go where not wanted. • *n* **intrusion**.

intruder /in-**troo**-der/ *n* **1** someone who intrudes. **2** a person who breaks into a house to steal, a burglar.

intrusive /in-**troo**-siv/ *adj* tending to intrude.

intuition /in-tyoo-**wi**-shun/ *n* **1** immediate knowledge of the truth gained without having to think. **2** the ability to know things in this way. • *adj* **intuitive**. • *vb* **intuit** to know or learn by intuition.

Inuit /in-yoo-wit/ *n* **1** original inhabitants of northern North America or Greenland or their descendants. **2** the language of this people.

inundate /i-nun-date/ *vb* **1** to flow over. **2** to flood, to come in very large amounts.

invade /in-**vade**/ *vb* **1** to enter as an enemy, to attack. **2** to interfere with.

invalid[1] /in-**va**-lid/ *adj* **1** not valid. **2** useless, unreliable.

invalid[2] /in-va-lid/ *adj* weak, sickly. • *n* a sick person. • *vb* to send away because of illness.

invalidate /in-**va**-li-date/ *vb* to make to have no value or effect.

invalidism /in-va-li-di-zum/ *n* the state of being an invalid, long-term ill health or disability.

invaluable /in-**val**-yu-bul/ *adj* of very great value or help.

invariable /in-**vay**-ree-ya-bul/ *adj* unchanging, constant. • *n* **invariability**.

invariant /in-**vay**-ree-ant/ *adj* constant, unchanging.

invasion /in-**vay**-zhun/ *n* **1** entry into a country by enemy forces. **2** interference. • *adj* **invasive**.

invent /in-**vent**/ *vb* **1** to think of and plan something new. **2** to make up. • *n* **inventor**.

invention /in-**ven**-shun/ *n* **1** a thing thought of and made for the first time. **2** the ability to think of new ideas.

inventive /in-**ven**-tiv/ *adj* good at thinking of new or unusual ideas.

inventory /in-ven-toe-ree/ *n* a list of goods or articles.

inverse /in-verse/ *adj* opposite or reverse.

inversion /in-ver-shun/ *n* **1** act of turning upside down. **2** a change in the usual order of words in a sentence.

invert /in-vert/ *vb* to turn upside down, to turn the other way round.

invertebrate /in-ver-te-brate/ *adj* having no backbone. • *n* an animal without a backbone.

invest /in-vest/ *vb* **1** to mark someone's entry to rank or office by clothing him or her with the robes belonging to it. **2** to surround a fort with an army. **3** to lend money so as to increase it by interest or a share in profits.

investigate /in-ve-sti-gate/ *vb* to examine, to find out everything about. • *n* **investigator**.

investigation /in-ve-sti-gay-shun/ *n* a careful examination, an inquiry.

investigative /in-ve-sti-ga-tiv/ *adj* inclined to investigate, involved in investigation.

investment /in-vest-ment/ *n* **1** the act of investing. **2** a sum of money invested. **3** the thing money has been invested in.

investor /in-ve-stor/ *n* someone who invests money.

inveterate /in-ve-trit/ *adj* **1** firmly fixed in a habit. **2** firmly established.

invincible /in-vin-si-bul/ *adj* that cannot be defeated. • *n* **invincibility**.

invisible /in-vi-zi-bul/ *adj* that cannot be seen. • *n* **invisibility**.

invite /in-vite/ *vb* **1** to ask politely, to ask to come, especially as a guest. **2** to attract. • *n* **invitation**.

inviting /in-vie-ting/ *adj* attractive.

invoice /in-voiss/ *n* **1** a list of goods sent to a buyer, with prices. **2** a list of work done and payment due. • *vb* to send an invoice.

invoke /in-voke/ *vb* **1** to bring into use or operation. **2** to call on God or a god in prayer. **3** to request or beg for. **4** to make an urgent request to.

involuntary /in-vol-un-te-ree/ *adj* unintentional, done without conscious effort or intention.

involve /in-volve/ *vb* **1** to include. **2** to mix up in. **3** to cause as a result.

involved /in-volvd/ *adj* complicated.

invulnerable /in-vuln-ra-bul/ *adj* that cannot be wounded.

inward /in-ward/ *adj* **1** inner. **2** having to do with the mind. • *adv* (*also* **inwards**) towards the inside.

inwardly /in-ward-lee/ *adv* on the inside, in the mind.

iodine /eye-o-deen/ *n* a chemical used in medicine to clean wounds, instruments, etc.

ion /eye-on/ *n* an electrically charged atom. • *adj* **ionic**.

ionosphere /eye-on-oe-sfeer/ *n* the outer part of the earth's atmosphere.

iota /eye-oe-ta/ *n* **1** a Greek letter. **2** a tiny amount.

IQ /eye-kyoo/ *abbr* = **Intelligence Quotient**: a person's level of intelligence as measured by a special test.

irate /eye-rate/ *adj* very angry, furious.

ire /ire/ *n* (*fml, lit*) anger.

iridescent /i-ri-des-ant/ *adj* coloured like the rainbow, brightly coloured, having or showing shifting colours. • *n* **iridescence**.

iris /eye-ris/ *n* **1** the coloured circle of the eye. **2** a flowering plant.

irk /urk/ *vb* to annoy, to bother.

irksome /irk-sum/ *adj* troublesome, tedious, annoying.

iron /eye-urn/ *n* **1** the most common of metals. **2** a tool or instrument made of iron, especially for smoothing clothes. **3** *pl* chains. • *adj* **1** made of iron. **2** strong, hard. • *vb* to smooth. • **to have too many irons in the fire** to be trying to do too many things at once.

ironic /eye-ron-ic/, **ironical** /eye-ron-ic-al/ *adjs* expressing irony.

irony /eye-ro-nee/ *n* **1** a remark made in such a way that the meaning is understood to be the opposite of what is said. **2** the result of an action that has the opposite effect to that intended.

irradiate /i-ray-dee-ate/ *vb* **1** (*fml or lit*) to make bright by throwing light on. **2** to treat with radiation. • *n* **irradiation** exposure to radiation, an irradiating of.

irrational /i-ra-shnal/ *adj* **1** not rational, not reasonable, not sensible. **2** not able to reason, not using reason. • *n* **irrationalism** irrational thought.

irregular /i-reg-yu-lar/ *adj* **1** not in agreement with the rules, not according to accepted standards. **2** not straight or even. **3** not happening, etc, regularly. • *n* **irregularity**.

irrelevant /i-re-le-vant/ *adj* having nothing to do with the subject, not to the point. • *n* **irrelevance, irrelevancy**.

irreplaceable /i-re-play-sa-bul/ *adj* not replaceable, that cannot be replaced.

irrepressible /i-re-pre-si-bul/ *adj* that cannot be kept down or held back.

irresistible /i-re-zi-sta-bul/ *adj* **1** that cannot be resisted. **2** very strong. **3** very attractive, charming.

irrespective /i-re-**spec**-tiv/ *adj* with disregard for, not troubling about.

irresponsible /i-re-**spon**-si-bul/ *adj* not caring about the consequences of actions.

irrigate /i-ri-gate/ *vb* to supply water to dry land by canals, etc. • *n* **irrigation**. • *adj* **irrigable**.

irritable /i-ri-ta-bul/ *adj* easily angered or annoyed. • *n* **irritability**.

irritant /i-ri-tant/ *n* something that irritates, annoys, angers, inflames, makes sore, etc.

irritate /i-ri-tate/ *vb* **1** to annoy, to anger. **2** to cause to itch, become inflamed, red, swollen, etc. • *n* **irritation**.

is /iz/ *vb* t of the verb **be** used with 'he', 'she', 'it', and 'one' or with singular nouns.

Islam /iz-lam/ *n* **1** the Muslim religion founded by Mohammed in which the god is called Allah. **2** all Muslims. **3** all the lands in which Islam is the main religion. • *adj* **Islamic**.

island /eye-land/ *n* a piece of land surrounded by water.

islander /eye-lan-der/ *n* a native of an island.

isle /ile/ *n* (*lit*) an island, especially a small island.

islet /eye-let/ *n* a very small island.

isolate /eye-so-late/ *vb* **1** to place apart or alone. **2** to cut off. **3** to separate. • *n* **isolation**.

isosceles /eye-**sos**-leez/ *adj* (*of a triangle*) having two sides equal.

issue /i-shoo/ *vb* **1** to go or come out. **2** to send out. **3** to flow out. **4** to give out. **5** to publish. • *n* **1** a flowing out. **2** (*fml*) children. **3** (*fml*) a result. **4** a question under discussion. **5** number of books, papers, etc, published at one time.

it /it/ *pron* the person, animal, or thing previously mentioned, also used as the subject to an impersonal verb (e.g. it is snowing).

IT /eye-**tee**/ *abbr* = **information technology**: the study or use of computers and telecommunication sytems.

italicize /i-ta-li-size/ *vb*, *also* **italicise** to print in italics.

italic(s) /i-ta-lics/ *n* in printing, letters in sloping type (e.g. *italics*). • *also adj*.

itch /itch/ *n* **1** an irritation of the skin that causes a desire to scratch. **2** a longing. • *vb* **1** to feel an itch. **2** to feel a strong desire. • *adj* **itchy**.

item /eye-tem/ *n* **1** a single one out of a list or number of things. **2** a piece of news. • *adv* **also**, in the same way.

itemize /eye-tem-ize/ *vb*, *also* **itemise** to specify the items of.

itinerant /eye-ti-ne-rant/ *adj* not settling in any one place, moving from place to place. • *n* one who is always on the move from place to place.

itinerary /eye-**ti**-ne-ra-ree/ *n* a note of the places visited or to be visited on a journey.

its /its/ *pron* that or those of or belonging to it, the possessive form of 'it'.

it's /its/ *contraction* shortened form of **it is** or **it has**.

I've *contraction* **I have**.

ivory /eye-vree/ *n* the hard white substance forming the tusks of elephants, etc. • *adj* of or like ivory, creamy white.

ivy /eye-vee/ *n* a climbing vine with a woody stem and evergreen leaves.

J

J, j /jay/ the tenth letter of the English alphabet.

jab /jab/ *vb* (**jabbed, jabbing**) to prod or poke suddenly. • *n* **1** a sudden prod or poke. **2** an injection.

jabber /ja-ber/ *vb* to chatter, to speak quickly and indistinctly.

jack /jack/ *n* **1** a tool for lifting heavy weights. **2** the small white ball aimed at in the game of bowls. **3** the knave in cards. **4** an electronic connection for an electric machine or telephone. • *vb* to raise with a jack. • **every man jack** (*inf*) every single one.

jackal /ja-cal/ *n* a doglike wild animal.

jackass /ja-cass/ *n* **1** a male donkey. **2** (*inf*) a fool.

jacket /ja-cet/ *n* **1** a short coat. **2** a loose paper cover for a book.

jack-of-all-trades /jack-of-awl-**traydz**/ *n* someone who is able to do any kind of job.

Jacuzzi /ja-**coo**-zee/ (*TM*) a kind of whirlpool bath with a system of underwater jets which massage the body.

jade /jade/ *n* a green precious stone.

jaded /jay-did/ *adj* tired, bored, uninterested.

jagged /ja-ged/ *adj* having rough edges or sharp points.

jaguar /jag-you-ar, ja-gwar/ *n* an animal like the leopard, found in South America.

jail /jale/ *n, also* **gaol** a prison.

jailer /jay-ler/ *n* a prison guard.

jam[1] /jam/ *n* fruit boiled with sugar to preserve it; jelly; preserve.

jam[2] /jam/ *vb* (**jammed, jamming**) **1** to squeeze in, to fix so tightly that movement is impossible. **2** to crowd full. **3** to prevent the receiving of radio messages by broadcasting sounds on the same wavelength. • *n* a pile-up of traffic.

jangle /jang-gl/ *n* a harsh ringing noise. • *vb* **1** to make or cause to make a jangle. **2** (*inf*) to irritate.

janitor /ja-ni-tor/ *n* in Scotland, someone who takes care of a building; a caretaker.

January /jan-yoo-a-ree/ *n* the first month of the year.

jar /jar/ *n* a glass or earthenware vessel with a wide mouth.

jargon /jar-gon/ *n* words special to a group or profession.

jasmine /jaz-min/, **jessamine** /jess-min/ *n* a climbing bush with sweet-smelling flowers.

jasper /ja-sper/ *n* a precious stone, yellow, red or brown in colour.

jaundice /jon-diss/ *n* an illness marked by yellowness of the eyes and skin.

jaundiced /jon-dist/ *adj* **1** suffering from jaundice. **2** full of envy, disappointment, etc, thinking of everything as bad or unlucky.

jaunt /jont/ *n* a short pleasure trip. • *vb* to go from place to place.

jaunty /jon-tee/ *adj* **1** cheerful-looking, confident. **2** pleased with oneself.

javelin /ja-ve-lin/ *n* a light throwing spear.

jaw /jaw/ *n* one of the bones in the mouth that hold the teeth.

jay /jay/ *n* a bird of the crow family with brightly coloured feathers.

jaywalk /jay-wawk/ *vb* to walk across the street carelessly or without obeying the rules of the road. • *n* **jaywalker**.

jazz /jazz/ *n* syncopated music and dancing of African-American origin.

jealous /je-luss/ *adj* **1** disliking rivals in love, having feelings of dislike for any possible rivals. **2** disliking another because he or she is better off than you in some way; envious. **3** (*fml*) very careful of. • *n* **jealousy**.

jean /jeen/ *n* a cotton cloth. • *npl* close-fitting trousers often made of denim.

Jeep /jeep/ (*TM*) a light truck, military or otherwise, for going over rough ground.

jeer /jeer/ *vb* to laugh or shout at disrespectfully, to mock. • *n* insulting words.

jehad /ji-had/ *see* jihad.

Jehovah /ji-ho-va/ *n* from the Old Testament of the bible, a name for God.

jelly /je-lee/ *n* **1** a type of preserved fruit; jam. **2** a food made from fruit juice boiled with sugar, from meat juices, or from gelatine. **3** a material that is in a state between solid and liquid.

jellyfish /je-lee-fish/ *n* a jellylike sea creature often with stinging tentacles.

jeopardize /je-par-dize/ *vb, also* **jeopardise** to put in danger, to risk.

jeopardy /je-par-dee/ *n* danger.

jerk /jerk/ *vb* **1** to give a sudden pull or push. **2** to move suddenly and quickly. • *n* a sudden, quick movement.

jerkin /jer-kin/ *n* a close-fitting jacket or short coat.

jerky[1] /jer-kee/ *adj* moving by jerks.

jerky² /jer-kee/ *n* a preserved dried meat.

jersey /jer-zee/ *n* **1** a fine wool. **2** a jumper.

jest /jest/ *n* a joke, something done or said in fun. • *vb* to joke.

jester /je-ster/ *n* (*old*) one paid to make jokes, as in a king's or nobleman's household.

Jesuit /je-zoo-it/ *n* a priest or brother in the Society of Jesus, a Roman Catholic religious order.

jet¹ /jet/ *n* a hard black substance, often used for ornamental purposes.

jet² /jet/ *n* **1** a stream of liquid or gas forced through a narrow opening. **2** a spout through which a narrow stream of liquid or gas can be forced. **3** a jet plane.

jet lag /jet lag/ *n* tiredness which results from travelling across several time zones.

jet plane /jet plane/ *n* an aeroplane that is jet-propelled, i.e., driven forward by the force of jets of gas forced out to the rear.

jetsam /jet-sum/ *n* goods thrown overboard to make a ship lighter.

jettison /je-ti-son/ *vb* **1** to throw. **2** to get rid of.

jetty /je-tee/ *n* **1** a pier. **2** a wall built to protect a harbour from high seas.

Jew /joo/ *n* a member of the people who are descendants of the ancient Hebrew people of Israel and whose religion is Judaism.

jewel /joo-ul/ *n* **1** a precious stone. **2** something valued highly.

jeweller /joo-u-ler/, **jeweler** (*US*) *n* someone who buys and sells jewels.

jewellery /joo-ul-ree/ *n*, *also* **jewelry** (*US*), jewels, personal ornaments, as rings, necklaces, etc.

Jewish /joo-ish/ *adj* having to do with Jews or Judaism.

jib /jib/ *n* **1** a triangular sail raised in front of a ship's foremast. **2** the arm of a crane. • *vb* to pull a sail round to the other side. • **to like the cut of someone's jib** to like someone.

jibe *same as* **gibe**.

jiffy /ji-fee/ *n* (*inf*) a moment, an instant.

jig /jig/ *n* a lively dance tune. • *vb* (**jigged**, **jigging**) **1** to dance a jig. **2** to move up and down quickly in a jerky way.

jigsaw /jig-saw/ *n* a picture that has been cut into different shapes and the puzzle is to try to fit them together again.

jihad /ji-had/ *n*, *also* **jehad** a holy war waged by Muslims against nonbelievers.

jilt /jilt/ *vb* to leave someone after promising to love or marry him or her.

jingle /jing-gul/ *n* a light ringing noise made by metal against metal, as by small bells or coins. • *vb* to ring lightly, to clink.

jitters /ji-terz/ *npl* (*inf*) great nervousness.

jittery /ji-te-ree/ *adj* (*inf*) nervous.

jive /jive/ *n* **1** a type of jazz music. **2** the way of dancing to it. • *also vb*.

job /job/ *n* **1** a piece of work. **2** someone's employment. **3** (*inf*) a crime.

jockey /jaw-key/ *n* a rider in horse races. • *vb* to struggle to gain an advantage over someone or to achieve something.

jocular /joc-yu-lar/ *adj* **1** intended to be humorous. **2** fond of joking.

jodhpurs /jod-purz/ *npl* riding breeches reaching to the ankle.

jog /jawg/ *vb* (**jogged**, **jogging**) **1** to nudge, to prod. **2** to walk or run at a slow, steady pace. • *n* **1** a nudge, a slight shake. **2** a slow walk or trot.

join /join/ *vb* **1** to put or fasten together. **2** to take part in with others. **3** to become a member of. • *n* a place where things join. • **join battle** to begin fighting.

joiner /joy-ner/ *n* a carpenter, a worker in wood, who makes furniture, etc.

joint /joint/ *n* **1** a place at which two things meet or are fastened together. **2** a place where two things are joined, but left the power of moving. **3** a large piece of meat containing a bone. **4** (*inf*) a particular kind of place. **5** (*inf*) a cigarette containing cannabis. • *adj* **1** shared between two or among all. **2** done by several together. • *also vb*.

jointed /join-ted/ *adj* having joints.

jointly /joint-lee/ *adv* together.

joist /joist/ *n* one of the beams of wood supporting the floor or ceiling.

jojoba /ho-ho-ba/ *n* an evergreen shrub from which oil is extracted for use in creams and shampoos.

joke /joke/ *n* something said or done to cause laughter. • *also vb*.

jollification /jol-i-fi-cay-shun/ *n* merrymaking and feasting.

jollity /jol-i-tee/ *n* gaiety, cheerfulness.

jolly /jol-ee/ *adj* merry, cheerful.

Jolly Roger /jol-ee raw-jer/ *n* the black pirate flag with the skull and crossbones.

jolt /joalt/ *vb* **1** to give a sudden jerk to. **2** to move along jerkily. • *n* **1** a sudden jerk. **2** a shock.

jonquil /jon-kwil/ *n* a small daffodil.

jostle /joss-ul/ *vb* to knock or push against.

jot /jot/ *n* a small amount. • *vb* (**jotted**, **jotting**) to write down in short form.

jotting /jot-ing/ *n* a short note.

journal /jur-nal/ *n* **1** (*usually in titles*) a daily newspaper. **2** a weekly or monthly magazine. **3** a record of the events of every day.

journalism /jur-na-li-zum/ *n* the work of preparing or writing for newspapers and magazines.

journalist /jur-na-list/ *n* someone whose job is journalism.

journalistic /jur-na-li-stic/ *adj* having to do with journalism.

journey /jur-nee/ *n* a distance travelled, especially over land. • *vb* (*fml or old*) to travel.

journeyman /jur-nee-man/ *n* a person who has served an apprenticeship to learn a craft or a trade and is now employed by another.

joust /joust/ *n* (*old*) a contest between two armed knights on horseback at a tournament. • *also vb*.

jovial /jo-vee-al/ *adj* merry, joyful, cheerful. • *n* **joviality**.

jowl /jowl/ *n* the jaw, the lower part of the cheek. • **cheek by jowl** very close together.

joy /joy/ *n* **1** delight, gladness. **2** a cause of great happiness.

joyful /joy-ful/, **joyous** /joy-us/ *adjs* full of joy.

joy ride /joy-ride/ *n* (*inf*) a drive for pleasure in a car. • *vb* **joy-ride**.

joystick /joy-stick/ *n* **1** the pilot's lever to control an aeroplane. **2** a control lever on a computer.

JP /jay pee/ *abbr* = **Justice of the Peace**.

jubilant /joo-bi-lant/ *adj* rejoicing greatly, triumphant, very glad.

jubilation /joo-bi-lay-shun/ *n* triumphant joy.

jubilee /joo-bi-lee/ *n* **1** a special anniversary of an event. **2** a celebration of this. • **golden jubilee** a 50th anniversary. • **silver jubilee** a 25th anniversary. • **diamond jubilee** a 60th anniversary.

Judaism /joo-day-iz-um/ *n* the religion of the Jewish people.

judge /judge/ *n* **1** someone who presides in a court of law giving advice on matters of law and deciding on the punishment for guilty persons. **2** someone asked to settle a disagreement. **3** someone able to distinguish what is good from what is bad. • *vb* **1** to act as judge in a court of law. **2** to decide, to give an opinion on. **3** to decide which is the best in a competition. **4** (*fml*) to criticize or blame someone.

judgement, judgment /judge-ment/ *n* **1** act or power of judging. **2** the decision given at the end of a law case. **3** good sense. **4** an opinion. • **Judgement** the Last Judgment of the Old Testament.

judicature /joo-di-ca-chur/ *n* all the judges or law courts of a country.

judicial /joo-di-shal/ *adj* having to do with a judge or court of law.

judiciary /joo-di-sha-ree/ *adj* having to do with a court of law. • *n* judges as a body.

judicious /joo-di-shus/ *adj* wise, showing good sense.

judo /joo-do/ *n* a Japanese system of unarmed combat adapted as a competitive sport from ju-jitsu.

jug /jug/ *n* a deep vessel for holding liquids, with a handle. • *vb* (**jugged, jugging**) to cook in a jar or jug.

juggernaut /ju-ger-not/ *n* **1** a large destructive force. **2** a very large lorry.

juggle /ju-gul/ *vb* **1** to keep on throwing things up, catching them and throwing them up again with great quickness of hand. **2** to try to deal satisfactorily with several activities at the same time. **3** to present facts in a way that makes them seem good or favourable. • *n* **juggler**.

jugular /ju-gyu-lar/ *adj* having to do with the neck or throat.

jugular vein /ju-gyu-lar vane/ *n* the large vein at the side of the neck.

juice /joos/ *n* the liquid of a fruit or plant. • *adj* **juicy**.

ju-jitsu /joo-jit-soo/ *n* a form of self-defence first used in Japan.

jukebox /jook-boks/ *n* a machine in a café, pub, etc. that automatically plays a selected record or compact disc when a coin is inserted.

July /joo-lie/ *n* the seventh month of the year.

jumble /jum-bul/ *vb* to mix in an untidy heap. • *n* a muddle.

jumble sale /jum-bul sale/ *n* a sale of second-hand goods, often to make money for a charity.

jumbo /jum-bo/ *n* something very large of its kind. • *adj* very large.

jump /jump/ *vb* **1** to push off the ground with the feet so that the whole body moves through the air. **2** to make a sudden quick movement or start, as when surprised. • *n* **1** a leap. **2** a sudden, quick movement. **3** an obstacle to be jumped over. • *n* **jumper** one who jumps. • **jump at** to accept willingly. • **jump to conclusions** to take things as true without waiting for them to be proved so.

jumper /jum-per/ *n* a close-fitting knitted garment put on over the head; a sweater.

jumpy /jum-pee/ *adj* (*inf*) nervous, anxious. • *n* **jumpiness**.

junction /jungk-shun/ *n* **1** (*fml*) a joining point. **2** a station where several railway lines meet.

juncture /**jungk**-chur/ *n* moment, point, stage.

June /**joon**/ *n* the sixth month of the year.

jungle /**jung**-gul/ *n* land especially in the tropics, covered with trees and matted undergrowth.

junior /**joon**-yer/ *adj* **1** younger. **2** lower in rank. • *also n.*

juniper /**joo**-ni-per/ *n* an evergreen shrub.

junk[1] /**jungk**/ *n* unwanted things, rubbish.

junk[2] /**jungk**/ *n* a Chinese sailing vessel.

junket /**jung**-ket/ *n* **1** the thickened part of sour milk sweetened with sugar. **2** a feast. • *vb* to feast.

junk food /**jungk** food/ *n* food which is low in nutritional value, often eaten as snacks.

junk mail /**jungk** mail/ *n* mail that you receive without having asked for it, usually containing advertisements.

junkyard /**jungk**-yard/ *n* a place used to store and eventually dispose of discarded objects such as old cars.

Jupiter /**joo**-pi-ter/ *n* the fifth planet from the sun.

juror /**joo**-ror / *n* a member of a jury.

jury /**joo**-ree/ *n* a number of persons who have sworn to give a fair and honest opinion of the facts related in a law case.

just /**just**/ *adj* **1** right and fair. **2** honest, fair, moral. **3** reasonable, based on one's rights. **4** deserved. • *adv* **1** exactly. **2** on the point of. **3** quite. **4** merely, only. **5** barely. **6** very lately or recently.

justice /**ju**-stiss/ *n* **1** fairness or rightness in the treatment of other people. **2** a judge.

Justice of the Peace /**ju**-stiss ov the **peess**/ *n* (*abbr* **JP**) a person appointed to help administer the law in a certain district.

justifiable /**ju**-sti-fie-a-bul/ *adj* that may be shown right, excusable.

justification /**ju**-sti-fi-**cay**-shun/ *n* a reason for doing something, a defence.

justify /**ju**-sti-fie/ *vb* to show that something is right, just, reasonable or excusable.

jut /**jut**/ *vb* (**jutted**, **jutting**) to stick out.

jute /**joot**/ *n* a fibre from the bark of certain plants, from which rope, canvas, etc, are made.

juvenile /**joo**-vi-nile/ *adj* **1** having to do with young people. **2** typical of young people, childish. • *n* a young person.

juxtapose /**juk**-sta-poaz/ *vb* to place side by side or close together, especially to show a contrast.

juxtaposition /**jux**-sta-po-**zi**-shun/ *n* a placing near, or side by side.

K

K, k /kay/ the 11th letter of the English alphabet.

kale /kale/ *n* a type of cabbage with dark, crinkled leaves.

kaleidoscope /ka-lie-do-scope/ *n* **1** a toy consisting of a tube in which quickly changing colours and shapes are seen through an eyehole. **2** a constantly and quickly changing pattern.

kaleidoscopic /ka-lie-do-**scop**-ic/ *adj* **1** with many changing colours. **2** quickly changing.

kangaroo /kang-ga-**roo**/ *n* an Australian mammal with a pouch for its young and long, strong hind legs by means of which it jumps along.

kapok /ka-pok/ *n* a light cottonlike fibre used for stuffing cushions, etc.

karaoke /ka-ree-o-kay/ *n* a type of entertainment in which a machine plays music while people take it in turns to sing the lyrics of songs which are shown on a screen.

karate /ka-**ra**-tay/ *n* a Japanese form of unarmed combat using the feet, hands and elbows.

kayak /**ka**-yak/ *n* an Inuit canoe, made from sealskin.

kebab /ke-**bab**/ *n* small pieces of meat and vegetables cooked on a metal or wooden skewer under a broiler or over flames.

kedgeree /**kedge**-e-ree/ *n* a dish made of rice, fish and eggs.

keel /keel/ *n* the long beam or girder along the bottom of a ship from which the whole frame is built up. • *vb* **keel over 1** to turn over to one side, to capsize. **2** (*inf*) to fall down, to collapse.

keen /keen/ *adj* **1** sharp. **2** eager, very interested. • *n* keenness.

keep /keep/ *vb* (*pt, pp* kept) **1** to have something without being required to give it back. **2** not to give or throw away, to preserve. **3** to remain in a certain state. **4** to have charge of, to look after. **5** to pay for and look after. **6** to hold back. **7** to carry out. **8** to go on doing. **9** (*inf*) to remain in good condition. • *n* **1** care. **2** a strong tower in the centre of a castle. **3** (*inf*) maintenance, food and lodging. • **keep at** to go on trying to do. • **keep body and soul together** to help to keep alive. • **keep one's hand in** to practise enough to remain good at.

keeper /**kee**-per/ *n* someone who keeps or looks after.

keeping /**kee**-ping/ *n* care, charge.

keepsake /**keep**-sake/ *n* a gift valued because of the giver.

keg /keg/ *n* a small barrel.

kelp /kelp/ *n* a type of seaweed.

ken /ken/ *n*. • **beyond one's ken** outside the extent of one's understanding.

kennel /ke-nel/ *n* **1** a house for dogs. **2** (*pl*) place where dogs are looked after temporarily.

kept *pt and pp of* keep.

kerb /kerb/ *n* the stone edging to a pavement.

kerchief /**ker**-chuf/ *n* a cloth for covering the head.

kerfuffle /ker-**fuf**-ul/ *n* unnecessary fuss and activity.

kernel /**ker**-nel/ *n* **1** the edible part in the centre of a nut or fruit stone. **2** the most important part.

kerosene /**ke**-ro-seen/ *n* (*US*) paraffin.

kestrel /**ke**-strel/ *n* a small falcon.

ketchup /**ke**-chup/ *n* a sauce, usually made of tomatoes, onions, salt and sugar.

kettle /**ke**-tul/ *n* a metal vessel, with a spout and handle, used for boiling water. • **a pretty kettle of fish** a great difficulty.

kettledrum /**ke**-tul-drum/ *n* a drum made of skin or parchment stretched across the mouth of a rounded metal frame.

key /kee/ *n* **1** an instrument for opening locks, winding clocks, etc. **2** one of the levers or buttons struck by the fingers on a piano, computer, etc. **3** the relationship of the notes in which a tune is written. **4** something that when known enables you to work out a code, problem, etc. **5** a translation. **6** a general mood, tone or style.

keyboard /**kee**-board/ *n* the set of levers or buttons struck by the fingers on a piano, computer, etc. • *vb* to use a keyboard.

keyhole /**kee**-hole/ *n* the hole through which a key is put in a lock.

kg /kay-jee/ *abbr* = kilogram.

khaki /ka-kee/ *adj* dust-coloured. • *n* yellowish brown cloth originally used in making army uniforms.

kibbutz /ki-**boots**/ *n* in Israel, a small community in which the members all live and work together.

kibbutznik /ki-**boots**-nik/ *n* a member of a kibbutz.

kick /kick/ vb **1** to strike with the foot. **2** (of a gun) to jerk back when fired. • n **1** a blow given with the foot. **2** the recoil of a gun. **3** (inf) a thrill, a feeling of pleasure. **4** strength, effectiveness.

kick-off /ki-cawff/ n the beginning of a game of football.

kid /kid/ n **1** (inf) a child. **2** a young goat. **3** goatskin leather. • vb (**kidded, kidding**) (inf) to deceive in fun.

kidnap /kid-nap/ vb (**kidnapped, kidnapping**) to carry off a person by force. • n **kidnapper**.

kidney /kid-nee/ n **1** one of two glands that cleanse the blood and pass the waste liquid out of the body. **2** the kidneys of certain animals used as food.

kill /kill/ vb **1** to put to death. **2** to put an end to. • n the animal(s) killed in a hunt. • **kill time** to make time seem to pass more quickly by occupying or amusing yourself in some way.

kiln /kiln/ n a furnace or oven for heating or hardening anything, especially bricks and pottery.

kilo- /kee-lo/ prefix one thousand.

kilogram /kee-lo-gram/ n a measure of weight = 1000 grams, abbr **kg**.

kilometre /ki-lom-i-ter/ n, also **kilometer** (US) a measure of length = 1000 metres, abbr **km**.

kilowatt /ki-lo-wat/ n a measure of electric power = 1000 watts.

kilt /kilt/ n a short pleated skirt worn by Scotsmen as part of Highland dress.

kimono /ki-mo-no/ n a Japanese long loose robe, tied with a sash, worn by women.

kin /kin/ n (fml) relatives, by blood or marriage.

kind /kined/ n **1** sort, type, variety. **2** nature, character. • adj thoughtful and friendly, generous. • n **kindness**. • **pay in kind** to pay by goods, etc, not money.

kindergarten /kin-der-gar-ten/ n a school for children ages four to six.

kindle /kin-dul/ vb **1** to set on fire, to light. **2** to stir up.

kindling /kin-dling/ n small pieces of wood used for lighting a fire.

kindly /kine-dlee/ adj kind, friendly. • also adv. • n **kindliness**.

kindred /kin-dred/ n **1** (fml) relatives, especially by blood. **2** relationship. • adj **1** related. **2** congenial.

kinetics /ki-ne-tics/ n the study of the connection between force and motion. • adj **kinetic**.

king /king/ n **1** the male ruler of a state. **2** a playing card with a king's picture. **3** a piece in chess.

kingdom /king-dom/ n a state ruled by a king.

kingfisher /king-fi-sher/ n a small brightly coloured bird that dives for fish.

kink /kingk/ n **1** a backward twist in a rope, chain, etc. **2** an unusual or strange way of thinking about things.

kinship /kin-ship/ n **1** a family connection. **2** any close connection.

kinsman /kinz-man/ n a male relative. • f **kinswoman**.

kiosk /kee-osk/ n **1** a small hut or stall for the sale of newspapers, sweets, etc. **2** a public telephone booth.

kipper /ki-per/ vb to preserve by splitting open, salting and drying. • n a fish so preserved, especially a herring, and used as food.

kirk /kirk/ n (Scot) a church.

kiss /kiss/ vb to touch with the lips as a sign of love or respect. • also n.

kit /kit/ n all the tools, etc, needed to do a job.

kitbag /kit-bag/ n a bag for necessary tools, clothes, etc, as carried by soldiers, sailors, etc.

kitchen /kit-chen/ n the room in which cooking is done.

kite /kite/ n **1** a type of hawk. **2** a toy made of paper or cloth stretched on a tight framework, flown in the air at the end of a string.

kitten /ki-ten/ n a young cat.

kiwi /kee-wee/ n **1** a wingless, tailless bird of New Zealand. **2** the fruit of an Asian vine.

Kleenex /klee-neks/ n (TM) tissue paper used as a handkerchief.

kleptomania /klep-toe-may-nee-a/ n an uncontrollable desire to steal things. • n **kleptomaniac**.

km abbr **kilometre**.

knack /nak/ n knowledge of the right way to do a thing, skill gained by practice.

knackered /nak-erd/ (inf) adj **1** extremely tired. **2** broken, useless.

knapsack /nap-sack/ n (old) a bag strapped to the back, worn by soldiers or travellers.

knave /nave/ n **1** a rascal, a dishonest rogue. **2** the third picture in a pack of cards, the jack.

knead /need/ vb to press into a dough or paste.

knee /nee/ n the joint between the upper and lower parts of the leg.

kneel /neel/ vb (pt, pp **knelt** or **kneeled**) to go down or rest on the knees.

knell /nell/ *n* (*fml or lit*) the sound of a bell, especially at a funeral. • *vb* **1** (*of a bell*) to ring a knell. **2** to summon by, or as by, a knell.

knelt *pt and pp of* **kneel**.

knew *pt of* **know**.

knickerbockers /ni-ker-bok-erz/ *npl* (*old*) loose breeches ending at the knee.

knickers /ni-kerz/ *npl* (*inf*) a woman's undergarment with elastic round the waist; panties.

knick-knack /nik-nak/ *n* a small or dainty ornament.

knife /nife/ *n* (*pl* **knives**) a tool with a sharp edge for cutting. • *vb* to stab with a knife.

knight /nite/ *n* **1** in olden days, someone of honourable military rank. **2** a rank awarded for service to society, entitling the holder to be called Sir. **3** a piece in chess. • *vb* to make (someone) a knight.

knight errant /nite er-ant/ *n* (*old*) a knight who travelled in search of adventure.

knighthood /nite-hood/ *n* the rank of a knight.

knightly /nite-lee/ *adj* **1** having the characteristics of a knight. **2** courageous, noble.

knit /nit/ *vb* (**knitted**, **knitting**) **1** to make woollen thread into garments by means of needles. **2** to join closely.

knitting /ni-ting/ *n* the thing knitted.

knitting needle /ni-ting nee-dul/ *n* a long needle used for knitting.

knives *pl of* **knife**.

knob /nob/ *n* **1** a rounded part sticking out from a surface. **2** the round handle of something. **3** a round control switch. **4** a small lump of something.

knobbly /nob-lee/ *adj* covered with lumps, bumpy.

knock /nok/ *vb* **1** to strike. **2** to rap on a door. **3** (*inf*) to criticize. • *n* **1** a blow. **2** a rap on the door.

knocker /nok-er/ *n* a hammer attached to a door for knocking.

knock-kneed /nok-need/ *adj* having knees that touch in walking.

knoll /nole/ *n* (*fml or lit*) a little rounded hill.

knot /not/ *n* **1** the twisting of two parts or pieces of string, etc, together so that they will not part until untied. **2** a hard piece of the wood of a tree, from which a branch grew out. **3** a small group of people. **4** a measure of speed at sea. • *vb* to tie in a knot.

knotty /not-ee/ *adj* difficult.

know /no/ *vb* (*pt* **knew**, *pp* **known**) **1** to be aware that. **2** to have information or knowledge about. **3** to have learned and remember. **4** to be aware of the identity of, to be acquainted with. **5** to recognize or identify.

knowing /no-wing/ *adj* showing secret understanding.

knowledge /nol-idge/ *n* **1** that which is known, information. **2** the whole of what can be learned or found out.

known *pp of* **know**.

knuckle /nu-cul/ *n* a finger joint. • *vb* **knuckle down** to start working hard. • **knuckle under** to be forced to accept the authority of someone, to give in to.

knuckle-duster /nu-cul du-ster/ *n* a blunt metal instrument fixed on to the hand as a weapon.

koala /ko-a-la/ *n* a small bearlike animal found in Australia.

kookaburra /koo-ka-bu-ra/ *n* an Australian bird.

Koran *or* **Qu'ran** /ku-ran/ *n* the holy book of Islam, the book of the Muslim religion.

kosher /ko-sher/ *adj* **1** of food that has been prepared according to the rules of Jewish law. **2** (*inf*) genuine, honest, legal.

kudos /koo-dos/ *n* glory, fame, credit.

kung fu /kung foo/ *n* a Chinese form of unarmed combat using the hands and feet, similar to karate.

L

L, l /el/ the 12th letter of the English alphabet.

lab /lab/ n short for **laboratory**.

label /lay-bel/ n a piece of paper or card fixed to something to give information about it. • vb (**labelled, labelling**) to fix a label to.

labia /lay-bee-a/ npl plural of **labium**.

labial /lay-bee-ul/ of or related to the lips or the labia.

labium /lay-bee-um/ n, **labia** /lay-bee-a/ npl 1 a lip-shaped structure. 2 a fold of the vulva.

labour /lay-bur/ n, also **labor** (US) 1 hard work. 2 childbirth. 3 all workers as a body. 4 (cap) the British Labour political party. • also adj. • vb 1 to work hard. 2 to be employed to do hard and unskilled work. 3 to do something slowly or with difficulty.

laboratory /la-bor-at-ree/ n a workshop used for scientific experiments.

laboured /lay-burd/ adj, also **labored** (US) showing a lot of effort or hard work.

labourer /lay-bu-rer/ n, also **laborer** (US) a person who does unskilled work.

lace /lace/ n 1 a cord used for tying opposite edges together. 2 an ornamental network of thread. • vb to fasten with a lace.

lacerate /la-se-rate/ vb 1 to tear, to wound. 2 to hurt badly. • n **laceration**.

lack /lak/ vb to want, to need, to be without. • n want, need.

lackey /la-kee/ n 1 (old) a servant. 2 someone who behaves like a servant.

lacklustre /lack-lu-ster/ adj, also **lackluster** (US) dull, lacking brightness.

laconic /la-con-ic/ adj using few words to express a meaning.

lacquer /la-ker/ n 1 a varnish. 2 a substance used to keep hair in place. • vb to paint with lacquer.

lacrosse /la-cross/ n a team ball game played with long-handled rackets.

lactic /lac-tic/ adj having to do with milk.

lacuna /la-coo-na/ n (pl **lacunae**) (fml) a gap, a blank.

lad /lad/ n a boy, a young man.

ladder /la-der/ n 1 a frame of two poles or planks, joined by short crossbars, used as steps for going up or down. 2 a tear that runs up or down a stocking or tights.

laden /lay-den/ adj loaded.

ladies /lay-diz/ npl 1 plural of **lady**. 2 (fml) a public toilet for women.

ladle /lay-del/ n a large long-handled spoon for lifting liquids. • vb to lift with a ladle.

lady /lay-dee/ n 1 a woman of rank or with good manners. 2 (fml) a woman; sometimes considered more polite than 'woman'. 3 (cap) the title of the wife of a knight or of a man of higher rank. • n **your /her Ladyship** the title used in speaking to or of a lady of high rank.

ladybird /lay-dee-burd/ n a small beetle, usually red with black spots.

lag /lag/ vb (**lagged, lagging**) 1 to go too slowly, not to keep pace with, to fall behind. 2 not to keep up with. • n (inf) an old convict.

lager /la-ger/ n a light, clear beer of German origin.

lagoon /la-goon/ n a shallow saltwater lake cut off from the sea by sandbanks or rocks.

laid /laid/ pt and pp of **lay**[2].

laid-back /laid-back/ adj relaxed, easygoing.

lain pp of **lie**.

lair /lair/ n a wild beast's den.

lake[1] /lake/ n a large stretch of water surrounded by land.

lake[2] /lake/ n a deep red colour.

lamb /lam/ n a young sheep.

lame /lame/ adj 1 unable to walk well because of an injured or badly formed leg. 2 not good, inadequate. • vb to make lame. • n **lameness**.

lament /la-ment/ vb 1 to show grief or sorrow for, to mourn for. 2 to express regret for. • n 1 the expressing of great grief. 2 a mournful song or tune. • n **lamentation**.

lamentable /la-men-ta-bul/ adj much to be regretted, extremely unsatisfactory.

laminate /la-mi-nate/ vb to put a thin layer (e.g. of plastic) over something. • also n.

lamp /lamp/ n a vessel for giving light.

lampoon /lam-poon/ n something written specially to make another seem foolish or wicked.

lance /lanse/ n a long spear used by horse soldiers. • vb 1 to wound or hit with a lance. 2 to cut open with a lancet.

lance-corporal /lanse-cawr-pral/ n the lowest appointed rank in the British Army, just below that of a corporal.

lancet /lan-set/ n a surgical knife with two sharp edges.

land /land/ n 1 the solid part of the earth's surface. 2 country. 3 ground, soil. • vb to bring, put, or go ashore; to touch down.

landed /lan-did/ adj possessing land.

landfall /land-fawl/ *n* **1** a ship's approach to land at the end of a voyage. **2** the land approached.

landfill site /land-fill site/ *n* a place where waste material is buried under layers of earth, often excavated for this purpose.

landing /lan-ding/ *n* **1** the act of going ashore. **2** a place for going on shore. **3** the corridor opening on to the rooms at the top of a flight of stairs.

landlady /land-lay-dee/ *n* **1** a woman who keeps an inn or boarding house. **2** a woman who rents out rooms, flats or houses.

landlord /land-lawrd/ *n* **1** a man who keeps an inn or boarding house. **2** a man who rents out rooms, flats or houses.

landmark /land-mark/ *n* **1** an easily recognized object from which travellers can tell where they are. **2** a very important event. • *also adj*.

landscape /land-scape/ *n* **1** a view of the country seen from one position. **2** a picture of the countryside.

landslide /land-slide/ *n* the falling of a mass of earth, etc, down the side of a mountain.

landslip /land-slip/ *n* a landslide.

landward /land-ward/ *adj and adv* towards land.

lane /lane/ *n* **1** a narrow road. **2** a narrow passage or alley between buildings, often found in place names. **3** any of the parallel parts into which roads are divided for a single line of traffic. **4** the route intended for or regularly used by ships or aircraft. **5** a marked strip of track, water, etc, for a competitor in a race.

language /lang-gwidge/ *n* **1** meaningful speech. **2** the speech of one people. **3** words.

languid /lang-gwid/ *adj* lacking energy, weak; slow-moving, relaxed.

languish /lang-gwish/ *vb* to lose strength, to become weak. **2** to experience long suffering.

lank /langk/ *adj* **1** tall and thin, lanky. **2** straight and limp.

lanky /lang-kee/ *adj* ungracefully tall and thin.

lanolin(e) /la-no-lin/ *n* a soothing ointment made from fat obtained from sheep's wool.

lantern /lan-tern/ *n* a case, usually of glass, that encloses and protects a light.

lap[1] /lap/ *n* **1** the seat formed by the knees and thighs of a person sitting. **2** one round of a course in a race.

lap[2] /lap/ *vb* (**lapped, lapping**) **1** to lick up. **2** to wash against in little waves. • *n* the sound made by small waves.

lapdog /lap-dog/ *n* a small pet dog.

lapel /la-pel/ *n* the folded back part of the breast of a coat or jacket.

lapis lazuli /la-pis la-zu-lee/ *n* a blue precious stone.

lapse /lapse/ *n* **1** a mistake, a small error or fault. **2** the passing (of time). • *vb* **1** to fall out of use. **2** to come to an end. **3** to pass gradually into a less active or less desirable state.

laptop /lap-top/ *n* a small, light computer that can be operated by battery and can be used on someone's lap.

larch /larch/ *n* a type of deciduous, cone-bearing tree.

lard /lard/ *n* the fat of pigs, prepared for use in cooking.

larder /lar-der/ *n* a room or cupboard for storing food.

large /large/ *adj* more than usual in size, number or amount, big. • **at large** free; on the run.

lariat /la-ree-at/ *n* **1** a rope. **2** a rope with a running knot for catching animals, like a lasso.

lark /lark/ *n* **1** a songbird. **2** something done for fun. • *vb* to play tricks.

larva /lar-va/ *n* (*pl* **larvae**) the form of an insect on coming out of the egg, a grub.

larynx /la-rinks/ *n* the upper part of the windpipe, containing the vocal chords which produce the voice.

lasagne /la-zan-ya/ *n* an Italian dish made from layers of flat, wide pasta, a meat or vegetable sauce and a cheese sauce.

laser /lay-zer/ *n* a device that produces a narrow beam of concentrated light.

lash /lash/ *n* **1** the cord of a whip. **2** a blow given with a whip. • *vb* **1** to whip, to strike hard or often. **2** to fasten by tying tightly.

lass /lass/ *n* a girl.

lasso /la-soo/ *n* (*pl* **lassos** *or* **lassoes**) a rope with a running knot for catching animals. • *vb* to catch with a lasso.

last[1] /last/ *adj* **1** coming after all others. **2** latest. **3** final. • *adv* at the last time or place. • **at last** in the end.

last[2] /last/ *n* a foot-shaped block on which shoes are made or repaired.

last[3] /last/ *vb* **1** to go on. **2** to continue.

lasting /la-sting/ *adj* **1** going on for a long time. **2** remaining in good condition.

latch /lach/ *n* a small piece of wood or metal for keeping a door shut. • *vb* to fasten with a latch.

latchkey /lach-kee/ *n* the key for the main door of a house.

late /late/ *adj* **1** arriving after the time fixed. **2** far on in time. **3** now dead. **4** recent. • *adv* after the time fixed. • *n* **lateness**. • **of late** (*fml*) recently.

lately /late-lee/ *adv* in recent times, recently.

latent /lay-tent/ *adj* present but not yet noticeable, not fully developed.

lateral /la-te-ral/ *adj* on, at or from the side.

lathe /lathe/ *n* a machine for turning around wood, metal, pottery, etc, while it is being shaped.

lather /la-ther/ *n* **1** froth of soap and water. **2** froth from sweat. • *vb* **1** to cover with lather. **2** to become frothy.

Latin /la-tin/ *n* the language of ancient Rome. • *adj* **1** having to do with the ancient Romans. **2** having to do with the peoples of France, Italy, Portugal and Spain.

latitude /la-ti-tood/ *n* **1** distance north or south of the equator. **2** freedom from controls.

latrine /la-treen/ *n* a lavatory, especially in a camp or institution.

latter /la-ter/ *adj* **1** near the end of a period of time. **2** second of two just mentioned.

latterly /la-ter-lee/ *adv* recently, lately, in the last part of a period of time.

lattice /la-tis/ *n* a network of crossed bars or strips as of wood. • *adj* **latticed**.

laugh /laf/ *vb* to make a sound expressing amusement or pleasure. • *n* the sound of laughing.

laughable /la-fa-bul/ *adj* causing people to laugh, ridiculous.

laughter /laf-ter/ *n* the act or sound of laughing.

launch /lawnch/ *vb* **1** to put into motion, to send on its course. **2** to cause. **3** to put into action, to set going. • *n* **1** the act of launching. **2** a large motorboat.

launder /lawn-der/ *vb* to wash and iron.

laundry /lawn-dree/ *n* **1** a place where clothes, etc, are washed and ironed. **2** clothes and other items that are in need of washing or are being washed.

laurel /law-rel/ *n* **1** a bay tree whose leaves are used for making wreaths of honour. **2** a special honour.

lava /la-va/ *n* the melted rock emitted by a volcano.

lavatory /la-va-toe-ree/ *n* a toilet; a room with a toilet.

lavender /la-ven-der/ *n* **1** a plant with sweet-smelling flowers. **2** a light purple colour.

lavish /la-vish/ *adj* **1** giving freely, generous. **2** given or spent in great quantities. • *vb* to give or spend lavishly.

law /law/ *n* **1** a rule or set of rules laid down for a people or a group of people by a person or persons with recognized authority. **2** in science, a statement of the way in which objects regularly behave.

law-abiding /law-a-bide-ing/ *adj* obeying the law.

lawful /law-ful/ *adj* allowed by law.

lawless /law-less/ *adj* not keeping the laws, wild.

lawn¹ /lawn/ *n* a stretch of carefully kept grass in a garden.

lawn² /lawn/ *n* a type of fine linen.

lawnmower /lawn-mo-wer/ *n* a machine for cutting grass.

lawsuit /law-soot/ *n* claiming before a judge that another has broken the law.

lawn tennis /lawn-te-nis/ *n* tennis played on a grass court.

lawyer /law-yer/ *n* someone skilled in the law.

lax /laks/ *adj* not sufficiently strict or severe.

laxative /lak-sa-tiv/ *n* a medicine that causes or helps the bowels to empty. • *also adj*.

lay¹ /lay/ *pt of* **lie**.

lay² /lay/ *vb* (*pt, pp* **laid**) **1** to cause to lie. **2** to place. **3** to make ready. **4** to produce eggs. **5** to bet. **6** (*inf*) to have sex with. • **lay by, lay up** to store for the future. • **lay oneself open to** to put yourself into the position of receiving.

lay³ /lay/ *n* (*old*) a poem or song.

lay⁴ /lay/ *adj* **1** having to do with people who are not members of the clergy. **2** not expert.

layer /lay-er/ *n* an even spread of one substance over the surface of another.

layman /lay-man/ *n* **1** someone who is not a clergyman. **2** someone who is not an expert or specialist.

laze /laze/ *vb* to be lazy, to do nothing.

lazy /lay-zee/ *adj* unwilling to work, liking to do nothing. • *n* **laziness**.

lb *abbr of* **pound¹**.

lead¹ /led/ *n* **1** a soft heavy metal. **2** the stick of black lead or graphite in a pencil. **3** a piece of lead attached to a cord for finding the depth of water. **4** *pl* **leads** /leds/ the sheets of lead used for covering roofs.

lead² /leed/ *vb* (*pt, pp* **led**) **1** to go in front to show the way, to guide. **2** to act as a chief or commander. **3** to influence. **4** to spend. • *n* **1** a guiding suggestion or example. **2** a chief part. **4** a cord, etc, for leading a dog. **5** a long piece of wire, usually covered in plastic, used to convey electricity to an appliance.

leader /lee-der/ *n* **1** someone who shows the way. **2** someone who gives orders or takes charge. **3** a person or thing that is ahead of others. **4** a newspaper article giving an opinion on a news item of interest (*also* **leading article**). • *n* **leadership**.

leading /lee-ding/ *adj* chief, most important.

leading question /lee-ding **kwes**-chun/ *n* a question asked in such a way as to suggest the answer desired.

leaf /leef/ *n* (*pl* **leaves**) **1** one of the thin, flat usually green blades growing out of the stem of a plant or the branch of a tree. **2** a single sheet of paper in a book with pages printed on both sides. **3** the movable part of a table-top or double door. • **turn over a new leaf** to begin to live or act in a better way.

leaflet /leef-let/ *n* a printed sheet of paper, usually folded and free of charge, containing information.

leafy /lee-fee/ *adj* full of leaves.

league[1] /leeg/ *n* a measure of distance.

league[2] /leeg/ *n* **1** a group of people or nations bound by agreement to help one another. **2** a group of sports clubs or players that play matches among themselves. **3** a level of ability, quality, etc. • *vb* (*fml*) to join together, to unite.

leak /leek/ *n* **1** a hole by which water escapes (e.g. from a pipe) or enters a dry place. **2** a small accidental hole or crack through which something flows in or out. **3** the accidental or intentional making public of secret information. • *vb* **1** to let water in or out. **2** to get out through a hole or crack. **3** to make public that which is secret.

leakage /lee-kage/ *n* act of leaking.

leaky /lee-kee/ *adj* (*inf*) having leaks.

lean[1] /leen/ *vb* (*pt, pp* **leaned** *or* **leant**) **1** to slope to one side. **2** to bend. **3** to rest against. **4** to have a preference for.

lean[2] /leen/ *adj* **1** not having much fat. **2** thin, healthily thin. • *n* meat without fat. • *n* **leanness**.

leaning /lee-ning/ *n* preference, liking.

leant *pt and pp of* **lean**.

leap /leep/ *vb* (*pt, pp* **leaped** *or* **leapt**) to jump. • *n* **1** a jump. **2** the height or distance jumped.

leapfrog /leep-frawg/ *n* a game in which one player leaps over the others while they are bent over.

leapt *pt and pp of* **leap**.

leap year /leep year/ *n* a year in which there are 366 days, occurring once every 4 years.

learn /lern/ *vb* (*pt, pp* **learned** *or* **learnt**) **1** to gain knowledge or skill, to find out how to do something. **2** to come to understand, to realize. **3** to memorize, to fix in the memory.

learned /ler-ned/ *adj* having much knowledge, gained by study.

learner /ler-ner/ *n* someone who is learning.

learning /ler-ning/ *n* knowledge gained by study.

learning disability /ler-ning dis-a-bil-i-tee/ *n* a problem that someone has in learning basic skills such as reading, which is caused by a physical condition.

learnt *pt and pp of* **learn**.

lease /leess/ *n* an agreement by which the use of house or land is given to another in return for a fixed annual amount or rent. • *vb* to give or take on lease.

leash /leesh/ *n* a cord or strap for leading animals. • *vb* to hold on a leash.

least /leest/ *adj* smallest. • *also n.* • *adv* in the smallest degree.

leather /le-ther/ *n* material made by preparing animal skins in a certain way. • *also adj.* • *vb* (*inf*) to beat, to thrash. • *adj* **leathery**.

leave /leev/ *n* **1** permission. **2** permitted absence. **3** holiday. **4** farewell. • *vb* (*pt, pp* **left**) **1** to give to another at your death. **2** to cause to be or remain in a particular state or condition. **3** to go without taking. **4** to depart. **5** to desert. **6** to entrust to another. **7** to allow to remain unused, untaken, uneaten, etc.

leaves *pl of* **leaf**.

lectern /lec-tern/ *n* a reading desk for standing at.

lecture /lec-cher/ *n* **1** a talk on a certain subject. **2** a scolding. • *vb* **1** to give a lecture. **2** to scold.

lecturer /lec-che-rer/ *n* **1** someone giving a talk. **2** someone who teaches in a college or university.

led /led/ *pt and pp of* **lead**[2].

ledge /ledge/ *n* **1** a narrow shelf. **2** a ridge.

ledger /le-jer/ *n* the chief account book of a business.

leech /leech/ *n* **1** a blood-sucking worm. **2** (*old*) a doctor.

leek /leek/ *n* a vegetable with broad flat leaves.

leer /leer/ *vb* to look at sideways in a sly or unpleasant way. • *also n.*

left[1] /left/ *pt and pp of* **leave**.

left[2] /left/ *n* **1** the side opposite to the right. **2** in politics, the Socialist party. • *also adj.* • **the extreme left** the Communist party.

left-handed /left-han-did/ *adj* better able to use the left hand than the right.

leg /leg/ *n* **1** one of the limbs on which an animal stands or moves. **2** a support for a table, chair, etc. • **on one's last legs** near the end of your power, life, etc.

• **pull a person's leg** to play a joke on someone.

legacy /le-ga-see/ n that which is left to someone by will.

legal /lee-gal/ adj **1** having to do with the law. **2** allowed by law.

legality /li-ga-li-tee/ n lawfulness.

legalize /lee-ga-lize/ vb, also **legalise** to make lawful.

legend /le-jend/ n **1** an ancient story passed on by word of mouth. **2** the words written under a picture, etc.

legendary /le-jen-da-ree/ adj **1** having to do with ancient legends, famous in story, existing only in story. **2** very famous.

leggings /le-gingz/ npl a thick covering for the lower leg.

leggy /le-gee/ adj (inf) having very long legs.

legible /le-ji-bul/ adj possible to read. • n **legibility**.

legion /lee-jun/ n **1** a Roman regiment or division (3000–6000 soldiers). **2** a great number.

legionary /lee-ju-ne-ree/ n a soldier belonging to a legion.

legislate /le-ji-slate/ vb to make laws.

legislation /le-ji-slay-shun/ n **1** the act of making laws. **2** the laws made.

legislative /le-ji-slay-tiv/ adj having the power or right to make laws.

legislator /le-ji-slay-tor/ n someone who makes laws.

legislature /le-ji-slay-chur/ n the part of a government that makes laws.

legitimate /li-ji-ti-mat/ adj **1** allowed by law, lawful. **2** born of married parents.

legume /lay-goom/ n a plant that bears seeds in pods (e.g. peas, beans, etc.).

leisure /lee-zhur/ n spare time, time free from work.

leisurely /lee-zhur-lee/ adj slow, unhurried. • also adv.

lemming /le-ming/ n a small ratlike animal of far northern regions.

lemon /le-mon/ n **1** a pale, yellow, sharp-tasting fruit. **2** the tree bearing this fruit. **3** a pale yellow colour.

lemonade /le-mo-nade/, **lemon squash** /le-mon skwash/ n a drink made from or tasting of lemon juice.

lemur /lee-mur/ n a nocturnal primate, native to Madagascar.

lend /lend/ vb (pt, pp **lent**) to give something to another on condition that it is returned after use. • n **lender**.

length /lenth/ n measurement from end to end of space or time. • **at length 1** at last. **2** taking a long time, in detail.

lengthen /lenth-en/ vb to make or become longer.

lengthways /lenth-waze/ adv, also **lengthwise** (US) /lenth-wize/ in the direction of the length.

lengthy /lenth-ee/ adj very long.

lenient /leen-yent/ adj **1** merciful. **2** not severe. • n **lenience**, **leniency**.

lens /lenz/ n a transparent substance, usually glass, with a surface curved in such a way that objects seen through it appear bigger or smaller.

Lent /lent/ n the period between Ash Wednesday and Easter during which Christ's fast in the desert is commemorated.

lentil /len-til/ n the edible seed of a pealike plant.

leopard /le-pard/ n a large, spotted animal of the cat family.

leper /le-per/ n a person with leprosy.

leprechaun /le-pre-con/ n in fairy tales, an elf, especially in Ireland.

leprosy /le-pru-see/ n an infectious disease that eats away the skin and parts of the body. • adj **leprous**.

lesion /lee-zhun/ n (fml) an injury, a wound.

less /less/ adj smaller, not so much. • n a smaller amount. • adv not so greatly, not so much.

lessen /le-sun/ vb to make or become less.

lesser /le-ser/ adj less, smaller.

lesson /le-sun/ n **1** something that is learned or taught. **2** a period of teaching. **3** a passage read from the Bible. **4** an example.

let /let/ vb (**let**, **letting**) **1** to allow. **2** to allow the use of for rent or payment. • n the act of letting for rent.

lethal /lee-thal/ adj causing death.

lethargic /le-**thar**-jic/ adj sleepy, slow-moving, lacking interest.

lethargy /le-thar-jee/ n lack of energy and interest.

letter /le-ter/ n **1** a sign standing for a sound. **2** a written message. **3** (fml) pl literature, learning. • **letter of credit** a letter allowing the holder to draw money when away from home. • **to the letter** exactly.

lettered /le-terd/ adj (fml) well read.

lettering /le-te-ring/ n letters that have been drawn, painted, etc.

lettuce /le-tus/ n a plant whose leaves are used in salads.

leukaemia /loo-kee-mee-a/, also **leukemia** (US) n a cancer of the blood, in which too many white blood cells are produced.

levee /le-vee/ n **1** (old) a morning party at which guests were introduced to the king or queen. **2** a raised bank at the side of a river.

level /le-vel/ *n* **1** a flat, even surface. **2** a general standard of quality or quantity. **3** a horizontal division or floor in a house, etc. • *adj* **1** flat. **2** even. **3** on the same line or height. • *vb* (**levelled, levelling** /le-ve-ling/) **1** to make flat. **2** to make equal. **3** to destroy, to demolish. **4** to aim.

level crossing /le-vel **craw**-sing/ *n* a place where a railway line crosses the surface of a road.

level-headed /le-vel-he-ded/ *adj* sensible.

lever /lee-ver/ *n* a bar for raising heavy objects.

leverage /lee-ve-rige/ *n* power gained by the use of a lever.

leveret /le-ve-ret/ *n* a young hare.

leviathan /li-vie-a-thin/ *n* **1** a sea monster. **2** anything very large.

levity /le-vi-tee/ *n* (*fml*) lack of seriousness.

levy /le-vee/ *vb* **1** to bring together men to form an army. **2** to collect money for a tax. • *n* **1** the soldiers thus assembled. **2** the money thus collected.

lewd /lood/ *adj* indecent, obscene. • *n* **lewdness.**

lexicographer /lek-si-**cog**-ra-fer/ *n* someone who prepares a dictionary.

lexicon /lek-si-con/ *n* a dictionary.

liability /lie-a-**bi**-li-tee/ *n* **1** debt. **2** the state of being liable. **3** something for which someone is responsible.

liable /lie-a-bul/ *adj* **1** likely to have to do or suffer from. **2** legally responsible for. **3** likely to get, be punished with, etc.

liaison /lee-ay-zon/ *n* **1** a close connection or working association. **2** (*fml*) an unlawful sexual relationship.

liar /lie-ar/ *n* someone who tells lies.

libel /lie-bel/ *n* something written that damages a person's reputation. • *also vb* (**libelled, libelling**).

libellous /lie-bel-us/ *adj* hurtful to someone's reputation.

liberal /lib-ral/ *adj* **1** generous. **2** ready to accept new ideas. **3** (*of education*) intended solely to develop the powers of the mind. • *n* someone who believes in greater political freedom.

liberality /li-ber-a-li-tee/ *n* (*fml*) readiness to give to others.

liberate /li-ber-ate/ *vb* to set free. • *n* **liberation.**

libertine /lib-er-teen/ *n* (*fml*) someone who openly leads a wicked, immoral life.

liberty /lib-er-tee/ *n* **1** freedom. **2** the right to do as you like. **3** too great freedom of speech or action.

librarian /lie-**bray**-ree-an/ *n* someone in charge of a library.

library /lie-bre-ree/ *n* **1** a collection of books. **2** a room or building in which books are kept.

libretto /li-bre-toe/ *n* (*pl* **libretti**) the book of words of an opera or musical work.

lice /lice/ *see* **louse.**

licence /lie-sense/ *n, also* **license** (*US*) **1** a written permission to do or keep something. **2** (*fml*) too great freedom of action.

license /lie-sense/ *vb* to give a licence to.

licensee /lie-sen-see/ *n* someone to whom a licence is given.

licentious /lie-sen-shus/ *adj* (*fml*) behaving in an immoral or improper way, indecent. • *n* **licentiousness.**

lichen /lie-ken/ *n* a moss that grows on rocks, tree trunks, etc.

licit /li-sit/ *adj* (*fml*) lawful.

lick /lick/ *vb* **1** to pass the tongue over. **2** to take. **3** (*inf*) to defeat. **4** (*inf*) to thrash. • *n* **1** act of passing the tongue over. **2** a blow.

licking /li-king/ *n* (*inf*) a thrashing.

licorice *n* US variant of **liquorice.**

lid /lid/ *n* the movable cover of a pot, box, etc.

lie[1] /lie/ *n* a statement that the maker knows to be untrue. • *vb* (**lied, lying**) to tell a lie.

lie[2] /lie/ *vb* (**lay, lying**) **1** to put the body full length upon. **2** to be or remain in a certain place. • *n* the way in which something lies.

liege /leedge/ *n* (*old*) **1** someone owing certain duties to a lord. **2** a lord.

lieu /loo/ *n*. • **in lieu of** instead of.

lieutenant /lef-ten-ant/ *n* **1** (*fml*) someone who does the work of another, deputy. **2** a naval or army officer.

life /life/ *n* (*pl* **lives**) **1** the state of being alive. **2** the force existing in animals and plants that gives them the ability to change with the passing of time. **3** liveliness, activity. **4** the time someone has been alive. **5** the story of someone's life.

lifebelt /life-belt/ *n* a belt of a material that floats easily and so helps to prevent the wearer sinking when in water.

lifeboat /life-boat/ *n* a boat that goes to the help of those in danger at sea.

lifebuoy /life-boy/ *n* an object that floats easily and to which shipwrecked people can hold until help arrives.

life cycle /life sie-cul/ *n* the series of forms into which a living thing changes during its development.

lifeless /life-less/ *adj* **1** dead. **2** dull. **3** not lively.

lifelike /life-like/ *adj* seeming to have life.

lifelong /life-long/ *adj* lasting through life.

life-size /life-size/, **life-sized** /life-siezd/ *adj* of the same size as the person or thing represented.

life span /life span/ *n* the length of time that someone is likely to live or something is likely to function.

lifestyle /life-stile/ *n* the way in which someone lives.

lifetime /life-time/ *n* the length of time a person lives.

lift /lift/ *vb* **1** to raise up higher. **2** to take up. • *n* **1** a machine by which people or goods are carried from floor to floor of a building. **2** a free ride in a private vehicle.

ligament /li-ga-ment/ *n* a band of tough substance joining bones together at joints.

ligature /li-ga-chur/ *n* **1** (*fml*) a bandage. **2** a cord for tying up the end of a blood vessel during an operation. **3** two letters joined together in type (e.g. fi, fl).

light[1] /lite/ *n* **1** that which makes it possible for the eye to see things. **2** anything that gives light, as the sun, a lamp, etc. **3** knowledge, understanding. **4** brightness in the eyes or face. • *adj* **1** clear, not dark. **2** not deep or dark in colour. • *vb* (*pt, pp* lit) to give light to, to set fire to.

light[2] /lite/ *adj* **1** not heavy. **2** not difficult. **3** not severe. **4** small in amount. **5** not serious, for entertainment. **6** graceful. **7** happy, merry.

light[3] /lite/ *vb* to come upon by chance.

light bulb, lightbulb /lite-bulb/ a glass bulb containing a wire (filament) or a gas that glows when it is supplied with electricity.

lighten[1] /lie-ten/ *vb* **1** to make bright. **2** to flash.

lighten[2] /lie-ten/ *vb* to make less heavy.

lighter[1] /lie-ter/ *n* a device for setting something (e.g. a cigarette) alight.

lighter[2] /lie-ter/ *n* a large boat, usually flat-bottomed, for carrying goods from ship to shore.

light-fingered /lite-fing-gerd/ *adj* (*inf*) thieving.

light-footed /lite-foo-ted/ *adj* nimble, quick on your feet.

light-headed /lite-he-ded/ *adj* giddy, dizzy.

light-hearted /lite-har-ted/ *adj* **1** merry, cheerful. **2** not serious.

lighthouse /lite-house/ *n* a tower with a light to guide ships.

lightning /lite-ning/ *adj* the electric flash seen before thunder is heard.

lightning conductor /lite-ning con-duc-tor/, *US* **lightning rod** /lite-ning rod/ *n* a metal rod that protects a building from lightning by conducting the flash to the earth.

lights /lites/ *npl* the lungs of an animal, such as a sheep, used as food.

lightship /lite-ship/ *n* an anchored ship with a light to guide other ships.

light year /lite year/ *n* the distance light travels in a year.

lignite /lig-nite/ *n* a type of brown coal.

like[1] /like/ *adj* nearly the same, resembling. • *prep* in the same way as. • *n* a person or thing nearly the same as or equal to another.

like[2] /like/ *vb* **1** to be pleased by. **2** to be fond of.

likeable, likable /like-a-bul/ *adj* attractive, pleasant.

likelihood /like-li-hood/ *n* probability.

likely /like-lee/ *adj* **1** probable. **2** suitable. • *adv* probably.

liken /like-en/ *vb* to compare.

likeness /like-ness/ *n* **1** resemblance. **2** a picture of a person.

likes /likes/ *npl* things that are pleasing to someone.

likewise /like-wize/ *adv* **1** in the same way. **2** also.

liking /like-ing/ *n* a fondness or preference for.

lilac /lie-lac/ *n* **1** a type of small tree with light purple or white flowers. **2** a light purple colour. • *adj* light purple.

lilt /lilt/ *vb* to sing cheerfully. • *n* **1** a regular pattern of rising and falling sound. **2** a cheerful song. **3** a tune with a strongly marked rhythm.

lilting /lil-ting/ *adj* having a strongly marked lilt.

lily /li-lee/ *n* a flower grown from a bulb, often white in colour.

lily of the valley /li-lee ov the va-lee/ *n* a flower with small white bells and a distinctive sweet smell.

limb /lim/ *n* **1** an arm, leg or wing. **2** a branch of a tree.

limber /lim-ber/ *adj* moving and bending easily, supple. • *vb* **limber up** to exercise in order to make more supple.

limbo /lim-bo/ *n* **1** a place where, it is supposed, the souls of those who die in complete ignorance of God spend eternity. **2** a place where someone is forgotten or neglected, a state of uncertainty.

lime[1] /lime/ *n* a white substance got by heating certain kinds of rock.

lime[2] /lime/ *n* **1** a small lemon-like, yellowish-green fruit. **2** the tree bearing this fruit. **3** the linden tree.

limelight /lime-lite/ *n*. • **in the limelight** in a position in which someone's actions are followed with interest by many people.

limerick /**lim**-e-rick/ *n* a humorous nonsense poem written in a special five-line stanza.

limestone /**lime**-stone/ *n* rock containing a lot of lime.

limit /**li**-mit/ *n* **1** a boundary. **2** that which you may not go past. **3** the greatest or smallest amount or number that is fixed as being correct, legal, necessary, desirable, etc. • *vb* to keep within bounds.

limitation /li-mi-**tay**-shun/ *n* **1** that which limits. **2** inability to do something, weakness.

limited /**li**-mi-ted/ *adj* **1** small in amount. **2** not very great, large, wide-ranging, etc.

limn /**lim**/ *vb* (*old*) to draw or paint.

limp[1] /**limp**/ *vb* to walk lamely. • *also n.*

limp[2] /**limp**/ *adj* **1** not stiff, drooping. **2** without energy or strength.

limpet /**lim**-pet/ *n* a shellfish that clings tightly to rocks.

limpid /**lim**-pid/ *adj* clear, transparent.

linchpin /**linch**-pin/ *n* **1** the pin passed through the end of an axle to keep the wheel on it. **2** a person who is very important to the running of a form or organization.

linden /**lin**-den/ *n* a kind of tree with yellow sweet-smelling flowers, the lime tree.

line /**line**/ *n* **1** a small rope or cord. **2** a thin mark made with a pen, pencil, etc. **3** a row of persons or things. **4** a row of words on a page. **5** a short letter. **6** a railway track. **7** ancestors and descendants. **8** a fleet of steamers, aeroplanes, etc, providing regular services. **9** (*inf*) the equator. **10** a telephone wire. **11** (*inf*) way of behaving or of earning your living. **12** *pl* the positions of an army ready to attack or defend. • *vb* **1** to mark with lines. **2** to arrange in a row or rows. **3** to cover on the inside.

lineage /**li**-nee-age/ *n* someone's ancestors.

lineal /**li**-nee-al/ *adj* passed down from father to son.

lineament /**li**-nee-a-ment/ *n* (*fml*) a noticeable feature of the face.

linear /**li**-nee-ar/ *adj* having to do with lines.

linen /**li**-nen/ *n* cloth made of flax.

liner /**lie**-ner/ *n* **1** a large ocean-going passenger ship. **2** something that lines.

linesman /**line**-zman/ *n* someone who assists an umpire or referee by signalling when a ball is out of play.

ling /**ling**/ *n* **1** a fish of the cod family. **2** heather.

linger /**ling**-ger/ *vb* **1** to delay before going. **2** to stay about, to last or continue for a long time.

lingerie /**lon**-je-ree/ *n* women's underclothing.

lingo /**ling**-go/ *n* (*inf*) a language.

lingua franca /**ling**-gwa **frang**-ka/ *n* a mixed language in which people of different languages may speak to one another.

lingual /**ling**-gwal/ *adj* (*fml*) **1** having to do with the tongue. **2** having to do with language.

linguist /**ling**-gwist/ *n* someone skilled in foreign languages.

linguistic /ling-**gwi**-stic/ *adj* having to do with the study of languages. • *n* **linguistics**.

liniment /**li**-na-ment/ *n* an ointment or oil rubbed into the body to prevent stiffness.

lining /**lie**-ning/ *n* the covering of the inside of something, such as a garment or box.

link /**lingk**/ *n* **1** one ring of a chain. **2** that which connects one thing with another. **3** in imperial measurements, $\frac{1}{100}$ part of a chain (= 7.92 inches). • *vb* to connect, to join.

links /**lingks**/ *npl* **1** flat sandy, grassy ground by the seashore. **2** a seaside golf course.

linoleum /li-**no**-lee-um/ *n* a floor covering made of cloth coated with linseed oil.

linseed /**lin**-seed/ *n* the seed of flax.

lint /**lint**/ *n* linen specially prepared for dressing open wounds.

lintel /**lin**-tel/ *n* the wood or stone across the top of a window or door.

lion /**lion**/ *n* **1** a large flesh-eating animal of the cat family. **2** a famous and important person. • *f* **lioness**. • **lion's share** the largest share.

lion-hearted /**lion**-har-ted/ *adj* very brave.

lionize /**lion**-ize/ *vb*, *also* **lionise** to treat a person as if he or she were famous.

lip /**lip**/ *n* **1** either of the edges of the opening of the mouth. **2** the edge or brim of anything.

lip-read /**lip**-reed/ *vb* to understand what a person is saying from the movements of his or her lips.

lipstick /**lip**-stick/ *n* a kind of pencil or crayon used to colour the lips.

liquefy /**li**-kwi-fie/ *vb* to make or become liquid. • *n* **liquefaction**.

liqueur /li-**cur**/ *n* a sweetly flavoured alcoholic drink.

liquid /**li**-kwid/ *adj* **1** in the form of a liquid. **2** clear. **3** (*of sounds*) smooth and clear, as the letter *r* or *l*. • *n* a substance that flows and has no fixed shape, a substance that is not a solid or gas.

liquidate /**li**-kwi-date/ *vb* **1** to pay debts. **2** to close down a business when it has too many debts. **3** to put an end to, to get rid of, to destroy. • *n* **liquidation**.

liquor /**li**-cur/ *n* **1** strong alcoholic drink, such as spirits. **2** the liquid produced from cooked food.

liquorice /li-crish, li-ker-iss/ *n, also* **licorice** (*US*) **1** a black sweet-tasting root used in making medicines and sweets. **2** a kind of sweet made from this.

lisp /lisp/ *vb* **1** to say the sound *th* for *s* when speaking. **2** to speak as a small child does. • *also n.*

list[1] /list/ *n* a series of names, numbers, etc, written down in order one after the other. • *vb* to write down in order.

list[2] /list/ *vb* to lean over to one side. • *also n.*

listed building /list-ed bild-ing/ *n* a building officially protected because of its historical or artistic importance.

listen /li-sen/ *vb* **1** to try to hear. **2** to pay attention to. • *n* **listener**.

listless /list-less/ *adj* lacking energy, uninterested.

lit *pt and pp of* **light**[1].

litany /li-ta-nee/ *n* a form of public prayer with responses given by the worshippers.

liter US variant of **litre**.

literacy /li-tra-see/ *n* the ability to read and write.

literal /li-tral/ *adj* **1** with each word given its ordinary meaning, word for word. **2** following the exact meaning without any exaggeration or anything added from the imagination. • *adv* **literally**.

literary /li-te-ra-ree/ *adj* having to do with literature or with writing as a career.

literate /li-te-rat/ *adj* **1** able to read and write. **2** having read a great deal.

literature /li-te-ra-chur/ *n* **1** the books, etc, written on a particular subject. **2** written works of lasting interest and of fine quality and artistic value.

lithe /lithe/ *adj* able to bend or twist easily and gracefully.

litmus /lit-mus/ *n* a blue dye turned red by acids.

litre /lee-ter/ *n, also* **liter** (*US*) in the metric system, a measure of liquid volume, *abbr* l.

litter /li-ter/ *n* **1** (*old*) a light bed that can be carried about, a stretcher. **2** bedding of straw, etc, for animals. **3** the young of an animal born at one time. **4** trash; scraps of paper and rubbish lying about. • *vb* **1** to throw away untidily. **2** (*of animals*) to give birth to.

little /li-tul/ *adj* **1** small. **2** short. **3** young. • *n* **1** a small amount. **2** a short time. • *adv* not much.

live[1] /liv/ *vb* **1** to have life, to exist, to be alive. **2** to continue to be alive. **3** to dwell, to have your home. **4** to behave in a certain way. **5** to keep oneself alive, obtain the food or goods necessary for life. **6** to

pass or spend one's life. • **live down** to live in a way that makes others overlook one's past faults.

live[2] /live/ *adj* **1** having life, alive. **2** full of energy, capable of becoming active. **3** heard or seen as the event takes place, not recorded. **4** burning.

livelihood /live-lee-hood/ *n* the work by which one earns one's living.

livelong /liv-long/ *adj* **1** seeming long. **2** (*fml*) whole.

lively /live-lee/ *adj* active, energetic, cheerful. • *n* **liveliness**.

liven /lie-ven/ *vb* to make more cheerful.

liver /li-ver/ *n* **1** an organ inside the body that helps to cleanse the blood. **2** this organ from certain animals used as food.

livery /li-ve-ree/ *n* a special uniform worn by servants in one household.

livestock /live-stock/ *n* animals kept on a farm.

live wire /live wire/ *n* **1** a wire through which an electric current is passing. **2** a person with a lot of energy.

livid /li-vid/ *adj* **1** discoloured, black and blue. **2** (*old*) pale. **3** (*inf*) very angry.

living /li-ving/ *n* **1** a means of providing oneself with what is necessary for life. **2** employment as a member of clergy in the Church of England.

lizard /li-zard/ *n* a four-footed reptile with a long tail.

llama /la-ma/ *n* a South American animal of the camel family.

lo /lo/ *interj* (*old or lit*) look!

load /load/ *vb* **1** to put a burden on the back of an animal. **2** to put goods into a vehicle. **3** to put a heavy weight on. **4** to put ammunition into a gun. **5** to put film into a camera. • *n* **1** that which is carried. **2** a weight. **3** a cargo.

loadstar *see* **lodestar**.

loadstone *see* **lodestone**.

loaf[1] /loaf/ *n* (*pl* **loaves**) bread made into a shape convenient for selling.

loaf[2] /loaf/ *vb* to pass time without doing anything, to laze around. • *n* **loafer**.

loam /loam/ *n* a sand and clay soil. • *adj* **loamy**.

loan /loan/ *n* that which is lent.

loath, loth /loath/ *adj* unwilling.

loathe /loathe/ *vb* to hate.

loathing /loathe-ing/ *n* hate, disgust.

loathsome /loathe-sum/ *adj* hateful, disgusting.

loaves *see* **loaf**.

lob /lob/ *vb* (**lobbed, lobbing**) to hit, kick or throw a ball gently in the air. • *also n.*

lobby /lob-ee/ *n* **1** an entrance hall. **2** a group of people trying to influence the decisions of the government. • *vb* to try to influence decisions of the government.

lobe /loab/ *n* the fleshy hanging part of the ear.

lobelia /lo-beel-ya/ *n* a kind of garden flower, often blue, white or red in colour.

lobster /lob-ster/ *n* a long-tailed jointed shellfish.

lobster pot /lob-ster pot/ *n* a baited basket for trapping lobsters.

local /lo-cal/ *adj* having to do with a particular place.• *n* **1** a person who lives in a particular place.

local colour /lo-cal cul-ur/ *n* in a picture or story, accuracy over details of place to make it more realistic.

locality /lo-cal-i-tee/ *n* a district, area, neighbourhood.

localize /lo-ca-lize/ *vb*, *also* **localise** to keep to one place or district.

locate /lo-cate/ *vb* **1** to find the place of. **2** to fix or set in a certain place.

location /lo-cay-shun/ *n* **1** place. **2** the place where a story is filmed.

loch /loch/ (*Scottish English*) *n* **1** a lake, especially in Scotland. **2** an arm of the sea.

lock /lok/ *n* **1** a fastening bolt moved by a key. **2** the part of a gun by which it is fired. **3** a section of a canal, enclosed by gates, in which the amount of water can be increased to raise a ship to a higher level, or vice versa. **4** a firm grasp. **5** a curl of hair. • *vb* **1** to fasten with lock and key. **2** to hold firmly. **3** to jam, to become fixed or blocked. • **lock, stock and barrel** altogether, completely.

locker /lok-er/ *n* a small cupboard with a lock.

locket /lok-et/ *n* a small metal case, often containing a picture, worn on a chain round the neck as an ornament.

lockjaw /lok-jaw/ *n* a condition in which the muscles of the jaw become so stiff that the mouth cannot be opened, usually a sign of tetanus.

locksmith /lok-smith/ *n* one who makes or repairs locks.

lock-up /lok-up/ *n* **1** a cell in a prison. **2** a garage in which a car can be locked away.

locomotive /lo-co-moe-tiv/ *n* a railway engine.

locust /lo-cust/ *n* a large grasshopper that feeds on and destroys crops.

lode /lode/ *n* a vein of metal in a crack in a rock.

lodestar, loadstar /lode-star/ *n* **1** the star by which one sets a course, the Pole star. **2** a guide or example to follow.

lodestone, loadstone /lode-stone/ *n* a stone containing magnetic iron, formerly used as a compass.

lodge /lodge/ *n* **1** a small house originally for a gatekeeper at the entrance to a park, church, etc. **2** the meeting place of a society (e.g. Freemasons) or the members meeting there. **3** a house for a hunting party. **4** a house or cabin used occasionally for some seasonal activity. • *vb* **1** to put in a certain place. **2** to stay in another's house on payment. **3** to fix in. • **lodge a complaint** to make a complaint before an official.

lodger /lod-jer/ *n* one who stays in hired rooms in another's house.

lodging /lod-jing/ *n* a place where one pays to stay.

loft /loft/ *n* **1** the space or room under the roof of a building. **2** a raised area over a barn. **3** a gallery in a hall or church. • *vb* to strike upward.

lofty /lof-tee/ *adj* **1** (*lit*) very high. **2** of high moral quality. **3** proud, haughty. • *n* **loftiness**.

log /log/ *n* **1** a piece sawn from the trunk or one of the large branches of a tree. **2** an instrument for measuring the speed of ships. **3** an official written record of a journey.

loganberry /lo-gan-be-ree/ *n* a fruit like a raspberry.

logarithms /law-ga-ri-thumz/ *n* numbers arranged in a table to help in calculations.

logbook /lawg-book/ *n* **1** a book in which the rate of progress of a ship is written daily. **2** an official record of a journey. **3** the registration document of a car.

loggerheads /law-ger-hedz/ *npl*. • **at loggerheads** quarrelling.

logic /law-jic/ *n* **1** the art or science of reasoning. **2** a particular way of thinking or reasoning. **3** (*inf*) reasonable thinking, good sense.

logical /law-ji-cal/ *adj* **1** having to do with logic. **2** well-reasoned. **3** able to reason correctly.

logician /law-ji-shun/ *n* one skilled in logic.

logo /lo-go/ *n* a special symbol or design that an organization uses on its products, notepaper, etc.

loin /loin/ *n* **1** a piece of meat cut from the back of an animal. **2** *pl* the part of the human back below the ribs. • **gird (up) one's loins** to prepare for action.

loin-cloth /loin-cloth/ *n* a piece of cloth worn round the loins.

loiter /loi-ter/ *vb* **1** to stand about idly. **2** to go slowly, often stopping.

loll /lol/ *vb* **1** to sit back or lie lazily. **2** (*of the tongue*) to hang out.

lollipop /law-lee-pop/ *n* a candy on a stick.

lollipop man, woman /law-lee-pop man, woo-man/ *n* a man (woman) whose job is to help people, particularly children, cross the road.

lone /lone/ *adj* alone, single, without others.

lonely /lone-lee/ *adj* sad because alone.

lonesome /lone-sum/ *adj* (*inf*) lonely.

long /long/ *adj* **1** not short, in time or space. **2** having length, covering a certain distance from one end to the other or a certain time. **3** (*of drinks*) containing little or no alcohol and served in a tall glass. • *adv* for a long time. • *vb* to want very much.

longboat /long-boat/ *n* the largest and strongest boat carried on board a ship.

longbow /long-bo/ *n* a bow, drawn by hand, for firing arrows. • (*old*) **draw the longbow** to tell untrue and improbable stories.

longevity /lan-je-vi-tee/ *n* very long life.

longing /long-ing/ *n* an eager desire.

longish /long-ish/ *adj* (*inf*) quite long.

longitude /lon-ji-tud/ *n* **1** length. **2** distance in degrees east or west of an imaginary line from pole to pole, running through Greenwich, London.

longitudinal /lon-ji-tood-nal/ *adj* having to do with length or longitude.

long-sighted /long-sie-ted/ *adj* able to see distant objects more clearly than near ones.

long-suffering /long-su-fring/ *adj* patient, ready to put up with troubles without complaint.

long-winded /long-win-ded/ *adj* speaking or writing in an unnecessarily roundabout way.

loo /loo/ *n* (*inf*) toilet.

loofa(h) /loo-fa/ *n* **1** a marrowlike plant. **2** the fibrous framework of the plant stripped of the fleshy part and used in washing as a sponge.

look /look/ *vb* **1** to turn the eyes towards so as to see. **2** to have a certain appearance. **3** to face in a certain direction. • *n* **1** act of looking. **2** a glance. **3** the appearance, especially of the face. • **look after** to take care of. • **look a gift-horse in the mouth** to say that one is not pleased with a present or to criticize it. • **look down on** to despise. • **look for 1** to try to find. **2** to hope for. • **look on** to watch. • **look out 1** to be careful. **2** to watch out for. • **look over** to examine.

looker-on /loo-ker-on/ *n* one who watches or spectates.

looking glass /loo-king glass/ *n* a mirror.

lookout /loo-kout/ *n* **1** watchman. **2** a post from which one watches. **3** a careful watch.

loom[1] /loom/ *n* a machine for weaving cloth.

loom[2] /loom/ *vb* **1** to appear gradually and dimly, as in the dark; to seem larger than natural. **2** to seem threateningly close.

loon /loon/ *n* a northern diving bird.

loop /loop/ *n* **1** a line that curves back and crosses itself. **2** a rope, cord, etc, that so curves. • *vb* **1** to make a loop. **2** to fasten in a loop. • **in the loop** (*inf*) part of a group that is dealing with something or is well-informed about something.

loophole /loop-hole/ *n* a way of escaping or avoiding something.

loose /looss/ *adj* **1** untied, not packed together in a box, etc. **2** free, at liberty. **3** not definite. **4** careless. **5** not tight. **6** indecent, immoral. • *vb* **1** to untie. **2** to set free.

loose cannon /looss ca-non/ *n* a person whose behaviour is unpredictable and often reckless.

loose-leaf /looss-leef/ *adj* describing a notebook that can hold pages with perforations which can be added or removed.

loosen /loo-sen/ *vb* to make or become loose or less tight.

loot /loot/ *n* that which is stolen or carried off by force.

lop[1] /lop/ *vb* (**lopped, lopping**) to cut off.

lop[2] /lop/ *vb* (**lopped, lopping**) to hang loosely.

lop-sided /lop-sie-ded/ *adj* leaning to one side.

lord /lawrd/ *n* **1** a master. **2** a ruler. **3** a nobleman. **4** a title of honour given to noblemen and certain high officials (e.g. judges). **5** an owner. • *n* (*cap*) God. • *vb* to rule strictly or harshly.

lordly /lawrd-lee/ *adj* **1** proud, grand. **2** commanding.

lordship /lawrd-ship/ *n* **1** the state of being a lord. **2** the power of a lord. **3** the title by which one addresses noblemen, judges, etc.

lore /lore/ *n* **1** (*old*) learning. **2** all that is known about a subject, usually that which is handed down by word of mouth.

lorry /law-ree/ *n* a truck.

lose /looz/ *vb* (*pt, pp* **lost**) **1** to cease to have. **2** to fail to keep in one's possession. **3** to be defeated in. **4** to fail to use, to waste. **5** to miss. **6** (*of a watch or clock*) to work too slowly. **7** to have less of. • **lose one's head** to become too excited to act sensibly.

loser /loo-zer/ *n* one who loses.

loss /loss/ *n* **1** act of losing. **2** that which is lost. **3** harm, damage. • **at a loss** not knowing what to do.

lost *pt and pp of* **lose.**

lot /lot/ *n* **1** one of a set of objects, a separate part. **2** a set of objects sold together at an auction. **3** the way of life that one has to follow. **4** a large number or quantity. **5** a piece of land.

loth *see* **loath.**

lotion /lo-shun/ *n* a liquid for healing wounds, cleansing the skin, etc.

lottery /lot-e-ree/ *n* a game of chance in which prizes are shared out among those whose tickets are picked out in a public draw.

lotus /lo-tus/ *n* a type of water-lily whose flower was once said to make those who ate it forget everything.

loud /loud/ *adj* **1** easily heard. **2** noisy. **3** unpleasantly bright, showy.

loudspeaker /loud-spee-ker/ *n* a radio apparatus by which sound is transmitted and made louder when necessary.

lough /laak/ *n* a lake, especially in Ireland.

lounge /loundge/ *vb* **1** to stand about lazily, to move lazily, to spend time in an idle way. **3** to sit or lie back in a comfortable position. • *n* **1** a sitting room. **2** a public room in a hotel. • *n* **lounger.**

lounge suit /loundge soot/ *n* a man's suit of clothes for everyday wear.

lour *see* **lower².**

louse /louss/ *n* (*pl* **lice**) a wingless insect that lives on the bodies of animals.

lousy /lou-zee/ *adj* **1** full of or covered with lice. **2** (*inf*) very bad, poor.

lout /lout/ *n* a rude and clumsy fellow.

lovable /lu-va-bul/ *adj* worthy of love.

love /luv/ *n* **1** a strong liking for. **2** a feeling of desire for. **3** the person or thing loved. **4** a term of endearment. **5** (in some games) no score. • *vb* **1** to be fond of, to like. **2** to be strongly attracted to, to be in love with. • *n* **lover.**

loveless /luv-less/ *adj* **1** with no love. **2** unloved.

lovelorn /luv-lawrn/ *adj* (*old*) sad because left by one's lover.

lovely /luv-lee/ *adj* **1** beautiful. **2** (*inf*) very pleasing. • *n* **loveliness.**

loving /lu-ving/ *adj* full of love, fond.

low¹ /lo/ *vb* **1** to bellow, as an ox. **2** to moo like a cow. • *n* **lowing.**

low² /lo/ *adj* **1** not far above the ground. **2** not tall, not high. **3** small in degree, amount, etc. **4** not high in rank or position. **5** cheap. **6** vulgar, coarse. **7** dishonourable.

8 soft, not loud. **9** sad, unhappy. • **low spirits** a sad mood.

lower¹ /loe-er/ *vb* **1** to make less high. **2** to let or bring down. **3** to make of less value or worth.

lower², **lour** /laoo-er/ *vb* **1** to frown. **2** to become dark.

lowland /lo-land/ *n* low-lying or level country.

lowlander /lo-lan-der/ *n* one born or living in lowlands.

lowly /lo-lee/ *adj* **1** (*fml or hum*) humble, not high in rank. **2** (*old or lit*) gentle in manner.

loyal /loy-al/ *adj* **1** faithful to one's friends, duty, etc. **2** true. • *n* **loyalty.**

loyalist /loy-a-list/ *n* one who supports the lawful government of the country.

lozenge /loz-endge/ *n* **1** a diamond-shaped figure. **2** a small sweet, or medicine in the form of a sweet.

lubricant /loo-bri-cant/ *n* oil or grease used to make machinery run smoothly.

lubricate /loo-bri-cate/ *vb* to apply oil or grease something to make it run smoothly. • *n* **lubrication, lubricator.**

lucid /loo-sid/ *adj* clear, easily understood. • *n* **lucidity.**

Lucifer /loo-si-fer/ *n* Satan.

luck /luck/ *n* **1** the good or bad things that happen by chance, fate, fortune. **2** something good that happens by chance, good fortune.

luckless /luck-less/ *adj* (*fml*) unfortunate.

lucky /lu-kee/ *adj* fortunate, having good luck.

lucrative /loo-cra-tiv/ *adj* bringing in much money or profit.

ludicrous /loo-di-crus/ *adj* funny, silly and laughable.

lug /lug/ *vb* (**lugged, lugging**) to pull, draw or carry with difficulty.

luggage /lu-gidge/ *n* a traveller's baggage.

lukewarm /luke-**wawrm**/ *adj* **1** quite warm, neither hot nor cold. **2** not eager.

lull /lull/ *vb* **1** to calm. **2** to send to sleep. • *n* an interval of calm.

lullaby /lu-la-by/ *n* a song sung to a baby to make it sleep.

lumbago /lum-**bay**-go/ *n* muscular pain in the lower part of the back.

lumbar /lum-bar/ *adj* having to do with the lower part of the back.

lumber /lum-ber/ *n* unused or useless articles. • *vb* **1** to move heavily and clumsily. **2** to give someone an unpleasant or unwanted responsibility or task.

lumberjack /lum-ber-jack/ *n* someone whose job it is to cut down trees.

luminary /loo-mi-na-ree/ *n* (*lit*) a body that gives light (e.g. the sun). **2** (*fml*) a person well-known for his or her knowledge, expertise or talent.

luminous /loo-mi-nuss/ *adj* shining, giving light.

lump /lump/ *n* **1** a shapeless mass. **2** a hard swelling. • *vb* to put together as one, to consider together.

lump sum /lump sum/ *n* a single large amount of money instead of several smaller payments.

lumpy /lum-pee/ *adj* full of lumps.

lunacy /loo-na-see/ *n* madness, great foolishness.

lunar /loo-nar/ *adj* having to do with the moon.

lunatic /loo-na-tic/ *n* **1** a person who behaves very foolishly. **2** (*formerly and often offensively*) a person suffering from severe mental illness. • *adj* very foolish.

lunch /lunch/ *n* a midday meal. • *vb* to take lunch.

lung /lung/ *n* one of the two bodily organs by means of which we breathe.

lunge /lundge/ *n* a sudden move or thrust forward. • *vb* to make a sudden onward movement.

lupin /loo-pin/ *n* a kind of garden plant with a tall stem covered in many flowers.

lurch /lurch/ *vb* to roll or sway to one side. • *n* a sudden roll. • **leave in the lurch** to leave (someone) in difficulty.

lure /loor/ *n* something that attracts or leads on. • *vb* to attract, to lead on, as by promise or gifts.

lurid /loo-rid/ *adj* **1** too brightly coloured, too vivid. **2** horrifying, shocking.

lurk /lurk/ *vb* **1** to remain out of sight. **2** to lie hidden, to exist unseen.

luscious /lu-shus/ *adj* very sweet in taste.

lush /lush/ *adj* **1** growing very plentifully, thick. **2** (*inf*) affluent, luxurious.

lust /lust/ *n* a strong or uncontrollable desire, especially for sexual pleasure. • *vb* to desire eagerly. • *adj* **lustful**.

lustre /lu-ster/ *n* **1** brightness. **2** glory. **3** dress material with a shiny surface.

lustreless /lu-ster-less/ *adj* dull.

lustrous /lu-struss/ *adj* bright, shining.

lusty /lu-stee/ *adj* **1** strong and healthy, full of energy. **2** strong or loud.

lute /loot/ *n* (*old*) a stringed musical instrument, rather like the guitar.

luxuriant /lug-zhoo-ree-ant/ *adj* growing in great plenty.

luxuriate /lug-zhoo-ree-ate/ *vb* to live in or enjoy great comfort.

luxurious /lug-zhoo-ree-uss/ *adj* **1** fond of luxury. **2** splendid and affluent.

luxury /luk-shu-ree/ *n* **1** great ease and comfort. **2** a desirable or pleasing thing that is not a necessity of life.

Lycra /lie-cra/ *n* (*TM*) a stretchy, shiny synthetic fabric used for swimsuits, sportswear, etc.

lying /lie-ing/ *pres p of* **lie**. • *also adj*.

lymph /limf/ *n* a colourless liquid in the body.

lynch /linch/ *vb* to seize someone, judge him or her on the spot and put him or her to death without a proper trial.

lynx /links/ *n* an animal of the cat family noted for keen sight.

lyre /lire/ *n* (*old*) a U-shaped stringed musical instrument similar to a harp, played by the ancient Greeks.

lyre-bird /lire-burd/ *n* a bird with a tail shaped like a lyre.

lyric /li-ric/ *n* **1** a short poem expressing the writer's feelings. **2** *pl* the words of a song.

lyrical /li-ri-cal/ *adj* **1** expressing feeling. **2** enthusiastic, effusive.

M

M, m /em/ the 13th letter of the English alphabet.

ma'am /mam/ n **1** madam. **2** in the UK, used when addressing the Queen or senior female officers in the police or army.

mac /mack/ n (short for **mackintosh**) a waterproof rain coat.

macabre /ma-**cab**/ adj horrible, causing a shudder of horror.

macaron /**mak**-a-ron/ (French) a cake made of two smooth meringue and ground-almond shells with a flavoured filling.

macaroni /ma-ca-**roe**-nee/ n a type of pasta in the shape of long tubes.

macaroon /ma-ca-**roon**/ n a small, rough cake containing ground almonds or coconut.

macaw /ma-**caw**/ n a large type of parrot.

mace /mase/ n **1** (old) a spiked club used as a weapon of war. **2** a heavy ornamental stick carried before certain officials as a sign of their office.

machete /ma-**shet**-ee/ n a large heavy knife sometimes used as a weapon.

machine /ma-**sheen**/ n **1** any apparatus for producing power or doing work. **2** a system under which the work of different groups is directed to one end.

machine gun n a gun that fires many bullets in a short time before it has to be reloaded.

machinery /ma-**shee**-ne-ree/ n **1** machines. **2** parts of a machine. **3** organization.

machinist /ma-**shee**-nist/ n a person who makes, looks after or operates machinery.

mackerel /**ma**-krel/ n an edible sea fish.

mackintosh /ma-kin-tosh/ see **mac**.

mad /mad/ adj **1** insane, seriously mentally ill. **2** out of your mind with anger, pain, etc. **3** (inf) very angry. **4** (inf) very unwise, crazy. **5** very enthusiastic about something.

madam /**ma**-dam/ n the title used in addressing a woman politely.

Madame /ma-**dam**/ n the French form of Mrs.

madcap /**mad**-cap/ n a wild or reckless person. • adj reckless, very thoughtless.

madden /**ma**-din/ vb to make mad. • adj **maddening**.

made /made/ pt an pp of make.

madly /**mad**-lee/ adv very much.

madman /**mad**-man/ n a man who is insane.

madness /**mad**-ness/ n **1** insanity. **2** folly.

Madonna /ma-**don**-a/ n **1** the Virgin Mary. **2** a picture or statue of the Virgin Mary.

maelstrom /**mail**-strom/ n **1** a powerful whirlpool. **2** something resembling the motion of a whirlpool.

magazine /ma-ga-**zeen**/ n **1** a store for firearms and explosives. **2** a weekly or monthly paper containing articles, stories, etc.

magenta /ma-**jen**-ta/ n a crimson dye. • adj crimson.

maggot /**ma**-got/ n the grub of certain insects, especially the fly or bluebottle.

Magi /**may**-jie/ npl in Christianity, the wise men from the East who visited the infant Jesus.

magic /**ma**-jic/ n **1** the art of controlling spirits, and so gaining knowledge of the future or commanding certain things to happen; witchcraft. **2** the art of producing illusions by tricks or sleight of hand. **3** fascination. • adj also **magical 1** having to do with magic. **2** (inf) marvellous, very good. • adv **magically**.

magician /ma-**ji**-shun/ n **1** a person who has magic powers. **2** a person who practises the art of producing illusions by tricks or sleight of hand.

magisterial /ma-ji-**sti**-ree-al/ adj **1** having the manner of a person who is used to giving commands. **2** having to do with magistrates.

magistracy /ma-**ji**-stra-see/ n the office of magistrate.

magistrate /**ma**-ji-strate/ n a person who has the authority to try and sentence those who break the law; a judge.

magnanimous /mag-**na**-ni-mus/ adj generous, especially to enemies or dependants; unselfish. • n **magnanimity**.

magnate /**mag**-nate/ n a person of great wealth or importance.

magnesia /mag-**nee**-sha/ n a white powder made from magnesium, used as a medicine.

magnesium /mag-**nee**-zee-um/ n a white metal that burns with a bright white light.

magnet /**mag**-net/ n **1** a piece of iron that attracts to it other pieces of iron and that when hung up points to the north. **2** a person or thing that attracts.

magnetic /mag-**net**-ic/ adj **1** acting like a magnet. **2** attractive.

magnetism /**mag**-ne-ti-zum/ n **1** the power of the magnet. **2** the science that deals with the power of the magnet. **3** personal charm or attraction.

magnificent /mag-**ni**-fi-sent/ *adj* splendid, grand. • *n* **magnificence**.

magnify /**mag**-ni-fie/ *vb* **1** to make appear larger, to exaggerate. **2** to praise.

magnifying glass /**mag**-ni-fie-ing glass/ *n* a glass with a curved surface that makes things appear larger.

magnitude /**mag**-ni-tood/ *n* **1** greatness of size or extent. **2** importance.

magnolia /mag-**nole**-ya/ *n* a tree with beautiful foliage and large pale-coloured flowers.

magnum /**mag**-num/ *n* a bottle holding twice the usual amount of one bottle.

magpie /**mag**-pie/ *n* a black-and-white bird of the crow family.

maharaja(h) /ma-ha-**ra**-ja/ *n* an Indian prince.

maharanee /ma-ha-**ra**-nee/ *n* an Indian princess.

mahatma /ma-**hat**-ma/ *n* an Indian title of respect for a very holy person.

mahogany /ma-**hog**-a-nee/ *n* a reddish-brown wood often used for furniture.

maid /made/ *n* **1** (*old*) a young girl. **2** a female servant. **3** a woman who is employed to clean other people's houses. **4** (*old*) a virgin.

maiden /**may**-den/ *n* (*old*) a young unmarried woman.

maidenly /**may**-den-lee/ *adj* modest, gentle.

maiden name /**may**-den name/ *n* the surname of a married woman before marriage.

maiden voyage /**may**-den **voy**-idge/ *n* the first voyage of a new ship.

mail[1] /male/ *n* **1** (*also* **post**) the postal service. **2** (*also* **post**) letters, parcels, etc, sent by mail. **3** email. • *vb* **1** (*esp US*) to send by mail. **2** send by email.

mail[2] /male/ *n* (*old*) armour.

mail order /male awr-der/ *n* a system of buying goods from a catalogue and having them delivered to your home.

maim /mame/ *vb* to disable.

main /mane/ *adj* chief, principal. • *n* **1** the greater part. **2** (*old*) the ocean. **3** a pipe under the street for water, gas, etc. **4** strength.

mainframe /**mane**-frame/ *n* a large fast computer that serves a lot of terminals.

mainland /**mane**-land/ *n* land, as distinct from nearby islands.

mainly /**mane**-lee/ *adv* chiefly.

mainstay /**mane**-stay/ *n* **1** the rope holding up the mast of a ship. **2** the chief support.

mainstream /**mane**-streem/ *n* the prevailing way of thinking or of doing something.

maintain /mane-**tain**/ *vb* **1** to feed and clothe. **2** to keep up. **3** to keep in good repair. **4** to defend a point of view.

maintenance /**mane**-ti-nanse/ *n* upkeep, support.

maize /maze/ *n*, *also* **corn** (*US*) a kind of cereal plant with large yellow seeds that are eaten as a vegetable.

majestic /ma-**je**-stic/ *adj* dignified, stately.

majesty /**ma**-je-stee/ *n* **1** grandeur, dignity. **2** the title given to a king or queen.

major /**may**-jor/ *adj* **1** the greater in number, size, or quantity. **2** the more important. • *n* an army officer just above a captain in rank.

majority /ma-**jaw**-ri-tee/ *n* **1** the greater number. **2** in voting, the amount by which the number of votes cast for one candidate exceeds that cast for another. **3** (*fml*) the age at which you have full civil rights.

make /make/ *vb* (*pt, pp* made) **1** to create. **2** to construct by putting parts or substances together. **3** to cause to be. **4** to force. **5** to add up to. **6** to earn. • *n* **1** the way something is made. **2** shape. • **make for** to go towards. • **make good** to succeed, to do well. • **make off** to run away. • **make out 1** to decipher. **2** (*inf*) to succeed. • **make up 1** to invent. **2** to put on paint, powder, etc. **3** to bring.

make-believe /**make**-bi-leev/ *n* pretence. • *also vb*.

make-over /**make**-oe-ver/ *n* the process of trying to improve the appearance of a person or place.

maker /**make**-er/ *n* a person who makes. • **your Maker** God.

makeshift /**make**-shift/ *adj* used or done because nothing better can be found or thought of. • *also n*.

make-up /**make**-up/ *n* **1** mascara, lipstick, and other substances used to enhance the appearance of the face. **2** your character.

malaria /ma-**ler**-ee-ya/ *n* a fever caused by a mosquito bite.

male /male/ *adj* **1** consisting of boys or men. **2** of or relating to the sex that can become a father. • *also n*.

malevolent /ma-**le**-vo-lent/ *adj* wishing harm to others, spiteful. • *n* **malevolence**.

malformed /mal-**fawrmd**/ *adj* out of shape, wrongly shaped. • *n* **malformation**.

malfunction /mal-**fung**-shun/ *vb* to fail to work correctly.

malice /**ma**-liss/ *n* pleasure in the misfortunes of others, spite, a desire to harm others.

malicious /ma-li-shus/ *adj* spiteful, full of malice.

malign /ma-line/ *vb* to speak ill of. • *adj* evil, harmful.

malignancy /ma-lig-nan-see/ *n* **1** great hatred. **2** a desire to do harm.

malignant /ma-lig-nant/ *adj* **1** able to cause death. **2** very harmful. **3** feeling great hatred.

mall /mawl/ *n* a large indoor shopping centre.

mallard /ma-lard/ *n* a wild duck.

mallet /ma-let/ *n* **1** a wooden hammer. **2** the stick used in croquet.

malnutrition /mal-noo-tri-shun/ *n* a state caused by eating too little food or food that does not supply the needs of the body.

malt /mawlt/ *n* **1** barley or other grain prepared for making beer or whisky. **2** malt whisky. • *vb* to make into or become malt. • *adj* malty.

malted milk /mawl-ted milk/ *n* milk, flavoured with malt, sometimes mixed with ice cream.

maltreat /mal-treet/ *vb* to treat badly, to ill-use. • *n* maltreatment.

malt whisky /mawlt whis-kee/ *n* a kind of whisky distilled from malted barley, made at one particular distillery.

mam(m)a /ma-ma/ *n* (*inf*) mother.

mammal /ma-mal/ *n* an animal that suckles its young.

mammoth /ma-moth/ *n* a type of large elephant, no longer existing. • *adj* huge.

man /man/ *n* (*pl* **men**) **1** the human race. **2** a human being. **3** a male human being. **4** (*inf*) a husband. **5** a male servant. • *vb* (**manned, manning**) to provide with people to go to or be in the place where a duty is to be performed.

manage /ma-nidge/ *vb* **1** to control, to be in charge of. **2** to succeed (in doing something).

manageable /ma-ni-ja-bul/ *adj* easily controlled.

management /ma-nidge-ment/ *n* **1** control, direction. **2** the group of persons who control or run a business.

manager /ma-na-jer/ *n* a person who controls a business or part of it.

managerial /ma-ni-jee-ree-al/ *adj* having to do with the management of a business.

mandarin /man-d(a-)rin/ *n* a variety of small orange.

Mandarin /man-d(a-)rin/ *n* a group of closely related dialects of the Chinese language.

mandate /man-date/ *n* **1** a command. **2** power given to one person, group, or nation to act on behalf of another (e.g. by voters to the governing party).

mandatory /man-da-toe-ree/ *adj* compulsory.

mandible /man-di-bul/ *n* the lower jawbone.

mandolin(e) /man-do-lin/ *n* a musical stringed instrument, like the guitar but with a rounded back.

mane /mane/ *n* the long hair on the neck of certain animals.

maneuver US variant of **manoeuvre**.

manful /man-ful/ *adj* brave. • *adv* **manfully**.

manganese /mang-ga-neez/ *n* a hard, easily broken grey metal.

mange /mainj/ *n* a skin disease of dogs, etc.

manger /main-jer/ *n* a raised box or trough out of which horses or cattle feed.

mangle /mang-gul/ *vb* to cut or tear so as to be unrecognizable.

mango /man-go/ *n* (*pl* **mangoes**) **1** an Indian fruit with a large stone. **2** the tree on which it grows.

mangrove /man-grove/ *n* a tropical tree that grows in wet or muddy ground.

mangy /main-jee/ *adj* **1** affected with mange. **2** shabby or dirty.

manhandle /man-han-dul/ *vb* **1** to move by hand. **2** to treat roughly.

manhole /man-hole/ *n* a hole in the ground or floor through which a person may enter an underground shaft or tunnel.

manhood /man-hood/ *n* the state of being a man or of having the qualities of a man.

mania /may-nee-ya/ *n* **1** madness. **2** a very great interest (in), an obsession.

maniac /may-nee-yac/ *n* a madman.

maniacal /ma-nie-a-cul/ *adj* completely mad.

manicure /ma-ni-cyoor/ *n* the care of the hands and fingernails. • *also vb*.

manicurist /ma-ni-cyoo-rist/ *n* a person whose job it is to care for hands and fingernails.

manifest /ma-ni-fest/ *adj* (*fml*) easily seen or understood, obvious. • *vb* to show clearly.

manifestation /ma-ni-fe-stay-shun/ *n* an open showing, a display.

manifestly /ma-ni-fest-lee/ *adv* clearly, obviously.

manifesto /ma-ni-fe-sto/ *n* a public announcement of future plans.

manipulate /ma-ni-pyu-late/ *vb* **1** to handle skilfully. **2** to manage skilfully. • *n* **manipulation**.

mankind /man-kinde/ *n* the human race.

manly /man-lee/ *adj* having the qualities of a man.

mannequin /ma-ni-kin/ *n* **1** a dummy used to display clothes in a clothes shop. **2** (*old*) another word for a fashion model.

manner /ma-ner/ *n* **1** the way in which anything is done or happens. **2** the way a person speaks or behaves to others. **3 manners** /ma-nerz/ courteous behaviour.

mannerism /ma-ne-ri-zum/ *n* a way of behaving, writing, etc, that has become a habit.

mannish /ma-nish/ *adj* like a man.

manoeuvre /ma-noo-ver/ *n, also* **maneuver** (*US*) **1** a planned movement of armies or ships. **2** a skilful or cunning plan intended to make another behave as you want him or her to. **3** *npl* practice movements of armies or ships. • *vb* **1** to move armies or ships. **2** to move or act cunningly to gain your ends.

manor /ma-ner/ *n* the land or house belonging to a lord. • *adj* **manorial**.

mansion /man-shun/ *n* a large dwelling house.

manslaughter /man-slaw-ter/ *n* the unlawful but unintentional killing of a person.

mantelpiece /man-tel-peess/, **mantel** /man-tel/ *n* the shelf above a fireplace.

mantilla /man-tee-ya/ *n* a lace veil used as a head covering.

mantle /man-tel/ *n* **1** (*old*) a loose sleeveless cloak. **2** a coating or covering.

manual /man-yoo-wul/ *adj* done by hand. • *n* **1** a small book containing all the important facts on a certain subject. **2** the keyboard of an organ. • *adv* **manually**.

manufacture /man-yoo-fac-chur/ *n* **1** the making of goods or materials. **2** an article so made. • *vb* to make, especially by machinery, in large quantities. • *n* **manufacturer**.

manure /ma-nyoor/ *n* dung or some other substance used to make soil more fertile. • *vb* to treat with manure.

manuscript /man-yoo-script/ *n* **1** a paper or book written by hand. **2** the written material sent by an author for publishing.

many /men-ee/ *adj* great in number. • *n* a large number.

Maori /maoo-ree/ *n* one of the original inhabitants of New Zealand. • *also adj*.

map /map/ *n* a plan of any part of the earth's surface. • *vb* (**mapped, mapping**) to make a map of. • **map out** to plan.

maple /may-pul/ *n* a tree from whose sap sugar is made.

mar /mar/ *vb* (**marred, marring**) to spoil, to damage.

marathon /ma-ra-thon/ *n* **1** a long race of about 26 miles (42 km) along roads. **2** something that takes a long time and requires a great deal of effort.

marauder /ma-raw-der/ *n* (*fml*) a robber. • *adj* **marauding**.

marble /mar-bul/ *n* **1** a type of hard stone

used for buildings, statues, etc. **2** a small ball of stone or glass used in children's games.

march /march/ *vb* to walk with a regular step. • *n* **1** movement of a body of soldiers on foot. **2** the distance walked. **3** music suitable for marching to. • *n* **marcher**.

March /march/ *n* the third month of the year.

mare /mare/ *n* a female horse.

margarine /mar-je-reen/ *n* a substance made from vegetable or animal fat, often used instead of butter.

margin /mar-jin/ *n* **1** (*fml*) edge, border. **2** the part of a page that is not usually printed or written on. **3** an amount more than is necessary, something extra.

marginal /mar-ji-nal/ *adj* **1** on or near the edge, border, or limit. **2** very small or unimportant. **3** (of a parliamentary or council seat) won by a very few votes. •*n* a parliamentary or council seat that was won by a very small number of votes. • *adv* **marginally**.

marginalize /ma-ji-na-lize/ *v* to treat someone or something as unimportant or inferior.

marigold /ma-ri-goald/ *n* a bright yellow or orange flower.

marijuana /ma-ri-wa-na/ *n* cannabis.

marina /ma-ree-na/ *n* a harbour for the use of yachts and small boats.

marine /ma-reen/ *adj* **1** having to do with the sea. **2** having to do with shipping. • *n* **1** shipping. **2** a soldier serving on board ship.

mariner /ma-ri-ner/ *n* (*fml*) a seaman.

marionette /ma-ree-u-net/ *n* a doll that can be moved by strings; a puppet.

marital /ma-ri-tal/ *adj* (*fml*) having to do with marriage.

maritime /ma-ri-time/ *adj* of or near the sea.

marjoram /mar-ju-ram/ *n* a sweet-smelling herb used in cooking.

mark[1] /mark/ *n* **1** a sign, spot, or stamp that can be seen. **2** a thing aimed at. **3** a number or letter indicating the standard reached. **4** an acceptable level of quality. **5** a stain or dent. **6** an indication, a sign. • *vb* **1** to make a mark on. **2** to indicate by a mark the standard reached. **3** (*old*) to watch closely, to pay attention to. **4** to show the position of. **5** to be a sign of. • **beside the mark** (*fml*) off the subject. • **mark time 1** to move the legs up and down as if walking, but without going backward or forward. **2** to fill in time.

mark[2] /mark/ *n* a former German currency.

marked /markt/ *adj* noticeable, important.

markedly /mar-kid-lee/ *adv* noticeably.

marker /mar-ker/ *n* **1** a person who keeps the score. **2** a person or thing used to mark a place.

market /mar-ket/ *n* **1** a public place for buying and selling, a coming together of people to buy and sell. **2** a demand or need. • *vb* to sell in a market.

marketable /mar-ke-ta-bul/ *adj* that can be sold.

marketing /mar-ke-ting/ *n* the promoting and selling of a product.

marketplace /mar-ket-place/ *n* the open space where a market is held.

market research /mar-ket ree-serch/ *n* the collection and study of data on which products or services people want.

marksman /marks-man/ *n* a person who shoots well.

marmalade /mar-ma-lade/ *n* a jam made from oranges or lemons.

marmoset /mar-mo-set/ *n* a type of small monkey.

marmot /mar-mot/ *n* a small squirrel-like animal.

maroon[1] /ma-**roon**/ *n* a brownish-crimson colour. • *adj* of this colour.

maroon[2] /ma-**roon**/ *vb* to abandon.

marquee /mar-**kee**/ *n* a large tent.

marquetry /mar-ke-tree/ *n* work in which a design is made by setting differently coloured pieces of wood into another piece of wood.

marriage /ma-ridge/ *n* **1** the ceremony of marrying or being married. **2** life together as husband and wife.

marrow /ma-roe/ *n* **1** a soft fatty substance filling the hollow parts of bones. **2** a large, long dark-green vegetable.

marry /ma-ree/ *vb* **1** to join together as husband and wife. **2** to take as husband or wife.

Mars /marz/ *n* **1** the fourth planet from the sun. **2** the Roman god of war.

marsh /marsh/ *n* low watery ground, a swamp. • *adj* marshy.

marshal /mar-shal/ *n* **1** an officer of high rank in the army or air force. **2** (*US*) a law enforcement officer. **3** an official who makes arrangements for public processions, etc, or who controls crowds etc at processions or sport events. • *vb* to arrange in order.

marshmallow /marsh-me-loe/ *n* a type of soft sweet confection.

marsupial /mar-**soo**-pee-al/ *n* an animal that carries its young in a pouch.

marten /mar-ten/ *n* a type of weasel valued for its fur.

martial /mar-shal/ *adj* having to do with war.

martin /mar-tin/ *n* a bird of the swallow family.

martyr /mar-tir/ *n* **1** a person who suffers death for his or her beliefs. **2** a person who suffers continuously from a certain illness. **3** (*hum, irony*) someone who makes a show of their misfortune to gain sympathy. • *vb* to put someone to death for refusing to give up his or her faith. • *n* **martyrdom**.

marvel /mar-vel/ *n* a wonder. • *vb* to wonder (at), to feel astonishment.

marvellous /mar-ve-lus/ *adj*, *also* **marvelous** (*US*) **1** wonderful, astonishing, extraordinary. **2** (*inf*) very good, excellent.

marzipan /mart-si-pan/ *n* a sweet made from ground almonds, sugar, etc.

mascara /ma-**sca**-ra/ *n* a substance used for darkening eyelashes.

mascot /ma-scot/ *n* a person, animal, or thing supposed to bring good luck.

masculine /ma-skyu-lin/ *adj* **1** of the male sex. **2** manly. **3** like a man.

mash /mash/ *vb* to crush food until it is soft. • *n* **1** a mixture of crushed grain, etc, given to animals as food. **2** mashed potato.

mask /mask/ *n* **1** a cover for the face or part of the face. **2** an animal or human face painted on paper, etc, and worn at parties or processions. **3** any means of concealing what is really going on. **4** (*usually called* **masque**) a poetical play. • *vb* **1** to cover with a mask. **2** to hide.

mason /may-son/ *n* **1** a person who is skilled in shaping stone or in building. **2** a Freemason. • *adj* **masonic**.

masonry /may-sun-ree/ *n* **1** stonework. **2** the skill or work of a mason. **3** Freemasonry.

masquerade /ma-ske-**rade**/ *n* a ball at which masks are worn. • *vb* **1** to go in disguise. **2** to pretend to be another.

mass /mass/ *n* **1** a lump or quantity of matter. **2** (*fml*) the quantity of matter in a body. **3** (*often pl*) a crowd. **4** the larger part. • *vb* **1** to gather into a mass. **2** to form a crowd.

Mass /mass/ *n* in the Roman Catholic Church, the celebration of the Lord's Supper.

massacre /ma-sa-cur/ *n* the killing of large numbers of men, women, and children. • *vb* to kill in large numbers.

massage /ma-**sazh**/ *n* rubbing and pressing the muscles to strengthen them or make them less stiff. • *also vb*.

masseur /ma-**soor**/ *n* a person who gives massages. • *f* **masseuse** /ma-**sooz**/.

massive /ma-siv/ *adj* huge, big and heavy.

mast /mast/ *n* on a ship, an upright pole on which sails may be set.

master /ma-ster/ *n* **1** a person who is in charge or gives orders. **2** a male teacher. **3** an expert. • *vb* **1** to gain complete knowledge of. **2** to overcome.

masterful /ma-ster-ful/ *adj* commanding, used to giving orders.

masterly /ma-ster-lee/ *adj* showing great skill.

mastermind /ma-ster-mind/ *n* **1** a very intelligent person. **2** a person who plans and organizes a complex scheme, especially a crime. • *vb* to plan and organize a complex scheme.

masterpiece /ma-ster-peess/ *n* the best piece of work done by an artist.

mastery /ma-ste-ree/ *n* **1** control, command. **2** thorough knowledge.

masticate /ma-sti-cate/ *vb* (*fml*) to chew. • *n* **mastication**.

mastiff /ma-stif/ *n* a large powerful dog.

masturbate /ma-stur-bate/ *vi* to manually stimulate one's sexual organs to achieve orgasm without sexual intercourse.

mat /mat/ *n* **1** a small piece of coarse cloth or plaited fibre used as a floor covering or foot-wiper. **2** a piece of cloth or other material placed under a plate or dish. • *adj* matt. • *vb* (**matted, matting**) to twist together, to entangle.

matador /ma-ta-dor/ *n* in Spain, the man who fights the bull in a bullfight.

match[1] /match/ *n* a small stick tipped with a substance that catches fire when rubbed on certain prepared surfaces.

match[2] /match/ *n* **1** a person or thing the same or nearly the same as another. **2** an equal. **3** a sporting contest or game. **4** a marriage. • *vb* **1** to be equal to. **2** to be like or to go well with something else.

matchbox /match-boks/ *n* a box for holding matches.

matchmaker /match-may-ker/ *n* a person who tries to arrange a marriage between others.

mate /mate/ *n* **1** a companion, a colleague. **2** (*inf*) a friend. **3** a husband or wife. **3** a ship's officer below the captain in rank. **4** a workman's assistant. **5** an animal with which another is paired for producing offspring. • *vb* to come together for breeding.

material /ma-tee-ree-al/ *adj* **1** made of matter. **2** worldly, not spiritual. **3** (*fml*) important. • *n* **1** the substance out of which a thing is made. **2** cloth.

materialism /ma-tee-ree-al-iz-um/ *n* **1** the belief that nothing exists but matter. **2** the state of being interested only in worldly things such as wealth.

materialist /ma-tee-ree-al-ist/ *n* **1** a person who believes in materialism. **2** a person who is concerned more with wealth and comfort than with ideas. • *adj* **materialistic**.

materialize, materialise /ma-tee-ree-al-ize/ *vb* **1** to become real, to happen. **2** to appear.

materially /ma-tee-ree-al-ee/ *adv* to a large extent, considerably.

maternal /ma-ter-nal/ *adj* of or like a mother.

maternity /ma-ter-ni-tee/ *n* motherhood.

maths /maths/ *n* (*inf*) mathematics.

mathematical /ma-thi-ma-ti-cal/ *adj* having to do with mathematics.

mathematics /ma-thi-ma-tics/ *n* the science of space and number. • *n* **mathematician**.

matinee /mat-nay/ *n* an afternoon performance in a theatre.

matriculate /ma-tri-cyu-late/ *vb* to enrol or be accepted as a student in a university or college. • *n* **matriculation**.

matrimony /ma-tri-moe-nee/ *n* (*fml*) the state of marriage. • *adj* **matrimonial**.

matrix /may-triks/ *n* (*pl* **matrices**) **1** in mathematics, the arrangement of a set of quantities in rows and columns. **2** a mould in which hot molten metal is shaped.

matron /may-tron/ *n* **1** (*old*) an older married woman. **2** a woman in a school in charge of medical care, etc.

matronly /may-tron-lee/ *adj* (*of a woman*) **1** middle-aged and rather plump. **2** dignified, serious.

matt(e) /mat/ *adj* dull, without gloss or shine.

matter /ma-ter/ *n* **1** that out of which all things are made. **2** a subject of conversation or writings. **3** affair. **4** the infected liquid contained in a wound or sore. • *vb* to be of importance.

matter-of-fact /ma-ter-ov-fact/ *adj* without imagination or exaggeration, containing or concerning facts only.

matting /ma-ting/ *n* material used as mats.

mattress /ma-tress/ *n* a flat bag filled with soft material and sometimes springs, placed under a sleeper for comfort.

mature /ma-choor/ *adj* **1** ripe. **2** fully grown. **3** fully developed in body or mind. • *vb* **1** to ripen. **2** to become mature. **3** to be due in full.

maturity /ma-choo-ri-tee/ *n* **1** ripeness. **2** full growth or development.

maul /mawl/ *vb* **1** to injure badly. **2** to handle roughly.

mausoleum /maw-zu-lee-um/ *n* a magnificent tomb.

mauve /mawv/ *n* a purple dye or colour.
• *adj* light purple.

maxim /mak-sim/ *n* a wise saying, a rule for behaviour.

maximize /mak-si-mize/ *vb, also* **maximise** to make as large or as important as possible.

maximum /mak-si-mum/ *n* the greatest possible number or amount. • *also adj.*

may[1] /may/ *vb* (*pt* **might**) used to express possibility or permission.

may[2] /may/ *n* hawthorn blossom.

May /may/ *n* the fifth month of the year.

maybe /may-be/ *adv* perhaps.

Mayday /may-day/ *n* the first day of May.

mayonnaise /may-u-naze/ *n* a salad dressing of eggs, oil, etc.

mayor /may-ur/ *n* the chief magistrate of a city or borough.

maze /maze/ *n* **1** a confusing system of paths or passages through which it is difficult to find your way. **2** a confusing network of streets, etc.

ME /em-ee/ *abbr* = **myalgic encephalomyelitis** /en-kef-a-low-my-ah-lie-tus/: a chronic condition that makes someone feel extremely tired and weak all the time, *also* **chronic fatigue syndrome (CFS).**

me /mee/ *pron* the form of 'I' used when the object of a sentence.

meadow /me-doe/ *n* rich grassland.

meagre /mee-ger/ *adj, also* **meager** (*US*) scanty, not enough.

meal[1] /meel/ *n* food taken at one time.

meal[2] /meel/ *n* grain ground to powder.

mean[1] /meen/ *adj* **1** nasty, unkind over small things. **2** unwilling to spend or give away. **3** (*old or lit*) poor. **4** (*old or lit*) of low birth or behaviour (*of mean birth*). • *n* **meanness.**

mean[2] /meen/ *vb* (*pt, pp* **meant**) **1** to intend. **2** to have a certain purpose. **3** to express a certain idea.

mean[3] /meen/ *adj* **1** middle. **2** halfway between numbers, amounts, extremes, etc; average. • *n* **1** the average. **2** a middle state. **3** (*pl*) see **means.**

meander /mee-an-der/ *vb* to follow a winding course, as a river over very flat land.

meaning /mee-ning/ *n* **1** the idea expressed by a word or words. **2** the sense in which something is intended to be understood. • *adjs* **meaningful, meaningless.**

means /meenz/ *npl* **1** that by which something is done or carried out. **2** money or property.

meantime /meen-time/ *n* the time between two events. • *adv* **meanwhile.**

meanwhile /meen-while/ *n* the time between two events, meantime. • *adv* **1** in or during the intervening time. **2** at the same time.

measles /mee-zulz/ *n* an infectious disease with a red rash.

measly /mee-zlee/ *adj* worthless, mean.

measure /me-zhur/ *n* **1** a unit used to express size, weight, etc. **2** size, weight, etc; so expressed. **3** an instrument used in finding size, weight, etc. **4** a course of action. **5** a law proposed but not passed. • *vb* **1** to find out size, quantity, etc, with an instrument. **2** to judge. **3** to weigh out. • *n* **measurement.**

measured /me-zhurd/ *adj* (*fml*) steady, regular.

meat /meet/ *n* the flesh of animals used as food.

meaty /mee-tee/ *adj* **1** full of meat. **2** full of information.

mechanic /me-ca-nic/ *n* a person who looks after a machine.

mechanical /me-ca-ni-cal/ *adj* **1** done or worked by machine. **2** having to do with machinery. **3** done by habit, done without awareness. • *adv* **mechanically.**

mechanics /me-ca-nics/ *n* the science of motion and force.

mechanism /me-ca-ni-zum/ *n* the machinery that makes something work.

medal /me-dal/ *n* a flat piece of metal with a picture or writing stamped on it, made to comemmorate a person or event or as a reward of merit. • *vb* (**medalled, medalling**) to win a medal, especially at a sporting event.

medallion /me-dal-yun/ *n* a large medal.

medallist /me-da-list/ *n* the winner of a medal.

meddle /me-dul/ *vb* to interfere. • *n* **meddler.**

meddlesome /me-dul-sum/ *adj* given to interfering.

media *n* **1** *pl* of **medium. 2** a means of reaching many people, such as through television, newspapers and radio.

mediaeval /med-di-ec-val/ *adj, also* **medieval** /med-dee-val/ having to do with the Middle Ages.

medial /mee-dee-al/, **median** /mee-dee-an/ *adj* (*fml*) in the middle.

mediate /mee-dee-ate/ *vb* to try to settle a dispute between others. • *n* **mediator.**

mediation /mee-dee-ay-shun/ *n* an attempt to settle a dispute between others.

medical /me-di-cal/ *adj* **1** having to do with medicine. **2** having to do with the work of a doctor, medicine, or healing. • *adv* **medically.**

medicate /me-di-cate/ *vb* (*fml*) **1** to give medicine to. **2** to soak in medicine.

medication /me-di-**cay**-shun/ *n* (*fml*) medicine, treatment by medicine.

medicine /me-di-sin/ *n* **1** the science of bringing the sick back to health. **2** any substance that cures or heals. **3** the science of curing or treating by means other than surgery. • *adj* **medicinal**. • *adv* **medicinally**.

mediocre /mee-dee-**oe**-car/ *adj* not very good, ordinary. • *n* **mediocrity**.

meditate /me-di-tate/ *vb* **1** to think deeply about. **2** to spend short regular periods in deep, especially religious, thought.

meditation /me-di-**tay**-shun/ *n* deep thought.

meditative /me-di-ta-tiv/ *adj* (*fml*) thoughtful.

medium /mee-dee-um/ *n* **1** (*pl* **media**) the means by which something is done. **2** (*pl*) a means by which news is made known. **3** (*pl* **mediums**) a person who is able to receive messages from spirits at a meeting held for that purpose. • *adj* middle or average in size, quality, etc.

medley /med-lee/ *n* **1** a mixture. **2** a selection of tunes played as one item.

meek /meek/ *adj* gentle, kind, unresisting. • *adv* **meekly**.

meet /meet/ *vb* (*pt, pp* **met**) **1** to come face to face with, often by chance. **2** to come together by arrangement. **3** to pay. **4** to satisfy. **5** to answer. • *n* a coming together of huntsmen on horseback with hounds for a hunt.

meeting /mee-ting/ *n* a coming together for a special purpose.

megabyte /me-ga-bite/ *n* in computing, a unit of storage capacity equal to approximately 1,000,000 bytes.

megaphone /me-ga-foan/ *n* a large device for making the voice louder.

melancholy /me-lan-col-ee/ *n* sadness, depression. • *also adj*.

mellow /me-loe/ *adj* **1** soft with ripeness. **2** made kindly by age. • *vb* to make or become mellow. • *n* **mellowness**.

melodic /me-lod-ic/ *adj* relating to melody.

melodious /me-loe-dee-us/ *adj* sweet-sounding.

melodrama /me-lo-dra-ma/ *n* a thrilling or sensational play, usually with an improbable plot.

melodramatic /me-lo-dra-ma-tic/ *adj* more like a play than real life, theatrical, exaggerated.

melody /me-lo-dee/ *n* **1** a tune. **2** the principal part in a piece of harmonized music.

melon /me-lon/ *n* a large juicy fruit that grows on the ground.

melt /melt/ *vb* **1** to make or become liquid by heat, to soften, to dissolve. **2** to disappear. **3** to make or become gentler.

member /mem-ber/ *n* **1** one of a society or group. **2** (*fml or old*) a limb of the body.

membership /mem-ber-ship/ *n* **1** the state of being a member. **2** all the members of a society.

membrane /mem-brane/ *n* a thin layer of skin covering or connecting parts inside the body.

memento /mu-men-toe/ *n* an object kept or given to remind you of a person or event.

memo *see* **memorandum**.

memoir /mem-war/ *n* **1** a written account of past events. **2** (*npl*) the story of a person's life.

memorable /mem-ra-bul/ *adj* worth remembering. • *adv* **memorably**.

memorandum /me-mu-**ran**-dum/ *n* (*pl* **memoranda**).

memorial /me-**moe**-ree-al/ *n* an object, often a monument, that helps people to remember a person or event.

memorize /me-mu-rize/ *vb*, *also* **memorise** to learn by heart.

memory /me-mu-ree/ *n* **1** the power of the mind to recall past events or to learn things by heart. **2** the mind's store of remembered things. **3** something remembered. **4** the part of a computer that stores information.

men /men/ *n pl of* **man**.

menace /me-nis/ *n* **1** a threat, a person or thing likely to cause harm or danger. **2** a threat, a show of hostility. • *vb* (*fml*) to threaten.

menacing /me-ni-sing/ *adj* **1** threatening to harm. **2** threatening-looking.

menagerie /me-**nadge**-ree/ *n* a collection of wild animals for public show.

mend /mend/ *vb* **1** to repair. **2** to improve. **3** (*inf*) to become well or healthy again. • *n* the hole or crack that has been mended.

menial /mee-nee-al/ *adj* humble, unskilled.

meningitis /me-nin-**jie**-tis/ *n* a serious disease affecting the membrane around the brain.

menstrual cycle /men-stroo-al **sie**-cul/ *n* a series of changes that take place in a woman's body, roughly over a 28-day period, which prepare her body for possible pregnancy.

menstruation /men-stroo-**way**-shun/ *n*, *also* **period** a monthly discharge of blood from a woman's womb at the end of the normal menstrual cycle if pregnancy does not take place. • *vb* **menstruate**. • *adj* **menstrual**.

mental /men-tal/ *adj* **1** having to do with the mind. **2** done in the mind without anything being written. • *adv* **mentally**.

mentality /men-**ta**-li-tee/ *n* **1** mental power. **2** the way of thinking typical of a person, the character of a person's mind.

menthol /men-thol/ *n* a substance made from mint and used as a medicine.

mention /men-shun/ *vb* **1** to speak of, to refer to, to say the name of. **2** to say briefly or indirectly. • *n* a remark about or reference to.

mentor /men-tawr/ *n* (*fml*) a wise adviser.

menu /men-yoo/ *n* **1** a list of foods that can be ordered for a meal in a restaurant. **2** a list of options on a computer display.

meow /mee-ow/ *see* **mew**.

MEP *abbr* = **Member of the European Parliament**.

mercenary /**merse**-(u)-ne-ree/ *adj* **1** working for money. **2** doing things only to obtain money, greedy for money. • *n* a soldier hired to fight for a country not his or her own.

merchandise /mer-chan-dize/ *n* goods bought and sold.

merchant /mer-chant/ *n* a person who buys and sells goods in large quantities.

merciful /mer-si-ful/ *adj* showing mercy, forgiving. • *adv* **mercifully**.

merciless /mer-si-less/ *adj* pitiless. • *adv* **mercilessly**.

mercurial /mer-**cyoo**-ree-al/ *adj* quickly changing mood.

mercury /mer-cyu-ree/ *n* a liquid silvery-white metal used in thermometers.

Mercury /mercury/ *n* the closest planet to the sun.

mercy /mer-see/ *n* kindness and pity, forgiveness, willingness not to punish.

mere /meer/ *adj* no more or less than.

merely /meer-lee/ *adv* only.

merge /merj/ *vb* **1** to join together to make one. **2** to become part of a larger whole.

merger /mer-jer/ *n* the joining together of two or more businesses.

meridian /me-ri-dee-an/ *n* an imaginary line encircling the earth from pole to pole.

meringue /mu-rang/ *n* a light sweet or cake made from sugar and white of egg.

merit /me-rit/ *n* **1** the quality of deserving praise or reward; worth; excellence. **2** good point. **3** *npl* good qualities. • *vb* to deserve.

mermaid /mer-maid/ *n* an imaginary sea creature, half woman and half fish. • *also* **merman**.

merry /me-ree/ *adj* joyous, happy, full of fun. • *adv* **merrily**. • *n* **merriment**.

merry-go-round /me-ree-go-round/ *n* a large revolving circular platform with seats in the shape of animals, etc, on which people may ride for amusement at an amusement park.

mesh /mesh/ *n* the space between the threads of a net.

mesmerize /mez-me-rize/ *vb*, *also* **mesmerise** **1** to hold the complete attention of and make seemingly unable to move or speak. **2** (*old*) to hypnotize.

mess[1] /mess/ *n* **1** a muddle. **2** a dirty or untidy state. • *vb* **1** to make dirty or untidy. **2** to do badly or inefficiently.

mess[2] /mess/ *n* **1** a company of people who take their meals together as in the armed services. **2** the place where they eat.

message /me-sidge/ *n* **1** information or news sent to another by word of mouth or in writing. **2** a piece of instruction, an important idea.

messenger /me-sin-jer/ *n* a person who bears a message.

Messiah /me-sie-ya/ *n* **1** the deliverer promised by God to the Jews. **2** Jesus Christ, believed by Christians to be the Messiah.

Messrs /me-surz/ *npl* plural of **Mr**, short for **Messieurs** /mus-**yur**/, usually found in addresses on envelopes.

messy /me-see/ *adj* dirty or untidy.

met /met/ *pt and pp of* **meet**.

metabolism /me-**ta**-bo-li-zum/ *n* the system of chemical changes in the cells of the body that provide energy. • *adj* **metabolic**.

metal /me-tal/ *n* a class of substances, such as gold, copper, iron, tin, etc.

metallic /me-**tal**-ic/ *adj* of or like metal.

metallurgy /me-**tal**-ur-jee/ *n* the art or study of working with metals. • *n* **metallurgist**.

metamorphosis /me-ta-**mawr**-fu-sis/ *n* (*pl* **metamorphoses**) **1** a change in form or kind. **2** a complete change.

metaphor /me-ta-fawr/ *n* a way of comparing two things by identifying them and speaking about one as if it were the other. • *adjs* **metaphoric**, **metaphorical**. • *adv* **metaphorically**.

metaphysics /me-ta-**fi**-zics/ *n* the study of the nature of existence and of the mind. • *adj* **metaphysical**.

mete /meet/ *vb* (*old*) to measure.

meteor /mee-tee-or/ *n* a shining body that can be seen moving across the sky, a shooting star.

meteoric /me-tee-**awr**-ic/ *adj* rapid but often short-lasting.

meteorite /mee-tee-u-rite/ *n* a meteor that falls to earth as a piece of rock.

meteorological /mee-tee-u-rol-**odge**-i-cal/ *adj* having to do with meteorology.

meteorology /mee-tee-u-**rol**-o-jee/ *n* the study or science of the earth's weather. • *n* **meteorologist**.

meter[1] /**mee**-ter/ *n* an instrument for measuring things.

meter[2] /**mee**-ter/ *n* US variant of **metre**.

methane /me-thane/ *n* a flammable gas produced by decaying matter and used as a fuel.

methinks /mee-**thingks**/ *vb* (*old or hum*) it seems to me.

method /me-thod/ *n* **1** a way of doing something. **2** an orderly way of arranging or doing things.

methodical /me-**thod**-ic-al/ *adj* orderly in following a plan or system. • *adv* **methodically**.

Methodist /me-thod-ist/ *n* a member of a Christian sect founded by John Wesley.

methyl /me-thil/ *n* a substance from which wood-alcohol can be made.

methylated spirits /me-thi-lay-tid **spi**-rits/ *n* a type of alcohol unfit for drinking but used for burning, cleaning, etc.

meticulous /me-ti-cyu-lus/ *adj* extremely careful about details or small matters.

metre[1] /**mee**-ter/ *n*, *also* **meter** (*US*) a measure of length (100 cm, 39.37 inches) in the metric system, *abbr* **m**.

metre[2] /**mee**-ter/ *n*, *also* **meter** (*US*) the systematic arrangement of stressed and unstressed syllables that give poetic rhythm.

metrical /me-tri-cal/ *adj* (*of poetry*) having a regular rhythm or metre.

metric system /me-tric **sis**-tem/ *n* a system of weights and measures in which each unit is divisible into 10 parts.

metronome /me-tro-nome/ *n* an instrument that can be set to mark time correctly for a musician.

metropolis /me-**trop**-lis/ *n* (*fml or hum*) a large city, especially the capital.

metropolitan /me-tro-**pol**-i-tan/ *adj* belonging to a metropolis.

mettle /me-tul/ *n* spirit, courage.

mew /myoo/, **miaow**, **meow** /mee-aoo/ *n* the cry of a cat. • *vb* to make a high-pitched cry like a cat.

mews /myooz/ *n* a row of houses or flats in a small street which have been converted from stables.

mezzo-soprano /met-so su-**pra**-noe/ *n* a female voice between soprano and contralto.

miaow *see* **mew**.

mice *pl of* **mouse**.

Michaelmas /**mi**-cal-mus/ *n* the feast of St Michael, September 29.

microbe /**mie**-crobe/ *n* a tiny living creature, especially one causing disease.

microchip /**mie**-cro-chip/ *n* a very small piece of a material, usually silicon, which acts as a semi-conductor and forms the base on which an electronic circuit is printed.

microcosm /**mie**-cru-caw-zum/ *n* a little world, a small copy.

microphone /**mie**-cru-fone/ *n* an instrument by which the sound of the voice is changed into electric waves, used to make sounds louder.

microscope /**mie**-cru-scope/ *n* an instrument containing an arrangement of curved lenses by means of which very tiny objects can be seen larger and studied.

microscopic /mie-cru-**scop**-ic/ *adj* **1** very small, tiny, seen only with the help of a microscope. **2** (*inf*) tiny.

microwave /**mie**-cro-wave/ *n* a microwave oven, an oven that cooks or heats up food very quickly using electromagnetic radiation. • *vb* to cook or heat in a microwave.

mid /mid/ *adj* having to do with the middle, in the middle of.

midday /mid-**day**/ *n* noon or the time about noon.

middle /**mi**-dul/ *adj* equally distant from the ends or limits. • *n* the centre, the middle part or point.

middle-aged /mi-dul-**ayjd**/ *adj* neither old nor young, between youth and old age.

Middle Ages /**mi**-dul ay-jez/ *npl* the period between AD 500 and AD 1500 in European history.

middle class /mi-dul **class**/ *n* those who are well enough off to live in comfort, but are neither wealthy nor of noble birth. • *adj* having to do with the middle class.

Middle East /**mi**-dul eest/ *n* Asian countries west of India and China.

middleman /**mi**-dul-man/ *n* a trader who buys goods in large quantities from the maker or producer and sells them again at a profit to store owners.

middleweight /**mi**-dul-wate/ *n* a boxer who fights in the class with a maximum weight of 160 lb (72.64 kg).

middling /mid-ling/ *adj* (*inf*) neither very good nor very bad, average.

midget /**mid**-jet/ *n* a very small person or thing.

midland /mid-land/ *adj* far from the coasts or borders of a country.

midnight /mid-nite/ *n* 12 o'clock at night.

midriff /mid-rif/ *n* the part of the body containing the muscles separating the stomach from the lungs.

midshipman /mid-ship-man/ *n* a low-ranking officer in the navy.

midst /midst/ *n* the middle.

midsummer /mid-su-mer/ *n* the middle of summer.

midway /mid-way/ *n* halfway. • *also adv*.

midwife /mid-wife/ *n* (*pl* **midwives**) a person who assists a mother at the birth of a baby.

midwifery /mid-wi-free/ *n* the knowledge or study of the work of a midwife.

midwinter /mid-**win**-ter/ *n* the middle of winter.

might[1] /mite/ *pt of* **may**[1].

might[2] /mite/ *n* power, strength.

mighty /mie-tee/ *adj* **1** powerful, strong. **2** huge. • *adv* very.

migraine /mie-grane, mee-grane/ *n* a severe headache, often accompanied by visual disturbances and a feeling of sickness.

migrant /mie-grant/ *n* a person or a bird that migrates. • *also adj*.

migrate /mie-grate/ *vb* **1** to move your home from one land to another, to go from one place to another. **2** (*of birds*) to move to another place at the season when its climate is suitable. • *n* **migration**. • *adj* **migratory**.

mike /mike/ *n* (*inf*) a microphone.

mild /milde/ *adj* **1** gentle, merciful, not severe. **2** calm. **3** (*of weather*) not cold. • *adv* **mildly**. • *n* **mildness**.

mildew /mil-doo/ *n* a tiny but destructive growth that appears and spreads on leaves or on damp paper, leather, etc.

mile /mile/ *n* a measure of length (= 1760 yards).

mileage, milage /mile-idge/ *n* distance in miles.

milestone /mile-stone/ *n* **1** a stone by the roadside telling the distance in miles to places in the neighbourhood. **2** an important stage in the development or progress of something.

militant /mi-li-tant/ *adj* **1** fighting, warlike. **2** active in a campaign. • *n* **militancy**.

militarism /mi-li-ta-ri-zum/ *n* belief in the use of armies or war in politics. • *n* **militarist**. • *adj* **militaristic**.

military /mi-li-ta-ree/ *adj* having to do with the armed forces. • *n* the armed forces.

militate /mi-li-tate/ *vb* **1** to act or stand. **2** to act as a reason against.

militia /mi-li-sha/ *n* a reserve army, consisting of people trained in the use of arms, and called out in an emergency. • *n* **militiaman**.

milk /milk/ *n* **1** the liquid produced by female mammals to feed their babies. **2** such milk produced by cows or goats and drunk by humans or made into butter and cheese. • *vb* to draw milk from (e.g. a cow).

milkmaid /milk-maid/ *n* a woman who milks cows.

milkman /milk-man/ *n* a man who sells or delivers milk.

milk shake /milk-shake/ *n* a cold frothy drink made from milk shaken up with flavouring and ice cream.

milk tooth /milk tooth/ *n* one of a child's first set of teeth.

milky /mil-kee/ *adj* **1** like milk. **2** containing a lot of milk.

Milky Way /mil-kee way/ *n* a bright band across the night sky, made up of countless stars.

mill /mill/ *n* **1** a machine for grinding corn, coffee, etc. **2** the building in which corn is ground into flour. **3** a factory. • *vb* **1** to grind. **2** to stamp a coin and cut grooves around its edge.

millennium /mi-len-ee-um/ *n* (*pl* **millennia** *or* **millenniums**) **1** a period of 1000 years. **2** according to the Bible, the 1000 years for which Christ will reign on the Earth.

miller /mi-ler/ *n* a person who keeps a corn mill.

millet /mi-let/ *n* a grass bearing edible grain.

mill hand /mil hand/ *n* a factory worker.

milligram /mi-li-gram/ *n* the thousandth part of a gram.

millimetre /mi-li-mee-ter/ *n*, *also* **millimeter** (*US*) the thousandth part of a metre.

milliner /mi-li-ner/ *n* a person who makes or sells ladies' hats.

millinery /mi-li-ne-ree/ *n* hats made or sold by a milliner.

million /mil-yun/ *n* **1** a thousand thousand (1,000,000). **2** (*inf*) a very great many.

millionaire /mil-yu-**nare**/ *n* a person who possesses a million or more pounds.

millipede /mi-li-peed/ *n* an insect with many feet.

millstone /mil-stone/ *n* **1** a heavy round stone used for grinding corn into flour. **2** a very heavy load or handicap.

millwheel /mil-wheel/ *n* the large wheel, turned by water power, that drives the machinery inside a mill.

mime /mime/ *n* **1** a play without words which is carried on by facial expressions, gestures and actions. **2** using actions without language. • *vb* **1** to mouth the words to a recorded song. **2** to act without speaking.

mimic /mi-mic/ *vb* (**mimicked, mimicking**) to imitate, especially in order to make fun of. • *n* a person who imitates.

mimicry /mi-mi-cree/ *n* imitation.

mimosa /mi-mo-sa/ *n* a tree with sweet-smelling flowers.

minaret /mi-na-ret/ *n* the tower of a Muslim mosque.

mince /minss/ *n* meat, often beef, that has been cut up into extremely small pieces. *vb* to cut into very small pieces. • **not to mince words** to speak the plain truth.

mincemeat /mince-meet/ *n* dried fruits, such as currants, etc, chopped up small and mixed with spices.

mind /minde/ *n* **1** the power by which human beings understand, think, feel, will, etc. **2** a person of great mental ability. **3** memory. • *vb* **1** to take care of. **2** to take heed, to be careful. **3** watch out for, be careful of **4** to object to. • **mind your p's and q's** to be careful what you say or do. • **mind your own business** not to interfere in another's affairs.

minded /mine-did/ *adj* desirous, inclined.

mindful /minde-ful/ *adj* not forgetful, paying attention to.

mindless /minde-less/ *adj* unthinking, stupid.

mine[1] /mine/ *poss pron* belonging to me.

mine[2] /mine/ *n* **1** a deep hole made in the earth so that minerals can be taken from beneath its surface. **2** a container filled with an explosive charge to blow something up. **3** a person or place from which much may be obtained. • *vb* **1** to make tunnels into and under the earth. **2** to dig for in a mine. **3** to place explosive mines in position. **4** to blow up with mines.

minefield /mine-feeld/ *n* **1** an area in which there are many mineral mines. **2** an area in which many explosive mines are placed. **3** something full of hidden dangers.

miner /mine-er/ *n* a person who works in a mine.

mineral /min-ral/ *n* an inorganic substance found naturally in the earth. • *adj* having to do with minerals.

mineralogy /mi-ne-rol-o-jee/ *n* the study of minerals. • *n* **mineralogist**.

mineral water /min-ral waw-ter/ *n* water that comes from a natural spring and contains minerals, sometimes still and sometimes carbonated.

mine-sweeper /mine-swee-per/ *n* a ship that clears an area of mines.

mingle /ming-gul/ *vb* **1** to mix together. **2** to mix with.

mini /mi-nee/ *adj* very small of its kind. • *n* a very short skirt.

mini- /mi-nee/ *prefix* very small of its kind.

miniature /mi-ni-chur/ *n* a very small painting. • *adj* very small, tiny.

minibus /mi-nee-bus/ *n* a small bus for a few passengers, often around ten or twelve

minim /mi-nim/ *n, also* **half note** (*US*) in music, a note having one-half the duration of a semibreve.

minimize /mi-ni-mize/ *vb, also* **minimise** **1** smaller or less. **2** to make seem less important.

minimum /mi-ni-mum/ *n* the smallest amount possible. • *also adj.* • *adj* minimal.

minion /min-yun/ *n* a slavelike follower or employee; a person who always does as his or her employer orders.

minister /mi-ni-ster/ *n* **1** a member of the clergy. **2** a person in charge of a government department. **3** the principal representative of a government in another country. • *vb* to give help, to serve.

ministerial /mi-ni-stee-ree-al/ *adj* having to do with a minister.

ministry /mi-ni-stree/ *n* **1** the clergy. **2** a department of government in charge of a minister.

mink /mingk/ *n* (*pl* **mink**) a small stoatlike animal valued for its fur.

minnow /mi-no/ *n* a very small freshwater fish.

minor /mie-nor/ *adj* **1** smaller, of less importance. **2** (*mus*) with certain intervals altered. • *n* **1** a person below the age when you have full civil rights. **2** (*mus*) a minor key, interval, or scale.

minority /mi-naw-ri-tee/ *n* **1** the state of being below the age when you have full civil rights. **2** the smaller number in a group or assembly, less than half.

minstrel /min-strel/ *n* **1** in olden times, a wandering singer and poet. **2** (*old*) a singer.

mint[1] /mint/ *n* **1** a place where coins are made, especially by the government. **2** (*inf*) a large amount. • *vb* to make coins.

mint[2] /mint/ *n* a sweet-smelling herb whose leaves are used as flavouring in cooking.

minuet /min-yu-et/ *n* (*old*) **1** a slow, graceful dance. **2** music for this dance.

minus /mie-nus/ *prep* **1** less. **2** (*inf*) not having. • *adj* less than zero. • *n* the sign of subtraction (-).

minuscule /mi-ni-scyool/ *adj* extremely small.

minute[1] /mi-nit/ *n* **1** the 60th part of an hour. **2** the 60th part of a degree. **3** a short time. **4** a written note or comment. **5** *pl* a short account of what was discussed and decided at a meeting. • *vb* to make a written note of.

minute² /mie-**nyoot**/ *adj* **1** very small. **2** exact.

minutiae /mie-**noo**-shee-eye/ *npl* small details.

minx /**mingks**/ *n* a forward or impertinent girl.

miracle /**mi**-ra-cul/ *n* **1** an extraordinary event believed by some to be brought about by the interference of God with the natural course of events. **2** any extraordinary event for which there is no known explanation.

miraculous /mi-**ra**-cue-lus/ *adj* **1** caused by a miracle, marvellous. **2** amazing, extraordinary. • *adv* **miraculously**.

mirage /mi-**razh**/ *n* imaginary objects.

mire /**mire**/ *n* (*fml or lit*) wet, muddy ground, mud.

mirror /**mi**-rur/ *n* a looking glass. • *vb* to reflect as in a mirror.

mirth /**mirth**/ *n* laughter, merriment. • *adj* **mirthful**, **mirthless**.

misadventure /mi-sad-**ven**-chur/ *n* (*fml or old*) an unlucky happening.

misanthrope /**mi**-san-thrope/, **misanthropist** /mi-**san**-thru-pist/ *n* (*fml*) a person who hates humankind. • *adj* **misanthropic**. • *n* **misanthropy**.

misapprehend /mi-sa-pri-**hend**/ *vb* (*fml*) to misunderstand. • *n* **misapprehension**.

misappropriate /mi-sa-**pro**-pree-ate/ *vb* (*fml*) to put to a wrong use, to use dishonestly for yourself.

misbehave /mis-bee-**have**/ *vb* to behave badly. • *n* **misbehaviour**, *also* **misbehavior** (*US*).

miscalculate /mis-**cal**-cyu-late/ *vb* to work out an answer or likely result wrongly. • *n* **miscalculation**.

miscarriage /mis-**ca**-ridge/ *n* the loss of a baby from the womb before it is able to survive. • **miscarriage of justice** a mistaken finding by a court that an innocent person is guilty of a crime.

miscarry /mis-**ca**-ree/ *vb* to have a miscarriage.

miscellaneous /mi-se-**lay**-nee-us/ *adj* mixed, of different kinds.

miscellany /mi-se-la-nee/ *n* (*fml*) a mixture, a collection of things of different kinds.

mischance /mis-**chanse**/ *n* (*fml*) an unlucky happening.

mischief /**mis**-chif/ *n* **1** (*fml*) harm done on purpose. **2** children's naughtiness.

mischievous /**mis**-chi-vus/ *adj* **1** harmful, intended to cause trouble. **2** naughty. • *adv* **mischievously**.

misconception /mis-con-**sep**-shun/ *n* a mistaken idea, misunderstanding.

misconduct /mis-**con**-duct/ *n* bad or wrong behaviour.

misconstrue /mis-con-**stroo**/ *vb* (*fml*) to give a wrong meaning or significance to. • *n* **misconstruction**.

miscreant /**mis**-cree-ant/ *n* (*fml*) a wicked person.

misdeed /mis-**deed**/ *n* (*fml*) a wrongful action, a crime.

misdemeanour /mis-di-**mee**-nor/ *n*, *also* **misdemeanor** (*US*) a fairly minor misdeed or act of misbehaviour.

misdirect /mis-di-**rect**/ *vb* to give wrong instructions to. • *n* **misdirection**.

miser /**mie**-ser/ *n* a person who dislikes spending money.

miserable /**miz**-ru-bul/ *adj* **1** very unhappy. **2** causing unhappiness or discomfort. **3** low in quality or quantity. • *adv* **miserably**.

miserly /**mie**-zer-lee/ *adj* very mean.

misery /**mi**-ze-ree/ *n* great unhappiness or suffering.

misfire /mis-**fire**/ *vb* **1** (*of guns*) to fail to go off. **2** to fail. • *also n.*

misfit /**mis**-fit/ *n* a person unsuited to his or her circumstances.

misfortune /mis-**fawr**-chun/ *n* **1** bad luck. **2** a piece of bad luck.

misgiving /mis-**gi**-ving/ *n* a feeling of fear, doubt, or mistrust.

misguided /mis-**gie**-did/ *adj* showing bad judgment.

mishandle /mis-**han**-dul/ *vb* (*fml*) to manage badly.

mishap /**mis**-hap/ *n* an unlucky event, usually not serious.

misinform /mi-sin-**fawrm**/ *vb* (*fml*) to give wrong information.

misinterpret /mi-sin-**ter**-pret/ *vb* to give a wrong meaning to. • *n* **misinterpretation**.

misjudge /mis-**judge**/ *vb* to judge wrongly, to form a wrong opinion.

mislay /mis-**lay**/ *vb* (*pt, pp* **mislaid**) to put.

mislead /mis-**leed**/ *vb* (*pt, pp* **misled**) to deceive, to give the wrong idea to.

mismanage /mis-ma-**nidge**/ *vb* to manage badly. • *n* **mismanagement**.

misnomer /mis-**no**-mer/ *n* a wrong or unsuitable name.

misogynist /mi-**sodge**-in-ist/ *n* a man who hates women.

misplace /mis-**place**/ *vb* to put in a wrong place.

misprint /**mis**-print/ n a mistake in printing. • also vb.

mispronounce /mis-pro-**nounse**/ vb to pronounce wrongly. • n **mispronunciation**.

misquote /mis-**kwote**/ vb to quote wrongly, to make mistakes in trying to repeat another's words. • n **misquotation**.

misread /mis-**reed**/ vb (pt, pp misread /miss-**red**/) to read wrongly.

misrepresent /mis-re-pri-**zent**/ vb to give an untrue account of another's ideas or opinions. • n **misrepresentation**.

misrule /mis-**rule**/ vb to rule or govern badly. • also n.

miss[1] /**miss**/ vb 1 to fail to hit, find, meet, catch, or notice. 2 to leave out. 3 to regret the loss or absence of. • n a failure to hit or catch.

miss[2] /**miss**/ n (pl **misses**) 1 (cap) the title of an unmarried woman. 2 (old) an unmarried woman, a girl.

missal /**mi**-sal/ n a Roman Catholic prayer book containing prayers, etc, for Mass.

misshapen /mis-**shay**-pen/ adj badly formed, deformed, ugly.

missile /**mi**-sile/ n 1 any object thrown or fired from a gun to do harm. 2 an explosive flying weapon with its own engine, which can be aimed at distant objects.

missing /**mi**-sing/ adj lost.

mission /**mi**-shun/ n 1 persons sent to carry out a certain task or discuss something, often overseas. 2 the task itself. 3 your chief aim in life. 4 a group of persons sent to a foreign land to teach their religion. 5 the building(s) in which they live.

missionary /**mi**-shu-ner-ee/ n a person who is sent to a foreign land to teach his or her religion. • also adj.

misspell /mis-**spel**/ vb (pt, pp misspelled or misspelt) to spell wrongly. • n **misspelling**.

misspend /mis-**spend**/ vb (pt, pp misspent) to spend wastefully or unprofitably.

mist /**mist**/ n 1 rain in fine, tiny drops. 2 a cloud resting on the ground.

mistake /mi-**stake**/ vb 1 to understand wrongly. 2 to confuse one person or thing with another. • n an error.

mistaken /mi-**stay**-ken/ adj in error, wrong.

mister /**mi**-ster/ n the title put before a man's name (usually written **Mr**).

mistime /mis-**time**/ vb to time badly, to do something at a wrong time.

mistletoe /**mi**-sul-toe/ n an evergreen plant with white berries.

mistreat /mi-**street**/ vb to treat badly.

mistress /**mi**-stress/ n 1 (cap, usually written **Mrs** /**miss**-eez/) the title put before the name of a married woman. 2 a woman having charge or control. 3 a woman teacher. 4 a woman who is the lover of a man and sometimes maintained by him but not married to him.

mistrust /mi-**strust**/ vb to suspect, to doubt. • also n.

misty /**mi**-stee/ adj 1 darkened or clouded by mist. 2 not clear.

misunderstand /mi-sun-der-**stand**/ vb (pt, pp **misunderstood**) to take a wrong meaning from.

misunderstanding /mi-sun-der-**stan**-ding/ n a disagreement, especially one due to failure to see another's meaning or intention.

misuse /mis-**yooz**/ vb to use in the wrong way, to use badly. • n improper or wrong use.

mite /**mite**/ n 1 a type of very small insect. 2 a small child. 3 a very small amount.

mitre /**mie**-ter/ n, also **miter** (US) 1 the tall pointed headgear worn by bishops. 2 a way of joining two boards meeting at right angles.

mitigate /**mi**-ti-gate/ vb to make less serious, to excuse to some extent. • n **mitigation**.

mitt /**mit**/, **mitten** /**mi**-ten/ n 1 a type of glove that covers the hand but not the fingers and thumb. 2 a glove without separate places for the fingers.

mix /**miks**/ vb 1 to put together to form one. 2 to go together or blend successfully. 3 to join in (with others).

mixed /**mikst**/ adj 1 made up of different things or kinds. 2 relating to people of different sexes.

mixture /**miks**-cher/ n the result of mixing things or people together.

mnemonic /ne-**mon**-ic/ adj helping the memory. • n something easily remembered that helps you to remember something else.

moan /**moan**/ vb 1 to make a low sound expressing sorrow or pain. 2 (inf) to complain. • also n.

moat /**moat**/ n a trench, often filled with water, around a castle or fort.

mob /**mob**/ n a disorderly crowd. • vb (**mobbed**, **mobbing**) to crowd around in a disorderly way.

mobile /**mo**-bile/ adj 1 that can be moved. 2 easily moved. 3 able to move easily, active. • n 1 /**mo**-beel/ a decoration that hangs from the ceiling by threads or wire and that has attached to it several small objects that move when the surrounding air moves. 2 a mobile phone.

mobile home /**mo**-bile **home**/ a large caravan which stays in one place and is used as a house.

mobile phone /mo-bile **foan**/ *n* a handheld, portable phone that works by means of radio networks; a cellphone.

mobility /mo-**bi**-li-tee/ *n* ability to move about.

mobilize /mo-bi-lize/ *vb, also* **mobilise** 1 to call upon to serve as soldiers. 2 to organize for a particular reason. • *n* **mobilization**, *also* **mobilisation**.

moccasin /mok-a-sin/ *n* a shoe or slipper made of deerskin or sheepskin.

mock /mock/ *vb* 1 to make fun of. 2 to imitate in order to make appear foolish. • *adj* false, not real.

mockery /mock-ree/ *n* 1 the act of mocking. 2 a person or thing mocked.

mockingbird /mok-ing-burd/ *n* a type of thrush that imitates the song of other birds, etc.

mode /mode/ *n* 1 (*fml*) the way of doing something. 2 (*old*) a fashion in clothing.

model /mo-del/ *n* 1 a person or thing to be copied. 2 a copy, usually smaller, of a person or thing. 3 a small copy of (e.g. a building or ship made from a plan to show what the finished object will look like). 4 a particular type or design of a product. 5 a living person who sits or stands still to let an artist draw him or her. 6 a person who is employed to display clothes by wearing them. • *adj* worth copying, perfect. • *vb* 1 to give shape to. 2 to make a model of. 3 to wear clothes to show to possible buyers.

modem /mo-dem/ *n* a piece of equipment that links a computer to the telephone system so that information can be sent to other computers.

moderate /mod-rit/ *adj* 1 not going to extremes. 2 within sensible limits. 3 average. • *vb* /mod-er-ate/ 1 to prevent from going to extremes. 2 to lessen. • *adv* **moderately**.

moderation /mod-e-ray-shun/ *n* avoidance of extremes, self-control.

modern /mod-ern/ *adj* 1 belonging to the present day. 2 belonging to recent centuries. 3 up-to-date. • *n* **modernity**.

modernize /mod-er-nize/ *vb, also* **modernise** to bring up-to-date.

modest /mod-est/ *adj* 1 not having too high an opinion of yourself. 2 not boastful. 3 decent. 4 not very large. • *adv* **modestly**. • *n* **modesty**.

modicum /mod-i-cum/ *n* (*fml*) a small amount.

modification /mod-i-fi-**cay**-shun/ *n* an alteration, a small change.

modify /mod-i-fie/ *vb* 1 to alter in part. 2 to make less severe.

modish /mod-ish/ *adj* (*fml*) fashionable.

modulate /maw-ju-late/ *vb* 1 to raise or lower the tone or pitch of the voice when speaking or singing. 2 in music, to change from one key to another. • *n* **modulation**.

module /maw-jul/ *n* 1 one of several parts that together form a larger structure. 2 a unit of a course of study.

mohair /mo-hair/ *n* 1 the silky hair of an Angora goat. 2 the wool or cloth made from it.

moist /moist/ *adj* slightly wet, damp.

moisten /moi-sen/ *vb* to make damp.

moisture /mois-chur/ *n* dampness; wetness caused by tiny drops of water in the atmosphere.

moisturizer /mois-chu-rie-zer/ *n, also* **moisturiser** cream or lotion applied to treat dry skin.

molar /mo-lar/ *n* one of the back teeth that grind food.

molasses /mo-la-siz/ *n* a thick sticky dark liquid left over when sugar is made from sugarcane.

mold US variant of **mould**.

molder US variant of **moulder**.

molding US variant of **moulding**.

moldy US variant of **mouldy**.

mole¹ /mole/ *n* a dark spot on the human skin.

mole² /mole/ *n* 1 a small furry burrowing animal. 2 a spy who works from within an organization, passing information to another organization.

molecular /mol-e-cyu-lar/ *adj* having to do with molecules.

molecule /mol-i-cyool/ *n* the smallest particle of a substance that can exist while still retaining the chemical qualities of that substance.

molehill /mole-hill/ *n* the heap of earth thrown up by a burrowing mole.

moleskin /mole-skin/ *n* a strong ribbed cotton cloth.

molest /mo-lest/ *vb* 1 to disturb or annoy. 2 to make a bodily, often sexual, attack upon. • *n* **molestation**.

mollify /mol-i-fie/ *vb* to make less angry, to calm down.

mollusc /mol-usk/ *n, also* **mollusk** (*US*) a soft-bodied animal with a hard shell, as a snail, oyster, etc.

mollycoddle /mol-ee-cod-ul/ *vb* to take too great care of.

molt US variant of **moult**.

molten /moal-ten/ *adj* 1 melted. 2 made by having been melted.

moment /mo-ment/ *n* a very short time.

momentarily /mo-men-**ter**-i-lee/ *adv* for a moment. **2** (*inf*) shortly.

momentary /mo-men-ter-ee/ *adj* lasting only a moment.

momentous /mo-**men**-tus/ *adj* very important.

momentum /mo-**men**-tum/ *n* the force of a moving body.

monarch /mon-ark/ *n* a single supreme ruler, a sovereign, a king or queen.

monarchist /mon-ar-kist/ *n* a person who believes in monarchy.

monarchy /mon-ar-kee/ *n* a state or system of government in which power is, in appearance or reality, in the hands of a single ruler.

monastery /mon-a-stree/ *n* a house for monks.

monastic /mu-**na**-stic/ *adj* having to do with monks or monasteries.

Monday /mun-day/ *n* the first day of the working week.

monetary /mon-i-te-ree/ *adj* having to do with money.

money /mu-nee/ *n* metal coins and printed banknotes used in making payments, buying and selling.

moneyed /mu-need/ *adj* rich.

moneylender /mu-nee-**len**-der/ *n* a person who lives by lending money on condition that interest is paid to him or her for the time of the loan.

mongoose /mong-goos/ *n* (*pl* **mongooses**) a small weasel-like animal that kills snakes.

mongrel /mong-grel/ *adj* of mixed breed or race. • *n* a dog of mixed breed.

monitor /mon-i-tor/ *n* **1** in school, a student who helps a teacher in some way. **2** a device for checking electrical transmission without interfering with it. **3** an instrument that receives and shows continuous information about the working of something. **4** a screen for use with a computer. **5** a small screen in a television studio showing the picture that is being broadcast at any given time. • *vb* to observe and check something regularly.

monk /mungk/ *n* a man who, with the intention of devoting his life to prayer, joins a religious society and spends his life in a monastery.

monkey /mung-kee/ *n* **1** a long-tailed animal resembling a human being in shape. **2** (*inf*) a mischievous child. • *vb* to play about (with).

monkey puzzle /mung-kee pu-zul/ *n* an evergreen tree whose branches are covered with short prickly leaves.

mono- /mon-oe/ *prefix* one.

monochrome /mon-oe-crome/ *adj* in one colour, or in black and white.

monocle /mon-i-cul/ *n* a single eyeglass.

monogamy /mo-**nog**-a-mee/ *n* marriage to one husband or wife only. • *n* **monogamist**. • *adj* **monogamous**.

monogram /mon-o-gram/ *n* letters, especially initials, written one on top of another to make a single design.

monolith /mon-o-lith/ *n* a single standing stone like a pillar or ornament. • *adj* **monolithic**.

monologue /mon-o-log/ *n*, *also* **monolog** (*US*) a scene or play in which only one person speaks.

monoplane /mon-o-plane/ *n* an aeroplane with only one pair of wings.

monopolize /mu-**nop**-lize/ *vb*, *also* **monopolise** **1** to have or obtain complete possession or control of. **2** to take up the whole of.

monopoly /mu-no-pu-lee/ *n* **1** complete control of the trade in a certain article by a single person or company. **2** possession of or control over something that is not shared by others.

monosyllable /mon-o-si-la-bul/ *n* a word of one syllable. • *adj* **monosyllabic**.

monotone /mon-o-tone/ *n* a single unvarying tone of voice when speaking.

monotonous /mu-**no**-ti-nus/ *adj* **1** dull from lack of variety. **2** in a monotone.

monotony /mu-**not**-nee/ *n* dullness, lack of variety, sameness.

monsoon /mon-**soon**/ *n* a south Asian wind, blowing from the southwest in summer and the northeast in winter, usually bringing heavy rain.

monster /mon-ster/ *n* **1** a huge frightening creature. **2** anything huge. **3** an unnaturally cruel or wicked person.

monstrosity /mon-**stros**-i-tee/ *n* something, usually large, that is very ugly.

monstrous /mon-struss/ *adj* **1** huge. **2** unnaturally cruel or wicked.

montage /mon-tazh/ *n* a picture made by putting together many separate images.

month /munth/ *n* one of the 12 periods of time into which the year is divided.

monthly /munth-lee/ *adj* happening once a month or every month. • *also adv*.

monument /mon-yu-ment/ *n* a statue, stone, etc, set up in memory of a person or event.

monumental /mon-yu-**men**-tal/ *adj* **1** huge. **2** outstanding.

mood /mood/ *n* **1** a state of the mind and feelings, a person's temper at a certain moment. **2** a state of bad temper. **3** in grammar, a verb form that tells whether the verb is used to express a command, desire, statement of fact, etc.

moody /moo-dee/ *adj* tending to change mood suddenly or often; often bad-tempered. • *adv* **moodily**. • *n* **moodiness**.

moon /moon/ *n* **1** the heavenly body that moves around the earth and reflects the light of the sun. **2** any smaller heavenly body that moves around a larger one. • *vb* (*inf*) to walk about in a dreamy way.

moonbeam /moon-beem/ *n* a ray of light from the moon.

moonlight /moon-lite/ *n* the light from the moon. • *adj* **moonlit**.

moonstone /moon-stone/ *n* a precious stone, bluish white in colour.

moor[1] /moor/ *n* a large extent of poor land on which only coarse grass, heather, etc, will grow; a heath.

moor[2] /moor/ *vb* to fasten a ship by ropes, cables, etc.

moorage /moo-ridge/ *n* a place for mooring a ship.

moorcock /moor-cock/, **moorfowl** /moor-foul/ *n* the red grouse.

moorhen /moor-hen/ *n* the water-hen.

mooring /moo-ring/ *n*, **moorings** /moo-ringz/ *npl* **1** the ropes, cables, etc, by which a ship is fastened. **2** the place where a ship is so fastened.

moorland /moor-land/ *n* a moor, moors.

moose /mooss/ *n* an elk, a type of large deer with large flat antlers found in North America.

moot /moot/ *vb* (*fml*) to put forward for discussion.

moot point /moot point/ *n* a matter on which two or more opinions may be upheld, an undecided matter.

mop /mop/ *n* strips of coarse cloth, yarn, etc, fixed together to a handle and used for washing floors, etc. • *vb* (**mopped**, **mopping**) to clean with a mop, to wipe.

mope /moap/ *vb* to be gloomy or sad.

moral /maw-ral/ *adj* **1** having to do with what is right or wrong in action. **2** living according to the rules of right conduct. • *n* **1** the lesson to be learned from a story. **2** (*pl*) your beliefs as to what is right or wrong in action. **3** standards of behaviour. • *adv* **morally**.

morale /mu-ral/ *n* belief in your ability to do what is asked of you; courage.

moralist /maw-ra-list/ *n* a person who studies questions of right and wrong.

morality /maw-ra-li-tee/ *n* **1** moral principles.

2 a particular system of moral principles. **3** the quality of an action, as estimated by a standard of right and wrong.

moralize /maw-ra-lize/ *vb*, *also* **moralise** to discuss questions of morals.

morbid /mawr-bid/ *adj* **1** unhealthy, diseased. **2** thinking too much about what is gloomy or disgusting. • *n* **morbidity**. • *adv* **morbidly**.

more /more/ *adj* greater in amount, number, etc. • *also n*. • *adv* **1** to a greater extent or degree. **2** again.

morgue /mawrg/ *n* a mortuary.

Mormon /mawr-mon/ *n* a member of the Church of Jesus Christ of the Latter-day Saints, founded by Joseph Smith in 1830. • *also adj*.

morn /mawrn/ *n* (*lit*) morning.

morning /mawr-ning/ *n* the early part of the day.

morning star /mawr-ning star/ *n* the planet Venus when seen before sunrise.

morocco /mo-roc-o/ *n* a fine goatskin leather originally prepared in Morocco.

moron /moe-ron/ *n* (*inf*) a very stupid person. • *adj* **moronic**.

morose /mo-rose/ *adj* gloomy and ill-natured.

morphia /mawr-fee-a/, **morphine** /mawr-feen/ *n* a drug made from opium that causes sleep and lessens pain.

morse /mawrss/ *n* a signalling code in which dots and dashes (or short and long sounds or flashes) represent the letters of the alphabet.

morsel /mawr-sel/ *n* a small piece, a bite.

mortal /mawr-tal/ *adj* **1** having to die. **2** causing death. • *n* a human being. • *adv* **mortally**.

mortality /mawr-ta-li-tee/ *n* **1** the state of being mortal. **2** the number who die from a certain cause.

mortar /mawr-tar/ *n* **1** a bowl in which substances are crushed into powder. **2** a gun with a short barrel. **3** a cement made of lime and sand and used in building.

mortar-board /mawr-tar-board/ *n* a square-topped cap worn with an academic gown.

mortgage /mawr-gidge/ *n* **1** a legal arrangement by which a bank or other organization lends you money to buy a house and you agree to pay back the money over a set number of years, on the understanding that the bank has the right to sell the property if you cannot pay the loan back. **2** the amount of money you borrow in the form of a mortgage • *vb* to give control over property to another to obtain a loan.

mortify /mawr-ti-fie/ *vb* to make ashamed. • *n* mortification.

mortise /mawr-tis/ *n* a hole cut in a piece of wood, etc, to fit part of another piece.

mortuary /mawr-chu-we-ree/ *n* a building in which dead bodies are kept until burial.

mosaic /mo-zay-ic/ *n* design made by placing together differently coloured pieces of glass, stone, etc.

mosque /mosk/ *n* a Muslim place of worship.

mosquito /mo-skee-toe/ *n* (*pl* mosquitoes) a stinging insect that sometimes carries the germs of malaria.

moss /mawss/ *n* a tiny flowerless plant growing on walls and tree trunks and in damp places.

mossy /maw-see/ *adj* overgrown with moss.

most /moast/ *adj* greatest in number, amount, etc. • *also n.* • *adv* 1 in or to the greatest degree or extent. 2 very.

mostly /moast-lee/ *adv* mainly.

MOT test /em-owe-tee test/ *abbr* = Ministry of Transport test: a test that all cars over three years old in the UK must pass in order to show that they are safe to be driven on the road.

motel /mo-tel/ *n* a hotel with special facilities for motorists.

moth /mawth/ *n* 1 a winged insect that flies by night. 2 the clothes moth.

mother /mu-ther/ *n* 1 a female parent. 2 the female head of a convent of nuns. • *vb* to care for, as would a mother.

motherhood /mu-ther-hood/ *n* the state of being a mother.

mother-in-law /mu-ther-in-law/ *n* (*pl* mothers-in-law) the mother of the person to whom you are married.

motherly /mu-ther-lee/ *adj* like a mother.

mother-of-pearl /mu-ther-ov-perl/ *n* the hard pearl-like lining of certain shells.

mother tongue /mu-ther tung/ *n* your native language.

motif /mo-teef/ *n* 1 a repeated theme in an artistic or a literary work. 2 a design or pattern used as a decoration.

motion /mo-shun/ *n* 1 act of moving. 2 a movement. 3 an idea put to a meeting so that it can be voted on. • *vb* to make a movement as a sign.

motionless /mo-shun-less/ *adj* unmoving.

motivate /mo-ti-vate/ *vb* to give a reason or urge to act. • *n* motivation.

motive /mo-tiv/ *n* a reason for doing something. • *adj* causing movement.

motor /mo-tor/ *n* an engine that by changing power into motion drives a machine. • *adj* causing movement or motion. • *vb* to travel by motor car.

motorbike /mo-tor-bike/ *n* a bicycle driven by a motor. • *similarly* motor-boat, motor car.

motorist /mo-tu-rist/ *n* a person who drives a motor car.

motorway /mo-tur-way/ *n* a road with multiple lanes to accommodate fast-moving traffic.

mottle /mot-ul/ *vb* to mark with spots or blotches.

motto /mot-oe/ *n* (*pl* mottoes) 1 a wise saying that can be used as a rule of life. 2 the word or words on a coat of arms. 3 a printed saying.

mould[1] /moald/ *n, also* mold (*US*) 1 a shaped vessel into which hot molten metal is poured so that when it cools, it has the same shape as the vessel. 2 a vessel used to shape food. • *vb* 1 to form in a mould. 2 to work into a shape. 3 to shape or influence.

mould[2] /moald/ *n, also* mold (*US*) a fluffy growth consisting of tiny plants on stale food or damp surfaces.

moulder /moal-der/ *vb, also* molder (*US*) to rot away, to crumble.

moulding /moal-ding/ *n, also* molding (*US*) 1 anything given shape in a mould. 2 an ornamental pattern on a wall or ceiling or on a picture frame.

mouldy /moal-dee/ *adj, also* moldy (*US*) 1 covered with mould. 2 (*inf*) of little value, unpleasant, dull.

moult /moalt/ *vb, also* molt (*US*) to lose the hair or feathers, to fall off.

mound /mound/ *n* 1 a low hill. 2 a heap of earth or stones.

mount /mount/ *n* 1 (*usually in names*) a hill, a mountain. 2 an animal, especially a horse, for riding. 3 a card or paper surrounding a painting or photograph. • *vb* 1 to go up, to climb. 2 to get on to. 3 to place in position. 4 to get on horseback.

mountain /moun-tin/ *n* 1 a high hill. 2 a large heap.

mountain ash /moun-tin ash/ *n* a type of tree, the rowan.

mountaineer /moun-ti-neer/ *n* a person who climbs mountains. • *n* mountaineering.

mountainous /moun-ti-nus/ *adj* 1 having many mountains. 2 huge.

mounted /moun-tid/ *adj* on horseback.

mourn /moarn/ *vb* to show sorrow, to feel grief, especially after a loss or death. • *n* mourner.

mournful /moarn-ful/ *adj* sad, sorrowful. • *adv* mournfully.

mourning /moar-ning/ *n* 1 sorrow, grief.

mouse /mouse/ *n* (*pl* mice) 1 a small rodent animal found in houses or in the fields.

2 (*comput*) (*pl* **mouses, mice**) a handheld device which allows the user to control some computer functions without the keyboard.

moustache /mus-**tash**/ *n, also* **mustache** /mus-tash/ (*US*) the hair growing on the upper lip.

mouth /mouth/ *n* **1** the opening in the face for eating and uttering sounds. **2** the opening into anything hollow. **3** the part of a river where it flows into the sea. • *vb* to twist the mouth into different shapes.

mouthful /mouth-ful/ *n* the amount placed in the mouth at one time.

mouthpiece /mouth-peess/ *n* **1** the part of a musical instrument or pipe placed in the mouth. **2** a person who speaks for others.

movable, moveable /moo-va-bul/ *adj* able to be moved. • *npl* property that can be moved, especially furniture.

move /moov/ *vb* **1** to cause to change place or position. **2** to go from one place to another. **3** to change houses. **4** to set in motion. **5** to stir up the feelings. **6** to rouse to action. **7** at a meeting, to put forward an idea to be voted on. • *n* **1** a change of position or place. **2** a change of house. **3** an action. **4** in chess, etc, the act of moving a piece.

movement /moov-ment/ *n* **1** act of moving. **2** change of position. **3** a number of people working for the same purpose. **4** a complete part of a long musical work.

movie /moo-vee/ *n* (*esp US*) a film. • *npl*: **the movies** a showing of a film.

moving /moo-ving/ *adj* stirring up the feelings.

mow /moe/ *vb* (*pp* **mown**) **1** to cut. **2** to knock down, to kill in large numbers.

mower /moe-er/ *n* a person or machine that mows.

MP /em-pee/ *abbr = member of parliament*: a member of the UK parliament.

mp3 /em-pee-three/ *abbr =* **MPEG** (Moving Picture Experts Group) **Layer-3**: is a file format for digital audio. • **mp3 player** a device on which you can store and play mp3s.

Mr *abbr* of **Mister**.

Mrs *abbr* of **Mistress**.

MSP /em-ess-pee/ *abbr =* **Member of the Scottish Parliament**.

much /much/ *adj* great in amount or quantity. • *n* a great amount. • *adv* greatly.

muck /muck/ *n* (*inf*) wet filth, dirt. • *vb* (*inf*) **1** to dirty. **2** to make a mess of. **3** to spoil. **4** to bungle.

mucky /mu-kee/ *adj* (*inf*) filthy.

mucous /**myoo**-cus/ *adj* producing mucus, slimy.

mucous membrane /**myoo**-cus mem-brane/ *n* the inner skin lining the nose, mouth, etc.

mucus /**myoo**-cus/ *n* the shiny liquid coming from the mucous membrane of the nose.

mud /mud/ *n* soft, wet earth.

muddle /mu-dul/ *vb* **1** to confuse. **2** to mix up. **3** to act without plan. • *n* confusion, disorder.

muddy /mu-dee/ *adj* covered with mud. • *vb* **1** to make dirty or muddy. **2** to make unclear.

mudguard /mud-gard/ *n* a metal shield over a wheel of a bicycle or motorbike to protect against mud and water thrown up from the road.

muesli /**myoo**-zlee/ *n* a breakfast cereal consisting of grains, nuts and dried fruit.

muff[1] /muff/ *n* a cover of warm material.

muff[2] /muff/ *vb* (*inf*) **1** to fail to hold. **2** to do badly.

muffin /mu-fin/ *n* **1** a small round individual cake, often containing fruit or chocolate. **2** a small thick bread roll, often eaten toasted with butter.

muffle /mu-ful/ *vb* **1** to wrap up to keep warm. **2** to deaden sound. **3** to make a sound less loud.

muffler /mu-fler/ *n* a warm scarf.

mug[1] /mug/ *n* **1** a drinking vessel with a handle and more or less straight sides. **2** (*inf*) someone who is easy to deceive.

mug[2] /mug/ *vb* (**mugged, mugging**) to attack and rob. • *n* **mugger**.

muggy /mu-gee/ *adj* unpleasantly warm and damp.

mulberry /mul-ber-ee/ *n* **1** a tree bearing dark red edible berries. **2** a dark reddish purple colour.

mule /myool/ *n* the offspring of an ass and a horse, supposedly famous for its stubbornness. • *adj* **mulish** stubborn. • *n* **mulishness**.

mull[1] /mull/ *vb*. • **mull over** to think carefully about.

mull[2] /mull/ *vb* to heat, sweeten and spice.

mullet /mu-let/ *n* an edible sea fish.

mullion /mul-yin/ *n* an upright bar between the divisions of a window.

multi- /mul-tee/ *prefix* many.

multicoloured /mul-tee-cu-lurd/ *adj* of many colours.

multilateral /mul-tee-lat-ral/ *adj* **1** having many sides. **2** (*fml*) concerning more than two groups.

multimedia /mul-tee-**mee**-dee-ya/ *adj* **1** using several different methods and media. **2** in computing, using sound and video images as well as data.

multiple /mul-ti-pul/ adj **1** having or affecting many parts. **2** involving many things of the same kind. • n a number that contains another an exact number of times.

multiplex /mul-ti-pleks/ n a building that contains several cinemas.

multiplier /mul-ti-plie-er/ n the number by which another is multiplied.

multiply /mul-ti-plie/ vb **1** to find the number obtained by adding a number to itself a certain number of times. **2** to increase.

multi-storey /mul-ti-sto-ree/ adj having several storeys.

multitude /mul-ti-tood/ n **1** (old) a crowd. **2** a great number.

multitudinous /mul-ti-tood-nus/ adj (fml or hum) very many.

mum /mum/ n (inf) mother. • adj silent.

mumble /mum-bul/ vb to speak in a low, indistinct voice.

mumbo-jumbo /mum-bo-jum-bo/ n meaningless talk.

mummy[1] /mu-mee/ n a human body kept from decay by being treated with certain drugs and wrapped tightly in cloth. • vb **mummify**.

mummy[2] /mu-mee/ n (inf) mother.

mumps /mumps/ n an infectious disease that causes swelling of the neck and face.

munch /munch/ vb to chew noisily, to crush with teeth.

mundane /mun-dane/ adj **1** (fml) having to do with this world. **2** ordinary, with nothing exciting or unusual.

municipal /myoo-ni-si-pal/ adj having to do with a city or town.

municipality /myoo-ni-si-pa-li-tee/ n a city or town with certain powers of self-government.

munificent /myoo-ni-fi-sent/ adj (fml) generous. • n **munificence**.

munitions /myoo-ni-shunz/ npl the guns, shells, etc, used in making war.

mural /myoo-ral/ n a painting that is painted directly on to the walls of a building.

murder /mur-der/ n act of unlawfully and intentionally killing another. • also vb. • n **murderer, murderess** /mur-de-ress/.

murderous /mur-de-rus/ adj **1** used to commit murder. **2** cruel, savage.

murky /mur-kee/ adj **1** dark, gloomy. **2** vague or obscure.

murmur /mur-mur/ n **1** a low, indistinct sound, as of running water. **2** a soft, low continuous sound. **3** a grumble. • vb **1** to make a low indistinct sound. **2** to talk in a low voice. **3** to grumble.

muscle /mu-sul/ n the elastic fibres in the body that enable it to make movements.

muscular /mu-skyu-lar/ adj **1** having well-developed muscles, strong. **2** having to do with muscles.

muse[1] /myooz/ n **1** in legend, one of the nine goddesses of the arts and learning. **2** (fml) inspiration to write (e.g. poetry).

muse[2] /myooz/ vb to think deeply about, to ponder.

museum /myoo-zee-um/ n a building in which objects of scientific, artistic, or literary interest are kept.

mushroom /mush-room/ n an edible plant with a soft whitish pulpy top. • vb to grow in size very rapidly.

music /myoo-zic/ n **1** the art of arranging sounds to give melody or harmony. **2** the sounds so arranged when played, sung, or written down.

musical /myoo-zi-cal/ adj **1** having to do with music. **2** pleasant-sounding. • n a play or a movie that includes a lot of songs. • adv **musically**.

musician /myoo-zi-shun/ n a person who is skilled in music.

musk /musk/ n a sweet-smelling substance obtained from the musk deer and used in making perfume.

musket /mus-ket/ n (old) a handgun formerly carried by soldiers.

musketeer /mus-ke-teer/ n (old) a soldier armed with a musket.

muskrat /musk-rat/ n a large water rat found in North America.

musky /mus-kee/ adj smelling of musk.

Muslim /muz-lim/ n a person who follows the religion of Islam. • also adj.

muslin /muz-lin/ n a fine, thin cotton cloth.

musquash /muz-kwawsh/ n the fur of the muskrat.

mussel n an edible shellfish enclosed in a hinged shell.

must /must/ vb to have to.

mustache US variant of **moustache**.

mustang /mus-tang/ n a wild horse native to the United States, descended from horses brought by the Spanish.

mustard /mus-tard/ n **1** a plant with hot-tasting seeds. **2** a type of seasoning made from these for flavouring food, especially meat.

musty /mu-stee/ adj stale.

mutable /myoo-ta-bul/ adj (fml) changeable.

mutation /myoo-tay-shun/ n a change in the genetic structure of an animal or plant that makes it different from others of the same kind. • *n* mutant.

mute /myoot/ *adj* 1 silent. 2 unable to speak. 3 not pronounced. • *n* 1 a dumb person. 2 an attachment that lessens or modifies the sound of a musical instrument.

muted /myoo-tid/ *adj* 1 having the sound altered by a mute. 2 subdued. 3 soft in hue, shade, etc.

mutilate /myoo-ti-late/ *vb* to damage seriously by removing a part, especially a limb. • *n* mutilation.

mutineer /myoo-ti-neer/ *n* a person who takes part in a mutiny.

mutinous /myoo-ti-nus/ *adj* 1 taking part in a mutiny. 2 obstinate and sulky, as if going to disobey.

mutiny /myoo-ti-nee/ *n* refusal to obey those in charge, especially a rising of people in the armed services against their officers. • *also vb*.

mutter /mu-ter/ *vb* to speak in a low voice, without sounding the vowels clearly, especially when grumbling or insulting. • *also n*.

mutton /mu-tun/ *n* the flesh of sheep as meat.

mutual /myoo-choo-wal/ *adj* 1 given and received in the same degree by those concerned. 2 common to, or shared by, two or more persons or parties. • *adv* mutually.

muzzle /mu-zul/ *n* 1 the mouth and nose of an animal. 2 a cage or set of straps fastened on an animal's mouth to prevent it biting. 3 the open end of a gun. • *vb* 1 to put a muzzle on an animal's mouth. 2 to prevent from speaking freely.

muzzy /mu-zee/ *adj* 1 dazed or confused. 2 blurred, indistinct.

my /mie/ *adj* belonging to me.

myalgic encephalomyelitis *see* ME.

myopia /mie-oe-pee-a/ *n* short-sightedness. • *adj* myopic short-sighted.

myriad /mi-ree-ad/ *n* a very large number. • *also adj*.

myrrh /mur/ *n* 1 a tree from which is obtained a sweet-smelling gum. 2 the gum so obtained.

myrtle /mur-tul/ *n* an evergreen shrub with sweet-smelling white flowers.

myself /mie-self/ *pron* (*used reflexively or for emphasis*) me.

mysterious /mi-stee-ree-us/ *adj* difficult to understand or explain. • *adv* mysteriously.

mystery /mi-ste-ree/ *n* 1 anything difficult to understand or explain. 2 a secret way of doing something, known only to a few.

mystic /mi-stic/ *adj* having to do with religious mysteries or secrets. • *n* a person who believes that through prayer or sympathy he or she has understood in part the mysteries of life and the existence of God.

mystical /mi-sti-cal/ *adj* mystic.

mysticism /mi-sti-si-zum/ *n* the beliefs or practices of a mystic.

mystify /mi-sti-fie/ *vb* to puzzle, to bewilder. • *n* mystification.

mystique /mi-steek/ *n* a mysterious quality.

myth /mith/ *n* 1 a story about the gods or goddesses of ancient peoples, especially one containing their beliefs about the facts of nature. 2 something that is popularly thought to be true but is not.

mythical /mi-thi-cal/ *adj* 1 existing in myths or legends. 2 imaginary, not real.

mythologist /mi-thol-o-jist/ *n* a person who studies myths.

mythology /mi-thol-o-jee/ *n* 1 a collection of myths. 2 the study of myths. • *adj* mythological.

N

N, n /en/ the 14th letter of the English alphabet.

nab /nab/ *vb* (*inf*) (nabbed, nabbing) **1** to catch or capture. **2** to arrest.

nag[1] /nag/ *n* a horse, especially a small, weak, or old one.

nag[2] /nag/ *vb* (nagged, nagging) to keep on annoying or finding fault with.

nail /nail/ *n* **1** the horny growth on the tips of the fingers or toes. **2** the claw of a bird or animal. **3** a thin piece of metal with a pointed end and a flattened head, used for joining together pieces of wood. • *vb* to fasten with a nail.

nail-biting /nail-bie-ting/ *adj* extremely tense and exciting, full of suspense.

nailbrush /nail-brush/ *n* a small, stiff brush for cleaning fingernails and toenails.

nail file /nail file/ *n* a small, flat file for smoothing and shaping fingernails and toenails.

nail head /nail hed/ *n* the flattened end of a nail.

naïve /nie-eev/ *adj* **1** simple and natural, innocent. **2** ignorantly simple, too trustful. • *n* naïveté. • *n* naïf a naïve person.

naked /nay-ked/ *adj* **1** wearing no clothes. **2** uncovered. **3** plain, unconcealed. • *n* nakedness.

name /name/ *n* **1** the word by which a person or thing is known. **2** reputation. • *vb* **1** to give a name to. **2** to speak about by name. • *adj* **1** having a good reputation. **2** carrying a name.

nameless /name-less/ *adj* **1** unknown. **2** having no name. **3** wanting his/her name to be concealed. **4** too bad to be mentioned by name.

namely /name-lee/ *adv* that is to say.

nameplate /name-plate/ *n* a metal, wooden or plastic plate on which the name of a person, firm, etc, is engraved.

namesake /name-sake/ *n* a person with the same name as another.

nan /nan/ *n* a kind of flat bread of India made with white flour.

nana /na-na/ *n* a child's term for grandmother.

nanny /na-nee/ *n* a person employed to take care of children, a children's nurse.

nanny goat /na-nee goat/ *n* a female goat.

nanogram /na-no-gram/ *n* one-billionth of a gram.

nanosecond /na-no-se-cond/ *n* one-billionth of a second.

nap[1] /nap/ *n* a short sleep, a doze. • *vb* (napped, napping) to take a short sleep. • caught napping taken by surprise.

nap[2] /nap/ *n* the woolly or hairy surface of cloth.

nape /nape/ *n* the back part of the neck.

napkin /nap-kin/ *n* a small cloth or paper used at the table to keep the clothes clean.

nappy /na-pee/ *n* (short for napkin) a piece of absorbent material or paper fastened around a baby's bottom to hold its urine and faeces. • *also* diaper (*US*).

narcissism /nar-si-si-zum/ *n* too much interest in a person's own appearance, comfort, importance, etc. • *adj* narcissistic. • *n* narcissist a person who is like this.

narcissus /nar-si-sus/ *n* (*pl* narcissi) a flower of the daffodil family, but with white petals.

narcotic /nar-cot-ic/ *n* a drug that causes sleep and eases pain. • *adj* causing sleep.

narrate /nar-rate/ *vb* to tell.

narration /nar-ray-shun/ *n* a story, the act of telling a story.

narrative /na-ra-tiv/ *adj* **1** telling a story. **2** having to do with storytelling. • *n* a story.

narrator /na-ray-tor/ *n* the teller of a story.

narrow /na-ro/ *adj* **1** not broad, measuring little from side to side. **2** (*also* narrow-minded) unwilling to accept new ideas or ways of doing things. **3** not extensive, not wide-ranging. **4** only just avoiding the opposite result. • *n* (*usually pl*) a narrow part of a river or sea. • *vb* to make or become narrow.

narrowly /na-ro-lee/ *adv* barely, only just.

narwhal /nar-wal/ *n* a type of whale with one large tusk.

NASA /na-sa/ *abbr* = National Aeronautics and Space Administration: the organization in the United States that deals with space travel and exploration.

nasal /nay-zal/ *adj* **1** having to do with the nose. **2** sounded through the nose. • *n* a vowel or consonant so sounded.

nasty /na-stee/ *adj* **1** unpleasant. **2** dirty. **3** disagreeable. **4** unkind. • *n* nastiness.

nation /nay-shun/ *n* all the people belonging to one country and living under the same government.

national /na-shnal/ *adj* **1** having to do with a nation. **2** of concern to all the people in a country.

nationalism /na-shna-li-zum/ *n* **1** devotion to, and pride in, a person's own country.

2 a belief in independence for one's country.

nationalist /na-shna-list/ *n* **1** a person who has great pride in and love of their country and considers it superior to others. **2** a person who believes in, and seeks, independence for their country.

nationality /na-shu-na-li-tee/ *n* membership of a particular nation.

nationalize /na-shna-lize/ *vb, also* **nationalise** to transfer ownership and control of land, resources, industry, etc. to the national government.

national monument /na-shnal mon-yu-ment/ *n* a natural feature or historic site that is preserved by the government for the public to visit.

national park /na-shnal park/ *n* an area of scenic beauty or historical interest that is preserved by the government for the public to visit.

nationwide /nay-shun-wide/ *adj* by or throughout the whole nation.

native /nay-tiv/ *adj* **1** of the place where one was born. **2** belonging to a country. • *n* a person who was born in a particular place.

Native American /nay-tiv ah-mer-i-can/ *n* one of the peoples, and their descendants, that originally occupied North and South America before Europeans began to settle there. • *also adj.*

nativity /na-ti-vi-tee/, **the Nativity** the birth of Jesus.

natter /na-ter/ *vb* (*inf*) to talk for a long time about nothing very important; to chat. • *also n.*

natural /na-chu-ral/ *adj* **1** not caused or altered by humans, occurring in nature. **2** born in a person. **3** normal. **4** real, genuine. **5** (*mus*) neither sharp nor flat. • *n* **1** (*inf*) a person who is naturally good at something. **2** (*mus*) a natural note and the mark by which it is shown.

natural gas /na-chu-ral gas/ *n* a gas that occurs naturally and is often used for fuel.

natural history /na-chu-ral hi-stree/ *n* the study of the earth and all that grows on it.

naturalism /na-chu-ra-li-zum/ *n* **1** action or thought based on natural desires. **2** the belief that the natural world is all that exists and that there is no spiritual world dealing with creation or control.

naturalist /na-chu-ra-list/ *n* one who studies plant and animal life.

naturalize /na-chu-ra-lize/ *vb, also* **naturalise** to accept someone as a member of a nation to which he or she does not belong by birth. • *n* **naturalization**, *also* **naturalisation**.

naturally /na-chu-ra-lee/ *adv* **1** in a natural way. **2** of course.

natural resource /na-chu-ral ri-zoarse/ *n* a form of wealth supplied by nature, such as coal, oil, water power, etc.

natural science /na-chu-ral sie-enss/ *n* any of the branches of knowledge and study of nature, which includes zoology, chemistry, geology, etc.

natural selection /na-chu-ral si-lec-shun/ *n* the process by which a kind of animal or plant will take on certain features and not others to help it adapt to its surroundings.

nature /nay-chur/ *n* **1** all existing and happening in the universe that is not the work of humans, such as plants, animals, mountains, lakes, etc. **2** the sum of those qualities that make any creature or thing different from others. **3** the character of a person. **4** kind, sort.

naught /nawt/ *n* (*old or lit*) nothing.

naughty /naw-tee/ *adj* mischievous, badly behaved. • *n* **naughtiness**.

nausea /naw-zee-ya/ *n* **1** a feeling of sickness, as if needing to vomit. **2** great disgust.

nauseate /naw-zee-ate/ *vb* **1** to sicken. **2** to disgust. • *adj* **nauseating**.

nauseous /naw-shess/ *adj* **1** feeling sick. **2** causing sickness. **3** disgusting, sickening.

nautical /naw-ti-cal/ *adj* having to do with the sea, sailors, or ships.

nautical mile /naw-ti-cal mile/ *n* a unit for measuring distance at sea; about 1.2 miles, or about 6076 feet (1.8 kilometres).

nautilus /naw-ti-lus/ *n* a sea creature living in a shell that twists round in a spiral.

naval /nay-vul/ *adj* having to do with a navy or warships.

nave[1] /nave/ *n* the main part of a church where people worship.

nave[2] /nave/ *n* the central part of a wheel.

navel /nay-vul/ *n* a little scar, sometimes shaped like a hollow, in the centre of the belly where, before birth, a baby was attached to its mother.

navigable /na-vi-ga-bul/ *adj* that can be steered, that ships can sail through.

navigate /na-vi-gate/ *vb* **1** to steer, to sail. **2** to work out the correct course for a ship, aircraft, etc, and direct it on that course.

navigation /na-vi-gay-shun/ *n* **1** the science of working out the course or position of a ship, aircraft, etc. **2** act of sailing a ship.

navigator /na-vi-gay-tor/ *n* a person who navigates.

navy /nay-vee/ *n* the warships of a nation, their crews, and their equipment.

navy blue /nay-vee blue/ *adj* very dark blue.

navvy /na-vee/ *n* an unskilled worker who does physical work.

Nazi /nat-see/ *n* the far-right Nationalist Socialist Party, or one of its followers, which controlled Germany under the leadership of Adolf Hitler between 1933 and 1945. • *also adj.*

Neanderthal /nee-an-der-tawl/ *adj* of a form of early human being. • *n* **1** a Neanderthal human being. **2** a crude, primitive person.

near /neer/ *adj* **1** close, not distant in time or place. **2** only just missed or avoided. • *prep* close to. • *adv* almost. • *vb* to approach.

nearby /neer-bie/ *adj*, *adv* near, close by.

nearer /nee-rer/ *adv*, *adj*, *prep* less distant from.

nearest /nee-rest/ *adv*, *adj*, *prep* least distant from.

nearly /neer-lee/ *adv* almost.

nearsighted /neer-sie-ted/ *adj* short-sighted.

neat /neet/ *adj* **1** tidily arranged. **2** skilfully done or made. **3** not mixed with anything, said of alcoholic drinks. • *n* **neatness**. • *vb* **neaten**.

nebula /ne-byu-la/ *n* (*pl* **nebulae**) **1** (*astron*) a cloud of gas and dust in outer space. **2** (*med*) a cloudy patch on the cornea. • *adj* **nebular**.

nebulous /ne-byu-lus/ *adj* not clear, cloudy.

necessary /ne-si-se-ree/ *adj* needed, unavoidable, that cannot be done without. • *adv* **necessarily**.

necessitate /ni-se-si-tate/ *vb* to make necessary.

necessity /ni-se-si-tee/ *n* **1** that which a person needs. **2** the condition of being necessary or unavoidable. **3** events forcing a person to act or behave in a certain way.

neck /neck/ *n* **1** the part of the body joining the head to the shoulders. **2** the narrow part near the mouth of a bottle. **3** a narrow strip of land joining two larger masses of land. • **neck and neck** exactly level.

neckband /neck-band/ *n* a band worn around the neck.

neckerchief /ne-ker-chif/ *n* a large handkerchief or scarf worn around the neck.

necklace /ne-cliss/ *n* a chain of gold, silver, etc or a string of beads or jewels worn around the neck.

neckline /ne-cline/ *n* the line formed by the edge of a piece of clothing around or nearest the neck.

nectar /nec-tar/ *n* **1** in Greek legend, the drink of the gods. **2** a sweet liquid found in flowers.

nectarine /nec-ta-reen/ *n* a type of peach with a smooth skin.

need /need/ *n* **1** a want. **2** that which one requires. **3** poverty. • *vb* **1** to be in want of, to require. **2** to have to.

needful /need-ful/ *adj* necessary.

needle /nee-dul/ *n* **1** a small, sharply pointed piece of steel used for drawing thread through cloth in sewing. **2** a short, pointed stick used for knitting wool. **3** a small metal pointer on a dial, compass, etc. **4** a very thin pointed piece of metal at the end of a syringe, used, for example, to administer drugs or draw blood. **5** the long pointed leaf of a pine tree, fir, etc.

needlepoint /nee-dul-point/ *n* decorative sewing done with thread on canvas used for pillow covers, decorative hangings, etc.

needless /need-less/ *adj* not needed, unnecessary.

needlework /nee-dul-wurk/ *n* sewing done by hand with a needle such as crocheting, embroidering, knitting, etc.

needy /nee-dee/ *adj* poor, living in want.

negate /ni-gate/ *vb* (*fml*) **1** to deny. **2** to cause to have no effect.

negation /ni-gay-shun/ *n* **1** a denial. **2** a word or phrase saying no.

negative /ne-ga-tiv/ *adj* **1** saying no. **2** criticizing, but putting forward no alternative plan or idea. • *n* **1** a word such as no, not, etc, expressing refusal or denial. **2** the image on a photographic film or plate in which light seems dark and shade light.

neglect /ni-glect/ *vb* **1** to fail to take care of. **2** to leave undone. **3** to pay no or little attention to, to give too little care to. • *n* want of care or attention.

neglectful /ni-glect-ful/ *adj* heedless, careless.

negligee /ne-gli-zhay/ *n* a woman's light, thin robe or dressing gown.

negligence /ne-gli-jense/ *n* carelessness, lack of proper care.

negligent /ne-gli-jent/ *adj* careless.

negligible /ne-gli-ji-bul/ *adj* too little to bother about, unimportant.

negotiable /ni-go-sha-bul/ *adj* **1** able to be settled or changed through discussion. **2** that can be exchanged for money. **3** able to be passed.

negotiate /ni-go-she-ate/ *vb* **1** to try to reach agreement, to bargain. **2** to arrange, usually after a long discussion. **3** to pass. • *n* **negotiation**. • *n* **negotiator**.

neigh /nay/ *n* the cry of a horse, a whinny. • *also vb*.

neighbour /nay-bur/ *n, also* **neighbor** (*US*) **1** a person living near. **2** a person living next door.

neighbourhood /nay-bur-hood/ *n, also* **neighborhood** (*US*) **1** the surrounding area or district. **2** a group of people and their homes forming a small area within a larger one.

neighbouring /nay-bu-ring/ *adj, also* **neighboring** (*US*) close at hand, near.

neighbourly /nay-bur-lee/ *adj, also* **neighborly** (*US*) friendly, helpful.

neither /nee-ther, neye-ther/ *adj, pron, conj and adv* not either.

Neolithic /nee-yo-li-thic/ *adj* having to do with the later Stone Age, during which people used polished stone tools, made pottery, reared stock, etc.

neon /nee-on/ *n* a gas that glows brightly when electricity passes through it.

nephew /ne-fyoo/ *n* the son of a person's brother or sister.

nepotism /ne-pu-ti-zum/ *n* unjust use of a person's power by giving good positions to relatives.

Neptune /nep-toon/ *n* **1** the eighth planet from the sun. **2** in Roman mythology, the god of the sea.

nerd /nurd/ *n* a person thought of as dull, awkward, etc, especially if they are overly interested in computers or schoolwork.

nerve /nerv/ *n* **1** one of the threadlike fibres along which messages pass to and from the brain. **2** courage. **3** (*inf*) self-confidence, cheek. **4** *pl* excitement, nervousness. • *vb* to give strength.

nerveless /nerv-less/ *adj* without strength or feeling.

nervous /ner-vus/ *adj* easily excited or upset, timid. • *n* **nervousness**.

nervous breakdown /ner-vus **brake**-down/ *n* an episode of mental illness.

nervous system /ner-vus **sis**-tem/ *n* all the nerve cells and tissues in a body that control responses and behaviour.

nervy /ner-vee/ *n* nervous, easily frightened.

nest /nest/ *n* **1** a place built by a bird in which it lays its eggs and brings up its young. **2** the home built by certain small animals and insects. **3** a comfortable shelter. **4** a set of things that fit one inside another. • *vb* to build a nest and live in it.

nest egg *n* /nest egg/ **1** a sum of money put aside for future use. **2** a real or fake egg put into a nest to get a hen to lay more eggs there.

nestle /ne-sul/ *vb* **1** to lie close to. **2** to settle comfortably.

nestling /ne-sling/ *n* a bird too young to leave the nest.

net¹ /net/ *n* **1** crisscrossing strings knotted together at the crossing places. **2** an extent of this used for catching fish, animals, etc, and for many other purposes. **3** a fabric made like this. • *vb* (**netted, netting**) **1** to catch in a net. **2** to cover with a net. **3** to hit or kick into a net.

net² /net/ *adj* left after one has subtracted the amount due for taxes, expenses, etc. • *vb* (**netted, netting**) to bring in as profit.

nether /ne-ther/ *adj* (*fml or hum*) lower.

nethermost /ne-ther-moast/ *adj* farthest down.

netting /ne-ting/ *n* **1** material made in the form of a net. **2** the act or process of making nets.

nettle /ne-tul/ *n* a weed covered with stinging hairs. • *vb* to anger, to annoy.

network /net-wurk/ *n* **1** anything in which lines, roads, railways, etc, cross and recross one another. **2** a widespread organization.

neural /nyoo-ral/ *adj* of a nerve, nerves, or the nervous system.

neurological /nyoo-ro-**lodge**-i-cal/ *adj* having to do with the nerves.

neurology /nyoo-**rol**-o-jee/ *n* the study of the nerves. • *n* **neurologist**.

neurosis /nyoo-ro-sis/ *n* a type of mental illness in which a person suffers from great anxiety, depression and/or fear.

neurotic /nyoo-**rot**-ic/ *adj* **1** in a nervous state, unreasonably anxious or sensitive. **2** suffering from a neurosis.

neuter /nyoo-ter/ *adj* having no sexual organ. • *n* an animal that has been spayed or castrated, an animal that has been fixed. • *vb* to spay, castrate, or fix an animal.

neutral /nyoo-tral/ *adj* **1** not taking sides, neither for nor against, impartial. **2** not strong or definite. • *n* a neutral person or party.

neutrality /nyoo-**tra**-li-tee/ *n* the state of being neutral.

neutralize, neutralise /nyoo-tra-lize/ *vb* to cause to have no effect, to make useless, to balance by an opposite action or effect.

never /ne-ver/ *adv* at no time, not ever.

nevermore /ne-ver-**more**/ *adv* never again.

never-never land /ne-ver-ne-ver land/ *n* an unreal place or situation.

nevertheless /ne-ver-the-**less**/ *adv* for all that, despite everything.

new /nyoo/ *adj* **1** never known before. **2** just bought or made, fresh. **3** changed from an earlier state, different. • *n* **newness**.

newborn /**nyoo**-bawrn/ *n* a recently born infant.

newcomer /**nyoo**-cu-mer/ *n* a person who has recently arrived.

newfound /nyoo-**found**/ *adj* newly gained.

newly /**nyoo**-lee/ *adv* recently.

newlywed /**nyoo**-lee-wed/ *n* a recently married person.

new moon /nyoo **moon**/ *n* the first phase of the moon when it is between the Earth and the sun with its dark side facing the Earth.

news /**nyooz**/ *n* **1** information about what is going on. **2** an account of recent events.

newsagent /**nyooz**-ay-jent/ *n* a person or shop that sells newspapers, magazines, etc and often cigarettes and sweets.

newsletter /**nyooz**-le-ter/ *n* a printed sheet of news sent to members of a group, organization, etc.

newspaper /**nyooz**-pay-per/ *n* a number of printed sheets (usually issued daily) containing the latest news, articles, advertisements, etc.

newsprint /**nyooz**-print/ *n* a cheap, low-grade paper used for printing newspapers.

newsreel /**nyooz**-reel/ *n* a film showing recent events.

newsstand /**nyooz**-stand/ *n* a stand at which newspapers, magazines, etc. are sold.

newsy /**nyoo**-zee/ *adj* (*inf*) containing a lot of news.

newt /**nyoot**/ *n* a small lizardlike creature that can live both on land and in water.

New Testament /**nyoo** tes-ta-ment/ *n* the part of the Christian Bible that deals with the life and teachings of Jesus.

next /**nekst**/ *adj* nearest, just before or just after in time, place, degree, or rank. • *also adv, prep, n.*

next-door /**neks(t)**-door/ *adj* in or at the next house or building.

next of kin /nek stov **kin**/ *n* someone's closest relative.

nib /**nib**/ *n* **1** the bill or beak of a bird. **2** the point of a pen.

nibble /**ni**-bul/ *vb* to take small bites at. • *also n.*

nice /**nice**/ *adj* **1** pleasing. **2** (*old*) particular when choosing, hard to please. **3** (*fml*) fine, delicate, precise.

nicety /**nie**-si-tee/ *n* **1** the quality or the state of being nice. **2** exactness, precise detail. **3** a very small difference.

niche /**nich, neesh**/ *n* **1** a hollow place in a wall for a statue, etc. **2** the work, place, or position for which a person or thing is best suited. **3** an area of the market specializing in a particular product.

nick /**nick**/ *n* **1** the small hollow left when a piece is cut or chipped out of something, a notch. **2** (*inf*) a police station, prison. **3** (*inf*) condition. • *vb* **1** to cut notches in. **2** (*inf*) to steal. • **in the nick of time** just in time.

nickel /**ni**-cel/ *n* a hard silver-white metal used for plating utensils and mixed with other metals because it doesn't rust.

nickname /**nic**-name/ *n* a name used instead of one's real name in friendship or mockery. • *vb* to give a nickname to.

nicotine /**ni**-co-teen/ *n* the toxic oily liquid from tobacco that is addictive.

niece /**neess**/ *n* the daughter of a person's brother or sister.

night /**nite**/ *n, also* **night time** the time between sunset and sunrise, darkness.

nightcap /**nite**-cap/ *n* **1** a cap worn in bed. **2** a drink taken last thing at night.

nightclothes /**nite**-cloathz/ *n* clothes worn in bed, pyjamas.

nightclub /**nite**-club/ *n* a place of entertainment open at night for eating, drinking, dancing, etc.

nightdress /**nite**-dres/ *n* a nightgown.

nightfall /**nite**-fawl/ *n* evening, the approach of darkness.

nightgown /**nite**-goun/ *n, also* **nightie** a loose gown worn to bed by women or girls.

nightingale /**nie**-ting-gale/ *n* a type of small bird that sometimes sings at night.

night light /**nite** lite/ *n* a small, faint light burning all night, as in a hallway or child's room.

nightly /**nite**-lee/ *adj* happening every night. • *adv* every night.

nightmare /**nite**-mare/ *n* a frightening dream.

night owl /**nite** owl/ *n* a person who works at night or who generally stays up late.

nightshirt /**nite**-shirt/ *n* a long, loose-fitting, shirt worn to bed.

night watch /**nite** watch/ *n* a watching or guarding during the night.

night watchman /**nite** watch-man/ *n* a man who looks after buildings, etc, by night.

nightwear /**nite**-ware/ *n* nightclothes.

nil /**nil**/ *n* nothing, zero.

nimble /**nim**-bul/ *adj* active, quick-moving. • *n* **nimbleness**.

nimbus /**nim**-bus/ *n* (*pl* **nimbi** *or* **nimbuses**) **1** a rain cloud. **2** the halo around the head of an angel in paintings.

nimby *acronym* = **not in my backyard** a person who protests against a new development if it is to be located near their own home. • *also adj.*

nine /nine/ *adj* the number between eight and ten.

nineteen /nine-teen/ *adj* ten more than nine.

nineteenth /nine-teenth/ *adj* preceded by 18 others in a series.

ninetieth /nine-tee-eth/ *adj* preceded by 89 others in a series.

nine-to-five /nine-to-five/ *adj* of or referring to the time between 9am and 5am, the period of business hours on a weekday.

ninety /nine-tee/ *n* the number between 89 and 91.

ninth /nine-th/ *adj* **1** preceded by eight others in a series. **2** any of the nine equal parts of something.

nip /nip/ *vb* (**nipped, nipping**) **1** to pinch. **2** to bite. **3** to stop the growth. • *n* **1** a pinch. **2** biting cold. **3** a small drink. • **nip in the bud** to destroy at an early stage.

nipple /ni-pul/ *n* **1** the point of the breast. **2** anything so shaped. **3** a rubber stopper with a small hole in it through which liquid may pass; a teat.

nippy /ni-pee/ *adj* able to move very quickly.

nirvana /nir-va-na/ *n* **1** in Buddhism, the state of being perfectly blessed after death and taken into the supreme spirit. **2** complete peace and happiness. **3** in Hinduism, a blowing out of the flame of life through reunion with Brahma, the god of creation.

nit /nit/ *n* a young louse or the egg of a louse or other small insect.

nitpick /nit-pick/ *vb* to find fault with someone or something in a manner that is finicky or minor.

nitrogen /nie-tro-jen/ *n* a colourless, odourless, and tasteless gas that makes up about four-fifths of the air. • *adj* **nitrogenous**.

nitroglycerin /nie-tro-**glis**-ren/ *n* an explosive.

nitty gritty /ni-tee **gri**-tee/ *n* the basic or most important details of something.

nitwit /nit-wit/ *n* a foolish, stupid, or silly person.

no[1] /noe/ *sentence substitute* to express denial; refusal; the opposite of **yes**; it cannot be so. • *n* the answer of 'no'.

no[2] /noe/ *determiner* not ever; not any; not at all.

nobility /no-**bi**-li-tee/ *n* **1** goodness of character. **2** the class of nobles of a country.

noble /no-bul/ *adj* **1** fine in character, honourable. **2** of high rank. **3** stately. • *n* a person of high rank. • *adv* **nobly**.

nobleman /no-bul-man/ *n* a man in the noble class.

noblewoman /no-bul-woo-man/ *n* a woman in the noble class.

nobody /no-bu-dee/ *n* **1** no one. **2** (*inf*) a person of no importance.

no-brainer /no-bray-ner/ *n* (*inf*) something so obvious or simple as to require little thought.

nocturnal /noc-**tur**-nal/ *adj* **1** (*fml*) happening at night. **2** active by night.

nocturne /noc-turn/ *n* **1** a dreamy piece of music. **2** a painting of a night scene.

nocuous /noc-yu-wus/ *adj* harmful, poisonous.

nod /nod/ *vb* (**nodded, nodding**) **1** to bow the head slightly. **2** to let the head drop forward in tiredness. • *n* a slight bow of the head.

nodal /no-dal/ *adj* of or like a node.

node /node/ *n* **1** the place where a leaf joins the stem. **2** the point at which a curve crosses itself. **3** a swelling or a roundish lump, as on a tree trunk or a person's body.

nodule /nod-jul/ *n* a small rounded lump. • *adj* **nodular**.

Noël /no-wel/ *n* Christmas.

noise /noyz/ *n* **1** a sound. **2** loud or unpleasant sounds, din. • *adj* **noisy**.

noiseless /noyz-less/ *adj* not making any sound.

nomad /no-mad/ *n* **1** a wanderer. **2** a member of a group of people that has no permanent home but moves around constantly in search of food, pastures, etc.

nomadic /no-ma-dic/ *adj* wandering.

no man's land /no-manz-land/ *n* **1** land that belongs to no one. **2** land lying between two opposing armies.

nominal /nom-in-al/ *adj* **1** existing in name but not in reality. **2** having to do with a noun or nouns. **3** very small compared to others.

nominate /nom-in-ate/ *vb* **1** to put forward another's name for a certain office. **2** to appoint. • *n* **nomination**.

nominative /nom-in-a-tiv/ *adj* **1** having the name of a person on it. **2** in grammar, of or in the case of the subject of a verb.

nominee /nom-i-nee/ *n* a person who is nominated.

non- /non/ *pref* not, the opposite of, used to give a negative meaning to a word.

nonagenarian /non-i-ji-**nay**-ree-an/ *n* a person who is 90 years old or between 90 and 100.

nonchalant /non-sha-lont/ *adj* calm, unexcited, showing little interest, cool, without warmth or concern. • *n* **nonchalance**.

nondescript /non-di-**script**/ *adj* not easily described, not very interesting.

none /nun/ *pron* not one, not anyone, no persons or things.

nonentity /non-**en**-ti-tee/ *n* a person of no importance, a person of little ability or character.

nonetheless /nun-thi-**less**/ *adv* in spite of that, nevertheless.

nonexistent /non-ig-**zi**-stant/ *adj* not existing.

nonflammable /non-**fla**-ma-bul/ *adj* not likely to catch fire or burn easily.

no-no /**no**-no/ *n* (*inf*) something that is forbidden or unwise to do.

no-nonsense /no-**non**-sense/ *adj* practical and serious.

nonplus /non-**plus**/ *vb* (**nonplussed, nonplussing**) to puzzle completely; to leave speechless.

nonsense /**non**-sense/ *n* foolish or meaningless words, ideas, etc.

nonsensical /non-**sen**-si-cal/ *adj* meaningless, absurd.

nonstop /**non**-stop/ *adj and adv* without any stop or pause.

noodle /**noo**-dul/ *n* a long thin strip of pasta used especially in Chinese or Italian cooking, often eaten with sauce or soup.

nook /nook/ *n* **1** a corner. **2** an out-of-the-way place.

noon /noon/ *n* midday, 12pm.

noose /nooss/ *n* a cord or rope with a loop at one end fastened by a running knot. • *vb* to catch in a noose.

nor /nor/ *conj, prep* **1** (preceded by **neither**) and not. **2** or not; not either.

norm /norm/ *n* the usual rule, an example or standard with which others may be compared.

normal /**nor**-mal/ *adj* usual, according to what is expected, average. • *n* **normality**.

normalize /**nor**-ma-lize/ *vb, also* **normalise** to make normal.

north /north/ *n* **1** one of the chief points of the compass; opposite south. **2** (*often cap*) the northern part of the country. **3** the northern regions of the world.

north /north/, **northern** /nor-then/, **northerly** /nor-ther-lee/ *adjs* **1** having to do with the north. **2** of or from the north.

northbound /**north**-bound/ *adj* travelling north.

northeast /north-**east**/ *n* the point of the compass halfway between north and east. • *also adj.* • *adj* **northeastern**.

northern /**nor**-thern/ *adj* in, of, to, towards, or facing the north.

northerner /**nor**-ther-ner/ *n* (*often cap*) a person living in or coming from the north.

northern lights /**nor**-thern **lites**/ *npl* bright rays of coloured light sometimes seen in the region of the North Pole; common name for *aurora borealis*.

northernmost /**nor**-thern-moast/ *adj* farthest to the north.

North Pole /north **pole**/ *n* the northernmost part of the Earth, in the middle of the Arctic regions.

northward /**north**-ward/ *adv* towards the north.

northwest /north-**west**/ *n* the point of the compass halfway between north and west. • *also adj.*

northwestern /north-**we**-stern/ *adj* in, of, to, towards, or facing the northwest.

nose /noze/ *n* **1** the part of the face between the eyes and mouth that allows people and animals to breathe and smell. **2** a sense of smell. **3** the part that juts out in the front of anything. • *vb* **1** to smell. **2** to find by smell. **3** to look or search around in. **4** to discover by searching. **5** to move slowly.

nosebleed /**noze**-bleed/ *n* a bleeding from the nose.

nose dive /**noze**-dive/ *n* **1** a nose-first dive earthward by an aeroplane. **2** a sudden and great fall or drop. • *vb* to take a nose dive.

nose ring /**noze**-ring/ *n* **1** a metal ring passed through the nose of an animal for leading it about. **2** a ring worn in the nose as a piece of jewellery.

nostalgia /nos-**tal**-ja/ *n* a longing or feeling of fondness for things past. • *adj* **nostalgic**.

nostril /**nos**-tril/ *n* one of the two openings of the nose.

nosy /**no**-zee/ *adj* (*inf*) curious about the affairs of others.

not /not/ *adv* in no manner, to no degree.

notable /**no**-ta-bul/ *adj* worthy of notice, deserving to be remembered. • *n* **notability**.

notation /no-**tay**-shun/ *n* a set of signs or symbols that stand for letters, numbers, notes in music, etc.

notch /notch/ *n* a small V-shaped cut. • *vb* to make a notch in.

note /note/ *n* **1** a short letter. **2** a short written account of what is said or done. **3** a written explanation. **4** a single musical sound or the sign standing for it. **5** fame, good reputation. **6** a piece of paper money. • *vb* **1** to put down in writing. **2** to take notice of.

notebook /**note**-book/ *n* a book into which notes may be written.

noted /**no**-tid/ *adj* famous, well known.

notepad /**note**-pad/ *n* a small pad of paper.

notepaper /**note**-pay-per/ *n* paper for writing notes or letters on.

noteworthy /**note**-wur-thee/ *adj* deserving to be noticed or remembered.

nothing /**nu**-thing/ *n* 1 no thing, not anything. 2 a thing of no importance.

notice /**no**-tiss/ *n* 1 a written or printed announcement. 2 warning. 3 attention. 4 advance information. • *vb* 1 to pay attention to. 2 to see. • *adj* noticeable.

notify /**no**-ti-fie/ *vb* to inform, to make known. • *n* notification.

notion /**no**-shun/ *n* 1 idea, opinion, view. 2 a sudden desire.

notoriety /no-tu-**rie**-i-tee/ *n* bad reputation.

notorious /no-**toe**-ree-us/ *adj* well known for something bad.

notoriously /no-**toe**-ree-us-lee/ *adv* as is well known for something bad.

nougat /**noo**-gat/ *n* a white toffeelike sweet containing nuts.

noun /**noun**/ *n* in grammar, a word that names a person, place, quality, or thing.

nourish /**nu**-rish/ *vb* 1 to feed, to give what is needed to grow or stay healthy. 2 to keep in the mind.

nourishment /**nu**-rish-ment/ *n* food, especially food of value to health.

nova /**no**-va/ *n* a type of star that suddenly increases in brightness and then decreases in brightness over time.

novel /**nov**-el/ *adj* new and often of an unusual kind. • *n* a long story of which all or some of the events are imaginary.

novelist /**nov**-list/ *n* a person who writes novels.

novelty /**nov**-el-tee/ *n* 1 newness, the quality of being novel. 2 a new or unusual thing. 3 an unusual, small, cheap object.

November /no-**vem**-ber/ *n* the eleventh month of the year.

novice /**nov**-iss/ *n* 1 a beginner. 2 a person who has newly joined a religious order but has not yet taken vows.

novitiate /no-**vi**-shate/ *n* 1 the time spent as a novice. 2 a novice.

now /**now**/ *n* 1 at the present time. 2 at once.

nowadays /**now**-a-daze/ *adv* in modern times.

nowhere /**no**-whare/ *adv* in no place.

noxious /**nok**-shus/ *adj* (*fml*) poisonous, harmful, hurtful.

nozzle /**noz**-ul/ *n* a spout or pipe fitted on to the end of a hose, etc, to direct the liquid.

nuance /**nyoo**-onse/ *n* a slight difference in meaning, colour, etc.

nub /**nub**/ *n* the most important point.

nuclear /**nyoo**-clee-ar/ *adj* having to do with the atomic nucleus.

nuclear bomb /**nyoo**-clee-ar **bom**/ *n* an atomic bomb or a hydrogen bomb, capable of destroying a large area.

nuclear energy /**nyoo**-clee-ar **en**-er-jee/ *n* the energy in an atomic nucleus.

nuclear family /**nyoo**-clee-ar **fa**-mi-lee/ *n* a basic family unit consisting of parents and their children living in one household.

nuclear physics /**nyoo**-clee-ar **fi**-zics/ *n* the science of the forces within the nucleus of the atom.

nuclear reactor /**nyoo**-clee-ar ree-**ac**-tor/ *n* a machine for producing atomic energy.

nucleus /**nyoo**-clee-us/ *n* (*pl* nuclei) 1 the central part of an atom, seed, etc. 2 the central part of anything around which the rest grows up.

nude /**nyood**/ *adj* naked, wearing no clothes. • *n* a naked person.

nudge /**nudge**/ *vb* to push with the elbow. • *also n*.

nudist /**nyoo**-dist/ *n* a person who believes that it is healthy to wear no clothes.

nudity /**nyoo**-di-tee/ *n* nakedness.

nugget /**nu**-get/ *n* a lump, as of gold, silver, etc.

nuisance /**nyoo**-sanse/ *n* a person, action, or thing that annoys.

null /**nul**/ *adj*. • null and void having no legal force.

numb /**num**/ *adj* unable to feel. • *vb* to take away the power of feeling sensations. • *adj* numbing.

number /**num**-ber/ *n* 1 a word or sign that tells how many. 2 a collection of several. 3 a single copy of a magazine, etc, printed at a particular time; an issue. 4 a piece of popular music or a popular song usually forming part of a longer performance. • *vb* 1 (*fml*) to reach as a total. 2 to give a number to. 3 to include.

numerable /**nyoom**-ra-bul/ *adj* that can be numbered or counted.

numeral /**nyoom**-ral/ *n* a word or figure standing for a number.

numerate /**nyoo**-me-rate/ *vb* (*fml*) to count. • *adj* /**nyoo**-me-rit/ able to do arithmetic and mathematics. • *n* numeration.

numerator /**nyoo**-mer-ay-tor/ *n* in fractions, the number above the line, which tells how many parts there are.

numerical /nyoo-**mer**-ic-al/ *adj* having to do with numbers.

numerous /**nyoo**-mer-uss/ *adj* many.

nun /**nun**/ *n* a woman who joins a convent and vows to devote her life to the service of God.

nunnery /**nu**-ni-ree/ *n* a convent, a house for nuns.

nuptial /**nup**-shal/ *adj* (*fml*) having to do with marriage. • *npl* **nuptials** a marriage.

nurse /nurss/ *n* a person trained to look after the young, sick, or aged. • *vb* **1** to look after as a nurse. **2** to give milk from the breast, to suckle. **3** to look after with great care. **4** to keep in existence.

nursemaid /**nur**-smade/ *n* a woman hired to take care of a child or children.

nursery /**nur**-si-ree/ *n* **1** a room in a house for children to sleep or play in. **2** a place where young children are looked after. **3** a place where young plants are grown for sale.

nursery rhyme /**nur**-si-ree rime/ *n* a short, rhymed poem for children.

nursery school /**nur**-si-ree skool/ *n* a school for young children of preschool age.

nursing /**nur**-sing/ *n* the duties of or care given by a nurse.

nursing home /**nur**-sing home/ *n* a care home or rest home for those unable to care for themselves.

nurture /**nur**-chur/ *n* care and training. • *vb* **1** to care for. **2** to help to grow or develop.

nut /nut/ *n* **1** a fruit with a hard outer shell and an edible kernel inside it. **2** the edible kernel. **3** a screw that is turned on to one end of a bolt to fasten it. • **in a nutshell** in a few words.

nutcracker /**nut**-cra-ker/ *n* an instrument for cracking nuts.

nutmeg /**nut**-meg/ *n* the hard seed of a certain kind of tree, used as a spice in cooking.

nutrient /**nyoo**-tree-ent/ *n* a substance in food that is good for the body.

nutriment /**nyoo**-tri-ment/ *n* food needed for life and growth.

nutrition /nyoo-**tri**-shun/ *n* **1** food, nourishment. **2** the process of giving or getting food.

nutritious /nyoo-**tri**-shus/ *adj* good for the health of the body.

nuzzle /**nu**-zul/ *vb* **1** to push or rub with the nose. **2** to press close up to.

nylon /**nie**-lon/ *n* a strong lightweight synthetic material.

nymph /nimf/ *n* in legend, a goddess of forests, rivers, trees, etc.

O

O, o /oh/ the 15th letter of the English alphabet.

oaf /oaf/ *n* a stupid or clumsy person.

oak /oak/ *n* a hardwood tree that bears acorns.

OAP /owe-ay-**pea**/ *abbr* = **old age pensioner**: *n* a person who is old enough to receive a state pension.

oar /oar/ *n* a pole with a flat broad end, used for rowing a boat.

oarlock /**oar**-lock/ *n* a U-shaped device on the side of a boat for keeping an oar in place.

oarsman /**oarz**-man/ *n* a rower. • *n* **oarsmanship**.

oasis /oa-**ay**-sis/ *n* (*pl* **oases**) a place in the desert where there is water and trees and plants grow.

oat /oat/ *n*, **oats** /oats/ *npl* a grain often used for food.

oatcake /**oat**-cake/ *n* a thin cake made of oatmeal.

oath /oath/ *n* **1** a solemn promise, especially one made in God's name. **2** a swear word.

oatmeal /**oat**-meel/ *n* oats ground to powder.

obedient /oa-**bee**-dee-ent/ *adj* willing to do what you are told. • *n* **obedience**.

obelisk /**ob**-el-isk/ *n* a tall four-sided stone monument, narrowing to a point at its top.

obese /oa-**beess**/ *adj* very fat. • *n* **obesity**.

obey /oa-**bay**/ *vb* **1** to do what you are told. **2** to carry out.

obituary /oa-**bi**-chu-we-ree/ *n* **1** a list of deaths. **2** a newspaper account of the life of a person who has recently died.

object /**ob**-ject/ *n* **1** anything that can be perceived by the senses. **2** aim, purpose. **3** in grammar, a word governed by a verb or preposition. • *vb* /ob-**ject**/ **1** to express dislike. **2** to speak against.

objection /ob-**jec**-shun/ *n* a reason against.

objectionable /ob-**jec**-shu-na-bul/ *adj* deserving to be disliked, unpleasant.

objective /ob-**jec**-tiv/ *adj* not depending on, or influenced by, personal opinions. • *n* aim, purpose. • *adv* **objectively**.

objector /ob-**jec**-tor/ *n* a person who objects.

obligation /ob-li-**gay**-shun/ *n* **1** a duty, a promise that must be kept. **2** gratitude due to another for kindness or help.

obligatory /o-**bli**-ga-toe-ree/ *adj* that which has to be done (e.g. as a duty), compulsory.

oblige /o-**blije**/ *vb* **1** to force or make it necessary to do. **2** to do a kindness to or service for.

obliging /o-**blie**-jing/ *adj* ready to help, kind.

oblique /o-**bleek**/ *adj* **1** slanting. **2** indirect, roundabout.

obliterate /o-**bli**-te-rate/ *vb* **1** to destroy utterly. **2** to blot out. • *n* **obliteration**.

oblivion /o-**bli**-vee-on/ *n* **1** the state of being unaware, forgetfulness. **2** the state of being forgotten.

oblivious /o-**bli**-vee-us/ *adj* unaware of, not paying attention to.

oblong /**ob**-long/ *n* **1** a four-sided figure with all angles right angles and one pair of sides longer than the other pair. **2** a figure or object so shaped. • *adj* having this shape.

obnoxious /ob-**nok**-shus/ *adj* very unpleasant, hateful.

oboe /**o**-bo/ *n* a wooden wind instrument. • *n* **oboist**.

obscene /ob-**seen**/ *adj* disgusting, indecent. • *adv* **obscenely**. • *n* **obscenity**.

obscure /ob-**scyoor**/ *adj* **1** not clear in meaning. **2** not well-known, not famous. • *vb* **1** to hide from view. **2** to make more difficult.

obscurity /ob-**scyoo**-ri-tee/ *n* the state of being obscure.

observance /ob-**zer**-vanse/ *n* **1** the act of observing. **2** the act of obeying.

observant /ob-**zer**-vant/ *adj* quick to notice things.

observation /ob-zer-**vay**-shun/ *n* **1** the act, power, or habit of observing. **2** a remark.

observatory /ob-**zer**-va-toe-ree/ *n* a place from which scientists study the stars, the planets, and the heavens.

observe /ob-**zerv**/ *vb* **1** to see, to notice. **2** to watch carefully. **3** to carry out. **4** to say, to make a remark.

observer /ob-**zer**-ver/ *n* **1** a person who observes. **2** a person whose job it is to take careful notice of what is going on.

obsess /ob-**sess**/ *vb* to take up all your thoughts and interest. • *adj* **obsessive**.

obsession /ob-**se**-shun/ *n* an idea or interest that takes up all your attention so that you never think about other things.

obsolete /ob-so-**leet**/ *adj* no longer in use, out-of-date.

obstacle /**ob**-sta-cul/ *n* that which is in the way and prevents progress.

obstacle race /**ob**-sta-cul race/ *n* a race in which the runners have to find their way under, over, or through certain objects placed on the course to hinder them.

obstetrician /ob-ste-**tri**-shun/ *n* a doctor who specializes in obstetrics.

obstetrics /ob-**stet**-riks/ *n* the branch of medicine concerned with childbirth.

obstinate /**ob**-sti-nit/ *adj* **1** determined to hold to your own opinions, etc; stubborn. **2** not easy to cure or remove. • *n* **obstinacy**.

obstruct /ob-**struct**/ *vb* **1** to stop up. **2** to prevent from moving or acting freely.

obstruction /ob-**struc**-shun/ *n* **1** a cause of delay. **2** an obstacle.

obstructive /ob-**struc**-tiv/ *adj* causing delay.

obtain /ob-**tane**/ *vb* to get.

obtainable /ob-**tay**-na-bul/ *adj* that can be gotten.

obtuse /ob-**tyoos**/ *adj* **1** stupid, slow to understand. **2** (*of an angle*) greater than a right angle.

obvious /**ob**-vee-us/ *adj* easily seen or understood. • *adv* **obviously**.

occasion /o-**cay**-zhun/ *n* **1** a particular time. **2** a special event. **3** (*fml*) a reason. **4** (*fml*) opportunity. • *vb* to cause.

occasional /o-**cay**-zhnal/ *adj* **1** happening now and then. **2** having to do with a particular event or occasion. • *adv* **occasionally**.

occult /o-**cult**/ *adj* secret, mysterious, having to do with magic.

occupancy /**ok**-yu-pan-see/ *n* **1** act of going to live in a house. **2** the time during which you live there.

occupant /**oc**-yu-pant/, **occupier** /**oc**-yu-pie-er/ *n* the person living in a house.

occupation /oc-yu-**pay**-shun/ *n* **1** act of occupying. **2** the time during which a place is occupied. **3** your job. **4** that which you are doing at a certain time. • *adj* **occupational**.

occupy /**oc**-yu-pie/ *vb* **1** to take possession of. **2** to live in. **3** to fill. **4** to keep busy. **5** to take up.

occur /u-**cur**/ *vb* (**occurred**, **occurring**) **1** to happen. **2** to come to the mind. **3** to be found here and there.

occurrence /u-**cu**-rense/ *n* a happening, an event.

ocean /**o**-shin/ *n* **1** the vast body of salt water surrounding the land on the earth. **2** a large sea. • *adj* **oceanic**.

ocelot /**oss**-uh-lot/ *n* a spotted wildcat found in parts of America

o'clock /u-**clock**/ *adv* according to the clock.

octagon /**oc**-ta-gon/ *n* a figure or shape with eight angles and sides.

octagonal /oc-**tag**-nal/ *adj* eight-sided.

octave /**oc**-tave/ *n* **1** (*mus*) a scale of eight notes beginning and ending with a note of the same tone but a different pitch. **2** a stanza of eight lines.

octet /oc-**tet**/ *n* a piece of music for eight singers or instruments.

October /oc-**toe**-ber/ *n* the tenth month of the year.

octogenarian /oc-ta-je-**nay**-ree-an/ *n* a person who is 80 years old or between 80 and 90.

octopus /**oc**-to-pus/ *n* a sea creature with eight arms.

odd /odd/ *adj* **1** (*of a number*) not even, that cannot be divided by two without leaving a remainder of one. **2** strange, unusual. **3** unmatched. • *adv* **oddly**.

oddity /**od**-i-tee/ *n* something strange or unusual, a strange person.

oddment /**od**-ment/ *n* a piece left over.

odds /odz/ *npl* the chances in favour of a certain happening or result. • **at odds with** on bad terms with. • **by all odds** in every way, without question. • **odds and ends** extra pieces or things of various kinds.

ode /ode/ *n* a poem in which the writer expresses his or her ideas or feelings on a certain subject at some length.

odious /**oe**-dee-us/ *adj* hateful, disgusting.

odium /**oe**-dee-um/ *n* (*fml*) hatred, widespread dislike or blame.

odor US variant of **odour**.

odorous /**oe**-du-rus/ *adj* having a smell, especially a characteristic one.

odour /**oe**-dur/ *n*, *also* **odor** (*US*) any smell, pleasant or unpleasant.

odourless /**oe**-dur-less/ *adj*, *also* **odorless** (*US*) having no smell.

odyssey /**od**-i-see/ *n* (*lit*) a long adventurous journey.

o'er /**oar**/ *prep*, *adv* (*lit*) over.

oesophagus /i-**sof**-a-gus/ *n*, *also* **esophagus** (*US*) the tube that goes from your throat to your stomach.

of /ov/ *prep* **1** belonging to. **2** relating to. **3** made of. **4** from.

off /off/ *adv* **1** away. **2** distant. • *adj* **1** not happening. **2** (*inf*) not fit to eat, bad, rotten. • *prep* away from, not on.

offal /**of**-al/ *n* the inner organs of an animal, sold as food or regarded as waste matter.

offence /o-**fense**/ *n*, *also* **offense** (*US*) **1** a wrongful act. **2** hurt done to the feelings, a feeling that you have been insulted.

offend /o-**fend**/ *vb* **1** to displease, to hurt someone's feelings. **2** (*fml*) to do wrong. **3** to be unpleasant or disagreeable.

offender /o-**fen**-der/ *n* **1** a person who does wrong. **2** a person who causes offence.

offense US variant of **offence**.

offensive /o-**fen**-siv/ *adj* **1** unpleasant. **2** insulting. **3** having to do with attack. • *n* an attack.

offer /**off**-er/ *vb* **1** to give someone the chance of taking. **2** to say that you are willing. **3** to give as a sacrifice. • *n* **1** act of offering. **2** the thing or amount offered.

offering /**off**-er-ing/ *n* **1** (*fml or hum*) a gift. **2** (*old*) that which is sacrificed to God. **3** a sum of money given at a religious service, used for the work of the church.

offhand /off-**hand**/ *adj* careless, thoughtless.

office /**off**-is/ *n* **1** a special duty. **2** a job, especially one in the service of the public. **3** a room or building in which business is carried on. **4** (*fml*) an act of kindness.

officer /**off**-i-ser/ *n* a person who holds a post with certain powers or duties, especially in the armed forces.

official /o-**fi**-shal/ *adj* **1** having to do with an office or the duties attached to it. **2** given out or announced by those with the right to do so. • *n* a person who holds a post with certain powers or duties. • *adv* **officially.**

officialdom /o-**fi**-shal-dom/ *n* **1** all those holding public office. **2** an unbending attitude of holding to regulations and routine.

off-licence /**off**-lie-sense/ *n* a shop that sells alcoholic drink to be drunk elsewhere.

off-peak /**off**-peek/ *adj* happening when, for example, the city is less busy.

off-putting /**off**-poo-ting/ *adj* discouraging.

offset /off-**set**/ *vb* (**offset, offsetting**) to make up for.

offshoot /**off**-shoot/ *n* **1** a branch or shoot growing out from the main stem of a plant. **2** something growing out of something else.

offshore /off-**shore**/ *adj* towards the sea. • *adv* **offshore.**

offside /off-**side**/ *adv, adj* in football, in a position disallowed by the rules when the ball was last kicked or struck.

offspring /**off**-spring/ *n* a child or children.

often /**off**-en/ *adv* frequently.

ogle /o-gul/ *vb* to look sidewise at, to look or stare at because of admiration or physical attraction.

ogre /o-gur/ *n* in fairy tales, a man-eating giant. • *f* **ogress.**

ohm /oam/ *n* the unit of measurement of electrical resistance.

oil /oil/ *n* a greasy liquid obtained from vegetable, animal, or mineral sources, and used as a food, fuel, lubricant, etc. • *npl* oil paints or painting. • *vb* to put or drop oil on, as on the parts of a machine to make them work smoothly.

oil painting /**oil** pane-ting/ *n* a picture done in oils.

oilskin /**oil**-skin/ *n* a cloth made waterproof with oil.

oily /oi-lee/ *adj* **1** covered with oil. **2** greasy.

ointment /**oint**-ment/ *n* an oily paste rubbed on the skin to heal cuts or sores.

OK /o-**kay**/ *adv, adj* (*inf*) all right.

old /oald/ *adj* **1** not new. **2** aged. **3** belonging to the past. **4** not fresh.

olden *adj* (*old*) of former times. • *npl* olden days.

old-fashioned /oald-fa-shund/ *adj* out-of-date.

olive /ol-iv/ *n* **1** an evergreen tree bearing a small, sharp-tasting fruit, from which oil can be obtained. **2** its fruit, used as food. • *adj* yellowish green. • *n* **olive oil.**

olive branch /ol-iv branch/ *n* a sign of peace.

olive-skinned /ol-iv-skind/ *adj* having a yellowish-brown skin.

Olympic /o-**lim**-pic/ *adj* having to do with Olympia in Greece, and the games held there every four years in ancient times.

Olympic Games /o-**lim**-pic **gaymz**/ *n* an international athletic contest held every four years, each time in a different country.

omelette /**om**-let/ *n, also* **omelet** (*US*) eggs beaten and fried in a pan, usually served folded in half.

omen /o-men/ *n* a sign of a future event, good or bad.

ominous /**om**-in-us/ *adj* signifying future trouble or disaster.

omit /o-**mit**/ *vb* (**omitted, omitting**) **1** to fail to do. **2** to leave out. • *n* **omission.**

omnibus /**om**-ni-bus/ *n* **1** (*old*) a bus. **2** a book containing several works by the same author or on the same subject.

omnivorous /om-**niv**-rus/ *adj* (*fml or hum*) eating all kinds of food.

on /on/ *adv* **1** being worn. **2** forward. • *adj* in operation. • *prep* on top of.

once /wunse/ *adv* **1** on one occasion only. **2** formerly. • **once and for all** once and never again. • **at once** immediately.

oncoming /on-cu-ming/ *adj* approaching.

one /wun/ *adj* **1** the number coming before two. **2** single. • *pron* a person.

one-off /wun-**off**/ *adj* happening or done only once. • *n* **1** something that is done or made only once. **2** (*inf*) someone who is completely different from other people.

one-sided /wun-**sie**-did/ *adj* favouring one party or point of view only.

one-way /wun-**way**/ *adj* of a street, allowing movement of traffic in one direction only.

ongoing /on-go-wing/ *adj* continuing, continuing to develop.

onion /un-yun/ *n* a strong-smelling edible bulb, often used in cooking.

online /on-**line**/ *adj* controlled by or connected to a central computer or connected to the Internet. • *also adv*.

onlooker /awn-loo-ker/ *n* a spectator, a person who looks at what is happening but takes no part in it.

only /oan-lee/ *adv* no more than. • *conj* except that.

only child /oan-lee childe/ *n* a person who has no brothers or sisters.

onomatopoeia /on-o-ma-to-pay-a/ *n* forming words by imitating sounds (e.g. hiss, bang). • *adj* **onomatopoeic**.

onrush /on-rush/ *n* a rapid advance.

onset /on-set/ *n* the first attack of or the beginning of.

onshore /on-shore/ *adj* towards the shore. • *adv* **onshore**.

onslaught /on-slot/ *n* a fierce attack.

onward /on-ward/ *adj* forward. • *adv* **onwards**.

onyx /aw-niks/ *n* a precious stone containing layers of different colours.

ooze /ooz/ *n* soft mud, slime. • *vb* **1** to flow very slowly. **2** to have flowing from.

opacity *see* **opaque**.

opal /oa-pal/ *n* a white precious stone that changes colour when turned in the light.

opaque /oa-**pake**/ *adj* that cannot be seen through, letting no light through. • *n* **opacity**.

open /oa-pen/ *adj* **1** not shut, uncovered. **2** ready for business. **3** not hidden. **4** free from obstructions. **5** public. **6** sincere. **7** clear. • *vb* **1** to make or become open. **2** to unlock. **3** to begin. • **in the open air** outside. • **open up** to build roads, etc, in a country to make progress possible.

open-handed /oa-pen-**han**-did/ *adj* (*fml*) generous.

opening /ope-ning/ *n* **1** beginning. **2** a gap, a way in or out. **3** an opportunity.

openly /oa-pen-lee/ *adv* publicly, not secretly.

open-minded /oa-pen-**mine**-did/ *adj* ready to consider new ideas, unprejudiced.

opera[1] /aw-pra/ *n* a musical drama in which all or some of the words are sung.

opera[2] *see* **opus**.

opera glasses /aw-pra gla-siz/ *npl* glasses used in the theatre to magnify the stage and players.

operate /aw-pe-rate/ *vb* **1** (*machine*) to work or to cause to work. **2** (*surgeon*) to cut the body in order to cure or treat a diseased part.

operatic /aw-pe-ra-tic/ *adj* having to do with opera.

operating system /aw-pe-ray-ting si-stem/ *n* the software that controls the operation of a computer.

operation /aw-pe-**ray**-shun/ *n* **1** action. **2** the way a thing works. **3** the cutting of the body by a doctor or surgeon to cure or treat a diseased or injured part.

operative /aw-pra-tiv/ *adj* **1** in action. **2** having effect. • *n* a worker in a factory.

operator /aw-pe-ray-tor/ *n* a person who looks after a machine.

operetta /aw-pe-re-ta/ *n* a short, not too serious, musical play.

ophthalmic /of-thal-mic/ *adj* having to do with the eye(s).

opinion /o-**pin**-yun/ *n* **1** that which you think or believe about something. **2** judgement.

opinionated /o-**pin**-yu-nay-tid/, **opinionative** /o-**pin**-yu-na-tiv/ *adjs* sure that your opinions are correct.

opium /o-pee-yum/ *n* a sleep-producing drug made from poppy seeds.

opossum /o-**poss**-um/ *n* a small animal that carries its young in a pouch.

opponent /o-**po**-nent/ *n* an enemy, a person whom you try to overcome in a game, argument, etc.

opportune /op-or-**toon**/ *adj* happening at the right time.

opportunist /op-or-**too**-nist/ *n* a person who takes advantage of opportunities that occur). • *adj* **opportunistic**.

opportunity /op-or-**too**-ni-tee/ *n* happening at the right time.

oppose /o-**poaz**/ *vb* **1** to act or speak against. **2** to resist.

opposite /**op**-u-zit/ *adj* **1** facing. **2** in the same position on the other side. **3** different in every way. • *n* something in every way different. • *adv*, *prep* across from.

opposition /op-u-**zi**-shun/ *n* **1** the act of going or speaking against, resistance. **2** (*often cap*) in politics, the party that criticizes or resists the governing party.

oppress /o-**press**/ *vb* **1** to govern harshly or unjustly, to treat cruelly. **2** to make gloomy or anxious. • *n* **oppression**.

oppressive /o-**pre**-siv/ *adj* **1** harsh and unjust. **2** (*of the weather*) hot and tiring.

opt /opt/ *vb* to choose. • **opt out** to choose not to do something.

optic /op-tic/, **optical** /**op**-ti-cal/ *adjs* having to do with sight or the eye(s).

optician /op-**ti**-shan/ *n* a person who makes or sells glasses for the eyes.

optics /**op**-tics/ *n* the science of light or sight.

optimal /op-ti-mal/ *adj* best.

optimism /**op**-ti-mi-zum/ *n* the belief that all

that happens is for the best, cheerful hope that all will go well.

optimist /op-ti-mist/ *n* a cheerfully hopeful person.

optimistic /op-ti-mi-stic/ *adj* having to do with or characterized by optimism. • *adv* **optimistically**.

optimum /op-ti-mum/ *adj, n* best.

option /op-shun/ *n* choice.

optional /op-shnal/ *adj* that may be done or not, by choice.

opulence /op-yu-lense/ *n* (*fml*) riches, wealth.

opulent /op-yu-lent/ *adj* (*fml*) rich, wealthy.

opus /oa-pus/ *n* (*pl* **opuses** *or* **opera**) **1** (*fml*) a work of art. **2** a musical work numbered in order of composition.

or /awr/ *conj* used to link alternatives.

oracle /aw-ra-cul/ *n* **1** in legend, the answer given to a question by or on behalf of a god. **2** the place where such answers were given. **3** a person who answers on behalf of a god. **4** (*often hum*) a wise or knowledgeable person.

oral /oar-al/ *adj* spoken, not written. • *adv* **orally**.

orange /aw-ranj/ *n* **1** a juicy fruit with a reddish yellow skin. **2** the tree bearing it. **3** its colour, reddish-yellow. • *adj* of orange colour.

orangutan /aw-rang-u-tan/ *n* a large man-like ape with long arms.

oration /aw-ray-shun/ *n* (*fml*) a formal public speech.

orator /aw-ra-tor/ *n* a skilled public speaker.

orb /awrb/ *n* (*lit*) a sphere, a round object.

orbit /awr-bit/ *n* the curved path of a planet, comet, rocket, etc, around a larger heavenly body. • *adj* **orbital**.

orchard /awr-chard/ *n* a field in which fruit trees are grown.

orchestra /awr-ke-stra/ *n* **1** a group of musicians skilled in different instruments who play together. **2** the place where they sit in a hall or theatre.

orchestral /awr-ke-stral/ *adj* suitable for performance by an orchestra.

orchestrate /awr-ke-strate/ *vb* **1** to arrange for an orchestra. **2** to organize or arrange. • *n* **orchestration**.

orchid /awr-kid/ *n* a showy flower with unusually shaped petals.

ordain /awr-dane/ *vb* **1** (*fml*) to order. **2** to admit to office as a priest or minister of religion.

ordeal /awr-deel/ *n* a difficult, painful experience.

order /awr-der/ *n* **1** a methodical arrangement. **2** a command. **3** rank, class. **4** obedience to law. **5** tidiness. **6** an instruction to make or supply something. **7** a body or brotherhood of people of the same profession, etc; a religious brotherhood obeying a certain rule. • *vb* **1** to arrange. **2** to command. **3** to give an instruction to make or supply.

orderly /awr-der-lee/ *adj* **1** tidy, well-arranged. **2** well-behaved. • *n* **1** a soldier who carries the orders and messages of an officer. **2** a hospital attendant.

ordinal /awr-di-nal/ *adj* showing the place in an order.

ordinance /awr-di-nanse/ *n* (*fml*) a law, a command.

ordinary /awr-di-ne-ree/ *adj* usual, common, not exceptional. • *adv* **ordinarily**.

ordination /awr-di-nay-shun/ *n* the act or ceremony of admitting to office as a priest or minister of religion.

ore /ore/ *n* rock from which metal is obtained.

oregano /aw-re-ga-no/ *n* the dried leaves of the herb marjoram, used in cooking.

organ /awr-gan/ *n* **1** part of an animal or plant that serves some special purpose. **2** a large musical instrument supplied with wind through pipes and played by a keyboard. **3** a means of conveying views or information to the public (e.g. a newspaper).

organic /awr-ga-nic/ *adj* **1** having to do with an organ. **2** produced by living organs. **3** grown without the use of artificial fertilizers. • *adv* **organically**.

organise *see* **organize**.

organism /awr-ga-ni-zum/ *n* **1** any living thing. **2** anything in which the parts all work together to serve one purpose.

organist /awr-ga-nist/ *n* a person who plays the organ.

organization /awr-ga-ni-zay-shun/ *n also* **organisation 1** orderly arrangement. **2** a group of people working systematically to carry out a common purpose. • *adj* **organizational**, *also* **organisational**.

organize /awr-ga-nize/ *vb*, *also* **organise 1** to put together in an orderly way, to make to work systematically. **2** to arrange. • *n* **organizer**, *also* **organiser**.

orgasm /awr-ga-zm/ *n* the climax of sexual excitement.

orgy /awr-jee/ *n* **1** a wild or drunken party, with excessive drinking and indiscriminate sexual activity. **2** a wild excess of something.

orient /aw-ree-ent/ *vb* to orientate.

Orient /aw-ree-ent/ *n* the East.

oriental /aw-ree-en-tal/ *adj* Eastern, Asian. • *n* a native of an Eastern or Asian country.

Orientalist /oa-ree-en-ta-list/ *n* a person who studies Eastern languages.

orientate /aw-ree-en-tate/ *vb* **1** to find out north, south, east, and west from the point where you are standing. **2** to arrange or direct towards. • *n* **orientation**.

orienteering /aw-ree-en-tee-ring/ *n* the sport of following a route on foot as quickly as possible, using a map and compass.

orifice /aw-ri-fiss/ *n* (*fml*) an opening.

origami /aw-ri-ga-mee/ *n* the Japanese art of paper-folding.

origin /aw-ri-jin/ *n* **1** the place or point at which a thing begins; the beginning. **2** the cause.

original /aw-ri-ji-nal/ *adj* **1** new, not thought of before. **2** first in order. **3** ready to think or act in a new way. **4** not copied. • *n* **1** an original work of art, etc. **2** a creative or eccentric person. • *adv* **originally**.

originality /aw-ri-ji-na-li-tee/ *n* the ability to think or act in a new way.

originate /aw-ri-ji-nate/ *vb* **1** to bring into being. **2** to come into being.

oriole /aw-ree-ole/ *n* a bird with golden-yellow feathers.

ornament /awr-na-ment/ *n* that which decorates or makes more attractive. • *vb* **ornament** to decorate. • *n* **ornamentation**.

ornamental /awr-na-men-tal/ *adj* decorative.

ornate /awr-nate/ *adj* with a great deal of ornament, richly decorated.

ornithology /awr-na-thol-o-jee/ *n* the study of birds. • *n* **ornithologist** *n* a person who studies birds.

orphan /awr-fan/ *n* a child whose parents are dead. • *vb* to cause to become an orphan. • *also adj*.

orphanage /awr-fa-nidge/ *n* a home for orphans.

orthodontist /awr-tha-dawn-tist/ *n* a dentist who straightens teeth.

orthodox /awr-tho-doks/ *adj* **1** having the same beliefs or opinions as most other people. **2** agreeing with accepted belief. • *n* **orthodoxy**.

orthopaedic /awr-tho-pee-dic/ *adj*, *also* **orthopedic** (*US*) having to do with injury or diseases of the bones or joints.

osprey /aw-spray/ *n* a hawk that feeds on fish.

ostensible /aw-sten-si-bul/ *adj* as far as can be seen, apparent. • *adv* **ostensibly**.

ostentatious /aw-sten-tay-shus/ *adj* showy, fond of display.

osteopath /aw-stee-o-path/ *n* a person who practises osteopathy.

osteopathy /aw-stee-op-a-thee/ *n* cure of pain or disease by massage or otherwise manipulating the bones.

ostracize /aw-stra-size/ *vb*, *also* **ostracise** to drive out of society, to refuse to have anything to do with. • *n* **ostracism**.

ostrich /aw-strich/ *n* a large swift-running bird valued for its feathers.

other /u-ther/ *adj* **1** one of two things. **2** addition. **3** those not mentioned, present, etc.

otherwise /u-ther-wize/ *adv* **1** in a different way. **2** if this were not so.

otter /aw-ter/ *n* a fish-eating animal of the weasel family.

ottoman /aw-to-man/ *adj* a sofa without back or arms.

ought /awt/ *vb* should.

ounce /ounse/ *n* **1** an imperial unit of weight ($^1/_{16}$ lb). **2** a small amount.

our /our/ *adj* belonging to us. • *poss prons* **ours, ourselves** /our-selvz/.

oust /oust/ *vb* to put out, to drive out.

out /out/ *adv* **1** not inside. **2** away. • *prep* out of, out through, outside. • *adj* **1** external. **2** asleep or unconscious. •

out-and-out /ou-tan-(d)out/ *adj* thorough.

outback /out-back/ *n* a remote area of Australia with very few inhabitants.

outbid /out-bid/ *vb* to offer a higher price than another.

outboard /out-board/ *adj* attached to the outside of a boat.

outbreak /out-brake/ *n* a sudden beginning, a breaking out.

outburst /out-burst/ *n* a bursting out, an explosion.

outcast /out-cast/ *adj* driven away from your home and friends. • *n* a person who is so driven away.

outcome /out-come/ *n* the result.

outcrop /out-crop/ *n* a layer of rock that shows above the surface of the earth.

outcry /out-cry/ *n* widespread complaint.

outdated /out-day-tid/ *adj* old-fashioned, out-of-date.

outdo /out-doo/ *vb* to do better than.

outdoor /out-dore/ *adj* done in the open air.

outdoors /out-doarz/ *adv* in the open air. • *also n*.

outer /ou-ter/ *adj* **1** farther out. **2** outside.

outermost /ou-ter-moast/ *adj* farthest out.

outer space /ou-ter space/ *n* space beyond the earth's atmosphere.

outfit /out-fit/ *n* **1** all the articles necessary for a certain job. **2** a set of articles of clothing.

outgoings /out-go-ingz/ *npl* the money spent.

outgrow /out-gro/ *vb* **1** to grow taller than. **2** to grow too big or too old for.

outing /ou-ting/ *n* a short trip made for pleasure.

outlast /out-last/ *vb* to last longer than.

outlaw /out-law/ *n* (*old*) someone whose person and property are no longer protected by the law. • *vb* **1** to declare an outlaw. **2** to declare not legal.

outlet /out-let/ *n* **1** an opening outward. **2** an activity that allows you to make use of your powers or of a particular ability.

outline /out-line/ *n* **1** a line showing the shape of a thing. **2** an account of the most important points, etc. • *vb* **1** to draw in outline. **2** to describe without giving details.

outlive /out-liv/ *vb* to live longer than.

outlook /out-look/ *n* **1** a view. **2** what seems likely to happen in future. **3** a point of view.

outmoded /out-mo-did/ *adj* out of fashion.

outnumber /out-num-ber/ *vb* to be greater in number than.

out-of-date /out-ov-date/ *adj* old-fashioned.

outpatient /out-pay-shent/ *n* a person who visits a hospital for treatment but does not stay there overnight.

outpost /out-poast/ *n* **1** a defended place close to enemy territory and in front of the main positions. **2** a settlement far from towns and main roads.

output /out-poot/ *n* the total amount produced by a machine, factory, worker, etc.

outrage /out-rage/ *n* **1** a violent and wicked deed. **2** a deed that shocks or causes widespread anger. • *vb* **1** to injure. **2** to insult. • *adj* **outrageous**.

outrider /out-rie-der/ *n* a person who rides on horseback or on a motorcycle beside or in front of a vehicle.

outright /out-rite/ *adv* **1** completely and at once. **2** openly, frankly. • *adj* complete.

outrun /out-run/ *vb* to run faster than.

outset /out-set/ *n* beginning.

outside /out-side/ *n* **1** the outer part or parts. **2** the part farthest from the centre. • *adj* **1** being on the outside, external. **2** outdoor. **3** slight. • *adv* on or to the outside. • *prep* on or to the exterior of, beyond.

outsider /out-sie-der/ *n* **1** a person who is not accepted as a member of a certain group. **2** a person who is believed to have little chance of winning.

outskirts /out-skirts/ *npl* the parts of a town or city farthest from the centre.

outsmart /out-smart/ *v* to outwit someone.

outsource /out-source/ *vb* to give work to, or obtain services from, people who are not employed within an organization.

outspoken /out-spo-ken/ *adj* saying just what you think, frank.

outstanding /out-stan-ding/ *adj* **1** exceptionally good. **2** still in existence.

outward /out-ward/ *adj* **1** on the outside or surface. **2** away from a place. • *adv* **outwards**, **outwardly**.

outwit /out-wit/ *vb* to outdo or overcome by greater cleverness, to deceive.

ova *see* **ovum**.

oval /oa-val/ *adj* egg-shaped. • *n* an oval shape or figure.

ovary /oa-va-ree/ *n* **1** a bodily organ in which eggs are formed. **2** the seed case of a plant.

ovation /oa-vay-shun/ *n* enthusiastic applause.

oven /u-ven/ *n* a small chamber heated by a fire or stove and used for cooking.

over /oa-ver/ *prep* **1** above. **2** across. **3** more than. • *adv* **1** above. **2** across. **3** from one side to the other or another. **4** more than the quantity assigned. **5** completed. **6** from beginning to end.

overalls /oa-ver-awlz/ *npl* a garment worn over your usual clothing to keep it clean.

overawe /oa-ver-aw/ *vb* to frighten into obeying or being silent, to fill with silent respect.

overbalance /oa-ver-ba-lanse/ *vb* **1** to lean too much in one direction and fall. **2** to cause to fall in this way.

overbearing /oa-ver-bay-ring/ *adj* proud and commanding.

overboard /oa-ver-board/ *adv* over the side of a ship.

overcast /oa-ver-cast/ *adj* clouded over.

overcharge /oa-ver-charge/ *vb* to ask for too great a price.

overcoat /oa-ver-coat/ *n* a warm outer garment.

overcome /oa-ver-cum/ *vb* **1** to defeat. **2** to get the better of.

overdo /oa-ver-doo/ *vb* **1** to do too much. **2** to cook for too long.

overdose /oa-ver-doass/ *n* too large a dose. • *also vb*.

overdraft /oa-ver-draft/ *n* the amount of money drawn from a bank in excess of what is available in an account.

overdraw /oa-ver-draw/ *vb* to take more from a bank than you have in your account.

overdress /oa-ver-dress/ *vb* to dress too well for the occasion.

overdue /oa-ver-dyoo/ *adj* after the time fixed or due.

overestimate /oa-ver-e-sti-mate/ *vb* to set too high a value on.

overexpose /oa-ver-ek-spoaz/ *vb* to expose a photographic film to too much light.

overflow /oa-ver-flo/ *vb* to flood, to flow over the edge or limits of. • *n* /oa-ver-flo/ **1** what flows over the sides. **2** the amount by which something is too much.

overgrown /oa-ver-groan/ *adj* grown beyond the normal size.

overhand /oa-ver-hand/ *adj* something done with your arm raised above your shoulder.

overhaul /oa-ver-**haul**/ *vb* to examine thoroughly and carry out necessary repairs or improvements. • *n* /oa-ver-haul/.

overhead /oa-ver-**head**/ *adj* and *adv* in the sky, above.

overheads /oa-ver-heads/ *npl* the cost of running a business.

overhear /oa-ver-**heer**/ *vb* to hear what you are not intended to hear.

overjoyed /oa-ver-**joyd**/ *adj* extremely happy.

overland /oa-ver-land/ *adv* across land (not sea). • *adj* passing by land.

overlap /oa-ver-**lap**/ *vb* to cover partly and go beyond.

overleaf /oa-ver-**leef**/ *adv* on the reverse side of a page.

overload /oa-ver-**load**/ *vb* to add too heavy a load.

overlook /oa-ver-**look**/ *vb* **1** to look down on from above. **2** to forgive, to let off without punishment. **3** not to notice, to miss.

overnight /oa-ver-**nite**/ *adv* during the night. • *adj* done in or lasting the night.

overpower /oa-ver-**pow**-er/ *vb* to defeat by greater strength.

overpowering /oa-ver-**pow**-er-ing/ *adj* too great to bear.

overrate /oa-ver-**rate**/ *vb* to think a person or thing better than he, she, or it really is.

override /oa-ver-**ride**/ *vb* to decide to pay no attention to.

overrule /oa-ver-**rool**/ *vb* to use your power to rule out the decision or judgment of another.

overrun /oa-ver-**run**/ *vb* **1** to spread over in large numbers. **2** to continue beyond the expected time.

oversaw *see* oversee.

oversea(s) /oa-ver-**see(z)**/ *adj* and *adv* across the sea.

oversee /oa-ver-**see**/ *vb* (*pt* **oversaw**, *pp* **overseen**) to direct the work of others. • *n* overseer.

overshadow /oa-ver-**sha**-doe/ *vb* **1** to make less happy. **2** to make seem less important.

overshoot /oa-ver-**shoot**/ (*pt, pp* **overshot**) *vb* to go beyond before stopping.

oversight /**oa**-ver-site/ *n* a mistake, a failure to do something.

oversleep /oa-ver-**sleep**/ *vb* (*pt, pp* **overslept**) to sleep later than intended.

overstep /oa-ver-**step**/ *vb* to go beyond the limits of.

overt /oa-**vert**/ *adj* done or said openly, not hidden. • *adv* overtly.

overtake /oa-ver-**take**/ *vb* **1** to pass while travelling in the same direction. **2** to

become larger in number or amount, more important, etc. **3** to affect someone suddenly.

overthrow /oa-ver-**throe**/ *vb* to defeat, to remove from power. • *also n*.

overtime /**oa**-ver-time/ *n* time worked beyond the regular hours. • *also adj and adv*.

overture /oa-ver-**choor**/ *n* **1** a proposal, an offer. **2** the music played by the orchestra before an opera, etc.

overturn /oa-ver-**turn**/ *vb* **1** to turn upside down. **2** to make fall, to defeat, to ruin.

overweight /oa-ver-**wate**/ *adj* weighing more than the proper amount. • *n* excess weight.

overwhelm /oa-ver-**whelm**/ *vb* **1** to defeat utterly. **2** to overcome all your powers, to make feel helpless. • *adj* overwhelming. • *adv* overwhelmingly.

overwork /oa-ver-**wurk**/ *vb* to work too hard. • *n* too much work.

ovoid /**oa**-void/ *adj* egg-shaped.

ovum /**oa**-vum/ *n* (*pl* ova) an egg.

owe /**oa**/ *vb* **1** to be in debt to. **2** to be obliged to (someone), to feel grateful to. • **owing to** because of.

owl /**owl**/ *n* a night bird of prey.

owlet /**ow**-let/ *n* a young owl.

own /**oan**/ *adj* belonging to yourself. • *vb* to possess. • **own up** to admit. • *n* owner. • *n* ownership.

ox /**oks**/ *n* (*pl* oxen) a bull or cow. • *npl* oxen cattle.

oxidation /ok-si-**day**-shun/ *n* compounding with oxygen.

oxide /**ok**-side/ *n* a compound of oxygen in another element.

oxidize /**ok**-si-dize/ *vb*, *also* oxidise to unite with oxygen.

oxygen /**ok**-si-jen/ *n* a gas without colour, taste, or smell that is present in air and water, and is necessary for all life.

oxygenate /**ok**-si-je-nate/, **oxygenize** /**ok**-si-je-nize/, *also* oxygenise *vb* to mix with oxygen.

oxymoron /ok-si-**mo**-ron/ *n* a figure of speech in which an adjective seems to contradict the noun it accompanies.

oyster /**oy**-ster/ *n* an edible shellfish with a double shell in which pearls are sometimes found.

oyster-catcher /**oy**-ster-ca-cher/ *n* a bird of the seashore.

ozone /**oa**-zone/ *n* **1** a kind of colourless gas with a chlorinelike smell. **2** (*inf*) clean, bracing air as found at the shore.

ozone layer /**oa**-zone lair/ *n* a layer of ozone in the stratosphere that absorbs ultraviolet rays from the sun.

P

P, p /pee/ the 16th letter of the English alphabet.

pace /payss/ *n* **1** a step with the foot. **2** the distance so covered. **3** speed. • *vb* **1** to walk slowly. **2** to measure by steps.

pacification /pa-si-fi-**cay**-shun/ *n* act of bringing peace.

pacifier /**pa**-si-fie-er/ *n* (*esp US*) a rubber teat given to babies to suck on; a dummy.

pacifism /**pa**-si-fi-zum/ *n* the belief that war is never right.

pacifist /**pa**-si-**fist**/ *n* someone who works for the end of all war.

pacify /**pa**-si-fie/ *vb* **1** to restore peace, to end a war in. **2** to calm, to soothe.

pack /pack/ *n* **1** a bundle of things fastened or strapped together. **2** a set of playing cards. **3** individual items grouped together into one package. **4** a number of animals acting or hunting together. **5** a gang. **6** a mass of floating pieces of ice. • *vb* **1** to make into a bundle, to put things into a case, etc. **2** to fill. **3** to fill to overflowing. **4** to fill with a person's own supporters.

package /**pa**-kidge/ *n* **1** a parcel, a bundle, usually sent by post. **2** a set of plans, proposals, services put forward or offered as a group. • *n* **package holiday** a holiday offered by a travel company at a fixed price covering both transport costs and accommodation costs.

packaging /**pa**-ka-jing/ *n* the materials in which objects are wrapped before being sold.

pack animal /pack a-ni-mal/ *n* an animal used for carrying loads.

packet /**pa**-kit/ *n* **1** a wrapped and sealed container, along with its contents. **2** a small parcel. **3** a mail boat.

pack-ice /pack-ice/ *n* a mass of floating pieces of ice.

packing /**pa**-king/ *n* the paper, cardboard, etc, used to protect goods being delivered.

pact /pact/ *n* an agreement.

pad[1] /pad/ *n* **1** a small cushion. **2** soft material used to protect or to alter shape. **3** sheets of paper fixed together. **4** the soft flesh on the foot of certain animals. • *vb* (**padded, padding**) **1** to fill out with soft material. **2** to make longer with unnecessary words.

pad[2] /pad/ *vb* to walk steadily and usually softly.

padding /**pa**-ding/ *n* **1** soft material used for stuffing or filling out. **2** words, sentences, etc, put in merely to make something longer.

paddle /**pa**-dul/ *n* a short oar with a broad blade, sometimes at each end. • *vb* **1** to row with a paddle. **2** to walk in water with bare feet.

paddle steamer /**pa**-dul stee-mer/ *n* a steamer driven by two large wheels turning in the water to make it move.

paddock /**pa**-dick/ *n* **1** a small enclosed field. **2** an enclosure in which horses are assembled before a race.

paddy field /**pa**-dee **feeld**/ *n* a field in which rice is grown.

padlock /**pad**-lock/ *n* a metal locking device that closes over two rings and thus fastens something. • *vb* to close with a padlock.

paediatrician /pee-dee-a-**tri**-shan/, *also* **pediatrician** (*US*) *n* a doctor specializing in children's illnesses.

paediatrics /pee-dee-**at**-riks/, *also* **pediatrics** (*US*) *n* the branch of medicine dealing with children's illnesss. • *adj* **paediatric**.

paedophile /**pee**-du-file/, *also* **pedophile** (*US*) *n* a person who is sexually attracted to children.

pagan /**pay**-gan/ *n* **1** someone who does not believe in any of the world's major religions. **2** someone who worships many gods. **3** someone who has no religion; heathen. • *n* **paganism**.

page[1] /paidge/ *n* **1** a boy servant, usually uniformed, in a hotel, club, etc. **2** a boy attendant on a bride at a wedding. **3** (*old*) a boy attendant of a knight or nobleman.

page[2] /paidge/ *n* one side of a sheet of paper in a book, etc.

pageant /**pa**-jint/ *n* **1** a performance or procession, often presenting scenes from history. **2** a fine display or show.

pageantry /**pa**-jin-tree/ *n* splendid display.

pagoda /pa-**goe**-da/ *n* a pyramid-shaped temple in Eastern countries.

paid *pt and pp of* **pay**.

pail /pail/ *n* an open vessel with a handle for carrying liquids.

pain /pain/ *n* **1** suffering of body or mind. **2** *pl* trouble, care. • *vb* (*fml*) to cause suffering to. • *adj* **painful, painless**. • **on pain of death** with death as a punishment.

painstaking /**pain**-stay-king/ *adj* **1** very careful. **2** taking great trouble.

paint /paint/ *n* a colouring substance spread over the surface of an object with a brush.

• *vb* **1** to put on paint. **2** to paint a picture. • *n* **painter**.

paintbrush /**paint**-brush/ *n* **1** a brush used for decorating a house with paint. **2** a brush used for painting pictures.

painting /**pain**-ting/ *n* a painted picture.

pair /**pair**/ *n* **1** two things of the same kind, a set of two. **2** a couple, two people, animals, etc, often one of either sex, who are thought of as being together. • *vb* **1** to arrange in twos. **2** to join one to another.

pal /**pal**/ *n* (*inf*) a friend, comrade.

pajamas US variant of **pyjamas**.

palace /**pa**-liss/ *n* a large and splendid house, especially the house of a king or queen. • *adj* **palatial**.

palaeolithic /pay-lee-o-li-thic/ *adj*, *also* **paleolithic** (*US*) having to do with the early Stone Age.

palaeontology /pay-lee-on-**tol**-uh-jee/ *n*, *also* **paleontology** (*US*) the study of fossils and ancient life forms.

palaeontologist /pay-lee-on-**tol**-uh-jist/ *n*, *also* **paleontologist** (*US*) someone who studies palaeontology.

palate /**pa**-lit/ *n* **1** the roof of the mouth. **2** the sense of taste, the ability to tell good food or wine from bad. **3** a taste or liking.

pale[1] /**pale**/ *adj* **1** lacking colour, whitish. **2** not dark in colour. • *vb* to make or become pale.

pale[2] /**pale**/ *n* a pointed stake of wood driven into the ground as part of a fence. • **beyond the pale** beyond the limit of proper behaviour.

paleolithic US variant of **palaeolithic**.

paleontology US variant of **palaeontology**.

paleontologist US variant of **palaeontologist**.

palette /**pa**-lit/ *n* a thin board on which an artist mixes paints.

palindrome /**pa**-lin-droam/ *n* a word or phrase whose letters when read from end to beginning spell the same word (e.g. noon).

palisade /pa-li-**sade**/ *n* (*old*) a defensive fence of stakes.

pallet /**pa**-let/ *n* **1** a wooden platform on which goods can be carried by a fork-lift truck. **2** (*old*) a bed of straw.

pallor /**pa**-lur/ *n* paleness.

palm[1] /**pahm**/ *n* the inner part of the hand between the wrist and fingers. • *vb* **palm off** to get to accept something worthless.

palm[2] /**pahm**/ *n* a tall tropical tree with a crown of long broad leaves at the top of the trunk.

palmist /**pah**-mist/ *n* a person who claims to tell someone's future from the lines on their hand. • *n* **palmistry**.

Palm Sunday /pahm **sun**-day/ *n* the Sunday before Easter.

palsy /**pawl**-zee/ *n* a disease causing trembling of the limbs. • *adj* **palsied**.

paltry /**pawl**-tree/ *adj* **1** contemptibly small, worthless. **2** mean.

pampas /**pam**-paz/ *npl* the vast grassy treeless plains of South America.

pamper /**pam**-per/ *vb* to spoil by trying to please too much.

pamphlet /**pam**-flit/ *n* a small paper-covered book.

pan /**pan**/ *n* **1** a metal pot used for cooking. **2** the tray of a balance or set of scales. • *vb* **1** to criticize severely. **2 pan out** to turn out, to result.

Pan /**pan**/ *n* in legend, the Greek god of nature and shepherds.

pan- /**pan**/ *prefix* all.

panacea /pa-na-**see**-ya/ *n* a cure for all diseases or evils.

panache /pa-**nash**/ *n* style, a dramatic show of skill, etc.

pancake /**pan**-cake/ *n* a thin cake of batter cooked in a pan or on a griddle.

pancreas /**pan**-cree-as/ *n* a gland in the body that produces a fluid that helps digestion and produces insulin that helps the body to use glucose. • *adj* **pancreatic**.

panda /**pan**-da/ *n* a large black-and-white animal found in China.

pandemonium /pan-di-**moe**-nee-um/ *n* a scene of noisy disorder, uproar.

pander /**pan**-der/ *vb* to give in to the desires of a person or group.

pane /**pane**/ *n* a single piece of glass in a window.

panel /**pa**-nul/ *n* **1** a thin board fitted into the framework of a door or on a wall or ceiling. **2** a group of people who discuss or answer questions put to them by others.

pang /**pang**/ *n* **1** a sudden sharp pain. **2** a sudden sharp feeling.

panic /**pa**-nic/ *n* **1** a sudden uncontrollable fear. **2** sudden fear spreading through a crowd and causing wild disorder. • *also adj*.

panic-stricken /**pa**-nic-**stri**-kin/ *adj* filled with panic.

panorama /pa-nu-ra-ma/ *n* **1** a wide view. **2** a general representation in words or pictures.

pansy /**pan**-zee/ *n* a large type of violet.

pant /**pant**/ *vb* **1** to take short quick breaths. **2** to long for. • *n* a gasp.

panther /**panth**-er/ *n* a leopard, especially the black variety.

panties /**pan**-tees/ *npl* women or children's underpants, knickers.

pantomime /**pan**-tu-mime/ *n* **1** a story told through mime. **2** (*Br*) an amusing Christmas play, popular with children, with music and songs, based on a well-known story or fairy tale.

pantry /**pan**-tree/ *n* **1** a small room for keeping food. **2** a room in which food, dishes, cutlery, etc, are stored.

pants /pants/ *npl* **1** underpants. **2** knickers.

paparazzi /pa-pa-**rat**-see/ *npl* (*sing* **paparazzo** /pa-pa-**rat**-so/) photographers who follow famous people (often intrusively) in order to take their photographs to sell to newspapers and magazines.

papaw, pawpaw /**paw**-paw/ *n* a North American tree with edible fruit.

papaya /pa-**pie**-ya/ *n* a yellow or orange, melonlike sweet-tasting tropical fruit.

paper /**pay**-per/ *n* **1** a material made from wood pulp, rags, etc, and used for writing, printing, wrapping and many other purposes. **2** a newspaper. **3** an essay. **4** a set of examination questions on a subject or part of a subject. • *vb* to cover with paper.

paperback /**pay**-per-back/ *n* a soft book with a cover of thin card.

paper chase /**pay**-per-chase/ *n* a cross-country run in which certain runners throw down a trail of paper for the others to follow.

paper money /**pay**-per **mu**-nee/ *n* banknotes.

paperweight /**pay**-per-wate/ *n* a heavy object placed on top of loose papers to keep them in place.

papier mâché /**pay**-per ma-shay, pa-pee-ay ma-shay/ *n* a substance consisting of paper pulp and used for making boxes, ornaments, etc.

paprika /pa-**pree**-ka/ *n* red pepper.

papyrus /pa-**pie**-rus/ *n* (*pl* **papyri**) **1** a reed from which paper was made in ancient times. **2** the paper thus made.

par /par/ *n* **1** the state of being equal. **2** the normal value, amount or degree of something. **3** in golf, the number of strokes that should be taken on a round by a good player.

parable /**pa**-ra-bul/ *n* a simple story made up to illustrate the difference between right and wrong.

parabola /pa-ra-bu-la/ *n* **1** a curved line so drawn that it is throughout its length the same distance from both a fixed point and a line. **2** a section obtained by cutting a cone by a plane parallel to its side.

parachute /pa-ra-**shoot**/ *n* an apparatus that opens like an umbrella and enables people to jump from an aeroplane and drop to the ground safely.

parade /pa-**rade**/ *n* **1** a public procession. **2** display, show. **3** soldiers, etc, standing in lines under the command of their officers. • *vb* **1** to show off. **2** to take up places in an orderly body (e.g. of soldiers). **3** to march in procession. **4** to walk up and down.

paradise /**pa**-ra-dice/ *n* **1** heaven. **2** the garden of Eden. **3** (*inf*) a place or state of great happiness.

paradox /**pa**-ra-doks/ *n* a statement that seems to contradict itself. • *adj* **paradoxical**.

paraffin /**pa**-ra-fin/ *n* a waxy substance obtained from shale or coal and used for making candles or made into oil for lamps, etc.

paragon /**pa**-ra-gon/ *n* a perfect example of some good quality.

paragraph /**pa**-ra-graf/ *n* a distinct division of a piece of writing beginning on a new line, often with its first word slightly in from the left-hand margin.

parakeet /**pa**-ra-keet/ *n* a small parrot.

parallel /**pa**-ra-lel/ *adj* **1** (*of lines*) at the same distance from each other at all points. **2** similar. • *n* **1** a like or similar example, a comparison. **2** one of the lines drawn on maps through all places at the same distance from the equator.

parallelogram /pa-ra-**lel**-lo-gram/ *n* a four-sided figure whose opposite sides are parallel.

paralyse /**pa**-ra-lize/ *vb*, *also* **paralyze** (*US*) **1** to make helpless or powerless. **2** to strike with paralysis.

paralysis /pa-**ra**-li-sis/ *n* a condition causing loss of feeling and the power to move in part of the body.

paralytic /pa-ra-**li**-tic/ *adj* suffering from paralysis. • *also n*.

paramedic /pa-ra-**med**-ic/ *n* a person who is trained to give someone a certain amount of medical treatment until the patient can be treated by a doctor.

parameter /pa-**ra**-mi-ter/ *n* a factor that determines the limits.

paramount /**pa**-ra-mount/ *adj* highest, greatest.

paranoia /pa-ra-**noy**-a/ *n* a form of mental illness that can result in delusions or feelings of persecution.

parapet /**pa**-ra-pit/ *n* a safety wall at the side of a bridge, at the edge of a roof, etc.

paraphernalia /pa-ra-fer-**nale**-ya/ *npl* a large collection of objects, often personal belongings, or all the tools necessary for a job or hobby.

paraphrase /pa-ra-fraze/ *vb* to express the sense of a passage by using other words. • *also n.*

parasite /pa-ra-site/ *n* **1** a plant or animal that lives on or in another. **2** someone who lives at another's expense. • *adj* **parasitic.**

parasol /pa-ra-sawl/ *n* a sunshade in the form of an umbrella.

paratroop(er) /pa-ra-troop(-er)/ *n* a soldier trained to drop from an aeroplane by parachute.

parboil /par-boil/ *vb* to boil slightly.

parcel /par-sul/ *n* **1** a small bundle or package. **2** a small piece of land, especially part of a large piece. • *vb* (**parcelled, parcelling**) **1** to divide into shares. **2** to wrap up in paper, etc.

parch /parch/ *vb* to dry up.

parched /parcht/ *adj* **1** dried out. **2** (*inf*) very thirsty.

parchment /parch-ment/ *n* **1** a skin prepared for writing on. **2** what is written on it.

pardon /par-dun/ *vb* to forgive, to let off without punishment. • *n* forgiveness.

pardonable /par-du-na-bul/ *adj* that can be forgiven.

pare /pare/ *vb* to cut off the skin or edge of.

parent /pay-rint/ *n* a father or mother.

parentage /pay-rin-tidge/ *n* parents and ancestors, birth.

parental /pa-ren-tal/ *adj* of a parent.

parenthesis /pa-ren-thi-sis/ *n* **1** a group of words put into the middle of a sentence interrupting its sense, often enclosed in brackets. **2** either of a pair of brackets. • *adj* **parenthetical.**

parish /pa-rish/ *n* **1** a district with its own church and priest or minister. **2** a division of a county for administrative purposes. • *adj* having to do with a parish.

paring /pay-ring/ *n* a piece of skin cut off.

parity /pa-ri-tee/ *n* equality, the state of being equal.

park /park/ *n* **1** an enclosed piece of ground for the use of the public. **2** a large enclosed space of open ground around a country house. • *vb* to leave.

parka /par-kah/ *n* a heavy jacket with a hood.

parliament /par-li-ment/ *n* **1** an assembly that discusses and makes laws. **2** (*cap*) in the United Kingdom, the House of Commons and the House of Lords. • *adj* **parliamentary.**

parlour /par-lur/ *n, also* **parlor** (*US*) **1** (*old*) a sitting room. **2** a shop providing some kind of personal service.

parody /pa-ru-dee/ *n* **1** a humorous imitation of a serious work of literature. **2** a weak and unsuccessful copy or absurd imitation. • *vb* **1** to make a parody of. **2** to imitate in order to make fun of.

parole /pa-role/ *n* the release of a prisoner before the end of his or her sentence on condition that he or she does not break the law.

parrot /pa-rut/ *n* a brightly coloured tropical bird able to imitate human speech.

parse /parss/ *vb* to tell what part of speech a word is and its relation to other words in the sentence. • *n* **parsing.**

parsley /par-slee/ *n* a garden herb used in cooking.

parsnip /par-snip/ *n* a vegetable with a yellow edible root.

parson /par-sun/ *n* a member of clergy.

part /part/ *n* **1** one of the pieces into which a thing can be divided. **2** some but not all. **3** the character played by an actor. **4** a person's contribution to an action. • *adj, adv* in part. • *vb* **1** to divide. **2** to separate. • *adv* **partly.** • **in good part** without being angry. • **part and parcel** a necessary part.

partake /par-take/ *vb* (*fml*) **1** to take a share in, to take part in. **2** to eat.

partial /par-shul/ *adj* **1** in part only. **2** favouring one side or person. **3** fond.

partiality /par-shee-a-li-tee/ *n* **1** (*fml*) the favouring of one more than others, unfairness. **2** liking.

participant /par-ti-si-pant/, **participator** /par-ti-si-pay-tor/ *n* someone who takes part in.

participate /par-ti-si-pate/ *vb* to take part in, to have a share in. • *n* **participation.**

participle /par-ti-si-pul/ *n* a part of the verb that does the work of an adjective.

particle /par-ti-cul/ *n* a very small part.

particular /par-ti-cyu-lar/ *adj* **1** different from others, special. **2** careful, exact. **3** difficult to please. • *n* a single fact, a detail.

particularize /par-ti-cyu-la-rize/ *vb, also* **particularise** to describe in detail.

parting /par-ting/ *n* **1** separation. **2** act of going away or leaving. **3** the division made when the hair is brushed in two directions. • *adj* done when going away, final.

partition /par-ti-shun/ *n* **1** a dividing wall or screen. **2** division. **3** a part divided off from the rest. • *vb* **1** to divide up. **2** to set up a dividing wall, etc.

partner /part-ner/ *n* **1** someone who works or plays with another in a certain undertaking, game, etc. **2** a husband or wife, someone with whom one lives or is in a long-term relationship. • *vb* to go with or give to as a partner.

partnership /part-ner-ship/ *n* **1** the state of being partners. **2** a group of people working together for the same purpose. **3** people playing on the same side in a game.

partridge /par-tridge/ *n* a game bird with grey, brown and white feathers.

part-time /part-**time**/ *adj* for some of the time only.

party /par-tee/ *n* **1** a group of people who have the same or similar beliefs and opinions. **2** a number of people meeting for enjoyment. **3** a person or organization taking part.

pass /pass/ *vb* **1** to go past. **2** to go on one's way. **3** to move. **4** to die. **5** (*of time*) to go by. **6** to spend. **7** to overtake. **8** to succeed at examination. **9** to recognize as good enough, to approve. **10** to utter. **11** to set up as by vote. **12** (*fml*) to be too great for. • *n* **1** a narrow valley between mountains. **2** a written permission to visit certain places. **3** success in an examination. • **a pretty pass** a bad state of affairs.

passable /pa-sa-bul/ *adj* **1** fairly good. **2** that can be crossed or travelled on.

passage /pa-sidge/ *n* **1** a way through. **2** act of passing. **3** a journey, especially by sea. **4** a corridor. **5** part of a book, poem, etc.

passbook /pass-book/ *n* a book showing the amounts paid into and drawn from a bank account.

passenger /pa-sin-jer/ *n* someone travelling in a ship, car, train, etc.

passe-partout /pa-spar-**too**/ *n* (*fml*) a sticky tape used in framing pictures, photographs, etc.

passer-by /pa-sur-**bie**/ *n* (*pl* **passers-by**) someone who is walking past.

passing /pa-sing/ *adj* **1** moving or going by. **2** lasting for a short time only.

passion /pa-shin/ *n* **1** a strong feeling, such as love. **2** anger. **3** great enthusiasm. **4** (*fml*) great suffering. • **the Passion** the last sufferings of Christ.

passionate /pash-nit/ *adj* **1** having or showing strong feelings. **2** very enthusiastic.

passion fruit /pa-shin-froot/ *n* an edible purple fruit of the passion flower.

passive /pa-siv/ *adj* **1** acted on. **2** showing no emotion, interest, etc. **3** unresisting. • *n* **passivity**.

passive smoking /pa-siv smo-king/ *n* the breathing in of other people's cigarette smoke.

Passover /pa-so-ver/ *n* a Jewish feast in memory of their escape from Egypt.

passport /pass-poart/ *n* a document giving a person permission to travel in foreign countries.

password /pass-wurd/ *n* **1** a secret word, that proves identity or allows access to something. **2** a sequence of characters that allows access to a computer.

past /past/ *adj* **1** gone by. **2** belonging to an earlier time. • *n* **1** time gone by. **2** one's earlier life. • *prep* **1** beyond. **2** after. • *adv* by.

pasta /pa-sta/ *n* an Italian food made from flour, eggs and water and formed into different shapes, such as spaghetti, often dried before use.

paste /paist/ *n* **1** flour mixed with water, etc, to make dough for cooking. **2** a sticky mixture used as an adhesive. **3** food crushed so that it can be spread like butter. **4** the material of which imitation gems are made. • *vb* to stick with paste.

pasteboard /paist-board/ *n* cardboard.

pastel /pa-stul/ *n* **1** a coloured chalk or crayon. **2** a drawing done with pastel. • *adj* soft, quiet, not bright.

pasteurize /pa-styu-rize/ *vb*, *also* **pasteurise** to heat in order to kill all harmful germs.

pastille /pa-stul/ *n* **1** a small sweet-smelling lozenge. **2** a lozenge containing medicine.

pastime /pa-stime/ *n* a hobby, a game, an interest for one's spare time.

past master /past ma-ster/ *n* an expert, someone with great skill.

pastor /pa-stur/ *n* the minister of a church.

pastoral /pa-stu-ral/ *adj* **1** (*fml*) having to do with the country or country life. **2** having to do with a member of the clergy or his or her duties. • *n* a poem describing country life.

past participle /past par-ti-si-pul/ *n* a form of verb, often ending in -ed or -en, that shows that an action happened in the past.

past perfect /past **per**-fect/ *n*, *also* **pluperfect** /plu-per-fect/ a tense indicating that an action took place before a past action (e.g. *I had written*).

pastry /pay-stree/ *n* **1** dough of flour, water etc, made crisp by baking. **2** a pie or tart.

pasture /pa-schur/ *n* grassland where farm animals graze. • *vb* **1** to put cattle to graze. **2** to eat grass on.

pasty[1] /pa-stee/ *n* a small piece of pastry filled with meat and vegetables.

pasty[2] /pay-stee/ *adj* white and unhealthy, pale.

pat /pat/ *n* **1** a tap, a light touch. **2** a small lump. • *vb* (**patted**, **patting**) to tap, to hit lightly. • *adj* ready, coming too easily.

patch /patch/ *n* **1** a piece of material sewed or put on to cover a hole. **2** a small piece of ground. • *vb* to mend by covering over.

patchwork /patch-wurk/ *n* many small pieces of material sewn together.

patchy /pa-chee/ *adj* 1 full of small areas of differing quality. 2 (*inf*) sometimes good, sometimes bad.

pâté /pa-tay/ *n* finely minced meat, such as liver, that can be spread on bread etc.

patent /pa-tint, pay-tint/ *n* 1 a written document giving someone the sole right to make or sell a new invention. 2 the granting of land titles by the government. • *adj* 1 protected by patent. 2 (*fml*) obvious, clear. • *vb* 1 to obtain a patent for. 2 to grant land titles by a patent.

patent leather /pay-tint le-ther/ *n* leather with a very high gloss.

paternal /pa-ter-nal/ *adj* 1 fatherly, like a father. 2 related by blood to one's father.

paternity /pa-ter-ni-tee/ *n* the state of being a father.

path /path/ *n* 1 a narrow way made by the treading of feet, a track. 2 the course followed by a person or thing.

pathetic /pa-thet-ic/ *adj* sad, causing pity.

pathological /pa-thu-lodge-ic-al/ *adj* 1 having to do with the study of disease. 2 (*inf*) unreasonable, unnatural.

pathology /pa-thol-u-jee/ *n* the study of diseases. • *n* **pathologist** a doctor who specializes in pathology, especially one who examines dead bodies to find out the cause of death.

pathos /pay-thos/ *n* the quality that excites pity or sadness.

pathway /path-way/ *n* a path.

patience /pay-shince/ *n* 1 the ability to suffer or wait long without complaining, calmness despite delay or difficulty. 2 a card game for one person, solitaire.

patient /pay-shint/ *adj* suffering delay, pain, irritation, etc quietly and without complaining. • *n* a person receiving treatment from a doctor.

patio /pa-tee-o/ *n* a paved area outside a house where people can sit, plants can be grown in containers, etc.

patriarch /pay-tree-ark/ *n* (*fml*) 1 the head of a tribe or family. 2 a senior bishop. 3 a head of the Greek church. 4 a very old man. • *adj* **patriarchal**.

patriot /pay-tree-ut/ *n* someone who loves his or her country. • *n* **patriotism**.

patriotic /pay-tree-ot-ic/ *adj* loving one's country.

patrol /pa-trole/ *n* 1 a group of men, ships, etc, sent out as a moving guard. 2 the act of patrolling. 3 a small group of

Scouts or Guides. • *vb* (**patrolled**, **patrolling**) to move about on guard or to keep watch.

patron /pay-trun/ *n* 1 someone who encourages, helps or protects. 2 a regular customer.

patronage /pay-tru-nidge/ *n*, *also* /pa-tru-nidge/ 1 the help or protection given by a patron. 2 the right of appointing to certain offices. 3 a manner that shows that one thinks oneself superior.

patronize /pa-tru-nize, *also* pay-tru-nize/ *vb*, *also* **patronise** 1 to behave to another as if superior to him or her. 2 to go somewhere regularly as a patron.

patron saint /pay-trun saint/ *n* a saint believed to give special protection.

patter[1] /pa-ter/ *vb* 1 to make a light tapping sound. 2 to run with quick light steps. • *n* the sound of pattering.

patter[2] /pa-ter/ *n* fast talk, especially persuasive talk.

pattern /pa-tern/ *n* 1 a model that can be copied. 2 an example. 3 a design as on cloth, a carpet, etc. 4 the way in which something happens or develops.

patty /pa-tee/ *n* a little pie.

paunch /pawnch/ *n* the belly, especially a large protruding one.

pauper /paw-per/ *n* a person too poor to support himself or herself.

pause /pawz/ *vb* to stop for a time. • *n* a short stop.

pave /pave/ *vb* to make a road or pathway by laying down flat stones. • **pave the way for** to prepare for.

pavement /pave-mint/ *n* a footpath at the side of a road.

pavilion /pa-vil-yun/ *n* a building or large tent put up quickly for a special purpose.

paw /paw/ *n* the foot of an animal that has claws. • *vb* 1 to scrape with the forefoot. 2 to handle clumsily and often in too familiar a way.

pawn[1] /pawn/ *n* 1 in chess, the piece of least value. 2 a person made use of by another to do his or her will.

pawn[2] /pawn/ *vb* to hand over in return for money lent. • *n* a thing handed over in return for a loan of money and returned when the loan is repaid. • **pawnbroker** *n* someone who lends money to those who pawn goods with him or her until the loan is repaid.

pay /pay/ *vb* (*pt*, *pp* **paid**) 1 to give money for goods, service, etc. 2 to suffer for faults, crimes, etc. 3 to give. 4 to produce a profit. 5 to let run out. • *n* wages, salary. • **pay**

through the nose (*inf*) to pay too much for something.

payment /pay-mint/ *n* **1** the act of paying. **2** the amount paid.

payroll /pay-role/ *n* a list of persons to be paid.

PC /pee-see/ *abbr* = **1 personal computer:** a computer designed to be used by one person. **2** *see* **politically correct. 3** police constable.

pea /pee/ *n* **1** a climbing plant with pods containing round edible seeds. **2** one of the seeds.

peace /peess/ *n* **1** quiet, calm. **2** freedom from war or disorder. **3** the agreement to end a war.

peaceful /peess-ful/ *adj* **1** quiet, calm, untroubled. **2** without war.

peach /peech/ *n* a juicy fruit with a rough stone and soft velvety skin.

peacock /pee-cock/ *n* a male peafowl.

peahen /pee-cock/ *n* a female peafowl.

peafowl /pee-fowl/ *n* a bird of the pheasant family, the male of which has a large brightly coloured spreading tail; the female's plumage is grey/brown. • *m* **peacock.** • *f* **peahen.**

peak /peek/ *n* **1** the highest point. **2** the pointed top of a mountain. **3** the jutting-out brim at the front of a cap. • *adj* connected with the time of greatest use or demand. • *vb* to reach the highest point.

peaked /peekt/ *adj* having a jutting-out brim in front.

peal /peel/ *n* **1** a sudden noise. **2** the loud ringing of bells. **3** a set of bells for ringing together. • *vb* to sound or ring loudly.

peanut /pee-nut/ *n* a type of edible nut.

pear /pare/ *n* a juicy fruit, narrower at one end than at the other. • **go pear-shaped** to go wrong, fail.

pearl /perl/ *n* **1** a shining white jewel found in shellfish, especially oysters. **2** (*inf*) something highly valued. **3** mother-of-pearl.

peasant /pe-zant/ *n* a person who works on the land, especially in a poor, primitive or underdeveloped area.

peasantry /pe-zan-tree/ *n* peasants, country people.

peat /peet/ *n* turf containing decayed vegetable matter, dried and used as fuel.

pebble /pe-bul/ *n* a small stone made round by the action of water. • *adj* **pebbly.**

peck¹ /peck/ *n* an imperial measure for grain, etc (= 2 gallons).

peck² /peck/ *vb* **1** to strike with the beak. **2** to pick up with the beak. **3** to eat slowly in small mouthfuls, to nibble.

peculiar /pi-cyool-yar/ *adj* **1** strange, odd. **2** belonging to one person, place or thing in particular and to no other.

peculiarity /pi-cyool-ya-ri-tee/ *n* **1** a quality, custom, etc, that belongs to a particular person, thing, etc. **2** an odd way of behaving.

pedal /pe-dal/ *n* a lever worked by foot to control the working of a machine. • *vb* (**pedalled, pedalling**) to work a pedal by foot.

pedant /pe-dant/ *n* **1** someone who shows off his or her learning. **2** someone who attaches too much importance to small details and unimportant rules. • *adj* **pedantic.**

pedantry /pe-dan-tree/ *n* **1** showing off one's learning. **2** over-insistence on rules, etc.

peddle /pe-dal/ *vb* to sell from door to door.

peddler, *also* **pedlar, pedler** /ped-ler/ *n* someone who travels about selling small objects.

pedestal /pe-di-stal/ *n* the block of stone at the base of a column or under a statue. • **put on a pedestal** to treat with very great, often too much, respect.

pedestrian /pi-de-stree-an/ *n* someone who goes on foot, a walker. • *adj* **1** going on foot. **2** dull, uninteresting. • *adj* of streets in which traffic is not allowed so that pedestrians can walk safely.

pedestrian crossing /pi-de-stree-an craw-sing/ *n* a specially marked area on a road at which people may safely cross.

pediatrician *see* **paediatrician.**

pediatrics *see* **paediatrics.**

pedicure /pe-di-cyoor/ *n* treatment for the feet to remove corns etc, or cosmetic treatment to improve their appearance.

pedigree /pe-di-gree/ *n* **1** a written table showing one's ancestors. **2** one's ancestors. • *adj* of good birth.

pediment /pe-di-ment/ *n* the triangular topmost part at the front of a building.

pedlar, pedler *see* **peddler.**

pedometer /pi-dom-i-ter/ *n* an instrument that measures distance walked.

pedophile *see* **paedophile.**

peel /peel/ *vb* **1** to strip off. **2** to cut the skin off a fruit or vegetable. **3** to come off, as does skin or the bark of a tree. • *n* skin, rind, bark.

peeling /pee-ling/ *n* a piece peeled off.

peep¹ /peep/ *vb* to chirp, to squeak. • *n* **1** a chirp or squeak. **2** any of various small sandpipers.

peep² /peep/ *vb* **1** to look at through a narrow opening. **2** to look at for a moment only. **3** to begin to appear. • *n* **1** a quick or secret look. **2** a look through a narrow opening. **3** a first appearance.

peephole /peep-hole/ *n* a small hole for looking through.

peer¹ /peer/ *vb* **1** to strain one's eyes to see. **2** to look closely.

peer² /peer/ *n* **1** an equal, one's equal in age, ability, rank. **2** a British nobleman. • *f* **peeress**.

peerage /pee-ridge/ *n* **1** all the noblemen of a country. **2** the rank or title of a British nobleman.

peerless /peer-less/ *adj* (*fml*) unequalled.

peevish /pee-vish/ *adj* irritable, full of complaints.

peg /peg/ *n* a nail, pin or fastener. • *vb* (**pegged, pegging**) to fasten with a peg. • **take down a peg** to humble, to humiliate.

pejorative *adj* (*of a word or phrase*) having unpleasant or deliberately negative connotations.

pelican /pe-li-can/ *n* a water bird with a large beak containing a pouch for storing fish.

pellet /pe-lit/ *n* **1** a small ball of anything. **2** one of a number of small lead balls packed in a cartridge and fired from a gun.

pell-mell /pel-mel/ *adv* in great disorder.

pelt¹ /pelt/ *n* the raw skin of an animal.

pelt² /pelt/ *vb* **1** to attack by throwing things at. **2** (*of rain*) to fall heavily.

pelvis /pel-vis/ *n* the bony frame and the lower end of the trunk, into which the hip bones fit.

pen¹ /pen/ *n* an instrument for writing in ink. • *vb* to write.

pen² /pen/ *n* a female swan.

pen³ /pen/ *n* a small enclosure, especially for animals. • *vb* (**penned, penning**) to shut up in a small space.

penal /pee-nal/ *adj* having to do with punishment.

penalize /pee-na-lize/ *vb*, *also* **penalise 1** to punish. **2** to put someone at a disadvantage, often unfairly.

penalty /pe-nal-tee/ *n* **1** due punishment. **2** a disadvantage of some kind that must be suffered for breaking the rules.

penance /pe-nanse/ *n* punishment willingly accepted as a sign of sorrow for sin.

pence /pense/ *see* **penny**.

penchant /pon-shont/ *n* (*fml*) a liking for, a preference for.

pencil /pen-sil/ *n* a writing or drawing instrument. • *vb* (**pencilled, pencilling**) to write or draw with a pencil.

pendant /pen-dant/ *n* **1** an ornament hanging from a necklace or bracelet. **2** an earring. **3** anything hanging (e.g. a lamp from a roof).

pending /pen-ding/ *adj* not yet decided. • *prep* waiting for.

pendulous /pen-ju-luss/ *adj* (*fml*) hanging.

pendulum /pen-ju-lum/ *n* a swinging weight, as in a large clock.

penetrable /pe-ni-tra-bul/ *adj* that can be penetrated.

penetrate /pe-ni-trate/ *vb* **1** to pass through. **2** to make a hole in or through. **3** to reach the mind of.

penetrating /pe-ni-tray-ting/ *adj* **1** sharp. **2** loud and clear.

penetration /pe-ni-tray-shun/ *n* **1** act of passing through or making a hole in. **2** clear understanding, intelligence.

pen friend /pen frend/ *n* a person one gets to know only through exchanging letters. • *also* **pen pal**.

penguin /pen-gwin/ *n* a web-footed bird with very short wings that it uses for swimming, not flying.

penicillin /pe-ni-si-lin/ *n* a medicinal drug used to treat infections caused by bacteria.

peninsula /pe-nin-su-la/ *n* a piece of land almost surrounded by water.

penis /pee-nis/ *n* the male reproductive and urinary organ in mammals and humans.

penitent /pe-ni-tent/ *adj* sorrowful for having done wrong. • *n* someone who is penitent. • *n* **penitence**.

penitential /pe-ni-ten-shal/ *adj* (*fml*) having to do with penitence.

penitentiary /pe-ni-ten-shree/ *n* a prison.

penknife /pen-nife/ *n* a folding pocket knife.

penmanship /pen-man-ship/ *n* the art of handwriting.

pen name /pen name/ *n* a name, other than his or her real name, under which an author writes.

pennant /pe-nant/, **pennon** /pe-nun/ *n* a long, narrow triangular flag.

penniless /pe-nee-less/ *adj* having no money.

penny /pe-nee/ *n* (*pl* **pennies, pence**) a British bronze coin worth one-hundredth of a pound. 100 pence = £1.

pen pal *see* **pen friend**.

pension /pen-shun/ *n* money paid regularly to someone for the rest of his or her lifetime after he or she has stopped working or after some misfortune. • *vb* to give a pension to.

pensioner /pen-shu-ner/ *n* someone who receives a pension.

pensive /pen-siv/ *adj* (*fml*) thoughtful.

pentagon /pen-ta-gon/ *n* a five-sided figure.

Pentagon /pen-ta-gon/ *n* the headquarters of the US Department of Defense.

Pentecost /pen-ta-cawst/ *n* a Christian and Jewish festival.

penthouse /pent-house/ *n* an apartment, usually luxurious, at the top of a building.

penultimate /pe-**nul**-ti-mit/ *adj* the last but one.

peony /**pee**-u-nee/ *n* a garden plant with large white or red flowers.

people /**pee**-pul/ *n* 1 persons in general. 2 (*pl* **peoples**) all those belonging to one nation or country. 3 the ordinary persons of a country and not their rulers, etc. • *vb* 1 to fill with people. 2 to inhabit.

pep /pep/ *n* vitality, high spirits.

pepper /**pe**-per/ *n* 1 a plant whose seeds are ground into a hot-tasting powder and used for flavouring food. 2 the powder so used.

peppercorn /**pe**-per-cawrn/ *n* the seed of the pepper plant.

peppermint /**pe**-per-mint/ *n* 1 a plant with sharp-tasting oil. 2 a sharp-tasting sweet.

peppery /**pe**-per-ee/ *adj* 1 like pepper, hot. 2 easily angered.

per /per/ *prep* 1 for each. 2 during each. 3 (*inf*) according to.

perceive /per-**seev**/ *vb* to know through one of the senses, to see, to understand.

percent, per cent /per-**sent**/ in each hundred (%).

percentage /per-**sen**-tidge/ *n* the number of cases in every hundred.

perceptible /per-**sep**-ti-bul/ *adj* able to be perceived.

perception /per-**sep**-shun/ *n* 1 the ability to perceive. 2 the ability to understand and notice things quickly.

perceptive /per-**sep**-tiv/ *adj* 1 quick to notice or understand. 2 showing the ability to notice or understand.

perch[1] /perch/ *n* a freshwater fish.

perch[2] /perch/ *n* 1 the bar on which a bird stands when resting. 2 a high place. • *vb* 1 to rest on a bar or high place. 2 to put or be in a high position.

perchance /per-**chanse**/ *adv* (*old*) perhaps.

percussion /per-**cu**-shun/ *n* 1 the striking of one thing against another. 2 the sound thus made. 3 the drums and cymbals section of an orchestra.

perdition /per-**di**-shun/ *n* 1 entire ruin. 2 condemnation to hell.

peremptory /pe-**remp**-tree/ *adj* short and commanding.

perennial /pe-**ren**-ee-yal/ *adj* 1 lasting forever, continual. 2 (*of a plant*) growing again year after year. • *n* a perennial plant.

perfect /**per**-fect/ *adj* 1 without fault, excellent. 2 exact. 3 complete, utter. • *vb* /per-**fect**/ to finish, to make perfect. • *n* **perfection**.

perforate /**per**-fu-rate/ *vb* to make a hole or row of holes through.

perforation /per-fu-**ray**-shun/ *n* a row of small holes, often to make tearing easy, as in sheets of stamps, etc.

perform /per-**fawrm**/ *vb* 1 to do, to carry out. 2 to show in a theatre. 3 to act in a play.

performance /per-**fawr**-manss/ *n* 1 act of doing or carrying out. 2 that which is done. 3 the acting of a play or part.

performer /per-**fawr**-mer/ *n* an actor, musician, etc.

performing /per-**fawr**-ming/ *adj* trained to act, do tricks, etc.

perfume /**per**-fyoom/ *n* 1 a sweet smell. 2 a sweet-smelling liquid, scent. • *vb* /per-**fyoom**/ 1 to apply perfume to. 2 to give a pleasant smell to.

perfumery /per-**fyoo**-mer-ee/ *n* 1 a place where perfumes are made or sold. 2 the art of making perfumes.

perfunctory /per-**fung**(k)-tree/ *adj* done carelessly or without interest, badly done.

perhaps /per-**haps**/ *adv* it may be, possibly.

peril /**pe**-ril/ *n* risk, danger.

perilous /**pe**-ri-lus/ *adj* dangerous.

perimeter /pe-**ri**-mi-ter/ *n* 1 the total length of the line(s) enclosing a certain space or figure. 2 the boundaries of a camp or piece of land.

perineum /pe-ri-**nee**-um/ *n* the area between the genitals and the anus.

period /**pee**-ree-ud/ *n* 1 a certain length of time. 2 an age in history. 3 the dot or full stop marking the end of a sentence. 4 a time of menstruation.

periodic /pee-ree-**od**-ic/ *adj* happening at regular intervals.

periodical /pee-ree-**od**-ic-al/ *n* a newspaper or magazine that appears at regular intervals (e.g. of a week, month, etc). • *adj* periodic.

periodic table /pee-ree-**od**-ic **tay**-bul/ *n* a chart showing the arrangement of chemical elements and their connections to one another.

periphery /pee-**ri**-free/ *n* a boundary line.

periscope /**pe**-ri-scope/ *n* an instrument in which mirrors are so arranged that one can see things on the surface of the land or sea when in a trench or submarine.

perish /**pe**-rish/ *vb* 1 to die. 2 to pass away completely. 3 to rot away.

perishable /**pe**-ri-sha-bul/ *adj* that will rot away under ordinary conditions.

perjury /**per**-ju-ree/ *n* the act of saying under oath that a statement is true when one knows it to be false.

perk[1] /perk/ *vb*. • **perk up** (*inf*) to cheer up.

perk[2] *n see* **perquisite.**

perky /per-kee/ *adj* lively, cheerful. • *n* **perkiness.**

perm /perm/ *n* an artificial wave in the hair.

permanent /per-ma-nent/ *adj* lasting. • *n* **permanence.**

permeable /per-mee-a-bul/ *adj* allowing liquid, gases, etc, to pass through.

permeate /per-mee-ate/ *vb* to pass through, to spread through every part of.

permissible /per-mi-su-bul/ *adj* that can be allowed.

permission /per-mi-shun/ *n* leave, consent.

permissive /per-mi-siv/ *adj* allowing freedom.

permit /per-mit/ *vb* (**permitted, permitting**) to allow. • *n* /per-mit/ a paper giving the holder the right to do certain things.

permutation /per-myoo-**tay**-shun/ *n* **1** all the ways in which a series of things, numbers, etc, can be arranged. **2** one of these ways.

pernickety /per-nik-i-tee/ *adj* fussy, being too concerned with small and unimportant details.

peroration /pe-ru-**ray**-shun/ *n* **1** (*fml*) the closing part of a speech. **2** a grand long speech, often meaningless.

peroxide /per-ok-side/ *n* **1** a mixture of oxygen with another element to contain the greatest possible amount of oxygen. **2** a substance used for bleaching, e.g. the hair.

perpendicular /per-pen-di-cyoo-lar/ *adj* **1** at right angles. **2** upright. • *n* a line at right angles to another.

perpetrate /per-pi-trate/ *vb* to commit, to do. • *n* **perpetration, perpetrator.**

perpetual /per-pe-chu-wal/ *adj* **1** lasting forever. **2** continuing endlessly, uninterrupted.

perpetuate /per-pe-chu-wate/ *vb* to cause to continue to exist for a long time. • *n* **perpetuation.**

perpetuity /per-pe-**choo**-wi-tee/ *n* (*fml*) everlasting time. • **in perpetuity** forever.

perplex /per-pleks/ *vb* to puzzle, to bewilder.

perplexity /per-plek-si-tee/ *n* puzzlement, bewilderment.

perquisite /per-kwi-zit/ *n* (*usually shortened to* **perk**) money, goods, etc, gained from a job in addition to wages or salary.

persecute /per-si-cyoot/ *vb* to ill-treat, especially because of someone's beliefs; to treat cruelly. • *n* **persecution.** • *n* **persecutor.**

perseverance /per-si-**vee**-ranse/ *n* the quality of continuing to try until one succeeds.

persevere /per-si-**veer**/ *vb* to keep on trying.

persist /per-sist/ *vb* **1** to keep on doing. **2** to last. **3** not to give in despite difficulty.

persistence /per-si-stense/ *n* the quality of persisting; obstinacy.

persistent /per-si-stent/ *adj* **1** keeping on trying, not giving in easily. **2** long, continuing.

person /per-sun/ *n* **1** a human being, a man, woman or child. **2** (*fml*) one's body.

personal /per-su-nal/ *adj* **1** concerning a person's own private life. **2** (*of remarks*) unkind. **3** done by a particular person and not someone acting for them.

personal identification number *see* **PIN.**

personality /per-su-na-li-tee/ *n* **1** the combination of qualities that makes someone's character different from those of other people. **2** a strong, distinct character. **3** a well-known person.

personally /pers-na-lee/ *adv* as far as one is concerned oneself.

personify /per-son-i-fie/ *vb* **1** to speak or write of a thing, quality, etc, as if it were a human being. **2** to be a perfect example of. • *n* **personification.**

personnel /per-su-nel/ *n* the persons employed in an organization.

perspective /per-spec-tiv/ *n* **1** the art of drawing objects on a flat surface so that they appear farther or nearer as they do to the eye. **2** a view. • **see in perspective** to see the real value or importance of things when compared with others.

Perspex /per-speks/ *n* (*TM*) tough transparent glasslike plastic.

perspicacious /per-spi-**cay**-shus/ *adj* quick to notice or understand.

perspicacity /per-spi-**ca**-si-tee/ *n* quickness or clearness of understanding.

perspire /per-spire/ *vb* to sweat. • *n* **perspiration.**

persuade /per-swade/ *vb* to convince a person or get him or her to do as one wants by argument.

persuasion /per-**sway**-zhun/ *n* **1** act of persuading. **2** (*fml*) a belief or set of beliefs.

persuasive /per-**sway**-siv/ *adj* good at gaining the agreement of others, able to influence others.

pert /pert/ *adj* forward, cheeky. • *n* **pertness.**

pertain /per-tain/ *vb* to belong, to have to do with.

pertinent /per-ti-nent/ *adj* to the point, having to do with the subject. • *n* **pertinence, pertinency** /per-ti-nen-see/.

perturb /per-turb/ *vb* to make worried or anxious, to disturb. • *n* **perturbation.**

perusal /pe-roo-zal/ *n* reading, study.

peruse /pe-**rooz**/ *vb* (*fml*) to read through, to examine carefully.

pervade /per-**vade**/ *vb* to spread through.

pervasive /per-**vay**-siv/ *adj* spreading through all parts.

perverse /per-**verse**/ *adj* **1** holding firmly to a wrong opinion. **2** continuing to do things that one knows to be wrong, unacceptable or forbidden.

perversion /per-**ver**-zhun/ *n* **1** putting to a wrong or evil use. **2** abnormal or unacceptable sexual behaviour.

perversity /per-**ver**-si-tee/ *n* the quality of being perverse.

pervert /per-**vert**/ *vb* **1** to put to a wrong use. **2** to teach wrong ways to. • *n* /**per**-vert/ someone whose sexual behaviour is abnormal or unacceptable.

peseta /pi-**say**-ta/ *n* a former Spanish coin.

pessimism /**pe**-si-mi-zum/ *n* the belief that things generally turn out for the worst. • *n* **pessimist**.

pessimistic /pe-si-**mi**-stic/ *adj* having to do with pessimism, gloomy.

pest /pest/ *n* **1** an annoying person, a nuisance. **2** a destructive animal, insect, etc.

pester /**pe**-ster/ *vb* to keep on annoying.

pesticide /**pe**-sti-side/ *n* a chemical substance used to kill pests, especially insects that are harmful to crops and other plants.

pestilence /**pe**-sti-lense/ *n* any deadly disease that spreads quickly, plague. • *adj* **pestilential**.

pestilent /**pe**-sti-lent/ *adj* causing pestilence or disease.

pestle /**pe**-sul/ *n* an instrument for pounding substances to powder.

pet /pet/ *n* **1** a favourite child. **2** a tame animal kept in the house as a companion. • *adj* best-loved, favourite. • *vb* (**petted, petting**) **1** to treat lovingly. **2** to fondle.

petal /**pe**-tal/ *n* the leaf-shaped part of a flower.

peter /**pee**-ter/ *vb*. • **peter out** to stop or disappear gradually.

petite /pi-**teet**/ *adj* tiny, dainty.

petition /pi-**ti**-shun/ *n* **1** a request. **2** a written request signed by a number of people. **3** a prayer. • *vb* **1** to make a request to someone able to grant it. **2** to put forward a written request. • *n* **petitioner**.

petrel /**pe**-trul/ *n* a sea bird.

petrifaction /pe-tri-**fac**-shun/ *n* **1** turning into stone. **2** terror, amazement.

petrify /**pe**-tri-fie/ *vb* **1** to turn into stone. **2** to terrify, to astound.

petrol /**pe**-trul/ *n* a liquid obtained from a mixture of gas and petroleum, used as a fuel for motor vehicles.

petroleum /pi-**tro**-lee-um/ *n* a heavy oil obtained from under the surface of the earth.

petrology /pi-**trol**-u-jee/ *n* the study of the formation, composition and erosion of rocks.

petticoat /**pe**-tee-coat/ *n* a woman's undergarment.

pettish /**pe**-tish/ *adj* sulky.

petty /**pe**-tee/ *adj* **1** small, unimportant, trivial. **2** mean-spirited.

petty cash /**pe**-tee **cash**/ *n* money held in readiness to meet small expenses.

petty officer /**pe**-tee **aw**-fi-ser/ *n* in the navy, a non-commissioned officer.

petulant /**pe**-chu-lant/ *adj* easily angered or annoyed, peevish. • *n* **petulance**.

petunia /pe-**toon**-ya/ *n* a flowering garden plant of various colours, often purple.

pew /pyoo/ *n* a seat in a church.

pewter /**pyoo**-ter/ *n* a mixture of tin and lead.

pH /pee-**aich**/ *n* the measurement of the acid or alkaline content of something.

phaeton /**fay**-u-tun/ *n* (*old*) an open four-wheeled carriage drawn by a pair of horses.

phalanx /**fa**-langks/ *n* **1** (*fml or old*) a body of foot soldiers standing close to each other in battle. **2** a body of persons or animals standing close to one another.

phantom /**fan**-tum/ *n* a ghost.

pharaoh /**fay**-ro/ *n* a king of ancient Egypt.

pharisee /**fa**-ri-see/ *n* (*inf*) a hypocrite.

pharmaceutical /far-ma-**soo**-ti-cal/ *adj* having to do with the making up of drugs or medicines.

pharmacy /**far**-ma-see/ *n* **1** the making up of drugs or medicines. **2** a shop in which medicines are made up and sold. • *n* **pharmacist**.

pharyngitis /fa-rin-**jie**-tis/ *n* inflammation of the pharynx.

pharynx /**fa**-rinks/ *n* the back part of the mouth.

phase /faze/ *n* **1** a distinct stage in growth or development. **2** apparent shape (e.g. of the moon).

pheasant /**fe**-zant/ *n* a large bird hunted for sport.

phenomenon /fi-**nom**-i-nun/ *n* (*pl* **phenomena**) **1** any natural happening that can be perceived by the senses. **2** anything unusual or extraordinary.

phenomenal /fi-**nom**-i-nal/ *adj* unusual, extraordinary.

phial /**fie**-al/ *n* a small glass bottle.

philander /fi-**lan**-der/ *vb* to flirt. • *n* **philanderer**.

philanthropy /fi-**lan**-thru-pee/ *n* love of humankind, shown by giving money, etc, to help those in need or to benefit the public. • *adj* **philanthropic**. • *n* **philanthropist**.

philately /fi-la-tu-lee/ *n* stamp collecting. • *n* **philatelist**.

philistine /**fi**-li-stine/ *n* an uncultured person.

philology /fi-**lol**-u-jee/ *n* the study of languages, their history and development. • *n* **philologist**.

philosopher /fi-**los**-u-fer/ *n* **1** someone who tries to find by reasoning the causes and laws of all things. **2** someone who treats life calmly.

philosophic(al) /fi-lu-**sof**-ic-al/ *adj* **1** having to do with philosophy. **2** calm, not easily annoyed.

philosophy /fi-**los**-u-fee/ *n* **1** the study of the causes and laws of all things. **2** a particular way of thinking.

philter /**fil**-ter/ *n* (*fml*) a magic drink supposed to make the drinker fall in love.

phlebitis /fli-**bie**-tus/ *n* inflammation of a vein of the body.

phlegm /**flem**/ *n* the thick, slimy liquid coughed up from the throat.

phlegmatic /fleg-**ma**-tic/ *adj* cool, not easily excited.

phlox /**floks**/ *n* a garden plant with brightly coloured flowers.

phobia /**foe**-bee-ya/ *n*. an unreasoning fear or dread.

phoenix /**fee**-niks/ *n* in ancient fables, a bird said to burn itself and rise again from its own ashes.

phone /**foan**/ *n* the common short form of **telephone**/.

phonetic /fu-**ne**-tic/ *adj* having to do with the sounds of speech or pronunciation. • *npl* the study of the sounds of speech.

phonic /**fon**-ic/ *adj* having to do with sound.

phonograph /**fon**-u-graph/ *n* (*old*) an instrument for recording sounds and playing them back.

phony /**foe**-nee/ *adj* (*inf*) not genuine, not sincere, unreal.

phosphate /**fos**-fate/ *n* a type of salt mixed into soil to make it more fertile.

phosphorescence /fos-fu-**re**-sense/ *n* a faint shining visible only in the dark.

phosphorescent /fos-fu-**re**-sent/ *adj* giving out a faint light in the dark.

phosphorous /**fos**-fu-rus/ *n* a yellow substance, easily set alight, giving out a faint light.

photo /**fo**-toe/ *n* the common short form of **photograph**.

photocopier /**fo**-toe-cop-ee/ *n* a (digital or analogue) machine that makes copies of written or graphic material. *See* **xerox**.

photocopy /**fo**-toe-cop-ee/ *n* a photographed reproduction made by a photocopier. • *vb* to make a photographed copy. *See* **xerox**.

photogenic /fo-toe-**jen**-ic/ *adj* suitable for photographing, looking particularly attractive in photographs.

photograph /**fo**-toe-graph/ *n* (*abbr* = **photo**) a picture taken with a camera by means of the action of light on film and developed on photographic paper; such a picture, taken digitally. • *vb* to take a photograph. • *n* **photographer**. • *adj* **photographic**.

photography /fo-**tog**-ra-fee/ *n* the art of taking photographs.

photometer /fo-**tom**-i-ter/ *n* an instrument for measuring intensity of light.

phrase /**fraze**/ *n* **1** a small group of connected words expressing a single idea. **2** (*mus*) a group of connected notes. • *vb* to express in words.

phraseology /fray-zee-**ol**-u-jee/ *n* a manner or style of expressing in words.

phrenology /fri-**nol**-u-jee/ *n* **1** the belief that a person's intelligence and abilities may be judged from the shape of his or her skull. **2** study of the shape of the skull based on this belief. • *n* **phrenologist**.

physical /**fi**-zi-cal/ *adj* **1** having to do with the body. **2** having to do with the natural world.

physiotherapy /fi-zee-oa-**ther**-a-pee/ *n* the use of exercise or massage to improve mobility after illness or injury.

physician /fi-**zi**-shun/ *n* a doctor, especially as opposed to a surgeon.

physicist /**fi**-zi-sist/ *n* a scientist who specializes in physics.

physics /**fi**-zics/ *n* the study of matter, its properties, and the forces affecting it (e.g. heat, electricity, etc).

physiology /fi-zee-**ol**-u-jee/ *n* the study of living bodies, their organs and the way they work. • *adj* **physiological**. • *n* **physiologist**.

physique /fi-**zeek**/ *n* **1** the structure of a person's body. **2** strength of body.

pianissimo /pee-a-**ni**-si-mo/ *adv* (*mus*) very softly.

pianist /**pee**-a-nist/ *n* someone who plays on a piano.

piano[1] /**pee**-a-no/, **pianoforte** /pee-a-no-**for**-tay/ *n* a musical instrument played by pressing down keys that cause little hammers to strike tuned strings.

piano[2] /**pee**-a-no/ *adv* (*mus*) softly.

piazza /pee-**at**-za/ *n* **1** an open square surrounded by buildings. **2** a path under a roof supported by pillars.

piccolo /**pi**-ca-lo/ *n* a small high-pitched flute.

pick[1] /**pick**/ *vb* **1** to choose. **2** to pull or gather. **3** to eat by small mouthfuls. **4** to open. • *n* choice, the best. • **pick holes in** to point out the faults in. • **pick up 1** to take up. **2** to learn as if by chance. **3** to come upon by chance.

pick² /pick/, **pickaxe** /pi-caks/ *n, also* **pickax** (*US*) a tool with a long pointed head, used for breaking up hard ground. etc.

picket /pi-cit/ *n* **1** a pointed wooden post. **2** a small group of soldiers acting as a guard. **3** a number of people on strike who try to prevent others from going to work. • *vb* to send out soldiers, strikers, etc, on picket.

pickle /pi-cul/ *n* **1** salt water or vinegar in which food is preserved. **2** (*inf*) a difficult or unpleasant situation. **3** *pl* vegetables, especially cucumber, preserved in vinegar. • *vb* to preserve by putting in salt water, vinegar, etc.

pickpocket /pic-poc-it/ *n* someone who steals from pockets.

picnic /pic-nic/ *n* an outing taken for pleasure, during which a meal is eaten out of doors. • *also vb*.

pictorial /pic-**toe**-ree-al/ *adj* told or illustrated by pictures.

picture /pic-chur/ *n* a painting, drawing, photograph or other likeness; a portrait. • *vb* **1** to imagine clearly. **2** (*fml*) to represent in a painting.

picturesque /pic-chu-**resk**/ *adj* that would make a good picture, striking in appearance, beautiful.

pie /pie/ *n* meat or fruit in or under a crust of pastry.

piece /peess/ *n* **1** a bit. **2** a distinct part. **3** a literary or musical composition. **4** a gun. **5** a short distance. **6** a coin. • *vb* **1** to put. **2** to patch.

piecemeal /peess-meel/ *adv* **1** in or by pieces. **2** little by little.

piecework /peess-wurk/ *n* work paid by the amount done, not by time.

pied /pied/ *adj* (*fml*) of different colours, spotted.

pier /peer/ *n* **1** a stone pillar supporting an arch, etc. **2** a wooden platform built out into the sea, often used as a landing place by boats.

pierce /peerss/ *vb* **1** to make a hole through. **2** to go through.

piercing /peer-sing/ *adj* **1** high-sounding. **2** bright and intelligent-looking, staring.

pig /pig/ *n* **1** a common farm animal. **2** a rough block or bar of smelted metal. • *vb* (**pigged, pigging**) to live in dirty or untidy surroundings. • **buy a pig in a poke** to buy something without examining it first.

pigeon /pi-jin/ *n* a bird like a dove, but slightly larger.

pigeon-hole /pi-jin-hole/ *n* one of several compartments in a desk for storing papers, letters, etc.

piggy bank /pi-gee bank/ *n* a small savings bank shaped like a pig.

pig-headed /pig-he-did/ *adj* foolishly stubborn.

pigment /pig-mint/ *n* any substance used for colouring.

pigmy *see* **pygmy.**

pigpen /pig-pen/ *n* an enclosure for pigs.

pig-sticking /pig-sti-king/ *n* hunting wild boar with spears.

pigtail /pig-tale/ *n* a plait of hair hanging down the back or from each side of the head.

pike¹ /pike/ *n* a large freshwater fish.

pike² /pike/ *n* (*old*) a long spear.

pilchard /pil-churd/ *n* a small edible sea fish.

pilates /pi-lat-ays/ *n* a series of gentle exercises, based on the principles of yoga and devised by Dr Joseph Pilates.

pile¹ /pile/ *n* **1** a heap. **2** (*inf*) a large and grand building. • *vb* to heap up.

pile² /pile/ *n* one of a number of wooden posts driven into the ground as the foundation for a building.

pile³ /pile/ *n* the soft woolly hair on cloth, carpets, etc.

pilfer /pil-fur/ *vb* to steal small amounts or articles of small value. • *n* **pilferer.**

pilgrim /pil-grim/ *n* someone who travels, often very far, to a holy place to worship.

pilgrimage /pil-gri-midge/ *n* a journey made by a pilgrim.

pill /pill/ *n* a tiny ball of medicine.

pillar /pi-lar/ *n* **1** an upright of stone, wood, etc, for supporting an arch, roof, etc. **2** any person or thing that gives support.

pillow /pi-lo/ *n* a soft cushion for the head.

pillowcase /pi-lo-case/ *n* the cover put over a pillow.

pilot /pie-lut/ *n* **1** someone who steers an aeroplane. **2** someone who guides a ship in and out of harbour. • *vb* **1** to steer an aeroplane. **2** to guide, to show the way.

pimple /pim-pul/ *n* a small swelling on the skin.

pimply /pim-plee/ *adj* (*inf*) covered with pimples.

pin /pin/ *n* **1** a short pointed bar of wire with a flattened head, used for fastening cloth, paper etc. **2** a wooden, metal, or plastic peg. **3** a bolt. **4** a narrow brooch. • *vb* (**pinned, pinning** /pi-ning/) **1** to fasten with pins. **2** to hold firmly (to). • **pins and needles** a tingling feeling in a limb as the blood starts to flow freely through it again.

PIN /pin/ *abbr* = **personal identification number**: a number, consisting of several digits, used to identify a person.

pinata /pi-nya-ta/ *n* a paper container full of treats, hung from the ceiling and hit with sticks until its contents spill out.

pincers /pin-surz/ *npl* **1** a tool for gripping things firmly, used especially for pulling out nails. **2** claws (e.g. as of a crab).

pinch /pinch/ *vb* **1** to take or nip between the finger and thumb. **2** to squeeze the flesh until it hurts. **3** (*inf*) to steal. • *n* **1** the amount that can be taken between the finger and thumb. **2** a small amount. **3** need, distress.

pine[1] /pine/ *n* a cone-bearing evergreen tree.

pine[2] /pine/ *vb* **1** to waste away with sorrow, pain, etc. **2** to long for.

pineapple /pine-a-pul/ *n* a pine-cone-shaped tropical fruit.

pine cone /pine-cone/ *n* the scaly fruit of the pine tree.

ping /ping/ *n* a sharp sound, as of a bullet striking something.

pink[1] /pingk/ *n* **1** a garden flower. **2** a light red colour. **3** the best of condition. • *also adj*.

pink[2] /pingk/ *vb* to cut a zigzag edge on cloth.

pinnacle /pi-na-cul/ *n* **1** a pointed tower or spire on a building. **2** a pointed mountain. **3** the highest point.

pinstripe /pin-stripe/ *n* a very thin stripe running through a material.

pint /pinte/ *n* in imperial measurement, the eighth part of a gallon, 0.568 litres.

pioneer /pie-u-neer/ *n* **1** someone who goes before the main body to prepare the way, someone who is the first to try out new ideas etc. **2** an explorer. • *vb* **1** to begin. **2** to explore.

pious /pie-us/ *adj* loving and worshipping God, religious. • *n* piety.

pip /pip/ *n* **1** seed of fruit. **2** the spot on a card, dice, domino, etc. **3** one of the badges worn on an army officer's shoulder to show his rank.

pipe /pipe/ *n* **1** a musical wind instrument. **2** a long tube. **3** a tube with a bowl at one end for smoking tobacco. **4** a shrill voice. **5** a bird's note. **6** (*fml*) a measure of wine. • *vb* **1** to play upon a pipe. **2** to make. **3** to speak in a shrill voice. **4** to whistle. • **piping hot** very hot.

pipeline /pipe-line/ *n* a long line of pipes to carry water, oil, etc. • **in the pipeline** in preparation.

piper /pie-per/ *n* someone who plays a pipe or bagpipes. • **pay the piper** to pay the bill.

piquant /pee-kawnt/ *adj* **1** sharp-tasting, appetizing. **2** witty, arousing interest. • *n* piquancy.

pique /peek/ *n* irritation, anger caused by wounded pride. • *vb* to wound the pride of, to offend.

pirate /pie-rit/ *n* **1** someone who attacks and robs ships at sea. **2** a person who does something without legal right. • *also vb*. • *n* piracy.

pirouette /pi-roo-wet/ *vb* to turn round on the points of the toes as in ballet. • *also n*.

pistachio /pi-sta-shee-o/ *n* a nut with a green kernel.

pistil /pi-stul/ *n* the seed-bearing part of a flower.

pistol /pi-stul/ *n* a small firearm fired with one hand.

piston /pi-stun/ *n* a plug that fits closely into a hollow cylinder inside which it moves up and down.

pit[1] /pit/ *n* **1** a deep hole in the earth. **2** the passageway leading down to a mine. **3** a mine. **4** the area in front of the stage in a theatre where the orchestra sits. **5** a trading area in a commodities exchange. • *vb* (**pitted**, **pitting**) **1** to lay in a pit. **2** to set against in order to outdo.

pit[2] /pit/ *n* the stone of fruits such as the peach, plum, or cherry.

pitch[1] /pitch/ *vb* **1** to set up. **2** to throw. **3** to fall heavily. **4** to set the keynote of. **5** (*of a ship*) to dip down headfirst after rising on a wave. • *n* **1** a throw. **2** the highness or lowness of a note in music. **3** the ground marked out for a game. • **pitched battle** a set battle between two prepared armies.

pitch[2] /pitch/ *n* a thick dark substance obtained from tar.

pitcher[1] /pi-cher/ *n* a container for liquids.

pitcher[2] /pi-cher/ *n* the person who throws the ball to the batter in baseball.

pitchfork /pitch-fawrk/ *n* a long-handled tool with prongs for moving hay. • *vb* **1** to move with a pitchfork. **2** to put suddenly into a new situation.

pitfall /pit-fawl/ *n* a trap.

pith /pith/ *n* **1** material just under the skin of an orange, etc. **2** the soft centre of the stem of a plant. **3** the most important part.

pithy /pith-ee/ *adj* short and to the point, forceful.

pitiable /pi-tee-ya-bul/ *adj* deserving pity.

pitta (**bread**) /pi-ta bred/ *n* an oval-shaped type of flat bread that can be opened to insert a filling.

pittance /pi-tanse/ *n* a small allowance or wage.

pitted /pi-tid/ *adj* marked with little hollows.

pity /pi-tee/ *n* sympathy for the pain or sorrow of others. • *vb* to feel sorry for. • *adjs* pitiful, pitiless /pi-tee-less/.

pivot /pi-vut/ *n* 1 the pin on which anything (e.g. a wheel) turns. 2 the central point of anything.

pivotal /pi-vu-tal/ *adj* holding a central or important position.

pixel /piks-ul/ *n* in computing or photography, one of many tiny dots that make up a larger picture.

pixie, pixy /pik-see/ *n* a fairy.

pizza /peet-sa/ *n* a baked circle of dough covered with cheese, tomatoes, etc.

pizzeria /peet-se-ree-a/ *n* a restaurant where pizzas are baked and sold.

placard /pla-card/ *n* a notice put up in a public place to announce or advertise something.

placate /pla-cate/ *vb* to make calm or peaceful.

place /place/ *n* 1 an open space in a town. 2 a particular area of space. 3 a village, town, etc. 4 the post or position held by someone. 4 rank in society. 5 a passage in a book. • *vb* 1 to put or set. 2 to decide from where a thing comes or where it ought to be. 3 to recognize. 4 to find a job for.

placebo /pla-see-bo/ *n* an ineffective medication given to a control group in an experiment, when members of another group are given a new medicine under trial.

placid /pla-sid/ *adj* calm, not easily angered or upset, gentle. • *n* placidity.

plagiarism /play-ja-ri-zum/ *n* the act of stealing from another author's works. • *n* plagiarist.

plagiarize /play-ja-rize/ *vb*, *also* plagiarise to use the words or ideas of another and pretend they are one's own.

plague /plaig/ *n* 1 a very infectious and dangerous disease. 2 (*inf*) a nuisance. • *vb* (*inf*) to keep on annoying, to pester.

plaice /place/ *n* an edible flat fish.

plaid /plaid/ *n* 1 a type of checked or tartan cloth. 2 a large woollen shawl-like wrap, often of tartan, worn as part of Scottish Highland dress.

plain /plain/ *adj* 1 clear, easily understood. 2 simple, bare, undecorated. 3 obvious. • *n* a stretch of level country. • plain sailing /plain say-ling/ *n* something easy.

plain-spoken /plain-spo-kin/ *adj* saying what one thinks, frank.

plaintiff /plain-tif/ *n* the person who brings a suit before a court of law.

plaintive /plain-tiv/ *adj* sad, expressing sorrow.

plait /plat/, /plate/, pleat /pleet/ *n* 1 a pigtail of intertwined hair. 2 a fold (e.g. in material). • *vb* to twist together into a plait.

plan /plan/ *n* 1 a drawing of the outlines made by an object on the ground, a map. 2 a scheme of what is to happen on a future occasion. • *vb* (planned, planning) 1 to draw a plan of. 2 to arrange beforehand what should happen. • *n* planner.

plane¹ /plane/ *n* 1 a smooth or level surface. 2 a carpenter's tool for giving wood a smooth surface. 3 a common short form of aeroplane. • *adj* level, smooth. • *vb* to make smooth.

plane², plane tree /plane tree/ *n* a tall broad-leaved tree.

planet /pla-nit/ *n* one of the heavenly bodies moving in orbit round the sun.

planetarium /pla-ni-tay-ree-um/ *n* 1 a model of the planetary system. 2 a type of museum in which you can learn about the universe.

planetary /pla-ni-te-ree/ *adj* having to do with the planets.

plank /plangk/ *n* a long, flat piece of timber.

plankton /plangk-tun/ *n* small living organisms found in the sea.

plant /plant/ *n* 1 anything growing from the earth and feeding on it through its roots. 2 the machinery and equipment used in a factory. • *vb* 1 to put in the ground to grow. 2 to set firmly.

plantain¹ /plan-tin/ *n* a type of plant with small green flowers and broad leaves.

plantain², plantain tree /plan-tin tree/ *n* a tropical tree with fruit like a banana.

plantation /plan-tay-shun/ *n* 1 a wood planted by man. 2 an estate on which a large amount of sugar, tea, cotton, etc, is cultivated.

planter /plan-ter/ *n* the owner or manager of a plantation.

plaque /plak/ *n* 1 an ornamental plate of metal, etc. 2 a deposit of saliva and bacteria that forms on the teeth.

plasma /plaz-ma/ *n* the liquid part of blood.

plasma screen /plaz-ma screen/ *n* a type of flat screen on a television set.

plaster /pla-ster/ *n* 1 a mixture of lime, water and sand spread over the walls of buildings to make them smooth. 2 an adhesive bandage used for dressing wounds, etc. • *vb* 1 to cover with plaster. 2 to spread over the surface of.

plaster cast /pla-ster cast/ *n* a rigid casing put around a broken limb for support while it is healing.

plasterer /pla-stu-rer/ *n* someone who plasters walls.

plastic /pla-stic/ *adj* easily shaped or moulded. • *n* **1** one of a group of man-made substances that can be moulded into any shape. **2** credit cards.

plastic surgery /pla-stic **sur**-ju-ree/ *n* the reshaping of part of the human body by surgery.

plate /plate/ *n* **1** a shallow dish for food. **2** a flat piece of metal, glass, etc. **3** gold and silver household articles. **4** a picture printed from an engraved piece of metal, etc. • *vb* to cover with a thin coat of metal.

plateau /pla-toe/ *n* (*pl* **plateaux** *or* **plateaus**) an extent of high level land, a tableland.

platform /plat-fawrm/ *n* **1** a raised part of the floor. **2** a bank built above ground level for those entering trains, etc. **3** statement of the aims of a group.

plating /play-ting/ *n* the art of covering articles with a thin coat of metal.

platinum /plat-num/ *n* a valuable heavy greyish white metal.

platonic love /pla-ton-ic **luv**/ *n* a non-sexual love between two human beings.

platoon /pla-**toon**/ *n* a small division of a company of infantry.

platter /pla-ter/ *n* a large flat plate or dish.

platypus /pla-ti-pus/ *n* an Australian mammal with jaws like a duck's bill.

plausible /plau-zi-bul/ *adj* that which sounds convincing, is seemingly true or truthful. • *n* plausibility.

play /play/ *vb* **1** to amuse oneself. **2** to take part in a game or sport. **3** to gamble. **4** to act a part in a drama. **5** to perform on a musical instrument. **6** to trifle with. • *n* **1** a drama. **2** things that people, such as children, do to amuse or entertain themselves. **3** gambling. **4** free movement.

player /play-er/ *n* **1** someone who takes part in a sport or drama. **2** a musical performer.

playful /play-ful/ *adj* fond of sport or amusement.

playground /play-ground/ *n* a piece of ground set aside for children to play in.

playhouse /play-house/ *n* a toy house large enough for children to play inside.

playmate /play-mate/ *n* a childhood companion.

plaything /play-thing/ *n* a toy.

playwright /play-rite/ *n* someone who writes plays.

plea /plee/ *n* **1** an excuse. **2** an earnest request. **3** the prisoner's answer to the charge in a law court.

plead /pleed/ *vb* (*pt*, *pp* **pled** *or* **pleaded**) **1** to request earnestly. **2** to put forward in excuse. **3** to present one's case or one's client's case in a court of law.

pleasant /ple-zant/ *adj* agreeable, enjoyable.

please /pleez/ *vb* **1** to make happy or content. **2** to seem good to. **3** to be so kind as to.

pleasurable /plezh-ra-bul/ *adj* giving pleasure.

pleasure /ple-zhur/ *n* **1** delight, joy. **2** will or choice.

pleat *see* **plait**.

plectrum /plec-trum/ *n* a small instrument for plucking the strings of stringed instruments.

pled *pt and pp of* **plead**.

pledge /pledge/ *n* **1** a solemn promise. **2** an object handed over to another to keep until a debt has been paid back to him or her. **3** a toast. • *vb* **1** to promise solemnly. **2** (*fml*) to give to keep until a debt has been repaid. **3** to drink to the health of.

plenitude /ple-ni-tood/ *n* an abundance, completeness.

plentiful /plen-ti-ful/ *adj* enough, more than enough.

plenty /plen-tee/ *n* all that is necessary, more than is necessary.

plethora /ple-tho-ra/ *n* more than enough of anything.

pliable /plie-a-bul/ *adj* **1** easily bent. **2** easily influenced. • *n* pliability.

pliant /plie-ant/ *adj* **1** easily bent. **2** easily influenced. • *n* pliancy.

pliers /plie-urs/ *npl* a small tool for gripping things firmly and for cutting wire.

plight[1] /plite/ *n* a difficult condition, situation.

plight[2] /plite/ *vb* (*old*) to promise.

plinth /plinth/ *n* the square slab at the foot of a pillar or under a statue.

plod /plod/ *vb* (**plodded**, **plodding**) to walk or work slowly and steadily.

plodder /plod-er/ *n* someone who, though not clever, makes progress by hard work.

plonk /plongk/ *n* (*inf*) cheap or low-quality wine. • *v* to put something down heavily or carelessly.

plot /plot/ *n* **1** a small piece of ground. **2** the planned arrangement of the events of a story, play, etc. **3** a secret plan against one or more persons. • *vb* (**plotted**, **plotting**) **1** to plan. **2** to form a plan against. **3** to mark out or set down on paper. • *n* plotter.

plough /plow/ *n*, *also* **plow** (*US*) an instrument for turning up soil before seeds are sown. • *vb* to turn up with a plough.

ploughman /plow-man/ *n* someone who ploughs, a farm labourer.

ploughshare /plow-share/ *n* the cutter or blade of a plough.

ploy /ploy/ *n* a devious tactic.

pluck /pluck/ *vb* **1** to pick or gather. **2** to snatch. **3** to pull off the feathers. • *n* courage.

plucky /plu-kee/ *adj* brave.

plug /plug/ *n* **1** an object that fits into a hole and stops it, a stopper. **2** a device with metal pins that connects an electrical appliance to the main electrical supply. • *vb* (**plugged**, **plugging**) **1** to stop with a plug. **2** (*inf*) to publicize.

plughole /plug-hole/ *n* a hole at the foot of a sink or bath through which the water drains and into which a plug fits.

plum /plum/ *n* a smooth-skinned, purple-coloured fruit with a pit. • *adj* **1** a dark, purple-red colour. **2** desirable.

plumage /ploo-midge/ *n* the feathers of a bird.

plumb /plum/ *n* a piece of lead on a string, lowered from the top of a wall to see that it is at right angles to the ground. • *adj* straight up and down. • *adv* **1** exactly. **2** straight up and down. • *vb* **1** to measure depth. **2** to study thoroughly.

plumber /plu-mer/ *n* a workman skilled in mending or fitting pipes, taps, etc.

plumbing /plu-ming/ *n* **1** the work of a plumber. **2** all the pipes, taps, etc, in a house.

plumbline /plum-line/ *n* the string by which a plumb is lowered.

plume /ploom/ *n* **1** a feather. **2** an ornament of feathers in a hat, etc. • **3** a cloud of something such as smoke, etc that rises up into the air.

plummet /plu-mit/ *vb* to drop down, to plunge.

plump[1] /plump/ *adj* fat and rounded. • *vb* to grow fat, to fatten. • *n* **plumpness**.

plump[2] /plump/ *vb* **1** to sit or fall suddenly. **2** to choose. • *adv* suddenly or directly.

plum pudding /plum poo-ding/ *n* a pudding containing currants, raisins, etc, flavoured with spices.

plunder /plun-der/ *vb* to steal by force, to rob. • *n* that which is taken away by force.

plunge /plunj/ *vb* **1** to thrust into water. **2** to jump or dive into water. **3** to rush. • *n* **1** a dive. **2** act of rushing.

pluperfect /ploo-per-fect/ *n see* **past perfect**.

plural /plu-ral/ *adj* more than one in number. • *n* the form(s) of a word indicating more than one.

pluralist /plu-ra-list/ *n* (*fml*) someone who holds more than one office.

plurality /plu-ra-li-tee/ *n* (*fml*) **1** a number consisting of more than one. **2** the majority.

plus /plus/ *prep* with the addition of. • *adj* **1** more than. **2** to be added, extra. • *n* the sign (+) of addition.

plush /plush/ *n* (*inf*) a velvety kind of cloth. • *adj* luxurious.

Pluto /ploo-to/ *n* originally classified as the ninth planet from the sun, since 2006 Pluto has been regarded as one of 44 dwarf planets (there are now deemed to be eight planets in the solar system).

ply[1] /plie/ *vb* **1** to work at. **2** to go regularly between two places. **3** to use skilfully.

ply[2] /plie/ *n* a layer.

plywood /plie-wood/ *n* strong board made up of several thin layers of wood stuck together.

p.m. /pee-em/ *abbr* = **post meridiem** /post mer-id-ee-em/: a Latin phrase, meaning after noon.

PMS /pee-em-ess/ *n abbr* = **premenstrual syndrome**: the physical and emotional effects that some women experience just before a period starts. • *sometimes* **PMT** *n abbr* = **premenstrual tension**.

pneumatic /noo-ma-tic/ *adj* filled with air, moved by air.

pneumonia /noo-moe-nee-a/ *n* an inflammation of the lungs.

poach[1] /poach/ *vb* to cook (fish, eggs, etc.) lightly in liquid.

poach[2] /poach/ *vb* to hunt unlawfully on another's land. • *n* **poacher**.

pocket /pock-it/ *n* **1** a small bag attached to a garment, billiard table, suitcase, etc. **2** a hollow in earth or rock filled with metal ore. • *vb* **1** to put into a pocket. **2** to steal. **3** to conceal.

pocketbook /pock-it-book/ *n* a small case for holding paper money, letters, etc.

pocket money /pock-it mu-nee/ *n* a small amount of money that parents give regularly to their children.

pockmarked /pock-markt/ *adj* marked with small hollows on the skin as a result of smallpox.

pod /pod/ *n* the covering of the seed of plants, such as peas, beans, etc.

podcast /pod-cast/ *n* an audio or video file, downloadable (usually for free) from a web site and playable on computers or mp3 players.

podgy /pod-jee/ *adj* (*inf*) short and fat.

poem /poa-em/ *n* a piece of writing set down in memorable language and in lines with a recognizable rhythm.

poet /poa-et/ *n* someone who writes poetry. • *f* **poetess**.

poetic /poa-et-ic/, **poetical** /poa-et-i-cal/ *adjs* **1** having to do with poetry. **2** suitable for poetry.

poetry /poa-e-tree/ *n* ideas, feelings, etc, expressed in memorable words and rhythmical language.

poignant /**poy**-nyant/ *adj* painful and deeply felt.

point /point/ *n* **1** the sharp end of anything. **2** a headland. **3** a dot. **4** the exact place or time. **5** the purpose for which something is said or written. **6** a single stage in an argument or list. **7** the unit of scoring in certain games. • *vb* **1** to show the direction of with a finger, stick, etc. **2** to sharpen. **3** to aim. **4** (*of dogs*) to show the direction of game with the nose. • **make a point of** to attach special importance to. • **on the point of** about to.

pointed /**poin**-tid/ *adj* **1** sharp. **2** meant to be understood in a certain way.

pointer /**poin**-ter/ *n* **1** a rod for pointing with. **2** a dog trained to point out game.

pointless /**point**-less/ *adj* having no meaning, having no sensible purpose.

poise /poiz/ *n* **1** balance. **2** calmness and good sense. • *vb* **1** to balance. **2** to hover.

poison /**poi**-zun/ *n* **1** any substance that when taken into a living creature (animal or vegetable) harms or kills it. **2** any idea, etc, that when spread through society causes standards of judgment to become lower. • *vb* **1** to give poison to. **2** to kill by poison.

poisonous /**poi**-zu-nuss/ *adj* **1** being or containing poison. **2** having a very harmful influence.

poke /poke/ *vb* to push with something pointed (e.g. a finger, stick, etc), to prod. • *n* a prod given with something pointed. • **poke fun at** to make fun of. • **poke one's nose into** to interfere in what does not concern one.

poker /**po**-ker/ *n* **1** a metal rod for stirring the coal, etc, in a fire. **2** a card game, usually played for money.

poky /**po**-kee/ *adj* (*inf*) small and cramped.

polar /**po**-lar/ *adj* of or near one of the poles of the earth.

polar bear /**po**-lar bare/ *n* the white bear of Arctic regions.

polarize /**po**-la-rize/ *vb*, *also* **polarise** to divide into groups based on two completely opposite opinions, attitudes, etc.

pole[1] /pole/ *n* **1** a long rod. **2** a long rounded post. **3** an imperial measure of length (= 5.03 metres).

pole[2] /pole/ *n* **1** one of the ends of the axis of the earth. **2** one of the points in the sky opposite the poles of the earth. **3** the end of either of the two arms of a magnet.

polecat /**pole**-cat/ *n* a weasel-like animal that throws out a foul-smelling liquid when attacked.

polestar, Pole Star /**pole**-star/ *n* a particular star at or near the celestial North Pole, used for finding directions.

police /pu-**leess**/ *n* a body of persons whose job is to keep public order and see that the law is kept. • *vb* to see that law and order are kept. • *n* **policeman, police officer, policewoman.**

policy /**pol**-i-see/ *n* **1** the methods or plans of a government or party. **2** a plan for a course of action. **3** a written agreement with an insurance company.

polish /**pol**-ish/ *vb* **1** to make smooth and shining by rubbing. **2** to improve, to refine. • *n* **1** a smooth, shiny surface. **2** any substance rubbed on to make smooth and shiny. **3** good manners, refinement.

polite /pu-**lite**/ *adj* well-mannered, refined. • *n* **politeness.**

political /pu-**li**-ti-cal/ *adj* having to do with politics.

politically correct /pu-li-tic-lee cu-**rect**/ *adj* of language that is designed to avoid giving offence to particular groups of people, usually people who are often discriminated against, often abbreviated to **PC**. • *n* **political correctness.**

politician /pol-i-**ti**-shun/ *n* **1** a statesman whose work is concerned with the public affairs or government of a country. **2** someone who seeks political office for selfish motives.

politics /**pol**-i-tics/ *n* the art or study of government; political matters.

polka /**pol**-ka/ *n* a quick lively dance.

poll /pole/ *n* **1** an election. **2** the number of votes. • *vb* **1** to record the vote of. **2** to receive a vote or votes.

pollen /**pol**-in/ *n* the yellow dust on a flower that when united to seeds makes them grow.

pollinate /**pol**-in-ate/ *vb* to make pollen unite with the seed. • *n* **pollination.**

pollutant /pu-**loo**-tant/ *n* something that pollutes.

pollute /pu-**loot**/ *vb* to make filthy or unfit for use. • *n* **pollution.**

polo /**po**-lo/ *n* a game like hockey played on horseback.

poltergeist /**pole**-ter-giest/ *n* a mischievous spirit or ghost.

poly- /**pol**-ee/ *prefix* many.

polyester /po-lee-**es**-ter/ *n* a synthetic fibre used to make fabric.

polythene /**pol**-i-theen/ *n* a man-made plastic material resistant to chemicals and moisture.

pomegranate /**pom**-e-gra-nit/ *n* a large thick-skinned fruit containing many red, juicy, edible seeds.

pomp /pomp/ n splendid show or display, grandeur.

pomposity /pom-**pos**-i-tee/ n act of being pompous.

pompous /pom-pus/ adj trying to appear dignified or important.

poncho /**pon**-sho/ n a circular or rectangular cloak with a hole in the middle to put the head through.

pond /pond/ n a large pool of standing water.

ponder /**pon**-der/ vb (fml) to think deeply, to consider carefully.

ponderous /**pon**-drus/ adj 1 (fml) very heavy. 2 slow, dull.

pong /pong/ n (inf) an unpleasant smell.

pontiff /**pon**-tif/ n 1 a bishop. 2 the pope. • **Supreme Pontiff** the pope.

pontifical /pon-**ti**-fi-cal/ adj 1 having to do with a bishop or the pope. 2 pompous.

pontificate /pon-**ti**-fi-cate/ vb 1 (fml) to state one's opinions pompously, as if stating undoubted facts. 2 to act as a pontiff. • n the office or reign of a pontiff.

pontoon[1] /pon-**toon**/ n a card game, usually played for money.

pontoon[2] /pon-**toon**/ n a flat-bottomed boat used as a support for a bridge. • n **pontoon bridge**.

pony /**poe**-nee/ n a small horse.

poo /poo/ (inf) n 1 faeces. 2 the passing of faeces. • vb to pass faeces.

poodle /**poo**-dul/ n a pet dog with curly hair, often clipped to leave part of its hair short.

pooh /poo/ interj an exclamation of contempt.

pooh-pooh /poo-**poo**/ vb (inf) to sneer at, to speak scornfully of.

pool[1] /pool/ n 1 a puddle. 2 a deep place in a stream or river. 3 an area of still water.

pool[2] /pool/ n 1 all the money bet on a certain game or event. 2 a collection of resources, money, etc, for sharing, communal use etc. • vb to put together the goods, etc, of individuals for use by the whole group.

poop[1] /poop/ n the back part of a ship, the stern.

poop[2] /poop/ vb to exhaust.

poop[3] /poop/ n (inf) 1 faeces. 2 the passing of faeces. • vb to pass faeces.

poor /poor/ adj 1 having little money. 2 unfortunate. 3 bad.

poorly /**poor**-lee/ adj unwell.

pop /pop/ n 1 a sharp, low sound. 2 pop music. • vb (popped, popping) 1 to make a sharp, low sound. 2 to move quickly or suddenly.

Pope /pope/ n the head of the Roman Catholic Church.

poplar /**pop**-lar/ n a tall slender tree.

pop music /pop myoo-zic/ n modern popular music, usually having simple tunes and a strong beat.

poppy /**pop**-ee/ n a plant with brightly coloured flowers.

populace /**pop**-yu-lis/ n (fml) the common people.

popular /**pop**-yu-lar/ adj 1 having to do with the people. 2 well-liked by most people.

popularity /pop-yu-**la**-ri-tee/ n the state of being liked by most people.

popularize /**pop**-yu-la-rize/ vb, also **popularise** to make popular.

populate /**pop**-yu-late/ vb to provide with inhabitants.

population /pop-yu-**lay**-shun/ n all the people living in a place.

populous /**pop**-yu-lus/ adj having many inhabitants.

porcelain /**pore**-su-lin/ n fine pottery.

porch /**poarch**/ n a roofed approach to a door.

porcupine /**pawr**-cyu-pine/ n an animal like the rat, covered with prickly quills.

pore[1] /pore/ n a tiny opening, especially in the skin.

pore[2] /pore/ vb. • **pore over** to study closely.

pork /poark/ n the meat obtained from a pig.

porous /**poe**-rus/ adj having small holes through which liquid may pass.

porpoise /**pawr**-poiz/ n a sea animal about 1.5 metres long.

porridge /**paw**-ridge/ n a food made from oatmeal boiled in water or milk and served hot for breakfast.

port[1] /port/ n 1 a harbour. 2 a place with a harbour.

port[2] /port/ n an opening in the side of a ship.

port[3] /port/ n the left side of a ship (looking forward), larboard (old).

port[4] /port/ n a dark sweet red wine.

portable /**pore**-ta-bul/ adj able to be carried about.

portal /**pore**-tal/ n (fml) a doorway, a gateway.

portcullis /port-**cu**-lis/ n a grating of crisscrossed iron bars that can be lowered suddenly to close the gateway of a castle against attackers.

porter /**pore**-tur/ n 1 someone who carries loads, baggage, etc, for others. 2 a person employed in a hospital to move patients from place to place. 3 a person in charge of the entrance to a hotel or other large building. 4 a dark brown beer.

portfolio /port-**foe**-lee-o/ n 1 a case for carrying loose papers, drawings, etc. 2 the office of a minister of state.

porthole /**poart**-hole/ n a small window in the side of a ship.

portico /pore-ti-co/ *n* (*pl* **porticoes** *or* **porticos**) **1** a roof supported by a row of pillars, jutting out at the front of a building. **2** a roofed approach to a door. **3** a path covered by a roof supported by pillars.

portion /pore-shun/ *n* **1** a share. **2** a helping, a serving. **3** the money and property given to a woman at the time of her marriage. **4** (*fml or old*) one's fate. **5** a part of something. • *vb* **1** to divide up. **2** to give a share to.

portly /port-lee/ *adj* stout.

portrait /pore-trait/ *n* **1** a picture of a person. **2** a good description.

portraiture /pore-tri-chur/ *n* **1** the drawing of portraits. **2** describing in words.

portray /pore-tray/ *vb* **1** to draw or paint. **2** to describe.

portrayal /pore-tray-al/ *n* the act of portraying.

Portuguese /pore-tyoo-geez/ *n* the language of Portugal and Brazil. • *adj* pertaining to the land or people of Portugal.

pose /poze/ *vb* **1** to put. **2** to put on or take up a certain attitude. **3** to pretend to be what one is not. • *n* **1** position, attitude. **2** a pretence of being what one is not. **3** a false manner or attitude.

posh /posh/ *adj* **1** expensive or luxurious. **2** upper-class.

position /pu-zi-shun/ *n* **1** place. **2** rank, grade. **3** job. **4** state of affairs. **5** a place occupied by troops during battle. • *vb* to place.

positive /pos-i-tiv/ *adj* **1** sure. **2** certain, definite. **3** confident. **4** greater than zero. **5** really existing. **6** active, leading to practical action.

positively /pos-i-tiv-lee/ *adv* completely, really.

posse /pos-ee/ *n* a group of people with a shared interest or purpose.

possess /pu-zess/ *vb* **1** to have as one's own. **2** (*fml*) to control the mind of. • *adj* **possessed**.

possession /pu-ze-shun/ *n* **1** the act of possessing. **2** ownership. **3** control by evil spirits.

possessive /pu-ze-siv/ *adj* **1** showing possession. **2** liking to possess or own, unwilling to share.

possessor /pu-ze-sur/ *n* someone who possesses.

possibility /paw-si-bi-li-tee/ *n* something possible.

possible /paw-si-bul/ *adj* **1** that may be true. **2** that may exist. **3** that can be done.

possibly /paw-si-blee/ *adv* perhaps, maybe.

post¹ /poast/ *n* a strong pole or length of wood stuck upright in the ground. • *vb* to put up on a post, noticeboard, etc.

post² /poast/ *n* **1** the official system by which letters, parcels, etc are sent from one place to another. **2** letters or parcels sent in this system. **3** one's place of duty. **4** one's job. **5** a military camp. **6** a settlement. • *vb* **1** to send by post. **2** to send to a certain place of duty. **3** (*old*) to travel on horseback changing horses at regular intervals. **4** to supply with the latest news.

post- /poast/ *prefix* after.

postage /poa-stidge/ *n* the charge for sending something by mail.

postbox /poast-boks/ *n* a metal box in a public place for putting letters to be sent by post.

postcard /poast-card/ *n* a card on which a message may be written and which can be posted without an envelope.

postcode *n* /poast-code/ a combination of letter and number to aid in addressing posted items.

postdate /poast-date/ *vb* to put on a date later than the actual one.

poster /poas-ter/ *n* a large printed notice for public display.

posterior /pu-sti-ree-ur/ *adj* (*fml*) **1** later. **2** placed behind.

posterity /pos-te-ri-tee/ *n* one's descendants, later generations.

posthumous /pos-chu-mus/ *adj* **1** happening after someone's death. **2** born after the father's death. **3** published after the author's death.

postman /poast-man/ *n* a man whose job is to deliver letters and parcels sent by post.

postmortem /poast-mawr-tum/ *adj* after death. • *n* an examination of a body after death to find out the cause of death. • *also* **autopsy** (*US*).

postnatal /poast-nay-tal/ *adj* after birth.

post office /poast awf-iss/ *n* **1** an office where stamps may be bought, letters posted, etc. **2 the Post Office** of the government department in charge of postal services.

postpone /poast-pone/ *vb* to put off until a later time. • *n* **postponement**.

postscript /poast-script/ *n* something extra written at the end of a letter after the signature, *abbr* **PS**.

posture /pos-chur/ *n* **1** a way of holding oneself. **2** an attitude. • *vb* **1** to hold oneself in a certain way. **2** (*fml*) to behave in a way not natural to oneself.

posy /poe-zee/ *n* a small bunch of flowers.

pot /pot/ *n* **1** a vessel for cooking in. **2** a vessel for holding plants, liquids, etc. • *vb* (**potted, potting**) **1** to put in a pot. **2** to shoot at and kill.

potash /pot-ash/ *n* a substance obtained from the ashes of certain plants.

potassium /pu-ta-see-um/ *n* the metallic base of potash.

potato /pu-tay-toe/ *n* (*pl* **potatoes**) a plant, the tubers of which are eaten as vegetables.

potency /poe-ten-see/ *n* power.

potent /poe-tent/ *adj* strong, powerful.

potential /pu-ten-shal/ *adj* existing but not made use of; possible. • *n* the unrealized ability to do something.

potentiality /pu-ten-shee-a-li-tee/ *n* unused or undeveloped power(s).

pothole /pot-hole/ *n* 1 a hole in the surface of a road. 2 a deep hole in limestone.

potholing /pot-hole-ing/ *n* the exploring of limestone potholes.

potion /po-shun/ *n* (*lit*) a dose, a liquid medicine.

pot luck /pot luck/ *n* 1 whatever food is available. 2 whatever is available.

potpourri /po-poo-ree/ *n* 1 a mixture of dried pieces of sweet-smelling flowers and leaves. 2 (*fml*) a selection of writings or pieces of music, a miscellany.

pottage /pot-idge/ *n* (*old*) a thick soup or porridge.

potter[1] /pot-er/ *n* someone who makes earthenware vessels.

potter[2] /pot-er/ *vb* work slowly and without much attention.

pottery /pot-er-ee/ *n* 1 cups, plates, etc, made of earthenware. 2 a potter's workshop.

pouch /pouch/ *n* a small bag.

pouffe /poof/ *n* a large firm cushion used as a seat or for resting your feet on.

poulterer /pole-tu-rer/ *n* someone who buys and sells poultry.

poultice /pole-tiss/ *n* a dressing containing some soft material, often heated, and placed on or over a sore part of the body. • *vb* to put a poultice on.

poultry /pole-tree/ *n* farmyard fowls.

pounce /pounse/ *n* 1 a sudden jump on. 2 the claw of a bird. • *vb* 1 to jump on suddenly. 2 to attack suddenly.

pound[1] /pound/ *n* 1 an imperial measure of weight (= 16 ounces or 0.454 kilograms), *abbr* **lb**. 2 a British unit of money (100 pence).

pound[2] /pound/ *vb* 1 to beat hard. 2 to crush into powder or small pieces. 3 to walk or run heavily.

pound[3] /pound/ *n* 1 a place for stray cats and dogs. 2 a place where cars that have been illegally parked are kept until the owners pay to get them back.

pour /pore/ *vb* 1 to cause to flow. 2 to flow strongly. 3 to rain heavily. 4 to move in great quantity or in large numbers.

pout /pout/ *vb* to thrust out the lips in displeasure, to look sulky. • *n* a sulky look.

poverty /po-vur-tee/ *n* lack of money or goods, want, the state of being poor.

poverty-stricken /po-vur-tee-stri-kin/ *adj* very poor.

powder /pow-der/ *n* 1 any substance in the form of tiny dry particles. 2 gunpowder. • *vb* 1 to make into a powder. 2 to put powder on.

powdery /pow-dree/ *adj* 1 dustlike. 2 covered with powder.

power /pow-er/ *n* 1 the ability to act or do. 2 strength, force. 3 influence. 4 control. 5 a strong nation. 6 mechanical energy. • *adj* **powerful, powerless**.

powerhouse /pow-er-house/ *n* (*inf*) a strong or energetic person, team, etc.

power station /pow-er stay-shun/ *n* a place where electrical power is generated.

powwow /pow-wow/ *n* 1 (*inf*) a friendly discussion. 2 (*old*) a conference among American Indians.

practicable /prac-ti-ca-bul/ *adj* that can be done, possible.

practical /prac-ti-cal/ *adj* 1 skilful in work, able to deal with things efficiently. 2 that can be carried out, useful. 3 concerned with action rather than with ideas. • *adv* **practically**.

practicality /prac-ti-ca-li-tee/ *n* usefulness.

practice /prac-tiss/ *n* 1 (*fml*) habit, frequent use. 2 the doing of an action often to improve one's skill. 3 a doctor or lawyer's business.

practise /prac-tiss/ *vb*, *also* **practice** (*US*) 1 to do frequently. 2 to do often in order to improve one's skill. 3 to carry on a profession.

practitioner /prac-tish-ner/ *n* someone who practises a profession.

pragmatic /prag-ma-tic/ *adj* concerned with practicalities rather than theories.

pragmatism /prag-ma-ti-zum/ *n* the judging of actions or events by their practical outcome.

prairie /pray-ree/ *n* an extent of level treeless grassland.

praise /praise/ *vb* 1 to speak well of, to speak in honour of. 2 to worship, as by singing hymns, etc. • *n* 1 an expression of credit or honour. 2 glory, worship expressed through song.

praiseworthy /praise-wur-thee/ *adj* deserving to be spoken well of.

pram /pram/ *n* a four-wheeled vehicle for pushing a baby in.

prance /pranss/ vb 1 to jump about. 2 to walk in a showy manner.

prank /prangk/ n a trick played in fun.

prattle /pra-tul/ vb to talk a lot and foolishly, to chatter like a young child. • n foolish or childish talk.

prawn /prawn/ n a small pink edible shellfish.

pray /pray/ vb 1 to beg for, to ask earnestly. 2 to speak to God in worship, thanksgiving, etc.

prayer /prare/ n 1 an earnest request. 2 words addressed to God in worship, thanksgiving, etc.

prayer book /prare book/ n a book containing prayers, order of services, etc.

pre- /pree/ prefix before.

preach /preech/ vb 1 to speak in public on a religious or sacred subject. 2 to give advice on how to behave correctly, especially in what is considered a boring or annoying way. 3 to recommend a particular way of behaving or thinking. • n preacher.

preamble /pree-am-bul/ n (fml) the introductory part of a statute or constitution, speech, piece of writing, etc.

prearrange /pre-a-range/ vb to arrange beforehand.

precarious /pri-cay-ree-us/ adj uncertain, dangerous.

precaution /pri-caw-shun/ n something done to prevent future trouble. • adj precautionary.

precede /pree-seed/ vb to come or go before in time, place or importance.

precedence /pre-si-dense/ n 1 being earlier in time. 2 greater importance. 3 order according to rank.

precedent /pre-si-dent/ n an earlier case that helps one to decide what to do in like circumstances.

preceding /pri-see-ding/ adj previous.

precinct /pree-singkt/ n 1 the land around and belonging to a building. 2 pl the grounds. 3 a part laid out for a particular use.

precious /pre-shus/ adj 1 of great worth or value. 2 too deliberate, too concerned with perfection or unimportant detail.

precipice /pre-si-piss/ n a very steep cliff.

precipitate /pri-si-pi-tate/ vb 1 to make happen at once. 2 to hasten. 3 to cause the solid matter in a liquid to sink to the foot. • adj /pri-si-pi-tit/ thoughtless, overhasty. • n /pri-si-pi-tit/ the solid matter that settles at the bottom of a liquid.

precipitation /pri-si-pi-tay-shun/ n the fall of water from the sky in the form of rain, hail, sleet or snow.

precise /pri-siess/ adj 1 exact, clearly expressed. 2 careful. 3 exact, particular, very. • n precision.

precocious /pri-co-shus/ adj (of a child) too clever for one's age, forward. • n precocity.

predator /preh-da-tor/ n an animal that hunts other animals for food.

predatory /preh-da-toe-ree/ adj living by killing or robbing others.

predecessor /pree-di-se-sur/ n someone who held a certain post before another.

predestination /pree-de-sti-nay-shun/ n the belief that God has settled beforehand everything that is to happen, including the fate of people in the afterlife.

predestine /pree-de-stin/ vb to settle or decide beforehand.

predetermine /pree-di-ter-min/ vb (fml) to decide beforehand.

predicament /pri-di-ca-ment/ n a difficulty, an unpleasant situation.

predicate /pre-di-cit/ n the part of sentence, containing a verb, which tells you what the subject or object does, or what is done to it.

predict /pri-dict/ vb to say what will happen in the future, to foretell. • n prediction.

predilection /pre-di-lec-shun/ n (fml) a preference.

predispose /pree-di-spoaz/ vb to influence, to make more likely to be affected by.

predisposition /pree-dis-pu-zi-shun/ n a tendency to be influenced or affected by.

predominance /pri-dom-in-anse/ n 1 control. 2 superiority in numbers, etc.

predominant /pri-dom-in-ant/ adj 1 outstanding. 2 largest.

predominate /pri-dom-in-ate/ vb 1 to have control over. 2 to be most or greatest.

preempt /pree-empt/ vb to take action to stop something from happening.

preen /preen/ vb 1 (of birds) to clean the feathers with the beak. 2 to tidy one's hair, clothes, etc.

prefabricate /pree-fa-bri-cate/ vb to make ready the parts.

preface /pre-fiss/ n an explanatory passage at the beginning of a speech or book. • vb to begin with some explanation or other remarks.

prefect /pree-fect/ n 1 in some countries, such as France, an officer responsible for an area of local government. 2 a senior pupil who helps to keep order in a school.

prefer /pri-fer/ vb (preferred, preferring) to like better; to choose before others.

preferable /pref-ra-bul/ adj more likable, chosen before others.

preference /pref-rense/ n a liking for one more than another.

preferential /pre-fe-**ren**-shal/ *adj* giving, receiving or showing preference.

prefix /**pree**-fiks/ *vb* to put at the beginning. • *n* a meaningful syllable or word put at the beginning of a word to alter its meaning.

pregnant /**preg**-nant/ *adj* 1 carrying unborn young within the body. 2 full of. 3 full of meaning. • *n* **pregnancy**.

prehensile /pree-**hen**-sul/ *adj* (*fml*) able to grasp or hold.

prehistoric /pre-hi-**stor**-ic/ *adj* before the time of written records.

prejudge /pre-**judge**/ *vb* to decide or form an opinion before hearing all the facts.

prejudice /**pre**-ju-diss/ *n* 1 an unreasonable feeling for or against. 2 an opinion formed without full knowledge of the facts. 3 (*fml*) harm, injury. • *vb* 1 to influence unreasonably for or against. 2 to harm, to spoil.

prejudicial /pre-ju-**di**-shal/ *adj* harmful.

preliminary /pri-**li**-mi-na-ree/ *adj* coming before what is really important, introductory. • *also n*.

prelude /**prel**-yood/ *n* 1 a piece of music played before and introducing the main musical work. 2 something done or happening before an event, helping to prepare one for it.

premature /**pree**-ma-choor/ *adj* 1 happening or done too soon. 2 before the natural or proper time.

premeditate /pree-**med**-i-tate/ *vb* to plan beforehand.

premeditation /pree-med-i-**tay**-shun/ *n* the act of thinking about something before doing it.

premier /pri-**myur**/ *adj* first, chief. • *n* the prime minister.

premiere /pri-**myur**/ *n* the first public performance of a play, film, etc. • *also vb*.

premise /**pre**-miss/ *n* 1 a statement accepted as true for the purpose of an argument based on it. 2 *pl* a building, its outhouses and grounds.

premium /**pree**-mee-um/ *n* 1 the amount paid for an insurance policy. 2 a reward, especially an inducement to buy. 3 something given free or at a reduced price with a purchase. • **at a premium** of greater value than usual, difficult to obtain.

premonition /pre-mu-**ni**-shun/ *n* a feeling that something particular is about to happen.

prenatal /pree-**nay**-tal/ *adj* before birth.

preoccupation /pree-oc-yu-**pay**-shun/ *n* a concern that prevents one thinking of other things.

preoccupied /pree-**oc**-yu-pide/ *adj* thinking of other things.

prepaid /**pree**-paid/ *adj* paid in advance.

preparation /pre-pe-**ray**-shun/ *n* 1 the act of preparing. 2 something done to make ready. 3 that which is made ready.

preparatory /pri-**pa**-ri-toe-ree/ *adj* helping to prepare, making ready for something that is to follow.

prepare /pri-**pare**/ *vb* 1 to make ready. 2 to get oneself ready.

preposition /pre-pu-**zi**-shun/ *n* a word showing the relation between a noun or pronoun and another word.

preposterous /pri-**pos**-truss/ *adj* completely absurd, foolish.

prerogative /pri-**rog**-a-tiv/ *n* a special power or right attached to a certain office.

prescribe /pri-**scribe**/ *vb* 1 (*fml*) to lay down what is to be done. 2 to order a certain medicine.

prescription /pri-**scrip**-shun/ *n* a written order by a doctor for a certain medicine.

prescriptive /pri-**scrip**-tiv/ *adj* indicating how something must be done.

presence /**pre**-zinss/ *n* 1 the state of being in the place required. 2 someone's appearance and bearing. • **presence of mind** ability to behave calmly in the face of difficulty or danger.

present[1] /**pre**-zent/ *adj* 1 in the place required or mentioned. 2 now existing or happening. • *n* the time in which we live.

present[2] /**pre**-zent/ *n* a gift. • *vb* /pri-**zent**/ 1 to give, to offer. 2 to introduce. 3 to show. 4 to put forward. 5 to point.

presentable /pri-**zen**-ta-bul/ *adj* fit to be seen or shown.

presentation /pre-zen-**tay**-shun/ *n* 1 the act of handing over a present, especially in public. 2 something given by a group of people to mark a special occasion. 3 the way in which things are shown or arguments put forward.

presently /**pre**-zent-lee/ *adv* soon.

preservation /pre-zer-**vay**-shun/ *n* 1 the act of preserving. 2 safeguarding.

preservative /pre-**zer**-va-tiv/ *n* an ingredient or application that prevents something from going bad. • *also adj*.

preserve /pri-**zerv**/ *vb* 1 (*fml*) to keep from harm. 2 to keep from rotting or decaying. 3 to keep safe or in good condition. • *n* 1 fruit, etc, treated so as to prevent it from going bad; jam. 2 a place where animals, birds, etc, are protected.

preside /pri-**zide**/ *vb* to control a meeting, to act as chairman.

presidency /pre-zi-den-see/ *n* the job or office of president.

president /pre-zi-dent/ *n* **1** the elected head of state of a republic. **2** the head of a company, etc; a chairman.

presidential /pre-zi-**den**-shal/ *adj* having to do with a president.

press¹ /press/ *vb* **1** to push on or against with force. **2** to squeeze. **3** to smooth and flatten. **4** to try to persuade. • *n* **1** a crowd. **2** a printing machine. **3** a machine for crushing or squeezing. **4** the newspapers.

press² /press/ *vb* (*old*) to force to serve in the armed forces.

press gang /press gang/ *n* (*old*) a body of seamen sent out to seize men and force them to serve in the navy. • *vb* **press-gang** **1** (*old*) to seize someone and force him or her to serve in the navy. **2** to make someone do something by forceful persuasion.

pressing /press-ing/ *adj* requiring immediate action, urgent.

pressure /pre-shur/ *n* **1** the act of pressing; force. **2** forceful influence. **3** stress.

prestige /pre-**steezh**/ *n* good name, high reputation.

presumably /pri-**zoo**-ma-blee/ *adv* apparently.

presume /pri-**zoom**/ *vb* **1** to take for granted, to accept as true without proof. **2** to act in a bold or forward way.

presumption /pri-**zum**-shun/ *n* **1** something supposed to be true. **2** forwardness, boldness of manner.

presumptive /pri-**zum**-tiv/ *adj* (*fml*) probable.

presumptuous /pri-**zum**-chu-wus/ *adj* overconfident, bold in manner.

presuppose /pree-su-**poaz**/ *vb* to take for granted.

pretence /pri-**tense**/ *n, also* **pretense** (*US*) **1** the act of pretending. **2** a deception. **3** a false claim.

pretend /pri-**tend**/ *vb* **1** to make believe by words or actions that one is other than one really is. **2** to behave as if one were in other circumstances. **3** to claim.

pretender /pri-**ten**-der/ *n* (*fml*) someone making a certain claim.

pretension /pri-**ten**-shun/ *n* **1** a claim, true or false. **2** pretentiousness.

pretentious /pri-**ten**-shus/ *adj* claiming much for oneself, too proud.

preterite /**pre**-tu-rite/ *n* the past tense of a verb.

pretext /**pree**-tekst/ *n* a pretended reason, an excuse.

pretty /**pri**-tee/ *adj* pleasing to the eye, attractive. • *adv* quite. • *n* **prettiness**.

prevail /pri-**vail**/ *vb* **1** to overcome, to prove better or stronger than. **2** to be in general use. **3** to persuade.

prevailing /pri-**vay**-ling/ *adj* **1** common, most widely accepted, etc. **2** (*of wind*) that usually blows over an area.

prevalent /**pre**-va-lent/ *adj* common, widespread. • *n* **prevalence**.

prevent /pri-**vent**/ *vb* to stop from happening. • *n* **prevention**.

preventive /pri-**ven**-tiv/ *adj* helping to prevent. • *also n*.

preview, prevue /**pree**-vyoo/ *n* an advance showing of a film, performance, etc. before its official opening

previous /**pree**-vee-us/ *adj* earlier, happening before.

prey /pray/ *n* **1** an animal or bird hunted and killed by another animal or bird. **2** someone who suffers (from). • *vb* **1** to hunt and kill for food. **2** to keep on attacking and robbing. **3** to trouble greatly.

price /price/ *n* **1** the money asked or paid for something on sale. **2** what is required to obtain something.

priceless /**price**-less/ *adj* of great value.

prick /prick/ *vb* **1** to stab lightly with the point of a needle, dagger, etc. **2** to make a tiny hole in. **3** to make to stand up straight. • *n* **1** a sharp point. **2** a tiny hole. **3** a sting. **4** a thorn.

prickle /**pri**-cul/ *n* a small sharp point growing out from a plant or an animal.

prickly /**pri**-clee/ *adj* covered with small sharp points.

prickly heat /**pri**-clee heet/ *n* skin inflammation causing severe itching.

pride /pride/ *n* **1** a feeling of pleasure at one's own abilities, deeds, etc. **2** too great an opinion of oneself, one's deeds, etc. **3** the most valuable person or thing. • **pride oneself on** to take pleasure in.

priest /preest/ *n* a clergyman, a minister of religion. • *f* **priestess**.

priesthood /**preest**-hood/ *n* **1** the office of priest. **2** priests in general.

prim /prim/ *adj* **1** stiff in manner, formal and correct. **2** neat, restrained.

primacy /**prie**-ma-see/ *n* **1** the office of archbishop. **2** the state of being first in time, order, rank, etc.

prima donna /pree-ma **don**-a/ *n* **1** the chief female singer in an opera. **2** someone who is prone to tantrums if his or her wishes are not met.

primal /**prie**-mal/ *adj* (*fml*) original, having to do with early times.

primary /**prie**-mer-ee/ *adj* **1** first. **2** chief. • *n* a preliminary US election in which the candidates are chosen. • *adv* **primarily**.

primary colours /prie-mer-ee **cu**-lurz/ *npl* the colours red, yellow and blue, from which other colours may be made.

primary school /prie-mer-ee **skool**/ *n* a school for children roughly between the ages of four and twelve.

primate /prie-mate/ *n* **1** an archbishop. **2** one of the highest kinds of animals, including humans and monkeys.

prime /prime/ *adj* **1** most important. **2** excellent in quality. **3** that cannot be divided by any smaller number. • *n* the best time. • *vb* **1** to provide with information. **2** to prepare.

prime minister /prime mi-ni-ster/ *n* the chief minister in a parliamentary government.

prime number /prime num-ber/ *n* a number that can be divided only by itself and the number 1.

primer /prie-mer/ *n* **1** the mechanism that sets off the explosive in a shell, etc. **2** (*old*) a child's first reading book. **3** (*old*) a simple book on any subject. **4** an undercoat of paint.

primeval /prie-**mee**-val/ *adj*, *also* **primaeval** having to do with the first ages of the world.

priming /prie-ming/ *n* the powder in a gun.

primitive /**pri**-mi-tiv/ *adj* **1** of the earliest times. **2** simple or rough.

primordial /prie-**mawr**-dee-al/ *adj* (*fml*) existing from the beginning.

primrose /prim-roze/ *n* **1** a pale yellow early spring flower. **2** a pale yellow colour. • *adj* pale yellow.

primula /prim-yu-la/ *n* a flowering plant of the primrose family.

prince /prinss/ *n* **1** a ruler. **2** the son of a king or emperor.

princely /prinss-lee/ *adj* **1** of or like a prince. **2** (*fml*) magnificent, splendid.

princess /prin-sess/ *n* **1** the wife of a prince. **2** the daughter of a king or emperor.

principal /prin-si-pal/ *adj* chief, most important. • *n* **1** the head of a school, college, etc. **2** a amount of money lent at interest.

principality /prin-si-**pa**-li-tee/ *n* a country ruled by a prince.

principally /prin-si-pa-lee/ *adv* chiefly.

principle /prin-si-pul/ *n* **1** a general truth from which other truths follow. **2** a rule by which one lives.

print /print/ *vb* **1** to make a mark by pressure. **2** to reproduce letters, words, etc, on paper by use of type. **3** to publish in printed form. **4** to write without joining the letters. **5** to stamp. **6** to stamp a design on cloth. **7** to produce a picture from a photographic negative. **8** to write in large clear lettering.

9 to export a computer file in the form of hard copy. • *n* **1** a mark made by pressure. **2** letters, words, etc, reproduced on paper by use of type. **3** a copy of a picture taken from a photographic negative or engraving. **4** cloth with a design stamped on it.

printer /prin-ter/ *n* **1** someone who prints books, newspapers, etc. **2** a machine connected to a computer which prints a record of computer information.

printing machine /prin-ting ma-**sheen**/, **printing press** /prin-ting **press**/ *n* a machine for printing with type.

prior[1] /prie-ur/ *adj* earlier, previous.

prior[2] /prie-ur/ *n* **1** the head of a house of monks. **2** a monk next in rank to an abbot.

prioress /prie-ur-ess/ *n* the head of a house of nuns.

priority /prie-**aw**-ri-tee/ *n* **1** the state or right of coming before others in position or time. **2** something or someone that must be considered or dealt with first.

priory /prie-ur-ee/ *n* a house of monks or nuns ruled by a prior(ess).

prise /prize/ *vb*, *also* **prize** to force open.

prism /pri-zum/ *n* **1** a solid body with ends the same in shape and size and parallel to one another, and sides that are parallelograms. **2** a triangular glass solid used for breaking up light into colours.

prismatic /priz-**ma**-tic/ *adj* **1** of or like a prism. **2** (*of colours*) very bright.

prison /pri-zun/ *n* a building in which criminals convicted of serious crimes are held.

prisoner /priz-ner/ *n* **1** someone kept in prison. **2** a person captured by the enemy in war.

pristine /pri-steen/ *adj* **1** former, of earlier times. **2** pure, undamaged, clean.

privacy /pri-va-see/ *n* **1** undisturbed quiet. **2** secrecy.

private /prie-vit/ *adj* **1** belonging to oneself only, not open to other people. **2** not public. **3** secret. • *n* a common soldier who has not been promoted.

privateer /prie-vi-**teer**/ *n* a privately owned ship licensed to carry arms and attack enemy vessels.

privation /prie-**vay**-shun/ *n* lack of food and comforts, hardships.

privatize /prie-vu-tize/ *vb*, *also* **privatise** to transfer something from public to private ownership. • *n* privatization, *also* privatisation.

privilege /priv-lidge/ *n* **1** a right or advantage allowed to a certain person or group only. **2** advantage possessed because of social position, wealth, etc. • *vb* to allow a privilege to.

prize[1] /**prize**/ *n* **1** something given as a reward for merit or good work. **2** that which is won by competition. **3** anything seized from an enemy. • *vb* to value highly.

prize[2] /**prize**/ *vb* variant spelling of **prise**.

prizefight /**prize**-fite/ *n* a boxing match for a prize.

pro- /**pro**/ *prefix* **1** before. **2** in favour of. • **pros and cons** reasons for and against.

proactive /pro-**ac**-tiv/ *adj* acting positively and taking the initiative so that you are in charge of a situation rather than reacting to it.

probability /prob-a-**bi**-li-tee/ *n* likelihood.

probable /**prob**-a-bul/ *adj* **1** likely to happen, likely to be true. **2** easy to believe.

probably /**prob**-u-blee/ *adv* very likely.

probate /**pro**-bate/ *n* proving before a court that a will has been properly and lawfully made. • *also vb*.

probation /pro-**bay**-shun/ *n* **1** the testing of a person's conduct, work or character. **2** a time of trial or testing, especially for a young person found guilty of a crime, but not sentenced on condition that his or her conduct improves.

probation officer /pro-**bay**-shun **aw**-fi-ser/ *n* someone whose duty it is to watch over young persons on probation.

probationary /pro-**bay**-shu-ne-ree/ *adj* being tested, on approval.

probationer /pro-**bay**-shu-ner/ *n* **1** someone whose fitness for certain work is being tested. **2** someone who is on probation.

probe /**probe**/ *n* a blunt metal instrument used by doctors when examining a wound closely. • *vb* **1** to examine with a probe. **2** to examine carefully, to inquire into thoroughly.

probity /**pro**-bi-tee/ *n* (*fml*) honesty, upright-ness.

problem /**prob**-lem/ *n* a question or difficulty to which the answer is hard to find.

problematic(al) /prob-lem-a-tic(-al)/ *adj* involving problems, difficult.

proboscis /pru-**boss**-iss/ *n* (*fml*) **1** the trunk of an elephant. **2** the tube through which certain animals or insects suck food to their mouths.

procedure /pro-**see**-jur/ *n* way of conducting business.

proceed /pru-**seed**/ *vb* **1** to move forward. **2** to go on doing, to continue. **3** (*fml*) to go to law. • *npl* /**pro**-seeds/ money made on a particular occasion.

proceedings /pru-**see**-dings/ *npl* **1** the official written report of a meeting, society, etc.

2 an event or series of events. **3** a legal action.

process /**pro**-sess/ *n* **1** the way in which a thing is done or made. **2** a series of actions, each of which brings one nearer to the desired end. **3** (*fml*) a legal case.

procession /pro-**se**-shun/ *n* a body of people moving forward in an orderly column.

processional /pro-**se**-shnal/ *adj* having to do with a procession. • *n* a hymn sung during a religious procession.

proclaim /pro-**claim**/ *vb* to announce publicly, to tell openly.

proclamation /pro-cla-**may**-shun/ *n* a public announcement.

procrastinate /pro-**cra**-sti-nate/ *vb* to put off until later.

procrastination /pro-cra-sti-**nay**-shun/ *n* delay, a habit of putting things off until later.

procreation /pro-cree-**ay**-shun/ *n* having sexual intercourse in order to reproduce.

prod /**prod**/ *vb* (**prodded, prodding**) **1** to push someone with something pointed. **2** to nudge. **3** to urge into action. • *also n*.

prodigal /**prod**-i-gal/ *adj* (*fml*) wasteful, spending too freely. • *n* a waster, a spendthrift.

prodigious /pru-**di**-jus/ *adj* (*fml*) **1** wonderful, extraordinary. **2** huge.

prodigy /**prod**-i-jee/ *n* **1** (*fml*) a wonder. **2** a person of extraordinary abilities.

produce /pro-**dyooss**/ *vb* **1** to bring forward, to bring into view. **2** to bear, to yield. **3** to cause or bring about. **4** to make or manufacture. **5** to give birth to. • *n* /**praw**-dyooss/ things grown, crops.

producer /pru-**dyoo**-ser/ *n* **1** a person or country that grows or makes certain things. **2** someone who gets a play or programme ready for performance.

product /**prod**-uct/ *n* **1** that which grows or is made. **2** result. **3** the number given by multiplying other numbers together.

production /pru-**duc**-shun/ *n* **1** the act of making or growing. **2** the amount produced. **3** a performance or series of performances of a programme, play, opera, etc.

productive /pru-**duc**-tiv/ *adj* **1** fertile. **2** having results.

productivity /praw-duc-**ti**-vi-tee/ *n* the rate of producing something.

profane /pro-**fane**/ *adj* **1** not showing respect for what is holy. **2** coarse or vulgar. • *vb* to treat irreverently.

profanity /pru-**fa**-ni-tee/ *n* **1** bad language. **2** lack of respect for what is holy.

profess /pru-**fess**/ *vb* **1** to say openly. **2** to claim skill or ability. **3** to declare one's beliefs. **4** to pretend.

professed /pru-**fest**/ *adj* openly admitted or declared.

profession /pru-**fe**-shun/ *n* **1** an employment requiring special learning. **2** the people involved in such employment. **3** a public declaration.

professional /pru-**fesh**-nal/ *adj* **1** having to do with a profession. **2** paid for one's skill. **3** done for a living. **4** of a very high standard. • *n* someone who makes his or her living by arts, sports, etc.

professor /pru-**fe**-sur/ *n* a teacher of the highest rank in a university or college.

professorial /pro-fi-**soe**-ree-al/ *adj* having to do with a professor.

proficient /pru-**fi**-shent/ *adj* highly skilled, expert. • *n* **proficiency**.

profile /**pro**-file/ *n* **1** an outline, a short description. **2** a head or an outline of it in side view.

profit /**prof**-it/ *n* **1** an advantage. **2** a gain, especially of money. • *vb* **1** to gain an advantage. **2** to be of use to.

profitable /**prof**-i-ta-bul/ *adj* **1** bringing profit or gain. **2** useful.

profiteer /prof-i-**teer**/ *n* someone who makes money by selling scarce goods at very high prices. • *vb* to make money thus.

profound /pru-**found**/ *adj* **1** deep. **2** showing much knowledge or intelligence. **3** intense.

profundity /pro-**fun**-di-tee/ *n* **1** depth. **2** the state of being profound.

profuse /pro-**fyoos**/ *adj* very plentiful.

profusion /pro-**fyoo**-zhun/ *n* great plenty.

prognosis /prog-**no**-sis/ *n* a forecast, especially of the progress of a disease.

program /**pro**-gram/ *n* a sequence of instructions put into a computer. • *vb* (**programmed**, **programming**) **1** to put a program into a computer. **2** to write a computer program.

programme /**pro**-gram/ *n*, *also* **program** (*US*) **1** a plan or scheme. **2** a list of the items in a concert, etc. **3** a scheduled radio or television broadcast. • *also vb* (**programmed**, **programming**).

progress /**pro**-gress/ *n* **1** movement forward, advance. **2** improvement. • *vb* /pru-**gress**/ **1** to advance. **2** to improve.

progression /pru-**gre**-shun/ *n* **1** onward movement. **2** a steady and regular advance.

progressive /pru-**gre**-siv/ *adj* **1** moving forward, advancing. **2** believing in trying new ideas and methods.

prohibit /pro-**hi**-bit/ *vb* **1** to forbid. **2** to prevent.

prohibition /pro-hi-**bi**-shun/ *n* **1** an order not to do something. **2** the forbidding by law of the making or selling of all strong drink in a country.

prohibitive /pro-**hi**-bi-tiv/ *adj* so high (in price) that people are unable to buy.

project /pro-**ject**/ *vb* **1** to throw. **2** to plan. **3** to stick out. **4** to make pictures appear on screen by using a projector. • *n* /**praw**-ject/ a plan.

projectile /pro-**jec**-tile/ *n* **1** something thrown. **2** something fired from a gun, a shell.

projection /pro-**jec**-shun/ *n* a part that sticks out.

projector /pro-**jec**-tur/ *n* **1** someone who forms plans. **2** an apparatus for showing pictures on a screen.

proletariat /pro-li-**tay**-ree-at/ *n* the lowest class in society, the working people. • *adj* **proletarian**.

prolific /pru-**li**-fic/ *adj* producing much.

prologue /**pro**-log/ *n*, *also* **prolog** (*US*) **1** an introduction. **2** some lines spoken to the audience before a play begins. **3** an event that leads to another.

prolong /pro-**long**/ *vb* to make longer. • *n* **prolongation**.

prolonged /pro-**longd**/ *adj* very long.

prom /prom/ *n* **1** *abbrev* = **promenade concert**. **2** (*esp US*) a formal dance in a high school or college.

promenade /prom-i-**nad**/ *n* (*fml*) a short walk for pleasure. • *vb* (*fml*) **1** to take a short walk. **2** to walk up and down.

promenade concert /prom-i-**nad** kon-surt/ *n* a concert at which many members of the audience remain standing up during the performance.

prominence /**prom**-i-nense/ *n* **1** the state or act of being prominent. **2** something that sticks out or is prominent.

prominent /**prom**-i-nent/ *adj* **1** easily seen. **2** well-known. **3** sticking out.

promiscuous /pru-**mi**-skyu-wus/ *adj* having many sexual relationships. • *n* **promiscuity**.

promise /**prom**-iss/ *vb* **1** to say that one will do or not do something, to give one's word. **2** to give hope of a good result. • *n* **1** act of giving one's word. **2** a sign of future success.

promising /**prom**-iss-ing/ *adj* likely to do well in the future.

promontory /**prom**-un-toe-ree/ *n* a headland.

promote /pru-**mote**/ *vb* **1** to raise to a higher position or rank. **2** to help on. **3** to help to start. • *n* **promoter**. • *n* **promotion**.

prompt /prompt/ *adj* **1** ready, quick to take action. **2** done without delay, quick. • *vb* **1** to cause another to take action. **2** to help someone (especially an actor) who cannot remember what he or she ought to say.

prompter /prom(p)-ter/ *n* someone whose job it is to whisper words to an actor who cannot remember them.

prone /prone/ *adj* **1** lying face downward. **2** inclined (to).

prong /prong/ *n* the spike of a fork, etc. • *adj* **pronged**.

pronoun /pro-noun/ *n* a word used instead of a noun.

pronounce /pru-nounse/ *vb* **1** to make the sound of. **2** to declare publicly. **3** to speak.

pronounced /pru-nounst/ *adj* very noticeable.

pronouncement /pru-nounse-ment/ *n* **1** a statement to an assembly. **2** a firm statement.

pronunciation /pru-nun-see-ay-shun/ *n* the way of making the sounds of a word or language.

proof /proof/ *n* **1** an argument, fact, etc, that shows clearly that something is true or untrue. **2** (*fml*) a test or trial. **3** (*in printing*) a first printing made solely for correction. **4** the statement of strength of some spirits, e.g. whiskey. • *adj* not affected by, able to resist.

proofreader /proof ree-der/ *n* someone whose job it is to read first printings and mark errors.

prop /prop/ *n* **1** a support. **2** a piece of stage equipment. • *vb* (**propped, propping**) to support, to hold up.

propaganda /prop-a-gan-da/ *n* the organized spreading of certain ideas, beliefs etc, to large numbers of people.

propagandist /prop-a-gan-dist/ *n* someone who spreads ideas, etc, by propaganda.

propagate /prop-u-gate/ *vb* **1** to spread widely. **2** to increase in numbers by sowing seeds or producing young. • *n* **propagation**.

propel /pru-pel/ *vb* (**propelled, propelling**) to drive or push forward.

propeller /pru-pe-lur/ *n* a revolving screw with sloping blades attached for moving forward ships, aeroplanes, etc.

propensity /pru-pen-si-tee/ *n* a natural leaning or tendency to behave in a certain way.

proper /prop-er/ *adj* **1** correct, suitable, decent, polite. **2** (*inf*) thorough, complete.

properly /prop-er-lee/ *adv* **1** correctly, suitably. **2** strictly.

property /prop-er-tee/ *n* **1** anything owned, that which belongs to one. **2** someone's land. **3** a building or buildings with any surrounding land. **4** a quality or characteristic. **5** (*abbr* = **prop**) an object

needed on the stage during a play.

prophecy /prof-i-see/ *n* **1** the foretelling of future events. **2** something foretold.

prophesy /prof-i-sye/ *vb* to tell what will happen in the future, to foretell.

prophet /prof-it/ *n* **1** someone who foretells the future. **2** someone who tells men a message or command from God. • *f* **prophetess**. • *adj* **prophetic(al)**.

proponent /pru-po-nent/ *n* someone who argues in favour of something.

proportion /pru-pore-shun/ *n* **1** the size of a part when compared with the whole. **2** the size of one object, number, etc, when compared with that of another. **3** a share. **4** *pl* size.

proportional /pru-pore-shnal/, **proportionate** /pru-pore-shu-nate/ *adj* in correct or proper proportion.

proposal /pru-poe-zal/ *n* **1** a suggestion or plan put forward. **2** an offer to marry.

propose /pru-poze/ *vb* **1** to put forward for consideration. **2** to intend. **3** to offer to marry.

proposition /prop-u-zi-shun/ *n* **1** a plan or suggestion put forward. **2** an offer. **3** a statement, a statement that is to be proved true. **4** (*in geometry*) a problem to be solved.

proprietary /pru-pri-u-tree/ *adj* **1** produced and marketed by a particular company under a registered trademark. **2** owned by a person or group of persons. **3** possessive.

proprietor /pru-prie-u-tur/ *n* an owner. • *f* **proprietress, proprietrix**.

propriety /pru-prie-u-tee/ *n* correctness of behaviour, fitness.

propulsion /pru-pul-shun/ *n* a driving or pushing forward.

prosaic /pro-zay-ic/ *adj* dull, commonplace, unpoetic.

proscribe /pro-scribe/ *vb* to forbid the use of. • *n* **proscription**.

prose /proze/ *n* **1** the language of ordinary speech and writing. **2** all writing not in verse.

prosecute /pros-i-cyoot/ *vb* **1** to accuse in a court of law. **2** (*fml*) to carry on. • *n* **prosecution**.

prosecution /pros-si-cyoo-shun/ *n* the lawyers, etc, in a court who try to prove that someone is guilty of a crime.

prosecutor /pros-si-cyoo-tur/ *n* the person who makes the accusation in a court of law.

prosody /proz-u-dee/ *n* (*fml*) rules for the writing of poetry.

prospect /pros-pect/ *n* **1** (*fml*) a view. **2** an idea of what the future may hold. **3** chance of future success. • *vb* to explore, to search for places where mines may be sunk for oil, metals, etc.

prospective /pru-**spec**-tive/ *adj* expected, probable.

prospector /pru-**spec**-tor/ *n* someone who searches for gold or other minerals.

prospectus /pru-**spec**-tus/ *n* a written description of some undertaking or of the training offered by a school.

prosper /**pros**-per/ *vb* to do well, to succeed.

prosperity /pru-**spe**-ri-tee/ *n* success, good fortune.

prosperous /**pros**-prus/ *adj* successful, well-off.

prostate /**pros**-tate/ *n, also* **prostate gland** a gland in males in front of the bladder.

prostrate /**pros**-trate/ *adj* **1** lying flat with the face to the ground. **2** exhausted. • *vb* /**pros**-**trate**/ **1** to throw flat on the ground. **2** to bow in reverence. **3** to tire out. • *n* **prostration**.

protagonist /pru-**ta**-gu-nist/ *n* **1** someone playing a leading part in a drama or in an exciting situation in real life. **2** a leader. **3** someone taking part in a contest.

protect /pru-**tect**/ *vb* to keep safe from danger, loss, etc; to defend.

protection /pru-**tec**-shun/ *n* **1** defence, watchful care. **2** the taxing of goods brought in from other countries so that goods made at home will be cheaper than them.

protectionist /pru-**tec**-shu-nist/ *n* someone who believes in taxing goods from abroad to protect home goods.

protective /pru-**tec**-tiv/ *adj* giving defence, care or safety.

protector /pru-**tec**-tur/ *n* a person or thing that protects.

protectorate /pru-**tec**-trit/ *n* a country that is defended and governed by another until it can look after itself.

protégé /**pro**-ti-zhay/ *n* someone under the care of another.

protein /**proe**-teen/ *n* a substance contained in certain foods (e.g. meat, eggs) that helps the body to grow and become stronger.

protest /pro-**test**/ *vb* **1** to object. **2** to strongly disapprove. **3** to declare. • *n* a statement of disagreement or disapproval.

Protestant /**prot**-i-stant/ *n* a member of one of the Christian groups which separated from the Roman Catholic Church at the Reformation. • *also adj*.

Protestantism /**prot**-i-stan-ti-zum/ *n* the Protestant religion.

protestation /prot-u-**stay**-shun/ *n* **1** an objection. **2** a declaration.

proto- /**pro**-to/ *prefix* first.

protocol /**pro**-to-col/ *n* **1** correct procedure or behaviour. **2** an international agreement or treaty.

proton /**pro**-ton/ *n* part of the nucleus of an atom that has a positive charge.

protoplasm /**pro**-to-pla-zum/ *n* the living substance from which plants and animals grow.

prototype /**pro**-to-tipe/ *n* the first model from which others are copied, a pattern.

protozoan /pro-to-**zo**-a/ *n* a tiny living creature, the lowest form of animal life. • *npl* **protozoans, protozoa**.

protract /pru-**tract**/ *vb* to make long, to make last longer.

protractor /pru-**trac**-tur/ *n* an instrument for measuring angles.

protrude /pru-**trood**/ *vb* to stick out, to stand out from. • *n* **protrusion**. • *adj* **protrusive**.

protuberance /pru-**troo**-ber-anse/ *n* a swelling, a part that bulges out.

protuberant /pru-**troo**-ber-ant/ *adj* bulging out.

proud /**proud**/ *adj* **1** having too high an opinion of oneself, one's deeds or possessions. **2** rightly satisfied with oneself and what one has done.

prove /**proov**/ *vb* **1** to show the truth of. **2** to turn out to be. **3** show your abilities, good qualities, etc.

proverb /**prov**-erb/ *n* a popular truth or belief expressed in a short memorable sentence.

proverbial /pru-**ver**-bee-al/ *adj* **1** well-known to all. **2** expressed in a proverb.

provide /pru-**vide**/ *vb* **1** to supply what is needed. **2** to make ready beforehand, to prepare for.

provided (that) /pru-**vie**-dd **(that)**/ *conj* on condition (that).

providence /**prov**-i-dense/ *n* **1** care for the future, foresight. **2** Christians' belief in God's care of his creatures. **3** fate.

provident /**prov**-i-dent/ *adj* (*fml*) **1** taking care of the future. **2** not spending too much.

province /**prov**-inss/ *n* **1** a division of a country. **2** the limits of one's powers, knowledge, etc. **3** *pl* all the parts of a country outside the capital.

provincial /pru-**vin**-shal/ *adj* **1** like or in a province. **2** having limited or local interests, unsophisticated.

provision /pru-**vi**-zhun/ *n* **1** something provided for the future. **2** *pl* food. • *vb* to supply with stores of food.

provisional /pru-**vizh**-nal/ *adj* for a time only, that may be changed.

provocation /prov-u-**cay**-shun/ *n* a cause of anger or annoyance.

provocative /pru-**voc**-a-tiv/ *adj* intended to anger or annoy, arousing the emotions or passions.

provoke /pru-**voke**/ *vb* **1** to make angry. **2** to give rise to.

prow /prow/ *n* the front part of a ship or boat.

prowess /prow-ess/ *n* skill or ability.

prowl /prowl/ *vb* to keep moving about as if searching for something, to move quietly about looking for the chance to do mischief.

prowler /prow-ler/ *n* someone who moves stealthily, especially a thief.

proximate /prok-si-mit/ *adj* (*fml*) nearest.

proximity /prok-**si**-mi-tee/ *n* nearness, neighbourhood.

proxy /prok-see/ *n* **1** the right to act or vote for another. **2** someone with the right to act or vote for another.

prude /prood/ *n* a person who makes a show of being very modest and correct in behaviour. • *n* **prudery.**

prudence /proo-dense/ *n* foresight, caution.

prudent /proo-dent/ *adj* thinking carefully before acting, wise, cautious.

prudery *see* **prude.**

prudish /proo-dish/ *adj* over-correct in behaviour.

prune[1] /proon/ *n* a dried plum.

prune[2] /proon/ *vb* **1** to cut off the dead or overgrown parts of a plant. **2** to shorten by cutting out what is unnecessary.

pry /prie/ *vb* to inquire closely, especially into the secrets of others; to examine closely.

psalm /sahm/ *n* a sacred song or hymn.

psalmist /sahm-ist/ *n* a writer of sacred songs.

pseudo /soo-doe/ *adj* false, not real.

pseudonym /soo-du-nim/ *n* a name used instead of one's real name (e.g. a pen-name).

psychiatry /sie-**kie**-u-tree/ *n* the treatment of diseases of the mind. • *n* **psychiatrist.**

psychic /sie-kik/, **psychical** /sie-ki-kal/ *adj* **1** having to do with the mind. **2** (*of influences and forces*) that act on the mind and senses but have no physical cause. **3** (*of a person*) sensitive to these influences. **4** able to communicate with spirits. • *n* someone who claims to be psychic, a clairvoyant.

psychoanalysis /sie-ko-a-**na**-li-sis/ *n* treatment of mental disease by questioning problems, fears, etc, that exist in the patient's mind without his or her being aware of them. • *n* **psychoanalyst.** • *vb* **psychoanalyse.**

psychology /sie-**kol**-u-jee/ *n* **1** the study of the human mind. **2** the mental processes of a person. • *adj* **psychological.** • *n* **psychologist.**

psychopath /sie-ko-path/ *n* someone with a personality disorder which can lead him or her to commit often violent acts without guilt.

pterodactyl /ter-u-**dac**-tul/ *n* a prehistoric winged reptile known of from fossils.

pub /pub/ *n* a building in which alcoholic drinks, and sometimes food, are served; a public house.

puberty /pyoo-bur-tee/ *n* the age by which a young person has fully developed all the characteristics of his or her sex.

public /pu-blic/ *adj* **1** open to all. **2** having to do with people in general. **3** well-known. • *n* the people in general.

publication /pu-bli-**cay**-shun/ *n* **1** the act of publishing. **2** a published book, magazine or paper.

public house /pub-lick howss/ *see* **pub.**

public school /pub-lick skool/ *n* **1** in England, a fee-paying private school for senior pupils who often live at the school. **2** in US and Scotland, a free government-run school.

publicity /pu-**bli**-si-tee/ *n* **1** making something widely known, advertising. **2** the state of being well-known. • *vb* **publicize,** *also* **publicise.**

publish /pu-blish/ *vb* **1** (*fml*) to make widely known. **2** to print for selling to the public.

publisher /pu-bli-sher/ *n* someone who publishes books, etc.

puck /puck/ *n* a small hard rubber disc used instead of a ball in ice hockey.

pucker /pu-ker/ *vb* to gather into small folds or wrinkles. • *n* a fold or wrinkle.

pudding /poo-ding/ *n* a sweet soft dessert served at the end of a meal.

puddle /pu-dul/ *n* a small pool of dirty water. • *vb* to make watertight with clay.

pudgy /pu-jee/ *adj* (*inf*) short and fat.

puff /puff/ *n* **1** a short sharp breath or gust of wind. **2** a small cloud of smoke, steam, etc, blown by a puff. **3** a soft pad for powdering the skin. **4** a kind of light pastry. • *vb* **1** to breathe quickly or heavily, as when short of breath. **2** to blow in small blasts. **3** to blow up, to swell. **4** to praise too highly.

puffin /pu-fin/ *n* a diving bird with a brightly coloured beak.

puffy /pu-fee/ *adj* blown out, swollen.

pug, pug dog /pug dawg/ *n* a type of small dog with an upturned nose.

pugnacious /pug-**nay**-shus/ *adj* quarrelsome, fond of fighting. • *n* **pugnacity.**

pug nose /pug noze/ *n* a short upturned nose. • *adj* **pug-nosed.**

puke /pyook/ *vb* (*inf*) to bring up the contents of the stomach, to vomit.

pule /pyool/ *vb* (*fml*) to whine, to cry peevishly.

pull /pool/ *vb* **1** to draw towards one, to draw in the same direction as oneself. **2** to bring along behind one while moving. **3** to remove. **4** to gather. **5** to row with oars. • *n* **1** act of pulling. **2** (*inf*) advantage, special influence.

pulley /poo-lee/ *n* a grooved wheel with a cord running over it used for raising weights.

pulmonary /pul-mu-ne-ree/ *adj* (*fml*) having to do with the lungs.

pulp /pulp/ *n* **1** the soft juicy part of a fruit. **2** soft substance obtained by crushing rags, wood, etc, and made into paper. • *vb* to make into pulp, to become pulpy.

pulpit /pool-pit/ *n* a raised platform enclosed by a half wall for preaching in a church.

pulsate /pul-sate/ *vb* to beat or throb. • *n* pulsation.

pulse[1] /pulss/ *n* **1** the throb of the heart or of the blood passing through the arteries. **2** a place on the body where the throb of the blood can be felt. • *vb* to beat or throb.

pulse[2] /pulss/ *n* any of the edible seeds of peas, beans, lentils, etc.

pulverize /pul-vu-rize/ *vb*, *also* pulverise **1** to make into dust or powder. **2** (*inf*) to defeat thoroughly.

puma /pyoo-ma/ *n* a large wild cat, the cougar.

pumice /puhm-iss/ *n* a light stone with a rough surface, used for cleansing or polishing.

pummel /pu-mul/ *vb* (pummelled /pu-muld/, pummelling; *also* pummeled, pummeling [*US*]) to strike repeatedly with the fist(s).

pump[1] /pump/ *n* **1** a machine for raising water from a well. **2** a machine for raising any liquid to a higher level. **3** a machine for taking air out of or putting air into things. • *vb* **1** to work a pump. **2** to raise with a pump. **3** (*inf*) to get information from someone by asking them constant questions.

pump[2] /pump/ *n* a light shoe for dancing, exercise etc.

pumpkin /pum(p)-kin/ *n* a large fleshy fruit with a thick yellow skin.

pun /pun/ *n* the witty or amusing use of a word like another in sound but different in meaning. • *vb* (punned, punning) to make a pun.

punch[1] /punch/ *vb* **1** to strike with the fist. **2** to herd or drive cattle. **3** to make a hole with a special tool or machine. • *n* **1** a blow with the fist. **2** a tool or machine for making holes.

punch[2] /punch/ *n* a drink made from wine or spirit mixed with sugar, hot water, fruit, etc.

punctual /pungk-chu-wal/ *adj* **1** on time, not late. **2** good at arriving at the correct time. • *n* punctuality.

punctuate /pungk-chu-wate/ *vb* **1** to divide up written work with full stops, commas, etc. **2** to interrupt repeatedly. • *n* punctuation.

puncture /pungk-chur/ *n* a hole made by a sharp point. • *vb* to make a hole in, to pierce.

pundit /pun-dit/ *n* (*fml*) an expert.

pungent /pun-jent/ *adj* **1** sharp to taste or smell. **2** sharp. • *n* pungency.

punish /pu-nish/ *vb* **1** to cause someone to suffer for doing wrong. **2** to deal roughly with.

punishment /pu-nish-ment/ *n* pain, loss, etc, inflicted on a wrongdoer.

punitive /pyoo-ni-tiv/ *adj* **1** done by way of punishment, inflicting punishment. **2** very high and expensive.

punster /pun-ster/ *n* (*inf*) someone who makes puns.

punt[1] /punt/ *n* a flat-bottomed boat moved by means of a pole. • *vb* to move a punt with a pole.

punt[2] /punt/ *vb* to kick a ball dropped from the hands before it touches the ground. • *also n.*

puny /pyoo-nee/ *adj* small and weak.

pup /pup/ *n* a puppy, a young dog.

pupa /pyoo-pa/ *n* (*pl* pupae *or* pupas) **1** a stage in the growth of an insect just before it develops wings. **2** an insect in this stage.

pupil /pyoo-pil/ *n* **1** someone being taught, a learner. **2** the round opening in the centre of the eye through which light passes.

puppet /pu-pit/ *n* **1** a doll whose movements are controlled by strings, etc. **2** someone who obeys without question all the orders given him or her by another.

puppet show /pu-pit show/ *n* a performance using puppets.

puppy /pu-pee/ *n* a young dog.

purchase /pur-chiss/ *vb* to buy. • *n* **1** the thing bought. **2** a position that allows one to apply all one's strength.

purchaser /pur-chi-ser/ *n* a buyer.

pure /pyoor/ *adj* **1** clear. **2** unmixed. **3** clean, free from dirt or harmful matter. **4** free from guilt or evil. **5** complete, absolute.

purée /pyoo-ray/ *n* food crushed to pulp and sometimes passed through a sieve.

purely /pyoor-lee/ *adv* **1** wholly. **2** only, merely. **3** in a pure manner.

purge /purge/ *vb* **1** to make pure and clean. **2** to get rid of unwanted persons. **3** to clear the body of waste matter, to empty the bowels.

purification /pyoo-ri-fi-**cay**-shun/ *n* **1** act of purifying. **2** a ceremonial cleansing.

purify /**pyoo**-ri-fie/ *vb* **1** to cleanse. **2** to make pure.

puritan /**pyoo**-ri-tan/ *n* someone who is very strict in matters of morals or religion. • *adj* puritanic(al). • *n* puritanism.

purity /**pyoo**-ri-tee/ *n* the state of being pure.

purl¹ /**purl**/ *n* the rippling sound made by a stream. • *vb* to ripple.

purl² /**purl**/ *n* a type of knitting stitch. • *also* *vb*.

purple /**pur**-pul/ *n* **1** a colour of red and blue mixed. **2** (*fml*) the purple robe of a king or cardinal. **3** (*fml*) the rank of king or cardinal. • *adj* of purple colour.

purpose /**pur**-puss/ *n* **1** the reason for an action, an intention or plan. **2** use or function. **3** determination. • *vb* to intend.

purposeful /**pur**-pus-ful/ *adj* **1** having a clear intention in mind. **2** determined.

purposely /**pur**-pus-lee/ *adv* intentionally, on purpose.

purr /**pur**/ *n* the low sound made by a cat when pleased. • *also vb*.

purse /**purss**/ *n* **1** a small leather or plastic bag used by women to carry coins, paper money, and sometimes credit cards. **2** a sum of money offered as a prize. • *vb* to pull in.

pursue /pur-**soo**/ *vb* **1** to follow in order to catch. **2** to carry on.

pursuer /pur-**soo**-er/ *n* someone who chases.

pursuit /pur-**soot**/ *n* the act of pursuing.

purvey /pur-**vay**/ *vb* (*fml*) to provide food or meals. • *n* purveyor.

pus /**puss**/ *n* yellow matter from an infected sore or wound.

push /**poosh**/ *vb* **1** to press against with force. **2** to move by force, to shove. **3** to try to make someone do something. **4** (*inf*) to promote, to advertise. • *n* **1** a shove. **2** a strong effort. **3** (*inf*) energy. **4** an attack by a large army.

pushchair /**poosh**-chare/ *n* a small folding chair on wheels on which a young child is pushed.

pushy /**poo**-shee/ *adj* extremely assertive or ambitious.

pusillanimous /pyoo-si-**la**-ni-muss/ *adj* timid, cowardly. • *n* pusillanimity.

puss /**pooss**/, **pussy** /**poo**-see/ *n* (*inf*) a cat.

pustule /**pus**-tchul/ *n* a small pimple containing infected matter.

put /**poot**/ *vb* (**put**, **putting**) **1** to set down in, or move into, a certain place. **2** to ask. **3** to express in words. **4** to throw from the shoulder with a bent arm. • *n* act of throwing a weight in sport. • **put by** to keep for future use. • **put up** to give accommodation to. • **put up with** to bear without complaining.

putative /pyoo-**tay**-tiv/ *adj* supposed, commonly believed to be.

putrefy /**pyoo**-tri-fie/ *vb* (*fml*) to become rotten, to decay. • *n* putrefaction.

putrid /**pyoo**-trid/ *adj* (*fml*) rotten, decayed. **2** (*inf*) very bad, poor.

putt /**putt**/ *vb* (**putted**, **putting**) (*in golf*) to hit the ball into the hole on the green. • *n* (*in golf*) a hit intended to send the ball into the hole.

putter /**pu**-ter/ *n* a golf club for putting.

putting green /**pu**-ting green/ *n* (*in golf*) the smooth green near a hole.

putty /**pu**-tee/ *n* a paste made from chalk and linseed oil, used for fitting glass in windows, etc. • *vb* to cement with putty.

puzzle /**pu**-zul/ *vb* **1** to present with a difficult problem or situation, to baffle, to perplex. **2** to think long and carefully about. • *n* **1** a difficult question or problem. **2** a game or toy intended to test one's skill or cleverness. • *n* puzzlement.

PVC /pee-vee-**see**/ *abbr* = **polyvinyl chloride**: a tough kind of plastic.

pygmy, **pigmy** /**pig**-mee/ *n* **1** a member of a race of very small people in Africa. **2** (*inf*) a very small person or animal. • *also adj*.

pyjamas /pa-**ja**-maz/ *npl*, *also* **pajamas** (*US*) a loose, lightweight set of trousers and shirt, worn in bed.

pylon /**pie**-lon/ *n* a hollow skeleton pillar for carrying overhead electric cables.

pyramid /**pi**-ra-mid/ *n* **1** a solid body with triangular sides meeting in a point at the top. **2** a monument of this shape.

pyre /**pire**/ *n* a pile of wood, etc, on which a dead body is placed for burning.

pyrotechnic /pie-ro-**tec**-nic/ *adj* having to do with fireworks.

pyrotechnics /pie-ro-**tec**-nics/ *n* the art of making or using fireworks.

Pyrrhic /**pi**-ric/ *adj*. • **Pyrrhic victory** a victory in which the victors suffer very heavy losses (King Pyrrhus of Epirus, suffered great casualties in defeating the Romans during the Pyrrhic War 280–275 BC).

python /**pie**-thon/ *n* a large nonpoisonous snake that crushes its prey in its coils.

Q

Q, q /kyoo/ the 17th letter of the English alphabet.

quack[1] /kwak/ *n* the harsh cry of a duck. • *vb* to make the cry of a duck.

quack[2] /kwak/ *n* **1** a person who pretends to have knowledge or skill that he or she does not have, especially in medicine. **2** (*inf*) a doctor. • *n* **quackery** the claims or methods of a quack.

quad /kwad/ *n* **1** *short for* **quadrangle** (of a school or college). **2** *short for* **quadruplet**. **3** *pl short for* **quadriceps**.

quadr- /kwad-r/ *prefix* four.

quadrangle /kwad-rang-gul/ *n* **1** a figure with four sides and four angles. **2** a square or rectangular courtyard enclosed by a building or buildings, especially at a school or college.

quadrant /kwad-rant/ *n* **1** the fourth part of a circle. **2** an instrument for measuring angles.

quadratic /kwad-ra-tic/ *adj* in algebra, having to do with the square of an unknown quantity, but with no higher power.

quadrennial /kwad-re-nee-al/ *adj* **1** happening every four years. **2** lasting for four years.

quadrennium /kwad-re-nee-um/ *n* a period of four years.

quadriceps /kwad-ri-seps/ *npl* the large muscles at the front of the thighs.

quadrilateral /kwad-ri-lat-rul/ *n* a four-sided figure.

quadrille /kwad-ril/ *n* **1** a dance for four couples, each forming the side of a square. **2** a kind of card game played by four people.

quadruped /kwad-ru-ped/ *n* an animal with four feet.

quadruple /kwad-roo-pul/ *adj* four times as great. • *vb* to make or become four times greater.

quadruplet /kwad-roo-plet/ *n* (*abbr* **quad**) one of four children born at one birth.

quaff /kwaf/ *vb* (*fml*) to drink a lot at one swallow.

quagmire /kwag-mire/ *n* soft, very wet ground, bog, marsh.

quail[1] /kwail/ *vb* to bend or draw back in fear.

quail[2] /kwail/ *n* a small bird of the partridge family.

quaint /kwaint/ *adj* unusual or old-fashioned in a pleasing way.

quake /kwake/ *vb* to shake, to tremble.

Quaker /kway-ker/ *n* a member of the religious group the Society of Friends.

qualification /kwal-i-fi-cay-shun/ *n* an ability, skill, etc, that fits a person for a certain position or job.

qualify /kwal-i-fie/ *vb* **1** to achieve the standards required before entering a business, filling a certain position, getting a job, etc. **2** to make fit. **3** to change but not alter completely.

qualitative /kwal-i-tay-tiv/ *adj* (*fml*) having to do with quality.

quality /kwal-i-tee/ *n* **1** a feature of a person or thing. **2** the degree to which something is good or excellent, a standard of excellence. **3** excellence. • *adj* **qualitative**.

qualm /kwahm/ *n* doubt; a fear that a person is about to do something that is wrong.

quandary /kwawn-dree/ *n* a state of uncertainty; doubt as to what a person ought to do.

quantify /kwan-ti-fie/ *vb* to express the amount of, to measure.

quantitative /kwan-ti-tay-tiv/ *adj* (*fml*) able to be measured, having to do with quantity.

quantity /kwan-ti-tee/ *n* **1** size, amount. **2** a large amount. **3** the length of a vowel sound.

quantum /kwawn-tum/ *n* an amount.

quarantine /kwaw-ren-teen/ *n* a period of time during which a person, animal, or ship that may carry infection is kept apart.

quarrel /kwaw-rel/ *n* an angry argument or disagreement. • *vb* (**quarrelled, quarrelling**; *also* **quarreled, quarreling** (*US*)) **1** to exchange angry words with, to fall out (with). **2** to disagree.

quarrelsome /kwaw-rel-sum/ *adj* fond of quarrelling.

quarry[1] /kwaw-ree/ *n* an intended prey.

quarry[2] /kwaw-ree/ *n* a place from which stone, slate, etc, may be cut. • *vb* to dig or cut from a quarry.

quart /kwawrt/ *n* an imperial measurement of liquid (1.136 litres, 2 pints, or 1/4 gallon).

quarter /kwawr-ter/ *n* **1** the fourth part of anything. **2** an imperial measure of weight, a quarter of a hundredweight (25 pounds). **3** one fourth of an hour. **4** a district in a town. **5** *pl* lodgings. • *vb* **1** to divide into four equal parts. **2** (*fml*) to provide with lodgings.

quartered /**kwawr**-terd/ *adj* divided into four parts.

quarterfinal /**kwawr**-ter-**fie**-nal/ *n* a match or game just before the semifinals in a contest. • *adj* having to do with quarterfinals.

quarter-hour /**kwawr**-ter-hour/ *n* 15 minutes.

quarterly /**kwawr**-ter-lee/ *adj* happening every three months. • *also n.* • *adv* once every three months.

quartet /kwawr-**tet**/ *n* **1** a piece of music written for four performers. **2** a group of four singers or players. **3** a set or group of four.

quartz /**kwawrts**/ *n* a type of mineral found in rocks, usually in the form of crystals.

quasar /**kway**-zar/ *n* a distant starlike heavenly body that emits light and radio waves.

quash /**kwawsh**/ *vb* **1** to set aside. **2** to put down, to put an end to.

quasi- /**kway**-zie/ *prefix* almost, to some extent but not really.

quassia /**kwa**-sha/ *n* a South American tree with a bitter-tasting bark used in medicines.

quatrain /kwaw-**train**/ *n* a poem or section of a poem of four lines, usually rhyming alternately.

quaver /**kway**-ver/ *vb* **1** to shake, to tremble. **2** to speak in a trembling, uncertain voice. • *n* **1** a trembling of the voice. **2** (*mus*) a note having the duration of a minim (also quarter note (*US*)).

quay /**kee**/ *n* a landing place for the loading and unloading of ships.

queasy /**kwee**-zee/ *adj* feeling sick, easily made sick.

queen /**kween**/ *n* **1** the wife of a king. **2** a female royal ruler of a country. **3** the female bee, ant, etc. **4** a picture playing card. **5** a piece in chess.

queenly /**kween**-lee/ *adj* like a queen.

queen mother /kween **mu**-ther/ *n* a former queen who is mother of the reigning king or queen.

queer /**kweer**/ *adj* strange, unusual.

quell /**kwell**/ *vb* **1** to put down completely, to crush. **2** to put an end to.

quench /**kwench**/ *vb* **1** to put out (e.g. water on a fire). **2** to satisfy.

querulous /**kwe**-ru-lus/ *adj* complaining.

query /**kwee**-ree/ *n* **1** a question. **2** a question mark (?). • *vb* **1** (*fml*) to ask a question. **2** to doubt.

quest /**kwest**/ (*fml or lit*) *n* a search. • *vb* to go in search of.

question /**kwes**-chun/ *n* **1** a request for news, information, knowledge, etc. **2** words spoken or arranged in such a way that an answer is called for. **3** a problem. **4** the matter under consideration. • *vb* **1** to ask questions. **2** to doubt. • *n* **questioner**.

questionable /**kwes**-chu-na-bul/ *adj* **1** doubtful. **2** open to suspicion.

question mark *n* a piece of punctuation, ?, that denotes a question.

questionnaire /kwes-chu-**nare**/ *n* a set of written questions chosen for a particular purpose.

queue /**cyoo**/ *n* a line of people waiting their turn for something. • *vb* to form a queue, to stand in a queue.

quibble /**kwi**-bul/ *n* an objection or argument, especially an unimportant objection or argument. • *vb* to argue about small, unimportant details.

quiche /**keesh**/ *n* an unsweetened egg custard baked in a tart with onions, cheese, bacon, etc.

quick /**kwick**/ *adj* **1** fast-moving. **2** clever. **3** done in a short time. **4** (*old*) living. • *n* the very tender flesh under the nails or just below the skin. • *adv* quickly.

quicken /**kwi**-ken/ *vb* **1** to give life to. **2** to become alive or lively. **3** to make or become faster.

quickly /**kwik**-lee/ *adv* at once, rapidly.

quicksand /**kwik**-sand/ *n* loose, wet sand into which anything of weight (e.g. ships, people) may sink.

quicksilver /**kwik**-sil-ver/ *n* mercury.

quiet /**kwie**-et/ *adj* **1** at rest. **2** noiseless, not noisy. **3** calm, peaceful, gentle. **4** (*of colours*) not bright. • *n* **1** rest, peace. **2** silence. • *vb* **1** to calm. **2** to make silent.

quill /**kwill**/ *n* **1** a large feather from a goose or other bird, used as a pen. **2** the hollow stem of a feather. **3** one of the prickles on the back of a porcupine.

quilt /**kwilt**/ *n* a bedcover padded with feathers, wool, etc. • *vb* to make a quilt.

quince /**kwinss**/ *n* **1** a sour pear-shaped fruit often used in jams. **2** a kind of fruit-bearing tree.

quintet /kwin-**tet**/ *n* **1** a piece of music written for five performers. **2** a group of five singers or players. **3** a set or group of five.

quintuple /kwin-**too**-pul/ *adj* five times as great. • *vb* to make or become five times greater.

quintuplet /kwin-**tu**-plet/ *n* (*abbr* **quin**) one of five children born at one birth.

quip /**kwip**/ *n* a joking or witty remark. • *vb* (**quipped, quipping**) to make such remarks.

quirk /**kwirk**/ *n* **1** a way of behaving or doing something peculiar to oneself. **2** a strange or unexpected happening.

quit /**kwit**/ *vb* (**quitted** *or* **quit, quitting**) **1** to leave. **2** to give up.

quite /**kwite**/ *adv* **1** completely, wholly. **2** fairly, rather.

quits /**kwits**/ *adj* on even terms, owing nothing to each other.

quiver[1] /**kwi**-ver/ *n* a case for carrying arrows.

quiver[2] /**kwi**-ver/ *vb* to tremble. • *n* a shudder, a slight trembling.

quixotic /kwik-**sot**-ic/ *adj* trying to achieve impossible or unrealistic aims, especially when these are to help others and bring danger to oneself.

quiz /**kwiz**/ *vb* (**quizzed, quizzing**) to examine by questioning. • *n* a number of questions set to test a person's knowledge.

quizzical /**kwi**-zi-cal/ *adj* as if asking a question, especially mockingly or humorously.

quota /**kwo**-ta/ *n* the share of the whole to which each member of a group has a right.

quotation /kwo-**tay**-shun/ *n* **1** the words or passage quoted. **2** a price stated.

quotation marks /kwo-**tay**-shun marks/ *npl* punctuation marks (" ' *or* " ") placed at the beginning and end of a written quotation.

quote /**kwoat**/ *vb* **1** to repeat or write down the exact words of another person, making it known that they are not anyone else's. **2** to say the price of. • *n* (*inf*) **1** a quotation. **2** a quotation mark.

quotidian /kwo-**ti**-dee-an/ *adj* (*fml*) daily.

quotient /**kwo**-shent/ *n* the answer to a division problem.

Qu'ran *see* **Koran**.

R

R, r /ar/ the 18th letter of the English alphabet.

rabbi /ra-bie/ *n* a person who is learned in the law and doctrine of the Jewish people, a Jewish leader and teacher.

rabbit /ra-bit/ *n* a small long-eared burrowing animal.

rabble /ra-bul/ *n* a noisy or disorderly crowd.

rabid /ra-bid/ *adj* **1** fanatical. **2** (*of dogs*) suffering from rabies.

rabies /ray-beez/ *n* a disease, usually caught from a bite from another infected animal, that causes madness, and often death, in dogs and other animals.

raccoon, racoon /ra-coon/ *n* an American animal of the bear family.

race¹ /race/ *n* **1** a contest to see who can reach a given mark in the shortest time. **2** a strong quick-moving current of water. • *vb* **1** to take part in a race. **2** to run or move very quickly.

race² /race/ *n* **1** any of the main groups into which human beings can be divided according to their physical characteristics. **2** the fact of belonging to one of these groups. **3** a group of people who share the same culture, language, etc. **4** ancestors, family.

racing car /race-ing car/ *n* a car designed to race and to travel at high speed.

race course /race coarss/ *n, also* **racetrack** /race-track/ (*US*) the ground on which races are run.

racehorse /race-hawrss/ *n* a horse bred for racing.

racial /ray-shul/ *adj* having to do with a race or nation.

racism /ray-si-zum/ *n* prejudice or discrimination against people on the grounds of race, sometimes accompanied by violent behaviour. • *adj, n* **racist**.

rack /rack/ *n* **1** a frame for holding articles. **2** (*old*) instrument for torturing people by stretching their joints. • *vb* to cause great pain or trouble to. • **rack your brains** to think as hard as possible.

racket¹ /ra-kit/ *n* a bat (usually a frame strung with crisscrossing cords) for playing tennis, badminton, etc.

racket² /ra-kit/ *n* **1** an uproar, a din. **2** a dishonest method of making a lot of money.

racketeer /ra-ki-teer/ *n* a person who makes money by dishonest or violent methods. • *n* **racketeering**.

racoon *see* **raccoon**.

radar /ray-dar/ *n* the sending out of radio signals to determine the position of ships, aeroplanes, etc.

radial /ray-dee-al/ *adj* **1** of or in rays. **2** arranged like spokes.

radiance /ray-dee-anse/ *n* brightness, brilliance.

radiant /ray-dee-ant/ *adj* **1** showing great joy or happiness. **2** sending out rays of light or heat. **3** glowing. **4** shining.

radiate /ray-dee-ate/ *vb* **1** to send out rays of light or heat. **2** to shine with. • *n* **radiation**.

radiator /ray-dee-ay-tur/ *n* **1** a metal device fixed to a wall through which hot water passes to warm a room. **2** an apparatus for cooling the engine of a car.

radical /ra-di-cal/ *adj* **1** having to do with the root or basic nature. **2** seeking great political, social, or economic change. **3** very thorough. • *n* a person who desires to make far-reaching changes in society or in methods of government. • *adv* **radically**.

radii *see* **radius**.

radio /ray-dee-o/ *n* **1** the sending or receiving of sounds through the air by electric waves. **2** an apparatus for receiving sound broadcast through the air by electric waves. **3** the radio broadcasting industry.

radioactive /ray-dee-o-ac-tiv/ *adj* giving off rays of force or energy which can be dangerous but that can be used in medicine, etc. • *n* **radioactivity**.

radiographer /ray-dee-og-ra-fer/ *n* a person who is trained to take X-ray photographs.

radiography /ray-dee-og-ra-fee/ *n* the obtaining of photographs by X-rays.

radiology /ray-dee-ol-u-jee/ *n* the study or use of radioactivity as a means of treating disease. • *n* **radiologist**.

radiotherapy /ray-dee-o-ther-a-pee/ *n* the treatment of disease by rays (e.g. X-rays). • *n* **radiotherapist**.

radish /ra-dish/ *n* a plant with an edible hot-tasting red root.

radium /ray-dee-um/ *n* a rare metallic substance that gives off rays of heat and light used in the treatment of disease.

radius /ray-dee-us/ *n* (*pl* **radii**) **1** a straight line from the centre of a circle to any point on the circumference. **2** a bone in the forearm.

radon /ray-don/ *n* a radioactive gas that can be produced from the earth and rock.

raffle /ra-ful/ n a sale in which people buy tickets for an article that is given to the person whose name or number is drawn by lottery. • vb to sell by raffle.

raft /raft/ n 1 logs fastened together to make a floating platform or a flat boat without sides. 2 a large number of things, a series.

rag /rag/ n a torn or tattered piece of cloth, a left-over piece of material. • npl old tattered clothes.

rage /rage/ n 1 violent anger, fury. 2 something very popular or fashionable at a certain time. • vb 1 to be furious with anger. 2 to behave or talk violently.

ragged /ra-gid/ adj 1 torn or tattered. 2 wearing old tattered clothing. 3 rough-edged.

ragtime /rag-time/ n a highly syncopated form of music of African-American origin, an early form of jazz.

raid /raid/ n a sudden quick attack made by a group intending to return to their starting point. • also vb. • n raider.

rail /rail/ n 1 a level or sloping bar of wood or metal linking up a line of posts, banisters, etc. 2 a strip of metal moulded to a certain shape and laid down as part of a railway track. 3 railways as a means of transport. • vb 1 to enclose with railings. 2 to send by railway.

railing /ray-ling/ n a fence made of posts some distance apart linked together by crossbars or a rail.

railway /rail-way/ n 1 a track laid with parallel metal strips so moulded that a train can run on them. 2 a system of tracks and trains.

rain /rain/ n moisture falling from the clouds in drops. • vb 1 to fall in drops. 2 to fall or throw down in large numbers. • n **raindrop, rainwater**.

rainbow /rain-bo/ n a semicircular coloured band that often appears in the sky when the sun shines through raindrops.

rainfall /rain-fawl/ n the amount of rain that falls in a certain place during a certain length of time.

rainforest /rain-faw-rest/ n a dense tropical forest where there is a high rainfall.

rainy /rain-ee/ adj wet, raining.

raise /raiz/ vb 1 to lift upward, to move to a higher position. 2 to breed. 3 to make higher. 4 to cause to grow, to cultivate. 5 to increase in amount, size, etc. 6 to begin to talk about. 7 to collect. 8 to make louder. 9 to give up.

raisin /ray-zin/ n a dried grape.

rake /rake/ n a metal or wooden toothed crossbar fixed to a pole and used for scraping the ground, pulling together cut grass or hay, smoothing the soil, etc. • vb 1 to scrape, pull together, smooth, etc, with a rake. 2 to search very carefully.

rally /ra-lee/ vb 1 to bring or come together again in one body. 2 to regain some of your strength, health, etc, after weakness or illness. • n 1 a coming together in large numbers. 2 recovery of strength, health, good spirits, etc.

ram /ram/ n 1 a male sheep. 2 any heavy instrument used for breaking down walls, doors, etc. • vb (**rammed, ramming**) 1 run into with great force. 2 to push down into or onto with great force. 3 (of a ship) to strike another ship head-on in order to make a hole in its side. 4 to strike violently.

RAM /ram/ abbr = **Random Access Memory**: memory that is lost when a computer is switched off.

Ramadan /ra-ma-dan/ n the ninth month of the Muslim year during which Muslims fast between the hours of sunrise and sunset.

ramble /ram-bul/ vb 1 to change from one subject to another in a foolish, purposeless way. 2 to walk as and where you like for pleasure. 3 to grow in all directions. • n a walk taken for pleasure.

rambler /ram-bler/ n 1 a wanderer, a person who rambles. 2 a climbing plant, especially a type of rose.

ramification /ra-mi-fi-cay-shun/ n a consequence, especially one of many and an indirect one.

ramp /ramp/ n a slope.

rampage /ram-page/ vb to rush about, to rage. • n great anger or excitement.

rampant /ram-pant/ adj 1 uncontrolled. 2 growing uncontrollably. 3 in heraldry, standing on the hind legs.

rampart /ram-part/ n a defensive wall or mound of earth.

ramshackle /ram-sha-kul/ adj broken-down, nearly falling down.

ranch /ranch/ n a large cattle farm.

rancher /ran-cher/ n a person who owns or works on a ranch.

rancid /ran-sid/ adj bad, unpleasant to taste or smell.

random /ran-dum/ adj without plan or purpose. • **at random** without plan or purpose.

rang pt of **ring**.

range /range/ vb 1 to extend. 2 to vary between certain limits. 3 to set in a line, to place in order. 4 (fml) to wander. • n 1 a variety. 2 extent. 3 a line or row, e.g. of mountains. **4** the distance between a gun and the fall of the shot, the distance over which an object can be sent or thrown, sound carried, heard, etc. **5** an area of land where animals roam and graze. **6** a piece of ground for firing practice. **7** an enclosed kitchen fireplace for cooking and baking.

ranger /rane-jer/ *n* a person in charge of a national park or forest.

rank[1] /rangk/ *n* **1** a position of authority; a level of importance. **2** a social class. **3** a row or line. **4** a row of soldiers standing side by side. • *vb* **1** to put or be in a certain class or in an order of merit. **2** to arrange in a row or line. • **rank and file** the common people.

rank[2] /rangk/ *adj* **1** very bad. **2** overgrown. **3** growing thickly and untidily.

rankle /rang-kul/ *vb* to go on causing anger or dislike.

ransack /ran-sack/ *vb* **1** to search thoroughly. **2** to plunder.

ransom /ran-sum/ *n* a sum of money paid to free someone from captivity. • *vb* to pay to obtain freedom, to redeem.

rant /rant/ *vb* to talk in a loud, uncontrolled, forceful manner. • *also n.* • *n* **ranter**.

rap /rap/ *n* **1** a quick light blow, a knock. **2** a style of popular music in which (usually rhyming) words are spoken in a rhythmic chant over an instrumental backing. • *vb* (**rapped, rapping**) **1** to give a rap, sense 1, to. **2** to chat, converse. **3** to perform a rap, sense **2**. • **take the rap** to be blamed or punished for something, often unfairly. • *n* **rapper**.

rape /rayp/ *vb* to force someone to have sex against their will. • *also n.*

rapid /ra-pid/ *adj* very quick-moving. • *n* (*usually pl*) a quick-flowing stretch of river running downhill. • *n* **rapidity**. • *adv* **rapidly**.

rapier /ray-pee-er/ *n* a long, thin sword.

rappel /ra-pel/ *vb* same as **abseil**.

rapport /ra-poar/ *n* a friendly relationship between people who understand one another.

rapt /rapt/ *adj* giving your whole mind.

rapture /rap-chur/ *n* delight, great joy.

rapturous /rap-chu-rus/ *adj* full of delight, very happy.

rare /rare/ *adj* **1** uncommon, unusual. **2** valuable. **3** very good. **4** very lightly cooked. **5** not thick. • *n* **rareness**.

rarefied /ray-ri-fied/ *adj* thin; (*of air*) with less oxygen than usual.

rarely /rare-lee/ *adv* seldom, not often.

rarity /ray-ri-tee/ *n* **1** a thing seldom met with. **2** rareness.

rascal /ra-scal/ *n* **1** a rogue, a scoundrel. **2** a naughty boy. • *adj* **rascally**.

rash[1] /rash/ *n* a redness of the skin caused by illness.

rash[2] /rash/ *adj* **1** acting without forethought. **2** hasty. **3** foolishly daring. • *adv* **rashly**. • *n* **rashness**.

rasher /ra-sher/ *n* a thin slice of bacon.

rasp /rasp/ *n* **1** a file with a very rough face. **2** a harsh, grating sound. • *vb* **1** to rub with a rasp. **2** to make a harsh, grating sound. **3** to say in a harsh, angry voice.

raspberry /rasp-be-ree/ *n* **1** a common shrub. **2** its edible red berry.

Rastafarian /ra-sta-fay-ree-an/ *n* a member of a religious group that originated in Jamaica and worships the late Ethiopian emperor Haile Selassie.

rat /rat/ *n* a gnawing animal like, but larger than, the mouse. • *vb* (**ratted, ratting**) to inform on someone.

ratchet /rat-chit/ *n* a toothed wheel with which a catch automatically engages as it is turned, preventing it from being turned in the reverse direction.

rate /rate/ *n* **1** the amount of one thing measured by its relation to another. **2** speed. **3** price. • *vb* **1** to consider. **2** to value. **3** to assign to a position on a scale. • *adj* **ratable**.

rather /ra-ther/ *adv* **1** preferably, more willingly. **2** fairly, quite. **3** more exactly, more truly.

rating /ray-ting/ *n* **1** value or rank according to some kind of classification. **2** in the navy, a sailor who is not an officer.

ratio /ray-sho/ *n* one number or amount considered in relation or proportion to another.

ration /ra-shun/ *n* **1** a fixed amount of something allowed every so often. • *npl* (*old*) food. • *vb* to limit to fixed amounts.

rational /ra-shnul/ *adj* **1** having the power to think things out. **2** reasonable, sensible. • *adv* **rationally**.

rationalist /ra-shna-list/ *n* a person who tries to find natural causes for all things, including miracles. • *n* **rationalism**.

rationalize /ra-shna-lize/ *vb, also* **rationalise** **1** to try to find reasons for all actions. **2** to explain as due to natural causes. **3** to reorganize a business firm in order to improve efficiency.

rat race /rat-race/ *n* the competitive, aggressive struggle to survive and be successful in the modern world.

rattle /ra-tul/ *vb* **1** to make a number of short quick noises one after the other. **2** to shake something so as to cause such noises. **3** to speak or say quickly. • *n* **1** an instrument or toy for rattling. **2** a rattling sound.

rattlesnake /ra-tul-snake/ *n* an American snake able to make a rattling sound with horny rings on its tail.

raucous /raw-cus/ *adj* hoarse, harsh-sounding.

ravage /ra-vidge/ *vb* to lay waste, to plunder, to destroy far and wide. • *n* damage, destruction.

rave /rave/ *vb* **1** to talk wildly or madly. **2** to praise very highly.

raven /ray-vin/ *n* a bird of prey of the crow family. • *adj* black.

ravenous /ra-vi-nus/ *adj* very hungry. • *adv* **ravenously**.

ravine /ra-veen/ *n* a narrow valley with steep sides.

ravioli /ra-vee-o-lee/ *n* an Italian dish consisting of small squares of pasta with a meat or vegetable filling.

ravish /ra-vish/ *vb* **1** to take or carry off by force. **2** to delight. **3** to rape.

ravishing /ra-vi-shing/ *adj* delightful, wonderful. • *adv* **ravishingly**.

raw /raw/ *adj* **1** uncooked. **2** in its natural state. **3** sore. **4** (*of part of the body*) uncovered by skin, scraped. **5** cold and damp.

ray[1] /ray/ *n* **1** a line of light, heat, etc, getting broader as it goes further from its origin. **2** a little, a very small amount.

ray[2] /ray/ *n* a species of flatfish.

rayon /ray-on/ *n* artificial silk.

raze /raze/ *vb* to destroy completely, to wipe out.

razor /ray-zor/ *n* an implement for shaving hair.

razorblade /ray-zor-blade/ *n* a very sharp blade for use in certain kinds of razor.

reach /reech/ *vb* **1** to stretch out. **2** to stretch out a hand or arm for some purpose. **3** to obtain by stretching out for. **4** to arrive at, to get as far as. **5** to pass with the hand. • *n* **1** the distance you can extend the hand from the body. **2** a distance that can be easily travelled. **3** a straight stretch of river.

react /ree-act/ *vb* **1** to act, behave, or change in a certain way as a result of something said or done. **2** to do or think the opposite.

reaction /ree-ac-shun/ *n* **1** action or behaviour given rise to by something said or done. **2** opposition to progress. **3** in chemistry, the change in a substance when certain tests are made on it.

reactionary /ree-ac-shun-ree/ *adj* wanting to return to things as they were before, opposed to progress. • *also n.*

read /reed/ *vb* (*pt, pp* **read** /red/) **1** to look at and understand. **2** to speak aloud what is written or printed. **3** in computing, to extract. **4** to be written or worded.

readable /ree-da-bul/ *adj* easy to read, interesting.

reader /ree-der/ *n* **1** a person who enjoys reading. **2** a person whose job it is to report on manuscripts sent in to publishers or to read and correct proofs. **3** a reading book for schools. • *n* **readership**.

readily /re-di-lee/ *adv* willingly, cheerfully.

reading /ree-ding/ *n* **1** the study of books. **2** words read out from a book or written paper. **3** an explanation of what is written. **4** the figure recorded on an instrument.

readjust /ree-a-just/ *vb* **1** to put right or in the proper place again. **2** to make changes needed for altered circumstances. • *n* **readjustment**.

ready /re-dee/ *adj* **1** prepared and fit for use. **2** quick. **3** willing. • *n* **readiness**.

real /reel/ *adj* **1** actually existing. **2** true, genuine, not false or fake. **3** utter, complete. • *adv* very.

real estate /reel i-state/ (*esp US*) *n* property consisting of lands and buildings.

realism /ree-li-zum/ *n* **1** the belief that only objects perceptible by the senses actually exist. **2** trying to make works of art as true to life as possible. **3** the habit of taking a sensible, practical view of life.

realist /ree-a-list/ *n* a person who believes in realism.

realistic /ree-a-li-stic/ *adj* **1** lifelike. **2** taking a sensible, practical view of life. • *adv* **realistically**.

reality /ree-a-li-tee/ *n* **1** that which actually exists. **2** truth. **3** things as they actually are.

realize /ree-a-lize/ *vb*, *also* **realise 1** to understand fully. **2** to make real. **3** to sell for money. • *n* **realization**, *also* **realisation**.

really /ree-lee/ *adv* **1** actually, in fact. **2** very.

realm /relm/ *n* **1** (*fml*) a kingdom. **2** one particular aspect or sphere of life.

reap /reep/ *vb* **1** to cut down.

reaper /ree-per/ *n* **1** a person who reaps. **2** a machine for reaping.

reappear /ree-a-peer/ *vb* to appear again. • *n* **reappearance**.

rear[1] /reer/ *n* **1** the part behind. **2** the back part of an army or fleet.

rear[2] /reer/ *vb* **1** to bring up. **2** to breed. **3** to stand on the hind legs. **4** to raise.

reason /ree-zun/ *n* **1** cause for acting or believing. **2** the power to think things out. **3** good sense. • *vb* **1** to think out step by step. **2** to try to convince by arguing.

reasonable /reez-na-bul/ *adj* **1** sensible. **2** willing to listen to another's arguments. **3** not excessive. • *adv* **reasonably**.

reasoning /ree-zu-ning/ *n* **1** use of the power of reason. **2** arguments used to convince.

reassure /ree-a-shoor/ *vb* to take away the doubts or fears of. • *n* **reassurance**.

rebate /ree-bate/ *n* part of a payment given back to the payer.

rebel /re-bel/ *n* a person who revolts against authority. • *vb* /ri-bel/. **2** to refuse to obey those in authority.

rebellion /ri-bel-yun/ *n* open resistance to or fighting against authority.

rebellious /ri-bel-yuss/ *adj* **1** ready to rebel, disobedient. **2** fighting against authority.

rebirth /ree-berth/ *n* a revival of something.

reboot /ree-boot/ *vb* to start a computer again.

rebound /ree-bound/ *vb* to bounce back off, to spring back. • *also n*.

rebuke /ri-byook/ *vb* to scold, to find fault with. • *n* a scolding.

rebut /ri-but/ *vb* (**rebutted, rebutting**) to refuse to accept as true. • *n* **rebuttal**.

recall /ri-cawl/ *vb* **1** to remember. **2** to call back. • *n* /ree-cawl/ an order to return.

recede /ri-seed/ *vb* **1** to move back. **2** to slope back.

receipt /ri-seet/ *n* **1** a written statement that a sum of money or an article has been received. **2** the act of receiving.

receive /ri-seev/ *vb* **1** to come into possession of, to get. **2** to welcome.

receiver /ri-see-ver/ *n* **1** a person who accepts stolen goods from a thief. **2** the earpiece of a telephone. **3** a radio set.

recent /ree-sint/ *adj* not long past. • *adv* **recently**.

receptacle /ri-sep-ti-cal/ *n* a place or vessel for holding things.

reception /ri-sep-shun/ *n* **1** the act of receiving or being received, the welcoming of guests. **2** a formal party. **3** welcome. **4** the desk or area in a hotel or other large organization where guests or visitors go first. **5** the quality of radio or television signals.

receptionist /ri-sep-shu-nist/ *n* a person who is employed by a hotel, doctor, business, etc, to receive guests, clients, callers, etc.

receptive /ri-sep-tiv/ *adj* quick to learn. • *n* **receptivity**.

recess /ree-sess/ *n* **1** a break from work or study. **2** part of a room set back into the wall.

recession /ri-se-shun/ *n* a period of reduced trade and business activity.

recipe /re-si-pee/ *n* instructions on how to make or prepare a certain dish.

recipient /ri-si-pee-ent/ *n* a person who receives.

recital /ri-sie-tal/ *n* **1** a detailed account. **2** a public musical performance, especially by one performer.

recitation /re-si-tay-shun/ *n* **1** a reciting of something. **2** that which is recited (e.g. a poem).

recite /ri-site/ *vb* to repeat aloud from memory.

reckless /reck-less/ *adj* rash, heedless of danger. • *adv* **recklessly**.

reckon /re-kun/ *vb* **1** to think or consider. **2** to guess, to estimate. **3** (*fml*) to count.

reckoning /re-ku-ning/ *n* **1** a calculation, estimate. **2** (*old*) a settlement of accounts, a bill.

reclaim /ri-claim/ *vb* **1** to demand the return of. **2** to bring under cultivation waste land, land covered by the sea, etc. • *n* **reclamation**.

recline /ri-cline/ *n* to sit or lie back at your ease, to rest.

recluse /ri-clooss/ *n* a person who prefers to live away from human society. • *adj* **reclusive**.

recognition /re-cug-ni-shun/ *n* **1** act of recognizing. **2** acknowledgment.

recognizable /re-kug-nie-za-bul/ *adj*, *also* **recognisable** that may be recognized.

recognize /re-kug-nize/ *vb*, *also* **recognise** **1** to know again. **2** to greet or salute. **3** to admit. **4** to accept. **5** to reward.

recoil /re-coil/ *vb* **1** to go suddenly backward in horror, fear, etc. **2** (*of a gun*) to move sharply backward on firing. • *n* /ree-coil/ **1** a shrinking backward. **2** the backward kick of a gun on firing.

recollect /re-cu-lect/ *vb* to remember.

recollection /re-cu-lec-shun/ *n* **1** memory. **2** something remembered.

recommend /re-cu-mend/ *vb* **1** to speak in praise of, to suggest that something or someone is good, suitable, etc. **2** to advise.

recommendation /re-cu-men-day-shun/ *n* **1** act of praising or speaking in favour of. **2** a letter praising a person's good points.

reconcile /re-con-sile/ *vb* **1** to make or become friendly again. **2** to make (yourself) accept something new or strange.

reconciliation /re-cun-si-lee-ay-shun/ *n* a renewal of friendship.

reconsider /ree-kun-**si**-der/ *vb* to think about again with a view to changing your mind. • *n* **reconsideration**.

reconstruct /ree-con-**struct**/ *vb* **1** to rebuild. **2** to try to build up a description or picture of, to work out exactly what happened when all the facts are not known. • *n* **reconstruction**.

record /ri-**cawrd**/ *vb* **1** to put down in writing. **2** to preserve sounds or images by mechanical means, on a CD, tape, etc. **3** to sing songs, play music, etc, which is recorded on a CD or tape. • *n* /**re**-curd/ **1** a recorded account. **2** a book containing written records, a register. **3** the best performance yet known in any type of contest. **4** a disc for playing on a CD player or phonograph. **5** what is known about a person's past. **6** a criminal record.

recorder /ri-**cawr**-der/ *n* **1** a person who keeps registers or records. **2** a judge in certain cities. **3** a simple form of flute.

recount /ri-**count**/ *vb* **1** to tell in detail. **2** to count again. • *n* /**ree**-count/ another counting, e.g. of votes after an election.

recoup /ri-**coop**/ *vb* to get back all or part of a loss.

recover /ri-**cu**-ver/ *vb* **1** to cover again. **2** to get back, to regain. **3** to make or become better after sickness or weakness.

recovery /ri-**cu**-vu-ree/ *n* **1** a return to health after sickness. **2** the regaining of anything after losing some or all of it.

recreation /rec-ree-**ay**-shun/ *n* **1** rest and amusement after work. **2** a sport, a pastime.

recriminate /ri-**cri**-mi-nate/ *vb* to accuse in return, to accuse your accuser.

recrimination /ri-cri-mi-**nay**-shun/ *n* the act of recriminating, a counteraccusation.

recruit /ri-**croot**/ *n* **1** a soldier who has just joined the army. **2** a new member. • *vb* to enlist new soldiers, employees, members. • *n* **recruitment**.

rectangle /**rec**-tang-gul/ *n* a four-sided figure with all its angles right angles and one pair of sides longer than the other. • *adj* **rectangular**.

rectify /**rec**-ti-fie/ *vb* **1** to put right, to correct. **2** (*chemistry*) to purify. • *n* **rectification**.

rectum /**rec**-tum/ *n* the part of the large intestine that leads to the anus.

recuperate /ri-**coo**-pe-rate/ *vb* to regain health or strength after illness. • *n* **recuperation**.

recur /ri-**cur**/ *vb* (**recurred**, **recurring**) to happen again and again. • *n* **recurrence**.

recurrent /ri-**cu**-rent/ *adj* happening or appearing again and again.

recycle /ri-**sie**-cul/ *vb* to put something through some kind of process so that it can be used again.

red /red/ *adj* **1** of a colour like blood. **2** of a colour that varies between a golden brown and a reddish brown. **3** (*inf*) communist or extremely left-wing. • *n* **1** the colour red. **2** a communist. • **see red** to become suddenly very angry.

Red Cross /red **crawss**/, **Red Crescent** /red **cress**-ent/ *n* an international organization that looks after sick and wounded people in time of war, and protects the rights of prisoners of war.

redden /**re**-den/ *vb* **1** to make or become red. **2** to blush.

reddish /**re**-dish/ *adj* slightly red.

redeem /ri-**deem**/ *vb* **1** to buy back. **2** to buy freedom for. **3** to carry out. **4** to make up for. **5** to save from the punishment due to sin.

redeeming /ri-**dee**-ming/ *adj* cancelling out bad by good.

redemption /ri-**dem**-shun/ *n* the act of redeeming.

red-handed /red-**han**-did/ *adj* in the very act of doing wrong.

redhead /**red**-hed/ *n* a person who has reddish brown hair.

red herring /red **herr**-ing/ *n* something mentioned that takes attention away from the subject being discussed.

redoubtable /ri-**dow**-ta-bul/ *adj* to be feared, deserving respect.

red tape /red **tape**/ *n* excessive attention to rules and regulations so that business is delayed.

reduce /ri-**dooss**/ *vb* **1** to make less, smaller, or less heavy. **2** to change into another, and usually worse state, form, etc. **3** to bring or force to do something less pleasant, etc, than usual. • *n* **reduction**.

redundant /ri-**dun**-dant/ *adj* **1** more than is necessary. **2** no longer employed by a firm because you are no longer needed. • *n* **redundancy**.

reed /reed/ *n* **1** a tall grasslike water plant with a hollow stem. **2** that part of certain wind instruments that vibrates and so causes the sound when the instrument is blown.

reedy /**ree**-dee/ *adj* **1** covered with reeds. **2** high-pitched and thin.

reef[1] /**reef**/ *n* **1** a ridge of rock or sand just above or just below the surface of the water. **2** a crack in a rock containing gold.

reef[2] /**reef**/ *n* one of the parts of a sail that can be rolled or folded up. • *vb* to roll or fold up the reefs of a sail.

reef knot /reef not/ *n* a symmetrically tied double knot.

reek /reek/ *n* a strong unpleasant smell. • *vb* **1** to give off a smell, especially an unpleasant one. **2** to show or suggest strongly something bad or unpleasant.

reel /reel/ *n* **1** a frame or roller around which string, thread, photographic film, etc, may be wound. **2** a lively Scottish dance. • *vb* **1** to wind on to a reel. **2** to stagger. • **reel off** to tell without stopping or hesitating.

refer /ri-fer/ *vb* (**referred, referring**) **1** to make mention of. **2** to advise to consult elsewhere. **3** to look up a certain item in a book. **4** to pass.

referee /re-fe-ree/ *n* **1** a person who is chosen to give a clear decision in case of doubt. **2** in games, a person who sees that the rules are kept. **3** a person who supplies information about the character, behaviour, etc of someone applying for a job.

reference /ref-rense/ *n* **1** mention. **2** directions as to where to find certain items, passages, etc, in a book. **4** a letter giving information about the character, behaviour, etc, of a person who applies for a job.

reference book /ref-rense book/ *n* a book (e.g. a dictionary like this one) that supplies information.

refill /ree-fill/ *vb* to fill again. • *n* /ree-fill/ **1** a replacement for the contents of a container. **2** a replacement filling. **3** an additional drink replacing one already drunk.

refine /ri-fine/ *vb* **1** to purify. **2** to make more polite and civilized. • *adj* **refined**.

refinery /ri-fie-ne-ree/ *n* a place for purifying sugar, oil, etc.

reflect /ri-flect/ *vb* **1** (*of a mirror*) to show the image of. **2** to throw back, especially rays of light or heat. **3** to think about carefully. **4** to be a cause (of praise or blame) for.

reflection /ri-flec-shun/ *n* **1** the image seen in a mirror, etc. **2** the act of reflecting. **3** a deep or careful thought. **4** blame.

reflective /ri-flec-tiv/ *adj* thoughtful.

reflector /ri-flec-tor/ *n* a polished surface for reflecting light or heat.

reflex /ree-fleks/ *adj* automatic. • *n* an unintentional movement of the body caused by something outside it.

reflex angle /ree-fleks ang-gel/ *n* an angle between 180 degrees and 360 degrees.

reform /ri-fawrm/ *vb* **1** to make or become better. **2** to give up bad habits. • *n* a change for the better. • *n* **reformer**.

reformation /re-fur-may-shun/ *n* **1** a thorough change for the better. **2** (*cap*) the religious changes that occurred in Europe in the sixteenth century that resulted in the establishment of the Protestant churches.

refract /ri-fract/ *vb* to change the direction of. • *n* **refraction**.

refrain[1] /ri-frain/ *vb* to hold back.

refrain[2] /ri-frain/ *n* a line or phrase that is repeated several times in a song or poem; a chorus.

refresh /ri-fresh/ *vb* to give new strength, energy, power, etc. • *adj* **refreshing**. • *adv* **refreshingly**.

refreshment /ri-fresh-ment/ *n* (*often pl*) a light meal, a snack, a drink.

refrigerate /ri-fri-je-rate/ *vb* to make cold, to freeze. • *n* **refrigeration**.

refrigerator /ri-fri-je-ray-tur/ *n* an apparatus for preserving food, etc, by keeping it cold.

refuel /ree-fyool/ *vb* (of an aircraft or a ship) to take on more fuel.

refuge /ref-yoodge/ *n* a place of shelter from danger or distress.

refugee /re-fyoo-jee/ *n* a person who is fleeing from danger, a person who leaves his or her country to seek shelter in another.

refund /ri-fund/ *vb* to repay. • *n* /ree-fund/ **1** the act of refunding. **2** the amount refunded.

refurbish /ri-fur-bish/ *vb* to redecorate or restore.

refusal /ri-fyoo-zal/ *n* act of refusing.

refuse[1] /ri-fyooz/ *vb* **1** not to accept. **2** to say that you will not do or give something.

refuse[2] /ref-yooss/ *n* waste material that has been thrown away; rubbish.

refute /ri-fyoot/ *vb* to prove that something is not the case. • *n* **refutation**.

regain /ri-gain/ *vb* **1** to get possession of again. **2** to reach again.

regal /ree-gal/ *adj* of or like a king, royal, magnificent.

regale /ri-gale/ *vb* **1** to supply with plenty of food and drink. **2** to entertain.

regalia /ri-gay-lee-a/ *npl* objects worn or carried as signs of royalty (e.g. a crown, etc.) or high office.

regard /ri-gard/ *vb* **1** to consider. **2** (*fml*) to look at. • *n* **1** respect. **2** (*fml*) attention. • *npl* good wishes.

regarding /ri-gar-ding/ *prep* concerning.

regardless /ri-gard-less/ *adv* paying no attention, not caring about.

regatta /ri-ga-ta/ *n* a race meeting for boats and yachts.

regency /ree-jen-see/ *n* **1** rule by a regent. **2** the office of regent. **3** the period during which a regent rules.

regenerate /ri-**je**-ne-rate/ *vb* to improve after a period of worsening, to give fresh faith or energy to. • *n* **regeneration**.

regent /**ree**-jent/ *n* a person who governs during the youth, absence, or illness of a monarch.

reggae /**re**-gay/ *n* a type of popular music of West Indian origin.

regime /ray-**zheem**/ *n* a method or system of government.

regiment /**re**-ji-ment/ *n* a body of soldiers commanded by a colonel, an army unit consisting of several battalions.

regimental /re-ji-**men**-tal/ *adj* having to do with a regiment.

regimentation /re-ji-men-**tay**-shun/ *n* strict organization and control.

region /**ree**-jun/ *n* **1** a part of a country, often a large area of land. **2** a particular part of someone's body. • **in the region of** approximately. • *adj* **regional**.

register /**re**-ji-ster/ *n* **1** an official list. **2** a book in which records (e.g. of births, deaths, school attendance, etc) are kept. **3** the distance from the highest to the lowest note of a singing voice or musical instrument. • *vb* **1** to write down in a register. **2** to give details to an official for writing in a register. **3** to pay extra postage to ensure that a letter or parcel reaches its destination safely. **4** to show.

register office *see* **registry office**.

registrar /**re**-ji-strar/ *n* an official who keeps a register.

registration /re-ji-**stray**-shun/ *n* act of registering.

registry office /**re**-ji-stree of-is/, *also* **register office** /**re**-ji-ster of-is/, a government building where civil marriages are performed and where official records of births, deaths, marriages, etc, are kept.

regress /ri-**gress**/ *vb* to move backward. • *adj* **regressive**.

regression /ri-**gre**-shun/ *n* backward movement, a falling away.

regret /ri-**gret**/ *vb* (**regretted**, **regretting**) **1** to be sorry for what one has said or done. **2** to remember with sorrow. • *n* sorrow, grief. • *adj* **regretful**. • *adv* **regretfully**.

regrettable /ri-**gre**-ta-bul/ *adj* unfortunate, unwelcome. • *adv* **regrettably**.

regular /**re**-gyu-lar/ *adj* **1** normal, usual. **2** done always in the same way or at the same time. **3** occurring acting, etc with equal amounts of space, time, etc. between. **4** belonging to the regular army. **5** the same on both or all sides. **6** ordinary, normal. • *n* **1** a habitual customer. **2** a

soldier of the regular army. • *n* **regularity**. • *adv* **regularly**.

regular army /**re**-gyu-lar **ar**-mee/ *n* that part of the army in which people who wish to make soldiering their career are kept in training.

regulate /**re**-gyu-late/ *vb* **1** to control. **2** to alter.

regulation /re-gyu-**lay**-shun/ *n* a rule, an order, an instruction. • *adj* as laid down in the rules.

regulator /**re**-gyu-lay-tur/ *n* **1** a lever by which you can control a machine. **2** a person who controls.

regurgitate /ri-**gur**-ji-tate/ *vb* **1** to throw up again from the stomach. **2** to repeat without change.

rehabilitate /ree-ha-**bi**-li-tate/ *vb* to bring back to a normal life or normal standards of behaviour by treatment or instruction. • *n* **rehabilitation**.

rehearsal /ri-**her**-sal/ *n* a practice before a performance.

rehearse /ri-**herss**/ *vb* **1** to practise, especially in preparation for public performance. **2** (*fml*) to repeat aloud, to give a list of.

reign /rane/ *n* **1** rule. **2** the time during which a king or queen has ruled. • *vb* **1** to rule as a sovereign. **2** to exist.

reimburse /ree-im-**burse**/ *vb* to repay what someone has lost or spent. • *n* **reimbursement**.

rein /rane/ *n* **1** the strap by which a driver or rider directs a horse. **2** control. • *vb* to check or control with the rein.

reindeer /**rane**-deer/ *n* a deer found in northern parts of America and Europe.

reinforce /ree-in-**force**/ *vb* **1** to make stronger. **2** to supply with more soldiers, helpers, etc.

reinforcement /ree-in-**foarss**-ment/ *n* the act of reinforcing. • *npl* more or fresh troops, etc.

reinstate /ree-in-**state**/ *vb* to put back in a former position. • *n* **reinstatement**.

reiterate /ree-i-te-rate/ *vb* to repeat again and again. • *n* **reiteration**.

reject /ri-**ject**/ *vb* **1** to refuse to accept. **2** to throw back or away. • *n* /**ree**-ject/ someone or something that has been rejected. • *n* **rejection**.

rejoice /ri-**joiss**/ *vb* to be glad or joyful, to make glad, to express your joy.

rejoicing /ri-**joy**-sing/ *n* a feeling or expression of joy. • *npl* celebrations.

rejuvenate /ri-**joo**-vi-nate/ *vb* to make feel young again. • *n* **rejuvenation**.

relapse /ri-**lapss**/ *vb* to fall back into evil or

sickness after improving. • *also n* /ree-lapse/.

relate /ri-**late**/ *vb* **1** to show or see the connection between. **2** to tell. • *adj* **related**.

relation /ri-**lay**-shun/ *n* **1** a person who belongs to the same family by birth or marriage. **2** a connection. • *n* **relationship**.

relative /**re**-la-tiv/ *adj* **1** considered in comparison with others. **2** having to do with. • *n* a person who belongs to the same family, by birth or marriage.

relatively /**re**-la-tiv-lee/ *adv* **1** quite. **2** when compared with others.

relative pronoun /**re**-la-tiv **pro**-noun/ (*grammar*) a pronoun, such as 'who' or 'which', referring to an earlier word in the sentence.

relax /ri-**laks**/ *vb* **1** to take a complete rest, to become less tense or worried. **2** to loosen. **3** to become or make less strict or severe.

relaxation /ree-lak-**say**-shun/ *n* **1** rest, amusement after work. **2** loosening. **3** making less severe.

relaxing /ri-**lak**-sing/ *adj* **1** restful. **2** causing a feeling of tiredness.

relay /**ree**-lay/ *n* **1** a supply of fresh people or horses to take over from tired ones. **2** a relay race. **3** the sending out of a radio or television signal or show that has been received from somewhere else. • *vb* /ree-**lay**/ to rebroadcast a radio message or show received from elsewhere.

relay race /**ree**-lay race/ *n* a team race in which each member of a team covers part of the whole distance.

release /ri-**leess**/ *vb* **1** to set free. **2** to let go. **3** to unfasten. **4** to make public. • *also n*.

relegate /**re**-li-gate/ *vb* to put down to a lower position.

relent /ri-**lent**/ *vb* to become less severe, to give way.

relentless /ri-**lent**-less/ *adj* without pity, unmerciful, continuous. • *adv* **relentlessly**.

relevant /**re**-li-vant/ *adj* having to do with the matter under consideration. • *n* **relevance**, **relevancy**.

reliability /ri-lie-a-**bi**-li-tee/ *n* trustworthiness.

reliable /ri-**lie**-a-bul/ *adj* able to be trusted. • *adv* **reliably**.

reliance /ri-**lie**-anse/ *n* trust, confidence.

reliant /ri-**lie**-ant/ *adj* relying on, depending on.

relic /**re**-lic/ *n* **1** something old-fashioned that still exists. **2** a part of the body or belongings of a holy person after their death.

relief /ri-**leef**/ *n* **1** complete or partial freeing from pain or worry. **2** money, etc, given to the poor or those who have lost everything in a disaster. **3** a person who takes another's place on duty. **4** forcing an enemy to end the siege of a town. **5** a piece of sculpture in which the design stands out just beyond a flat surface. **6** a clear outline.

relieve /ri-**leev**/ *vb* **1** to set free from or lessen. **2** to give help to. **3** to take another's place on duty. **4** to force an enemy to end the siege of a town.

religion /ri-**li**-jun/ *n* **1** belief in and worship of a god or gods. **2** a particular system of this belief and worship.

religious /ri-**li**-jus/ *adj* **1** referring to religion. **2** believing strongly in your religion and obeying its rules. **3** careful and regular. • *adv* **religiously**.

relinquish /ri-**ling**-kwish / *vb* to give up.

relish /**rel**-ish/ *vb* **1** to enjoy the taste of. **2** to like or enjoy. • *n* **1** a taste, flavour. **2** enjoyment. **3** a sharp-tasting sauce.

relive /ree-**liv**/ *vb* to remember (an experience) in detail as if living through it again.

reluctant /ri-**luc**-tant/ *adj* unwilling. • *n* **reluctance**. • *adv* **reluctantly**.

rely /ri-**lie**/ *vb* **1** to trust in. **2** to depend on.

remain /ri-**main**/ *vb* **1** to stay on in a place. **2** to be left over. **3** to continue to be.

remainder /ri-**main**-der/ *n* that which is left over or behind.

remains /ri-**mainz**/ *npl* **1** that which is left. **2** (*fml*) a dead body.

remand /ri-**mand**/ *vb* to send back to prison while further inquiries are being made. • *n* **1** act of remanding. **2** the state of being remanded.

remark /ri-**mark**/ *vb* **1** to say. **2** to comment. • *n* **1** something said. **2** (*fml*) notice, attention.

remarkable /ri-**mar**-ka-bul/ *adj* worthy of notice, extraordinary. • *adv* **remarkably**.

remedial /ri-**mee**-dee-al/ *adj* intended or helping to cure.

remedy /**re**-mi-dee/ *n* **1** a cure. **2** a medicine. **3** any way of putting right what is wrong. • *vb* **1** to cure. **2** to put right.

remember /ri-**mem**-ber/ *vb* **1** to keep in mind. **2** to recall to the mind. **3** to give greetings from another.

remembrance /ri-**mem**-branss/ *n* **1** memory. **2** a souvenir.

remind /ri-**minde**/ *vb* to cause to remember.

reminder /ri-**mine**-der/ *n* something that helps you to remember.

reminisce /re-mi-**niss**/ *vb* to tell stories of your past.

reminiscence /re-mi-**ni**-sense/ *n* **1** a memory

of your past. **2** the remembering of the past.
• *npl* stories about your past.

reminiscent /re-mi-**ni**-sent/ *adj* **1** remembering the past. **2** tending to remind you of someone.

remiss /ri-**miss**/ *adj* careless, not doing your duty properly.

remission /re-**mi**-shun/ *n* **1** the reduction of a prison sentence. **2** a period when an illness is less severe.

remnant /**rem**-nant/ *n* a small piece or part left over, especially of fabric.

remorse /re-**mawrss**/ *n* great sorrow for having done wrong. • *adj* **remorseful**. • *adv* **remorsefully**.

remorseless /re-**mawrss**-less/ *adj* feeling no remorse, pitiless. • *adv* **remorselessly**.

remote /ri-**mote**/ *adj* **1** distant, far away, out of the way. **2** not closely related. **3** not friendly, withdrawn. **4** slight. • *adv* **remotely**.

remote control /ri-**mote** cun-**trole**/ *n* **1** a system that allows a device or machine to be controlled from a distance, using electrical, electronic, or radio signals. **2** *also* (*inf*) **remote** a handheld device that enables the user to operate a television set, etc from a distance.

removal /ri-**moo**-val/ *n* **1** act of removing. **2** moving house, the transfer of furniture and other belongings from one house to another.

remove /ri-**moov**/ *vb* **1** to take from its place. **2** to take off. **3** to dismiss. • *adj* **removable**.

Renaissance /ri-nay-**sanss**/ *n* a revival, especially of interest in arts and learning, as in the 15th century.

render /**ren**-der/ *vb* **1** to give. **2** to perform in a certain way. **3** to translate. **4** to cause to be.

rendering /**ren**-dring/ *n* **1** a translation. **2** a particular performance.

rendezvous /**ron**-day-voo/ *n* **1** an agreed meeting place. **2** a meeting.

rendition /ren-**di**-shun/ *n* a particular performance.

renew /ri-**noo**/ *vb* **1** to make valid again for a further period. **2** to begin again. **3** to replace something old or broken. • *adj* **renewable**. • *n* **renewal**.

renounce /ri-**nounss**/ *vb* **1** to give up. **2** to state that you will have nothing more to do with. • *n* **renunciation**.

renovate /**re**-nu-vate/ *vb* to make like new, to repair and clean. • *n* **renovation**.

renown /ri-**noun**/ *n* fame, glory.

renowned /ri-**nound**/ *adj* famous.

rent[1] /**rent**/ *n* a payment made for the use of land, a house, etc. • *vb* **1** to get the use

of by paying rent. **2** to let or hire out for rent.

rent[2] /**rent**/ *n* (*fml*) a tear, a split.

rental /**ren**-tal/ *n* rent, the sum paid in rent.

rent boy /**rent** boy/ *n* (*sl*) a young man who has sex with men for money.

repair /ri-**pair**/ *vb* **1** to mend. **2** to put right, make up for. **3** (*fml*) to go. • *n* **1** returning to good condition, mending. **2** a mended place. **3** condition for using.

repay /ri-**pay**/ *vb* **1** to pay back. **2** to treat in a like way.

repayment /ri-**pay**-ment/ *n* **1** the act of repaying. **2** the sum repaid.

repeal /ri-**peel**/ *vb* to withdraw, to set aside, to abolish. • *also n*.

repeat /ri-**peet**/ *vb* **1** to do or say again. **2** to speak aloud something learned by heart. • *n* a television show that is broadcast again.

repeatedly /ri-**pee**-tid-lee/ *adv* again and again.

repel /ri-**pel**/ *vb* (**repelled, repelling**) **1** to cause dislike. **2** to drive back.

repellent /ri-**pe**-lent/ *adj* causing dislike or disgust. • *n* that which is able to repel or drive away something.

repent /ri-**pent**/ *vb* to feel sorry for having said or done something. • *n* **repentance**. • *adj* **repentant**.

repertoire /**re**-per-twar/ *n* **1** a performer's stock of musical pieces, poems, etc. **2** a company's stock of plays that are ready for acting.

repetition /re-pi-**ti**-shun/ *n* **1** act of repeating. **2** saying from memory. • *adj* **repetitious**. • *adj* **repetitive** occurring again and again.

repetitive strain injury /re-**pe**-ti-tiv strain in-ju-ree/ *n see* **RSI**.

replace /ri-**place**/ *vb* **1** to put back in place. **2** to take the place of.

replacement /ri-**place**-ment/ *n* **1** act of replacing. **2** a person or thing that takes the place of another.

replenish /ri-**ple**-nish/ *vb* to fill up again. • *n* **replenishment**.

replica /**re**-pli-ca/ *n* **1** an exact copy of a work of art. **2** a reproduction, especially of a smaller size.

replicate /**re**-pli-cate/ *vb* to make an exact copy of.

reply /ri-**plie**/ *vb* to answer. • *n* an answer.

report /ri-**poart**/ *vb* **1** to give as news or information, to tell. **2** to write an account of, especially for a newspaper. **3** to make a complaint about for having done wrong. **4** to tell someone in authority. • *n* **1** a spoken or written account of work performed (e.g. by a committee, a student). **2** an account of something that has been said or done, especially when written for a newspaper. **3** a rumour. **4** a loud noise.

reporter /ri-**poar**-ter/ *n* a person who reports for a newspaper or television/radio broadcast.

repose /ri-**poaz**/ (*fml*) *vb* **1** to lay at rest, to lie at rest. **2** to place. • *n* **1** rest, sleep. **2** calmness.

represent /re-pri-**zent**/ *vb* **1** to stand for, or make to stand for, as a sign or likeness. **2** to be a picture or statue of. **3** to have the right to speak or act for. **4** to describe or declare, perhaps falsely. **5** to be, to constitute. **6** to be the representative of.

representation /re-pri-zen-**tay**-shun/ *n* **1** the act of representing or being represented. **2** an image or likeness. **3** a protest or objection.

representative /re-pri-**zen**-ta-tiv/ *adj* typical, standing for others of the same class. • *n* **1** a person who acts for another. **2** a person who sells goods for a business firm. **3** an elected member of the US House of Representatives.

repress /ri-**press**/ *vb* to keep under control, to keep down, to restrain.

repression /ri-**pre**-shun/ *n* strict control, restraint.

repressive /ri-**pre**-siv/ *adj* (*fml*) intended to keep down or restrain.

reprieve /ri-**preev**/ *vb* to let off punishment, to pardon. • *also n*.

reprimand /**re**-pri-mand/ *n* a severe scolding. • *vb* to scold severely.

reprint /ree-**print**/ *vb* to print again. • *n* /**ree**-print/ a new printing or edition.

reprisal /ri-**prie**-zal/ *n* something done by way of punishment or revenge.

reproach /ri-**proach**/ *vb* to accuse and blame, to scold, usually with a suggestion of sadness or disappointment. • *n* **1** scolding, blame. **2** something that brings shame.

reproachful /ri-**proach**-ful/ *adj* accusing, shameful.

reproduce /ree-pru-**dooss**/ *vb* **1** to cause to be heard, seen, or done again. **2** to increase by having offspring. • *n* **reproduction**. • *adj* **reproductive**.

reptile /**rep**-tile/ *n* a class of cold-blooded animals that crawl or creep (e.g. snake, lizard).

republic /ri-**pub**-lic/ *n* a state entirely governed by elected persons, there being no sovereign.

republican /ri-**pu**-bli-can/ *adj* having to do with a republic. • *n* a person who prefers republican government.

Republican /ri-**pu**-bli-can/ *n* a member or supporter of the Republican Party of the USA. • *also adj*.

repugnance /ri-**pug**-nanse/ *n* disgust.

repugnant /ri-**pug**-nant/ *adj* very unpleasant, disgusting.

repulse /ri-**pulss**/ *vb* **1** to drive back, to defeat. **2** to refuse sharply. • *n* **1** a defeat. **2** a refusal.

repulsion /ri-**pul**-shun/ *n* dislike, disgust.

repulsive /ri-**pul**-siv/ *adj* hateful, disgusting.

reputable /**re**-pyu-ta-bul/ *adj* having a good name, respectable.

reputation /re-pyu-**tay**-shun/ *n* **1** your good name, your character as seen by other people. **2** fame.

repute /ri-**pyoot**/ *n* reputation. • *vb* to consider to be.

reputed /ri-**pyoo**-tid/ *adj* supposed.

reputedly /ri-**pyoo**-tid-lee/ *adv* as is commonly supposed.

request /ri-**kwest**/ *vb* to ask for. • *n* **1** the act of asking for something. **2** a favour asked for.

requiem /**re**-kwee-em/ *n* **1** a church service in which prayers are said for a dead person. **2** a musical composition for the dead.

require /ri-**kwire**/ *vb* **1** to need. **2** to demand by right, to order.

requirement /ri-**kwire**-ment/ *n* **1** a need, something needed. **2** a necessary condition.

rerun /**ree**-run/ *n* (*chiefly US*) a repeat of a TV show.

rescue /**re**-scyoo/ *vb* to save from danger or evil. • *n* act of rescuing. • *n* **rescuer**.

research /ree-**search**/ *n* careful study to discover new facts. • *also v*.

resemble /ri-**zem**-bul/ *vb* to be like. • *n* **resemblance**.

resent /ri-**zent**/ *vb* to be angered by, to take as an insult.

resentful /ri-**zent**-ful/ *adj* showing anger, full of annoyance. • *adv* **resentfully**.

resentment /ri-**zent**-ment/ *n* anger, indignation.

reservation /re-zer-**vay**-shun/ *n* **1** something kept back. **2** land set aside for some special purpose (e.g. as a place for Native Americans to live). **3** a booked place or seat. **4** a feeling or expression of doubt.

reserve /ri-**zerv**/ *vb* **1** to keep back for future use. **2** to order or book for future use. • *n* **1** something kept back for future use. **2** land set aside for some special purpose. **3** shyness, unwillingness to show your feelings. • *npl* troops kept out of battle for use where and when needed.

reserved /ri-**zervd**/ adj shy, not showing what you are thinking or feeling.

reservoir /**re**-zerv-war/ n 1 a place where the water supply of a city is stored. 2 a store.

reside /ri-**zide**/ vb to dwell, to live (in).

residence /**re**-si-denss/ n dwelling, house.

residency /**re**-si-den-see/ n the house of an official, e.g. a governor.

resident /**re**-si-dent/ n a person who lives somewhere. • also adj.

residential /re-si-**den**-shal/ adj 1 suitable for living in. 2 (of a district) having many dwelling houses.

residual /ri-**zi**-ju-wal/ adj (fml) left after the rest has been taken.

residue /**re**-zi-doo/ n the remainder, what is left over.

resign /ri-**zine**/ vb 1 to give up. 2 to give up an office or a post. 3 to accept with complaint. • n **resignation**.

resigned /ri-**zined**/ adj accepting trouble without complaint; patient.

resilient /ri-**zil**-yint/ adj 1 able to spring back to a former position after being bent. 2 having good powers of recovery. • n **resilience**.

resin /**re**-zin/ n a sticky substance that oozes from certain plants, e.g. firs, pines, etc. • adj **resinous**.

resist /ri-**zist**/ vb 1 to stand against, to fight against, to oppose. 2 to face or allow yourself not to accept.

resistance /ri-**zis**-tanse/ n the act or power of resisting, opposition.

resistant /ri-**zis**-tant/ adj offering resistance.

resolute /**re**-zu-loot/ adj determined, bold, having the mind made up. • adv **resolutely**.

resolution /re-zu-**loo**-shun/ n 1 determination. 2 a firm intention. 3 a proposal for a meeting to vote on. 4 the decision of a meeting on a certain matter. 5 (fml) the act of solving.

resolve /ri-**zolv**/ vb 1 to determine. 2 to break up into parts or elements. 3 to solve. • n 1 a fixed purpose. 2 determination.

resonant /**re**-zu-nant/ adj 1 echoing. 2 deep-sounding. • n **resonance**.

resort /ri-**zawrt**/ vb to make use of, to turn to. • n 1 a place to which you go frequently. 2 a place where many people go on vacation. • as a last resort as a last possibility.

resound /ri-**zound**/ vb to echo, to give back the sound of.

resounding /ri-**zoun**-ding/ adj 1 echoing. 2 very great.

resource /ri-**zoarss**/ n 1 a means of obtaining help, something turned to in time of need.

2 (often pl) a source of economic wealth, especially of a country.

resourceful /ri-**zoarss**-ful/ adj full of clever plans.

respect /ri-**spect**/ vb 1 to think highly of. 2 to pay attention to. • n 1 honour. 2 care or attention. • npl good wishes.

respectability /ri-spec-ta-**bi**-li-tee/ n 1 state of deserving respect. 2 decency.

respectable /ri-**spec**-ta-bul/ adj 1 deserving respect, decent. 3 large enough, good enough, etc. • adv **respectably**.

respectful /ri-**spect**-ful/ adj showing respect or honour to. • adv **respectfully**.

respecting /ri-**spec**-ting/ prep (fml) having to do with.

respective /ri-**spec**-tiv/ adj each to their own, proper to each.

respectively /ri-**spec**-tiv-lee/ adv belonging to each in the order already mentioned.

respiration /re-spi-**ray**-shun/ n (fml) breathing.

respirator /**re**-spi-ray-tor/ n a mask with a filter worn over the nose and mouth to purify the air breathed in.

respiratory /**resp**-ra-toe-ree/ adj having to do with breathing.

respond /ri-**spond**/ vb 1 to answer. 2 to do as a reaction to something that has been done.

respondent /ri-**spon**-dent/ n (fml) the defendant in a lawsuit, especially in divorce.

response /ri-**sponss**/ n 1 an answer, a reply. 2 a reaction.

responsible /ri-**spon**-si-bul/ adj 1 able to be trusted. 2 having to say or explain what you have done. 3 being the cause of something. • n **responsibility**. • adv **responsibly**.

responsive /ri-**spon**-siv/ adj quick to react.

rest[1] /rest/ n 1 a pause in work. 2 inactivity. 3 sleep. 4 a support or prop. • vb 1 to cease from action. 2 to stop work for a time. 3 to be still or quiet. 4 to sleep or repose. 5 to be supported.

rest[2] /rest/ n that which is left, the remainder.

restaurant /**re**-strawnt/ n a place where one may eat and buy meals.

restaurateur /re-stu-ra-**tur**/ n a person who keeps a restaurant.

restful /**rest**-ful/ adj peaceful, quiet.

restive /**re**-stiv/ adj unable to keep still, impatient.

restless /**rest**-liss/ adj 1 always on the move. 2 not restful, giving no rest.

restore /ri-**store**/ vb 1 to bring back. 2 to put back. 3 to make strong again. 4 to bring back to an earlier state or condition. • n **restoration**.

restrain /ri-**strain**/ *vb* to hold back, to check.

restraint /ri-**straint**/ *n* **1** self-control. **2** lack of freedom.

restrict /ri-**strict**/ *vb* to set limits to, to keep down.

restriction /ri-**stric**-shun/ *n* a rule or condition that lessens freedom.

restrictive /ri-**stric**-tiv/ *adj* lessening freedom, keeping under control.

result /ri-**zult**/ *n* **1** that which happens as the effect of something else, the outcome. **2** the final score in a sports contest. **3** (*inf*) a favourable or successful result. • *vb* **1** to follow as the effect of a cause. **2** to end (in).

resume /ri-**zoom**/ *vb* **1** to begin again. **2** (*fml*) to take back.

résumé /**re**-zu-may/ *n* **1** a summary. **2** (*US*) a CV.

resumption /ri-**zum**-shun/ *n* the act of resuming.

resurgence /ri-**sur**-jinse/ *n* a rising again.

resurrect /re-zu-**rect**/ *vb* **1** to raise or bring back again. **2** to raise to life again after death.

resurrection /re-zu-**rec**-shun/ *n* **1** the act of resurrecting. **2** a rising again from the dead.

resuscitate /ri-**su**-si-tate/ *vb* to bring back to life or consciousness. • *n* resuscitation.

retail /**ree**-tail/ *vb* **1** to sell direct to the public in small amounts. **2** to sell. • *n* the sale of goods in small quantities. • *n* retailer.

retain /ri-**tain**/ *vb* **1** to continue to use, have, remember, etc. **2** to hold back. **3** to engage someone's services by paying a fee in advance.

retainer /ri-**tay**-ner/ *n* **1** (*old*) a follower. **2** an advance fee for someone's services.

retaliate /ri-**ta**-lee-ate/ *vb* to return like for like, to get your own back. • *n* retaliation.

retard /ri-**tard**/ *vb* to make slow or late, to make go more slowly, to delay. • *n* retardation.

retch /**retch**/ *vb* to try to vomit. • *also n.*

retention /ri-**ten**-shun/ *n* (*fml*) act of retaining.

reticent /**re**-ti-sent/ *adj* unwilling to speak to others, silent. • *n* reticence.

retina /**re**-ti-na/ *n* the inner layer of the eye to which are connected the ends of the nerves that enable us to see.

retire /ri-**tire**/ *vb* **1** to leave your work forever because of old age, illness, etc. **2** to go to bed. **3** to go back or away.

retired /ri-**tierd**/ *adj* having given up your business or profession.

retirement /ri-**tire**-ment/ *n* **1** the act of retiring. **2** the time after you have finished your working life.

retiring /ri-**tie**-ring/ *adj* shy, not fond of company.

retort /ri-**tawrt**/ *vb* to reply quickly or sharply. • *n* **1** a quick or sharp reply. **2** a thin glass bottle with a long bent-back neck, used for heating chemicals.

retrace /re-**trace**/ *vb* to go back over again.

retract /ri-**tract**/ *vb* to say that a previous opinion was wrong, to take back what you have said. • *n* retraction.

retreat /ri-**treet**/ *vb* **1** to go back. **2** (of an army) to move back away from the enemy. • *n* **1** act of retreating. **2** a quiet, out-of-the-way place, a place of peace and safety. **3** a period of rest, meditation, prayer, etc.

retribution /re-tri-**byoo**-shun/ *n* just punishment for wrong done.

retrieve /ri-**treev**/ *vb* **1** to find again. **2** to find and bring back. **3** to undo harm or loss undergone.

retriever /ri-**tree**-ver/ *n* a dog trained to fetch birds shot by hunters.

retro- /**re**-troe/ *prefix* backward.

retro /**re**-troe/ *adj* (*inf*) involving styles or designs from the recent past.

retrospect /**re**-troe-spect/ *n* looking back to the past.

retrospection /re-troe-**spec**-shun/ *n* a looking-back to the past.

retrospective /re-troe-**spec**-tiv/ *adj* looking back to the past.

return /ri-**turn**/ *vb* **1** to come or go back. **2** to give or send back. • *n* **1** a coming or going back. **2** what is given or sent back. **3** profit. **4** a written statement of certain facts, expenses, figures, etc. • **return ticket** a ticket paid for a journey from one place to another and back again.

reunion /ri-**yoon**-yun/ *n* a meeting again of old friends or colleagues.

reunite /ri-yoo-**nite**/ *vb* to join together again.

re-use /ree-**yooz**/ *vb* to use again. • *also n.* • *adj* reusable.

rev /**rev**/ *n* (*inf*) revolution per minute. • *npl* revolutions per minute. • *vb* (**revving revved**) to increase the speed of a motor. • **rev up**.

Rev, Rev. /**rev**/ *abbr* = **1** Reverend. **2** (*Bible*) Revelation.

reveal /ri-**veel**/ *vb* **1** to show what was hidden. **2** to make known.

reveille /re-**va**-lee/ *n* a morning call on the bugle, etc, to waken soldiers.

revel /**re**-vul/ *n* merrymaking, a noisy feast.

• *vb* **1** (*old*) to make merry. **2** to take great delight (in). • *n* **reveler**.

revelation /re-ve-**lay**-shun/ *n* **1** act of making known. **2** a surprising discovery or piece of information.

revelry /**re**-vel-ree/ *n* noisy feasting or merrymaking.

revenge /ri-**venj**/ *n* making someone suffer for a wrong done to another, repaying evil with evil. • *also vb*. • *adj* **revengeful**.

revenue /**re**-vi-noo/ *n* money made by a person, business, or state.

reverberate /ri-**ver**-bi-rate/ *vb* to echo. • *n* **reverberation**.

revere /ri-**veer**/ *vb* to feel great respect for.

reverence /**rev**-rense/ *n* respect and admiration.

Reverend /**rev**-rend/ *n* (*abbr* = **Rev**, **Rev**.) a title given to a member of clergy.

reverent /**rev**-rent/ *adj* showing or feeling great respect.

reverential /re-ve-**ren**-shal/ *adj* full of reverence.

reverse /ri-**verse**/ *vb* **1** to turn back to front or upside down. **2** to go or move backward. **3** to change to the opposite. • *n* **1** a defeat. **2** a failure. **3** the opposite. **4** the back of a coin, medal, etc. • *adj* **1** opposite. **2** back.

reversible /ri-**ver**-si-bul/ *adj* **1** able to be reversed. **2** that which can be turned inside out.

revert /ri-**vert**/ *vb* **1** to go back to a former condition, custom, or subject. **2** to return or be returned to the previous owner or member of his/her family.

review /ri-**vyoo**/ *vb* **1** to look over again, to consider with a view to changing. **2** to inspect. **3** to write your opinion of. • *n* **1** a looking back on the past. **2** reconsideration or revision. **3** an article in a newspaper, magazine, etc, giving an opinion on a book, play, etc. **4** a magazine that reviews books, plays, etc.

reviewer /ri-**vyoo**-er/ *n* a person who writes reviews, a critic.

revile /ri-**vile**/ *vb* to speak insultingly about or to.

revise /ri-**vize**/ *vb* **1** to go over again and correct, improve or update. **2** to study again, usually for an exam. • *n* **reviser**.

revision /ri-**vi**-zhun/ *n* the act of revising.

revitalize /ree-**vie**-ta-lize/ *vb, also* **revitalise** to put new life or strength into.

revival /ri-**vie**-val/ *n* **1** the act of reviving. **2** the arousing of fresh enthusiasm for religion.

revivalist /ri-**vie**-va-list/ *n* a person who tries to arouse fresh enthusiasm for religion.

revive /ri-**vive**/ *vb* **1** to bring back to life, health, or consciousness. **2** to bring back to use or an active state. **3** to give new vigour or energy to. **4** to produce an old play in the theatre.

revoke /ri-**voke**/ *vb* to do away with, to withdraw. • *n* **revocation**.

revolt /ri-**voalt**/ *vb* **1** to rebel. **2** to shock or disgust. • *n* a rebellion, a rising against the government.

revolting /ri-**vole**-ting/ *adj* disgusting, shocking.

revolution /re-vu-**loo**-shun/ *n* **1** one complete turn of a wheel, etc. **2** a complete change. **3** a movement or rebellion as a result of which a new method of government is introduced.

revolutionary /re-vu-**loo**-shun-ree/ *adj* desiring to bring about a complete change. • *n* a person who works for a complete change of government.

revolutionize /re-vu-**loo**-shu-nize/ *vb, also* **revolutionise** to bring about a complete change in.

revolve /ri-**volv**/ *vb* **1** to turn around and around. **2** to move around a centre or axis.

revolver /ri-**vol**-ver/ *n* a pistol able to fire several shots without reloading.

revue /ri-**vyoo**/ *n* a light theatrical entertainment with music, songs, dances, etc.

revulsion /ri-**vul**-shun/ *n* a sudden complete change of feeling, disgust.

reward /ri-**wawrd**/ *n* **1** something given in return for work done, good behaviour, bravery, etc. **2** a sum of money offered for finding or helping to find a criminal, lost or stolen property, etc. • *vb* to give as a reward. • *adj* **rewarding**.

rhapsodize /**rap**-su-dize/ *vb, also* **rhapsodise** to talk in an excited, disconnected manner.

rhapsody /**rap**-su-dee/ *n* **1** a piece of writing, music or speech full of excited feeling and therefore not following the usual rules of composition. **2** (*usually pl*) an expression of excited approval.

rhetoric /**re**-tu-ric/ *n* **1** the art of speaking and writing well. **2** words that sound well but say little of importance. • *n* **rhetorician**.

rhetorical /ri-**tawr**-ic-al/ *adj* high-sounding.

rhetorical question /ri-**tawr**-ic-al **kwes**-chun/ *n* a question asked for effect where no answer is expected.

rheumatism /**roo**-ma-ti-zum/, **rheumatics** /roo-**ma**-tics/ *n* a disease causing painful swelling in the joints. • *adj* **rheumatic**.

rhinoceros /rie-**nos**-rus/ *n* a large thick-skinned animal with a horn (or two horns) on its nose.

rhododendron /ro-du-**den**-drun/ *n* an evergreen shrub with large brightly coloured flowers.

rhombus /**rom**-bus/ *n* (*pl* **rhombuses** *or* **rhombi**) a parallelogram with equal sides but angles that are not right angles.

rhubarb /**roo**-barb/ *n* a garden plant with juicy stalks edible when cooked, and roots sometimes used in medicines.

rhyme /rime/ *n* **1** sameness of sound at the ends of words or lines of poetry. **2** a word that rhymes with another. **3** a poem with rhymes. • *vb* **1** to find words ending in the same sound(s). **2** to end in the same sound(s) as. **3** to write poetry. • **without rhyme or reason** foolish, unreasonable.

rhythm *n* **1** the regular beat of words or sounds. **2** a regular repeated pattern of movements, graceful motion.

rhythmic /**rith**-mic/, **rhythmical** /**rith**-mi-cal/ *adjs* having a regular beat, regular. • *adv* **rhythmically**.

rib /rib/ *n* **1** one of the curved bones of the breast. **2** a low, narrow ridge or raised part of a material. **3** a curved piece of wood attached to the keel of a ship and going up to the deck.

ribald /**ri**-bald/ *adj* coarse, indecent, vulgar.

ribaldry /**ri**-bald-ree/ *n* coarse talk.

ribbon /**ri**-bun/ *n* a narrow decorative band of silk or other material.

rice /rice/ *n* a white edible grain often grown in hot countries, especially in river valleys.

rice paper /**rice** pay-per/ *n* **1** a kind of fine paper. **2** a special form of this that can be eaten and is used in cookery.

rich /rich/ *adj* **1** having much money, wealthy. **2** fertile. **3** valuable. **4** plentiful. **5** containing much fat or sugar. **6** deep, strong. • *n* **richness**.

riches /**ri**-chiz/ *npl* wealth.

richly /**rich**-lee/ *adv* **1** in a rich manner. **2** with riches.

rick /rick/ *n* a heap or stack of hay, etc.

rickety /**ri**-ki-tee/ *adj* shaky, unsteady.

rickshaw /**rik**-shaw/ *n* a light two-wheeled carriage pulled by a person.

ricochet /**ri**-cu-shay/ *n* the skimming of a bullet off a flat surface. • *vb* to hit something and bounce away at an angle.

rid /rid/ *vb* (**rid** *or* **ridded**, **ridding**) to make free from, to clear.

ridden *pp* of **ride**.

riddle[1] /**ri**-dul/ *n* a puzzling question.

riddle[2] /**ri**-dul/ *n* a large sieve. • *vb* **1** to sift. **2** to fill with holes.

ride /ride/ *vb* (*pt* **rode**, *pp* **ridden**) **1** to be carried on the back of an animal or on a vehicle. **2** to be able to ride on and control a horse, bicycle, etc. • *n* a trip on an animal's back or in a vehicle.

rider /**rie**-der/ *n* **1** a person who rides. **2** something added to what has already been said or written.

ridge /ridge/ *n* **1** a long, narrow hill. **2** the raised part between two lower parts. **3** a mountain range.

ridicule /**ri**-di-cyool/ *n* mockery. • *vb* to mock, to make fun of.

ridiculous /ri-**di**-cyu-lus/ *adj* deserving to be laughed at, absurd. • *adv* **ridiculously**.

riding habit /**rie**-ding ha-bit/ *n* the clothes worn for riding.

rife /rife/ *adj* found everywhere or in large numbers or quantities, extremely common.

rifle[1] /**rie**-ful/ *n* a handgun with a grooved barrel that makes the bullet spin in flight. • *vb* to make grooves in a gun barrel.

rifle[2] /**rie**-ful/ *vb* to search through and steal anything valuable.

rift /rift/ *n* **1** a disagreement between two friends. **2** a split or crack in the ground.

rig /rig/ *vb* **1** (*inf*) to provide clothing for. **2** to provide tools or equipment. **3** to provide (*a ship*) with ropes, sails, etc. **4** to set up. **5** to arrange wrongfully to produce a desired result, often an unfair or unlawful one. • *n* the particular way in which a ship's masts, sails, etc, are arranged.

rigging /**ri**-ging/ *n* a ship's spars, ropes, etc.

right /rite/ *adj* **1** correct. **2** true. **3** just, morally correct. **4** straight. **5** on the side of the right hand. **6** in good condition. **7** suitable, appropriate. **8** total, complete. • *vb* **1** to put back in position, to set in order. **2** to mend, to correct. • *n* **1** that which is correct, good, or true. **2** something to which you have a just claim. **3** the right-hand side. **4** in politics, the party or group holding the more traditional, conservative beliefs. • *adv* **1** straight. **2** exactly. **3** to the right-hand side.

right angle /**rite** ang-gul/ *n* an angle of 90 degrees.

righteous /**rie**-chus/ *adj* **1** having just cause. **2** good-living, virtuous. • *adv* **righteously**. • *n* **righteousness**.

rightful /**rite**-ful/ *adj* lawful, just. • *adv* **rightfully**.

right-handed /rite-**han**-ded/ *adj* better able to use the right hand than the left.

rightly /**rite**-lee/ *adv* **1** justly. **2** correctly.

rigid /**ri**-jid/ *adj* **1** that cannot be bent. **2** stern, strict, not willing to change. **3** not to be changed. • n **rigidity**. • adv **rigidly**.

rigmarole /rig-ma-role/ n long and confused or meaningless talk.

rigour /ri-gur/ n, also **rigor** (US) strictness, severity, harshness. • adj **rigorous**. • adv **rigorously**.

rile /rile/ vb to make angry.

rim /rim/ n 1 the outer hoop of a wheel. 2 the outer edge, brim.

rime[1] /rime/ n white or hoar frost.

rime[2] /rime/ another spelling of **rhyme**.

rind /rinde/ n 1 the skin of some fruits. 2 the skin of bacon, cheese, etc.

ring[1] /ring/ n 1 a hoop of gold or other metal for the finger. 2 anything in the form of a circle. 3 a space enclosed by ropes for a boxing match. • vb (pt, pp **ringed**) to surround, to encircle.

ring[2] /ring/ vb (pt **rang**, pp **rung**) 1 to make a clear sound as a bell. 2 to cause a bell to sound. 3 to echo. 4 to phone someone. • n 1 the sound of a bell. 2 a phone call.

ringleader /ring-lee-der/ n the leader of a gang.

ringlet /ring-let/ n a curl of hair.

ringtone /ring-tone/ n the sound made by a mobile phone to show that there is an incoming call.

rink /ringk/ n 1 a level stretch of ice for skating or curling. 2 a floor for roller-skating.

rinse /rinss/ vb 1 to wash by pouring water over. 2 to dip in water and wash lightly. 3 to put in clean water to remove soap.

riot /rie-ut/ n 1 a noisy or violent disorder caused by a crowd. 2 (inf) something or someone that is very funny. 3 a bright and splendid show. • **read the riot act** to give clear warning that unruly behaviour must stop. • **run riot** to go wild, to go out of control.

riotous /rie-u-tuss/ adj noisy, disorderly.

rip /rip/ vb (**ripped, ripping**) to tear or cut open; to strip off. • n a tear, a rent.

ripe /ripe/ adj 1 ready to be gathered or picked, ready for eating. 2 suitable or ready for. • n **ripeness**.

ripen /rie-pin/ vb 1 to become ripe. 2 to cause to become ripe.

ripple /ri-pul/ n 1 a little wave. 2 the sound of shallow water running over stones. 3 a sound resembling this. • vb 1 to flow in ripples. 2 to cause tiny waves to appear on. 3 to flow with a murmuring sound.

rise /rize/ vb (pt **rose**, pp **risen**) 1 to get up from bed. 2 to stand up. 3 to go upward. 4 to increase. 5 to rebel. 6 to move to a higher position. 7 (of a river) to have its source or beginning. • n 1 an increase in number, amount, value. 2 an increase in pay. 3 an increase in power, importance or popularity. 4 upward slope. 5 a small hill. • **give rise to** to cause or bring about. • **rise to the occasion** to do all that is necessary at a difficult time. • **take a rise out of** (inf) to play a joke or trick on.

rising /rie-zing/ n 1 the act of rising. 2 a rebellion.

risk /risk/ n 1 danger. 2 possible harm or loss. • vb 1 to put in danger, to lay open to the possibility of loss. 2 to take the chance of something bad or unpleasant happening.

risky /ri-skee/ adj dangerous.

risotto /ri-zot-o/ n an Italian rice dish cooked with meat, vegetables, etc.

rite /rite/ n an order or arrangement of proceedings fixed by rule or custom.

ritual /ri-chu-wal/ adj having to do with or done as a rite. • n 1 a set of rites. 2 ceremonies performed to worship God. • adv **ritually**.

rival /rie-val/ n 1 a person who is trying to do better than another. 2 a competitor for the same prize. • vb to be as good or nearly as good as. • n **rivalry**.

river /ri-ver/ n a large running stream of water.

rivet /ri-vit/ n a bolt driven through metal plates, etc, to fasten them together and then hammered flat at both ends. • vb 1 to fasten with rivets. 2 to fix.

rivulet /ri-vyu-lit/ n a small stream.

road /road/ n 1 a prepared public way for travelling on. 2 a street. 3 a way.

roadhog /road-hog/ n (inf) a dangerously reckless motorist.

road rage /road rage/ n extreme anger, often leading to violent or dangerous behaviour, resulting from a driver's reaction to the actions of another driver or pedestrian.

roam /roam/ vb to wander about.

roar /roar/ vb to give a roar. • n 1 a loud shout or cry. 2 the full loud cry of a large animal.

roast /roast/ vb to cook before a fire or in an oven. • n roasted meat.

rob /rob/ vb (**robbed, robbing**) 1 to steal from. 2 to cause someone not to get what he or she ought to get. • n **robber**.

robbery /rob-er-ee/ n the act of robbing.

robe /robe/ n a long, loose-fitting garment. • npl **robes** clothes worn as a sign of rank or position. • vb to put on robes, to put robes on someone else.

robin /rob-in/ n 1 a small red-breasted songbird related to the thrush. 2 a north

American thrush about the size of a pigeon.

robot /ro-bot/ *n* **1** a machine made to carry out certain tasks usually done by people. **2** a person who does his or her work mechanically without thinking or asking questions. • *adj* **robotic**.

robust /ro-**bust**/ *adj* **1** healthy and strong. **2** vigorous, rough. • *adv* **robustly**. • *n* **robustness**.

rock[1] /rock/ *vb* **1** to move from side to side, or backward and forward in turn. **2** to sway from side to side. • *n* a type of loud popular music with a strong beat.

rock[2] /rock/ *n* **1** the hard, solid part of the earth's crust. **2** a large mass or piece of stone.

rock and roll, rock 'n' roll /rock-in-**roll**/ *n* a type of popular dance music that originated in the 1950s.

rock climbing /rock clime-ing/ *n* a sport that involves the climbing of steep cliffs and rock faces, usually with ropes.

rocker /rock-er/ *n* a curved piece of wood fastened to the foot of a chair, cradle, etc, to enable it to rock.

rockery /rock-er-ee/ *n* part of a garden consisting of a heap of earth and large stones or small rocks with plants growing between them.

rocket /rock-it/ *n* **1** a cylinder that is propelled through the air by a backward jet of gas. **2** a spacecraft launched in this way. **3** a firework that flies up into the air as it is burning out, often used as a signal.

rocking chair /rock-ing chair/ *n* a chair on rockers.

rocking horse /rock-ing hawrss/ *n* a toy horse on rockers.

rock salt /rock sawlt/ *n* common salt found in solid lumps in the earth.

rocky /rock-ee/ *adj* **1** shaky. **2** unstable, in difficulties. **3** full of rocks. **4** hard as rock.

rod /rod/ *n* a straight slender stick or bar.

rode *pt of* ride.

rodent /roe-dint/ *n* any animal that gnaws, e.g. a mouse or rat.

rodeo /roe-dee-o/ *n* a display of riding skill by cowboys.

roe[1] /roe/ *n* **1** a female deer. **2** a small type of deer.

roe[2] /roe/ *n* all the eggs in a female fish.

roebuck /roe-buck/ *n* a male roe deer.

rogue /roag/ *n* **1** a dishonest person. **2** a naughty, mischievous child.

roguish /roe-gish/ *adj* **1** dishonest. **2** mischievous, teasing.

role /role/ *n* **1** the part played by an actor. **2** your actions or duties.

role model /role mod-él/ *n* a person whom others admire and try to copy.

roll /role/ *vb* **1** to move by going around and around, like a wheel or ball. **2** to rock or sway from side to side. **3** to flatten with a roller. **4** to make a loud long noise. • *n* **1** paper, cloth, etc, rolled into the form of a cylinder. **2** a list of names. **3** a turning or rocking movement. **4** a long-drawn-out noise.

roll call /role cawl/ *n* the calling over of a list of names.

roller /roe-ler/ *n* **1** anything made in the form of a cylinder so that it can turn around and around easily. **2** a long swelling wave.

Rollerblade /roe-ler-blade/ *n* (*TM*) a type of roller skate that has the wheels set in one straight line. • *n* **rollerblading**.

roller coaster /roe-ler coe-ster/ *n* a fairground ride like an elevated railway with steep sharp curves.

roller skate /roe-ler skate/ *n* a skate mounted on small wheels for skating on hard surfaces. • *vb* **roller-skate**.

rollicking /ro-li-king/ *adj* noisy and merry.

rolling pin /roe-ling pin/ *n* a roller for making pastry flat and thin before it is cooked.

Roman /roe-man/ *adj* having to do with Rome.

Roman Catholic /roe-man cath-lic/ *n* a member of that part of the Christian Church that is governed by the Pope, the Bishop of Rome.

romance /roe-manss/ *n* **1** a love affair. **2** a love story. **3** a story of wonderful or fanciful events. • *adj* /roe-manss/ (*of a language*) derived from Latin.

Roman numerals /roe-man nyoom-e-ralz/ *npl* numbers represented by letters (e.g. IV, V, VI for 4, 5, 6, etc.).

romantic /roe-**man**-tic/ *adj* **1** showing feelings of love. **2** dealing with love. **3** imaginative, fanciful. • *adv* **romantically**.

roman type /roe-man tipe/ *n* ordinary upright type (not italics).

romp /romp/ *vb* **1** to play roughly or noisily. **2** to do swiftly and easily. • *n* rough or noisy play.

romper /rom-per/ *n* a one-piece garment for a small child.

roof /roof/ *n* **1** the outside upper covering of a house, building, vehicle, etc. **2** the upper part of the mouth. • *vb* to cover with a roof.

rook /rook/ *n* **1** a piece in chess. **2** a black bird of the crow family. • *vb* to cheat someone.

room /room/ *n* **1** an apartment in a house.

2 space. **3** space for free movement. **4** scope. • *npl* lodgings.

roomy /roo-mee/ *adj* having plenty of space.

roost /roost/ *n* the pole on which birds rest at night. • *vb* to rest or sleep on a roost.

rooster /roo-ster/ *n* a cockerel, a cock.

root /root/ *n* **1** the part of a plant that is fixed in the earth and draws nourishment from the soil. **2** the beginning or origin, a first cause from which other things develop. **3** a word from which other words are formed. **4** a factor of a number that when multiplied by itself gives the original number. • *vb* **1** to fix firmly. **2** to search about for.

rope /rope/ *n* a strong thick cord, made by twisting together strands of hemp, wire, etc. • *vb* **1** to fasten with a rope. **2** to mark off with a rope.

rosary /roe-za-ree/ *n* in the Roman Catholic Church, a series of prayers, or a string of beads each of which represents a prayer in the series.

rose[1] /roze/ *n* **1** a beautiful, sweet-smelling flower growing on a thorny shrub. **2** a shrub bearing roses. **3** a light red or pink colour. **4** a nozzle full of holes at the end of the spout of a watering can.

rose[2] *pt of* **rise**.

rosemary /roze-me-ree/ *n* an evergreen sweet-smelling shrub used as a herb in cooking.

rosette /roe-zet/ *n* **1** a badge, like a rose in shape, made of ribbon. **2** a rose-shaped ornament carved in stone, etc.

rosewood /roze-wood/ *n* a hard dark-coloured wood smelling of roses when fresh cut.

Rosh Hashana /rosh ho-za-na/ (or **Hashanah**) *n* the Jewish New Year festival, held in September or October.

rosy /roe-zee/ *adj* **1** red, pink. **2** giving cause for hope.

rot /rot/ *vb* (**rotted, rotting**) **1** to go bad from age or lack of use, to decay. **2** to cause to decay. • *n* **1** decay. **2** (*inf*) nonsense.

rota /roe-ta/ *n* a list which shows when each of a group of people has to do a particular task.

rotary /roe-ta-ree/ *adj* turning around on an axle.

rotate /roe-tate/ *vb* **1** to turn around a centre or axis. **2** to move like a wheel.

rotation /roe-tay-shun/ *n* **1** movement around a centre or axis. **2** a regular order repeated again and again.

rotten /rot-in/ *adj* **1** decaying, having gone bad. **2** (*inf*) mean.

Rottweiler /rot-wie-ler/ *n* a breed of very large, strong dog with a black and brown coat.

rotund /roe-tund/ *adj* round, fattish. • *n* **rotundity**.

rouble *see* **ruble**.

rouge /roozh/ *n* red colouring for the cheeks.

rough /ruf/ *adj* **1** not smooth, uneven. **2** wild, stormy. **3** not polite. **4** not gentle. **5** coarse, violent. **6** badly finished. **7** not exact. • *n* a violent, badly behaved person. • *adv* **roughly**. • *n* **roughness**.

roughage /ru-fidge/ *n* food that contains a lot of fibre, which aids digestion.

roughen /ru-fin/ *vb* to make or become rough.

roulette /roo-let/ *n* a gambling game played on a revolving board with a ball that falls into one of a number of holes when the board ceases spinning.

round /round/ *adj* like a ball or circle in shape. • *n* **1** a round object. **2** a duty visit to all the places under your care. **3** a part song in which singers join at different times and begin again when they have finished. **4** a shell or bullet for firing. **5** a division of a boxing match. **6** a complete part of a knock-out competition (e.g. in football). **7** a game of golf. **8** a spell or outburst. • *adv* **1** in the opposite direction. **2** in a circle. **3** from one person to another. **4** from place to place. • *prep* **1** on every side of. **2** with a circular movement about. • *vb* **1** to give a round shape to. **2** to go around.

roundabout /roun-da-bout/ *n* a meeting place of roads with a central circle around which vehicles must go until they turn off. • *adj* **1** indirect. **2** using too many words.

roundly /round-lee/ *adv* plainly.

round trip /round trip/ *n* a journey to a place and back again.

roundup /round-up/ *n* **1** the gathering of cattle or other farm animals for market. **2** a gathering of something. **3** the gathering together of a particular group of people.

rouse /rouz/ *vb* **1** to awaken. **2** to stir up to action.

rousing /rou-zing/ *adj* stirring, exciting.

rout /rout/ *vb* to defeat and put to disordered flight. • *n* **1** a disorderly and hasty retreat after a defeat. **2** a complete defeat.

route /root/ *n* a way from one place to another.

routine /roo-teen/ *n* a regular way or order of doing things. • *adv* **routinely**.

rove /rove/ *vb* **1** to wander about. **2** to move around.

rover /roe-ver/ *n* **1** a wanderer. **2** (*old*) a pirate.

row¹ /roe/ *n* a line of people or things.

row² /roe/ *vb* to move a boat by means of oars. • *n* **1** a spell of rowing. **2** a trip in a boat moved by oars.

row³ /row/ *n* **1** noise, disturbance. **2** a quarrel. **3** a public argument. • *vb* (*inf*) to quarrel.

rowdy /row-dee/ *adj* noisy and quarrelsome. • *n* **rowdiness**. • *n* **rowdyism**.

royal /roy-al/ *adj* **1** having to do with a king or queen. **2** splendid, kingly. • *adv* **royally**.

royalist /roy-a-list/ *n* a supporter of a king or queen.

royalty /roy-al-tee/ *n* **1** a royal person or persons. **2** a share of the profits paid to authors, inventors, etc, for the use of their work.

RSI /ar-ess-eye/ *abbrev* = **repetitive strain injury**: regular pain in the hands, arms etc, caused by doing the same job, and so using the same muscles, a lot of the time.

rub /rub/ *vb* (**rubbed**, **rubbing**) to move one thing to and fro against another. • *n* act of rubbing. • **rub out** to remove or erase, especially with a rubber.

rubber /ru-ber/ *n* **1** a tough elastic substance made from the juice of certain tropical trees. **2** a piece of rubber used to remove marks by rubbing. • *adj* **rubbery**.

rubbish /ru-bish/ *n* **1** things of no value that you would throw away. **2** nonsense.

rubble /ru-bul/ *n* broken pieces of bricks or stones.

ruble /roo-bul/ *n*, *also* **rouble** the main unit of currency of Russia, Belarus, Abkhazia, South Ossetia and Transnistria.

ruby /roo-bee/ *n* a red precious stone. • *adj* **1** containing rubies. **2** red.

ruck /ruck/ *n* the mass of ordinary people.

rucksack /ruck-sack /*n* a bag carried on the back with straps over the shoulder to hold it in place.

rudder /ru-der/ *n* a flat hinged plate at the stern of a ship or the tail of an aircraft, used for steering.

rude /rood/ *adj* **1** impolite. **2** referring to sex or parts of the body in a way that some people find offensive or embarrassing. **3** sudden and unpleasant. **4** (*old*) uncivilized, untaught, vulgar. • *adv* **rudely**. • *n* **rudeness**.

ruff /ruff/ *n* a stiff frilled collar worn in olden times.

ruffian /ru-fee-an/ *n* a rough brutal fellow, a violent lawbreaker.

ruffle /ru-ful/ *vb* **1** to disturb the smoothness of, to disarrange. **2** to anger or annoy. • *n* a frill.

rug /rug/ *n* **1** a mat for the floor. **2** a thick woollen coverlet or blanket.

rugby /rug-bee/ *n* a form of football in which the ball, oval in shape, may be carried in the hands.

rugged /ru-gid/ *adj* **1** rough, uneven. **2** strongly built.

ruin /roo-in/ *n* **1** destruction. **2** downfall, overthrow, state of having lost everything of value. **3** (*often pl*) remains of old buildings. • *vb* **1** to destroy. **2** to cause to lose everything of value.

rule /rool/ *n* **1** government. **2** a regulation or order. **3** an official or accepted standard. **4** the usual way that something happens. • *vb* **1** to govern, to manage. **2** to give an official decision. **3** to draw a straight line with the help of a ruler.

ruler /roo-ler/ *n* **1** a person who governs or reigns. **2** a flat rod for measuring length.

ruling /roo-ling/ *adj* greatest, controlling. • *n* a decision.

rum /rum/ *n* spirit made from sugar cane.

rumba /rum-ba/ *n* a dance of Cuban origin.

rumble /rum-bul/ *vb* to make a low, rolling noise. • *also n*.

ruminant /roo-mi-nant/ *adj* chewing the cud. • *n* an animal that chews the cud.

ruminate /roo-mi-nate/ *vb* **1** to chew the cud. **2** to think deeply.

rummage /ru-midge/ *vb* to search thoroughly but untidily. • *also n*.

rumour /roo-mur/ *n*, *also* **rumor** (*US*) **1** a widely known story that may not be true. **2** common talk, gossip.

rump /rump/ *n* **1** the end of an animal's backbone. **2** the buttocks. **3** a piece left over from something much larger.

rumple /rum-pul/ *vb* to crease, to spoil the smoothness of.

rumpus /rum-pus/ *n* a noisy disturbance or quarrel, an uproar.

run /run/ *vb* (*pt* **ran**, **running**, *pp* **run**) **1** to move quickly. **2** to move from one place to another. **3** to take part in a race. **4** to flow. **5** to organize or manage. **6** to smuggle. **7** to last or continue. **8** to compete in a competition or an election. • *n* **1** act of running. **2** the length of time for which something runs. **3** a widespread demand for. **4** an enclosed place for animals or fowls. • **run down 1** to say bad things about. **2** to stop working because of lack of power (e.g. because a spring is unwound). • **run over 1** to read or repeat quickly. **2** to knock over in a vehicle.

runaway /ru-na-way/ *n* a person who runs away from their home or an institution. • *adj* **1** (of an animal or vehicle) out of control. **2** leaving home without telling anyone. **3** happening in a very fast and easy manner.

rung[1] /**rung**/ *n* a step of a ladder.

rung[2] *pp of* **ring**.

runner /**ru**-ner/ *n* **1** a person who runs. **2** a messenger. **3** a long spreading stem of a plant. **4** a long narrow cloth for a table or carpet for a stair. **5** any device on which something slips or slides along.

runner-up /**ru**-ner-up/ *n* (*pl* **runners-up**) the person or team second to the winner.

running /**ru**-ning/ *adj* **1** going on all the time. **2** in succession. • *n* **1** the act of moving quickly. **2** that which runs or flows. • **in the running** with a chance of success.

running mate /**ru**-ning mate/ *n* in the US, a candidate for the lesser of two political posts, such as vice-president.

runny /**ru**-nee/ *adj* liquid, flowing.

runway /**run**-way/ *n* a flat road along which an aircraft runs before taking off or after landing.

rupee /**roo**-pee/ *n* the main unit of currency in India and Pakistan.

rupture /**rup**-chur/ *n* **1** a clean break. **2** a quarrel or disagreement. **3** the thrusting of part of the intestine through the muscles of the abdomen. • *vb* **1** to break or burst. **2** to quarrel. • **rupture yourself** undergo a rupture in the body.

rural /**roo**-ral/ *adj* having to do with the country or its way of life.

ruse /**rooz**/ *n* a trick.

rush[1] /**rush**/ *vb* **1** to move quickly and with force. **2** to do hastily. **3** to make someone hurry. **4** to capture by a sudden quick attack. • *n* **1** hurry. **2** a fast and forceful move. **3** a sudden demand. **4** a sudden advance.

rush[2] /**rush**/ *n* a tall grasslike plant growing in damp or marshy ground.

rust /**rust**/ *n* the red coating formed on iron and steel left in a damp place. • *vb* to decay by gathering rust.

rustic /**ru**-stic/ *adj* having to do with the country or country people.

rustle[1] /**ru**-sul/ *vb* to make a low whispering sound. • *also n.*

rustle[2] /**ru**-sul/ *vb* to steal. • *n* **rustler**.

rusty /**ru**-stee/ *adj* **1** covered with rust. **2** out of practice.

rut /**rut**/ *n* a deep track made by a wheel. • **in a rut** so tied by habits and customs that you are no longer interested in new or better methods.

ruthless /**rooth**-less/ *adj* cruel, merciless, showing no pity. • *adv* **ruthlessly**. • *n* **ruthlessness**.

rye /**rie**/ *n* **1** a grain used for making bread. **2** rye bread.

rye bread /**rie** bred/ *n* bread made with rye flour.

rye grass /**rie** grass/ *n* a type of grass used as fodder for animals.

S

S, s /ess/ the 19th letter of the English alphabet.

Sabbath /sa-buth/ *n* **1** the seventh day of the week, Saturday, set aside for rest and worship, observed by Jews and some Christian groups. **2** Sunday.

saber /say-ber/ *n* a heavy sword with a slightly curved blade.

sable /say-bul/ *n* **1** a type of weasel with dark-coloured fur. **2** its fur. • *adj* black, dark.

sabotage /sa-bu-tazh/ *n* the destroying, wasting, or ruining of something on purpose. • *also vb.* • *n* **saboteur** a person who destroys, wastes, or ruins something on purpose.

sac /sac/ *n* a small bag of liquid inside an animal or plant.

saccharine /sa-ca-rin/ *n* a very sweet substance used instead of sugar. • *adj* **saccharine** too sweet or syrupy.

sachet /sa-shay/ *n* a small, sealed bag or packet.

sack¹ /sack/ *n* a bag made of coarse cloth for holding flour, wool, etc. • *vb* (*inf*) to dismiss someone from his or her job.

sack² /sack/ *vb* to rob and destroy a town after capturing it. • *also n.*

sacred /say-crid/ *adj* holy, set apart for the service of God.

sacrifice /sa-cri-fice/ *n* **1** an offering to a god or God. **2** the act of giving up something desirable. **3** something given up in this way. • *vb* **1** to make an offering to God or a god. **2** to give up something that is important to you. • *adj* **sacrificial.**

sacrilege /sa-cri-lidge/ *n* disrespectful or insulting treatment of something holy. • *adj* **sacrilegious.**

sacrosanct /sa-cro-sangt/ *adj* **1** very holy. **2** to be treated only with great respect.

sad /sad/ *adj* sorrowful, unhappy.

sadden /sa-den/ *vb* to make sad.

saddle /sa-dul/ *n* **1** a seat for a rider on a horse or bicycle. **2** meat taken from an animal's back. • *vb* **1** to put a saddle on. **2** to give. • **in the saddle** in control.

sadist /say-dist/ *n* a person who takes pleasure in giving pain to another. • *n* **sadism.** • *adj* **sadistic.**

safari /sa-fa-ree/ *n* a hunting trip, especially one in Africa.

safe /safe/ *adj* **1** out of harm or danger. **2** not likely to cause harm, danger, or risk. • *n* a strong box or room for valuables. • *adv* **safely.**

safeguard /safe-gard/ *n* any person or thing that protects. • *also vb.*

safekeeping /safe-kee-ping/ *n* a keeping or being kept in safety.

safety /safe-tee/ *n* freedom from danger, harm, or loss.

safety belt /safe-tee belt/ *n* a belt that attaches a driver or passenger to the seat in a car, plane, etc for reasons of safety.

safety pin /safe-tee pin/ *n* a pin bent back on itself so as to cover the point when fastened.

saffron /saf-ron/ *n* **1** a crocus flower. **2** the stamens of the crocus used to colour or flavour food. • *adj* deep yellow colour.

sag /sag/ *vb* (**sagged, sagging**) **1** to sink in the middle. **2** to droop, to hang down. • *adj* **saggy.**

saga /sa-ga/ *n* **1** a Scandinavian story of heroes, customs, battles, etc. **2** a very long adventure story.

sage¹ /saydge/ *adj* wise. • *n* a wise person.

sage² /saydge/ *n* **1** a sweet-smelling plant, used as a herb in cooking. **2** a greyish green colour.

sago /say-go/ *n* a type of flour, used in certain puddings.

said /sed/ *pt and pp of* say.

sail /sale/ *n* **1** a canvas spread to catch the wind. **2** a trip in a boat moved by sails. **3** the arm of a windmill. • *vb* **1** to travel on water by way of a sail. **2** to move along without effort.

sailboard /sale-board/ *n* a board, used in windsurfing, similar to a surfboard with a sail attached to it.

sailing /say-ling/ *n* **1** the act of a thing or person that sails. **2** the sport of managing a sailing boat, as for racing.

sailing boat /say-ling boat/ *n* a boat or ship that has sails, by which it moves through the water.

sailor /say-lor/ *n* a person who makes a living by sailing.

saint /saint/ *n* **1** a person who is very good, patient, helpful, etc. **2** a title given to an especially holy person by certain Christian churches. • *adj* **saintly.** • *adj* **sainted.**

sainthood /saint-hood/ *n* the status or rank of a saint.

sake¹ /sake/ *n.* • **for the sake of** to get. • **for my sake** to please me.

sake² /**sah**-kee/ *n* a Japanese alcoholic drink made from rice.

salaam /sa-**lom**/ *n* **1** a greeting, meaning peace, used among Muslims. **2** in India, a greeting made by bowing low with the palm of the right hand on the forehead.

saleable /**say**-la-bul/ *adj* that can be sold.

salacious /sa-**lay**-shus/ *adj* indecent, obscene.

salad /**sa**-lad/ *n* a dish of lettuce and other vegetables, mostly raw but sometimes cooked and sometimes including meat, fish, cheese, or fruit, usually served with a dressing.

salamander /sa-la-**man**-der/ *n* a lizardlike animal that can live both on land and in water.

salami /sa-**la**-mee/ *n* a highly spiced, salted sausage of pork or beef.

salary /**sal**-ree/ *n* the fixed sum of money paid to someone for work over an agreed length of time, usually a month or a year.

sale /**sale**/ *n* **1** the act of selling. **2** the exchange of anything for money. **3** a selling of goods more cheaply than usual.

salesman /**saylz**-man/, **saleswoman** /**saylz**-woo-man/, **salesperson** /**saylz**-per-sun/, **sales assistant** /**saylz**-a-**sis**-tant/ *n* a person engaged in selling products.

salesmanship /**saylz**-man-ship/ *n* skill in selling things.

sales tax /**saylz** taks/ a tax on things that are sold, usually a percentage.

salient /**sale**-yent/ *adj* **1** sticking outward. **2** most important. • *n* in war, a narrow strip of land jutting into enemy territory.

saline /**say**-leen/ *adj* containing salt. • *n* a salt lake or spring.

salinize /**sa**-lin-nize/ *vb, also* **salinise** to put salt into.

saliva /sa-**lie**-va/ *n* the liquid that keeps the mouth moist; spittle. • *adj* **salivary**.

salivate /**sa**-li-vate/ *vb* to produce excess saliva.

sallow¹ /**sa**-lo/ *n* a type of willow tree.

sallow² /**sa**-lo/ *adj* having a slightly yellow skin.

salmon /**sa**-mun/ *n* a large fish with pinkish flesh and silver scales, greatly valued for food and sport.

salmonella /sal-mu-**ne**-la/ *n* a kind of bacteria that can cause sickness in people or animals.

salon /**sa**-lon/ *n* **1** a public room in a home, hotel, etc, where people gather. **2** a building or room used for a particular business, such as hairdressing, the selling of fashionable clothes, etc.

saloon /sa-**loon**/ *n* **1** a large public room in a passenger ship. **2** a kind of bar, a place where alcoholic drinks are sold and drunk.

salsa /**sal**-sa/ *n* **1** a type of Latin American dance music. **2** a spicy tomato sauce eaten with Mexican food.

salt /**sawlt**/ *n* **1** a white mineral, obtained from sea water or by mining, used to give flavour to or to preserve food. • *vb* to flavour or preserve with salt. • *adj* containing or tasting of salt. • *adj* **salty**.

salt-and-pepper /sawl-tand-**pe**-per/ *adj* dotted or specked with black and white.

saltcellar /**sawlt**-se-ler/ *n* a small container for salt, often with a top that has a hole in it for shaking over food.

saltire /**sawl**-tire/ *n* a Saint Andrew's cross (X).

saltwater /**sawlt**-waw-ter/ *adj* having to do with salt water or the sea.

salutation /sal-yu-**tay**-shun/ *n* a greeting.

salute /sa-**loot**/ *vb* **1** to greet. **2** to make a gesture of respect by raising the right hand to the forehead or cap, firing guns, etc. • *n* **1** the gesture of respect made by saluting. **2** the firing of guns as a welcome or mark of respect.

salvage /**sal**-vidge/ *n* **1** the saving of a ship or its cargo from loss. **2** the saving of property from any sort of destruction. **3** property saved in this way. • *vb* to save from destruction, shipwreck, fire, etc.

salvation /sal-**vay**-shun/ *n* the saving or being saved from danger, evil, difficulty, destruction, etc.

salve /**salv**/ *n* a medicine applied to wounds, burns, etc, to sooth or heal.

samba /**sam**-ba/ *n* **1** a South American dance of African origin. **2** music for this dance.

same /**same**/ *adj* in no way different. • *n* the same person or thing. • *adv* in a like manner.

sameness /**same**-ness/ *n* lack of change or variety.

same-sex /**same**-seks/ *adj* of or relating to people of the same sex.

sampan /**sam**-pan/ *n* a small flat-bottomed boat used in China.

sample /**sam**-pul/ *n* a part or piece given to show what the whole is like. • *vb* to try something to see what it is like.

sampler /**sam**-pler/ *n* a cloth sewn with designs, words, etc, in different types of stitches to show a beginner's skill.

samurai /**sa**-mu-rie/ *n* a member of the Japanese military class of people.

sanatorium /sa-na-**toe**-ree-um/ *n, also* **sanitarium** /sa-ni-**ter**-ee-um/ (*US*) a quiet resort where people go to rest and regain their health, usually taking advantage of natural resources such as mineral springs.

sanctify /sang-ti-fie/ *vb* to make holy or sacred. • *n* **sanctification.**

sanctimonious /sang-ti-mo-nee-us/ *adj* pretending to be holy or religious. • *n* **sanctimony.**

sanction /sang-shun/ *n* **1** permission. **2** a punishment imposed to make people obey a law. • *vb* to permit.

sanctity /sang(k)-ti-tee/ *n* holiness.

sanctuary /sang(k)-che-wer-ee/ *n* **1** a place where a person is safe from pursuit or attack. **2** a place providing protection, such as a reserve for wildlife. **3** a holy place such as a church or temple.

sanctum /sang(k)-tum/ *n* **1** a person's private room where he or she is not to be bothered. **2** a sacred place.

sand /sand/ *n* **1** loose, gritty pieces of tiny particles of rock, shell, etc. **2** *pl* stretches of sand on the seashore. • *vb* to rub with sandpaper to make smooth.

sandal /san-dal/ *n* a type of shoe to protect the sole, leaving the upper part of the foot largely uncovered except by straps, etc.

sandalwood /san-dal-wood/ *n* any of several kinds of sweet-smelling wood.

sandbag /sand-bag/ *n* a bag filled with sand and used for protection against enemy attack or to protect against floods.

sandbar /sand-bar/ *n* a ridge of sand formed in a river or along a shore by the currents or tides.

sandpit /sand-pit/ *n* an area filled with sand in which children can play.

sander /san-der/ *n* a person or tool that sands.

sand hopper /sand hop-er/ *n* any of the various tiny animals that jump like fleas on beaches.

sandiness /san-dee-ness/ *n* a sandy state or quality.

sandman /sand-man/ *n* a fairy-tale person who is thought to make children sleepy by dusting sand in their eyes.

sandpaper /sand-pay-per/ *n* paper made rough by a coating of sand, used for smoothing and polishing.

sandpiper /sand-pie-per/ *n* a wading bird of the snipe family.

sandstone /sand-stone/ *n* a stone made up of sand pressed together.

sandstorm /sand-stawrm/ *n* a windstorm in which large amounts of sand are blown about in the air near the ground.

sandwich /san(d)-wich/ *n* two slices of bread with meat, cheese, salad, etc, in between them. • *vb* to fit between two other things.

sandy /san-dee/ *adj* **1** covered with sand, full of sand. **2** the colour of sand, a reddish yellow.

sane /sane/ *adj* **1** having a normal, healthy mind. **2** sensible.

sang *pt of* **sing.**

sangria /sang-gree-ya/ *n* a punch made with wine, fruit juice, pieces of fruit, and soda water.

sanitary /sa-ni-tree/ *adj* having to do with health or cleanliness.

sanitary towel /sa-ni-tree taoo-el/ *n* a cotton-filled pad worn by women during menstruation.

sanitation /sa-ni-tay-shun/ *n* **1** the process or methods of keeping places clean and healthy. **2** a drainage or sewage system.

sanitize /sa-ni-tize/ *vb, also* **sanitise** to make sanitary.

sanity /sa-ni-tee/ *n* **1** the condition of being sane. **2** good sense.

sank *pt of* **sink.**

sans /sanz/ *prep* without, lacking.

Sanskrit /san-skrit/ *n* an ancient language of India. • *also adj.*

sap /sap/ *n* the juice that flows in plants, trees, etc, and feeds the various parts. • *vb* (**sapped, sapping**) to weaken gradually.

sapling /sap-ling/ *n* a young tree.

sapphire /sa-fire/ *n* **1** a precious stone of a rich blue colour. **2** its colour. • *also adj.*

sarcasm /sar-ca-zum/ *n* a mocking remark intended to hurt another's feelings.

sarcastic /sar-ca-stic/ *adj* **1** given to sarcasm. **2** mocking, scornful.

sarcophagus /sar-caw-fa-gus/ *n* (*pl* **sarcophagi**) a stone coffin.

sardine /sar-deen/ *n* a small fish of the herring family.

sardonic /sar-don-ic/ *adj* bitterly sneering, mocking.

sari /sa-ree/ *n* the dress of women in India, Pakistan, etc, consisting of a long piece of cloth wrapped around the body to form an ankle length skirt with the other end draped across the chest, over the shoulder, and sometimes over the head.

sarong /sa-rong/ *n* an item of clothing consisting of a length of often brightly coloured cloth worn wrapped around the waste like a skirt by both men and women.

sarsaparilla /sar-spa-ri-la/ *n* **1** any of a number of tropical, woody vines of the lily family with fragrant roots and heart-shaped leaves. **2** the dried roots of these plants, formerly used in medicine. **3** a sweetened, carbonated drink flavoured with sarsaparilla.

sash[1] /sash/ *n* a scarf worn around the waist or across the body over one shoulder.

sash[2] /sash/ *n* a window frame.

sashay /sa-**shay**/ *vb* to move, walk, etc. in such a way as to attract attention or show off.

sassafras /**sa**-sa-fras/ *n* **1** a small eastern North American tree having a pleasant smelling bark. **2** the dried root bark of this tree used as a flavouring.

sat *pt and pp of* **sit**.

Satan /**say**-tin/ *n* in Christian belief, the enemy of humankind and of goodness, the devil.

satanic /sa-**tan**-ic/ *adj* of, like, or having to do with the devil.

Satanism /**say**-ta-ni-zum/ *n* worship of Satan.

satay /sa-**tay**/ *n* a dish consisting of chunks of flavoured meat broiled on sticks and dipped in a spicy peanut sauce.

satchel /**sa**-chel/ *n* a small bag worn on the shoulder or back for carrying books, clothes, etc.

sate /**sate**/ *vb* to satisfy a want fully.

satellite /**sa**-tu-lite/ *n* **1** a body, launched by man or there naturally, that moves through the heavens around a larger body. **2** a person who depends completely on another. **3** a country that is totally in the power of another.

satellite dish /**sa**-tu-lite dish/ *n* bowl-shaped device on the outside of a building for receiving television signals sent by a satellite.

satellite television /**sa**-tu-lite tel-le-**vizh**-un/ *n* the broadcasting of television programmes via satellite rather than by television masts on land.

satiate /**say**-shee-ate/ *vb* **1** to satisfy fully. **2** to give more than enough.

satiety /su-**tie**-i-tee/, **satiation** /**say**-shee-**ay**-shun/ *n* **1** the state of having more than enough. **2** over-fullness.

satin /**sa**-tin/ *n* a silk or nylon cloth that is shiny on one side.

satire /**sa**-tire/ *n* a piece of writing in which persons, customs, actions, etc, are mocked and made to appear foolish. • *adj* **satirical**.

satirist /**sa**-ti-rist/ *n* a person who writes satires.

satirize /**sa**-ti-rize/ *vb, also* **satirise** to make seem foolish in satire.

satisfaction /sa-tis-**fac**-shun/ *n* **1** contentment. **2** the feeling of having enough.

satisfactory /sa-tis-**fac**-tree/ *adj* **1** good enough. **2** quite good.

satisfy /**sa**-tis-fie/ *vb* **1** to give all that is requested or expected. **2** to be enough. **3** to convince.

sat nav /sat nav/ *abbr* = **satellite navigation**: a piece of electronic equipment in a vehicle giving information via satellite as to location and best route.

satsuma /sat-**soo**-ma/ *n* a small, loose-skinned kind of orange.

saturate /**sa**-chu-rate/ *vb* to soak something so thoroughly that it cannot take in any more liquid. • *n* **saturation**.

Saturday /**sa**-tur-day/ *n* the seventh day of the week.

Saturn /**sah**-turn/ *n* the sixth planet away from the sun.

satyr /**say**-tur/ *adj* a mythical creature, half man, half goat.

sauce /saws/ *n* **1** a liquid poured on foods to improve or bring out the flavour. **2** (*inf*) rash or impudent talk.

saucepan /**saws**-pan/ *n* a small pot with a lid and handle.

saucer /**saw**-ser/ *n* a small plate placed under a cup.

saucy /**saw**-see/ *adj* **1** rude. **2** stylish or smart.

sauerkraut /**sa**-wer-krout/ *n* chopped cabbage soaked in its own juice and salt.

sauna /**saw**-na/ *n* a bath of dry, hot air produced by dropping small amounts of water onto very hot stones, usually followed by a plunge into icy cold water.

saunter /**sawn**-ter/ *vb* to walk slowly, to stroll. • *also n*.

sausage /**saw**-sidge/ *n* a roll of minced meat and seasonings in a thin skin.

sauté /saw-**tay**/ *adj* to fry quickly in a pan with a small amount of oil.

savage /**sa**-vidge/ *adj* **1** wild, untamed, or uncivilized. **2** fierce, cruel. • *n* a very cruel person.

savagery /**sa**-vidge-ree/ *n* **1** cruelty. **2** the state of being wild or uncivilized.

savanna(h) /sa-**van**-a/ *n* a grassy, treeless plain.

save /save/ *vb* **1** to rescue from danger or harm. **2** to keep for future use. **3** to keep money instead of spending it. • *prep* except.

savings /**say**-vingz/ *npl* money put aside for future use.

saviour /**save**-yur/ *n, also* **savior** (*US*) a person who saves from danger or harm.

savour /**say**-vur/ *n, also* **savor** (*US*) taste, flavour. • *vb* **1** to taste. **2** to have a taste of, to suggest the idea of.

savoury /**say**-vu-ree/ *adj, also* **savory** (*US*) **1** salty, meaty, or sharp, rather than sweet. **2** pleasant, morally acceptable. • *n* an appetizing dish served at the beginning or end of dinner or as a snack at a party, etc.

savoy /sa-**voy**/ *n* a type of cabbage with crinkled leaves.

savvy /sa-vee/ (*inf*) *n* shrewdness, understanding, know-how.

saw¹ /saw/ *n* a tool with a toothed edge used for cutting wood, etc. • *vb* to cut with a saw.

saw² /saw/ *n* a wise old saying.

saw³ /saw/ *pt of* **see**.

sawdust /saw-dust/ *n* small fragments of wood made by sawing.

sawmill /saw-mill/ *n* a mill with a mechanical saw for cutting wood.

sax /saks/ *n* short for saxophone.

saxophone /sak-su-fone/ *n* a brass wind instrument with a single reed and keys.

say /say/ *vb* (*pt* **said**) **1** to utter in words, to speak. **2** to state. • *n* the right to give an opinion.

saying /say-ing/ *n* a proverb, something commonly said.

scab /scab/ *n* a crust that forms over a healing sore. • *adj* **scabby**.

scabbard /sca-bard/ *n* the case of a sword.

scabies /scay-beez/ *n* an itchy skin disease.

scaffold /sca-foald/ *n* the platform on which people stand during the erecting, repairing, or painting of a building, etc.

scallywag /sca-li-wag/ *n* a rascal.

scald /scawld/ *vb* to burn with hot liquid. • *n* a burn caused by hot liquid.

scale¹ /scale/ *n* one of the thin flakes or flat plates on the skin of fish, reptiles, etc. • *vb* to remove the scales from. • *adj* **scaly** covered with scales, like a fish.

scale² /scale/ *n* a balance or weighing machine.

scale³ /scale/ *n* **1** a series of successive musical notes between one note and its octave. **2** the size of a map compared with the amount of area it represents. **3** a measure. **4** a system of units for measuring. **5** a system of grading. **6** range, extent. • *vb* to climb.

scalene /scay-leen/ *adj* (*of a triangle*) having unequal sides and angles.

scallop /sca-lup/ *n* **1** an edible shellfish, the shell of which has an uneven and toothed edge. **2** a series of even curves. • *vb* to cut in scallops. • *adj* **scalloped** with an edge shaped like that of the scallop shell.

scalp /scalp/ *n* the skin and hairs on top of the head. • *vb* to cut off the scalp.

scalpel /scal-pul/ *n* a light, very sharp knife used by a surgeon.

scam /scam/ *n* a swindle, cheat, or fraud. • *also vb*.

scamp /scamp/ *n* a rascal.

scamper /scam-per/ *vb* to run quickly or hurriedly, as if afraid. • *n* a quick or hurried run.

scampi /scam-pee/ *n* a large shrimp broiled or fried with its tail on and served hot.

scan /scan/ *vb* (**scanned, scanning**) **1** to look at closely or carefully. **2** to obtain an image of an internal part (of the body) by using X-rays, ultrasonic waves, etc. • *n* a medical examination in which part of the body is scanned.

scandal /scan-dal/ *n* **1** widespread talk about someone's wrongdoings, real or supposed. **2** a disgrace. **3** disgraceful behaviour that gives rise to widespread talk.

scandalize /scan-da-lize/ *vb, also* **scandalise** to shock.

scandalous /scan-da-luss/ *adj* disgraceful.

scanner /sca-ner/ *n* a person or thing that scans.

scant /scant/ *adj* barely enough, very little.

scanty /scan-tee/ *adj* barely enough, very little.

scapegoat /scape-goat/ *n* a person who is given the blame for wrong done by others.

scar¹ /scar/ *n* the mark left by a healed wound. • *vb* (**scarred, scarring**) to leave or cause a scar.

scar² /scar/ *n* a cliff.

scarab /sca-rab/ *n* a beetle considered sacred in ancient Egypt.

scarce /scayrss/ *adj* **1** few and hard to find. **2** not enough.

scarcely /scare-slee/ *adv* hardly; surely not.

scarcity /scare-si-tee/ *n* shortage, lack of what is necessary.

scare /scare/ *vb* to frighten. • *n* a fright, panic.

scarecrow /scare-croe/ *n* **1** anything (e.g. a dummy man) set up to frighten away birds. **2** someone dressed in rags.

scaremonger /scare-mung-ger/ *n* a person who purposely scares people.

scarf /scarf/ *n* (*pl* **scarfs** *or* **scarves**) a strip of material worn around the neck and over the shoulders.

scarify /scay-ri-fie/ *vb* to make many scratches or small cuts in the skin, as for surgery.

scarlet /scar-let/ *n* a bright red colour. • *also adj*.

scarlet fever /scar-let fee-ver/ *n* a very infectious disease causing a red rash on the skin, sore throat, and fever.

scarp /scarp/ *n* a steep slope.

scarves *pl of* **scarf**.

scary /skay-ree/ *adj* causing alarm, frightening.

scathe /skathe/ *vb* to injure.

scathing /skay-thing/ *adj* hurtful, bitter, harsh.

scatter /sca-ter/ *vb* **1** to throw about on all sides. **2** to go away or drive in different directions.

scatterbrain /sca-ter-brane/ *n* a foolish

person, a person not capable of serious thinking. • *adj* **scatterbrained**.

scatty /**sca**-tee/ *adj* rather silly, disorganized and forgetful.

scavenger /**sca**-vin-jer/ *n* an animal or person that searches for or lives on discarded or decaying material. • *vb* **scavenge**.

scenario /si-**nar**-ee-yo/ *n* **1** an outline of the main incidents in a play or film. **2** an outline for any planned series of events.

scene /**seen**/ *n* **1** the place where something happens. **2** what a person can see from a certain viewpoint. **3** a distinct part of a play. **4** a painted background set up on the stage to represent the place of the action. **5** a quarrel or open show of strong feeling in a public place. • **behind the scenes** in private.

scenery /**seen**-ree/ *n* **1** the painted backgrounds set up during a play to represent the places of the action. **2** the general appearance of a countryside.

scenic /**see**-nic/ *adj* **1** having to do with scenery. **2** picturesque.

scent /**sent**/ *n* **1** a smell, especially a pleasant one. **2** the smell of an animal left on its tracks. **3** the sense of smell. • *vb* **1** to smell. **2** to find by smelling. **3** to make something smell pleasant.

sceptic /**skep**-tik/ *adj*, *also* **skeptic** (*US*) a person who doubts things that others believe are true. • *adj* **sceptical**, *also* **skeptical** (*US*).

sceptre /**sep**-ter/ *n*, *also* **scepter** (*US*) the staff held by a ruler as a sign of authority.

schedule /**she**-jul/ *n* a list of details, a timetable. • *vb* to plan.

scheme /**skeem**/ *n* **1** a plan of what is to be done. **2** a plot. • *vb* **1** to plan. **2** to plot. • *n* **schemer**. • *adj* **scheming** given to planning schemes.

schism /**skism**/ *n* a dispute or division between two groups.

schizophrenia /skits-oh-**free**-nee-a/ *n* a severe mental disorder in which a person's thoughts and feelings are not based on reality. •*adj* **schizophrenic** relating to schizophrenia. **2** (*inf*) having opposing or contradictory elements, opinions or attitudes.

scholar /**skoll**-ar/ *n* a learned person.

scholarly /**skoll**-ar-lee/ *adj* learned.

scholarship /**skoll**-ar-ship/ *n* **1** learning. **2** wide knowledge. **3** a grant of money given to students to help pay for their education.

scholastic /sku-**lass**-tic/ *adj* having to do with schools or scholars.

school[1] /**skool**/ *n* **1** a place where children are educated. **2** a place where instruction is given in a particular subject. **3** a group of writers, thinkers, painters, etc, having the same or similar methods, principles, aims, etc. • *vb* to train.

school[2] /**skool**/ *n* a large number of fish of the same kind swimming together.

schoolbook /**skool**-book/ *n* a book used for study in schools.

schooling /**skoo**-ling/ *n* training or education.

schoolroom /**skool**-room/ *n* a room in which students are taught.

schoolteacher /**skool**-tee-cher/ *n* a person whose job it is to teach in a school.

schoolwork /**skool**-wurk/ *n* lessons worked on in classes for school or done as homework.

schooner /**skoo**-ner/ *n* **1** a large sailing ship with two masts. **2** a kind of large glass.

sciatic /see-**ya**-tic/ *adj* having to do with the hip or with the nerve (**sciatic nerve**) that goes down the back of the thigh.

sciatica /see-**ya**-ti-ca/ *n* pain in the hip or thigh, caused by pressure on the sciatic nerve.

science /**sie**-ense/ *n* **1** all that is known about a subject, arranged in a systematic manner. **2** the study of the laws and principles of nature. **3** trained skill.

science fiction /sie-ense **fic**-shun/ *n* a form of fiction that deals with imaginary scientific developments or imaginary life on other planets, often abbreviated to **sci-fi**.

scientific /sie-en-**ti**-fic/ *adj* **1** having to do with science. **2** done in a systematic manner.

scientist /**sie**-en-tist/ *n* a person learned in one of the sciences.

sci-fi /**sie**-fie/ *see* **science fiction**.

scissors /**si**-zurz/ *n* a cutting tool consisting of two blades moving on a central pin.

scoff /**scoff**/ *vb* **1** to mock (at). **2** to eat very quickly. • *n* mocking words, a jeer.

scold /**scoald**/ *vb* to find fault with angrily.

scone /**scon**, **scoan**/ *n* a round, sweet tea bread, made of flour, butter, baking powder, eggs and milk, served with butter or cream and jam.

scoop /**scoop**/ *vb* **1** to gather and lift up, as with the hands. **2** to hollow with a knife, etc. • *n* **1** a deep shovel for lifting grain, earth from a hole, etc. **2** a piece of important news known only to one newspaper.

scoot /**scoot**/ *vb* to go or move quickly.

scooter /**scoo**-ter/ *n* **1** a child's toy for riding on with a footboard, wheels at either end, and a raised handlebar for steering, moved by pushing off the ground with one foot. **2** a light motorcycle.

scope /**scope**/ *n* **1** the range of matters being dealt with. **2** opportunity.

scorch /scawrch/ *vb* **1** to burn the outside of. **2** to singe or blacken by burning.

scorcher /scawr-cher/ *n* **1** (*inf*) a very hot day.

score /score/ *n* **1** a set of 20. **2** a mark or line cut on the surface of. **3** a note of what is to be paid. **4** in games, the runs, goals, points, etc, made by those taking part. **5** a piece of music written down to show the parts played by different instruments. • *vb* **1** to make marks or scratches on the surface of. **2** to gain an advantage. **3** to keep the score of a game. **4** to arrange music in a score. • **score off** to get the better of. • *n* **scorer**.

scoreboard /score-board/ *n* a large board for posting the score and other details of a game.

scorekeeper /score-kee-per/ *n* a person who keeps score at a game or contest.

scorn /scawrn/ *vb* **1** to feel dislike for. **2** to refuse to have anything to do with. • *n* dislike, complete lack of respect for.

scornful /scawrn-ful/ *adj* mocking, full of dislike.

scorpion /scawr-pee-on/ *n* a small creature related to the spider with eight legs and a lobsterlike tail containing a poisonous sting, found in warm regions.

scoundrel /scoun-drel/ *n* a thoroughly wicked person, a rascal.

scour[1] /scour/ *vb* to clean or brighten by rubbing.

scour[2] /scour/ *vb* to go back and forward over, searching carefully.

scourge /scurdge/ *n* **1** a whip. **2** a cause of great trouble or suffering. • *vb* **1** to whip. **2** to make suffer greatly.

scourings /scou-ringz/ *n* dirt or remains removed by scouring.

scout /scout/ *n* **1** a person sent in front to see what lies ahead and bring back news. **2** a person employed to find new talent. • *vb* **1** to go out as a scout. **2** to search or explore.

Scout /scout/ *n* a member of the Scout Association, a youth organization that stress ability and skill in a wide range of activities.

scowl /scowl/ *vb* to lower the brows and wrinkle the forehead in anger or disapproval. • *also n*.

scrabble /scra-bul/ *vb* **1** to scratch, scrape, or paw as though looking for something. **2** to move quickly and awkwardly.

scraggy /scrag-ee/ *adj* thin and bony.

scram /scram/ *vb* to leave or get out, especially in a hurry.

scramble /scram-bul/ *vb* **1** to climb using both hands and feet. **2** to move awkwardly or with difficulty. **3** to struggle to obtain. **4** to throw together randomly, to collect without any method. • *n* a pushing and struggling for something.

scrap /scrap/ *n* **1** a small piece. **2** a picture, often cut to shape, for pasting in a book. **3** *pl* what is left over. • *vb* (**scrapped**, **scrapping**) to throw away as no longer useful.

scrapbook /scrap-book/ *n* a book for keeping scraps, cuttings from newspapers, pictures, etc.

scrape /scrape/ *vb* **1** to clean by rubbing with an edged instrument. **2** to make a harsh, unpleasant sound by rubbing along. **3** to save or gather with difficulty. **4** to scratch by rubbing, as if by a fall. • *n* **1** a scratch. **2** something caused by scraping or its sound. **3** (*inf*) a small fight. **4** (*inf*) a difficult situation.

scrap heap /scrap-heep/ *n* a place for waste material, a rubbish heap.

scraping /scray-ping/ *n* the act of a person or thing that scrapes; the sound of this.

scrappy /scra-pee/ *adj* made up of bits and pieces, incomplete.

scratch /scratch/ *vb* **1** to mark or wound the surface with something pointed. **2** to rub with the fingernails to stop itching. **3** to tear with the fingernails or claws. **4** to rub out or cross off. **5** to withdraw from a competition or contest. • *n* a slight mark or wound, especially one made by scratching. • *adj* **1** without a plus or minus handicap. **2** put together hastily. • **up to scratch** as good as usual.

scratchy /scratch-ee/ *adj* that scratches, scrapes, itches, etc.

scrawl /scrawl/ *vb* to write untidily or carelessly. • *n* untidy or careless handwriting.

scrawny /scraw-nee/ *adj* very thin, skinny, bony, small, etc.

scream /screem/ *vb* to shout in a loud, high-pitched voice, to shriek. • *also n*.

screamer /scree-mer/ *n* a person who screams.

scree /scree/ *n* loose stones, etc, on a slope or at the foot of a cliff.

screech /screech/ *vb* to utter a loud, high-pitched cry. • *also n*.

screed /screed/ *n* a long and uninteresting written statement.

screen /screen/ *n* **1** a movable piece of furniture, similar to a section of fence, that can be used to block a draught, to conceal part of a room, etc. **2** a surface on which films are shown. **3** a frame covered with mesh of wire or plastic and fixed into windows or doors so that when they are open no insects can get in. **4** the front glass surface of a television, computer, etc, on which pictures or items of information are shown. **5** a sieve for separating smaller pieces of coal, stones, etc, from larger. • *vb* **1** to protect. **2** to hide. **3** to put through a test. **4** to carry out medical tests on a large number of people to check whether they have a particular disease or not. **5** to show on film or television.

screenplay /**screen**-play/ *n* the script from which a film is produced.

screen saver /**screen** say-ver/ *n* a program that prolongs the life of a computer monitor.

screenwriter /**screen**-rie-ter/ *n* the writer of a script for a film.

screw /scroo/ *n* **1** a type of nail with a spiral thread so that it can be twisted into wood, etc, instead of hammered. **2** a twist or turn. • *vb* **1** to fasten by means of a screw. **2** to twist. **3** (*inf*) to have sex with. **4** (*inf*) to cheat or swindle.

screwdriver /**scroo**-drie-ver/ *n* a tool that can fit into the slot on the head of a screw and turn it into wood, plaster, etc.

scribble /**scri**-bul/ *vb* to write carelessly or hurriedly. • *n* something written quickly or carelessly. • *n* **scribbler** a person who writes carelessly.

scribe /scribe/ *n* **1** a person whose job it was to copy books, pamphlets, poems, etc, by hand before the invention of the printing machine. **2** a writer or author.

scrim /scrim/ *n* a light, sheer, loosely woven cloth used for curtains, linings, etc.

scrimmage /**scri**-midge/ *n* a confused fight or struggle.

scrimp /scrimp/ *vb* to give or use too little of.

script /script/ *n* **1** handwriting. **2** a printing type like handwriting. **3** a written outline of the actions, speaking, etc, in a film. **4** the text of a show, film, or play.

scripture(s) /**scrip**-chur(z)/ *n* a holy book or set of writings, such as the Bible, the Koran, etc. • *adj* **scriptural**.

scrotum /**scro**-tem/ *n* the bag that contains the testicles.

scrounge /scrounj/ *vb* to try to get something for free.

scrub[1] /scrub/ *vb* (**scrubbed**, **scrubbing**) **1** to clean by rubbing hard, especially with a stiff brush. **2** (*inf*) to cancel, to remove.

scrub[2] /scrub/ *n* small stunted bushes or trees, brushwood. • *adj* **scrubby**.

scrubland /**scrub**-land/ *n* land or a region that has much scrub plant life.

scruff /scruff/ *n* the back of the neck.

scruffy /**scru**-fee/ *adj* shabby, untidy.

scrumptious /**scrum**-chus/ *adj* very pleasing, attractive, etc, especially to the taste, delicious.

scrutinize /**scroo**-ti-nize/ *vb*, *also* **scrutinise** to look at closely or carefully. • *n* **scrutinizer**, *also* **scrutiniser**.

scrutiny /**scroo**-ti-nee/ *n* a close or careful look.

scuba /**scoo**-ba/ *abbr* = **self-contained underwater breathing apparatus**: worn by divers for breathing underwater, usually consisting of air tanks strapped to the back and connected by a hose to a mouthpiece.

scud /scud/ *vb* (**scudded**, **scudding**) to move quickly.

scuff /scuff/ *vb* **1** to scrape with the feet. **2** to wear a rough place or places on the surface of.

scuffle /**scu**-ful/ *n* a confused or disorderly struggle.

scull /scull/ *n* one of a pair of short oars. • *vb* **1** to row with sculls. **2** to move a boat by rowing with one oar at the front.

sculpt /sculpt/ *vb* to carve or model a figure, design, image, etc.

sculptor /**sculp**-tur/ *n* a person skilled in sculpture.

sculpture /**sculp**-chur/ *n* **1** the art of carving or modelling in wood, stone, clay, etc. **2** a work of sculpture.

scum /scum/ *n* **1** dirt and froth that gathers on the surface of liquid. **2** wicked or worthless people. • *adj* **scummy**.

scurf /scurf/ *n* small dry flakes of skin.

scurrilous /**scu**-ri-lus/ *adj* **1** using bad or indecent language. **2** very insulting.

scurry /**scur**-vee/ *vb* to run hurriedly. • *also n*.

scurvy /**scur**-ee/ *n* a disease caused by lack of fresh fruit or vegetables. • *adj* mean, nasty.

scuttle[1] /**scu**-tul/ *n* a box or bucket for keeping coal at the fireside.

scuttle[2] /**scu**-tul/ *n* a hole with a lid in the deck or side of a ship. • *vb* to sink (a ship) by making a hole in it.

scuttle[3] /**scu**-tul/ *vb* to run away hurriedly.

scythe /sythe/ *n* a tool consisting of a long, curving, very sharp blade set at an angle to a long handle, used for cutting grass, etc. • *vb* to cut with a scythe.

sea /see/ *n* **1** the salt water that covers much of Earth's surface. **2** a large extent of this. **3** a large amount or extent of anything. • **at sea** confused and uncertain.

seabed /**see**-bed/ *n* the ocean floor, especially the areas with rich mineral or oil deposits.

seabird /**see**-bird/ *n* a bird living on or near the sea.

seaboard /**see**-board/ *n* land or coastal region near the sea.

seafood /**see**-food/ *n* food prepared from or consisting of saltwater fish or shellfish.

seagull /see-gull/ *n* a kind of bird that lives along the seacoast.

sea horse /see hawrse/ *n* a kind of small, tropical, bony fish with the head and nose looking somewhat like those of a horse.

seal[1] /seel/ *n* 1 wax with a design, etc, stamped on it, used to fasten shut envelopes, boxes, etc. 2 a stamp with a design, initials, etc, engraved on it. 3 a substance or thing that closes, fixes, or prevents leakage. • *vb* 1 to fasten with a seal. 2 to close firmly. 3 to make airtight. 4 to confirm.

seal[2] /seel/ *n* a sea animal valued for its oil and fur.

sealant /see-lant/ *n* any substance used for sealing, such as wax, plastic, etc.

sea level /see le-vel/ *n* the level of the sea's surface at half-tide.

sea lion /see lie-un/ *n* a large seal.

sealskin /seel-skin/ *n* 1 the skin or pelt of the seal. 2 an article of clothing made from this.

seam /seem/ *n* the line made by two pieces of something joined together, such as the stitching joining two pieces of cloth.

seamless /seem-less/ *adj* made without a seam.

seamstress /seem-stress/ *n* a woman who makes her living by sewing.

séance /say-onss/ *n* a meeting, especially of people who believe they can call up the spirits of the dead.

seaplane /see-plane/ *n* an aeroplane with floats that enable it to take off from or land on water.

sear /seer/ *vb* 1 to burn with sudden powerful heat. 2 to have a very strong and painful or unpleasant effect on. • *adj* dry, withered.

search /serch/ *vb* to look for, to explore, to try to find. • *n* act of looking for. • *n* **searcher**.

search engine /serch en-jin/ *n* computer software designed to locate items on a given topic.

searching /ser-ching/ *adj* thorough, testing thoroughly.

searchlight /serch-lite/ *n* a powerful electric lamp able to throw a beam of light on distant objects.

seasick /see-sick/ *adj* sick because of the rocking of a ship at sea.

seaside /see-side/ *n* the land near or beside the sea.

season[1] /see-zun/ *n* 1 one of the four divisions of the year (e.g. winter, summer). 2 a time of the year noted for a particular activity.

season[2] /see-zun/ *vb* 1 to make (*wood*) hard and fit for use by drying gradually. 2 to add something to food to give it a good taste.

seasonable /seez-na-bul/ *adj* suitable to the season of the year.

seasonal /seez-nal/ *adj* having to do with one or all of the seasons.

seasoning /seez-ning/ *n* anything added to food to bring out or improve its taste.

season ticket /see-zun ti-ket/ a ticket that can be used many times over a stated period.

seat /seet/ *n* 1 anything on which a person sits. 2 a piece of furniture for sitting on. 3 a place for a person to sit in a vehicle, hall, etc. 4 a parliamentary constituency. 5 a person's bottom. 6 large country house belonging to an aristocratic family. • *vb* 1 to place on a seat. 2 to have or provide seats for.

seat belt /seet belt/ *n* a belt worn across the lap and sometimes chest to keep a person in place while driving, flying, riding, etc.

sea urchin /see ur-chin/ *n* a sea creature living in a round prickly shell.

seaweed /see-weed/ *n* sea plants.

secede /si-seed/ *vb* to break away from.

secession /si-se-shun/ *n* act of seceding. • *n* **secessionist** a person who favours or takes part in a secession.

seclude /si-clood/ *vb* to keep away from others, to make private or hidden.

secluded /si-cloo-did/ *adj* 1 out of the way. 2 private, quiet.

seclusion /si-cloo-zhun/ *n* quietness and privacy.

second[1] /se-cund/ *adj* coming immediately after the first. • *n* 1 a person who comes after the first. 2 a person who supports and assists another in a fight or duel. 3 *npl* goods that because of some flaw are sold more cheaply. • *vb* 1 to support. 2 to assist. • *vb* /se-**conned**/ to transfer from normal duties to other duties.

second[2] /se-cund/ *n* the 60th part of a minute.

secondary /se-cun-de-ree/ *adj* 1 of less importance. 2 coming after that which is first in a series of events, states, etc.

secondary school /se-cun-de-ree skool/ *n* a school for pupils who are over the age of 11 or 12.

second-guess /se-cund-**gess**/ *vb* try to predict what is likely to happen by guesswork.

secondhand /se-cund hand/ *adj* not new, having been used by another.

second hand /se-cund hand/ *n* the hand on a clock or watch that times the seconds.

second nature /se-cund nay-chur/ *n* habits fixed so deeply that they seem a part of a person's nature.

second-rate /se-cund-rate/ *adj* not of high quality.

second sight /se-cund site/ *n* the ability to see things happening elsewhere or to foresee the future.

second wind /se-cund **wind**/ *n* the ability to breathe smoothly again after having been out of breath.

secrecy /see-cre-see/ *n* **1** the habit of keeping information to oneself. **2** concealment.

secret /see-cret/ *adj* **1** hidden from others. **2** known or told to few. **3** private. • *n* **1** a piece of information kept from others. **2** privacy. **3** a hidden reason or cause.

secretarial /sec-re-ter-ee-al/ *adj* having to do with the work of a secretary.

secretary /sec-re-ter-ee/ *n* **1** a person whose job it is to deal with letters and help to carry out the day-to-day business of his or her employer. **2** a high government official or minister.

secrete /si-creet/ *vb* **1** to hide away. **2** to produce a substance or fluid within the body by means of glands or other organs.

secretion /si-cree-shun/ *n* **1** the act of secreting. **2** the substance or fluid secreted (e.g. saliva).

secretive /see-cri-tiv/ *adj* **1** keeping information to oneself. **2** fond of concealing things.

sect /sect/ *n* a body of persons holding the same beliefs, especially in religion.

sectarian /sec-ter-ee-an/ *adj* **1** having to do with a sect or sects. **2** concerned with or relating to the interests of a person's own group, etc.

section /sec-shun/ *n* **1** a distinct part. **2** a part cut off. • *adj* **sectional**.

sector /sec-tor/ *n* **1** a section of a circle. **2** one of the parts into which an area is divided. **3** part of a field of activity. • *adj* **sectorial**.

secular /se-cyu-lar/ *adj* **1** having to do with this world, not with a faith or religion; not sacred. **2** having to do with lay, not church, affairs. • *n* **secularity** the state or quality of being secular. • *vb* **secularize**, *also* **secularise** to change from religious to civil ownership or use. • *n* **secularism**.

secure /si-cyoor/ *adj* **1** free from care or danger. **2** safe. • *vb* **1** to make safe. **2** to fasten securely. **3** to seize and hold firmly.

security /si-cyoo-ri-tee/ *n* **1** safety. **2** precautions taken to protect someone or something from attack, crime, danger, etc. **3** something given as proof of a person's willingness or ability to repay a loan. **4** *pl* documents stating that a person has lent a sum of money to a business, etc, and is entitled to receive interest on it.

sedan /si-dan/ *n* a car with either two or four doors, a full-sized rear seat, and a hard top.

sedate /si-date/ *adj* calm, quiet, and relaxed. • *vb* to give someone a drug to to make them calm or sleepy.

sedation /si-day-shun/ *n* the act or process of reducing excitement or nervousness.

sedative /se-da-tiv/ *adj* having a calming effect. • *n* a sedative drug.

sedentary /se-den-ter-ee/ *adj* inactive, requiring much sitting.

sediment /se-di-ment/ *n* the particles of matter that sink to the bottom of liquid. • *adj* **sedimentary** of, having the nature of, or containing sediment.

sedition /se-di-shun/ *n* words or actions intended to stir up rebellion against the government. • *adj* **seditious**.

seduce /si-dooss/ *vb* **1** to persuade someone to do what is wrong or immoral. **2** to persuade to have sex. • *n* **seducer**.

seduction /si-duc-shun/ *n* the act of seducing.

seductive /si-duc-tiv/ *adj* **1** tempting, attracting to do wrong. **2** sexually attractive.

see[1] /see/ *vb* (*pt* **saw**, *pp* **seen**) **1** to look at with the eye. **2** to notice. **3** to understand. **4** to visit or interview. • **see about** to attend to. • **see off** **1** to go so far with a person who is leaving. **2** (*inf*) to get rid of. • **see through** **1** to keep on with to the end. **2** to understand thoroughly. • **seeing that** since, because.

see[2] /see/ *n* the district over which a bishop has control.

seed /seed/ *n* **1** the grain or germ from which, when placed in the ground, a new plant grows. **2** the beginning of something. • *vb* to produce seed, to plant seeds. • **go to seed**, **run to seed** **1** (*of a plant*) to shoot up too quickly. **2** to grow careless and lazy. **3** to become weak.

seedbed /seed-bed/ *n* a bed of soil, usually covered with glass, in which seedlings are grown.

seedling /seed-ling/ *n* a young plant grown from a seed.

seedy /see-dee/ *adj* **1** shabby. **2** unwell. **3** containing many seeds.

seeing /see-ing/ *n* the sense or power of sight, the act of using the eyes to see.

seek /seek/ *vb* (*pt*, *pp* **sought**) **1** to look for. **2** to try to get, to ask.

seem /seem/ *vb* to appear to be, look as if.

seeming /see-ming/ *adj* having the appearance of, apparent.

seemly /seem-lee/ *adj* proper, fitting, decent.

seen *pp of* **see**.

seep /seep/ *vb* to leak, drip, or flow slowly out through small openings. • *n* **seepage** the act or process of seeping, the liquid that seeps.

seer /seer/ *n* a person who foresees the future, a prophet.

seersucker /**seer**-su-ker/ *n* a crinkled fabric of linen, cotton, etc, usually with a striped pattern.

seesaw /**see**-saw/ *n* **1** a plank that is balanced in the middle and on which children sit at either end so that when one end goes up the other end goes down. **2** the act of moving up and down or back and forth. • *adj* moving up and down like a seesaw. • *vb* **1** to play on a seesaw. **2** to move up and down or back and forth.

seethe /**seethe**/ *vb* **1** to boil. **2** to be full of anger, excitement, etc.

see-through /**see**-throo/ *adj* that can be seen through, more or less transparent.

segment /**seg**-ment/ *n* **1** a piece cut off. **2** part of a circle cut off by a straight line. • *vb* to cut into segments. • *adj* **segmental**.

segmentation /seg-men-**tay**-shun/ *n* a dividing or being divided into segments.

segregate /**seg**-ri-gate/ *vb* to set apart or separate from others. • *n* **segregation**.

seismic /**size**-mik/ *adj* having to do with earthquakes.

seismograph /**size**-mo-graf/ *n* an instrument showing the force of an earthquake and the direction in which it has occurred.

seismology /size-**mol**-u-jee/ *n* the science of earthquakes.

seize /**seez**/ *vb* **1** to take by force. **2** to take firm hold of.

seizure /**see**-zhur/ *n* **1** act of taking by force. **2** a sudden attack of illness, especially a stroke or epileptic fit.

seldom /**sel**-dum/ *adv* rarely.

select /se-**lect**/ *vb* to choose, to pick out. • *adj* specially chosen. • *n* **selector** the person or thing that selects.

selection /se-**lec**-shun/ *n* **1** act of choosing. **2** what is chosen.

selective /se-**lec**-tiv/ *adj* choosing carefully, rejecting what is not wanted.

self /**self**/ *n* (*pl* **selves**) a person's own person or interest.

self- /**self**/ *prefix* of oneself or itself.

self-awareness /self-a-**ware**-ness/ *n* awareness of oneself as an individual.

self-centred /self-**sen**-turd/ *adj* selfish, thinking chiefly of oneself and one's interests.

self-confident /self-**con**-fi-dent/ *adj* sure of oneself and one's powers.

self-conscious /self-**con**-shus/ *adj* thinking about oneself too much, shy because one thinks others are watching.

self-contained /self-cun-**taind**/ *adj* **1** keeping to oneself, not showing one's feelings. **2** (*of a house*) complete in itself and separate from other houses.

self-control /self-cun-**trole**/ *n* the ability to control one's temper, excitement, etc.

self-destruct /self-di-**struct**/ *vb* to destroy itself automatically. • *n* **self-destruction**. • *adj* **self-destructive**.

self-employed /self-im-**ployd**/ *adj* working for oneself, with direct control over work, services, etc.

self-esteem /self-i-**steem**/ *n* one's opinion of oneself, self-respect.

self-help /self-**help**/ *n* care of or betterment of oneself by one's own efforts.

self-important /self-im-**pore**-tant/ *adj* full of one's own importance, pompous. • *n* **self-importance**.

selfish /**sel**-fish/ *adj* thinking only of oneself and one's own advantage. • *n* **selfishness**.

selfless /**self**-less/ *adj* concerned about other's welfare or interests and not one's own. • *n* **selflessness**.

self-respect /self-re-**spect**/ *n* proper care of one's own character and reputation.

self-righteous /self-**rie**-chus/ *adj* too aware of what one supposes to be one's own goodness.

self-sacrificing /self-**sa**-cri-fie-sing/ *adj* ready to give up one's own desires for the good of others.

self-service /self-**ser**-viss/ *adj* (*of a shop, restaurant, etc*) helping oneself. • *also n*.

self-sufficient /self-su-**fi**-shent/ *adj* needing no help from others.

sell /**sell**/ *vb* (*pt, pp* **sold**) to give in exchange for money.

seller /**se**-ler/ *n* a person who sells.

sellout /**se**-lout/ *n* **1** a performance or sports event of some kind for which all the tickets have been sold. **2** the act of betraying someone or something, a person who betrays someone or something.

selves /**selvz**/ *pl of* **self**.

semantic /se-**man**-tic/ *adj* of or regarding meaning, especially meaning in language.

semaphore /**sem**-ah-fore/ *n* a system of conveying messages using flags.

semblance /**sem**-blanse/ *n* outward appearance.

semester /si-**mes**-ter/ *n* a college or university term of about 18 weeks.

semen /**see**-men/ *n* the white fluid produced by the reproductive organs of male mammals, also called sperm.

semi- /**se**-mee/ *prefix* half.

semicircle /**se**-mee-sir-cul/ *n* a half circle. • *adj* **semicircular**.

semicolon /**se**-mee-**co**-lon/ *n* a mark of punctuation (;).

semi-detached /**se**-mee-di-**tacht**/ *adj* (*of*

a house) joined to another house by a communal wall.

semifinal /se-mee-**fie**-nal/ *adj* coming just before the final match, as in a tournament. • *n* such a match.

seminar /se-mi-nar/ *n* a group of students working together under the guidance of a teacher.

seminary /se-mi-ne-ree/ *n* a school or college, especially one training people to be priests, ministers, rabbis, etc.

Semite /se-mite/ *n* **1** a member of any of the peoples who speak a Semitic language, including the Hebrews, Arabs, Assyrians, etc. **2** used loosely, a Jewish person.

Semitic /se-mi-tic/ *adj* **1** having to do with Semites.

senate /se-nit/ *n* **1** a group of officials elected to make laws. **2** (*cap*) one of the two houses of the United States Congress. **3** the governing body of certain universities.

senator /se-ni-tor/ *n* a member of a senate. • *adj* **senatorial**.

send /send/ *vb* (*pt, pp* sent) **1** to have taken from one place to another. **2** to order to go. • *n* **sender**.

senile /see-nile/ *adj* weak in the mind from old age. • *n* **senility**.

senior /seen-yur/ *adj* **1** older. **2** higher in rank or importance. **3** for older people. • *n* **1** one who is older. **2** a senior pupil in a school. • *n* **seniority**.

sensation /sen-say-shun/ *n* **1** the ability to perceive through the senses, feeling. **2** a feeling that cannot be described. **3** great excitement. **4** an event that causes great excitement.

sensational /sen-say-shnal/ *adj* causing great excitement. • *vb* **sensationalize**, *also* **sensationalise**.

sensationalism /sen-say-shna-li-zum/ *n* a liking for exciting news and events.

sense /senss/ *n* **1** one of the five powers (sight, hearing, taste, smell, touch) by which people and animals gain knowledge of things outside themselves. **2** wisdom in everyday things. **3** understanding. **4** meaning.

senseless /senss-less/ *adj* **1** foolish, pointless. **2** unconscious.

sensibility /sen-si-bi-li-tee/ *n* **1** the ability to feel emotions strongly. **2** delicacy of feeling.

sensible /sen-si-bul/ *adj* **1** having or showing good judgment, wise. **2** aware. **3** practical.

sensitive /sen-si-tiv/ *adj* **1** quick to feel things. **2** easily hurt or damaged. **3** able to feel emotions strongly. • *n* **sensitivity**.

sensor /sen-sawr/ *n* a tool designed to detect, measure, or record things such as heat, temperature, pressure, etc.

sensory /sen-sree/ *adj* having to do with the senses.

sensual /sen-shwal/ *adj* **1** having to do with the pleasures of the body. **2** fond of the pleasures of the body. • *n* **sensuality**.

sensuous /sen-shwus/ *adj* **1** having to do with the senses. **2** pleasing to the senses.

sent *pt and pp of* send.

sentence /sen-tense/ *n* **1** a group of words, containing at least a subject and a verb, that is grammatically correct and makes complete sense. **2** a judgment given in a court of law. **3** the punishment given to a wrongdoer by a judge. • *vb* to state the punishment given to a wrongdoer.

sentient /sen-shent/ *adj* having the power of feeling. • *n* **sentience** ability to feel.

sentiment /sen-ti-ment/ *n* **1** what a person feels or thinks about something. **2** an expression of feeling. **3** tender or kindly feeling.

sentimental /sen-ti-men-tal/ *adj* **1** showing, causing, etc, excessive tender feeling or emotion. **2** concerning the emotions rather than reason. • *n* **sentimentality**.

sentinel /sen-ti-nel/ *n* a person or animal that guards a group.

sentry /sen-tree/ *n* a soldier on guard.

sentry box /sen-tree boks/ *n* a shelter for a sentry.

separate /sep-a-rate/ *vb* **1** to put apart. **2** to go away from. **3** to stop living together. **4** to go different ways. **5** to divide into parts. • *adj* /sep-rit/ unconnected, distinct, apart. • *adj* **separable**.

separation /se-pe-ray-shun/ *n* **1** act of separating. **2** an agreement by a married couple to live apart from each other.

separatism /se-pra-ti-zum/ *n* the condition of political, religious, or racial separation. • *n* **separatist** a person who believes in separatism.

sepia /see-pee-ya/ *n* a dark, reddish brown dye or colour made from fluid obtained from the cuttlefish.

September /sep-tem-ber/ *n* the ninth month of the year.

septic /sep-tic/ *adj* infected and poisoned by germs.

septic tank /sep-tic-tangk/ *n* an underground tank for waste matter to be stored and broken down.

septuagenarian /sep-twa-je-ner-ee-an/ *n* one who is 70 years old or between 70 and 80.

septuplet /sep-tu-plet/ *n* one of seven babies born at a single birth.

sepulchral /se-**pul**-cral/ *adj* **1** having to do with a tomb. **2** (*of a voice*) deep and gloomy.

sepulture /se-pul-chur/ *n* (*fml*) burial.

sequel /**see**-kwel/ *n* **1** that which follows, a result or consequence. **2** a novel, film, etc, that continues the story of an earlier one.

sequence /**see**-kwense/ *n* a number of things, events, etc, following each other in a natural or correct order.

sequential /si-**kwen**-shal/ *adj* of, relating to, or forming a sequence.

sequin /**see**-kwin/ *n* a tiny disc of bright metal sewn onto a dress for ornament, usually one of many. • *adj* **sequined** decorated with sequins.

sequoia /see-**kwoh**-ya/ *n* a large redwood tree.

seraph /se-raf/ *n* (*pl* **seraphs** *or* **seraphim**) an angel of the highest rank.

seraphic /se-ra-fic/ *adj* angelic, pure.

serenade /se-ra-**nade**/ *n* a musical work played outside at night, especially by a lover under the window of his sweetheart. • *vb* to sing or play a serenade.

serendipity /se-ren-**di**-pi-tee/ *n* a seeming gift for finding something good accidentally.

serene /se-**reen**/ *adj* calm, undisturbed.

serenity /se-**re**-ni-tee/ *n* calmness, peace.

serf /serf/ *n* a slave, a person bound to his or her master's land and transferred with it to any new owner.

serge /serge/ *n* a strong woollen cloth.

sergeant /**sar**-jint/ *n* **1** a rank in the army or air force. **2** in the police, an officer just below a captain or lieutenant.

serial /**see**-ree-al/ *n* a story published or broadcast in parts or instalments. • *adj* **1** happening in a series. **2** in successive parts.

series /**see**-reez/ *n* (*pl* **series**) a number of things arranged in a definite order.

serious /**see**-ree-us/ *adj* **1** thoughtful. **2** important. **3** likely to cause danger.

sermon /**ser**-mun/ *n* **1** a talk given by a priest, minister, or rabbi on a religious subject. **2** a talk containing advice or warning. • *vb* **sermonize**, *also* **sermonise**.

serpent /**ser**-pent/ *n* a snake.

serrate /se-**rate**/, **serrated** /se-**ray**-tid/ *adj* having notches like the edge of a saw.

serration /se-**ray**-shun/ *n* the condition of being serrate.

serum /**see**-rum/ *n* **1** the watery part of the blood. **2** liquid taken from the blood of an animal and injected into a person's blood to protect against a disease. **3** the thin, watery part of plant fluid.

servant /**ser**-vant/ *n* **1** a person who works for and obeys another. **2** a person employed to do tasks about the house.

serve /serv/ *vb* **1** to work for and obey. **2** to hand food to at the table. **3** to supply with. **4** to be helpful. **5** (*in tennis, volleyball, etc*) to hit the ball into play. • **serves you right** that is just what you deserve.

server /**ser**-ver/ *n* **1** a person who serves. **2** the central computer in a network to which other computers are connected so that software and files can be shared.

service /**ser**-viss/ *n* **1** the work of a servant or employee. **2** time spent in the armed forces, police, etc. **3** use, help. **4** a religious ceremony. **5** a set of dishes for use at table. **6** in tennis, the hit intended to put the ball into play. **7** *pl* the armed forces. **8** *pl* service station.

serviceable /**ser**-vi-sa-bul/ *adj* useful.

service station /**ser**-vis stay-shun/, **services** *n* a place that sells petrol, oils, some other car requirements and often drinks and snacks, and usually provides toilet facilities.

servile /**ser**-vul/ *adj* behaving like a slave, too ready to obey. • *n* **servility**.

servitude /**ser**-vi-tood/ *n* slavery, the condition of being a slave, serf, etc.

sesame /**se**-sa-mee/ *n* a plant whose seeds are used in cooking and from which an oil, used in cooking and salads, is obtained. • **open sesame** a sure means of gaining admission.

session /**se**-shun/ *n* a meeting of a group or sitting of a court or assembly.

set /set/ *vb* **1** to put out. **2** to fix in position. **3** to put to music. **4** to become hard or solid. **5** (*of the sun, etc.*) to sink below the horizon. • *n* **1** a number of things of the same kind. **2** a group of people with similar interests. **3** a group of games in a tennis match. • *adj* fixed, regular. • **set off**, **set out** to begin a journey. • **set upon** to attack.

setback /**set**-back/ *n* something that keeps a person from doing something or from carrying out a plan.

set point /**set** point/ *n* in a game such as tennis, when the next point scored by a player decides the winner of the set.

settee /se-**tee**/ *n* a small sofa.

setting /**se**-ting/ *n* **1** surroundings. **2** background. **3** music written to go with certain words.

settle /**se**-tul/ *n* a bench with arms and a high back. • *vb* **1** to set up home in a certain place. **2** to come to rest on. **3** to put an end to by giving a decision or judgment. **4** to make or become quiet or calm. **5** to pay. **6** to sink to the bottom of.

settlement /se-tul-ment/ *n* **1** a decision or judgment that ends an argument. **2** money or property given to someone under certain conditions. **3** payment of a bill. **4** a colony.

settler /set-ler/ *n* someone who makes his or her home in a new colony or land that has not previously been occupied.

set-to /set-too/ *n* a fight.

setup /se-tup/ *n* **1** the way in which something is set up. **2** a contest or plan that is arranged to go a certain way.

seven /se-ven/ *n* the number between six and eight.

sevenfold /se-ven-foald/ *adj* **1** having seven parts. **2** having seven times as much or as many.

seventeen /se-ven-teen/ *n* seven more than 10.

seventeenth /se-ven-teenth/ *adj* coming after 16 others.

seventh /se-venth/ *adj* coming after six others.

seventieth /se-ven-tee-eth/ *adj* coming after 69 others.

seventy /se-ven-tee/ *n* the number between 69 and 71.

sever /se-ver/ *vb* **1** to cut or tear apart or off. **2** to break. • *n* **severance**.

severable /sev-ra-bul/ *adj* that can be severed.

several /sev-ral/ *adj* **1** more than two, but not very many. **2** separate, various.

severe /se-veer/ *adj* **1** strict, harsh. **2** plain and undecorated. **3** very cold. • *n* **severity**.

sew /so/ *vb* (*pt* **sewed**, *pp* **sewn**) to join by means of needle and thread. • *n* **sewer** a person or thing that sews.

sewage /soo-widge/ *n* waste matter of a house or town.

sewer /soo-wer/ *n* an underground drain to carry away water, waste matter, etc.

sewerage /soo-ridge/ *n* a system of underground drains or sewers.

sex /seks/ *n* **1** the state of being male or female. **2** the qualities by which an animal or plant is seen to be male or female. **3** sexual intercourse.

sexagenarian /sek-se-je-nair-ee-an/ *n* someone who is 60 years old, or between 60 and 70.

sexism /sek-si-zum/ *n* the treatment of someone in a different, often unfair way on the grounds of that person's sex, especially against women. • *adj*, *n* **sexist**.

sextet /sek-stet/ *n* **1** a piece of music written for six. **2** a group of six singers or players. **3** a set or group of six.

sextuplet /sek-stoo-plet/ *n* one of six babies born at a single birth.

sexual /sek-shwal/ *adj* having to do with sex.

sexual intercourse /sek-shwal in-ter-coarse/ *n* sexual contact whereby the male's penis is inserted into the female's vagina to produce an orgasm.

sexuality /sek-shu-wa-li-tee/ *n* the state or quality of being sexual.

sexy /sek-see/ *adj* **1** sexually attractive. **2** sexually aroused. **3** exciting or intended to excite sexual desire. • *n* **sexiness** *n* a sexy state or quality.

sh /sh/ *interj* used to urge or request silence.

shabby /sha-bee/ *adj* **1** untidy through much wear, threadbare, dressed in threadbare or untidy clothes. **2** mean, ungenerous. • *n* **shabbiness**.

shack /shack/ *n* a hut, small house, cabin.

shackle /sha-cul/ *vb* **1** to fasten with a chain. **2** to limit freedom of action or speech. • *npl* chains for fastening the limbs.

shade /shade/ *vb* **1** to protect from light or sun. **2** to darken. **3** to colour. • *n* **1** any device that protects from light or sun. **2** a place in a shadow cast by the sun, half-darkness. **3** a slight difference. **4** a little.

shadiness /shay-dee-ness/ *n* a shady state or quality.

shading /shay-ding/ *n* the effects used to suggest darkness in a picture.

shadow /sha-doe/ *n* **1** a dark patch on the ground caused by the breaking of rays of light by a body. **2** shade. **3** someone who follows another around. **4** a ghost. • *vb* to follow someone closely without his or her knowing it.

shadowy /sha-doe-wee/ *adj* **1** in shadow, shaded, dark. **2** dark and unclear.

shady /shay-dee/ *adj* **1** protected from light or sun. **2** dishonest, untrustworthy. • *adv* **shadily** in a shady manner.

shaft /shaft/ *n* **1** the long handle of any tool or weapon. **2** an arrow. **3** a connecting rod in a machine, one of the poles of a carriage to which a horse is tied. **4** the main part of a pillar. **5** a deep tunnel leading down to a mine. **6** a ray of light.

shag /shag/ *n* **1** a kind of haircut that is shorter in front and longer in back with many layers. **2** heavy, rough woollen cloth.

shaggy /sha-gee/ *adj* **1** having rough, long hair. **2** rough.

shake /shake/ *vb* (*pt* **shook**, *pp* **shaken**) **1** to move quickly up and down or to and fro. **2** to tremble. **3** to make weaker or less firm. • *n* **1** trembling. **2** a sudden jerk. **3** a shock. **4** short for milk shake.

shaker /shay-ker/ *n* **1** a person or thing that shakes. **2** (*cap*) a member of the United

Society of Believers, an American religious community which believes in living with simplicity.

shaky /shay-kee/ *adj* **1** not steady. **2** weak after illness.

shale /shale/ *n* a soft rock that was formed by the hardening of clay and that breaks apart easily. • *adj* **shaly.**

shall /shall/ *aux vb, pt* **should** will; especially used in formal writing. *See* **will.** (**Shall** was used for the first person of the verb and **will** for second and third person. This usage has become very old fashioned.)

shallot /sha-lot/ *n* a small onion.

shallow /sha-lo/ *adj* **1** not deep. **2** not thinking deeply. • *n* a place where water is not deep.

shalom /sha-lom/ *n* a greeting meaning peace, used among Jewish people.

sham /sham/ *n* **1** a person pretending to be what he or she is not. **2** a thing made to look like something else. **3** a trick or fraud. • *adj* not real, pretended. • *vb* (**shammed, shamming**) to pretend.

shaman /shay-man/ *n* a priest or medicine man, especially among some Asian people, who is believed to be able to heal and to tell the future by contacting good and evil spirits.

shamanism /shay-ma-ni-zum/ *n* the religion of certain peoples believing in good and evil spirits that can be contacted by a shaman.

shamble /sham-bul/ *vb* to walk clumsily. • *also n.*

shambles /sham-bulz/ *npl* a scene of great disorder and confusion.

shame /shame/ *n* a feeling of sorrow for wrongdoing or for the inability to do something; disgrace; a painful feeling of having lost the respect of others. • *vb* to make ashamed, to disgrace.

shamefaced /shame-faist/ *adj* showing shame or embarrassment.

shameful /shame-ful/ *adj* disgraceful, shocking, bringing or causing shame.

shameless /shame-less/ *adj* not easily made ashamed, bold.

shampoo /sham-poo/ *vb* to wash and rub the head and hair. • *n* **1** act of shampooing. **2** a preparation used for shampooing.

shamrock /sham-rock/ *n* a small plant with three leaves on each stem, the national symbol of Ireland.

shank /shangk/ *n* **1** the leg from the knee to the ankle. **2** the long handle or shaft of certain tools.

shanty /shan-tee/ *n* a poorly built hut, a shack.

shantytown /shan-tee-town/ *n* the section of a city where there a many shanties or small, rundown shacks.

shape /shape/ *n* **1** the form or outline of anything. **2** (*inf*) condition, state. • *vb* **1** to form. **2** to give a certain shape to. • **in good shape** in good condition.

shapeless /shape-less/ *adj* ugly or irregular in shape.

shapely /shape-lee/ *adj* well-formed.

shard /shard/ *n* a piece of broken pottery or glass.

share /share/ *n* **1** part of a thing belonging to a particular person. **2** one of the equal parts of the money of a company or business, lent by persons who may then receive a part of the profits. **3** the cutting part of a plough. • *vb* **1** to divide among others. **2** to receive a part of.

shareholder /share hole-der/ *n* a person who owns shares in a company or business.

shareware /share-ware/ computer software that is provided for free for a limited time, with an option to buy.

sharia, shariah /sha-ree-ah/ *n* the religious law of Islam.

shark /shark/ *n* **1** a large meat-eating fish. **2** (*inf*) one ready to use unfair means to get as much money as possible.

sharp /sharp/ *adj* **1** having a thin edge for cutting with; having a fine point. **2** quick and intelligent. **3** hurtful, unkind. **4** stinging, keen. **5** (*mus*) higher than the correct note. **6** rather sour. • *n* a musical sign to show that a note is to be raised half a tone (#). • *adv* (*of time*) exactly. • *n* a needle.

sharpen /shar-pen/ *vb* to make sharp.

sharper /shar-per/ *n* a person who cheats, especially at cards.

sharp-tongued /sharp-tungd/ *adj* using severe or harshly critical language.

sharp-witted /sharp-wi-tid/ *adj* quick and clever.

shatter /sha-ter/ *vb* **1** to break into pieces, to smash. **2** to put an end to.

shatterproof /sha-ter-proof/ *adj* that will resist shattering.

shave /shave/ *vb* **1** to cut off hair with a razor. **2** to cut strips off the surface. **3** to pass very close to without touching. • *n* **1** act of shaving, especially the face. **2** a close hair cut. **3** a narrow escape.

shaven /shay-ven/ *adj* closely trimmed, shaved.

shaver /shay-ver/ *n* a person or instrument that shaves.

shaving /shay-ving/ *n* a thin strip cut off the surface.

shawl /shawl/ *n* a cloth folded and worn loosely over the shoulders, especially by women.

she /she/ *pron* the woman, girl, female animal, or sometimes the thing referred to as female (as a boat) referred to.

sheaf /sheef/ *n* (*pl* **sheaves**) a number of things in a bundle.

shear /sheer/ *vb* (*pp* **shorn**) **1** to cut with shears. **2** to clip the wool from. **3** to cut or cause to break. • *npl* a pair of large scissors.

shearer /shee-rer/ *n* a person who shears.

shearing /shee-ring/ *n* the action of cutting with or as with shears.

sheath /sheeth/ *n* a close-fitting case or container.

sheathe /sheethe/ *vb* to put into a sheath.

sheaves *pl of* **sheaf**.

shebang /shi-bang/ *n* an affair, business, thing, etc.

shed[1] /shed/ *vb* (**shed, shedding**) **1** to let fall down or off. **2** to spread about.

shed[2] /shed/ *n* a hut, a small building used for storage.

sheen /sheen/ *n* brightness, shininess.

sheep /sheep/ *n* (*pl* **sheep**) **1** a farm animal valued for its wool and its meat. **2** a person who follows the lead of others without question.

sheepdog /sheep-dawg/ *n* a dog trained to look after and herd sheep.

sheepish /sheep-ish/ *adj* awkward or embarrassed because of having done something wrong.

sheepskin /sheep-skin/ *n* the skin of a sheep, especially one dressed with the fleece on it, as for a coat.

sheer[1] /sheer/ *adj* **1** very steep. **2** (*of material*) very fine or transparent. **3** thorough, complete.

sheer[2] /sheer/ *vb* to swerve, to move suddenly in another direction.

sheet /sheet/ *n* **1** a broad thin piece of anything. **2** a bedcovering of linen, cotton, etc. **3** a broad stretch of water, flame, ice, etc. **4** a rope tied to the lower corner of a sail.

sheik(h) /sheek/ *n* an Arab chief of a family, tribe, or village.

shekel /shek-el/ *n* **1** *pl* (*inf*) money. **2** the unit of currency in Israel.

shelf /shelf/ *n* (*pl* **shelves**) **1** a board fixed to a wall or fastened in a cupboard, used for placing things on. **2** a ledge, a long flat rock or sandbank.

shell /shell/ *n* **1** a hard outer covering. **2** a thick metal case filled with explosive and fired from a gun. • *vb* **1** to take the shell off. **2** to fire shells at.

she'll /sheel/ *contraction* shortened form of *she will* or *she shall*.

shellac /sheh-lac/ *n* a type of resin used for making varnish. • *vb* to apply this to something.

shellfish /shell-fish/ *n* a fish with a shell covering.

shelter /shel-ter/ *n* **1** a place that gives protection from the weather or safety from danger. **2** protection. • *vb* to protect, to go for protection.

shelve /shelv/ *vb* **1** to place on a shelf. **2** to put aside for a time. **3** to slope.

shelves *pl of* **shelf**.

shelving /shel-ving/ *n* **1** material for shelves. **2** a set of shelves.

shepherd /shep-urd/ *n* a person who looks after or herds sheep. • *f* **shepherdess**. • *vb* to guide a flock or group.

shepherd's pie /shep-urdz pie/ *n* a meat pie with a layer of mashed potatoes serving as a top crust.

sherbet /sher-bet/ *n* **1** a sweet consisting of fruity powder that fizzes in the mouth. **2** (*US*) a frozen, fruit-flavoured dessert.

sheriff /sher-if/ *n* **1** in the US, the chief law officer or judge of a county. **2** in Scotland, a judge who presides over a lower court. **3** in England and Wales, a senior officer representing the king or queen in a county or some cities.

sherry /sher-ee/ *n* a Spanish wine.

shield /sheeld/ *n* **1** a piece of metal or strong leather held in front of the body to defend it against sword strokes, etc. **2** a protector or protection. • *vb* to defend, to protect.

shift /shift/ *vb* **1** to change. **2** to move. **3** to remove, get rid of. • *n* **1** a change. **2** a group of workers who carry on a job for a certain time and then hand over to another group. **3** the period during which such a group works. **4** a simple dress or nightgown.

shifty /shif-tee/ *adj* untrustworthy, deceitful.

shiitake /shee-tak-ee/ *n* an edible Japanese mushroom.

shimmer /shi-mer/ *vb* to shine with a flickering light. • *also n*.

shimmy /shi-mee/ *n* a to move quickly, shaking your hips and shoulders.

shin /shin/ *n* the front part of the leg below the knee. • *vb* (**shinned, shinning**) to climb, gripping with the legs.

shine /shine/ *vb* (*pt, pp* **shone**) **1** to give off light. **2** to direct a light or lamp. **3** to polish. **4** (*inf*) to be very good at. • *n* brightness, polish.

shingle /shing-gul/ *n* **1** a thin, wedge-shaped piece of wood, slate, etc laid with others in a series of overlapping rows as a covering for roofs and the sides of houses. 2 a mass of small round pieces of stone on a beach.

Shinto /shin-toe/ *n* the native religion of Japan.

shiny /shie-nee/ *adj* bright, glossy, as if polished. • *n* **shininess**.

ship /ship/ *n* a large seagoing boat. • *vb* (**shipped, shipping**) 1 to put or take, as on board ship. 2 to go on board a ship.

shipbuilding /ship-bil-ding/ *n* the act of making ships.

shipmate /ship-mate/ *n* a fellow sailor on the same ship.

shipment /ship-ment/ *n* 1 the sending of goods by ship. 2 the goods put on board a ship.

shipping /shi-ping/ *n* 1 all the ships of a port, country, etc. 2 ships in general. 3 the act or business of sending goods.

shipshape /ship-shape/ *adj* in good order, neat and tidy.

shipwreck /ship-reck/ *n* the loss or destruction of a ship at sea. • *also vb*.

shipyard /ship-yard/ *n* a place where ships are built or repaired.

shire /shire/ *n* a county.

shirk /shirk/ *vb* to avoid. • *n* **shirker**.

shirt /shurt/ *n* a kind of upper garment.

shiva /shi-va/ *n* in Judaism, the mourning period of seven days after someone has died.

shiver /shi-ver/ *vb* 1 to tremble. 2 to break into small pieces. • *n* 1 a shaking or trembling. 2 a small piece.

shivery /shi-ve-ree/ *adj* trembling, as with cold or fear.

shoal[1] /shoal/ *n* a shallow place in the sea, a sandbank.

shoal[2] /shoal/ *n* 1 a large number of fish swimming together. 2 (*inf*) a crowd.

shock[1] /shock/ *n* a mass of long untidy hair.

shock[2] /shock/ *n* 1 the sudden violent striking of one thing against another (e.g. in a collision). 2 weakness of body or confusion of mind caused by a violent blow or collision. 3 sorrow or a state of upset caused by sudden bad news, etc. 4 an involuntary movement of the body, caused by passing electricity through it. • *vb* 1 to cause sudden pain or sorrow. 2 to horrify, to disgust.

shocker /shock-er/ *n* a person or thing that shocks.

shocking /shock-ing/ *adj* very bad, disgusting, indecent.

shockproof /shock-proof/ *adj* able to absorb shock without being damaged.

shoddy /shod-ee/ *adj* cheap, of poor quality. • *n* cheap cloth made up from the clippings of other material.

shoe /shoo/ *n* 1 a covering for the foot. 2 a U-shaped metal plate nailed to the hoof of a horse. • *vb* to fit a horse with shoes.

shoehorn /shoo-hawrn/ *n* a curved piece of horn, metal, etc, to help the foot to slip easily into a shoe.

shoelace /shoo-lace/ *n* a length of cord, leather, etc, used for tying a shoe.

shone *pt and pp of* **shine**.

shoo /shoo/ *interj* go away, get out.

shoo-in /shoo-in/ *n* a person who is expected to win easily an election, contest, etc.

shook *pt of* **shake**.

shoot /shoot/ *vb* (*pt, pp* **shot**) 1 to fire a bullet from a gun. 2 to let fly. 3 to move suddenly or quickly. 4 to hit or kill with a bullet from a gun. 5 (*in games*) to kick or hit at goal. 6 to begin to grow. 7 to make a film. • *n* 1 a young branch or bud. 2 a sloping way down which water may flow or objects slide. 3 an outing for shooting and hunting.

shooter /shoo-ter/ *n* a person or thing that shoots.

shooting /shoo-ting/ *n* the act of shooting a gun.

shooting gallery /shoo-ting ga-lu-ree/ *n* a place where people can safely practise shooting guns at targets.

shooting star /shoo-ting star/ *n* what looks like a moving star but is really a glowing fragment of a heavenly body flying through space.

shootout /shoo-tout/ *n* a battle with handguns.

shop /shop/ *n* 1 a place where goods are sold. 2 a place where work is done with tools or machines. • *vb* (**shopped, shopping**) to visit shops to buy things. • **talk shop** to talk about work.

shop assistant /shop a-sis-tant/ *n* a person who sells goods in a shop.

shopkeeper /shop-kee-per/ *n* a person who owns or runs a shop where goods are sold.

shoplifter /shop-lif-ter/ *n* a person who steals from the shops he or she is visiting. • *vb* **shoplift**.

shopper /shop-er/ *n* a person who shops.

shore[1] /shore/ *n* the land beside the sea, a river, lake, etc.

shore[2] /shore/ *n* a wooden prop or support. • *vb* to prop up or support.

shoreline /shore-line/ *n* the edge of a body of water.

shorn /shawrn/ *pp of* **shear**.

short /shawrt/ *adj* 1 not long or tall. 2 not enough. 3 without enough of. 4 not lasting long. 5 quick and almost impolite. 6 (*of* *pastry, etc.*) crumbling easily. • *adv* **shortly** briefly, soon. • *npl* trousers reaching not lower than the knees. • **in short** in a few words.

shortage /shawr-tidge/ *n* a lack of, not enough of.

shortbread /shawrt-bred/ *n* a biscuit-like cake made of flour, butter, and sugar.

shortcake /shawrt-cake/ *n* a crisp, light cake or biscuit served with fruit and whipped cream as a dessert.

short circuit /shawrt sir-kit/ *n* the touching of two electric wires so that current passes from one to the other instead of straight on, usually accidental and causing damage.

shortcoming /shawrt-cu-ming/ *n* a falling short of what is needed.

shortcut /shawrt-cut/ *n* a quicker way.

shorten /shawr-ten/ *vb* to make less in length or time.

shortening /shawrt-ning/ *n* fat for making pastry, etc.

shorthand /shawrt-hand/ *n* a type of writing, featuring symbols, in which a person can write as fast as a speaker speaks.

short-handed /shawrt-**han**-did/ *adj* not having the number of helpers or workers required.

short-lived /shawrt-livd/ *adj* living or lasting for a short time only.

shorts *see* **short**.

short-sighted /shawrt-**sie**-tid/ *adj* **1** unable to see clearly things that are distant. **2** lacking foresight.

short-tempered /shawrt-**tem**-perd/ *adj* easily angered.

shot[1] /shot/ *vb*, *pt and pp of* **shoot**. • *n* **1** the firing of a gun, etc. **2** small lead bullets. **3** a solid metal ball fired from a gun. **4** a person able to shoot. **5** (*inf*) a single attempt at doing something. **6** a series of pictures of a scene taken at one time by a camera. **7** (*inf*) an injection.

shot[2] /shot/ *adj* having threads of a different colour interwoven.

shotgun /shot-gun/ *n* a kind of gun usually used in hunting small animals.

shot put /shot put/ *n* a contest in which a heavy metal ball is thrown as far as possible from the shoulder.

should /shood/ *vb* used to express duty, what a person is supposed to do.

shoulder /shole-der/ *n* **1** the joint connecting an arm, wing, or foreleg to the body. **2** anything jutting out like a shoulder. • *vb* **1** to push with the shoulder. **2** to put on to the shoulder. **3** to bear, to accept, to take on.

shoulder blade /shole-der blade/ *n* the broad flat bone of the shoulder.

shout /shout/ *vb* to utter a loud cry. • *n* a loud cry, a call.

shove /shuv/ *vb* (*inf*) to push. • *also n*.

shovel /shu-vel/ *n* a spade with a broad blade for lifting earth, gravel, etc. • *vb* (**shovelled**, **shovelling**; *also* **shoveled**, **shoveling** (*US*)) to move with a shovel.

show /show/ *vb* **1** to let be seen, to display. **2** to point out. **3** to be in sight. **4** to prove. • *n* **1** a display. **2** a performance or entertainment. **3** a gathering at which flowers, animals, etc, are displayed to the public.

show business /show biz-ness/ *n* the world of entertainment, e.g. theatre, films, television.

shower /shou-er/ *n* **1** a short fall of rain. **2** a great number of things falling or arriving at one time. **3** a piece of bathroom equipment that produces a spray of water so that people standing underneath it can wash themselves. • *vb* **1** to give to or let fall on in large numbers. **2** to take a shower.

showerproof /shou-er-proof/ *adj* waterproof against light rain only.

showery /shou-ree/ *adj* rainy, marked by many showers.

showroom /shoa-room/ *n* a room or shop in which things are on display to the public.

shrapnel /shrap-nel/ *n* **1** a shell packed with bullets or pieces of metal that are scattered when it explodes. **2** a fragment of the case of a bomb or shell.

shred /shred/ *vb* (**shredded**, **shredding**) to tear or cut into small pieces. • *n* a scrap, a rag, a piece cut or torn off. • *n* **shredder** a person or thing that shreds.

shrew /shroo/ *n* **1** a small mouse-like animal. **2** a bad-tempered or sharp-tongued woman.

shrewd /shrood/ *adj* clever in practical matters, cunning, good at judging.

shriek /shreek/ *vb* to scream. • *also n*.

shrift /shrift/ *n* the confession of sins to a priest. • **short shrift** little mercy or sympathy.

shrill /shrill/ *adj* high and piercing in sound.

shrimp /shrimp/ *n* **1** a small edible shellfish. **2** (*inf*) a very small person. • *vb* to fish for shrimps.

shrine /shrine/ *n* **1** a box or tomb containing something connected with a holy person or thing. **2** a place revered because of a connection with a holy person or event.

shrink /shringk/ *vb* **1** to make or become smaller. **2** to go back in fear, horror, etc.

shrinkage /shring-kidge/ *n* the amount by which something becomes smaller.

shrink-wrap /shringk-rap/ *vb* to wrap in a tough, clear plastic material that shrinks to size when heated.

shrive /shrive/ *vb* (*pt* **shrove** *or* **shrived**, *pp* **shriven**) (*fml or old*) to hear the confession and forgive the sins of.

shrivel /shri-vel/ *vb* (**shrivelled, shrivelling**; *also* **shriveled, shriveling** (*US*)) **1** to dry up and become smaller. **2** to become wrinkled.

shroud /shroud/ *n* **1** a garment or covering for a dead body. **2** *pl* the set of ropes supporting a mast of a ship. • *vb* **1** to put in a shroud. **2** to cover, to hide.

shrub /shrub/ *n* a short treelike bush with a short trunk.

shrubbery /shru-bree/ *n* a place where many shrubs are growing close together.

shrug /shrug/ *vb* (**shrugged, shrugging**) to raise and drop the shoulders to express indifference.

shrunken /shrung-kin/ *adj* grown smaller, shriveled.

shudder /shu-der/ *vb* to tremble from fear, etc, to shiver with cold. • *also n.*

shuffle /shu-ful/ *vb* **1** to make a noise by moving the feet on the ground. **2** to mix cards before giving them out. • *also n.*

shun /shun/ *vb* (**shunned, shunning**) to avoid; to keep away from.

shunt /shunt/ *vb* **1** (*of a railway engine or train*) to move on to a different track or side line. **2** to move or turn to the side, to turn the other way.

shush /shush/ *interj* used to tell another to be quiet.

shut /shut/ *vb* (**shut, shutting**) to close.

shut-eye /shu-tie/ *n* (*inf*) sleep.

shutter /shu-ter/ *n* a covering that can be placed or closed over a window or other opening to keep out light.

shuttle /shu-tul/ *n* **1** the part of a weaving or sewing machine that carries the thread to and fro. **2** a travelling back and forth over an often short route, as by train, bus, aeroplane, etc. • **space shuttle** an aircraft that can go into space and return to Earth.

shuttlecock /shu-tul-cock/ *n* a cork rounded at one end and stuck with feathers, used for a ball in badminton.

shy[1] /shie/ *adj* timid, easily frightened, keeping to oneself in front of others. • *vb* to jerk or jump to the side in fear, etc. • *n* **shyness**.

shy[2] /shie/ *vb* to throw. • *n* a throw.

sibling /sib-ling/ *n* a brother or sister.

sibyl /si-bul/ *n* in ancient times, a prophetess or fortune teller.

sick /sick/ *adj* **1** (*esp US*) ill. **2** bringing up food from the stomach by vomiting, about to vomit. **3** tired of something through having too much of it .

sickbed /sick-bed/ *n* the bed in which a sick person stays.

sicken /si-ken/ *vb* **1** to make or become sick. **2** to disgust. • *adj* **sickening** causing sickness or nausea, disgusting or revolting.

sickle /si-cul/ *n* a knife with a curved blade for cutting corn, etc.

sickly /si-clee/ *adj* **1** often ill. **2** pale. **3** oversentimental.

sickness /sick-ness/ *n* **1** illness. **2** vomiting.

side /side/ *n* **1** one of the surfaces of a body, the part of the body between either shoulder and thigh. **2** edge, border. **3** slope. **4** one of two opposing parties or teams. • *adj* on, at, or towards the side. • *vb* to support one party against another.

sideboard /side-board/ *n* a piece of furniture for storing dishes, cutlery, linen, etc.

sideburns /side-burnz/ *n* the hair on a man's face just in front of the ears, especially when the rest of the beard is shaved.

side effect /side ef-ect/ *n* a negative effect of taking medication.

sidekick /side-kick/ *n* a close friend, a partner.

sideline /side-line/ *n* an activity carried on in addition to a person's real job.

sidelight /side-lite/ *n* one of the two small lights next to the headlights on a car.

sidelong /side-long/ *adj* to the side, slanting. • *also adv.*

sideshow /side-shoa/ *n* a less important show at a fair, circus, exhibition, etc.

sidetrack /side-track/ *vb* to turn someone away from what he or she was about to do.

sideways /side-wayz/ *adv* on or towards one side.

siding /sie-ding/ *n* **1** a covering for an outside wall of a building. **2** a short railway track off the main line, used for shunting, etc.

siege /seej/ *n* surrounding a fort, town, etc, with an army to take it or make its garrison surrender.

sienna /see-ye-na/ *n* an earthy colouring matter, yellowish brown in the natural state and reddish brown when burned.

sierra /see-ye-ra/ *n* a range of mountains with pointed peaks.

siesta /see-ye-sta/ *n* a nap or rest taken after lunch, especially in Spain and some Latin American countries.

sieve /siv/ *n* a container with a net bottom or a bottom full of holes, used for separating small particles of anything from larger pieces. • *vb* to pass through a sieve.

sift /sift/ *vb* **1** to pass through a sieve. **2** to examine closely. • *n* **sifter**. • **sift out** to separate good from bad.

sigh /sie/ *vb* a long, deep, easily heard breath expressing pain, sadness, unreturned love, etc. • *vb* **1** to draw such a breath. **2** (*lit*) to long (for).

sight /site/ *n* **1** the power of seeing. **2** that which is seen. **3** something worth seeing. **4** the area within which things can be seen by someone. **5** (*often pl*) a device attached to a gun to make it easier to aim straight. • *vb* to see, to notice. • **out of sight** too far away to be seen.

sighting /sie-ting/ *n* an observation of something rare or unusual.

sightseeing /site-see-ing/ *n* going around the places of interest in a town, district, etc. • *n* **sightseer**.

sign /sine/ *n* **1** a mark, movement, gesture, etc, representing an accepted meaning. **2** a mark by which a person or thing can be recognized. **3** a notice to give directions or advertise. • *vb* **1** to write a person's name on. **2** to convey meaning by a movement of the head, hands, etc.

signal /sig-nal/ *n* **1** a sign to give information, orders, etc, from a distance. **2** a tool used to give such signs to drivers of railway engines. **3** a message conveyed by such signs. • *adj* notable, important. • *vb* (**signalled, signalling;** *also* **signaled, signaling** (*US*)) to make signals to. • *n* **signaller**, *also* **signaler** (*US*).

signatory /sig-na-toe-ree/ *n* a person who has signed an agreement.

signature /sig-ni-chur/ *n* a person's name written by him or herself.

significance /sig-ni-fi-canse/ *n* meaning, importance.

significant /sig-ni-fi-cant/ *adj* full of meaning, important.

signify /sig-ni-fie/ *vb* **1** to show by a sign. **2** to mean. **3** to be important.

sign language /sine lang-gwidge/ *n* a method of communication using the hands, used especially to communicate with deaf people.

signpost /sine-poast/ *n* a post indicating the direction and sometimes also the distance to a place.

Sikh /seek/ *n* a member of an Indian religion called **Sikhism** /see-ki-zum/, originally connected with Hinduism, but now based on a belief that there is only one God.

silage /sie-lidge/ *n* green food for farm animals, kept in a silo.

silence /sie-linss/ *n* lack of sound, quietness. • *vb* to cause to be quiet.

silencer /sie-lin-ser/ *n* a device for reducing the noise of an engine, gun, etc.

silent /sie-lint/ *adj* **1** making no sound. **2** not talking, speaking little. **3** with no noise or sound.

silhouette /si-lu-wet/ *n* the dark outline and flat shape of an object, especially of a face from the side, as seen with a light behind it.

silica /si-li-ca/ *n* the dioxide form of silicon (SiO_2), a glassy, hard, colourless mineral found as quartz or in an agate, etc.

silicon /si-li-con/ *n* a chemical element found in rocks and minerals, with symbol Si.

silk /silk/ *n* **1** the fine thread produced by the silkworm. **2** a soft material woven from this.

silken /sil-ken/ *adj* (*lit*) made of silk.

silkworm /silk-wurm/ *n* a caterpillar that spins silk thread to enclose its cocoon.

silky /sil-kee/ *adj* **1** made of silk. **2** soft, smooth.

sill /sill/ *n* the ledge of stone or wood at the foot of a window.

silly /si-lee/ *adj* foolish, unwise.

silo /sie-lo/ *n* a tower or pit in which green fodder (grass, etc) is stored until needed as food for animals.

silt /silt/ *n* the earth, sand, etc, deposited by a moving river. • *vb* to block or become blocked with silt. • *adj* **silty**.

silver /sil-ver/ *n* **1** a precious metal of shining white colour. **2** coins, dishes, etc, made of silver. **3** (*old*) money. • *adj* made of silver. • *vb* to coat with silver. • *adj* **silvery 1** like silver. **2** clear in tone.

silver wedding /sil-ver wed-ding/ *n* the twentieth-fifth anniversary of a wedding.

silverware /sil-ver-ware/ *n* dishes and utensils made of silver.

simian /si-mee-an/ *adj* like a monkey or ape.

similar /si-mi-lar/ *adj* like, resembling.

similarity /si-mi-la-ri-tee/ *n* likeness, resemblance.

simile /si-mi-lee/ *n* a striking comparison of one thing with another.

simmer /si-mer/ *vb* to keep on boiling slowly without boiling over.

simper /sim-per/ *vb* to smile in a silly or insincere way. • *also n*.

simple /sim-pul/ *adj* **1** unmixed, without anything added, pure. **2** not complicated. **3** plain. **4** trusting, innocent, and inexperienced. **5** foolish, easily tricked. • *n* (*old*) a herb used as medicine.

simplicity /sim-pli-si-tee/ *n* **1** easiness. **2** sincerity. **3** plainness. **4** innocence.

simplification /sim-pli-fi-cay-shun/ *n* the act of making easier to do or understand.

simplify /sim-pli-fie/ vb to make easier to do or understand.

simply /sim-plee/ adv 1 in a clear way. 2 absolutely. 3 plain. 4 just, merely.

simulate /sim-yu-late/ vb (fml) to pretend. • n simulation.

simultaneous /si-mul-tay-nee-us/ adj taking place at the same time.

sin /sin/ n 1 a thought, word, or action that breaks the law of God. 2 a wicked act. • vb (sinned, sinning) 1 to do wrong. 2 to commit sin. • n sinner.

since /sinse/ prep from. • adv ago. • conj 1 from the time that. 2 because.

sincere /sin-seer/ adj real, genuine, meaning what is said, frank.

sincerity /sin-se-ri-tee/ n honesty of mind, genuineness.

sinew /sin-yoo/ n a tendon, a tough cordlike substance that joins muscle to bone; muscular power.

sinewy /sin-yoo-wee/ adj strong, tough.

sinful /sin-ful/ adj full of sin, wicked.

sing /sing/ vb (pt sang, pp sung) to make music with the voice, with or without words. • n singer.

singe /sinj/ vb to burn slightly, to burn the surface or ends of. • also n.

single /sing-gul/ adj 1 one only, alone. 2 unmarried. • vb to pick out one. • n a ticket for a journey from place to another, but not valid for the return journey.

single-handed /sing-gul-han-did/ adj 1 having only one hand. 2 using or needing the use of only one hand. 3 without help, done or working alone.

single-minded /sing-gul-mine-did/ adj concentrating on one main purpose.

singlet /sing-glet/ n a vest or similar garment.

singly /sing-glee/ adv one by one, one at a time.

singular /sing-gyu-lar/ adj 1 (fml) remarkable, unusual, odd, strange. 2 (in grammar) referring to one only.

singularity /sing-gyu-la-ri-tee/ n 1 peculiarity, strangeness. 2 an unusual feature.

singularly /sing-gyu-lar-lee/ adv (fml) strangely, remarkably.

sinister /si-ni-ster/ adj 1 evil looking. 2 threatening harm or evil.

sink /singk/ vb (pt sank, pp sunk) 1 to go slowly down. 2 to go below the surface of water. 3 to become worse or weaker. 4 (of an idea) to be understood gradually. 5 to dig. 6 to cause to go underwater. • n a basin with a drainpipe leading from it, used when washing.

sinker /sing-ker/ n a weight attached to a fishing line.

sinner /si-ner/ n a person who commits a sin.

sinus /sie-nus/ n a small hollow in a bone, especially that connecting the nose with the skull.

sip /sip/ vb (sipped, sipping) to drink in small mouthfuls. • also n.

siphon /sie-fun/ n, also **syphon** 1 a bent tube for drawing liquids out of one vessel into another. 2 a bottle of aerated water in which the liquid is forced out up a tube by the pressure of the gas.

sir /sur/ n 1 a word of respect used to men. 2 the title given to a knight or baronet.

sire /sire/ n 1 father. 2 male parent of a horse or other animal. 3 a title of respect used when addressing a king. • vb (of animals) to procreate.

siren /sie-run/ n 1 a mythical creature, half-woman, half-bird, who by the beauty of her song lured sailors to destruction. 2 an attractive but dangerous woman. 3 a loud horn sounded as a time signal or as a warning of danger.

sirloin /sir-loin/ n the upper part of a loin of beef.

sister /si-ster/ n 1 a girl or woman born of the same parents as another person. 2 nun. 3 a woman fellow member of the same race, church, profession, etc.

sisterhood /si-ster-hood/ n 1 the state of being sisters. 2 a society of women, usually carrying out religious or charitable works.

sister-in-law /si-ster-in-law/ n 1 the sister of a husband or wife. 2 the wife of a person's brother.

sisterly /si-ster-lee/ adj like a sister.

sit /sit/ vb (pt, pp sat; sitting) 1 to take a rest on a seat. 2 to rest upon eggs to hatch them. 3 (of government, courts, etc.) to meet to do business. 4 to rest upon. 5 to take an exam in. • sit up 1 to sit straight. 2 to stay out of bed when it is time to sleep.

sitar /si-tar/ n an Indian stringed instrument with a long neck and gourdlike bottom.

sit-down /sit-down/ n a strike in which the strikers stay inside a factory, etc, refusing to leave or to work.

site /site/ n the ground on which a building or number of buildings stands or is to stand. • vb to choose a place for.

sit-in /si-tin/ n a method of protesting against the government, a business, etc. in which people sit in a public place and refuse to leave.

sitter /si-ter/ n 1 a person who visits an artist to have his or her portrait done. 2 short for babysitter, a person who watches children while parents or guardians are away.

sitting /si-ting/ *n* **1** a single uninterrupted meeting. **2** a single visit to an artist doing one's portrait. **3** the act or position of one that sits.

sitting room /si-ting room/ *n* the room in which a family sits when not working; a living room.

situate /si-chu-wate/ *vb* to put in a certain place. • *adj* **situated** placed.

situation /si-chu-way-shun/ *n* **1** a place or position. **2** (*fml*) a job. **3** circumstances.

sit-up /si-tup/ *n* a stomach exercise in which a person lies flat on the back and rises to a sitting position without using the hands.

six /siks/ *adj* one more than five.

sixfold /siks-foald/ *adj* having six parts, having six times as much or as many.

sixteen /sik-steen/ *adj* six more than 10.

sixteenth /sik-steenth/ *adj* coming after 15 others.

sixth /siksth/ *adj* coming after five others.

sixtieth /sik-stee-ith/ *adj* coming after 59 others.

sixty /sik-stee/ *adj* the number between 59 and 61.

sizeable, sizable /sie-za-bul/ *adj* quite large or bulky.

size[1] /size/ *n* **1** bigness, bulk, the overall measurement of something. **2** a standard measurement for an item of clothing, etc. • *vb* to arrange in order according to size. • **size up** to form an opinion about.

size[2] /size/ *n* a thin glue used as a varnish on paper, cloth, etc.

sizzle /si-zul/ *vb* to make a hissing or spluttering sound, as when frying.

skate[1] /skate/ *n* a steel blade fastened to a boot to allow a gliding movement on ice. • *vb* to move on skates or roller skates.

skate[2] /skate/ *n* a large edible flatfish.

skateboard /skate-board/ *n* a short narrow board on small wheels on which a person stands and moves rapidly or performs jumps and stunts. • *n* **skateboarding**.

skating rink /skay-ting ringk/ *n* an area of ice prepared for skating.

skedaddle /ski-da-dul/ *vb* (*inf*) to run off or run away, to leave in a hurry.

skeleton /ske-le-tun/ *n* **1** the bony framework of a body. **2** an outline of a plot or plan. • **skeleton in the closet** something in a person's past life that he or she keeps secret for fear of disgrace.

skeleton key /ske-le-tun kee/ *n* a key that will open a number of different locks of a similar pattern.

skeleton staff /ske-le-tun staff/ *n* the least number of people needed to keep a factory, etc, working.

sketch /sketch/ *n* **1** a rough drawing or painting, sometimes to be finished later. **2** an outline or short account. **3** a short amusing play. • *vb* **1** to make a quick or rough drawing. **2** to give a short account or outline of; to draw.

sketchbook /sketch-book/ *n* a book of drawing paper for making sketches.

sketchy /sket-chee/ *adj* incomplete, leaving out details.

skew /skyoo/ *vb* to affect something in a way that makes it inaccurate, unfair, etc.

skewer /skyoo-ur/ *n* a wooden or metal pin for fastening meat in shape while cooking.

ski /skee/ *n* a long strip of wood, metal, etc, fixed to the feet to allow gliding movement over snow. • *n* **skier, skiing.** • *also vb* to glide over snow on skis.

skid /skid/ *n* **1** a sort of runner fixed to the under part of an aeroplane. **2** a sideways movement of a wheel on the ground. • *vb* (**skidded, skidding**) **1** to move sideways on wheels that fail to turn. **2** to stop turning by placing a block under (a wheel).

skill /skill/ *n* ability gained by practice; natural cleverness at doing something.

skilled /skild/ *adj* expert.

skilful /skil-ful/ *adj*, *also* **skillful** (*US*) expert, clever. • *adv* **skilfully,** *also* **skillfully** (*US*).

skim /skim/ *vb* (**skimmed, skimming**) **1** to remove anything floating on the surface of a liquid. **2** to pass quickly over the surface of. **3** to read quickly and without attention.

skimmed milk /skimd milk/ *n*, *also* **skim milk** (*US*) /skim milk/ milk from which the cream has been removed.

skimp /skimp/ *vb* to give less than is needed, to give or use sparingly.

skimpy /skim-pee/ *adj* barely or not quite enough.

skin /skin/ *n* **1** the natural outer covering of animals or vegetables. **2** a thin layer or covering. **3** a container made of skin. • *vb* (**skinned, skinning**) to take the skin off.

skinny /skin-ee/ *adj* (*inf*) very thin.

skintight /skin-tite/ *adj* clinging closely to the body.

skip[1] /skip/ *vb*. • *n* **1** a light jump. **2** a large open container for collecting and carrying away large, heavy items of waste, such as builders' rubbish.

skip[2] /skip/ *n* the captain of a curling or bowling team.

skipper /**skip**-er/ *n* the captain of a ship or team.

skirmish /**skir**-mish/ *n* **1** a fight in which the main armies are not engaged. **2** a short period of fighting or argument. • *vb* to fight in small parties.

skirt /skirt/ *n* **1** the part of a garment below the waist. **2** a woman's garment stretching from the waist down. **3** the border or outer edge. • *vb* to pass along the edge or border.

skirting board /**skirt**-ing bored/ *n* a long narrow piece of wood along the bottom of the wall of a room.

skit /skit/ *n* a piece of writing in which persons, events, etc, are imitated in a way that makes fun of them.

skittish /**skit**-ish/ *adj* easily excitable.

skive /skive/ *vb* to avoid work by staying away without permission or good reason. • *n* **skiving.**

skivvy /**skiv**-ee/ *n* a person who does all the unpleasant chores in a house.

skulk /skulk/ *vb* to try to keep out of sight for fear or with evil intentions.

skull /skull/ *n* the bony case that contains the brain.

skullcap /**skull**-cap/ *n* a light, close-fitting, brimless cap usually worn indoors.

skunk /skungk/ *n* **1** a black-and-white animal that sprays a bad-smelling fluid when attacked. **2** (*inf*) a mean or contemptible person.

sky /skie/ *n* the space around Earth as visible to our eyes.

sky blue /skie **bloo**/ *adj* light blue, azure.

sky dive /skie dive/ *vb* to jump from a plane and fall for as long as possible without opening a parachute.

skylark /**skie**-lark/ *n* a small bird that sings as it flies upward. • *vb* to play about noisily, to play tricks.

skylight /**skie**-lite/ *n* a window in the roof of a building.

skyline /**skie**-line/ *n* the horizon.

skyscraper /**skie**-scray-per/ *n* a very tall building.

skywards /**skie**-wurdz/ *adv* upward from the earth.

slab /slab/ *n* a large flat piece of anything.

slack[1] /slack/ *adj* **1** loose, not tight. **2** careless, lazy. **3** not busy. • *n* the loose part of a rope, etc. • *vb* **1** to work lazily or carelessly. **2** to lose speed.

slack[2] /slack/ *n* coal dust and tiny pieces of coal.

slacken /**sla**-ken/ *vb* **1** to loosen. **2** to lose force or speed. **3** to become less.

slacker /**sla**-ker/ *n* (*inf*) a person who does not work hard.

slackness /**slack**-ness/ *n* **1** looseness. **2** carelessness.

slacks /slacks/ *npl* loose-fitting trousers.

slain *pp of* **slain.**

slake /slake/ *vb* **1** to satisfy. **2** to mix lime with water.

slalom /**sla**-lum/ *n* a skiing race downhill over a zigzag course marked by poles.

slam /slam/ *vb* (**slammed, slamming**) to shut or put down noisily. • *n* a bang.

slander /**slan**-der/ *n* an untrue story written or said to injure a person's character. • *vb* to spread such a story.

slanderous /**slan**-druss/ *adj* harmful to the reputation.

slang /slang/ *n* words and phrases in common use but not accepted as good English.

slant /slant/ *n* slope. • *vb* **1** to slope or cause to slope. **2** to express or describe something in such a way as to emphasize a certain point or show favour towards a particular point of view.

slap /slap/ *n* a blow with the open hand. • *vb* (**slapped, slapping**) to strike with the flat of the hand or anything flat.

slapdash /**slap**-dash/ *adj* careless, done in a hurry. • *adv* carelessly.

slapstick /**slap**-stick/ *adj* causing laughter by silly actions, such as falling down or bumping into things. • *also n.*

slash /slash/ *vb* **1** to make a sweeping cut at with a knife, etc; to make long cuts in. **2** to reduce sharply. • *n* a long cut.

slat /slat/ *n* a thin strip of wood, etc.

slate[1] /slate/ *n* **1** a type of rock that splits easily into thin layers. **2** a shaped piece of slate for covering a roof or for writing on. • *vb* to cover with slate.

slate[2] /slate/ *vb* to criticize severely.

slaughter /**slaw**-ter/ *n* **1** killing in great numbers. **2** the act of killing. • *vb* **1** to kill in great numbers. **2** to kill for food.

slaughterhouse /**slaw**-ter-house/ *n* a place where animals are killed for food, an abattoir.

slave /slave/ *n* **1** a person who is the property of another person and has to work for him or her. **2** a person who has to do the dirty or unpleasant work. • *vb* to work very hard.

slavery /**slave**-vu-ree/ *n* **1** the state of being a slave, the owning or keeping of slaves as a practice. **2** hard, unpleasant, and badly paid work. **3** lack of all freedom.

slave trade /**slave** trade/ *n* the buying and selling of people as slaves.

slay /slay/ *vb* (*pt* **slew,** *pp* **slain**) to kill.

sleazy /slee-zee/ adj shoddy, shabby, morally low. • n **sleaze**.

sledge /sledge/ n, also **sled** (US) a vehicle on runners for use in the snow. • vb to ride on a sledge, to carry on a sledge. • n **sledging** riding or carrying on a sledge.

sledgehammer /sledge-ha-mer/ n a long-handled, heavy hammer usually held with two hands.

sleek /sleek/ adj 1 smooth and shiny. 2 well-fed and cared for.

sleep /sleep/ vb, (pt, pp **slept**) to rest the body, with the eyes shut, unaware of the surroundings. • n a complete rest for the body, as at night. • adv **sleepily** in a drowsy, sleepy manner.

sleeper /slee-per/ n 1 a person or animal who is asleep. 2 a long rectangular block that supports railway lines. 3 a coach on a train with bunks for sleeping passengers.

sleeping bag /slee-ping bag/ n a large, warmly lined, zippered bag in which a person can sleep, especially outdoors.

sleeping pill /slee-ping pill/ n a drug that makes a person sleepy and drowsy, so as to help him or her to sleep.

sleepless /sleep-less/ adj 1 unable to sleep. 2 without sleep.

sleepover /sleep-oa-ver/ n (inf) 1 a party where (usually) children spend the night at a place other than home. 2 a night spent by children at someone else's house.

sleepwalker /sleep-waw-ker/ n a person who walks about in his or her sleep. • vb **sleepwalking**.

sleepy /slee-pee/ adj wanting to sleep, drowsy.

sleet /sleet/ n falling snow mixed with rain or hail. • adj **sleety**.

sleeve /sleev/ n 1 the part of a garment that covers the arm. 2 a tube or tubelike part fitting over or around another part. 3 a thin paper or plastic cover for protecting something.

sleigh /slay/ n a vehicle on runners for use in snow, a sledge.

sleight /slite/ n cunning or craft used to trick.

sleight of hand /slite ov hand/ n quickness with the hands, jugglery.

slender /slen-der/ adj 1 slim. 2 thin, scanty, only just enough.

slept pt and pp of **sleep**.

sleuth /slooth/ n a detective.

slew[1] /sloo/ n a large number, a group.

slew[2] /sloo/ pt of **slay**.

slice /slice/ vb 1 to cut into thin pieces. 2 to strike a ball in a glancing blow that makes it spin. • n 1 a thin, broad piece cut off. 2 a flat utensil for serving food.

slick /slick/ adj 1 quick and clever. 2 smart but not trustworthy.

slide /slide/ vb (pt, pp **slid**) 1 to move smoothly over a surface, as of ice, to slip. 2 to become gradually lower or worse. • n 1 a slope or track for sliding on. 2 a small glass plate with an object to be examined through a microscope or a picture to be shown on a screen.

slight /slite/ adj 1 small, lightly built. 2 small, not great, not serious. • n an insult. • vb to treat as unimportant, to treat insultingly. • adj **slighting**.

slim /slim/ adj 1 thin in an attractive way, lightly built. 2 slight, small. • vb (**slimmed**, **slimming**) to reduce weight by exercises, not eating certain foods, etc.

slime /slime/ n any soft, moist, slippery, sometimes sticky matter.

slimy /slie-mee/ adj 1 covered with slime, slippery. 2 untrustworthy.

sling /sling/ vb (pt, pp **slung**) 1 to throw with the outstretched arm. 2 to cause to hang from. • n 1 a strap or band used for hurling stones. 2 a bandage hanging from the neck to support an injured arm. 3 a band passed around something to help to lift or support it.

slink /slingk/ vb (pt, pp **slunk**) to go away quietly as if ashamed.

slinky /sling-kee/ adj of a dress, close-fitting so that it shows off the figure.

slip /slip/ vb (**slipped**, **slipping**) 1 to move smoothly along. 2 to go quietly unseen. 3 to lose footing. 4 to escape (the memory). • n 1 the act of slipping. 2 a careless mistake. 3 a narrow piece of paper. 4 a twig. 5 a loose cover (e.g. a pillowcase). 6 a woman's undergarment or petticoat. 7 a prepared downward slope along which ships can slide into the sea. • **give the slip to** to go away from without being noticed.

slipcase /slip-case/ n a boxlike container for a book or set of books, open at one end to show the spine(s) of the book(s).

slipcover /slip-cu-ver/ n a removable, fitted cloth cover for a chair, sofa, etc.

slipknot /slip-not/ n a knot that can be moved.

slippage /sli-pidge/ n the act of slipping, the amount of slipping.

slipper /sli-per/ n a loose shoe for wearing in the house.

slippery /sli-pree/ adj 1 hard to stand on without sliding or falling. 2 hard to hold without the grip sliding. 3 (inf) untrustworthy.

slipshod /slip-shod/ adj careless, untidy.

slit /slit/ vb (**slitted**, **slitting**) to make a long cut in. • *n* a long narrow cut or opening.

slither /sli-ther/ *vb* to slide clumsily or without control, to slip or slide on.

sliver /sli-ver/ *n* a thin piece cut off, a splinter.

slob /slob/ *n* a lazy, untidy person.

slobber /slob-er/ *vb* to let saliva run or fall from the mouth.

slog /slog/ *vb* (**slogged, slogging**) **1** to hit hard. **2** to work hard. • *n* **slogger**.

slogan /slo-gan/ *n* **1** a war cry. **2** a party cry or catchword. **3** an easily memorized saying used to advertise a product or campaign.

sloop /sloop/ *n* a small sailing boat with one mast.

slop /slop/ *vb* (**slopped, slopping**) to spill through, carelessness; to overflow a little at a time. • *n* **1** a puddle of spilled liquid. **2** (*usually pl*) dirty or waste water. **3** (*usually pl*) liquid food.

slope /slope/ *n* **1** a rise or fall from the level. **2** a slant. • *vb* **1** to rise or fall from the level. **2** to slant.

sloppy /slop-ee/ *adj* (*inf*) **1** wet, muddy. **2** careless and untidy. **2** foolishly sentimental.

slosh /slosh/ *vb* to shake a liquid; to apply a liquid; to splash through water.

slot /slot/ *n* a narrow opening or hole, especially one made to receive coins.

sloth /slawth/ *n* **1** laziness. **2** a slow-moving South American animal that lives in trees.

slothful /slawth-ful/ *adj* very lazy.

slouch /slouch/ *vb* to stand, walk, or sit with bent back and head and shoulders sloping inward. • *n* a lazy, unhealthy, and improper way of standing and walking. • *adj* **slouchy**.

slough /sluf/ *n* the cast-off skin of a snake. • *vb* **1** to cast off. **2** to throw off.

slovenly /slu-ven-lee/ *adj* dirty and untidy, very careless.

slow /sloa/ *adj* **1** not quick or fast. **2** taking a long time to do things. **3** not clever. **4** behind the correct time. • *vb* to go or cause to go less quickly.

sludge /sludge/ *n* soft, thick mud.

slug[1] /slug/ *n* a shell-less snail that is harmful to plants.

slug[2] /slug/ *vb* (**slugged, slugging**) **1** to shoot. **2** to hit hard. • *n* a small solid metal bullet.

sluggish /slu-gish/ *adj* slow-moving.

slum /slum/ *n* part of a town in which poor people live in overcrowded, dirty, and unhealthy houses.

slumber /slum-ber/ *vb* to sleep. • *n* sleep.

slump /slump/ *n* a sudden fall in prices, wages, etc. • *vb* **1** to go suddenly down in price, etc. **2** to fall suddenly or heavily.

slung *pt and pp of* **sling**.

slunk *pt and pp of* **slink**.

slur /slur/ *vb* (**slurred, slurring**) **1** to pass over quickly or without attention. **2** to make (sounds) unclear by running them together. • *n* **1** a bad point in a person's character or reputation. **2** (*mus*) a curved mark over two or more notes to be played smoothly one after the other.

slurp /slurp/ *vb* to drink or eat noisily.

slush /slush/ *n* **1** half-melted snow. **2** (*inf*) foolishly sentimental writing or talk. • *adj* **slushy**.

sly /slie/ *adj* cunning, tricky, doing things in a secret and untrustworthy way. • **on the sly** secretly.

smack[1] /smack/ *vb* **1** to hit with the flat of the hand. **2** to part the lips so as to make a sharp noise. • *n* **1** a slap. **2** a loud kiss.

smack[2] /smack/ *n* a taste, a flavour or suggestion of. • *vb* **1** to taste. **2** to remind of, to suggest.

smack[3] /smack/ *n* a small fishing boat with sails.

small /smawl/ *adj* **1** little. **2** not much. • *n* the lower part of the back.

small intestine /small in-**tess**-tin/ *n* the part of the digestive system where nutrients are absorbed from food and passed into the bloodstream.

smallpox /**smawl**-poks/ *n* a dangerous infectious disease that leaves little pocks on the skin.

small talk /smawl tok/ *n* conversation about unimportant matters.

smart /smart/ *adj* **1** quick, clever. **2** well-dressed. • *vb* to feel or cause a quick keen pain.

smarten /smar-ten/ *vb* to make smart or smarter.

smash /smash/ *vb* to break into pieces. • *n* **1** act of breaking into pieces. **2** the noise caused by breakage. **3** an accident involving one or more vehicles. **4** a disaster, downfall. • **smash and grab** a theft carried out by smashing a shop window and taking articles behind it.

smear /smeer/ *vb* **1** to spread. **2** to smudge, to make or become blurred. • *n* **1** a dirty mark, a blot. **2** a story intended to harm a person's good name. • *adj* **smeary**.

smell /smell/ *n* **1** the sense that enables animals to become aware of by breathing in through the nose. **2** scent, odour. • *vb* (*pt, pp* **smelled**) **1** to perceive by smell. **2** to give off an odour. • **smell a rat** to be suspicious.

smelly /smel-ee/ *adj* having an unpleasant odour.

smelt[1] /smelt/ *vb* to melt metal out of rock. • *n* **smelter**.

smelt² /smelt/ *n* a small edible fish of the salmon family.

smile /smile/ *vb* 1 to show joy, amusement, etc, by an upward movement of the lips. 2 to be favourable. • *n* a look of pleasure or amusement. • *adj* smiley.

smirk /smurk/ *vb* to smile in a silly or unnatural manner. • *n* a smug or scornful smile.

smite /smite/ *vb* (*pt* smote, smiting; *pp* smitten) (*old or fml*) 1 to strike hard. 2 to cause to suffer from.

smith /smith/ *n* a craftsperson who works in metals.

smock /smock/ *n* 1 a loose overall worn to protect a person's clothes. 2 a woman's loose dress.

smog /smog/ *n* a smoky fog, pollution.

smoke /smoke/ *n* the sooty vapour rising from a burning substance. • *vb* 1 to give off smoke. 2 to draw in the tobacco smoke from a cigarette, pipe, etc. 3 to preserve in smoke. 4 to drive out by smoke. • *adj* smoky.

smoker /smo-ker/ *n* a person who smokes tobacco.

smoke screen /smoke screen/ *n* 1 thick clouds of smoke sent out to conceal movements. 2 something intended to conceal activities.

smokestack /smoke-stack/ *n* the chimney of a steamer or factory.

smote *pt of* smite.

smoulder /smole-der/ *vb, also* smolder (*US*) to burn and smoke without flame.

smooth /smooth/ *adj* 1 having an even surface, not rough. 2 free from difficulties. 3 having good yet not pleasing manners. • *vb* to make smooth or level.

smooth-tongued /smooth-tungd/ *adj* able to speak in a very polite or flattering manner.

smother /smu-ther/ *vb* to kill by keeping air from.

smudge /smudge/ *n* a dirty mark, a stain. • *vb* 1 to make a dirty mark on. 2 to make or become blurred or smeared. • *adj* smudgy.

smug /smug/ *n* self-satisfied, too pleased with oneself.

smuggle /smu-gul/ *vb* 1 to bring goods into the country secretly, without paying customs duties on them. 2 to bring in or pass secretly.

smuggler /smu-gler/ *n* a person who smuggles goods.

smut /smut/ *n* 1 a flake of soot. 2 a dirty mark or stain. 3 dirty or indecent talk. • *adj* smutty.

snack /snack/ *n* something small, such as a piece of fruit or biscuit, eaten between meals. • *vb* to eat between meals.

snag *n* an unexpected difficulty. • *vb* to damage or tear something by getting it caught on something sharp.

snail /snail/ *n* a slow-moving soft-bodied creature with a shell on its back.

snail mail /snail mail/ *n* the ordinary postal service, as opposed to email.

snake /snake/ *n* 1 a long creature that slithers along the ground with no legs and a scaly skin, a serpent. 2 an untrustworthy or deceitful person.

snap /snap/ *vb* (snapped, snapping) 1 to bite or seize suddenly. 2 to break with a sharp sound. 3 to speak in a quick, angry manner. 4 to take a photograph of with a hand camera. • *n* 1 a sudden bite. 2 a short, sharp sound. 3 a lock that springs shut when released. 4 a spell of weather. 5 a card game. 6 a snapshot.

snapdragon /snap dra-gun/ *n* a plant with a showy white, yellow, red, or purple flower.

snappish /sna-pish/ *adj* irritable, short-tempered.

snappy /sna-pee/ *adj* 1 snappish. 2 (*inf*) quick.

snapshot /snap-shot/ *n* 1 a quick shot. 2 a photograph taken with a hand camera.

snare /snare/ *n* 1 a kind of musical drum. 2 a trap for catching birds or animals, especially one made with a running noose. 3 a temptation. • *vb* to catch by a snare.

snarl /snarl/ *vb* 1 to growl angrily and show the teeth. 2 to speak rudely or angrily. • *also n*.

snatch /snatch/ *vb* to seize quickly or suddenly. • *n* 1 a sudden seizing. 2 a small part.

sneak /sneek/ *vb* 1 to go quietly, as a thief. 2 to take secretly and often dishonestly or illegally. 3 to tell of another's wrongdoing to a person in authority. • *n* a tell-tale.

sneaking /snee-king/ *adj* secret.

sneaky /snee-kee/ *adj* doing things in a secret, underhand way.

sneer /sneer/ *vb* to show scorn by a look or remark. • *n* a mocking smile or remark.

sneeze /sneez/ *vb* to expel air noisily through the nose and mouth in a sudden, explosive action. • *n* the act or sound of sneezing.

snicker /sni-ker/ *vb* to laugh under the breath or secretly, to giggle nervously or unpleasantly. • *also n*.

snide /snide/ *adj* cutting, slyly mean, nasty.

sniff /sniff/ *vb* 1 to breathe noisily inward. 2 to smell. • *n* 1 the act or sound of sniffing. 2 a slight smell. • sniff at to show scorn for.

sniffle /sni-ful/ *vb* to sniff repeatedly, as when a person has a cold or the flu. • *n* the sniffles a cold.

snigger /sni-ger/ same as **snicker**.

snip /snip/ vb (**snipped, snipping**) to cut as with scissors, to cut off with one sharp movement. • n **1** the act or sound of scissors closing to cut. **2** a small piece cut off. **3** (inf) a bargain.

snipe[1] /snipe/ n a game bird with a long bill, found in marshy places.

snipe[2] /snipe/ vb to shoot at from a hiding place. • n **sniper**.

snippet /sni-pit/ n **1** a small piece cut off. **2** a short item of news.

snivel /sni-vul/ vb (**snivelled, snivelling**) **1** to run at the nose. **2** to go on crying or complaining, to whimper.

snob /snob/ n a person who looks down on others because they are less wealthy or of lower rank in society. • n **snobbery**. • adj **snobby**.

snobbish /snob-ish/ adj behaving like a snob.

snooker /snoo-ker/ n a billiards game in which players have to knock, with a white cue ball, 15 red and then, in order, six coloured balls into pockets on a table.

snoop /snoop/ vb to go about secretly or stealthily to find out something. • n **snooper**.

snooty /snoo-tee/ adj (inf) haughty, proud, distant in manner.

snooze /snooz/ n (inf) a short, light sleep. • vb to take a short nap.

snore /snore/ vb to breathe noisily while asleep, as if grunting. • n the noise so made.

snorkel /snawr-kul/ n a tube that extends above the water through which a person can breathe while swimming just below the surface of the water.

snort /snawrt/ vb to blow air out noisily through the nose. • also n.

snot /snot/ n (inf) the mucus of the nose.

snout /snout/ n **1** the long nose and mouth of an animal. **2** the nozzle of a pipe.

snow /sno/ n vapour frozen in the air and falling in flakes. • vb to fall as snow, to cover as with snow. • adj **snowy**.

snowball /sno-bawl/ n snow pressed into a hard ball.

snowboard /sno-board/ n a long, wide board with bindings for the feet on which people slide down slopes. • n **snowboarding**.

snowdrift /sno-drift/ n snow heaped up by the wind to form a bank.

snowdrop /sno-drop/ n a small white flower that grows in early spring.

snowfall /sno-fawl/ n a falling of snow.

snowflake /sno-flake/ n a single piece of snow.

snow line /sno-line/ n the level above which snow never melts.

snowplough /sno-plow/ n, also **snowplow** (US) an implement for clearing snow from roads or railways.

snowshoe /sno-shoo/ n a light, broad frame worn on the feet for walking on snow.

snub /snub/ vb (**snubbed, snubbing**) to show dislike or disapproval of a person by taking no notice of or speaking rudely to him or her. • n rude lack of notice, an unfriendly act or speech. • adj (of a nose) short and turned up.

snuff[1] /snuff/ vb to sniff powdered tobacco, etc, up the nose. • n tobacco powdered for sniffing up the nose.

snuff[2] /snuff/ vb **1** to cut off the burnt part of the wick of a candle, to put out a candle. **2** to put an end to something. • n **snuffer** a tool used to put out a candle.

snuffbox /snuff-boks/ n a box for carrying snuff in the pocket.

snuffle /snu-ful/ vb to breathe noisily through your nose, making sniffing noises.

snug /snug/ adj warm and comfortable, cosy.

snuggle /snu-gul/ vb to lie close for warmth, to settle comfortably.

so /so/ adv **1** in this or that manner. **2** to that extent. **3** thus. **4** very. • conj therefore.

soak /soak/ vb **1** to wet thoroughly. **2** to steep. **3** to suck up.

soap /soap/ n **1** a substance made of oil or fat and certain chemicals, used in washing. **2** a **soap opera**. • vb to rub with soap. • adj **soapy** having to do with or containing soap.

soapbox /soap-boks/ n **1** a box or crate for soap. **2** a platform used by a person making an informal speech to people on the street.

soap opera /soap op-ra/ n a radio or television drama serial that deals with the day-to-day lives and problems of the same group of characters.

soar /soar/ vb **1** to fly upward. **2** to tower up.

sob /sob/ vb (**sobbed, sobbing**) to draw in the breath noisily when weeping or short of breath. • also n.

sober /so-ber/ adj **1** not drunk. **2** serious, quiet. **3** dark in colour.

sobriety /so-brie-i-tee/ n the state of being sober.

so-called /so-cawld/ adj given a name or title to which a person has no right.

soccer /sock-er/ n a game played with a round ball by two teams of 11 players on a field with a goal at either end, the ball being moved by kicking; football.

sociable /so-sha-bul/ adj fond of company.

social /so-shal/ *adj* **1** having to do with society. **2** living in an organized group.

socialism /so-sha-li-zum/ *n* the belief that all means of producing national wealth (e.g. mines, etc.) are the property of the community and should be used for the benefit of all.

socialist /soe-sha-list/ *n* a person who believes in socialism.

social science /so-shal sie-inss/ *n* the study of people living together in groups, families, etc.

social security /so-shul si-cure-i-tee/ *n* a government programme that pays money to people who are not working or who are unable to work.

social work /so-shal wurk/ *n* (*sometimes cap*) any service designed to improve the welfare of the community and the individual through various services.

society /suh-sie-u-tee/ *n* **1** a group of people living together in a single organized community. **2** a group of people who meet regularly for a special purpose, mixing with other people. **3** the wealthy or high-ranking members of a community.

sociology /so-see-ol-u-jee/ *n* the study of the nature, growth, and problems of human society. • *n* **sociologist**. • *adj* **sociological**.

sock /sock/ *n* a short stocking, a cloth covering of the foot.

socket /sock-it/ *n* a hole or hollow for something to fit into or turn in.

sod /sod/ *n* a piece of earth held together by the roots of the grass growing in it.

soda /so-da/ *n* **1** a powder used in washing, baking, etc. **2** soda water.

soda water /so-da wa-ter/ *n* water containing soda and made fizzy by gas.

sodden /sod-en/ *adj* wet through, soaking.

sodium /so-dee-um/ *n* an element found in salt, with the chemical symbol Na.

sofa /so-fa/ *n* a couch with a cushioned seat, back, and arms.

sofa bed /so-fa-bed/ *n* a sofa that can be opened into a bed.

soft /soft/ *adj* **1** not hard. **2** easily reshaped by pressing. **3** not loud. **4** (*of colour*) not bright. **5** gentle. **6** not strict. **7** not alcoholic. **8** foolishly kind. • *adv* quietly, gently.

soft drink /soft drink/ *a* non-alcoholic drink, such as lemonade or cola.

soften /sawf-en/ *vb* **1** to make or become soft. **2** to become less harsh or angry. • *n* **softener** something that softens.

software /soft-ware/ *n* the programs used in computers.

soggy /sog-ee/ *adj* soft and wet.

soil /soil/ *n* the ground, earth, especially that in which plants are grown. • *vb* to dirty, to spoil.

solace /sol-iss/ *vb* to cheer, to comfort. • *n* that which gives cheer or comfort.

solar /so-lar/ *adj* having to do with the sun.

solarium /su-lay-ree-um/ *n* a glassed-in porch, roof, etc, where people sun themselves, as in treating illness.

solar system /so-lar sis-tem/ *n* the sun and the planets that move around it.

sold /soald/ *pt and pp of* **sell**.

solder /sole-dur/ *n* a metal alloy that when melted can be used for cementing together pieces of metal. • *vb* to join with solder.

soldier /sole-jur/ *n* a person serving in an army. • *n* **soldiery** a group of soldiers, the profession of being a soldier.

sole[1] /sole/ *n* the underside of the foot, stocking, or shoe. • *vb* to put a sole on.

sole[2] /sole/ *n* a small flatfish.

sole[3] /sole/ *adj* only, single. • *adv* **solely**.

solemn /sol-um/ *adj* **1** serious in manner or appearance. **2** slow, stately.

solemnity /su-lem-ni-tee/ *n* seriousness.

sol-fa /sole-fa/ *n* the use of the sounds *doh, ray, me, fah, soh, lah, te* in singing the scale. • *also adj*.

solicit /su-li-sit/ *vb* to ask earnestly or repeatedly. • *n* **solicitation**.

solid /sol-id/ *adj* **1** not hollow, consisting of hard matter throughout. **2** not liquid or gaseous. **3** firm. **4** reliable. • *n* a body consisting of hard matter throughout.

solidarity /sol-i-da-ri-tee/ *n* sameness of interests, complete unity.

solidify /su-li-di-fie/ *vb* to make or become solid.

soliloquy /su-li-lu-kwee/ *n* (*fml*) a speaking to oneself.

solitaire /sol-i-tair/ *n* **1** a single diamond or other gem set by itself in a ring. **2** a game of cards for one player, patience.

solitary /sol-i-tree/ *adj* **1** alone, without companions. **2** living or being alone by habit or preference. **3** single. • *n* a person who lives alone and away from others.

solitude /sol-i-tyood/ *n* loneliness, being alone, a lonely place.

solo /so-lo/ *n* **1** a piece of music for a single performer. **2** a performance by one person. **3** a single person's unaccompanied flight in an aeroplane. • *adv* unaccompanied, alone.

soloist /so-lo-ist/ *n* a solo singer or performer.

solstice /sol-stiss/ *n* the time when the sun is farthest north (June 21) or south (December 21), giving in the Northern Hemisphere the longest and shortest days, respectively.

soluble /sol-yu-bul/ *adj* **1** able to be melted or dissolved in liquid. **2** (*fml*) to which an answer or solution can be found. • *n* **solubility**.

solution /su-loo-shun/ *n* **1** a liquid containing another substance dissolved in it. **2** the answer to or explanation of a problem, etc.

solvable /sol-va-bul/ *adj* that can be solved.

solve /solv/ *vb* to find the right answer to or explanation of.

solvent /sol-vent/ *adj* **1** able to pay your debts. **2** able to dissolve. • *n* a liquid able to dissolve another substance.

sombre /som-bur/ *adj*, *also* **somber** (*US*) dark, gloomy, cheerless.

sombrero /sum-bre-ro/ *n* a broad-brimmed felt or straw hat.

some /sum/ *adj* a certain number or amount. • *pron* **1** certain people. **2** a little. • *n and pron* **someone, something**.

somebody /sum-bod-ee/ *n and pron* **1** some person. **2** a person of importance.

somehow /sum-how/ *adv* in some way or other.

somersault /su-mer-sawlt/ *n* a leap or roll in which the heels turn completely over the head.

sometime /sum-time/ *adj* (*fml*) former.

sometimes /sum-tiemz/ *adv* now and then.

somewhat /sum-what/ *adv* in some degree, a little.

somewhere /sum-whare/ *adv* in some place.

son /sun/ *n* a male child.

sonar /so-nar/ *n* a machine that finds objects underwater by reflecting sound waves.

sonata /su-na-ta/ *n* a piece of music in several movements, usually for a solo instrument.

song /song/ *n* **1** words set to music for the voice. **2** the sounds uttered by a bird. **3** a short poem, poetry.

songbird /song-burd/ *n* a bird that sings or a woman who sings.

songbook /song-book/ *n* a book containing a collection of songs, both the words and the notes.

sonic /son-ic/ *adj* of or having to do with sound.

son-in-law /sun-in-law/ *n* the man married to a person's daughter.

sonnet /son-et/ *n* a poem of 14 lines, usually following fixed rhyming patterns. • *n* **sonneteer** a person who writes sonnets.

soon /soon/ *adv* **1** in a short time. **2** early. **3** willingly.

soot /soot/ *n* black particles that rise with the smoke from burning matter.

sooth /sooth/ *adj* true or real, fact.

soothe /soothe/ *vb* to calm, to comfort.

sooty /soo-tee/ *adj* **1** like soot. **2** black.

sophisticated /su-fi-sti-cay-tid/ *adj* **1** (*fml*) not natural, complicated. **2** having a great deal of experience and wordly wisdom, knowledge of how to dress elegantly, etc. • *n* **sophistication**. • *vb* **sophisticate**.

soporific /sop-u-rif-ic/ *adj* (*fml*) causing sleep. • *n* a drug that causes sleep.

soppy /sop-ee/ *adj* foolishly sentimental.

soprano /su-pran-o/ *n* **1** the highest female or boy's singing voice. **2** a singer with such a voice.

sorbet /sawr-bay/ *n* a tart ice, as of fruit juice, served as a dessert or sometimes between meals.

sorcerer /sore-su-rer/ *n* a person who works magic. • *f* **sorceress**.

sorcery /sore-su-ree/ *n* magic, witchcraft.

sordid /sawr-did/ *adj* mean, dirty, disgusting.

sore /sore/ *adj* painful, hurtful. • *n* a painful cut or growth on the body.

sorely /sore-lee/ *adv* **1** very much. **2** painfully.

sorority /su-raw-ri-tee/ *n* a group of women or girls joined together by common interests, for fellowship, etc.

sorrel /saw-rel/ *n* **1** a plant with sour-tasting leaves. **2** a reddish brown colour. **3** a horse of that colour.

sorrow /sor-o/ *n* sadness caused by loss or suffering, grief. • *vb* to mourn, to grieve. • *adj* **sorrowful**.

sorry /sor-ee/ *adj* **1** feeling pity or regret, sad because of wrongdoing. **2** wretched.

sort /sawrt/ *n* a kind, class, or set. • *vb* to arrange in classes or sets. • **out of sorts** not well.

soufflé /soo-flay/ *n* a light dish made from beaten egg whites.

sought /sawt/ *pt and pp of* **seek**.

soul /sole/ *n* **1** the spiritual part of a person. **2** (*inf*) a person. **3** a kind of rhythm-and-blues music.

soulful /sole-ful/ *adj* full of feeling.

soulless /sole-less/ *adj* **1** without soul; without spirit. **2** mean-spirited.

soul mate /sole-mate/ *n* a person with whom a person has a deeply personal relationship.

sound[1] /sound/ *adj* **1** healthy. **2** strong. **3** without serious error or weakness. • *adv* completely.

sound[2] /sound/ *n* **1** a noise. **2** that which is heard. • *vb* **1** to make a noise. **2** to touch or strike so as to cause a noise.

sound[3] /sound/ *n* a long narrow piece of water between two land masses, a strait. • *vb* **1** to find depth by lowering a lead weight on a cord. **2** to try to discover someone's opinion by questioning.

soundproof /**sound**-proof/ *adj* that keeps sound from coming through.

soundtrack /**sound**-track/ *n* the part of a film on which sounds are recorded.

sound wave /**sound** wave/ *n* a vibration that carries a sound through a substance, for example, the air.

soup /**soop**/ *n* a liquid food made by boiling meat, vegetables, etc. together. • *adj* **soupy**.

sour /**sour**/ *adj* 1 sharp or bitter in taste. 2 ill-tempered and hard to please. • *vb* to make sour.

source /**soarss**/ *n* 1 that from which anything begins. 2 the spring from which a river flows. 3 origin or cause.

sousaphone /**soo**-za-foan/ *n* a brass instrument of the tuba family.

south /**south**/ *n* 1 one of the points of the compass, opposite north. • *adj* being in the south, facing south. • *also adv.* • *adj and adv* **southward**, **southbound**.

southeast /**sou**-theest/ *n* the point midway between south and east. • *also adj.* • *adj* **southeasterly**, **southeastern**, **southeastward**.

southerly /**su**-ther-lee/ *adj* lying towards or coming from the south.

southern /**su**-thern/ *adj* in or of the south. • *n* **Southerner** a person living in or coming from the South.

Southern Hemisphere /**su**-thern **hem**-iss-feer/ *n* the half of the earth south of the equator.

southernmost /**su**-thern-moast/ *adj* farthest south.

South Pole /**south pole**/ *n* the place on Earth that is the absolutely farthest south.

southwest /**south**-west/ *n* the point midway between south and west. • *also adj.* • *adj* **southwesterly**, **southwestern**, **southwestward**.

souvenir /**soo**-vin-ir/ *n* an object kept to remind a person of another person or past event.

sovereign /**sov**-rin/ *adj* above all others, chief. • *n* ruler, a king or queen.

sovereignty /**sov**-rin-tee/ *n* supreme power.

sow[1] /**sou**/ *n* a female pig.

sow[2] /**soe**/ *vb* (*pp* **sown**) 1 to scatter. 2 to plant with seeds.

soya bean /**soy**-uh been/ *n*, *also* **soybean** /**soy**-been/ (*US*) a type of bean used for making flour or oil, as fodder for cattle, and in food that is free of meat or dairy products, such as **soya milk** /**soy**-uh milk/.

soy sauce /**soy** sawss/ *n* a dark, salty sauce made from soya beans and generally used in Chinese and Japanese dishes.

spa /**spa**/ *n* 1 a place at which natural mineral waters may be drunk or bathed in for better health, a health resort at a mineral spring. 2 a place where people go for health and beauty treatments.

space /**space**/ *n* 1 the whole extent of the universe not occupied by solid bodies. 2 the distance between one body or object and another. 3 the place occupied by a person or thing. 4 a length of time. • *vb* to arrange with intervals between.

spacecraft /**space**-craft/ *n* a vehicle used for space travel.

spaceship /**space**-ship/ *n* a spacecraft in which people travel.

spacing /**spay**-sing/ *n* the arrangement of spaces.

spacious /**spay**-shus/ *adj* roomy, having or giving more than enough room.

spade /**spade**/ *n* 1 a tool with a broad blade, used for digging. 2 *pl* a suit of playing cards. • **call a spade a spade** to say exactly what a person thinks.

spadework /**spade**-wurk/ *n* the hard work needed to start an enterprise.

spaghetti /spa-**ge**-tee/ *n* long thin strings of pasta.

spam /**spam**/ *n* 1 a kind of tinned meat product, containing ham. 2 unsolicited, and often unwanted, email or text messages.

span /**span**/ *n* 1 the distance between the tip of the thumb and the little finger fully extended. 2 the spread of an arch. 3 the distance from end to end of a bridge. 4 a space of time. 5 a number of horses or oxen yoked together to draw a cart, etc. • *vb* (**spanned**, **spanning**) 1 to extend from one point in space or time to another. 2 to measure with outstretched fingers.

spangle /**spang**-gul/ *n* a small, glittering metal ornament.

spaniel /**span**-yul/ *n* a sporting or pet dog with long silky hair and drooping ears.

Spanish *n* the language of Spain, Mexico and countries of South and Central America • *adj* relating to Spain, the country, the language and the people.

spank /**spangk**/ *vb* 1 to slap with the hand. 2 to move along quickly.

spanner /**span**-ner/ *n* a tool fitted to the head of a nut and used for tightening or loosening it.

spar[1] /**spar**/ *n* 1 a long piece of wood. 2 a pole attached to the mast, used for holding sails in position.

spar[2] /**spar**/ *vb* (**sparred**, **sparring**) to box, to fight with the fists, to argue.

spare /spare/ *adj* **1** scarce. **2** thin. **3** more than is needed, kept in reserve. • *vb* **1** to let off punishment or suffering, to show mercy to. **2** to do without. **3** to use up slowly and carefully. • *n* an item kept in case another like it gets broken, lost, etc.

spare ribs /spare ribz/ *n* a cut of meat, especially pork, consisting of the thin end of the ribs with most of the meat cut away.

spark /spark/ *n* **1** a tiny piece of burning matter. **2** a tiny flash made by electricity passing from one wire to another. **3** a small amount of something. • *vb* to give off sparks. • *adj* **sparky**.

sparkle /spar-kul/ *vb* **1** to throw off sparks, to gleam or shine in flashes, to glitter or glisten. **2** to be lively and intelligent. • *also n*. • *n* **sparkler 1** someone or something that sparkles. **2** a kind of hand-held firework.

spark plug /spark plug/ a device for causing an electric spark to ignite the gas that drives an engine.

sparrow /spa-ro/ *n* a common small bird.

sparse /sparse/ *adj* **1** thinly scattered. **2** scanty, scarcely enough. • *n* **sparsity**.

spasm /spa-zum/ *n* **1** a sudden movement of the body not done on purpose, caused by a tightening of muscles, as in a cramp; a fit. **2** a feeling or activity that does not last long.

spasmodic /spaz-**mod**-ic/ *adj* done occasionally for short periods.

spat /spat/ *n* a brief, petty quarrel.

spatial /spay-shal/ *adj* (*fml*) having to do with space.

spatter /spa-ter/ *vb* to throw or scatter.

spatula /spa-chu-la/ *n* a broad thin blade used in spreading or scraping plaster, paint, ointment, food, etc.

spawn /spawn/ *n* the eggs of fish, frogs, etc. • *vb* **1** to produce spawn. **2** to produce, usually in large numbers.

speak /speek/ *vb* (*pt* spoke, *pp* spoken) **1** to utter words, to talk. **2** to make a speech. **3** to pronounce.

speaker /spee-ker/ *n* **1** a person who speaks. **2** an official who controls debates and discussion in parliament. **3** loudspeaker.

spear /speer/ *n* a weapon with a long straight handle and a pointed metal head. • *vb* to pierce with a spear.

spearhead /speer-hed/ *n* **1** the pointed head of a spear. **2** the leading person in a military attack.

special /spe-shal/ *adj* **1** having to do with one particular thing, person, or occasion. **2** not common or usual, distinctive. • *n* **speciality**, *also* **specialty** (*US*). • *adv* **specially** in a special manner.

specialist /spe-shlist/ *n* a person who makes a particular study of one subject or of one branch of a subject.

speciality /spesh-i-al-i-tee/ *n*, *also* **specialty** (*US*) **1** a type of food or dish for which a restaurant or person is well-known. **2** a field of work or study that you have a lot of knowledge about and experience in.

specialty /spesh-ul-tee/ *n* **1** (*US*) speciality. **2** a branch of medicine.

specialize /spe-sha-lize/ *vb*, *also* **specialise** to make a particular study of.

species /spee-sheez/ *n* kind, sort, a group of things (e.g. plants, animals) with certain features in common.

specific /spe-si-fic/ *adj* **1** definite. **2** exact. **3** particular. • *n* a remedy for a particular disease.

specification /spe-si-fi-**cay**-shun/ *n* an exact statement of the details of a piece of work to be done.

specify /spe-si-fie/ *vb* to state exactly or in detail.

specimen /spe-si-men/ *n* a sample, a part taken as an example of the whole.

speck /speck/ *n* a tiny particle, spot, or stain.

speckle /spe-cul/ *n* a small spot on a differently coloured background.

speckled /spe-culd/ *adj* marked with speckles.

specs /specs/ *n* (*inf*) spectacles, glasses.

spectacle /spec-ta-cul/ *n* **1** something worth looking at, a wonderful or magnificent sight. **2** *pl* glasses worn in front of the eyes to assist the eyesight.

spectacular /spec-**ta**-cyu-lar/ *adj* **1** magnificent, wonderful, or splendid to look at. **2** impressive, dramatic.

spectator /spec-tay-tur/ *n* a person who looks on. • *vb* **spectate** to be a spectator at an event.

spectral /spec-tral/ *adj* ghostly.

spectre /spec-ter/ *n*, *also* **specter** (*US*) a ghost.

spectrum /spec-trum/ *n* **1** band of colours, as in a rainbow, produced by passing light through a prism. **2** a range of radio or sound waves. **3** a wide rage of opinions, attitudes, beliefs etc, going from one extreme to the other.

speculate /spe-cyu-late/ *vb* **1** to think about, to guess without having the necessary facts. **2** to buy shares in the hope of selling them later at a profit.

speculation /spec-cyu-**lay**-shun/ *n* **1** act of speculating. **2** a guess or theory.

speculative /spec-yu-la-tiv/ *adj* **1** risky. **2** hesitant, uncertain. **3** given to trying to think out the reasons for things.

speculator /spec-yu-lay-tur/ *n* a person who

buys things (especially of uncertain value) in the hope of making a large profit on them.

sped *pt and pp* of **speed**.

speech /speech/ *n* **1** the ability to speak. **2** a talk given in public.

speechless /speech-less/ *adj* unable to speak for love, surprise, fear, etc.

speed /speed/ *n* **1** quickness of movement. **2** haste. • *vb* (*pt, pp* **sped**) **1** to go fast. **2** to drive a car, truck, etc very fast, often illegally fast. **3** to succeed or make succeed.

speedboat /speed-boat/ *n* a motorboat built for speed.

speedometer /spi-**dom**-i-ter/ *n* a tool to show how fast a car, motorcycle, etc, is travelling.

speedwell /speed-well/ *n* a plant with small blue flowers.

speedy /spee-dee/ *adj* fast, quick-moving.

spell[1] /spell/ *vb* (*pt, pp* **spelt** *or* **spelled**) to say or write the letters of a word in order. • *n* **speller** a person who spells words. • *n* **spelling** the act of a person who spells.

spell[2] /spell/ *n* certain words uttered in order to make something happen by magic; a charm, a strange or magical power.

spell[3] /spell/ *n* **1** a length of time. **2** a turn at doing work.

spellbound /spell-bound/ *adj* fascinated, made still by wonder or magic. • *vb* **spellbind**.

spell-checker /spell-che-cker/ *n* a computer program that checks a document for misspelled words.

spelling bee /spe-ling bee/ *n* a spelling contest.

spelunker /spi-**lung**-ker/ *n* a person who explores caves as a hobby. • *n* **spelunking**.

spelt *pt an pp* of **spell**.

spend /spend/ *vb* (*pt, pp* **spent**) **1** to pay out. **2** to use or use up. **3** to pass.

spender /spen-der/ *n* a person who spends, especially someone who spends too much.

spendthrift /spend-thrift/ *n* a person who spends money wastefully and carelessly.

spent[1] /spent/ *adj* **1** tired out. **2** used up.

spent[2] /spent/ *pt and pp* of **spend**.

sperm /sperm/ *n* **1** a male reproductive cell. **2** semen.

spew /spyoo/ *vb* **1** (*inf*) to vomit. **2** to come out in a flood.

sphere /sfeer/ *n* **1** a ball. **2** a sun, star, or planet. **3** the extent of a person's work, knowledge, influence, etc.

spherical /sfe-ri-cal/ *adj* round like a sphere.

sphinx /sfinks/ *n* a winged mythical monster, half-woman, half-lion.

spice /spice/ *n* **1** a sharp-tasting substance used to flavour food. **2** something exciting or interesting. • *vb* to flavour with spice, etc.

spicy /spie-see/ *adj* **1** sharp-tasting. **2** lively and witty.

spider /spie-der/ *n* an eight-legged creature that spins a web to catch insects for food.

spidery /spie-de-ree/ *adj* like a spider, long and thin like a spider's legs.

spike /spike/ *n* **1** a short piece of pointed metal, a large nail. **2** an ear of corn. **3** many small flowers forming a single head along a stalk. • *vb* **1** to fasten with spikes. **2** to pierce with a spike. **3** to put a gun out of action by driving a spike into it.

spiky /spie-kee/ *adj* having spikes, shaped like a spike.

spill[1] /spill/ *vb* (*pt, pp* **spilled** *or* **spilt**) to let run out or overflow. • *n* **1** a fall. **2** something spilled.

spill[2] /spill/ *n* a thin strip of wood or twisted paper for lighting cigarettes, candles, etc.

spillage /spi-lidge/ *n* the thing that is spilled.

spillover /spi-lo-ver/ *n* the act of spilling over.

spin /spin/ *vb* (**spun**, **spinning**) **1** to draw out (wool, cotton, etc) and twist into threads. **2** to turn quickly around one point. **3** (*inf*) to make up. • *n* **1** a short or rapid trip. **2** a dive made by an aeroplane as it turns around at the same time. **3** the presenting of information in such a way that it seems favourable or acceptable.

spinach /spi-nich/ *n* a vegetable whose leaves are eaten as food.

spinal /spie-nal/ *adj* having to do with the spine.

spinal cord /spie-nal cawrd/ *n* the thick cord of nerves that runs down the spine.

spindle /spin-dul/ *n* in a spinning machine, the bar onto which the newly made thread is wound.

spindly /spin-dlee/ *adj* very long and thin.

spin doctor /spin doc-tor/ *n* someone employed, particularly by the government, to put a favourable interpretation on something that has happened.

spine /spine/ *n* **1** the backbone. **2** a pointed spike on an animal or fish. **3** a thorn.

spineless /spine-less/ *adj* **1** having no spine. **2** weak, lacking courage or willpower.

spine-tingling /spine-ting-gling/ *adj* very moving, thrilling, or terrifying.

spinning /spi-ning/ *n* **1** the act of making thread or yarn. **2** the act of fishing with a certain kind of rod. • *adj* that spins or used in spinning.

spinning wheel /spi-ning-wheel/ *n* a home spinning machine operated by a wheel driven by a pedal.

spinster /**spin**-ster/ *n* a woman who has never been married.

spiny /**spie**-nee/ *adj* full of prickles or thorns.

spiral /**spie**-ral/ *adj* winding around like the thread of a screw. • *also n.*

spire /**spire**/ *n* a tall tower, tapering to a pointed top.

spirit /**spi**-rit/ *n* **1** the soul. **2** a ghost. **3** courage, liveliness. **4** mood. **5** the intention. **6** *pl* strong alcoholic liquor. • *vb* to remove in a mysterious way.

spirited /**spi**-ri-tid/ *adj* **1** lively. **2** showing courage.

spiritless /**spi**-rit-less/ *adj* without courage or liveliness.

spirit level /**spi**-rit le-vul/ *n* a tool for making surfaces level consisting of a sealed tube filled with alcohol and containing an air bubble that is stationary in the middle of the tube when it is level.

spiritual /**spi**-ri-chu-wal/ *adj* **1** having to do with the soul or spirit. **2** religious, holy. • *n* an American religious song, originating among Southern blacks in the 18th and 19th centuries, combining African and European styles of music.

spiritualism /**spi**-ri-chu-wa-li-zum/ *n* the belief that only the soul or spirit has real existence, the belief that it is possible to communicate with the souls of the dead. • *n* **spiritualist**.

spirituality /spi-ri-chu-**wa**-li-tee/ *n* concern with religion and matters of the soul.

spit[1] /**spit**/ *n* **1** a long, thick pin on which meat is roasted over a fire. **2** a long piece of lowland running out into the sea. • *vb* (**spitted, spitting**) to put on a spit, to pierce.

spit[2] /**spit**/ *vb* (**spat, spitting**) **1** to blow from the mouth. **2** to put saliva, etc, out of the mouth. • *n* a quantity of saliva put out of the mouth.

spite /**spite**/ *n* ill-feeling against another, a desire to hurt or harm another. • *vb* to do something to hurt or harm another. • **in spite of** without paying attention to.

spiteful /**spite**-ful/ *adj* desiring or intended to hurt or harm another.

spitfire /**spit**-fire/ *n* a quick-tempered person.

spittle /**spit**-ul/ *n* saliva.

splash /**splash**/ *vb* to throw or scatter drops of mud or liquid onto. • *n* **1** act of splashing. **2** the sound made by a body striking water. **3** a spot of mud or liquid.

splashdown /**splash**-down/ *n* a spacecraft's soft landing in the sea.

splat /**splat**/ *n* a wet, slapping sound.

splatter /**spla**-ter/ *n* spatter or splash of a sticky or thick liquid. • *also vb.*

splay /**splay**/ *vb* to slope or turn outward. • *adj* (*of feet*) turned outwards and flat.

spleen /**spleen**/ *n* **1** an organ near the stomach that helps purify the blood. **2** ill-temper, gloom.

splendid /**splen**-did/ *adj* **1** bright, shining, brilliant. **2** excellent.

splendour /**splen**-dur/ *n, also* **splendor** (*US*) brightness, magnificence.

splice /**splice**/ *vb* **1** to join the ends of two ropes together by interweaving their strands. **2** to fit one piece of wood into another so as to join them. • *n* a joint so made.

splint /**splint**/ *n* a piece of wood to keep a broken bone in position.

splinter /**splin**-ter/ *n* a sharp-edged or pointed piece of glass, wood, metal, etc, broken off a larger piece. • *vb* to break into small pieces.

split /**split**/ *vb* (**split, splitting**) **1** to cut or break from end to end. **2** to separate into parts or smaller groups. • *n* **1** a long break or crack. **2** a division. **3** *pl* the trick of going down upright on the ground with the legs spread out at each side at right angles to the body.

splurge /**splurge**/ *vb* an excessive spending, spending by way of treating oneself.

splutter /**splu**-ter/ *vb* **1** to utter confused, indistinct sounds. **2** to make a spitting noise. • *also n.*

spoil /**spoil**/ *vb* (*pt, pp* **spoiled** *or* **spoilt**) **1** to make or become useless or unpleasant. **2** make something less pleasant or enjoyable. **3** to harm someone's character by always allowing him or her his or her own way. • *n* things stolen or taken by force.

spoilsport /**spoil**-spoart/ *n* a person who spoils the pleasure of others.

spoke[1] /**spoke**/ *pt of* **speak**. • *pp* **spoken**.

spoke[2] /**spoke**/ *n* one of the bars running from the hub to the rim of a wheel.

spokesman /**spoaks**-man/, **spokeswoman** /**spoaks**-woo-man/, **spokesperson** /**spoaks**-per-sun/ *n* a person who speaks for others.

sponge /**spunge**/ *n* **1** a type of sea animal. **2** a kind of light, absorbent washcloth made from or to be like the soft frame of a sponge. **3** one who lives on the money or favours of another. • *vb* **1** to wipe with a sponge. **2** to live on the money or favours of another.

spongy /**spun**-jee/ *adj* soft and absorbent; soft, squishy.

sponsor /**spon**-sur/ *n* **1** a person who introduces someone or something and takes responsibility for it. **2** a business that pays for an event, show, etc, in return for advertising. **3** a person who agrees to pay someone money for charity if he or she completes a specified activity. • *vb*

1 to put forward and support. **2** act as a sponsor.

spontaneous /spon-**tay**-nee-us/ *adj* **1** done willingly. **2** not caused by an outside agency. **3** done without previous thought. • *n* **spontaneity.**

spoof /spoof/ *n* (*inf*) a humorous imitation of a serious, book, film, etc.

spook /spook/ *n* (*inf*) a ghost.

spooky /spoo-kee/ *adj* of, like, or suggesting a spook; eerie; easily fearful.

spool /spool/ *n* a reel on which thread, film, etc, may be wound.

spoon /spoon/ *n* **1** a domestic tool consisting of a shallow bowl and a handle, used in cooking, eating, or feeding. **2** a wooden golf club. • *vb* to lift or scoop with a spoon.

spoonful /**spoon**-ful/ *n* the amount that a spoon contains.

spore /spore/ *n* the seed of a flowerless plant.

sport /spoart/ *n* **1** outdoor or athletic indoor games in which certain rules are obeyed. **2** one of these games. **3** (*fml*) something done for fun or amusement. **4** (*fml*) a person fond of fun or amusement. • *vb* to play, to have fun.

sporting /**spore**-ting/ *adj* **1** fond of sports. **2** used in sport. **3** fair-minded and generous, especially in sports.

sportsman /**spoarts**-man/, **sportswoman** /**spoarts**-woo-man/, **sportsperson** /**spoarts**-per-sun/ *n* **1** a person who takes part in a sport. **2** a person who likes to see every person or group given an equal chance of success. • *adj* **sportsmanlike.**

sportsmanship /**spoarts**-man-ship/ *n* the spirit of fair play.

sportswear /**spoarts**-ware/ *n* the clothing made for and worn while playing sports.

spot /spot/ *n* **1** a small mark, stain, or blot. **2** a tiny piece. **3** the exact place where something happened. **4** a pimple. • *vb* (**spotted, spotting**) **1** to stain. **2** to see or catch sight of.

spotless /**spot**-less/ *adj* unmarked, very clean.

spotlight /**spot**-lite/ *n* a strong beam of light shone on a particular person or place.

spotty /**spot**-ee/ *adj* **1** covered with spots. **2** irregular, uneven.

spouse /spouss/ *n* a husband or wife.

spout /spout/ *n* **1** a long tube sticking out from a pot, jug, pipe, etc, through which liquid can flow. **2** a jet or gush of liquid. • *vb* **1** to gush or make to gush in a jet. **2** (*inf*) to talk at length.

sprain /sprain/ *n* the painful twisting of a joint in the body, causing damage to muscles or ligaments. • *vb* to twist a joint in such a way.

sprang *pt of* **spring.**

sprawl /sprawl/ *vb* **1** to sit or lie with the limbs spread out awkwardly. **2** to be spread out untidily.

spray¹ /spray/ *n* **1** a twig or stem with several leaves or flowers growing out from it. **2** an arrangement of flowers.

spray² /spray/ *n* **1** a cloud of small drops of liquid moving through the air. **2** liquid to be sprayed under pressure. **3** a can or container holding this. • *vb* to sprinkle with fine drops of liquid.

spread /spred/ *vb* (*pt, pp* **spread**) **1** to lay out over an area. **2** to grow bigger, so covering more space. **3** to make or become more widely known or believed. **4** to affect more people. • *n* **1** an area covered, extent. **2** a good meal, a feast.

spreadsheet /**spred**-sheet/ *n* a computer program that organizes information.

spree /spree/ *n* **1** a lively activity. **2** a period of drinking. • **spending spree** a period of reckless spending of money.

sprig /sprig/ *n* **1** a small shoot or twig. **2** a small nail without a head.

sprightly /**sprite**-lee/ *adj* lively. • *n* **sprightliness.**

spring /spring/ *vb* (*pt* **sprang,** *pp* **sprung**) **1** to jump. **2** to flow up from under the ground. **3** to be caused by. **4** to suddenly appear or develop. **5** to cause (a mine) to explode. • *n* **1** a jump. **2** a piece, or coil, of metal that, after being compressed, returns to its earlier shape or position. **3** water flowing up from under the ground. **4** the season following winter when plants begin to grow again. • **spring a leak** to have a hole through which water can come in. • **spring a surprise** to give a surprise.

springboard /**spring**-board/ *n* a springy board for jumping or diving from.

spring-cleaning /spring-**clee**-ning/ *n* a thorough cleaning of the entire house, as is sometimes done in the spring.

spring onion /spring un-yun/ *n* a type of onion with a small white round part and a long green stem, usually eaten raw in salads.

springtime /**spring**-time/ *n* the season of spring.

spring tide /spring tide/ the high tide at new and full moon.

springy /**spring**-ee/ *adj* **1** having elasticity, having a light bounciness. **2** light on the feet.

sprinkle /**spring**-kul/ *vb* to scatter in small drops or tiny pieces.

sprinkler /**spring**-kler/ *n* a person or thing that sprinkles.

sprinkling /spring-kling/ *n* a very small number or quantity.

sprint /sprint/ *vb* to run as fast as possible for a short distance. • *n* 1 a short foot race. 2 a short fast run.

sprite /sprite/ *n* an elf or fairy.

spritzer /sprit-ser/ *n* a drink made of wine and soda water.

sprout /sprout/ *vb* to begin to grow, to bud. • *n* a young plant, a shoot of a plant.

spruce[1] /sprooss/ *adj* neat, smart and tidy.

spruce[2] /sprooss/ *n* a type of fir tree, valued for its white timber.

sprung *pp of* **spring.**

spume /spyoom/ *n* froth, foam.

spunk /spungk/ *n* (*inf*) courage, spirit, live-liness. • *adj* **spunky.**

spur /spur/ *n* 1 a pointed instrument or spiked wheel attached to a horse-rider's heel and dug into the horse's side to make it move more quickly. 2 anything that urges on to greater effort. 3 the sharp point on the back of the legs of certain birds. 4 a ridge or line of hills running out at an angle from a larger hill or hills. • *vb* (**spurred, spurring**) 1 to prick with a spur. 2 to urge to greater effort. • **on the spur of the moment** without previous thought.

spurious /spyoo-ree-us/ *adj* false.

spurn /spurn/ *vb* 1 to push away, as with the foot. 2 to refuse with scorn.

spurt /spurt/ *vb* to burst out in a jet. • *n* 1 a gush of liquid. 2 a special effort. 3 a sudden short burst of extra speed.

sputter /spu-tter/ *vb* 1 to spit when speaking. 2 to throw out small drops of liquid. 3 to make spitting and hissing noises.

spy /spie/ *n* 1 a person who tries to obtain secret information about a country on behalf of an enemy country. 2 a person who tries to find out another's secrets. • *vb* 1 to catch sight of. 2 to act as a spy.

spyglass /spie-glass/ *n* a small telescope.

squabble /skwob-ul/ *vb* to quarrel noisily over unimportant matters. • *also n.*

squad /skwod/ *n* a small party of soldiers or workers.

squadron /skwod-run/ *n* a military force consisting of a group of aircraft or ships.

squalid /skwol-id/ *adj* dirty and unpleasant, wretched.

squall /skwol/ *vb* to scream loudly. • *n* 1 a loud scream. 2 a sudden violent gust of wind, a brief, violent windstorm.

squally /skwol-ee/ *adj* gusty, stormy and windy.

squalour /skwol-ur/ *n*, *also* **squalor** (*US*) excessive dirt, filth, the condition of being squalid.

squander /skwon-der/ *vb* to spend wastefully, to use up needlessly.

square /skware/ *adj* 1 having four equal sides and four right angles. 2 forming a right angle. 3 just, fair. 4 even, equal. • *n* 1 a square figure. 2 an open space in a town with buildings on its four sides. 3 the number obtained when a number is multiplied by itself. 4 an L- or T-shaped instrument for drawing right angles. • *vb* 1 to make square. 2 to pay money due. 3 to bribe. 4 to multiply (a number) by itself. 5 to agree with.

square dance /skware-danse/ *n* a lively dance with various steps, figures, etc in which the couples are grouped in a particular form.

square root /skware root/ *n* the number that must be multiplied by itself to obtain a given number.

squash[1] /skwosh/ *vb* 1 to crush, to press or squeeze into pulp. 2 to speak sharply or rudely to someone to silence him or her. • *n* 1 a crowd, a crush. 2 a indoor game similar to tennis played with a rubber ball.

squash[2] /skwosh/ *n* a fruit of the gourd family eated as a vegetable.

squat /skwot/ *vb* (**squatted, squatting**) 1 to sit down on the heels. 2 to make one's home on a piece of land or in a building to which one has no legal right. • *adj* short and broad. • *n* 1 a squatting position. 2 a building occupied by squatters.

squatter /skwot-er/ *n* a person who settles on land or in a building without legal right to do so.

squawk /skwawk/ *vb* to utter a harsh cry. • *also n.*

squeak /skweek/ *vb* to utter a short, high-pitched sound. • *also n.*

squeal /skweel/ *vb* to cry with a sharp shrill voice. • *also n.*

squeamish /skwee-mish/ *adj* 1 easily made sick, feeling sick. 2 easily shocked or upset.

squeeze /skweez/ *vb* 1 to press from more than one side. 2 to hug. 3 to push through a narrow space. • *n* 1 the act of squeezing. 2 a hug. 3 a tight fit.

squelch /skwelch/ *vb* to make a sucking noise, as when walking over sodden ground. • *also n.*

squib /skwib/ *n* a small firework.

squid /skwid/ *n* a cuttlefish, a long slender sea creatures with eights arms and two tentacles.

squint /skwint/ *vb* 1 to look or peer with the eyes partly closed, as when the light is too strong. 2 to look sideways without turning the head. 3 to be cross-eyed. • *n* 1 the act of looking with eyes partly closed. **2** eyes looking in different directions. **3** (*inf*) a quick look.

squirm /skwirm/ *vb* to wriggle about, to move by wriggling.

squirrel /skwurl/ *n* a small bushy-tailed animal living in trees.

squirt /skwurt/ *vb* to force or be forced out in a thin, fast stream. • *n* **1** a jet. **2** an instrument for throwing out a jet of liquid.

squish /skwish/ *vb* to squash. • *n* the sound of something being squashed.

squishy /skwi-shee/ *adj* making a squishing sound.

stab /stab/ *vb* (**stabbed, stabbing**) to wound with a pointed weapon. • *n* **1** a wound made with a pointed weapon. **2** a thrust with a dagger or pointed knife. **3** a sharp feeling.

stability /sta-bi-li-tee/ *n* steadiness, security.

stabilize /stay-bu-lize/ *vb*, *also* **stabilise** to make firm or steady. • *n* **stabilizer** *also* **stabiliser** a thing that makes something firm or steady.

stable[1] /stay-bul/ *n* a building or shelter for horses, cattle, etc. • *vb* to keep in a stable.

stable[2] /stay-bul/ *adj* **1** firm, secure, not easily moved, upset, or changed. **2** likely to behave reasonably.

stablemate /stay-bul-mate/ *n* any of the horses sharing a stable.

stabling /stay-bling/ *n* buildings available as stables.

staccato /stu-ca-toe/ *adj* (*mus*) having each note sounded clearly and distinctly. • *also n*.

stack /stack/ *n* **1** a large orderly pile of hay, wood, papers, etc. **2** a group of chimneys built in together. **3** a very tall chimney. • *vb* to pile together.

stadium /stay-dee-um/ *n* (*pl* **stadia** *or* **stadiums**) a large ground for sports and athletics.

staff /staff/ *n* **1** a stick or rod used as a support. **2** a stick as a sign of office. **3** the set of five parallel lines on and between which musical notes are written. **4** a group of officers chosen to assist a general. **5** any body of employees. • *vb* to provide with workers or employees.

staff officer /staff-of-i-ser/ *n* a member of a general's staff.

stag /stag/ *n* a male red deer.

stage /stage/ *n* **1** a raised platform for actors, performers, speakers, etc. **2** the theatre. **3** a halting place. **4** the distance that may be travelled after paying a certain fare. **5** a certain point in development or progress. • *vb* to produce.

stagecoach /stage-coach/ *n* formerly, a horse-drawn coach providing a regular service for passengers.

stage fright /stage frite/ *n* the nervousness felt on appearing on the stage in public.

stagger /sta-ger/ *vb* **1** to walk unsteadily, to lurch to the side, to reel. **2** to amaze. **3** to arrange breaks, holidays, etc, so that they do not begin and end at the same times as those of others. • *adj* **staggering**.

stagnant /stag-nant/ *adj* **1** not flowing and often dirty. **2** not developing or growing, inactive.

stagnate /stag-nate/ *vb* **1** to cease to flow. **2** to cease to develop or make progress. **3** to become dull. • *n* **stagnation**.

stag night /stag nite/ *n* a party held before a man's wedding which is attended by his male friends and relatives.

staid /staid/ *adj* serious, steady, unwilling to move with the times.

stain /stain/ *vb* **1** to make dirty. **2** to change the colour of. **3** to make marks of a different colour on. **4** to spoil, to disgrace. • *n* **1** a dirty mark or discolouration that cannot be removed. **2** a paint or dye. **3** disgrace.

stained glass /staind glass/ *n* coloured glass, held together by lead strips, used for church windows, decorations, lamp shades, etc.

stainless /stain-less/ *adj* **1** not easily stained or rusted. **2** without fault or disgrace.

stair /stare/, **staircase** /stare-case/, **stairway** /stare-way/ *n* a series of connected steps, usually with a railing, leading from one place to another on a different level.

stairwell /stare-well/ *n* a vertical shaft in a building that contains a staircase.

stake[1] /stake/ *n* **1** a stout piece of wood pointed at one end for driving into the ground. **2** formerly, the post to which was tied a person condemned to death by burning. • *vb* to mark with stakes.

stake[2] /stake/ *n* the amount of money, or anything else of value, bet or risked. • *vb* to bet (money), to risk. • **at stake** able to be lost.

stalactite /sta-lac-tite/ *n* a mass of mineral matter hanging like an icicle from the roof of a cave.

stalagmite /sta-lag-mite/ *n* a mass of mineral matter rising like a spike from the floor of a cave.

stale /stale/ *adj* **1** not fresh. **2** not new. **3** uninteresting.

stalemate /stale-mate/ *n* **1** in chess, a position from which neither player can win. **2** a situation or argument in which neither side can gain an advantage over the other.

stalk[1] /stock/ *n* **1** the stem of a plant. **2** a tall chimney. • *adj* **stalky**.

stalk[2] /stock/ *vb* **1** to walk holding oneself stiffly upright. **2** to approach an animal quietly and without being seen when hunting it. • *n* **stalking**, **stalker**.

stall /stawl/ *n* **1** a division of a stable in which one animal is kept. **2** a counter on which goods are laid out for sale. **3** a small, sometimes temporary, shop set up in an open place. **4** a ground-floor seat in a theatre. **5** a seat in the choir of a church. • *vb* **1** (*of an aeroplane*) to lose speed and get out of control. **2** (*of a motor car engine*) to stop working. **3** to avoid giving a direct answer.

stallion /stal-yun/ *n* a male horse, especially one kept for breeding.

stamen /stay-men/ *n* one of the little pollen-bearing stalks in the middle of a flower.

stamina /sta-mi-na/ *n* staying power, ability to endure.

stammer /sta-mer/ *vb* to have difficulty in uttering the sounds at the beginning of words, sometimes attempting them several times before succeeding. • *n* such difficulty in speaking.

stamp /stamp/ *vb* **1** to strike the foot forcefully or noisily downward. **2** to print a mark on. **3** to put a postage stamp on. • *n* **1** a forceful or noisy downward movement of the foot. **2** a mark or paper affixed to a letter or package to show that postage has been paid. **3** a mark consisting of letters, numbers, a pattern, etc, printed on paper, cloth, coins, etc. **4** a machine for making such a mark.

stampede /stam-peed/ *n* a sudden panic-stricken rush of many people or animals. • *vb* to take sudden flight.

stance /stanse/ *n* the way a person or animal stands.

stand /stand/ *vb* (*pt, pp* **stood**) **1** to be upright on the feet, legs, or end. **2** to rise up. **3** to set upright. **4** to stop moving. **5** to stay motionless. **6** to be in a certain place. **7** to bear, to put up with. **8** to become a candidate for election. • *n* **1** a halt. **2** a small table, rack, etc, on which things may be placed or hung. **3** a structure with seats arranged in tiers for spectators. **4** a base or support on which an object may be placed upright. **5** resistance to an attack. • **stand by** to support, to be ready to help. • **stand down** to withdraw. • **stand fast** to remain firm. • **stand out 1** to be prominent or noticable. **2** to refuse to give in. • **stand up** to get to the feet. • **stand up for** to defend. • **stand up to** to resist.

standard /stan-dard/ *n* **1** a fixed measure. **2** an average level of accomplishment with which other work is compared. **3** an upright post, etc. used for support. • *adj* **1** fixed. **2** fixed by rule. **3** usual. **4** standing upright.

standardize /stan-dar-dize/ *vb, also* **standardise** to see that all things are made or done in the same way.

standard lamp /stan-dard lamp/ *n* a tall lamp that is placed on the floor.

standby /stand-bie/ *n* a person or thing that can always be depended on and ready to be put into service when needed.

standing /stan-ding/ *n* rank, position, reputation. • *adj* **1** upright. **2** not flowing. **3** permanent, fixed.

standpoint /stand-point/ *n* a point of view.

standstill /stand-still/ *n* a stoppage.

stank[1] *pt of* **stink**.

stank[2] /stank/ *n* **1** a drain (*dial, Scot*). **2** a pool.

stanza /stan-za/ *n* in poetry, a number of lines arranged in a certain pattern that is repeated throughout the poem.

staple /stay-pul/ *n* **1** a U-shaped nail or pin. **2** a principal product or article of trade. **3** a main item. • *adj* chief, principal.

stapler /stay-pler/ *n* a tool used to drive staples into papers, wood, etc. to bind them or attach them.

star /star/ *n* **1** a heavenly body seen as a twinkling point of light in the night sky. **2** any object like a twinkling star in shape. **3** an asterisk (*). **4** a leading actor or actress. • *vb* to have a leading part in a play or a film. • *adj* **starry** full of stars; like stars.

starboard /star-board/ *n* the right-hand side of a ship as one faces the bows. • *also adj*.

starch /starch/ *n* **1** a vegetable substance found in potatoes, cereals, etc. **2** a white powder mixed with water and used to make cloth stiff.

starchy /star-chee/ *adj* **1** containing starch. **2** stiff with starch. **3** stiff or unfriendly in manner.

stardom /star-dum/ *n* fame as an entertainer, sportsman, etc.

stardust /star-dust/ *n* a cluster of stars too far away to be seen separately with the naked eye.

stare /stare/ *vb* to look at fixedly, to look at with wide-open eyes. • *also n*.

starfish /star-fish/ *n* a star-shaped sea creature.

stark /stark/ *adj* **1** bare or simple, often in a severe way. **2** utter, complete. • *adv* completely.

starless /star-less/ *adj* with no stars visible.

starlet /star-let/ *n* 1 a small star. 2 a young actress being promoted as a future star.

starlight /star-lite/ *n* the light given off by stars.

starling /star-ling/ *n* a bird, with black-brown feathers, of the crow family.

start /start/ *vb* 1 to begin. 2 to set in motion. 3 to jump or make a sudden movement. • *n* 1 a beginning. 2 a sudden sharp movement. 3 the distance certain runners are allowed to start a race in front of the others.

starter /star-ter/ *n* 1 a device for starting a motor engine. 2 a person who gives the signal to begin. 3 a person who takes part in a race. 4 a small amount of food eaten as the first course of a meal.

startle /star-tul/ *vb* to frighten, to give a sudden surprise to.

starve /starv/ *vb* 1 to die of hunger, to suffer greatly from hunger. 2 to keep without food. 3 to suffer for want of something necessary. • *n* **starvation**.

state /state/ *n* 1 condition, circumstances, situation. 2 the people of a country organized under a form of government. 3 the governmental institutions of a country. 4 (*fml*) pomp or ceremonious display. • *adj* 1 having to do with the government. 2 public. • *vb* 1 to say as a fact. 2 to put clearly into words, spoken or written.

stately /state-lee/ *adj* dignified, grand in manner or behaviour.

statement /state-ment/ *n* 1 a clear spoken or written account of facts. 2 an account of money due or held.

state-of-the-art /state-ov-thi-art/ *adj* using the most modern, advanced methods.

statesman /stayts-man/, **stateswoman** /stayts-woo-man/ *n* 1 a person skilled in the art of government. 2 a person who has held high political office.

static /sta-tic/ *adj* motionless, at rest.

station /stay-shun/ *n* 1 (*old*) position, rank. 2 a regular stopping place for trains, buses, etc. 3 a headquarters from which a public service is operated. • *vb* to put in or send to a certain place.

stationary /stay-shu-ne-ree/ *adj* fixed, not moving.

stationer /stay-shu-ner/ *n* a person who sells stationery.

stationery /stay-shu-ne-ree/ *n* paper, pens, and all other writing materials.

station wagon /stay-shun wag-on/ *n* a car with a large storage area where the trunk would usually be.

statistician /sta-ti-sti-shun/ *n* a person who compiles or studies statistics.

statistics /sta-tis-tics/ *n* 1 the science of turning facts into figures and then classifying them. 2 the study of figures to deduce facts. 3 figures giving information about something.

statue /sta-choo/ *n* the carved or moulded figure of a person or animal in stone, etc.

statuesque /sta-choo-esk/ *adj* 1 like a statue. 2 motionless, not showing changes in expression.

statuette /sta-choo-et/ *n* a small statue.

stature /sta-chur/ *n* 1 height of the body. 2 importance, reputation.

status /stay-tus/ *n* rank, social position.

status quo /stay-tus-kwoe/ *n* an unchanged state of affairs.

status symbol /stay-tus **sim**-bul/ *n* a possession that seems to mark a higher social position.

statute /sta-choo/ *n* a law.

statutory /sta-chu-toe-ree/ *adj* required by law or statute.

staunch[1] /stawnch/ *adj* loyal, firm, reliable. • *vb see* **staunch**[2].

staunch[2] /stawnch/, **stanch** /stanch/ *vb* to stop blood flowing from a cut, etc.

stave /stave/ *n* 1 one of the strips of wood forming the sides of a barrel. 2 the set of five parallel lines on and between which musical notes are written. 3 a verse of a song, a stanza. • *vb* to break inward. • **stave off** to keep away, to put off.

stay /stay/ *vb* 1 to remain. 2 to live in a place for a time. 3 (*fml*) to delay, to stop. • *n* 1 time spent in a place. 2 a delay. 3 one of the ropes supporting the mast in its upright position.

steadfast /sted-fast/ *adj* loyal, firm, unmoving.

steady /ste-dee/ *adj* 1 firm. 2 not easily changing. 3 regular. 4 reliable, sensible. • *n* **steadiness**.

steak /stake/ *n* a slice of meat or fish for cooking.

steakhouse /stake-house/ *n* a restaurant that specializes in beef steaks.

steal /steel/ *vb* (*pt* **stole**, *pp* **stolen**) 1 to take what belongs to another. 2 to move slowly and quietly.

stealth /stelth/ *n* 1 secrecy. 2 acting quietly or slyly so as not to be seen or heard.

stealthy /stel-thee/ *adj* quiet, sly, secretive.

steam /steem/ *n* the vapour of hot liquid, especially water. • *vb* 1 to give off steam. 2 to cook in steam. 3 to move driven by steam power. • *adj* **steamy** of or like steam, covered or filled with steam.

steamboat /steem-boat/, **steamer** /stee-mer/, **steamship** /steem-ship/ *n* a ship driven by steam power.

steam engine /steem en-jin/ *n* an engine driven by steam power.

steamroller /steem-ro-ler/ *n* a steam-driven vehicle with wide, heavy wheels, used for flattening road surfaces.

steed /steed/ *n* (*old*) a horse.

steel /steel/ *n* **1** an alloy consisting of iron hardened by carbon. **2** a steel bar on which knives may be sharpened. • *adj* made of steel. • *vb* to harden, to strengthen.

steely /stee-lee/ *adj* hard, unsympathetic.

steep[1] /steep/ *adj* having a rapid slope up or down. • *n* a cliff or precipice.

steep[2] *vb* to soak, to leave in water for a time.

steeple /stee-pul/ *n* a tall church tower, sometimes tapering to a point.

steeplechase /stee-pul-chase/ *n* a cross-country race over obstacles for horses or runners.

steeplejack /stee-pul-jack/ *n* a person who climbs steeples, tall chimneys, etc, to repair them.

steer[1] /steer/ *n* a bullock.

steer[2] /steer/ *vb* to keep a moving object pointed in the right direction; to guide or control.

stegosaurus /ste-gu-**saw**-rus/ *n* a kind of dinosaur that has a small head and bony plates and sharp spikes down the backbone.

stellar /ste-lar/ *adj* having to do with the stars.

stellular /stel-yu-lar/ *adj* shaped like a star; covered with small stars or starlike spots.

stem[1] /stem/ *n* **1** the trunk of a tree, the stalk of a flower, leaf, etc. **2** the front part of a ship. **3** the main unchanging part of a word, prefixes and suffixes left out. • *adj* **stemmed** referring objects that have a stem or stemlike object, such as a goblet.

stem[2] /stem/ *vb* (**stemmed, stemming**) to check, to delay, to stop (something) flowing.

stench /stench/ *n* a foul smell.

stencil /sten-sil/ *n* **1** a thin plate or card with a design cut through it so that patterned markings can be painted or printed on a surface beneath. **2** a waxed paper from which copies of typewritten material can be printed. • *vb* (**stenciled, stenciling**) to make a design or copy by using a stencil.

step /step/ *n* **1** a pace taken by one foot. **2** the distance covered by such a pace. **3** a footprint. **4** the sound of a footfall. **5** a complete series of steps in a dance. **6** one of a series of rungs or small graded platforms that allow a person to climb or walk from one level to another. **7** *pl* a flight of stairs. **8** *pl* a stepladder. • *vb* (**stepped, stepping**) to walk. • **out of step 1** out of time with others in performing a regular movement.

2 behaving or thinking differently from others • **step out** to move boldly or quickly forward. • **step up** to increase. • **take steps** to take action.

stepchild /step-childe/ *n* the child of a husband or wife by a previous marriage. • *also* **stepdaughter, stepfather, stepmother, stepson, stepfamily.**

stepladder /step-la-der/ *n* a portable self-supporting ladder.

steppe /step/ *n* in Russia or Asia, a vast treeless uncultivated plain.

stereo /ste-ree-o/ *n* a device used to play music in stereoscopic sound. • *also adj.*

stereoscopic sound /ste-ree-o-**scop**-ic **sound**/ *n* sound relayed from two transmitters so that it seems to come from an area and not one point.

stereotype /ste-ree-o-tipe/ *n* **1** a metal plate on which type is reproduced so that it may be reprinted over and over again. **2** an idea, image, etc, that has become fixed and unchanging.

stereotyped /ste-ree-o-tiped/ *adj* fixed and unchanging.

sterile /ste-rul/ *adj* **1** bearing no fruit or children, barren. **2** germ-free. • *n* **sterility.**

sterilize /ste-ri-lize/ *vb, also* **sterilise 1** to make sterile. **2** to get rid of germs.

sterling /ster-ling/ *adj* genuine, of worth.

stern[1] /stern/ *adj* severe, strict, harsh.

stern[2] /stern/ *n* the back part of a ship.

sternum /ster-num/ *n* a thin, flat bone to which most of the ribs are attached in the front of the chest.

stethoscope /ste-thu-scoap/ *n* an instrument by means of which a person can listen to the sound of another's breathing or heartbeats.

stew /stoo/ *vb* to boil slowly in little liquid in a closed vessel. • *n* **1** stewed meat and vegetables. **2** (*inf*) a state of anxiety. • *adj* **stewed** cooked by stewing.

steward /stoo-wurd/ *n* **1** a person paid to manage another's land or property. **2** a manservant on a ship or aeroplane. **3** an official at a concert, race, meeting, show, etc. • *f* **stewardess.**

stick[1] /stick/ *vb* (*pt, pp* **stuck**) **1** to pierce or stab. **2** to fasten or be fastened to, as with glue. **3** to be unable to move.

stick[2] /stick/ *n* **1** a rod, a long, thin piece of wood, especially one carried when walking. **2** something shaped like a stick.

stickball /stick-bawl/ *n* a game like baseball played by children in city streets with a stick, such as a broom handle, and a soft rubber ball.

sticker /sti-ker/ n a small piece of paper with an illustration that sticks on to a surface.

stickler /sti-kler/ n a person who is fussy about details or unimportant matters.

sticky /sti-kee/ adj 1 smeared with glue, etc, for fixing to other things. 2 tending to fasten on by sticking. 3 (inf) difficult.

stiff /stiff/ adj 1 hard to bend. 2 firm. 3 unable to move easily. 4 cold and severe in manner.

stiffen /sti-fen/ vb to make or become stiff.

stifle /stie-ful/ vb 1 to smother, to choke, to cut off the supply of air. 2 to prevent from expressing. 3 to keep down by force. • also adj.

stigma /stig-ma/ n (pl stigmas) 1 a mark of shame or disgrace. 2 the part of a flower that receives the pollen. 3 (pl stigmata) marks like those of the wounds on Jesus's body.

stigmatic /stig-ma-tic/ adj of, like, or having a stigma.

stigmatize /stig-ma-tize/ vb, also **stigmatise** to blame as being shameful or disgraceful.

stile /stile/ n a set of steps over a fence or wall.

stiletto /sti-le-toe/ n 1 a small dagger. 2 a small, sharp tool used for making small holes in cloth. 3 a type of heel on a ladies' shoe.

still¹ /still/ adj 1 at rest, motionless. 2 calm, silent. 3 not carbonated. • n a single photograph out of a series taken by a moving camera. • vb to make still. • adj 1 even so. 2 up to this moment.

still² /still/ n a device for distilling spirits, or making alcoholic drinks.

stillbirth /still-burth/ n the birth of a stillborn baby.

stillborn /still-bawrn/ adj born dead.

still life /still-life/ n (pl still lifes) nonliving objects (e.g. fruit, ornaments, etc.) as subjects for painting; paintings of such objects.

stilt /stilt/ n one of a pair of poles with footrests so that a person can walk some height above the ground.

stilted /stil-tid/ adj 1 unnatural or pompous in manner. 2 awkwardly expressed.

stimulant /sti-myu-lant/ n something that increases energy for a time. • also adj.

stimulate /sti-myu-late/ vb 1 to rouse or make more alert, active, etc. 2 to stir up, cause. • adj **stimulating**.

stimulus /sti-myu-lus/ n (pl stimuli) something that arouses a person's feelings or excites a person to action.

sting /sting/ n 1 a sharp-pointed defensive organ of certain animals or insects by means of which they can inject poison into an attacker. 2 in plants, a hair containing poison. 3 the pain caused by a sting. 4 any sharp pain. • vb (pt, pp **stung**). 1 to pierce or wound with a sting. 2 to pierce painfully with a sharp point. 3 to drive or provoke.

stingray /sting-ray/ n a kind of flat fish that has a long, whiplike tale that can sting its enemies.

stingy /stin-jee/ adj mean, unwilling to spend or give money.

stink /stingk/ vb (pt **stank** or **stunk**, pp **stunk**) to give an unpleasant smell. • n an unpleasant smell.

stint /stint/ vb to give or allow only a small amount of. • n limit, a set amount of work.

stipple /sti-pul/ vb to paint or draw in very small dots instead of lines.

stipulate /sti-pyu-late/ vb to lay down conditions in advance.

stipulation /sti-pyu-lay-shun/ n conditions demanded as part of an agreement.

stir /stir/ vb (**stirred**, **stirring**) 1 to move or set in motion. 2 to arouse. • n excitement, noisy movement, a sensation.

stir-fry /stir-frie/ vb to fry very quickly in a wok with a little oil while stirring constantly. • n a dish prepared this way.

stirring /sti-ring/ adj rousing, exciting.

stirrup /sti-rup/ n a metal foot support hung from the saddle for a horse-rider.

stitch /stitch/ n 1 a single complete movement of the needle in knitting, sewing, etc. 2 the thread, wool, etc, used in such a movement. 3 a sharp pain in the side as a result of running, etc. • vb to join by stitches.

stock /stock/ n 1 the main stem of a plant, the trunk of a tree. 2 the wooden handle of a gun. 3 the families from which a person is descended. 4 goods kept for selling. 5 shares in a business. 6 the animals of a farm. 7 a liquid made from the boiling of bones, vegetables, herbs and spices in water, which is subsequently used in soups and sauces. 8 a sweet-smelling garden flower. 9 pl (old) a frame with holes for the hands and feet into which lawbreakers could be fastened for punishment. 10 pl the wooden frame on which a ship rests while being built. • adj always in use or ready for use. • vb to provide with necessary goods, to keep a store of. • **take stock** 1 to list and check goods. 2 to consider all the aspects of a situation.

stockade /stock-ade/ n a fence of strong posts built for defence.

stockbroker /stock-bro-ker/ n a person who buys and sells shares in business companies on behalf of others.

stock car /stock car/ n a normal automobile adapted for racing with.

stock exchange /stock eks-change/, **stock market** /stock mar-kit/ n a place where shares are bought and sold.

stockholder /stock-hole-der/ n a person owning stock in a given company.

stocking /stock-ing/ n a close-fitting covering for the foot and leg.

stockist /stock-ist/ n a person or establishment that keeps stock to sell.

stockpile /stock-pile/ n a supply of goods for use in case of a shortage.

stocktaking /stock-tay-king/ n the checking of all the goods held in a store.

stocky /stock-ee/ adj short and broad.

stodgy /stodge-ee/ adj 1 dull. 2 (of food) heavy or hard to digest.

stoic /stoe-ic/ n a person who accepts good and bad, pleasure and pain without excitement or complaint. • adj stoical. • n stoicism.

stoke /stoke/ vb to put fuel on a fire.

stole[1] /stole/ n 1 a band of cloth worn around the neck by a clergyman during services. 2 a long scarf worn around the shoulders by women.

stole[2] /stole/ pt of steal.

stolen /stoe-len/ pp of steal. • also adj.

stomach /stuh-mac/ n 1 the baglike bodily organ that receives and digests food. 2 courage. • vb to bear with, to put up with.

stomp /stomp/ n a jazz tune with a lively rhythm and a strong beat. • vb to dance to this music.

stone /stone/ n 1 a hard mass of rock. 2 a piece of rock, a pebble. 3 the hard centre of some fruits. 4 a piece of hard matter that forms in the body in certain diseases. 5 a precious stone or gem. 6 an imperial unit of weight made up of 14 lbs. • adj made of stone. • vb 1 to throw stones at. 2 to remove the stones from. • leave no stone unturned to do everything possible.

Stone Age /stoe nayj/ n an early period in history during which humans made tools, weapons, etc, of stone.

stonemason /stone-may-sun/ n a person who cuts stone to shape and uses it to make walls, buildings, etc.

stoneware /stone-ware/ n a coarse pottery with a glazed finish.

stonewashed /stone-wawsht/ adj (usually of material) washed with rough stones to cause fading and make softer.

stonework /stone-wurk/ n the art or process of working in stone, as in masonry or jewellery.

stony /stoe-nee/ adj 1 like stone. 2 covered with stones. 3 hard, unsympathetic.

stood /stood/ pt and pp of stand.

stooge /stooj/ n 1 a person made a fool of. 2 a person who does unpleasant work for another, a person who takes the blame due to others.

stool /stool/ n a low, backless seat.

stoop /stoop/ vb 1 to bend forward and downward. 2 to agree to do something unworthy, to give in. • n a downward bending of the head and shoulders.

stop /stop/ vb (stopped, stopping) 1 to cease or prevent from moving or doing something. 2 to come to or bring to a standstill. 3 to block or close up. • n 1 a pause. 2 a place where a bus, etc, halts to pick up passengers. 3 time spent standing still or doing nothing. 4 one of the knobs controlling the flow of air in the pipes of an organ, thereby regulating the sounds produced.

stopper /stop-er/ n something closing a small hole (e.g. in the neck of a bottle).

stopwatch /stop-wach/ n a watch, used for timing events, that can be started or stopped at will.

storage /sto-ridge/ n 1 the putting of goods in warehouses, etc, until they are required. 2 the charge for storing goods.

store /store/ n 1 a large quantity. 2 a supply of goods that can be drawn on when necessary. 3 a room or building where such goods are kept. 4 a shop selling many different kinds of articles. • vb 1 to keep for future use. 2 to put in warehouses, etc. • set store by to regard as valuable.

storey /sto-ree/ n, also **story** (US) a level of a building.

stork /stawrk/ n a white wading bird of the heron family, with long legs and bill.

storm /stawrm/ n 1 a spell of very bad weather (e.g. rain, wind, snow, etc.). 2 a display of violent emotion; public anger. • vb 1 to make a sudden violent attack on a defended place. 2 to rage. • take by storm to capture by sudden violent attack.

stormy /stawr-mee/ adj 1 of, like, or troubled by storms. 2 violent, marked by angry feelings.

story /sto-ree/ n 1 an account of events, real or imagined. 2 (inf) a lie.

storybook /sto-ree-book/ n a book of stories, especially those for children.

storyteller /sto-ree-te-ler/ n a person who tells stories.

stout /stout/ adj 1 strong or thick. 2 fat. 3 brave. • n a strong dark beer.

stove /stove/ *n* a closed-in fireplace or metal device for warming a room, cooking, etc.

stow /stoe/ *vb* to put away, to pack tightly.

stowaway /stoe-a-way/ *n* a person who hides on a ship, etc, so as to travel without paying the fare.

straddle /stra-dul/ *vb* **1** to spread the legs wide apart. **2** to sit or stand with a leg on either side of.

straggle /stra-gul/ *vb* **1** to move in widely scattered formation. **2** to fall behind the main body.

straggler /stra-gler/ *n* a person who wanders from the main body.

straggly /stra-glee/ *adj* spread out in an irregular way.

straight /strate/ *adj* **1** not curving or crooked. **2** honest. • *adv* directly, at once. • *vb* **straighten** to make straight.

straightaway /stray-ta-way/ *adv* at once.

straightforward /strate-fawr-ward/ *adj* **1** simple, easy to understand. **2** honest.

strain¹ /strain/ *vb* **1** to stretch tightly. **2** to make the utmost effort. **3** to harm by trying to do too much with. **4** to put in a sieve to draw liquid off. • *n* **1** violent effort. **2** harm caused to muscles, etc, by straining them. **3** manner or style of speaking or writing. **4** a tune.

strain² /strain/ *n* **1** breed, stock. **2** an element of character. **3** a tune.

strained /straind/ *adj* **1** stretched too far. **2** not natural.

strainer /stray-ner/ *n* a small sieve or filter.

strait /strait/ *adj* narrow, strict. • *n* **1** a narrow strip of water between two land masses. **2** *pl* distress, difficulties.

strait-jacket /strait-ja-ket/ *n* a strong, tightly fitting garment that can be laced onto violent persons to make them helpless or to people with a back injury for support.

strait-laced /strait-layst/ *adj* having strict rules of behaviour for oneself and others.

strand¹ /strand/ *n* (*fml*) the shore. • *vb* **1** to run aground. **2** (*usually passive*) to leave helpless without money, friends, etc.

strand² /strand/ *n* one of the threads of a rope or string.

strange /straynj/ *adj* **1** unusual, odd. **2** unfamiliar. **3** (*lit*) foreign. **4** peculiar, uncomfortable, unwell.

strangeness /straynj-ness/ *n* the state or quality of being strange.

stranger /strane-jer/ *n* **1** a person previously unknown. **2** a new arrival to a place, town, etc. **3** a person who is unfamilar with or ignorant of something.

strangle /strang-gul/ *vb* to kill by pressing the throat tightly, to choke.

strap /strap/ *n* **1** a narrow band of leather or other material. **2** a leather belt. • *vb* (**strapped**, **strapping**) **1** to fasten with a strap. **2** to beat with a strap.

strapless /strap-less/ *adj* having no strap.

strapping /stra-ping/ *adj* tall and strong.

strata *pl of* **stratum**.

stratagem /stra-ta-jum/ *n* a trick intended to deceive.

strategic(al) /stra-tee-jic(-al)/ *adj* having to do with strategy.

strategist /stra-te-jist/ *n* a person skilled in strategy.

strategy /stra-te-jee/ *n* **1** the art of dealing with a situation in such a way as to gain from it the greatest advantage possible. **2** in war, the planning of a campaign.

stratify /stra-ti-fie/ *vb* to form into or set out in layers. • *n* **stratification**.

stratosphere /stra-tu-sfeer/ *n* a layer of Earth's atmosphere (5–10 miles up) in which temperature does not become lower as a person goes higher.

stratum /stra-tum/ *n* (*pl* **strata**) **1** a layer of rock, earth, etc, forming part of Earth's surface. **2** a level.

straw /straw/ *n* **1** the dried stalks of corn, etc. **2** one such stalk or something resembling it. **3** something of no worth.

strawberry /straw-ber-ee/ *n* **1** a wild or garden plant. **2** the juicy red fruit it bears.

stray /stray/ *vb* to wander, to lose the way. • *adj* **1** lost, off the right path. **2** occasional. • *n* a lost or wandering person, animal, or thing.

streak /streek/ *n* **1** a long, narrow mark or stain, a stripe, a narrow band. **2** part of a person's character. • *vb* to mark with streaks.

streaky /stree-kee/ *adj* consisting of or marked with streaks.

stream /streem/ *n* **1** a current of any liquid or gas. **2** a small river. **3** a succession of people moving in one direction. • *vb* **1** to move in a stream. **2** to flow freely.

streamer /stree-mer/ *n* **1** a long, narrow flag. **2** a narrow strip of ribbon or coloured paper for flying in the wind.

streamline /streem-line/ *vb* **1** to build so as to offer minimum resistance to air or water. **2** to make more efficient.

street /street/ *n* a public road lined with buildings in a city or town.

streetlight /street-lite/ *n* a light mounted on a tall pole used to light up a street.

streetwise /street-wise/ *adj* knowing how to cope with difficulties and trouble common in some cities and large towns.

strength /strength/ *n* 1 bodily power. 2 might, force. 3 the number of persons of a class, army, etc, present or on the roll.

strengthen /streng-then/ *vb* to make or become stronger.

strenuous /stren-yu-wus/ *adj* requiring much energy.

stress /stress/ *vb* 1 to point out the importance of. 2 to emphasize with the voice. • *n* 1 importance. 2 strain, pressure. 3 the special emphasis given to particular syllables, words, etc, when speaking.

stressed /strest/, **stressed-out** /strest-out/ *adj* tired, nervous, or depressed as a result of overwork, pressure, etc.

stretch /stretch/ *vb* 1 to make or become longer or broader by pulling. 2 to draw out to the fullest extent. 3 to reach out. 4 to exaggerate, to make seem more important, bigger, etc, than in actuality. • *n* a full length of time or space.

stretcher /stret-cher/ *n* a light frame for carrying a sick or wounded person.

stretchy /stret-chee/ *adj* that can be stretched.

strew /stroo/ *vb* (*pp* **strewn**) to scatter about, to spread at intervals over.

stricken /stri-ken/ *adj* affected by.

strict /strict/ *adj* 1 severe. 2 demanding that others obey the rules.

stricture /stric-chur/ *n* 1 blame, unfavourable criticism of a person. 2 limit.

stride /stride/ *vb* (*pt* **strode**) to walk with long steps. • *n* a long step.

strident /strie-dent/ *adj* loud and harsh in sound.

strife /strife/ *n* open disagreement, arguing, fighting.

strike /strike/ *vb* (*pt, pp* **struck**) 1 to hit. 2 (*of a clock*) to sound the hours or quarters. 3 to stop work to try to make employers grant better pay or conditions. 4 to come suddenly to mind. 5 to make and stamp. 6 to take down. 7 to light. • *n* a stopping of work.

striking /strie-king/ *adj* attracting attention because of being fine or unusual.

string /string/ *n* 1 a cord or strong thread. 2 the cord or wire of a musical instrument. 3 a number of persons or things, one following the other. • *vb* 1 to put on a string. 2 to put a string into.

string bean /string been/ *n* a long, thin, green, edible bean pod.

stringent /strin-jent/ *adj* 1 severe, strict, laying down exact rules to be obeyed. 2 marked by severe lack of money or by firm control. • *n* **stringency**.

stringy /string-ee/ *adj* 1 like string. 2 thin and muscular.

strip /strip/ *vb*. 3 to take everything from. • *n* a long, narrow piece.

stripe /stripe/ *n* 1 a band or streak of different colour from those on either side of it. 2 a stroke from a whip, rod, etc. • *adj* **stripy**, **striped** marked with stripes.

strive /strive/ *vb* (*pt* **strove** *or* **strived**, *pp* **striven**) to try as hard as possible, to struggle.

strobe light /strobe-lite/ *n* a light that gives off very bright, rapid flashes.

stroke[1] /stroke/ *n* 1 a blow. 2 a sudden turn of luck, good or bad. 3 a sudden attack of illness, especially one affecting arteries in the brain. 4 a line made by a pen, pencil, etc. 5 one sound from a bell. 6 in a boat, the oarsman with whom the others keep time when rowing.

stroke[2] /stroke/ *vb* to rub gently with the hand in one direction.

stroll /strole/ *vb* to walk in a leisurely way. • *n* a short leisurely walk.

stroller /stroa-ler/ *n* 1 a person who strolls. 2 a baby pushchair.

strong /strong/ *adj* 1 powerful. 2 healthy. 3 possessing bodily power.

stronghold /strong-hoald/ *n* 1 a fort. 2 a place difficult to capture by attack.

strove *pt of* **strive**.

struck *pt and pp of* **strike**.

structure /struc-chur/ *n* 1 a building. 2 anything consisting of parts put together according to a plan. 3 the way in which a thing is put together. • *adj* **structural**.

struggle /stru-gul/ *vb* 1 to try hard. 2 to fight. • *n* 1 a hard effort. 2 a fight.

strum /strum/ *vb* (**strummed, strumming**) 1 to play a tune carelessly. 2 to play on a stringed instrument by plucking the strings.

strut[1] /strut/ *vb* (**strutted, strutting**) to walk stiffly, as if trying to look important. • *also n*.

strut[2] /strut/ *n* a supporting bar, a prop or support.

strychnine /stric-neen/ *n* a highly poisonous drug.

stub /stub/ *n* 1 a short piece left when the rest is cut off or used up. 2 the retained section of a ticket, etc. • *vb* (**stubbed, stubbing**) to strike (the toes) against something by accident.

stubble /stu-bul/ *n* 1 the stumps of the corn stalks left in the ground after reaping. 2 the short bristly hairs that grow after a person has shaved.

stubborn /stu-burn/ *adj* unwilling to change point of view, not ready to give in.

stubby /stu-bee/ *adj* short and broad, short and thick.

stuck *pt and pp of* **stick**[1].

stud[1] /**stud**/ *n* **1** a nail with a large head or knob. **2** a fastener with a head at each end for linking two buttonholes. **3** one of the supporting wooden beams in a wall. • *vb* (**studded, studding**) **1** to decorate with many small ornaments. **2** to cover with. • *adj* covered with studs.

stud[2] /**stud**/ *n* a number of horses kept for breeding.

student /**styoo**-dent/ *n* a person who studies, a person who goes to school.

studied /**stu**-deed/ *adj* done with care, deliberate.

studio /**styoo**-dee-o/ *n* **1** the room in which a painter, sculptor, photographer, etc, works. **2** a building in which films are made. **3** a workshop in which records are made or from which programmes are broadcast. **4** a one-room apartment.

studious /**stoo**-dee-us/ *adj* of, given to, or engaged in study.

study /**stu**-dee/ *vb* **1** to read about or look at to obtain knowledge. **2** to examine closely, to think deeply about. • *n* **1** the obtaining of information, especially by reading. **2** a subject studied. **3** an office, a room set aside for reading and learning. **4** a work of art done to improve a person's skill.

stuff /**stuff**/ *n* **1** the material or substance of which something is made. **2** anything said, done, written, composed, etc. **3** cloth. • *vb* **1** to fill full or tightly. **2** to fill something hollow with another material.

stuffing /**stu**-fing/ *n* **1** material used to stuff something hollow. **2** a mixture of breadcrumbs, seasoning, etc, put inside chickens, etc, when cooking.

stuffy /**stu**-fee/ *adj* hot and airless.

stumble /**stum**-bul/ *vb* **1** to trip and nearly fall. **2** to make an error, to do wrong. **3** to come upon by chance. • *n* a trip, a false step when walking, nearly causing a person to fall.

stump /**stump**/ *n* **1** the part of a tree left above ground when the rest is cut down. **2** the part of a limb left after the rest has been amputated. • *vb* **1** to walk heavily. **2** to ask someone a question that he or she is unable to answer.

stumpy /**stum**-pee/ *adj* short and thick, short and broad.

stun /**stun**/ *vb* (**stunned, stunning**) **1** to knock senseless. **2** to amaze. • *n* **stunner** a person or thing that is extremely attractive. • *adj* **stunning** extremely attractive.

stung *pt and pp of* **sting**.

stunk *pt and pp of* **stink**.

stunt[1] /**stunt**/ *vb* to prevent the full growth of.

stunt[2] /**stunt**/ *n* **1** a trick to display special skill or daring. **2** anything done to attract attention or gain publicity.

stunted /**stun**-tid/ *adj* undersized.

stupefaction /styoo-pi-**fac**-shun/ *n* (*fml*) amazement.

stupefy /**styoo**-pi-fie/ *vb* **1** to make stupid, to make the senses less acute. **2** to amaze.

stupendous /styoo-**pen**-dus/ *adj* extraordinary, so large or powerful that it amazes.

stupid /**styoo**-pid/ *adj* foolish, not intelligent, slow to understand. • *n* **stupidity**.

stupor /**styoo**-pur/ *n* temporary inability to think clearly, confusion of mind.

sturdy /**stur**-dee/ *adj* strong, well-built.

sturgeon /**stur**-jin/ *n* a large fish from whose eggs caviar is made.

stutter /**stu**-ter/ *vb* to repeat the first sound of a word several times before saying the whole word. • *n* a stammer.

sty[1] /**stie**/ *n* an enclosure or a pen in which pigs are kept.

sty[2], **stye** /**stie**/ *n* a swelling on the edge of the eyelid.

style /**stile**/ *n* **1** manner of doing anything. **2** a way of writing, painting, etc, by which works of art can be recognized as the work of a particular artist, school, or period. **3** a fashion. **4** elegance.

stylish /**stie**-lish/ *adj* well-dressed, smart, fashionable.

stylist /**stie**-list/ *n* a person who designs, creates, or advises on current styles of clothing, hair, etc.

stylistic /stie-li-stick/ *adj* having to do with style.

stylistics /stie-li-sticks/ *n* the study of style as a way of figuring out meaning.

stylize /**stie**-lize/ *vb, also* **stylise** to make part of one particular style.

suave /**swav**/ *adj* agreeable in manner, especially in an insincere way. • *n* **suavity**.

sub- /**sub**/ *prefix* under, below.

subconscious /sub-**con**-shus/ *adj* not fully aware of what one is doing. • *n* mental processes that go on without a person being fully aware of them.

subdivide /**sub**-di-vide/ *vb* to divide into smaller parts or groups. • *n* **subdivision**.

subdue /sub-**dyoo**/ *vb* to conquer, to force to be tame or obedient.

subdued /sub-**dyood**/ *adj* not bright, not loud.

subject /**sub**-jict/ *adj* **1** ruled by another. **2** liable to. • *n* **1** a person who owes loyalty to a ruler or government. **2** that about which something is said or written. **3** something studied. **4** in a clause or sentence, the word

with which the verb agrees grammatically.
• *vb* /sub-**ject**/ **1** to bring under the power of. **2** to expose to.

subjection /sub-**jec**-shun/ *n* control, the state of being under another's rule or power.

subjective /sub-**jec**-tiv/ *adj* having to do with a person's own ideas and feelings rather than with objects outside.

sublet /sub-**let**/ *vb* to rent to another what one is already paying rent for. • *also n.*

sublime /su-**blime**/ *adj* noble, awe-inspiring, grand and lofty.

subliminal /su-**bli**-mi-nal/ *adj* not quite at a conscious level.

sublimity /su-**bli**-mi-tee/ *n* greatness of feeling or expression.

submarine /sub-ma-**reen**/ *adj* under the surface of the sea. • *n* a ship that can travel under the surface of the sea.

submerge /sub-**merj**/ *vb* to put or sink under water. • *n* **submergence**.

submersion /sub-**mer**-shun/ *n* the act of putting or sinking under water.

submission /sub-**mi**-shun/ *n* **1** surrender, obedience, the act of giving in or yielding. **2** a proposal or opinion.

submissive /sub-**mi**-siv/ *adj* willing to accept orders, ready to give in without fighting back.

submit /sub-**mit**/ *vb* (**submitted, submitting**) **1** to give in. **2** to put forward for consideration.

subordinate /su-**bawr**-di-nit/ *adj* **1** less important. **2** of lower rank. • *n* a person who is lower in rank, a person who is working under the orders of another. • *vb* /su-**bawr**-di-nate/ **1** to place in a lower rank, to put under the command of. **2** to regard as less important. • *n* **subordination**.

subpoena /su-**pee**-na/ *n* an order to appear as a witness in a court of law.

subscribe /sub-**scribe**/ *vb* **1** to sign the name under. **2** to agree with. **3** to give or promise to give money to a fund or collection. **4** to give money to receive a weekly, monthly, etc, magazine, newspaper, etc. • *n* **subscriber**.

subscription /sub-**scrip**-shun/ *n* a sum of money given to a fund, collection, magazine, newspaper, etc.

subsequent /sub-si-kwent/ *adj* following, later.

subservient /sub-ser-vee-ant/ *adj* ready to do all one is told to gain favour.

subside /sub-**side**/ *vb* **1** to sink gradually down. **2** to become less, to disappear gradually.

subsidence /sub-**sie**-dense/ *n* a gradual sinking down, especially of land.

subsidiary /sub-si-**dee**-a-ree/ *adj* of less importance.

subsidize /**sub**-si-dize/ *vb, also* **subsidise** to pay a subsidy to.

subsidy /**sub**-si-dee/ *n* money paid by the government to certain groups, trades, etc, to enable them to provide the public with necessary services without losing money.

subsist /sub-**sist**/ *vb* to live or exist, to have the means of living.

subsistence /sub-si-stense/ *n* existence, being, that which is necessary to support life.

substance /**sub**-stanse/ *n* **1** the material of which a thing is made. **2** that which really exists (not what is imagined). **3** the chief ideas in a speech or written work. **4** (*fml*) wealth.

substantial /sub-**stan**-shal/ *adj* **1** really existing. **2** solid. **3** fairly large or important.

substantiate /sub-**stan**-shee-ate/ *vb* to prove the truth of.

substitute /**sub**-sti-toot/ *vb* to put in place of. • *n* a person or thing put in the place of another. • *also adj.* • *n* **substitution**.

subterranean /sub-tu-**ray**-nee-an/ *adj* underground.

subtitle /**sub**-tie-tul/ *n* **1** a second, less important, title of a book. **2** explanatory comments, etc, printed on silent or foreign-language films.

subtle /**su**-tul/ *adj* **1** cunning, clever, not obvious. **2** difficult to understand completely. **3** faint or delicate.

subtlety /**su**-tul-tee/ *n* **1** skill, cleverness. **2** refinement.

subtract /sub-**tract**/ *vb* to take (one number) from another. • *n* **subtraction**.

suburb /**su**-burb/ *n* an outlying part of a city. • *adj* **suburban**.

subversive /sub-**ver**-siv/ *adj* intended or likely to overthrow or destroy, directed against the government, management, organization, etc.

subvert /sub-**vert**/ *vb* (*fml*) to overthrow, to try to destroy. • *n* **subversion**.

subway /**sub**-way/ *n* **1** an underground passage. **2** an underground railway.

succeed /suc-**seed**/ *vb* **1** to do what a person has attempted or desired to do. **2** to come after, to follow in order and take the place of.

success /suc-**sess**/ *n* **1** the doing of what a person has attempted or desired to do. **2** a favourable result or outcome. **3** a person or thing that does as well as was hoped or expected. • *adj* **successful**.

succession /suc-se-shun/ *n* **1** a number of persons or things following one another in order. **2** the order in which people may inherit a title when it becomes available.

successive /suc-se-siv/ *adj* coming in order, following one after another.

successor /suc-se-sur/ *n* a person who comes after or takes the place of another.

succinct /suc-sinct/ *adj* short and to the point, concise.

succour /su-cur/ *vb, also* **succor** (*US*) (*fml*) to help when in difficulty. • *n* aid, help.

succulent /su-cyu-lent/ *adj* juicy.

succumb /su-cum/ *vb* **1** to give way to, to be overcome. **2** to die.

such /such/ *adj* **1** of a like kind or degree, similar. **2** so extreme, so much, so great, etc. • *adv* to so great a degree.

suck /suck/ *vb* **1** to draw into or in with the mouth. **2** to draw the liquid from the mouth or something in it with the tongue. • *also n*.

sucker /su-ker/ *n* (*inf*) **1** a foolish or gullible person. **2** a cup-shaped rubber item that sticks to things by suction.

suckle /su-cul/ *vb* to allow to suck milk from the breast.

suckling /su-cling/ *n* a baby or animal still feeding from its mother's breast.

suction /suc-shun/ *n* the act of sucking, the drawing up of a fluid into a tube, etc, by expelling the air so that the fluid fills where the air once was.

sudden /su-den/ *adj* happening without warning, unexpected, hurried.

sudden infant death syndrome *or* **SIDS** *n* a sudden unexplained death of a baby in its sleep; familiarly known as cot death.

suds /sudz/ *npl* the froth on soapy water. • *adj* **sudsy**.

sue /soo/ *vb* **1** to bring a case against in a court of law. **2** (*fml*) to beg for.

suede /swade/ *n* a soft kind of leather that is brushed and buffed so that it has a soft, furry feel. • *also adj*.

suet /soo-it/ *n* a hard fat from cattle and sheep, used in cooking.

suffer /su-fer/ *vb* **1** to undergo pain or great anxiety. **2** to experience or undergo. **3** to put up with. • *n* **suffering** the bearing of pain, distress, etc.

suffice /su-fise/ *vb* (*fml*) to be enough.

sufficiency /su-fi-shen-see/ *n* a big enough supply.

sufficient /su-fi-shent/ *adj* enough.

suffix /su-fiks/ *n* a syllable added to the end of a word (e.g. -ness, -ly) to change its use or meaning.

suffocate /su-fu-cate/ *vb* **1** to choke for lack of air. **2** to kill by preventing from breathing. • *n* **suffocation**.

suffrage /su-fridge/ *n* (*fml*) the right to vote in elections. • *n* **suffragist** a person who believes in giving people the right to vote.

suffragette /su-fri-jet/ *n* in the 19th century, a woman who claimed and obtained the right for women to vote.

suffuse /su-fyooz/ *vb* (*fml*) to spread over. • *n* **suffusion**.

sugar /shoo-gar/ *n* a sweet substance manufactured from sugar cane, beets, etc. • *vb* **1** to sweeten with sugar. • *adj* **sugary**.

sugar beet /shoo-gar beet/ *n* a plant with a root from which sugar is obtained.

sugar cane /shoo-gar cane/ *n* a tall, stiff reed from which sugar is obtained.

suggest /su-jest/ *vb* **1** to put forward. **2** to hint. **3** to cause an idea to come into the mind.

suggestion /su-jes-chun/ *n* **1** a proposal. **2** a hint.

suggestive /su-jes-tiv/ *adj* **1** putting ideas into the mind. **2** rather indecent.

suicide /soo-i-side/ *n* **1** the killing of oneself on purpose. **2** a person who kills himself or herself on purpose. • *adj* **suicidal**.

suit /soot/ *vb* **1** to please or satisfy. **2** to go well with. **3** to look good or attractive on. • *n* **1** a set of clothes of the same material. **2** attentions paid to a lady with the intention of marrying her. **3** one of the four sets of playing cards.

suitable /soo-ta-bul/ *adj* what is wanted for the purpose, fitting the occasion.

suitcase /soot-case/ *n* a travelling bag for clothes.

suite /sweet/ *n* **1** a set of rooms or furniture. **2** all the attendants who wait upon a certain person. **3** a series of connected pieces of music. **4** a group of connected rooms.

suitor /soo-tur/ *n* **1** a person making a request or asking for a favour. **2** a man paying attention to a lady with the intention of marrying her.

sulk /sulk/ *vb* to behave in an ill-humoured, unfriendly way, to refuse to speak to others because of ill-temper.

sulky /sul-kee/ *adj* ill-natured, not mixing with others because of ill-humour.

sullen /su-len/ *adj* ill-natured, silently bad-tempered, gloomy, sad.

sulphate /sul-fate/ *n, also* **sulfate** (*US*) a salt of sulphuric acid.

sulphur /sul-fur/ *n, also* **sulfur** (*US*) a yellow non-metallic element.

sulphuric /sul-few-ric/ *adj, also* **sulfuric** (*US*) having to do with or containing sulphur.

sulphurous /sul-fur-uss/ *adj, also* **sulfurous** (*US*) having to do with or like sulphur.

sultan /sul-tan/ *n* the ruler of a Muslim country, especially of the former Ottoman Empire.

sultana /sul-**ta**-na/ *n* **1** the wife of a sultan. **2** a kind of seedless raisin used in baking.

sultry /sul-tree/ *adj* very hot and close.

sum /sum/ *n* **1** the answer obtained by adding several numbers together. **2** the total or entire amount, especially of money. **3** a problem in arithmetic. • *vb* (**summed**, **summing**) to add up. • **sum up** to summarize.

summarize /su-ma-rize/ *vb*, *also* **summarise** to give a brief account of the main points.

summary /su-ma-ree/ *n* a brief account of the main points. • *adj* **1** short. **2** done quickly or by a short method.

summation /su-**may**-shun/ *n* the act or process of summing up or of finding a total.

summer /su-mer/ *n* the warmest season of the year, in the Northern Hemisphere, generally June, July, and August. • *adj* summery of or like summer.

summit /su-mit/ *n* **1** the highest point, the top. **2** a meeting of heads of government, or other high-ranking officials, of several countries to discuss matters of great importance.

summon /su-mun/ *vb* **1** to call upon to appear before an official. **2** to call upon to do something.

summons /su-munz/ *n* an order to appear for trial by a court of law. • *vb* to present with such an order.

sumo wrestling /soo-mo ress-ling/ *n* a Japanese form of wrestling, performed by very large men. • *n* sumo wrestler.

sump /sump/ *n* a hole or hollow in which liquid collects (e.g. an oil sump in an engine).

sumptuous /sum-shu-wus/ *adj* splendid, very expensive, luxurious.

sun /sun/ *n* **1** (*often cap*) the heavenly body that gives light and heat to the Earth and other planets in the same solar system. **2** the warmth or light given by the sun.

sunbathe /sun-bathe/ *vb* to lie out in the sun.

sunblock /sun-block/ *n* sunscreen.

sunburn /sun-burn/ *n* a reddening of the skin's colour caused by exposure to the sun. • *also vb.*

suncream /sun-creem /*n* sunscreen.

sundae /sun-day/ *n* ice cream served with fruit, nuts, syrup, etc.

Sunday /sun-day/ *n* the first day of the week.

sundial /sun-dile/ *n* an instrument that tells the time by casting the shadow of an indicator on a face marked with the hours.

sun-dried /sun-dried/ *adj* dried by the sun.

sunflower /sun-flour/ *n* a tall plant with a large yellow flower.

sung *pp of* **sing.**

sunglasses /sun-gla-siz/ *n* tinted glasses to shade the eyes from the brightness of the sun.

sunk *pp of* **sink.**

sunlight /sun-lite/ *n* the light of the sun. • *adj* sunlit.

sunny /su-nee/ *adj* **1** brightly lit by the sun. **2** cheerful, happy.

sunrise /sun-rize/ *n* the appearance of the sun above the horizon in the morning.

sunscreen /sun-screen/ *n* a cream or oily substance worn on the skin to protect it from the sun's rays.

sunset /sun-set/ *n* the disappearance of the sun below the horizon in the evening.

sunshine /sun-shine/ *n* **1** the light or warmth of the sun. **2** cheerfulness.

sunstroke /sun-stroke/ *n* a severe illness caused by the effect of the sun's heat on the body.

suntan /sun-tan/ *n* a darkening of the skin caused by the sun.

sunward /sun-ward/ *adj* facing the sun.

sup /sup/ *vb* (**supped**, **supping**) **1** (*old*) to take supper. **2** to eat or drink in small mouthfuls. • *n* a small mouthful.

super /soo-per/ *adj* outstanding, great, wonderful.

super- /soo-per/ *prefix* above, over.

superb /soo-perb/ *adj* magnificent, excellent.

superbug /soo-per-bug/ *n* (*inf*) a bacterium that is resistant to most antibiotics.

supercilious /soo-per-si-lee-us/ *adj* **1** overproud, having a scornful manner, looking down on others. **2** disdainful, scornful.

superficial /soo-per-fi-shal/ *adj* **1** on the surface. **2** not deeply felt or thought about. **3** shallow, incapable of deep thought or feeling. • *n* superficiality.

superfluous /soo-**per**-floo-us/ *adj* more than enough, unnecessary. • *n* **superfluity.**

superhero /soo-per-hee-ro/ *n* an all-powerful hero of a kind found in comic books.

superhuman /soo-per-hyoo-man/ *adj* more than human, extraordinary, divine.

superimpose /soo-per-im-poaz/ *vb* to lay on top of something else.

superintend *vb* to manage something.

superintendent /soo-per-in-ten-dent/ *n* **1** one who superintends. **2** a person in charge of a department, group, school, etc.

superior /soo-**pir**-ee-ur/ *adj* **1** higher in rank. **2** better. • *n* **1** a person higher in rank. **2** a person better than others. **3** the head of a monastery or convent. • *n* superiority.

superlative /soo-per-la-tiv/ *adj* **1** excellent, above all others in quality. **2** expressing the highest degree.

superman /soo-per-man/ *n* a man of extraordinary powers, the imagined perfect human being of the future.

supermarket /soo-per-mar-kit/ *n* a large store selling (usually by self-service) food and household goods.

supernatural /soo-per-**nach**-ral/ *adj* **1** not to be explained by natural causes. **2** caused by direct divine intervention in human affairs.

supernova /soo-per noe-vah/ *n* an exploding star giving off millions of times more light than the sun.

supersede /soo-per-**seed**/ *vb* to take the place of, to put another in the place of.

supersonic /soo-per-**son**-ic/ *adj* faster than sound.

superstition /soo-per-**sti**-shun/ *n* **1** a tendency to believe that certain human beings or objects have more than natural powers. **2** belief in magic, luck, etc. • *adj* **superstitious.**

supervise /**soo**-per-vize/ *vb* **1** to watch others to see that they do their work properly. **2** to be in charge of. • *n* **supervision.** • *n* **supervisor.**

supper /su-per/ *n* a light evening meal.

supple /su-pul/ *adj* **1** (*fml*) easily bent. **2** bending or moving easily and gracefully.

supplement /su-pli-mint/ *n* **1** something added to make up what is lacking. **2** an addition. • *vb* to make additions to.

supplementary /su-pli-**men**-ta-ree/ *adj* given in addition, given to make up what is lacking.

suppliant /su-plie-ant/ *adj* (*fml*) begging for as a favour. • *n* (*fml*) a person humbly asking for a favour.

supply /su-**plie**/ *vb* to provide what is needed. • *n* **1** a store of what is needed. **2** *pl* stores.

support /su-**poart**/ *vb* **1** to help to hold up. **2** to give help or encouragement to. **3** to provide the necessities of life for. **4** to put up with. • *n* **1** a prop. **2** assistance, encouragement. **3** a person or thing that supports. • *adj* **supportive.**

supporter /su-**poar**-ter/ *n* a person who helps or encourages.

suppose /su-**poaz**/ *vb* **1** to believe to be true without sure evidence. **2** to imagine. **3** to think probable. • *adv* **supposedly** according to what is, was, or may be supposed.

supposition /su-pu-**zi**-shun/ *n* **1** a guess. **2** something taken as true or imagined.

suppress /su-**press**/ *vb* **1** to put down, to crush. **2** to prevent from being known. • *n* **suppression.**

suppressant /su-**press**-ant/ *n* something, especially a drug, that suppresses an action, condition, etc.

supremacist /soo-**prem**-a-sist/ *n* a person who believes that one group is superior to others.

supremacy /soo-**prem**-a-see/ *n* the highest power or authority.

supreme /soo-**preem**/ *adj* **1** highest in power or authority. **2** greatest.

surcharge /sur-charge/ *n* an extra charge.

sure /shoor/ *adj* **1** certain. **2** convinced of. **3** unfailing.

surely /**shoor**-lee/ *adv* without doubt.

surf /surf/ *n* the foamy water caused by waves breaking on a sloping shore.

surfboard *see* **surfing.**

surface /**sur**-fiss/ *n* **1** the outside or top part of anything. **2** outside appearance. • *vb* to rise to the surface.

surfeit /**sur**-fut/ *n* too much of anything. • *vb* to overfeed.

surfing /**sur**-fing/ *n* **1** the sport of riding on the crest of large waves while standing on a long, narrow board with a rounded or pointed front end, called a **surfboard** /**surf**-board/. **2** the act of moving from site to site on the Internet looking for something interesting. • *vb* **surf.**

surge /surge/ *n* the rising of a wave, the up-and-down movement of the surface of the sea. • *vb* to rise, to well up, as a wave.

surgeon /**sur**-jin/ *n* a doctor skilled in surgery.

surgery /**sur**-je-ree/ *n* **1** the art or science of curing disease by cutting the body open to fix whatever is wrong. **2** a place where a doctor sees patients.

surgical /**sur**-ji-cal/ *adj* having to do with surgery.

surly /**sur**-lee/ *adj* gloomy and ill-humoured. • *n* **surliness.**

surname /**sur**-name/ *n* a person's family name, last name.

surpass /sur-**pass**/ *vb* to do better than.

surpassing /sur-pa-sing/ *adj* excellent.

surplus /**sur**-plus/ *n* the amount by which anything is more than is required.

surprise /sur-**prize**/ *n* **1** the feeling caused by what is sudden or unexpected. **2** a sudden or unexpected event, gift, piece of news, etc. • *vb* **1** to come upon when not expected. **2** to take unawares, to startle, to astonish. • *adj* **surprising.**

surreal /su-**reel**/ *adj* bizarre, strange, of or related to surrealism.

surrealism /su-**ree**-ul-iz-um/ *n* an artistic style that focuses on the unconscious mind, dreams, and fantastic, irrational subject material. • *adj* **surrealistic.**

surrender /su-**ren**-der/ *vb* **1** to stop fighting and accept the enemy's terms, to give up. **2** to hand over. • *also n.*

surrey /**su**-ree/ *n* a light, four-wheeled carriage of the late 19th and early 20th centuries.

surrogate /**su**-ru-gate/ *n* **1** a substitute. **2** a woman who, by agreement, has the baby of another woman who cannot for some reason bear the child. • *also adj.* • *n* **surrogacy** the fact or condition of being a surrogate.

surround /su-**round**/ *vb* to go, put, or be on all sides of.

surroundings /su-**round**-dingz/ *npl* the objects or country around a person or place.

surveillance /sur-**vay**-lanse/ *n* a careful watch.

survey /sur-**vay**/ *vb* **1** to look over. **2** to look at carefully. **3** to measure an area of land and make a plan of it. **4** to examine and report on the condition of a building. • *n* /**sur**-vay/ **1** a general view. **2** the measuring of a piece of land. **3** a plan made of a piece of land. **4** a report on the condition of a building.

surveyor /sur-**vay**-ur/ *n* a person who surveys land or who reports on the condition of a building.

survival /sur-**vie**-val/ *n* **1** act of surviving. **2** a person or thing that has lived on from a past age. • **survival of the fittest** the belief that only those kinds of plants, animals, etc, live on that are adapted to their surroundings.

survivalist /sur-**vie**-va-list/ *n* a person who is determined to survive.

survive /sur-**vive**/ *vb* **1** to live on after. **2** to continue to live or exist.

survivor /sur-**vie**-vur/ *n* a person who has lived on, especially after a disaster.

susceptible /su-**sep**-ti-bul/ *adj* easily influenced or affected by. • *n* **susceptibility**.

sushi /**soo**-shee/ *n* a Japanese dish of small cakes of cold rice served with raw or cooked fish, vegetables, etc.

suspect /su-**spect**/ *vb* **1** to think something is the case but have no proof. **2** to mistrust, to doubt the truth of. **3** to believe to be guilty. • *n* /**sus**-pect/ a person who is suspected. • *adj* /**sus**-pect/ doubtful, not worthy of trust.

suspend /su-**spend**/ *vb* **1** to hang from. **2** to cause to stop for a time.

suspenders /su-**spen**-derz/ *n pl* a pair of straps attached to a belt and fastened to the tops of stockings to keep them up.

suspense /su-**spense**/ *n* uncertainty or anxiety about what may happen in the future.

suspension /su-**spen**-shun/ *n* the state of being suspended.

suspension bridge /su-**spen**-shun bridge/ *n* a bridge suspended by chains or steel ropes from towers or arches.

suspicion /su-**spi**-shun/ *n* a feeling of doubt or mistrust.

suspicious /su-**spi**-shus/ *adj* doubtful, mistrustful.

suss /sus/ *vb* (*inf*) to discover or underand the truth about something.

sustain /su-**stane**/ *vb* **1** to keep up, to support. **2** to give strength to. **3** to keep in existence over a long period. **4** to undergo.

sustainable /su-**stay**-na-bul/ **1** able to continue for a long time. **2** able to continue without for a long time without causing damge to the environment.

sustenance /**su**-sti-nanse/ *n* food, nourishment.

suture /**soo**-chur/ *n* the act of joining together as by sewing. • *vb* to join together by sewing.

svelte /svelt/ *adj* slender and graceful, polished, sophisticated.

swab /swob/ *n* **1** a pad of cotton (sometimes wrapped around a stick) used for cleansing wounds, applying medicines, etc. **2** a mop for cleaning decks, etc. • *vb* (**swabbed**, **swabbing**) to clean with a swab.

swagger /**swa**-ger/ *vb* to walk proudly, to behave boastfully. • *also n.*

swallow[1] /**swaw**-loe/ *vb* **1** to draw down the throat and into the stomach. **2** to enclose in the middle of something bigger. **3** to believe without question. • *n* the act of swallowing.

swallow[2] /**swaw**-loe/ *n* a bird with long wings and a forked tail.

swamp /swomp/ *n* wet, marshy ground. • *vb* **1** to flood. **2** to overwhelm by greater numbers or strength.

swampy /**swom**-pee/ *adj* soft and wet, marshy.

swan /swon/ *n* a long-necked bird of the duck family.

swank /swangk/ *n* a stylish display of dress, behaviour, etc. • *adj* **swanky**.

swap /swop/ *vb* (**swapped**, **swapping**) to exchange.

swarm /swawrm/ *n* **1** a large number of insects (e.g. bees) moving as a group. **2** a large, closely packed crowd. • *vb* **1** to come together in large numbers. **2** (*of bees, etc*) to leave the hive in a body.

swarthy /**swawr**-thee/ *adj* dark-skinned.

swastika /**swos**-ti-ca/ *n* an ancient symbol of a cross with four equal arms each bent at right angles. Found throughout history, but during the 20th century it was used to symbolize Nazi Germany and Nazi beliefs.

swat /swot/ *vb* (**swatted**, **swatting**) to hit sharply, to crush.

swatch /swotch/ *n* a sample piece of cloth.

swathe /swathe/ *vb* to wrap up in bandages or clothing. • *n* **swathe** *or* **swath**.

sway /sway/ *vb* **1** to move with a rocking motion from side to side or backward and forward. **2** to rule, to have influence over. • *n* **1** a rocking movement. **2** control, rule.

swear /sware/ *vb* (*pt* **swore**, *pp* **sworn**) **1** to promise to tell the truth. **2** to declare something is true. **3** to use bad words or bad language, to use words that are considered offensive and socially unacceptable.

sweat /swet/ *n* the moisture that oozes from the body when it is overheated, perspiration. • *vb* **1** to perspire. **2** to work very hard. **3** (*inf*) to be very anxious or worried about something.

sweater /swe-ter/ *n* a jumper.

sweaty /swe-tee/ *adj* (*inf*) damp with perspiration.

sweep /sweep/ *vb* (*pt*, *pp* **swept**) **1** to clean with a brush or broom. **2** to move over swiftly and smoothly. **3** to remove with an extensive or curving movement. • *n* **1** an extensive or curving movement. **2** a quick look over. **3** a person who cleans chimneys. • **sweep the board** to win everything offered or at stake.

sweeping /swee-ping/ *adj* **1** wide, extensive. **2** not taking sufficient account of exceptions.

sweet /sweet/ *adj* **1** tasting like honey or sugar. **2** having a pleasing smell. **3** pleasing to the senses. **4** gentle and likable. **5** pretty. • *n* **1** a candy. **2** a dessert, a pudding. • *adv* **sweetly.** • **have a sweet tooth** to like eating sweet-tasting things.

sweeten /swee-ten/ *vb* to make or become sweet. • *n* **sweetener** a thing that makes something sweet. • *n* **sweetening** the process of making something sweet.

sweetcorn /sweet-cawrn/ *n* **1** a type of maize consisting of juicy yellow kernels growing on thick stems. **2** the kernels eaten as a vegetable.

sweetheart /sweet-hart/ *n* a person dearly loved, a lover.

sweet pea /sweet pee/ *n* a garden plant with sweet-smelling flowers.

sweet potato /sweet pu-tay-toe/ *n* a plant whose orange-coloured root is used as a vegetable.

swell /swell/ *vb* (*pp* **swollen**) **1** to grow larger. **2** to make or become louder. **3** to bulge out. **4** (*of the sea*) to rise and fall in large waves that do not break. • *n* **1** movement of the sea in large waves that do not break. **2** (*inf*) a very well-dressed person.

swelling /swe-ling/ *n* a lump raised for a time on the body by a bruise, infected cut, etc.

swelter /swel-ter/ *vb* to be very hot, to be uncomfortable because of great heat. • *adj* **sweltering.**

swept *pt and pp of* **sweep.**

swerve /swerv/ *vb* to turn or move suddenly to one side. • *also n.*

swift /swift/ *adj* quick-moving, speedy.

swig /swig/ *vb* (**swigged**, **swigging**) to drink in large mouthfuls • *n* (*inf*) a large mouthful.

swim /swim/ *vb* (**swam**, **swimming**, *pp* **swum**) **1** to move through the water by moving the arms and legs. **2** to float in or on top of. **3** to be dizzy. • *n* act of swimming. • *n* **swimmer.** • **in the swim** knowing what is going on, knowing important people.

swimmingly /swi-ming-lee/ *adv* smoothly, with great success.

swimsuit /swim-soot/ *n* a bathing suit, garment worn for swimming.

swimwear /swim-ware/ *n* garments worn for swimming.

swindle /swin-dul/ *vb* to cheat. • *n* a deception intended to cheat people, a fraud.

swindler /swin-dler/ *n* a cheat, a person who tricks people out of money.

swine /swine/ *n* (*pl* **swine**) **1** a pig. **2** (*inf*) a very nasty person.

swing /swing/ *vb* (*pt*, *pp* **swung**) **1** to move to and fro, especially when suspended from above. **2** to whirl around. **3** to turn around when at anchor. **4** to walk quickly with a swaying movement. • *n* **1** a seat suspended by ropes, etc, on which a person can swing to and fro. **2** a swinging movement. **3** a type of jazz music. **4** a long-range blow given with a curved arm. • **in full swing** in progress.

swingeing /swinj-ing/ *adj* extreme, severe.

swinging /swing-ing/ *adj* **1** moving to and fro. **2** done with a swing; lively, fashionable.

swipe /swipe/ *vb* **1** to hit hard with a swinging movement. **2** (*inf*) to steal. • *n* a hard, sweeping blow.

swipe card /swipe card/ *n* a small plastic card containing coded information which is passed through an electronic device which reads this information.

swirl /swirl/ *vb* to flow or move with a circular motion. • *n* a circular motion of water.

swish /swish/ *n* the sound made by a light or thin object moving through the air. • *vb* to move through the air with a swish. • *adj* smart and expensive.

switch /switch/ *n* **1** an easily bent stick. **2** a small lever for turning on and off electric current. • *vb* **1** to hit with a switch. **2** to turn electric current on or off. **3** to change suddenly.

switchboard /switch-board/ *n* a board at which connection can be made between one telephone line and another.

swivel /swi-vul/ *n* a ring that turns freely around a stable pin. • *vb* (**swivelled**, swivelling; *also* swiveled, swiveling (*US*)) to turn around, as on a swivel.

swollen *pp of* **swell**.

swoon /swoon/ *vb* to faint. • *n* a fainting turn.

swoop /swoop/ *vb* **1** to fly down upon with a sudden swift movement. **2** to come upon swiftly and suddenly. • *n* **1** a sudden downward rush. **2** a sudden attack.

sword /sawrd/ *n* a weapon with a long blade and sharp point for cutting or thrusting.

swordfish /sawrd-fish/ *n* a large fish whose upper jaw sticks out and comes to a point like a sword.

swore *pt of* **swear**.

sworn *pp of* **swear**.

swot /swot/ *vb* to study hard. • *n* someone who spends a great deal of time studying.

swung *pt and pp of* **swing**.

sycamore /si-ca-more/ *n* a large tree, of the same family as the maple and fig tree.

sycophant /si-cu-fant/ *n* a person who flatters another to gain his or her favour. • *adj* **sycophantic**.

syllable /si-la-bul/ *n* a part of a word or a word containing one vowel sound. • *adj* **syllabic**.

syllabus /si-la-bus/ *n* a plan for a course of study, giving subjects to be studied, times of classes, etc.

symbol /sim-bul/ *n* **1** an emblem or sign made to stand for or represent something else. **2** a sign that all recognize as bearing a certain meaning.

symbolic /sim-bol-ic/ *adj* standing for or representing something else. • *adv* **symbolically**.

symbolism /sim-bu-li-zum/ *n* the use of symbols.

symbolize /sim-bu-lize/ *vb, also* **symbolise** to stand as a sign for.

symmetrical /si-met-ri-cal/ *adj* **1** having a balanced or regular design. **2** graceful because the parts are in pleasing proportion to one another and to the whole.

symmetry /si-mi-tree/ *n* **1** sameness between the two halves of a design. **2** a pleasing similarity or contrast between parts, beauty resulting from graceful proportions.

sympathetic /sim-pa-thet-ic/ *adj* showing or feeling understanding or pity.

sympathize /sim-pa-thize/ *vb, also* **sympathise** **1** to feel with and for another. **2** to be in agreement with.

sympathy /sim-pa-thee/ *n* **1** understanding of the sorrow or distress of another, pity. **2** agreement with the opinion of another.

symphony /sim-fu-nee/ *n* **1** a piece of music written for a full orchestra. **2** (*lit*) a pleasant

unison of sounds, colours, etc. • *adj* **symphonic**.

symptom /sim(p)-tum/ *n* **1** a sign or mark by which something can be recognized. **2** one of the signs by which a doctor is able to recognize the disease affecting a patient. • *adj* **symptomatic**.

synagogue /si-nu-gog/ *n* a place where Jewish people go to worship.

synchronize /sing-cru-nize/ *vb, also* **synchronise** **1** to happen or cause to happen at the same time. **2** to set to exactly the same time.

syncopate /sing-cu-pate/ *vb* to change the rhythm of music by beginning or ending notes slightly sooner or later than expected. • *n* **syncopation**.

syndicate /sin-di-kit/ *n* **1** a group of persons or companies who are working together for business reasons or financial gain. • *vb* /sin-di-cate/ **1** to join together in a syndicate. **2** to sell for publication in more than one journal, newspaper, etc.

syndrome /sin-drome/ *n* a number of symptoms occurring together making up a specific disease or condition.

synonym /si-nu-nim/ *n* a word having the same or nearly the same meaning as another word.

synonymous /si-non-im-us/ *adj* having the same meaning.

synopsis /si-nop-sis/ *n* a summary; a short account of the main happenings or ideas in a book.

syntax /sin-taks/ *n* the putting of words in a sentence in order and in the correct relation to each other. • *adjs* **syntactic(al)**.

synthesis /sin-thi-sis/ *n* the putting together of parts to make a whole.

synthetic /sini-thet-ic/ *adj* made or put together by artificial means, not naturally.

syphon /sie-fun/ *n same as* **siphon**.

syringe /si-rinj/ *n* a tube filled with a piston by means of which fluid can be drawn up or squirted out. • *vb* to squirt or spray with a syringe.

syrup /si-rup/ *n* **1** any thick, sweet-tasting liquid. **2** the thick liquid obtained when refining cane sugar.

system /si-stum/ *n* **1** a method by which a number of parts of different kinds are made to work together as a unified whole. **2** a regular method of doing things. **3** a plan.

systematic /si-stu-mat-ic/ *adj* methodical, arranged in an orderly or reasonable manner, following a pre-arranged plan.

systematize /si-stu-ma-tize/ *vb, also* **systematise** to reduce to a system.

T

T, t /**tee**/ the 20th letter of the English alphabet.

tab /**tab**/ *n* a small piece of paper, fabric, etc, sticking out from something larger, a small flap.

tabby /**ta**-bee/ *n* a grey or brown striped cat.

tabernacle /**ta**-ber-na-cul/ *n* a place of worship.

table /**tay**-bul/ *n* **1** an article of furniture with legs and a flat top, used for placing or resting things on. **2** a list of figures, names, facts, etc, arranged in columns. • *vb* to put forward for discussion. • **turn the tables on** to begin doing to another what he or she has been doing to you.

tableau /**ta**-blo/ *n* (*pl* **tableaux**) a scene in which people stand motionless as if figures in a picture.

tablecloth /**tay**-bul cloth/ *n* a piece of material that is spread over a dining table.

table manners /**tay**-bul man-ers/ *npl* good behaviour while at the dinner table.

tablespoon /**tay**-bul-spoon/ *n* a large spoon used for serving at the table or as a measure in cooking.

tablet /**ta**-blet/ *n* **1** a piece of cardboard or flat piece of metal or stone with some writing or signs on it. **2** a small flat slab. **3** a pill.

table tennis /**tay**-bul te-nis/ *n* a game like tennis, played with paddles and a light plastic ball on a table with a net across the middle.

tabloid /**ta**-bloid/ *n* a small-format newspaper, usually with emphasis on photographs and news in condensed form.

taboo, tabu /ta-**boo**/ *adj* set apart so as not to be touched or used, forbidden for religious reasons or because it is against social custom. • *n* an order not to touch or use something.

tabular /**ta**-byu-lar/ *adj* set out in columns or tables.

tabulate /**tab**-yoo-late/ *vb* to arrange in columns or tables in a systematic way. • *n* **tabulation, tabulator**.

tacit /**ta**-sit/ *adj* thought or intended, but not spoken.

taciturn /**ta**-si-turn/ *adj* speaking little, silent by nature. • *n* **taciturnity**.

tack /**tack**/ *n* **1** a small sharp nail with a broad head. **2** a long, loose stitch. **3** the zigzag course of a sailing ship when sailing against the wind. • *vb* **1** to nail with tacks. **2** to sew with long, loose stitches. **3** (*of a sailing ship*) to change course to catch the wind. **4** to add on. • **on the wrong tack** on the wrong trail.

tackle /**ta**-cul/ *n* **1** all the equipment needed for some sport or game. **2** all the things necessary for a task. **3** a series of ropes, pulleys, etc, for raising weights, sails, etc. • *vb* **1** to struggle with, to seize and pull down. **2** (*in football*) to prevent from advancing with the ball. **3** to try to do. **4** to speak to or put questions to.

tacky[1] /**ta**-kee/ *adj* sticky. • *n* **tackiness**.

tacky[2] /**ta**-kee/ *adj* (*inf*) cheap, in bad taste. • *n* **tackiness**.

tact /**tact**/ *n* the ability to speak or behave without hurting the feelings of others, consideration. • *adj* **tactful, tactless**. • *adv* **tactfully, tactlessly**.

tactical /**tac**-ti-cul/ *adj* having to do with tactics. • *adv* **tactically**.

tactician /tac-ti-**shun**/ *n* **1** a person who is skilled in tactics. **2** a person who is quick to see a possible advantage.

tactics /**tac**-tics/ *npl* **1** the art of moving armies or other warlike forces during battle. **2** any actions intended to gain an immediate advantage.

tactile /**tac**-tile/ *adj* having to do with the sense of touch.

tadpole /**tad**-pole/ *n* the young of a frog, toad, etc, just after it has come out of the egg.

taffeta /**ta**-fi-ta/ *n* a shiny silk material.

tag[1] /**tag**/ *n* **1** the metal point at the end of a shoe-lace. **2** an address label. **3** a common quotation or saying. • *vb* (**tagged, tagging**) to fasten on.

tag[2] /**tag**/ *n, also* **tig** a children's game in which one person chases the others, tapping on the shoulder the first one caught, who then becomes the chaser.

tail /**tail**/ *n* **1** a long hanging part of an animal's body, situated at the end of the spine. **2** the back part of anything.

tailcoat /**tail**-coat/ *n* a man's coat, short in front, long and divided down the middle at the back.

tail end /**tail** end/ *n* the last or back part.

tailgate /**tail**-gate/ *n* a board for closing the back of a cart or truck. • *vb* to drive too closely to another vehicle.

tail light /**tail** lite/ *n* the light at the back of a vehicle.

tailor /**tay**-lor/ *n* a person who makes clothing, especially for men. • *vb* to make clothing.

tails /**tailz**/ *npl* **1** the reverse side of a coin. **2** a tailcoat.

taint /**taint**/ *vb* to spoil or make bad. • *n* **1** a stain, an evil element that spoils the rest. **2** a mark of shame or disgrace.

take /take/ *vb* (*pt* **took**, *pp* **taken**) **1** to seize or grasp. **2** to receive or accept. **3** to capture. **4** to carry. **5** to travel by. **6** to eat. **7** to require. • **take after** to be like. • **take down** to write. • **take for** to think to be. • **take heart** to become braver. • **take in 1** to deceive. **2** to understand. **3** to make. • **take on** to agree to play or fight against. • **take over** to get control of. • **take place** to happen. • **take to** to begin to like. • **take up** to begin to do or study. • **take up with** to begin to go about with.

take-away /tayk-a-way/ *n* **1** ready-cooked food bought from a restaurant or store to be eaten elsewhere. **2** a restaurant selling such food.

taken *pp of* **take**.

takeover /take-oa-ver/ *n* an instance of getting control of something, especially a business.

talc /talc/ *n* **1** a glasslike mineral. **2** a fine powder for the skin made from this.

talcum powder /tal-cum pow-der/ *n* a fine, perfumed powder made from talc.

tale /tale/ *n* a story.

talent /ta-lent/ *n* special ability or skill.

talented /ta-len-tid/ *adj* very clever.

talisman /ta-liz-man/ *n* (*pl* **talismans**) an object, word or words supposed to possess magic powers.

talk /tawk/ *vb* to speak. • *n* **1** a conversation. **2** a lecture. **3** gossip. • **talk over** to discuss. • **talk (someone) around** to convince. • **talk to** to scold.

talkative /taw-ka-tiv/ *adj* fond of talking.

tall /tawl/ *adj* **1** high. **2** above the usual height.

tallow /ta-lo/ *n* the melted fat of animals.

tally /ta-lee/ *n* **1** an account. **2** a score or count. • *vb* to agree with, to fit.

Talmud /tal-mood/ *n* the Jewish system of law.

talon /ta-lon/ *n* the claw of a bird of prey.

tambourine /tam-bu-reen/ *n* a small one-sided drum with rattling metal discs around its sides, played by hand.

tame /tame/ *adj* **1** not wild. **2** trained to be obedient. **3** not exciting, dull. • *vb* to make tame.

tamper /tam-per/ *vb* to meddle with, to interfere with dishonestly or unlawfully.

tampon /tam-pon/ *n* a plug of absorbent material inserted in the vagina during menstruation.

tan /tan/ *n* **1** bark of trees crushed for use in preparing leather. **2** a light brown colour. **3** suntan. • *vb* (**tanned, tanning**) **1** to treat animal skins so as to turn them into leather. **2** to make or become brown from exposure to the sun. • *adj* light brown in colour.

tandem /tan-dem/ *adj* one behind the other. • *n* a bicycle for two persons, one sitting behind the other.

tandoori /tan-doo-ree/ *n* an Indian way of cooking meat in a clay pot.

tang /tang/ *n* **1** a sharp taste. **2** a characteristic flavour.

tangent /tan-jent/ *n* a straight line touching a circle but not cutting it. • **go off at a tangent** to begin talking about something quite different.

tangible /tan-ji-bul/ *adj* **1** able to be touched. **2** real, actual. • *adv* **tangibly**.

tangle /tang-gul/ *vb* **1** to interweave in a confused way that is difficult to undo. **2** to muddle. • *n* **1** a mass of confusedly interwoven thread, string, etc. **2** a muddle, a complication.

tango /tang-go/ *n* a South American dance.

tank /tangk/ *n* **1** a large container for storing water, oil, etc. **2** a fighting vehicle protected by thick metal plates and moving on caterpillar tracks.

tankard /tang-kard/ *n* a large metal drinking mug.

tanker /tang-ker/ *n* a cargo ship with tanks for carrying oil.

tanned /tand/ *adj* **1** made brown by the sun. **2** made into leather.

tannery /ta-ne-ree/ *n* a place where leather is made.

tannic /ta-nic/ *adj* having to do with tannin.

tannin /ta-nin/ *n* a substance found in the bark of the oak and certain other trees, used in tanning leather.

tantalize /tan-ta-lize/ *vb*, *also* **tantalise** to torment by raising false hopes.

tantrum /tan-trum/ *n* a fit of bad temper or ill-humour.

tap[1] /tap/ *n* **1** a stopper. **2** a device for regulating the flow of a liquid from a pipe. • *vb* (**tapped, tapping**) **1** to fit with a tap. **2** to draw liquid out of. **3** to obtain information from.

tap[2] /tap/ *vb* (**tapped, tapping**) **1** to strike lightly. **2** to knock gently. • *also n.*

tap-dance /tap-danse/ *vb* to dance with shoes with metal plates on the soles, making elaborate tapping sounds on the floor. • *n* **tap-dancer, tap-dancing**.

tape /tape/ *n* **1** a long, narrow strip of cloth, paper, or sticky material. **2** a sensitized strip for recording and transmitting sound or pictures. • *also vb.*

tape measure /tape-me-zhur/ *n* a strong tape of cloth, metal, etc, used for measuring.

taper /tay-per/ *n* a long wick coated with wax, like a thin candle. • *vb* to become narrow or thinner at one end.

tape recorder /tape ri-cor-der/ *n* a machine for recording and transmitting sounds on magnetic tape. • *n* **tape-recording**.

tapestry /ta-pe-stree/ *n* a large piece of cloth in which different coloured threads are worked together to make a picture, sometimes hung on walls as a decoration.

tapeworm /tape-wurm/ *n* a long tapelike worm sometimes found in the intestines.

tapioca /ta-pee-yo-ca/ *n* **1** an edible grain obtained from a West Indian plant. **2** a pudding made from it.

tapir /tay-pir/ *n* a piglike animal of South America.

tar /tar/ *n* **1** a thick, black, sticky substance obtained from wood or coal. **2** (*old*) a sailor. • *vb* (**tarred**, **tarring**) to coat with tar.

tarantula /ta-ran-chu-la/ *n* a large poisonous spider.

tardy /tar-dee/ *adj* (*old*) slow, late. • *n* **tardiness**.

target /tar-git/ *n* **1** something set up for aiming or shooting at. **2** a goal or result that you hope to achieve. • *vb* to make someone the object or focus of something.

tariff /ta-rif/ *n* **1** the tax to be paid on an imported commodity. **2** a list of the taxes to be paid on imported goods. **3** a list of charges.

tarnish /tar-nish/ *vb* **1** to make less bright, to discolour. **2** to spoil.

tarpaulin /tar-paw-lin/ *n* strong cloth or canvas covered with tar to make it waterproof.

tarragon /ta-ra-gon/ *n* a plant with leaves that are used to add flavour in cooking.

tarry[1] /tahr-ee/ *adj* coated with tar.

tarry[2] /tar-ee/ *vb* (*old or lit*) to stay, to delay, to wait behind.

tart[1] /tart/ *n* a pastry containing jam or fruit.

tart[2] /tart/ *adj* **1** sharp-tasting. **2** sour, biting, sarcastic.

tartan /tar-tan/ *n* a cloth with stripes and squares of different colours, especially when worn as part of Scottish Highland dress.

tartar /tar-tar/ *n* **1** a crust of lime left by wine in a barrel. **2** a hard substance that forms on the teeth. **3** a hot-tempered person, a person who is hard to manage.

task /task/ *n* a piece of work to be done. • *vb* to lay upon as a burden.

task force /task-foarss/ *n* a group of people brought together to deal with a particular problem.

taskmaster /task-ma-ster/ *n* (*old*) a person who sets work to be done and sees that it is done properly.

tassel /ta-sel/ *n* an ornamental knot with loose threads hanging down from it.

taste /tayst/ *n* **1** the sense by which you judge whether food is pleasant or unpleasant. **2** the ability to distinguish what is fine, beautiful, or correct from what is not so. **3** the flavour of food when eaten. **4** a small portion of food for testing. • *vb* **1** to eat to see whether pleasant or unpleasant. **2** to have a flavour.

tasteful /tayst-ful/ *adj* showing good taste or judgment. • *adv* **tastefully**.

tasteless /tayst-less/ *adj* **1** having no flavour. **2** showing bad taste or judgment.

tasty /tay-stee/ *adj* having a pleasing flavour.

tattered /ta-terd/ *adj* ragged.

tatters /ta-terz/ *npl* ragged clothing.

tattoo[1] /ta-too/ *vb* to make a coloured design on the skin by pricking holes in it and filling them with coloured matter. • *also n*.

tattoo[2] /ta-too/ *n* **1** beating of a drum, blowing of a bugle, etc, to recall soldiers to camp at night. **2** a night display of military drill, exercises, etc, to music.

tatty /ta-tee/ *adj* shabby, worn.

taught /tawt/ *pt of* **teach**.

taunt /tawnt/ *vb* to make fun of in order to hurt; to mock, to sneer at. • *n* a mocking or hurtful remark.

taut /tawt/ *adj* stretched tight.

tautology /taw-tol-o-jee/ *n* saying the same thing again in different words. • *adj* **tautological**.

tavern /ta-vern/ *n* (*old*) an inn, a pub.

tawdry /taw-dree/ *adj* showy but cheap or of bad quality. • *n* **tawdriness**.

tawny /taw-nee/ *adj* yellowish brown.

tax /taks/ *n* money paid to the government to help pay for public services. • *vb* **1** to raise a tax. **2** to charge a tax on. **3** to accuse. **4** to be a hard test for. • *adj* **taxable**.

taxation /tak-say-shun/ *n* **1** all the taxes paid. **2** the charging of taxes.

taxi /tak-see/ *n* a car with driver for hire, especially one fitted with a machine (**taximeter**) showing the amount to be paid as a fare. • *also* **taxicab**. • *vb* (*of an aeroplane*) to run along the ground.

taxidermist /tak-si-der-mist/ *n* a person who is skilled in taxidermy.

taxidermy /tak-si-der-mee/ *n* the art of stuffing the skins of dead animals to make them look like living animals.

tea /tee/ *n* **1** a shrub found in India and China. **2** its leaves, dried. **3** a drink made by pouring boiling water on dried tea leaves. **4** a light afternoon or evening meal.

teach /teech/ *vb* (*pt, pp* **taught**) **1** to give information about. **2** to show how to do something. **3** to give lessons to. • *n* **teaching**.

teacher /tee-cher/ *n* **1** a person who teaches. **2** a person who teaches in a school.

teak /teek/ *n* an Indian tree producing very hard wood.

teal /teel/ *n* a small freshwater wild duck.

team /teem/ *n* **1** a number of persons working together for the same purpose. **2** a set of players on one side in a game. **3** a number of horses, oxen, etc, harnessed together.

teamwork /teem-wurk/ *n* united effort for the common good.

tear[1] /tear/ *n* a drop of water appearing in or falling from the eyes.

tear[2] /tare/ *vb* (*pt* **tore**, *pp* **torn**) **1** to pull apart or into pieces. **2** to pull with violence. **3** (*inf*) to rush. • *n* a hole or division made by tearing.

tearful /teer-ful/ *adj* weeping. • *adv* **tearfully**.

tear gas /teer gas/ *n* a gas that makes your eyes water, sometimes used to disperse a crowd.

tease /teez/ *vb* **1** to annoy by making fun of. **2** to pull apart wool, etc, into separate strands. **3** to comb wool or hair to give it a hairy surface. • *n* a person who annoys another by teasing.

teaser /tee-zer/ *n* a difficult problem.

teaspoon /tee-spoon/ *n* a small spoon for use with tea or as a measure in cooking.

teat /teet/ *n* **1** the part of the breast from which milk may be sucked or drawn. **2** a rubber attachment through which a baby sucks milk from a bottle.

technical /tec-ni-cal/ *adj* having to do with a particular art, science, or craft.

technicality /tec-ni-**ca**-li-tee/ *n* **1** a technical word or phrase. **2** a small detail or rule.

technically /**tek**-ni-cal-lee/ *adv* strictly speaking.

technician /tek-**ni**-shan/ *n* a person who is skilled in a particular art or craft.

technique /tek-**neek**/ *n* the method of doing something that requires skill.

technology /tek-**nol**-o-jee/ *n* the use of practical sciences to change and improve human environments such as solve problems, manufacture, develop communications, etc. • *adj* **technological**. • *n* **technologist**.

teddy /te-dee/, **teddy bear** /te-dee bare/ *n* a child's toy bear.

tedious /tee-dee-us/ *adj* long and boring, tiresome.

tedium /tee-dee-um/ *n* boredom; long, drawn-out dullness.

tee /tee/ *n* **1** the starting place for each 'hole' in golf. **2** a peg or small mound on which the ball may be placed for the first shot at each hole in golf.

teem /teem/ *vb* to be full of.

teenager /tee-nay-jer/ *n* a person who is between the ages of 13 and 19. • *adj* **teenage**.

teens /teenz/ *npl* the ages from 13 to 19.

teepee *see* **tepee**.

teeth *pl of* **tooth**.

teethe /teethe/ *vb* to grow your first teeth.

teetotal /tee-**toe**-tal/ *adj* taking no alcoholic drinks. • *n* **teetotaller**, *also* **teetotaler** (*US*).

tele- /te-lee/ *prefix* far, at, or to a distance.

telecommunications /te-li-cu-myoo-ni-**cay**-shunz/ *n* the technology or industry involved in transmitting information electronically over long distances by means of wires, radio signals, satellite, etc.

telegram /te-li-gram/ *n* a message sent by telegraph.

telegraph /**te**-li-graf/ *n* an apparatus for sending messages over a distance, especially by means of electricity. • *vb* to send by telegraph. • *adj* **telegraphic**. • *n* **telegraphy**.

telepathy /ti-le-pa-thee/ *n* the power to pass thoughts to or receive them from another, without the use of words or signs.

telephone /te-li-foan/ *n* (*abbr* = **phone**) an apparatus by means of which you may speak with a person at a distance. • *vb* to speak with or communicate by telephone.

telephonist /te-**le**-fu-nist/ *n* a person who operates a telephone switchboard; **operator**.

telephoto lens /tel-uh-**foe**-toe-lens/ *n* a lens on a camera enabling it to take pictures from a great distance.

telescope /te-le-scope/ *n* an instrument consisting of lenses set in a tube or tubes that, when looked through, makes distant objects appear larger. • *vb* **1** to slide together, one section fitting into another, as with a telescope. **2** to become shorter by one part sliding over the other.

telescopic /te-le-**scop**-ic/ *adj* **1** having to do with a telescope. **2** able to be seen only by means of a telescope. **3** something that telescopes.

televise /te-le-vize/ *vb* to transmit by television.

television /te-le-**vi**-zhun/ *n* the transmitting of pictures by sound waves so as to reproduce them on a screen.

tell /tell/ *vb* (*pt*, *pp* **told**) **1** to give an account of. **2** to let another know of by speaking. **3** to count. **4** to have an effect.

teller /tel-er/ *n* **1** a bank clerk who receives and pays out cash. **2** a person who is appointed to count votes.

telling /te-ing/ *adj* very effective.

telltale /tel-tale/ *adj* **1** giving information. **2** revealing what was meant to be secret. • *n* a person who tells what another has done to get him or her into trouble.

temerity /te-**mer**-i-tee/ *n* boldness, rashness.

temper /**tem**-per/ *n* 1 anger. 2 mood, state of mind. 3 the correct hardness of metal. • *vb* 1 to make less severe. 2 to harden. 3 to mix in proper proportions.

temperament /**tem**-pra-ment/ *n* 1 your character. 2 the usual state of your mind or feelings.

temperamental /tem-pra-**men**-tal/ *adj* easily excited, changing mood quickly. • *adv* **temperamentally**.

temperate /**tem**-prit/ *adj* 1 taking neither too much nor too little. 2 neither too hot nor too cold.

temperature /**tem**-pri-chur/ *n* degree of heat or cold. • **take your temperature** to find the degree of heat of your body.

tempest /**tem**-pest/ *n* a violent storm.

tempestuous /tem-**pes**-chu-wus/ *adj* 1 very stormy. 2 violent.

template /**tem**-plit/ *n* a pattern or mould used as a guide for shaping things.

temple[1] /**tem**-pul/ *n* 1 a place of worship. 2 a church.

temple[2] /**tem**-pul/ *n* the side of the head above the end of the cheekbone and between the ear and the forehead.

tempo /**tem**-po/ *n* (*pl* **tempos** or **tempi**) the speed at which a piece of music is played.

temporal /**tem**-pral/ *adj* 1 (*fml*) having to do with time. 2 worldly. 3 having to do with life on earth.

temporary /**tem**-pra-ree/ *adj* lasting for a time only, not permanent. • *adv* **temporarily**.

tempt /**tem**(p)t/ *vb* 1 to try to get someone to do what he or she ought not to do. 2 to arouse desire in. • *n* **tempter**, **temptress**.

temptation /tem(p)-**tay**-shun/ *n* attraction to what is wrong or forbidden.

tempting /**tem**(p)-ting/ *adj* 1 attractive. 2 arousing desire.

ten /ten/ *n, adj* the number 10. • **tenth** *adj and n*.

tenacious /ti-**nay**-shus/ *adj* 1 holding on firmly. 2 not giving in easily, stubborn. • *adv* **tenaciously**. • *n* **tenacity**.

tenancy /**te**-nan-see/ *n* 1 the renting of property. 2 property for which a rent is paid. 3 the time during which you rent property.

tenant /**te**-nant/ *n* a person who occupies rented property.

tend[1] /**tend**/ *vb* 1 to incline to. 2 to have a leaning towards.

tend[2] /**tend**/ *vb* to care for, to look after.

tendency /**ten**-den-see/ *n* a leaning towards, an inclination, liability to do certain things more than others.

tender[1] /**ten**-der/ *adj* 1 soft, gentle, and loving. 2 easily hurt. • *adv* **tenderly**. • *n* **tenderness**.

tender[2] /**ten**-der/ *vb* (*fml*) to offer or present. • *n* an offer, especially one to do work at a certain price.

tender[3] /**ten**-der/ *n* 1 a small boat carrying stores, etc, to a larger one. 2 a wagon or truck attached to a locomotive to carry coal, water, etc, for it.

tendon /**ten**-don/ *n* a strong cord-like band joining a muscle to a bone.

tendril /**ten**-dril/ *n* 1 a slender curling shoot by which some plants cling to supports when climbing. 2 a wispy curl of hair.

tenement /**te**-ni-ment/ *n* a large old building divided into flats, especially one in a city.

tennis /**te**-nis/ *n* a game played across a net by striking a ball to and fro with rackets.

tenor /**te**-nor/ *n* 1 the higher men's singing voices in the ordinary range. 2 the general meaning.

tense[1] /**tense**/ *n* a set of forms of the verb that indicate time.

tense[2] /**tense**/ *adj* 1 stretched tight. 2 strained. 3 excited from expectation. • *adv* **tensely**.

tension /**ten**-shun/ *n* 1 act of stretching. 2 tightness, strain. 3 excitement due to expectation.

tent /**tent**/ *n* a portable shelter of canvas, supported by a pole or poles and stretched and held in position by cords.

tentacle /**ten**-ta-cul/ *n* a slender boneless limb of various creatures, used for feeling, gripping, or moving.

tentative /**ten**-ta-tiv/ *adj* done as an experiment or trial. • *adv* **tentatively**.

tenterhooks /**ten**-ter-hooks/ *npl* hooks used to hold cloth taught on a frame. • **on tenterhooks** anxious or excited because of doubt or suspense.

tenth *see* **ten**.

tenuous /**ten**-yu-wus/ *adj* thin, slender.

tenure /**ten**-yur/ *n* the holding or conditions of holding land, office, etc.

tepee /**tee**-pee/, *also* **teepee** *and* **tipi** *n* a cone-shaped Native American tent made of skins.

tepid /**te**-pid/ *adj* lukewarm.

term /**term**/ *n* 1 a limited period of time. 2 a word or phrase used in a particular study. 3 a time when law courts are dealing with cases. 4 a division of the school year. • *vb* to name, to call. • *npl* conditions, charge, price. • **come to terms** to make an agreement. • **on good terms** friendly.

terminal /**ter**-mi-nal/ *adj* having to do with the end or last part. • *n* 1 the station at the end of a railway line or route. 2 an airport building where passengers arrive and depart from. **3** one of the screws to which an electric wire is attached to make a connection. **4** a computer monitor and keyboard for entering data. • *adv* **terminally**.

terminate /**ter**-mi-nate/ *vb* to bring or come to an end.

termination /ter-mi-**nay**-shun/ *n* **1** end, ending. **2** a medical procedure to end a pregnancy at an early stage; an abortion.

terminology /ter-mi-**nol**-o-jee/ *n* the words, phrases, etc, special to a particular branch of study.

termite /**ter**-mite/ *n* a white ant.

tern /**tern**/ *n* a sea bird like a gull, but smaller.

terrace /**te**-riss/ *n* **1** a raised bank of earth with a flat area on top. **2** a row of houses.

terraced /**te**-rist/ *adj* having terraces.

terracotta /te-ra-**cot**-a/ *n* **1** a reddish brown pottery. **2** its colour. • *also adj*.

terrain /te-**rain**/ *n* a stretch of country.

terrapin /**te**-ra-pin/ *n* a type of tortoise.

terrestrial /te-**re**-stree-al/ *adj* having to do with the Earth.

terrible /**te**-ri-bul/ *adj* **1** frightening, causing dread. **2** very bad. • *adv* **terribly**.

terrier /**te**-ree-er/ *n* a small dog that is good at hunting.

terrific /te-**ri**-fic/ *adj* **1** exceptionally good. **2** frightening, causing dread. • *adv* **terrifically**.

terrify /**te**-ri-fie/ *vb* to make very frightened.

territorial /te-ri-**toe**-ree-al/ *adj* having to do with a certain district or piece of land.

territory /**te**-ri-toe-ree/ *n* a district or piece of land, especially one that belongs to a person, a nation, etc.

terror /**te**-ror/ *n* **1** great fear, dread. **2** terrorism.

terrorism /**te**-ror-i-zum/ *n* the use of, or the threat of, extreme violence for political purposes.

terrorist /**te**-ror-ist/ *n* a person who uses, or threatens to use, extreme violence for political purposes.

terrorize /**te**-ror-ize/ *vb*, *also* **terrorise 1** to make very frightened. **2** to make do what is desired by causing fear.

terror-stricken /**te**-ror-stri-ken/ *adj* full of fear or dread.

terse /**terss**/ *adj* short and to the point. • *adv* **tersely**. • *n* **terseness**.

test /**test**/ *n* an examination or trial intended to reveal quality, ability, progress, etc. • *vb* **1** to try the quality of. **2** to examine.

testament /**tes**-ta-ment/ *n* **1** in law, a person's will. **2** one of the two main divisions of the Bible.

testator /tes-**tay**-tor/ *n* a person who leaves a will at death. • *f* **testatrix**.

testicle /**tes**-ti-kl/ *n* either of the two male reproductive glands that produce semen.

testify /**te**-sti-fie/ *vb* **1** to give evidence. **2** to say publicly what you believe to be true.

testimonial /te-sti-**moe**-nee-al/ *n* **1** a letter stating a person's good qualities and abilities. **2** a gift presented as a sign of respect.

testimony /**te**-sti-mo-nee/ *n* evidence, a public statement of belief.

test pilot /**test** pie-lot/ *n* a person who tests an aircraft by making it perform difficult manoeuvres.

test tube /**test**-toob/ *n* a glass tube open at one end, used for scientific experiments.

testy /**te**-stee/ *adj* irritable, easily angered.

tetanus /**tet**-nus/ *n* a disease causing cramp in the muscles and making the jaw so stiff that it cannot move.

tête-à-tête /te-ta-**tet**/ *n* a private talk between two people.

tether /**te**-ther/ *vb* to tie an animal by a rope to a stake or peg. • *n* a stake, etc. • **at the end of your tether** at the end of your strength or endurance.

tetra- /**te**-tra/ *prefix* four.

tetragon /**te**-tra-gon/ *n* a four-sided figure.

tetrahedron /te-tra-**hee**-dron/ *n* a solid figure with four sides shaped like a pyramid.

text /**tekst**/ *n* **1** the words actually written by the author (not including notes, drawings, etc.). **2** a short passage from the Bible. **3** subject, topic. **4** a text message. • *vb* to send a text message to.

textbook /**tekst**-book/ *n* a book about a subject written for those studying it.

textile /**tek**-stile/ *n* a fabric made by weaving. • *adj* having to do with or made by weaving.

text message /**tekst** meh-sidge/ *n* a message typed into a mobile phone and sent to another mobile phone. • *also* **SMS** = short message service.

texture /**teks**-chur/ *n* **1** the way in which a fabric or cloth, etc, is woven. **2** the quality of woven cloth.

than /**than**/ *conj* compared with.

thank /**thangk**/ *vb* to express pleasure to another for something done, etc, to express gratitude.

thankful /**thangk**-ful/ *adj* grateful, full of gratitude. • *adv* **thankfully**.

thankless /**thangk**-less/ *adj* ungrateful, for which you will receive no thanks.

thanks /**thangks**/ *npl* an expression of gratitude.

thanksgiving /thangks-gi-ving/ *n* **1** the act of giving thanks, especially to God at harvest time. **2** (*cap*) a national holiday in the US (November) and Canada (October) for giving thanks to God for health and harvest.

that /that/ *adj, pron, pl* **those** being the person or thing there. • *pron* who or which. • *conj* introduces a statement, a wish, etc.

thatch /thatch/ *n* straw used as a cover for the roof of a house. • *vb* to put thatch on. • *n* **thatcher**.

thaw /thaw/ *vb* **1** to melt. **2** to become more friendly. • *n* a state or time of thawing.

the /thi/, /thee/ *definite article* referring to a particular person or thing.

theatre /thee-a-tor/ *n, also* **theater** (*US*) **1** a building or hall in which plays are acted. **2** a lecture hall. **3** a scene of action. **4** a room in a hospital where surgeons perform operations.

theatrical /thee-a-tri-cal/ *adj* **1** having to do with plays or the theatre. **2** behaving as if acting in a play. • *adv* **theatrically**.

theatricals /thee-a-tri-calz/ *npl* dramatic performances.

thee /thee/ *pron* (*old*) you.

theft /theft/ *n* act of stealing.

their /thayr/, **theirs** /thayrz/ *poss adj and pron* belonging to them.

theism /thee-iz-um/ *n* belief in the existence of God. • *n* **theist**.

them /them/ *n* the form of 'they' used when the object of a sentence.

theme /theem/ *n* **1** subject, topic. **2** a set of notes played several times in a piece of music.

theme park /theem park/ *n* an amusement park based around a particular theme.

themselves /them-selvz/ *pron* the reflexive form of 'they'.

then /then/ *adv* **1** at that time. **2** after that. **3** therefore.

thence /thenss/ *adv* **1** from that time or place. **2** for that reason.

theologian /thee-ol-oaj-ee-an/ *n* an expert in or a student of theology.

theological /thee-ol-odge-ic-al/ *adj* having to do with theology.

theology /thee-ol-odge-ee/ *n* the study of the existence of God and people's beliefs about God.

theorem /thee-ur-em/ *n* an idea that can be proved true by reasoning.

theoretical /thee-ur-et-i-cal/ *adj* based on ideas, not on practice. • *adv* **theoretically**.

theorize /thee-ur-ize/ *vb, also* **theorise 1** to suggest explanations. **2** to put forward theories.

theory /thee-ur-ee/ *n* **1** an explanation that seems satisfactory but has not been proved true. **2** a set of ideas or rules on how something should be done.

therapeutic /ther-a-pyoo-tic/ *adj* having to do with therapy.

therapy /ther-a-pee/ *n* the treatment and cure of disease. • *n* **therapist**.

there /thare/ *adv* in that place.

thereafter /thay-raf-ter/ *adv* after that.

thereby /thare-bie/ *adv* by that means.

therefore /thare-fore/ *adv* for this or that reason.

thermal /ther-mal/ *adj* having to do with heat, hot.

thermodynamics /ther-mo-die-na-mics/ *n* the study of heat as a source of power.

thermometer /ther-mom-e-ter/ *n* an instrument for measuring degree of heat.

Thermos bottle /ther-mus/ *n* (*TM*) a flask for keeping hot liquid hot or cold liquid cold.

thermostat /ther-mu-stat/ *n* an instrument that mechanically controls temperature and keeps it steady.

thesaurus /thi-sawr-us/ *n* a reference book containing synonyms and antonyms.

these /theez/ *pl of* **this**.

thesis /thee-sis/ *n* **1** an opinion to be defended in writing or discussion. **2** an essay on a subject submitted for a higher university degree.

they /thay/ *pron* the people or things already mentioned.

they'd /thayd/ *contraction* they had.

they'll /thayl/ *contraction* they will.

they're /thayr/ *contraction* they are.

they've /thayv/ *contraction* they have.

thick /thick/ *adj* **1** broad. **2** fat. **3** not easily seen through. **4** slow to understand. • *n* the most crowded part. • *adv* **thickly**. • *n* **thickness**.

thicken /thi-ken/ *vb* to make or become thicker.

thicket /thi-ket/ *n* a group of trees, shrubs, etc, growing close together.

thick-skinned /thick-skind/ *adj* slow to feel or resent insults.

thief /theef/ *n* (*pl* **thieves**) a person who steals.

thieve /theev/ *vb* to steal things.

thievish /thee-vish/ *adj* given to stealing.

thigh /thie/ *n* the part of the leg above the knee.

thimble /thim-bul/ *n* a metal or plastic cap to protect the finger in sewing.

thin /thin/ *adj* **1** not thick. **2** not fat; lean, skinny, slim. **3** not crowded. **4** not convincing. • *vb* to make or become thin. • *adv* **thinly**. • *n* **thinness**.

thing /thing/ *n* **1** any single existing object. **2** whatever may be thought of or spoken about. **3** a happening. • *npl* your belongings.

think /thingk/ *vb* (*pt, pp* **thought, thinking**) **1** to form ideas in the mind, to consider. **2** to believe, to hold as an opinion.

thinker /thing-ker/ n **1** a person who thinks. **2** a person who tries to work out an explanation of life, etc, for himself or herself.

thinking /thing-king/ adj able to think or reason.

thin-skinned /thin-skind/ adj quick to feel or resent insults, easily upset.

third /thurd/ adj coming after second. • n one of three equal parts.

thirst /thurst/ n **1** the need or desire to drink. **2** a strong desire for anything. • vb**1** to feel thirst. **2** to desire strongly.

thirsty /thur-stee/ adj **1** wanting or needing a drink. **2** dry. **3** causing thirst. • adv **thirstily**.

thirteen /thur-teen/ n, adj the number 13. • adj and n **thirteenth**.

thirty /thur-tee/ n, adj the number 30. • adj and n **thirtieth**.

this /this/ adj, pron, pl **these** being the person or thing here.

thistle /thi-sul/ n a prickly plant with a purple head, the national emblem of Scotland.

thong /thong/ n **1** a strap of hide or leather. **2** a sandal consisting of a sole and straps from either side that pass between the first and second toe. **3** a woman's undergarment for the lower body that leaves the buttocks uncovered.

thorn /thawrn/ n **1** a prickle on the stem of a plant. **2** a bush or plant with prickles. • **thorn in the flesh** a cause of trouble or difficulty.

thorny /thawr-nee/ adj **1** prickly. **2** difficult, troublesome.

thorough /thu-ro/ adj **1** complete. **2** doing work with great care. • adv **thoroughly**. • n **thoroughness**.

thoroughfare /thu-ro-fare/ n a road open to the public and to traffic.

those /thoaz/ pl of **that**.

though /thoa/ prep despite the fact that.

thought /thawt/ pt of **think**. • n **1** the power or act of thinking. **2** what you think, an idea.

thoughtful /thawt-ful/ adj **1** given to thinking. **2** considerate, thinking of others. • adv **thoughtfully**. • n **thoughtfulness**.

thoughtless /thawt-less/ adj **1** not thinking before acting. **2** inconsiderate, not thinking of others. • adv **thoughtlessly**. • n **thoughtlessness**.

thousand /thou-zand/ adj and n ten hundred.

thrash /thrash/ vb **1** to beat hard, to flog. **2** to move around in an uncontrolled way.

thrashing /thra-shing/ n a hard beating, a flogging.

thread /thred/ n **1** a fine strand of any substance (e.g. cotton, wool, etc.) drawn out and twisted to make a cord. **2** the spiral ridge running around a screw, etc. **3** the main connected points running through an argument. • vb **1** to pass thread or fine cord through. **2** to make your way through.

threadbare /thred-bare/ adj (of clothing) having the fluffy surface worn off, shabby, frequently used, and so no longer fresh or new.

threat /thret/ n **1** a promise to hurt or punish another in future. **2** a warning of harm to come.

threaten /thre-ten/ vb **1** to make threats to. **2** to be a sign of coming harm, evil, etc. • adj **threatening**. • adv **threateningly**.

three /three/ adj and n the number 3.

thresh /thresh/ vb to separate grains from the rest of the plant by beating it or putting it through a machine.

threshing machine /thre-shing-ma-sheen/ n a machine that separates seed from straw.

threshold /thresh-hoald/ n **1** the plank or stone you cross when passing through a door. **2** the beginning.

threw /throo/ pt of **throw**.

thrice /thrice/ adv three times.

thrift /thrift/ n care in spending or using up, the habit of saving and not wasting.

thrifty /thrif-tee/ adj careful in spending, saving. • adv **thriftily**.

thrill /thrill/ n a sudden feeling of excitement or emotion. • vb to excite, to cause a thrill in.

thriller /thri-ler/ n a story written to excite or horrify.

thrilling /thri-ling/ adj very exciting.

thrive /thrive/ vb **1** to do well. **2** to be or become strong or successful.

throat /throat/ n **1** the front of the neck. **2** the opening downward at the back of the mouth and the pipe leading down from it.

throb /throb/ vb **1** to beat, as the heart. **2** (of pain) to increase and decrease at short regular intervals. • also n.

throne /throan/ n the chair occupied by a monarch or bishop.

throng /throng/ n a crowd. • vb to go in crowds, to crowd together.

throttle /throt-ul/ n **1** the throat or windpipe. **2** a lever working a valve that controls the supply of steam, petrol, etc, to an engine. • vb **1** to choke or strangle. **2** to cut down the supply of steam, etc, by using a throttle.

through /throo/ prep **1** from end to end. **2** from beginning to end. **3** by means of. **4** because of. • adv from end to end. • adj going all the way without requiring changes.

throughout /throo-out/ adv in every way or part. • prep all the way through.

throw /thro/ vb (pt **threw**, pp **thrown**) **1** to fling or cast. **2** to make to fall on the ground (e.g. in wrestling). • *n* **1** act of throwing. **2** the distance to which something can move or be flung through the air.

thrum /thrum/ *vb* (**thrummed, thrumming**) **1** to play (a musical instrument) carelessly. **2** to play by pulling the strings of.

thrush[1] /thrush/ *n* a songbird.

thrush[2] /thrush/ *n* a fungal infection that can affect the mouth, throat and genitals.

thrust /thrust/ *vb* **1** to push with force. **2** to stab at or into. **3** to push forward. • *n* **1** a sudden or violent push. **2** a stab.

thud /thud/ *n* a low dull sound, as of a muffled blow. • *also vb.*

thug /thug/ *n* a ruffian.

thumb /thum/ *n* the shortest and thickest of the fingers. • *vb* to turn over pages with your thumb. • **rule of thumb** a rough rule based on practice. • **thumb a lift** *to* signal with the thumb that you would like a lift in a passing vehicle. • **under someone's thumb** under the control or influence of someone.

thump /thump/ *n* a dull heavy blow. • *vb* to beat heavily.

thunder /thun-der/ *n* **1** the sound that follows lightning. **2** any loud rumbling noise. • *vb* **1** to make thunder. **2** to make a loud noise. • *adj* **thundery** (*of weather*) hot and close, as before a thunderstorm.

thunderbolt /thun-der-boalt/ *n* a flash of lightning.

thunderclap /thun-der-clap/ *n* a peal of thunder.

thunderous /thun-der-us/ *adj* like thunder, very loud.

thunderstorm /thun-der-stawrm/ *n* a spell of thunder, lightning, and heavy rain.

thunderstruck /thun-der-struck/ *adj* amazed, astonished.

Thursday /thurz-day/ *n* the fifth day of the week.

thus /thus/ *adv* in this way.

thwack /thwack/ *vb* to beat hard. • *n* a heavy blow.

thwart /thwawrt/ *vb* to prevent from succeeding.

thyme /time/ *n* a herb with sweet-smelling leaves, used in cooking.

tiara /tee-ya-ra/ *n* a jeweled band, like a small crown, worn on the head by ladies.

tibia /ti-bee-ya/ *n* the shin bone.

tic /tic/ *n* an involuntary movement of a muscle, especially in the face.

tick[1] /tick/ *n* **1** the sound made by a watch or clock. **2** a mark made when checking or correcting. • *also vb.*

tick[2] /tick/ *n* a small blood-sucking insect.

ticket /ti-ket/ *n* **1** a marked card giving its possessor the right to do something (e.g. travel by train, enter a theatre, etc). **2** a label.

tickle /ti-cul/ *vb* **1** to cause discomfort or make laugh by touching or prodding lightly a sensitive part of the body. **2** (*inf*) to please, to amuse.

ticklish /ti-clish/ *adj* **1** easily tickled. **2** difficult, requiring careful management.

tidal /tie-dal/ *adj* having to do with tides.

tidal wave /tie-dal-wave/ *n* a **tsunami**.

tide /tide/ *n* **1** the regular rise and fall, or ebb and flow, of the sea. **2** time, season.

tidings /tie-dingz/ *npl* (*old or fml*) news.

tidy /tie-dee/ *adj* neatly arranged, orderly. • *vb* to arrange neatly. • *adv* **tidily**. • *n* **tidiness**.

tie /tie/ *vb* **1** to fasten with cord, rope, etc. **2** to make a knot in. **3** (*in a game or contest*) to be equal (with). • *n* **1** a connection, bond. **2** a draw. **3** a match in a knockout competition. **4** a narrow band of coloured cloth worn round the neck, mostly by men, but also by women and children as part of a uniform.

tie breaker /tie brake-ur/ *n* an extra game played to decide between participants in a game that has resulted in a **tie**, sense **3**.

tier /teer/ *n* one of a series of rows, of seats, e.g., arranged on a slope, so that each row is slightly higher than the one below it.

tiff /tiff/ *n* a slight quarrel.

tig *see* **tag**[2].

tiger /tie-ger/ *n* a large fierce striped animal of the cat family. • *f* **tigress**.

tiger lily /tie-ger li-lee/ *n* a lily with spotted orange flowers.

tight /tite/ *adj* **1** close-fitting. **2** closely packed. **3** (*inf*) difficult, especially because of shortage of money. **4** (*inf*) drunk.

tighten /tie-ten/ *vb* to make or become tight. • *adv* **tightly**. • *n* **tightness**.

tightrope /tite-rope/ *n* a tightly stretched rope on which an acrobat walks and performs tricks.

tights /tites/ *npl* a light, close-fitting garment covering the lower trunk and legs.

tigress *see* **tiger**.

tile /tile/ *n* a thin slab of baked clay or other suitable material for covering roofs, floors, etc. • *vb* to cover with tiles.

till[1] /till/ *prep* up to the time of. • *conj* up to the time when.

till[2] /till/ *n* in a store, a drawer for money.

till[3] /till/ *vb* to plough and prepare for seed.

tiller /ti-ler/ *n* the handle of a rudder, a blade at the back of a boat by means of which it is steered.

tilt /tilt/ *vb* to make to slope to one side, to lean. • *n* a slant, a sloping position.

timber /**tim**-ber/ *n* **1** wood for building, carpentry, etc. **2** trees from which such wood can be obtained. **3** a wooden beam used in the framework of a house or ship.

time /**time**/ *n* **1** the measure of the passage of past, present, and future. **2** the moment of the hour, day, year, etc. **3** a season. **4** an occasion. **5** the rhythm of a piece of music. • *vb* **1** to see how long something lasts. **2** to see that something happens at the right moment. • **for the time being** meanwhile.

timekeeper /**time**-kee-per/ *n* a person who notes the times at which something begins and ends.

timely /**time**-lee/ *adj* (*inf*) happening at the right time.

timepiece /**time**-peess/ *n* (*old*) a watch or clock.

timer /**tie**-mer/ *n* a device used for timing something.

times /**tiemz**/ *prep* multiplied by.

timetable /**time**-tay-bul/ *n* **1** a list of classes, giving times when they begin and end. **2** a list giving the times of arrival and departure of trains, buses, etc.

timid /**ti**-mid/ *adj* easily made afraid, shy. • *adv* **timidly**. • *n* **timidity**.

timorous /**ti**-mu-russ/ *same as* **timid**.

timpani /**tim**-pa-nee/ *npl* kettledrums.

tin /**tin**/ *n* **1** a soft, light white metal. **2** a small metal container. • *adj* **tinned** preserved in a tin.

tincture /**tinc**-chur/ *n* **1** a shade of colour. **2** a slight taste or flavour of something. **3** a drug dissolved in alcohol.

tinder /**tin**-der/ *n* an easily lit substance that catches light from a spark.

tinge /**tinge**/ *vb* **1** to colour slightly. **2** to have a slight effect on. • *n* **1** a shade, a slight colour. **2** a small amount.

tingle /**ting**-gul/ *vb* to feel a prickly or thrilling sensation.

tinker /**ting**-ker/ *n* **1** a person who goes from door to door, mending pots, kettles, etc. **2** a vagabond. • *vb* **1** to mend roughly. **2** to work at unskilfully.

tinkle /**ting**-kul/ *vb* to make soft, bell-like sounds. • *also n*.

tinned /**tind**/ *see* **tin**.

tinny /**ti**-nee/ *adj* sharp and harsh in sound.

tin-opener /**tin**-o-pe-ner/ a device for opening tins of food etc.

tinsel /**tin**-sel/ *n* **1** thin strips, threads, discs, etc, of shiny metal, used for decoration. **2** anything showy but of little value.

tint /**tint**/ *n* **1** a shade of colour. **2** a faint colour. • *vb* to colour slightly.

tiny /**tie**-nee/ *adj* very small.

tip /**tip**/ *n* **1** a narrow end or point. **2** a light blow. **3** money given as a present or for special help. **4** a helpful hint. **5** a place where rubbish is left. **6** a very dirty or untidy place. • *vb* (**tipped, tipping**) **1** to put a tip on. **2** to make to tilt. **3** to give a money tip to. **4** to give a useful hint to. **5** to throw out.

tipi *see* **tepee**.

tipple /**ti**-pul/ *vb* (*inf*) to make a habit of taking strong liquor, to drink alcohol often. • *n* a small amount of alcohol.

tipsy /**tip**-see/ *adj* slightly drunk.

tiptoe /**tip**-toe/ *n* the point of the toe. • *vb* **1** to walk on the points of the toes. **2** to walk very quietly.

tiptop /**tip-top**/ *adj* splendid, excellent.

tirade /**tie**-rade/ *n* a long, angry speech, a violently critical speech.

tire /**tire**/ *vb* to make or become weary. • *adj* **tiring**. • *n* US variant of **tyre**.

tired /**tierd**/ *adj* weary.

tireless /**tire**-less/ *adj* not easily wearied, having much energy. • *adv* **tirelessly**.

tiresome /**tire**-sum/ *adj* boring, annoying.

tiring /**tie**-ring/ *see* **tire**[1].

tissue /**ti**-shoo/ *n* **1** any fine woven material. **2** substance (fat, muscle, etc.) of which the parts of animals and plants are made. **3** a complete connected set. **4** a paper handkerchief.

tissue paper /**ti**-shoo pay-per/ *n* thin soft paper for wrapping.

tit[1] /**tit**/ *n* a small bird.

tit[2] /**tit**/ *n* (*sl*) the female breast.

titanic /tie-**ta**-nic/ *adj* huge, gigantic.

titanium /tie-**tay**-nee-yum/ *n* a silver-grey metal that is used to make alloys.

titbit /**tit**-bit/ *n* a tasty piece of food.

titillate /**ti**-ti-late/ *vb* **1** to tickle. **2** to give pleasure to. • *n* **titillation**.

titivate /**ti**-ti-vate/ *vb* to make neat or smart.

title /**tie**-tul/ *n* **1** the name of a book, piece of writing or music, picture, etc. **2** a name or word used in addressing someone, to indicate rank, office, etc. **3** a claim to ownership, a right.

titled /**tie**-tuld/ *adj* being a member of the nobility.

title role /**tie**-tul role/ *n* the part of a character in a play whose name is the same as that of the play, e.g. Macbeth in *Macbeth*.

titter /**ti**-ter/ *vb* to giggle. • *also n*.

tittle-tattle /**ti**-tul-ta-tul/ *n* gossip, foolish talk.

titular /**ti**-chu-lar/ *adj* **1** relating to a title. **2** having rank or title but no powers.

to /**too**/ *prep* used to show movement towards.

toad /**toad**/ *n* a froglike animal that lives both on land and in water.

toadstool /**toad**-stool/ *n* a poisonous fungus, like a mushroom in shape.

toady /**toa**-dee/ *n* (*inf*) a person who flatters another in order to gain his or her favour. • *vb* to flatter or try to please in order to gain favour.

toast /toast/ *vb* **1** to dry and brown by heat. **2** to warm at the fire. **3** to drink the health of. • *n* **1** sliced bread browned by heat. **2** an act of raising glasses at a social gathering and drinking in honour of a person. **3** person whose health is drunk. **4** a sentiment or thing to which you drink.

toaster /**toa**-ster/ *n* an electrical appliance for toasting bread.

tobacco /tu-**ba**-co/ *n* the dried leaves of the tobacco plant, used for smoking or taken as snuff.

tobacconist /tu-**ba**-cu-nist/ *n* a person who sells tobacco, cigarettes, etc.

toboggan /tu-**bog**-an/ *n* a narrow sledge for sliding down snow-covered slopes. • *vb* (**tobogganed, tobogganing**) to go on a toboggan.

today /to-**day**/ *adv* on this day.

toddle /**tod**-ul/ *vb* to walk with short unsteady steps, as a small child.

toddler /**tod**-ler/ *n* a small child just beginning to walk.

toddy /**tod**-ee/ *n* a mixture of spirits, sugar, and hot water.

toe /toe/ *n* one of the five fingerlike members at the end of the foot. • **toe the line** to behave as you are told.

toffee /**taw**-fee/ *n* a kind of sweet made of sugar and butter.

toga /**toe**-ga/ *n* in ancient times, the garment of a Roman citizen.

together /to-**ge**-ther/ *adv* with another or others, in company.

toil /toil/ *vb* to work hard. • *n* hard work. • *n* **toiler**.

toilet /**toi**-let/ *n* **1** (*old*) the act of making yourself clean and tidy. **2** a large bowl in which people urinate or defecate before the waste matter is flushed away. **3** a room with such a bowl, a lavatory. • **toilet soap** *n* soap for washing the body.

token /**toe**-ken/ *n* **1** a mark or sign. **2** an object used to help to remember. **3** something used instead of money.

told /toald/ *pt and pp of* **tell**.

tolerable /**tol**-ra-bul/ *adj* able to be put up with. • *adv* **tolerably**.

tolerance /**tol**-er-anse/, **toleration** /tol-er-ay-shun/ *n* **1** patience. **2** readiness to allow what is displeasing, strange, or different to continue to exist.

tolerant /**tol**-er-ant/ *adj* ready to tolerate, broad-minded.

tolerate /**tol**-er-ate/ *vb* **1** to put up with. **2** to allow.

toll[1] /tole/ *n* a tax charged for the use of a bridge, road, etc.

toll[2] /tole/ *vb* to ring slowly, as a bell at a funeral. • *n* a single stroke of a large bell.

tomahawk /**tom**-a-hawk/ *n* an axe once used as a tool or a weapon by Native American peoples.

tomato /tom-**a**-toe/ *n* (*pl* **tomatoes**) **1** a plant with a soft edible fruit. **2** the fruit of the tomato.

tomb /toom/ *n* **1** a grave. **2** a cellar in which dead bodies are placed.

tomboy /**tom**-boy/ *n* an energetic girl who is fond of boyish games and sports.

tombstone /**toom**-stone/ *n* a stone placed over a grave giving the name, etc, of the person buried underneath.

tome /tome/ *n* a large, heavy book.

tommy gun /**tom**-ee-gun/ *n* a small machine gun.

tomorrow /to-**mor**-ow/ *adv* the day after today.

ton /tun/ *n* **1** an imperial measure of weight (= 20 hundredweight, 2000 lbs). **2** a metric tonne = 1000 kg.

tone /tone/ *n* **1** a sound. **2** the quality or pitch of a voice or sound. **3** the prevailing spirit or atmosphere. **4** a shade of colour. • *vb* to fit in with. • **tone down** to soften, to make less harsh. • *adj* **tonal**.

tongs /tongz/ *npl* an instrument with two arms between which things can be gripped for moving.

tongue /tung/ *n* **1** an organ in the mouth with the help of which you speak or taste. **2** anything shaped like a tongue (e.g. a leather flap in a shoe). **3** a language. **4** the clapper of a bell. • **hold your tongue** to remain silent.

tongue-tied /**tung**-tied/ *adj* unable to speak because of excitement or nervousness.

tongue-twister /**tung**-twi-ster/ *n* a group of words that it is difficult to pronounce quickly.

tonic /**ton**-ic/ *adj* **1** strengthening, giving vigour or health. **2** having to do with musical tones. **3** a soft drink. • *n* a strengthening medicine.

tonight /to-**nite**/ *adv* on this night.

tonnage /**tu**-nidge/ *n* the weight of goods a ship can carry.

tonne /tun/ *n* a metric ton (=2204.6 lbs, 1000 kg).

tonsil /**ton**-sil/ *n* one of the two glands at the back of the mouth.

tonsillitis /ton-si-**lie**-tis/ *n* a disease causing the tonsils to become swollen and sore.

too /too/ *adv* **1** also. **2** excessively.

took /took/ *pt of* **take**.

tool /tool/ *n* **1** an instrument for working with. **2** a person who does exactly what another wants him or her to do.

toot /toot/ *n* the sound of a horn. • *also vb.*

tooth /tooth/ *n* (*pl* **teeth**) **1** one of the bony projections rooted in the jaw, used for biting or chewing. **2** any tooth-shaped projection, as on a saw, comb, etc. • **have a sweet tooth** to like eating sweet things. • **long in the tooth** (*inf*) old. • **tooth and nail** with great violence or fury.

toothache /tooth-ake/ *n* a pain in a tooth.

toothbrush /tooth-brush/ *n* a brush for cleaning the teeth.

toothpaste /tooth-paste/ *n* a paste for cleaning the teeth.

toothpick /tooth-pick/ *n* a small stick used for removing anything stuck in or between the teeth.

toothy /too-thee/ *adj* having or showing large or sticking-out teeth.

top /top/ *n* **1** the highest part or place. **2** the summit. **3** a toy for spinning. **4** a garment worn on the upper body, e.g. a sweater or a T-shirt. • *adj* **1** highest. **2** most important. • *vb* (**topped, topping**) **1** to be at the top of. **2** to hit the top of. **3** to do better than.

topaz /to-paz/ *n* a precious stone.

top hat /top-hat/ *n* a tall cylindrical hat covered with silk.

top-heavy /top-he-vee/ *adj* so heavy at the top that it may fall over.

topic /top-ic/ *n* a subject of discussion.

topical /top-ic-al/ *adj* having to do with events of the present day.

topmost /top-moast/ *adj* highest.

topping /top-ing/ *n* a sauce or garnish that is put on the top of a hamburger, ice cream, etc.

topple /top-ul/ *vb* **1** to fall over, to overbalance. **2** to cause to fall.

topsy-turvy /top-see-tur-vee/ *adj* confused, upside-down.

torch /tawrch/ *n* **1** (*old*) a piece of blazing wood carried or stuck up to give light. **2** a small electric lamp for carrying in the hand.

tore /tore/ *pt of* **tear**.

toreador /taw-ree-ya-dore/ *n* a Spanish bullfighter.

torment /tawr-ment/ *n* **1** great suffering or agony. **2** great anxiety. • *vb* /tor-ment/ **1** to cause distress or suffering to, to torture. **2** to tease. • *n* **tormentor**.

torn /toarn/ *pp of* **tear**.

tornado /tor-nay-doe/ *n* (*pl* **tornadoes**) a violent swirling wind or hurricane.

torpedo /tor-pee-doe/ *n* (*pl* **torpedoes**) a long fish-shaped shell that can be fired through the water to hit another ship and explode on touching it. • *vb* to hit or damage with a torpedo.

torpid /tawr-pid/ *adj* lacking energy, numb, inactive, dull.

torrent /taw-rent/ *n* **1** a rushing stream. **2** a heavy downpour.

torrential /taw-ren-shal/ *adj* flowing with great violence, falling heavily and steadily.

torrid /taw-rid/ *adj* **1** extremely hot. **2** dried up by heat.

torso /tawr-so/ *n* the body not including the head or limbs.

tortilla /tawr-tee-ya/ *n* a thin pancake made with cornmeal or wheat flour and wrapped around a filling, used in Mexican cooking.

tortoise /tawr-toyz/ *n* a four-limbed reptile almost entirely covered in a hard shell. • *see also* **turtle**.

tortoiseshell /tawr-tus-shell/ *n* the shell of a type of sea turtle used to make combs, rims of spectacles, etc, coloured brown and yellow.

tortuous /tawr-choo-wus/ *adj* crooked, twisting.

torture /tawr-chur/ *vb* **1** to cause great suffering or anxiety to. **2** to cause pain to as a punishment or in order to obtain information from. • *n* extreme pain or anxiety. • *adj* **torturous**.

toss /tawss/ *vb* **1** to throw upward, to jerk upward. **2** (*of a ship*) to roll about in rough seas. **3** to drink. • *n* a throw. • **toss up** to throw up a coin to decide something by chance.

tot /tot/ *n* a small child.

total /toe-tal/ *adj* **1** whole. **2** complete. • *n* **1** the whole amount. **2** the result when everything has been added up. • *vb* **1** to add up. **2** to add up to. • *adv* **totally**.

totalitarian /toe-ta-li-tay-ree-un/ *adj* allowing only one political party.

totality /toe-ta-lity/ *n* the complete amount.

totem /toe-tem/ *n* an animal or plant taken by a tribe as an emblem and regarded as mysteriously connected with the tribe. • **totem pole** /toe-tem pole/ *n* a pole on which the totem or symbols of it are carried.

totter /tot-er/ *vb* to stand or walk unsteadily, to stagger.

toucan /too-can/ *n* a South American bird with a huge bill.

touch /tuch/ *vb* **1** to come to rest against any part of the body, especially the hand. **2** to be in contact. **3** to cause to feel emotion.

4 to make a difference to, to concern. • *n* **1** act of coming against or being in contact with. **2** the ability to do really well something requiring skill. **3** the sense of feeling. **4** (*in football*) the ground at the side of the marked field of play. • **touch on** to mention briefly. • **touch up** to improve by making small changes.

touching /tu-ching/ *adj* moving the feelings, causing pity.

touchline /tuch-line/ *n* (*in sports*) the side lines of the marked field of play.

touchstone /tuch-stone/ *n* something by comparison with which you judge other things, ideas, etc.

touchy /tu-chee/ *adj* easily angered or hurt. • *n* **touchiness**.

tough /tuff/ *adj* **1** hard to cut, tear, or chew. **2** hardy and strong. **3** rough-mannered. **4** difficult to deal with. • *n* a street ruffian.

toughen /tu-fen/ *vb* **1** to make tough. **2** to make better able to resist.

tour /toor/ *n* a journey, made for pleasure, to various places, usually ending up at the starting point. • *vb* to go for a tour, to travel here and there.

tourism /too-ri-zum/ *n* the providing of hotels, routes, etc, for tourists.

tourist /too-rist/ *n* a person who travels for pleasure, a sightseer.

tournament /toor-na-ment/ *n* **1** a series of games between different competitors to see which is the best player or team. **2** (*old*) a display of fighting on horseback in which the warriors carried blunted arms.

tourniquet /toor-ni-ket/ *n* a bandage twisted tightly around a limb to prevent the flow of blood from a cut artery.

tousle /tou-zel/ *vb* to disarrange, to make untidy, especially the hair.

tout /tout/ *vb* to go about looking for customers or buyers. • *n* a person who touts.

tow¹ /toe/ *vb* to pull along with a rope, chain, etc. • *n* the act of towing.

tow² /toe/ *n* fibres of flax or hemp.

towards /toow-ords/ *prep* in the direction of.

towel /taoo-el/ *n* a cloth for drying the body. • *vb* to rub with a towel.

tower /taoo-wer/ *n* **1** a building much higher than it is broad. **2** a high part of another building, projecting above it. **3** a fortress. • *vb* to rise high into the air.

towering /taoo-wer-ing/ *adj* **1** very high or tall. **2** very great.

town /taoon/ *n* a group of houses, stores, etc, larger than a village but smaller than a city.

toxic /tok-sic/ *adj* poisonous. • *n* **toxicity**.

toxicology /tok-si-**col**-o-jee/ *n* the study of poisons. • *n* **toxicologist**.

toxin /tok-sin/ *n* a poison.

toy /toy/ *n* a plaything. • *vb* to play with.

trace /trace/ *n* **1** a mark left behind. **2** a footstep. **3** a sign of something that has happened or existed. • *vb* **1** to copy a drawing on to transparent paper laid on top of it. **2** to follow the tracks of. • *adj* **traceable**.

tracery /tray-se-ree/ *n* stone carved to form an open design, as in the windows of old churches.

tracing /tray-sing/ *n* a drawing made by copying another drawing on to transparent paper laid on top of it.

track /track/ *n* **1** a footprint. **2** the mark or rut left by a wheel. **3** a path made by coming and going. **4** a railway line. **5** a course for races. • *vb* **1** to follow the marks left by. **2** to pursue or search for someone or something until found.

track-and-field /track-and-**feeld**/ *adj* of sports events, referring to sports such as running and jumping. •*n* athletics.

tract /tract/ *n* **1** a wide area of land. **2** a short booklet, especially one about religion.

traction /trac-shun/ *n* **1** the drawing of vehicles. **2** treatment of an injured limb by pulling on it gently with a device using weights and pulleys.

traction engine /trac-shun en-jin/ *n* a steam engine for dragging loads on roads.

tractor /trac-tor/ *n* a heavy motor vehicle used for drawing other vehicles or farm implements.

trade /trade/ *n* **1** the buying and selling of goods. **2** the exchanging of goods in large quantities. • *vb* **1** to buy and sell. **2** to exchange in large quantities.

trademark /trade-mark/ *n* an officially registered mark or name of manufactured goods to protect their ownership and use. Often shown by the symbols ® and ™.

trader /tray-der/ *n* a person who buys and sells goods, a merchant.

tradesman /traydz-man/, **tradesperson** /traydz-per-sun/ *n* **1** a skilled manual worker. **2** a shopkeeper.

tradition /tra-di-shun/ *n* **1** the handing down of knowledge, customs, etc, from age to age by word of mouth. **2** any story, custom, etc, so handed down.

traditional /tra-di-shnal/ *adj* according to or handed down by tradition. • *adv* **traditionally**.

traffic /tra-fic/ *n* **1** the coming and going of persons, vehicles, etc, between places. **2** trade. **3** the carrying of goods or persons in vehicles, etc. **4** all the vehicles on the roads. • *vb* (**trafficked, trafficking**) to trade.

tragedy /tra-je-dee/ *n* **1** a sad event, a disaster. **2** a play showing the suffering caused by man's inability to overcome evil.

tragic /tra-jic/ *adj* **1** having to do with tragedy. **2** very sad. • *adv* **tragically**.

trail /trail/ *n* **1** the track or scent left by a moving creature. **2** a path or track made by coming and going. • *vb* **1** to drag along the ground. **2** to draw along behind. **3** to walk wearily. **4** to follow the tracks of.

trailer /tray-ler/ *n* **1** a vehicle without an engine towed by another. **2** a short part of a film shown in advance advertisement. **3** a climbing plant.

train /train/ *vb* **1** to prepare or make to prepare by constant practice or teaching. **2** to aim. **3** to make to grow in a particular direction. • *n* **1** railway carriages or wagons drawn by an engine. **2** part of a dress that trails behind the wearer. **3** a series. • *n* **trainee**.

trainer /tray-ner/ *n* a person who teaches animals or people to do something, often a sport, well.

training /tray-ning/ *n* education, practice.

trait /trate/ *n* a special characteristic by which you may know a person.

traitor /tray-tor/ *n* a person who helps an enemy against his or her own country friends. • *adj* **traitorous**.

trajectory /tra-jec-tree/ *n* the path of a moving body (e.g. a bullet, a comet, etc.).

tram /tram/, **tramcar** /tram-car/ a vehicle running on rails laid in the street.

tramp /tramp/ *vb* to walk with heavy steps. • *n* **1** a long or difficult journey on foot. **2** a person who has no home and walks about the countryside begging. **3** the sound of heavy steps or many steps together.

trample /tram-pul/ *vb* to walk heavily on top of.

trampoline /tram-pu-leen/ *n* a large piece of canvas or strong nylon joined to a metal frame by springs, used for jumping on.

trance /transs/ *n* a state in which you are unconscious of your surroundings.

tranquil /tran-kwil/ *adj* **1** calm, peaceful. **2** still. • *n* **tranquillity**, *also* **tranquility** (*US*).

tranquilize /tran-kwi-lize/ *vb*, *also* **tranquilise** to calm (someone) down.

tranquilizer /tran-kwi-lie-zer/ *n*, *also* **tranquiliser** anything (e.g. a pill) that calms a person down.

transact /tran-zact/ *vb* (*fml*) to carry on or put through.

transaction /tran-zac-shun/ *n* a piece of business. • *npl* a written record of the doings of a society.

transatlantic /tran-zat-lan-tic/ *adj* across or crossing the Atlantic.

transcend /tran-send/ *vb* **1** to rise above. **2** to be superior to.

transcendent /tran-sen-dent/ *adj* mavellous.

transcendental /tran-sen-den-tal/ *adj* beyond human understanding, supernatural.

transcribe /tran-scribe/ *vb* to copy in writing.

transcript /tran-script/ *n* a written copy.

transept /tran-sept/ *n* one of the two parts representing the arms in a cross-shaped church.

transfer /tran-sfer/ *vb* (**transferred, transferring**) to send or remove from place or owner to another. • *n* /tran-sfer/ **1** the act of transferring. **2** a design that can be pressed from one surface onto another.

transferable /tran-sfe-ra-bul/ *adj* that can be transferred.

transference /tranz-fe-rense/ *n* act of transferring.

transfigure /tranz-fi-gyur/ *vb* **1** to change in form, shape, or appearance. **2** to make more beautiful or splendid. • *n* **transfiguration**.

transfix /tranz-fiks/ *vb* **1** to pierce through. **2** to cause to be unable to move.

transform /tranz-fawrm/ *vb* **1** to change the form of. **2** to change completely. • *n* **transformation**.

transformer /tranz-fawr-mer/ *n* a machine for changing the voltage of an electric current.

transfuse /trans-fyooz/ *vb* to transfer from one thing to another (e.g. by pouring).

transfusion /trans-fyoo-zhun/ *n* **1** the act of transfusing. **2** the passing of the blood of one person into another.

transient /tran-zee-ent/ *adj* **1** not lasting for long, passing quickly. **2** not staying for long. • *n* **transience**.

transistor /tran-zis-tor/ *n* a simple radio receiving set in which the current is produced by sensitive wires in contact with a crystal. • *adj* **transistorized**, *also* **transistorised**.

transit /tran-zit/ *n* **1** going or being moved from one place to another. **2** the passing of a planet between the sun and the earth.

transition /tran-zi-shun/ *n* changing from one state or condition to another. • *adj* **transitional**.

transitive /tran-si-tiv/ *adj* (*gram*) describing a verb taking a direct object. • *compare with* **intransitive**.

transitory /tran-zi-toe-ree/ *adj* passing quickly, not lasting for long.

translate /tranz-**late**/ vb to give the meaning of what is said or written in one language in another language. • n **translator**.

translation /tranz-**lay**-shun/ n a turning from one language into another.

translucent /tranz-**loo**-sent/ adj allowing light to pass through.

transmission /tranz-**mi**-shun/ n 1 the act of sending messages, etc. 2 a radio or television broadcast.

transmit /tranz-**mit**/ vb (**transmitted, transmitting**) 1 to send (a message, news, etc.). 2 to send by radio or television. 3 to send or pass from one person to another.

transmitter /tranz-**mi**-ter/ n a radio apparatus able to send messages or make broadcasts.

transmute /tranz-**myoot**/ vb (fml) to change from one form into another. • n **transmutation**.

transom /tran-sum/ n a window over a door.

transparent /tran-**spa**-rent/ adj 1 that can be clearly seen through. 2 obvious. • n **transparence, transparency**.

transpire /tran-**spire**/ vb 1 to become known. 2 to happen. 3 to exhale.

transplant /tran-s**plant**/ vb 1 to uproot and plant in another place. 2 to replace an organ of the body by one belonging to someone else. • n **transplant, transplantation** /transplan-**tay**-shun/.

transport /tran-**sport**/ vb 1 to carry from one place to another. 2 (old) to convey to another country as a punishment. 3 (fml) to fill with emotions, anger, etc. • n /tran-spoart/ 1 any means of carrying persons or goods from one place to another. 2 a ship for carrying troops. 3 (fml) great delight, ecstasy. • n **transportation**.

transpose /tran-**spoaz**/ vb 1 to interchange the places of. 2 to change the order of. • n **transposition**.

transverse /tranz-**verse**/ adj lying across.

trap /trap/ n 1 an instrument or device for catching wild animals and holding them alive or dead. 2 any device that, by its appearance, deceives you into advancing or progressing into unseen difficulties. 3 an S-shaped bend in drainpipes to prevent foul air rising. 4 a light two-wheeled horse carriage. • vb (**trapped, trapping**) 1 to catch in a trap or snare. 2 to deceive.

trapdoor /trap-dore/ n a door in a floor, ceiling, or roof.

trapeze /tra-**peez**/ n a bar suspended from two swinging ropes, some distance above the ground, and used in gymnastic or acrobatic exercises.

trapezium /tra-**pee**-zee-um/ n a four-sided

figure of which two sides are parallel and unequal in length.

trapper /tra-per/ n a person who traps animals, especially for their furs.

trappings /tra-pingz/ npl 1 finery, decoration. 2 an ornamental harness for a horse.

trash /trash/ n 1 (esp US) rubbish, waste material. 2 nonsense. 2 (inf) something of very poor quality. • vb (inf) to cause a lot of damage, to destroy something. • adj (inf) **trashy** very poor quality.

trauma /**traw**-ma/ n a shock that has a long-lasting effect. • adj **traumatic**. • adv **traumatically**.

travel /**tra**-vel/ vb 1 to make a journey. 2 to move on your way. • also n. • vb, adj **travelled, travelling**; also **traveled, traveling** (US).

travel agent /**tra**-vel-ay-jent/ n a person who makes travel arrangements for customers. • n **travel agency**.

traveller /**trav**-ler/ n, also **traveler** (US), also **travelling salesman** 1 a person who journeys. 2 a person who goes from place to place trying to obtain orders for a business firm.

traverse /tra-**verse**/ vb to go across.

travesty /tra-ve-stee/ vb to imitate in such a way as to make appear ridiculous. • n a silly imitation.

trawl /trawl/ n a large wide-mouthed net for deep-sea fishing. • vb to fish by drawing a trawl through the water.

trawler /**traw**-ler/ n a fishing boat using a trawl.

tray /tray/ n a flat piece of wood, metal, etc, with a rim, used for carrying dishes, etc.

treacherous /**tre**-che-rus/ adj 1 faithless, disloyal, deceitful. 2 dangerous, but seeming safe.

treachery /**tre**-che-ree/ n unfaithfulness to those who have placed trust in you; disloyalty.

treacle /**tree**-cul/ a dark-coloured syrup obtained when refining sugar.

tread /tred/ vb (pt trod, pp **trodden** or **trod**) 1 to step or walk. 2 to walk heavily on. • n 1 a step. 2 your way of walking. 3 the sound of walking. 4 the flat part of the step of a stair. 5 the part of a tire that touches the ground.

treadle /**tre**-dul/ n a pedal used for operating a machine.

treadmill /**tred**-mill/ n 1 a millwheel turned by persons treading on steps sticking out from it. 2 an exercise machine with an endless belt on which you walk or run.

treason /**tree**-zun/ n disloyalty to your country or ruler.

treasonable /**tree**-zu-na-bul/ adj having to do with treason.

treasure /**tre**-zhur/ *n* **1** something greatly valued. **2** a store of great wealth. • *vb* to value greatly.

treasurer /**tre**-zhu-rer/ *n* a person who is in charge of the money of a society, business firm, etc.

treasure trove /**tre**-zhur trove/ *n* treasure found hidden and ownerless.

treasury /**trezh**-ree/ *n* **1** (*cap*) the government department in charge of a nation's finances. **2** a place where valuable objects or money is kept. **3** (*old*) a book containing a collection of facts, poems, etc.

treat /**treet**/ *vb* **1** to deal with. **2** to act towards. **3** to talk or write about. **4** to try to cure by certain remedies. **5** to pay for another's entertainment. **6** to discuss conditions for an agreement. • *n* **1** an entertainment. **2** something that gives great pleasure.

treatise /**tree**-tiss/ *n* a piece of writing giving information on a certain subject.

treatment /**treet**-ment/ *n* the way of treating anything.

treaty /**tree**-tee/ *n* an agreement between two nations.

treble /**tre**-bul/ *adj* threefold, three times. • *vb* to multiply by three. • *n* the highest part in singing; soprano.

tree /**tree**/ *n* a plant with a trunk and branches of wood.

trek /**trek**/ *vb* (**trekked**, **trekking**) to journey on foot, often wearily. • *also n.*

trellis /**tre**-liss/ *n* a light framework of crisscrossing bars of wood or metal for supporting climbing plants.

tremble /**trem**-bul/ *vb* **1** to shake with fear, cold, fever, etc. **2** to feel great fear.

tremendous /tri-**men**-dus/ *adj* **1** huge. **2** very great, impressive. • *adv* **tremendously**.

tremor /**tre**-mur/ *n* a slight shaking or shivering.

trench /**trench**/ *n* a long, narrow hole or ditch dug in the ground, especially one to shelter soldiers from enemy gunfire.

trenchant /**tren**-chant/ *adj* (*of remarks*) sharp and forceful.

trend /**trend**/ *n* **1** a tendency. **2** a general inclination towards.

trendy /**tren**-dee/ *adj* (*inf*) very fashionable.

trepidation /tre-pi-**day**-shun/ *n* fear.

trespass /**tress**-pass/ *vb* **1** to go unlawfully on another's land. **2** (*old*) to sin. • *also n.* • *n* **trespasser**.

tress /**tress**/ *n* a lock of hair. • *npl* **tresses** long hair worn loose.

trestle /**tre**-sul/ *n* a frame that supports a bridge or railway track.

tri- /**trie**/ *prefix* three.

trial /**trie**-al/ *n* **1** the examining of a prisoner in a court of law. **2** a test. **3** hardship or distress undergone.

triangle /**trie**-ang-gul/ *n* **1** a figure with three sides and three angles. **2** a musical instrument consisting of a triangle-shaped steel rod, played by striking it with a small rod.

triangular /trie-**ang**-gyu-lar/ *adj* having three sides and three angles.

triathlon /trie-**ath**-lon/ *n* an athletic contest consisting of three events, usually swimming, cycling, and running.

tribe /**tribe**/ *n* a group of people or families living together under the rule of a chief. • *adj* **tribal**. • *n* **tribesman**.

tribulation /tri-byoo-**lay**-shun/ *n* great suffering or trouble.

tribunal /trie-**byoo**-nal/ *n* **1** a court of justice. **2** a body appointed to look into and report on a matter of public interest.

tribune /**tri**-byoon/ *n* a Roman magistrate chosen by the people.

tributary /**tri**-byu-ta-ree/ *n* a stream that flows into a larger stream or river

tribute /**tri**-byoot/ *n* **1** deserved praise. **2** money paid by a defeated nation to its conquerors.

trice /trice/ *n.* • **in a trice** in a moment.

trick /**trick**/ *n* **1** something said or done in order to deceive. **2** something done quickly and skilfully in order to amuse. **3** a special way of doing something. **4** cards played and won in a round. • *vb* to deceive, to cheat.

trickery /**trik**-ree/ *n* cheating, deceitful conduct.

trickle /**tri**-cul/ *vb* to flow very slowly. • *n* a thin stream of liquid.

tricky /**tri**-kee/ *adj* **1** cunning, crafty. **2** requiring skill. **3** difficult.

tricycle /**trie**-si-cul/ *n* a three-wheeled cycle.

trident /**trie**-dent/ *n* a spear with three prongs.

tried /**tried**/ *pt, pp of* **try**. • *adj* reliable, proved good.

trifle /**trie**-ful/ *n* **1** a thing of little value or importance. **2** a small amount. **3** a pudding consisting of sponge cake, fruit, and cream. • *vb* **1** to treat without seriousness. **2** to idle.

trifling /**trie**-fling/ *adj* **1** of no value or importance. **2** very small.

trigger /**tri**-ger/ *n* a small lever that when pulled fires a gun. • *vb* to cause something to happen.

trigonometry /tri-gu-**nom**-et-ree/ *n* the science dealing with the measurement of triangles, and the relation between their sides and angles.

trillion /**trill**-yun/ *n* **1** a million million (10^{12}; 1,000,000,000,000) **2** (*inf*) a very large number.

trilogy /**tri**-lo-jee/ *n* a series of three connected plays, novels, etc.

trim /trim/ *vb* (**trimmed, trimming**) **1** to make neat, especially by cutting. **2** to decorate. **3** to rearrange cargo so that a ship is properly balanced. **4** to make ready for sailing. • *adj* neat, tidy. • **in good trim 1** in good condition. **2** well-prepared.

trimester /trie-**mes**-ter/ *n* **1** an academic term. **2** three months. **3** one third of the length of a human pregnancy.

trimming /**tri**-ming/ *n* something added as an ornament.

trinity /**tri**-ni-tee/ *n* a union of three in one. • **the Trinity** the Christian belief that in one God there are three persons – the Father, Son, and Holy Spirit.

trinket /**tring**-ket/ *n* an ornament of little value, a piece of cheap jewellery.

trio /**tree**-yo/ *n* **1** a set of three, especially three musicians who play together. **2** a piece of music for three performers.

trip /trip/ *vb* (**tripped, tripping**) **1** to stumble or fall over. **2** to cause to stumble or fall. **3** (*fml*) to move with quick light steps. • *n* **1** a stumble. **2** a short journey or outing.

tripe /tripe/ *n* **1** part of the stomach of a sheep, cow, etc, prepared as food. **2** (*inf*) nonsense, rubbish.

triple /**tri**-pul/ *adj* made up of three parts, threefold. • *vb* to make or become three times as large or as many.

triplet /**tri**-plit/ *n* one of three children born at one birth.

triplicate /**tri**-pli-kit/ *adj* threefold. • *n*: **in triplicate** with three copies.

tripod /**trie**-pod/ *n* a three-legged stand or support (e.g. for a camera).

tripper /**tri**-per/ *n* (*old inf*) a person who is on holiday or on an outing for pleasure.

trite /trite/ *adj* often used, commonplace.

triumph /**trie**-yumf/ *n* **1** joy at success or victory. **2** a great success or victory. • *vb* to gain a great success or victory.

triumphal /trie-**yum**-fal/ *adj* having to do with a victory.

triumphant /trie-**yum**-fant/ *adj* **1** successful, victorious. **2** extremely pleased at success or victory. • *adv* **triumphantly**.

triumvirate /trie-**yum**-vi-rit/ *n* a group of three people sharing the power of government.

trivet /**tri**-vet/ *n* a three-legged stand for a pot, kettle, etc.

trivia /**tri**-vee-ya/ *npl* (*now often regarded as a singular noun*) facts of small importance.

trivial /**tri**-vee-yal/ *adj* of small importance, trifling. • *n* **triviality**.

trod *pt and pp of* **tread** (*pp also* **trodden**).

troglodyte /**trog**-la-dite/ *n* a cave-dweller.

troll /**trole**/ *n* a dwarfish elf or goblin.

trolley /**trol**-ee/ *n* (*pl* **trolleys**) **1** a kind of large metal basket on wheels for transporting goods in a supermarket or baggage at an airport. **2** a small table on wheels for serving food.

trombone /trom-**bone**/ *n* a deep-toned type of trumpet with a sliding tube moved in and out when it is being played.

troop /**troop**/ *n* **1** a collection or group of people or animals. **2** an organized group of soldiers, scouts, etc. • *vb* to move or gather in large numbers. • *npl* soldiers.

trooper /**troo**-per/ *n* a cavalryman, *see* **cavalry**.

trophy /**troe**-fee/ *n* something given or kept as a reward for or reminder of success or victory.

tropic /**trop**-ic/ *n* one of two imaginary lines around the earth marking the farthest distance north and south of the equator at which the sun rises and sets during the year. • *npl* the hot regions north and south of the equator.

tropical /**trop**-ic-al/ *adj* **1** having to do with the tropics. **2** very hot.

trot /trot/ *vb* (**trotted, trotting**) **1** (*of a horse*) to go at a pace between a walk and a gallop. **2** to run with short steps. • *n* a medium pace.

troth /troth/ *n.* • **plight your troth** (*old*) to promise to marry.

trotter /**trot**-er/ *n* the foot of a pig or sheep.

trouble /**tru**-bl/ *vb* **1** to cause anxiety, difficulty, or distress to. **2** to disturb. • *n* **1** worry, anxiety, distress. **2** difficulty.

troublesome /**tru**-bl-sum/ *adj* causing trouble.

trough /troff/ *n* **1** a long, narrow vessel to hold water or food for animals. **2** a hollow (e.g. between two waves).

trounce /**trounss**/ *vb* to beat severely.

troupe /**troop**/ *n* a company of actors or other performers.

trousers /**trou**-zers/ *npl* a garment with two tube-shaped pieces of material joined at the top, worn to cover the legs.

trousseau /**troo**-so/ *n* (*pl* **trousseaux** *or* **trousseaus**) a bride's outfit.

trout /trout/ *n* an edible freshwater fish.

trowel /**trow**-el/ *n* **1** a tool with a flat blade used for spreading mortar, plaster, etc. **2** a tool with a curved blade used in gardening.

troy /troy/, **troy weight** *n* a system of measures used in weighing precious metals or gems.

truant /**troo**-ant/ *n* a child who stays off school without leave. • **play truant** to stay off school without leave. • *n* **truancy**.

truce /**trooss**/ *n* an agreement to stop fighting for a time.

truck[1] /**truck**/ *n* a large motor vehicle for carrying goods, a lorry.

truck[2] /**truck**/ *n* dealings.

truculent /**tru**-cyu-lent/ *adj* quarrelsome, trying to find a cause for quarrelling or fighting. • *n* **truculence**.

trudge /**trudge**/ *vb* to walk, especially with heavy steps, to walk in a tired manner. • *also n*.

true /**troo**/ *adj* **1** in agreement with fact, not false. **2** genuine. **3** honest. **4** faithful, loyal. **5** exact, close. • *adv* **truly**.

truffle /**tru**-ful/ *n* **1** an edible fungus that grows underground. **2** a soft creamy chocolate sweet.

truism /**troo**-i-zum/ *n* a remark that is obviously true and therefore unnecessary.

trump /**trump**/ *n* one of a suit of cards that, in a particular hand, beats a card of any other suit. • *vb* to play a trump on a card of another suit. • **trump up** to make up, to invent.

trump card /**trump** card/ *n* a means of ensuring success.

trumpet /**trum**-pet/ *n* a metal wind instrument. • *vb* **1** to make known far and wide. **2** to make a noise, as e.g. an elephant.

trumpeter /**trum**-pe-ter/ *n* a person who plays the trumpet.

truncate /**trung-cate**/ *vb* to cut off, to cut short.

truncheon /**trun**-chun/ *n* **1** a club carried by a police officer. **2** a short staff carried as a sign of authority.

trundle /**trun**-dul/ *vb* to roll, push, or bowl along.

trunk /**trungk**/ *n* **1** the main stem of a tree. **2** the body not including the head or limbs. **3** the long tubelike nose of an elephant. **4** a box or chest for clothing, etc. **5** the storage place for luggage at the back of an automobile.

trunks /**trungks**/ *npl* men's shorts worn for swimming or other sports.

truss /**truss**/ *n* **1** a bundle of hay or straw. **2** a supporting bandage. • *vb* **1** to tie. **2** to tie up (a fowl) for cooking.

trust /**trust**/ *n* **1** a firm belief that another person or a thing is what it claims or is claimed to be; confidence. **2** a union of several firms to advance their business interests. **3** the holding and controlling of money or property for the advantage of someone. **4** care or responsibility. • *vb* **1** to rely upon, to have faith in. **2** to hope. • **take on trust** to accept without examination.

trustee /tru-**stee**/ *n* a person who is appointed to hold and look after property on behalf of another. • *n* **trusteeship**.

trustful /**trust**-ful/, **trusting** /**trust**-ing/ *adj* ready to trust.

trustworthy /**trust**-wur-thee/ *adj* deserving trust or confidence, reliable.

trusty /**tru**-stee/ *adj* (*fml*) that can be trusted, reliable.

truth /**trooth**/ *n* that which is true. • *adj* **truthful**. • *adv* **truthfully**.

try /**trie**/ *vb* (*pt and pp* **tried**, **trying**). **1** to attempt. **2** to test. **3** to examine and judge in a court of law.

trying /**trie**-ing/ *adj* difficult, worrying, annoying.

tsar, tzar *see* **czar**.

tsetse /(**t**)**set**-see/ *n* an African fly whose bite is fatal to horses, cattle, etc, and which carries the disease of sleeping sickness.

T-shirt /**tee**-shirt/ *n* a short-sleeved collarless shirt or vest.

tsunami /(**t**)soo-**na**-mee/ *n* a huge sea wave produced by an underwater earthquake.

tub /**tub**/ *n* **1** a large open container used for bathing, washing clothing, growing things, etc. **2** a bathtub.

tuba /**too**-ba/ *n* a low-pitched brass wind instrument.

tubby /**tu**-bee/ *adj* (*inf*) round and fat.

tube /**tyoob**/ *n* **1** a pipe. **2** a hollow cylinder.

tuber /**tyoo**-ber/ *n* a swelling on the root of a plant (e.g. a potato).

tuberculosis /tyoo-ber-cyu-**lo**-sis/ *n* a wasting disease caused by the growth of tubercles on the lungs or other organs; consumption. • *adj* **tubercular**.

tubing /**too**-bing/ *n* **1** a length of tube. **2** a series of tubes.

tubular /**tyoo**-byu-lar/ *adj* **1** like a tube. **2** consisting of tubes.

tuck /**tuck**/ *vb* **1** to push, to stuff. **2** to put in a secure or private place. • *n* a fold in a garment. • **tuck in 1** to cover up comfortably. **2** (*inf*) to eat hungrily.

Tuesday /**tyooz**-day/ *n* the third day of the week.

tuft /**tuft**/ *n* **1** a bunch or clump of grass, hair, etc, growing together. **2** a bunch of threads, etc, held together.

tufty /**tuf**-tee/ *adj* growing in tufts.

tug /**tug**/ *vb* (**tugged**, **tugging**) **1** to pull with effort. **2** to pull sharply. • *n* **1** a strong sharp pull. **2** a small boat used to pull larger ones.

tug-of-war /tu-guv-**wawr**/ *n* a contest in which two teams pull opposite ways on a rope until one is pulled across a mark.

tuition /tyoo-**wi**-shun/ *n* teaching.

tulip /**tyoo**-lip/ *n* a plant growing from a bulb and having a single brightly coloured flower.

tumble /**tum**-bul/ *vb* **1** to fall. **2** to move in an uncontrolled, headlong way. **3** to decrease rapidly in amount or value. • *n* a fall.

tumbler /**tum**-bler/ *n* **1** a drinking glass. **2** (*old*) an acrobat.

tumbleweed /**tum**-bul-weed/ *n* a plant broken away from its roots in the autumn and rolled about by the wind.

tummy /**tu**-mee/ *n* (*inf*) a stomach.

tumour /**tyoo**-mur/ *n, also* **tumor** /**too**-mur/ (*US*) a mass of diseased cells in the body causing swelling.

tumult /**tyoo**-mult/ *n* **1** noisy confusion, uproar. **2** disorderly behaviour by a crowd.

tumultuous /tyoo-**mul**-chu-wus/ *adj* noisy and disorderly.

tuna /**choo**-na/ *n* a large edible fish of the mackerel family.

tundra /**tun**-dra/ *n* a wide plain of frozen marshy land in northern Siberia or North America.

tune /**tyoon**/ *n* **1** the melody or air of a piece of music. **2** a short pleasing piece of music. **3** the correct relation of one musical note to others. • *vb* **1** to ensure that an instrument is adjusted to play the correct notes. **2** to adjust a radio, etc, until it is receiving as clearly as possible.

tuneful /**tyoon**-ful/ *adj* having a pleasing air or melody. • *adv* **tunefully**.

tungsten /**tung**-sten/ *n* a rare metallic element, used for filaments in electric light bulbs.

tunic /**tyoo**-nic/ *n* **1** a loose upper garment covering the body, sometimes to below the waist. **2** a soldier's uniform jacket.

tuning fork /**tyoo**-ning fawrk/ *n* a two-pronged fork that, when struck, gives a musical note to which instruments can be adjusted.

tunnel /**tu**-nel/ *n* an underground passage, especially one that enables a road or railway to pass under or through an obstacle.

turban /**tur**-ban/ *n* a headdress, made by winding a band of fabric around and around the head.

turbine /**tur**-bine/ *n* a type of wheel that, when moved by steam or water power, drives an engine.

turbot /**tur**-but/ *n* a large edible flatfish.

turbulent /**tur**-byu-lent/ *adj* **1** moving violently and irregularly. **2** disorderly, hard to control or rule, rebellious. • *n* **turbulence**.

tureen /tyoo-**reen**/ *n* a large deep dish for soup.

turf /**turf**/ *n* earth covered thickly with short grass. • *vb* to cover with turf. • **turf out** (*inf*) to throw out someone out, to evict or dismiss someone.

turkey /**tur**-kee/ *n* a large farmyard fowl.

Turkish bath /**tur**-kish **bath**/ *n* **1** a treatment in which you sit in a room of steam to induce a sweat and then follow it with a shower and massage. **2** the place where you would go for a Turkish bath.

turmoil /**tur**-moil/ *n* noisy confusion, disorder.

turn /**turn**/ *vb* **1** to move or cause to move around. **2** to shape wood by cutting it as it revolves. **3** to change. **4** (*of milk*) to become sour. • *n* **1** a change of direction. **2** (*of a wheel*) a revolution. **3** a bend. **4** an act. **5** a short walk. **6** a sudden feeling of sickness. • **turn down** to refuse. • **turn in** (*inf*) to go to bed. • **turn out 1** to have. **2** to attend a meeting, etc. • **turn over a new leaf** to change yourself for the better. • **turn turtle** to turn completely over, to capsize. • **turn up** to appear unexpectedly. • **turn upon** to attack suddenly. • **in turn** one after the other, in the proper order.

turning /**tur**-ning/ *n* **1** a bend in the road. **2** a corner leading off to another road.

turnip /**tur**-nip/ *n* a plant of the mustard family with a thick edible root.

turnout /**tur**-nout/ *n* the number of people in an assembly.

turnover /**tur**-no-ver/ *n* in business, the amount of money paid in and out in a certain period.

turnpike /**turn**-pike/ *n* a gate or bar across a road at which travellers must pay a tax for the use of the road.

turnstile /**turn**-stile/ *n* a revolving gate through which only one person can pass at a time.

turntable /**turn**-tay-bul/ *n* **1** a revolving platform for turning round railway engines, etc. **2** a round spinning surface on a phonograph on which the record is placed.

turpentine /**tur**-pen-tine/ *n* **1** a resin obtained from certain trees. **2** an oil made from this.

turquoise /**tur**-kwoiz/ *n* a greenish-blue precious stone or its colour. • *also adj*.

turret /**tu**-ret/ *n* **1** a small tower forming part of a building. **2** a revolving tower to protect guns and gunners on a warship or in a fort.

turtle /**tur**-tul/ *n* **1** a reptile with four flipper-like limbs, almost entirely covered by a hard shell. **2** (*US*) a tortoise.

turtle dove /**tur**-tul duv/ *n* a dove with a soft, cooing note.

turtle neck /**tur**-tul nek/ *n* **1** a high collar that turns down and fits closely around the neck. **2** a sweater or shirt with such a collar.

tusk /**tusk**/ *n* a long, pointed tooth sticking out from the mouth, as in a walrus, etc.

tussle /**tu**-sul/ *n* a short struggle, a disorderly fight. • *vb* to struggle.

tut /tut/ *interj* an exclamation expressing disappointment or disapproval.

tutor /tyoo-tur/ *n* a private teacher. • *vb* to teach, to act as tutor.

tutorial /tyoo-toe-ree-al/ *adj* having to do with a tutor or teaching. • *n* 1 a group of students who study with a tutor. 2 study time spent with a tutor.

tutu /too-too/ *n* a very short stiff skirt worn by a female ballet dancer.

TV /tee-vee/ *n* television.

twaddle /twod-ul/ *n* nonsense, foolish talk.

twang /twang/ *n* 1 the sound made by plucking a tightly stretched string or wire. 2 a tone that sounds as if you were speaking through your nose. • *vb* to pluck a tightly stretched string or wire.

tweak /tweek/ *vb* to twist sharply, to pinch. • *also n.*

tweed /tweed/ *n* a rough woollen cloth, suitable for outer garments.

tweezers /twee-zerz/ *npl* small pincers for pulling out hairs, lifting tiny things, etc.

twelve /twelv/ *n, adj* the number 12. • *adj and n* **twelfth**.

twenty /twen-tee/ *n, adj* the number 20. • *adj and n* **twentieth**.

twice /twice/ *adv* two times.

twiddle /twi-dul/ *vb* to play with.

twig /twig/ *n* a small shoot or branch of a tree or shrub.

twilight /twie-lite/ *n* the faint light just after sundown.

twill /twill/ *n* a strong cloth with ribbed lines or ridges running from end to end.

twin /twin/ *n* 1 one of two children born at one birth. 2 a person or thing that looks exactly the same as another. • *adj* 1 born at one birth. 2 double. 3 consisting of two like parts or things. • *vb* (**twinned**, **twinning**) to pair together.

twine /twine/ *n* strong string. • *vb* 1 to twist or wind around. 2 to twist together.

twinge /twinge/ *n* a sudden sharp pain.

twinkle /twing-kul/ *vb* to sparkle. • *n* 1 a gleam of light. 2 a quick look of amusement.

twinkling /twing-kling/ *n* a moment.

twirl /twirl/ *vb* to spin or turn around rapidly. • *also n.*

twist /twist/ *vb* 1 to turn quickly out of shape or position. 2 to wind strands around each other. 3 to put a wrong meaning on. • *n* 1 something made by twisting. 2 a sudden turning out of shape or position.

twister /twi-ster/ *n* a tornado.

twitch /twich/ *n* 1 a jerk. 2 a sudden quick movement. • *vb* 1 to pull sharply. 2 to make a quick movement unintentionally.

twitter /twi-ter/ *vb* to chirp, as a bird. • *n* 1 a chirp. 2 a state of nervous excitement.

two /too/ *adj, n* one more than one; the number 2.

two-faced /too-fayst/ *adj* deceitful.

tycoon /tie-coon/ *n* a very successful and influential businessman, a business magnate.

type /tipe/ *n* 1 a class or kind. 2 a person or thing possessing most of the qualities of a certain group, class, nationality, etc. 3 a letter or symbol cut in metal, etc, and used for printing. 4 the kind and size of a set of letters used in printing. • *vb* to use a keyboard to write something.

typescript /tipe-script/ *n* typewritten material.

typeset /tipe-set/ *vb* to set a written piece of work in a typed form. • *n* **typesetter**. • *adj* **typeset**.

typewriter /tipe-rie-ter/ *n* a machine operated by keys that, when struck, cause letters or symbols to be printed through an inked ribbon on to paper.

typhoid /tie-foid/ *n* an infectious disease causing acute pain in the intestines.

typhoon /tie-foon/ *n* a violent storm of wind and rain, especially in the China seas.

typical /ti-pi-cal/ *adj* 1 characteristic. 2 serving as an example of a class or group. • *adv* **typically**.

typify /ti-pi-fie/ *vb* to serve as an example of.

typist /tie-pist/ *n* a person who uses a typewriter.

typography /tie-pog-ra-fee/ *n* the art of printing. • *n* **typographer**.

tyrannical /ti-ran-ic-al/, **tyrannous** /ti-ran-us/ *adjs* cruel, ruling unjustly.

tyrannize /ti-ra-nize/ *vb, also* **tyrannise** to use power cruelly or unjustly.

tyrannosaurus /ti-ran-o-saw-rus/ *n* a very large meat-eating dinosaur that walked on its hind legs and had two small front legs.

tyranny /ti-ra-nee/ *n* cruel or unjust use of power.

tyrant /tie-rant/ *n* 1 a person who uses power cruelly. 2 an unjust ruler.

tyre /tire/ *n, also* **tire** (*US*) a ring of iron or rubber around the outside rim of a wheel.

tzar /zar/ *see* **tsar**. • *f* **tsarina**.

U

U, u /yoo/ the 21st letter of the English alphabet.

ubiquitous /yoo-**bi**-kwi-tus/ *adj* being or seeming to be in more than one place at the same time, seemingly occurring everywhere. • *n* **ubiquity**.

U-boat /**yoo**-boat/ *n* a German submarine.

udder /**u**-der/ *n* the organ containing the milk-producing gland of a cow, sheep, etc.

UFO /yoo-ef-**oa**/ *abbr* = **unidentified flying object**: a strange, unidentified object seen in the sky, believed by some people to be an alien spacecraft.

ugly /**ug**-lee/ *adj* **1** unpleasant to see or hear. **2** unpleasant, dangerous. • *n* **ugliness**.

ukulele /yoo-ca-**lay**-lee/ *n* a stringed musical instrument similar to a guitar played by plucking the strings.

ulcer /**ul**-sur/ *n* an open, painful sore on the skin, or inside the mouth or stomach.

ulcerated /**ul**-su-ray-tid/, **ulcerous** /**ul**-su-russ/ *adj* having an ulcer or ulcers.

ulna /**ul**-na/ *n* the larger of the two bones of the forearm in humans, on the opposite side from the thumb.

ulterior /ul-**ti**-ree-ur/ *adj* further, secret, hidden.

ulterior motive /ul-**ti**-ree-ur **mo**-tiv/ *n* a reason for action that one does not make known to others.

ultimate /**ul**-ti-mit/ *adj* **1** last, final. **2** greatest or highest possible.

ultimately /**ul**-ti-mit-lee/ *adv* in the end.

ultimatum /ul-ti-**may**-tum/ *n* (*pl* **ultimatums** *or* **ultimata**) a last offer of conditions, to be followed, if refused, by action without more discussion.

ultra- /**ul**-tra/ *prefix* **1** very, extremely. **2** beyond.

ultramarine /ul-tra-ma-**reen**/ *n* a deep blue colour. • *also adj*.

ultrasound /**ul**-tra-sound/ *n* the use of ultrasonic waves to form images of inside the body.

ultraviolet /ul-tra-**vie**-lit/ *adj* having to do with a kind of radiation present in sunlight that is harmful to the eyes and skin, the wavelengths of which are shorter than violet light.

ultravirus /**ul**-tra-vie-rus/ *n* a virus so small that it can pass through even the finest filters.

umber /**um**-ber/ *n* a reddish brown colour.

umbilicus /um-**bi**-li-cus/ *n* (*pl* **umbilici**) the navel. • *adj* **umbilical**.

umbrage /**um**-bridge/ *n*: **take umbrage** to be offended or made angry by.

umbrella /um-**bre**-la/ *n* a folding frame covered with waterproof material that can be opened out and held over the head at the end of a stick as protection against rain.

umpire /**um**-pire/ *n* a person who acts as judge in a dispute or contest, a referee.

umpteen /**um**-teen/ *adj* a great number of, a great many. • *adj* **umpteenth**.

un- /un/ *prefix* not.

unabashed /u-na-**basht**/ *adj* not ashamed, not put off, confident.

unable /u-**nay**-bul/ *adj* not able; lacking the ability, means or power to do something.

unabridged /u-na-**bridgd**/ *adj* not shortened, complete.

unacceptable /un-ak-**sep**-ta-bul/ *adj* unwelcome, not good enough to be acceptable.

unaccommodating /un-a-**com**-a-day-ting/ *adj* not ready to oblige.

unaccountable /u-na-**coun**-ta-bul/ *adj* that cannot be explained.

unaccustomed /u-na-**cu**-stumd/ *adj* not usual.

unacknowledged /u-nak-**nol**-idgd/ *adj* not recognized, ignored.

unaffected /u-na-**fec**-tid/ *adj* **1** simple, sincere. **2** unmoved.

unanimous /yoo-**na**-ni-mus/ *adj* **1** being all of the same opinion. **2** agreed to by all present.

unapproachable /u-na-**pro**-cha-bul/ *adj* unfriendly in manner.

unarmed /u-**narmd**/ *adj* having no weapons, especially firearms or armour.

unassuming /u-na-**soo**-ming/ *adj* modest, not boastful.

unauthorized /un-**aw**-thu-riezd/ *adj*, *also* **unauthorised** done without permission.

unaware /u-na-**ware**/ *adj* not knowing, ignorant.

unawares /u-na-**wayrz**/ *adv* unexpectedly.

unbearable /un-**bay**-ra-bul/ *adj* that cannot be borne; that cannot be accepted or allowed.

unbecoming /un-bi-**cu**-ming/ *adj* not suitable, not proper, unattractive.

unbeliever /un-bi-**lee**-ver/ *n* a person who does not believe in the accepted religion.

unbend /un-**bend**/ *vb* **1** to make straight. **2** to behave in a more friendly way.

unbiased /un-**bi**-ast/ *adj* fair to all parties, just.

unblock /un-**block**/ *vb* to remove a block from.

unbounded /un-**boun**-did/ *adj* great, without limits.

unbridled /un-**brie**-duld/ *adj* uncontrolled.

unburden /un-**bur**-din/ *vb* **1** (*fml*) to take a load off. **2** to tell about something that has caused worry or anxiety.

unbutton /un-**bu**-tin/ *vb* to unfasten the button or buttons of something.

uncalled-for /un-**cawld**-fawr/ *adj* not required; unnecessary and rude.

uncanny /un-**ca**-nee/ *adj* strange, mysterious.

uncap /un-**cap**/ *vb* to remove the cap from.

uncertain /un-**ser**-tin/ *adj* **1** not sure. **2** doubtful. • *n* **uncertainty**.

uncharitable /un-**cha**-ri-ta-bul/ *adj* harsh, severe, unkind, ungenerous.

unclasp /un-**clasp**/ *vb* to unfasten the clasp of.

uncle /un-**cul**/ *n* **1** the brother of a person's father or mother. **2** the husband of a person's aunt.

uncoil /un-**coil**/ *vb* to unwind.

uncomfortable /un-**cumf**-ta-bul/ *adj* **1** uneasy. **2** giving no comfort.

uncommunicative /un-cu-**myoo**-ni-cay-tiv/ *adj* not speaking much to others.

uncomplimentary /un-com-pli-**men**-tree/ *adj* critical, insulting.

uncompromising /un-**com**-pru-mise-ing/ *adj* firm, not ready to give in.

unconcerned /un-cun-**sernd**/ *adj* **1** unmoved. **2** uninterested.

unconditional /un-cun-**dish**-nal/ *adj* without conditions.

unconscious /un-**con**-shus/ *adj* **1** not knowing, unaware. **2** stunned, as by a blow to the head, and so unaware of what is going on.

unconstitutional /un-con-sti-**too**-shnal/ *adj* against the principles of the constitution of a country or the rules of an organization.

unconventional /un-cun-**ven**-shnal/ *adj* not bound by custom, natural, free and easy.

uncouth /un-**cooth**/ *adj* rough in manner, awkward, clumsy.

uncover /un-**cu**-ver/ *vb* to make known, to reveal.

uncultivated /un-**cul**-ti-vay-tid/ *adj* **1** not prepared for crops. **2** uncivilized, crude.

undaunted /un-**dawn**-tid/ *adj* bold, fearless.

undecided /un-di-**sie**-did/ *adj* not having made up the mind, doubtful.

undemonstrative /un-di-**mon**-stra-tiv/ *adj* not showing feelings, calm by nature.

undeniable /un-di-**nie**-a-bul/ *adj* that cannot be argued against, certain.

under /un-der/ *prep* **1** below. **2** beneath. **3** subject to. **4** less good than. • *adv* in a lower condition, degree, or place. • *pref* **under-** in, on, to, or from a lower place or side, beneath or below.

underachieve /un-der-a-**cheev**/ *vb* to fail to do as well as expected, as in school classes.

underage /un-der-**ayj**/ *adj* below the age required by law.

underarm /un-der-**arm**/ *adj* of, for, in, or used on the area under the arm or the armpit.

underbelly /**un**-der-be-lee/ *n* **1** the lower part of an animal's belly. **2** any unprotected area.

undercarriage /**un**-der-ca-ridge/ *n* the wheels or other parts on the underside of an aircraft needed for landing.

underclothes /**un**-der-cloathz/, **underclothing**, /**un**-der-cloathe-ing/ *n* clothes worn under others or next to the skin; underwear.

undercoat /**un**-der-coat/ *n* **1** a layer of short hair or fur under the longer hair or fur on an animal's coat. **2** *also* **undercoating** a coating, like a primer, which prepares a surface for another layer of paint, varnish etc.

undercover /un-der-**cu**-ver/ *adj* acting or carried out in secret.

undercurrent /**un**-der-cu-rint/ *n* **1** a current, as of air or water, flowing beneath the surface. **2** an influence or popular feeling that cannot easily be noticed.

undercut /un-der-**cut**/ *vb* to offer to sell at a lower price.

underdog /**un**-der-dawg/ *n* a person or group that is expected to lose.

underdone /un-der-**dun**/ *adj* not sufficiently cooked, lightly cooked.

underestimate /un-der-e-sti-mate/ *vb* to have too low an opinion of.

undergo /un-der-**go**/ *vb* to bear, to suffer.

undergraduate /un-der-**gra**-ju-wit/ *n* a university student who has not yet earned a degree. • *also adj*.

underground /un-der-**ground**/ *adj and adv* **1** beneath the ground. **2** secret. • *n* /**un**-der-ground/ **1** a place below the surface of the earth. **2** a railway running through underground tunnels.

undergrowth /**un**-der-groath/ *n* shrubs and low bushes growing among trees.

underhand /un-der-**hand**/ *adj* sly, secret, dishonest.

underline /**un**-der-line/ *vb* **1** to draw a line under. **2** to emphasize.

undermine /un-der-**mine**/ vb **1** to make holes underground. **2** to destroy gradually, to seek to harm by underhand methods.

underneath /un-der-**neeth**/ adv under, below, beneath, on the underside.

underpants /un-der-pants/ n underwear for the lower part of the body, long or short, with two openings for the legs.

underpass /un-der-pass/ n part of a road or footpath that goes underneath a road or railway.

underrate /un-der-**rate**/ vb to have too low an opinion of.

undersell /un-der-**sell**/ vb to sell at a lower price.

undersized /un-der-**siezd**/ adj less than the normal size, very small.

understand /un-der-**stand**/ vb (pt, pp **understood**) **1** to see the meaning of. **2** to know thoroughly. **3** to work out the truth from what has been said.

understanding /un-der-**stan**-ding/ n **1** intelligence, powers of judgment. **2** an agreement, especially an unwritten one. • adj sympathetic and kind.

understate /un-der-**state**/ vb to talk of something as smaller or less important than it really is. • n **understatement**.

understudy /**un**-der-stu-dee/ n an actor or actress who learns the same part as another to be able to take his or her place if necessary.

undertake /un-der-**take**/ vb (**undertook**, **undertaken**) to take upon oneself to do, to attempt.

undertaker /**un**-der-tay-ker/ n a funeral director.

undertaking /un-der-**tay**-king/ n **1** a task. **2** a promise.

undertow /**un**-der-toe/ n the backward flow of water after a wave breaks on the shore, an undercurrent.

underwear /**un**-der-ware/ n underclothes.

underworld /un-der-wurld/ n **1** the mythical place to which the spirits of people go after death. **2** those members of society who live by violence and crime.

undid pt of **undo**.

undies /**un**-deez/ n (inf) underwear.

undisguised /un-dis-**giezd**/ adj open, not hidden.

undisturbed /un-di-**sturbd**/ adj calm, tranquil.

undo /un-**doo**/ vb (**undid**, **undone**)to reverse what has been done, to untie or unfasten, to ruin.

undoing /un-**doo**-ing/ n ruin.

undone /un-**dun**/ pp of **undo**. • adj **1** not done. **2** ruined.

undoubted /un-**dou**-tid/ adj certain, undeniable.

undress /un-**dress**/ vb **1** to take your clothes off. **2** to take off the clothes of.

undue /un-**dyoo**/ adj greater than is necessary.

undulate /**un**-ju-late/ vb **1** to rise and fall like waves. **2** to have a wavy appearance.

unduly /un-**dyoo**-lee/ adv more than is necessary, excessively.

unearth /un-**erth**/ vb **1** to discover by searching. **2** to dig up.

unearthly /un-**erth**-lee/ adj weird, supernatural, ghostly.

uneasy /un-ee-zee/ adj uncomfortable, worried, anxious.

unemployed /un-im-**ployd**/ adj having no paid job, out of work.

unemployment /un-im-**ploy**-mint/ n the state of not having a job.

unequivocal /un-i-**kwi**-vu-cal/ adj clear, that cannot be misunderstood.

unerring /un-**er**-ing/ adj true, going straight to the target.

uneven /un-ee-vin/ adj **1** not flat, not smooth. **2** sometimes not as good as at other times.

unfailing /un-**fay**-ling/ adj sure, reliable.

unfamiliar /un-fa-**mil**-yar / adj strange.

unfasten /un-fa-sin/ vb to undo, to unfix, to set loose.

unfathomable /un-fa-thu-ma-bul/ adj **1** very deep. **2** mysterious.

unfetter /un-**fet**-ur/ vb to free from restraint of any kind. • adj **unfettered**.

unforeseen /un-fur-seen/ adj unexpected.

unfortunate /un-fawr-chew-nit/ adj unlucky.

unfounded /un-**foun**-did/ adj not based on fact.

unfurl /un-**furl**/ vb to spread out.

ungainly /un-**gane**-lee/ adj clumsy, awkward.

ungodly /un-**god**-lee/ adj not religious, sinful, wicked.

ungrateful /un-**grate**-ful/ adj not showing due thanks.

unhappiness /un-ha-pee-ness/ n misfortune, misery.

unhappy /un-**ha**-pee/ adj **1** miserable, sad. **2** unlucky.

unhealthy /un-**helth**-ee/ adj **1** not having good health. **2** bad for health. **3** having a bad influence.

uni- /**yoo**-nee/ prefix having or consisting only of one.

unicorn /**yoo**-ni-cawrn/ n in fables, an animal like a horse with a single straight horn on its head.

unicycle /yoo-ni-sie-cul/ *n* a one-wheeled cycle straddled by the rider who pushes its peddles.

uniform /yoo-ni-fawrm/ *adj* 1 unchanging. 2 of one kind, shape, size, etc. • *n* distinctive clothing worn by all members of the same organization, institution, etc.

unify /yoo-ni-fie/ *vb* to unite, to form into one. • *n* unification.

unilateral /yoo-ni-la-tu-rul/ *adj* affecting one side or party only.

unintentional /un-in-ten-shnal/ *adj* not done on purpose.

union /yoon-yun/ *n* 1 a putting together to make one. 2 act of joining together. 3 a trade union.

unique /yoo-neek/ *adj* being the only one of its kind, unequalled.

unisex /yoo-ni-seks/ *adj* designed for use by both men and women, not for one particular sex.

unison /yoo-ni-sun/ *n* agreement. • **in unison** all at the same time together.

unit /yoo-nit/ *n* 1 the number one. 2 a single person, thing, or group. 3 a fixed amount, etc, taken as a standard in measuring.

unite /yoo-nite/ *vb* 1 to make or become one. 2 to join, to act or work together.

unity /yoo-ni-tee/ *n* 1 oneness. 2 agreement.

universal /yoo-ni-ver-sal/ *adj* 1 total, whole. 2 affecting all, done by everyone. • *adv* universally.

universality /yoo-ni-ver-sa-li-tee/ *n* the state of being universal.

universe /yoo-ni-verse/ *n* 1 the whole of creation. 2 the world.

university /yoo-ni-ver-si-tee/ *n* a place of higher education in which advanced study in all branches of knowledge is carried on, and by which degrees are awarded to those showing proper achievement in their subjects.

unjust /un-just/ *adj* unfair, dishonest, not just.

unkempt /un-kempt/ *adj* (of hair) uncombed.

unlawful /un-law-ful/ *adj* against the law, illegal.

unleaded /un-led-id/ *adj* not containing lead compounds, said of petrol.

unleavened /un-le-vend/ *adj* not mixed with yeast.

unless /un-less/ *conj* if not, except that.

unlimited /un-li-mi-tid/ *adj* as much as is wanted, that cannot be used up.

unload /un-load/ *vb* to remove the load or burden from.

unlucky /un-lu-kee/ *adj* unfortunate.

unmask /un-mask/ *vb* to remove a mask or disguise from.

unmentionable /un-men-shna-bul/ *adj* unfit to be mentioned, especially in polite conversation.

unmitigated /un-mi-ti-gay-tid/ *adj* complete, with no good qualities, thorough.

unmoved /un-moovd/ *adj* firm, calm, not affected.

unnerve /un-nerv/ *vb* to take away the strength or courage of.

unobtrusive /un-nub-troo-siv/ *adj* not attracting attention, modest.

unoccupied /un-oc-yu-pied/ *adj* empty.

unorthodox /un-or-thu-doks/ *adj* holding unusual views, differing from the accepted view.

unpack /un-pack/ *vb* to open and removed the packed contents of.

unpalatable /un-pa-la-ta-bul/ *adj* 1 unpleasant to taste. 2 unpleasant.

unpopular /un-pop-yu-lar/ *adj* widely disliked.

unparalleled /un-par-a-leld/ *adj* that has no equal, unmatched.

unprecedented /un-pre-su-den-tid/ *adj* without a previous example of the same kind.

unprejudiced /un-pre-ju-dist/ *adj* fair, showing favour to no one.

unpremeditated /un-pree-med-i-tay-tid/ *adj* done without forethought.

unprepossessing /un-pre-pu-ze-sing/ *adj* unattractive at first sight.

unpretentious /un-pri-ten-shus/ *adj* modest, not attracting attention.

unprincipled /un-prin-si-puld/ *adj* immoral, wicked, recognizing no standards of right or wrong.

unproductive /un-pru-duc-tiv/ *adj* 1 yielding no crops, etc. 2 giving no profit.

unprofessional /un-pru-fesh-nal/ *adj* against the rules or customs of a profession.

unqualified /un-kwawl-i-fied/ *adj* 1 not having the necessary training or skill. 2 complete.

unquestionable /un-kwes-chu-na-bul/ *adj* undoubted, certain.

unravel /un-ra-vel/ *vb* 1 to untangle. 2 to solve.

unrelenting /un-ri-len-ting/ *adj* refusing to yield.

unrelieved /un-ri-leevd/ *adj* 1 without relief. 2 lacking variety.

unremitting /un-ri-mi-ting/ *adj* without pause, ceaseless.

unrequited /un-ri-kwie-tid/ *adj* not rewarded, not returned.

unresolved /un-ri-**zolvd**/ *adj* not settled, undecided.

unrest /un-**rest**/ *n* discontent, rebellion.

unruly /un-**roo**-lee/ *adj* disorderly, badly behaved.

unsavoury /un-**save**-ree/ *adj*, *also* **unsavory** (*US*) unpleasant, nasty, unacceptable.

unscathed /un-**scaythd**/ *adj* unhurt.

unscrupulous /un-**scroo**-pyu-lus/ *adj* having no standards of good and evil, wicked.

unseemly /un-**seem**-lee/ *adj* not fitting, improper.

unsettle /un-**se**-tul/ *vb* to upset, to disturb.

unsheathe /un-**sheethe**/ *vb* to draw from a sheath or holder.

unsightly /un-**site**-lee/ *adj* ugly, unpleasant to look at.

unskilled /un-**skild**/ *adj* having no special skill or training.

unsociable /un-**so**-sha-bul/ *adj* avoiding others, not sociable, unfriendly.

unsolicited /un-su-**li**-si-tid/ *adj* not asked for.

unsophisticated /un-su-**fi**-sti-cay-tid/ *adj* simple, natural, innocent.

unsound /un-**sound**/ *adj* **1** not healthy. **2** faulty.

unspeakable /un-**spee**-ca-bul/ *adj* better or worse than can easily be expressed in words.

unstudied /un-**stu**-deed/ *adj* natural, without having tried, not got by study.

unsuspecting /un-su-**spec**-ting/ *adj* free from fear of danger or evil, trusting.

untangle /un-**tang**-gul/ *vb* to free from a snarl, to free from confusion.

unthinkable /un-**thing**-ka-bul/ *adj* beyond the ability to understand or imagine.

unthinking /un-**thing**-king/ *adj* showing lack of thought, attention, or consideration.

untie /un-**tie**/ *vb* to loosen, undo, or unfasten something tied or knotted.

until /un-**til**/ *prep* up to the time of. • *conj* up to the time when.

untimely /un-**time**-lee/ *adj* happening at a wrong or an inconvenient time.

untold /un-**toald**/ *adj* **1** not related, not told. **2** vast.

untouchable /un-**tu**-cha-bul/ *n* **1** a person or thing that cannot be touched. **2** a member of the lowest Hindu caste, whom a higher-caste Hindu may not touch.

untoward /un-tu-**wawrd**/ *adj* awkward, unsuitable, undesirable.

untrue /un-**troo**/ *adj* **1** not true. **2** not loyal, faithless.

untruth /un-**trooth**/ *n* (*fml*) a lie, a falsehood.

untruthful /un-**trooth**-ful/ *adj* given to lying.

unusual /un-**yoozh**-wal/ *adj* rare, peculiar, strange.

unutterable /un-**u**-tu-ra-bul/ *adj* that cannot be described in words.

unveil /un-**vale**/ *vb* to uncover, to reveal, to disclose to view.

unwelcome /un-**wel**-cum/ *adj* not gladly received.

unwell /un-**wel**/ *adj* ill; sick.

unwieldy /un-**weel**-dee/ *adj* **1** huge. **2** hard to move. **3** clumsy.

unwilling /un-**wi**-ling/ *adj* not willing, reluctant.

unwind /un-**winde**/ *vb* to undo, to straighten out, to make relaxed or less tense.

unwitting /un-**wi**-ting/ *adj* not knowing.

unworldly /un-**wurld**-lee/ *adj* **1** not interested in things in this life. **2** lacking experience of public life.

unworthy /un-**wur**-thee/ *adj* **1** not deserving. **2** dishonourable.

unwrap /un-**rap**/ *vb* to open, to take off the wrapping.

unzip /un-**zip**/ *vb* to open a zip, to separate the edges by opening a zip.

up /up/ *adv* **1** in or to a higher place, amount, etc. **2** above. • *prep* to, towards, or at a higher place on or in.

up- /up/ *prefix* combining form to suggest an upward movement.

up-and-coming /up-and-**cu**-ming/ *adj* gaining in importance or status, promising.

upbeat /up-**beet**/ *n* **1** an upward trend. **2** in music, an unaccented beat, especially on the last note of a bar. • *adj* positive, optimistic, cheerful.

upbringing /**up**-bring-ing/ *n* a person's early training at home and school.

upcoming /**up**-cum-ing/ *adj* happening soon.

upcountry /up-**cun**-tree/ *adj* of or located in the central part of a country, inland.

update /up-**date**/ *vb* to bring up to date, to make aware of the most recent facts. • *also n* /**up**-date/.

upend /up-**end**/ *vb* to set or turn on end.

upfield /up-**feeld**/ *adv*, *adj* into, towards, or in the opposite end of the field.

upfront /up-**frunt**/ *adj* very honest and open.

upgrade /**up**-grade/ *n* **1** an upward slope, especially in a road. **2** an improvement of the position or status of something. • *also vb*.

upheaval /up-**hee**-val/ *n* **1** the pushing up of part of the earth's surface by forces below it. **2** a great change.

uphill /up-**hill**/ *adv* in an upward direction. • *adj* **1** sloping upward. **2** very difficult:

uphold /up-**hoald**/ *vb* **1** to support. **2** to defend as correct.

upholster /up-**hole**-ster/ *vb* to provide (chairs, sofas, etc.) with springs, stuffing, covering, etc. • *n* **upholstery**. • *n* **upholsterer**.

upkeep /up-keep/ *n* **1** the money needed to keep anything in good condition. **2** the act of keeping in good health or condition.

upland /up-land/ *n* land above other land, as along a river.

uplift /up-lift/ *vb* **1** to raise. **2** to make to think of higher things. • *n* /**up**-lift/ the act or process of lifting up.

upload /up-load/ *vb* to load or transfer a file or program from a personal computer to a central computer.

upon /up-**on**/ *adv* on, used only for completing a verb.

upper /up-er/ *adj* higher in place or rank. • *n* the upper part of a shoe.

uppercase /up-er-**case**/ *n* capital-letter type used in printing, rather than lower case or small letters.

uppercut /up-er-cut/ *n* in boxing, a short, swinging blow directed upward towards the chin.

uppermost /up-er-moast/ *adj* highest in place or rank.

upright /up-rite/ *adj* **1** standing straight up. **2** honest. • *n* a vertical post.

uprising /up-rie-zing/ *n* the action of rising up, as in a rebelling against the government.

upriver /up-ri-ver/ *adj*, *adv* towards the source of a river.

uproar /up-roar/ *n* loud, confused noise. • *adj* **uproarious**.

uproot /up-**root**/ *vb* to tear up by the roots.

upset /up-set/ *vb* **1** to overturn, to knock over. **2** to spoil completely. **3** to cause to be sad, worried, etc. • *adj* **1** worried. **2** ill. • *n* /up-set/ **1** disturbance. **2** trouble. **3** a sudden misfortune.

upset price /up-set **price**/ *n* the minimum price something can be sold for at an auction.

upshot /up-shot/ *n* result, outcome.

upside /up-side/ *n* the upper side or part.

upside-down /up-side-**down**/ *adv* with the top down and the bottom upward.

upstage /up-**stage**/ *adv* towards or at the rear of a stage. • *also adj*. • *vb* to draw the attention of the audience away from a fellow actor/actress and put the focus on oneself.

upstairs /up-**stares**/ *adv* on an upper floor of a house with stairs.

upstanding /up-**stan**-ding/ *adj* **1** standing straight. **2** upright in character and behaviour.

upstart /**up**-start/ *n* a person who has risen quickly to a position of wealth or importance.

upstream /up-**streem**/ *adv*, *adj* in the direction against the current of a stream.

uptight /up-**tite**/ *adj* tense and worried.

up-to-date /up-tu-**date**/ *adj* containing the most recent information.

upward /**up**-ward/ *adj*, *adv* towards a higher place, position, degree, amount, etc.

uranium /yoo-**ray**-nee-um/ *n* a heavy, white, radioactive metal.

Uranus /**yoo**-ra-nus/ *n* the seventh planet away from the sun.

urban /**ur**-ban/ *adj* having to do with a city or city life.

urbane /ur-**bane**/ *adj* polite, refined, smooth. • *n* **urbanity**.

urchin /**ur**-chin/ *n* **1** (*old*) a ragged, poor street boy. **2** a sea creature with a prickly shell.

urethra /yoo-**ree**-thra/ *n* the duct through which urine is passed through the body in most mammals.

urge /**urge**/ *vb* **1** to press to do. **2** to suggest strongly.

urgent /**ur**-jent/ *adj* requiring to be done quickly or at once, needing immediate attention. • *n* **urgency**.

urinal /**yoo**-ra-nul/, /yoo-**rie**-nul/ *n* a place for passing urine.

urinate *vb* to pass fluid from the bladder.

urine /**yoo**-rin/ *n* fluid passed from the kidneys and bladder. • *adj* **urinary** having to do with urine.

urn /urn/ *n* **1** a vase for the ashes of the dead. **2** a large container with a tap for making and serving tea or coffee.

us *pron* **1** the speaker adn one or more other people. **2** (*inf*) me (*give us a clue*). **3** ourselves.

usable /**yoo**-za-bul/ *adj* that can be used.

usage /**yoo**-sidge/ *n* treatment.

use /**yooz**/ *vb* **1** to do something with for a purpose. **2** to employ. **3** to consume. • *n* /**yooss**/ **1** the act of using, the state of being used. **2** advantage, benefit, value. **3** the power of using. **4** permission to use, the right to use. • **use up** to consume or exhaust, leaving nothing.

useful /**yoos**-ful/ *adj* **1** of help. **2** able to be used.

useless /**yoos**-less/ *adj* **1** of no help. **2** not any use.

user /**yoo**-zer/ *n* a person or thing that uses something.

user-friendly /yoo-zer-**frend**-lee/ *adj* designed to be used easily by a wide range of people who are not experts.

usher /u-sher/ *n* a person who meets people at the door (of a church, hall, etc.) and shows them to their seats. • *vb* to show in. • *f* **usherette**.

usual /**yoo**-zhoo-wal/ *adj* common, normal.

usurer /**yoo**-zhu-rer/ *n* a person whose business consists of lending money at high interest.

usurp /yoo-**surp**/ *vb* to seize power or property to which one has no right. • *n* **usurpation**. • *n* **usurper**.

usury /**yoo**-zhu-ree/ *n* (*fml*) the lending of money at high interest.

utensil /yoo-**ten**-sil/ *n* a vessel or object in common household use, such as a fork or knife.

uterine /**yoo**-te-rine/ *adj* **1** of the uterus. **2** born of the same mother but not the same father, as in half-brother.

uterus /**yoo**-te-rus/ *n* a female organ in mammals in which babies are developed; womb.

utilitarian /yoo-ti-li-**tay**-ree-an/ *n* a person who considers that a thing or action is good only if it is useful. • *also adj*.

utilitarianism /yoo-ti-li-**tay**-ree-a-ni-zum/ *n* the belief that only what is useful is good.

utility /yoo-**ti**-li-tee/ *n* **1** usefulness. **2** benefit. **3** a public service.

utilize /**yoo**-ti-li-tize/ *vb*, *also* **utilise** to make use of.

utmost /**ut**-moast/ *adj* **1** the farthest. **2** the greatest.

utopia /yoo-**toe**-pee-ya/ *n* an imaginary state in which everything is perfect.

utopian /yoo-**toe**-pee-yan/ *adj* perfect but impossible to achieve.

utter[1] /**u**-ter/ *adj* complete, total.

utter[2] /**u**-ter/ *vb* to speak, to pronounce.

utterance /**u**-ter-anse/ *n* **1** something said. **2** a way of speaking.

uttermost /**u**-ter-moast/ *adj* **1** farthest. **2** greatest.

U-turn /**yoo**-turn/ *n* **1** a turn made so as to head in the opposite direction. **2** a complete change in policy, ideas, etc.

uvula /**yoo**-vyu-la/ *n* a small piece of flesh hanging inside the back of the mouth.

V

V, v /**vee**/ the 22nd letter of the English alphabet.

vacancy /**vay**-can-see/ *n* **1** an empty space. **2** a job to be filled.

vacant /**vay**-cant/ *adj* **1** empty, not occupied. **2** unthinking. • *adv* **vacantly**.

vacate /vay-**cate**/ *vb* **1** to leave empty. **2** to give up.

vacation /vay-**cay**-shun/ *n* **1** (*esp. US*) a holiday. **2** a period when university students take a break from their studies.

vaccinate /**vac**-si-nate/ *vb* to inject with vaccine or with fluids giving protection against diseases. • *n* **vaccination**.

vaccine /**vac**-seen/ *n* **1** fluid taken from a cow infected with cowpox and injected into a person's bloodstream to cause a mild attack of smallpox and so protect against worse attacks later. **2** a substance made from the germs that cause a particular disease and given to someone to prevent the disease.

vacillate /**va**-si-late/ *vb* to keep on changing your mind, to hesitate to come to a decision. • *n* **vacillation**.

vacuous /**va**-cyu-wus/ *adj* **1** empty, meaningless. **2** without expression.

vacuum /**va**-cyoom/ *n* a space from which all the air has been taken.

vacuum cleaner /**va**-cyoom clee-ner/ *n* a machine that cleans carpets, etc, by sucking dust into a bag.

vacuum flask /**va**-cyoom flask/ *see* **Thermos bottle**.

vagabond /**va**-ga-bond/ *n* a person who wanders aimlessly from place to place. • *adj* wandering.

vagary /**vay**-ga-ree/ *n* a piece of odd or unexpected behaviour.

vagina /va-**jeye**-na/ *n* in female mammals and humans, the canal connecting the uterus and the external sex organs.

vagrant /**vay**-grant/ *adj* wandering. • *n* a wanderer or tramp. • *n* **vagrancy**.

vague /**vage**/ *adj* not clear, not definite. • *adv* **vaguely**. • *n* **vagueness**.

vain /**vain**/ *adj* **1** having no meaning or value. **2** too proud of yourself. **3** useless. • *adv* **vainly**. • **in vain** without result or effect.

valance /**va**-lanse/ *n* a short piece of cloth hanging from a couch, bedstead, etc to the floor.

vale /**vale**/ *n* (*fml*) a valley.

valediction /va-li-**dic**-chun/ *n* (*fml*) a farewell. • *adj* **valedictory**. • *n* **valedictorian** (*US, Can*) one who makes a farewell speech at a graduation ceremony, *also adj*.

valency /**vay**-lin-see/ *n* the power of chemical elements to combine.

valentine /**va**-lin-tine/ *n* **1** a person who is chosen as a lover or beloved on St Valentine's Day, February 14. **2** a card expressing love sent on this day.

valet /**va**-lay/ *n* a man's personal servant.

valiant /**va**-lee-ent/ *adj* brave. • *adv* **valiantly**.

valid /**va**-lid/ *adj* **1** correct according to law. **2** good, sound. • *n* **validity**.

validate /**va**-li-date/ *vb* to make valid, to prove that something is true or correct.

valley /**va**-lee/ *n* the low ground between neighbouring hills or mountains, often watered by a river.

valour /**va**-lur/ *n*, *also* **valor** (*US*) bravery, courage. • *adj* **valorous**.

valuable /**val**-yu-bul/ *adj* **1** of great worth or importance. **2** costly.

valuables /**val**-yu-bulz/ *npl* precious things.

valuation /val-yu-**way**-shun/ *n* the estimated worth, price, or importance of a thing.

value /**val**-yoo/ *n* **1** worth, importance. **2** price, cost. • *npl* the standards by which you judge the worth of things. • *adj* **valueless**.

valuer /**val**-yoo-er/ *n* a person who estimates the value of things.

valve /**valv**/ *n* **1** a device that, when opened, allows gas, air, fluid, etc, to pass through in one direction only. **2** in old radio sets, a device by which you can control the power of waves transmitted or received.

vamp /**vamp**/ *n* the upper part of a boot or shoe. • *vb* to play music made up as you play.

vampire /**vam**-pire/ *n* **1** in old stories, a ghost supposed to suck the blood of the living. **2** a bloodsucking bat.

van[1] /**van**/ *n* a covered wagon for goods or animals.

van[2] /**van**/ short for **vanguard**.

vandal /**van**-dal/ *n* a person who purposefully and pointlessly destroys or damages public buildings or other property. • *n* **vandalism**. • *vb* **vandalize**, *also* **vandalise**.

vane /**vane**/ *n* **1** a weathercock. **2** the blade of a windmill, propeller, etc.

vanguard /**van**-gard/ n (abbr = **van**) **1** the front part of an army or fleet. **2** those leading the way.

vanilla /va-**ni**-la/ n a flavouring prepared from a tropical plant. • adj **1** having the flavour of vanilla. **2** ordinary, uninteresting.

vanish /va-nish/ vb **1** to disappear. **2** to pass out of sight.

vanity /va-ni-tee/ n **1** lack of meaning or value. **2** too great pride in yourself, conceit.

vanquish /vang-kwish/ vb to defeat completely.

vantage /van-tidge/ n (old) advantage.

vantage point /van-tidge point/ n a good position.

vapid /va-pid/ adj lacking in spirit, dull.

vaporize /vay-pu-rize/ vb, also **vaporise** to turn into vapour.

vapour /vay-pur/ n, also **vapor** (US) **1** the gas given off by a body when sufficiently heated. **2** mist.

variable /vay-ree-a-bul/ adj **1** quick to change. **2** changing often or easily.

variance /vay-ree-anse/ n: • **at variance with** in disagreement with.

variant /vay-ree-ant/ n a different or alternative form. • adj different.

variation /vay-ree-ay-shun/ n change, difference.

varicose /va-ri-coas/ adj. • **varicose veins** swollen veins.

varied /vay-reed/ adj including many different things.

variegate /vay-ree-u-gate/ vb to mark with different colours. • adj **variegated**.

variety /va-rie-i-tee/ n **1** the state of being different. **2** a collection of different or slightly different things. **3** a class or species. **4** a theatre show with performers of different kinds.

various /vay-ree-us/ adj of several different types.

varnish /var-nish/ n a clear, sticky liquid used to give a shiny surface to wood, metal, paper, etc. • vb to coat with varnish.

vary /vay-ree/ vb to make or become different, to change.

vase /vahz/ n a vessel used for holding flowers or as an ornament.

vasectomy /vas-ek-tom-ee/ n a surgical operation to cut the duct carrying a man's sperm from the testicles, as a means of sterilization.

Vaseline /va-su-leen/ n (TM) a jelly made from petroleum, used on the skin as an ointment.

vassal /va-sal/ n (old) in the feudal system, a person who held land from a lord on condition that he performed certain services for the lord.

vast /vast/ adj **1** of great extent. **2** huge. • adv **vastly**. • n **vastness**.

vat /vat/ n a large tub or tank.

Vatican /va-ti-can/ n the Pope's palace in Rome.

vaudeville /vawd-vil/ n an entertainment including songs and dances, usually comic; a light variety entertainment.

vault[1] /vawlt/ n **1** an arched roof. **2** a room, usually underground, with an arched roof (e.g. a cellar, a tomb, etc).

vault[2] /vawlt/ vb to jump over while resting the hand on something for support. • n a leap.

v-chip /vee-chip/ n a device that can be attached to a television to block unsuitable shows from being viewed.

VCR /vee-see-ar/ n video cassette recorder.

VDU /vee-dee-yoo/ n visual display unit.

veal /veel/ n the flesh of a calf.

veer /veer/ vb to change direction.

vegan /vee-gan/ n a person who eats no food made from animal products.

vegetable /vedge-ta-bul/ n a plant grown for food.

vegetarian /ve-ji-tay-ree-an/ n a person who eats no meat. • n **vegetarianism**.

vegetate /ve-ji-tate/ vb **1** to live a plant's life. **2** to lead a dull, inactive life.

vegetation /ve-ji-tay-shun/ n **1** plants in general. **2** the plants of a particular region.

vehement /vee-i-ment/ adj **1** full of strong feeling, passionate. **2** having a forceful way of speaking. • n **vehemence**. • adv **vehemently**.

vehicle /vee-i-cul/ n **1** any type of carriage, cart, etc, used on land for carrying people or things. **2** a means of doing something. • adj **vehicular**.

veil /vale/ n **1** a cloth worn over the face to hide or protect it. **2** something that hides or conceals. • vb **1** to conceal. **2** to cover.

vein /vane/ n **1** one of the blood vessels through which blood flows back to the heart. **2** a sap tube or small rib of a leaf. **3** a layer of mineral in a rock. **4** a mood.

Velcro /vel-cro/ (TM) n a type of fastening for clothing, etc, consisting of two strips of fabric that stick to each other when pressed together.

veld, **veldt** /velt/ n in South Africa, a wide expanse of grassy country with few trees.

velocity /vu-los-i-tee/ n speed.

velour /vu-loor/, **velours** /vu-loor/ n a material like velvet.

velvet /vel-vet/ *n* a thick, silk or synthetic fabric, with a soft pile on one side.

velvety /vel-vi-tee/ *adj* soft and smooth, like velvet.

venal /vee-nal/ *adj* ready to take bribes, corrupt. • *n* venality.

vendetta /ven-de-ta/ *n* a feud between two families in which each is bound to revenge the death of any of its members killed by the other.

vending machine /ven-ding ma-sheen/ *n* a machine from which certain items can be bought by putting coins in it.

vendor /ven-dur/ *n* a person who sells.

veneer /vu-neer/ *n* **1** a thin layer (of fine wood, plastic, etc) glued on the surface of another inferior one. **2** something that appears fine but is not deep or lasting. • *vb* to cover with veneer.

Venetian /vu-nee-shin/ *adj* from or of Venice.

venetian blind /vu-nee-shin blind/ *n* a window blind made from horizontal strips of thin wood, plastic, etc.

vengeance /ven-jinse/ *n* harm done in return for harm or injury received; revenge. • **with a vengeance** with a great deal of force and effort.

vengeful /venj-ful/ *adj* desiring revenge.

venison /ve-ni-sun/ *n* the flesh of deer.

venom /ve-num/ *n* **1** poison. **2** spite.

venomous /ve-nu-mus/ *adj* **1** poisonous. **2** spiteful.

vent /vent/ *n* **1** a hole or opening through which air, smoke, etc, can pass. **2** an outlet. **3** expression. • *vb* to give free expression to.

ventilate /ven-ti-late/ *vb* **1** to allow fresh air to pass into or through. **2** to discuss freely. • *n* ventilation.

ventilator /ven-ti-lay-tur/ *n* any device to let in fresh air.

ventriloquist /ven-tri-lu-kwist/ *n* a person who is able to speak without moving his or her lips, in such a way that the voice seems to come from another person. • *n* ventriloquism.

venture /ven-chur/ *n* a business activity that is potentially very risky. • *vb* **1** to dare. **2** to risk.

venturesome /ven-chur-sum/ *adj* (*fml*) ready to take risks, daring.

venue /ven-yoo/ *n* the place appointed for a public event.

Venus /vee-nus/ *n* **1** the Roman goddess of love. **2** the second planet away from the sun.

veranda, verandah /vu-ran-da/ *n* a covered platform or open balcony along the wall of a house.

verb /verb/ *n* a word that tells of the action or state of the subject of a sentence.

verbal /ver-bal/ *adj* **1** of or in words. **2** by word of mouth. **3** word for word. • *adv* verbally.

verbatim /ver-bay-tim/ *adv* word for word.

verbose /ver-boass/ *adj* (*fml*) using too many words, using more words than are necessary. • *n* verbosity.

verdict /ver-dict/ *n* **1** the decision of a jury. **2** a considered opinion or judgment.

verdigris /ver-di-gree/ *n* the green rust on metals of various kinds.

verge /verj/ *n* **1** the edging of a road, etc. **2** edge, brink. • *also vb*.

verger /ver-jer/ *n* a church attendant or usher.

verify /ve-ri-fie/ *vb* **1** confirm. **2** to prove to be true. • *n* verification.

veritable /ve-ri-ta-bul/ *adj* (*fml or hum*) true, real, actual.

verity /ve-ri-tee/ *n* (*fml*) truth.

vermicelli /ver-mi-chel-ee/ *n* long, thin threads of pasta.

vermilion /ver-mil-yun/ *n*, *also* vermillion a bright red colour.

vermin /ver-min/ *npl* small animals or insects that do harm (e.g. to crops) or carry disease, as rats, mice, etc.

vernacular /ver-na-cyu-lar/ *n* the language spoken from infancy by the people of a certain country or district.

verruca /vu-roo-ca/ *n* a plantar wart on the sole of the foot.

versatile /ver-sa-tile/ *adj* able to do many different kinds of things. • *n* versatility.

verse /verss/ *n* **1** poetry. **2** writing set down in the form of poetry. **3** a stanza. **4** a short division of a chapter of the Bible.

versed /verst/ *adj* skilled, having knowledge.

version /ver-shun/ *n* **1** an account or description peculiar to a particular person. **2** a translation.

versus /ver-sus/ *prep* against.

vertebra /ver-ti-bra/ *n* (*pl* vertebrae) one of the bones of the spine.

vertebrate /ver-ti-brit/ *adj* having a backbone. • *n* a living creature having a backbone.

vertex /ver-teks/ *n* (*pl* vertices) the highest point, the top.

vertical /ver-ti-cal/ *adj* upright, at right angles to the bottom or ground level, running straight from top to bottom.

vertigo /ver-ti-go/ *n* dizziness, giddiness.

verve /verv/ *n* enthusiasm, liveliness.

very /ve-ree/ *adv* extremely. • *adj* true, real.

vespers /ve-spers/ *npl* evening service in church.

vessel /ve-sul/ *n* **1** a container for holding things. **2** a ship or boat.

vest /vest/ *n* a collarless shirt with or without sleeves worn under an outer shirt, blouse, etc. • *vb* to place (*power, rights*) with something or someone. • **vested interests** /ve-stid in-trests/ rights that have been long held and will not readily be given up.

vestibule /ve-sti-byool/ *n* a porch or small compartment between the outer and inner front doors of a house; a small entrance hall.

vestige /ve-stidge/ *n* **1** a mark or trace. **2** a very small amount.

vestment /vest-ment/ *n* a garment or robe, especially that worn by a priest or official.

vestry /ve-stree/ *n* a room in a church where the robes of priests, etc, are kept.

vet[1] /vet/ *abbr* = **veterinary surgeon**: someone who is qualified to give medical treatment to sick and injured animals.

vet[2] /vet/ *vb* (**vetted, vetting**) to approve, to pass as sound.

veteran /ve-te-ran/ *n* **1** a person having long experience of something. **2** a soldier, sailor, etc who has served in a war. • *also adj*.

veterinary /ve-tu-ri-nay-ree/ *adj* having to do with the diseases of domestic animals.

veterinary surgeon *see* **vet**[1].

veto /vee-toe/ *n* (*pl* **vetoes**) the right to refuse or forbid. • *vb* to forbid, to refuse to allow discussion of.

vex /veks/ *vb* to make angry, to annoy. • *n* **vexation**.

vexatious /vek-say-shus/ *adj* annoying, troublesome.

via /vee-a/ *prep* by way of.

viable /vie-a-bul/ *adj* **1** able to exist or survive. **2** workable. • *n* **viability**.

viaduct /vie-a-duct/ *n* a long arched bridge carrying a road or railway over a valley, etc.

vibrant /vie-brant/ *adj* **1** quivering. **2** full of energy. **3** bright, shining. • *n* **vibrancy**. • *adv* **vibrantly**.

vibrate /vie-brate/ *vb* **1** to move quickly backward and forward. **2** to shake, to quiver. • *n* **vibration**.

vicar /vi-car/ *n* the priest or minister in charge of a parish.

vicarage /vic-ridge/ *n* the house of a vicar.

vicarious /vie-cay-ree-us/ *adj* **1** suffered or undergone in place of another. **2** enjoyed or experienced through the medium of other people.

vice[1] /vice/ *n* **1** immoral or wicked behaviour. **2** criminal behaviour, often involving sex or drugs.

vice[2] /vice/ *n, also sometimes* **vise** (*US*) an instrument for holding something (a piece of wood, metal, etc.) steady while you are working on it.

vice[3] /vice/ *prep* in place of.

vice- /vice/ *prefix* in the place of, next in order to.

viceroy /vice-roy/ *n* a person who rules in behalf of a king or queen.

vice versa /vie-si ver-sa/ *adv* the other way around.

vicinity /vi-si-ni-tee/ *n* neighbourhood.

vicious /vi-shus/ *adj* wicked, evil, ill-tempered. • *adv* **viciously**. • *n* **viciousness**.

vicious circle /vi-shus sir-cul/ *n* a series in which each bad event or action or argument leads on to a worse one.

victim /vic-tim/ *n* **1** a person who has been injured or killed as the result of a crime or an accident. **2** a person who suffers because of something bad that happens to them.

victimize /vic-ti-mize/ *vb, also* **victimise** to make to suffer, to treat unfairly. • *n* **victimization**, *also* **victimisation**.

victor /vic-tur/ *n* a person who wins or conquers.

victorious /vic-toe-ree-us/ *adj* successful in a war, battle, contest, or match.

victory /vic-tree/ *n* the winning of a battle, contest, or game.

victuals /vi-tulz/ *npl* food.

video /vi-dee-oe/ *n* the transmission or recording of television shows or movies using a television set and a **video cassette recorder** and **videotape**. • *also vb*.

video game /vi-dee-oe game/ *n* an electronic game with images that you can manipulate on a video screen.

vie /vie/ *vb* to try hard to do better than, to compete with.

view /vyoo/ *n* **1** all that can be seen at one look or from one point, a scene. **2** opinion. **3** intention. • *vb* **1** to look at. **2** to examine, to consider.

viewer /vyoo-wer/ *n* a person who watches something, e.g. television.

viewpoint /vyoo-point/ *n* **1** a place from which you can see the surroundings well. **2** the way in which you consider or think of something.

vigil /vi-jil/ *n* an act of staying awake all night or of remaining watchful.

vigilance /vi-ji-lanse/ *n* watchfulness, care.

vigilant /vi-ji-lant/ *adj* watchful, careful. • *adv* **vigilantly**.

vigilante /vi-ji-**lan**-tee/ *n* a member of an unauthorized group who try to prevent, or who punish, crime in their neighbourhood.

vigour /**vi**-gur/ *n*, *also* **vigor** (*US*) strength and energy, power of mind.

vigorous /**vi**-gu-rus/ *adj* full of strength or energy, active. • *adj* **vigorously**.

Viking /**vie**-king/ *n* a Norse pirate or sea rover of the 8th to 10th centuries.

vile /vile/ *adj* **1** wicked, evil. **2** disgusting, horrible.

vilify /**vi**-li-fie/ *vb* to speak ill of. • *n* **vilification**.

villa /**vi**-la/ *n* **1** a country house. **2** in a town, a house with a garden in a residential area. **3** a house rented for a holiday, often in southern Europe.

village /**vi**-lidge/ *n* a group of houses, stores, etc, smaller than a town.

villager /**vi**-li-jer/ *n* a person who lives in a village.

villain /**vi**-lin/ *n* a bad or wicked person, a scoundrel.

villainous /**vi**-li-nus/ *adj* wicked.

villainy /**vi**-li-nee/ *n* wickedness.

vim /vim/ *n* energy, strength, force.

vindicate /**vin**-di-cate/ *vb* **1** to show that charges made are untrue, to free from blame. **2** to prove that something is true or right, to justify. • *n* **vindication**.

vindictive /vin-**dic**-tiv/ *adj* eager to obtain revenge, spiteful.

vine /vine/ *n* a climbing plant that bears grapes.

vinegar /**vi**-ni-gar/ *n* a sour liquid, dilute acetic acid, made from wine or malt and used in cooking or for seasoning.

vinegary /**vi**-ni-gree/ *adj* sour.

vineyard /**vin**-yard/ *n* a field or area in which vines are cultivated.

vintage /**vin**-tidge/ *n* **1** the number of grapes or amount of wine obtained from one vineyard in a year. **2** all the wine made from the grapes grown in a certain year. • *adj* **1** of a good vintage. **2** classic, the best of its kind. **3** of a time gone by.

vinyl /**vie**-nil/ *n* a kind of strong plastic that can bend easily, used to make wall and floor coverings, etc, and, especially formerly, records.

viola[1] /vee-**oe**-la/ *n* a large type of violin.

viola[2] /vie-**oe**-la/ *n* a family of plants, including the violet, pansy, etc.

violate /**vie**-u-late/ *vb* **1** to break a rule or formal agreement. **2** to treat someone without respect. **3** to rape. • *n* **violation**. • *n* **violator**.

violence /**vie**-lense/ *n* **1** great force. **2** harm, injury.

violent /**vie**-lent/ *adj* **1** strong. **2** using force. • *adv* **violently**.

violet /**vie**-let/ *n* **1** a small bluish-purple flower. **2** a bluish-purple colour. • *adj* bluish-purple.

violin /vie-u-**lin**/ *n* a four-stringed musical instrument played with a bow. • *n* **violinist**.

violoncello /vie-u-li-**che**-lo/ *n* (*abbr* = **cello** /**che**-lo/) a large violin giving deep notes. • *n* **violoncellist**.

viper /**vie**-per/ *n* **1** a poisonous snake. **2** (*lit*) a treacherous or spiteful person.

virago /vi-**ra**-go/ *n* (*pl* **viragoes** *or* **viragos**) a bad-tempered scolding woman.

virgin /**vir**-jin/ *adj* **1** pure, without any sexual experience. **2** untouched, still in its original condition. • *n* someone who has never had sex. • *n* **virginity**. • *adj* **virginal**.

virile /**vi**-rile/ *adj* manly, strong. • *n* **virility**.

virtual /**vir**-chal/ *adj* being so in fact but not in name or title. • *adv* **virtually**.

virtual reality /vir-chal ree-a-li-tee/ *n* the computer simulation of three-dimensional images that seems to surround the viewer and that allows interaction.

virtue /**vir**-choo/ *n* **1** goodness of life or character. **2** a good quality, power, strength.

virtuoso /vir-choo-**wo**-so/ *n* (*pl* **virtuosi** *or* **virtuosos**) an exceptionally highly skilled musician or other artist. • *n* **virtuosity**.

virtuous /**vir**-choo-wus/ *adj* morally good, of good character, leading a good life. • *adv* **virtuously**.

virulent /**vir**-yu-lent/ *adj* **1** powerful, dangerous. **2** full of hatred, spiteful. • *n* **virulence**.

virus /**vie**-rus/ *n* any of various types of germ that are smaller than bacteria and cause infectious diseases in the body.

visa /**vee**-za/ *n* a permit stamped on a passport, giving the owner the right to enter or leave a particular country.

visage /vi-**zazh**/ *n* (*fml*) the face.

vis-à-vis /vee-za-**vee**/ *prep* (*fml*) with regard to.

viscose /**vis**-coass/ *n* a kind of rayon made from viscous cellulose.

viscount /**vie**-count/ *n* a nobleman of the rank below an earl.

viscous /**vis**-cuss/ *adj* sticky. • *n* **viscosity**.

visibility /vi-zi-**bi**-li-tee/ *n* **1** clearness to sight. **2** the state of weather, atmosphere, etc, as they affect your ability to see clearly.

visible /**vi**-zi-bil/ *adj* able to be seen. • *adv* **visibly**.

vision /**vi**-zhun/ *n* **1** the ability to see, sight. **2** something imagined as in a dream. **3** something seen that has no bodily existence. **4** the power to foresee consequences.

visionary /vi-zhin-ree/ *adj* **1** existing only in the imagination. **2** full of fancies or hopes of perfection. • *n* a person who believes in ideals that cannot be achieved in his or her lifetime.

visit /vi-zit/ *vb* **1** to go to see or stay with. **2** to call upon. • *n* **1** a call upon. **2** a short stay.

visitation /vi-zi-tay-shun/ *n* **1** an official visit. **2** suffering believed to be sent by God as punishment.

visitor /vi-zi-tur/ *n* a person who visits.

visor /vie-zur/ *n* **1** (*old*) a movable part of a helmet, protecting the face when closed. **2** the peak of a cap.

vista /vi-sta/ *n* a narrow view, as seen between rows of houses, trees, etc.

visual /vi-zhu-wal/ *adj* of the sense of sight. • *adv* **visually**.

vital /vie-tal/ *adj* **1** very important. **2** unable to be done without, necessary to life. • *adv* **vitally**.

vitality /vie-ta-li-tee/ *n* energy, vigour, liveliness.

vitals /vie-talz/ *npl* the organs of the body necessary to life.

vitamin /vi-ta-min, vie-ta-min/ *n* one of several substances found in food, necessary to the health of the body.

vitreous /vi-tree-us/ *adj* of or like glass.

vitriol /vi-tree-ole/ *n* **1** sulphuric acid. **2** hostile language.

vitriolic /vi-tree-ol-ic/ *adj* using violent language, full of hatred.

vivacious /vi-vay-shus/ *adj* lively, bright, and talkative. • *adv* **vivaciously**.

vivacity /vi-va-si-tee/ *n* liveliness.

vivid /vi-vid/ *adj* **1** bright, striking. **2** appearing true to life. • *adv* **vividly**.

vivisection /vi-vi-sec-shun/ *n* the cutting up of a living animal to assist scientific experiment.

vixen /vik-sun/ *n* a female fox.

vizier /vi-zeer/ *n* a high political official in some Muslim countries.

vocabulary /vu-ca-byu-la-ree/ *n* **1** all the words used by a certain person or in a certain work. **2** a list of words with their meaning.

vocal /vo-cal/ *adj* **1** having to do with the voice, spoken or sung. **2** intended to be heard. • *adv* **vocally**.

vocal cords /vo-cal cawrds/ *npl* two membranes in the throat that produce vocal sounds.

vocalist /vo-ca-list/ *n* a singer.

vocation /vo-cay-shun/ *n* **1** your employment, profession, or trade. **2** the particular work you feel you are specially fitted for.

vocational /vo-cay-shnal/ *adj* concerned with your profession or trade.

vociferous /vu-si-frous/ *adj* **1** noisy. **2** expressing opinions loudly or openly.

vodka /vod-ka/ *n* a kind of strong alcoholic liquor, made from grain or potatoes, originating in Russia.

vogue /voag/ *n* a popular or passing fashion.

voice /voiss/ *n* **1** the sound produced through the mouth when speaking or singing. **2** a vote, an opinion. **3** the right to speak or express an opinion. **4** (*gram*) a grouping of forms of the verb according to whether they are active or passive. • *vb* **1** to say. **2** to express.

voicemail /voiss-male/ *n* an electronic system for storing telephone messages so that they can be listened to later.

void /void/ *adj* **1** empty. **2** having no effect, having no force. • *n* empty space.

volatile /vol-a-tile/ *adj* **1** easily changing into gas. **2** able to evaporate readily. **3** changing moods or ideas often. • *n* **volatility**.

volcano /vol-cay-no/ *n* (*pl* **volcanoes**) a mountain with an opening at its summit through which molten rock, metals, etc, are occasionally forced up in a red-hot stream from beneath the surface of the earth. • *adj* **volcanic**.

vole /vole/ *n* the water-rat.

volition /vu-li-shun/ *n* willpower.

volley /vol-ee/ *n* **1** the firing of several guns or throwing of many things at the same time. **2** the speaking of a number of words in quick succession. **3** in tennis, the hitting of a ball before it touches the ground. • *vb* **1** to send a volley. **2** to hit (a ball) before it touches the ground.

volleyball /vol-ee-bawl/ *n* a game in which two teams volley a ball back and forth over a net.

volt /voalt/ *n* the unit used in measuring electrical power or force.

voltage /voal-tidge/ *n* electrical power measured in volts.

voluble /vol-yu-bul/ *adj* speaking much. • *n* **volubility**.

volume /vol-yoom/ *n* **1** a book. **2** one of a series in a set of books. **3** the amount of space taken up by anything. **4** a large mass or amount. **5** level of sound.

voluminous /vu-lyoo-mi-nus/ *adj* **1** taking up much space. **2** very big, holding a lot.

voluntary /vol-un-tree/ *adj* done of your own free will, not forced. • *n* an organ solo before or after a church service.

volunteer /vol-un-teer/ *n* a person who offers to do something without being asked or ordered. • *vb* **1** to offer your services without pay. **2** to give.

voluptuous /vu-lup-choo-wus/ *adj* **1** having a full, rounded figure. **2** tempting to bodily pleasures. **3** giving pleasure to the senses.

vomit /vom-it/ *vb* **1** to throw up from the stomach through the mouth, to be sick. **2** to put out in large clouds, e.g. of smoke.

voodoo /voo-doo/ *n* a primitive and degraded form of worship, witchcraft.

voracious /vu-ray-shus/ *adj* very greedy. • *adv* **voraciously**. • *n* **voracity**.

vortex /vawr-teks/ *n* **1** a whirlpool. **2** a whirlwind.

vote /vote/ *n* **1** an expression of opinion for or against a proposal. **2** the support given by an individual to a person contesting an election. • *vb* **1** to give a vote. **2** to decide by vote. • *n* **voter**.

vouch /vouch/ *vb* to speak.

voucher /vou-cher/ *n* **1** a paper handed over in exchange for goods instead of cash. **2** a receipt.

vouchsafe /vouch-safe/ *vb* (*fml*) to be good enough to give or grant.

vow /vow/ *n* a solemn promise, a promise made to God. • *vb* to promise solemnly.

vowel /vow-el/ *n* **1** a simple sound (*a*, *e*, *i*, *o*, *u*) made by the voice without obstruction to the air passage. **2** the letter representing it.

voyage /voy-idge/ *n* a long journey, especially by sea.

vulcanize /vul-ca-nize/ *vb*, *also* **vulcanise** to treat rubber with sulphur.

vulgar /vul-gar/ *adj* **1** coarse in manners or behaviour; rude. **2** relating to sex or certain body parts and likely to cause offence to some people; rude. **3** (*old*) having to do with ordinary people; low. • *adv* **vulgarly**.

vulgar fraction /vul-gar frac-shun/ *n* a fraction other than a decimal fraction (e.g. $5/8$).

vulgarity /vul-ga-ri-tee/ *n* rudeness, coarseness.

vulnerable /vuln-ra-bul/ *adj* **1** able to be wounded or hurt. **2** weakly defended against attack. • *n* **vulnerability**.

vulture /vul-chur/ *n* a large bird that feeds on the flesh of dead animals.

vulva /vul-va/ *n* the external genitals of human females.

W

W, w /**du**-bul-yoo/ the 23rd letter of the English alphabet.

wacky /**wa**-kee/ *adj* (*inf*) mad or eccentric.

wad /wod/ *n* **1** a lump of soft fibrous material for padding garments, stopping holes, etc. **2** a bundle.

wadding /wod-ing/ *n* soft material used for padding, etc.

waddle /**wod**-ul/ *vb* to walk, rolling from side to side, as a duck. • *also n.*

wade /wade/ *vb* **1** to walk through water. **2** to walk slowly and with difficulty. **3** to read through with difficulty.

wader /**way**-der/ *n* any long-legged bird that wades in water in search of food.

waders /**way**-derz/ *npl* high waterproof boots worn by fishermen, etc.

wafer /**way**-fer/ *n* a very thin cake or cracker.

waffle[1] /**woff**-ul/ *n* a batter cake with a grid pattern, baked in a waffle iron

waffle[2] /**woff**-ul/ *vb* (*inf*) to talk in a rambling way.

waft /waft/ *vb* to bear along gently through the air.

wag /wag/ *vb* (**wagged, wagging**) to shake up and down or to and fro. • *n* **1** a wagging movement. **2** a person who is fond of telling jokes or making amusing comments.

wage /wayj/ *n* money paid regularly for work done. • *vb* to carry on.

wager /**way**-jer/ *n* a bet. • *vb* to bet.

waggle /**wa**-gul/ *vb* to wag.

wagon /**wa**-gun/ *n* **1** a four-wheeled vehicle used to carry loads. **2** a large open container pulled by a train for carrying goods.

wagtail /**wag**-tail/ *n* a small bird with a long tail that it wags constantly.

waif /waif/ *n* a homeless child or animal.

wail /wail/ *vb* to cry aloud in grief or distress. • *n* a loud cry of grief, a moaning cry.

waist /waist/ *n* the narrowest part of the human trunk, just below the ribs.

waistcoat /**waist**-coat/ *a* sleeveless garment worn by men under a suit coat.

wait /wait/ *vb* **1** to stay in a place in the hope or expectation of something happening. **2** to serve at table. • *n* time spent waiting.

waiter /**way**-ter/ *n* a person employed to serve food at table. • *f* **waitress**.

waiting list /**way**-ting list/ *n* a list of people who are waiting for something.

waiting room /**way**-ting room/ *n* a room where people may wait.

waitress *see* **waiter**.

waive /waiv/ *vb* to give up, not to insist on.

wake[1] /wake/ *vb* (*pt* **woke**, *pp* **woken**) **1** to arouse from sleep. **2** to return to full consciousness after sleep. • *n* a watch kept over a dead body until the time of burial, sometimes with feasting.

wake[2] /wake/ *n* the track left on water by a moving ship. • **in the wake of** behind, following.

wakeful /**wake**-ful/ *adj* not sleeping.

waken /**way**-kin/ *vb* to wake.

walk /wawk/ *vb* **1** to advance step by step. **2** to go on foot. • *n* **1** an outing on foot. **2** your manner of walking. **3** a road or path. • **walk of life** your rank or work in life.

walking stick /**waw**-king stick/ *n* a stick carried when walking.

walkover /**waw**-koa-ver/ *n* **1** an easy victory. **2** a victory granted because there has been no opposition.

wall /wawl/ *n* **1** a barrier of stone, brick, etc. **2** one of the sides of a building, room, etc. • *vb* to provide with a wall.

wallaby /**waw**-la-bee/ *n* a small marsupial of the kangaroo family.

wallet /**waw**-let/ *n* a small flat case for holding money and credit cards.

wallflower /**wawl**-flour/ *n* **1** a sweet-smelling garden flower. **2** a person who is not dancing because he or she has no partner.

wallop /**waw**-lup/ *vb* to thrash soundly, to strike heavily. • *also n.*

wallow /**waw**-lo/ *vb* **1** to roll about in mud, dirt, etc. **2** to enjoy what is dirty or unpleasant.

wallpaper /**wawl**-pay-per/ *n* coloured or decorative paper covering the walls of rooms.

walnut /**wawl**-nut/ *n* **1** a tree whose wood is much used for making furniture. **2** its edible nut.

walrus /**wawl**-rus/ *n* a large tusked sea mammal that can live on both land and sea.

waltz /wawltz/ *n* **1** a ballroom dance for two people. **2** music for such a dance. • *vb* to dance a waltz.

wan /wan/ *adj* pale, sickly-looking. • *adv* **wanly**. • *n* **wanness**.

wand /wawnd/ *n* **1** a long, thin stick. **2** the rod of a magician or conjurer.

wander /wawn-der/ *vb* **1** to go purposelessly from place to place. **2** to lose your way. **3** to talk in a disconnected manner. **4** to go off the point. • *n* **wanderer.**

wane /wane/ *vb* **1** to grow less or smaller. **2** to lose strength or power. • **on the wane** growing less.

wangle /wang-gul/ *vb* to arrange cleverly or by trickery.

want /wawnt/ *n* **1** need. **2** longing. **3** shortage. **4** poverty. • *vb* **1** to lack. **2** to need. **3** to desire.

wanting /wawn-ting/ *adj* **1** not as good as required. **2** lacking. **3** foolish-minded.

wanton /wawn-tun/ *adj* **1** immoral. **2** malicious. • *n* an immoral person.

war /wawr/ *n* **1** a state of fighting and enmity between nations or within a nation. **2** an active campaign against something. • *vb* (**warred, warring**) to make war.

warble /wawr-bul/ *vb* to sing, as a bird.

warbler /wawr-blur/ *n* a songbird.

ward /wawrd/ *vb* (*with* **off**) **1** to defend oneself against. **2** to defeat.

-ward /wurd/ *suffix* in the direction of.

warden /wawr-din/ *n* **1** a person who guards or helps to protect. **2** the head of a college or hostel.

warder /wawr-der/ *n* a guard in a prison.

wardrobe /wawr-droab/ *n* **1** a cupboard for hanging clothing. **2** all of a person's clothing.

ware /ware/ *n* articles manufactured out of some material. • *npl* goods for sale.

warehouse /ware-houss/ *n* a building for storing goods.

warfare /wawr-fare/ *n* the carrying-on of fighting in war.

warlock /wawr-lock/ *n* a person who has magical powers.

warm /wawrm/ *adj* **1** quite hot. **2** affectionate. **3** sincere. • *vb* to make or become warm. • *adv* **warmly.**

warm-hearted /wawrm-**har**-tid/ *adj* kindly, generous.

warmth /wawrmth/ *n* **1** gentle heat. **2** excitement. **3** sincerity.

warn /wawrn/ *vb* **1** to advise against possible danger or error. **2** to tell to be careful.

warning /wawr-ning/ *n* **1** advice to be careful. **2** advice that danger or trouble lies ahead.

warp /wawrp/ *vb* **1** to twist or bend out of shape. **2** to become twisted or bent. **3** to spoil the nature or character of. • *n* **1** the lengthwise threads in a loom.

warrant /wawr-rant/ *n* a written document giving the right to do certain things. • *vb*

1 to give the right or permission to. **2** to be good reason for, to justify.

warren /wawr-rin/ *n* many rabbit burrows in one piece of land.

warrior /wawr-yur/ *n* **1** a person who is good at fighting. **2** a soldier.

wart /wawrt/ *n* a hard dry growth on the skin.

wary /way-ree/ *adj* careful, cautious, not rushing into danger.

was *pt of* **be** used with 'I', 'he', 'she', 'it' and singular nouns. *See also* **is, are, were.**

wash /wawsh/ *vb* **1** to clean with water. **2** to flow against or over. **3** to carry away. **4** to colour lightly. • *n* **1** the act of cleaning with water. **2** a washing, the flow or dash of water. **3** a healing liquid. **4** a thin coat of colour. • **wash your hands of** to refuse to have anything more to do with. • *adj* **washable.**

washer /wawsh-er/ *n* a ring of metal, rubber, etc, to keep a bolt, etc, firmly in position.

washing /wawsh-ing/ *n* **1** dirty clothing or linen to be washed. **2** clothing or linen newly washed.

washing machine /wawsh-ing ma-sheen/ *n* a machine for washing clothing and linen.

washing-up /wawsh-ing-up/ *n* **1** dirty dishes, cutlery etc to be washed. **2** the washing of dishes, cutlery, etc.

washstand /wawsh-stand/ *n* a table for a basin of water, formerly used to wash the hands and face.

wasp /wawsp/ *n* a stinging winged insect, with black and yellow stripes on its body.

waspish /waw-spish/ *adj* sharp-tempered, spiteful.

wastage /way-stidge/ *n* that which is lost by waste.

waste /waste/ *vb* **1** to fail to put to a useful purpose. **2** to spend or use foolishly. **3** to destroy, to damage. **4** to make or become weaker. • *adj* **1** left over. **2** uncultivated, undeveloped. • *n* **1** what is left over as useless. **2** useless spending.

wasteful /waste-ful/ *adj* spending foolishly or uselessly.

waste paper /waste pay-per/ *n* paper thrown away as useless.

waste pipe /waste pipe/ *n* a pipe to carry away dirty water.

waster /way-ster/, **wastrel** /way-stril/ *n* (*inf*) a lazy useless person.

watch /wawch/ *vb* **1** to look at or observe with care. **2** to look at. **3** to guard. **4** to look after. • *n* **1** a guard. **2** a careful look-out. **3** a four-hour spell of duty for half the crew on board a ship. **4** a clock carried in the pocket or on the wrist.

watchdog /wawch-dawg/ *n* **1** a dog used to guard a house or other building. **2** a person or group who watches out for wrongdoing, especially by a business firm.

watchful /wawch-ful/ *adj* keeping a lookout, observant, alert.

watchmaker /wawch-may-kur/ *n* a person who makes or repairs watches.

watchman /wawch-man/ *n* a man employed to look after a building or site when it is unoccupied.

watchword /wawch-wurd/ *n* **1** a word known only to members of a group so that by using it they may be recognized as members. **2** a motto.

water /waw-ter/ *n* **1** the clear liquid that falls as rain and flows in streams and rivers. **2** a large area of water, as a lake, sea, etc. • *vb* **1** to supply with water. **2** to pour or sprinkle water on. **3** (of eyes) to fill with tears. **4** (of the mouth) to fill with saliva. **5** to dilute a drink with water.

watercolour /waw-ter-cu-lur/ *n*, *also* **watercolor** (*US*) **1** colouring matter to be mixed with water, not oil. **2** a painting in watercolours.

watercress /waw-ter-cress/ *n* an edible water plant.

waterfall /waw-ter-fawl/ *n* a stream falling over steep rocks or stones to a lower level.

water-lily /waw-ter-li-lee/ *n* a plant with floating flowers and leaves, found in ponds, etc.

waterlogged /waw-ter-logd/ *adj* soaked or filled with water.

watermark /waw-ter-mark/ *n* the faint trademark on a piece of paper.

watermelon /waw-ter-mel-on/ *n* a large juicy type of melon with red flesh.

water polo /waw-ter po-lo/ *n* a ball game for swimmers.

water power /waw-ter pow-ur/ *n* mechanical power got from running water.

waterproof /waw-ter-proof/ *adj* able to keep out water, that water cannot pass through. • *n* **1** waterproof cloth. **2** waterproof raincoat.

watershed /waw-ter-shed/ *n* **1** a ridge or hill separating two river valleys. **2** a point at which events take a different turn.

water-ski /waw-ter-skee/ *n* a board on which a person can stand and be towed over water by a speedboat. • *also vb.* • *n* **water-skier.** • *n* **water-skiing.**

waterspout /waw-ter-spout/ *n* a column of water sucked up by a whirlwind.

watertight /waw-ter-tite/ *adj* so tight that water can pass neither in nor out.

waterworks /waw-ter-wurks/ *n* an apparatus for supplying water through pipes to a town, etc.

watery /waw-ter-ee/ *adj* **1** full of water. **2** tasteless, weak, thin.

watt /wat/ *n* a unit of measurement of electric power. • *n* **wattage.**

wattle /wat-ul/ *n* **1** a fence made of twigs woven together. **2** an Australian tree.

wave /wave/ *n* **1** a moving ridge of water rising above the surface of the sea and then sinking down again. **2** any movement resembling this. **3** one of several ridges in the hair. **4** a moving of the hand as a signal. • *vb* **1** to move or make to move up and down or to and fro. **2** to shake in the air as a sign. **3** to put waves in hair. **4** to signal with your hand.

waveband /wave-band/ *n* a band of radio waves between specific limits.

wavelength /wave-length/ *n* the distance in water, air etc, between the crest of one wave and that of the next.

waver /way-ver/ *vb* **1** to be uncertain, to hesitate. **2** to move unsteadily. **3** to flicker.

wavy /way-vee/ *adj* **1** rising and falling in waves. **2** covered with waves.

wax[1] /waks/ *n* **1** a sticky yellow substance made by bees. **2** any material resembling this. **3** a substance used to seal letters, packets, etc.

wax[2] /waks/ *vb* (*old*) **1** to grow larger. **2** to become.

waxen /wak-sin/ *adj* like wax.

waxwork /waks-wurk/ *n* the image of a famous person made in wax for showing to the public. • *npl* (*functioning as sing.*) a museum where waxworks are exhibited.

way /way/ *n* **1** a track, path, or road. **2** a method of doing something. **3** distance travelled. **4** the route to a place. **5** a custom or habit. • **have a way with you** to be attractive in character. • **under way** in movement. • **ways and means** methods.

wayfarer /way-fay-rer/ *n* a traveller, especially on foot.

waylay /way-lay/ *vb* to hide and wait for in order to surprise or attack.

wayside /way-side/ *n*. • **fall by the wayside** not to continue.

wayward /way-ward/ *adj* fond of having your own way, not heeding the advice or orders of others.

WC /du-bul-yoo-see/ *abbr* = **water closet** a toilet.

we *subjective pron* **1** refers to the speaker, or writer, and one other or several other people. **2** a formal word for I, e.g. used by royalty.

weak /week/ *adj* **1** not strong, feeble. **2** giving in too easily to others. **3** not good at. • *adv* **weakly**.

weaken /wee-kin/ *vb* to make or become weak.

weakling /week-ling/ *n* a person who is weak in body or character.

weakly /week-lee/ *adj* not strong, not having good health.

weakness /week-ness/ *n* **1** lack of strength or determination. **2** a bad point in your character. **3** a foolish liking for.

weal /weel/ *n* a raised mark on the skin caused by a blow from a whip, thin stick, etc.

wealth /welth/ *n* **1** riches. **2** plenty.

wealthy /wel-thee/ *adj* very rich.

wean /ween/ *vb* **1** to change from feeding.

weapon /wep-un/ *n* any instrument that can be used in fighting or attack.

wear /ware/ *vb* (*pt* **wore**, *pp* **worn**) **1** to have on the body as clothing. **2** to put or stick on your clothing for show. **3** to damage or waste by rubbing or use. • *n* **1** clothing. **2** damage caused by rubbing or use. • *n* **wearer**. • **wear away** to become gradually less, to rub or be rubbed away. • **wear off** to become gradually less. • **wear on** to pass slowly. • **wear out 1** to exhaust. **2** to make useless by using too often.

wearisome /wee-ree-sum/ *adj* tiring, boring.

weary /wee-ree/ *adj* **1** tired by continued effort, exhausted. **2** fed up, bored. • *adv* **wearily**.

weasel /wee-zul/ *n* a small reddish-brown animal that eats frogs, mice, birds, etc.

weather /weth-er/ *n* the general conditions of the atmosphere (e.g. sunshine, rain, wind, etc) at any particular time. • *vb* **1** to come safely through. **2** to be damaged or discoloured by the effects of weather. • **make heavy weather of** to find difficulty in doing. • **under the weather** feeling unwell.

weather-beaten /weth-er-bee-tin/ *adj* marred or coloured by the effects of the weather.

weather vane /weth-er vane/ *n* a pointer that turns around to show the direction from which the wind is blowing.

weave /weev/ *vb* (*pt* **wove**, *pp* **woven**) **1** to form cloth by intertwining threads. **2** to put together sticks, twigs, etc, by interlacing them. **3** to make up. • *n* **weaver**.

web /web/ *n* **1** cloth made by weaving. **2** the net of fine threads made by a spider. **3** the skin between the toes of water birds. **3** (*cap*) short for the World Wide Web, the Internet. • *adj* **webbed**.

webbing /web-ing/ *n* a narrow band of strong material used for belts, etc.

webcam /web-cam/ *n* a video camera connected to a computer so that the images can be viewed on the Internet.

web-footed /web-foo-tid/ *adj* having skin between the toes.

weblog *see* **blog**.

web page /web payj/ *n* a computer file accessed on the Internet or World Wide Web.

web site /web site/ *n* an Internet location that consists of a number of related documents or files.

wed /wed/ *vb* (**wedded**, **wedding**) to marry.

we'd /weed/ *contraction* we had.

wedding /wed-ing/ *n* a marriage.

wedge /wedge/ *n* a piece of wood, metal, etc, thick at one end and narrowing to a sharp edge at the other. • *vb* to split open, fix, or fasten with a wedge.

wedlock /wed-lock/ *n* the married state.

Wednesday /wed-anz-day/ *n* the fourth or middle day of the week.

weed /weed/ *n* **1** a useless plant growing in a garden or field. **2** (*inf*) a weak or very thin person. **3** (*inf*) cannabis. • *vb* **1** to clear of weeds. **2** to pull up weeds.

weeds /weedz/ *npl* the black clothing worn by a widow in mourning.

weedy /wee-dee/ *adj* thin and weak-looking.

week /week/ *n* a period of seven days.

weekday /week-day/ *n* any day of the week except Sunday and often Saturday.

weekend /week-end/ *n* the period from the time your work ceases on Friday or Saturday until you begin it again on Monday.

weekly /week-lee/ *adj* happening once a week. • *n* a newspaper or magazine published once a week.

weep /weep/ *vb* (*pt*, *pp* **wept**) **1** to shed tears, to cry. **2** to mourn. • *adj* **weepy**.

weeping /wee-ping/ *adj* **1** crying. **2** (*of a tree*) having drooping branches.

weevil /wee-vil/ *n* a type of beetle that destroys stored grain.

weft /weft/ *n* the cross-threads of a piece of cloth.

weigh /way/ *vb* **1** to measure the heaviness of. **2** to raise. **3** to be of a certain heaviness. • **weigh down** to trouble. • **weigh up** to consider carefully. • **weigh with** to seem important to.

weight /wate/ *n* **1** heaviness. **2** a piece of metal, etc, of known heaviness, used in finding how heavy another object is or in fitness training. **3** importance, influence.

4 a heavy load. • *adj* **weightless**. • *n* **weightlessness**.

weightlifting /wate-lif-ting/ *n* the sport of lifting heavy weights.

weight training /wate tray-ning/ *n* a kind of fitness training involving the use of light weights.

weighty /way-tee/ *adj* **1** heavy. **2** important, deserving careful consideration.

weir /weer/ *n* a barrier built across a stream to make the water approaching it deeper.

weird /weerd/ *adj* **1** odd, very strange. **2** strange, eerie, unearthly. • *adv* **weirdly**. • *n* **weirdness**.

welcome /wel-cum/ *adj* **1** pleasing. **2** allowed to use or take at any time. • *n* a kindly greeting or reception. • *vb* **1** to greet kindly. **2** to receive or hear with pleasure. • **make welcome** to make (a guest) feel at home.

weld /weld/ *vb* to join two pieces of metal by heating them and hammering them together. • *n* **welder**.

welfare /wel-fare/ *n* **1** happiness, success. **2** health, good living conditions. **3** payments provided by the government for those in need.

well[1] /well/ *adv* **1** in a good way or style. **2** thoroughly. **3** rightly. **4** with approval. • *adj* **1** in good health. **2** all right. • **as well as** in addition to.

well[2] /well/ *n* **1** a spring of water. **2** a hole in the ground from which water can be drawn. **3** a pit made in the ground to reach oil. **4** a fountain. • *vb* **1** to come up as from a spring. **2** to gush out.

we'll /weel/ *contraction* we will.

well-being /well-bee-ing/ *n* success, happiness.

well-informed /well-in-**fawrmd**/ *adj* having much knowledge.

well-known /well-**noan**/ *adj* famous.

well-nigh /well-nie/ *adv* (*old or fml*) almost.

well-off /well-**awf**/ *adj* rich.

well-read /well-**red**/ *adj* having read much.

well-spoken /well-**spoe**-kin/ *adj* always pronouncing clearly with a pleasing, educated accent.

well-wisher /well-wi-sher/ *n* a friendly supporter.

well-worn /well-**woarn**/ *adj* much worn, much used.

welter /well-ter/ *n* a confused mass, disorder.

welterweight /well-ter-wate/ *n* a boxer between middleweight and heavyweight.

wench /wench/ *n* (*old*) a young woman.

wend /wend/ *vb* (*old*) to go, to make.

were /wer/ *pt of* **be**, used with 'we', 'you' or 'they' or with plural nouns

we're /weer/ *contraction* we are.

went *pt of* **go**.

wept *pt and pp of* **weep**.

west /west/ *n* one of the four principal points of the compass, the direction in which the sun sets.

westerly /west-er-lee/ *adj* from or towards the west.

western /west-ern/ *adj* in or from the west. • *n* a movie, usually about cowboys and American Indians, set in the west of North America during the 19th or early 20th century.

westward /west-ward/ *adv* towards the west.

wet /wet/ *adj* **1** covered or soaked with water or other liquid. **2** not dry, moist. **3** rainy. • *n* rainy weather. • *vb* (**wet** *or* **wetted**, **wetting**) to make wet. • *n* **wetness**.

we've /weev/ *contraction* we have.

whack /whack/ *vb* (*inf*) to strike sharply, to beat severely. • *n* **1** a blow. **2** a share. **3** an attempt.

whale /whale/ *n* a large sea mammal. • *vb* to hunt whales. • *n* **whaling**.

whalebone /whale-bone/ *n* an elastic horny substance got from the jaw of a whale.

whaler /whay-ler/ *n* a ship engaged in whale hunting.

wharf /whawrf/ *n* (*pl* **wharfs** *or* **wharves**) a platform or quay at which ships are loaded and unloaded.

what /whawt/ *adj and pron* used to ask for information about someone or something.

whatever /whaw-**te**-ver/ *pron* no matter what, any thing concerned.

whatnot /whawt-nawt/ *n* an object not easily described or defined.

wheat /wheet/ *n* the grain from which bread flour is obtained.

wheaten /whee-tin/ *adj* made from wheat.

wheedle /whee-dul/ *vb* to try to please a person in order to get him or her to do something; to coax.

wheel /wheel/ *n* a round frame, often strengthened by spokes, turning on an axis. • *vb* **1** to move on wheels. **2** to turn like a wheel. **3** to change direction by a wheeling movement when marching in line.

wheelbarrow /wheel-ba-ro/ *n* a handcart, usually with one wheel, two legs, and handles.

wheelchair /wheel-chair/ *n* a chair with wheels for people who are unable to walk.

wheelwright /wheel-rite/ *n* a maker of wheels and carts.

wheeze /wheez/ *vb* to breathe with a hoarse or hissing sound. • *also n.* • *adj* **wheezy**.

when /when/ *adv and conj* at what or which time.

whence /whenss/ *adv and conj* from what place.

whenever /whe-ne-ver/, **whensoever** /when-so-ev-er/ *adv and conj* at no matter what time.

where /whare/ *adv and conj* at, to, or in what place.

whereabouts /whay-ra-bouts/ *n* the place you are in.

whereas /whay-raz/ *conj* since, although.

whereby /whare-bie/ *adv and conj* by which.

wherefore /whare-fore/ *adv and conj* for which or what reason.

whereupon /whare-up-awn/ *adv* after which.

wherever /whare-ev-er/ *adv and conj* at, to, or in whatever place.

whet /whet/ *vb* **1** to sharpen. **2** to make.

whether /whe-ther/ *conj* if. • *pron* which of two.

whey /whay/ *n* the watery part of the milk, separated from the curd.

which /which/ *adj and pron* what particular.

whiff /whiff/ *n* **1** a puff of air or smoke. **2** a quick or slight smell. • *vb* **1** to puff. **2** to smell.

while /while/, *also* **whilst** *n* a space of time. • *conj* during the time that. • *vb* to pass.

whilst *conj see* **while**.

whim /whim/ *n* a sudden strange desire or idea, a passing fancy.

whimper /whim-per/ *vb* to cry brokenly, to whine. • *also n.*

whimsical /whim-zi-cal/ *adj* full of whims, odd, unusual, fantastic.

whimsy /whim-zee/ *n* whim. • *n* **whimsicality**. • *adv* **whimsically**.

whine /whine/ *n* a long cry of complaint, a wail. • *vb* **1** to utter a sad or complaining cry. **2** to speak in a complaining voice.

whinny /whi-nee/ *n* the high-pitched cry of a horse. • *also vb.*

whip /whip/ *n* a cord attached to a stick for beating or driving animals. • *vb* (**whipped**, **whipping**) **1** to strike with a whip. **2** to beat eggs, cream, etc, into a froth. **3** to take or move.

whippet /whi-pit/ *n* a dog like a greyhound used for racing.

whir(r) /whir/ *vb* (**whirred**, **whirring**) to move through the air or spin with a buzzing or clicking sound. • *also n.*

whirl /whirl/ *vb* to move quickly around and around, to spin quickly. • *n* a quick round-and-round movement, confusion.

whirlpool /whirl-pool/ *n* a current of water turning around and around with a circular motion.

whirlwind /whirl-wind/ *n* a violent wind blowing around and around in a circle.

whisk /whisk/ *vb* **1** to knock or brush with a quick light movement. **2** to beat lightly into a froth. **3** to take with a quick movement. • *n* **1** a quick or jerky movement. **2** an implement for beating eggs, etc. **3** a bunch of hair, etc, for brushing away flies, dust, etc.

whisker /whi-sker/ *n* **1** the hair growing on the cheeks, the stiff hairs growing on the cheeks of men. **2** the stiff hairs growing above the mouth of certain animals.

whiskey /whi-skee/ *n* a strong alcoholic drink made in Ireland or North America from barley, rye, etc.

whisky /whi-skee/ *n* a strong alcoholic drink made in Scotland from barley.

whisper /whi-sper/ *vb* **1** to speak very softly, using the breath instead of the voice. **2** to rustle. • *n* **1** a very soft voice. **2** what is whispered. **3** a rumour.

whist /whist/ *n* a game of cards for four persons.

whistle /whi-sul/ *vb* **1** to make a high, shrill sound with the lips or a special instrument. **2** to play a tune by whistling. • *n* **1** a shrill sound made with the lips or a special instrument. **2** an instrument that makes a whistling sound when blown.

whit /whit/ *n* a tiny piece.

white /white/ *adj* **1** of the colour of clean snow or milk. **2** pale. **3** having a pale skin. • *also n.*

White House /white howss/ *n* the official residence of the president of the USA in Washington, DC.

white lie /white lie/ *n* a lie told for what is believed to be a good purpose.

whiten /white-en/ *vb* to make or become white.

whitewash /white-wawsh/ *n* a mixture of lime or chalk and water used for painting walls, etc, white. • *vb* **1** to paint with whitewash. **2** to try to make what is wrong appear blameless, to try to make a guilty person seem innocent.

whither /whi-ther/ *adv and conj* to which or what place.

whiting /whie-ting/ *n* a small edible sea fish.

whittle /whi-tul/ *vb* **1** to pare off short strips with a knife. **2** to make smaller or thinner. **3** to cut down or reduce a little at a time.

whiz(z) /whizz/ *vb* (**whizzed**, **whizzing**) to make a hissing or swishing sound when moving through the air. • *also n.*

whizkid or **whizzkid** /whiz-kid/ *n* (*inf*) a young person who is exceptionally successful at something, often in business.

who /hoo/ *pron* which person.

whoever /hoo-ev-er/ *pron* no matter who, any person concerned.

whole /hole/ *adj* **1** complete, entire. **2** unharmed. • *n* the total, all.

wholefood /hole-food/ *n* food which has not been refined or processed very much and which does not contain artificial substances.

wholehearted /hole-har-tid/ *adj* enthusiastic, keen. • *adv* **wholeheartedly**.

wholemeal /hole-meel/ *adj* of flour or bread, made from the complete grain of wheat, including the husk.

wholesale /hole-sale/ *n* the selling of goods in large quantities to those who will resell them to others. • *adj* on a large scale. • *n* **wholesaler**.

wholesome /hole-sum/ *adj* **1** having a good effect on health. **2** healthy, morally healthy.

wholly /hole-lee/ *adv* completely.

whom /hoom/ *pron* the form of 'who' used when the object of a sentence or following a preposition.

whoop /whoop/ *n* a loud shout. • *vb* to make a whoop.

whooping cough /whoo-ping coff/ *n* a disease, chiefly of children, with long fits of coughing, during which the breath is taken in again with a gasping sound.

whorl /whawrl/ *n* **1** a ring of leaves around a stem. **2** one turn of a spiral shell.

whose /hooz/ *pron* belonging to whom.

why /whie/ *adv and conj* for what reason.

wick /wick/ *n* the thread in a candle; in an oil lamp or oil heater, the band of cloth that draws up the oil and is burned to give light.

wicked /wi-kid/ *adj* bad, sinful, evil. • *adv* **wickedly**. • *n* **wickedness**.

wicker /wi-ker/ *n* a willow twig. • *adj* made of willow twigs woven together.

wickerwork /wi-ker-wurk/ *n* basket work.

wicket /wi-kit/ *n* a small gate, a small door in or near a larger one.

wide /wide/ *adj* broad, extending far in all directions. • *adv* **1** missing the target by passing beside it. **2** fully. • *adv* **widely**.

widen /wie-den/ *vb* to make or become wide.

widespread /wide-spred/ *adj* occurring or found far and wide.

widow /wi-doe/ *n* a woman whose husband is dead.

widower /wi-doe-wer/ *n* a man whose wife is dead.

width /width/ *n* breadth.

wield /weeld/ *vb* **1** to use with the hands. **2** to use or put into practice.

wife /wife/ *n* (*pl* **wives**) a married woman.

wifely /wife-lee/ *adj* like a wife.

wifi *see* **wireless**.

wig /wig/ *n* an artificial covering of hair for the head.

wiggle /wi-gul/ *vb* to wag, to shake from side to side.

wigwam /wig-wam/, also **wickiup** *n* a domed tent dwelling of a Native American.

wild /wilde/ *adj* **1** not tamed or civilized. **2** not cultivated. **3** savage. **4** uncontrolled. **5** very excited. • *n* a desert area, an area unaltered by man. • *adv* **wildly**.

wildcat /wilde-cat/ *n* **1** a fierce wild animal of the cat family. **2** a fierce person. • *adj* foolish, reckless, risky.

wildebeest /wil-di-beest/ *n* a gnu.

wilderness /wil-der-ness/ *n* a desert, an uncultivated or uninhabited area.

wildfire /wilde-fire/ *n*. • **spread like wildfire** to spread very quickly.

wild-goose chase /wilde-goos-chase/ *n* an undertaking that cannot possibly succeed.

wildlife /wilde-life/ *n* animals, birds, and insects, and sometimes plants, which live in their natural environment.

wile /wile/ *n* a trick.

will[1] /will/ *aux vb, pt* **would** (*with a noun or pronoun*) **1** to express the future (*he will, she will, they will*). **2** to express a command (*you will do this*). **3** to express a desire (*I will succeed*). **4** to express expectation (*it will happen*). *See also* **shall**.

will[2] /will/ *n* **1** your power to make decisions or choices, self-control. **2** desire. **3** a written document made by a person to say what is to be done with his or her property after death. • *vb* to leave property to others by a signed will.

wilful /will-ful/ *adj*, *also* **willful** (*US*) always wanting your own way; done deliberately. • *adv* **wilfully**, also **willfully** (*US*).

willing /wi-ling/ *adj* ready, eager. • *adv* **willingly**.

willow /wi-loe/ *n* a tree with slender, easily bent branches.

willowy /wi-lo-wee/ *adj* **1** easily bent. **2** slender, graceful.

willpower /will-pow-er/ *n* determination to control what you do.

wilt /wilt/ *vb* **1** to droop. **2** to lose freshness or vigour.

wily /wie-lee/ *adj* cunning.

wimple /wim-pul/ *n* (*old*) a headdress, fitting closely around the face, worn by nuns.

win /win/ *vb* (**won, winning**) **1** to be successful in a match or contest, to be victorious. **2** to obtain in a competition. • *n* **1** a success. **2** a victory. • *n* **winner**.

wince /winss/ *vb* **1** to make a quick movement back because of pain or fear. **2** to twist the face from pain.

winch /winch/ *n* **1** a handle for turning a wheel. **2** a device for moving a heavy object by winding a rope attached to it around a drum or wheel, so drawing the object up or along.

wind¹ /wind/ *n* **1** air moving. **2** a current of air, a breeze or gale. **3** breath. • *vb* (*pt, pp* **winded**) to put out of breath by a blow in the stomach.

wind² /wynd/ *vb* (*pt, pp* **wound**) **1** to twist. **2** to coil. **3** to gather up by turning. **4** to follow a twisting course. • **wind up 1** to turn a handle to tighten a spring in a machine. **2** to bring to an end. **3** (*inf*) to joke with in order to irritate.

windbag /wind bag/ *n* (*inf*) a person who talks too much.

windfall /wind-fawl/ *n* **1** fruit blown down. **2** a piece of unexpected luck, an unexpected gift of money.

windfarm /wind-farm/ *n* a collection of turbines, for generating electricity, that are driven by wind power.

wind instrument /wind in-stru-mint/ *n* a musical instrument, such as the flute, played by blowing into it.

windmill /wind-mill/ *n* a mill with sails driven by wind.

window /win-doe/ *n* an opening in the wall of a house, etc, to let in light (usually filled with a sheet of glass).

windpipe /wind-pipe/ *n* the air passage from the mouth to the lungs.

windscreen /wind-skreen/ *n* the glass panel at the front of a motor car that acts like a shield.

windsurfing /wind-sur-fing/ *n* a sport involving moving along the surface of the sea or a stretch of water while standing on a board with a sail attached to it. • *n* **windsurfer**.

windward /wind-ward/ *n* the direction from which the wind is blowing. • *also adj*.

windy /win-dee/ *adj* open to the winds, breezy, gusty.

wine /wine/ *n* an alcoholic drink made from the fermented juice of grapes.

wing /wing/ *n* **1** the limb with the help of which birds, insects, etc, fly. **2** a side part or extension of a building, stage, etc. **3** the supporting parts of an aeroplane. **4** the side part of an army when drawn up for battle. **5** the far right or left of a sports field, such as a football pitch. **6** the part of a car above the wheel. • *vb* **1** to fly. **2** to wound in the wing or arm. • *adj* **winged**. • *adj* **wingless**. • **on the wing** in flight.

wink /wingk/ *vb* **1** to shut and open one eyelid with a quick movement. **2** to flicker, to twinkle. **3** (*fml*) (*usually with* **at**) to pretend not to see. • *n* **1** the act of winking. **2** a hint given by winking. • **forty winks** a nap, a short sleep.

winner *see* **win**.

winning /wi-ning/ *adj* **1** successful. **2** charming. • *npl* money that you have won.

winnow /win-noe/ *vb* to separate the grain from the chaff by a draught of air.

winsome /win-sum/ *adj* (*fml*) attractive, pleasant.

winter /win-ter/ *n* the coldest season of the year. • *vb* to spend the winter.

wintry /win-tree/ *adj* like winter; cold, stormy, or snowy.

wipe /wipe/ *vb* to clean or dry by gentle rubbing. • *n* a rub intended to clean or dry. • **wipe out** to destroy, to cause to cease to exist.

wiper /wie-per/ *n* a device for wiping rain from a car windscreen.

wire /wire/ *n* a thread or cord of metal. • *vb* to provide with wire or wires. • *n* **wiring**.

wireless *adj* **1** having no wire. **2** of telecommunications devices transmitting electromagnetic waves. **3** of computer networking, *abbr* **wifi**. •*n* (*old, Brit*) the radio.

wiry /wie-ree/ *adj* thin but muscular.

wisdom /wiz-dum/ *n* **1** the ability to make good use of your knowledge and experience. **2** good sense.

wisdom tooth /wiz-dum tooth/ *n* a back tooth that grows when you are a young adult.

wise /wize/ *adj* **1** having or showing wisdom. **2** sensible.

-wise /wize/ *suffix* (*fml*) with regard to.

wish /wish/ *vb* to have a desire, to want (to do), to long. • *n* **1** a desire. **2** the thing wanted.

wishful thinking /wish-ful thing-king/ *n* something believed in spite of the facts because you want it to be true.

wishy-washy /wi-shee-waw-shee/ *adj* weak and pale, feeble.

wisp /wisp/ *n* a small bundle of straw, hay, etc. • *adj* **wispy**.

wistful /wist-ful/ *adj* thoughtful, longing. • *adv* **wistfully**.

wit /wit/ *n* **1** the ability to say things shortly, neatly, and cleverly, often in a way that makes them amusing. **2** a person who has this ability. **3** intelligence, understanding. • **at your wit's end** so worried that you do not know what to do next. • **to wit** namely, that is to say.

witch /witch/ *n* **1** a woman believed to have magical powers granted by the devil. **2** an ugly old woman.

witchcraft /witch-craft/ *n* magic performed with the aid of the devil.

witch-doctor /witch-doc-tor/ *n* among certain African tribes, a man believed to be able to control evil spirits and cure illness by magic.

with /with/ *prep* **1** in the company of. **2** having.

withdraw /with-draw/ *vb* **1** to draw or pull back, to retreat. **2** to take back. **3** to take money, etc, from your bank or stock. • *n* **withdrawal**.

withdrawn /with-drawn/ *adj* shy or unfriendly.

wither /wi-ther/ *vb* to make or become dry and faded, to shrivel, to rot away.

withering /wi-ther-ing/ *adj* **1** drying, fading. **2** hurtful, sarcastic.

withers /wi-therz/ *npl* the ridge between the shoulder blades of a horse.

withhold /with-hoald/ *vb* to refuse to grant or give, to keep back.

within /wi-thin/ *prep* inside. • *adv* **1** indoors. **2** inwardly.

without /with-out/ *prep* not having.

withstand /with-stand/ *vb* to resist, to oppose.

witless /wit-less/ *adj* (*fml*) foolish, stupid.

witness /wit-ness/ *n* **1** a person who sees an event taking place. **2** a person who tells in a court of law what took place on an occasion at which he or she was present. **3** (*fml*) evidence pointing to the truth. • *vb* **1** to see happening. **2** to sign a document to confirm that another has signed it in your presence. • **bear witness** to give evidence.

witticism /wi-ti-si-zum/ *n* a clever or humorous saying, shortly and neatly expressed.

wittingly /wi-ting-lee/ *adv* with knowledge or understanding of what you are doing.

witty /wi-tee/ *adj* able to say clever things briefly and often amusingly. • *adv* **wittily**.

wives *pl of* **wife**.

wizard /wi-zard/ *n* **1** a man who claims magical powers. **2** a conjurer.

wizardry /wi-zard-ree/ *n* **1** magic. **2** great skill.

wizened /wi-zend/ *adj* dried up and wrinkled.

wobble /wob-ul/ *vb* to sway from side to side, move unsteadily. • *also n*.

wobbly /wob-lee/ *adj* unsteady.

woe /woe/ *n* (*fml*) grief, sorrow, misery.

woebegone /wo-bi-gawn/ *adj* (*fml*) full of sorrow or grief.

woeful /wo-ful/ *adj* **1** sad. **2** deplorably bad. • *adv* **woefully**.

wok /wok/ *n* a large bowl-shaped cooking pan used for stir-frying.

woke /woke/ *pt of* **wake**. • *pp* **woken**.

wolf /woolf/ *n* (*pl* **wolves**) a fierce wild animal of the dog family. • *vb* to eat greedily.

woman /woo-man/ *n* (*pl* **women** /wi-min/) a grown-up female human being.

womanhood /woo-man-hood/ *n* the state or qualities of a woman.

womanish /woo-ma-nish/ *adj* **1** having the qualities of a woman. **2** unmanly.

womankind /woo-man-kiend/ *n* women in general.

womanly /woo-man-lee/ *adj* having the good qualities of a woman, gentle.

womb /woom/ *n* the female organ in which the young are kept and fed until birth.

wombat /wom-bat/ *n* a pouched Australian animal, like a small bear.

women *pl of* **woman**.

women's movement /wi-minz moov-mint/ *n* a movement whose aim is to improve the position of women in society and obtain equality with men.

won /wun/ *pt of* **win**.

wonder /wun-der/ *n* **1** great surprise or astonishment. **2** anything giving rise to such feelings, a marvel or miracle. • *vb* **1** to think about the reasons for something. **2** to feel surprise or astonishment.

wonderful /wun-der-ful/ *adj* very surprising, extraordinary. • *adv* **wonderfully**.

wonderment /wun-der-ment/ *n* surprise, astonishment.

wondrous /wun-druss/ *adj* (*old*) wonderful.

wont /wawnt/ *n* custom, habit. • *adj* accustomed.

won't /woant/ *contraction* will not.

woo /woo/ *vb* **1** to try to make someone love you, to seek to marry. **2** to try to get someone's support or custom. • *n* **wooer**.

wood /wood/ *n* **1** a large collection of growing trees. **2** the hard substance of which the trunks and branches of trees are made.

woodcut /wood-cut/ *n* a print made from a picture carved on wood.

wooded /woo-did/ *adj* covered with trees or woods.

wooden /woo-din/ *adj* **1** made of wood. **2** dull, lacking feeling.

woodland /wood-land/ *n* country covered with trees or woods.

woodpecker /wood-pe-ker/ *n* a bird that taps holes in trees with its long pointed beak and takes out insects from them with its tongue.

woodwind instrument /wood-wind in-stru-mint/ *n* a wind instrument usually made of wood, such as the clarinet.

woodwork /wood-wurk/ *n* **1** the art of making objects out of wood. **2** objects so made.

woodworm /wood-wurm/ *n* a grub that eats its way into wood and destroys it.

woody /woo-dee/ *adj* **1** made of wood. **2** covered with woods.

woof /woof/ *n* the sound that a dog makes when it barks.

wool /wool/ *n* **1** the soft, wavy hair covering the body of certain animals (e.g. sheep, goats, etc.). **2** thread or cloth made from wool.

woollen /woo-len/ *adj*, *also* **woolen** (*US*) made of wool. • *also n*.

woolly /woo-lee/ *adj* **1** covered with wool. **2** like wool.

word /wurd/ *n* **1** a sound or group of sounds expressing an idea. **2** a message, information. **3** a promise. • *vb* to express in words. • **have words with** to quarrel with. • **word for word** in exactly the same words as those used before.

wording /wur-ding/ *n* the way that something is expressed in words.

word-perfect /wurd-per-fect/ *adj* able to say without an error the words of something learned.

word processor /wurd pro-se-sur/ *n* a computer system used for writing, editing and printing documents.

wordy /wur-dee/ *adj* using more words than are necessary.

wore /wore/ *pt of* wear.

work /wurk/ *n* **1** effort. **2** a task, tasks. **3** that which you do for a living. **4** a book, picture, piece of music, etc. • *vb* **1** to labour, to toil. **2** to be in a job. **3** to make to do work. **4** to have the desired effect or result. **5** to cause, to bring about. **6** to give shape to. • *npl* **works 1** a factory. **2** the parts of a machine that make it go. • **work up** to excite.

workable /wur-ka-bul/ *adj* that can be done or used.

worker /wur-ker/ *n* **1** a person who works. **2** an insect (e.g. a bee) that does all the work.

workforce /wurk-foarss/ *n* the number of people who work in a particular firm, place, industry, etc.

workman *n* /wurk-man/ a worker who is emplowed as a craftsman or manual labourer.

workmanship /wurk-man-ship/ **1** skill of a worker. **2** the quality of a piece of work.

workout /wurk-out/ *n* a session of physical exercise or training. • *vb* work out.

workshop /wurk-shap/ *n* a building or room in which work is carried on.

world /wurld/ *n* **1** the Earth on which we live. **2** any planet or star. **3** the universe and all created things. **4** all human beings. **5** any sphere of activity, study, etc. **6** a great amount.

worldly /wurld-lee/ *adj* **1** having to do with this world or life. **2** interested only in the things of this life.

worldwide /wurld-wide/ *adj* spread throughout or found everywhere in the world.

World Wide Web /world wide web/ *n* (*abbr* = **WWW**) the Internet network that stretches across the world.

worm /wurm/ *n* **1** a small creeping animal without a backbone or legs. **2** the thread of a screw. **3** (*inf*) a despicable person. • *vb* **1** to wriggle or crawl along. **2** to do something slowly and secretly. **3** to persuade to tell by persistent questioning.

worn /woarn/ *pp of* wear. • *adj* showing signs of wear.

worn-out /woarn-out/ *adj* **1** exhausted. **2** overused or worn.

worry /wu-ree/ *vb* **1** to feel anxiety. **2** to trouble, to vex. **3** to tear with the teeth. • *n* **1** anxiety, trouble. **2** a cause of anxiety.

worse /wurss/ *adj* more bad, less good, more sick. • *adv* more badly.

worsen /wur-sin/ *vb* to make or become worse.

worship /wur-ship/ *n* **1** prayers and praise offered to God. **2** a religious service. **3** great love or reverence for. • *vb* (**worshipped**, **worshiping**) **1** to pray to. **2** to honour greatly. **3** to join in a religious service. • *n* **worshiper**.

worst /wurst/ *adj* most bad or sick. • *adv* most badly. • *n* the greatest evil or ill possible. • *vb* to defeat.

worth /wurth/ *adj* **1** equal in value to. **2** deserving of. **3** having such-and-such an amount of money or property. • *n* **1** value. **2** price. **3** merit, excellence.

worthless /wurth-less/ *adj* of no use or value. • *n* **worthlessness**.

worthwhile /wurth-while/ *adj* profitable, repaying the money, work, etc, expended.

worthy /wur-thee/ *adj* deserving, deserving respect.

would /wood/ *pt of* **will**.

would-be /wood-be/ *adj* wishing to be, intending.

wound /woond/ *n* a hurt, cut, or bruise, an injury. • *vb* **1** to injure, to cause a wound to. **2** to hurt the feelings of.

wound /wound/ *pt, pp of* **wind**. • **wound-up** over-excited.

wove /wove/ *pt of* **weave**. • *pp* **woven**.

wraith /raith/ *n* (*fml*) a ghost.

wrangle /rang-gul/ *vb* to quarrel, to argue angrily. • *n* a quarrel, a dispute. • *n* **wrangler**.

wrap /rap/ *vb*. • *n* **1** a shawl, a loose cloak. **2** a sandwich consisting of some kind of rolled-up thin bread with a filling inside. • *n* **wrapping**.

wrapper /ra-per/ *n* a cover for books, etc.

wrath /rath/ *n* great anger, rage.

wrathful /rath-ful/ *adj* very angry.

wreak /reek/ *vb* to carry out, to put into effect.

wreath /reeth/ *n* **1** flowers, leaves, etc, woven together to form a ring or crown. **2** a curling or spiral cloud.

wreathe /reethe/ *vb* to put a wreath on or around.

wreck /reck/ *n* **1** destruction, especially of a ship at sea. **2** a ruin. **3** the remains of a ship destroyed by the sea. **4** a person weakened by ill health or evil living. • *vb* to ruin, to destroy.

wreckage /re-kidge/ *n* the broken parts of a wrecked ship.

wren /ren/ *n* a very small songbird.

wrench /rench/ *n* **1** a violent twist. **2** the sorrow caused by parting from or giving away. **3** a tool for gripping and turning nuts, bolts, etc. • *vb* **1** to give a sudden twist or pull to. **2** to sprain.

wrest /rest/ *vb* to twist, to pull violently from.

wrestle /re-sul/ *vb* **1** to struggle with another by gripping and trying to throw down. **2** to try hard to solve.

wrestler /re-sler/ *n* a person who wrestles for sport.

wrestling /re-sling/ *n* the sport of wrestling.

wretch /rech/ *n* **1** a very unfortunate or miserable person. **2** a wicked or worthless person.

wretched /rech-ed/ *adj* **1** miserable. **2** worthless.

wriggle /ri-gul/ *vb* **1** to twist from side to side. **2** to move with a wriggling movement. • *also n.* • *adj* **wriggly**.

-wright /rite/ *suffix* worker at, maker of.

wring /ring/ *vb* (*pt, pp* **wrung**) **1** to squeeze hard, to twist tightly. **2** to get by pressure or persuasion.

wringer /ring-er/ *n* a machine for squeezing the water out of clothing.

wrinkle /ring-cul/ *n* a fold or furrow in the skin, or in cloth, etc. • *vb* to make wrinkles in.

wrist /rist/ *n* the joint between the hand and the arm.

wristwatch /rist-wawch/ *n* a watch attached to a band worn around the wrist.

writ /rit/ *n* a written order from a law court to do or not to do certain acts.

write /rite/ *vb* (*pt* **wrote**, *pp* **written**) **1** to make marks standing for sounds, letters, or words on paper, etc, with a pen or pencil. **2** to make up stories, poems, etc, for publication. **3** to write a letter to.

writer /rie-ter/ *n* **1** an author. **2** a person who writes.

writhe /rithe/ *vb* to twist and turn the body about.

writing paper /rie-ting pay-per/ *n* paper for writing letters on.

writings /rie-tingz/ *npl* the written works of an author.

written *pp of* **write**.

wrong /rong/ *adj* **1** not correct, false. **2** incorrect in your opinion, etc. **3** not good, not morally right, evil. • *vb* **1** to treat unjustly. **2** to do harm to. • *n* **1** an injustice. **2** harm. • *adv* **wrongly**.

wrongdoer /rong-doo-er/ *n* a criminal, a sinner. • *n* **wrongdoing**.

wrongful /rong-ful/ *adj* **1** unjust. **2** criminal, wrong. • *adv* **wrongfully**.

wrote /rote/ *pt of* **write**.

wrought /rawt/ *old pt of* **work**. • *adj* beaten or rolled into shape. • *also adj.*

wrought iron /rawt eye-urn/ *n* hammered iron. • *also adj.*

wrung *pt and pp of* **wring**.

wry /rie/ *adj* **1** twisted, turned to one side. **2** slightly mocking. • *adv* **wryly**. • *n* **wryness**.

www *abbr* = **World Wide Web**.

X

X, x /eks/ **1** the 24th letter of the English alphabet. **2** (*algebra*) the first unknown quantity. **3** (*math*) the first coordinate.

xenophobia /ze-nu-**fo**-bee-ya/ *n* hatred of foreigners and their ways.

xerox /**zee**-roks/ *vb* (*TM*) to make photograph copies by machine. • *n* such a copy.

Xmas /eks-mas/ short for **Christmas**.

X-rays /eks-raze/ *npl* electric rays that are able to pass through solid substances and so can be used in photographing broken bones, or other objects hidden behind a solid surface. • *n* **X-ray** an X-ray photograph. • *vb* **X-ray** to make an X-ray photograph of.

xylophone /**zie**-lu-fone/ *n* a musical instrument of hanging wooden bars that give notes when struck with a wooden hammer.

Y

Y, y /why/ **1** the 25th letter of the English alphabet. **2** (*algebra*) the second unknown quantity. **3** (*math*) the second coordinate.

yacht /yot/ *n* a ship, especially a sailing ship, used for pleasure or racing. • *n* **yachting**.

yachtsman /yots-man/, **yachtswoman** /yots-woo-man/ *n* a person who sails a yacht.

yak /yak/ *n* a type of ox with long silky hair, found in Tibet.

yam /yam/ *n* a tropical plant with an edible root; a sweet potato.

yank /yangk/ *vb* to move suddenly or with a jerk.

Yankee /yang-kee/ *n* a citizen of the North of the United States.

yap /yap/ *vb* (**yapped, yapping**) to yelp; to bark shrilly.

yard /yard/ *n* **1** an imperial measure of length (= 3 feet or 0.9144 metres). **2** a pole fixed across a mast for supporting a sail. **3** an enclosed piece of ground near or behind a building. **4** a piece of ground enclosed for a particular purpose.

yardstick /yard-stick/ *n* a standard by which you measure or judge other things.

yarn /yarn/ *n* **1** any type of spun thread. **2** (*inf*) a made-up or improbable story.

yashmak /yash-mak/ *n* a veil worn by Muslim women in public.

yawn /yawn/ *vb* **1** to open the mouth wide because of tiredness or boredom. **2** to be wide open. • *n* the act of yawning.

ye /yee/ *pron* (*old*) you (*pl*).

yea /yay/ *adv* yes.

yeah /yeh/ *sentence substitute* (*inf*) yes.

year /yeer/ *n* the time taken by the earth to travel once around the sun; 365 days, especially from January 1 to December 31; 12 months.

yearling /yeer-ling/ *n* a one-year-old animal.

yearly /yeer-lee/ *adj* **1** happening once a year. **2** happening every year. • *also adv*.

yearn /yurn/ *vb* to desire greatly, to long.

yearning /yur-ning/ *n* a strong desire, a longing.

yeast /yeest/ *n* a frothy substance used for making bread rise and in making beer, etc.

yell /yell/ *vb* to scream, to shout loudly and suddenly. • *also n*.

yellow /ye-lo/ *n* a bright golden colour, as of daffodils. • *adj* **1** of golden colour. **2** (*inf*) cowardly.

yellow fever /ye-lo fee-ver/ *n* a dangerous tropical disease spread by mosquitoes.

yelp /yelp/ *vb* to utter a sharp cry, as a dog in pain. • *also n*.

yen[1] /yen/ *n* (*pl* **yen**) the currency of Japan.

yen[2] /yen/ *n* (*inf*) desire.

yeoman /yoe-man/ *n* a farmer, one who owns a small farm of his own.

yesterday /ye-ster-day/ *n* the day before today. • *also adv*.

yes *sentence substitute* used to express the affirmative. • *n* an answer of 'yes'.

yet /yet/ *adv* **1** still. **2** in addition. **3** up to the present. **4** however. **5** all the same.

yeti /**ye**-tee/ *n* a legendary very large creature said to live in the Himalayas.

yew /**yoo**/ *n* a large evergreen tree often grown in churchyards.

Yiddish /**yid**-ish/ *n* a language, partly German and Hebrew, spoken by some Jewish people.

yield /**yeeld**/ *vb* **1** to produce. **2** to give in, to surrender. **3** to give way. • *n* **1** the amount produced or made in profit. **2** a crop.

yielding /**yeel**-ding/ *adj* giving in easily, easily influenced or managed.

yodel /**yo**-dul/ *vb* (**yodelled, yodelling**) to sing with frequent changes from one's ordinary voice to a higher-pitched one. • *n* **yodeler**.

yoga /**yo**-ga/ *n* a Hindu belief that by prayer and complete control over the body and its desires, you may become one with God.

yogi /**yo**-gee/ *n* a person who practises yoga.

yogurt, yoghurt /**yo**-gurt/ *n* a food made from fermented milk.

yoke /**yoke**/ *n* **1** the part of a garment that fits over the shoulders and round the neck. **2** a frame of wood that fits over the necks of two oxen, making them work together when pulling a plough, cart, etc. **3** something that forces people to do something. • *vb* **1** to put together under a yoke. **2** to link together.

yokel /**yo**-kul/ *n* (*derog*) someone from the country.

yolk /**yoke**/ *n* the yellow part of an egg.

Yom Kippur /yom ki-**poor**/ *n* the Day of Atonement, a Jewish festival involving fasting and repenting.

yon /**yon**/, **yonder** /**yon**-dur/ *adjs* (*old*) that (one) over there. • *adv* **yonder** over there.

yore /**yore**/ *n* (*old*) olden times. • **of yore** in olden times.

you /**yoo**/ *pron, pl* **you** the person or people being addressed.

young /**yung**/ *adj* not old, not grown up, childish, youthful. • *n* **1** all the children or offspring. **2** young people in general.

youngster /**yung**-ster/ *n* a young person.

your /**yoor**/ *adj* belonging to you.

yours /**yoorz**/ *pron* something belonging to you.

yourself /yoor-**self**/ *pron* (*pl* **yourselves**) the reflexive form of 'you'.

youth /**yooth**/ *n* **1** the early part of one's life. **2** a young man. **3** young people.

youthful /**yooth**-ful/ *adj* young, young-looking. • *adv* **youthfully**.

yowl /**yowl**/ *vb* to cry or howl like a dog. • *also n*.

yo-yo /**yo**-yo/ *n* a toy consisting of a double disc that you move up and down on a string.

Yule /**yool**/ *n* Christmas.

Yuletide /**yool**-tide/ *n* the Christmas season.

Z

Z, z /zee, zed/ **1** the 26th letter of the English alphabet. **2** (*algebra*) the third unknown quantity. **3** (*math*) the third coordinate.

zany /zay-nee/ *adj* crazy.

zap /zap/ *vb* **1** to destroy or kill, especially in computer games. **2** to change television channel using a remote control.

zeal /zeel/ *n* keenness, eagerness, enthusiasm.

zealot /zel-ut/ *n* a person who is so keen on a cause or idea that he or she can talk of nothing else.

zealous /zel-uss/ *adj* very keen, eager. • *adv* **zealously**.

zebra /zeh-bra/ *n* a striped horselike animal found in Africa.

zenith /ze-nith/ *n* **1** the point of the heavens directly overhead. **2** the highest point.

zephyr /ze-fur/ *n* (*lit*) a gentle breeze.

zero /zee-ro/ *n* **1** the figure 0. **2** the 0-mark on a measuring scale.

zero hour /zee-ro our/ *n* the time fixed for the beginning of something, such as a military attack.

zest /zest/ *n* keen enjoyment, enthusiasm. • *adj* **zestful**.

zigzag /zig-zag/ *adj* turning sharply to the left, following a straight line, then turning sharply to the right, and so on. • *n* a zigzag line or course. • *also vb*.

zinc /zingk/ *n* a bluish white metal.

Zionism /zie-u-ni-zum/ *n* the movement to found and develop Israel. • *adj and n* **Zionist**.

zip /zip/ *vb* (**zipped**, **zipping**) **1** (*inf*) to whiz. **2** to fasten with a zip. • *n* a sliding fastener that causes two strips of metal teeth to engage in or disengage from each other as it moves.

zip code /zip code/ *n* a number identifying a postal area of the US.

zither /zi-ther/ *n* a flat stringed musical instrument played with the fingers.

zodiac /zo-dee-ac/ *n* the band of the heavens within which the sun, moon, and planets seem to move, and containing the 12 groups of stars known as the signs of the zodiac.

zone /zone/ *n* **1** a belt or stripe. **2** any region with distinctive characteristics of its own. **3** one of the five great belts running around the earth (e.g. *Arctic zone*).

zoo /zoo/ *n* a park in which animals are kept in cages, enclosures, ponds, etc, for show.

zoological /zoo-u-lodge-ic-al/ *adj* having to do with the study of animals.

zoological gardens /zoo-u-lodge-ic-al gardenz/ *n* a zoo.

zoologist /zoo-ol-u-jist/ *n* a person who studies animals.

zoology /zoo-ol-u-jee/ *n* the study of animals.

zoom /zoom/ *vb* **1** to climb rapidly at a steep angle. **2** (*inf*) to increase rapidly. **3** (*inf*) to move very quickly.

zoom lens /zoom lenz/ *n* a camera lens that is adjusted for focusing on close or distant objects.

zucchini /zoo-kee-nee/ (*esp. US*) *n* a courgette.

Zulu /zoo-loo/ *n* **1** a member of an African tribe. **2** its language.